BRITAIN
The Ultimate Guide

Managing editor: Donna Wood
Project editor: Sandy Draper
Page layout: Tracey Butler
Picture research: Carol Walker
Verifier: Jane Smith
Proofreader: Jennifer Wood
Image retouching and repro: Sarah Montgomery
Cartography produced by the Mapping Services department of AA Publishing

Produced by AA Publishing
© AA Media Limited 2007. Reprinted 2008.
This edition revised and updated 2010. Reprinted January 2011.
Previously published as *The Great Britain Guide*.

Published by AA Publishing (a trading name of AA Media Limited, whose registered office is Fanum House,
Basing View, Basingstoke, Hampshire RG21 4EA; registered number 06112600).

 This product includes mapping data licensed from the Ordnance Survey® with the permission
of the Controller of Her Majesty's Stationery Office. ©Crown Copyright 2011. All rights reserved.
Licence number 100021153.

A04661

ISBN: 978-0-7495-6600-5
ISBN: 978-0-7495-6633-3 (The Works)
ISBN: 978-0-7495-6607-4 (Special Sales)
ISBN: 978-0-7495-6781-1 (Baker & Taylor)

A CIP catalogue record for this book is available from the British Library.

The contents of this book are believed to be correct at the time of printing. Nevertheless, the publishers cannot
be held responsible for any errors or omissions or for changes in the details given in this book or for the
consequences of any reliance on the information it provides. We have tried to ensure accuracy in this book, but
things do change and we would be grateful if readers would advise us of any inaccuracies they may encounter.
This does not affect your statutory rights.

We have taken all reasonable steps to ensure that the walks and cycle rides in this book are safe and achievable
by people with a realistic level of fitness. However, all outdoor activities involve a degree of risk and the publishers
accept no responsibility for any injuries caused to readers whilst following these walks and cycle rides. For advice
on walking and cycling in safety, see the walking and cycling in safety pages. Some of the information, walks, cycle
rides and tours may appear in other AA books and publications.

theAA.com/shop

Colour separation by AA Digital Department
Printed in China by Leo Paper Group

Title page images:
Opposite Dove Crag, Northumberland National Park
Previous Ladybower Reservoir, Peak District National Park

BRITAIN
The Ultimate Guide

CONTENTS

URQUHART CASTLE, LOCH NESS

SCOTLAND
1 CLACKMANNANSHIRE
2 DUNDEE
3 EAST AYRSHIRE
4 EAST DUNBARTONSHIRE
5 EAST LOTHIAN
6 EAST RENFREWSHIRE
7 EDINBURGH
8 FALKIRK
9 GLASGOW
10 INVERCLYDE
11 MIDLOTHIAN
12 NORTH LANARKSHIRE
13 RENFREWSHIRE
14 SOUTH AYRSHIRE
15 SOUTH LANARKSHIRE
16 WEST DUNBARTONSHIRE
17 WEST LOTHIAN

WALES
18 BLAENAU GWENT
19 BRIDGEND
20 CAERPHILLY
21 CARDIFF
22 ISLE OF ANGLESEY
23 MERTHYR TYDFIL
24 NEATH PORT TALBOT
25 NEWPORT
26 RHONDDA CYNON TAFF
27 TORFAEN
28 VALE OF GLAMORGAN

ENGLAND
29 BRISTOL
30 ISLE OF MAN
31 ISLE OF WIGHT
32 RUTLAND
33 TYNE & WEAR
34 WIRRAL

SOUTHWEST
SOUTHEAST
CENTRAL
WALES
NORTH
SCOTLAND

WESTERN ISLES

HIGHLANDS

MORAY

ABERDEEN

ABERDEENSHIRE

ANGUS

PERTH & KINROSS

ARGYLL & BUTE

STIRLING

1
2
8
7
5
17
11

16
4
10
13 9 12
6

NORTH AYRSHIRE

15

BORDERS

3

14

DUMFRIES & GALLOWAY

NORTHUMBERLAND

33

DURHAM

CUMBRIA

30

NORTH YORKSHIRE

EAST RIDING OF YORKSHIRE

LANCASHIRE

WEST YORKSHIRE

LIVERPOOL

GREATER MANCHESTER

SOUTH YORKSHIRE

34

22

CONWY

FLINTS

DENBGS

WREXHAM

CHESHIRE

DERBYS

NOTTS

LINCOLNSHIRE

GWYNEDD

STAFFS

SHROPSHIRE

LEICS

32

NORFOLK

POWYS

BIRMINGHAM

WORCS

WARWKS

NHANTS

CAMBS

SUFFOLK

CERDGN

HEREFS

BEDS

PEMBKS

CARMTH

GLOUCS

OXON

BUCKS

HERTS

ESSEX

SWANSEA

24
23 18
26 20 27
19 25
21
28

MONS

29

WILTSHIRE

BERKSHIRE

GREATER LONDON

SOMERSET

HAMPSHIRE

SURREY

KENT

DEVON

DORSET

WEST SUSSEX

EAST SUSSEX

31

CORNWALL

INTRODUCTION

BOSCOMBE BEACH, BOURNEMOUTH

Introduction

The abiding beauty of Britain is its astounding diversity and contrast, that and an ability to cram a huge amount into what is, comparatively, a small space. The whole country is not unlike a miniature work of art, in which the brush strokes detail its most minute aspects and set them against a rich background of history, tradition and heritage.

At one extreme, Britain – England, Scotland and Wales – has great swathes of largely uninhabited, sometimes bleak and barren, open moorland and rugged mountainous terrain, where those with a yearning for adventure and the 'outdoor' life have long found a welcome niche. At the other end of the scale, the country has arguably the richest heritage of stunning architectural buildings and striking monuments in the world covering many periods from prehistoric to modern and more than 20 of them have been awarded World Heritage Site status.

This matchless historical pedigree spans centuries, and in itself is one of the country's finest and most precious assets. Britain today exists as a country for all ages and all interests, and responds both to leisurely appreciation of its buildings and culture, as well as far more involved exploration on foot, cycle, horseback, in a car and even on the flotilla of boats and barges that gently cruise the country's inland canals and quiet waterways.

The mantle of history lies across the whole country from the striking pomp and circumstance of glittering ceremonial to the localised celebrations that commemorate less widely known causes and events. Take almost any part of Britain at random, and you will discover some defining moment in the calendar of Man's cultural and social awakening that occurred there: Kent saw the building of Canterbury cathedral, seat of the Anglican church in Britain; Oxford, the so-called 'City of the dreaming spires', was the foundation of nationwide higher education provision that today has no equal, and not a few stunning buildings and museums; Cumbria boasts the superb stone circle at Castlerigg, an ancient monument that pre-dates other circles like Stonehenge and Avebury, and is the birthplace and home-base of one of Britain's leading poets of the 19th century, William Wordsworth; Shropshire, and the Iron Bridge gorge in particular, carved by the Severn, Britain's longest river, has long been regarded as the cradle of the industrial revolution; Warwickshire is the home of the bard, William Shakespeare, and Worcestershire the birthplace of the great British composer, Edward Elgar; Glasgow, surprisingly, was the unlikeliest of places from which Britain's renowned and prized tea shop tradition arose, while the great castle at Caernarfon in North Wales, long resounding to a note of discord between the English and the Welsh, is nevertheless the site of investiture of the Princes of Wales and one of the finest castles in Britain.

ROCKFORD COMMON

The natural beauty of Britain is equally unrivalled, a compact miscellany of landscapes rich and verdant, gentle and inspiring, rugged and wild, and none more so than the coast, tormented and constantly fashioned by the Irish and North seas. In places subdued by the trappings of Victorian seaside leisure ideology, elsewhere the coast of Britain is untamed and simply breathtaking, from Land's End to John o'Groats. To follow the coast, along many stretches defined as 'heritage coast', is to experience a constantly changing scene, from Norfolk and Suffolk, around the white cliffs of Dover – where at South Foreland lighthouse Marconi tested the first ship-to-shore radio – along the undulating coast of the South Downs, around the sea cliffs of Cornwall and Devon, and by way of the shores of Pembrokeshire, Ceredigion and Gwynedd, to the Lake District and the superb but infrequently visited west coast of southern Scotland.

Further north, the borders of Scotland reach out to remote rugged headlands like Ardnamurchan, the westernmost point of Britain, and like much of what lies beyond serves to underline the fact that the British mainland is an island among many islands. Mull, Skye, the Western Isles, Orkney and Shetland are all a part of Britain, but have evolved their own cultures and traditions that are colourful threads in a remarkable and ancient tapestry.

Britain actively conserves and protects its landscape heritage through the mechanism of 15 National Parks. Forty smaller but no less vital areas have been designated as Areas of Outstanding Natural Beauty, an accolade that is not given lightly, and a description that means exactly what it says: the parks are beautiful, they are entirely natural and they are outstanding.

National Parks in contrast are not nationally owned, but rather parks for the nation, which are truly special places, each notably different from the others. The newest of them, the South Downs, created in 2010, and the New Forest, the smallest of all the national parks, in 2005. North of the border, the high tundra-like mountains and ancient pine woods of the Cairngorms were made a national park in 2003 only a year after the designation of the Loch Lomond National Park, a place of rolling lowland landscapes and high mountains with lochs and rivers, forests and woodlands.

The compactness of Britain brings another welcome dimension, that of ease of access. So well developed is Britain's air, road and rail infrastructure that there are few places that are not easily accessible, and those that remain are all the more rewarding for being just a little awkward to get to. Moreover, that accessibility continues throughout the year, and there are few parts of Britain that cannot be reached whatever the season.

Spring and autumn reveal natural Britain at its most colourful, the one with the burgeoning blues and greens of a ripening countryside, the other with the warm, golden hues that herald winter. Indeed winter snows may hinder exploration for a while, but such inconvenience is short-lived, and, in any case, adds a whole new quality to the year-round appreciation of a truly remarkable country.

This informative guide to Britain has everything you need for your visit, from walks and cycle rides to car tours complete with information along the way. There are details of the main annual events in each region and some great pubs and cosy tea rooms to stop at and enjoy the local fare. This guide will help you make the most of your trip.

WALKING & CYCLING IN SAFETY

WALKS & CYCLE RIDES

Each walk and cycle ride has a panel giving information for the walker and cyclist, including the distance, terrain, nature of the paths, and where to park your car.

WALKING

All of the walks are suitable for families, but less experienced family groups, especially those with younger children, should try the shorter walks. Route-finding is usually straightforward, but the maps are for guidance only and we recommend that you always take the relevant Ordnance Survey map with you.

RISKS

Although each walk has been researched with a view to minimizing any risks, no walk in the countryside can be considered to be completely free from risk. Walking in the outdoors will always require a degree of common sense and judgement to ensure that it is as safe as possible, especially for young children.

• Be particularly careful on cliff paths and in upland terrain, where the consequences of a slip can be serious.
• Remember to check tidal conditions before walking on the seashore.
• Some sections of route are by, or cross, busy roads. Remember traffic is a danger even on minor country lanes.
• Be careful around farmyard machinery and livestock.
• Be prepared for the consequences of changes in the weather and check the forecast before you set out.
• Ensure the whole family is properly equipped with suitable clothing and a good pair of boots or sturdy walking shoes.

• Take waterproof clothing with you and a torch if you are walking in the winter months.
• Remember the weather can change quickly at any time of the year, and in moorland and heathland areas, mist and fog can make route-finding much harder. In summer, take account of the heat and sun by wearing a hat and sunscreen, and carrying enough water.
• You should carry a mobile phone, whistle and, if possible, a survival bag on walks away from centres of population. If you do have an accident requiring emergency services, make a note of your position as accurately as possible and dial 999.

CYCLING

In devising the cycle rides in this guide, every effort has been made to use designated cycle paths, or to link them with quiet country lanes and waymarked byways and bridleways. In a few cases, some fairly busy B-roads have been used to join up with quieter routes.

RULES OF THE ROAD

• Ride in single file on narrow and busy roads.
• Be alert, look and listen for traffic, especially on narrow lanes and blind bends. Be extra careful when descending steep hills, as loose gravel or a poor road surface can lead to an accident.
• In wet weather make sure that you keep an appropriate distance between you and other riders.
• Make sure you indicate your intentions clearly.
• Brush up on The Highway Code before venturing out onto the road.

OFF-ROAD SAFETY CODE OF CONDUCT

• Only ride where you know it is legal to do so. Cyclists are not allowed to cycle on public footpaths, marked in yellow. The only 'rights of way' open to cyclists are bridleways (blue markers) and unsurfaced tracks, known as byways, which are open to all traffic and waymarked in red.
• Canal towpaths: you need a permit to cycle on some stretches of towpath (www.waterscape.com). Remember that access paths can be steep and slippery so always push your bike under low bridges and by locks.
• Always yield to walkers and horses, giving adequate warning of your approach, and dismount if necessary.
• Don't expect to cycle at high speeds.
• Keep to the main trail to avoid any unnecessary erosion to the area beside the trail and to prevent skidding, especially in wet weather conditions.
• Remember to follow the Country Code.

WALK & CYCLE RIDE MAP LEGEND

PREPARING YOUR BICYCLE

Check the wheels, tyres, brakes and cables. Lubricate hubs, pedals, gear mechanisms and cables. Make sure you have a puncture repair kit, pump, a bell, a rear rack to carry useful panniers, and a set of lights.

EQUIPMENT

• A cycling helmet provides essential protection.
• Make sure you are visible to other road users, by wearing light-coloured or luminous clothing in daylight and sashes or reflective strips in failing light and darkness.
• Take extra clothes with you, depending on the season, and a wind/waterproof jacket.
• Carry a basic tool kit, a pump, a strong lock and a simple first aid kit.
• Always carry enough water for your outing.
• Tell somebody of your planned route.

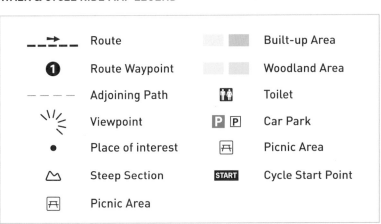

Route			Built-up Area
Route Waypoint			Woodland Area
Adjoining Path			Toilet
Viewpoint			Car Park
Place of interest			Picnic Area
Steep Section			Cycle Start Point
Picnic Area			

QUEEN ELIZABETH COUNTRY PARK, HAMPSHIRE

Southwest England

Southwest England

The West Country of Britain is a land of diverse terrain that stretches from the hills and vales of the Mendip Hills in the east to the tip of the Cornish peninsula that points west out to the big rollers of the Atlantic, not forgetting the flower-filled meadows of the Isles of Scilly, and the rugged moors of Dartmoor and Exmoor in between.

Parts of its coastline, stretching from Devon to Dorset, bears witness to prehistoric times with the fossil-strewn Jurassic coast, and there is evidence of ancient civilisations dotted all over the countryside. Inland, Somerset is famous for the delicious cider that has been produced here for hundreds of years and the Cotswolds dotted with picture-postcard villages of pale stone-built cottages.

Cities, towns and villages of note include Exeter, with its grand cathedral, and Plymouth, famous for its noble seafaring history and architecture influenced by wealthy merchants, to St Ives, threaded with a labyrinth of small cobbled streets and Selworthy, in Somerset, renowned for its many lovely thatched cottages set amid woodland.

Wherever you go in this part of the region you'll see marvellous contrasts in its beautiful and varied countryside, find fantastic beaches and resorts, and travel through market towns and tiny villages where West Country traditions are still upheld.

Cornwall

CLOCKWISE FROM TOP LEFT: NEWQUAY HARBOUR; WATERGATE; MULLION COVE; WHIPSIDDERY

BEDRUTHAN STEPS MAP REF 398 D6

Access to the beach at Bedruthan has been difficult over the years because of the crumbling nature of the cliffs, but the National Trust has built a secure stairway from the clifftop at Carnewas. The famous 'Steps' are the weathered rock stacks that stand in bold isolation amidst the sand. Bedruthan Steps are the result of sea erosion on the caves and arches in the friable slate cliffs. According to local legend, a mythical giant, Bedruthan, was reputed to use the stacks as stepping stones; but to nowhere in particular it seems. There is a National Trust shop and café on the clifftop in what was the office building of the old Carnewas iron mine. This is a delightful spot to indulge, as cream teas and other Cornish treats are the order of the day.

BODMIN MOOR MAP REF 398 E6

Cornwall's largest area of high moorland has been bisected by the A30, but the moor falls naturally into contrasting east and west sectors. The eastern side seems less wild and rugged than the undulating hills and rocky ridges of Brown Willy and Rough Tor to the west, while around the remote village of Minions it has all the raw beauty of wild country. The moor has been torn apart in places. The ragged, gaping hole of Cheesewring Quarry above Minions is the result of a moorland industry that was as vigorous as the copper mining

industry that left behind great engine houses like nearby Phoenix United Mine. Cheesewring's granite was used to build Devonport Dockyard, Birkenhead Docks and part of Copenhagen Harbour, and was included in the materials used in the Thames Embankment and Westminster and Tower bridges. The quarry's name comes from the remarkable formation of layered granite that stands at its western edge, named after its similarity to a cider press used to squeeze the 'cheese' or juice from apples. It is formed by erosion of the weaker horizontal joints in the granite.

Close to the southwestern edge of the quarry is the reconstructed cave dwelling of Daniel Gumb, who was a stone-cutter in the 18th century. He built a much larger original cave dwelling here for himself and his family. Gumb was blessed with considerable intellectual gifts. He was known as 'the Mountain Philosopher' and was said to be well versed in astronomy and mathematics. Gumb's original cave was destroyed in the 1870s when Cheesewring Quarry was extended, but the roof of the present one is part of the original and has on its surface a carving of one of Euclid's theorems. Minions Heritage Centre, in a Cornish engine house, has displays on the history of the landscape from the Stone Age up until the present day.

Bodmin Moor is much older than its mining industry. Close to Minions village is a cluster of interesting early Bronze

Age (2500–1500 BC) monuments, including the stone circles of the Hurlers and their adjacent standing stones. Craddock Moor to the west is peppered with burial mounds from the Bronze Age, hut circles of the Iron Age, and medieval field systems. North of Minions is Twelve Men's Moor and the rocky ridges of Kilmar Tor and Bearah Tor. Further north, a broad sweep of moorland runs through marshy ground to Fox Tor and then washes up against the asphalt boundary of the A30. To the west, the River Fowey flows from near Bolventor and Jamaica Inn, through a long, shallow valley. There are reservoirs with the characteristics of natural lakes at Colliford and Siblyback, and where the Fowey turns to the west at Draynes Bridge it pours through deep woods and moss-shrouded boulders at Golitha Falls. North of Minions, the moor drops suddenly into the deeply wooded valley of the River Lynher, with peaceful hillside villages, such as North Hill.

BUDE MAP REF 398 E5

There are few more exhilarating beaches than Bude's Summerleaze when the sea rolls on to the sand in long, unbroken waves. The Bude Canal shaped much of the immediate hinterland of Bude Harbour and is now a popular attraction for boating, walking and watching wildlife. The canal was built in the early 19th century to carry calcium-rich sand to inland farms,

where it was used to enrich the soil. Bude Canal reached nearly to Launceston, but its full potential was never realized and its use declined by the middle of the 19th century. Much of the history of the canal is illustrated in the Bude-Stratton Museum at the Old Forge on the Lower Wharf.

Bude is a busy, friendly town – The Strand and Belle Vue are the main shopping streets. There is a good visitor centre in the car park near the harbour. A series of easily accessible and attractive beaches stretches north from Bude: Crooklets, Northcott Mouth and Sandy Mouth. The last two are almost covered at high tide. There are some pleasant walks along the coast path to the north where the clifftop area is level, cropped grassland. To the south of Bude, via a scenic road, is the vast expanse of Widemouth Bay.

Bude has few traditional buildings. The town evolved in the 19th century from a small fishing port through the grafting on of functional buildings, first for commerce, then for tourism. Just inland is Stratton. This medieval market town with a history that pre-dates Anglo-Saxon times was once the chief settlement of the area.

CADGWITH MAP REF 398 D8

Thatched and slate-roofed cottages crowd together at Cadgwith between encroaching hillsides and cliffs. A slim shingle beach runs to either side of a rocky promontory called the Todden. Cadgwith is best visited

CADGWITH

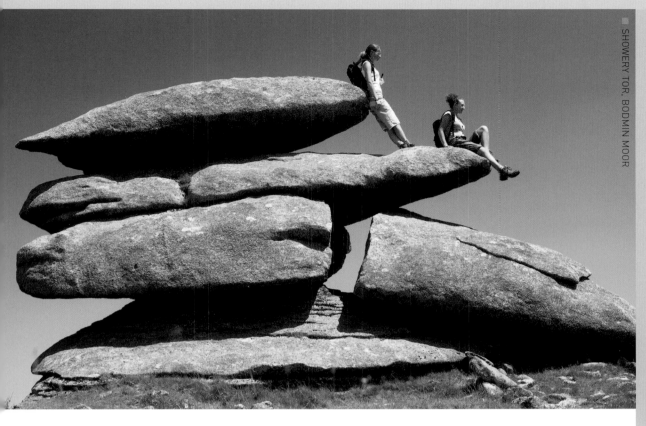

SHOWERY TOR, BODMIN MOOR

Visit
KIT HILL
The magnificent granite dome of Kit Hill rises to just over 1,000 feet (305m) above the town of Callington, about 4 miles (6.4km) northwest of Calstock. It stands in splendid isolation, as if torn between the granite masses of Bodmin Moor to the west and Dartmoor to the east. For centuries Kit Hill was quarried for stone and delved into for tin, copper, zinc, lead and even silver, but it is now a country park. The hill is crowned by an 80-foot (24m) chimney stack built in 1858 as part of the engine house of the Kithill Consols mine. There are several pathways around the hill, including both a waymarked walking trail and a pleasant heritage trail.

Activity
FALMOUTH AFLOAT
Various river and sea cruises are available from Falmouth's Prince of Wales Pier and from other boarding points around the estuary. Ferries leave for Flushing and St Mawes, and when the tide allows, there are cruises upriver to Malpas from where a five-minute bus ride connects with Truro. There are also trips along the coast and then up the Helford River; evening cruises on the Fal are another option, especially during the summer months, along with sea-angling trips from the Prince of Wales Pier.

Visit
LIZARD LAKES
Cornwall has few natural lakes but there are some reservoirs. The Argal Waterpark and College is about 2 miles (3km) from Falmouth along the A394. The reservoir is tree-fringed and peaceful, with much birdlife and paths skirting the shoreline. Coarse fishing is available all year and the fly-fishing season is from March to October. Stithians Lake is also within easy reach of Falmouth and Helston along the A394. There is a car park on the east side of the lake near the dam and another situated at its north end.

Activity
OTTER SANCTUARY
The Tamar Otter Park and Wildlife Centre is in North Petherwin, which is reached by turning west off the B3254 at Langdon Cross, about 3 miles (4.8km) north of Launceston. Here, the Otter Trust's aim is to rehabilitate and breed otters for introduction to the wild. Dormice and several species of deer feature here also.

---

on foot; there is a car park on the high ground above the village, from where a path leads down to the village. Fishing boats still work from Cadgwith's beach, where pilchards were once landed in vast quantities until the decline of the fishery in the early 20th century. Today Cadgwith's many fishermen use inkwell-shaped pots to catch lobster and crab, and gill nets to catch cod, pollack, monkfish and other species. The old buildings, known as cellers, where the pilchards were salted and pressed for oil, have been carefully converted for modern use.

The small building on the cliff to the north of the cove was a coastguard watch house that was built more than 100 years ago. The coast path to the south of Cadgwith (with the sea on your left) leads to the spectacular Devil's Frying-Pan, a huge gulf in the vegetated cliffs where a sea cave collapsed centuries ago leaving an arch of rock connecting both sides.

The rugged Lizard area is especially noted for the extensive variety and value of its plant life. Pink thrift, the powder-blue squill, cliff bluebells and kidney vetch grow in profusion here, but seemingly insignificant-looking plants may well be rare and vulnerable. Visitors are asked not to pick even the most prolific wild flowers and to take care while walking.

CRACKINGTON HAVEN MAP REF 398 E5
The mighty and dramatic bulwark of cliff at Crackington is best viewed from the southern approach. It seems to dwarf the cove and beach, its twisted and folded shale mellowed by swathes of grass and sedge. Crackington was a haven of sorts during

the 19th century, but it was a port in the most basic sense – small vessels simply ran on to the sand as the tide dropped to offload coal and to load slates.

The coast path from Crackington Haven leads north to Castle Point. Take a deep breath for the climb out of the cove. There are the remnants of Iron Age embankments at Castle Point. A mile or so further on is Dizzard Point, where an old oak wood clings to the slopes.

FALMOUTH MAP REF 398 D8
Vessels of all types and sizes still bustle in and out of Falmouth harbour, lending excitement and atmosphere to one of the world's largest natural harbours. Falmouth developed as a port after Henry VIII built Pendennis and St Mawes castles, the guardians of the Fal Estuary. Both are built in the distinctive clover-leaf design and St Mawes is renowned as a fine example of military architecture. Visitors here can explore the dungeons, barrack rooms and cannon-lined castle walls.

During the late 17th century the port became a packet station, from where small, fast-sailing brigantines took mail to northwest Spain, and in later years as far as North America, the West Indies and South America. Gold and silver bullion was carried and the packets provided a passenger service. By the 1830s over 40 packets worked out of Falmouth. They were well-armed against privateers, French naval hostility and even Algerian pirates. The crews supplemented their meagre wages with smuggling and by carrying unofficial goods; tales of swashbuckling abound. The packet service

had transferred to Southampton by 1850 but Falmouth's position as a major port was secured by a vigorous pilchard fishery, the development of Falmouth docks and a thriving shipbuilding industry. Ship repair, bunkering, cargo handling and yacht-building industries still continue today.

Falmouth's rather straggling form gives it less unity than might be expected of a port, as the town follows the riverside through a chain of linking main streets, but this makes it intriguing to explore. It is centred on The Moor, once just a muddy creek and now emphatically urban, and it is here that you will find the Falmouth Art Gallery, well worth a visit, on the upper floor of the old Passmore Edwards Free Library. As well as changing exhibitions there are permanent displays of paintings including those of Henry Scott Tuke, the Victorian painter who spent his last years near Falmouth. From The Moor, Webber Street leads to the Prince of Wales Pier.

Some of Falmouth's many engaging features include the 111-step Jacob's Ladder that leads up from The Moor, and watch out for the recurring theme of Falmouth's 'Opes', the passageways running between the town's buildings.

The National Maritime Museum Cornwall, on Falmouth's busy waterfront, includes the delightful National Small Boat Collection of more than one hundred boats. There is also a unique tidal gallery with windows that reveal the rise and fall of the tide, and breathtaking views across Falmouth Harbour from the top of a 95-foot (29m) tower. Use the aptly-named Park & Float in summer and sail over to the museum on a classic ferry.

FOWEY

FOWEY MAP REF 398 E7

Buildings crowd out Fowey's waterfront but there is a wonderful sense of unity within the jumble of narrow streets and there is access to the harbour and quay from various points. Fowey (pronounced 'Foy') was a major port from the earliest times. More than 700 seamen from the town and its surrounding parishes took part in the Siege of Calais in 1346, when the town supplied 47 vessels compared to London's 25. In return, Fowey was attacked and burnt by the French in 1380 and in 1467. It was the Port of Cornwall in every sense and its seamen earned the title 'the Fowey Gallants'. These outstanding sailors were known for their arrogance and contempt for the law, and their energies soon turned to lucrative piracy. When Edward IV took a grip on the port, Fowey turned to equally

lucrative, but honest, trade. China clay and the enterprise of the Treffry family brought prosperity, and today ocean-going ships pass upriver to Golant' quays from where clay is still exported.

Fowey draws you in from the long descent of Lostwithiel Street to Trafalgar Square, then on round the Town Quay and Webb Street. The buildings crowd in from all sides and even the dark-stoned Church of St Fimbarrus with its decorated tower seems to overhang.

The true face of Fowey is seen from the river or from Polruan on the opposite shore. Tall houses rise sheer from the waterfront, and when night falls in summer the boat-bobbing river is starred with lights. From the bottom of Lostwithiel Street, the Esplanade leads southwest to Readymoney Cove, where a small

sandy beach lies below tree-shrouded St Catherine's Point. St Catherine's Castle crowns the Point; built between 1538 and 1542 as part of the chain of defences set up along the coast by Henry VIII in response to hostility from France and the Holy Roman Empire. The castle can be reached up steep steps from the beach or by a leisurely track.

Driving through Fowey should be avoided at the busiest times. The main car park at the entrance to the town is signed from the A3082. You will find a good mix of shops lining the bustling streets, along with fine galleries, craft and antique shops. Fowey's pubs are full of a sea-going atmosphere and there are several good restaurants. The museum is in the town hall at Trafalgar Square and the Tourist Information Centre is at the far end of Fore Street.

Overlooking the town is Place, the historic home of the Treffry family (not open to the public). The original 15th-century house was rebuilt in Regency Gothic style during the 19th century and it is certainly a delightfully eccentric building. Impressive, tree-shrouded Golant lies 1.5 miles (2.4km) north of Fowey and is reached from the B3269. In this charming village the small but absorbing Church of St Sampson commemorates one of Cornwall's great Celtic saints.

GORRAN HAVEN MAP REF 398 D7

Gorran Haven lies just south of Mevagissey at the seaward end of a shallow valley. A labyrinth of narrow, steep lanes and passageways climbs from the harbour and an intriguing little chapel built on solid rock dates from the 15th century. South of Gorran Haven, the mighty Dodman Point thrusts its bull's head into the seaway. The Dodman, as it is commonly known, is 373 feet (114m) high. The Iron Age earthworks that enclose the seaward area of the Dodman are more than 2,000 feet (609m) long and 20 feet (6m) high.

GRIBBIN HEAD MAP REF 398 E7

Southwest of Fowey, Gribbin Head (National Trust) shoulders out the western sea preventing it from having too much influence on sheltered Fowey. The headland, always referred to by locals as The Gribbin, is crowned with a bizarre monolith – the 84-ft (25m) Daymark tower painted in barber-shop red and white. The Daymark was erected in 1832 in order to distinguish The Gribbin from St Anthony's Head at the entrance to Falmouth Bay. The two headlands look similar from the seaward approach and sailors regularly mistook The Gribbin for St Anthony's Head, with catastrophic results when they sailed blindly into the shallows

of St Austell Bay instead of the safer, deep waters of Falmouth Bay.

Inland of The Gribbin is Menabilly, where author Daphne du Maurier made her home and drew on her surroundings for inspiration for a number of her novels. In the eastern shelter of The Gribbin is Polridmouth Cove, with adjoining beaches and an ornamental lake.

The Gribbin can be reached on foot from a car park at Menabilly Barton, a mile (1.6km) inland. To the west, the tiny Polkerris faces into St Austell Bay. There is a car park halfway down the tree-shaded approach, from where it is just a short walk to the pleasant beach.

HELFORD MAP REF 398 D8

There is irresistible romance attached to Helford and its tree-shrouded river and creeks. The price is that the area can become uncomfortably busy during popular holiday periods. Lovely though the village is, the dense nature of this serene landscape rewards those who explore further than Helford itself. The countryside is more tame, compared with the extremes of the coast, and though access along the riverbank is limited in places, there are a number of fine walks to be enjoyed from Helford.

To the west lies Frenchman's Creek, romanticized by both authors Sir Arthur Quiller-Couch and Daphne du Maurier and still enchanting today, even when the falling tide reveals a plain of mud. A path leads east from Helford to the coast at Dennis Head and to St Anthony and Gillan, with great views over to Falmouth. These quiet places are best visited on foot as parking spaces are difficult to find.

A seasonal passenger ferry from Helford sails to Helford Passage on the north bank, from where the National Trust's Glendurgan Garden and the adjacent Trebah Garden can be visited. Glendurgan is one of the great subtropical gardens of the Southwest, situated on the banks of the Helford River near Mawnan Smith. Hydrangeas, camellias and rhododendrons flourish amidst lovely woodland and there is an engaging maze. Trebah Garden has, among its attractions, a fine water garden. The smaller garden at Penjerrick, just over a mile (1.6km) north of Mawnan Smith, is where Chilean firebushes, magnolias, with their delicate blooms, and azaleas flourish.

ISLES OF SCILLY MAP REF 398 A8

The Isles of Scilly are famously known as the 'Fortunate Islands' or the 'Sunshine Islands'. These ancient islands deserve the superlatives, though their beauty and uniqueness require no exaggeration.

The hundred or so islands and islets that make up the archipelago lie just 28 miles (45km) west-southwest of Land's End as the crow flies. Only five islands are inhabited – St Agnes, Bryher, St Mary's, St Martin's, and Tresco – and together they offer a rare combination of seascapes, golden beaches and crystal-clear sea, with quiet green corners inland.

Bryher lies amidst the northwestern group of islands that include Tresco. It is 1.5 miles (2.4km) long and barely half a mile (0.8km) across at its widest point. Bryher faces Tresco across the narrow channel of New Grimsby Sound and island life is focused on the beaches that fringe the Sound. Here boats draw up at a granite quay, or at the jetty, built as one of Anneka Rice's famous television 'challenges' to extend landing times on Bryher and now known as 'Annequay'.

Just over 1 mile (1.6km) wide, is the island of St Agnes. This island has a special atmosphere of serenity. It is the most southerly of the group and is separated from St Mary's by the deep water channel of St Mary's Sound. The Turk's Head Inn and the Post Office are at the hub of the community. To the east the main island is

linked by a narrow sandbar to the smaller tidal 'island' of Gugh and off its western shore is the protected bird island of Annet. Further out to sea, beyond Annet lie the dramatic Western Rocks – reefs that end at the Bishop Rock Lighthouse.

The most northerly island in the group, St Martin's, is 2 miles (3.2km) in length and just over half a mile (800m) wide. Landing on St Martin's can be adventurous at certain states of the tide, when walking the plank to reach the sandy shore from launches is necessary. Walking here is exhilarating, though the lure of magnificent beaches such as Great Bay on St Martin's northern shore tends to distract.

St Mary's is the largest of the Isles of Scilly. Its main settlement of Hugh Town is the marine metropolis of the islands, and it is from Hugh Town Quay that the passenger launches leave for the exciting sea trips that are an essential part of holidaying on Scilly. There are beaches on the north and south side of Hugh Town, the southern bay of Porth Cressa being particularly delightful. A footpath follows the coastline for a 9-mile (14.5km) circuit, passing several well-preserved prehistoric sites on the way. Early flower

growing developed in Scilly from the late 1860s. Daffodils and narcissi are still exported from the islands, but the trade has declined in recent years.

Attractive Tresco lies at the sheltered heart of the islands. It is much more of a show-place than the rest of Scilly, a private domain where there is an atmosphere of carefully regulated life and of gentle pace. The exquisite subtropical gardens surrounding Tresco Abbey House are the main focus of the island. A priory to St Nicholas was established by Benedictine monks during the 12th century; the scant ruins which remain are now incorporated into the Abbey Gardens, where examples of Burmese Honeysuckle, Australian Scarlet Bottle-brush, gigantic ice plants, Aloes, Dracaenas, Mimosa, and a host of other exotics line the terraced pathways. Tresco has a heliport from where connections can be made to Penzance. Dogs must be kept on leads on Tresco.

KYNANCE COVE MAP REF 398 C8

Victorian visitors first visited Kynance with their painting kits and sketch books, and the cove was visited by a poet, Tennyson, and a prince, Albert. Kynance satisfied

perfectly the romantic ideal of the picturesque in Nature. The whole of the beach is awash at high tide and emerges fresh and shining as each day dawns. Huge gnarled monoliths of serpentine rock that rise up from the beach create a beautiful seascape. One of the largest of these is Asparagus Island, with Steeple Rock and the Sugar Loaf lying between it and the mainland. For some, part of the charm of Kynance lies in its unexpectedness, hidden as it is below the flatness of the Lizard Peninsula.

The cove and the cliff land to the east are in the care of the National Trust, which has provided a car park above Kynance and a viewpoint for visitors with disabilities. Descent to the cove is steep, and the return is quite strenuous. Care should be taken if swimming off the cove – the tide comes in rapidly and the currents close to shore are dangerous.

The Kynance area is of great biological importance. Rare species grow in the area, including sedges and tiny liverworts. Spiders, moths and even a rare European woodlouse are also found here. The mild climate and a maritime environment partly explain the diversity of the local wildlife.

LANHYDROCK MAP REF 398 E7

Magnificent Lanhydrock lies about 2.5 miles (4km) north of Lostwithiel via the B3268, or can be reached from Bodmin via the A30. It is approached along an avenue of stately beech trees, which leads through the beautiful parkland. On first sight the house gives every impression of being wholly Tudor. In fact, all that remains of the original house, built between 1630 and 1642 for wealthy Truro merchant Sir Richard Robartes, is the gatehouse, entrance porch and north wing. The east wing was removed, and the rest fell victim to a terrible fire in 1881, but the house was rebuilt to match the surviving part. The interiors are very grand, notably the Long Gallery, and there are lavish furnishings throughout the house. Of all the 50 rooms that are open, visitors tend to find the 'below stairs' sections of most interest, including the kitchen, larders, bakehouse, dairy, cellars and servants' quarters.

Lanhydrock is surrounded by beautiful grounds, with some pleasant rides and paths to stroll along. Adjoining the house are formal gardens with clipped yews and bronze urns, while the higher garden is famed for its lovely magnolias and magnificent rhododendron blooms.

LISKEARD MAP REF 398 E7

With Bodmin Moor to the north, and Looe to the south, Liskeard makes an ideal choice as a holiday centre. Liskeard was a Coinage town from medieval times and Coinage endowed the town with a status and prosperity that encouraged other business; copper mining during the 19th century further increased the town's wealth. When mining declined, Liskeard continued to thrive as the important focus point of road and rail communications throughout east Cornwall and is still the northern terminus of the branch railway that connects with Looe.

Today Liskeard's attractive townscape reflects its prosperous history. The streets, quite narrow in places, are flanked by tall buildings. Fine individual examples include the notable Victorian Webb's Hotel, hip-roofed and stolid, which overlooks the Parade, whilst the Guildhall's Italianate tower dominates Market Street. In Well Lane, off Market Street, is the ancient Pipe Well; unfortunately, the water is now considered unfit to drink and the well is gated. Liskeard's Church of St Martin, the second largest church in Cornwall after St Petroc's at Bodmin, suffered some heavy-handed Victorian restoration and is rather dull because of it. Liskeard is a busy shopping centre, in keeping with its commercial traditions. On market days, the country comes to town, bringing a refreshing bustle to the streets.

LIZARD PENINSULA MAP REF 398 D8

The Lizard Downs are rich in ancient artefacts that date from a time when early man found reasonable grazing on this area's poorly drained soil. The serpentine soil also supports a remarkable variety of rare plants. The Lizard's mild climate encourages these plants but the main reason for the area's unique botanical nature is that the Lizard was joined to the European land mass thousands of years ago, when these plants spread effortlessly and flourished on what are now the peninsula's coastal fringes.

There are subtle distinctions between species and a specialist's knowledge is required to identify many of the plants, but everyone can recognize and enjoy the attractive Cornish Heath, Erica Vagans, a type of heather found in substantial quantities only on The Lizard. It has dark green leaves and spikes of small pink or lilac flowers. Closer to the clifftops, blue spring squill, pink thrift and sea campion contribute to a mosaic of wild flowers in spring and summer.

Lizard village is a convenient base from which to explore Lizard Point, the most southerly point in Britain, and its adjoining coastline. You can park at the Point, where there is an old lifeboat station that has long been superseded by the modern station at Kilcobben Cove situated to the northeast. The view seaward is exhilarating and the air can be mild even in midwinter, but when the tide is out, swathes of pungent smelling seaweed may dull the edge of the bracing sea air. Choughs returned to breed in Cornwall on Lizard Point in 2001 after an absence of more than 50 years and the RSPB operates a Chough Watchpoint in spring. The coast path leads west above high cliffs. To the east the path passes through a green, sheltered landscape above cliffs draped with the invasive Hottentot Fig, or mesembryanthemum.

The Lizard's position has long made it dangerous to seagoing vessels. For a mile (1.6km) seaward off Lizard Point the sea tumbles in frightening overfalls during stormy weather. To the northeast lies the promontory of Black Head and beyond here the deadly Manacles Reef.

The Lizard Lighthouse dominates the coast to the east. A warning light was first established here in 1612. Today's powerful light flashes every three seconds and can be seen in clear weather from up to 29 miles (46.7km) away. The fog signal is delivered by siren every 60 seconds.

About 1.5 miles (2.4km) east of Lizard Point is Church Cove, and its attractive little church of Landewednack. The cove is reached on foot from the car park past thatched cottages. A short walk south along the coast path takes you straight to the remarkable cliffside site of the Lizard-Cadgwith lifeboat house.

LIZARD POINT

LOOE MAP REF 398 E7

Tourism came early to Looe. It is said that the bathing machine came to Looe beach as early as 1800, when war with France sent the leisured classes to southwest England in search of a home-grown alternative to French resorts. But it was the arrival of the railway that led to the growth of the tourism that sustains Looe today.

The old town of East Looe is a delight. There is something of a French style in its ordered layout and in the way that the tall buildings seem to accentuate the narrowness of streets and passageways. The houses are painted in a variety of colours. The old pilchard-curing cellars by the quay are built from unadorned stone and many of the cottages have an outside stone staircase indicating that the ground floors were used as pilchard processing cellars and net stores. There is an interesting museum of local history in the Old Guildhall in Higher Market Street. Looe is Cornwall's second largest fishing port and the fishing industry brings a maritime bustle to the harbour and quayside at East Looe. Looe's viewpoint, Banjo Pier, can be reached from the quay and the East Looe Bay beach adjoins it.

West Looe was always the smaller settlement. It has a lovely outlook across the harbour to East Looe and the older parts of the town around Fore Street and Princes Square have some pleasant features. There is a big car park on the west side of the river at Millpool, where there is a Discovery Centre.

The delightful Kilminorth Woods are reached easily from the Millpool car park. Waymarked walks lead through a splendid oak wood and alongside the West Looe River. The woods and river are rich in plant, insect and bird life. These include herons, which nest in the trees on the opposite bank. Further information can be obtained at the Discovery Centre.

ALONG BUDE BAY

The windswept coastal grasslands of north Cornwall seem unlikely havens for plant life, but, around Bude, the cliff edges especially provide a unique refuge for wild flowers. This walk follows the flat cliff land north of Bude with an inland section on the return. Along the way you'll find numerous wild flowers that turn the cliff-top into a riot of colour in spring and early summer, and butterflies. Look out for the meadow brown, probably Britain's commonest butterfly, the common blue, a small butterfly with an almost lilac tinge, and for the glamorous painted lady, with its tawny-orange wings and black and white markings.

DISTANCE/TIME 5 miles (8km) 2h30 **MAP** OS Explorers 111 Bude, Boscastle & Tintagel and 126 Clovelly & Hartland **START** Crooklets Beach car park; grid ref: SS 204071 **PATHS** Excellent throughout. Grassy coast path, field paths and metalled lanes **THE PUB** The Inn on the Green, Flexbury. Tel: 01288 356013

1 From Crooklets Beach car park, go towards the beach, turn right to cross a bridge and head for some steps. Pass behind some beach huts, then turn left along a stony track between walls. Go up some steps and on to the coast path, signposted 'Maer Cliff'. Follow the coast path.

2 Go through a gate then along a track behind a white building, called Northcott House. Bear off to the left, by a signpost, down a path to reach the sea at Northcott Mouth beach. From here, bear right along a track that will take you back inland, past a group of houses on the left, and continue uphill to pass some more houses.

3 Where the track bends round to the right, leave it and keep ahead to a gateway. Keep walking along a banked bridle path ahead.

4 Reach a field gate and follow a track through fields. Keep ahead at a junction with another track, then continue to a T-junction with a public road. Turn left and walk down the road, with care, to Sandy Mouth.

5 Pass the National Trust information kiosk and descend towards the beach, then go left and uphill and follow the coast path back to Northcott Mouth beach, and a lifeguard hut passed earlier on your route.

6 Follow the roadside path just past the lifeguard hut and then retrace your steps towards Northcott House, which you passed earlier. Go along the track behind the building and then keep ahead along a broad track with a field hedge on your left.

7 As buildings come into view ahead, turn left over a stile with a footpath sign in a wall corner. Follow the field-edge ahead into a hedged-in path. Continue walking between trees to a lane by a house at Rosemerrin. Continue until you reach the road.

8 Turn right along the road, with Maer Lake Nature Reserve down to your left. Follow the road to a crossroads and turn right to return to the car park.

AROUND CADGWITH

This wandering route between coast and countryside leads inland to the sleepy village of Ruan, from where a narrow lane leads down to the Poltesco Valley. From Carleon Cove the coast path is followed pleasantly to the tiny fishing village of Cadgwith. Beyond the village the coast path leads to the Devil's Frying Pan, a vast gulf in the cliffs caused by the collapse of a large section of coast. From here the path closely follows the edge of the steep cliffs before turning inland to the Church of the Holy Cross at Grade. Beyond the church is the ancient St Ruan's Well and the road back to the start of this ramble.

DISTANCE/TIME 4.5 miles (7.2km) 3h **MAP** OS Explorer 103 The Lizard **START** Cadgwith car park, about 350 yards (320m) from Cadgwith. Busy in summer; grid ref: SW 720146 **PATHS** Good although coast path occasionally rocky in places. Rock can be slippery when wet **THE PUB** The Cadgwith Cove Inn, Cadgwith Cove. Tel: 01326 290513; www.cadgwithcoveinn.com

1 Go left along a grassy ride below the car park, to reach a stile. Continue through a gate and into woodland. Turn right at a lane, then on the corner, go up a track and continue to the main road at Ruan Minor.

2 Go left and, just beyond the shop, turn left down a surfaced path. Rejoin the main road by a thatched cottage (there are toilets just before the road). Cross diagonally right, then go down a lane past the Church of St Ruan.

3 In 0.3 mile (500m), just past an old mill and a bridge, go right at a T-junction to reach the car park at Poltesco. From the far end of the car park follow a track, signposted 'Carleon Cove'. Go right at a junction.

4 Go over a wooden bridge above the cove, then turn left at a T-junction and again turn left in 0.25 mile (400m) where the path branches. Go through a kissing gate and continue along the cliff-edge path to Cadgwith. At the road, turn left.

5 Follow a narrow path, which is signposted 'Coast Path'. By a house gateway, go left up a surfaced path, signposted 'Devil's Frying Pan'. At an open area turn left, pass Townplace Cottage, cross a meadow and reach the Devil's Frying Pan itself.

6 Keep on the coast path and at a junction, just past a chalet studio, follow a path inland to a T-junction with a rough track. Turn left and then, at a public lane, go left again and after 0.5 mile (800m) turn right along a track to Grade Church.

7 Follow the left-hand field-edge behind the church, then go over a stile into the next field to reach a lane. St Ruan's Well is opposite diagonally left. Turn right for 200yds (182m), then branch off right between stone pillars to return to the car park at Cadgwith.

A COASTAL ROUTE FROM CRACKINGTON HAVEN

Crackington Haven has given its name to a geological phenomenon, the Crackington Formation, a fractured shale that has been shaped into contorted forms. Along the open cliff south from Crackington the remarkable geology unfolds. Looking back from Bray's Point, you see the contortions in the high cliff face of Pencannow Point on the north side. Soon the path leads above Tremoutha Haven and up to the cliff edge beyond the headland of Cambeak. A short distance further on you arrive above Strangles Beach, where again you look back to such fantastic features as Northern Door. The second part of the walk turns inland and descends into East Wood and the peaceful Trevigue Valley, much of which is a nature reserve.

1 From the Crackington Haven car park entrance go left across a bridge, and then turn right at a telephone kiosk. Follow the broad track round to the left, between a signpost and an old wooden seat, then go through kissing gate on to the coast path, signed 'Cambeak'.

2 Eventually, a stile leads to steep stepped descent to the footbridges below Cambeak and a path junction. Keep to the left and follow the path up a sheltered valley on the inland side of the steep hill, then continue walking straight ahead along the cliff path.

3 Where a stretch of low inland cliffs begins, pass a coast path post marked 'Trevigue'. Turn left at the next path to reach a road by a National Trust sign for 'The Strangles'.

4 Go left, walking past a farm entrance to Trevigue, then, in just a few paces, turn right

down a drive by the Trevigue sign. Then bear off to the left to walk across grass and go through a gate with a yellow arrow.

5 Go directly down the field, keeping left of a telegraph pole, to reach a stile. Continue walking downhill to reach a stile on the edge of a wood. Continue walking down the tree-shaded path to reach a junction of paths in a shady dell by the river.

6 Turn sharp left here, following a signpost towards Haven, and continue on the obvious path down to reach the wooded river valley.

7 Cross a footbridge, then turn left at a junction with a track. Cross another footbridge, and continue to a gate by some houses. Follow the track and then a surfaced lane to reach the main road. Turn left to reach the car park.

DISTANCE/TIME 3.5 miles (5.6km) 1h45 **MAP** OS Explorer 111 Bude, Boscastle & Tintagel **START** Crackington Haven car park or Burden Trust car park, along B3263 to Wainhouse; grid ref: SX 145969 **PATHS** Good coastal footpath and woodland tracks. Can be very wet and muddy **THE PUB** The Coombe Barton Inn, Crackington Haven. Tel: 01840 230345

WALK 4

FROM FOWEY TO POLKERRIS

Explore the coast and countryside near Fowey – also known as Daphne du Maurier country. The walk starts from Readymoney Cove and follows inland lanes and tracks and then the coastal path, where a minor roller-coaster hike takes you to St Catherine's Point. There is then a steep descent back to to Readymoney Cove.

1 From the bottom end of the car park walk down St Catherine's Parade and then turn right towards Readymoney Cove. Continue walking to the end of the road, above the beach, and then follow the rocky Love Lane up on Saints Way. Go past the first junction, ignoring the options by an NT sign for 'Covington Woods'.

2 Turn left at the next junction and then climb up some wooden steps to reach Allday's Fields. Follow the right-hand field-edge and, at a field gap, follow an obvious grassy track ahead to reach a lane end at Coombe Farm. Continue walking to follow the lane ahead.

3 At a road, turn right and continue walking to Lankelly Farm. Pass a junction on the right and then follow Prickly Post Lane for a few paces. Turn off left on to a gravel drive, then keep to the left and walk along a narrow fenced-in path.

4 After the barn conversions at Trenant, cross the lane, then a stile. Keep ahead alongside the field-edge and follow the path to a kissing gate into the field below Tregaminion Farm. Go up the field to a gate. Continue between buildings and turn right,

then left to a T-junction with a road by the entrance gate to the Church of Tregaminion.

5 Turn right and then, in 100yds (91m), go left into a field, and continue walking to reach a junction on the edge of some woods. (For an enjoyable diversion, take the right-hand branch to the beach and cove at Polkerris.) On the main route, keep left along the field-edge and follow the well-defined coast path for 1.25 miles (2km) to reach Gribbin Head.

6 Enter the wooded National Trust property of Gribbin. Keep left at a junction. Go through a gate and cross to Gribbin Daymark. Go left and down a faint grassy track, then follow the coast path along to Polridmouth.

7 Follow the coast path and, at open ground, follow the seaward field-edge. Go steeply in to, and then out of, Coombe Haven. Enter Covington Wood and keep left at immediate junction, to pass the Rashleigh Mausoleum.

8 Turn right at a junction to reach St Catherine's Castle. Return along the path then go down some steps at the first junction on the right. Go down some wooden steps to reach Readymoney Beach. Return to the car park via St Catherine's Parade.

DISTANCE/TIME 7.5 miles (12km) 4h **MAP** OS Explorer 107 St Austell & Liskeard **START** Readymoney Cove car park; grid ref: SX 118511 **PATHS** Field paths, rough lanes and coastal footpath. Can be very muddy on inland tracks during wet weather; 10 stiles **THE PUB** The Rashleigh Inn, Polkerris. Tel: 01726 813991; www.rashleighinnpolkerris.co.uk

MARAZION MAP REF 398 C8

Marazion is a town first and foremost. It was the main trading port of Mount's Bay until Penzance developed its own markets and port during the 16th century. But Marazion has remained as distinctive as its lovely name, which derives, rather plainly, from the Cornish word for market. There is an informative little museum at the town hall in Market Square, antique and craft shops to browse and pleasant pubs, restaurants and cafés.

Marazion Beach offers safe bathing and is a glorious suntrap. It offers good windsurfing, especially during spring and autumn, when conditions are breezy. A few miles east lies Prussia Cove, a secluded rocky inlet of great charm reached most rewardingly by a pleasant 2-mile (3.2km) walk along the coast path.

The great complement to Marazion is the castellated Isle of St Michael's Mount (cared for by the National Trust), the most romantic offshore island in Britain and a matching image to Mont St Michel off the Normandy coast. The Mount was dedicated to St Michael after claims of miraculous sightings of the saint by 5th-century fishermen. Even today shafts of celestial light seem drawn to St Michael's Mount, although a view of angels is perhaps less likely. In its day the Mount has been a monastery, a prison, and a castle-under-siege. The Mount is defined as a part-time island by successive high tides, during which it may be reached by a pleasant boat trip. At low tide the approach is on foot along a fine cobbled causeway.

MEVAGISSEY MAP REF 398 D7

Mevagissey tucks into the land and guards itself within the folded arms of its inner and outer harbours. It is one of Cornwall's most popular resorts, a fishing village whose simple charm attracts tourists in their thousands. It became a leading pilchard fishing port in Tudor times and continued as such into the 21st century. For many years it supplied the navy with pilchards, which became known as Mevagissey Ducks. Today there is still a fishing fleet based here but, as modern fishermen, one that is far more diverse. Like most Cornish fishing villages Mevagissey has great character, especially in the old part of the village that lies between the Fountain Inn and the Battery on the eastern side of the harbour. The aquarium at the old lifeboat house on the South Quay gives an insight into life in deeper waters (the profits go to the upkeep and improvement of Mevagissey harbour). There is a little museum of local history on the East Quay and, engagingly for this sea-going town, there is a model railway museum in Meadow Street.

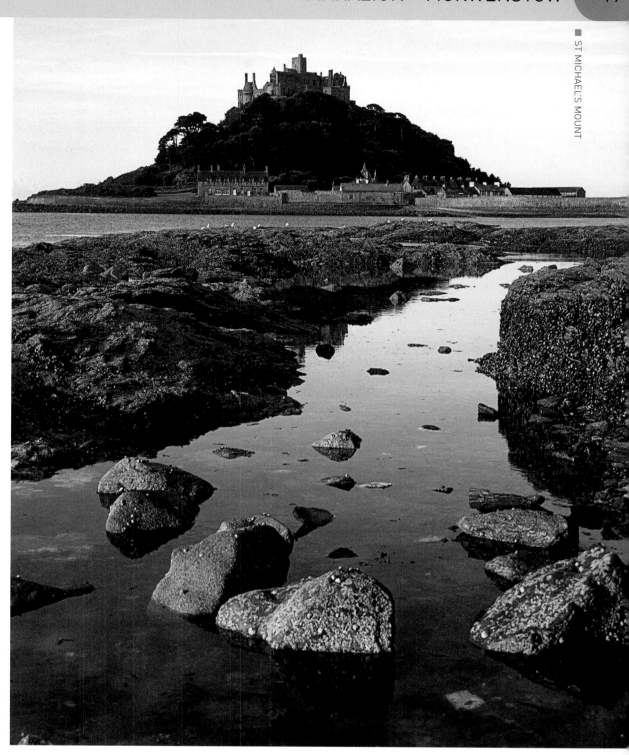

Heligan was once a lost garden, but now has been well and truly found. It lies northwest of Mevagissey and can be reached from the B3273 St Austell road. Restored Victorian features include lakes and ponds, an Italian Garden, an extensive valley garden with a splendid collection of tree ferns, and huge productive gardens and extensive fruit houses.

MORWENSTOW & COOMBE
MAP REF 398 E5

The delightful parish of Morwenstow lies at the northern extreme of Cornwall in the narrow corridor of land that the infant Tamar River withholds from its Devon neighbour. Its coast is awesome, yet unexpected, when approached across fields that enc without much warning at the edge of 300-foot (91.5m) cliffs. This is the land of the famous Culm Measures, great twisted slabs of shale that rise from remote boulder beaches that are ribbed with fins of sea-washed rock.

Its natural beauty apart, Morwenstow owes much of its fame to the reputation of the Victorian parson, eccentric and poet, Robert Stephen Hawker, who was vicar at the Church of St Morwenna for many years. The church has good Norman features and is beautifully situated among trees in a shallow combe that leads towards the sea. The interior of the church is pleasantly melancholic, especially at dusk, when there is a wonderful feeling of isolation. Make sure you visit Morwenstow with time to spare as the pretty land around the church, and the stretch of cliffs to the west, is owned and conserved by the National Trust and worth a visit.

Southwards from Morwenstow is Coombe hamlet, set in a wooded valley that is eagually as peaceful. The river reaches the sea at Duckpool, where the pebble beach has built up to dam a small pool of fresh water. Just north of Coombe, the coast path passes just above Lower Sharpnose Point, where spectacular natural piers of rock jut out into the sea like the massive walls of ruined temples.

Inland, the large satellite dishes of the Cleave Camp Satellite Station seem alien amidst such raw natural beauty, and dominate the view for miles around.

The Eden Project

Built in a china clay pit approaching the end of its working life, in the heart of Cornwall's clay mining country, the Eden Project is the story of man's dependence on plants, connecting plants, people and places. Dominated by the futuristic-looking biome structures, which have the appearance of giant-sized bubble wrap, the Project is much more than just a green theme park. Sure, it's all about plants, but it's a story told in a very special and unique way. Eden is a living demonstration of regeneration and aims to reconnect people with their environments locally and globally. This is not a place that pretends to have all the answers, but one that prefers people to explore their world with a fresh eye.

Life on Earth after all depends on the survival of the plants that surround us – each day of our lives, we use plants from every continent, often without realising it. To help explain the importance of plants, the Eden Project offers a cathartic passageway into a fascinating interactive world of plants and people; a living drama, one that explores our global garden inheritance, displaying plants as you may never have seen them before.

The vision of the first horticultural directors of Eden, Philip McMillan Browse and Peter Thoday, was to re-create the major elements of the world's flora, and to integrate a particular focus on the relationship people have with plants...and that doesn't just mean talking to them! The fact that the site chosen for Eden was a clay pit is itself a key element in the overall story. Gardeners everywhere will realize that it is a mere bagatelle, just a few days' work, to build a garden many tens of thousands of square metres in size that portrays the diverse and rich flora of the world – well almost – but quite another to do so in the soil-less crater prone to flooding that was Bodelva. On the plus side, the site was south facing and sheltered.

The project opened to the public in March 2001 and three months later had already welcomed its millionth visitor. What makes the Eden Project so special is that it successfully combines ecology, horticulture, science, art and architecture. It provides

an informative and enjoyable experience, while simultaneously promoting ways of maintaining a sustainable future in terms of human global dependence on plants and trees. The exhibits include over one hundred thousand plants, representing five thousand species from many of the climate zones of the world.

The site is huge, and you cannot visit Eden without being stunned by the sheer magnitude of it all. The incredible biome structures are the biggest conservatories in the world, and are split into a 'Rainforest Biome' and a 'Warm Temperate Mediterranean Biome'. Another world record reflects the 230 miles (370km) of free-standing scaffolding poles used during construction of the Rainforest Biome, which today contains thousands of plant species. The bubbles are made of inflated hexagonal, transparent 'plastic' windows, and flimsy as they may seem each hexagon is tough enough to take the weight of an entire rugby team.

The Rainforest Biome is 787 feet (240m) long, 361 feet (110m) wide and 164 feet (50m) high, easily tall enough to accommodate trees from the tropical rainforests; in fact, they tell you, this is the largest rain forest in captivity! The biome contains more than 1000 plant species at an air temperature between 18° and 35°C; waterfalls and mist sprays help to keep the air moist.

In the Rainforest Biome, you experience the sights, smells and sheer scale of the rainforest, typical of the Oceanic Islands, Malaysia, West Africa and tropical South America, but without the many and varied rainforest inhabitants that can make you very poorly, or dead. Rainforests have up to 60 inches of rain in a year, but in the tropical biome the soil is kept moist by a soil irrigation system.

In this beautifully controlled environment there are insects, butterflies and some lizards. Here, too, you can find plants like palms and bananas, rubber trees, rice, coffee, sugar, pineapples, bamboo, and lilies.

BELOW LEFT Lemon trees are among the many tropical fruits that thrive in the perfect growing conditions created in the Mediterranean Biome.

BELOW MIDDLE The King Protea (Protea cyanaroides), is found on moist sandstone slopes throughout the Cape Peninsula in South Africa.

RIGHT Originating from Sumatra, Indonesia, the 'Corpse plant' (*Amorphallus Titanum*) is the biggest flower in the world – and the smelliest when it blooms! Its yellow spike is wrapped in a single leaf and when the plant prepares for pollination, the spike heats up and gives off a putrid smell which attracts insects.

BOTTOM & OPPOSITE An alliance of the faith and the fortunes of two construction company giants, Sir Alfred and Robert McAlpine, enabled the 18-month creation of The Eden Project and its spectacular domes. The latest addition to the site is 'The Core', a £15 million education centre that was designed using nature's growth pattern, and elements of a tree, as inspiration.

The air in the Mediterranean Biome is a little cooler, and maintained between a comfortable range 15° and 25°C in the summer and a minimum of 10°C in the winter. Warm temperate zones include the Mediterranean regions, parts of California and South Africa, Southwest Australia and Chile, where plants thrive on drought and poor thin soils. Summers are hot and dry, whereas winters are cool and wet. Plants in the Mediterranean Biome include tobaccos, grape vines, cotton, varieties of olives and luscious Mediterranean fruits and peppers.

Within the unique experience of Eden, you encounter stories that demonstrate the ways in which man uses plants for food and medicine, and even for construction and entertainment. It also covers how plants affect the air we breathe and a whole lot more, and provides information on the relationship between plants and the development of our diverse global cultures.

Eden offers a glimpse, too, into the future, explaining the use of plants in new designs and technologies. For everyone there is a chance to be involved, to feel, taste and use plants on themed tours and in a wide range of workshops.

But it's not just plants and more plants. Eden has been voted the UK's best rock music venue and the arts generally are integral to how the Eden project gets its message across. In fact, the whole site is liberally dotted with thought-provoking artworks and installations. Eden's in-house creative team encourages world-renowned theatre companies to use Eden as a venue and you can see plays as well as rock and pop concerts, and even go clubbing.

The Eden project is continuously developing and will probably never be completely finished. 'The Edge', one of the next big constructions, is part of the evolution of Eden, having its roots in an ambition to have a biome that focuses on desert regions. It will concentrate on the challenges of water use and water security, energy use and energy security, and the climate change brought about by these factors.

In a nutshell, Eden is about man's delicate but often complex relationship with plants and is a showcase for questions and some, but not all, of the answers. Eden is about education and communication of the principal environmental issues of the day, all presented in an engaging, accessible, hands-on, and sometimes humorous way.

MOUSEHOLE MAP REF 398 C8

'Mouz'l', as it should be pronounced, is a fishing village of strong character, though the days are long gone when its harbour was crammed with pilchard-fishing boats. The name derives from obscure roots. Its old Cornish name is Porth Enys, meaning 'the landing place by the island'. The small island offshore from Mousehole is called St Clement's after a hermit who is said to have maintained a warning light.

Tempting alleyways and passages wriggle between sturdy cottages in Mousehole and the harbourside Ship Inn rounds things off with a flourish. The far end of Mousehole's tiny harbour has a splendid inner wall of irregular granite blocks, a perfect subject for imaginative photography. There are some shops, cafés and restaurants. Mousehole was not built for the motor car and is best explored on foot – there is a car park by the harbour and another on the outside of the village on the road from Newlyn.

A steep hill takes you inland from Mousehole to the village of Paul, where the Church of St Pol de Leon has some impressive features. These include a memorial to the Mousehole crew of the local lifeboat, the *Solomon Browne*. They died heroically near Lamorna during an appalling storm in December 1981 after repeated attempts to save the eight people aboard the wrecked cargo vessel *Union Star*. The road out of Mousehole to the west leads up the steep Raginnis Hill. Part way up is the famous Mousehole Bird Hospital, a refuge for countless injured birds, many of which are the victims of oil pollution. The recovery cages often contain several very vocal birds.

MULLION MAP REF 398 C8

Mullion is a large village a short distance inland from the harbour at Mullion Cove. There is a lovely sense of anticipation on first approaching Mullion and the village lives up to expectations – a bustling place with an excellent variety of shops, art and craft galleries and some good pubs. The Church of St Melanus has a remarkable collection of wooden bench-ends depicting characters, including a jester and a monk. Mullion Cove is fascinating and dramatic in winter high seas. Big cliffs and sea stacks, gold-leafed with yellow lichen, enclose the narrow inlet and its substantial piers. Offshore lies the bulky mass of Mullion Island, flickering with seabirds.

The coast to the south is pleasantly remote, especially around Predannack Head and Vellan Head, with delightful coast walks to either side of the cove. Just to the north of Mullion is Polurrian Cove, where there is a large sandy beach and further north again is the popular Poldhu Cove with its sandy dunes.

NARE HEAD MAP REF 398 D7

Nare Head is the focus of a beautiful stretch of coastline that borders the little parishes of Gerrans, Veryan and St Michael Caerhays, between the Roseland Peninsula and Dodman Point. The easiest approach to the area is along the A3078 then on an unclassified road that leads to the village of Veryan, noted for its unique and elegant church and for its remarkable thatched round houses. The Church of St Symphorian is impressive, with a dark tower of mottled stone. There are a number of beaches along the shores of Gerrans Bay and Veryan Bay. The best beaches are at Pendower and Carne, where there is good parking and access to Nare Head. To the east is the quiet little village of Portloe, which has a small car park at its eastern end. Further east again is a beach at Porthluney below Caerhays Castle. The castle is a picturesque, 19th-century replacement for an older building, which has a fine woodland garden.

NEWQUAY MAP REF 398 D7

Newquay is geared unashamedly to its splendid beaches, of course, and in places there seem to be more hotels and guest houses than breathing space. But there is still a strong sense of the 'old' Newquay. Sea-angling trips are available; a good way of appreciating the marine environment and the sea-going traditions of this Cornish town.

The town is lively. The beaches and broad, busy streets with shops, pubs and clubs make Newquay the epitome of bright and breezy holiday-making. Yet there are quiet corners in flower-filled parks and gardens. Attractions include a zoo, fun pools and a swimming pool at the Water World in Trenance Leisure Park, off Edgcumbe Avenue.

The Elizabethan manor house of Trerice (National Trust) lies just 3 miles (4.8km) southeast of Newquay. It is an exquisite building. The Elizabethan gardens have long since disappeared but the Trust has laid out the south side of the old garden with fruit trees in a classic 17th-century pattern. There is a restaurant in the Barn and a hayloft has a collection of interesting antique lawnmowers.

PADSTOW MAP REF 398 D6

Padstow is a likeable, good-natured town in a fine position on the Camel Estuary. Its maritime history is a noble one, though it was often tragic. The shifting sand bar across the mouth of the estuary, the Doom Bar, is extremely dangerous at certain states of the tide and in heavy seas. Records show that over 300 vessels were wrecked here between 1760 and 1920. At low tide, a vast expanse of sand sweeps away from Padstow, shading to gold towards the sea and to honey-coloured mud towards the inner estuary and Little Petherick Creek. Padstow's busy harbour has been modernized, but in keeping with

traditional style. The buildings that cluster around it have great variety, and the maze of streets and narrow passageways behind it are pleasantly cool on sunny mornings. Padstow was a busy trading port from the earliest times, and Welsh and Irish saints of the Dark Ages landed here. St Petroc arrived from Wales in the 6th century and stayed for 30 years, founding a monastery, which thrived until AD 981 when it was destroyed by marauding Vikings. The present Church of St Petroc is pleasantly sombre within its shaded churchyard. The route of the old railway line, closed in 1967, is now the Camel Trail, a walking and cycle route. North of Padstow is Stepper Point, the fine headland at the entrance to the estuary.

The Saints' Way, 'Forth an Syns' in Cornish, is a 28-mile (45km) route from Padstow to Fowey. It is a delightful route that can be walked in two days and is best started at the Church of St Petroc.

PENZANCE MAP REF 398 C8

Penzance has a sunny, friendly character gained from its south-facing position on the most sheltered part of Mount's Bay and from the bustle of its many attractive streets. It has the only promenade in Cornwall and it is a rather lengthy one,

with wonderful views. The open-air, art deco Jubilee Swimming Pool rounds off the harbour end of the promenade. Penzance harbour is small but has a busy atmosphere and a mix of vessels from fishing boats to visiting yachts; the passenger boat to the Isles of Scilly leaves from the outer pier.

A pleasant approach to the harbour, from the busy Market Place, is down the diverting Chapel Street, where there are antique and craft shops, pubs and eating houses. Penzance's attractive main street, Market Jew Street, is enhanced further by a raised granite terrace. There are shops of all kinds here, and in the pedestrianized Causewayhead that leads inland from Market Place. Towards the sea, and to either side of Morrab Road, are Morrab Gardens and Penlee Park; the former is a lovely ornamental garden, while the latter houses the Penlee House Gallery and Museum. The gallery stages excellent temporary exhibitions, often of work by the 19th- and early 20th-century Newlyn-based painters, such as Stanhope and Elizabeth Forbes, Walter Langley and 'Lamorna' Birch, who lived in the area from 1880 to 1940. The museum has good displays of local archaeology, social and local history, and the environment.

To the west, Penzance merges with Newlyn, the major fishing port in the southwest. Newlyn harbour is full of life and colour. Scores of fishing boats of all types and sizes work from here in spite of the increasing difficulties of the modern international industry. The large fish market bustles with activity in the early morning as boats land a remarkable variety of fish. Parking at Newlyn is difficult, and most visitors find that a walk along Penzance's spacious promenade and on along the seafront to Newlyn is a pleasant alternative, which can be combined with a visit to the interesting Newlyn Art Gallery along the way.

Just outside Penzance is the National Trust's Trengwainton Garden, a superb complex of five walled gardens set amid mature woodland, which is at its best during the spring and early summer months. Trengwainton Garden can be reached via Heamoor, or from Tremethick Cross on the St Just road.

Penzance has a summer festival called Golowan that lasts for eight days in late June and involves numerous cultural events and entertainment. It culminates in Mazey Day, when the streets of Penzance are closed to traffic and the main street, Market Jew Street, hosts a street fair.

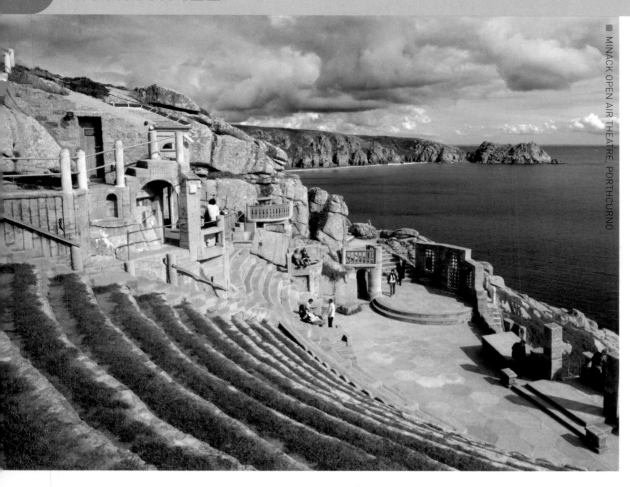

PORTHCURNO & MINACK THEATRE
MAP REF 398 C8

The pure, golden sand of Porthcurno's beaches and the crystal clear clarity of its sea supports Cornwall's claim to be an alternative to the Mediterranean. Under a blazing summer sun, the comparison is apt. Granite towers and pinnacles lie embedded in the steep vegetated slopes that encircle the bay and the superb sand lies deeply against the shoreline. Some of the adjoining beaches are covered at high tide but the main Porthcurno beach is always available, sparkling and luxurious.

For many years Porthcurno was the centre of international cable telegraphy. From here, undersea telegraph cables communicated with the rest of the world and, at one time, the Cable and Wireless Company ran a training college in the Porthcurno Valley. In 1994, the company donated Porthcurno beach and its adjacent cliff land to the National Trust, as the company had relocated its main training facilities to Coventry. There is a fascinating telegraph museum housed in underground chambers within the old Porthcurro college complex just inland from the large car park.

You are really spoiled for choice when you visit Porthcurno. The main beach is marvellously persuasive for wriggling the toes and to either side lie lovely coastal walks. Eastward is the famous Logan Rock, a vast monolith that once rocked at the touch of a finger but is less

responsive now, and westward is the well-known Minack Theatre, lovely Porth Chapel beach and the little Church of St Levan. St Levan can also be reached along the narrow road that climbs steeply uphill from Porthcurno. There is a car park by the church. All around Porthcurno Bay you will find sheltered coves, such as Penberth, and exquisite tidal beaches, and the eastern side is flanked by the magnificent headland of Treryn Dinas.

ROSELAND PENINSULA
MAP REF 398 D7

This beautiful peninsula seems quietly detached from mainstream Cornwall. Flanked on its eastern side by a craggy, rock-fringed coast curving north into Gerrans Bay, it is bordered on the west by the River Fal, with Mylor and Feock set opposite. The very tip of the Roseland Peninsula is pierced by the twisting Percuil River that cuts deeply inland to create even smaller peninsulas. The area is famous for St Mawes, St Mawes Castle and for the peaceful Church of St Just-in-Roseland. A pleasant alternative to the A3078 route out on to the peninsula, is to take the A39 southwards from Truro, the B3289, past Trelissick Gardens and then cross the Fal by the King Harry Ferry. Another approach is to take the passenger ferry from Falmouth to St Mawes.

St Just-in-Roseland is an exquisite place. The church stands on the banks of a small creek, its mellow stonework

embedded in a garden of shrubs and graceful trees that include palms as well as indigenous broad leaves.

On the promontory of land between Carrick Roads and the Percuil River stands St Mawes, deservedly popular and besieged with moored yachts in summer. On Castle Point to the west is Henry VIII's majestic St Mawes Castle, a quiet triumph of good Tudor design over function and renowned for its symmetry and decoration. The outer arm of the Roseland terminates at St Antony Head (one of the properties cared for by the National Trust on the peninsula) where there is a lighthouse and gun battery with an interesting history. On the east coast, further north, is Portscatho, open to the sea and with excellent sandy beaches nearby.

ST IVES MAP REF 398 C7

St Ives' rare character springs from its fishing traditions, its artistic inheritance, and its tourism industry. There is a clash of style amongst all three at times, but St Ives has survived such competing interests. Not only is the town the archetypal Cornish fishing port, it also has magnificent beaches of silken sand that offer both safe family bathing and surf to sing about. The town has aimed determinedly upmarket in recent years and has benefited greatly from the opening of the modern Tate St Ives in 1993. The gallery stands above Porthmeor Beach, its curves and crests are as white as the waves below. The paintings on

display are by leading artists of the St Ives School including Patrick Heron, Peter Lanyon and Terry Frost. It is a joy to find such paintings within the very landscape that inspired them. The view seaward from the gallery's roof terrace is worth crossing the world for. Before the Tate opened, the Barbara Hepworth Museum and Sculpture Garden was the most important artistic attraction here and still remains popular.

St Ives is a delight because of its narrow, canyon-like streets, ubiquitous granite cobbles, and clear, sea-mirrored light. The parish church of St Ia is one of the finest in Cornwall. St Ives harbour area, known locally as 'Downlong', is a maze of exquisite vernacular granite buildings where you catch satisfying glimpses of shady courtyards and passageways. And there are always those beaches to escape to: Porthminster to the south is sheltered and calm; Porthmeor to the north is a bit more lively and popular with the surfing crowd – through winter and summer.

There are several smaller beaches at the harbour and in the lee of the Island, (which is the breezy, green promontory that juts out to sea from a low-lying neck of land). The price of all this is potential overcrowding at the busiest holiday periods. Avoid dawdling through St Ives by car and be prepared for close-quarters humanity in the narrow Fore Street and along the busy harbour front. There is a useful park-and-ride scheme at Trenwith, above the town, and another at Lelant Station, southeast of the town, which uses a little branch line. Artistic ambience – and, at times, pretension – means that St Ives has numerous art galleries and craft shops. There is an excellent town museum at Wheal Dream, and most of the town's numerous restaurants, tea rooms and pubs are of quality and character.

TINTAGEL MAP REF 398 E6

Tintagel should not be missed, even if a visit is fleeting. The focus of this relentlessly 'themed' village is the ruined castle moulded to the blunt summit of 'the Island' of Tintagel Head and approached across a narrow neck of land. The castle is 13th century, but the romance of the site has attracted competing claims for its origins: Iron Age enclosure, Celtic monastery, Roman signal station and, of course, the court of King Arthur. The prominence of the Island suggests that it was used as a defensive site from the earliest times, face-on to the Atlantic.

Barras Nose to the north and Glebe Cliff to the south are in the care of the National Trust. It is tempting to say that the hinterland is in the care of the King Arthur industry, but Tintagel village offers much more than that. The wonderfully antiquated Old Post Office (National Trust) at the heart of the village is a delightful building. It is actually a small 14th-century manor house, with a central hall rising the full height of the building, and became a post office only in Victorian times. King Arthur's Great Halls in Fore Street is a remarkable token of dedication to a theme. The building was completed in the early 1930s and is devoted to Arthurian memorabilia, including a collection of stained-glass windows.

TRURO MAP REF 398 D7

Truro's great cathedral catches the eye from all quarters. It rises from the heart of the city, its honey-coloured stone and lancet windows reflecting the sun, its great Gothic towers piercing the sky. There is no trace of the Norman castle that once stood at Truro, nor of the Dominican friary that stood near the low ground by the river, but the cathedral makes up for their loss.

Truro's fortunes rose and fell over the years, but by the late 18th century it had become the political and cultural centre of Georgian Cornwall. It was during the last years of the 18th century that such famous features as Boscawen Street and Lemon Street were built. Today Boscawen Street is a broad, cobbled space, entered at both ends from narrow thoroughfares. The granite facade of the City Hall graces

Boscawen Street, and Lemon Street survives as one of the finest examples of a late Georgian street in Britain, its houses perfectly aligned to either side of a broad avenue that climbs uphill.

There are hidden glories in Truro amid the modern developments. From the Moorfield car park, a lane leads to Victoria Square, but parallel and to its right is the elegant Georgian crescent of Walsingham Place. Throughout the heart of Truro, the lanes connecting the main streets are lined with attractive shops, cafés and restaurants. From the west end of Boscawen Street, King Street leads up to the pedestrianized area of High Cross in front of the cathedral. The stylish Assembly Rooms, with a facade of Bath stone, stands nearby.

Seen from its forecourt the cathedral seems crowded in by buildings, instead of being the dominating presence that commands the view from outside the city. But the west front and its soaring towers is exhilarating. The foundation stones of the cathedral were laid in 1880 and the western towers were finally dedicated in 1920. Truro's cathedral is thus a Victorian building. Its design is mainly Early English Gothic but with strong French influences that are seen in the great spires. The interior is glorious. It is vaulted throughout and pillars and arches are in elegant

proportion, the air light beneath the great roofs. There are beautiful individual features such as the exquisite baptistry. All that remains of the old parish church of St Mary's is incorporated into the south aisle. Those with an eye for ancient stonework may find the outer wall of the old church a reassuring contrast to the smooth planes of the Victorian cathedral.

Pydar Street runs northwards from the cathedral and serves as a pleasant pedestrian concourse. A short distance away is the stylish Crown Court, and just below here are the pleasant Victoria Gardens. Boscawen Park, by the Truro River, is reached along the road to Malpas. The Royal Cornwall Museum in River Street has an excellent collection of minerals and there are exhibitions covering archaeology and mining. The little art gallery has works by John Opie, the 18th-century portrait painter, who was born near St Agnes. Truro is an excellent shopping centre with numerous shops offering a great variety of quality goods.

ZENNOR MAP REF 398 C7

Storm-tumbled cliffs and wheeling gulls guard Penwith's wild, Atlantic shoreline. The sleepy village of Zennor with its rough tawny hills slope, down towards the echoing sea cliffs. Between hills and sea lies a narrow coastal plateau of small

irregular fields whose Cornish 'hedges' of rough granite date from the Iron Age. Because of its antiquity, this long-farmed landscape has earned Zennor protected status for ecological and archaeological reasons. Such vulnerability should be taken into account when visiting Zennor and its surrounding countryside. Below the car park is the Wayside Museum; it is crammed with exhibits about different ways of farming, mining, archaeology and folklore. Zennor's Church of St Senara stands proud over the village.

Zennor has an endearing myth of a mermaid. The mermaid was said to have seduced a local chorister into the deep, dark waters below the lofty Zennor Head. On quiet evenings, the smooth heads of seals bobbing in the sea perpetuate the legend and an attractive bench-end motif in the church encourages the tale.

Access to Zennor Head and to the coast path is on foot down a narrow lane that starts behind the Tinner's Arms. Zennor Head has a flat top, but its western flank is spectacular. Towering cliffs plunge into a narrow gulf, the sea crashes white against the shoreline far below. If you can tear yourself away from thoughts of mermaids, it is an invigorating 6-mile (9.6km) walk eastwards to St Ives along some of the most remote coastline in Cornwall, with some truly spectacular coastal scenery.

ST IVES

HELFORD ESTUARY

The Helford River is enduringly popular with land-based visitors and leisure sailors alike, yet the area manages somehow to absorb it all. The pelt of trees that line the estuary and its creeks plays a great part of muffling this human racket so that you can enjoy this circuit of the peaceful tidal creeks.

1 Turn left along the path, signed 'Coast Path'. Go through a metal gate and follow the sunken track. Descend some steps, then turn right along the lane. At a steep right-hand bend, bear off ahead along the track. Follow this permissive path through the trees, passing some fine little beaches along the way.

2 Leave the wooded area via a metal gate, then turn left along the field-edge to a stone stile. Follow the bottom edge of the next two fields. Go through a field gap beside a white pole and post and triangle (navigation marks). Follow the field-edge ahead. Go through a kissing gate, and then follow the field-edge (seat and viewpoint on left). Go through a kissing gate. Go left to the start of a wide grassy track between gorse and low trees. (For a short circuit of Dennis Head, follow the track to a stile on the left.)

3 To continue walking along the main route, turn sharply right at the start of a wide track and follow the left-hand field-edge and then a path across the open field. Join a track behind a house, then go through a kissing gate and descend to reach St Anthony-in-Meneage Church. (The church has some fine features if you have time to explore.) Follow

the road alongside Gillan Creek. Partway along is a National Trust path along the creek edge.

4 Just past where the road curves round the bay, go up right and through a gate by a public footpath sign. Follow the broad track through the trees to reach the houses at Roscaddon. Keep ahead along the track that leads to Manaccan at a T-junction opposite Manaccan Church.

5 Cross the churchyard and then go through a gate to the road. Keep walking ahead to reach a junction, New Inn is on the left, then go up right, past a school. Keep uphill, then turn left along Minster Meadow, go over a stile, and through a field to the road.

6 Go diagonally left to a stile opposite, cross the field, then go left following signposts to reach some woods. Follow the path ahead. Reach a junction with track going up to the left. Go over the stile ahead and reach another junction.

7 Bear down to the right and follow a broad track through trees to some buildings at Helford. Keep ahead at a surfaced road and follow the road uphill to the car park.

DISTANCE/TIME 5 miles (8km) 3h **MAP** OS Explorer 103 The Lizard **START** Helford village car park (busy in summer); grid ref: SW 759261 **PATHS** Good woodland paths and tracks, field paths, short section of quiet lane; 10 stiles **THE PUB** The Shipwright's Arms, Helford. Tel: 01326 231235

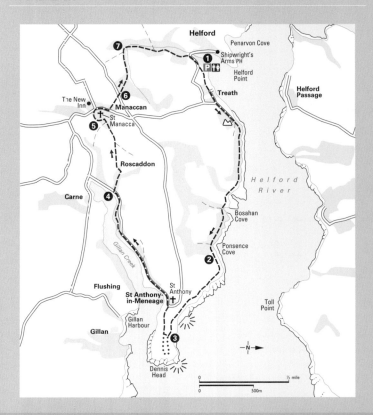

WALK 6

A COASTAL WALK NEAR ST IVES

This delightful walk starts from the maritime heart of St Ives and heads west along the glorious coastline. This is a very remote and wild part of the west Cornwall coast, a landscape of exquisite colours in spring and summer.

1 Walk along the harbour to Smeaton's Pier. Before the pier entrance, turn left, signed 'St Ives Museum'. Where the road bends, keep ahead into Wheal Dream. Turn right past St Ives Museum and follow the walkway to Porthgwidden Beach.

2 Cross the car park above beach and then climb to the National Coastwatch lookout. Go down some steps, behind the building at the back, then follow footway to Porthmeor Beach. Go along the beach to the car park.

3 Go up steps beside the public toilets and right along a track past bowling and putting greens. Continue to the rocky headlands of Carrick Du and Clodgy Point.

4 From Clodgy Point walk uphill and follow the path round to the right. Continue along a boggy, rocky path. In 0.5 mile (800m) go left at a junction by a small acorn signpost and big yellow-lichened boulder.

5 At a T-junction, with a track just past a National Trust sign for 'Hellesveor Cliff', turn right and follow the coast path. (Shorter version of walk goes left and inland.)

6 Keep right at the junction and continue walking past an old mine stack and a shed (heading inland). Continue to River Cove. On

the other side of the cove, climb to a junction and continue to follow the inland path.

7 At a junction, go left through a kissing gate and follow signs past Trevail Mill. Go through a kissing gate and climb steadily.

8 Cross a track and follow the hedged-in path, signposted 'Bridleway'. In 40yds (36m) go left over a stile by black and white pole. Follow the field-edges ahead over stiles.

9 Keep in the field with a granite upright. Cross a stile. Where the field hedge bends sharply right, head towards two gates. Cross a stile and continue to another at Trevalgan Farm. Go between buildings and in 50yds (46m), turn left at a gate, bear right and cross a stile. Continue to Trowan Farm.

10 At the farm, pass a granite post; continue between houses, go through a field gate. Follow field paths over several stiles.

11 Cross a lane, then a stile and follow the left-hand edges of fields. Pass a gap, left, and turn left before a rusty gate. Cross two stiles then between high hedges to a lane.

12 Turn right (Burthallan Lane) to reach a T-junction. Turn left and follow the main road back to Porthmeor Beach.

DISTANCE/TIME 8 miles (12.9km) 4h **MAP** OS Explorer 102 Land's End **START** Upper Trenwith car park, St Ives or Porthmeor Beach; grid ref: SW 522408 **PATHS** Coastal path, can be quite rocky. Field paths; many stiles **THE PUB** The Sloop Inn, St Ives. Tel: 01736 796584

DISTANCE/TIME 10 miles (16.1km) 2h **MAP** OS Explorer 106 Newquay & Padstow **START** The Quarryman Inn, Edmonton; grid ref: SW 964727 **TRACKS** Well-surfaced former railway track

THE PUB The Quarryman Inn, Edmonton. Tel: 01208 816444

DISTANCE/TIME 7 miles (11.3km) 1h30; including optional extension 10 miles (16.1km) 2h30 **MAP** OS Explorer 105 Falmouth & Mevagissey **START** Pentewan Valley Cycle Hire; grid ref: SX 017473 **TRACKS** Mainly well-surfaced track, some woodland paths and a little onroad **THE PUB** The Ship Inn, Pentewan. Tel: 01726 842855; www.staustellbrewery.co.uk

THE CAMEL TRAIL: EDMONTON TO PADSTOW

Fabulous views, wonderful birdlife and unusual maritime plants make this section of the Camel Trail a delight at any time of year. If you want to keep away from the crowds, turn round on the edge of Padstow, or just dive in quickly for an ice cream.

1 The Quarryman Inn is a fascinating place. Behind the pub are two terraces of stone cottages, originally homes for workers at the quarries (Point 3); when these fell into disuse in the early 20th century the building became a TB isolation hospital. Today it is a very welcoming pub. From the car park turn right. At the crossroads turn left and enjoy a lovely downhill run, with increasingly good views over towards the River Camel and farmland beyond. The Camel was known as the Allen River until 1870, thought to derive from the Irish word 'alain', for beautiful: it's clear to see why. Pass through the hamlet at Tregunna and follow the lane over a bridge until you get to its end. Turn right down a narrow earthy path to reach the trail.

2 Turn right and follow the trail along the edge of the estuary. At low tide it's almost like cycling along the edge of a beach as the river is flanked by broad expanses of sand and the views are superb. The creeks and sandbanks attract wintering wildfowl – widgeon, goldeneye, long-tailed duck – as well as many divers and waders, spring and autumn migrants. En route, look out for curlew, oystercatcher, shelduck and little egret. One of the main reasons for constructing the railway was to transport sea sand, which is rich in lime, from the estuary to fertilize farmland away from the coast. Granite, slate, tin, iron and copper from mines on Bodmin Moor were exported.

3 A long cutting ends at the spoil heaps of the old slate quarries, with rounded, wooded Cant Hill opposite. The estuary is widening as it approaches the sea; there's a glimpse of Padstow ahead on the left bank. The mouth of the Camel Estuary is marred by the notorious Doom Bar, a shifting sandbank responsible for more than 300 shipwrecks from 1760 to 1920. If you're gently cycling along the Camel Trail on a sunny day it's difficult to imagine such disasters.

4 Continue past Pinkson Creek – you may see herons – and continue on to pass the parking area at Oldtown Cove. Once through the next cutting you'll get fantastic views towards Rock, on the other side of the estuary, with Brea Hill and Daymer Bay beyond, and out to the open sea. The trail bears away from the estuary through a cutting.

5 Cross the bridge over Little Petherick Creek. The Saints' Way, a 30-mile (48km) walking route, links Fowey on the south coast with Padstow's St Petroc's Church. It runs along the edge of the creek and past the obelisk (commemorating Queen Victoria's jubilee in 1887) on Dennis Hill, seen ahead. The creek is also an important habitat for little egret and a good range of wading birds.

6 Follow the trail past a lake on the left and then past houses on the edge of Padstow, with moored boats on the water on the right. Rock, opposite, is a popular sailing and watersports venue, and there's always masses to watch on the water. The trail ends at the quay and car park; you should dismount at this point to explore the town. Retrace your tracks along the Camel Trail to Edmonton.

THROUGH THE PENTEWAN VALLEY

A ride along the banks of the St Austell River, with an optional extension to the Lost Gardens of Heligan. This pleasant route follows the line of the old Pentewan railway along the tranquil St Austell river.

1 From the village car park return towards the B3273 and pass through the parking area for Pentewan Valley Cycle Hire. Go round a staggered barrier on to the trail, which emerges from shady woods on to the banks of the St Austell River.

2 Turn right and follow the trail along the riverbank.

3 Note the turn-off left across the river to the Lost Gardens of Heligan. Pass a small parking area into King's Wood (Woodland Trust), and follow the trail as signed left back on to the riverbank. Dip into woodland again, then bear right on to a lane.

4 Turn left; pass a small parking area to meet a tarmac lane on a bend. Bear right as signed. Turn left opposite 'Brooklea' and continue on a wooded path, with a caravan site left. The track bears left at Molingey – with London Apprentice across the river – then right to run along the right bank of the river again. Continue to follow this tarmac way as it bears right through fields, then left to reach the edge of the water treatment works. Turn left for 50yds (46m) to meet the B3273. Turn right to walk along the pavement.

5 Cross the lane to Tregorrick, and take the second lane on the right (Sawles Road – unsigned). Follow this lane to its end. For St Austell turn left uphill to cross the A390. To reach Pentewan, either turn around here, or turn right and cycle steeply uphill through countryside. Drop to a T-junction and turn right, steeply downhill, through Tregorrick. At the B3273 turn left to return to Pentewan on the outward route.

6 Heligan extension: After passing Point 3, turn right to cross the river on the footbridge (dismount). At the B3273, turn left. Pass the touring park on the left, then turn right to cross the road as signed. Turn left, then continue on a track. Climb steadily uphill for 0.75 mile (1.2km), levelling off as the track passes beneath a road. Bear left to reach a fork. Keep left to meet the road; turn left for 0.5 mile (800m); Heligan is on the left.

7 On leaving Heligan, turn right along the road. Cycle downhill, with great views over St Austell Bay. Turn left on the first narrow lane, steeply downhill. At the next minor road, turn left, even more steeply, to meet the B3273 opposite Pentewan Sands Holiday Park. Turn left towards the Esso garage, then right into Pentewan village.

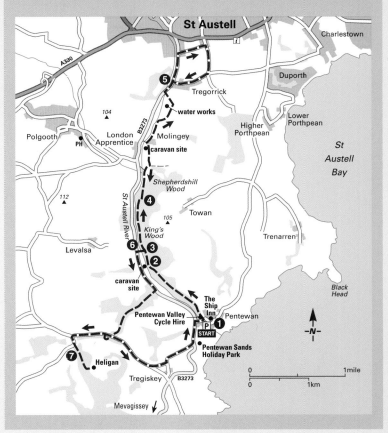

DISTANCE/TIME 5 miles (8km) 1h30 **MAP** OS Explorer 102 Land's End **START** The Godolphin Arms car park, Marazion; grid ref: SW 516306 **TRACKS** Short stretch of road, track generally level. Rough and bumpy in places **THE PUB** The Godolphin Arms, Marazion. Tel: 01736 710202; www.godolphinarms.co.uk

DISTANCE/TIME 10 miles (16.1km) 2h **MAP** OS Explorer 104 Redruth & St Agnes **START** The beach car park, Portreath; grid ref: SW 654453 **TRACKS** Well-surfaced track, some road sections **THE PUB** The Basset Arms, Portreath. Tel: 01209 842077

MARAZION TO PENZANCE

Enjoy an easy ride along one of south Cornwall's most beautiful bays. This level, easy, there-and-back route along the edge of Mount's Bay, with spectacular views over stunning St Michael's Mount, is an ideal option for families with young children. With just a short road stretch at the start and finish, the ride runs along the back of the huge expanse of sands that lie between Marazion and Penzance.

1 This ride is part of the First and Last Trail, the first stretch of the Cornish Way long-distance cycle route, which starts at Land's End and runs for 180 miles (290km) through the county. Marazion, where this ride starts, is Cornwall's oldest charter town, dating from 1257. Its unusual name comes from the Cornish 'marghas yow' – meaning 'Thursday market'. Marazion was the main trading port in Mount's Bay until Penzance overtook it in the 16th century. It's worth having a look around this attractive village before you set off. From the pub car park cycle uphill (away from the beach) on to West End. (The Godolphin Arms can be found by turning right.) Turn left along West End and cycle out of the village. There is a parking area on the left along much of this road, so look out for people opening their car doors suddenly. Marazion Marsh lies to the right.

2 Where the road bears right to cross the main Penzance to Exeter railway line, keep straight ahead through a parking area, with the Pizza Shack (and toilets behind) on the right. Take care cycling through the car park.

3 Keep ahead and leave the car park to the left of the old station (now the Station pub), to join a level track that runs along the back of the beach. Follow this track, passing public toilets on the right.

4 Take care where the track drops down to meet an entrance road to a beachside car park (there are warning notices 'Give way to traffic'). Pass through the parking area and continue along the track, with the railway close by on the right.

5 Go past the heliport, from which helicopters fly regularly to the Isles of Scilly, which lie more than 17 miles (27km) southwest of Land's End (day trips are available). Pleasant views open up ahead towards Penzance.

6 On approaching the station, the track narrows into a concrete walkway and becomes busier, so look out for pedestrians. Follow the track into the car park by Penzance railway and bus station, with the Tourist Information Centre to the right. There's lots to see in Penzance, which developed as an important pilchard-fishing centre in medieval times. The arrival of the Great Western Railway in Victorian times gave the town another boost and it is now the main centre in the area known as Penwith (the far western part of Cornwall). The pretty harbour is full of interest, and it is from here that the RMV *Scillonian* makes regular sailings to the lovely Isles of Scilly. When you've had your fill of this busy little harbour, relocate the Tourist Information Office, where you should turn round and return to Marazion. The First and Last Trail actually runs along the road to Newlyn, but the extended route is pretty busy in terms of traffic and therefore is not recommended for families with young children.

PORTREATH TRAMROAD

This ride ambles into the heart of old industrial Cornwall, following a trail that crosses the county for 11 miles (17.7km) to Devoran on Restronguet Creek.

1 From the car park turn left, pass the Portreath Arms Hotel then bear left along Sunny Vale Road. As it bears right, bear left on to the tramway. Go through woodland, over the access road to a reservoir, through more woodland then fields, until you reach a white cottage on the left. Go along a lane to a minor road. Cross the road at Cambrose.

2 Turn left along the pavement and follow the road past Elm Farm. After 500yds (455m), turn right on a lane to a T-junction at Lower Forge. Cross the road and keep ahead until the next T-junction to go back on to the tramway. Follow this to North Downs (1.75 miles/2.8km); turn left to a road. Turn right on the pavement to the roundabout.

3 Turn left across the road and follow the pavement. Cycle uphill, pass another small roundabout and a café on the left. At the top of the hill turn right to cross the A30.

4 Over the bridge turn left down a rough track. Bear left at Boscawen Farm and follow the track past Boscawen Mine. Pass Wheal Busy chapel left, to a lane junction. Keep ahead; 109yds (100m) on, turn right down a bridleway, then right on a track at the bottom. Go downhill, keep ahead, cross a lane, then go uphill. Bear left to meet a road.

5 Cross over and follow a track through a parking area and downhill past Killifreth Mine's Hawke's Shaft pumping house. Enter Unity Woods; keep left at the fork and follow the bumpy track downhill to a junction.

6 Turn right, rejoining the tramway. Follow the track out of the woods, with a road (B3298) left. Cross the road and continue to the left of the road. At the junction, turn left along the pavement. After 109yds (100m) turn right to cross the road, passing to the right of the Fox and Hounds pub. At the next road turn left and pass under the railway bridge. At the T-junction by the Crossroads Motel, cross the A30 and rejoin the outward route.

passageways, called 'drangs', between them. You'll have to breathe in to get through the narrowest passageway, Squeeze Belly Alley.

6 Leave Port Isaac and then descend steeply to Portgaverne. Ascend steeply, then continue to the B3314. Turn left, signed 'Delabole', and continue for 1.75 miles (2.8km) to a junction with the B3267. Turn right, signed 'St Teath'. Keep ahead through St Teath, signed 'Camelford'. Descend steeply to a T-junction with the A39 and turn left, signed 'Bude, Camelford'. Go through Camelford and continue along the A39 for 2 miles (3.2km), then turn right, signed Roughtor, Altarnun, Crowdy Reservoir'. After a mile (1.6km) turn right, signed 'Crowdy Reservoir', and follow the road (a one-time air strip), passing Crowdy Reservoir. At a crossroads, turn left, and soon after you reach a car park below the impressive granite ridge of Rough Tor.

This is a chance to get out of the car and stretch your legs. Leaving the car park, you can take one of several paths towards the top of the Tor. You should come prepared for a muddy walk in wet weather.

7 Return to the crossroads, turn right, pass Crowdy Reservoir again, then, at a junction, turn right, signed 'Altarnun'. Continue for about 5 miles (8km) to pass the Rising Sun Inn. Keep left and continue ahead, ignoring all side roads. After 3.5 miles (5.6km) pass Polyphant and reach the A30. Turn left and return to Launceston.

BODMIN MOOR & THE NORTH COAST

This drive takes in the wildest and loveliest parts of Bodmin Moor, with a visit to the north coast by way of contrast. The Minions area is dominated by ruined mine engine houses, Cheesewring Quarry, and by the rounded bulk of Caradon Hill, while the fine granite ridge of Rough Tor (pronounced 'Row Tor') dominates the western side of Bodmin Moor. The moorland slopes have numerous remains of Bronze Age circles and prehistoric field boundaries.

Route Directions

Start at Launceston, once a Norman fortified town and now home to fine architecture and interesting little streets.

1 Leave Launceston on the A388 (A30), signed 'Bodmin'. Go under the A30 then, at a roundabout, take the third exit, signed 'South Petherwin B3254'. Pass through South Petherwin and keep on the B3254 to a crossroads with the B3257 at Congdon's Shop (there's a war memorial opposite). Keep ahead for 5 miles (8km), passing through Middlewood and Darleyford, to a crossroads at Upton Cross. Turn right on to an unclassified road, signed 'Minions, Siblyback Lake'. Pass through Minions. Keep ahead at the next junction, signed 'St Cleer', passing a road on the right to Siblyback Watersports Centre.

Siblyback Watersports Centre on Siblyback Lake is a great place to go windsurfing, kayaking, canoeing, sailing, rafting, rowing, power boating or even angling. The centre offers tuition with fully qualified instructors for all levels of ability and the prices are pretty reasonable.

2 Continue on the main route, passing King Doniert's Stone on the left (parking). At the next junction, turn right, signed 'Draynes, Golitha Falls'. After 300yds (273m), a left turn over a bridge leads to a convenient car park (toilets). From here, it is only a short walk to the spectacular Golitha Falls, a National Nature Reserve.

3 Continue to Bolventor. Just before a junction is Daphne du Maurier's Smugglers at Jamaica Inn Centre. At the junction turn left to Jamaica Inn, then left opposite the Inn, signed 'Dozmary Pool'. In 1.5 miles (2.4km), pass Dozmary Pool and around the edge of Colliford Lake (park at Colliford Dam). At a junction turn right, signed 'Bodmin'. Continue to the A30. Turn left, to 'Bodmin'.

If you can, take a brief detour to Dozmary Pool, said to be the final resting place of King Arthur's legendary sword Excalibur.

4 After 7 miles (11.3km), bear left on to the A389, signed 'Bodmin'. Keep ahead for Bodmin, ignoring left-hand routes, then turn right at a junction, signed 'Bodmin

A389'. At a mini-roundabout, go right and along Pool Street and on through Bodmin following signs for Wadebridge, A389. At a junction, turn right by a clock tower, signed 'Wadebridge' and continue on the A389 for 6 miles (9.6km). At a roundabout take the first exit signed 'Rock, Polzeath'. Turn right at the next roundabout on to the B3314, signed 'Rock, Polzeath'. Cross the Trewornan Bridge, then after 2 miles (3.2km) turn left, signed 'Rock, Trebetherick'. Continue for 2 miles (3.2km), then opposite a garage turn right into Trewint Lane, signed 'Trebetherick, Polzeath'. In 0.75 miles (1.2km), turn left at the next junction, signed 'Trebetherick, Polzeath'. Pass through Trebetherick and descend steeply into Polzeath, then ascend even more steeply.

If you are a surfer, you might like to make a detour to the surfing beaches of Polzeath, where wet-suited surfers gather year-round.

5 In 1.25 miles (2km) pass a turn-off to New Polzeath. Pass a left turn to Portquin, then keep left off the bend, signed 'St Endellion, Port Isaac'. Soon join the B3314 and go left. Continue through St Endellion, then turn left on to the B3267, signed 'Port Isaac'. Go through the upper part of Port Isaac (park here to visit the village – toilets).

Attractive little Port Isaac is really popular with visitors and, because the car is sidelined, can truly claim to be 'unspoilt'. The houses are tightly crowded together with only narrow

HELFORD RIVER & THE LIZARD

An absorbing drive past some lovely lakes and on through the popular Helford River area, with its quiet tidal creeks, to The Lizard, Britain's most southerly point. The south side of the Helford Estuary is a delightful landscape of wood-fringed creeks and inlets. Helford is worth a diversion from the main route of the tour, although access is down narrow lanes and driving can become quite restricted especially during busy holiday periods.

Route Directions

The tour starts in Helston, a pleasant market town which was once a port (until the silting of the River Cober landlocked the town).

1 Leave Helston on the B3297, signed 'Redruth'. After 6 miles (9.6km), having passed via Wendron and the access to Poldark Mine, turn right on to an unclassified road, signed 'Carnmenellis'. After 2 miles (3.2km), at a T-junction turn left, signed 'Stithians'. Continue ahead, with Stithians Reservoir situated on the right.

The reservoir is a good place for watersports and has superior birdlife so remember to take your binoculars with you.

2 Pass the Golden Lion Inn and continue across a causeway. At the next junction turn right, signed 'Stithians', and continue through Goonlaze. (Note: access road to Stithians dam and car park, just after Goonlaze.) Continue to drive through Stithians (toilets just past the church), then, on the other side of the village at a crossroads, go straight across and down Tregonning Road, signed for 'Mabe'. Follow a very narrow lane for 1.25 miles (2km) then take a right turning at a T-junction, signed 'Longdowns'. In 0.75 miles (1.2km), just after you pass a quarry, go left at a T-junction. Soon you will reach the A394. Turn left here, signed 'Falmouth'. Only a short distance up ahead, and just past a garage, branch right. Reach Mabe Burnthouse and, at a junction at the village centre, bear right, signed 'Mawnan' and 'Constantine'. Keep left at the next junction, signed 'Mawnan Smith'.

A short distance further on, a side road branches right down to the Argal Water Park. There is a car parking area here and some lovely waterside walks.

3 On the main route, follow signs for Mawnan Smith. Go directly over a crossroads, signed 'Mawnan Smith and Helford Passage' and continue for approximately 2 miles (3.2km) to reach Mawnan Smith, a pleasant village within lovely surroundings. Keep right by the Red Lion Inn, signed 'Budock Vean', and then follow the signs for Helford Passage and Constantine. Carry on, passing Glendurgan Garden, a delightful woodland valley garden of 40 acres (16ha), then pass the equally fine Trebah Gardens.

The gardens are filled with subtropical plants in an area covering more than 25 acres (10ha) with plenty to amuse children of all ages and to interest adults. Careful planting has ensured colour year-round.

4 Follow signs for Porth Navas and Constantine along a winding and often narrow lane (with passing places). Pass through Porth Navas and follow the signs for Constantine. When you reach a T-junction, go left through Constantine. On the far side of the village ignore the first left turn signed 'Vicarage Terrace, Gweek' and take the next left turn signed 'Gweek'. Pass through Brill and turn left at the next junction signed 'Gweek'. Go through Gweek. (Just past the Gweek Inn and before a bridge, a road to the left, called 'Meneth', leads to the National Seal Sanctuary.)

Gweek, just beyond Culdrose, is the home of the National Seal Sanctuary, Europe's largest rescue centre for seals. Injured seal pups are diligently cared for at the hospital and returned to the sea when they are fit and healthy. Those that are too badly disabled are given a new home at the sanctuary.

5 Go left by a thatched house, signed 'Mawgan' and 'St Keverne'. Continue through a wooded area and, at a roundabout, go left, signed 'Mawgan'. Drive carefully through Mawgan, keeping left at a junction, signed 'Manaccan and Helford', pass Mawgan church and then follow signs for Manaccan and Helford along a narrow and winding road with some steep inclines and sharp bends. Pass through St Martin and reach Newtown-in-St Martin. The main route goes right at a junction, just past the Prince of Wales pub. (For a diversion to Helford, keep past this junction to reach a junction with a road leading left, signed 'Manaccan, Helford'.) On the main route, continue onwards until you get to a junction with the B3293. Here, turn left, signed 'St Keverne'. Continue on and pass the Goonhilly Satellite Earth Station.

Goonhilly is a complex of giant communication antennas and claims to be the world's largest and oldest satellite station.

6 A few hundred yards beyond the Earth Station turn right, signed 'Cadgwith and Kennack Sands', and follow along this

arrow-straight road to reach Kuggar. At a junction, turn right signed 'The Lizard'. At the next crossroads go forward, signed 'St Ruan and Cadgwith'. Continue through the village of St Ruan and after about half a mile (800m) pass a side road leading left. (300yds/273m down this side road is a large car park for Cadgwith.) On the main route keep ahead, and continue following signs for The Lizard. At a junction with the A3083, turn left for Lizard Point (toilets). Return along the A3083 to Helston, passing Culdrose Naval Air Base on the way back to Helford.

Devon

CLOCKWISE FROM TOP LEFT: PEBBLES AT BUDLEIGH SALTERTON; TORQUAY; GREAT WESTERN CANAL AT TIVERTON; STATUE OF RICHARD HOOKER AT EXETER CATHEDRAL; DAWLISH WARREN BEACH; SURFING AT SAUNTON SANDS

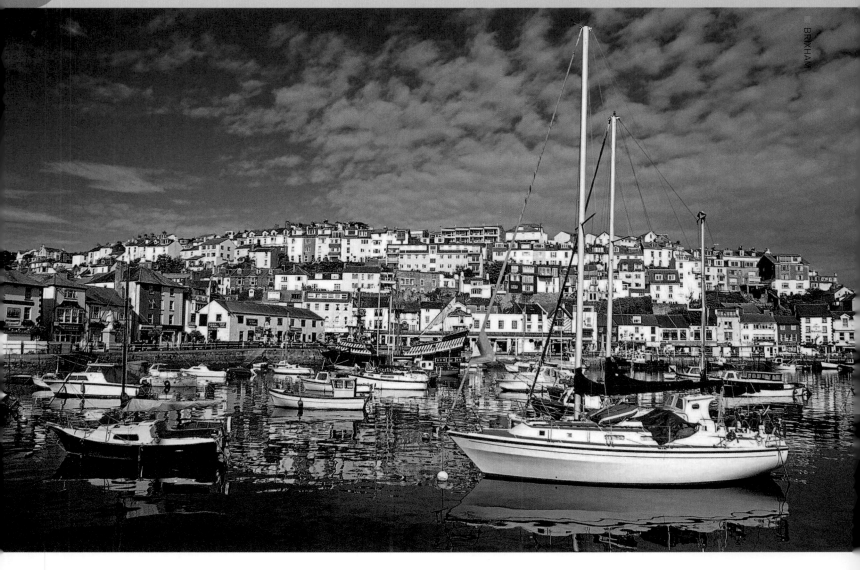

BRIXHAM

BARNSTAPLE MAP REF 398 F4

Barnstaple has attractive little alleyways, quiet corners and some fine buildings. These include the covered Pannier Market, built in the mid-19th century, where traditional markets as well as craft and antiques markets are held. Part of the same development is Butcher's Row, built to house 33 butchers' shops, though it has now been infiltrated by greengrocers, fishmongers and delicatessens.

One of the most historic sites in Barnstaple is the huge mound created by the Normans as a vantage point for their castle (only fragments of the original wall remain). But Barnstaple's history goes back further; records show that it was already the commercial centre for north Devon when it was first granted a charter in AD 930. It continued to prosper, becoming a major port for trade with America, and the ornate Queen Anne's Building down by the river dates from that era. Extensively renovated, it is now open to the public and contains the excellent Barnstaple Heritage Centre, portraying the history of the town with interactive displays and 'face-to-face' speaking models of figures from the town's past. These include the Elizabethan town clerk Adam Wyatt, whose book *Lost*

Chronicle is on sale in the Heritage Centre shop, and Mistress Grace Beaple, who, during the Civil War, sheltered Prince Charles (later Charles II). There are also reconstructions of the interior of a merchant's ship, a Civil War trench and scenes from earlier eras.

Near the bridge, the Museum of North Devon has lively and imaginative exhibits, including a room which takes visitors into an underwater world, complete with sound effects, with giant turtles and large fish mounted on a realistic marine background. The display of north Devon pottery is spectacular and, of course, Tarka the Otter is never very far away (the Tarka Trail passes through the town).

North of the town are the famous Marwood Hill Gardens, which occupy about 20 acres (8ha) of a sheltered valley. Pathways lead down between the hillside trees and shrubs to a series of lakes, inhabited by some enormous koi carp.

BEER MAP REF 399 H6

The lovely little fishing village of Beer occupies one of the most sheltered positions along this coast and its fishermen gained a reputation for hardy seamanship because they could put to

sea when others were kept at home by the pounding waves. Beer is known also for having the most westerly chalk cliffs in England, contrasting vividly with the deep red cliffs nearby and the lush green of the surrounding countryside. It was once home to a fine lace-making industry, established here by refugees from the Netherlands, and the quality of the work rivalled the more famous Honiton lace.

The Beer Quarry Caves offer a totally different experience, with an hour-long tour of these man-made caverns that extend for a quarter of a mile (400m) in each direction. The Romans worked these quarries nearly 2,000 years ago, and the vast caverns, with vaulted roofs connected with natural stone pillars, were hewn by hand over the intervening centuries. The Cretaceous limestone quarried at Beer was highly prized by stonemasons. Soft and easy to carve when it first comes out of the ground, it hardens when it is exposed to the elements; examples of the carved stone can be seen in Exeter Cathedral.

BRANSCOMBE MAP REF 399 H6

Branscombe is gorgeous. It stretches along one of the prettiest combes on the south coast, with picture-book thatched

cottages – complete with roses all around the door – lovely inns and an ancient church. St Winifred's dates back to just after the Norman Conquest and its tower contains a priest's room, from the time when the priest lived in the church.

Until 1987, the village bakery was the last traditional bakery in use in the county. Along with the old forge, Manor Mill and some farms and cottages, it has now been preserved by the National Trust and visitors can see the large faggot-fired oven, the great dough bins and traditional baking equipment in the baking room.

The drive from the village to the beach is along a narrow lane that goes steeply up and then down again to the sheltered bay. Much of the land to either side, including farmland and foreshore in places, is in the care of the National Trust and there are lovely walks, including one from the village. The pebble beach has rock pools at low tide and is good for swimming.

BRIXHAM MAP REF 399 G7

The least commercialized part of Torbay, Brixham is home to a pretty harbour surrounded by some fine old buildings and a handful of pretty colour-washed cottages. Here the fish and chip shops, inexpensive cafés and other typical seaside outlets seem to try to blend in with their traditional surroundings. This is very much a seafaring community, as evidenced by the replica of Francis Drake's ship the *Golden Hind* in the harbour (open to the public) and the aquarium and trawling exhibition on the dockside. Fishing continues today but only on a small scale. The Brixham Museum, New Road, traces the ebb and flow of the town's maritime fortunes over nine centuries of seafaring; you can get right up to date by visiting the nearby marina.

There are some fine beaches in the area – St Mary's Bay is large and sandy and excellent for families – but the rest are small shingle or pebble shores, good for walking and relatively peaceful and undeveloped. Just to the east of the town lies Berry Head Country Park, a splendid nature reserve, ideal for walking and for enjoying the views from the headland. The remains of a huge Napoleonic fort can also be visited here.

BUDLEIGH SALTERTON
MAP REF 399 H6

Budleigh Salterton became a resort in the wake of royal visits to nearby Sidmouth in Georgian and Victorian times, but it was – and remains – a quiet place, free of much of the bustle and amusements often associated with seaside holidays. It occupies a position on the west side of the Otter estuary (it was originally called Ottermouth), where one of the main industries used to be salt-panning, hence the 'Salterton' part of the name.

The beach at Otterhead (the mouth of the River Otter) is all pebbles, which shelve quite steeply into the sea, but swimming is safe enough in calm weather. If you prefer sand on your beach, walk westwards along the coast path to Littleham Cove, which is small and sheltered from the elements.

Many fine old buildings remain in the town, including Fairlynch in Fore Street, now a small but interesting museum that has displays on local history, the natural history of the River Otter and the Budleigh Salterton Railway, as well as a beautiful display of Devon lace and a fine costume collection. The Grade II listed building itself is of interest, being one of only a handful of thatched museums in the country, with many original features.

A little way inland is Otterton, a particularly pretty village made more so by its many thatched cottages. The watermill is the last working mill on the River Otter and you can see it in operation – milling takes place about once a fortnight. There are various displays on milling, as well as a craft shop, a gallery, a Devon food shop and a restaurant, plus live music on some evenings.

BURGH ISLAND   MAP REF 398 F7

One of the many curiosities of Devon, Burgh Island is a tiny rock covering just 28 acres (11ha) and can be seen clearly from the headland at Bigbury-on-Sea. Until the mid-19th century Burgh Island was a prosperous pilchard-fishing community. A lookout was stationed here and when the great shoals of pilchards were spotted he would shout to the local fishermen.

Burgh Island is in fact only an island at high tide. At other times you can walk or drive – 'England 282 metres', says the sign! The most novel way to arrive, however, is at high tide, aboard the extraordinary Burgh Island sea tractor, which, with its passenger compartment raised high above the waves, can safely cross in up to 7 feet (2m) of water.

CLOVELLY   MAP REF 398 E5

Of all Devon's pretty villages, this is surely the most famous and the most visited – which can make it too crowded for comfort at the height of the season. You need real stamina to visit Clovelly. Its single cobbled street has an alarming gradient which drops some 400 feet (122m) over the course of half a mile, and traffic is banned, so visitors have to park at the top of the hill and explore on foot. Two things you should be aware of: first, because of the steep cobbles, wear sensible footwear; second, visitors enter the village through the visitor centre and pay an admission fee. But if all this strikes you as commercialized, don't be put off, because Clovelly is well worth it. As if the narrow cobbled street weren't picturesque enough, the colour-washed 16th-century cottages that cluster along its slopes are decked with flowers and shrubs, and at the bottom is the lovely little harbour.

If you find walking back up the street a trial, spare a thought for those who live here – everything, from food to fuel and furniture, has to be carried down this street, or lowered on sleds. For those who may be weak of leg and short of breath, there is a Land Rover service from Easter to October to the car park by a back route. On the way to Clovelly along the A39 near Bucks Mills is Hobby Drive. It was constructed as a hobby (hence the name) in the 19th century by a wealthy local landowner. It is closed to traffic now, but offers a 3-mile (4.8km) walk through wooded slopes above the coastline.

CLOVELLY

DARTMOUTH MAP REF 399 G7

The ancient town and deep-water port of Dartmouth enjoys an unrivalled setting at the mouth of the picturesque River Dart, with steep green hills to either side and a busy, colourful estuary. The Embankment is a lovely uncluttered promenade, free of tourist trappings, and the attractive houses of Kingswear, many built for Dartmouth's wealthy merchants and sea captains, dot the far bank. Neither major road nor railway link has ever reached Dartmouth and this has undoubtedly helped the centre of town – a tiny web of criss-crossing cobbled streets and narrow alleyways – to retain its atmosphere and to protect it from the onslaught of modern traffic that blights many coastal towns.

In the very centre is the Boatfloat, a charming inner harbour only accessible to small craft. In the tourist information office, on the corner of the car park, is Thomas Newcomen's Atmospheric Steam Engine, invented in 1712, which is claimed to be the first ever successful steam engine. Also just off the Boatfloat, on Duke Street, is the 17th-century Butterwalk, a four-storey arcaded house decorated with wood carvings, its three upper floors supported by 11 granite pillars. It now houses shops and the delightful small Dartmouth Museum, with a whole flotilla of model ships and original 17th-century plaster and panelling. Further along Duke Street is the old cobbled market square

and building, erected in 1829, now home to various permanent shops but still the site of the weekly market.

Two buildings that have survived from the 14th century are the Cherub pub, Dartmouth's oldest building (1380) and Agincourt House. The prettiest part of town, however, is the charming cobbled quayside of Bayard's Cove. The Pilgrim Fathers put into this cove in 1620 en route to the New World and around five centuries earlier the Crusaders departed from here. You can explore the shell of a fortress, which was built in 1510 to protect the entrance to the harbour. Near the mouth of the river is Dartmouth Castle (English Heritage), a small fortification built in 1481 to stop sea raids on the town.

DAWLISH MAP REF 399 G6

This pleasantly old-fashioned seaside resort, once the haunt of authors, is famous for its landscaped gardens, known as the Lawn. These stretch back from the front, flanked by two peaceful streams which are home to black swans. Around here you'll find some fine Regency, Georgian and Victorian buildings, and there is a small local museum on Barton Terrace. One curious feature is that the mainline train runs alongside the beach. As many nostalgic local photographs confirm, this was a stirring sight in the days of steam and for most people it was the only way to get to the seaside.

EXETER MAP REF 399 G6

Exeter has just about everything you could wish for in a city. It has magnificent old buildings, fascinating places to visit, a lively arts programme and a new area with shops and restaurants, Princesshay, as well as a few surprises. Where else, for instance, can you explore the tunnels of a medieval water supply?

At its heart is the spectacular cathedral, which rises up from spacious lawns. The earliest part, the two great towers, dates from 1110, but most of the building is of the 14th century, including the beautiful west front, with its carved figures of apostles, prophets and soldiers. Inside the cathedral, the first thing that catches your eye is the roof of the central aisle. Dating from 1369, it is the longest unbroken Gothic vault in the world and can be studied using the magnifying mirrors provided.

The choir, with its magnificent oak carving, is in the centre of the cathedral. The bishop's throne, dating from 1312, is undoubtedly the finest in the country, and the 49 canopied stalls, dating from the 19th century, reflect its style. The cathedral has magnificently decorated tombs and monuments, delightful features among the carvings and peaceful little chapels, where there is no need to hurry.

One of the city's other major attractions is the revitalized historic quayside, where it is easy to imagine the wool-trading

vessels moored up alongside the quay. Here you can discover 2,000 years of Exeter's history in the Quay House Visitor Centre, where lively displays explain the history and development of the area. Then take your time to browse around a few of the antiques and craft shops.

Before extensive bombing in World War II changed the city, it was essentially medieval, and a number of old timbered buildings still exist, particularly along West Street and Stepcote Hill. Exeter's Guildhall has been used as the meeting place of the council since 1330 and visitors can see its remarkable timber roof and the collection of portraits, guild crests and civic silver.

The remains of St Nicholas's Priory, off Fore Street, date back to 1070. On the special 'Living History' days, 17th-century daily life is recreated. A most impressive reminder of Victorian Exeter exists in the extensive Royal Albert Memorial Museum, built in flamboyant Gothic style and housing rich collections.

EXMOUTH MAP REF 399 G6

There was a medieval settlement and port here at the mouth of the River Exe, but because of the tendency to silting at this eastern side of the river, Exmouth eventually could not compete as a port with Topsham or Exeter. The docks built at the western end of the Esplanade in the mid-19th century have been developed and now feature a smart marina and modern

Visit

DAWLISH WARREN NATURE RESERVE

More than 450 plant species are protected at this 500-acre (200ha) nature reserve, including a number of orchids and the famous Warren crocus, only found here. A large hide looks out over the estuary, where sanderling, oystercatchers and terns can be seen. In midwinter the estuary is host to Brent geese and a flock of wintering avocets. There is a visitor centre where guided walks start from.

housing complex, the latter enjoying superb sea views. As a resort, Exmouth began to develop at the end of the 18th century and today it is a popular spot, with long sandy beaches where there are rock pools to explore at half-tide.

Approximately 2 miles (3.2km) north is A La Ronde (National Trust), a 16-sided thatched house that was built in 1796 for spinster cousins Jane and Mary Parminter. Both the house and its contents are the result of their Grand Tour of Europe, and the interiors mirror their particular eccentricities. The rooms are arranged around an octagonal hall, and the Shell Gallery is decorated with shells, feathers and other natural materials.

GREAT TORRINGTON MAP REF 398 F5

This is a delightful little town with a great deal to see and do. Turn off the through-road going into the town centre and you will discover the heart of the place – a charming square that is most people's idea of what a real town centre should be. There is a lovely old inn, which has Civil War connections, a fine town hall and a market hall, and just around the corner from the square the Plough Arts Centre has a lively programme of jazz, theatre, film and stand-up comedy.

Great Torrington is set high on a hill overlooking lush agricultural land. On three sides it is bordered by common land, preserved by an Act of Parliament, and below it flows the wide River Torridge. The Dartington Crystal factory was established in the town in the 1960s, when Swedish craftsmen were brought here to train a local workforce in the difficult art of glass-blowing. The company rapidly expanded, exporting its fine crystal all over the world, but its operation here is very much geared to the large number of visitors it receives. The factory tours are fascinating, and walkways enable visitors to look down over the teams of craftsmen and witness their glass-blowing skills. Every stage in the production, from furnace

to packing case, can be seen. There is a very good video introduction and a display of glassware in the entrance hall, as well as the opportunity to buy from a range of glassware in the showroom.

Just south of the town on the B3220 Exeter road, RHS Rosemoor Gardens have long been famous and are continuing to expand and develop new areas of cultivation. The original 8 acres (3.2ha) were created by Lady Anne Barry to surround her home, but in 1988 she gave them, along with a further 32 acres (13ha) of land, to the Royal Horticultural Society, which has wasted no time in making full use of the golden opportunity provided. A National Garden has been thoughtfully created here, and the previously uncultivated land has been planted with a number of gardens.

There are two rose gardens, wonderful herbaceous borders, a lovely herb garden and potager, colour-themed gardens, an extensive stream and bog garden centred on an ornamental lake, a cottage garden and a foliage garden. Fruit and vegetable cultivation is featured and exciting new developments are always under way. There is a good visitor centre with a restaurant and shop, and plants for sale.

HARTLAND POINT MAP REF 398 E5

To many people, Hartland Point is more dramatic than Land's End. It looks out over one of the most treacherous stretches of water in Britain, with strong currents and huge jagged rocks. Even on the calmest of days, the waters swirl menacingly around the headland. Just to the east is lovely, unspoilt Shipload Bay (National Trust), practically inaccessible since the steps leading to the beach were damaged. Hartland Quay is 3 miles (4.8km) in the other direction, accessible by road.

The village of Hartland, inland, is pleasant, but its parish church at nearby Stoke is a real treasure, its size out of all proportion to the local community. Also nearby, you'll find Hartland Abbey, an 18th-century Gothic-style mansion.

HONITON MAP REF 399 H5

This town is easy to explore because just about everything is in the High Street, a charming wide thoroughfare lined with Georgian buildings. Its unity of style is due to a series of fires during the 18th century, which destroyed much of the original town that had stood here since about 1200. The straightness of its main street is due to the fact that the town was originally built astride an old Roman road. High Street is one of those streets that just begs you to get out of your car and wander up and down for a while, to browse around the variety of little shops, many of them selling antiques, and explore the courtyards and alleyways that run off at right angles. The old Pannier Market has been converted into an attractive little parade of shops.

Of course, what Honiton is most famous for is lace, and there is a wonderful collection in the Allhallows Museum, housed in Honiton's oldest building, a 13th-century chapel beside St Paul's Church. The museum also has lace-making demonstrations and displays which relate to the town's pottery and lace-making industries.

LUNDY MAP REF 398 E4

Lundy has an enormous variety of things to see and do. It is reached by boat, the MS *Oldenburg*, from either Bideford or Ilfracombe, and the trip takes 2 hours. There is also a year-round helicopter service available.

Just over 3 miles (4.8km) long and about half a mile (800m) across at its widest point, Lundy has steep granite cliffs rising to over 400 feet (122m) and the land varies from rough grazing in the north to fertile farm land in the south. Although once famous for its successful breeding colony of puffins, numbers fell significantly. Thankfully, after a gap of several years and conservation work by the RSPB, puffins bred again on Lundy in 2005. Visitors will see many other kinds of birds, as well as seals, basking sharks, sika deer, Soay

sheep, mountain goats and Lundy ponies. There is also a great deal of evidence of the island's fascinating history to see also, including an ancient burial chamber and a cave that was used as a prison. You can also see the cannons which were fired in Georgian times as a fog warning and a chasm that opened up when tremors from the Lisbon earthquake in 1755 reached Lundy. The real hub of the island's social life is the Marisco Tavern, a friendly pub serving Lundy beer.

All of Lundy is beautiful, but the most spectacular views can be enjoyed from the west side. If wild plants are your particular interest, explore the eastern side, and if you are a climber there are more than 60 challenging rock faces which can be tackled; many are closed during the seabird breeding season (April to July).

OTTERY ST MARY MAP REF 399 H6

This pleasant little town lies on the River Otter and was the birthplace in 1772 of the poet Samuel Taylor Coleridge, whose father was vicar of St Mary's Church. The church may seem too grand for a sleepy little Devon town, and it certainly had more modest beginnings in the 13th century, but in 1340 Bishop John de Grandisson had it enlarged, with Exeter Cathedral much in his mind. The interior is rich in medieval craftsmanship and there is an ancient astronomical clock, which is still in working order.

Not far away from Ottery is Cadhay, a classic Tudor manor house which was enlarged and remodelled in Georgian style. It is an interesting house with a history of mixed fortunes – one minute a social honeypot, the next declining as the owners fell into debt after supporting the wrong side in the Civil War. In the 18th century, a new owner raised its status once more, only for it to become a boarding house for agricultural workers in the 19th century. Fortunately, Cadhay was rescued and restored in 1909 and is now a fascinating and charming place to visit.

PAIGNTON MAP REF 399 G7

Around a century ago, Paignton was described as 'a neat and improving village and bathing place'. It remains a popular bathing place but is no longer a village, and, due to its amusement arcades, inexpensive cafés and discount stores, is often regarded as a poor relation to neighbouring Torquay. Paignton, however, is unabashed, and performs its role as provider of cheap holidays very effectively.

The beaches, some of the best in the Southwest, are the main draw, particularly Goodrington Sands, which has the region's largest water park. Although the town itself may appear devoid of high culture, there are historic houses to visit. Oldway Mansion, built by Isaac Singer (founder of the sewing-machine empire) in 1874, is now used as council offices, but the best rooms are open to the public. Just outside town is Compton Castle (National Trust), a fortified manor house built between 1340 and 1520 and home to the descendants of Sir Humphrey Gilbert, who colonized Newfoundland. Paignton Zoo, in 75 acres (30ha) a mile (1.6km) from the town, is one of the largest zoos in the country, with all the favourites – lions, tigers, elephants, rhinos, monkeys and giraffes. For many visitors the finest thing to come out of Paignton is the Paignton and Dartmouth Steam Railway, which steams along to Kingswear by the Dart estuary.

SALCOMBE MAP REF 399 G7

The blue saucer of Salcombe Bay, aflutter with white triangular sails, surrounded by the green hills of the South Hams and fringed by golden pocket-handkerchief beaches, is one of south Devon's finest sights. Salcombe is among the largest yachting centres in England and several old wharf houses are workshops for boat makers and marine engineers.

The tiny golden beach of North Sands is adjacent to the picturesque ruin of Salcombe Castle/Fort Charles, which was built in 1544 but was destroyed during the Civil War. Continue on to South Sands and Splat Cove or catch a ferry to one of the beaches on the other side of the bay.

About 1.5 miles (2.4km) southwest of Salcombe, at Sharpitor, is Overbecks Museum and Garden (National Trust), a charming Edwardian house which is largely dedicated to local maritime affairs. Overbecks' beautifully landscaped 6-acre (2.4ha) garden, set high above the estuary, is full of rare and exotic specimens which flourish in the area's mild micro-climate and is worth a visit for its views alone.

SAUNTON SANDS & BRAUNTON BURROWS MAP REF 398 F4

Saunton Sands is one of the best beaches in Devon, a 3-mile (4.8km) curve of golden sands backed by grassy dunes. Towards the northern end of the beach is a little car park

with a small shop, toilets and a beach bar and café. It is at this end that most visitors congregate, particularly surfers and those with young families. If you walk further on you will have a quieter beach experience, and an interrupted walk across the sand to the sea. Be warned, though, that the very southern end of the beach has treacherous sea currents which make swimming here very dangerous.

It is better to turn inland here and explore the Braunton Burrows. This incorporates one of the largest sand dune systems in Britain and is famous for its plant and animal life, receiving Biosphere status from UNESCO in 2002. Marram grass holds the sands in place, and where the ground has stabilized, other plants, such as stonecrop, viper's bugloss and evening primrose, carpet the ground with splashes of colour. In the damper areas there are the marsh varieties of marigolds, orchids and helleborines. Flocks of wading birds populate the estuary, migrating birds rest here and there is also a huge variety of moths and butterflies. The Ministry of Defence leases an area of the reserve for training; red warning flags are flown when exercises are in progress.

SIDMOUTH MAP REF 399 H6

This is a quiet and genteel resort, and has been since it was favoured by royal patronage in the early 19th century. Much

of its architecture goes back to Regency days, with elegant wrought-iron balconies and white-painted facades, and colourful gardens and floral displays enhance the scene. One of these imposing Regency buildings, in Church Street, houses the Sid Vale Heritage Centre, with interesting collections and detailed information about local history; guided walks depart from here two mornings a week. Visitors with a scientific bent should check out the Norman Lockyer Observatory on Salcombe Hill, with its planetarium, library, radio and weather stations, and historic telescopes.

A complete transformation comes over (or overcomes) Sidmouth during the first week in August, when singers, dancers and musicians from all over the world descend on the town for its famous music festival. Organized events are staged at various venues around the town, not to mention the impromptu ones that occur whenever two or more performers find themselves in any previously peaceful pub, street corner, park or bit of beach. Sitting in the sun listening to some good live music is a bonus for some holidaymakers.

SLAPTON MAP REF 399 G7

Slapton Sands is an uncommercialized 2-mile (3.2km) long windswept shingle ridge, a favourite spot for walking. Slapton Ley, which is divided from the beach by the road, is a freshwater lake, famous for its wildfowl. This is a National Nature Reserve and a public hide, for birdwatching, is situated in the Torcross car park.

Slapton (0.5 mile/800m inland and not to be confused with Torcross, at the southernmost part of Slapton Sands) has a fine medieval church. The impressive tower to the north of the church is all that remains of the College of Chantry Priests, founded in 1373. North of Slapton Sands is sandy Blackpool Sands, perhaps the best beach in the South Hams.

START POINT MAP REF 399 G7

The dramatic southwesterly tip of the South Hams, Start Point has cliffs rising over 100 feet (30.5m) high. On the south side they are almost sheer and streaked by quartz veins which run through the dark rock. A lighthouse (tours available) warns shipping off the dangerous bank known as the Skerries. In Elizabethan times, pirates were hung in chains here as a warning to other lawless seafarers.

From Start Point the coast path heads west along to Prawle Point, the most southern extremity of Devon. The latter, which can be lashed by the full fury of

the waves in stormy weather, has been chiselled and chipped into an almost vertical drop, plunging into the sea beneath the coastguard lookout station.

TEIGNMOUTH MAP REF 399 G6

The red cliffs with a verdant fringe and the red-sand beaches of Teignmouth (which should be pronounced 'Tin-muth') create a distinctive Devon seafront; the picture complete with an old-fashioned pier.

The town became a fashionable holiday resort in the late 18th and early 19th centuries and if you look along Powderham Terrace or the Den, or just up above the fronts of the many cafés and tourist shops, you will see that it retains a good deal of its Georgian and early Victorian architecture. The Quays are full of character; this is the old harbour area, which has for centuries shipped huge quantities of Bovey ball clay and Dartmoor granite. A small fishing fleet also operates from here. You can learn more about the town's local and maritime history if you go to the museum in French Street.

A narrow bridge connects Teignmouth to pretty Shaldon village. There the houses, many of which date back to Georgian

times, are packed so closely together that the only sensible way of visiting the village is by ferry from Teignmouth, a service that dates back to Elizabethan times.

There's a fine church to see but the favourite attraction is the charming Shaldon Wildlife Trust. It is a breeding centre for rare and endangered species of small mammals, exotic birds and reptiles and because of its tiny size many of its inmates are very tame. Close by, the erroneously named 'Smuggler's tunnel' leads down to Shaldon's own beach, the Ness, backed by a bold red cliff. Looking out from the top of the cliff there are marvellous views of Teignmouth and across the Teign estuary.

TIVERTON MAP REF 399 G5

For a town to prosper these days, its proximity to the motorway network is of considerable importance. In times gone by it was the rivers that provided a lifeline. Tiverton, with its two rivers, the Grand Western Canal and the M5 just a short distance away, has always been advantaged and it remains a lively centre. Tiverton's appearance owes much to the prosperity of its textile and clothing

industries in the 16th and 17th centuries, when rich wool merchants endowed their town with such splendid buildings as St Peter's Church, Blundell's School, the fine Great House and three sets of almshouses. St George's Church, built in 1773, is thought to be one of the finest Georgian churches to be built in Devon.

Tiverton's history is documented in the town museum in St Andrew Street. It includes the Heathcoat Lace Gallery, an agricultural section, two waterwheels and a railway gallery. Tiverton's two rivers are the Exe and the Lowman (Tiverton means 'two-ford town'), and the former is overlooked by Tiverton Castle. Dating from 1106, all that remains of the original building is one circular tower.

North of Tiverton is Knightshayes Court (National Trust), which is well worth taking time out to visit. This ornate 19th-century mansion was built for Sir John Heathcoat-Amory. Designed by William Burges, it features rich Gothic-style decoration, painted ceilings and wall stencilling. The house is more than equally matched by the wonderful grounds that surround it, comprising pleasing formal gardens, woodland and ornamental shrubs.

SIDMOUTH

Visit
PREHISTORIC RESIDENTS

As far as we know, the earliest human occupation of the British Isles was around 400,000 years ago and Kents Cavern provides evidence to this effect. At Torquay a layer of conglomerate limestone revealed simple tools and signs of stone working from that date, as well as the earlier remains of animals such as sabre-toothed tigers and mammoths.

Visit
A FLAVOUR OF HISTORIC SHALDON

Every Wednesday during the summer months, Shaldon turns the clock back to 1785 with traders dressed in period costume, special craft stalls and evening entertainment.

Visit
TWO ANCIENT WATERING HOLES

Walk to the top of Fore Street in Totnes, then up into the Narrows, turn left into Leechwell Street to the town's oldest pub, 17th-century Kingsbridge Inn. To the left, Leechwell Lane runs down to an ancient well with three granite troughs. This well was once thought to have had medicinal properties.

TORQUAY MAP REF 399 G7

Torquay is south Devon at its most continental – a balmy climate, palm trees sparkling with coloured lights and millionaires' yachts basking in the marina. The large number of English-language students and foreign tourists adds an exotic chatter to the town. Yet this is also the capital of the English Riviera.

From humble beginnings as a fishing village, the town's resort career began during Napoleonic times, and during the height of the Victorian era its mild winters were attracting consumptives and fashionable visitors on doctors' orders. By 1850 it was proclaiming itself 'Queen of the Watering Holes' and today it is still a popular seaside resort.

The centre of town is the lively marina and harbour, including the copper-domed Edwardian Pavilion, which houses an excellent shopping centre. Eastwards the cliffs rise up to Daddy Hole Plain, a great chasm in the cliff where the plain meets the sea, and the views from here are superb. Continue east to the point at Hope's Nose for more sea panoramas.

The beaches, though not as broad and sandy as those to be found at neighbouring Paignton, are numerous and spread well apart, which helps to dissipate the summer crowds. The most attractive of the major beaches is Oddicombe, with its backdrop of steep sandstone cliffs topped by lush woodland. The descent is steep and a cliff railway runs down 720 feet (220m) to the shingle below.

The Oddiccmbe/Babbacombe area is also home to Torquay's best tourist attractions. Kents Cavern forms one of the most important prehistoric sites in Europe, where a half a mile (800m) guided tour takes you back through two million years of history. More cave finds can be seen at the Torquay Museum on Babbacombe Road. The museum has a wide range of galleries and some fascinating displays.

Another excellent wet-weather option, in the charming St Marychurch parish, is Bygones, a life-size re-creation of a Victorian street, illustrating shops and dwellings, including an ironmonger, grocer, sweet shop and apothecary. Visit the giant model railway and the 'Trench Experience' of World War I. A further option, and one of Torquay's main attractions is Babbacombe Model Village, an outstanding piece of design.

Next to the harbour is Torre Abbey, from where the town derives its name. Constructed in the 12th century, the abbey was dissolved and subsumed into a 16th-century mansion, itself remodelled in the Georgian period. It now holds the municipal art gallery and history collection. In the grounds are monastic ruins, the well-preserved abbey gatehouse, exotic gardens and a splendid 12th-century tithe barn, known as the Spanish Barn, since it was used in 1588 to hold around 400 Armada prisoners who had been captured by Sir Francis Drake.

About one mile (1.6km) west of the centre of town is the chocolate-box village of Cockington, a delightful crossroads gathering of thatched cottages with an old smithy, working waterwheel, village stocks and a mill pond. The grounds and gardens of 19th-century Cockington Court are open to the public and include a craft centre, cafés and gallery.

WATERSMEET MAP REF 399 G4

This renowned beauty spot, now in the care of the National Trust, can be reached on footpaths from Lynmouth or by car. Once at Watersmeet, the network of riverside paths expands to give walkers plenty of choice. The waters that meet here are the East Lyn River and Hoaroak Water, both of which take the form of a series of pools, with water tumbling from one to another over the rocks. The steep sides of the valley are heavily wooded, mostly sessile oak, with some beech and larch, with an undergrowth of ferns, mosses and an abundance of wild flowers. The National Trust has an information centre, shop and tea rooms at Watersmeet House.

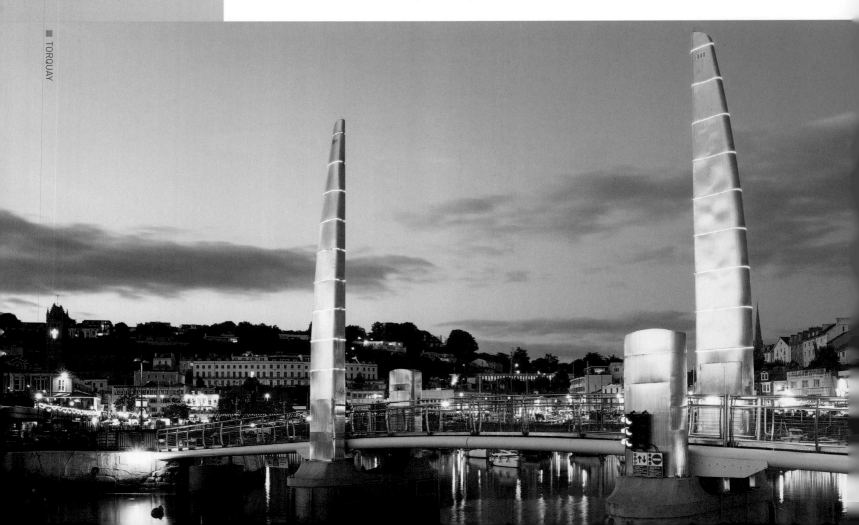

BICKLEIGH & THE EXE VALLEY

Leave the crowds behind at picturesque Bickleigh Bridge and explore the lovely Exe Valley along leafy country lanes and wildflower-strewn tracks. Bickleigh Castle, on the banks of the River Exe, is approached along a quiet lane, shaded by huge oak, ash and beech trees. Bickleigh Mill, the working watermill, has craft shops and a restaurant.

DISTANCE/TIME 5.75 miles (9.2km) 2h15 **MAP** OS Explorer 114 Exeter & the Exe Valley **START** Bickleigh Mill, just off A396, at Bickleigh Bridge; grid ref: SX 938075 **PATHS** Country lanes, one long steep track **THE PUB** The Fisherman's Cot, Bickleigh. Tel: 01884 855237

1 From the laneside near Bickleigh Mill go back, with care, to the A396 and cross the bridge. Turn left down the A3072, following the brown tourist sign for Bickleigh Castle. Take the first lane left, running along the edge of the flood plain on the Exe Valley Way (EVW). Bickleigh Castle will soon be found on the right. Go straight on along the lane.

2 Pass Way Farm and take the next lane right to leave the Exe Valley Way, roughly signposted 'Lee Cross & Perry Farm'. Take care along here, this is a very narrow lane, carrying traffic from local farms. Keep walking along the lane as it climbs steeply uphill and after 700yds (637m) you'll reach the farm at Lee Cross. Keep ahead up the lane to pass Perry Farm. Eventually the lane bears sharp left and then right.

3 Turn left on a green lane and walk uphill, with increasingly good views over the Exe Valley and back to Bickleigh. Pass a restored chapel – St Martins – on the left, and keep ahead; at last the track levels off.

4 Where the green lane meets the tarmac lane, turn left and proceed steeply downhill

(EVW). The views over the River Exe, and to Silverton church beyond, are glorious. Follow the lane down until you see Tray Mill Farm on the right.

5 The way home is straight on, but it's worth making a short detour to the river here. Turn right through the farmyard and pass through a metal gate on to a concrete standing. Cross the field, aiming for the suspension bridge ahead. Cross over (not for the faint-hearted!) to reach the dismantled railway track. Do not turn left along the track – although it would take you back to your car– it is privately owned and has no public right of way.

6 The path goes straight on here to meet the A369. You can do that, turn left, then eventually right to walk through Bickleigh village to the mill, but it is a busy road and you would be better advised to retrace your steps to Tray Mill Farm and take the quieter route back to Bickleigh Mill.

7 Back on the lane by Tray Mill Farm, turn right and walk straight along the lane, past Bickleigh Castle, turning right at the A3072, and right again over the bridge to return to your car.

WALK 8

BIGBURY-ON-SEA & BURGH ISLAND

This short walk, initially inland through farmland, returns to Bigbury-on-Sea via the dramatic coastal path. Just off Bigbury beach, 307yds (279m) from shore, lies craggy Burgh Island, which can still be reached by giant sea tractor whenever the tide is in. When the tide is out, however, you can simply stroll across the sand.

DISTANCE/TIME 4 miles (6.4km) 1h45 **MAP** OS Explorer OL20 South Devon **START** Huge car park at Bigbury-on-Sea; grid ref: SX 652442 **PATHS** Fields, tracks (muddy in winter) and coast path, 3 stiles **THE PUB** The Pilchard Inn, Burgh Island. Tel: 01548 810514

1 Leave the car park through the entrance. Follow the coast path signs right (low tide route along beach to seasonal ferry to Bantham), then left towards the road and right on to the cliffs. Turn left before some bungalows, then left to the road. Cross over, then go through a kissing gate and turn right uphill, passing through two big gates, to a path junction near Mount Folly Farm.

2 Turn left along a track, signed 'Ringmore'. At the top of the field there is junction of paths; go through the kissing gate and keep ahead downhill, signed 'Ringmore', with a fence right. Pass through a metal gate, drop down through a kissing gate, and keep ahead to another on a farm track. Walk up the next field, crossing a stile on to the lane.

3 Cross over, following signs for 'Ringmore', through a metal gate. Walk down into the next combe, keeping the hedge bank to the right. Cross a stream at the bottom on a concrete walkway, and over a stile. Ignore the path left, but go straight ahead, uphill, through a plantation and through a gate on to a narrow path between a fence and a hedge.

4 Pass through a kissing gate, bear right then turn immediately left uphill to reach a

path junction, then pass through kissing gate and follow the path to Ringmore. Turn right at the lane, then left at the church. Journey's End Inn is on the right.

5 From here, turn right down a narrow lane which gives way to a footpath. It winds round gardens to meet a tarmac lane. Turn left downhill. Walk straight down the track, eventually passing Lower Manor Farm, and continue past the 'National Trust Ayrmer Cove' notice. After a small gate and a stream crossing keep ahead at a path junction.

6 Go through a kissing gate and walk towards the cove on a grassy path above the combe on the left. Pass through gates and over a stile to gain the beach.

7 Follow coast path signs, 'Challaborough' left over a small footbridge then climb very steeply uphill to the cliff top and great views over Burgh Island. Cliffs are unstable here – take care. The path then leads to Challaborough – a huge holiday park.

8 Turn right along the beach road and take a track uphill along coast towards Bigbury-on-Sea. Go straight on to a tarmac road, then bear right on the coast path to the car park.

EAST PORTLEMOUTH TO LIMEBURY POINT

Follow this coastal stroll from the hamlet of East Portlemouth, which has some of the best views in the area. From Limebury Point you can see across the estuary to Overbecks (National Trust), an elegant Edwardian house in a magnificent setting above South Sands. A ferry connects East Portlemouth and Salcombe.

DISTANCE/TIME 4 miles (6.4km) 2h   **MAP** OS Explorer OL20 South Devon   **START** Near phone box in East Portlemouth or in small parking bay; grid ref: SX 746386   **PATHS** Good coast path, field paths and tracks   **THE PUB** The Victoria Inn, Salcombe. Tel: 01548 842604; www.victoriainn-salcombe.co.uk

1 Park on the verge near the phone box at East Portlemouth (or in the parking area – village hall fund contributions). Walk across the parking area and then go steeply downhill on a narrow tarmac footpath signposted to 'Salcombe', which gives way to steep steps.

2 When you reach the lane at the bottom of the steps, turn right if you want to stop for refreshments at The Venus Café and catch the ferry to Salcombe. To continue with the walk, turn left along the lane as it follows the edge of the estuary. This is the official route of the coast path and it passes some very exclusive residences.

3 The lane leads to the pretty, sandy beach at Mill Bay. Carefully follow the acorn coast path signs for Gara Rock through a sycamore wood, with lovely views across the estuary, and glimpses of inviting little coves.

4 At Limebury Point you reach open cliff, from where there are great views to South Sands and Overbecks, opposite, and craggy Bolt Head. The coast path now bears eastwards below Portlemouth Down.

5 The path along this stretch undulates steeply, and is rocky in places. Keep going

until you reach the bench and a superb viewpoint over the beach at Rickham Sands. Just beyond this, as the coast path continues to the right (there is reasonable access to the beach), take the left-hand fork and climb steeply up below the lookout to reach a signpost by the site of the old Gara Rock Hotel (demolished in 2006).

6 Turn left to reach the hotel drive and walk straight on up the lane. After 250yds (228m) turn left through a gate in the hedge ,signposted 'Mill Bay'. Walk straight ahead through a gate and across the field, bearing right to a gate; note Malborough church in the distance. Go through a small copse, then a gate and across the farm track. Go through a gate down the public bridleway.

7 This runs gradually downhill beneath huge, ancient, pollarded lime trees, with a grassy combe to the right. The path leads past the car park to reach Mill Bay.

8 Turn right along the lane. If you want to avoid the steps, look out for a footpath sign pointing right, up a narrow, steep, path to regain East Portlemouth and your car; if not, continue along the lane and retrace your route up the steps.

ALONG CLIFFS TO DARTMOUTH CASTLE

This is an easy round walk along the cliffs to Blackstone Point and Dartmouth Castle – and a ferry ride to the pub. Cared for by English Heritage, 15th-century Dartmouth Castle, which occupies a fine position at the mouth of the Dart, was built to protect the homes and warehouses of the town's merchants.

DISTANCE/TIME 3.5 miles (5.6km) 2h **MAP** OS Explorer OL20 South Devon **START** National Trust car park at Little Dartmouth; grid ref: SX 874491 **PATHS** Easy coastal footpath and green lanes; 1 stile **THE PUB** The Royal Castle Hotel, Dartmouth. Tel: 01803 833033; www.royalcastle.co.uk. Drive to Dartmouth or take the ferry from Stumpy Steps.

1 The car parks at Little Dartmouth are signposted off the B3205 (from the A379 Dartmouth-to-Stoke Fleming road). Go through the right-hand car park, following the signs 'Coast Path Dartmouth'. Continue through a kissing gate, keeping the hedge to your right. Walk through the next field, then through a gate and another kissing gate to join the coast path.

2 Turn left; there are lovely views west to Start Point and east towards the Day Beacon above Kingswear. The coast path runs a little inland from the cliff edge, but you can always walk out on to Warren Point (a plaque reveals that the Devon Federation of Women's Institutes gave this land to the National Trust in 1970).

3 From Warren Point follow the coast to pass above Western Combe Cove (with steps down to the sea) and then Combe Point (take care – it's a long drop to the sea from here).

4 Rejoin the coast path through an open gateway in a wall and follow it above Shinglehill Cove. The path turns inland, passes a pond and follows a track, then bears right along the back of Willow Cove. It passes above woods (with a field left) and then climbs to pass through a gate. Follow

the yellow arrow ahead to reach a footpath post, then turn sharp right down the valley, bearing right at the bottom to a stile as signed. Follow the path on, and through a gate near Compass Cove.

5 Follow the coast path left over a footbridge, and continue towards Blackstone Point. The path turns inland to run along the side of the estuary through deciduous woodland.

6 The path meets a surfaced lane opposite Compass Cottage; keep ahead on to the lane and immediately right again steeply downhill. Follow coast path signs right to zig-zag steeply down then up steps to reach a turning space, then go right down steps to reach the castle and café.

7 Retrace your route up the steps, then turn left up the lane to Point 6, then left to pass Compass Cottage, and continue straight on up the steep lane (signposted 'Little Dartmouth') and through a kissing gate on to National Trust land.

8 The path runs along the top of a field and through a five-bar gate on to a green lane. Go through a gate and the farmyard at Little Dartmouth and ahead on a tarmac lane to the car park.

DISTANCE/TIME 11 miles (17.7km) 2h15 **MAP** OS Explorer 128 Taunton & Blackdown Hills and 114 Exeter & the Exe Valley **START** Sampford Peverell; grid ref: ST 030142 **TRACKS** Canalside path, most gritty **THE PUB** Globe Inn, Sampford Peverell. Tel: 01884 821214; www.the-globeinn.co.uk

DISTANCE/TIME 12 miles (19.3km) 2h15 **MAP** OS Explorer 114 Exeter & the Exe Valley and 110 Torquay & Dawlish **START** The Quay, Exeter; grid ref: SX 920920 **TRACKS** Mainly well-surfaced path **THE PUB** Turf Hotel, Exminster. Tel: 01392 833128; www.turfpub.net

ALONG THE GRAND WESTERN CANAL TO TIVERTON

This peaceful ride along the banks of the old Grand Western Canal passes through the Grand Western Canal Country Park and the beautiful countryside of mid-Devon before finally reaching the centre of Tiverton. The canal provides ideal wildlife habitats and it's a wonderful place for wild flowers and butterflies, too.

1 From the back of the car park, pass the tennis court (left), bear left round a gate and uphill to the towpath (don't go too fast or you might easily overshoot!). Construction of the canal began in 1810, part of a scheme to link the English and Bristol Channels via Exeter and Bristol, but only the Tiverton and Taunton stretch was completed, in 1814. Competition from the railways eventually forced the closure of the canal, although this section was still being used to transport limestone from quarries in the area around Westleigh to Tiverton as late as 1924. Turn left along the towpath, passing The Globe Inn. Pass under Sampford Peverell bridge (best to dismount) and continue along a short stretch of quiet lane. Where that bears left, keep ahead along the canalside and you will find yourself immediately out in the countryside, with good views of the wooded Blackdown Hills to the left – you may well feel as if you're miles away from anywhere.

2 Continue to pass under Battens Bridge, then Rock Bridge. The next bridge is constructed from metal. These – look out for them along the route – were originally wooden swing bridges, which allowed the passage of barges and linked farmers' land where it was split by the canal.

3 Continue cycling along an embanked stretch to pass under the Greenway Bridge (car park) and then Sellake Bridge. Note how the canal takes a wide sweep to the left; this is known as the Swan's Neck, and was necessary to avoid the village of Halberton.

4 Next stop is Tiverton Road Bridge (car park and picnic area), where you may see canoes and kayaks. There was once a stone-crushing yard here; the journey from a quarry 8 miles (12.9km) away at Whipcott took 2.5 hours, with two horses pulling three 10-ton barges. Note milestone III on the left; it's only 3 miles (4.8km) further to the basin at Tiverton. Keep on to Crownhill Bridge, once known as Change Path. Horses had to change to the right bank here; you do the same by crossing the bridge and turning left.

5 Cross the brick aqueduct of the Bristol and Exeter Railway line, built in 1847; the Tiverton branch closed to passenger traffic in 1964. Three more bridges bring you to neat hedges and bungalows marking the edge of Tiverton. Tidcombe Bridge (look out for milestone I) marks another loop, made necessary by the Bishop of Exeter's refusal to allow the canal within 100yds (91m) of his home, grand Tidcombe Hall, nearby.

6 Built in 1842, Tiverton Canal Basin makes an excellent focus for this ride. You can buy refreshments en route at the thatched 16th-century Canal Tearooms, below the basin or from the floating Barge Canal shop. Look out, too, for the old lime kilns to the right. Until the late 19th century limestone was burned here to produce fertilizer. Farmers are said to have travelled up to 30 miles (48km) each way by horse and cart to collect it. To return to the start point at Sampford Peverell, simply retrace your steps back along the canal towpath to the car park.

EXETER SHIP CANAL

Follow the banks of the historic Exeter Ship Canal from the city's hub: the old quayside. The route runs through a lovely stretch of 'inner city' countryside before striking south along the canal through nature reserves and marshes to reach the Turf hotel, situated on the Exe estuary.

1 From Saddles & Paddles cross the quay to the riverside. Turn right and cycle upstream to Cricklepit Bridge (built in 1905). From here turn right over the bridge and right again on the other side. Cycle along the riverside walkway and keep ahead to cycle between the river on the left and canal basin (originally called The New Cut) on the right. Pass Trew's Weir, and the Port Royal on the opposite bank, to reach the canal.

2 Turn left over the canal; turn right along the tarmac way between the canal and the flood prevention 'trough'. Where the path forks, keep left. Look for yellow flag iris and purple loosestrife below left. Pass playing fields on the right bearing right at the end to reach the canal by a small car park (right).

3 Do not cross the canal; turn left on a tarmac cycle track that parallels the canal. The track bears away from the canal to pass to the left of the Double Locks pub, built in 1702. Continue to a fork just before the A379, passing the Double Locks Wetlands on the left, a managed area of reedbeds and a haven for wild flowers, birds and insects.

4 Take the right fork; cross the A379 at the traffic lights (note the swing bridge over the canal). On the other side, the track becomes (initially) narrower and tougher. Pass a small parking area (right) then cycle under the M5; from now on you're out in peaceful countryside. The Exe Estuary silted up during the 14th century, and the canal – the earliest working ship canal in England – was started around 1564, linking Exeter to Trenchard's Sluice (which entered the river by the M5 viaduct). The canal was extended to Topsham (a port since Roman times, seen across the canal and river to the left) in 1676. In the early 19th century – under the engineer James Green – it reached the Turf Lock. Its fortunes deteriorated after Brunel's railway reached Exeter in 1844, and then Exmouth (on the east side of the estuary) in 1861.

5 Arrive at the basin at the Turf Lock where the canal reaches the Exe estuary and you have lovely views ahead towards the sea. The building housing The Turf Hotel was built around the same time, and probably accommodated visiting boat crews. Horse-drawn barges then transported goods up the canal to Exeter.

6 Cycle back to Exeter. Exminster Marshes (this side) and Bowling Green marshes (on the other side of the estuary) are RSPB reserves, so keep an eye out for birdlife. It is also an important place for migrant birds.

DISTANCE/TIME 11 miles (17.7km) 1h30 **MAP** OS Explorer 139 Bideford, Ilfracombe & Barnstaple **START** Braunton car park (contributions); grid ref: SS 486365 **TRACKS** Level tarmac and gritty former railway track **THE PUB** The Williams Arms, Wrafton. Tel: 01271 812360; www.williams-arms.co.uk

DISTANCE/TIME 11 miles (17.7km) 2h30 **MAP** OS Explorer 126 Clovelly & Hartland **START** Car park on Great Torrington Common; grid ref: SS 485193 **TRACKS** Level former railway track, now smooth tarmac **THE PUB** The Puffing Billy, Great Torrington. Tel: 01805 623050

BRAUNTON TO BARNSTAPLE

Visiting Barnstaple by car at the height of the tourist season can be something of a trial, as this North Devon market town can get pretty choked by traffic. So what better way to get into the heart of Barnstaple than by cycling from Braunton via the Tarka Trail, along the edge of the Taw estuary.

1 The car park marks the site of the old Braunton railway station, closed in 1965. Bear left and leave the car park by the police station (right). Bear right on to Station Road and cycle down it, passing the cycle hire on the left. Turn right into Station Close and then immediately left down a tarmac way. At the end cross the lane; keep ahead through black bollards to cross another lane, with a roundabout right.

2 Follow signs left to pick up the old railway line. Pass a wetland conservation area (left) and a barrier to cross a lane (fences mark the boundary of RAF Chivenor).

3 To visit The Williams Arms turn left, cycle to the end of the lane, cross the A361; the pub is on the other side.) Otherwise Cycle on to reach a roundabout at the entrance to RAF Chivenor. Cross the road by the roundabout and continue into a wooded section.

4 Emerge suddenly from woodland on to the Taw Estuary, with far-reaching views. Listen for the oystercatcher's piping call, and watch out for curlew, easily identified by its curving bill. In winter thousands of migrant birds feed on the broad sandbanks here. Pass castellated Tarka Inn on the left, a refuge for Royalists in the Civil War. Continue cycling along the banks of the Taw and eventually pass the football club.

5 Cross arched Yeo Bridge, a swing bridge over a tributary of the Taw, and pass the Civic Centre on the left (cyclists and pedestrians seperate here). Bear left away from the river to meet the road. Turn right along the cycle path past old Barnstaple Town Station on the right (the railway reached the south side of the river in 1854, and this side in the early 1870s). Bear right as signed, then carry on left along the quay (take note: there is no wall along the edge; cycle with care).

6 Continue to pass Barnstaple Heritage Centre (left), with its statue of Queen Anne. The Riverside Café (with cycle racks) lies a few yards along on the left, just before Barnstaple's Long Bridge over the Taw (there has been a bridge here since the 13th century). There is evidence of a settlement at Barnstaple from early Saxon times and Queen Anne's Walk marks the site of the Great and Little Quays, once bustling with ocean-going ships. After exploring, retrace your route to return to the start.

GREAT TORRINGTON TO BIDEFORD

This ride, part of the Tarka Trail, from Great Torrington to Bideford, along the broad banks of the River Torridge, is one of three options, and can easily be linked to the route from Instow to Barnstaple.

1 Turn right along the A386 and descend to pick up the Tarka Trail on the right before Rolle Bridge. The trail runs between The Puffing Billy – the old station building – and cycle hire found in the goods yard opposite. Turn left along the trail to pass the pub and garden (cycle racks) located on the left.

2 Pause at the next river crosing to look at Beam Weir; as you cross the river for the third time look left towards Beam Aqueduct. Part of the railway utilized the bed of the former Rolle canal, involved in a scheme to link with the Bude Canal, in north Cornwall; only a 6-mile (9.7km) section was completed, in 1827. Pass a picnic area left, and continue between the A386 and the Torridge (right).

3 Where the Torridge takes a wide loop east cycle through Landcross Tunnel (lit), then through a cutting by Landcross Bridge. Now with the River Yeo on the left, cycle on to meet the old iron railway bridge over the Torridge.

4 The whole feel of the route changes here: the river is wide and slow, with large expanses of sa.tmarsh and reedbed. The bridge overlooks the Pool of the Six Herons (mentioned in the novel *Tarka*) – look out for herons, lapwing, redshank and curlew. Saltmarsh plants (specially adapted to seawater inundations) and reedbeds protect the river banks from erosion, and the mudflats support millions of invertebrates, food for wading birds. Limestone was shipped in from South Wales for burning in the limekiln left of the bridge; local woodland supplied timber for charcoal.

5 Continue along the right bank of the Torridge, with good views of Bideford, a significant port in medieval times, but today a busy market town and working port. Its 24-arched stone bridge recalls the town's early prosperity – it is said that each arch was funded by a local parish, and the size of the arch reflects their respective wealth!

6 Turn-around is at old Bideford Station – 220.5 miles (355km) from Waterloo! The Tarka Trail goes on to Instow. Refreshments are available from the Railway Carriage Visitor Centre. If you have time, after the ride, look around historical Great Torrington.

Dartmoor & Tamar Valley

CLOCKWISE FROM TOP LEFT: CLIMBING ON HAYTOR, DARTMOOR; OKEHAMPTON CASTLE; DARTMOOR PONIES; BUCKLAND IN THE MOOR

DARTMOOR & TAMAR VALLEY

BOVEY TRACEY MAP REF 399 G6

Bovey Tracey is a market town which bills itself as the Gateway to Dartmoor, because of its location at the busy southeastern corner of the moor. It is definitely worth a stop to explore the woodland and riverside walks of the Parke Estate (National Trust), half a mile (800m) west of the town. Parke is also the headquarters of the Dartmoor National Park Authority.

Back in the centre of Bovey Tracey is the beautifully restored Riverside Mill building – never actually used as a mill. It was built in 1850 as stables and the waterwheel simply scooped water from the river to a cistern used by the stables and adjacent house. It now houses a showcase for the members of the Devon Guild of Craftsmen, who produce some of the finest contemporary arts and crafts in the country, including jewellery, textiles, prints, ceramics and furniture.

Nearby is the Teign Valley Glass and House of Marbles centre, a shop in the former Bovey Tracey Pottery buildings selling marbles and glassware, games and toys. This is a major wet-weather attraction but the real interest is in the free demonstrations of glass-blowing. Three museums on the site explain the history of the Bovey potteries.

Near Bovey Tracey there are a number of tors – naturally formed granite rock towers, often weathered into strange shapes by the forces of erosion. Huge Haytor Rocks are the most accessible; the 30-feet (9m) high Bowerman's Nose is the most curiously shaped, resembling a face when looked at in profile. According to one legend, it is a local man who defied the injunction to rest on the Sabbath, went out hunting and was turned to stone; another story in local folklore has it that he disturbed a coven of local witches, who subsequently petrified him and his hounds (Hound Tor). Nearby lies the Hound Tor Deserted Medieval Village, the scant remains of dwellings, stables and grain stores of farmsteads abandoned at the time of the Black Death in the 14th century.

BUCKLAND IN THE MOOR
MAP REF 399 G6

Although, you may not know it, you have probably already seen Buckland in the Moor. Its thatched cottages, nestling on the edge of the moor – it is the perfect English rural retreat – have starred on countless calendars, a thousand jigsaws and biscuit tins by the score.

Another building in Buckland in the Moor that deserves the time for a visit is the interesting 15th-century church – however, not because it is an outstanding example of Early English architecture (parts of it date back to the 12th century), or because of its fine Norman font (most visitors don't even see its superb screen). The big attraction of the church is its clock face, on which the numerals have been replaced by the twelve letters M Y D E A R M O T H E R – a superb example of English sentimentality in a perfect setting.

DARTMEET MAP REF 398 F6

Dartmoor's two principal rivers are the East Dart and the West Dart. Dartmeet, not surprisingly, is where they come together and is a popular beauty spot with a characteristic Dartmoor clapper bridge spanning the river. Like many such places in the area, Dartmeet can get very busy in the high season, but a short walk – going north along the river is a good bet – will soon take you through the valley where you can enjoy spectacular scenery away from the crowds.

HAYTOR & FOX TOR
MAP REFS 399 G6 & 398 F6

Dartmoor is dotted with huge lumps of granite known as tors and Haytor is a particularly stunning example, situated close to the Devon village of Haytor Vale, and can be spotted on the skyline from as far away as Exeter. Haytor attracts many visitors and is a popular spot for walkers and hikers throughout the year. Rising to 1,500 feet (457m), Haytor stands on the eastern edge of Dartmoor, from where there are far-reaching views out to the coastline and the beautiful surrounding countryside. You can also enjoy views of the Teign estuary from its formidable summit. Although not a difficult climb, the summit is a popular challenge for climbers, and especially with schoolchildren.

Fox Tor is a much more modest beauty spot but the surrounding swampland was the inspiration behind a location in the well-known novel, *The Hound of the Baskervilles* by Sir Arthur Conan Doyle.

IVYBRIDGE MAP REF 398 F7

This small, often overlooked town on the River Erme most probably takes its name from the picturesque 13th-century humpbacked bridge which still spans the river today. There's nothing of great interest in the town but a walk north along the river is recommended. At Longtimbers Wood (a few minutes away) you will see some impressive granite pillars – all that remains of the viaduct that Brunel built in 1848 for the Great Western Railway.

Northwest of Ivybridge at Sparkwell is the popular Dartmoor Zoological Park. This entertaining zoo park, set in beautifully landscaped countryside has plenty to see and features a wide variety birds of prey, lions, tigers and bears among its collection of around 250 species.

OKEHAMPTON MAP REF 398 F6

Okehampton is the main town of north Dartmoor, with a range of shops for locals as well as for tourists, including a quaint Victorian covered arcade. Its main street, Fore Street, is dominated by the fine 14th-century tower of the Chapel of St James. At the opposite end of this street, tucked away in a charming cobbled courtyard adjacent to the White Hart Inn, is the excellent Museum of Dartmoor Life.

This is housed in an early 19th-century mill complete with a working waterwheel and is bristling with a range of weird and wonderful old objects relating to Dartmoor crafts and industries.

A short walk from the centre are the ruins of Okehampton Castle (English Heritage), the largest castle in Devon. Some parts of the castle date back to Norman times, though most of what remains today was built in the early 14th century by Hugh Courtenay, the Earl of Devon. Following the execution of the Earl in 1538 the castle was destroyed by Henry VIII. Today just enough remains to give a good idea of what it must have looked like. An entertaining personal stereo tour guides visitors around the buildings, at the same time outlining a supposed day in the life of the lady of the castle in medieval times. The setting, high on a hill overlooking the river and the beautiful woodlands which were once used as a royal deer park, is majestic.

PLYMOUTH MAP REF 398 F7

Plymouth's seafaring legacy is legendary. The port was naturally blessed with one of Europe's finest deep-water anchorages and, with the patronage of Sir Francis Drake and Sir John Hawkins, established its supremacy in the 16th century. It was, of course, from here in 1588 that Drake sailed to crush the Armada. In 1620 a more peaceable crew, the Pilgrim Fathers, set off from Plymouth aboard the *Mayflower* to make a new life in North America and lay the foundation for New England. In later years Captain Cooke launched his voyages of discovery from here, while in the 19th century hundreds of colonists and convicts set sail to Australia from Plymouth. Recent history has not been so kind – the city was devastated during World War II and the city centre has been completely rebuilt, but much of the old harbour area survived.

Start your visit on the grassy Hoe (the word 'hoe' means 'high place' or 'hill') for a marvellous view over Plymouth Sound and its busy shipping lanes. Smeaton's Tower, the archetypal and unmissable red-and-white lighthouse in the middle of the Hoe, was built in 1759 and once stood out on the treacherous Eddystone Rocks, 14 miles (22.5km) out to sea. It was replaced in 1882 by a bigger lighthouse and was reassembled here. Climb to the top for panoramic views. Just below the lighthouse is the wonderful and huge art deco Tinside Lido pool, open all day in the summer (weather permitting), which is a great place to swim on a sunny day.

Next to the Hoe is the Royal Citadel, a powerful star-shaped fortress built between 1666 and 1675. It is now home to a commando regiment but guided tours in summer (tickets available from the Dome) show the most interesting buildings, including the Royal Chapel of St Katherine (rebuilt in 1845). Just below the Citadel you'll find the National Marine Aquarium, one of the city's major visitor attractions and Britain's biggest aquarium, with more than 3,000 marine animals on display.

Keep walking down the hill and you will reach the Barbican, Plymouth's old harbour area. Several pleasure trips set off from here, the most popular being a one-hour tour around the dockyards. The oldest part of the Barbican is New Street, a cobbled street built in 1581, lined with timber-framed and jettied houses, including the atmospheric Elizabethan House, a rare surviving Tudor house which once belonged to a local sea captain. Also on New Street is a charming small Elizabethan garden.

On Barbican Quay you will find the exciting Mayflower Centre, where you can learn all about the history of the Barbican and experience the amazing story of the Pilgrim Fathers and the fascinating journey of the *Mayflower*.

Visit
THE GREAT BARN

The architectural highlight of the Buckland Abbey estate is the fine 14th-century Great Barn. It has a superb arch-braced roof, measures 159 feet (48m) long by 32 feet (10m) wide and, to the ridge, 60 feet (18m) high, thus making it one of the largest barns in the country.

Visit
BUCKLAND'S TEN COMMANDMENTS

Just to the east of Buckland in the Moor is Buckland Beacon, the West Country's answer to Mount Sinai. You will find a version of the Ten Commandments carved in 1928, on a granite block, to mark Parliament's rejection of the proposed new Book of Common Prayer.

Visit
DARTMOOR PONIES

At the Dartmoor Pony Heritage Centre at Brimpts Farm, near Dartmeet, you can get a close look at this delightful native breed. The centre was set up by the DPH Trust in 2006 to educate visitors on the history and heritage of the native Dartmoor Pony.

In the modern centre of town, just a short walk north, some old buildings survived the wartime bombing. On Finewell Street is the Prysten House (also known as Yogges House – visit by appointment only), a merchant's home and the oldest (1498) dwelling in the city, built around three sides of a galleried courtyard. Nearby is the Merchant's House, a classic four-storey Elizabethan building now housing a lively museum and a fully stocked apothecary's shop. The City Museum and Art Gallery has an outstanding collection of fine and decorative arts and holds temporary exhibitions throughout the year.

PRINCETOWN MAP REF 398 F6

Princetown is Dartmoor at its bleakest, greyest and grimmest. No wonder, then, that this spot was chosen for Dartmoor Prison. It was built in 1806 to house French prisoners captured during the Napoleonic Wars, and between 1812 and 1814 it confined Americans taken during the War of Independence. Conditions were grim and overcrowded and around 1,000 Frenchmen and Americans died here from jail fever. From 1816 to 1850 the prison stood empty, until it was revived for criminal offenders. Displays at the Prison Heritage Centre, which is housed in converted prison stables, give a fascinating history of Dartmoor Prison.

At 1,400 feet (427m) above sea level, Princetown claims to be the highest town in England (though in fact it is very little more than a village). However, its altitude makes it the natural centre of the 'High Moorland' and there is a Dartmoor National Park Visitor Centre and excellent information point in the restored early 19th-century Old Duchy Hotel. Princetown is also home to the Dartmoor Brewery and the appropriately named Jail Ale.

TAVISTOCK MAP REF 398 F6

Tavistock today is little more than a pleasant market town but it was once home to the most powerful abbey in southwest England. Parts of the Benedictine structure still stand, the abbey gateway has been incorporated into the town hall and opposite its infirmary dining hall is now a chapel. Betsey Grimbal's Tower, the abbey's west gatehouse, stands next to the Bedford Hotel and part of the cloisters is retained in the yard of the handsome 15th-century Church of St Eustace.

The town's second great period of wealth came in the 13th century with tin mining, when Tavistock became the largest of Devon's four stannary towns. By the time the supply of tin was exhausted in the 17th century, a thriving cloth trade was prospering in Tavistock and then along came the great 'copper rush' of the mid

to late 19th century when a rich lode was discovered locally. As boom turned to bust Tavistock's population dropped from 9,000 to 6,000 and the market town returned to its original role. Today Tavistock's Victorian covered Pannier Market is worth a visit and also hosts a fortnightly farmers market.

Tavistock's most famous son is Francis Drake, who was born in 1542 at Crowndale Farm just south of the town. There's nothing to see there, but there is a fine statue at the end of Plymouth Road in the town centre. This is the original (cast in 1883) of the famous one on Plymouth Hoe, which is a copy.

WIDECOMBE IN THE MOOR
MAP REF 398 F6

This picturesque Dartmoor village, set among rolling green hills, surrounded by high granite-strewn ridges, attracts thousands of visitors in summer and its natural charm can be somewhat overwhelmed. However, despite the pubs, tea rooms and tourist paraphernalia, little has changed here over the centuries. The famous fair is still celebrated on the second Tuesday in September, but its remit has grown from the simple horse-trading fair it once was to accommodate the coachloads who now descend upon it. The impressive spire of the local Church of St Pancras, 'the Cathedral of the Moors', is a landmark

for miles. The church was built in the 14th century and enlarged over the course of the subsequent two hundred years. It is more than 100 feet (30.5m) in length, and its most notable feature is its fine roof bosses. Look out for the interesting and unusual sign of the three rabbits. Ironically this docile emblem, linked to alchemy, was adopted by the tin miners. A less docile crowd you could never wish to meet; Sir Walter Raleigh, in his capacity as Warden of the Stannaries (tin mines), described them as 'the roughest and most mutinous men in England'.

The adjacent Church House, owned by the National Trust, dates back to 1537, when it was a brewhouse. The Church House was also a rest house for outlying farming families who had a very long distance to travel to Widecombe for services. The house later became almshouses, then it became a school and it now serves as the village hall. It also hosts the village's monthly market. The adjacent Sexton's Cottage is now a National Trust and Dartmoor information centre and shop. If you want to drink in the real atmosphere of Widecombe the pleasant main village pub, the Old Inn, dates back to the 14th century, but it has been much altered and is often packed with visitors. Walk a little way past the church and you'll find the ancient Rugglestone Inn.

WIDECOMBE IN THE MOOR

AROUND BRENT TOR

This is a steady climb up to the 13th-century Church of St Michael de Rupe at Brent Tor. Lying just inside the large national park boundary, the strange natural formation of Brent Tor is a remnant of the mass of lava that furiously poured out on to the seabed here 300 million years ago, when the area was just a shallow sea.

DISTANCE/TIME 4.5 miles (7.2km) 2h **MAP** OS Explorer 112 Launceston & Holsworthy **START** Lay-by past cattlegrid outside Mary Tavy on moorland road to North Brentor village; grid ref: SX 492800 **PATHS** Tracks and green lanes, open fields and lanes **THE PUB** Elephant's Nest, Horndon (off A386 north of Tavistock). Tel: 01822 810273

1 Walk straight ahead from your car towards Brent Tor, which positively invites you to visit it. Where the lane bears right turn left along an unfenced lane (dead end sign). Go gently downhill to pass Blacknor Park (left), then a cattle grid. The lane becomes rocky before passing Wortha Mill and crossing the disused railway line.

2 The track runs steeply uphill, before levelling off. At the next T-junction of tracks turn left to pass South Brentor Farm and a lane on the right, and keep straight on slightly uphill – under beech trees – to pass 'Hillside' on the left.

3 Pass Brennen Cottage (left); a few paces later the lane bends sharp left. Turn right through a gate and keep ahead up the right edge of the field on a permitted footpath. Turn right through a gate at the top, later bearing left going steeply uphill to reach Brent Tor church.

4 From the church door follow the path right then left to a gate, then downhill, bearing left to the road opposite the car park (toilets).

5 Turn right along the road – take care – eventually passing the (closed) Brentor Inn.

6 When you reach two white cottages on either side of the road, turn right down a tarmac lane signposted 'Brentor and Mary Tavy'. The lane runs gently downhill, with the moor rising steeply up behind the village ahead. This western edge of the moor is very different from the eastern side, where there is usually a long drive-in along wooded river valleys. At the edge of the houses go straight on, keeping the old chapel on the right, until you reach the World War I memorial.

7 Turn right slightly downhill to pass the phone box, church and village hall. Follow the lane as it bears right to cross the old railway line. You can see the old station complete with platform canopy below you to the right. Pass over the cattle grid on to the open moor, and up the lane.

8 Where the lane bends right just past the gateway to Wortha Farm, cut left over the edge of Gibbet Hill on an indistinct grassy track. The lane leads back to the car, but this is a more pleasant route. Once over the crest of the hill you will see the route that you need to follow back to your car on the lane below to the right.

WALK 12

BRIDFORD & THE TEIGN VALLEY

A lovely walk in springtime, when you can enjoy the sight of many tiny wild daffodils covering the river banks of the Teign.

DISTANCE/TIME 5 miles (8km) 2h45 **MAP** OS Explorer 110 Torquay & Dawlish **START** Free car park at Steps Bridge; grid ref: SX 803884 **PATHS** Woodland paths, open fields and country lanes; 3 stiles **THE PUB** The Bridford Inn, Bridford. Tel: 01647 252250

1 From the car park cross the road, following the signs to the former youth hostel. Turn right up the concrete track, then left as signed towards the building; the path bears right, and is signed for Heltor Farm. The steep path leads uphill through delightful oak, then beech woodland. At the top of the wood cross a ladder stile as signed.

2 Follow footpath posts straight up the field and through a small gate. Keep up the left edge of the next field; pass through a gateway and look to the left to see Heltor Rock.

3 At the end of the field turn left as signed through a gate into a plantation; follow the path to meet a gate on to a lane. Turn left and walk uphill to meet a tarmac lane.

4 Turn left (signs for Bridford). After 200yds (182m) turn left over a stile up the narrow fenced permissive path to Heltor. Retrace your steps to the road and turn left.

5 After about 1 mile (1.6km) the lane bears left, then right, to the edge of Bridford. Turn right down a small steep lane signed 'Parish Hall & Church'. Follow the church wall path, down steps and right to the Bridford Inn.

6 Turn left from the pub and follow the lane through the centre of the village. Take the fourth turning (Neadon Lane) on the right, by

a telephone box. Just past where a bridleway joins (from the left) the lane dips to the right, downhill; take the left fork ahead to pass Birch Down Farm on the left. Keep straight on at Westbirch Farm; turn left as signed to Lowton Farm on a fenced path, which bears right to a kissing gate; pass through and up the right edge of the next field to a stile in the top corner. Then cross a tumbledown granite wall and continue through an area of gorse bushes. Cross a stile by some beech trees.

7 Follow the fenced path along the top of two fields, and down a green lane to reach Lower Lowton Farm. Turn right as signed before the farm on a permissive bridlepath, which descends (with a stream, right) then rises to the next signpost; turn right for Steps Bridge down the narrow green lane, passing through a small gate. Continue down the deeply banked green lane until you reach a surfaced lane though a gate.

8 Turn left through the middle gate, signed 'Byway to Steps Bridge'. At the edge of Bridford Wood (by the National Trust sign) turn right following footpath signposts. The path is fairly narrow and quite steep. Go left, then right, to cross a track, keeping downhill. The path drops down steps then runs to the left, now high above the river, to Steps Bridge where it meets the road opposite the former café. Turn left here to return to your car.

VIEWPOINT FROM HUNTER'S TOR

A beautiful route to up Hunter's Tor for a superb 360-degree view. To the south you can see the coast of Teignmouth and pick out the familiar outline of Haytor, then Hound Tor (resembling a pack of hounds), Hayne Down and Bowerman's Nose.

DISTANCE/TIME 4.75 miles (7.6km) 2h30 **MAP** OS Explorer OL28 Dartmoor **START** By side of lane at Hammerslake; grid ref: SX 775816 **PATHS** Steep rocky ascents/descents, rough paths and woodland **THE PUB** Kestor Inn, Water Tel: 01647 221626; www.kestorinn.com

1 From the parking area walk north up the lane (heading away from the pretty village of Lustleigh) and turn left up a narrow rocky path between houses 'Logan Stones' and 'Grove', signed 'Cleave for Water'. At a gate go straight ahead, signed 'Hunters Tor', and climb steeply up to the top.

2 Turn right through woodland to eventually reach open ground then follow the path straight on over the highest part of the ridge and across the remains of an Iron Age fort to reach Hunter's Tor.

3 Pass through a gate to the right of the tor and follow the signed path right down to another signed path, left. Walk down through a gate, then right through another and down to Peck Farm. Go through a gate on the left of the farm and on down a concrete drive.

4 Shortly after, turn left through a gate signed 'Foxworthy Bridge' and along a wooded track to Foxworthy; turn right.

5 At path junction go left, signed 'Horsham'. Follow the track into woodland through a gate. After five minutes follow signs right for 'Horsham for Manaton & Water', to the River Bovey. Follow the river bank left for few paces to a crossing (on boulders) at Horsham Steps. To avoid crossing Horsham Steps, don't turn left for 'Horsham' at Point 5, go right, down a drive, which crosses the river. Take the first footpath on the left and keep ahead to rejoin the main route at Point 6; turn right uphill.

6 Cross, taking care, and walk downstream to enter Bovey Valley Woodlands. Follow the path steeply uphill (the path avoiding Horsham Steps comes in from the right) and over a stile. Keep ahead to pass through a gate by some cottages (note the tree-branch porch). Keep on up the track, following signs for 'Water' through Letchole Plantation.

7 At a track crossroads turn right ('Manaton direct') to a lane by Water Mill. Take the second lane right to reach Kestor Inn, a welcoming pub serving good food.

8 Return to the crossroads. Descend, signed 'Bovey Valley', to a split in the track. Keep left, eventually passing through a gate and down a steep path. Cross the river on a bridge and proceed steeply uphill to a signpost. Go left, signed 'Lustleigh via Hammerslake', and left again at the next signpost (very steep). At the junction keep ahead uphill; where path forks keep right to a gate. Turn right down the rocky path back to lane at start.

DARTMOOR'S HIGHEST TOWN

At 14,000 feet (4,267m) above sea level, Princetown is the highest town on Dartmoor, its name derived from 'Prince's town' from the early 19th century, when the then Prince of Wales decreed that a prison be built on the moor to hold prisoners captured in the Napoleonic Wars. The area is famous for its ghost sightings and features prominently in the folklore and legends of the area.

DISTANCE/TIME 7.5 miles (12.1km) 3h **MAP** OS Explorer OL28 Dartmoor **START** Main car park in Princetown; grid ref: SX 588735 **PATHS** Tracks, leat-side paths and rough moorland **THE PUB** The Plume of Feathers, Princetown. Tel: 01822 890240

1 Leave the car park past the toilets and turn right to pass the High Moorland Visitor Centre. Cross the road and follow the lane between the two pubs and their car parks behind. After 100yds (91m) a small gate leads to a broad track which ascends gently to South Hessary Tor with superb views.

2 Follow the track as it drops down gently, passing boundary stones. It crosses two other tracks (look left to spot the Devonport Leat) before dropping down to Nun's Cross (2.5 miles/4km from the start). The thatched Nun's Cross Farm can be seen to the left.

3 Turn 90 degrees right at the cross to pick your way through old tin workings and find the end of the tunnel where the leat emerges. It's near the remains of a building under a beech tree. Walk along the right bank of the leat, soon passing a granite cross.

4 Eventually meet a track by Older Bridge, cross the leat, and continue along the left bank, with wonderful views of Burrator reservoir to the left. Follow the leat on; there are various crossing places and you should cross back to the right bank before descending to the valley of the Meavy; the leat picks up speed as it rushes downhill here, and the path is steep and rocky.

5 The Meavy is crossed via an aqueduct and the leat turns left. Take the grassy path right leading slightly uphill away from the river (the tin working evidence in the valley is worth exploring). Climb steeply uphill aiming for Black Tor on the hilltop.

6 Go straight on past the Logan Stone, one of several on Dartmoor balanced in such a way that they can be rocked on their base, and on across open moorland to the road, with views of Brentor, Swelltor Quarries and the disused railway line ahead. Turn right at the road.

7 Pass a blocked-off parking place and continue along the verge. The road descends past a small parking space; as it rises again bear left across rough grassland, aiming to the right of the mast on North Hessary Tor.

8 At the railway track turn right and walk back to the edge of town. The path splits, so keep left, eventually passing a small gate to join a tarmac road, with the Dartmoor Brewery left. Bear right to the car park.

DISTANCE/TIME 5 miles (8km) 1h45 **MAP** OS Explorer OL28 Dartmoor **START** Princetown car park; grid ref: SX 588735 **TRACKS** Rocky former railway track and one particularly steep and rough section **THE PUB** Dartmoor Inn, near Princetown. Tel: 01822 890340

DISTANCE/TIME 7 miles (11.3km) 2h **MAP** OS Explorer OL20 South Devon **START** Steamer Quay (or Longmarsh) car park; grid ref: SX 809596 **TRACKS** Country house drive, rough woodland path, tarmac lane **THE PUB** Durant Arms, Ashprington. Tel: 01726 842855; www.thedurantarms.com

THE PRINCETOWN RAILWAY

There's a long history of granite quarrying on wild Dartmoor. It began around 1820 at Haytor Quarry and (in direct competition) at Swelltor and Foggintor. The old quarry workings are now flooded and provide a pleasant and peaceful picnic spot. This is a tough ride through the landscape of Dartmoor, along the old route of the Princetown to Yelverton railway.

1 Turn left out of the car park along a stretch of rough road. Just past the fire station (left) bear left as signed (disused railway/Tyrwhitt Trail) on a narrow fenced path, which then bears right. Go through the gate. The path then widens into a gritty track and passes a coniferous plantation (right).

2 Suddenly you're out in the open on a long embankment, looking towards the forests around Burrator Reservoir ahead right, below Sheeps Tor and Sharpitor (right). Continue along the contours of the hill – it's quite rough – and as you progress look ahead left to the railway winding its way towards Ingra Tor. This is the old Plymouth and Dartmoor railway line, the brainchild of Sir Thomas Tyrwhitt, who was a friend of and private secretary to the Prince Regent. Originally a tramway with horse-drawn wagons, it opened in 1823. The line was part of Tyrwhitt's plans to exploit the area's natural resources (granite), while at the same time enabling materials such as coal and lime to be brought to Princetown more easily. The Princetown Railway Company (a subsidiary of the Great Western Railway) took it over in 1881; it reopened as a steam railway in 1883, but was not profitable and closed in 1956. However, it makes a great cycle track.

3 Reach the edge of Foggintor Quarry (right), with Swelltor Quarry on the hill ahead; a track crosses the trail. The site of King Tor Halt (1928), from where a siding led to Foggintor, is nearby. Keep straight ahead, almost immediately taking the left fork (the track becomes grassier). Look right towards the spoil heaps of Foggintor Quarry. Follow the track on – look left towards Merrivale Quarry (Dartmoor Inn is just out of sight below) – and try to spot the Bronze Age Merrivale stone rows. Follow the track as it bears left round the hill (below King's Tor Quarry), to enjoy views right over Vixen Tor, almost 1,050ft (320m) high, home to one of the moor's most evil folklore characters, the witch Vixana. Pass through a cutting – there is another branch that joins in from the right – and keep cycling on to another fork.

4 Keep right along the lower track; views change again, with the wooded Walkham Valley below right and – on a good day – the sparkling waters of Plymouth Sound in the distance. About 50yds (46m) beyond the fork look left to see a pile of dressed stone on the upper track: 12 granite corbels, cut in 1903 for work on London Bridge, but excess to requirements. Pass the spoil heaps of Swelltor Quarry; the track is now fenced on the right, with views ahead to the bridge en route for Ingra Tor.

5 Where the track starts to curve sharp right, turn left opposite an old gate. Push your bike up a rough, rocky track to regain the outward route near Foggintor Quarry.

6 Turn right and make your way bumpily back to Princetown. The building of the infamous prison in 1806, originally for French prisoners from the Napoleonic Wars, was also down to Thomas Tyrwhitt. Since 1850 it has been a civilian establishment.

ALONG THE DART VALLEY TRAIL

The ideal escape route from the hustle and bustle of Totnes – which can get very busy in holiday times – to the peaceful, beautiful valley of the River Dart. The ride undulates through parkland and meadows of the Sharpham Estate overlooking the meandering Dart, before a tough climb through woodland. The lovely village of Ashprington, and the Durant Arms provide a great focus.

1 From the car park follow the road back towards Totnes. Turn left on to Seymour Road, then left over Totnes Bridge (built to replace a smaller one in 1838, and a toll bridge until 1881) – the lowest crossing point of the Dart – to reach the roundabout at the bottom of Fore Street. Turn left along the Plains, at one time an area of tidal marsh; the old riverside warehouses have now been converted into stylish accommodation. Keep ahead along New Walk to reach the Steam Packet Inn on the left.

2 As the road bends sharp left turn right up the narrow tarmac Moat Hill. After about 20yds (18m) turn left signed 'Ashprington', on a gritty, fenced track, gently uphill.

3 At the end bear right then left on to the old driveway to Sharpham House, initially walled. Pass out into the open briefly – look back for good views over the river at Totnes – then back into woodland. Continue uphill to cross a cattle grid in woodland. There follows a lovely downhill run through parkland, with fantastic views ahead left over reedbeds fringing the river. The drive runs uphill into woodland again and passes into the Sharpham Estate via a gate. Continue through two more gates and back into parkland – watch out for cowpats beneath your wheels and cows in front of you! A long downhill run, with Pinhay Plantation right, leads towards the river. Eventually, pass through a gate and out on to a track to reach a signpost.

4 Turn right along a narrow gritty track that runs uphill away from the river. Follow this as it bears left with the hedge and continues uphill. Pass over a cattle grid, at which point cyclists are asked to dismount. Continue up the rough, rooty track – Leafy Lane – through Lower Gribble Plantation – it's quite a slog. Pass through a staggered barrier; the track levels off and reaches a lane, with the entrance to Sharpham House left. Sharpham House was built in the late 18th century – replacing an Elizabethan building – for Captain Philemon Pownall of HMS *Favourite*, funded by prize money from the capture of a Spanish treasure ship. His grandson later lost Sharpham when he gambled away the family fortune. Situated on the warm south-facing slopes above the Dart, the estate now hosts a working vineyard and cheese dairy, and a shop and café.

5 Turn right along the narrow – but quiet – lane for 0.5 mile (800m). A pleasant downhill run ends in the centre of Ashprington. The Durant Arms, an inn since 1725 and renamed in honour of the Durant family of Sharpham, is on the left.

6 To return to Totnes, it is possible to follow a different route along the undulating country lanes. To do this, turn right at the war memorial in Ashprington and follow the lane to Ashprington Cross. Turn right and follow that lane all the way back to meet Moat Hill and turn right for New Walk. However, as Devon lanes are usually narrow and twisty, with high hedges and poor visibility, it is safer to return via the outward route you cycled out on.

DARTMOOR & TAMAR VALLEY

DARTMOOR & THE TAMAR VALLEY

This drive skirts the northwestern edge of Dartmoor before climbing on to its most spectacular, granite-dotted open moorland. From the most southerly point of the drive, the return is through the beautiful countryside of the Tamar Valley. The drive begins in Okehampton, which has an attractive wide main street, flanked by some fine old buildings. Just off the main street is a cobbled courtyard housing a Victorian tea room, a tourist information centre and the Museum of Dartmoor Life. The impressive ruins of Okehampton Castle are on the southwestern edge of the town.

Route Directions

1 From the traffic lights in the town centre take the B3260, signposted 'Tavistock'. In 3 miles (4.8km) cross a road bridge and turn right on to the A30, signposted 'Launceston'. In 1 mile (1.6km) take the A386, signed 'Tavistock' and 'Plymouth', and continue for 9 miles (14.5km) to Mary Tavy.

Mary Tavy, a peaceful village now, was once famous for its tin- and copper-mining industry. The preserved remains of Wheal Betsy engine house are passed just before reaching the village.

2 Continue for 3.75 miles (6km), making sure you make the most of the fine views of Dartmoor on the left, to reach Tavistock.

Tavistock is one of four stannary towns around the moor and is essentially a product of 19th-century prosperity. It still has a thriving covered market (the town was granted a market charter in 1105) and bustling main street and is one of the most attractive 'working' towns in the county.

3 Just before reaching the town centre, make a left turn on to the B3357, which is signposted 'Princetown'. The road soon climbs on to open moorland with huge outcrops of granite all around, including Coxtor on the left.

4 In 6.5 miles (10.5km) turn right, signed 'Princetown', and continue for 1 mile (1.6km) to Princetown, with sombre views down over the prison to the left. Pass the Dartmoor Prison Museum and the excellent National Park Visitor Centre, then turn right at a roundabout on to the B3212, which is signed 'Yelverton, Plymouth', a road which has some of the most spectacular views on the moor. In 6.25 miles (10km) reach a roundabout and take the first exit on to the A386, signposted 'Plymouth'. In half a mile (800m) turn right, signposted 'Crapstone, Buckland Monachorum, Milton Combe', with brown tourist signs to The Garden House and Buckland Abbey. In 1.25 miles (2km) detour left to visit Buckland Abbey.

Leave enough time to visit this splendid former monastic foundation which later became the home of Sir Francis Drake.

5 Continue on the main route, passing The Garden House in half a mile (800m) on the right. In another half mile (800m) turn left, signposted 'Milton Combe' and 'Bere Alston'. After a further half mile (800m) turn right, signposted 'Bere Alston', descending through a delightful wooded valley to cross the River Tavy at a picturesque stone bridge, following signs for 'Bere Alston'. Ascend a 1-in-5 (20%) hill and in 2 miles (3.2km) turn right, signed 'Gulworthy' and 'Tavistock'. In another 2.5 miles (4km) detour left for a mile (1.6km) to visit Morwellham Quay.

This once thriving copper mine and port has been accurately renovated and carefully restored to form a splendid open-air museum, staffed by craftsmen and other workers in period costume.

6 On the main route continue for 1.5 miles (2.4km) to meet the A390. Keep ahead over the roundabout, signed 'Chipshop', 'Lamerton' and 'Milton Abbot'. In 4.75 miles (7.6km) cross the B3362, then in 1.25 miles (2km) turn right, signposted 'Brentor'. In a further mile (1.6km) continue straight on at crossroads, signed 'Brentor'. In 1.5 miles (2.4km) reach the car park for Brent Tor Church on the right.

Perched atop a high grassy mound with great rocks strewn all around, the church has panoramic views from all sides.

7 Shortly after the car park, turn left signed 'Brentor' and 'Lydford'. In about 3 miles (4.8km) you will pass the first entrance to Lydford Gorge on the left.

This beautiful wooded gorge, owned by the National Trust, has a 3.5-mile (5.6km) walk with a waterfall at one end and the spectacular Devil's Cauldron at the other.

8 Continue for 1.5 miles (2.4km) to reach Lydford Castle, a great square stone keep which dates from 1195. In 0.75 miles (1.2km) turn left on to the A386, signposted 'Okehampton'. In 5.75 miles (9.2km) turn right on to the A30, signed 'Okehampton' and 'Exeter'. In half a mile (800m) turn left, signed 'Okehampton', and follow the B3260 for 2.5 miles (4km) back to the town centre.

Exmoor & the Quantocks

CLOCKWISE FROM TOP: PORLOCK VILLAGE; DUNKERY BEACON; EXMOOR NATIONAL PARK;
THE QUANTOCKS; CROWCOMBE

BRENDON HILLS MAP REF 399 G4

The Brendon Hills form an elongated ridge located to the east of the main part of Exmoor. Unlike the uplands of Exmoor and the Quantocks, the Brendon Hills are characterized by extensive cultivation. For centuries the Hills were mined for minerals, mainly ironstone, an activity that reached its zenith during the 19th century when a railway was built to take the ore to Watchet and onward to Ebbw Vale for smelting. The mines were eventually worked out by the turn of the century. A miners' chapel remains at Beulah, along with ruins of cottages and the steep mineral railway incline that steadfastly served the mines.

These lovely hills merge into the eastern side of Exmoor, and are within Exmoor National Park. The highest point is Lype Hill at 1,388 feet (423m). The terrain is broken by a series of streams and rivers running roughly southwards to meet Wimbleball Lake or River Haddeo.

CULBONE MAP REF 399 G4

Culbone village, originally a centre for charcoal burners and once supporting a colony of lepers, is today renowned for its little church, only accessible by a long walk. Reputedly the smallest in England, although St Olaf's in Wasdale in the Lake District would justifiably have something to say about that, Culbone's church has a chancel merely 13'6" x 10' (4m x 3m), and a nave 21'6" x 12'4" (6.4m x 3.6m). This diminutive place of worship has an overall length of just 35 feet (10.6m). Dedicated to St Beuno and set in a small clearing, it seats a congregation of about 30 people in some companiable and intimate degree of discomfort, and nestles in an endearing valley about 3 miles (4.8km) from Porlock. The church has Saxon parts, and there are numerous legends surrounding its history. To get there you trace the delicate fretwork of a green English woodland, with glimpses of the sea far below through a break in the foliage. Luxuriant ferns grow on the hillside along which the path is etched. Except for a rustle of leaves and a whisper of wind blown up from the sea, you can walk along here in reflective silence, far removed from the world below.

The nearby Culbone Stone is an early medieval standing stone which is about one metre high was discovered in 1940. The stone lies in woodland close to the parish boundary, and has an incised wheeled cross, suggesting that it dates originally from the 7th to the 9th century.

Samuel Taylor Coleridge, one of the 'Lake Poets', knew Somerset and Culbone well. On one visit he followed a zig-zag path from Porlock Weir to Culbone, passing through ancient woodland that 'abounded in wild deer, foxes, badgers and martin cats'. Whortleberries made a carpet beneath the trees, and the sound of the waves breaking below and distant views across to Wales filled him with 'pleasure and astonishment'. For Coleridge, Culbone was one of Somerset's holy places. If anyone ever needs time to be alone with their thoughts, Culbone is the place to come.

DUNKERY BEACON MAP REF 399 G4

At 1,702 feet (519m), Dunkery Beacon is the highest hill on Exmoor, and also the highest point in Somerset. The shortest route of ascent goes from Dunkery Gate, a brief haul of 0.6 miles (1km) and height gain of 433 feet (132m). With little to interrupt the view, those from the summit include the Bristol and English Channel coastlines, the Brecon Beacons, Bodmin Moor, Dartmoor, as well as the Severn Bridges. It is claimed you can see Cleeve Hill, 86 miles (138km) away in Gloucestershire. But from the top of Dunkery Beacon the horizon is 55 miles (88.5km) away, making this unlikely.

The hill is a lush carpet of heather, and in summer a richly deep purple. For the botanist, the Beacon area and adjacent woodland make this a fascinating place; ling and bell heather grow in abundance, along with gorse, sessile oak, ash, rowan, hazel, bracken, mosses, lichens and ferns, as well as whitebeam. This is a good spot, too, to see robust Exmoor ponies, shy red deer and birds of many varieties including dippers, snipe, skylarks and kestrels, while the nearby Horner Woods often yield redstart, pied flycatchers, wood and willow warblers, chiffchaff and lesser spotted woodpeckers. Horner Woods are also the home to 14 of the 16 UK bat species, which include the very elusive barbastelle and Bechstein bats. There are now thought to be only about 1,000 Exmoor ponies remaining in the world, which, if true, means they are rarer than the Giant Panda. About 150 live on the upland expanses of Exmoor.

CROWCOMBE, QUANTOCKS

The area around Dunkery Beacon is scattered with several Bronze Age burial mounds at or near the summit, notably Rowbarrows, Kit Barrows, Joaney How and Robin How.

The beacon was the site of a former fire beacon, and is still used occasionally for celebratory bonfires.

DUNSTER MAP REF 399 G4

On the eastern edge of Exmoor, Dunster is one of the most picturesque medieval villages in Somerset, complete with a huge Norman castle that dominates the entire area. Now in the care of the National Trust, Dunster Castle was substantially altered in the early 17th century and further work was carried out in 1868, but its core medieval character was preserved to a large extent. The oak-panelled halls have magnificent ceilings and there are many reminders of the Luttrell family, who called this home for some 600 years until 1950.

The village is one of the loveliest in Britain, its medieval character perfectly preserved. The main street of pretty little shops and tea rooms sits cosily between two high wooded hills, one topped by the castle, and is distinguished by the octagonal Yarn Market, a relic of its days as an important wool centre.

EXFORD MAP REF 399 G4

This tiny village, reputedly the smallest on Exmoor, is sometimes referred to as the capital of Exmoor. It has a small green draped around a medieval stone bridge. As the name suggests, Exford sits on the River Exe and has been the site of a ford or bridge for hundreds of years. The small village has a couple of traditional inns set around the green and its Crown Hotel is one of the best known hostelries in Exmoor. The church of St Salvyn stands to the east of the village, and has a fine wooden screen and a 16th-century tower

PORLOCK MAP REF 399 G4

Nestled quaintly in the embrace of the Exmoor hills, there has been a village on the existing site since ancient times. Indeed, there is evidence of a Stone Age settlement on the land nearby. Today's coastal village edges on to a saltmarsh nature reserve, created in the late 20th century by the breach of some low-lying land. This area has protected status.

Porlock is a traditional, attractive Exmoor village, with everything a working community could need in the way of services and shopping, as well as pubs, restaurants and hotels that appeal to visitors and locals.

Always popular, Porlock was a favourite of the 18th-century poet Coleridge (who actually lived a short distance away at Nether Stowey), and part of a walk from the Quantocks to Exmoor is named after him. Another of the Romantic poets fond of Porlock was William Wordsworth.

Insight
HUNTING THE EARL

If you are in Combe Martin over the Spring Bank Holiday, you will witness the Hunting of the Earl of Rone, a ceremony with its roots in pagan times but which has been adapted over time to incorporate some other historical events. The original Hobby Horse procession is now preceded by a chase through the woods in pursuit of the 'Earl', who is then placed on a donkey backwards and led in the main procession to the beach, where he is then dumped into the sea.

Insight
LORNA DOONE

The combes and heathery moorland around Malmsmead and Oare are the setting for R. D. Blackmore's story of the tragic heroine Lorna Doone and her lawless family. It is based on the exploits of a real-life family of Scottish outlaws who came to Exmoor, failed at farming and turned instead to a life of crime.

THE QUANTOCKS MAP REF 399 H4

Running in a gently curving line northwest to southeast from near Watchet on the Bristol Channel to the northern reaches of Taunton, the Quantock Hills form a wide spread of rolling heather moorland, brackeny hills and wooded combes. Designated in 1956 as the first of England's Areas of Outstanding Natural Beauty (AONB), the whole region is hugely popular for walking, and rightly so. With narrow lanes and homogeneous hamlets huddled in hollows this is a classically English landscape, much admired by Wordsworth and Coleridge, both of whom lived here. Because of the special nature of the Quantocks, much of it is covered by a designation of Site of Special Scientific Interest (SSSI) from the geologically interesting coastline to the maritime heathlands on the northern hills. There are archaeological remains on the higher parts of the hills, notably Bronze Age barrow mounds and an Iron Age hill fort. The hills are famous for their views which reputedly embrace nine counties.

For so small an area, the landscape shows great variety, its heights offering a remarkable air of solitude and wildness. Underlying rocks range from the ominously named Hangman Grits on the tops, to the undulating shales and distinctive red sandstone of the West Country. Eastward, long broad valleys form an enclosed landscape of copses and hedgerows that spill away towards the Somerset Levels.

The heathland and sessile oak woodlands of the AONB are nationally important wildlife habitats, and native red deer still roam here. Much of southern Britain's heathland has vanished or survives as fragments, making the AONB's extensive heaths particularly valuable.

SELWORTHY MAP REF 399 G4

On first impression, the thatched, cream-coloured stone cottages that flank the hill rising to the 15th-century church in Selworthy seem completely in harmony, part of the rural landscape. But, unlike neighbouring villages, Selworthy was substantially rebuilt in 1828 by Sir Thomas Acland of Killerton, a philanthropist who sought to provide homes for the pensioners on his Holnicote Estate. The houses, today in National Trust ownership but privately tenanted, are built using traditional materials and designs to produce what is an intentionally old-fashioned village, a modest variation on the vernacular architecture with typically tall chimneys and deep thatched eaves. The church sits at the top of the village and provides a lovely view over a rash of thatched roofs and tidy cottage gardens across the Vale of Porlock to the heathery heights of Dunkery Beacon.

The wider Holnicote Estate covers a large part of Exmoor National Park including the high tors of Dunkery and Selworthy Beacons. Selworthy is just one of the villages within the estate, which also embraces Allerford, Bossington, Horner and Luccombe, in addition to 4 miles (6.4km) of coastline between Porlock Bay and Minehead, where the South West Coast Path begins. There are over 100 miles (160km) of footpaths through the fields, dense woods, moors and pretty villages of the estate.

TARR STEPS MAP REF 399 G4

The Tarr Steps are an ancient bridge between Withypool and Dulverton over the River Barle, just where Little River joins the main valley. The bridge is an especially fine 'clapper bridge', hundreds of years old, and consists of 15 large, unmortared slabs, or 'stepping stones', resting on each other, and each weighing around 2 tons. The actual age of the bridge is still unknown, but it has clearly been restored over the years. Tarr Steps is a scheduled ancient monument but, although once thought to be prehistoric, it is now accepted as of medieval origin.

The River Barle is particularly attractive and joins the Exe south of Dulverton, and both the river and Tarr Steps are popular tourist attractions. The river and valley woodlands are Sites of Special Scientific Interest, and are rich in wildlife.

The term 'clapper' bridge is thought to derive from the Latin *claperius*, meaning pile of stones. The surrounding woodland is a National Nature Reserve that mainly consists of oak woodland with ash, hazel and sycamore, and beech in some of the drier areas. The woodland is however, particularly important for moss species, liverwort and lichen, while springtime brings a blanket of bluebells.

WILLS NECK MAP REF 399 H4

Wills Neck, the highest point of the Quantock Hills, is a heather-covered dome rising to 1260 feet (384 metres). Not surprisingly, the views from the top are absolutely amazing, with the entire Quantocks seen end-on in both directions, of course. To the northeast the Bristol Channel spreads across the distant horizon, with the town of Bridgwater in view away to the east. The Mendips, Wells and Glastonbury Tor can also be seen, and, on the clearest of days, even the Severn Bridges spanning the Bristol Channel, and linking England with Wales.

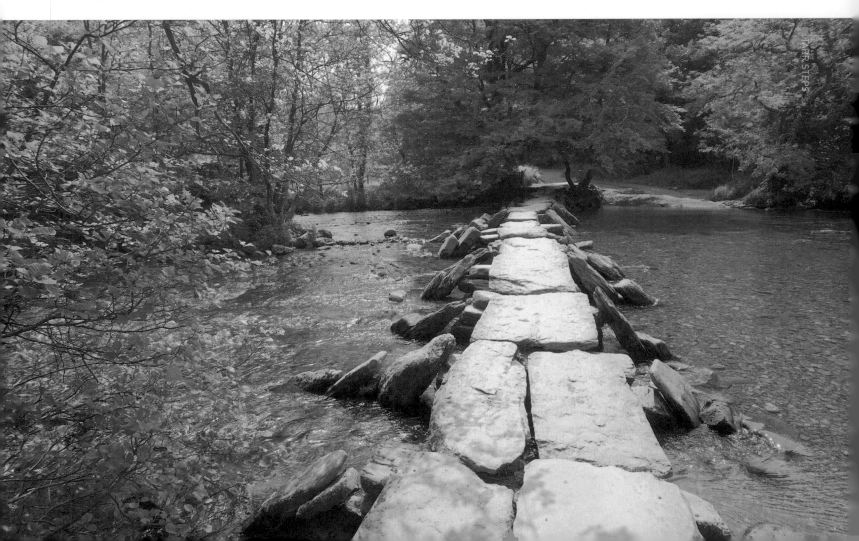

TARR STEPS

EXMOOR & THE NORTH COAST'S WOODED COMBES

This tour takes in the beautiful wooded valleys of the coast, the rolling pastures of its hinterland and the wild open moorland of western Exmoor, before visiting the beauty spot of Watersmeet. The early part of the drive is on steep, narrow roads with hairpin bends. It is slow going and you'll need to take care, but the scenery is well worth the time it takes.

Route Directions

1 Set out with Lynton town hall and tourist information office on your right, and follow signs for the Valley of Rocks, which you will reach shortly after leaving the town.

This beautiful dry valley has huge, fascinating sandstone rock formations created by freeze-thaw action during the Ice Age, and is populated by wild goats. From the road there are glimpses of the sea and a walk here will be even more rewarding. There is a picnic area on the left at the start of the valley and a large parking area, the last until the end of the valley, on the right.

2 The road passes into the pretty Lee Valley Estate and continues past Lee Abbey Christian Community, where a small toll is payable. Follow the narrow road downhill, then uphill as it turns away from the coast, winding its way through steep, wooded combes, for 0.75 mile (1.2km). At the next junction keep straight ahead, signposted 'Woody Bay'. Pass the Woody Bay Hotel and later a National Trust car park on the left, then in a mile (1.6km) at a T-junction turn right. In another mile (1.6km) – having passed through Martinhoe, and just past a telephone box – take the right fork downhill, signed 'Hunter's Inn, Heddons Mouth, Trentishoe'. Turn left at Hunter's Inn up a narrow lane. In 2.25 miles (3.6km) meet the A39 and turn right, signposted 'Barnstaple'. After 3.25 miles (5.2km) turn left on to the A399 at Blackmoor Gate, signposted 'South Molton'. Turn right instead at Blackmoor Gate if you want to visit Arlington Court: turn right, then left, signed 'Barnstaple', and continue for 3.25 miles (5.2km) before turning right, signposted 'Arlington Court'.

This charming house (National Trust) dates from 1822 and contains some fascinating collections and beautiful architectural details, such as the impressive Victorian staircase, which has natural light from three stained-glass windows.

3 On the main route, continue with hilly agricultural land on both sides of the road. In another 2.25 miles (3.6km) detour right to visit the lovely Exmoor Zoological Park.

The zoo specializes in small exotic animals. You can see wolves, Arctic foxes, lemurs, gibbons and even cheetah.

4 Return to the A399 and turn right. In 10 miles (16km) at a roundabout, take the 2nd exit, signposted 'South Molton' and continue for 1.5 miles (2.4km) into the town.

South Molton, where you can see some particularly elegant Georgian buildings dotted along the main street, still enjoys a position very much at the heart of the surrounding farming community.

5 From the main street in South Molton, pass the market hall and museum, and the health centre on the right and turn left into Station Road, signposted 'North Molton', with lovely views as you leave the town. In just under a mile (1.6km), meet the A361 and turn right, then immediately left, still signposted 'North Molton', and continue for 2.25 miles (3.6km) into the village. Just as you pass a petrol station on the left, turn left, following the signs for 'Heasley Mill' and 'Simonsbath', turning left again at the square. After travelling for 1 mile (1.6km) bear left, signposted 'North Heasley' and 'Simonsbath'. In half a mile (800m) at a crossroads continue forward, signposted 'Simonsbath' and then after 1.75 miles (2.8km) turn right at a T-junction, signposted 'Simonsbath' and 'Exford' to climb steadily on to Exmoor. In 5.25 miles (8.4km) turn left on to the B3223, signposted 'Lynton'. In 6 miles (9.7km) turn right on to the A39, which is signposted 'Lynmouth and Watersmeet'.

Watersmeet is one of the county's premier beauty spots. The confluence of the East Lyn River and Hoaroak Water and set in a beautiful, deep, wooded valley, with a wonderful network of footpaths, it also has that all-important National Trust tea room.

6 Continue down the wooded valley to return to Lynmouth, attractively set around the pretty river valley and tiny harbour, and Lynton, looking out from the cliff top. The two towns are linked by the famous cliff railway.

WIMBLEBALL LAKE WOODLAND WATER

Natural and artificial landscapes merge beautifully on this route through peaceful wooded valleys, heathland and across the Wimbleball Dam. The reservoir here was created in the 1970s and covers an area of nearly 380 acres (157ha). The water is a hive of activity year round, popular with every type of watersports enthusiast as well as ornithologists curious to see the many birds it attracts.

DISTANCE/TIME 6 miles (9.7km) 3h **MAP** OS Explorer OL9 Exmoor **START** Frogwell Lodge car park, Haddon Hill; grid ref: SS 969285 **PATHS** Rough descent, long climb, easy track between; 2 stiles **THE PUB** The Rock Inn, Waterrow. Tel: 01984 623293

1 Leave the car park by a kissing gate overlooking the reservoir. Follow the earth path ahead until it crosses another earth track, and runs down towards the reservoir to meet a tarred track. (Left down this track leads to the dam, Point **3**.) Cross and turn right, walking on a rough track contouring to the right. After 350yds (318m) this enters scattered birches. Turn down left, on a smaller path, to meet a stony track just above the reservoir.

2 Turn left on this. It emerges into open grassland and starts rising to the left. Watch out for a stile down on the right, into woodland. Across this, turn left on a small path that emerges near the Wimbleball Dam. A side-trip on to the dam gives fine views of Hartford Bottom below.

3 Return along the dam and turn right into a descending tarmac lane signed 'Bury 2.5'. At the bottom keep ahead on a concrete path signed 'Bridleway'. With a bridge ahead, bear left on to a grass track, this time signposted 'Bridleway to Bury'. It leads to a ford, so watch out for the footbridge on the right. Once across, take a track between houses, to turn left out into Hartford.

4 Turn left ('Bury 2') on a well-used track. It passes through woods of oak and beech beside the River Haddeo. The track becomes tarmac as it enters the village of Bury.

5 Turn left to the packhorse bridge beside the road's ford. Ignore a riverside track on the left and continue for 180yds (164m) to turn left at a bridleway sign, 'Haddon Hill'. Here pass between houses and ahead into a sunken track. This climbs steeply, with a stream at the bottom that flows over orange bedrock. At the top it continues as a green (or brown) track between grown-out hedges, before turning left for another short climb to reach Haddon Farm.

6 Pass to the left of the farmhouse, on its access track. After 0.25 mile (400m) this reaches the corner of a wood. As the track is concreted on a steep section, look out for a stile above leading into the wood. Go up the left-hand side of the wood to reach a gate on to the open hill at its top corner.

7 Take a track bearing left to cross the crest of the hill. Turn sharp right, on a wide track and continue downhill, on a wide track through open moor to the car park.

WALK 16

TARR STEPS BRONZE AGE TRACKWAYS

On this walk you will be able to visit one of the world's 'oldest' bridges, just south of Withypool. This ancient stone causeway spans the River Barle, as part of an ancient track that meanders through woodland, and draws crowds year on year. Known as a prehistoric 'clapper bridge' the stones are thought to date back to 1000 BC and probably weigh upwards of 2 tons.

DISTANCE/TIME 5.25 miles (8.4km) 2h30 **MAP** OS Explorer OL9 Exmoor **START** Car park just over 0.25 mile (400m) east of Tarr Steps (parking at Tarr Steps for disabled drivers only); grid ref: SS 872323 **PATHS** Riverside paths and field tracks, some open moor; no stiles **THE PUB** The Crown Hotel, Exford. Tel: 01643 831554; www.crownhotelexmoor.co.uk

1 Leave the bottom of the car park by the left-hand junction, signposted 'Scenic Path'. This path leads down to the left of a road to Little River, crossing two footbridges on the way to the famous Tarr Steps crossing over the River Barle, ahead.

2 Cross Tarr Steps, turning upstream at the far side ('North Barton Wood'). Follow the wide river bank path past an ingenious device for intercepting floating trees in times of flood. After 0.75 mile (1.2km) cross a side-stream on bridge (mini Tarr Steps), to reach a footbridge over river.

3 Cross the river, and then continue walking upstream, with the river now on your left. After 0.75 mile (1.2km) the path crosses a small wooden footbridge, and then divides at a signpost.

4 Turn right, uphill, signed 'Winsford Hill'. The wide path goes up through the woods with the stream on its right. Where it meets a track turn briefly right to ford the stream, then continue uphill on a narrower signed path. At a low bank with beech trees turn right to reach a gate and follow the foot of a field to tarred lane. Go along the lane to

cross a cattle grid on to the open moor. Here, bear right on a faint track that heads up between gorse bushes. After 250yds (227m) it reaches a four-way signpost.

5 Turn right, signed 'Knaplock', and slant down to the hedge corner. The route follows the foot of open moor, but is about to divert up left to avoid some bog. After 170yds (155m) a sign points back down to the moor-foot banking. Beech bank crosses ahead: aim for a gate at lower end of this, where the soft track leads forward, with occasional blue paint-spots. After 0.25 mile (400m) the track turns downhill, then back to left. It becomes firmer and drier as it reaches Knaplock Farm.

6 Among farm buildings turn downhill signed 'Tarr Steps', to exit on a muddy farm track. This becomes a steep, narrow, stony track, Watery Lane. After its initial descent it is a smooth path down to the River Barle. Turn left, downstream. When the path rises a little above the river, look out for a fork on the right, signed 'Footpath'. This rejoins the river to pass through an open field. Cross the road and a small footbridge, then turn left up the path to reach your car.

PORLOCK WILDWOOD & SEA VIEWS

A stiff climb through the wildwood for a sudden sea view. Set as it is in the vale of the hills of Exmoor on three of its four sides, Porlock is undeniably pretty and the coastline seems to add that finishing touch. The landscape has inspired many poets to write romantic verse, including Wordsworth and Coleridge.

DISTANCE/TIME 6 miles (9.7km) 3h15 **MAP** OS Explorer OL9 Exmoor **START** Porlock central car park; grid ref: SS 885468 **PATHS** Initial stiff climb then smooth, well-marked paths, no stiles **THE PUB** The Ship Inn, Porlock. Tel: 01643 862507; www.shipinnporlock.co.uk

1 Leave the car park at its top end, then turn left. Just before the church turn right into Parsons Street. At a small parking area a bridleway sign for Hawkcombe points upstream to a footbridge.

2 The path climbs through bamboo and laurel, to join another bridleway. This zig-zags steeply up through the wood, to pass below a wall with a small inset bench. At the top of this low wall, the paths then divide.

3 Turn left, still climbing, and at once bear left, signposted 'Hawkcombe', into a sunken path. Emerging at a white house, called Halsecombe, keep ahead to a field gate marked with a blue spot. Follow the left edge of a field, to the right-hand of two gates; the next gate ahead leads back into woodland. Take the bridleway track ahead, gently descending. It becomes a terraced path, running near the top edge of the wood for a mile (1.6km) to reach a track.

4 Turn left down the track for just a few paces, and then turn right up a path between gorse bushes; it then runs through bracken and heather with views into the head of Hawk Combe. As the path enters a thicket

of hawthorns bear right to reach the road signpost at Whitstone Post.

5 Cross the A39 into a parking area, and turn right down a heather path parallel with the road. After 110yds (100m) turn left down a broad track. Where it turns left, turn right on to a smaller track. This contours through gorse and heather, then rejoins the A39 at a cattle grid.

6 Turn left, then right on a track signposted to Hawkcombe. Cross two cattle grids to reach Point **4** of the outward route. Keep on the track for another 125yds (114m), then turn left into a small, terraced path. This runs gently downhill for 0.25 mile (400m), to meet a wider path. Turn sharp right down to the stream.

7 A broad path runs downstream. On reaching some houses it becomes a tarred lane and descends through a wood. At a high wall on the right a footpath sign points to a footbridge. Over this, the path ascends gently through the woods for 220yds (200m). Bear left on a crossing path and gently descend to a street. Turn left to cross the stream, then turn right into Parsons Street and Porlock.

ALONG THE QUANTOCK COASTLINE

This stimulating walk overlooking the coastline takes in Tudor villages, breezy cliffs, industrial remnants and interesting geology underfoot. Places of interest that are also en route include the oil retort house, which is near to the beach at Kilve, and was built during the time when oil was extracted from the shale there.

DITANCE/TIME 3 miles (4.8km) 1h30 **MAP** OS Explorer 140 Quantock Hills & Bridgwater **START** Pay-and-display car park at the end of Sea Lane; grid ref: ST 144442 **PATHS** Tracks, field paths, and grassy cliff top; 4 stiles **THE PUB** The Hood Arms, Kilve. Tel: 01278 741210

1 From the car park head back along the lane to the ruined chantry. Turn into the churchyard through a lychgate. Such gates were built to shelter coffins and their bearers: this one is too small for its purpose, so must be a modern reconstruction. Pass to the left of the church, to a kissing gate.

2 A signposted track crosses a field to a gate; bear right to another gate and pass along the foot of East Wood. (At its far end, a stile allows wandering into the wood, from April to August only.) Ignoring the stile on the left, keep ahead to a field gate with a stile and a track crossing a stream.

3 The track bends left past gardens and ponds of East Quantoxhead to reach a tarred lane. Turn right, towards the Tudor Court House, but before its gateway bear left into a car park. Pass through to a tarred path and a kissing gate. In an open field this bears right, to St Mary's Church.

4 Return to the kissing gate but don't go through, instead bear right to a field gate, and cross the field to a distant gate and a lane. Turn right and, where the lane bends left, keep ahead into a green track. At its top, turn right at a 'Permissive path' noticeboard.

5 Follow field-edges, with hedges on your right, down to the cliff top, and turn right. A clifftop path leads to a kissing gate before a sharp dip, with a ruined lime kiln opposite. This was built around 1770 to process limestone, shipped from Wales, into lime for the fields and for mortar. The foreshore below the kiln is limestone, but it was easier to bring it by sea across the Bristol Channel.

6 Turn around the head of the dip, and back left to the cliff top. Here an iron ladder descends to the foreshore: you can see alternating layers of blue-grey lias (a type of limestone) and grey shale. Fossils can be found here, but be aware that the cliffs are unstable – hard hats are now standard wear for geologists. Alternatively, given a suitably trained dog and the right sort of spear, you could pursue the traditional sport of 'glatting' – hunting conger eels in the rock pools. Continue along the wide clifftop path until a tarred path bears off to the right, crossing the stream studied by Coleridge. As you come into the car park, on your left is the brick chimney of a short-lived Oil Retort House (for oil distillation) from 1924; there is oil in the grey shale, but it's probably less trouble to get it from Texas.

Somerset & the Mendips

CLOCKWISE FROM TOP: CHEDDAR GORGE; WELLS CATHEDRAL; GLASTONBURY TOR

AXBRIDGE MAP REF 399 J4

The early inhabitants of the area around Axbridge were almost certainly the Romans, who are known to have mined lead on the top of the Mendips. Earlier still, prehistoric man fashioned draughty homes from the local caves, and his primitive flint tools have been found scattered widely across the slopes of the hills of the surrounding area.

But the documented history of Axbridge can be traced only to the time of King Alfred (849–899), ruler of the West Saxons, when it served as part of the Saxons' defence system for Wessex against the Vikings. Axbridge appears in the Domesday survey of 1086 as Alse Bruge, meaning 'the ash tree bridge', and was part of the royal manor of Cheddar.

The town was granted a Royal Charter in 1202, when King John sold most of the royal manor of Cheddar to the Bishop of Bath and Wells. As an important centre for cloth manufacture and trade, Axbridge flourished and developed during the Tudor period, and this was reflected in its early royal charters allowing it to hold markets and fairs, and to then become a royal borough. For a period of time, Axbridge even boasted its own mint and coinage bearing the town's own symbol, that of the Lamb and Flag.

Later, the town's importance waned, leading to stagnation, and the need to preserve many of the historic buildings in the town centre. These include King John's Hunting Lodge, a misleadingly named three-storey, 15th-century timber-framed house situated on the corner of the market place, jettied over the street in a double overhang, and by its date clearly much too late for King John (1199–1216). This historical house is now used as a small museum of local history.

Axbridge is a very old borough and sent members to parliament in the reigns of Edward I (1272–1307) and Edward III (1327–77), but it was a costly privilege, and so the burgesses prayed to be excused. As a result, Axbridge ceased to have a voice in the legislature.

BURRINGTON COMBE
MAP REF 399 J4

Burrington Combe is a carboniferous limestone gorge near the village of Burrington, on the north side of Beacon Batch in the Mendip Hills. 'Combe' or 'coombe' is a word of Celtic origin that occurs in several forms throughout different parts of Britain, and denotes a steep-sided valley or hollow. The gorge contains the entrances to many of the caves of the Mendip Hills, including Aveline's Hole and Goatchurch Cavern.

Augustus Montague Toplady (1740–78), an Anglican vicar, was inspired to compose the poem 'Rock of Ages' while evading a thunderstorm by sheltering below a rock in the combe. The alleged rock remains a prominent and frequently visited feature situated on the opposite side of the road from the car park.

Archaeological excavation of early cemeteries, notably at Aveline's Hole (a Mesolithic burial vault, thought to be the earliest scientifically dated cemetery in Britain), has revealed evidence of human occupation of the combe and its caves from Bronze Age times. The human bone fragments unearthed in the cemetery came from about 21 individuals, and are thought to be more than 10,000 years old, coincidental with the end of the last Ice Age when the present period of warm climate was beginning. Moreover, a further study has revealed a series of inscribed crosses on the wall of Aveline's Hole, in a style comparable with others discovered from Northern France, Germany and Denmark, giving, scientists now believe, a wider context for the finds of the period, and a rare suggestion of what may have been a basic means of communication used in those times. In recognition of its biological and geological interest, a large area within and around the combe became a Site of Special Scientific Interest in 1952.

CHEDDAR MAP REF 399 J4

Distinguished for its deep limestone gorge, Cheddar is unique. The gorge is no mere stripling, but Britain's largest gorge. The Cheddar Yeo in Gough's Cave is Britain's biggest underground river, and the Gorge Cliffs the highest inland limestone cliffs. Quite a tally for so compact an area.

Not surprisingly, the Cheddar Gorge is a Site of Special Scientific Interest, mainly because of the calcareous grassland, limestone buttresses and horseshoe bats that find the caves much to their liking. Pairs of Peregrines nest on the cliff face and an efficient Ground Force team of Soay sheep keep the scrubland mown.

Gough's Cave is an internationally famous archeological site because of finds some 12 to 13,000 years old, and Britain's oldest complete skeleton a mere 9,000 years old. The cave lies within the Mendip Hills Area of Outstanding Natural Beauty and is worth a visit.

The village of Cheddar has a long history, and was an important Roman and Saxon centre. As early as 1130, the Gorge was claimed as one of the 'Four Wonders of England', but historically, Cheddar's wealth came from farming and making the eponymous cheese. Legend has it that cheese was a chance discovery after a milkmaid left a pail of milk in the nearby caves, returning later to find that the milk had turned into a tasty substance, and so Cheddar cheese was born. Would that it were so simple.

Certainly cheese making was well established more than 800 years ago. Henry II (1154–89) declared Cheddar cheese to be the best in Britain, and the Court financial

CHEDDAR GORGE

records show that in 1170 the King bought 10,240lb (4,465kg) of Cheddar at a cost of a farthing per pound.

As elsewhere in Britain, popular tourism began with the arrival of the railway, in this case the Cheddar Valley Railway, which opened in 1869–70, providing workers from surrounding towns with the opportunity to make the most of bank holidays by visiting other towns in the area. The railway was popularly known as the Strawberry Line, because it passed close by the strawberry-growing fields that adorned the southwest-facing slopes on the Cheddar side of the valley. Until the Beeching Axe fell on British rail lines in 1965, 'Strawberry Special' trains carried the fruit across the country.

EBBOR GORGE MAP REF 399 J4

The Ebbor Gorge National Nature Reserve is a largely wooded site on the southern escarpment of the Mendip Hills. It forms part of the Mendip Woodlands Special Area of Conservation. The scarp is split by two valleys: Ebbor Gorge, a dry limestone gorge, and Hope Wood valley, which has a stream. There are two geologically important caves on the site with deposits that include bones of Ice Age mammals.

While the bulk of the reserve is comprised of ash and maple woodland, a number of woodland glades and areas of limestone grassland appear.

Hope Wood valley, which is quite humid, is ideal for ferns and fungi, and over 250 species of mosses, liverworts and lichens have been recorded at the site. Areas of coppice have also been cut in order to improve the reserve for woodland butterflies, particularly the rare white letter hairstreak, making this one of the most fascinating areas in the region for those interested in natural history.

GLASTONBURY MAP REF 399 J4

What is it about the town of Glastonbury and its Tor that excites so much fervour, anguish and passion?

In the past, Glastonbury Tor and surrounding land was an island joined to dry land by a narrow peninsular, but surrounded by marshes. In Neolithic times, transitory people inhabited lake villages near the island, which from the earliest days appears to have been treated as a sacred place.

From the shadows of pre-history come legends of this Isle of Avalon, a place of the dead, a sacred burial ground. Although primarily thought of in connection with King Arthur, Christians believe that the first British church was erected here (at the behest of Joseph of Arimathea) about 30 years after the death of Jesus, to shelter the Holy Grail. Legend also claims that

Visit
WILLOWS AND WETLANDS VISITOR CENTRE

The Somerset Levels are renowned for their excellent reed-growing conditions and expert weavers have been coming to this area for their materials for years. As well as the specialist raw material, the reeds are also processed and used to make charcoal for use by artists. The reeds are harvested in the spring each year and the processing of the willows can be seen at the Willows and Wetlands Visitor Centre in Stoke St Gregory.

Insight
FLYING VISITORS

The Somerset Levels and the surrounding moors are an important habitat for small mammals, plants, insects and birds. Waterfowl come here throughout the winter and it is also an important breeding area for wading birds, such as lapwing and redshanks. Indeed the lapwing population here is being carefully monitored because its numbers are still in decline, despite recent efforts to create a perfect breeding habitat. You may also be lucky enough to spot some birds of prey such as kestrels and barn owls.

Joseph had earlier visited Glastonbury along with Jesus as a child. The English poet, William Blake believed this story, and wrote the poem that became the words to the most patriotic of English songs, 'Jerusalem'. Later spin-doctoring of the various storylines contends that Joseph of Arimathea himself came to Britain and became the first bishop of Christianity.

Today, Avalon is commonly associated with present-day Glastonbury, and there is undoubtedly something other-worldly about the place. King Arthur and Guinevere are said to lie buried here, and it was home to medieval saints. This numinous hill, preternaturally cloaked in mystery, legend, beliefs and half-beliefs, dominates the surrounding countryside, and, more prosaically, provides outstanding views over Somerset, Dorset and Wiltshire. At the summit, excavation has exposed plans of two superimposed churches of which only a 15th-century tower remains. Of course, everyone knows that Glastonbury Tor is home to Gwyn ap Nudd, King of the Fairies, who kindly allows it to be managed by the National Trust. It is an agreeable walk up the Tor, especially if you want to distance yourself from the brew of rival faiths fermenting in the town.

In the Middle Ages, when the great Benedictine abbey was founded here, the region was described as England's 'holyest earthe'; many feel that nothing has changed. In spite of all the attention, Glastonbury is a bustling and energetic small town, a place with rich traditions, a cosmopolitan community with an eye to the future. It nestles against a backdrop of soft, green, rolling hills, and has been a pilgrimage place for many for thousands of years, and continues to be so.

Today the town, a unique, atmospheric community, also hosts the world-renowned Glastonbury Festival – the music festival being the number one event of the year for some – pilgrimages, musical events, a carnival, several conferences and other events. People visit from the world over, searching for something – inner peace, spiritual enlightenment, the meaning of life – and producing a mixture of locals and incomers in which threads of paganism and mysticism are woven together with those of Christianity.

PRIDDY MAP REF 399 J4

High on the plateau-like landscape of the Mendip Hills, southeast of Cheddar, Priddy village is built around a large green that is used each summer in August for a traditional sheep fair. It is thought that the fair was moved from Bath in the 14th century because of the plague, although there appear to be records of a sheep fair in Priddy earlier than this.

Each year, in February, Priddy holds a folk festival, claimed to be the friendliest folk festival in Britain. Quite what the criteria for 'friendliness' are is not clear.

The Mendip Hills Area of Outstanding Natural Beauty was designated in 1972 and enfolds the western and central area of the Mendip Hills range which reaches from Bleadon in the west to Chewton Mendip in the east. The soft, undulating Carboniferous limestone plateau is the main feature of the area which today is predominantly pastoral and criss-crossed by drystone walls largely dating from the 18th-century enclosure laws.

The Mendip Hills have a rich archaeological heritage, from Mesolithic cave deposits to historic World War II military features. The landscape appears to have had ritual importance in Neolithic times, with mortuary enclosures such as Ashen Hill barrow cemeteries and the enigmatic Priddy Circles.

The four Priddy Circles, huge circular formations crossing a number of field boundaries, have been interpreted as henge monuments created for ritual purposes. Their form is different from other known henge monuments, however, and their function is unknown. They appear to have been in some way linked to some of the other ritual monuments nearby, like the Priddy Nine Barrows.

GLASTONBURY

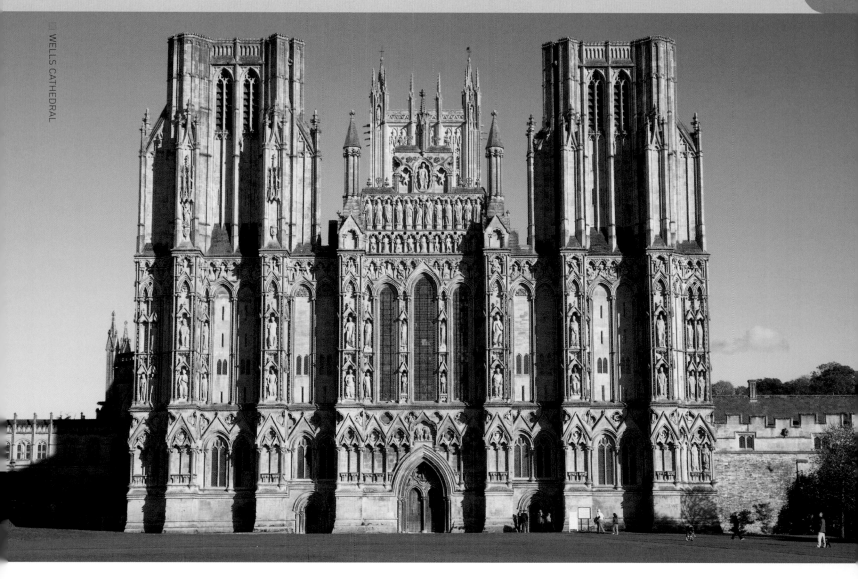

WELLS CATHEDRAL

SHEPTON MALLET MAP REF 399 J4

The small, mainly stone-built, town of Shepton Mallet has interest way beyond its size. Rich in history, in the centre of town is an elaborate market cross dating from the 1500s, and the town has England's oldest prison, first used in 1610, and still in use having had a chequered history and seen a number of prisoners executed. The prison is a Grade II listed building, one of its finer points probably not appreciated by the inmates. During World War II, many national treasures, such as the Domesday Book, were kept safe here.

Archaeologists uncovered a significant number of Roman artefacts in the early 1990s at a site adjacent to the nearby Fosse Way, including a Chi-Rho amulet, held to be among the earliest evidence of Christianity in England.

Somerset is famous for cider, and Shepton Mallet is home to Europe's largest cider plant, Gaymer Cider Company. This is where they produce Diamond White and Gaymer's Olde English cider.

SOMERSET LEVELS MAP REF 399 J4

At the heart of gentle Somerset, lies an amorphous, beautiful and quite remarkable area known as the 'Levels and Moors', an area that has international significance as one of the most important wetlands certainly in Europe and quite possibly in the world.

All of the levels and moors in Somerset were submerged until about 6,500 years ago, when peat deposits began to form in the salt marsh, fens and raised bogs. To cross these wetlands and reach dry islands of rock in the valleys, prehistoric people constructed wooden tracks, the oldest of which, Sweet Track, is a raised walkway built nearly 6,000 years ago, and still existing today.

The Somerset Levels are a haven to migrating and resident birds. Part of the moors is drier agricultural land and part is made up of wetland nature reserves and wilder areas. Throughout history, water levels have risen and fallen and, in recent centuries, the Levels have been artificially drained. Mining of peat over the last century has left pools and lakes, favourable for water birds.

STREET MAP REF 399 J4

On the southwest edge of Glastonbury, the village of Street has a history dating to Roman times, but played second fiddle to Glastonbury until 1829 when the Clark brothers started their shoe factory and began a business that is today multinational. Clarks Shoes still have their headquarters in Street today; the original factory is now a show museum.

Clarks, like many other benevolent industrialists, built terraces of model homes for their workers, and provided the village with a civic hall, library, open-air swimming pool and theatre, which are all still in use today.

WELLS MAP REF 399 J4

England's smallest city is a real gem, with one of the finest cathedrals in Britain. History oozes from the buildings, and the market place seems to have buildings in almost every architectural style. Vicar's Close is said to be the most complete medieval street in Europe.

The Market Place provides a link between the cathedral, the Bishop's Palace and the High Street, and has numerous attractive shops. Market days (Wednesday and Saturday) see a thriving outdoor market with a variety of stalls.

Wells is the home town of athlete Mary Rand, who, on 14th October 1964 at the Olympic Games, with a leap of 22ft 2¼ins (6.76m), became the first woman athlete ever to jump over 22 feet (6.7m). With that gold medal she became the first British woman track and field athletics champion in Olympic history. The actual length of her jump is marked out in brass markers close to Penniless Porch, found just off the Market Place.

WOOKEY HOLE MAP REF 399 J4

Wookey Hole has been fashioned by the River Axe, creating the most fascinating underground scenery. The name 'Wookey' is thought to derive from the Old English wocig, meaning an animal trap. The village is principally known for its show caves, a paper mill and a museum.

A visit to Wookey Hole is ideal for all the family, and all ages, and tours take visitors through the history of man and caves, including legend and folklore, where the first cave dive was attempted, and the spot where the mythical Witch of Wookey was turned to stone.

Nearby Glencot Country House Hotel, a late Victorian mansion built in Grand Jacobean style, is a Grade II listed building dating from 1887. The attractive 18th-century Bubwith farmhouse is also a Grade II building, as is the town's attractive high street post office.

POLDEN HILLS: EDGE OF THE LEVELS

This walk takes you from Polden's edge down on to the Somerset Levels and back up again. The Polden Hills run parallel almost to the Mendip Hills and lying in between is an area of little-populated, marshy wetland along the coastline and inland an area of moor, called the Somerset Levels. The hill ridge has been a well-trodden route as it was once the line of a Roman road, and its western extremes can be traced as a Saxon route.

DISTANCE/TIME 4.5 miles (7.2km) 2h15 **MAP** OS Explorer 141 Cheddar Gorge **START** Car Park at Street Youth Hostel, just off B3151, other car park on south side of the road; grid ref: ST 480345 **PATHS** Initially steep then easy tracks and paths; 3 stiles **THE PUB** Castlebrook Inn, Compton Dundon. Tel: 01458 443632

1 From the parking area on the youth hostel side, cross and turn right on a woodland path. After 100yds (91m) a smaller path descends on the left by some steps. At the foot of the wood turn right, and at a field corner go down to reach a track. This runs along the base of the wood to a lane.

2 Go down to the entrance of Lower Ivy Thorn Farm, and turn left onto a track. After 0.5 mile (800m) this reaches the corner of an unsurfaced road, where you turn right. After 0.25 mile (400m) the track turns left into a field. Follow its edge, with the ditch and fence to the left, to a gate at the field corner. In the next field continue alongside a ditch to the corner. The former footbridge is derelict under brambles. Take a gate on the left-hand side, then turn right. The field-edge zig-zags to pass to the left of Hurst Farm, leading to tarred lane.

3 Turn right to reach a bridleway sign on your left. Follow this green track until it joins Ham Lane. Follow the lane to reach the crossroads of B3151 in Compton Dundon, with Castlebrook Inn to your right.

4 Cross the busy B3151 and pass between the market cross (right) and the granite Victorian obelisk (left) into Compton Street. At the first junction keep round left, towards the Hood Monument above. As the street starts to climb, turn right and left up a lane beyond, signed 'Butleigh'. Where it reaches woodland bear right, up a steep fenced path, ignoring stiles on the left. The path slants up into a wood. Then, some 35yds (32m) before it arrives at a road, turn left along the top of steep ground, to Hood Monument.

5 Continue down through the wood to a minor road, with the main road 50yds (46m) away on your right. Ignore a path descending opposite but turn right for a few steps to a footpath sign and kissing gate. A grass path heads gently up the crest of Collard Hill.

6 From the summit go down to a stile and the signposted crossroads of B3151. Cross both roads. Ridge road is signed for the youth hostel, but your path is just to its right. Cross a glade into woodland. Keep to the right of some hummocky ground to the wood's edge, and follow the path to the car park.

EBBOR GORGE: COLERIDGE'S INSPIRATION

This sublime limestone gorge is thought to have inspired works by the founder of the Romantic movement Samuel Taylor Coleridge (1772–1834). This deep ravine, cutting into the limestone of the northern Mendips, contains huge caverns that were once home to an earlier group: the Stone Age hunter-gatherers.

DISTANCE/TIME 4.75 miles (7.6km) 2h30 **MAP** OS Explorer 141 Cheddar Gorge **START** Car park on the lane above Wookey Hole (optional small fee); grid ref: ST 521484 **PATHS** Small paths and field edges, with a rugged descent; 10 stiles **THE PUB** The Wookey Hole Inn, Wookey Hole. Tel: 01749 676677; www.wookeyholeinn.com

1 From the noticeboard at the top end of the car park descend on a stepped path. After a clearing, turn left, signposted 'The Gorge'. This wide path crosses the stream to reach a junction.

2 Turn right, away from the gorge down a valley to reach a road. Turn left, to pass through Wookey Hole village. At its end, the road bends right; take the kissing gate on your left with 'West Mendip Way' post. After two more kissing gates turn left up a spur to a stile and the top of Arthur's Point.

3 Bear right for 60yds (55m) into woods again. The path now bears right to a stile. Go down left to a kissing gate back into the wood. At once, and before a lime kiln just ahead, turn up left between boulders to pass between high quarry crags. Bear right along the wood's foot to join a short track ahead. It leads to four-track junction with a waymarker post standing in a stone plinth.

4 Turn sharp left, onto a tarred track that bends right then left through Model Farm, to reach Tynings Lane. Turn left for 85yds (77m) to reach a signposted stile on your

right. Go up with a fence on your right; bear left to a gate with a stile. Go straight up the next field, aiming for the gateway below the top left corner with tractor ruts running into it. This track leads up through a wood and a field. From the gate at its top slant upwards in the same direction to reach another gate next to a stile 100yds (91m) below the field's top left corner.

5 A small path runs along the tops of three fields with a long view across the Levels away to your left. With the stile on your right and a gate and horse trough in front, turn downhill keeping the fence on your right; follow it to a stile leading into Ebbor Gorge Nature Reserve.

6 A second stile leads into a wood. At a junction with a red arrow and sign marked 'Car Park' pointing forward, turn right into the valley and go down it – this narrows to an exciting, rocky gully. At the foot of the gorge turn right, signposted 'Car Park'. You are now back at Point **2** of the outward walk. After crossing the stream turn left at a T-junction to the wood edge, and back right to car park.

Dorset & the Purbecks

CLOCKWISE FROM TOP: MUPE BAY; DURDLE DOOR; CORFE IN THE MIST; BOATS ON THE BEACH

DORSET & THE PURBECKS

BOURNEMOUTH MAP REF 400 D7

Bournemouth is the queen of the south coast holiday resorts, with its 6 miles (9.7km) of fine golden sands, its pier complete with striped deck chairs and theatre for nostalgic summer shows (rebuilt several times), its orderly winter gardens, its parks lined with palms and compact town centre dedicated to serious shopping, as well as a vast hinterland of suburban sprawl.

Unlike its more serious neighbour, Poole, Bournemouth has never really been anything other than a resort. It was a small village in the early 19th century, at the time when many of the pine trees that now scent the air were first planted. Blessed with a mild climate, and a south-facing location in a sheltered cleft, the settlement boomed towards the end of the 19th century, and most of the town's central buildings date from this period, with Victorian buildings interspersed with some later art deco. New luxury blocks of offices and modern accommodation may have changed the skyline forever, but the town's heart has a comfortable, still old-fashioned feel that remains appealing to many holiday-makers.

The town centre is shaped around the Lower, Centre and Upper Gardens, a long, leafy park around the flowing Bourne stream, with magnificent island flowerbeds, scenic tethered balloon flights, an aviary, a mini-golf centre and various refreshment stops. Around the upper end and the Square cluster all the main shopping streets, with arcades leading off the largely pedestrianized Old Christchurch Road. The most appealing of these is the glazed 1866 Victorian Arcade housing well-known Dingles department store and designer outlets including Gucci and Karen Millen. Beales is Bournemouth's large independent department store. Opposite, is St Peter's Church, with Arts and Crafts wall paintings, a chapel dedicated to the Oxford Movement reformer John Keble, the grave of novelist Mary Shelley and the heart of her brother in the churchyard.

The lower end of the park runs past the Pavilion Theatre, under the main road and out on to the seafront, with the pier just ahead. Bournemouth's pier is a functional affair, reinforced with ugly concrete that has seen it survive when others along this coastline have been washed away. Photographs at the far end show how it was partly demolished during World War II to prevent its use in a possible German invasion. Now it has a pier theatre and amusements, and great views back to the town, and the western beaches with their beach huts tucked under the sandy cliffs. The aquarium is also a popular attraction, while a land train offers transport up and down the seafront. Set behind this, on East Cliff, you will find the interestingly turreted Russell-Cotes Art Gallery and Museum, which is home to a collection of fine Victorian paintings and treasures from around the world.

Bournemouth's newest attraction is the submerged Surf Reef, located to the east of Boscombe Pier, one of only four artificial reefs worldwide, which mimics the effects of a natural reef and increases the size of the waves.

CHESIL BEACH MAP REF 399 J6

This deep shingle strip runs for 18 miles (29km) east of Lyme Bay, from Burton Bradstock to Portland.

CORFE CASTLE MAP REF 400 C8

Corfe is the best-known village on the Isle of Purbeck, and is packed with pubs, tea rooms and little shops that make it a magnet for visitors, especially walkers.

The huge and toothy ruin of Corfe Castle seems to fill the gap in the wall of the Purbeck Hills with its presence. It has a grim history. In AD 978 a youthful King Edward (the Martyr) was murdered here by his stepmother; his body was buried without ceremony at Wareham, while his half-brother took the throne as Ethelred II (the Unready). However, stories of miracles soon resulted in the exhumation of Edward's body. The body was then transported to Shaftesbury, where an abbey grew up in his honour.

Around 1106 the big square Norman keep was built, to defend against raiders from the sea and to impress the local populace. King John used it as a lifelong prison for his niece Eleanor, a potential threat to his throne. Edward II, deposed by his wife, was imprisoned here briefly.

During the Civil War the castle's owner, Sir John Bankes, eventually sided with the king, leaving his spirited wife Mary, with a handful of women and just five men, to fight off a siege in 1642. History books state that the 500-strong Parliamentarian army stripped all the lead from the church roof to make their bullets, and stored their gunpowder and shot in the organ pipes, but they failed to take the castle. After a second siege, the castle was betrayed in 1646, and after it was abandoned it was destroyed to prevent its use again.

South of Corfe, Worth Matravers is a picturesque village of lichen-encrusted grey cottages, complete with duck pond. Men from here have worked in the local quarries for centuries, and Purbeck marble (in fact a type of limestone) from this area was famously sent inland for the building of Salisbury Cathedral. The Square & Compass, an old fashioned pub with smoked beams and a big stone hearth, is a favourite with walkers. On the nearby cliffs stands 800-year-old St Adhelm's Chapel, a sturdy, buttressed brown cube, that has only one tiny little window. Near the coastguard station is a steel memorial to the brilliant work of radar developers here in 1940–42.

LULWORTH COVE MAP REF 400 C8
Lulworth Cove is an almost perfectly circular bay in the rolling line of limestone cliffs that form Dorset's southern coast.

It provides a safe anchorage for small fishing boats and pleasure craft, and a place of safe water for summer bathers. The wave-polished grey, black and red pebbles of the shingle beach, from wren's egg to ostrich egg in size, are reminiscent of childhood jars of pebble sweets. To the west, along the South West Coast Path, lie rolling, chalky downs and the landmark of Durdle Door, below the cliffs. To the east lie Worbarrow and Mupe bays.

The geology of the area is intriguing, and a visit to the Heritage Centre in the village will help you to identify the various rock formations. The oldest layer is the gleaming white Portland stone, much employed by Christopher Wren in his rebuilding of London. It is a finely grained oolite around 140 million years old, consisting of tightly compressed fossilized shells, and occasionally throws up giant flat-coiled ammonites, called a titanite, which may be seen incorporated decoratively into many house walls across Purbeck. Above this is a thick layer of Purbeck marble, a rich limestone where dinosaur, reptile and fish fossils are usually found. The soft layer above this consists of Wealden beds – a

belt of colourful sedimentary clays, silts and sands that are unstable and prone to landslips when exposed. Crumbly white chalk overlays this, the remains of microscopic sea creatures and shells deposited over a long period of time when a deep sea covered much of Dorset, some 75 million years ago.

The Fossil Forest in the sea cliffs east of Lulworth Cove is an intriguing oddity, but don't go looking for stone trees. What you see are the stone rings where sediment has bubbled up around the tree-trunks that rotted away millions of years ago. Together with the fossilized soil discovered beneath the tree boles, they give an insight into Jurassic life here, 135 million years ago.

Lulworth Castle Park at nearby East Lulworth was an impressive hunting lodge, built four-square in 1608 with pepperpot towers. Unfortunately, it was gutted by fire in 1929, but it is now a handsome shell, still only partly restored. Other attractions on the estate include an interesting circular chapel, an animal farm, an adventure playground for children and summer jousting events.

Nearly 200 rescued and endangered apes and monkeys have found a new, welcoming home at Monkey World, a few miles north of the small village of Wool. The park has 65 acres (26ha) of woodland, where the monkeys can recuperate in a safe environment that was built especially for them.

LYME REGIS MAP REF 399 H6
The cliff exposures along the Dorset and East Devon coast provide an almost continuous sequence of Triassic, Jurassic and Cretaceous rock formations spanning the Mesozoic Era, and record 185 million years of Earth history. Here there is a range of internationally important fossil localities which have produced some well-preserved and diverse evidence of life during Mesozoic times.

This is why the Dorset coast holds World Heritage status, granted in 2001, and why Lyme Regis is perfectly placed to experience this geological antiquity. The town, a pretty seaside resort, features in John Fowles' classic novel *The French Lieutenant's Woman*, which is set in the town in the 19th century.

STUDLAND MAP REF 400 D7

The glorious sands in Studland Bay are justly famous, and attract over a million visitors a year, so it's worth getting up early to have them to yourself. You are unlikely to be alone for long, though.

As you progress up the beach, getting warmer, you can shed your clothes with impunity, for the upper stretch opens its arms to naturists – and even on a bright winter's morning you'll spot brave souls sunbathing naked in the shelter of the marram-covered dunes. Off shore, big, sleek motor boats let rip as they emerge from the constraints of Poole Harbour. Watch out, too, for the orange and blue of the Poole lifeboat on manoeuvres, and the yellow and black pilot boat nipping out to lead in the tankers. Jet-skiers zip around the more sedate sailing yachts, all dodging the small fishing boats. It's a perfect seaside harmony, complete with wheedling, soaring gulls.

Behind the beach lies the old rugged heath, part of the same nature reserve that is in the care of English Nature and the National Trust. They are currently working together on a programme of restoration, reclaiming heath that had become farmland, and clearing scrub and maintaining controlled grazing to prevent it all reverting to woodland. All six of Britain's reptiles – common lizard, sand lizard, smooth snake, adder, grass snake, slow worm – live on the heath.

SWANAGE MAP REF 400 D8

In the early 19th century Swanage was a small, bustling industrial port shipping stone from the 60 or more quarries in the area. A growing fashion for sea-bathing would in time change the focus of the town forever. The real changes to the face of Swanage came with the extraordinary collecting habit of a man called George Burt, who was a contractor with an eye for ornate architecture.

With his uncle John Mowlem, a local stonemason and philanthropist, Burt shipped marble from the old quarries of Purbeck up to London, where many old buildings were being knocked down to make way for new construction. He was reluctant to see such fine stonework discarded, so Burt salvaged large whole pieces, transported them back to Dorset as ballast, and re-erected them in his home town, giving Swanage an 'instant' architectural heritage.

The Town Hall is a prime example of Burt's influence. He had donated a reasonably plain and simple building to the town in 1872; but in 1883 he added a facade by Wren, which he had rescued from the Mercers' Hall in London's Cheapside. In a park near the pier you

can see a grand archway removed from Hyde Park Corner, and three statues and some columns rescued from Billingsgate Market. There is also an absurd but rather elegant clock tower, removed from the south end of London Bridge in 1867, where it had been set as a memorial to the Duke of Wellington.

Durleston Castle is an original folly by Burt dating from 1887, designed from the start as a cliff-top restaurant on Durleston Head. Facts and figures from around the world are carved into enormous stone slabs set into the walls below. Burt added an unusual large, segmented stone globe of the world. It is grey and rather disappointing, but nevertheless in

a beautiful spot where you can sit during the evening, watching the sunset fade the sea into the sky, with the lonely shape of the lighthouse at the end of the Needles winking from across the water.

At Studland Museum and Heritage Centre you can learn more about the area, including tales of smuggling and the actual development of Purbeck's stone-quarrying industry. And for a nominal fee, try the delights of Swanage's Victorian pier, which announces penny-in-the-slot machines and 'Wot the butler saw' – no seaside visit can be complete without it. The Victorian pier suffered in the past from neglect and threat of demolition, but has now been restored to its former glory.

WEYMOUTH MAP REF 399 J6

Facing out into Portland Harbour, Weymouth is an ancient port, dating from medieval times, but given fashionable credentials after George III took to staying there in the 18th century, effectively making Weymouth one the first tourist destinations in Britain.

The attractive seafront esplanade overlooking the wide sandy bay is comprised almost exclusively of terraces constructed in the Georgian and Regency periods between 1770 and 1855.

During World War II, Weymouth played a key role in the D-Day landings in Normandy – a memorial on the esplanade records the events of 1944 and 1945.

60 MILES (96KM)

POOLE & THE ISLE OF PURBECK

The Isle of Purbeck is the fascinating area to the west of Poole, a landlocked island of high hills and sea cliffs. The route entails a complete circuit of Poole Harbour, with a short ferry ride at the end. On the way you will see lovely villages and a deserted village, sheltered bays, a ruined castle, seaside resorts, a seaside pier and the long sandy beach of Studland.

Route Directions

Explore the quaint and busy quayside at Poole, with its shops, pubs and the Poole pottery factory outlet, then begin the drive.

1 Leave Poole town centre and follow the signs for Hamworthy and Poole Bridge. Cross the bridge, by the Sunseeker boatyard, and continue towards Hamworthy and Rockley Park. After 2.5 miles (4km) pass under two railway bridges, with Upton Park signed to your left. Continue through Upton, and at the double roundabout by the clock tower turn left, signed 'Lytchett Minster'. Pass through Lytchett Minster. At the roundabout with the A35, go straight ahead, signed 'A351 Wareham'. Continue ahead across several roundabouts and through traffic lights, following signs to Wareham. Go straight on at the next roundabout, signed 'Corfe Castle', and bear left at the next roundabout, following signs for Wareham.

Make sure you stop off to explore the historic town of Wareham, which is on the banks of the River Frome.

2 In Wareham continue down the High Street, then cross the river. Continue to Stoborough and bear right, following signs for Creech. At the junction with the A351 turn left and immediately right, signed 'Creech, Steeple and Kimmeridge'. After this, turn right on to a minor road, looking for signs to East and West Lulworth.

The route passes through an area of farmland and open heath that is typical of the area, with pine forests, and parkland at East Holme. There is a stunning view of the long chalk ridge of the Purbeck Hills to your left.

3 After 2.5 miles (4km), turn left for East Lulworth. Look out for tanks crossing (this is the Lulworth army training area). Continue through the village of East Lulworth. At the T-junction turn left and continue through West Lulworth village to Lulworth Cove.

Park on the right, by the heritage centre, to explore beautiful Lulworth Cove and walk part of the South West Coast Path.

4 Retrace your route for 3 miles (4.8km) back up the hill and almost to the gates of Lulworth Castle. Turn right here, and take the next narrow turning right, signed 'Tyneham Village'.

This winding road rises along the back of the ridge and up to the crest, with superb views across the country inland.

5 After 4.5 miles (7.2km), you'll come across Whiteways Viewpoint on your right.

At the viewpoint you can enjoy views down over the coast and Kimmeridge Bay, and also right across to Poole Harbour.

6 Continue on the same road and to a turning circle on the left which marks the tight right turn down to Tyneham village. Follow the road down to the church.

Here you can explore the deserted Purbeck village of Tyneham, which was evacuated during World War II in 1943. It is now used by the Army as a firing range.

7 Go back up the road to the turning circle and turn right. Just before another viewpoint turn right towards Steeple and Kimmeridge. The narrow road descends sharply. Turn right, signed to Kimmeridge and the sea. The road crosses a valley and goes up a ridge before descending to pass by Smedmore House. Finally, it zig-zags down through Kimmeridge village. Note: a toll is payable if you want to continue down to the beach car park on Kimmeridge Bay.

The pebble beach here, with its long rock ledges and numerous rock pools, is popular with families and watersports enthusiasts. You can find people canoeing here at most times of the year.

8 Retrace your route back across the valley and turn right, signed 'Church Knowle and Corfe Castle'. After 1.5 miles (2.4km) pass through Church Knowle. Continue towards Corfe Castle and turn right to Swanage on the A351. Make your way through the centre of Corfe Castle village. On the other side of the village turn right, signed 'Langton Matravers'. Cross the Common. Follow the road left, and soon turn right, which is signed 'Worth Matravers'. Continue for a mile (1.6km), passing the quarry on your right. Park your car in the car park just above Worth Matravers.

Walk down the hill and bear right if you want to visit the duck pond and the church of St Nicholas in Worth Matravers.

9 Turn left at the Square and Compass pub, at the sign to Langton Matravers. Turn right at the main road and descend to Langton Matravers. At the junction with the A351 turn right and then follow signs for Swanage town centre and to the beach.

The traditional seaside resort of Swanage has a gently shelving sandy beach and a Victorian pier. In summer the beach is particularly crowded with families.

10 Leave Swanage on the coast road, signed 'Studland, Poole and Bournemouth' via toll ferry. After 3 miles (4.8km) turn right for Studland on the B3351. Continue to the ferry crossing Studland Heath.

The toll ferry crossing to Sandbanks takes about 10 minutes only, but expect to queue for some time in high season. Follow the B3369 coast road, past Compton Acres, back into the centre of Poole.

CORFE CASTLE CIRCUIT

This is a loop to Kingston from the ruins of Corfe Castle. The route takes in Corfe Common and part of the Purbeck Way incorporating downland, heath and village streets. The Common is crisscrossed by narrow bridlepaths and walkways.

DISTANCE/TIME 9 miles (14.5km) 3h45 **MAP** OS Explorer OL15 Purbeck & South Dorset
START Corfe Castle village car park (fee); grid ref: SY 974776 **PATHS** Village lanes, rocky lanes (slippery after rain), moorland tracks, grassy paths, steep cliff path with steps; 16 stiles
THE PUB The Greyhound Inn, The Square, Corfe Castle Tel: 01929 480205

1 Turn right down the street and soon go right, up a path by a fingerpost. Turn left through one gate, then a further two, walking behind the village. Turn right at the end, cross the wall and continue down the next field. At the bottom bear left over the stile, walking down a narrow cutting.

2 Cross two stiles and turn right on to the Purbeck Way. Follow the track up the valley, bending left at Coombe Bottom and right through a gate and up a hill. Go through the gate at the top, then bear right on to a track. At the farm turn left then right to meet the road. Cross and turn left down the track, signed 'Purbeck Way'. Stay on this to the bottom of the hill passing through a kissing gate part way down. By some fir trees turn left, cross a footbridge and turn right. Pass a farm as you go through three more gates and head straight down on to the heath.

3 After a footbridge, go straight on over Corfe Common towards the castle. Bear left at a marker, and right to a gate. Cross the B3069, go through a gate and straight on, later bearing right behind houses. Go through a gate and follow the path towards the village centre. After it narrows turn right, through a gate, and go across fields into a playground. Turn left then right into West Street to the square.

4 Turn left by the castle on the path below the walls. Go left up the road and soon left again by a gate and over a stile. Cross the fields to a car park. Here bear right then right again on to West Street. At the end, go straight on over a cattle grid. Bear left on a path across the heath. Cross duckboards and go uphill, bearing right, as you near the top, between a stone block and a tumulus. Go straight down the other side and through a gate. Cross two bridges and continue between trees and over a stile. Then go ahead across a field, over another stile and into a green droving lane. Cross another field, go straight over a road and up the hill. Walk up the next field, heading towards Kingston church tower.

5 At the top, go through a gate, and turn right. Immediately after a junction of lanes, turn left, up through some trees, then bear left to a road. Turn right, soon taking the track on the left, signposted 'Houns Tout'. Follow this to the sea and along the exposed cliff tops. Descend steps, then cross a stile at the bottom. Head inland to a road. Turn right and follow it round, bearing left on to a track signed 'Coastal Path'. Beside a house bear right, downhill. Go through a gate and continue up the road. Where this swings right, bear left up to Beacon Bottom. After 0.25 mile (400m) turn right over the stile and retrace your steps to the car park.

DURDLE DOOR & LULWORTH COVE

An exhilarating walk on a stunning stretch of coastline visiting Durdle Door, a spectacular natural rock arch in the sea, and Lulworth Cove some 2 miles (4km) along the coast, before turning inland and skirting the village of West Lulworth. The white chalk that breaks through the soil here underlies Dorset's famous downland and is seen in the exposed soft, eroded cliffs at White Nothe. West Lulworth is also the starting point for many who wish to go looking for fossils on Dorset's Jurassic Coast world heritage site.

DISTANCE/TIME 6.75 miles (10.9km) 3h **MAP** OS Explorer OL15 Purbeck & South Dorset
START Car park (fee) above Durdle Door; grid ref: SY 821800 **PATHS** Stone path, grassy tracks, tarmac, mudcy field path; 4 stiles **THE PUB** The Castle Inn, West Lulworth. Tel: 01929 400311; www.thecastleinn-lulworthcove.co.uk

1 Find the gate at the back of the car park. Pass through this to take the broad, paved footpath that leads up some shallow steps to the top of the first hill. Continue along the brow, and down the other side. Pass below a caravan park and through a gate.

2 Reach the cove of Durdle Door, almost enclosed from the sea by a line of rocks. A flight of steps leads down to the sea here, but carry on walking straight ahead on the coast path and the natural stone arch of the Door itself is revealed in a second cove below you. The mass of Swyre Head looms close and yes, that is the path you're going to take, ascending straight up the side. Walk down to the bottom then climb back up to Swyre Head. The path leads steeply down again on the other side, to a short stretch overlooking Bat's Head. Climb the next steep hill. Continue along the path behind the cliffs, where the land tilts away from the sea.

3 The path climbs more gently up the next hill. Pass a navigation obelisk on the right, and follow the path as it curves round the contour above West Bottom.

4 At a marker stone, marked 'Whitenothe' ahead, turn right, through a gate, and then follow a fence inland. The path curves round so you are walking parallel with the coast on level greensward. Pass three stone embrasures with shell sculptures inside, and a second obelisk. Go through a gate. Now keep straight ahead along the top of the field and across a crossing of paths, signed to Daggers Gate. Go through a gateway and straight on. The path starts to descend gently. In the next field the path becomes more of a track. Bear right to pass close by a tumulus and reach a gate.

5 Cross this and walk along the top of the field, above Scratchy Bottom. Cross a stile into a green lane leading to Newlands Farm. Follow it round to the right, and turn right into the caravan park. Go straight ahead on the road through here. At the far side go through a gate and turn left, signed to West Lulworth. Stay along the field-edge and walk above a farm lane, around the end of the hill. Keep straight on at the fingerpost and reach the gate above the car park. Turn left and retrace your route back to the start.

Salisbury & Plains

CLOCKWISE FROM TOP: STONEHENGE; SALISBURY CATHEDRAL; CATHEDRAL CLOSE; WILTON HOUSE

OLD SARUM MAP REF 400 D6

Old Sarum's history dates back to a time long before records were made, and the giant earthwork is founded on an Iron Age camp that covered around 56 acres (23ha). The earliest settlers were followed by Romans, Anglo-Saxons, Danes and Normans – William the Conqueror is said to have reviewed his troops here in 1070. A Norman castle and cathedral were erected, but water was scarce on this plain, and the military and ecclesiastical factions could not agree who should take precedence. Accordingly, in 1220 a new cathedral was planned to the south in nearby New Sarum – or Salisbury – using stones from the old one. It seems that the spirit went out of Old Sarum in more ways than one, as the castle fell into decay, and the town was gradually abandoned. There's not much left to see of this once-thriving settlement today, but for the excavated foundations of the old cathedral and fragments of the castle.

MARLBOROUGH DOWNS
MAP REF 400 D5

The Marlborough Downs are just one part of the North Wessex Downs Area of Outstanding Natural Beauty, although the name 'North Wessex' is not a traditional one, the area being better known by a series of overlapping local names, including the Marlborough Downs. Beyond the town of Marlborough, the Downs sweep in a wide semi-circle to the south around the headwaters of the River Kennet, and are extensively used for training race horses often providing an exciting spectacle on the Downs gallops.

Characteristically, the Downs form high, large-scale rolling chalk downland with a dramatic scarp on the northern edge and intensive arable farming, sparse woodland cover and few hedgerows.

ROMSEY MAP REF 400 E6

This small town on the River Test is dominated by its magnificent Abbey Church of 1120–70, a handsome Norman building with a low, square tower, massive walls, a splendid south doorway and an interior of beautifully carved Norman arches. It contains two remarkable Saxon stone carvings from earlier churches on the site, and its treasures include the Romsey Psalter (a 15th-century illuminated manuscript), and a monument to the noted economist Sir William Petty (1623–87), born in Romsey and a founder member of the Royal Society. Lord Mountbatten of Burma (1900–79), the one-time confidant to Prince Charles, is buried here in the abbey.

Romsey is an attractive place with many pleasing streets of Georgian and later houses. It centres on spacious Market Place, which has a statue in the middle of Lord Palmerston, the Victorian statesman who lived at nearby Broadlands.

SALISBURY MAP REF 400 D6

Salisbury feels comparatively spacious and regular – it was planned and built on a grid structure, beside the River Avon. Many old streets are named after the goods that were sold there – Fish Row, Butchers Row, and so on. Some have been pedestrianized, and highlights to look for include the 16th-century facade of Joiner's Hall on St Ann Street and the 18th-century Guildhall. The Poultry Cross in Silver Street dates from the 15th century.

Unusually, the Gothic cathedral was built in almost one go, the majority of it being completed by 1258, at a cost of around £27,000. The main exception is its soaring spire, 404 feet (123m) high, which was added in the 14th century and is the structure's most identifiable feature, painted most memorably by John Constable from across the water meadows in 1823. A climb up 332 steps and through the cathedral's roof spaces takes you to the top of the tower for far-reaching views over the city and around.

Salisbury cathedral's interior was drastically remodelled in the 18th century by James Wyatt, who 'decluttered' it by clearing screens and tombs and throwing out some of the old stained glass. Wyatt also covered over the 13th-century roof painting in the choir, but this was later restored. Nowadays, the most striking glass is the intense blue 'Prisoners of Conscience Window' in the Trinity Chapel.

Two of the cathedral's most prized possessions are the clock of 1386, the oldest in England, and an original copy of the Magna Carta, the 'great document' forced by rebellious barons on King John at Runnymede in 1215, to limit the monarch's more arbitrary powers. It's surprisingly small for such a significant document, about A3 in size.

A stroll around the extensive cathedral close is essential, including gracious old houses such as the Old Deanery, and the King's House, now home to the interesting Salisbury and South Wiltshire Museum, which includes finds from Stonehenge, watercolours by Turner, history relating to Old Sarum, and the Warminster Jewel. Mompesson House is a gem in Queen Anne style, with notable plasterwork and a pretty walled garden, and played a starring role in the 1995 film of Jane Austen's Sense and Sensibility. The Wardrobe contains a military museum.

The 17th-century Palladian mansion of Wilton House, home of the Earl of Pembroke, lies west of the town, and is well worth a look for its famous Single and Double Cube Rooms and its elegant gardens. The house was also the most unlikely setting for the D-Day landings headquarters during World War II; much more recently, scenes from the movies The Madness of King George, Mrs Brown and the 2005 movie Pride and Prejudice were all filmed here.

Visit
CATHEDRAL CHOIR

There has been a choir at Salisbury Cathedral for around 800 years, and today the cathedral choir is famous for admitting girls as well as boys. In 1991, on the 900th anniversary of the founding of the boys' choir, the cathedral decided to found the girls' choir. Girls and boys as young as seven years old can now join the choir school. The children take part in regular school lessons alongside their twice-daily singing practices. You can go along to hear the choristers rehearsing at evensong during term time and at special services held throughout the year. You can find out about concerts at the cathedral at the website www.salisburycathedral.org.uk

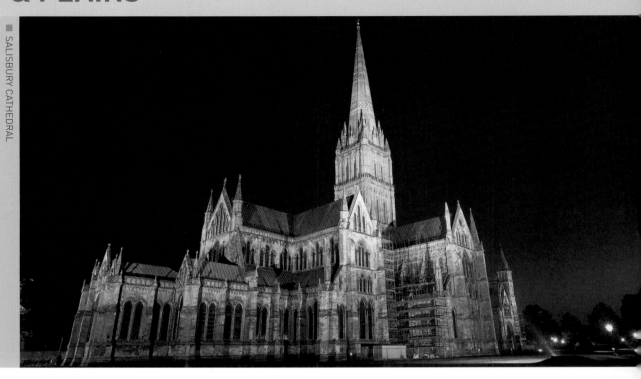

SALISBURY CATHEDRAL

STOCKBRIDGE MAP REF 400 E6

Lying deep in the broad Test valley, and spanning that many-streamed river on an artificial causeway constructed in Roman times, Stockbridge consists of a gracious wide street lined with an attractive variety of little houses and shops, with open views eastwards to the hills. It feels as if it should be the main thoroughfare of a sizeable town, but it is not, and behind the elegant facades, the gift and antiques shops, the art galleries and the hotels are the broad water meadows of the River Test. Some of the river's streamlets, teeming with trout, flow under and alongside the main street.

The most prestigious of English angling clubs, The Houghton, has its headquarters at the Grosvenor Hotel, Stockbridge's most impressive building, with a great pillared porch that juts out into the street and a room above. The town was on a main drovers' route between Wales, Surrey and Kent, and sheep fairs were held here from Tudor times until the early 20th century.

Stockbridge Common Marsh is ancient land in the care of the National Trust, as is the open Stockbridge Down, where there is a large Bronze Age cemetery.

Northwest of Stockbridge, on the A343, is the Museum of Army Flying at Middle Wallop airfield, which celebrates the history of army aviation. Exhibits include an Argentine Huey helicopter, captured during the Falklands War, and there are hands-on games and activities.

STONEHENGE MAP REF 400 D6

There was a henge at Stonehenge around 5,000 years ago, but it was little more than a ditch and bank around an open space. About 4200BC, the Beaker People appeared and began building a double ring of stones inside the henge.

These 'bluestones' were brought several hundred miles from Preseli in South Wales. Transporting the stones was an impressive achievement; most weigh more than 4 tons, and were brought to Salisbury Plain by boat and sledge, a process that must have taken decades.

Impressive it may have been, but the stones were barely in position before they were demolished, and may even have been moved to another building site. Speculation among archaeologists is that there was a shift in the power balance of the area, and the Beaker People were ousted by a local revolt. A new circle was erected, this time using more easily obtainable 'Sarsen' stones from the Marlborough Downs, to form an inner horseshoe surrounded by a circle. This is today's famous circle.

But what is Stonehenge? Is it an astronomical observatory? A Druid temple, perhaps? The truth is, no-one knows.

Current favourite is that Stonehenge was a form of multipurpose ceremonial centre, relating to fertility, death and rebirth.

WILTON MAP REF 400 D6

A small village of thatched cottages and a duck pond, Wilton is renowned for its windmill. The only working windmill in Wessex, the Wilton Mill was built in 1821 after construction of the Kennet and Avon canal, and was operational for 100 years, until the introduction of steam roller mills and fast production of cheap bread made it redundant. But in 1976, the mill was fully restored and is today managed by the Wilton Windmill Society.

Built as a traditional tower mill with a fantail to turn the cap, to ensure that the sails always point into the wind, the mill has four sails; it is fully operational, and produces stoneground wholemeal flour as a souvenir of your visit.

STONEHENGE

Cotswolds

CLOCKWISE FROM TOP: LAVENDER AT SNOWSHILL; GUITING POWER; IRIS AT HIDCOTE MANOR GARDEN; ULEY BURY; PITTVILLE PUMP ROOM

BLOCKLEY MAP REF 404 D7

This handsome village, situated along the fast-flowing Blockley Brook, is less well known than many of its neighbours but has a subtle appeal undoubtedly worthy of attention. Blockley was a silk town and by 1880, just before the failure of the industry in the area, the six mills here employed some 600 people. Many of the weavers' cottages remain; the older ones towards the village centre, the 19th-century silk workers' cottages terraced along the northern edge. One of the old mills can be seen beyond a pool near the church, while the village, with its pretty mill stream, is dotted with houses of varying ages and appeal. A beautiful garden, Mill Dene, has been created around one of the old mills.

BOURTON-ON-THE-WATER
MAP REF 400 D3

The busiest honeypot in the area is this attractive village, watered by the River Windrush, which flows proudly along the main street beneath a succession of five graceful footbridges, earning for Bourton the title 'the Venice of the Cotswolds'. A tourist mecca, and to be avoided if rural calm is what you yearn for, the village does have a lot to offer in the way of attractions. Birdland is a sanctuary for birds, with a remarkable collection of penguins in stream-side gardens. There is also a model village (Bourton in miniature), a perfume factory, a motor museum, the Dragonfly Maze, and a model railway exhibition, all within walking distance of each other and of the main street. Just off the main street is Bourton's church, St Lawrence's, a mixture of elements, with a medieval chancel, Victorian nave and distinctive domed Georgian tower, complete with skull on the exterior, a salutary reminder of our mortality.

Bourton can be best appreciated in the evenings after the crowds have dispersed, when a walk around its back streets and along the meandering river is a very pleasant experience.

Just to the east of Bourton are a series of gravel pits which, now filled with water, have become sanctuaries for waterfowl and make a very pleasant walk by following the path across Station Road from the car park. West of Bourton is a group of interesting villages – Notgrove, Cold Aston, Turkdean and Hazleton – that are well worth a visit.

BURFORD MAP REF 400 D4

Just off the main Oxford road, Burford is all but invisible to passing motorists. Drive north from the roundabout, however, and almost immediately, from the brow of the ridge, Burford slips away before you in a cascade of handsome inns and charming cottages. The wide main street, lined with shops and pubs, passes the church to the right before crossing the Windrush on a medieval bridge of 1322, by the old mill.

Burford's prosperity over the centuries has depended on three factors – wool, quarrying and coaching. There were burgesses here in the 13th century and the town developed rapidly to become an important wool centre.

The nearby quarries at the Barringtons, Upton and especially Taynton produced some of the most notable stone in the Cotswolds. Much of that stone was used in the construction of some of England's finest buildings – Blenheim Palace, St Paul's Cathedral and various Oxford colleges. The Barringtons also produced the Strongs, a family of masons – Sir Thomas Strong was Christopher Wren's master mason in the construction of St Paul's Cathedral. Another eminent family of masons, the Kempsters, came from Upton and Burford.

A fillip for Burford came with the dawn of the coaching era from the 18th century, when the town was an important stop on the route to Oxford and London. This, however, came to an end with the railway, which happened to bypass Burford.

Burford is a delight to stroll about. While the High Street is the main thoroughfare, Sheep Street to the west, and Witney Street and Church Lane to the east, have much to offer. Along Sheep Street there are some fine inns – the Bay Tree Hotel and the Lamb Inn (the old brewery next door houses the Tourist Information Centre) – while Witney Street boasts perhaps the finest building in the town, the 17th-century Great House. From Witney Street, Guildenford leads to Church Lane where a row of almshouses (1457), are close to St John the Baptist church.

The 15th-century parish church is impressive. Among the chapels and monuments, perhaps the finest is the one erected in 1628 to Sir Lawrence Tanfield, Lord Chief Baron of the Exchequer to James I. Another fine memorial, to Edmund Harman, barber-surgeon to Henry VIII, includes the first representation in Britain of Amazonian Indians from the New World. On the rim of the font the autograph of a Leveller, one of 340 Roundhead mutineers kept here for three days during the Civil War, is inscribed: 'Anthony Sedley prisner 1649' (sic). From the High Street, near the bridge, Priory Lane takes you past the handsome building of the Elizabethan Priory and round to Falkland Hall built in 1558.

BURFORD

CASTLE COMBE

Back on the High Street, on the corner of Sheep Street, is the pillared Tolsey, a Tudor house where wool merchants used to meet and which now houses a museum of considerable interest. Further down is the wide arch of the old George Hotel where Charles I used to stay with Nell Gwynn and which later became an important coaching inn. Their son was created Earl of Burford.

Approximately 3 miles (4.8km) south of Burford are the Cotswold Wildlife Park and Gardens, set in the grounds of a delightful 19th-century mansion.

CASTLE COMBE MAP REF 400 C5
Generally considered one of the loveliest villages in the Cotswolds, Castle Combe is very popular and can get crowded. Parking is a problem here and visitors are asked to use the car park. The perfection of this pretty village means that it is also used by film producers.

Like many other Cotswold villages, Castle Combe's wealth came from the sheep and wool industry. Most of its houses here were weavers' houses, and it was allowed to hold a fair for trading sheep and wool. The 14th-century Market Cross, with the old water pump beside it, forms the centre of the village. The nearby Butter Cross was dismantled during the 19th century. A favourite view of the village is from the old weavers' cottages, across the bridge. The museum contains many items of local interest.

Outside the village is the motor-racing circuit, which continued to host national championship races until the 1990s. Motor-racing test-drives and other automotive events are still held here.

CHELTENHAM MAP REF 400 C3
Built against the base of the Cotswold escarpment, overlooked by Cleeve and Leckhampton Hills, Cheltenham is ideal for visiting not only the Cotswolds but also the Severn Vale, the Forest of Dean and the Wye Valley. It is also the scene for several festivals: a Folk Festival in February; the National Hunt Festival when the Gold Cup is run; Jazz in April; the June Science Festival; the Summer Cricket Festival in the grounds of the Boys' College and the Music Festival in July; and the ever popular Literature Festival in October.

Cheltenham is usually associated with the Regency period, when a market town of insignificance became a fashionable watering hole. The ensuing building boom has left a town of considerable elegance, of handsome, wide streets lined with Regency-style villas and terraces.

The town centre is fairly compact and can easily be explored on foot. The original town ran along the current High Street, now home to major chain stores and two shopping arcades. The Regency town spread southwards along the Promenade, one of the finest town thoroughfares in the country, today lined with elegant shops. The magnificent terrace at the northern end, built to accommodate those coming to take the waters, now houses the Municipal Offices and the Tourist Information Centre. In front is the Neptune Fountain and a statue to Edward Wilson, the Cheltenham botanist who accompanied Captain Scott on his ill-fated expedition to the South Pole. The Promenade continues uphill to reach the imposing facade of the Queens Hotel, built on the site of the Imperial Well.

The road narrows between the shops here. It is worth walking along Queens Circus towards Fauconberg Road, on the right, a short way. On the right, here, is Cheltenham Ladies' College, part of which conceals the original Royal Well; on the left is one of Cheltenham's loveliest streets, Montpellier Street, which is lined with interesting shops raised from the road behind wide pavements. A small alleyway on the left from Montpellier Street leads back towards the main road passing old Montpellier Arcade to the left. At the top of the road is the Rotunda, now a bank although originally the Montpellier Spa, its design was apparently based on the Pantheon in Rome. The well-preserved interior is well worth a look.

If you have the time there is plenty more Regency architecture to see and appreciate in the area close to Montpellier, notably in Lansdowne, which is just to the west of Montpellier. Heading southeast will take you to Suffolk Square, beyond which, along Suffolk Parade and Suffolk Road, are some antique and curio shops.

North of the High Street is Pittville and its showpiece, the Pittville Pump Rooms. The Pump Rooms constitute a magnificent architectural ensemble and were designed between 1825 and 1830 by a local man, John Forbes. They were to be the focal point of Joseph Pitt's Pittville Estate. His legacies are the Pump Rooms, Pittville Park, with its lake surrounded by villas in an array of fantastic styles, Pittville Lawn, and Clarence Square and Wellington Square. In the Pump Rooms, which are often used for concerts and recitals, you can taste the waters or visit the museum on the upper floor.

Visit
DECORATIVE IRONWORK
Cheltenham is noted for its ironwork, which decorates many of the early buildings of the town. Balconies of finely wrought iron adorn the elegant buildings, adding a continental atmosphere to the streets and squares. Particularly fine examples can be found along Oxford Parade, Royal Parade and Suffolk Square.

Visit
BIRDLAND
Birdland was established by the late Len Hill, who purchased two small islands in the South Atlantic. These islands, part of the Falkland Islands group, are inhabited by penguins and a considerable variety of other birds, some of which can be seen at Birdland, along with macaws, parrots and cockatoos, in varied habitats on the banks of the River Windrush at Bourton-on-the-Water. You can watch the penguins zipping through the water via the glass-sided pool.

Visit
CHELTENHAM RACECOURSE
A visit to the racecourse is a 'must' for anyone interested in watching the world's top chasers and hurdlers. The track is best known for the National Hunt Festival in March, the top three-day meeting of the season which features the Gold Cup and Champion Hurdle and attracts more than 50,000 spectators. The Hall of Fame tells the story of the history of the racecourse.

CHIPPING CAMPDEN MAP REF 404 D7

The loveliest village in the Cotswolds is a gilded masterpiece. The main street curves in a shallow arc lined with houses each grafted to the next but each with its own distinctive embellishments.

As the name suggests ('Chipping' means market), Chipping Campden was a market town, one of the most important of the medieval wool towns in the Cotswolds. The town then dozed for centuries until Charles Robert Ashbee moved his Guild of Handicraft here from London in 1902. The Court Barn Museum displays some of his work and that of other craftsmen.

Campden's church, at the north end of the town, is perhaps the finest wool church in the Cotswolds, with a magnificent tower and a spacious interior that contains the largest brass, to William Grevel, that exists in the county. The Gainsborough Chapel houses the fine 17th-century marble tomb of Sir Baptist Hicks and his wife, who built the nearby stone almshouses in 1612, as well as Campden House, which was razed during the Civil War.

Grevel House, on the High Street opposite Church Street, once belonged to William Grevel, a wool merchant largely responsible for the church in its current form and who, it is supposed, was the original model for the merchant in Chaucer's *Canterbury Tales*.

Just off Leysbourne, which is the northern extension of the High Street, is the Ernest Wilson Memorial Garden, a charming little botanical enclave snug in the shadow of the church. The garden commemorates the eccentric plant collector who was born here in 1876. In the middle of the village, on stone pillars, is the 1627 Market Hall.

CHIPPING NORTON MAP REF 400 D3

This busy market town, the highest in Oxfordshire at 646 feet (197m), is distinguished at its outskirts by the large Victorian tweed mill, now converted to flats, that sits in a fold to the west of the town. The Bliss Tweed Mill, built in 1872 by the Lancashire architect George Woodhouse, closed in 1980 and is an unusual reminder, in the Cotswolds, of the Industrial Revolution; and yet there is something disconcertingly memorable about this example of the Victorian age.

The heart of Chipping Norton has to be the Market Square which is dominated by the 19th-century Town Hall, with its Tuscan-style portico. Opposite the Town Hall steps is the museum, which has displays on local history. Around the town you'll find a varied collection of shops, hotels and houses dating back to the 17th century, though most are 18th century.

From the square, the town slopes down Church Street past a row of almshouses dating back to 1640, towards St Mary's, a Perpendicular church containing some fine brasses and impressive tombs. Its most unusual feature is the hexagonal porch with a vaulted ceiling. Behind the church are the motte-and-bailey earthworks that show that the town was already of some importance in the Norman period.

CIRENCESTER MAP REF 400 D4

Now a busy market town, Cirencester was once the most important city in England after London, during the Roman occupation. Called Corinium Dubunnorum and founded as a military headquarters in AD 49, a number of important roads radiated from the city – the Fosse Way, Ermin Street and Akeman Street. The Saxons renamed Corinium 'Cirencester' (which from 'Coryn', means the 'top part', in reference to the River Churn, the highest source of the Thames; and 'Ceastre', which means 'fort') but practically destroyed the town, preferring instead to build smaller settlements outside the walls. Only in the Middle Ages did Cirencester regain something of its former glory when it became the premier of the Cotswold wool towns. Markets still take place each Monday and Friday.

The town is most easily explored on foot. There are a number of well-signposted car parks within easy reach of the city centre, while the market square is the most convenient place to begin discovery of the town. The 15th-century parish church, one of the largest in England, is the main feature. Its magnificent Perpendicular tower was built with the reward given by Henry IV to a group of local earls who foiled a rebellion. Its fine roof is illuminated by clerestory windows, while the east and west windows are filled with medieval stained glass. The best-known feature of the exterior, however, is the three-storeyed south porch, overlooking the market square, which was built by some of the abbots in the late 15th century as an office for the abbey and which became the Town Hall after the Dissolution. It was one of the finest in the country and was only returned to the church in the 18th century.

Opposite the church is the Victorian Corn Hall, on the Market Square, which has been beautifully restored and hosts several markets during the week. Cricklade Street, running south from the square, is the site of the Brewery Arts Centre, where craft studios are currently housed in the old brewery.

On Park Street, close to Cirencester Park, is Corinium Museum, which brings to life many aspects of local history and displays its various finds, including the mosaics that were made in the area from the Roman and later eras. It also houses the Tourist Information Centre.

Close by is Thomas Street, the location of the 15th-century Weavers Hall almshouse (also known as St Thomas's Hospital) and also Coxwell Street, lined with merchants' houses. Farther north is Spitalgate Lane, with the arcade of the nave of St John's Hospital, and another group of almshouses. Due east from here is the mysterious-looking Spital Gate, all that remains of the old abbey. From here a walk through the Abbey Grounds, where the remnants of the Roman walls can be seen at the eastern boundary, will take you back to the town centre.

No visit to Cirencester would be complete without a glimpse, at the very least, of Cirencester Park, probably the finest example of geometric landscaping in the country. It is approached up Cecily Hill, one of the prettiest streets in Cirencester, which leads to the wrought-iron entrance gates. The park was the conception of the 1st Lord Bathurst in the early 18th century and the house (not open to the public), behind one of the largest yew hedges in the world, was built to his own design. The park was landscaped with the help of the poet Alexander Pope, among others, who has celebrated the construction of the park in verse. In fact there is a corner known as Pope's Seat near the polo ground.

It is an excellent place for walking (the grounds are privately owned but open to walkers and riders), especially along the Broad Ride, which stretches out from the entrance almost to Sapperton.

Apart from the wall in the Abbey Garden, the only other surviving Roman souvenir is the superb 2nd-century Roman Amphitheatre, which is one of the largest and best preserved in the country. It is found on Cotswold Avenue.

COLN VALLEY MAP REF 400 D4

The River Coln, a tributary of the Thames, is arguably the loveliest of the many rivers that ripple peacefully through the Cotswolds. It rises on the escarpment not far from Cheltenham then gently descends the slopes, passing through a number of pretty villages en route.

Withington has an unusually large church with a fine Norman doorway and a handsome wall monument to Sir John and Lady Howe of Compton Cassey. The 17th-century mansion of Compton Cassey is now a magnificent farmhouse, lying in splendid isolation in the middle of the valley, forcing the Yanworth road to curve around it. As you approach it you may see a large sculpture in a field close by. If so it will be the product of the artist's gallery, Compton Cassey Gallery, which now occupies the house.

Near here the river passes close to Chedworth Roman Villa and thence to Fossebridge, a steep point on the Roman Fosse Way where an ancient inn continues to attract passing customers. On the other side of the road the Coln furrows across the meadows of Coln St Dennis, a small, silent village built around a green, with a small Norman church. Look for the inscription to Joan Burton on the interior wall of the tower, as well as the Norman corbel stones that line the nave.

Further on is the pretty hamlet of Calcot and then almost immediately Coln Rogers with a church remarkable for its Saxon plan and Saxon window north of the chancel. At the old mill in Winson, where the road zig-zags, there are charming gardens and towards the centre of the village you'll find some converted barns. The compact green is overlooked by a classical-looking manor house. After Winson come Ablington and Bibury.

Finally, before going on to Fairford and Lechlade, the Coln arrives at Coln St Aldwyns, where the green is shaded by a magnificent horse chestnut tree and the New Inn is a fine pub. A pretty churchyard surrounds the church, which has memorial windows commemorating John Keble, the 19th-century reformer, and his father. It is possible to walk along the Coln from here to Bibury.

THE GUITINGS MAP REF 400 D3

The valley running east of Winchcombe is sprinkled with some charming villages. There are two Guitings, for example – the intriguingly named Temple Guiting and Guiting Power. Temple Guiting takes its name from the Knights Templar who owned the manor from the 12th century, and is a pretty village among trees at the edge of the stream. The church has fragmentary remains of the Norman construction, the tower, pulpit and windows are 18th century, with 16th-century stained glass.

Guiting Power, a couple of miles to the south of Temple Guiting, is clustered around a small green, and is a perfect example of an English village.

The church to the south of the village, also once owned by the Knights Templar,

has an exceptionally fine Norman south doorway, although the interior is rather uninspiring. The foundations of a Saxon chapel have been discovered just to the north of the existing church. East of Temple Guiting is the popular Cotswold Farm Park.

HIDCOTE MANOR GARDEN
MAP REF 404 D7

Four miles (6.4km) northeast of Chipping Campden, in the hamlet of Hidcote Bartrim, is the National Trust property of Hidcote Manor, famous above all for its series of scenic gardens that have transformed a 17th-century property of comparative mediocrity into an inspiration for modern gardeners.

The 11-acre (4.5ha) garden, a mix of formal design and seemingly haphazard planting, was created over the course of 40 years after Hidcote was purchased in 1907 by the great horticulturist Major Lawrence Johnston. In fact, there are a number of separate gardens, each created to a different design and producing different colours of flowers and shrubs. The effect is heightened by the use of walls and hedges of copper and green beech, box, holly, hornbeam and yew, which protect the plants, many of which are rare or unique, from the severe Cotswold winds. Within the hedges are the formal Bathing Pool Garden, the Fuchsia Garden, and the White Garden as well as the Kitchen Garden and a less formal creation by a stream. In addition there is a beech avenue, a lime alley, and visitors can enjoy magnificent views of hill and vale.

Kiftsgate Court Gardens, near Hidcote Manor, are on a wooded slope from where there are views across the Oxfordshire wolds. The house is largely Victorian, while the gardens were created after World War I by Heather Muir. The terraced areas above the scarp are a paradise of colourful flower beds and shrubs, while the slope is covered in pines. The gardens are famous for a collection of roses, including Rosa filipes 'Kiftsgate', believed to be the largest rose in the United Kingdom at almost 60 feet (18.3m) high.

KELMSCOTT MAP REF 400 D4

Kelmscott is a small village, the fame of this is inseparable from the 19th-century poet and artist, William Morris. On the facade of a terrace of cottages on the main street, there he is in carved relief seated in the shade of a tree, knapsack and hat at his side. Kelmscott Manor, on the edge of the village, was his home from 1871 until his death in 1896. Morris is buried in the local churchyard in a grave, designed by Philip Webb and which was modelled on a Viking tomb.

Kelmscott Manor (limited public opening) was built in the late 16th century. Morris only rented it but it now contains a fine collection of items associated with the man and with his craft, most notably those comparatively simple, domestic artefacts that he strove to see reinvigorated through the Arts and Crafts Movement. It also contains some pictures by Rossetti and Burne-Jones. This village came to mean much to him, and he named his private printing press in London after it.

RIVER COLN

LECHLADE ON THAMES
MAP REF 400 D4

This is another town with the peculiar quality that derives more from its rivers, notably the Thames, than from the Cotswolds. In the Middle Ages the town was on the Salt Way but Lechlade is very much a river town. At the confluence of three rivers – the Coln, the Leach and the Thames – it was at Lechlade that stone quarried at Taynton was loaded on to wagons before setting out for London, to be used in the construction of St Paul's Cathedral. From 1789 the Thames was linked to the Severn via the Thames and Severn Canal, which started to the southeast at Inglesham, where the old round house, built for the canal lengthmen (who were responsible for the maintenance of certain lengths of the canal, hence the name), still stands.

Inevitably, wherever there are rivers there are bridges. Just south of the town, the A361 crosses the Thames with the old tollbridge, the 18th-century Halfpenny (or Ha'penny) Bridge; while to the east the

A417 crosses the Thames by means of the 13th-century St John Bridge where a statue of Father Thames presides close to the Thames' highest lock and from where there is a fine view of the town.

Lechlade is built about its pretty Market Square, and its wool church. The square, and the streets that radiate from it – Burford Street, High Street and St John Street – are overlooked by a collection of fine 17th- to 19th-century buildings. The church, with its distinctive spire, dates from the late 15th century when it was built largely from the same quarries at Taynton that later provided the stone for St Paul's Cathedral. The church contains an east window from 1510 and the brass of wool merchant John Townsend, as well as a fine chancel roof.

The bustle of commercial river life has long gone from Lechlade, although pleasure craft still bring colour and movement to the river and it is possible to hire small boats from the boatyard near the Ha'penny Bridge. The walk along the Thames, southwest from the Ha'penny

Bridge, is very enjoyable and at Inglesham there is the pretty church of St John the Baptist, 30 feet (10m) from the river, which was salvaged by William Morris.

Just to the southeast of Lechlade is Buscot Park, a handsome 18th-century house, with a well-known series of paintings by Burne-Jones in the saloon, and a trio of Rembrandts among many other works of art reflecting the taste of the 1st Lord Faringdon.

PAINSWICK MAP REF 400 C4

'Queen of the Cotswolds' sits more or less at the point of transition from the northern to the southern Cotswolds. Perched regally at the edge of the steep slopes of the Painswick Valley, the town is a hive of activity about the network of lanes around the church.

Like other important towns in this part of the Cotswolds, Painswick's prosperity reached its peak in the 17th and 18th centuries when the stream below was harnessed to work the mills producing wool cloth. The water purity also meant

that cloth dyeing became important. The character of the village depends considerably on the fine houses built by the wealthy wool merchants of the era.

But the most striking feature of Painswick is the graceful 17th-century spire of the church. The church itself is mainly 15th-century and contains some interesting monuments, although it is the churchyard for which Painswick is especially noted. There are two reasons for this. Interesting features include the colonnades of yew, which have graced the churchyard since 1792. There are said to be only 99, since the Devil always kills off the hundredth, and indeed, it is now impossible to count them with ease since some are intertwined with each other. The other distinction are table tombs from the 17th and 18th centuries, many of which were carved by a local mason, Joseph Bryan, and his two sons.

Stroll around the heart of the town and along Bisley Street, the original main street and the oldest part of the town. Here you will find the Little Fleece, now a National Trust bookshop in a largely 17th-century house that was built on to the 14th-century Fleece Inn.

Just outside the town, on the Gloucester road, is Painswick Rococo Garden, the landscaped 18th-century garden around Painswick House. It is utterly charming, particularly in early spring when snowdrops flower in abundance.

THE SLAUGHTERS MAP REF 400 D3

These two villages with unlikely names ('slaughter' means muddy, which they are no longer) are, like Bourton-on-the-Water, synonymous with the Cotswolds. Upper Slaughter, partly clustered around the fine 17th-century manor (now an hotel) and the 12th-century church, is the more pastoral of the two. Beyond the church (which contains a monument to F E Witts, 19th-century rector and lord of the manor, who wrote *Diary of a Cotswold Parson*) the scene is absurdly picturesque, with the forded River Eye bubbling in the shade of an oak tree below some wonderful stone cottages.

Lower Slaughter, about a half-mile (800m) walk away, is somewhat different in character. The River Eye is spanned by a number of flattish footbridges. The 19th-century corn mill, with its working waterwheel and steam chimney, has an interesting museum and has demonstrations to show the workings of a Victorian flour mill. Among its collection is one of only three unused millstones left in the country. There is an award-winning craft and gift shop and riverside tea room, and free tastings of their handmade organic ice-creams in the summer.

LOWER SLAUGHTER

SNOWSHILL MAP REF 400 D3

Pronounced (according to who you speak to), 'Snowzzle', or even 'Snozzle', this charming and comparatively remote village is famous, above all, for Snowshill Manor, an interesting National Trust property from the Tudor period that once belonged to the wealthy and eccentric sugar plantation owner, Charles Wade.

An ardent collector of anything that was crafted, he filled the manor house with his finds, living, meanwhile, in the Priest's House set in the lovely terraced garden, but without any comforts or conveniences and sleeping in an old Tudor bed. The fame of Snowshill Manor spread, so that eminent people – John Buchan, John Betjeman, J B Priestley, and Queen Mary who apparently declared that the finest thing in the house was Charles Wade – were frequent visitors.

SOUTH CERNEY MAP REF 400 D3

South Cerney, which is 3 miles (4.8km) southeast of Cirencester, is situated on the banks of the River Churn, where you will find rows of attractive cottages along Silver Street and Church Lane. The church has a Norman south doorway above which are some sculptures reflecting Heaven and Hell, while within are the remains of a 12th-century crucifix, one of the earliest wood carvings in the country.

The old Thames and Severn Canal passes just to the north of the village and walks along the towpath are possible; but the village is best known, nowadays, for a series of flooded gravel pits that make up the Cotswold Water Park. Broadly speaking there are two sections, one between Cricklade and Kemble (where South Cerney is situated), the other between Fairford and Lechlade, which provide facilities for nature lovers, bird watchers and sportsmen alike. There are eight nature reserves and the wetlands attract more than 20,000 wildfowl, particularly in the winter. The various activities coexist happily on 170 lakes.

STANTON MAP REF 403 J6

Stanton has a fine collection of farmhouses and cottages, most of which were built during the 17th century, the golden period of Cotswold vernacular architecture. A village of quite ridiculous perfection, it seems almost to have been preserved in aspic; and indeed is regularly used as the backdrop for period films. It owes its peculiar 'frozen-in-time' quality to the man who bought much of the village before World War I, the architect Sir Philip Stott from Oldham in Lancashire.

Living in Stanton Court, he was determined to restore the village. This he did, introducing modern conveniences

in the process, but ensuring by means of a covenant, that the more unsightly features of the 20th century were not allowed to disfigure the village. A place to stroll around (making use of the car park around the corner of the Broadway road), the church, St Michael's, is delightful and well worth a visit. It has a handsomely slender spire, and a number of 12th-century features in the north arcade and also two pulpits, one 14th century, one Jacobean. It also has some 15th-century stained glass, which came from Hailes Abbey near Winchcombe. The village's fine pub, the Mount Inn, is at its far end in the shadow of Shenbarrow Hill, with its Iron Age earthworks and magnificent views.

STANWAY MAP REF 400 D3

No more, really, than a hamlet, Stanway is dominated by Stanway House and its quite beautiful gatehouse. Just off the B4077 Stow road, Stanway House is reached by passing the striking St George and Dragon, a bronze war memorial by Alexander Fisher on a plinth by Sir Philip Stott, 'saviour' of nearby Stanton.

For a long time the 17th-century gatehouse was thought to have been designed by Inigo Jones. This theory has been superseded by the belief that it is the work of Timothy Strong, the mason from the Barringtons whose family worked with Sir Christopher Wren on St Paul's Cathedral. The glow of the stone is breathtaking, particularly at sunset.

The house itself, a Jacobean building with medieval origins, has changed hands only once in more than 1,000 years and definitely warrants a visit. Still inhabited by the owner, Lord Niedpath, whose aristocratic presence is much in evidence, the house wears an attractive lived-in aspect; and although it contains many items of interest and value, some even unique, a less-fossilized atmosphere in a house is hard to imagine.

In the grounds there is a magnificent tithe barn, which was built about 1370. The old water gardens have been superbly restored and pride of place must go to the fountain, the tallest in Britain, which rises to over 300 feet (91m). The old brewhouse has been revived and the coopers are built over log fires, making this one of the few log-fired breweries in the country. Several beers are produced, the most popular is Stanny, available in many local pubs.

Situated next to the house is the church with a Jacobean pulpit. Near by is a delightful, thatched wooden cricket pavilion set on saddle stones, presented to the village by J M Barrie, author of children's classic, Peter Pan. Barrie, a keen cricketer, was a frequent visitor to Stanway in the early 20th century.

TEWKESBURY MAP REF 400 C3

Tewkesbury's considerable historical significance was largely governed by its location on the banks of the rivers Severn and Avon, which were instrumental in the 16th-century cloth and mustard trade and the later flour trade. Its importance depended, too, on its medieval Benedictine monastery of which only the magnificent church remains. The monastery was built by the Norman, Robert Fitzhamon, who used the Severn to import stone from Normandy for its construction. After his death the 'Honour of Tewkesbury', as the patronage came to be known, passed on to an illegitimate son of Henry I and then to the de Clare family.

The abbey became one of the most powerful religious centres in the kingdom, owning large areas of sheep-grazing land and constructing many fine tithe barns in the process – some of these survive, for example, at Stanway. The abbey was dissolved in 1539 but Tewkesbury's citizens bought the church for the total sum of £483. Its location, however, close to two rivers, which tend to flood, meant the town was unable to expand and folded in on itself. Throughout the 17th and 18th centuries this was achieved by building around narrow alleyways, several of which have survived (Machine Court, Fish Alley, Fryzier Alley) off the main streets – Barton Street, Church Street and High Street. Its half-timbered and brick houses present one of the country's finest historical ensembles. The Heritage Centre, Out of the Hat, is an entertaining way to start any visit to the city. It is also the location of the Tourist Information Centre.

However, the town is dominated by the Abbey Church of St Mary and the eye filled by its great 148-foot (45m) square Norman tower. Inside, one of the most striking features is the set of 14 Norman pillars which support the 14th-century roof. The choir is illuminated by some 14th-century stained glass windows, while around it radiate six chapels containing monuments to the wealthy families that have influenced both the church and the town. The west front exterior is notable for its dramatic Norman arch, of almost unsurpassed grandeur.

There is a lot to enjoy in the town. A circular walk includes, in dry weather, a stroll across the Ham – an enormous meadow that separates the Mill Avon from the Severn and which invariably floods each winter – to the river.

Opposite the church is the handsome Bell Hotel. From here Mill Street leads you down to Abel Fletcher's Mill (Abbey Mill), so called because it is thought to have played a role in the Victorian novel, John Halifax, Gentleman, much of which is set

Activity
THE COTSWOLD WAY

The Cotswold Way is a challenging long-distance footpath of 103 miles (166km), which runs between Bath and Chipping Campden. It takes about nine days to complete the distance if you attempt it in one go, otherwise you can walk short sections of the route at a time.

Visit
COTSWOLD FARM PARK

At the Cotswold Farm Park, the home of rare breeds conservation, there are nearly 50 breeding flocks and herds of ancient breeds of British cattle, horses, pigs, sheep, goats, poultry and waterfowl. Newborn lambs and goat kids can be seen in April, spring calves in May, foals in June and cute piglets throughout the year.

in the fictional town of Norton Bury, which was modelled on Tewkesbury. From here you can either walk along St Mary's Road, with its attractive timbered cottages, or cross the River Avon and strike out across the Severn Ham. Every year the grass of the Ham, which is owned by the town, is cut and auctioned off according to a local, centuries-old tradition.

At the Severn turn right to walk along by the weir and return across the meadow this side of the flour mills. You can cross the old mill bridge and then walk along the River Avon. At King John's Bridge recross the river and turn right into the High Street. St Michael's Tower is built on the site of the medieval High Cross that was razed by Puritans in 1650.

On your left, Barton Street will take you to the fascinating Tewkesbury Museum, located in a 17th-century building. The museum features a model of the Battle of Tewkesbury. Church Street, to your right, takes you past the distinctive Royal Hop Pole Hotel, which featured famously in Charles Dickens' novel The Pickwick Papers. Beyond this is a row of restored 15th-century cottages built by wealthy medieval merchants. One, known as the Merchant's House, is presented exactly as it would have looked in its heyday. Another, the John Moore Countryside Museum, takes its name from the local writer whose stories were based on Tewkesbury, and the countryside and villages around nearby Bredon.

On the right, an alleyway leads down to the Old Baptist Chapel and Court. Although the actual building dates back to the 15th century, it became a chapel only in the 17th century.

ULEY MAP REF 399 K2

Uley is a large and pretty village of 18th-century houses scuttling down the hillside into a deep valley, which became prosperous through wool dyeing. There is still a functioning brewery, while the Crown is a fine pub. Old Uley Bury overlooks the town – it is a classic site for a hillfort, being a flat 32-acre (13ha) plateau surrounded by steep slopes.

North of Uley, towards Frocester Hill, is Hetty Pegler's Tump – the unusual name comes from the 17th-century landowner's wife. This 180-foot (55m) Neolithic barrow, surrounded by a stone wall, has a long central chamber that can be entered, with some discomfort, by obtaining the key from a nearby cottage. It may be wise to take a torch. East of Uley, within reasonable striking distance by foot, is Owlpen Manor, a beautifully sited and picturesque 15th-century manor house, which has an intersting collection of Arts and Crafts furniture. Also close by is the 19th-century church and 18th-century mill.

About a mile (1.6km) east of Owlpen is a most tranquil garden at Kingscote called Matara. Both Eastern and Western ideas of garden design are blended to produce a very restful place.

WINCHCOMBE MAP REF 400 D3

The capital of the Saxon kingdom of Mercia, Winchcombe is a town of considerable interest, with several legacies of its past that deserve investigation. There was an important abbey here during the Middle Ages, but all that now remains is the wall on one side of Abbey Terrace (behind which is private property) and the abbey church, now Winchcombe parish church. The handsome church, built between 1465 and 1468, owes its present form to wealthy local woolmen. Of note here are the 40 or so gargoyles, the Winchcombe Worthies, on the exterior, said to represent unpopular monks, a sign of dissatisfaction with the abbey at the time.

Strung all along the main street are an assortment of interesting buildings (including the fine Jacobean old school on Abbey Terrace), as well as the Railway Museum and the Winchcombe Folk and Police Museum located in the town hall.

Sudeley Castle, Gardens and Exhibitions, entered down Vineyard Street, is superb. Little remains of the original medieval castle, but of the 15th-century reconstruction undertaken by Ralph Botelar, St Mary's Chapel, the ruined banqueting hall, the tithe barn and the Portmare Tower are extant.

WINDRUSH VALLEY MAP REF 400 D3

The lush and beautiful Windrush rises near Taddington, south of Snowshill, and then wanders gently through several charming Cotswold villages. Beyond Bourton it widens as it approaches the Thames and continues through a number of villages to the north of the A40, to join the Thames.

A pleasant walk, the Windrush Way goes from Winchcombe to the enduringly popular Bourton-on-the-Water.

Sherborne, on a tributary of the Windrush, has been for centuries part of the Sherborne estate; before that the land was owned by the Abbots of Winchcombe, whose sheep were sheared on the banks of the river every summer. Sherborne House, allegedly haunted by its former owner, John 'Crump' Dutton, the Royalist hunchback, was rebuilt in the 19th century. It now belongs to the National Trust and, although it is not open to the public, there are waymarked walks through the woods and parkland. Lodge Park, an elaborate grandstand for deer-coursing in the 17th century, is open to the public.

The next village to the east is Windrush, with a church topped by a fine Perpendicular tower and a magnificent Norman south doorway surrounded by beakheads, bird-like grotesques of mysterious origin. Then come the Barringtons, first Little, then Great, once renowned for their stone quarries and the local families of masons, the Kempsters and the Strongs, who worked them. No evidence remains of the old subterranean quarries and Little Barrington is a quiet little village, its cottages very prettily clustered about its village green. The Fox Inn nearby, is by a bridge over the river, built by local master mason Thomas Strong, principal contractor of St Paul's and regarded by Christopher Wren as the leading builder of the day. Great Barrington, to the north, has a Norman church with some fine monuments by the well-known 18th-century sculptor Joseph Nollekens, while the country house and landscaped gardens of Barrington Park are to the east of it.

East of Great Barrington lies Taynton, another village that once supplied London and Oxford with its famous prime building stone, it was transported overland to Lechlade and thence by barge to London. Beyond it is Burford and then Widford church, the poignant remains of a once-thriving village that simply disappeared, probably as a result of the plague. The 13th-century church, built on the site of a Roman villa, stands on a raised mound overlooking the river, and is worth a look for its box pews, and the wall paintings that date from the 14th century.

A short way from Widford is Swinbrook, a village associated with the famous Mitford family, particularly five of Lord Redesdale's daughters – Nancy, Diana, Unity, Jessica and Deborah. Unity went on to become a close friend of Adolf Hitler, Diana married the British fascist leader, Sir Oswald Moseley, Deborah became the Duchess of Devonshire, while Nancy and Jessica became well-known writers. Nancy, Pamela, Diana and Unity are buried in the graveyard of the church, which contains the wonderful triple-decker monument to the Fettiplace family who once owned a mansion here.

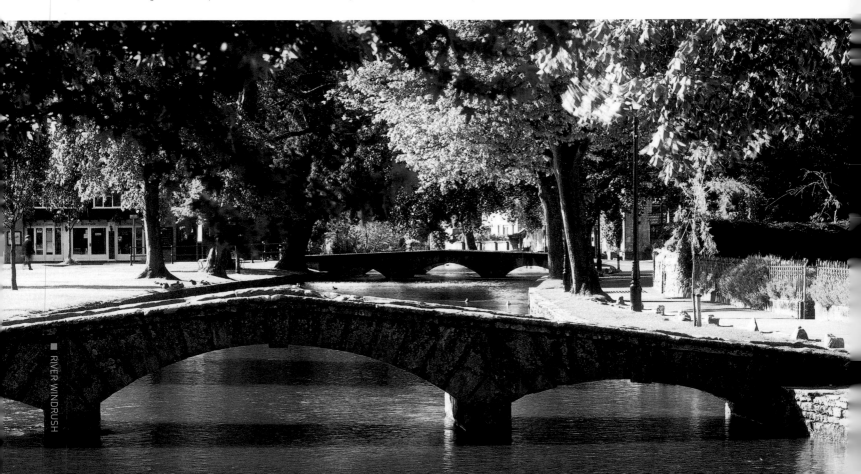

RIVER WINDRUSH

BLOCKLEY, BATSFORD & THE ARBORETUM

This walk starts in the unspoilt village of Blockley then passes through Batsford village at the gates of Batsford Park with its 90 species of magnolia, maples, cherry trees and conifers, stunning in autumn but colourful throughout the spring and summer too. The arboretum also has a falconry centre. Blockley is a pretty village that prospered in the 19th century and its fast-flowing stream, which once powered six silk mills, is now a delightful feature of the village.

DISTANCE/TIME 5 miles (8km) 2h15 **MAP** OS Explorer OL45 The Cotswolds **START** On the edge of the churchyard, just off the main street at Blockley; grid ref: SP 165348 **PATHS** Lanes, tracks and fields, 7 stiles **THE PUB** The Crown Inn, Blockley. Tel: 01386 700245

1 Leave the churchyard by the tower and walk through the village, turning left at School Lane. Follow this down across a stream and up to the main road. Turn left and, just before Lower Brook House, turn right on to a lane walking up for 0.25 mile (400m) until the lane bears left.

2 Continue ahead to pass to the right-hand side of a barn. In the next field follow its right-hand boundary to another gate. Pass through this to stay on the left side of the next field. Pass into yet another field and then after 0.3 miles (500m) go half right to a gate leading out to a road.

3 Go straight on and follow the road down to a crossroads. Turn right to pass through Batsford to a junction from where you can visit the church on the right. After visiting the church retrace your steps to the junction (there is no public access to the Arboretum from the village) and walk down the lime avenue. At the next junction, turn right.

4 After 100 paces turn right on to a footpath and then continue to follow this through a succession of fields, negotiating stiles and gates where they arise. Magnificent Batsford House will be visible above you to the right.

5 Finally, go through a gate into a ribbed field and turn right to a gate and kissing gate just left of a gate lodge at a drive. Cross this (the entrance to Batsford Arboretum), pass through a gate and follow the path up the field to a stile. Cross and continue to a track. Follow this up until where it bears left. Turn right on to a path and almost immediately left at a wall, to continue the ascent with the park wall on your right. Keep going until you reach a stile to a road.

6 Cross the road on to a track, then go through a gate and pass through two fields until you come to a path among trees. Turn left, go through another gate, and, after 140 paces, turn right over a stile into a field with Blockley below you. Continue down to a stile at the bottom. Cross into the next field and pass beneath Park Farm on your right. Go to the right of a pond to descend to a gate and stile, then follow a lane along the Duck Paddle, until you come to a road. Turn right and return to your starting point in the village.

WALK 24

AROUND CUTSDEAN & FORD

A lovely walk through open countryside once the focus of England's most valued export, wool. Look out for horses being exercised on 'The Gallops' along the way.

DISTANCE/TIME 6 miles (9.7km) 2h30 **MAP** OS Explorer OL45 The Cotswolds **START** Cutsdean village or beside lane to the east; grid ref: SP 088302 **PATHS** Tracks, fields and lane; 5 stiles **THE PUB** The Plough Inn, Ford. Tel: 01386 584215; www.theploughinnatford.co.uk

1 With the Church of St James to your right-hand side and, after a few paces, a telephone box away in a lane to your left, walk out of the village of Cutsdean past Stoneley. Continue uphill on this straight country road for just over a mile (1.6km), until you come to a T-junction with another road.

2 Cross this to enter another lane past a 'No Through Road' sign, at the margin of woodland. Beyond a second wood, where the track veers left towards a house, go straight on along a stony track.

3 Eventually you come to a gate. Through this continue along the track, initially a wood to your right, to another gate, ignoring a footpath to the left at the brow of the hill. Through the gate the path has a stone wall on the left for a field and a half, the path then goes quarter right over the brow of a slope to head for a plantation.

4 Emerging beyond the plantation turn immediately right at a track junction and right again; the plantation now on your right. Follow this track for 1.5 miles (2.4km), passing through Ford Hill Farm, all the way to a road.

5 Across the road go through a gate, signed 'Jackdaw's Castle' and follow a tarmac lane running to the left of 'gallops' used for training racehorses. Keep straight on where the track veers left into a neighbouring field.

6 Soon after passing the stables of Jackdaw's Castle across to your right, turn sharp right at a footpath sign across the gallops (watch out for horses) to join a tarmac track, where you turn left. The track descends gently for just under a mile (1.6km), the gallops and greensward to your left. Keep descending until you are near the bottom, at the beginning of Ford. If you walk into the village, the Plough Inn is ahead.

7 Otherwise turn right and, at a bend, turn right again to cross a car parking area to a stile. Over this walk along a grassy path, a post and rail fence to your right, a stream in a steep valley to your left, soon passing through a gate. The path leaves the fence and then descends through the copse to a stile.

8 Cross the stile into a field and then go half right across it. Go down a bank, across a rivulet (possibly dried up in summertime) and up the bank on the other side to a stile. Cross into a field and turn left along the side of the field towards Cutsdean. Pass to the right of the church, which sits back across a wall to your left. At the edge of the village come to a stile: cross this to join a track. After 25 paces emerge on to the main street through the village to your car.

DISTANCE/TIME 20 miles (32.2km) 4h; shorter route 15 miles (24.1km) 3h **MAP** OS Explorer 155 Bristol & Bath and 156 Chippenham & Bradford-on-Avon **START** Bradford-on-Avon railway station (pay car park); grid ref: ST 825606 **TRACKS** Gravel towpath, some road sections

THE PUB The George, Mill Lane, Bathampton. Tel: 01225 425079

DISTANCE/TIME 11.25 miles (18.1km) 2h30 **MAP** OS Explorer OL45 The Cotswolds **START** Coln St Aldwyns; grid ref: SP 145052 **TRACKS** Minor lanes **THE PUB** The Swan, Southrop. Tel: 01367 850205

FROM BRADFORD-ON-AVON ALONG THE KENNET & AVON CANAL

The Kennet and Avon Canal is ideal for cyclists and passes through picturesque countryside. You can turn around at the riverside pub at Bathampton although the locks you pass on the way into Bath are well worth seeing.

1 Leaving the station car park, turn right along the main road in the direction of Frome. Continue past a mini-roundabout to the Canal Tavern and Lock Inn Café. Go between them to join the towpath and follow it past Grange Farm with its massive 600-year-old tithe barn. The River Avon runs below to the right, containing Barton Farm Country Park's picnic and wildlife areas within the intervening spit of land. Beyond a gate, continue beside the canal to Avoncliff.

2 The canal now makes an abrupt turn across the Avon Valley, carried above both the river and railway on an imposing aqueduct. Do not cross, but at a sign to Dundas just before, drop steeply right towards the Cross Guns pub, then double back left underneath the bridge, climbing left to gain the opposite towpath. Tacked along the wooded valley, the waterway runs pleasantly on, harbouring an assortment of ducks, coots and moorhens. Turning a corner opposite Limpley Stoke, pass beneath a road bridge, then look out on the left for a glimpse of a viaduct taking the A36 across the Midford Brook valley.

3 Another sharp turn heralds the Dundas Aqueduct, beyond which is the last remnant of the Somerset Coal Canal. The track just before it leads to Brassknocker Basin, with a small exhibition. The route, however, continues ahead, signed 'Bath and Claverton', behind a maintenance building and a derrick and onto the opposite bank. About a mile (1.6km) further on, immediately beyond a bridge, a track drops across the railway to the river where there is a restored pump house (Claverton Pumping Station), built in 1813. There are views to Bathford and Batheaston as you pedal the final 1.75 miles (2.8km) to Bathampton and The George.

4 To extend the ride, continue beside the canal, the eastern suburbs of Bath rising on the opposite side of the valley. Eventually the city comes into view. There are a couple of short tunnels to pass through at Sidney Gardens, where you should dismount. Between them, two ornate cast-iron bridges span the canal, which, together with the elaborate facade of the second tunnel beneath Cleveland House, were added to placate the owners of Sidney Park, who disapproved of the cargo barges passing through their land.

5 Emerging below Cleveland House, the towpath doubles back on to the opposite bank, passes former warehouses, now a marina, and rises to a road. Taking care, diagonally cross and drop back to the towpath, here negotiating steps. Beyond, the canal falls through a succession of locks, the path periodically rising to cross a couple of roads and a track before meeting the River Avon. To explore Bath, carry on a little further by the river to emerge on the road beside Churchill Bridge in the city centre. As the city is busy, it is perhaps wise to secure your bikes while you wander around. The return is back the way you came, but remember you have to climb steps to the road at Bathwick Hill and dismount through the tunnels at Sidney Gardens, or you can return by train.

THE LEACH & COLN VALLEYS

Many Cotswold villages, content in their anonymity tucked away off the tourist trail, offer a quiet escape from hectic modern life and are attracting many new inhabitants from out of the cities. This pleasant ride meanders through villages such as these, crossing the gently rolling downs between the pretty Coln and Leach valleys. The route starts in the picturesque village of Coln St Aldwyns, with its ivy-clad cottages, which is pleasantly surrounded by pastureland and lies close to the hamlet of Hatherop.

1 The crossroads in the middle of Coln St Aldwyns is marked by a sturdy spreading chestnut tree. Begin the ride along the lane signed to Quenington and Fairford, which passes by The New Inn. On leaving the village, cycle over the River Coln and climb to a crossroads at the edge of Quenington village. Go left on to Fowlers Hill and then drop back into the valley, following the signs to Southrop and Lechlade as you bend past a junction to re-cross the River Coln. After a bit of a pull, the lane rises up over open downland and then follows the line of an ancient salt way for a little while. Pedal for a further 2.5 miles (4km), following signs for Southrop past some junctions, before losing height down to a 'Give Way' junction.

2 Go left, gaining height along a gentle fold in the rolling hillside. Stay with the main lane as it later turns to rise over the hill, winding down on the other side into Southrop. Carry on past the village hall and The Swan, the street slotted between high-kerbed pavements and now signed to Filkins.

3 After dropping away and crossing the second river that features on this journey, the Leach, turn off left to the villages of Fyfield and Eastleach. Keep cycling left again as the lane splits at Fyfield, following the gently rising valley all the way to Eastleach. There are two separately named halves to the village and the lane ends at a junction by the church in Eastleach Martin. Here, go left, and re-cross the Leach to enter the neighbouring parish, swinging left again beneath a massive willow tree, from which a track leads off to Eastleach Turville's church.

4 The main lane winds its way on past the village cross and then past a row of almshouses before it reaches a junction below The Victoria pub. Keep cycling straight ahead, the way signed 'Hatherop and Burford', climbing shortly to a second junction where you should go right in the direction of Burford and Westwell. Undulate onwards across open hills that are interspersed with sporadic clumps of copse. Stay to the left at successive turnings to curve above the higher reaches of the Leach valley. The signs you come across on this part of the route should now be directing you to the villages of Hatherop and Coln St Aldwyns.

5 For 1.25 miles (2km), the way follows the course of Akeman Street, a Roman road, passing a turn off signed to Dean Farm before breaking away from the line of the ancient thoroughfare into Hatherop village itself. When you reach a junction, take a right towards Coln St Aldwyns, winding down to leave the village past Hatherop School. From this point, it is then only a short ride back to the start point at Coln St Aldwyns.

CORSHAM & CORSHAM PARK

This walk explores Corsham where 15th-century Flemish gabled cottages and baroque-pedimented 17th-century Hungerford Almshouses mix with larger Georgian residences. The walk continues through adjacent Corsham Park.

DISTANCE/TIME 4 miles (6.4km) 2h **MAP** OS Explorer 156 Chippenham & Bradford-on-Avon **START** Long-stay car park, Newlands Lane, Corsham; grid ref: ST 871704 **PATHS** Field paths and country lanes; 10 stiles **THE PUB** The Flemish Weaver, Corsham. Tel: 01249 701929

1 Turn left out of the car park, then left again along Post Office Lane to reach the High Street. Turn left, pass the tourist information centre and turn right into Church Street. Pass the impressive entrance to Corsham Court, on your left, and enter St Bartholomew's churchyard.

2 Follow the path left to a gate and walk ahead to join the main path across Corsham Park. Turn left and walk along the south side of the park, passing Corsham Lake, to reach a stile and gate. Keep straight on along a fenced path beside a track to a kissing gate and proceed across a field to a stile and lane.

3 Turn left, pass Park Farm, a splendid stone farmhouse on your left, and shortly take the waymarked footpath right along a drive to pass Rose and Unicorn House. Cross a stile and follow the right-hand field-edge to a stile, then bear half left to a stone stile in the field corner. Ignore the path arrowed right and head straight across the field to a further stile and lane.

4 Take the footpath opposite, bearing half left to a stone stile to the left of a cottage.

Maintain your direction, passing to the right of a spring and then go through a field entrance to follow the path along the left-hand side of a field to a stile in the corner. Turn left along the road for 0.5 mile (800m) to reach the A4.

5 Go through the gate in the wall on your left and follow the worn path right, across the centre of parkland pasture to a metal kissing gate. Proceed ahead to reach a kissing gate on the edge of woodland. Follow the wide path to a further gate and bear half right to a stile.

6 Keep ahead on a worn path across the parkland and along the field-edge to a gate. Continue to a further gate with fine views right to Corsham Court. Follow the path right along the field-edge, then where it curves right, bear left to join the path beside the churchyard wall to a stile.

7 Turn left down the avenue of trees to a gate and the town centre, noting the stone almshouses on your left. Turn right along Lacock Road and then right again along the pedestrianized High Street. Turn left back along Post Office Lane to the car park.

WALK 26

SEVERNSIDE AT ASHLEWORTH & HASFIELD

This is a fine walk along the banks of the River Severn, visiting a preserved tithe barn. The barn, and Ashleworth Court next to it, dates from the late 15th century.

DISTANCE/TIME 7.25 miles (11.7km) 3h15 **MAP** OS Explorer 179 Gloucester, Cheltenham & Stroud **START** Ashleworth Quay; limited parking on grass verges in the vicinity of the tithe barn; grid ref: SO 818251 **PATHS** Tracks, fields, lanes and river bank; 20 stiles **THE PUB** The Queen's Arms, Ashleworth. Tel: 01452 700395

1 From the tithe barn walk along the road towards the River Severn, passing the Boat Inn on your left-hand side.

2 At Ashleworth Quay turn left over a stile to walk along the river bank. Follow it for a little over 3 miles (4.8km). In general the path is obvious, but where it sometimes appears to pass through gates, you may find they are locked and that you should instead be using a stile closer to the river. Sandhurst Hill will come and go across the river, followed by The Red Lion pub (sadly also out of reach across the river).

3 Eventually you will pass Haw Farm. Immediately after it follow a track that leads left, away from the river, and then passes to the left of a number of houses and cottages. The track becomes a lane and the Haw Bridge will appear before you.

4 Just before the lane goes left turn left over a stile into a field. Walk straight on and then, as the field opens up at a corner, bear half left to arrive at a wooden stile in a wire fence. Go half right to a stile and green metal gate crossing a drainage channel. Continue straight on across two fields.

5 This will bring you to a lane where you turn left. Within 400yds (366m) turn right along another lane, until you reach Great House Farm.

6 Stay on the lane as it bears left. Then, after passing two houses, cross left into a field. Head downhill, half right, to a corner and rejoin the lane.

7 Turn left and then continue walking into Hasfield, keeping left for Ashleworth. Turn left to visit the church and return to carry on through the village, still heading towards Ashleworth.

8 Before a row of cottages on the right, turn right at a footpath sign. Follow a good farm track, soon crossing a stile to walk parallel with it to Colways Farm. Beyond it, begin with a hedge to your left, later drifting right to cross two footbridges, then stiles over wire fences and beside a pylon. At a lane go over a stile just left of the road opposite. Head across to a gap. Now follow the path on the right side of fields all the way back to a point just before the tithe barn. Reward your efforts by stopping at The Queen's Arms for some well-earned refreshments.

turn right for Icomb. Turn right at Icomb war memorial and then left at a T-junction towards Little Rissington. Cross the A424 and continue for almost a mile (1.6km) to turn right at the crossroads. Drive through Little Rissington and then Bourton-on-the-Water.

7 Head for the A429, where you turn left. Soon fork right on to the A436 and after about 2 miles (3.2km), turn right for Aylworth. Continue through Aylworth to a crossroads, turning left on the B4068 towards Cheltenham. Join the A436 and then soon turn right following signs to Hawling and Winchcombe. Continue to Hawling and, some way past the church, turn right at a T-junction for Roel and Winchcombe. On reaching the crossroads at Roel turn left for Charlton Abbots. Continue for about 1.5 miles (2.4km) with some fine views along the way. Bypass Charlton Abbots and then at the next T-junction turn right for Winchcombe. Keep going towards Winchcombe, passing the Neolithic barrow Belas Knap, and Sudeley Castle down on the right.

There are good views from Belas Knap, one of the best-preserved Neolithic barrows in the UK. Sudeley Castle is also well worth a visit.

8 Eventually you come to the B4632 – turn right here to drive through Winchcombe, which was the capital of Saxon Mercia.

In Winchcombe look out for the Winchcombe Worthies, the carved gargoyles that embellish the facade of the little parish church.

9 Drive for 3 miles (4.8km) to a roundabout and take the 3rd exit on to the B4077, following signs for Stow. Continue for a mile (1.6km), then turn left at the war memorial for Stanton. Pass Stanway, then after about 1.5 miles (2.4km) turn right. Drive through Stanton, following signs to Broadway, to rejoin the B4632. Turn right here following the B4632 Stratford signs. Turn right, and then turn left through Broadway, continuing to follow the signs for the village centre.

Broadway's wide main street is lined with horse chestnut trees and a mixture of period houses and stone cottages.

10 In Broadway continue to the roundabout on the A44. Take the 2nd exit off the roundabout, still following the B4632 'Stratford' signs to Willersey. Drive through Willersey to a roundabout. Turn right here and continue towards Weston Subedge. Go through Weston Subedge and then turn right by the Seagrove Arms for Dover's Hill. Continue up Dover's Hill, with fine views, to a major crossroads, then go forward and down the hill to return to Chipping Campden and the start of the tour.

A TOUR OF THE NORTHERN COTSWOLDS

Starting from Chipping Campden, the finest of the Cotswold wool towns with a magnificent church and pretty houses, this superb circular car tour takes in many of the highlights of the northern Cotswolds as well as several worthy, though much less frequently visited, places in the area.

Route Directions

It's worth lingering for a while in Chipping Campden. For many, this town represents Cotswold charm at its best and it is possibly one of the area's most attractive towns.

1 From the Market Hall on Chipping Campden's High Street head for Mickleton on the B4081, and turn right just after the end of the speed restrictions. Soon turn right again for Hidcote Boyce. At a crossroads turn left to Hidcote Bartrim, Mickleton and Hidcote Gardens. Follow signs for Hidcote Gardens and Kiftsgate Court Gardens.

Both Hidcote Gardens and Kiftsgate Court Gardens are well worth a visit.

2 Drive past Kiftsgate, signed for Quinton and Stratford, to reach a T-junction. Turn right and continue to Ilmington village which has a charming manor house and church.

3 Just after entering Ilmington turn right signed 'Chipping Campden', then left for Shipston, keeping left at the war memorial. Pass the Red Lion pub, continuing in the direction of Stratford. At the end of the village

turn right and drive to Armscote, where you pass the Fox and Goose, and turn right for Blackwell and Tredington. Soon, just after a thatched barn and a pond, turn left for Tredington. Continue to reach the A429 and turn left signed 'Stratford, Warwick'. At a roundabout take the third exit to join the A3400, signed 'Tredington, Oxford'.

In the porch floor of St John the Baptist Church in the village of Tredington are the fossilized remains of a prehistoric marine reptile similar to an ichthyosaurus.

4 About a mile (1.6km) beyond Tredington turn left for Honington, through some pineapple-topped gates. Drive through Honington and then turn right at a junction for Barcheston. After a further 0.5 mile (800m) go left at a T-junction opposite farm buildings for St Dennis and Tysoe. Pass a crossroads for St Dennis Farm and continue for about a mile (1.6km) to reach another crossroads; go forward, signed 'Tysoe', and continue, to join another road at a corner. Turn right here and then fairly soon go left towards Compton Wynyates house, and Epwell. Follow the Epwell signs. Turn right at

a crossroads, and continue in the direction of Banbury and Sibfords. Continue to the B4035 and take a right turn, soon arriving at Lower Brailes. Drive past the George Hotel and then turn left, just after a school sign, into Sutton Lane for Stourton, Cherington and Long Compton.

The little village of unusually-named Sutton-under-Brailes has a pretty village green overlooked by cottages and houses.

5 Halfway through Sutton-under-Brailes turn left for Stourton, Cherington and Long Compton. Drive through Stourton, then Cherington and continue to follow signs for Long Compton until meeting the A3400. Turn left here and drive through Long Compton. Ignore the first sign for Little Rollright almost at the end of the village, but take the second turning, after about a mile (1.6km) on the right, for Little Rollright, to see the famous Rollright Stones.

These ancient standing stones consist of two stone circles and a monolith. They are believed to date from the Bronze Age.

6 Continue to the A44, turn right and then immediately left on to the A436, passing Chastleton House. Continue following signs for Stow then, after 4 miles (6.4km), turn left along the B4450 signed 'Bledington'. Keep going to cross a bridge and then immediately

80 MILES (129KM)

ALONG THE ROMANTIC ROAD

This drive, beginning and ending in the splendidly preserved Regency town of Cheltenham will take you through some delightful, but lesser-known areas of the Cotswolds as well as through pretty Burford and Cirencester. The route passes through some of the most beautiful villages in the Cotswolds, some of which, such as Bibury and Sheepscombe, inspired artists and authors alike.

Route Directions

Explore the heart of Cheltenham. This Regency town (it received the royal approval of George III) is renowed for its handsome terraces and its horse racing.

1 From Cheltenham take the A40 London road to pass through Charlton Kings, where author Lewis Carroll was inspired to write *Alice Through the Looking Glass*, and then pass by Dowdeswell Reservoir, built to supply drinking water to Cheltenham. Shortly afterwards, turn right to Dowdeswell, to climb fairly steeply up the Cotswold escarpment. Follow this country lane, crossing three sets of crossroads, towards Withington. Go through the village, pass the Mill Inn and turn right at a sign for Chedworth Villa and Yanworth. Follow a narrow country lane around the solitary manor farmhouse and gallery of Compton Cassey, until the road breaks off for the Roman villa.

The remains of Chedworth Villa, excavated in 1864 and considered to be the finest in the country, are set in a pretty wooded combe. There are fine 4th-century mosaics, two bathhouses, a hypocaust (underfloor heating system) and a good museum.

2 After visiting the villa, pass through Yanworth village and then head onwards for Northleach. Drive through the Market Place, and into the High Street and, soon after, make a left turn. At the next T-junction, turn right to go towards Farmington. Drive through Farmington village and then follow the lanes along the delightfully named Windrush Valley and its quiet villages of Sherborne (Sherborne House is said to be haunted) and Windrush. Turn right towards Little Barrington.

With its picture-postcard post office and large village green, Little Barrington is situated at the heart of stone-producing country and was once the home of Thomas Strong, who was the master mason for St Paul's Cathedral.

3 Pass through Little Barrington, continue to the A40 and turn left. Bypass Burford by continuing across a roundabout and then, after about a mile (1.6km), turn sharp left and then make a right turn for Widford and then for Swinbrook.

Swinbrook is a pretty village associated with the five Mitford sisters, two of whom are buried in the churchyard.

4 Leave Swinbrook and take the first left after the church. Proceed along a single-track road to a reach a junction with A361, turn left and left again at a mini-roundabout to cross a medieval bridge into Burford.

Burford, one of the loveliest of Cotswold villages, slopes down to the Windrush and has a plethora of shops, inns and delightful houses. The High Street runs down to a narrow three-arched bridge over the River Windrush. Take a leisurely stroll through the town and you'll stumble across a host of historic treasures – especially in the little side streets that run off the High Street. For example the Great House in Witney Street, built around 1690, and The Tolsey Museum (1500). Situated just south of the town is the popular Cotswold Wildlife Park.

5 Drive up the main street to a roundabout on the A40 and go straight across on the A361 in the direction of Lechlade. Continue for 4 miles (6.4km) then bear left to Filkins.

Visit the village of Filkins, home to Swinford Museum, which depicts west Oxfordshire's fascinating rural heritage.

6 At the far end of the village, rejoin the A361 to Lechlade. From Lechlade bear right on the A417 towards Fairford.

Fairford is known for its large RAF base. The village church contains the finest set of medieval stained glass in England.

7 Cross over the river and turn right for Quenington and on to Coln St Aldwyns. Pass the New Inn on the right and, at the end of the village, go straight over the staggered crossroads, signed 'Bibury', and shortly turn left following the signs.

Bibury was famously described by artist and designer William Morris as 'the most beautiful village in the Cotswolds'.

8 From Bibury, take the B4425 and continue on, passing through Barnsley.

9 Continue to drive straight ahead until you reach one of the principal towns in the Cotswolds, Cirencester.

In Roman times, this town was second in importance only to London. You could easily spend a day here exploring the church, Corinium Museum and pleasant shops and cafés. Market days are Monday and Friday.

10 Take the A419 towards Stroud, looking for a small road on the right in the direction of Sapperton after driving for about 3 miles (4.8km). Follow this road to the Daneway pub, near the entrance to the Thames and Severn Canal Tunnel. From here take the road, on a corner on the left, which climbs up towards Bisley. To get there fork left, then right and follow the road through Waterlane until you come to a crossroads at a main road just outside Bisley. Cross carefully and go down to the main thoroughfare of this handsome village. Turn right, then left opposite the post office. Pass the Bear Inn and, at Stancombe Lane, turn right towards The Camp and Birdlip. Immediately after The Camp take the left turn at an electricity generator, in the direction of Sheepscombe.

11 Cross the B4070 then fork right for the village, passing the village hall and pub. Keep on this narrow road until you reach the A46, where you turn left for Painswick.

Known as the 'Queen of the Cotswolds', Painswick slopes down to Painswick Brook where you can see the old textile mills.

12 From Painswick, you return along the A46 heading towards Cheltenham. Continue through several miles of beech woodland, passing by Prinknash Abbey on the left, and Cooper's Hill on the right.

Cooper's Hill is the scene of the dangerous annual Whitsun cheese-rolling event, which probably dates from the 16th century.

13 Descend to the vale, and continue to drive, via a roundabout, through the village of Shurdington, and back to Cheltenham.

PAINSWICK & WASHPOOL VALLEY

This is an enjoyable walk from Painswick through the Washpool Valley.

DISTANCE/TIME 7.25 miles (11.7km) 3h30 **MAP** OS Explorer 179 Gloucester, Cheltenham & Stroud **START** Car park (pay and display) near library, just off main road in Painswick; grid ref: SO 865095 **PATHS** Fields, tracks, golf course and a green lane; 20 stiles
THE PUB The Fa.con Inn, Painswick Tel: 01452 814222; www.falconinn-cotswolds.co.uk

1 From the car park turn right on the main street. Turn left along Gloucester Street, join another road and continue uphill, then right on to Golf Course Road. Bear left on a track, joining the Cotswold Way, through the car park. Turn left into a lane. After 50 paces go left into woodland and across a fairway.

2 Keep to the left of a cemetery, then cross another fairway to a woodland path. Continue to a road. After 50 paces turn right, leaving the track shortly to walk along the left edge of the golf course to the top of a promontory. Descend and turn left on a path. At a track go left to a road, aiming for a gap in the trees.

3 Turn right to descend to a bus stop. Cross to find a path. Take it, and, beyond a gate, turn left down a track to Spoonbed Farm, and descend bearing right at a track junction. Pass the farm to a gate, then take a path into a field. In a second field keep left to a stile. After a copse and another stile cross a field to the right of an electricity pole. Keep right of Upper Holcombe Farm to a stile.

4 Turn left on a lane to reach Holcombe Farm. Here, continue along a track, passing gates (left). Continue and, at a stile, go left into the field. Cross a stile and bear right to another. Over this turn right into a lane to a footbridge. Bear right along the stream and soon bear left uphill through trees to a stile. Follow the left-hand field-edge up to a stile.

5 Turn left along a track towards Edge Farm and then fork right at farm buildings to a gate. Over a stone stile cross two fields to another gate soon arriving at a road. Bear right at a Y-junction. Opposite a house turn left over a stile, bear half right to another stile and on to a path between a hedge and a fence to enter Edge.

6 Turn left, then sharp right at the post-box and go past the village hall. Before the farmhouse turn left over a stile, then another and descend along the field-edge to a footbridge. Over this ascend a field to a stile in the opposite hedge, then head for a gate at a track, to the right of a farm. Go through this then another gate opposite and then along the field edge to a kissing gate on to a lane. Turn left and, after 30 paces, turn right via a gate on to a track. The track becomes a path to a stile. Cross fields on the same line, then over stile and quarter left to a field gate then another, passing right by a house to a road.

7 Turn left, descend to cross the A46 and walk along Pincot Lane. At Primrose Cottage turn left over a stile and cross to another. Descend to cross a footbridge, climb and cross the field to a gate, left of Sheephouse. Walk along the drive and where it forks go left down to King's Mill. Bear right through a gate and over the weir, then a stile, and alongside the stream to a lane, via two more stiles. Turn left to return to Painswick.

WINCHCOMBE & SUDELEY CASTLE

A rewarding walk above the thriving Cotswold village of Winchcombe with its fine 'wool church', financed through income from the medieval wool trade. Sudeley Castle chapel is the burial place of Henry VIII's sixth queen, Catherine Parr.

DISTANCE/TIME 4 miles (6.4km) 2h **MAP** OS Explorer OL45 The Cotswolds **START** Long stay car park on Back Lane, Winchcombe; grid ref: SP 024282 **PATHS** Fields and lanes; 13 stiles
THE PUB The White Hart Inn, Winchcombe. Tel: 01242 602 359; www.the-white-hart-inn.com

1 From the parking area, walk towards the town centre past a bank and turn right, down Castle Street. Where it levels out, cross a river bridge and after a few paces bear right to leave the road near the Sudeley Castle Country Cottages and ascend to a kissing gate. Follow the path through the middle of a long field to a kissing gate. At a track, with the castle visitor centre ahead, turn right for 50 paces, then left through a gate.

2 Walk between fences to a kissing gate. Follow the left fence past Sudeley Castle, then across its parkland (guide posts). Over a stile in the far corner turn left and shortly cross a stile to walk along the left-hand field-edge, then right at the corner alongside a fence. At the willows go left over stile and walk uphill beside hedging towards a cottage.

3 Through a gate turn left on to a lane and follow this to a junction, turning left. After about 50 paces and just before Sudeley Hill Farm turn right and over a stile. Head half left uphill and over another stile. Over this cross the middle of the field, then bear to the left of a cottage to a stile.

4 Over this you see St Kenelm's Well, a 17th- to 19th-century building in a fenced enclosure. Pass to the left of this along a

track. Cross a stream and go through a gate (or over the stile) and climb half right towards a gate at the right end of woodland.

5 At a woodland fence corner turn left, short of the gate, and go left alongside the fence, over two stiles alongside a small fenced field. Beyond this the path drops, fairly close to the woods on your right, and curves left to a gate. Through this continue alongside the wood, then a line of trees, to a gate and stile in the far corner.

6 Descend half right towards Winchcombe, heading to the furthest corner. Over a stile descend, a fence on your right. At the fence corner continue half right across the field. Through the hedge in the next field continue half left towards a gate. Over the nearby stile cross the field corner to another stile and a footbridge. Half left in the next field head for the gap to the right of a cottage. Through the gate turn right on to a lane, passing a heavily buttressed kitchen garden wall on your left.

7 After 100yds (91m) turn left through a kissing gate and head across the field towards Winchcombe church tower. Then veer left to a kissing gate by a cottage. Follow this path to Castle Street and turn right over the river bridge and back into the town centre.

Forest of Dean

CLOCKWISE FROM RIGHT: RIVER WYE, SYMONDS YAT; BLUEBELLS IN THE FOREST OF DEAN

COLEFORD MAP REF 403 G7

The small market town of Coleford, one of the oldest existing communities in the Forest of Dean, lies some 4 miles (6.4km) east of the Welsh border, close to the Wye Valley. Coleford takes its name from one of the two rivers that merge in its centre, at what was once a busy fording point.

The town has a rich history, first recorded as Colevorde in 1275 when it was part of the royal hunting forest. It was in Coleford in the 1800s that the process of making steel was invented, at a furnace built by David Mushet senior.

The town's buildings are mainly Georgian in appearance, although many of the facades cover much older buildings. The tang of coaching days lingers in the large arched entrance to 'The Angel' pub, while the free-standing Clock Tower was formerly attached to an attractive octagonal church, demolished when it was considered too small for the local population; only the tower was left intact. The town also has an interesting octagonal church which was built in 1821.

Today, the town's excellent location at the heart of the Forest, makes it hugely popular with canoeists, walkers and cyclists. Coleford is a thriving community and administrative centre of the Forest of Dean, one of the most distinctive areas of Britain. The beautiful region has a persuasive charm and character that is unique. The magnificent landscapes and stunning scenery have inspired artists, craftspeople, inventors, poets and playwrights alike. This ancient royal forest of oak and beech covers an area of about 26,000 acres (10,500ha) between the Severn and Wye. It became a National Forest Park in 1938. Forest residents (known as 'commoners') retain their ancient feudal rights of sheep pasturage and hold their Verderers' Court, something of a judicial anachronism, at Speech House in Coleford. It became the place one went to talk or to make a speech, hence the name. Today it is a hotel.

GOODRICH MAP REF 400 B3

Sitting on a neck of land where the River Wye loops around wooded Coppet Hill, Goodrich is particularly famed for its castle, today a romantic ruin built in the 13th century to a square design, with large rounded towers at the corners.

Goodrich stands majestically on a wooded hill commanding the Wye at the point where it enters the valley of Symonds Yat. Work on the castle started in the late 11th century, by the English thegn, Godric, who gave it his name. Later, the splendid square keep which still forms the core you see today, was added, probably in the time of the Earl of Pembroke and Lord of Goodrich (1148–76).

During the Civil War, Goodrich was held by both sides. The Royalists eventually surrendered in 1646 when threatened with undermining and bombardment by a huge Parliamentarian mortar, the famous 'Roaring Meg', the only surviving Civil War mortar in Britain, now returned to the castle after more than 350 years.

LYDNEY MAP REF 400 B4

There are records of a community in this area and on this site since Roman times. Not surprising since its position is ideal for a market town to flourish in, being between the Forest of Dean and the wide River Severn. Nowadays the busy town covers an area just under 9 square miles (23sq km) and is bordered by the A48 road, which joins Gloucester to Chepstow, and is on the Gloucester to Cardiff rail route. The town is known also as the terminus of the Forest of Dean Railway, which runs between Lydney and Norchard.

The town also stretches to Lydney harbour and docks, which have been the subject of a regeneration scheme and are being restored to their former working glory. Built by the Romans, the harbour's importance grew as it was vital for transporting the iron ore being mined in the Forest of Dean. The town became a centre of trading and the harbour's ability to take sea-going ships made it ever more popular and useful. As a consequence of this, nearby Porlock canal was built to take the cargo further inland, providing an efficient way of moving iron ore and coal as the roads at that time were poor.

Lydney is also known for Lydney Park, situated just west of the town itself, which has some Roman ruins within the estate grounds. The house was originally the home of Sir William Wintour, who was Admiral to the Fleet during the reign of Queen Elizabeth I in 1588. Many of the ships that went to battle with the Spanish Armada were built at Lydney using timber felled from the nearby Forest of Dean.

The Roman remains at Lydney Park include a temple thought to be dedicated to a Celtic god, and the structure itself seems to resemble a shrine or maybe even a healing place.

SYMONDS YAT MAP REF 400 B3

The wonder with Symonds Yat Rock, an internationally renowned viewpoint and the site of an Iron Age hill fort, is that it simply doesn't crumble under the weight of the thousands of enthralled visitors that scramble over it each year. The cliffs are populated by peregrine falcon that soar above the Wye valley below, and the viewpoint is a perfect place from which to watch and photograph them. Elsewhere fallow deer are often glimpsed in the surrounding woodlands, usually in the early morning or dusk; badgers and foxes are plentiful, too. Otters have been spotted on stretches of the River Wye.

Peregrines have made their homes in the limestone cliffs of Coldwell Rocks for two decades or more, and the many

TINTERN ABBEY

parts of South Wales, etc. relative chiefly to Picturesque Beauty; made in the summer of the year 1770. It was (and is) a classic book, and an inspiration to the country's early tourists.

Today you can enjoy the Wye Valley for its unrivalled scenery, which is at its best when the colours are lush green in spring or mellow red and gold in autumn. The valley and the area around Symonds Yat is a delight to be discovered on foot, by canoe or by bicycle.

TINTERN ABBEY MAP REF 399 J2

Founded by Walter de Clare, Lord of Chepstow, in 1131, Tintern Abbey is on the River Wye in Monmouthshire, only the second Cistercian foundation in Britain, and the first in Wales. The abbey was almost entirely rebuilt and enlarged between 1220 and 1287, and the building finally completed, except for minor additions, in the early 14th century. The abbey was dissolved in 1537, and its property granted to the then Lord of Chepstow. Although the cruciform church is today without its roof (it was plundered for its lead very soon after the Dissolution) and the nave is damaged, many vital details of a style transitional from Early English to Decorated Gothic are preserved.

The remains of Tintern we see today, are a mish-mash of building endeavour spanning the 400-year period between 1136 and 1536. Little remains of the original buildings, and much of what was built later was demolished in 1537 during the Dissolution of the Monasteries, although a few sections of walling were embraced into later buildings. However, the two recessed cupboards on the east side of the cloisters date from this time.

Immortalized by William Wordsworth in his poem 'Tintern Abbey', this is one of the most spectacular ruins in Britain and not only inspired Wordsworth but more than one painting by Turner, and a poem by a less well-known contemporary of Wordsworth, Edmund Gardner. In his poem, more fully titled 'Lines composed a few miles above Tintern Abbey, on revisiting the banks of the Wye during a tour in July 13, 1798', Wordsworth perfectly sets the scene; one of

> steep and lofty cliffs,
> That on a wild secluded scene impress
> Thoughts of more deep seclusion; and connect
> The landscape with the quiet of the sky.

In time Tintern Abbey established two daughter houses, Kingswood in Gloucester (1139) and Tintern Parva, which is situated west of Wexford in the southeast of Ireland (1203). The Cistercians were clearly one of the most progressive and successful orders in both the 12th and 13th centuries.

crevices in the rock face are equally desirable nesting sites for ravens and jackdaws. Other birds of prey – goshawks and buzzards – are also often present. On a warm summer's evening, grass snakes and adders can sometimes be spotted basking in the sunlit clearings. Dragonflies and damselflies (including white-legged damselflies) frequent the banks of the River Wye, while the exquisite holly blue butterflies and

the hummingbird hawkmoth are often found around the viewing point. Not surprisingly, Symonds Yat Rock is a Site of Special Scientific Interest, and because of its European importance it has the status of a Special Area of Conservation, too. What underscores this important designation is the rare lime and yew woodland. With so much natural interest, it is no wonder the Wye Valley is an Area of Outstanding Natural Beauty.

In the 18th century, the river was used to ferry goods from Chepstow to Hereford, an activity that generated a number of boat-building yards along the route. The Valley also became popular at this time, when poets, artists and well-to-do gentlemen of leisure came to follow the 'Wye Tour' a high priority in their pursuit of the picturesque. Cleric William Gilpin was among these, and in 1782 he published *Observations on the River Wye and several*

Bath

LISTINGS 92

CLOCKWISE FROM RIGHT:
ROYAL CRESCENT; ROMAN BATHS

BATH MAP REF 399 K3

One of the most magnificent towns in Europe, and a UNESCO world heritage centre, Bath is known chiefly for its Roman baths and for its elegant Georgian architecture, the result of its fashionable re-emergence as a spa in the 18th century. Most of the buildings are of mellow Cotswold stone, and archaeological evidence indicates that the first settlement here, *Aquae Sulis*, was Roman. Later, an important Saxon abbey was built here, and then later still, a Norman cathedral. The famous waters continued to be used, but it was not until the 17th century that the fashion for medicinal waters led to new building under the sponsorship of Master of Ceremonies, Richard 'Beau' Nash, architect John Wood and, later, City Surveyor, Thomas Baldwin.

The town is dramatically situated among the surrounding hills, presenting a magnificent aspect. There is a great deal to see in Bath but you can enjoy many of the highlights on foot. Since parking can be a problem, use the park-and-ride system. Bus services run frequently to the city centre from Odd Down in the south, Newbridge in the west, and Lansdown in the north.

The centre of Bath can be divided into four – the oldest part is the city centre around the abbey and baths, the Upper Town was built as the town expanded, while Kingsmead is the liveliest area at night.

Bathwick and Widcombe are west of the Pulteney Bridge. The following walk takes in part of the first three areas; places not featured are described afterwards. Queen Square was John Wood's first important work and takes its name from Queen Caroline, consort of George II. The obelisk in the centre was built to honour the visit of the Prince and Princess of Wales in 1738. Wood's masterpiece, the Circus, begun in 1754, is at the top of Gay Street, which runs north along the east side of Queen Square and passes the Jane Austen Centre on the right. The Circus is a design of great originality, the facade of each of the three floors is framed in a series of columns, from bottom to top, Doric, Ionic and Corinthian.

From here it is a stroll west along Brock Street to another magnificent ensemble, the Royal Crescent, begun by John Wood's son in 1767. Number 1, which is open to the public, has been restored to look as it would have done some 200 years ago. A longer walk would take you further north to a number of other crescents, those of Somerset Place, Camden, Cavendish and Lansdown. Behind Lansdown Crescent is Beckford's Walk, replete with the splendid follies placed there by the eccentric millionaire William Beckford. Gravel Walk, opposite Upper Church Street, descends through parkland and shortly turns left, past the Georgian Garden, to Queen's Parade Place. Turn left, then left again to

re-enter Gay Street and then turn right into George Street and right again into Milsom Street. Continue into Burton Street as it becomes Union Street and turn left into Northumberland Place. Pass through this little alley of shops to the High Street and cross over to the Guildhall.

Beyond the Guildhall is the covered market. On the far side of the market is Grand Parade and the River Avon and to the left the magnificence of Pulteney Bridge, designed by Robert Adam in 1769. On the other side of the bridge is a marvellous vista down Great Pulteney Street towards the Holburne Museum and steps down to the riverside walk.

Turning right along Grand Parade will bring you to Orange Grove. Pass the east end of the abbey and continue down Terrace Walk. By the Huntsman Inn, turn right down North Parade Passage to Sally Lunn's House, built in 1622 and one of the oldest houses in Bath. Here Sally Lunn created her famous Bath buns and the original faggot oven and period kitchenware are still exhibited. Although it is still a coffee house, it is also a museum and the medieval and Roman excavations are the largest on show in Bath.

North Parade Passage emerges at Abbey Green. Turn right here for the abbey itself, the third to be built on this site. The first was built in the 8th century by Offa, King of Mercia. The 12th-century Norman abbey fell into disrepair and was

replaced by this smaller version. Inside, after passing a manned desk where 'voluntary' payment is expected, there is much to admire – its magnificent ceiling and windows, and array of plaques. The Heritage Vaults tell the story of the abbey and include some detailed Saxon and Norman stonework and a reconstruction of the Norman cathedral.

In the courtyard, a favourite place with buskers and other performers, the National Trust shop is in Marshall Wade's House, the oldest Palladian-style building in Bath. Opposite are the Roman baths, the best-preserved Roman religious spa from the ancient world. The remains of a temple can be seen here, as well as objects discovered in the area of the baths over the centuries. Next door are the elegant Pump Rooms, which are a great venue for a coffee, lunch or even a glass of the fairly unpleasant-tasting mineral water – and all can be taken accompanied by period music played by the Pump Rooms Trio. The atmosphere of course, is extremely civilized.

From Abbey Church Yard turn left into Stall Street, then right along Bath Street to Cross Bath, a delightful example of Bath's former hot mineral water sources, housed in an 18th-century building and with the Thermae Bath Spa to the left. Beyond, on the right of Cross Bath, is the entrance to St John's Hospital, a medieval foundation, still offering sheltered housing.

ROMAN BATHS

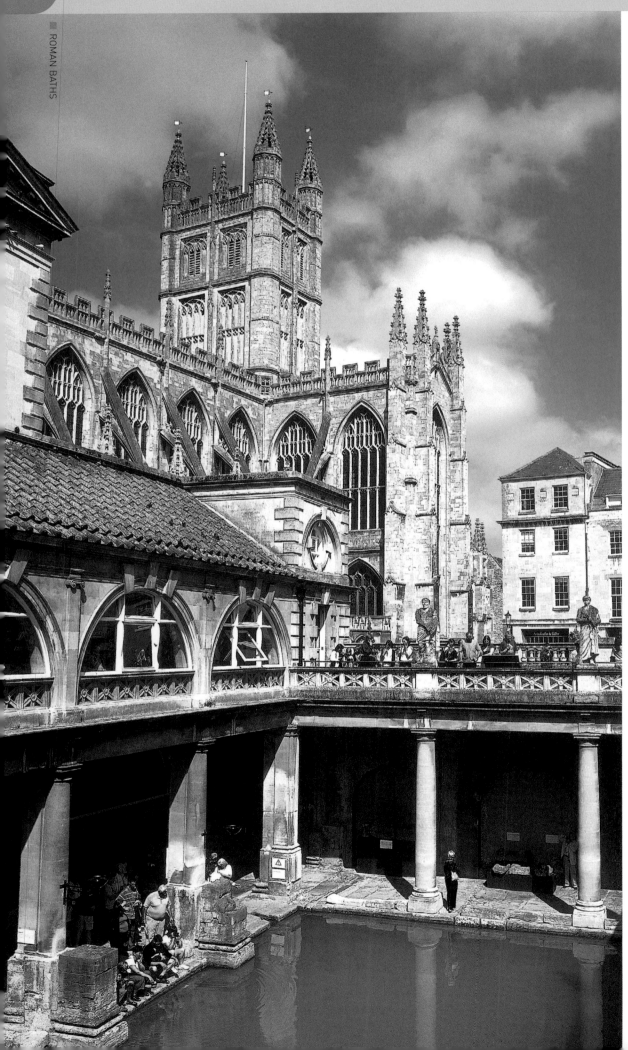

Take the wide pavement further to the right of Cross Bath, turning left by Chandos Buildings, and continue past the back of the Hospital to the road and Westgate Buildings. Turn right until you reach Sawclose to the right. Before continuing up there have a look at Kingsmead Square on the left, where Rosewell House is a rare example of the baroque style in this Georgian city. Continue up Sawclose where the Theatre Royal, opened in 1805, is on the left. Next door is the former home of Beau Nash. Cross the road to enjoy a good view of the theatre and then turn right down Upper Borough Walls.

Along Upper Borough Walls are the remnants of the medieval city wall opposite the Royal National Hospital for Rheumatic Diseases. After the wall turn left down a narrow lane and then left into Trim Street, where General Wolfe's former residence is marked with a memorial plaque. Turn right through Trim Bridge arch to Queen Street and then left by the junction with Quiet Street into Wood Street, which will bring you back to Queen Square.

Bath has many museum collections. In Upper Town the Assembly Rooms, on Bennett Street, were built to complement the Pump Room. This elegant building houses the Museum of Fashion, which covers the history of clothes from the 16th century to present day. Close by, near the Circus, is the Museum of East Asian Art, which covers 7,000 years of history including beautiful exhibits of jade, bamboo and lacquer.

On the Paragon, in the Countess of Huntingdon's Chapel, you'll find the Building of Bath Museum, which shows how the city was created. Not far from the Assembly Rooms, in Julian Road, is the Museum of Bath at Work, which tells the story of the city's trades and industries.

The Victoria Art Gallery is on Bridge Street. It has important paintings by British and European Masters, as well as fascinating scenes of early Bath life. There are also collections of porcelain, watches and other decorative items.

The Holburne Museum of Art, in a Palladian villa, is home to the city's finest collections, particularly silverware, porcelain, furniture and paintings. These treasures are displayed along with examples of 20th-century items. Among the interesting places in the area is Beckford's Tower, standing on the summit of Lansdown. It was built in 1825 to house part of William Beckford's art collection and now holds a museum devoted to his life. Two miles (3.2km) southeast of Bath, the restored American Museum at Claverton Manor, a 19th-century house, illustrates typical American life from the 17th to 19th centuries.

CORNWALL

■ TOURIST INFORMATION

Bodmin
Shire Hall, Mount Folly
☎ 01208 76616; www.bodminlive.com

Bude
The Crescent Car Park
☎ 01288 354240; www.visitbude.info

Falmouth
11 Market Strand, Prince of Wales Pier
☎ 01326 312300;
www.discoverfalmouth.co.uk

Fowey
5 South Street ☎ 01726 833616;
www.fowey.co.uk

Isles of Scilly
Hugh Street, St Mary's
☎ 01720 424031; www.simplyscilly.co.uk

Liskeard
Foresters Hall, Pike Street
☎ 01579 349148; www.liskeard.gov.uk

Looe
The Guildhall, Fore St, East Looe
☎ 01503 262072

Mevagissey
St Georges Square ☎ 01726 844857;
www.mevagissey-cornwall.co.uk

Newquay
Municipal Buildings, Marcus Hill
☎ 01637 854020; www.visitnewquay.org

Padstow
North Quay ☎ 01841 533449;
www.padstowlive.co.uk

Penzance
Station Approach ☎ 01736 362207;
www.visit-westcornwall.co.uk

St Ives
The Guildhall, Street-an-Pol
☎ 01736 796297

Truro
Municipal Buildings, Boscawen Street
☎ 01872 274555;
www.tourismtruro.gov.uk

■ PLACES OF INTEREST

Barbara Hepworth Museum
& Sculpture Garden
Barnoon Hill, St Ives
☎ 01736 796226; www.tate.org.uk/stives

Bude-Stratton Museum
Lower Wharf, Bude ☎ 01288 353576

Eden Project
Bodelva, St Austell
☎ 01726 811911; www.edenproject.com

Falmouth Art Gallery
Municipal Buildings ☎ 01326 313863;
www.falmouthartgallery.com.

Fowey Museum
Town Hall, Trafalgar Square, Fowey
☎ 01726 8333513

King Arthur's Great Halls
Fore Street, Tintagel ☎ 01840 770526;
www.kingarthursgreathall.com

Lost Gardens of Heligan
Pentewan ☎ 01726 845100;
www.heligan.com

Marazion Town Museum
Town Hall, The Square ☎ 01736 711061

Mevagissey Aquarium
South Quay ☎ 01726 843305

Minack Theatre
Porthcurno ☎ 01736 810181;
www.minack.com

Minions Heritage Centre
Minions ☎ 01579 362350

Mousehole Wild Bird Hospital
& Sanctuary
Raginnis Hill ☎ 01736 731386;
www.chycor.co.uk/mousehole-sanctuary

National Maritime Museum Cornwall
Discovery Quay, Falmouth
☎ 01326 313388; www.nmmc.co.uk

Newlyn Art Gallery
New Road, Newlyn, Penzance
☎ 01736 363715;
www.newlynartgallery.co.uk

Old Guildhall Museum
Higher Market Street, East Looe
☎ 01503 263709

Pendennis Castle
Falmouth ☎ 01326 316594

Porthcurno Telegraph Museum
Porthcurno ☎ 01736 810966;
www.porthcurno.org.uk

St Ives Museum
Wheal Dream ☎ 01736 796005

St Michael's Mount
Marazion ☎ 01736 710265/710507;
www.stmichaelsmount.co.uk

Southeast Cornwall Discovery Centre
Millpool, West Looe ☎ 01503 262777

Tate St Ives
Porthmeor, St Ives ☎ 01736 796226;
www.tate.org.uk/stives

Tintagel Castle
☎ 01840 770328;
www.tintagelcastle.co.uk

Trelissick Garden
Feock, near Truro ☎ 01872 862090

Tresco, Isles of Scilly
Abbey Garden and Valhalla Museum
☎ 01720 424105; www.tresco.co.uk

■ FOR CHILDREN

Newquay Zoo
Trenance Leisure Park, Newquay
☎ 01637 873342;
www.newquayzoo.org.uk

World of Model Railways
Meadow Street, Mevagissey
☎ 01726 842457;
www.model-railway.co.uk

■ SPORTS & ACTIVITIES

ANGLING

Coarse fishing
Argal Reservoir, Penryn, Falmouth
☎ 01209 860301
Porth Reservoir, nr Newquay
☎ 01566 771930
South West Lakes Trust ☎ 01566 780536;
www.southwestlakestrust.org

Tamar Lakes Water Park, near Bude
Permit required ☎ 01409 346522

Fly fishing
East and West Looe rivers. Permits from
Looe sub Post Office ☎ 01503 262110
Siblyback Watersports Centre. Fishing
permits available on site.
☎ 01579 342366

Sea fishing
Day and half-day trips from Fowey, Looe
and Polruan. Shark-fishing from Looe
☎ 01503 264355;
www.looechandlery.co.uk
Mevagissey Shark Angling Centre
☎ 01726 843430
National Boatmen's Association,
Newquay ☎ 01637 876352
Various trips from Padstow harbour;
enquire locally.

BOAT TRIPS

Bude
Rowing boats and canoes for hire at
Bude Canal.

Falmouth
Prince of Wales Pier. Regular passenger
ferries to St Mawes and Flushing.
River cruises to Roseland Peninsula
and Truro.

Fowey
River cruises and motor boat hire.
Fowey TIC for details.

Looe
Sea cruises from harbour.

Padstow
Pleasure trips available from the harbour.

Isles of Scilly
Steamship Company. Day trips to
Isles of Scilly ☎ 0845 710 5555;
www.islesofscilly-travel.co.uk

St Ives
Sea cruises from the harbour.

Truro
Enterprise Boats. River trips from Town
Quay or Malpas to Falmouth.
☎ 01326 374241/ 313234;
www.enterprise-boats.co.uk

CYCLE HIRE

Bodmin
Bodmin Bikes, Dennison Road
☎ 01208 73192

Bude
North Coast Cycles, 2 Summerleaze
Avenue ☎ 01288 352974

Liskeard
Liskeard Cycles, Pig Meadow Lane
☎ 01579 347696

Looe
Looe Mountain Bike Hire
☎ 01503 263871

Mevagissey
Pentewan Valley Cycle Hire, 1 West End,
Pentewan ☎ 01726 844242;
www.pentewanvalleycyclehire.co.uk

Newquay
Cycle Revolution, 7 Beach Road
☎ 01637 872634

Padstow
Padstow Cycle Hire Ltd, South Quay
☎ 01841 533533;
www.padstowcyclehire.com

Penzance
The Cycle Centre, New Street
☎ 01736 351671
Pedals Bike Hire, Kiosk 17, Wharfside
Shopping Centre ☎ 01730 360600

GOLF COURSES

Falmouth
Falmouth Golf Club, Swanpool Road
☎ 01326 311262;
www.falmouthgolfclub.com

Mullion
Mullion Golf Club, Cury
☎ 01326 240685;
www.mulliongolfclub.co.uk

■ ANNUAL EVENTS & CUSTOMS

Gig racing is still a popular sport in
Cornwall. Races are held throughout
the summer at venues such as Cadgwith
and Porthleven.

Bodmin
Riding and Heritage Day, Jul.

Bude
Jazz Festival, end of Aug.

Falmouth
Falmouth Regatta Week, Aug.
www.falmouthweek.co.uk
Various maritime events including racing
of Falmouth classic yachts and dinghies.

Fowey
Daphne du Maurier Festival, May.
Fowey Regatta, Aug.

Isles of Scilly
Camel Rock Festival, Aug.
Gig racing throughout the summer
from St Mary's Quay.
World Pilot Gig Racing Championships,
early May.

Liskeard
Carnival Week & Agricultural
Show, Ju..

Looe
Carnival Week, Jul/Aug.

Mevagissey
Mevagissey Feast Week, Jun.

Mousehole
Sea, Salts & Sail Festival, Jul.

Newquay
Run to the Sun Festival, May.
Surf, Skate and Music Festival, Aug.
English National Surfing
Championships, Jul.
Newquay Fish Festival, Sep.

Padstow
May Day Festival.

Penzance
Golowan Festival and Mazey Day, Jun.
www.golowan.co.uk

St Ives
St Ives Feast Day, early Feb.
St Ives Festival of Music, early Sep.

DEVON

■ TOURIST INFORMATION

Barnstaple
North Devon Museum, The Square
☎ 01271 375000;
www.staynorthdevon.co.uk

Brixham
The Old Market House, The Quay
☎ 01803 211211;
www.englishriviera.co.uk

Budleigh Salterton
Fore Street ☎ 01395 445275;
www.visitbudleigh.com

Dartmouth
The Engine House, Mayor's Avenue
☎ 01803 834224;
www.discoverdartmouth.org.uk

Dawlish
The Lawn ☎ 01626 215665;
www.visitsouthdevon.co.uk

Exeter
Dix's Field ☎ 01392 665700;
www.exeter.gov.uk

Exmouth
Alexandra Terrace ☎ 01395 222299;
www.exmouth-guide.co.uk

Honiton
Dowell Street East Car Park
☎ 01404 43716;
www.discoverdevon.com

Ottery St Mary
☎ 01404 813964;
www.otterytourism.org.uk

Paignton
The Esplanade ☎ 01803 558383;
www.englishriviera.co.uk

Salcombe
Council Hall, Market Street
☎ 01548 843927;
www.salcombeinformation.co.uk

Sidmouth
Ham Lane ☎ 01395 516441;
www.visitsidmouth.co.uk

Teignmouth
The Den Sea Front ☎ 01626 215666;
www.southdevon.org.uk

Tiverton
Phoenix Lane ☎ 01884 255827;
www.discovertiverton.co.uk

Torquay
Vaughan Parade ☎ 01803 296296;
www.englishriviera.co.uk

■ PLACES OF INTEREST

A La Ronde
Summer Lane, Exmouth ☎ 01395
265514; www.nationaltrust.org.uk

Allhallows Museum
High Street, Honiton ☎ 01404 44966;
www.honitonmuseum.co.uk

Barnstaple Heritage Centre
Queen Anne's Walk, The Strand
☎ 01271 373003

Beer Quarry Caves
Quarry Lane, Beer ☎ 01297 680282;
www.beerquarrycaves.fsnet.co.uk

Brixham Museum
Brixham ☎ 01803 856267;
www.brixhamheritage.org.uk

Cadhay
Ottery St Mary ☎ 01404 812299;
www.cadhay.org.uk

Clovelly
☎ 01237 431781; www.clovelly.co.uk

Cockington Country Park
Torquay ☎ 01803 606035;
www.countryside-trust.org.uk

Dartington Crystal
Great Torrington ☎ 01805 626262;
www.dartington.co.uk

Dartmouth Castle
Dartmouth ☎ 01803 833588;
www.english-heritage.org.uk

Dartmouth Museum
6 Butterwalk, Dartmouth
☎ 01803 832923;
www.devonmuseums.net

Exeter Cathedral
www.exeter-cathedral.org.uk

Fairlynch Museum
Budleigh Salterton ☎ 01395 442666;
www.devonmuseums.net

Hartland Abbey & Gardens
Hartland ☎ 01237 441264;
www.hartlandabbey.com

Hartland Quay Museum
Hartland ☎ 01288 331353

Knightshayes Court
Bolham, near Tiverton
☎ 01884 254665
www.nationaltrust.org.uk

Marwood Hill Gardens
Barnstaple ☎ 01271 342528;
www.marwoodhillgarden.co.uk

Museum of Barnstaple & North Devon
The Square, Barnstaple ☎ 01271 346747;
www.devonmuseums.net

Norman Lockyer Observatory
Salcombe Hill, Sidmouth
☎ 01395 579941;
www.normanlockyer.org

Oldway Mansion
Torquay Road, Paignton
☎ 01803 207933

Overbeck's Museum & Garden
Sharpitor ☎ 01548 842893;
www.nationaltrust.org.uk

Paignton Zoo
Totnes Road, Paignton
☎ 01803 697500
www.paigntonzoo.org.uk

Paignton & Dartmouth Steam Railway
Torbay Road, Paignton ☎ 01803 555872;
www.paignton-steamrailway.co.uk

Quay House Visitor Centre
Exeter ☎ 01392 271611;
www.exeter.gov.uk

RHS Garden Rosemoor
Great Torrington ☎ 01805 628810

Royal Albert Memorial Museum
Queen Street, Exeter ☎ 01392 265858;
www.exeter.gov.uk

Sid Vale Heritage Centre
Church Street, Sidmouth
☎ 01395 516139

Tiverton Castle
☎ 01884 253200;
www.tivertoncastle.com

Torquay Museum
529 Babbacombe Road, Torquay
☎ 01803 293975;
www.torquaymuseum.org

Torre Abbey Historic House & Gallery
The Kings Drive, Torquay
☎ 01803 293593;
www.torre-abbey.org.uk

Torrington Museum & Archive
High Street, , Great Torrington ☎ 01805
624324; www.great-torrington.com

■ SPORTS & ACTIVITIES
ANGLING
Coarse fishing
Grand Western Canal, Tiverton. Day and
season tickets from tackle shops.

Fly fishing
Bellbrook Valley Trout Fishery, Oakford,
Tiverton. Book in advance.
☎ 01398 351292;
www.bellbrookfishery.co.uk

CYCLE HIRE
Barnstaple
Biketrail, Fremington Quay
☎ 01271 372586; www.biketrail.co.uk

Exeter
Saddles & Paddles, King's Wharf, The
Quay ☎ 01392 424241; www.sadpad.com

Exmouth
Knobblies, 107 Exeter Road
☎ 01395 270182

Great Torrington
Torridge Cycle Hire, The Station
☎ 01805 622633

Sidmouth
Sidmouth Cycles, 110 High Street
☎ 01395 579786

Tiverton
Abbotshood Cycle Hire, Greenway,
Halberton ☎ 01884 820728;
www.abbotshoodcyclehire.co.uk

Torquay
Simply The Bike, Belgrave Road
☎ 01803 200024;
www.simplythebike.co.uk

DARTMOOR & TAMAR VALLEY
■ TOURIST INFORMATION
Dartmoor National Park Authority
Parke, Bovey Tracey ☎ 01626 832093;
www.dartmoor-npa.gov.uk

Okehampton
White Hart Courtyard ☎ 01837 53020;
www.okehamptondevon.co.uk

Tavistock
Bedford Square ☎ 01822 612938;
www.tavistock-devon.co.uk

OTHER INFORMATION
Bovey Tracey
Lower car park ☎ 01626 832047;
www.boveytracey.gov.uk

Ivybridge
The Watermark ☎ 01752 892220;
www.ivybridgedevon.co.uk

■ PLACES OF INTEREST
Dartmoor Zoological Park
Sparkwell ☎ 01752 837645

Devon Guild of Craftsmen
Riverside Mill, Bovey Tracey
☎ 01626 832223; www.crafts.org.uk

Museum of Dartmoor Life
West Street, Okehampton
☎ 01837 52295; www.
museumofdartmoorlife.eclipse.co.uk

Okehampton Castle
Okehampton ☎ 01837 52844;
www.english-heritage.org.uk

■ SPORTS & ACTIVITIES
ANGLING
Fly fishing
Drakelands Trout Fishing, Hemerdon
☎ 01752 344691
Milemead Fisheries, Mill Hill, Tavistock
☎ 01822 610888;
www.milemeadfisheries.com

■ ANNUAL EVENTS & CUSTOMS
Okehampton
Okehampton Show, Aug
Okehampton Carnival, mid-Oct.

Tavistock
Goosey Fair, mid-Oct.

Widecombe in the Moor
Widecombe Fair 2nd Tue Sep.

EXMOOR & THE QUANTOCKS
■ TOURIST INFORMATION
Exmoor National Park Authority
Cross Street, Coombe Martin
☎ 01271 883319;
www.visitcoombemartin.com

Porlock
West End ☎ 01643 863150;
www.porlock.co.uk

■ PLACES OF INTEREST
Dovery Manor Museum
Porlock ☎ 01643 862420

Dunster Castle
Dunster ☎ 01643 821314;
www.nationaltrust.org.uk

Dunster Watermill
Dunster ☎ 01643 821759;
www.dunsterwatermill.co.uk

■ SPORTS & ACTIVITIES
COUNTRY PARKS & NATURE RESERVES
Dunster Forest
☎ 01398 323665;
www.exmoor-nationalpark.gov.uk

SOMERSET & THE MENDIPS

■ TOURIST INFORMATION
Cheddar
The Gorge ☎ 01934 744071
Glastonbury
The Tribunal, 9 High Street
☎ 01458 832954;
www.glastonburytic.co.uk
Shepton Mallet
48 High Street ☎ 01749 345258:
www.visitsomerset.co.uk

DORSET & THE PURBECKS
■ TOURIST INFORMATION
Bournemouth
Westover Road ☎ 0845 051 1700;
www.bournemouthandpoole.co.uk
Swanage
The White House, Shore Road
☎ 01929 422885; www.swanage.gov.uk

■ PLACES OF INTEREST
Corfe Castle
☎ 01929 481294;
www.nationaltrust.org.uk
Lulworth Castle & Park
East Lulworth, Wareham
☎ 01929 400352; www.lulworth.com
Monkey World
Wool, near Wareham ☎ 01929 462537;
www.monkeyworld.org

■ SPORTS & ACTIVITIES
ANGLING
Poole Sea Angling Centre
Rear of 5 High Street, Poole
☎ 01202 676597;
www.pooleseaanglingcentre.co.uk
CYCLE HIRE
First Floor, Dolphin Shopping Centre,
Poole ☎ 01202 680123/669490;
www.cycle-paths.co.uk
WALKING
Ghost Walks of Old Poole Town
Meet at Scaplen's Court Museum,
Sarum Street, Poole ☎ 07977 969080
WATERSPORTS
FC Watersports Academy
4 Banks Road, Poole ☎ 01202 708283;
www.fcwatersports.co.uk

■ ANNUAL EVENTS & CUSTOMS
Bournemouth
Classic Cars on the Prom,
Sun from 4pm, mid-Apr to mid-Sep.
Carnival, first week Aug.
Swanage
Regatta & Carnival Week, late Jul, early
Aug.

SALISBURY & PLAINS
■ TOURIST INFORMATION
Salisbury
Fish Row ☎ 01722 334956

■ PLACES OF INTEREST
Mompesson House
Cathedral Close, Salisbury
☎ 01722 335659;
www.nationaltrust.org.uk
Museum of Army Flying
Middle Wallop, Stockbridge
☎ 01264 784421;
www.flying-museum.org.uk
Old Sarum
Castle Road, Salisbury ☎ 01722 335398;
www.english-heritage.org.uk
Salisbury Cathedral
Cathedral Close ☎ 01722 555120;
www.salisburycathedral.org.uk
Salisbury & South Wiltshire Museum
The King's House, 65 The Close,
Salisbury ☎ 01722 332151;
www.salisburymuseum.org.uk
Wilton House
Wilton, Salisbury ☎ 01722 743810;
www.wiltonhouse.com

■ SPORTS & ACTIVITIES
CYCLE HIRE
Hayball Cyclesport
The Black Horse Chequer, Salisbury
☎ 01722 411378; www.hayball.co.uk

■ ANNUAL EVENTS & CUSTOMS
Salisbury
St George's Day, 23 Apr. Street theatre,
pageantry and dragons. International
Arts Festival, mid-May to mid-Jun.

COTSWOLDS
■ TOURIST INFORMATION
Burford
The Brewery, Sheep Street
☎ 01993 823558
Cheltenham
Cheltenham Municipal Offices,
77 The Promenade ☎ 01242 522878;
www.visitcheltenham.gov.uk
Chipping Campden
High Street ☎ 01386 841206
Chipping Norton
The Guildhall, Goddards Lane
☎ 01993 861326
Cirencester
Corinium Museum, Park Street
☎ 01285 654180
Painswick
The Library, Stroud Road
☎ 01452 813552
Tewkesbury
100 Church Street ☎ 01684 295027;
www.tewkesburybc.gov.uk
Winchcombe
The Town Hall, High Street
☎ 01242 602925

■ PLACES OF INTEREST
Birdland
Rissington Road, Bourton-on-the-Water
☎ 01451 820480; www.birdland.co.uk

Chedworth Roman Villa
Yanworth, near Cheltenham
☎ 01242 890256;
www.chedworthromanvilla.org
Chipping Norton Museum
High Street, Chipping Norton
☎ 01608 641712
**Cotswold Motoring Museum,
Toy Collection**
The Old Mill, Bourton-on-the-Water
☎ 01451 821255;
www.cotswold-motor-museum.co.uk
Cotswold Perfumery
Bourton-on-the-Water ☎ 01451 820698;
www.cotswold-perfumery.co.uk
Cotswold Wildlife Park
Burford ☎ 01993 823006;
www.cotswoldwildlifepark.co.uk
**Gloucestershire & Warwickshire
Railway**
Toddington Station, Winchcombe
☎ 01242 621405; www.gwsr.com
Hailes Abbey
Winchcombe ☎ 01242 602398;
www.english-heritage.org.uk
John Moore Countryside Museum
41 Church Street, Tewkesbury
☎ 01684 297174;
www.johnmooremuseum.org
Mill Dene Garden
Blockley ☎ 01386 700457;
www.milldenegarden.co.uk
Model Village
Old New Inn, Rissington Road,
Bourton-on-the-Water ☎ 01451 820467;
www.theoldnewinn.co.uk
Old Mill Museum
Mill Lane, Lower Slaughter
☎ 01451 820052;
www.oldmill-lowerslaughter.com
Owlpen Manor
Uley ☎ 01453 860261;
www.owlpen.com
Pittville Pump Room & Museum
Pittville Park, Cheltenham
☎ 01242 523852
Railway Museum
Gloucester Street, Winchcombe
☎ 01242 609305
Snowshill Manor
Snowshill, near Broadway
☎ 01386 852410;
www.nationaltrust.org.uk
Stanway House
Stanway ☎ 01386 584469;
www.stanwayfountain.co.uk
Sudeley Castle
Winchcombe ☎ 01242 602308;
www.sudeleycastle.co.uk
Tewkesbury Abbey
Church Street, Tewkesbury
☎ 01684 850959
Tewkesbury Museum
64 Barton Street, Tewkesbury
☎ 01684 292901;
www.tewkesburymuseum.org

Winchcombe Folk & Police Museum
Town Hall ☎ 01242 609151;
www.winchcombemuseum.org.uk

■ FOR CHILDREN
Dragonfly Maze
Bourton-on-the-Water ☎ 01451 822251

■ SPORTS & ACTIVITIES
CYCLING
Cheltenham Spa Railway
Compass Holidays, Station, Queens Road
☎ 01242 250642

■ ANNUAL EVENTS & CUSTOMS
Burford
Annual Levellers Day, May.
Cheltenham
Folk Festival, Feb.
National Hunt, Cheltenham Racecourse,
Mar.
Jazz Festival, Apr/May.
Science Festival, Jun.
International Festival of Music, Jul.
Literature Festival, Oct.
Chipping Campden
Dover's Hill Olimpick Games and
Scuttlebrook Wake, Spring Bank Holiday.
Cirencester
Cotswold Country Fair, Jul.
Cooper's Hill
Cheese Rolling, Spring Bank Holiday.
Guiting
Guiting Festival, Jul.
Painswick
Church Clipping Ceremony, Sep.
Tewkesbury
Food Festival, May.
Medieval Festival, Jul.

BATH
■ TOURIST INFORMATION
Abbey Chambers, Abbey Churchyard
☎ 01225 477101; www.visitbath.co.uk

■ PLACES OF INTEREST
Bath Abbey Heritage Vaults
☎ 0906 711 2000 (50p/min)
Jane Austen Centre
Gay Street, Bath ☎ 01225 443000;
www.janeausten.co.uk
Number 1, Royal Crescent
☎ 01225 428126
Roman Baths Museum
Stall Street, Bath ☎ 01225 477785;
www.romanbaths.co.uk
Thermae Bath Spa
Hot Bath Street, Bath ☎ 01225 331234;
www.thermaebathspa.com

■ ANNUAL EVENTS & CUSTOMS
Literature Festival, Feb/Mar.
Music Festival, May/Jun.
Childrens Literary Festival Sep/Oct.
Jane Austen Festival, late Sep.
Mozartfest Nov.

PUBS
CORNWALL
Bay View Inn
Widemouth Bay, Bude EX23 0AW
☎ 01288 361273;
www.bayviewinn.co.uk
Savour a pint of real ale on the sun deck, absorb the view across the glorious sandy beach – just two reasons to visit this free house on Cornwall's north coast. Add a lively, candlelit bar, imaginative, freshly prepared food using locally sourced produce, and stylish bedrooms.

Cadgwith Cove Inn
Cadgwith, Ruan Minor, Helston
TR12 7JX ☎ 01326 290513;
www.cadgwithcoveinn.com
An unspoilt hamlet of thatched cottages is the setting for this old-fashioned, bustling local. Crab sandwiches and a pint of Sharp's Doom Bar provide the perfect lunch, best enjoyed on the sunny terrace with views across the cove.

Shipwrights Arms
Helford, Helston TR12 6JX
☎ 01326 231235
Stunningly located on the banks of the Helford Estuary, the narrow approach road is restricted to pedestrians only. This is a pretty thatched pub with a terraced garden and picnic benches on the water's edge. The bar is traditional, with rustic furnishings and plenty of nautical bits and pieces. Summer buffet lunches and evening barbecues draw the crowds.

Star Inn
Fore Street, St Just TR19 7LL
☎ 01736 788767
St Just's oldest pub has a low-beamed bar, a polished slate floor, glowing coal fires and walls packed with mining and seafaring memorabilia. Pop in to experience the homely, unspoilt atmosphere and the St Austell beer.

Tinners Arms
Zennor, St Ives TR26 3BY
☎ 01736 796927;
www.tinnersarms.com
A former tin miners' local, it is now an oasis for walkers tackling the St Ives to Zennor coastal walk. Two open fires warm the bar, filled with flagstones and pine tables, where you can rest and refuel on Sharp's ales and fresh fish.

DEVON
Churston Court
Churston, Brixham TQ5 0JE
☎ 01803 842186;
www.churstoncourt.co.uk
A visit to this huge Grade I listed inn is an extraordinary experience, as it used to be a Saxon manor and was once the haunt of sea captains and smugglers. Large, attractive inglenook fireplaces, flagstone floors, weaponry (and the odd suit of armour) fill every room. On the menu is fresh fish.

The Double Locks Hotel
Canal Banks, Exeter EX2 6LT
☎ 01392 256947; www.youngs.co.uk
This no-nonsense pub, renowned for its good food, real ales and extensive garden, is great on a sunny day. In a cute lock-keeper's cottage on the banks of the Exeter Ship Canal, the pub is a popular choice for outdoor enthusiasts and families. The food here is reasonably priced, and has choices ranging from steak and ale pie to haddock fishcakes.

The Masons Arms
Branscombe EX12 3DJ
☎ 01297 680300;
www.masonsarms.co.uk
This Grade II listed inn, originally a 1360 cider house, is in the pretty village of Branscombe. Food is a serious business here: where possible, all ingredients are grown or reared locally, with lobster and crab from Branscombe beach, so expect excellent restaurant-style meals.

The Mountpleasant Inn
Nomansland, Tiverton EX16 8NN
☎ 01884 860271; www.mpli.ltd.co.uk
A bustling, friendly, family-run pub that welcomes everyone, especially other families. Set in the heart of the county, this popular inn dates from the 18th century, when it began life as a simple ostler's house. Today there is an attractive restaurant in the former blacksmith's forge, which serves a variety of reasonably priced food.

The Puffing Billy
Station Hill, Great Torrington EX38 8JD
☎ 01805 623050
A pub with a difference, in a partially converted station on the old Barnstaple railway line, now the route of the Tarka Trail. The pub is full of railway memorabilia and has a small garden next to the track. The pub serves a wide range of food to suit most tastes and also sells locally brewed Cavalier ale.

The Tower Inn
Slapton, near Dartmouth TQ7 2PN
☎ 01548 580216;
www.thetowerinn.com
A mile from Slapton Sands, this inn was built as cottages to house the men working on the Collegiate Chantry of St Mary. Expect church-pew seating, a lovely garden and a sophisticated menu.

DARTMOOR & TAMAR VALLEY
The Elephant's Nest Inn
Horndon, Mary Tavy, Tavistock
PL19 9NQ ☎ 01822 810273
A pub since the mid-19th century, the building dates back to the 16th century, when it was used to accommodate tin and copper miners. There's a beamed bar with an open fire, two dining rooms and a pretty garden. The menu includes plenty of lighter options, such as tasty baguettes and lighter snacks, as well as a range of seafood, meat and vegetarian options.

EXMOOR & THE QUANTOCKS
The Crown Hotel
Exford, Somerset TA24 7PP
☎ 01643 831554;
www.crownhotelexmoor.co.uk
Set in the heart of the Exmoor National Park, this 17th-century coaching inn is thought to be the oldest working inn on the moor. It is especially popular for equine enthusiasts, as it has plenty of stabling and is set in three acres of gardens and woodlands. There is also an excellent bar menu available.

DORSET & THE PURBECKS
The Bankes Arms Hotel
Watery Lane, Studland BH19 3AU
☎ 01929 450225; www.bankesarms.com
Once the haunt of smugglers, this creeper-clad inn is renowned for its large menu of fresh fish and seafood, including fresh mussels, crab gratin and lobster dishes. There are meat options, too, such as lamb noisettes in mint, honey and orange sauce. Each year the pub hosts a beer festival, with around 60 real ales on tap accompanied by music, Morris dancing and stone carving in the garden.

The Castle Inn
Main Road, West Lulworth BH20 5RN
☎ 01929 400311
This beautiful thatched and beamed atmospheric free house close to Lulworth Cove, is perfectly placed for walkers. There's an extensive tiered garden, which fills up quickly on summer days, and is especially popular with families. Dogs are permitted too. The menu includes well-cooked staples such as chicken stroganoff, fillet and tuna steak, and plenty of vegetarian options.

SALISBURY & PLAINS
The Haunch of Venison
1–5 Minster Street, Salisbury SP1 1TB
☎ 01722 411313
Craftsmen working on the cathedral spire were some of the early customers of this atmospheric pub, which dates back to 1320. A restaurant in summer serves an excellent choice of lunch and dinner options with a range of well-cooked dishes, ranging from traditional cottage pie to pan-fried sea bass.

The Mayfly
Testcombe, Stockbridge SO20 6AZ
☎ 01264 860283
A firm favourite with fly-fishermen, this lovely old country pub looks onto the fast-flowing River Test. A selection of hot and cold meats, quiches and pies is laid out buffet-style, along with a few hot daily specials. Beers include Ringwood Best and Wadworth 6X.

COTSWOLDS
The Bell at Sapperton
Sapperton GL7 6LE ☎ 01285 760298;
www.foodatthebell.co.uk
The 300-year-old Bell is elegant in an understated way – all stone walls and fresh flowers on scrubbed tables. Enjoy a range of inexpensive lunchtime dishes and a gourmet menu of dishes in the evening, including home-made burger of Welsh Black beef, slow-braised veal and sea bass. Eat inside or in the pretty garden or courtyard.

Eight Bells
Church Street, Chipping Campden
GL55 6JG ☎ 01386 840371
This is the oldest inn in Chipping Campden and is near the famous church. It has two cosy bars, a smart dining room and a very pleasant terrace at the back. They serve a good range of local food at lunchtime and in the evenings.

FOREST OF DEAN
The Saracens Head Inn
Symonds Yat HR96JL ☎ 01600 890435;
www.saracensheadinn.co.uk
Formerly a cider mill, this attractive riverside inn sits on the east bank of the Wye where the river flows through a picturesque gorge. At just over a mile from the Welsh border, the inn is in a great location for exploring this unspoiled area. Choose from dishes such as Welsh mountain lamb, seafood casserole or roasted butternut squash and goat's cheese risotto.

BATH
The Old Green Tree
12 Green Street BA1 2JZ
☎ 01225 448259
This charming 18th-century, three-roomed, oak-panelled pub, is loved by the locals and visitors for its faded splendour, dim and atmospheric interior and a front room decorated with World War II Spitfire pictures. The menu includes soup and bangers and mash (probably the best sausages in Bath!).

TEA ROOMS

CORNWALL

Carnewas Tea Room and Garden
Bedruthan, St Eval, Wadebridge
PL27 7UW ☎ 01637 860701
The dramatic coastline at Bedruthan is renowned for its cliff-top views. Take in the view with a cream tea or a plate of cakes from the National Trust tea room on the cliff top, which is housed in the office building of the Carnewas iron mine.

Charlotte's Tea House
Coinage Hall, 1 Boscawen Street, Truro
TR1 2QU ☎ 01872 263706
This lovingly restored tea house is on the first floor of the Coinage Hall. Victorian uniforms, china cups and antiques add to the charm. The menu offers sandwiches and delicious set teas – cream teas with light, home-made scones and high teas with sandwiches and irresistible cakes.

Crumpets Tea Shop
1 Fore Street, Polruan, Fowey PL23 1PQ
☎ 01726 870806
Just a five-minute boat trip across the estuary from Fowey, Crumpets is a traditional tea shop decked out in yellow and blue, with sea-related prints on the walls. Just the ticket for light lunches, home-cooked cakes or a delicious cream tea, served with home-made jam.

Minnie Moon
Cadgwith Cove, Helston TR12 7JX
☎ 01326 290539
The owner is dedicated to fresh crab and you'll find her tiny shop-cum-café smack beside the beach and the boats that supply her with the crab that she sells from the shop window. Buy it by the pound or have it made into a crab sandwich. She'll also prepare you a cream tea – eat at tables by the beach.

Miss Peapod's Kitchen Café
Jubilee Wharf, Penryn TR10 8FG
☎ 01326 374424;
www.misspeapod.co.uk
An eco-eaterie in Jubilee Wharf, a new wind- and sun-powered eco-development on Penryn's revitalized waterfront. The furniture is recycled but the river views from the alfresco decking, and the food, are the stars, with excellent breakfasts, coffee, cakes and lunches prepared.

Polpeor Café
Lizard Point, The Lizard, TR12 7HJ
☎ 01326 290939
At Britain's most southerly café, perched high on the cliffs on the spectacular Lizard Point, you can watch waves crashing onto rocks and choughs wheeling around the cliffs while you tuck into a local crab salad and sandwiches or a traditional cream tea. On fine summer days, the suntrap terrace right on the cliff edge is the place to eat.

Rick Stein's Café
10 Middle Street, Padstow PL28 8AP
☎ 01841 532700; www.rickstein.com
The most relaxed of Rick Stein's restaurants is a casual café-with-rooms decked out with a nautical theme. It's open all day, so call in for breakfast or an excellent cappuccino and peruse the papers, or arrive early for deliciously simple lunches and dinners – salt and pepper prawn, whole grilled mackerel with tomato and onion salad, or chickpea, parsley and salt cod stew.

DEVON

Canal Tea Room and Garden
Lime Kiln Cottage, Grand Western Canal,
Tiverton EX16 4AQ ☎ 01884 252291
Enjoy home-made cakes, scones and ice cream at this lovely tea garden attached to a thatched cottage with a pond and covered seating. It's situated just below the basin of the Grand Western Canal.

The Cosy Teapot
13 Fore Street, Budleigh Salterton
EX9 6NH ☎ 01395 444016
The cries of seagulls accompany you on a visit to this traditional, genteel tea shop just a few minutes' walk from the beach. Floral-patterned china, sumptuous cakes, a range of sandwiches and tasty lunches all add to the homely atmosphere. If you dare, try the Black Forest Cream Tea – cherry jam, clotted cream and a chocolate scone. Gluten-free options are also available.

Four & Twenty Blackbirds Tea Shoppe
43 Gold Street, Tiverton EX16 6QB
☎ 01884 257055
Low beams, vases of flowers, and antique furniture create a homely atmosphere at this traditional tea shop near the clock tower. Choose from different 'teas': Maid's (apple tart), King's (cheese and chutney), Queen's (egg), Jenny Wren's (scones, jelly, ice cream) and Blackbird's (sandwiches and cake).

The Sea Shanty
Branscombe Beach EX12 3DP
☎ 01297 680577
The thatched Sea Shanty is right on Branscombe's beach, and has been serving refreshments for more than 70 years. It's the ideal setting for a cream tea or a light lunch, with crab, lobster and fish straight off the beach. With a walled sun-trap courtyard, an open fire inside, tables by the beach and wonderful views.

Soar Mill Cove Hotel
Near Salcombe, Devon TQ7 3DS
☎ 01548 561566
A single storey building of local stone and slate, the hotel overlooks the beach and cove without impacting on this area of outstanding natural beauty. Tea is served in the lounge, on the deck or out in the lovely garden.

DARTMOOR & TAMAR VALLEY

Brimpts Farm
Dartmeet, Dartmoor PL20 6FG
☎ 01364 631450;
www.brimptsfarm.co.uk
Brimpts Farm has a spectacular setting above Dartmeet and overlooking Yar Tor. Their cream teas have been justly renowned since 1913; the menu includes dishes made from fresh local produce.

EXMOOR

Lewis's Tea Rooms, 13 The High Street,
Dulverton TA22 9HB ☎ 01398 323850
This instantly welcoming tea shop, on the southern fringes of Exmoor National Park, occupies a pair of 18th-century cottages. At either end fires blaze in the winter and, in summer, the flower-filled courtyard tempts visitors outside. When it comes to tea time, speciality loose-leaf teas and fat scones with strawberry jam and clotted cream are always winners.

SOMERSET & MENDIPS

Grosvenor Hotel
High Street, Stockbridge SO20 6EU
☎ 01264 810606
Enjoy a cream tea, or toasted tea cakes with a choice of teas and coffees, in the comfort of this grand old fishing hotel, which juts into the High Street.

Lillie Langtry's
High Street, Stockbridge SO20 6HF
☎ 01264 810754
This old building on the main street was once an inn frequented by actress Lillie Langtry. Today it is a homely tea room, serving crumpets dripping with butter and home-made jam, and scones with clotted cream from a neighbouring Jersey herd. Lunches can be served on the shady terrace by the stream.

DORSET & THE PURBECKS

The Tea Shop
11a Trinity Street, The Harbourside,
Weymouth DT4 8TW ☎ 01305 788052
The Tea Shop is well known for its scrumptious selection of cakes and tasty afternoon tea favourites; don't leave without trying the Dorset apple cake. Coeliac and diabetic dietary needs are catered here. A selection of local produce is also for sale.

SALISBURY & PLAINS

The Polly Tea Rooms
8 St Thomas's Square, Salisbury
SP1 1BA ☎ 01722 336037
Just a short walk from the cathedral, The Polly Tea Rooms is in the ideal location to stop for a break. In winter the cosy decor inside is very inviting and in summer the little tables outside provide the perfect place to watch the world go by whilst tucking into a delicious afternoon tea.

COTSWOLDS

Badgers Hall
High Street, Chipping Campden
GL55 6HB ☎ 01386 840839;
www.badgershall.com
A true taste of the Cotswolds: the building is 15th-century, honey-coloured stone with exposed oak beams, mullioned windows and open fireplaces. Home-made cakes, scones and pastries are freshly baked on the premises using local produce. They also have charming bedrooms available.

Black Cat
High Street, Lechlade on Thames, GL7
3AD ☎ 01367 252273
This extended snug tea room is in Lechlade's busy high street. The interior is simplicity itself with white painted walls and tableware. There is a breakfast, lunch and afternoon tea menu.

Juri's Olde Bakery & Teashoppe
High Street, Winchcombe GL54 5LJ
☎ 01242 602469;
www.juris-tearoom.co.uk
On the High Street of this lovely village, Juri's traditional stone tea room is run by a Japanese family who are dedicated to maintaining high standards. Their freshly made cakes are first class. The patio garden and conservatory are delightful.

The Mad Hatter
Riverside, Bourton-on-the-Water
GL54 2BX ☎ 01451 821508;
www.the-mad-hatter-tearoom.co.uk
This lovely 18th-century building beside the River Windrush is a treat to visit. Enjoy their cream teas, delicious home-made cakes and lovely garden.

BATH

Sally Lunn's
4 North Parade Passage, Bath
☎ 01225 461634;
www.sallylunns.co.uk
The famous Sally Lunn Bun was originally baked in Georgian times and is still on offer in this historic tea shop in the oldest house in Bath. Come here for breakfast, lunch or a magnificent cream tea.

Southeast England

Southeast England

The gentle landscape of the southeast encompasses chalk downland ridges that stretch away to the west; deep beech woods that shelter herds of timid roe deer; towering white cliffs that form a stunning backdrop along the coast and myriad thatched cottages nestled around their village greens. The region includes The New Forest, an area well-known for its wildlife conservation projects and its unspoilt natural beauty. One of Britain's newer national parks, it is a haven for walkers, cyclists and wildlife lovers.

Nearby is Winchester, the ancient capital of England, with its medieval cathedral and links with Jane Austen and the mythical King Arthur and his round table. The surrounding North Downs and their counterparts, the South Downs in Sussex, are now protected as part of the South Downs National Park, designated in 2010.

And within striking distance of all this is London, the country's capital and one of the most famous cityscapes in the world, where the cultural life encompasses world-class opera, theatre, cinema, street festivals, art exhibitions and much more. But here, too, you'll find a number of beautiful parks that are like green oases amid the hustle and bustle of city life.

The New Forest

CLOCKWISE FROM TOP: BUCKLERS HARD LEADING TO THE BEAULIEU RIVER; NEW FOREST PONY; FALLOW DEER HINDS GRAZE ON BACKLEY PLAIN

BEAULIEU MAP REF 400 E7

The pretty village of Beaulieu is now synonymous with the National Motor Museum, the private passion of the then Lord Montagu. His forefathers acquired the Beaulieu estate in Tudor times, with its Cistercian abbey founded in 1204.

The abbey was torn down as part of the Dissolution of the Monasteries countrywide, but the fine cloisters survived and now contain a re-created monastic garden, the refectory became the parish church, and the Domus, the lay brothers' apartments, now houses an exhibition about abbey life. The Tudor house created from the 14th-century gatehouse was reconstructed in the 19th century as the present Palace House, and today shows the domestic workings of a Victorian household. During World War II the estate became the top-secret training school for those involved in the Special Operations Executive (SOE), where agents prepared for operations behind enemy lines in occupied France and Europe, and this story is told in the Secret Army Exhibition.

Lord Montagu first opened this lovely Palace House to the public in 1952, and the brilliant motor museum is dedicated to the memory of his father. It was, in fact, John Montagu who had successfully petitioned parliament to abolish the 12mph (19kph) speed limit, among other notable achievements. Today there are more than 250 vintage beauties and stars of the car world to admire in this famous collection, ranging from world record breakers such as 'Bluebird' and 'Golden Arrow' to TV favourites including Mr Bean's green Mini, and James Bond's Lotus submarine car from the movie *The Spy Who Loved Me*. A trip on the 'Wheels' pod ride transports you through a century of motoring history, and you can explore the site on a replica 1912 bus or the high-level monorail. Look out for the special events and exhibitions that take place throughout the year.

BREAMORE MAP REF 400 D6

Breamore (pronounced 'Bremmer') is an unspoiled village in the northeast corner of the New Forest, with many attractive redbrick, thatched cottages grouped tranquilly around its village green. It's a scene jealously guarded from change, and even the village stocks still stand, opposite the Bat and Ball pub. Little St Mary's Church, which dates from about 1000, is one of the most interesting Saxon survivals in Hampshire. The 12th-century porch contains part of the Saxon rood screen, a fine piece of carving, though the figures have been damaged.

The redbrick Elizabethan manor house of Breamore, built on the hillside in 1583, was purchased by Queen Anne's physician, Sir Edward Hulse, in the 18th century, and is still a family home with collections of paintings, furniture, needlework and porcelain. The Great Hall has its original carved stone fireplace, and in the Victorian kitchen hangs gleaming copperware.

In the old farmyard the Countryside Museum has full-size replicas of the village shops that would have made the estate self-sufficient, including a wheelwright's, a blacksmith's and a brewery.

BROCKENHURST MAP REF 400 D7

Brockenhurst is a big, pleasant village set amid wooded countryside. On the northern outskirts are two of the largest and loveliest of the New Forest 'lawns', Butts Lawn and Balmer Lawn, the latter overlooked by an elegant hotel.

New Forest churches tend to stand aloof from their villages and ancient Brockenhurst's St Nicholas' church, hidden away to the east, is no exception. It is reputedly the oldest in the forest, and it was the only one recorded in the 1086 Domesday survey. The yew tree that almost smothers the building has a girth of more than 20 feet (6m) and is known to be more than 1,000 years old.

To the northwest of Brockenhurst the Rhinefield Ornamental Drive features coniferous trees, including very large redwoods. Forest walks on either side of the drive include a 'Tall Trees Walk'. Further on, Bolderwood Drive passes close to the ancient Knightwood Oak, and the deer sanctuary whose platforms offer a view of deer roaming in the forest.

BUCKLERS HARD MAP REF 400 E7

Two redbrick, terraced rows of Georgian houses face each other across a wide open space that slopes gently down to the Beaulieu River, on the Beaulieu estate. The area is kept free of cars and presents a peaceful rural scene. Yet Bucklers Hard, originally called Montagu Town, was the shipyard that built many of the men-of-war for Nelson's fleet, including his favourite ship, *Agamemnon*. The yard was busy, but overreached itself and folded in 1811. During World War II Bucklers Hard revived its shipbuilding tradition, and some parts of a Mulberry Harbour for the

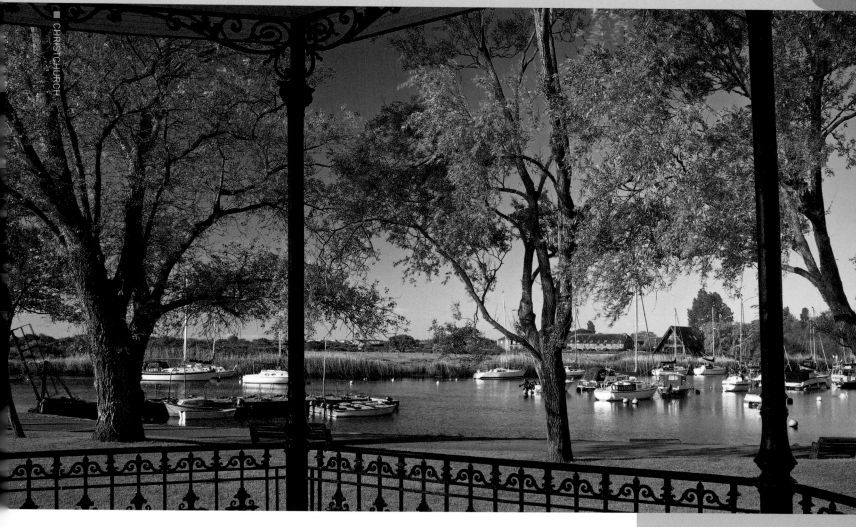

CHRISTCHURCH

D-Day landings were constructed here. In the Maritime Museum are models of the ships built here, and reconstructed cottage interiors offer an insight into the life of 18th-century shipyard workers.

Today, pleasure craft ride the tranquil waters of the Beaulieu River and, in summer, cruises set off from the quay. A riverside walk leads to Beaulieu village.

BURLEY MAP REF 400 D7

Burley is an excellent centre for walking, horse riding and mountain biking. This attractive village is set high above the River Avon amid the bleak heathlands of the western New Forest, where ponies and cattle roam freely. Burley Beacon is the village's high point, reached by the gravel track from Pound Lane, and from it the view expands westwards over the Avon Valley. Even better is the view from Castle Hill, topped by an Iron Age camp, at nearby Burley Street. Red deer roam in the grounds of grand Burley Manor.

During the 1950s, Burley had its own resident witch, called Sybil Leek, who dressed in black robes with a jackdaw perched on her shoulder. Despite her 'white' tendencies, local resentment caused her to flee to America. Since then the village has specialized in witchcraft shops as well as the usual range of antiques and souvenirs. A window in the

little church commemorates Constance Applebee, who died in 1981 at the ripe old age of 107. Burley is also home to New Forest Cider, a cider farm with a shop and an exhibition to show how it is made.

CHRISTCHURCH MAP REF 400 D7

This ancient town lies on the south coast where the rivers Stour and Avon pour into the bay. At the time of the Domesday survey there were only 21 houses here and it was named Twynham. The church was started later in the 11th century, and became an Augustinian priory around 1150. All that remains is the Priory Church, looming gold above the town, and worth exploring inside for its carvings. Look out for the Norman turret in the north transept, and the superb carving of the Salisbury Chantry. Nearby Place Mill, mentioned in the Domesday Book, was used for fulling (cleaning and thickening cloth) and corn grinding until 1808, and now has displays of old milling items, with an art and crafts gallery upstairs.

One of Christchurch town's most unusual sights is its surviving ducking stool, reached via a flagged alleyway beside the Olde George Inn – a wooden stool on the end of a pole which can be swung out into the chilly millstream, in a scolds' punishment revived with good humour in 1986. The town's Red House Museum is

a collection of local and natural history, housed in an appealing old Georgian house with a lovely garden.

Across the estuary, the pastel-coloured rows of beach huts on Mudeford's sandy peninsula are a cheerful throwback to childhood bucket-and-spade holidays of the early 20th century. This windswept peninsula has an archaeological record dating back 12,500 years, when Stone Age hunter-gatherers left a campsite on its seaward edge. Some 10,500 years later, Iron Age folk settled and built up a trading port on the inner shore, where Barn Field stands today. The great Double Dikes date from this period, built to shelter a village of timber-framed dwellings.

Barn Field has been untouched by farming since the Romans left in around AD 410 and its rare status is protected by conservationists. It's an area of low, acid grassland gripping onto thin soil, maintained by the salt-laden winds and the teeth of the rabbit population. Decimation of the rabbits by myxomatosis in the 1950s allowed gorse and bramble to take hold, but scrub clearance and controlled cattle grazing has done much to restore the original balance. Today it is an important site for ground-nesting birds such as the skylark and meadow pipit, and adorned with heath bedstraw, autumn hawkbit and harebell.

Activity
THE HAMPSHIRE AVON

The River Avon rises to the east of Devizes in Wiltshire and flows southwards for 48 miles (77km) to the English Channel at Christchurch. In its upper chalky reaches it is a noted clear trout stream, but where it flows through Hampshire past Breamore and Fordingbridge the acid soils of the New Forest change its nature and it becomes a river for coarse fishing. Below Ringwood it is renowned for salmon. The waymarked Avon Valley Path, opened in 1992, follows the river for 34 miles (54.5km) from Salisbury to Christchurch and the coast.

Insight
NEW FOREST PONIES

New Forest ponies may roam freely, but they are not strictly wild – they belong to the commoners. The Victorians 'improved' the hardy ponies that had grazed the forest for centuries, surviving on a diet of gorse, bracken and brambles, by inter-breeding them with Arab stallions – and now they mainly eat grass. Every autumn the ponies are rounded up for branding and marking, and several times a year ponies are sold at Beaulieu Road Station.

ELING MAP REF 400 E7

The Saxon village of Eling, on a little tidal creek off Southampton Water, was a shipbuilding village until the end of the 19th century. Before that it was a small port from where Henry I is said to have sailed to Normandy in 1130.

The creek, a sheltered little harbour for sailing craft, is crossed by a fast causeway with sluice gates to hold back the high tides and, in the little building on the northern shore, the power of Southampton Water's famous double tides is harnessed and used to produce wholemeal flour.

Eling Tide Mill is one of the few surviving tide mills regularly milling pure stoneground flour. The Domesday Book of 1086 records a mill here. The manor of Eling was later part of the endowment to Winchester College in 1385 and even at this time the mill and causeway had long been a ruin, but it was not until 1415 that the Wardens and Fellows of the college sought to find a means of rebuilding and maintaining the mill and causeway. The solution was to let the mill to Thomas Midlyngton of Southampton for a term

of 50 years at a fee of 13 shillings and 4 pence. In return he was required to restore the mill within two years and to maintain it, assisted by a grant of 20 marks (approximately £13.30p) and, as a charitable act "for the salvation of his soul", to rebuild and maintain the causeway "to last for a hundred years", although he was also granted the right to "remove sand and clay for his own convenience". The present building dates from the 18th century. It was restored in 1980 and milling demonstrations are given, depending on the tides. You can learn more about Eling and neighbouring Totton in the heritage centre by the mill.

The causeway across the creek at Eling carries is the only remaining toll road in Hampshire, which records show has been in operation since at least 1418.

EMERY DOWN MAP REF 400 D7

Emery Down is a pretty little village, full of character, just outside Lyndhurst within the New Forest National Park.

The New Forest had a famous snakecatcher, Henry 'Brusher' Mills

(1840-1905). He was born at Emery Down and lived in a charcoal burner's makeshift hut. In his time he is said to have caught 30,000 snakes and 3,500 adders, some of which he sold to zoos, but others were less fortunate – he made them into an ointment as a cure for rheumatism. The pub in which he used to drink at Brockenhurst is today called The Snakecatcher.

The artist Sven Berlin, one of the characters who made up the artistic community of St Ives, has been described as 'England's most important neglected artist'. He moved to the New Forest in a horse-drawn gypsy caravan in 1953 and painted a portfolio of paintings documenting the last days of the Forest gypsies. The celebrated English composer, Ralph Vaughan Williams, visited Berlin at his Emery Down home and collected songs from the gypsies.

EXBURY MAP REF 400 E7

This pleasant estate village nestling on the Beaulieu River is famed for the magnificent rhododendron gardens at Exbury House. They were the creation of banker Lionel de Rothschild, whose passion was gardening – and he gardened on a magnificent scale.

Rothschild started here in the 1920s, with 600 acres (243ha) of wooded slopes overlooking the river. He split the land into 250 acres (101ha) of gardens and 350 acres (142ha) of arboretum. He imported more than 1,000 varieties of rhododendron, then created 452 more by careful crossing.

The mild climate of the Beaulieu River valley ensures a long flowering season, with absolutely breathtaking displays of fabulous colour between April and June. Camellias, azaleas and magnolias contribute to the glory of an Exbury spring. Other gardens here include a daffodil meadow, rock garden, rose garden, herbaceous garden and water garden. A miniature steam railway offers a 20-minute tour of the Summer Lane Garden, leading to the American Garden. Dogs on a short lead are welcome.

FURZEY GARDENS MAP REF 400 D7

Designed by Hugh Dalrymple, Furzey Gardens was established in 1922 and has much to hold the attention of budding horticulturists. Located deep in the middle of the New Forest in the pretty village of Minstead, the informal gardens have a wonderful collection of rhododendrons and azaleas, that create an amazing display of colour when in full bloom.

Other parts of the garden are given over to many varieties of heathers and an extensive range of winter and summer flowering shrubs, as well as a separate sensory garden. For walkers, there is a lake to amble round.

LYMINGTON MAP REF 400 D7

Lymington is a busy sailing town at the mouth of the Lymington River. It received its charter in 1200 and became a free port, flourishing as the closest mainland harbour to the Isle of Wight, to which ferries still run. In the Middle Ages Lymington rivalled Southampton as a major port – and the numerous creeks around here were much frequented by smugglers well into the 18th century. Today the tidal salt marshes stretch for 10 miles (16km), and are protected as a national nature reserve.

For many years the town's prosperity depended on the production of salt, but sadly this trade eventually died out and Lymington briefly became a fashionable bathing place. By the end of the 19th century it had developed as a sailing centre, and today the town has an excellent yacht basin and is the headquarters of two sailing clubs. There is boat building too and, as with many ports, it is famed for its inns – reputedly there were once 45.

The wide Georgian and Victorian High Street, which climbs the hill from the quay to the church, bursts into life on Saturdays when there is a vibrant 700-year-old market, with a great variety of stalls laid out along both sides of the street. Enjoy views from the hilltop back down across the river, then take a look at the Church of St Thomas, which looks 18th century, with its jaunty white cupola and galleried interior, but is actually medieval. The town's St Barbe Museum is dedicated to the history of the New Forest coast, including hands-on displays for children, while its art gallery offers an ever changing range of exhibitions of world-class artworks.

To the north of Lymington is lovely Spinners, a beautiful woodland garden cultivating rhododendrons, magnolias, Japanese maples and much more. To the south, on Hurst Spit, stands Hurst Castle, one of Henry VIII's defences against possible Spanish invasion with its characteristic sturdy design. It was part of the modern coastal artillery defences in both world wars and in use until 1956.

LYNDHURST MAP REF 400 D7

The 'Capital of the New Forest' is a fairly sizeable town, and is the only one within the historical confines of the forest. It was designated the New Forest's administrative centre in 1079 by William I, and it continues to be the seat of the ancient Court of Verderers formed to protect the rights of the commoners. The Court Room and the Forestry Commission offices are housed in the beautiful 17th-century Queen's House where the Verderers meet every two months. All New Forest animals are under their jurisdiction, while patrolling the forest is the remit of four 'Agisters' – a medieval

FURZEY GARDENS

word meaning 'collector'. The Forestry Commission manages the woodland of the New Forest.

Lyndhurst is a town of narrow streets leading off the main High Street, which snarls up with traffic during peak holiday times. It is full of tourist shops and eating places, with Victorian and Edwardian architecture to admire. The 1860 church, on the site of two earlier ones, dominates the High Street with its 160-foot (49m) spire. It contains windows by Burne-Jones and a fresco, *The Parable of the Virgins*, by Lord Leighton. In the village churchyard lies Mrs Hargreaves, who died in 1934. As the little Alice Liddell, she was the real inspiration for Lewis Caroll's *Alice in Wonderland*. The town is the home of the New Forest Visitor Centre and Museum.

Lyndhurst's central position makes it an ideal base for exploring the forest, which still presses up close to the town's boundaries. To the west of Lyndhurst sits the picturesque thatched hamlet of Swan Green, formerly the site of an important pony fair, and Emery Down, famed for its Portuguese fireplace, which stands alone in the open air. It was constructed of cobble stones on the site of a building that was occupied by Portuguese troops during World War I, and it serves as a memorial to them. The New Forest Reptile Centre, 2 miles (3.2km) south west of Lyndhurst, is a conservation and education facility dedicated to rare native species, where you can also explore the circular Reptile Trail. To the east Bolton's Bench car park is an excellent starting point for walks over White Moor Heath.

STONEY CROSS MAP REF 400 D7

Stoney Cross airfield was built late in 1942 on an area anciently occupied by man; there is still a megalithic Round Barrow, surrounded by a ditch, a short distance from the Janesmoor Pond car park on the A31. The airfield made a significant contribution to World War II and was used by both the Royal Air Force and the United States Air Force. At one time, the Ninth Air Force had 472 American personnel based there. Following the end of hostilities in Europe, Stoney Cross was used as a staging post for RAF transports flying to the Far East.

The airfield was closed in 1946 and for a period following the war, the airfield was abandoned and quickly became overgrown. In the 1960s, the Forestry Commission created tree plantations and the site was developed to meet the needs of public recreation. Stoney Cross has now been returned to managed heathland and the facilities include fishing for under 17s and radio-controlled boating.

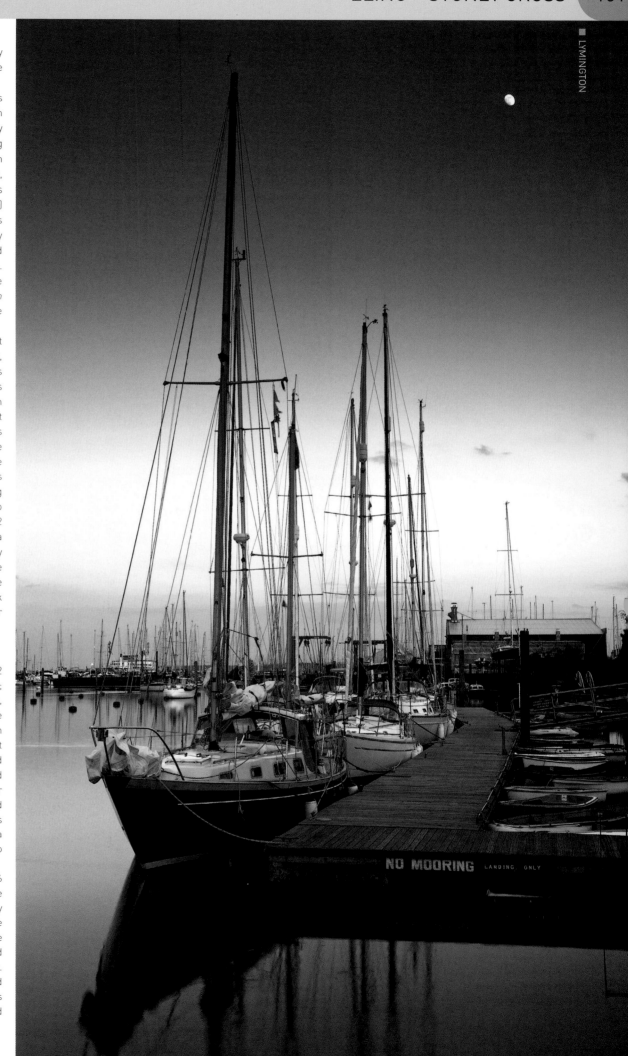

LYMINGTON

THE NEW FOREST

WALK 29

A FOREST WALK FROM FRITHAM

A walk from a hidden hamlet and the site of a former gunpowder factory, through woodland and open heathland. Look out for nests of wood ants beside the tracks, the mounds will be feverish with activity on dry warm days, and listen for the distinctive 'yaffle' of the green woodpecker, which feeds on the wood ants.

DISTANCE/TIME 5.5 miles (8.8km) 3h **MAP** OS Explorer OL22 New Forest **START** Forestry Commission car park beyond Royal Oak pub; grid ref: SU 230141 **PATHS** Gravel forest tracks, heathland and woodland paths **THE PUB** The Royal Oak, Fritham. Tel: 02380 812606

1 Turn left out of the Forestry Commission car park and head downhill along the road.

2 Keep ahead at the foot of the hill, leaving Eyeworth Pond on your right, and follow the short gravel track to a low wooden barrier at Oak Tree Cottage. Leave the barrier on your left, take the narrow path that heads north into Eyeworth Wood, and follow it for 0.5 mile (800m).

3 At length, the path leads on to a tree-studded heath, with far-reaching views. Continue for a further 550yds (500m) across Homy Ridge, as far as a stocky Scots pine tree at the edge of a small wood on your right.

4 The path divides here. Take the left-hand fork, and walk through the shallow valley to the car park at Telegraph Hill.

5 Turn left beside the B3078 for 20yds (18m), before turning left again on to the gravel track directly opposite Hope Cottage. The track bears left soon after passing a small, seasonal pond at Studley Head. After 250yds (227m), the path dives briefly beneath holly and oak trees before breaking back out on to the heath.

6 Continue past a deep pool on your right, just a few paces beyond the low mound of a tumulus. Follow the track south towards Amberwood Inclosure, ignoring the path that branches off to your right near Ashley Bottom. A little further on, look for the small brick shelter located on your right.

7 Turn left at a waymarked junction with the cycle track on the edge of Amberwood Inclosure, and dive steeply down the well-made gravel track into the woods. Ignore all turnings, and follow the waymarked route through the forest and over the Latchmoor Brook. The trees gradually drop behind as the cycle track winds its way up through Gorley Bushes, and there are glimpses of Eyeworth Lodge away to your left. A steady climb brings you to the green at Fritham. Turn right to return to the car park.

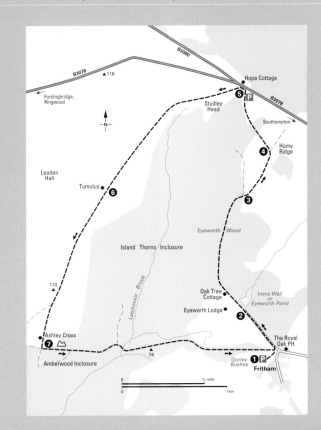

WALK 30

NEW FOREST TRAILS AROUND BANK

Ancient oaks, towering conifers and historic inclosures (managed woodland where young trees are protected from deer and ponies) are on the route.

DISTANCE/TIME 8 miles (12.9km) 4h **MAP** OS Explorer OL22 New Forest **START** Brock Hill Forestry Commission car park; grid ref: SU 266057 **PATHS** Grass and gravel forest tracks, heathland paths, some roads **THE PUB** The Oak Inn, Pinkney Lane, Bank. Tel: 02380 282350

1 Take the gravel path at the southern end of the car park (beyond the information post), parallel with the road. In 100yds (91m) turn right before a bench seat and descend to a gravel track. Cross over; then, where the path curves left, keep ahead to a gate and the A35. Cross the A35 (take care), go through a gate and keep to the path, uphill to a junction. Turn right and follow the path to Knightwood Oak car park, then follow the sign to the Knightwood Oak.

2 Return to the car park and bear right along the road. Turn right again after a few paces, on to a path into woodland. Cross a stream and soon reach a gravel track. Bear right and keep to this trail, passing red marker posts, to a fork. Keep left to a gate and road. Turn right to the Portuguese Fireplace.

3 Return through Holidays Hill Inclosure to the fork of tracks. Bear left and follow this to the New Forest Reptile Centre. Walk along the access drive past a cottage then, at a barrier (left), descend to a path and follow it across a bridge.

4 Keep to the main path for 0.75 mile (1.2km), skirting the walls to Allum Green and several clearings, then climb through trees to a defined crossing of paths and turn right. Shortly, bear half right across a clearing and footbridge, then continue through the woodland edge to an electricity pole. Bear right for 20yds (18m), then left through a gate to the A35.

5 Turn left, then almost immediately right across the road to a gate. Walk ahead to a garden boundary and turn right, the path leading to a lane in Bank. Turn right, pass the Oak Inn and walk through the hamlet.

6 Just beyond the cattle grid, turn right through a gate on to a gravelled track towards Brockenhurst. Follow this track for nearly a mile (1.6km) to a junction at a green.

7 Fork right towards Brockenhurst, and enter Hursthill Inclosure at a gate. Drop down past a turning on the right, then climb again and bear left at a fork. Keep to the waymarked track as it drops past another turning on the right and leaves Hursthill Inclosure at a gate. Walk along the track to the bridge over Highland Water, and follow the track round to the right. Soon a gate leads the waymarked trail into Poundhill Inclosure, and another straight section brings you to a five-way junction at waymark post 24.

8 Turn right here. Ignore all turnings, and follow the track as it turns sharp right and winds its way to a junction with the Ornamental Drive. Turn left for the last 100yds (91m) back to the car park.

AROUND ROMAN ROCKBOURNE

Through fields and dense woodland, this walk discovers Rockbourne, which has one of Hampshire's prettiest village high streets and is home to one of the most interesting Roman villa complexes in the country. The walk continues to Whitsbury, where foundations of another Roman building lie over Iron Age settlements.

DISTANCE/TIME 4.5 miles (7.2km) 2h15 **MAP** OS Explorer OL22 New Forest **START** Rockbourne village hall car park; grid ref: SU 113184 **PATHS** Field paths, woodland bridleways and tracks; 9 stiles **THE PUB** The Rose and Thistle, Rockbourne. Tel: 01725 518236

1 Turn left out of the village hall car park and shortly take the lane right towards Manor Farm. Turn right, signed to the church, and cross the gravel drive to a stepped path to St Andrew's Church. Continue along the right-hand edge of the churchyard to a junction of paths. Keep ahead behind houses, ignoring three paths right, then cross a stile and turn immediately right to go through a gate.

2 Follow the field-edge down to a junction of paths. Turn left and cross a stile to a gate, then cross a stile, go through a gate and along the field-edge. In the far corner of the field, zig-zag right and left over a stile and keep along the edge of a meadow to a stile. Pass in front of a thatched cottage to reach a gate and track, opposite Marsh Farm.

3 Bear left, then right through a gate and continue along the right-hand field-edge to a gate. Continue to another gate, then turn left along the field-edge, passing through a gate to a stile and lane. To visit the Roman Villa, turn right to a T-junction, and turn right, then left to the entrance. Retrace your steps.

4 Take the track opposite. Enter a copse, then at a junction of tracks, take the arrowed path left up a steep bank into a field. Follow the path parallel to the field-edge to reach a stile at the corner of a wood. Cross a track, and continue downhill inside the woodland edge to a lane.

5 Turn right, then left along a bridleway, and gently climb through Radnall Wood. At a junction bear left (follow the blue arrow) and pass behind Whitsbury House to a lane. Turn left, then right along a track between properties to a lane. Turn right, then bear off right (by a fingerpost) along the bridleway through Whitsbury Wood.

6 At a junction with a track, bear left and walk beside paddocks to a bungalow. Turn left along a track between paddocks towards Whitsbury church. Turn left at the T-junction and shortly enter the churchyard. Go through the gate opposite the church door and descend to the lane.

7 Turn left for the Cartwheel Inn. Otherwise turn right, then left on a farm drive and ahead, bearing left, then right between paddocks, uphill to a gate. Turn left along the field-edge, then cross the field to a track.

8 Turn right and follow the track left to a junction of tracks. Go through the gate opposite, then back to Rockbourne church. Retrace your steps to the village hall.

WALK 32

EXBURY – HAMPSHIRE'S GREAT GARDEN

Spectacular year-round displays await in the superb 200-acre (80ha) gardens, from brilliant spring and summer flowers to the wonderful autumnal displays of the maples. There is a steam railway ride through the gardens and exhibitions and events, including craft demonstrations.

DISTANCE/TIME 6.5 miles (10.4km) 3h **MAP** OS Explorer OL22 New Forest **START** Pay-and-display car parks at Lepe Country Park; grid ref: SZ 455985 **PATHS** Fields, woodland and foreshore paths, some roads; 4 stiles **THE PUB** The Master Builders House Hotel, Bucklers Hard Tel: 01590 616253; www.themasterbuilders.co.uk

1 Walk west from the shore car park along the road. Keep left along the path above the foreshore, and pass the distinctive black-and-white painted Watch House. Then, at a small lighthouse, turn right to meet the lane. Turn left then, as the road curves left, cross the stile on the right. Walk along the field-edge, then bear left over a bridge.

2 Keep alongside the fence to a stile and proceed straight across the field. Briefly pass beside some woodland and follow the path to a gap in the hedge near a telegraph pole. Follow the path across the next field and into the woodland ahead. Continue through the trees, bearing right beyond a footbridge, then right with a waymarker post to join a fenced bridleway arrowed to the left.

3 Pass East Hill Farm, keeping on the farm track until it curves sharp left. Turn right through a gate. Follow the path to enter a field and bear right to follow the field-edge to T-junction. Turn left to a stile and lane.

4 Turn right, continue through a gate beside a cattle grid and take the footpath left through a gate (by another cattle grid) to join a track to Gatewood Farm. Bear right at the fork, walk around the farm complex, and remain on the track for 0.75 mile (1.2km) to a gate and lane. Cross over for Exbury Gardens.

5 On leaving Exbury Gardens, turn right then, where the road bends left, keep ahead, signed 'Inchmery Lane'. Continue to a waymarked path and stile on the left.

6 Cross the stile then the grassland into woodland, following the path right, through the trees. At a crossing of paths, turn left over a plank bridge. On leaving the trees, turn right along the field-edge beside the woodland to a gap in the hedge near a 3-way signpost. Keep the woodland edge on your right until the path bears right over a footbridge into the woods. Two more footbridges lead to a kissing gate onto a lane.

7 Turn left and follow the lane to the shore. Keep along the foreshore (follow the fingerpost) close to the high tide line and continue below Inchmery House. Pass Lepe House and rejoin your outward route back to Lepe Country Park. The final stretch along the foreshore may be impassable at high tide, so keep to the lane around Inchmery House, then, just before the road junction, turn right beside a barrier down to the foreshore to pick up the path past Lepe House.

DISTANCE/TIME 6 miles (9.7km) 1h **MAP** OS Explorer OL22 New Forest **START** Public pay car park, Burley; grid ref: SU 211030 **TRACKS** Busy village centre, quiet lanes and an old railway route **THE PUB** The Queen's Head, Burley, Ringwood. Tel: 01425 403423

DISTANCE/TIME 7 miles (11.3km) 1h45 **MAP** OS Explorer OL22 New Forest **START** Spring Bushes car park, on the road that runs west from Emery Down, near Lyndhurst, just north of Ringwood; grid ref: SU 196107 **TRACKS** Gravelled forest tracks, two short sections on rural lanes **THE PUB** The High Corner Inn, Linwood. Tel: 01425 473973

A NEW FOREST LOOP FROM BURLEY

This route takes you through the heart of Burley, with its antiques shops, tea rooms and horse-drawn wagon rides, then joins the Castleman cycle trail where you can experience the surrounding heathland from a level stretch of old railway line. There are good opportunities for birdwatching on the route.

1 Turn right out of the car park, stop at the next road junction, and then continue straight ahead. Fork left at the war memorial into Pound Lane, which is signed to Bransgore. Cycle past the Forest Teahouse and cider shop, then follow the lane out over the heath until you get to Burbush Hill.

2 Fork left just before the old railway bridge, following the waymarked off-road cycle track through the Forestry Commission's car park and continue down on to the old railway line. The Castleman Trail sets out from a lovely sandy cutting, which is smothered with brilliant purple heather during late summer. Soon the old line emerges from the cutting on to a low embankment, where there are good views out over the boggy heath. You'll often see horse riders in the area and birdwatchers should look out for green woodpeckers, as well as for wetland birds like lapwings, curlews and redshanks, which nest on the heath in early summer. The trail then rises briefly to the broken brickwork of Greenberry Bridge, which survived the closure of the railway, only to be demolished in 1995 when it became unsafe. Continue forward to the low wooden barriers that guard the minor road crossing at Holmsley Passage, where you can still see sections of the original railway lines embedded in the road.

3 If you wish, you can shorten the ride by turning left here and returning to the start point. Otherwise, to complete the full route, cross the road and continue along the old railway line. The trail becomes much more shaded as it follows a perfectly straight line through an avenue of lovely oak trees. The track then crosses over two small bridges that herald the approach to Holmsley Station. Here, look out for the old brick platform situated over to your right before dismounting your bicycle at the wooden gate that marks the end of the cycle track.

4 Beyond the gate and across the road, the Old Station Tea Rooms are well worth a visit for morning coffee, lunch or a cream tea. There's a pleasant garden, as well as a gift shop where you can buy a souvenir of your visit to this unusual refreshment stop. Turn here and retrace your outward route to Holmsley Passage (Point 3). Turn right on to the quiet lane. Follow the lane up the hill and then stop at the 5-way junction.

5 Cross straight over towards Burley Lawn and zig-zag left, then right, past The White Buck Inn and into Bennetts Lane.

6 Bear left when you eventually reach the next junction leading into Beechwood Lane and keep cycling straight on through Lester Square until you finally reach a T-junction. Turn left here towards Burley, and continue cycling past the pretty little brick-built church of St John the Baptist for the final 400-yd (364m) stretch that takes you back to the car park in Burley village.

A CIRCUIT AROUND LINWOOD

This ride offers a good chance of some peace and quiet, and the opportunity to see the New Forest at its best. You'll follow the waymarked Forestry Commission off-road cycle tracks deep into the heart of the Forest for the majority of the ride, with two short sections on tarred roads

1 Turn right out of the car park and continue straight on, passing the end of the gravel track that leads up to The High Corner Inn.

2 At Woodford Bottom bear left at the wooden barrier on your right and pass the ford across the Dockens Water stream, also on your right. Keep to the waymarked cycle route as it closely follows the gravelled track that winds across the open heath, past a few scattered houses and the tree-capped mound of Black Barrow. A few smaller tracks lead off of the main track to the left and to the right, but the main gravelled trail is easy enough to follow. Keep cycling straight on as a similar track leads in from your left near the thatched Bogmyrtle Cottage, until you join a tarred lane. Almost at once the lane turns sharp left through a tiny ford and climbs gently up to the road junction located near to The Red Shoot Inn.

3 Turn left opposite the post-box, still following the waymarked cycle route, and continue to cycle uphill until the road levels off and swings round to the left at Amie's Corner. Fork right here, sticking with the waymarked cycle route as it eventually joins a gravelled forest track. The trail then dives into Milkham Inclosure through wooden gates situated beside an attractive whitewashed cottage, then the trail drops down a way to a bridge over the Linford Brook.

4 A few yards further on turn left at the numbered waymark post 5, then follow the track as it winds through open mixed woodland and then re-crosses the Linford Brook. Continue as the track bears right at the next waymark post, then right again in front of a pair of wooden gates where you enter an area of mainly coniferous woodland. Another pair of wooden gates punctuates your progress to the top of the hill, where further gates lead you out into the Forestry Commission's Milkham car park. Go through here, cross the car park, and stop at the road junction.

5 Turn left towards Linwood and follow the narrow tarred lane for 500yds (455m) until it bears away to the left. Fork right here on to the waymarked cycle trail that follows the gravel track towards Broomy Lodge and Holly Hatch. Here your route crosses the high heathland plateau of Broomy Plain. This is a good spot to see Dartford warblers, meadow pipits and stonechats, and you'll also enjoy good long views towards Cranborne Chase and the Wiltshire Downs. Bear right at the next fork and then follow the trail down into Holly Hatch Inclosure.

6 At the foot of the hill, numbered waymark post 3 stands at the forest crossroads. Turn left here, on to a lovely tree-shaded track with soft green verges that leads you through the oak woods. Two pairs of wooden gates mark your progress through the inclosure, and at length the oaks give way to conifers. Follow the waymarked trail until you rejoin your outward route at a low wooden barrier. Turn left here, and climb the short hill back to The High Corner Inn.

Isle of Wight

CLOCKWISE FROM TOP LEFT: SAILING BOATS AT COWES WEEK; ISLE OF WIGHT; ENTRANCE GATEHOUSE AT CARISBROOKE CASTLE; MEDUSA MOSAIC, BRADING ROMAN VILLA

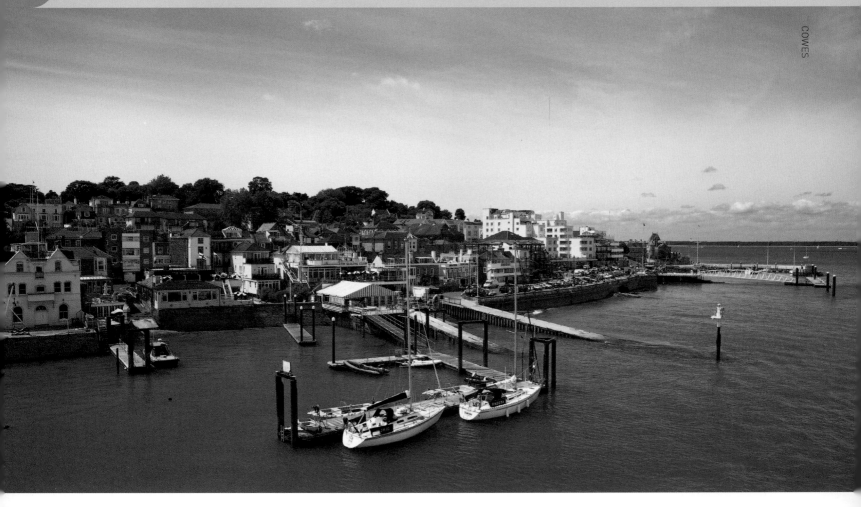

BRADING MAP REF 400 E7

In Roman times Bembridge Down was an island and Brading faced it across a tidal channel. In about AD 300 the Romans built a villa here, one of the best in Britain with fabulous mosaics. A vineyard on the slopes near the villa continues a tradition of wine-making begun in Roman times. In 1338 an embankment was built at Yar Bridge, creating a harbour to connect Bembridge Down with the rest of the Isle of Wight. Brading was an important port, but the harbour here, too, experienced increased silting. It was reclaimed in 1878–80 and is now an area of marshy meadows, a breeding ground for birds.

As well as the vineyard and Roman Villa, Brading is also home to the interesting Lilliput Museum of Antique Dolls and Toys, which has more than 2,000 exhibits. In the town centre, look out for the whipping post and stocks outside the Old Town Hall. For walkers, nearby Brading and Arreton Downs are great places for a walk, with breathtaking sea views. The pretty Church of St Mary, the Isle of Wight's oldest church, is believed to mark the spot where St Wilfred converted the island to Christianity, and a chapel contains the tombs of the Oglander family, important in affairs of the island for 800 years.

To the northwest, Nunwell House, seat of the Oglanders, is where Charles I spent his last night on the island.

CARISBROOKE MAP REF 400 E7

Carisbrooke, once the capital of the Isle of Wight, is inland above the Medina River to the west of the modern capital, Newport, and is overlooked by its impressive castle. The High Street is pleasant, and narrow Castle Street leads up from an old ford and a streamside footpath to get to the castle. St Mary's Church, with its lofty 15th-century tower, was the church of a priory dissolved as long ago as 1415.

Carisbrooke Castle is a big, well-preserved Norman fortress built high on an artificial mound. The oldest parts are the keep and the surviving sections of curtain walls, which were constructed in the 12th century and strengthened at the end of the 16th century. A head for heights is needed to walk the ramparts, but you will be rewarded with excellent views of the interior of the castle and the surrounding countryside. A very popular attraction is the well, 161 feet (49m) deep, with a 16th-century wheel to draw up the water in buckets. It is worked today by donkeys – learn more of this at the Donkey Centre. The castle also houses the Isle of Wight Museum.

COWES MAP REF 400 E7

Cowes, on the island's northern tip, is divided by the River Medina. On the west bank is the sailing capital of Britain, on the east is a residential and industrial area,

where high-speed ships, flying boats and seaplanes were built during World War II, and the Hovercraft was developed. Beyond all this lies the peace of Osborne House, Queen Victoria's favourite residence.

West Cowes, home of the Royal Yacht Squadron, has an attractive winding High Street and a good array of shops. You can see ships and boats of all sorts from the Victoria Parade. The inaugural Cowes Regatta took place between naval vessels in 1776, and the yacht club was founded in 1815. In 1856 Cowes Castle became the Squadron's headquarters, and the 22 brass guns from the *Royal Adelaide*, King William IV's yacht, were positioned in front of the castle to start races and salute victorious yachts – as they still do. There have always been Royal yachtsmen – including Edward VII, George IV, George V, Prince Philip and Prince Edward – and during Cowes Week in August the little town is alive with the great and the good of the yachting fraternity.

Cowes has a good Maritime Museum, a military history museum, as well as the Sir Max Aitken Museum, which has nautical instruments and paintings.

FRESHWATER MAP REF 400 E7

The southwest tip of the Isle of Wight which ends in the jagged sea-girt chalk pinnacles of The Needles is known as the Freshwater Peninsula. The village of Freshwater itself is large and bustling,

and was made famous by poet Alfred, Lord Tennyson who came to reside at Farringford – now a hotel – in 1853, soon after he was proclaimed Poet Laureate. The famous portrait photographer Julia Margaret Cameron settled here also, in the 1860s. Her home, Dimbola Lodge, on Terrace Lane, is now a museum.

THE NEEDLES & ALUM BAY
MAP REF 400 D7

The soaring, spiky chalk outcrops of The Needles are the Isle of Wight's most famous landmark. They sport a red-and-white striped lighthouse, topped by a small helicopter landing platform, which is best seen via boat trips from Alum Bay.

Set at right angles to the chalk, the cliffs at Alum Bay produce the island's most unusual souvenirs: clear glass novelty items that display the distinctive 12 shades of sand. The colours range from pink and gold to orange and brown, and are all found naturally in the cliffs here.

The sandstone strata of the cliffs are vertical, and were formed some 50 million years ago. You can view them from a spectacular chairlift ride down the cliffs to the beach at the bottom.

On the cliff edge is a monument to the Italian physicist and inventor, Marconi, who set up a wireless and telegraph station here at the end of the 19th century.

The Needles Old Battery at Totland is a

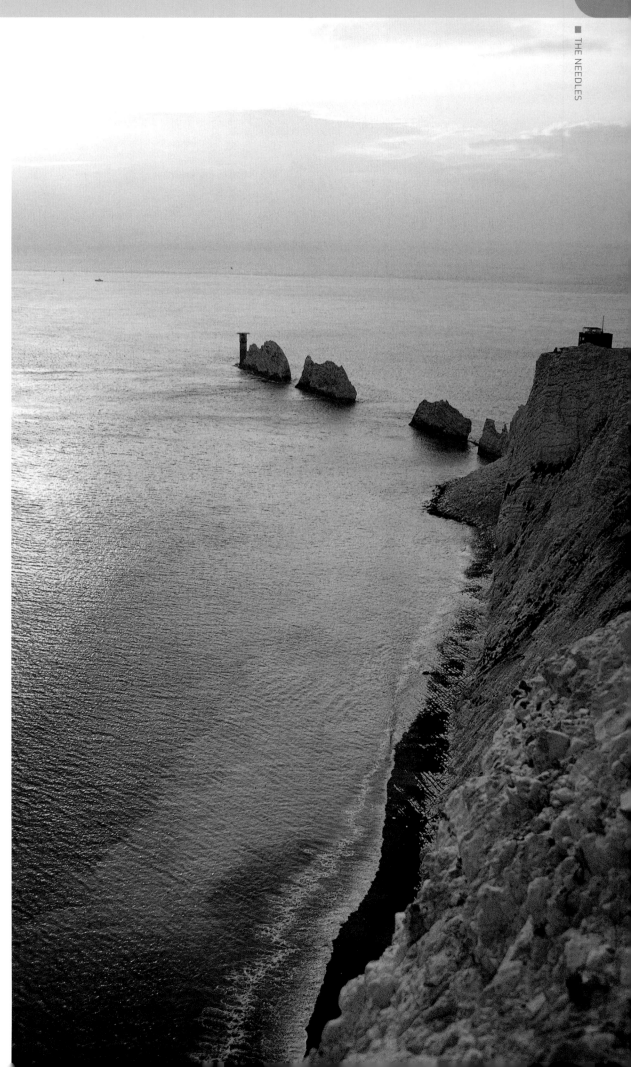

gun battery and fort with wonderful views over the Needles. It was built in 1863 as part of the defences for the large naval base at Portsmouth. Exhibitions tell the story of the fort during the world wars.

NEWPORT MAP REF 400 E7

Newport, the capital of the Isle of Wight, is a venerable old market town on the River Medina. Its squares and narrow, twisting streets may hide the river from view, but boats still ply their trade at the rejuvenated quay. Here, too, is the arts centre in a large converted warehouse. The pleasant High Street has many attractive buildings, and is dominated by the Guildhall, with its fine Ionic portico market designed by John Nash, now home to the Museum of Island History. St Thomas' Church has a beautiful marble monument designed by Marochetti to Princess Elizabeth, the youngest daughter of Charles I. She died of a fever aged 14 while she was a prisoner in Carisbrooke Castle.

A Roman villa, dating from the 3rd century AD, was discovered here in 1926. The villa has been excavated and is open to the public. Three of the public rooms have tessellated floors, and the largest also has a fireplace – this was an unusual feature in a Roman house. There is also a reconstructed Roman herb garden.

Northwest of the town is Parkhurst Prison, beyond which is Parkhurst Forest, the remaining glades and woodlands of a former royal hunting forest. This ancient woodland has been threaded by waymarked paths and is now one of the last remaining refuges of the red squirrel.

RYDE MAP REF 400 E7

When island visitors disembark at Ryde from the ferry, ex-London Transport underground trains take them down the 0.5-mile (800m) long pier, necessary because the coast shelves so gently that vessels can get no closer.

Ryde was developed in the late 18th century and is the largest town on the island, with some 24,000 residents. It has the usual seaside amusements as well as a 5-mile (8km) sandy beach. Ryde's summer carnival is a spectacular event.

Southwest of Ryde is Brickfields Horse Country, with horses of all sizes, wagon rides and pig-racing. At Ashey, Rosemary Vineyard, the largest of the island's three, offers tours, tastings and a shop. At Fishbourne, to the west, is Quarr Abbey, a modern foundation (1907–14) of Benedictine monks near the ruins of the earlier Cistercian Abbey. The Isle of Wight Steam Railway puffs out of Smallbrook Junction, just south of Ryde on its journey past Havenstreet to Wootton.

SANDOWN & SHANKLIN

MAP REF 400 E7 & 400 E8

The honky-tonk seaside neighbour of more sedate Shanklin, Sandown was founded as a resort in about 1800 and faces southeastwards out to sea across Sandown Bay. It is built at beach level, with the huge chalk walls of Culver Cliff to the north and the cliffed coast of Shanklin and Luccombe to the south. Sandown is a popular venue for family holidays, with its 6 miles (9.6km) of sandy beach and an esplanade and amusement park, a pier of 1878, cinema, zoo specializing in tigers and lemurs, and the fascinating Dinosaur Isle, a museum displaying life-size dinosaurs and offering guided fossil walks. At the Garlic Farm, near Newchurch, you can buy and learn more.

Shanklin, Sandown's quieter southern neighbour, is a resort that developed with the coming of the railway in 1891, and now has the best collection of beach huts on the island. You reach the beach by a lift from the clifftop, which has a superb view around Sandown Bay to the gleaming white heights of Culver Cliff. Inland is Shanklin Old Village, a former fishing village close to the winding glen of Shanklin Chine. This 300-feet (91.5m) deep, wooded and ferny fissure was much beloved of earlier tourists, including the poet, John Keats, who stayed at the Old Village in 1819 and composed part of 'Endymion' here. The Victorians flocked to tread its winding path past the 40-foot (12m) waterfall to the beach. Today, Shanklin Chine still pulls the crowds – its rare flora is of great interest – and the resort also has two theatres and seaside amusements.

VENTNOR MAP REF 400 E8

This south coast resort climbs the sheer cliff beneath flat St Boniface Down (the highest point on the island), as a series of terraces behind the sandy beach, so that the mainly Victorian buildings are built-up in layers and are joined by steep zig-zagging roads with corkscrew turns. There is something Mediterranean in this arrangement, and Ventnor has been dubbed 'the English Madeira'. Also the climate, too, is very good. Protected by the bulk of St Boniface Down, it basks in subtropical conditions.

Ventnor was a small fishing village up until 1841 – albeit much involved in smuggling – but in that year, a famous doctor, Sir James Clarke, publicly sang its praises and visitors started to come. The railway arrived in 1866, meaning Ventnor's development as a health resort was assured, attracting, among others, authors Macaulay, Dickens and Thackeray. Later it was the site of the Royal National Hospital for Consumption and Diseases of the Chest. The town's history is explained in Ventnor's Heritage Museum which has an extensive archive.

Ventnor divides into two parts, the elegant 'town' on the cliff face, where Ventnor ales are still brewed, and the seaside resort at the foot of the cliff.

The extraordinary climate is manifest in the Ventnor Botanic Gardens, which were planted in the 1970s, where some 3,500 species include palms and cork trees. The interesting Smuggling Museum, hidden in subterranean caverns beneath the Botanic Garden, has a large collection of fascinating relics, vividly illustrating the days when Ventnor was the unofficial 'headquarters' of illicit trade. Near by is the ancient village of St Lawrence with the Rare Breeds and Waterfowl Park. Isle of Wight Glass produces an exciting range of award-winning glassware.

The southern coast between Ventnor and St Catherine's Point is a region of landslides, where great masses of sandstone rock have been, and continue to be, carried down into the sea on a lubricating layer of blue clay. In fact, Ventnor has the biggest urban landslide problem in Britain. The Undercliff, a ledge which extends along the cliffs, is actually the top of an ancient landslide block. To appreciate the coast to the full, walk along part of the coastal path between Shanklin and Blackgang. From Shanklin the path first lies close to, and then on, the shore until you reach Ventnor and beyond. At St Lawrence, the path climbs up beyond the road and affords good views to the south before you reach Blackgang.

Nearby Blackgang Chine is an extraordinary theme park that combines static displays with fast fairground rides and lovely gardens. In fact the gardens were the initial inspiration for the park, created to attract Victorian vacationers.

WROXALL MAP REF 400 E8

The village of Wroxall was once no more than a small hamlet but the construction of the railway through a 0.75mile (1.2km) tunnel changed that and many of the old cottages in the main street were built to house the railway workmen. The village nestles in the downs and has a handsome Victorian church built from stone excavated in the tunnel workings. From Wroxall there are lovely walks to Ventnor, Shanklin, Whitwell and Godshill. The most notable attraction in Wroxall is Appuldurcombe House, once the most imposing house on the Isle of Wight and home to the Worsley family for 300 years. It then had a chequered history and the majority of the house was left as an impressive shell surrounded by 'Capability' Brown landscape. Now managed by English Heritage the front section of the building has been re-roofed and glazed and a portion of the interior has been recreated in all its 18th century baroque glory. This is open to the public from April to September. Appuldurcombe House also has an Owl and Falconry Centre.

YARMOUTH MAP REF 400 E7

The Lymington–Yarmouth ferry is the picturesque way of entry to the Isle of Wight, for Yarmouth is a compact little town with narrow streets and attractive houses, and a small harbour busy with yachts and a flourishing boatbuilder's yard. During the Middle Ages it was the most important Isle of Wight town, but decline set in and by 1800 it had only a few hundred inhabitants.

Yarmouth's sturdy castle was built against the French in 1547 by Henry VIII, and it remained in use until the 1870s.

It is hidden down an alley by the ferry, on King's Land, and is easy to miss. The pier near the lifeboat station was built in 1876 and was originally the landing stage for the Lymington ferry, but now it is a pleasant walkway.

Yarmouth's church, rebuilt 1614–26, contains an intriguing monument to Sir Robert Holmes, Governor of the Isle of Wight during the reign of Charles II. The figure was originally intended as a statue of the French 'Sun King', Louis XIV. The statue was being transported by sea so that the sculptor would be able to complete the head from life, but Holmes captured the ship carrying it, took the statue and had his own likeness attached to it instead. Holmes entertained Charles II at his house on the quay in Yarmouth, now the George Hotel.

West of Yarmouth is the 50-acre (20ha), wooded, Fort Victoria Country Park, based around the remains of a fort which was built in 1855. The many parts of the park afford superb views of the River Solent, and there are guided walks, a maritime heritage exhibition, a marine aquarium, a planetarium and a little model railway.

VENTNOR

FRESHWATER BAY

This ramble encapsulates the contrasting landscapes, from the wildlife-rich tidal estuary of the River Yar and the wetland habitat of freshwater marshes housing wild birds, to farmland and the magnificent chalk headlands.

1 From the car park, turn right along the road, then left before the bus shelter along a metalled track, signed 'Coastal Path'. After 50yds (46m) bear right through a gate and follow the well-walked path through a gateway and up to the memorial cross at the summit of Tennyson Down.

2 Continue down the wide grassy swathe, which narrows between gorse bushes, to reach the replica of the Old Nodes Beacon. Here, turn very sharp right down a chalk track. At a junction (car park right) keep straight on up the narrow path.

3 The path widens, then descends to a gate leading into woodland. Proceed close to the woodland fringe before emerging into more open countryside. Just beyond a disused pit on your right, fork left at a waymark post down a narrower path. Cross a stile, then follow the enclosed path as it turns sharp left to another stile. Cross the next field to a stile and turn right to walk along the field-edge to a further stile.

4 Cross a farm track, go through a gate and walk along the track (F47) beside Farringford Hotel. Pass beneath a wooden footbridge and continue downhill to a gate and the road. (Turn left if you wish to visit the hotel). Turn right; then, opposite the thatched church,

turn left down Blackbridge Road. Just before Black Bridge, turn left into Afton Marshes Nature Reserve.

5 Join the nature trail, following it across a footbridge and beside the stream to the A3055 (this can be very wet in winter). Turn left and almost immediately cross over to join a bridleway (F61) along the course of the old railway. In 0.5 mile (800m) reach the Causeway. Turn left here to visit Freshwater church and the Red Lion.

6 On this shorter walk turn right and continue to the B3399. Turn left and shortly cross on to unmetalled Manor Road. In a few paces, bear left , signed 'Freshwater Way', and ascend across grassland towards Afton Down.

7 Keep ahead at a junction of paths beside the golf course, soon to follow the gravel track right to the clubhouse. Go through a gate and pass in front of the building to reach the access track, keeping left to the A3055. Turn right downhill into Freshwater Bay.

DISTANCE/TIME 5.75 miles (9.2km) 3h **MAP** OS Explorer OL29 Isle of Wight **START** Ferry terminal or pay-and-display car park opposite, Freshwater; grid ref: SZ 346857 **PATHS** Downland, field and woodland paths, some road walking and stretch of disused railway; 4 stiles

THE PUB The Red Lion, Church Place, Freshwater. Tel: 01983 754925

WALK 34

BLACKGANG CHINE & THE PEEPING PEPPERPOT

This intriguing ramble is around an area steeped in tales about shipwrecks, smuggling and three lighthouses. Before you lies the broad sweep of Chale Bay and high upon St Catherine's Hill to your right is a curious octagonal tower, known locally as 'the Pepperpot', all that remains of a medieval lighthouse or beacon.

1 From the car park, cross the road and climb steps to a gate. Bear left, signposted towards 'St Catherine's Oratory'. Pass a broken stile and steadily climb up the grassy downland to a stile. Walk up to the old lighthouse, known locally as 'the Pepperpot'. Ignore the stile by the trig point just beyond; then, keeping the fence on your right, continue downhill and bear left to a gate.

2 Go through the gate and proceed ahead on the broad grassy swathe to Hoy's Monument. Return for 80yds (73m) and take the bridleway left. Descend steeply through trees and bear left with the main path downhill to a gate. Follow the bridleway left, then bear right along the driveway.

3 Proceed ahead at a crossing of tracks (Downcourt Farm drive is to the right), heading downhill to a gate by a house. Walk along the right-hand field-edge to a gate and head downhill on a hedged path. At a T-junction, turn right and go through a gate, the path soon emerging into a field.

4 Keep to the left-hand field-edge, beside an overgrown gully, and cross the first stile on the left. In a few paces, turn right, then take the path left just before another gate. Head through the trees, cross a concrete

bridge and keep right. Gradually ascend a stony path, which is very wet in winter, and which bears left then steepens to a stile.

5 Follow the defined path uphill beside a hedge to two stiles in the field corner. Cross the right-hand stile and immediately turn right, down on to a path that heads diagonally uphill across the face of Head Down to a stile. Turn left to a stile and track.

6 Turn left, then almost immediately right along a hedged bridleway. Head downhill, the path becoming metalled as it enters Niton. Just before the lane, bear right into the churchyard. (Turn left, then first right, for the White Lion). Keep left, exit the churchyard by a small gate and then turn right alongside the A3055.

7 Take the footpath beside the last house on the left and climb up steeply through trees to a stile. Walk ahead across grassland to a stile and follow the left-hand field-edge to a kissing gate.

8 Turn right along the coastal path, through two kissing gates and soon emerge on to open cliff top. Remain on this narrow path close to the cliff edge for nearly a mile (1.6km) back to the car park.

DISTANCE/TIME 5.5 miles (8.8km) 2h **MAP** OS Explorer OL29 Isle of Wight **START** Viewpoint car park above Blackgang Chine; grid ref: SZ 490767 **PATHS** Field paths, downland tracks, coast path; 8 stiles **THE PUB** The White Lion, Niton. Tel: 01983 528479

Cowes Week

More than a century old, and part of our heritage, Cowes Week is the premier sailing event in Britain. But then Cowes Week is all about boats: big boats, little boats, fast boats, slow boats, expensive boats, and some very, very expensive boats.

So successful has the event become that today it is the longest-running regatta in the world, the first official regatta taking place in 1812, on the Isle of Wight, accompanied by a review of the Trinity House Pilots. That first race was not for money, but for a gold cup with a value of £100.

Many believe that Cowes owes its name as the yachting capital of the world to the building of a small boat for Elizabeth I. Royal patronage was sure to start a trend, but it took a while for sailing as a leisure pastime to catch on. In fact, although the Dutch developed leisure yachting in the meantime, 260 years and nine monarchs were to go by before the interest of the then Prince of Wales was to flourish into organized yachting after his succession to the throne. In 1826 the Royal Yacht Squadron formally organized three whole days of racing in the waters of the Solent.

Cowes Regatta itself had been going before The Yacht Club (as the Squadron was first known) was founded in 1815, and was based around the local Pilot Cutters receiving their licences. The event we know today has been held during the first week in August continuously every year except during the world wars. Now, Cowes Week hosts more than 1,000 competing boats.

Until 1914 big cutters raced, but the inter-war years saw the introduction of cruiser handicap classes, although the 6–8 and 12 metre boats attracted the most racing interest. After 1946, when for a few years there was a revival of big yacht racing, ocean racing classes started to predominate, especially after the first competitive race for the Admiral's Cup in 1957. The two ocean races that start and finish the week – the Channel and Fastnet races – began to gain in popularity. Because the Fastnet Race is held in odd-numbered years only, another offshore course is sailed in even years to attract ocean racers to the regatta.

After World War II yachting changed from being solely the province of the rich to a sport for the enthusiast. Today it is, arguably, a sport mainly for rich enthusiasts, but it remains no less exciting to see the Solent crowded, sometimes perilously, with hundreds of tiny spectator boats.

Despite being a regatta for thousands of sailors, Cowes Week is a huge moment in the British social calendar, taking place after the Goodwood and Ascot horse-racing festivals.The event maintains the same traditions of glittery yacht club balls, dinners, cocktail parties and concerts throughout the week, almost 200 years on.

The Solent is a unique stretch of water characterized by its tides and challenges, and during Cowes Week this busy waterway is filled with hundreds of racing boats and up to 300 bobbing spectator boats. All the races take place on the Solent, the sheltered waters and irregular tides of which invariably produce challenging, unusual and unpredictable conditions for the competitors. It gives even the most experienced helmsman and crew plenty of 'moments' and a non-stop sequence of problems to solve.

TOP LEFT The ABN AMRO ONE crew are seen concentrating and hard at work on the gruelling seventh day of racing.

TOP MIDDLE Competing is the name of the game at Cowes Week, whether it be in the races or the Timberland Tug of War.

TOP RIGHT Perhaps the most famous yachtswoman, Dame Ellen MacArthur, assisted on this occasion by her sailing partner Giles Chichester, sails in to Cowes at the helm of the legendary and newly restored *Gipsy Moth IV*.

LEFT The Class 1 fleet makes an awe-inspiring spectacle as it gets underway on sparkling water and under blue skies.

BELOW An exciting moment as the fleet of racers assembles on the start line off the Royal Squadron.

OPPOSITE A Sigma 33 broaches dangerously as she goes all out to reach the finish line on a blustery day at Skandia Cowes Week.

Despite the name, Cowes 'Week' actually runs for eight days, with at least 35 starts each day from the Royal Yacht Squadron, and around 1,000 racing boats taking part in the same number of classes. Each class is made up using the International Rating System which ranks the yachts' individual measurements. Traditionally, Class Zero has the largest boats (which are up to 98ft/30m long) and Class Seven, the smallest. The creation of a Super-Zero class in 2007, with its own race series, is a shrewd move intended to entice the owners and skippers of the world's largest and fastest ocean-racing yachts to compete.

This very British regatta is open to seasoned sailors and amateurs alike. More than 8,000 people are on the water each day, competing in dozens of different classes. To help further pack the overcrowded Solent, Cowes Week also hosts visiting foreign warships, sail training vessels and celebrated high profile maxi and round-the-world yachts.

For landlubbers, the highlight of the week's evening activities is the famous fireworks display held on the final Friday, and attracting a crowd of over 170,000 people. Princes Green is the place to be, if watching rather than messing about on boats is your preference. Claim a space early, take refreshments, a blanket, warm clothing, a woolly bobble hat, a cuddly toy or a loved one, and watch the yachts battle it out to the finish line. Don't go home too early: there will often be events on the water after the main racing has finished late in the afternoons.

For the non-expert, Cowes Week is a magical mystery mélange of rigging, canting keels, multihulls, monohulls, success, failure and champagne. But like most spectator sports, you don't have to fully understand what's going on to have fun.

DISTANCE/TIME 8 miles (12.9km) 1h45 **MAP** OS Explorer OL29 Isle of Wight **START** Medina Road pay-and-display car park, West Cowes; grid ref: SZ 499956 **TRACKS** Back streets of Cowes, tarred and level cycle track **THE PUB** The Bargeman's Rest, Newport. Tel: 01983 525828; www.bargemansrest.com

DISTANCE/TIME 16 miles (25.7km) 1h45 **MAP** OS Explorer OL29 Isle of Wight **START** Shalfleet village car park; grid ref: SZ 415895 **CYCLE HIRE** Wavells Cycle Hire, Yarmouth. Tel: 01983 813813 **TRACKS** Country lanes, old railway tracks, bridleways **THE PUB** New Inn, Shalfleet. Tel: 01983 531314; www.thenew-inn.co.uk

A LINEAR RIDE FROM COWES TO NEWPORT

This ride makes a relaxed day out, with easy access from the mainland. There is a lot to see from the safe, level trail, which follows the National Cycle Network route along the former Cowes-to-Newport railway line. You'll enjoy lovely views across the River Medina, with plenty of birdwatching on the way.

1 From Medina Road turn into Bridge Road, signposted 'Newport via cycleway'. Follow the road to the mini-roundabout at the top of the hill and turn left into Arctic Road, still following the signposted cycle route. Pass the UK Sailing Academy on your left and continue to the very end of the road.

2 Zig-zag right and left as the cycle route joins the old railway line, which edges its way clear of industrial Cowes through a tunnel of trees. Pass the signposted footpath to Northwood on your right and, a little further on, look for the remains of an old bridge.

3 Beyond the bridge, look for a tall spire and pinnacles above the trees across the river. Around 0.5 mile (800m) from the gates of Osborne House, St Mildred's church was remodelled in the mid-18th century for use by the royal family. Continue on the track.

4 Now the views really open up, and between Pinkmead and Stag Lane you'll spot the old Ryde paddle steamer slowly rusting at Island Harbour Marina on the opposite bank. The hedges are thick with blackthorn, dog rose and crab apple, and in summer you'll see red admiral butterflies and dragonflies. Listen for the plaintive call of curlews.

5 The trail crosses the old trestle viaduct that once carried the railway line over Dodnor Creek. This area of open water, marshland and woodland was created in the 1790s when the creek was dammed to provide power for a proposed tide mill. Today the creek is a local nature reserve and you may see reed warblers, coots, moorhens and grey herons. Beyond the creek the cycleway climbs across Dodnor Lane and approaches industrial buildings on the edge of Newport. Look for a pair of concrete tracks that cross the trail and lead to a pair of slim concrete jetties built out into the river. A rolling gantry loads industrial products on to waiting barges. The facility was specially designed to minimize disturbance to the birds feeding on the mudflats of this protected wildlife site. Soon, reach the white gate at the end of the traffic-free route. Continue straight ahead as far as the post-box on the corner of Hurstake Road. Turn left to The Bargeman's Rest, and bear right at the bottom of the hill for the final 300yds (273m) to the pub.

6 Take a break before retracing your route to Cowes.

EXPLORING WEST WIGHT

The countryside between the high chalk hills of Compton and Brighstone Downs and Newtown Creek on the north coast is a joy to explore by bike.

1 Turn right out of the car park and return down the lane to the pub and road junction. Bear right, then left along Church Street, following the lane to a T-junction. Turn left, pass the post office and follow the lane for just under 1 mile (1.6km) to a second T-junction. Turn left, then right along Wellow Road, signposted 'Wellow and Thorley', and remain on this road for 2 miles (3.2km) to a T-junction beyond Thorley.

2 Turn right towards Yarmouth and near the outskirts, take the waymaked bridleway left, signposted Freshwater, and join the old railway track. Just past the former railway station, take the tarmac path right to visit Yarmouth, soon to turn left along Station Road, then right along Mill Road into the town. Retrace the route back to the old railway track. Follow this delightful trail beside the River Yar for 1.5 miles (2.4km) to the Causeway. Turn right to visit Freshwater church, otherwise turn left to reach the B3399.

3 Turn left and follow this open and wide road, which can be busy (great care to be taken), for 3 miles (4.8km) below Compton Down. Descend to a crossroads and turn left, signed to Newbridge. After a short climb the road levels and look out for a waymarked bridleway along the concrete drive to Eades Farm. (For the shorter route – keep on the lane to a T-junction and cross straight over to follow a bridleway for 0.5 mile (800m) to a road. Turn right and retrace your route back to Shalfleet and the New Inn).

4 For the longer route, turn right for Eades Farm, pass barns, keep left along a track and soon follow the narrow tarmac lane past houses to a T-junction on the edge of Newbridge. Turn right, then left for Lower Mill and Five Houses. Keep straight on at a T-junction, signed 'Five Houses', soon to follow the narrow lane left to the A3054.

5 Turn right, then left just beyond the bus park to follow a narrow unsigned lane. At the staggered crossroads, go across, signed 'Newtown'. Pass Waiter's Copse and soon turn sharp left to enter Newtown. Keep ahead past a distinctive house (Noah's Ark) and the Old Town Hall and drop downhill to cross a bridge. At the T-junction turn right, then take the first turning right, a lane, signed 'Coastal Path'. Bear right at the end. Follow the path across a footbridge and past a mill to reach a lane. Turn left to the car park.

Winchester & North Downs

CLOCKWISE FROM TOP LEFT: ALRESFORD STATION; SHOP SIGN, WINCHESTER; BOOKSHOP IN BROAD STREET, ALRESFORD; THE 13TH-CENTURY FULLING MILL IN ALRESFORD; CEILING OF WINCHESTER CATHEDRAL

ALRESFORD MAP REF 400 E6

Lovely Alresford, with its wide streets of Georgian houses of brick and stucco, lies in the broad valley of the River Alre, hence the name (pronounced 'Allsford'). It is really two places – Old Alresford to the north of the river, which is now no more than a village with an adjoining park, and New Alresford, the attractive busy market town to the south which was 'new' in about 1200. Sitting between the two is Alresford Pond, created by Godfrey de Lucy, Bishop of Winchester, in the 13th century. Its dam, the Great Weir, is the largest non-military medieval earthwork in England and the only one that still serves this original dual purpose of dam and road causeway. Today

its 30 acres (12ha) are a haven for wildlife and also feed the famous ancient local watercress beds.

New Alresford retains its medieval street plan, with a T-shape formed by the spacious elegant Broad Street and West and East Streets; the old Winchester–London road. A borough by 1294, New Alresford was one of England's greatest wool markets. Two mills survive: the Town Mill and the old Fulling Mill. Fires devastated the town between the early 15th century and 1689, which accounts for its mainly Georgian appearance.

Approach from Old Alresford or from Bishop's Sutton for the most attractive introduction to the town – the south

approach from Cheriton leads through less inviting modern suburbs. Strolling through New Alresford is a delight. The town has a variety of interesting shops and some excellent craft workshops, and Broad Street, with its line of lime trees and pretty old-fashioned lamps, is one of Hampshire's finest streets.

Mary Russell Mitford, author of the classic *Our Village*, was born at 27 Broad Street in 1787 and lived there until she was ten, when she moved with her father to Three Mile Cross near Reading – the village of her book. She later wrote, 'Alresford is or will be celebrated in history for two things: the first, to speak modestly, is my birth, the second is cricket'. Few

today would associate Alresford with cricket, but Taylor of Alresford, a member of the famous Hambledon Club was born here, and cricket writer and commentator John Arlott once lived at the Old Sun. Today Alresford is better known for its watercress beds and its steam railway, Mid-Hants Railway (the Watercress Line).

North of Alresford, Northington Grange is the dramatic empty shell of a neoclassical mansion, where the 1999 movie *Onegin* was filmed.

CHAWTON MAP REF 400 F6

Jane Austen's house at Chawton has become an international literary shrine, helped by popular TV and feature-film adaptations of her novels. Once on a busy road junction between Guildford, Winchester and Portsmouth, the unspoiled village of Chawton today is even quieter than it was in Jane Austen's time, but you can easily imagine her walking out along the lanes to visit neighbours.

Jane's brother Edward installed his widowed mother and sisters, Jane and Cassandra, at Chawton in 1809; his improvements for the house included the sash window with its Gothic arches on the right of the entrance. The women settled into a domestic routine whereby Cassandra kept house and her mother looked after the garden. This left Jane, whose main duty was preparing breakfast, free to write at her tiny 12-sided table, alerted to visitors by a creaking door that was deliberately left un-oiled. It was here that Jane revised *Sense and Sensibility* and the much-loved *Pride and Prejudice*, published in 1811 and 1813, and wrote *Mansfield Park*, *Emma* and *Persuasion*.

The rooms and gardens are as they would have been in Regency times, with a 'square piano' that visitors are very welcome to play and numerous family mementoes: the family teapot, the patchwork quilt made by the three ladies with tiny lozenge-shaped patches, family letters and portraits, and the donkey carriage that took them shopping in the nearby market town of Alton. Perhaps most evocative for devotees of the novels are Jane and Cassandra's topaz crosses, presents from their sailor brother Charles. Fanny Price, heroine of *Mansfield Park*, also receives an amber cross from her seafaring brother, and suffers much social embarrassment about the choice of gold chain to wear with it.

SELBORNE MAP REF 400 F6

Gilbert White's House takes up a long section of Selborne's characterful High Street, as befits the home of its most celebrated resident. Gilbert White (1720–93) is best known for his *Natural History*

THE WATERCRESS LINE, ALRESFORD

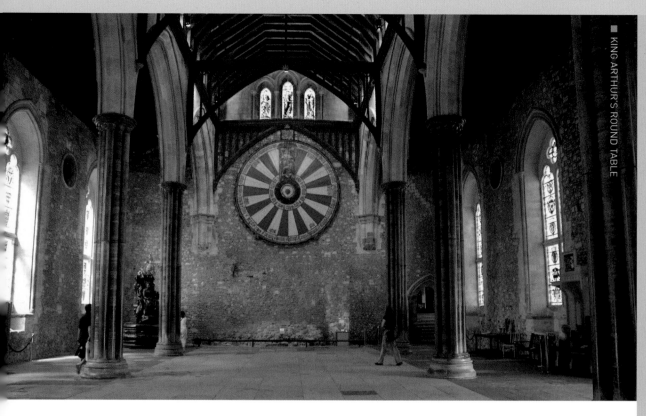

KING ARTHUR'S ROUND TABLE

and Antiquities of Selborne, observations of the natural world recorded in the form of a series of letters. It has never been out of print since 1789. At the same time readable and ground-breaking, White's works inspired both the scientific observations of Charles Darwin and the more poetic traditions of English nature writing. He was the first to describe the importance of earthworms in what we now call the ecosystem, and he helped to prove the phenomenon of bird migrations where previously people had speculated that birds hibernated in holes in the ground.

As was still possible in the 18th century, Gilbert White managed to be in the forefront of knowledge in more than one field. He was an antiquarian, as well as an active clergyman and an innovative gardener, doing the best he could on a modest clergy income to follow the horticultural and landscaping advances of his day. His garden, now restored to the form he created, is a delight, with walks meandering round the different areas, right up to the woods. The house re-creates the rooms as they would have been in the 18th century: the study has a dissected bird, grasses, a mouse nest and a deer skull alongside leather-bound volumes, drafts of sermons and a seed catalogue. Downstairs, you can see the original manuscript of the *Natural History*.

Also on the site, the Oates Museum commemorates Captain Lawrence Oates a member of Captain Scott's ill-fated Antarctic Expedition, and his uncle Frank Oates, a naturalist who died young in Africa. Robert Washington Oates, their descendant, helped with the purchase of the Gilbert White House in 1954.

Selborne offers some easy walks into the woods and valleys that White observed so closely, such as the stroll through the churchyard to the enticing grassy valleys of Short Lythe and Long Lythe (National Trust), surrounded by beech woods.

The remains of the Selborne Yew, thought to be around 1,400 years old, stand covered by honeysuckle in the churchyard. Felled by a gale in 1990, this much-loved landmark was replanted but sadly failed to survive. A highly polished section from its largest branch is on display in the church porch, with dates back to 1509 marked on the tree rings. The church door with its ironwork scrolls is even older, dating from the 13th century. Inside, the church is wide and plain, dating from about 1180. The black slab in front of the altar commemorates the life of Gilbert White's grandfather; White himself is buried in the northeast corner of the churchyard, where his simple headstone is almost sunk into the ground.

Selborne has a pottery and a unique gallery showing the work of mouth and foot artists who have attained high artistic standards; the Hampshire Artists Cooperative share the same gallery.

SHIRRELL HEATH   MAP REF 400 E6
Shirrell Heath is an outlying spur of the extensive North Downs, 250 feet (76m) above sea-level. It is well wooded on the north and east slopes, and on the summit are several houses, including a convalescent home. From its isolated position, Shirrell Heath commands a magnificent view of the Hamble and Meon valleys, with the blue hills of the Isle of Wight on the horizon.

WINCHESTER   MAP REF 400 E6
Physically, Winchester is relatively small. Spiritually, emotionally and historically it is large indeed. It was founded shortly before the Romans arrived in Britain, at an important crossing point on the River Itchen. A glance at a map shows how Roman roads radiate from the city like the spokes of a wheel, and certainly Roman Winchester – Venta Belgarum – was as important as this road pattern suggests.

Winchester's influence declined when the Romans left, so that when the shires were created in the 8th century, it did not give its name to the new county. Within a century the situation had been reversed and 'Vintanceastir', as Bede called it, was again ascendant. Alfred the Great made it capital of the West Saxons in AD 871 – Hamo Thorneycroft's statue of him stands in the High Street – and Winchester remained the capital of Wessex and, in a sense, of England, well into Norman times.

The city's prestige began to dwindle again once the Treasury moved to London, but the aura of past greatness lingers and it has been said that Winchester's High Street has 'a greater wealth of historical associations than any other street in England'. Here you will find the Buttercross, the Guildhall of 1713 (now a bank) with its overhanging City Clock, the arcaded, timbered row known as the Pentice, and the 14th-century Westgate, a small fortified gateway that once served as a debtors' prison. Explore the little alleyways off here for a feel of the old medieval city – Abbey Passage, just below the Victorian Guildhall, is one of the best.

Winchester Castle, where both kings Henry III and Henry VIII's elder brother,

Arthur, were born, was destroyed during the Civil War and only the Great Hall remains. The great painted round table-top which hangs on the west wall has been linked to King Arthur, but it was probably made in Tudor times.

The mighty cathedral does not dominate the city, but sits long and low among the trees and lawns of its lovely close. The present solid, squat Norman building was begun in 1097 by Bishop Wakelin on a floating foundation of logs, for the site was half swamp. In the 14th century Bishop William of Wykeham transformed it into the cathedral we see today, replacing the flat roof with great ribs and detailed mouldings, adding tall clustered columns around the original piers, and introducing vast, spacious, elegant fan vaulting.

Winchester Cathedral is dedicated to St Swithun (died AD 862), who was bishop here, and his tomb lies in the cathedral. Also here is the tomb of William II (Rufus) and a plain slab to the novelist, Jane Austen, who died near by in College Street in 1817. Look out for delights such as the richly patterned medieval floor tiles, and a stained glass window in memory of Izaak Walton, the famous angler. During school term time, evensong is sung by the cathedral choir at 5.30pm, Monday to Saturday, and 3.30pm Sunday. Parts of Winchester cathedral doubled as the Vatican for the 2006 blockbuster movie based on Dan Brown's *The Da Vinci Code*.

The cathedral close contains part of the priory destroyed by Henry VIII's officers, and the City Museum, while near by lie the ruins of the enormous Bishops' Palace, Wolvesey, largely demolished in 1800. The buildings of Winchester College, England's oldest public school, founded in 1387, lie at the end of College Street, and may be toured. A mile away to the south, and overlooking the River Itchen, you'll find the beautiful Hospital of St Cross – fine almshouses that date from the 12th century, with a superb Norman church and an ancient tradition of providing beer and bread for wayfarers, still given today on request.

Winchester is not all history though, but is a living city, with excellent shopping, including interesting smaller shops, many good museums including a restored water mill, and a lively arts scene.

South of Winchester, Marwell Wildlife is a family favourite zoological park with lots of animals, including lemurs, monkeys, giraffes, penguins, lions and tigers, and more. Free road trains make getting around the vast 100-acre (40.5ha) park easy, and there are animal shows and 'meet the keeper' sessions during the summer months.

In Romsey, visit King John's Hunting Lodge, now a heritage centre, and pick up a copy of a town trail to assist your exploration.

7 Return to the Broadlands roundabout and turn left for Winchester. Stay on the A3090, passing a turning on the left for Hillier Gardens. Continue through Ampfield and Hursley, a blend of real and mock-Tudor, to Standon. Now retrace your outward route back into the centre of Winchester.

ALONG THE ROMANTIC ROAD

This circular route links the historic centres of Winchester and Salisbury, with their fine cathedrals, and the market towns of Stockbridge and Romsey, set deep in the beautiful Test Valley. The drive takes you through rolling countryside and passes many pretty villages. Along the way you will pass some of the area's most attractive houses and gardens and, if you have time, it's worth stopping at one or two places along the way to stretch your legs and appreciate all that these magnificent homes and their attractive gardens have to offer.

Route Directions

1 Leave the centre of Winchester, following signs for Romsey and the A3090. Pass the hospital, go straight on at a roundabout, and bear right at the next, signed to Romsey. Pass a golf course, left, go through Pitt and down a long hill, to turn right just before the village of Standon, signed to Farley Mount and Sparsholt. Very soon turn left, signed 'Farley Mount', and follow this narrow country lane through trees to the open hilltops for 2 miles (3.2km) to reach Farley Mount Country Park. Keep heading left.

There are several car parks on your right where you can stop and visit the country park. The folly monument is up to your left.

2 The road descends steadily through beautiful chalky landscape. Drive through the pretty village of Ashley with its white-painted church and old well. Bear left at the end of the village for Kings Somborne and Romsey. At the next junction bear left, and pass through the village of Kings Somborne with its pretty thatched houses. Turn right at the end, and right again in front of the Crown Inn on to the A3057. Follow this for 3 miles (4.8km) to a junction on the edge of Stockbridge and turn left at the roundabout, signed Salisbury. Drive through Stockbridge, cross the River Test and immediately turn

left on to a minor road, signed 'Houghton'. This road now runs along largely parallel with the river.

The village of Houghton is long and spread out. Look out for Houghton Lodge, on your left, with its glorious gardens and lawns sweeping down to the peaceful River Test.

3 Continue past the black-and-white timbered Boot Inn. After 2.5 miles (4km) reach a junction. Turn right for Dunbridge, and keep going straight ahead for Mottisfont. Continue on this narrow road through rolling farmland into Mottisfont village. Stop in the village to see the Grade 1 listed St Andrew's Church. Then go on through to visit the famous Abbey and gardens.

Mottisfont Abbey (NT) is adapted from a 12th-century priory. In the gardens are the National Collection of old-fashioned roses.

4 Retrace your route through the village and turn left on Bengers Lane, signed to Dunbridge and Broughton. At the junction with the B3084 turn left down Hatt Hill and go downhill into Dunbridge. Cross over the river and railway line and then turn right, signed to Lockerley. At the junction in Lockerley turn right, signed 'East Tytherley', pass under the railway and then turn left

after the church, for East and West Dean. Pass through Lockerley Green. The hamlet of Lockerley Green is built around a large village green.

5 Cross the railway, pass through East Dean village, and West Dean with its lumber yard and thatched cottages. Turn left by the old brick bridge, signed 'East Grimstead and Salisbury'. Go straight ahead at the junction for East Grimstead, then go under the railway and soon you enter East Grimstead, with its neat little flint church. Turn left, signed to West Grimstead and Salisbury, and keep straight on this road, proceeding through wooded Alderbury. At the junction turn right for Salisbury, and continue downhill to meet the A36. Turn left and follow this into the middle of Salisbury, following signs round the ring road to the Central Car Park.

Explore the medieval city on foot (it is quite compact) taking in the cathedral and the museums that are housed in some of the historic buildings in Cathedral Close.

6 Leave Salisbury on the A36, signed to Southampton. Once you get to the end of the dual carriageway, look out for the viewpoint of Pepperbox Hill to your left. Descend to traffic lights and turn left on the A27, signed to Romsey and Whiteparish. Pass through Whiteparish, with its handsome old houses, and a string of hamlets that follow including Sherfield English. Look out for the bulky Abbey on your left as you descend further towards Romsey. At the junction turn left, signed 'Romsey and Winchester'. Cross the River Test and, when you reach the roundabout by Broadlands, make a left turn to Romsey town centre.

A WALK AROUND THE ALRESFORDS

New Alresford is one of Hampshire's most picturesque small towns. Much of the architecture is Georgian, and a stroll around the three principal streets reveals traditional country-town shops plus outlets selling specialist clothes, antiquarian books and crafts. Close to both Old and New Alresford you will find a network of crystal-clear chalk streams, rivulets and channels that form the rivers Arle and Itchen and the Candover Stream. Since Victorian times these springs and rivers have played a vital role in making Alresford the 'Watercress Capital' of England, and the steam railway once transported watercress across the country.

DISTANCE/TIME 4 miles (6.4km) 2h **MAP** OS Explorer 132 Winchester **START** Pay car park off Station Road, New Alresford; grid ref: SU 588325 **PATHS** Riverside paths, tracks, field, woodland paths and roads **THE PUB** The Bell, New Alresford. Tel: 01962 732429

1 From the car park walk down Station Road to the T-junction with West Street. Turn right, then left down Broad Street and keep left at the bottom along Mill Hill. Half way down turn left into Ladywell Lane and soon join the river bank and pass the attractive, timbered and thatched Fulling Mill Cottage which straddles the River Arle.

2 Continue to the bottom of Dean Lane and then keep to the riverside path. Cross a footbridge over the river, and ascend to pass some cottages. Shortly, a lane merges from your right; follow it for 50yds (46m), then fork right onto the Wayfarer's Walk and continue until you reach a junction of tracks. Bear right uphill to a lane.

3 Turn left, descend to Fobdown Farm and take the track on the right beside the farm buildings. On reaching a T-junction of tracks, turn right and follow the established track for just over 0.5 mile (800m), gently descending into Old Alresford.

4 Pass the lush watercress beds on your right and follow the now metalled lane left, past houses. Turn right beside the green to reach the B3046. Cross over and follow the pavement right to a lane opposite to St Mary's Church.

5 Having visited the church, cross the road and turn left along the pavement to a grass triangle by a junction. Bear right along the lane and take the footpath ahead over a stream and beside watercress beds back to Mill Hill and Broad Street.

WINCHESTER

Explore the ancient town of Winchester with its historic streets and shops, attractive and restful Cathedral Close and Winchester College. Then venture into the countryside along the River Itchen and enjoy the tranquillity of river walks contrasting with the bustle of the city centre.

DISTANCE/TIME 4 miles (6.4km) 2h **MAP** OS Explorer 132 Winchester **START** Pay-and-display car parks in city centre; grid ref: SU 485294 **PATHS** Established riverside paths through water-meadows, 3 stiles **THE PUB** The Westgate Hotel, Winchester. Tel: 01962 820222

1 From King Alfred's statue on the Broadway, walk towards the city centre, passing the Guildhall (tourist information centre) on your left. Join the High Street, then in 100yds (91m), turn left along Market Street. Continue ahead on to Cathedral Green to pass the cathedral's main door.

2 Turn left down a cloister (signed to Wolvesey Castle), then right through the Close, to Cheyney Court and exit via Prior's Gate. Turn left though Kingsgate, with the tiny Church of St Swithun above, then turn left down College Street and shortly pass the entrance to Winchester College. Beyond the road barrier, turn right along College Walk, then turn right at the end of the wall, along a college access road.

3 Go left by a private entrance to reach the college. Follow the path beside the River Itchen for 0.5 mile (800m) to reach a gate and road bridge. Cross over and follow the pleasant riverside gravel path to a gate and then cross open meadow towards the Hosptial of St Cross.

4 Keep left alongside the wall and through an avenue of trees to a stile. Keep ahead on the gravel path to two further stiles and join a farm

track leading to a traffic-free lane. Turn left and continue across the River Itchen to reach a junction of metalled paths by the M3.

5 Turn left along a path. Go under an old railway and pass a gate on your right (access to St Catherine's Hill). Keep left at a fork and drop down to follow a narrow path by the Itchen Navigation. Go through the car park to the road.

6 Turn left across the bridge and take the footpath immediately right. Keep to the path beside the water, disregarding the path left (College nature reserve). Soon cross over the bridge by some rowing sheds to join a metalled track.

7 Turn left, then left again at the road. Follow it right along College Walk and turn right at the end on to a metalled path. Pass the Old Bishops Palace (Wolvesey Castle) and follow the path beside the Itchen to Bridge Street, opposite the National Trust's City Mill. Turn left to King Alfred's statue.

Surrey Heaths

CLOCKWISE FROM TOP: VIEW FROM BOX HILL; GUILDFORD HIGH STREET; FLY AGARIC MUSHROOM, DEVIL'S PUNCHBOWL; GIBBET HILL, DEVIL'S PUNCHBOWL

BOX HILL MAP REF 401 G5

Box Hill, an outstanding area of woodland and chalk downland now in the care of the National Trust, has been a popular and renowned beauty spot for more than 200 years, attracting such literary notables as Jane Austen, Robert Louis Stevenson and John Keats. Its height may be modest at 400 feet (122m) but the views are magnificent. It is the best known summit of the North Downlands, and a rare, natural open space in such close proximity to London, and in summer has a good spread of orchid species to compliment the fine old oaks and beeches. The hill is an extremely good place for walkers, with routes of varying lengths shooting off from the information centre on the summit.

FARNHAM MAP REF 400 F6

A planned settlement, Farnham streets were laid out on a grid pattern in the 12th century, the attractive brick-built town of Farnham nevertheless has a strong Georgian air about it, having been virtually rebuilt on the back of the immense wealth generated by its 18th-century corn market, the largest in England.

Remains of Roman and Saxon dwellings have been found around Farnham, clearly pointing to a community here before the Norman arrivals. And there is evidence that men of the Old Stone or Palaeolithic Age (400,000 years BP) followed the gravel ridge above the present town. In time, Farnham found itself at a crossroads with ancient trails arriving from all directions, and as a result settlement continued and spread during the Bronze and Iron Ages.

In more recent centuries, it became a notable market town and a place that successfully combines the old with the new. Behind the Georgian fronts of some buildings, structures of Tudor and even earlier times are frequently found. The original core of the town has grown and spread over the centuries, and as you walk through its attractive streets today there is a palpable sense of antiquity tastefully blended with modernity.

Farnham Castle, a Norman motte and bailey, first built in 1138 by the Bishop of Winchester, is a fine backdrop to the town and can be seen on the town's approaches. Now in the care of English Heritage, little is known of the first castle other than it had a tower. This was demolished in 1155 on the orders of Henry II, but recent archaeological excavations have revealed the large basement and foundations of the original tower at the centre of the motte. Major rebuilding work took place in the 12th and 13th centuries, with the earlier motte entirely surrounded by a keep. The castle remained a residence of the Bishops of Winchester through to the early 20th century, and much of what is seen today dates from the 15th to 17th centuries. Mary Tudor in fact stayed at the castle on her way to marry Philip of Spain at Winchester Cathedral, and Elizabeth I came to the castle on several occasions.

GODALMING MAP REF 400 F6

Godalming has existed since Saxon times and is even mentioned in the will of Alfred the Great. The name clearly has Saxon origins, 'Godhelms Ingus' roughly meaning 'the family of Godhelm', probably a reference to one of the first lords of the manor. By the time of the Domesday survey, Godalming had a population of 400 people. Then, the manor belonged to the King, but later, ownership was granted to the Bishop of Salisbury by Edward I.

The considerable history of Godalming can be traced in its architecture, from its parish church, which combines a Saxon chancel and Norman tower, to its 19th century town hall, an odd construction nicknamed the Pepperpot, for obvious reason when you see it. The town has more than 200 listed buildings, providing an architectural legacy that embraces everything from Tudor timbers to 17th-century brickwork. Other noteworthy buildings are Edwin Lutyens 'Red House', and a significant English public school, Charterhouse, around a mile (1.6km) from the town on Charterhouse Hill. George Mallory, the British mountaineer who took part in the first three British Expeditions to Everest in the early 1920s, was a teacher at Charterhouse.

Godalming came to world attention in 1881, when it became the first town in the United Kingdom to have a public electricity supply installed. All was not well, however, and for a time the town reverted to gas lighting, before returning to the new system in 1904.

In 1887 Godalming was the birthplace of Chad 'Jack' Demaray, the Senior Wireless Officer on board the maiden voyage of the *Titanic*, and in 1894, of the writer Aldous Huxley, author of *Brave New World*. Television personality of the 1950s and actor, Terry-Thomas, byname of Thomas Terry Hoar Stevens, the mustachioed, gap-toothed comic noted for his film roles as a pretentious, scheming twit, died in Godalming in 1990.

GUILDFORD MAP REF 400 F5

The ancient capital of Surrey, busy Guildford is beautifully located at an ancient ford where the River Wey pushes its way through the North Downs. The town is believed to have been founded by Saxons following the departure of the Romans in AD 410. Just like Godalming, Guildford town was mentioned in the will of Alfred the Great, but grew to prominence with the rebuilding of its castle during the reign of King Henry II.

The modern town is bright and bustling, and has an intriguing menu of architectural styles. Dominated by the 17th-century Guildhall, the town also boasts Abbot's Hospital (1619), Guildford House (1660), and the Royal Grammar School, one of only a few places in Britain with a chained library. As well as a Norman castle there are several other historic buildings of note in Guildford, especially along its axial High Street. On Stag Hill is the modern cathedral (1936–68) designed by Sir Edward Maufe, the second newly sited Anglican cathedral built in England since the Reformation

Genesis, the British progressive rock group noted for their atmospheric sound in the 1970s and extremely popular albums and singles of the 1980s and '90s, was founded in Guildford in 1967 by boyhood schoolmates at the Charterhouse public school in Godalming. Genesis were first known for their songwriting talents and lead singer, Peter Gabriel's uniquely theatrical onstage performances. After their lineup stabilized with the addition of drummer Phil Collins and guitarist Steve Hackett in 1970, the group developed a style that featured heavy synthesizers and musical arrangements emphasizing intricate group performance over the individual pyrotechnics favoured by many of the other progressive rock groups.

Charles Dodgson (better known as Lewis Carroll) (1832-1898), author of *Alice's Adventures in Wonderland* and *Through the Looking-Glass*, used to live in Guildford and is buried in the Mount Cemetery. Other authors from the town include PG Wodehouse (1881), comic novelist, short-story writer, lyricist, and playwright, best known as the creator of Jeeves, the supreme 'Gentleman's gentleman', and Gerald Seymour, who wrote *Harry's Game*.

HASLEMERE MAP REF 400 F6

The small market town of Haslemere lies in a lovely location in a wooded valley near the uplands of Blackdown and Hindhead. Surrey has many charming small towns and villages, but Haslemere has a unique flavour. Situated on the borders of Hampshire and West Sussex, this historic town with its brick and timber, tile-hung houses and cottages, is one of the highlights of the Surrey Hills Area of Outstanding Natural Beauty.

Haslemere is an isolated town. In 1394, Richard II granted the town a charter to hold a weekly market; apart from agriculture, Haslemere had important glass, leather and iron smelting industries. Elizabeth

I declared the town a borough with the right to send two Members to Parliament. Elizabeth also issued a new charter in 1596 confirming the right to hold a weekly market, and granted the right to hold two annual fairs. The town commemorates the charter by holding a biennial Charter Fair in the High Street.

The Dolmetsch family, under the direction of Arnold Dolmetsch, originally from Le Mans in France, were internationally known as performers of early music on authentic instruments, and came to settle in Haslemere in 1916 where they subsequently founded a centre for the study of early music, and an annual summer festival in 1925.

HINDHEAD MAP REF 400 F6

At 800 feet (243m), Hindhead is Surrey's highest village, and enjoys fabulous views. In particular, it is well known for its famous beauty spot the 'Devil's Punch Bowl'. Now a Site of Special Scientific Interest, it was once the haunt of highwaymen and robbers who, not infrequently, met an ignominious end above the Devils Punch Bowl on Gibbet Hill where their remains were hung in chains as a warning to other

would-be robbers. Surrounded by National Trust managed land and with Hindhead Common stretching to the east this is a beautiful and diverse landscape of rolling chalk downs, flower rich grasslands, acid heaths and ancient woodlands that provides some of the best walking in southern England.

John Tyndall (1820-1893), physicist and mountaineer, and an avid promoter of science, died in Hindhead. Tyndall discovered that water vapour absorbs much more radiant heat than the gases of the atmosphere and argued the consequent importance of atmospheric water vapour in moderating the Earth's climate – that is, in the natural greenhouse effect. A man who had climbed Mont Blanc three times, Tyndall claimed that the air around Hindhead was as pure as in Switzerland. Whether for that reason or not is unrecorded, but both Sir Arthur Conan Doyle and George Bernard Shaw lived in Hindhead.

Improved roads and the railway made Hindhead a popular residential choice for a number of eminent Victorians and there are many splendid villas as well as imposing Arts and Crafts houses to admire around the town.

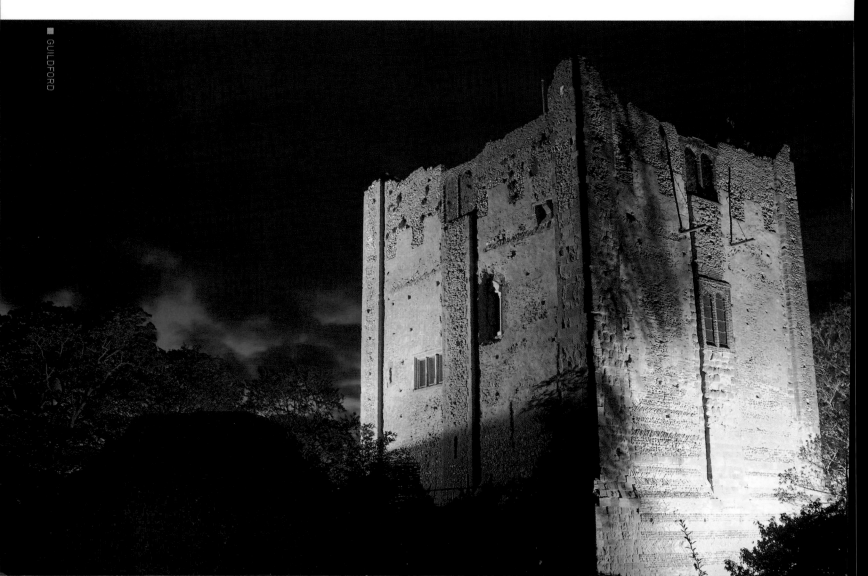

GUILDFORD

BOX HILL

This country park is worth visiting year-round and it is spectacular in the autumn when its trees put on a fine display of fiery colours. As well as its famous box trees, which cling to the steep cliff-face, it was where John Logie Baird, inventor of television, conducted some of his experiments.

DISTANCE/TIME 4 miles (6.4km) 2h   **MAP** OS Explorer 146 Dorking, Box Hill & Reigate
START National Trust car park, Fort Cottages, Box Hill Country Park; grid ref: TQ 178513
PATHS Woodland tracks, with two sections on minor roads **THE PUB** The Running Horses, Mickleham. Tel: 01372 372279

1 Turn left out of the car park, cross over, and follow the roadside path for 0.5 mile (800m). Shortly after you set out, you'll see a path leading down to the viewpoint, built in memory of Leopold Salomons of Norbury Park. The commanding views of Dorking and across the beautiful Mole Valley are well worth the short diversion.

2 A few paces short of the Smith & Western Bar, re-cross the road and then turn off to the left on to the signposted public bridleway. Follow this peaceful signposted route as it drops down through Juniper Bottom to reach Headley Lane.

3 The next few hundred paces are very steep indeed. As an alternative, you can turn left on to Headley Lane, and rejoin the route by turning left on to the Old London Road. This will cut out Mickleham village, and shorten your walk by 0.75 mile (1.2km). Otherwise, cross straight over onto the public footpath and climb up a long flight of rustic steps. Just beyond the top of the steps the path bears right and the gradient eases slightly.

Soon you will come to a bench seat. There are splendid views down the Mole Valley and across to Denbies vineyard from here. Now follow the National Trust's 'long walk' waymarks as you bear left and left again at the next waymark signpost No 6 and drop down over a footpath crossroads with the Thames Down Link, marked by red arrows as a byway open to all traffic. Cross the stile at the foot of the hill, and continue past the church into the village of Mickleham. Turn left, and follow the Old London Road. There's a pavement on the right-hand side to begin with, which at times transforms itself into a pleasant rural path running just a few paces away from the road. By the time you reach the junction with the Zig Zag Road, it's just an ordinary pavement again.

4 Cross over to the junction with the Zig Zag Road, and join the signposted bridleway that climbs steadily all the way back up the hill to the National Trust centre. Near the top, you'll see the old Victorian fort on your right. Turn right at the top of the hill for the last 60yds (55m) back to the car park.

WALK 38

GUILDFORD THROUGH THE LOOKING GLASS

Lewis Carroll, real name Charles Dodgson, author of *Alice's Adventures in Wonderland* and *Through the Looking-Glass*, rented The Chestnuts in Guildford as a family home for his six sisters. Although Dodgson didn't live in the town himself, he visited his sisters regularly and knew Guildford well.

DISTANCE/TIME 4.25 miles (6.8km) 2h   **MAP** OS Explorer 145 Guildford & Farnham
START Farnham Road car park, next to Guildford railway station; grid ref: SU 991494
PATHS Paved streets, downland tracks and riverside towpath **THE PUB** The Red Lion, Shamley Green, Guildford Tel: 01483 892202

1 Leave the car park via the footbridge at Level 5, cross Farnham Road, and turn right. Just beyond the railway bridge drop into the subway on your left, and follow the signposts to the 'Town Centre via Riverside Walk'. Follow the riverside walk to The White House pub. Turn left over the bridge, continue into High Street, and turn first right into Quarry Street. Pass Guildford Museum and turn immediately left through Castle Arch. Your route forks right here, into Castle Hill, but a quick diversion up the pedestrian path straight ahead brings you to the Looking Glass statue in the small garden through an iron gateway on your right. Retrace your steps, and follow Castle Hill past The Chestnuts. Turn left at the top, walk down South Hill, and turn right into Pewley Hill. Climb steadily past the Semaphore House on the corner of Semaphore Road; this was the next station down the line from Chatley Heath. At the end of the road, continue along the bridleway and follow it until you reach the striking viewpoint pillar on the summit of Pewley Down.

2 Fork right at the viewpoint and follow the path off the ridge, keeping the hedge on your left. Soon you'll enter a tunnel of trees, and emerge between hedges. Keep straight on at the crossroads by the Pewley Down information board, and continue uphill for 300yds (273m) until the path meets the North Downs Way National Trail at a blue bridleway marker.

3 Turn right here and follow the waymarked North Downs Way past South Warren Farm to the residential street called Pilgrims' Way. Turn left and follow the road past the junction with Clifford Manor Road.

4 Continue along Pilgrims' Way to the A281. Cross over and walk across Shalford Park, signposted towards Godalming and Shalford. Beyond the trees you'll reach the River Wey; cross the footbridge, and follow the towpath towards Guildford, with the river on your right. Cross the lattice girder footbridge at Millmead Lock, and continue past the 'Alice' statue on the little green near The White House pub. Next, just follow the river bank until you reach the prominent 1913 Electricity Works (now the Electric Theatre) on the opposite bank. Turn left, climb the steps, and retrace your route through the subway to the car park.

South Downs

CLOCKWISE FROM TOP: BUTSER HILL; DITCHLING; SOUTH DOWNS WAY; AMBERLEY CHURCH

ALFRISTON MAP REF 401 H7

With its worn market cross and a flint church on a spreading village green, known as the Tye, Alfriston looks like the ideal English village. The High Street with its narrow pavements has a selection of speciality shops, pubs and tea rooms.

The thatched, half-timbered Clergy House that lies by the green near the churchyard survived thanks to a far-sighted act of conservation in 1896, when it became the very first building bought by the National Trust. It is a classic example of a Wealden Hall, meticulously restored inside and with a delightful strip of cottage garden abutting the river.

The light chalky soils and dry, sunny slopes of the South Downs make for excellent wine-growing conditions. The English Wine Centre, just off the A27 near Alfriston, stocks a good selection of 160 varieties of English wine alongside local preserves, fruit wines and beers and there are tutored wine tastings.

AMBERLEY MAP REF 401 G7

With its thatched houses and idyllic position by water meadows, this village presents a picture of rare perfection. A 10-minute walk from the rail station, it has plenty to fill a day, with walks on to the downs and along the River Arun, and an outstanding industrial museum. There's a view of the extremely imposing curtain wall of the medieval castle (now a smart hotel) from its north side if you walk down to the edge of the village from where the great wetland of Amberley Wild Brooks spreads.

This is an area of water meadows that's now managed as a nature reserve by the Sussex Wildlife Trust and is a prized habitat for dragonflies and, during winter flooding, various wildfowl such as Bewick's swans. A footpath from the village penetrates the reserve and offers a good walk, floods allowing, to Greatham Bridge – a multi-arched stone bridge dating from the 16th century and joined to a metal span over the River Arun. Water meadows like these were created with ditches and sluices, which were flooded in winter, to enrich the farmland with silt. There are trips to here from Arundel during the summer.

Amberley Museum, just outside the village and next to Amberley station, is an open-air industrial museum in a disused chalk pit, with a series of buildings that include a foundry and an old telephone exchange, vintage Southdown buses, resident craftspeople (such as a printer, a potter and a clay-pipe maker), and outdoor displays celebrating the industrial heritage and crafts skills of the southeast. Run by volunteers, it succeeds admirably in bringing the region's working past to life, and there's a lively calendar of events too.

ARUNDEL MAP REF 401 G7

The massive castle towers over Arundel. It was restored and is still occupied by the Dukes of Norfolk, whose ancestors have owned it since 1138. The castle's grounds take up half the hill on which the compact town sits, and you might feel almost on your knees yourself as you approach up steepening pathways.

Today, however, you can visit the castle and explore Arundel's other attractions – enjoyable small shops in the historic centre, a spectacular Victorian cathedral in the French Gothic style and more echoes of France in the shady avenue of Mill Road, popular for parking and picnicking and close to the starting point for river trips to Amberley and the Black Rabbit pub. Beyond here is the Arundel Wetland Centre with its remarkable birdlife and wild flowers.

Arundel's sloping, tapered square with its attractive cobbles and simple war memorial is surrounded by a smart group of individual-looking businesses. Tarrant Street, running off the High Street, has artisan and specialist shops, some in converted Victorian industrial buildings, such as the Old Print Works. Further uphill, Maltravers Street is an elegant mix of 18th-century town houses, with the road running on two levels. On the High Street is the Tourist Information Centre (offering a town audio tour). Nearby Arundel Ghost Experience, in the Old Town Hall, is likely to chill spines of all ages with its ghost stories and sinister prison cells.

Clustered at the top of town is a remarkable collection of religious buildings that could be said to embody Arundel's extraordinary religious history. St Nicholas', Arundel's 14th-century Church of England parish church, backs on to the Fitzalan Chapel (access via the castle grounds), bought by the castle when Henry VIII dissolved its religious foundation and to this day still Catholic.

Arundel Cathedral soars almost opposite. Completed in 1873 by the 15th Duke of Norfolk to celebrate Britain's mid-Victorian Catholic revival, it is an almost perfect-looking re-creation of the French Gothic style of about 1400, with strong vertical lines in honey-coloured Bath stone, flying buttresses and a great rose window. Inside a stained glass window depicts the Earl of Arundel, Philip Howard, who was made a saint in 1970, alongside his faithful wife and dog.

Arundel Castle succeeds in giving a good impression of what entering the castle gates of the country's most powerful Duke might have felt like. The oldest part of the building is the keep, reached by many narrow steps, which has tableaux bringing the Civil War siege to life. Portcullis mechanisms are on view, and there are tremendous panoramas over the town, cathedral, coastal plain and Downs beyond. Of the occupied rooms on show, the Regency Gothic library is perhaps the finest, with its exuberant gilt balconies and plush red velvet sofas. Elsewhere, paintings by Canaletto, Constable, Turner and Van Dyck hang almost casually among hundreds of other works of art, and photographs of the ducal family meeting VIPs, such as popes and royalty, decorate the tabletops.

Outside, near the Fitzalan Chapel, a tea terrace set in beautiful gardens looks across to the cathedral. There's free access to the network of footpaths in the extensive park, which spreads over the Downs and features a large lake.

ARUNDEL CASTLE

BIGNOR MAP REF 400 F7

Tucked in deep countryside beneath a lushly wooded stretch of downs, Bignor village's square of streets boasts some marvellously unchanged old houses, including the Yeoman's House (or Old Shop), a thatched and half-timbered 15th-century cottage with an attractive overhanging upper storey.

Bignor is best known for its Roman villa. At first sight, what you see is a set of thatched buildings. These are shelters, which themselves have become historic structures, put up to protect the Roman remains in the early 19th century by John Hawkins, the landowner. He had the site excavated and transformed it into an early tourist attraction. Inside you can view some of the finest Roman mosaics in Britain, depicting glorious scenes from the lives of gladiators and mythical subjects, and in places you can even walk on the still-durable surface of a Roman floor.

What survives above ground is mainly from the 4th century AD. There's a full-scale bath suite with a cold plunge pool and a heated changing room, warm and hot rooms and a hot bath.

The discovery of Bignor was among the earliest evidence for Roman-style 'civilized' living in the countryside. Many other villas have since been discovered across southern England, usually in the same kind of position with a fine view.

CUCKMERE VALLEY MAP REF 401 H7

Winding its way slowly through the verdant South Downs to finally flow into the sea off the East Sussex coast, the River Cuckmere lies in a valley of beautiful countryside and threads through an area of great ecological importance. However, there are plans to allow the natural flooding of this entire valley as the costs of preventing soil erosion has become prohibitive. This would mean the loss of an Area of Outstanding Natural Beauty, but could be beneficial to the biosphere in the long run.

DITCHLING MAP REF 401 G7

The photogenic old village of Ditchling looks out to one of the choicest, most-frequented parts of the South Downs. The Bull and a couple of tea rooms make good stopping points in the village. The former Victorian school, near the church the Ditchling Museum has a local collection and changing exhibitions. It also remembers the work of pioneer calligraphers Eric Gill and Edward Johnston (who devised the distinctive sans serif script used by London Transport). Gill came here with his apprentice in 1907, and soon a community of craftsmen and artists was established, who adhered to principles of the Arts and Crafts movement; they set up workshops and a chapel, and the community continued until 1989, after which the complex was

demolished. From the village, a road climbs up to Ditchling Beacon, at 813 feet (248m) the highest point on the South Downs. It's a great place to come to for a picnic, fly a kite, paraglide, walk a stretch of the South Downs Way, or just drink in the big view over the Weald and across to the high ridge of greens and hills that include the prominent escarpment of Black Down, the highest point in Sussex at 919 feet (280m). The landscape hereabouts contains all sorts of evidence of prehistoric settlers, including burial mounds and ancient systems, and a stroll eastwards along the top of the escarpment leads close to the site of a Bronze Age settlement at Plumpton Plain.

GLYNDE MAP REF 401 H7

This is still very much an estate village, owned by Glynde Place, the Elizabethan manor house just north. As well as a tea room and pub with a large garden (the Trevor Arms), the village also has its own smithy. Bearing the date of 1907 by its horseshoe-shaped doorway, this has an assortment of tools hanging over a pair of brick-built hearths; the smith makes various types of ironwork.

A signposted path leading off from a stile roughly opposite the Little Cottage Tea Room on Ranscombe Lane takes visitors up Mount Caburn. You will often see paragliders hovering over this summit,

which looks down the Ouse valley towards the sea. Here. chalk-loving wild flowers carpet the slopes, and the site is encircled with Saxon and Iron Age ramparts.

Glynde Place is screened from the road by the stable block situated next to a Palladian-style church. The flint gables and brick chimneys at the front are from Tudor times, the back section was added in 1760. Knowledgeable guides introduce visitors to the family history, and with a welcome absence of roping-off you can get up close to all the details, including miniatures and embroidery. The walls are hung with old masters brought back from an Italian Grand Tour – the efforts of 300 years of collecting by the (related) Morley, Trevor and Brand families. Stone wyverns crown the gates beyond the Coach House, where the tea room has a cobbled courtyard shaded by fruit trees.

North of the village is Glyndebourne Opera House, home to Britain's top country house opera company.

HERSTMONCEUX MAP REF 401 H7

The science of astronomy provides the link between here, Greenwich and the Canary Islands. The Royal Observatory, established in the reign of Charles II to record the position of the stars to aid navigation for sailors, moved out from Greenwich, London, in 1946, because the light and air pollution was making it too difficult to observe the night sky. For more than 30 years the Herstmonceux Castle estate was the home of British astronomical observations, but it moved its main telescope to the island of La Palma in 1984. The former complex, with its striking domes, is now home to the Observatory Science Centre – a place full of appeal to all ages. It's best to visit on a dry day, as the large-scale interactive exhibits in the adventure playground-like Discovery Park outside are part of the fun, but there's also plenty indoors, with exhibits on optics, medieval machines, time, force and gravity, and more.

The romantic-looking 15th-century Herstmonceux Castle stands in a wide moat, and is the oldest brick building on such a scale in England. Henry VI's Treasurer, Sir Roger Fiennes, modelled it on French chateau designs and it was completed in 1446. Abandoned in the 1700s when the owners stripped it out to build a new mansion, Herstmonceux Place, near by, it became a picturesque ruin and was restored from 1910. It is now the International Study Centre for Queen's University, Ontario. You can take guided tours inside to see the beautiful courtyard and some of the very modern lecture rooms – these overlook the moat, and have Jacobean panelling, a dungeon with a stone toilet and a resident ghost.

The Elizabethan gardens and grounds move from the formal to the wild, rising gently up from the castle. Within a high brick wall, robust yew hedges enclose rhododendron, rose and herb gardens and a giant tilted steel sundial. Outside the wall, paths lead over rough meadows to a folly, a lily-filled lake and woods known for their carpets of bluebells.

KINGLEY VALE NATIONAL NATURE RESERVE MAP REF 400 F7

Yew forests are extremely rare, and this one, found on the South Downs between Stoughton and West Stoke – is Europe's largest, although tests involving pollen analysis suggest there were yew forests elsewhere in the area during prehistoric times, as at Mount Caburn near Lewes.

It's a marvellously eerie place, like some Tolkienesque fantasy, which is at its most spectacularly creepy and magical in the yew grove. Follow the path from the car park near West Stoke, keep forward at the next path junction, then go through a gate, to join the circular nature trail. Gnarled tree trunks have fallen over or twisted and continued to grow, creating a dark, gloomy canopy under which little else thrives. The luscious-looking berries are poisonous to us, but not to the hungry birds such as nuthatches, goldcrests and thrushes which feed on them. As you reach the top, the view opens out dramatically across Chichester Harbour – with the tall spire of Chichester Cathedral in view. The tall grassy hillocks up here are burial mounds consisting of a mound and ditch (or 'bell barrows') erected in the Bronze Age, doubtless for the view.

MEON VALLEY MAP REF 400 E6

Izaak Walton, known as the father of angling, loved to fish in the River Meon, still regarded today as one of Britain's best trout rivers. He famously penned his appreciation of the pastoral pastime in *The Compleat Angler*, published in 1653. Travelling between Wickham in the south to East Meon, you'll see the signs for trout fisheries where you can try your hand at the sport and get the idea of what it was that enthused Walton so much.

With some notable exceptions, the scenery here is pleasantly mild rather than dramatic. The valley's disused railway line, running from West Meon to Wickham, is now the particularly attractive Meon Valley Trail, a level route for walkers, horse-riders and cyclists. You can enjoy pottering around on a bike along the narrow lanes that connect the villages on the east side of the valley.

Further south, the Forest of Bere, a 865-acre (350ha) fragment of an ancient royal hunting forest, has numerous fine waymarked trails and picnic areas; there are also three designated car parks (West Walk, Woodend and Upperford Copse), and an exciting mountain bike trail that begins from West Walk.

One of Hampshire's most photogenic villages, East Meon has the infant river running along the middle of its quaint main street, lined with attractive brick and half-timbered houses, some thatched, and there's still a village smithy here – in operation for over a century. On a rise, the Church of All Saints dates from the mid-12th century and has mighty rounded Norman arches at the crossing of the chancel and the nave, and a wonderful Tournai font. Just across the road you can glimpse the medieval Court House, where the Bishops of Winchester once held court. Today the building is occasionally used for theatrical performances.

Old Winchester Hill National Nature Reserve is a dramatic stretch of chalk downland, where the steep slope has managed to escape modern farming, enabling a great range of wildlife to flourish. There are badgers, roe deer and dormice in the woodland, while more than 30 species of butterfly (including silver spotted skippers and speckled wood) can be found, and chalk-loving wild flowers such as orchids grow in profusion on the grasslands. From the main car park, an easy level track leads towards the fascinating Iron Age hill fort of Winchester Hill, within the ramparts of which are Bronze Age burial mounds, or barrows, which have never been excavated. There's also a very pleasant waymarked circular walk (it takes up to 2 hours) that leads downhill and along the hillside through woodland. For more detailed information, pick up a leaflet at the car park and consult the interpretative boards. The nature reserve is signposted from the A32 at Warnford; the road gets more scenic as you travel towards the Royal Navy communications school at HMS *Mercury*.

PETWORTH MAP REF 400 F6

The town of Petworth is dominated by the 17th-century Petworth House – its upper windows peering over near the church, and its great wall squeezing the A272 traffic uncomfortably close to the town's fine stone, half-timbered and tile-hung buildings. Petworth's shops are scattered around the streets near the square, some dotted along picturesquely cobbled Lombard Street. Petworth Cottage Museum at 346 High Street, takes you to 1910 when Mary Cummings, seamstress of Petworth House, lived there.

Petworth House (National Trust) can be reached on foot via an entrance near to the church, or from a car park north of the town. Another car park located a mile (1.6km) or so to the north gives free access to the grounds, where cyclists are welcomed. The hilly parkland here represents 18th-century landscaping by the great 'Capability' Brown on an enormous scale, set against which the house itself can seem oddly restrained. Its flat classical frontage in creamy grey stone seems a little sunken into the ground and the pasture goes right up to the windows.

Inside, the main rooms of the house have immensely different characters, from the gilt mirrors and oil paintings in the Square Drawing Room to the Marble Hall with its black-and-white floor, cool sage-green paint and authentic Roman statuary. One highlight is the Carved Room, decorated in c1692 by Grinling Gibbons and the Petworth carpenter John Selden, with its astonishing carvings in limewood. The festoons of flowers, beads, birds, musical instruments, cherubs and lace have been created in three dimensions, and tend to rather upstage the four Turner landscapes which hang beneath Tudor family and royal portraits. The art here is the finest

Insight
SOUTH DOWNS NATIONAL PARK
The South Downs National Park is the newest member of the national parks and was officially designated at midnight on 31 March 2010. This chalky range of hills stretches 100 miles (160km) from the historic city of Winchester to the dizzying heights of Beachy Head, and covers huge areas of woodland, heathland, downland and cliffs, and supports a huge variety of trees, plants, birds and wildlife as well as being home to 180,000 people.

WEALD & DOWNLAND MUSEUM

of any National Trust House; the North Wing Gallery includes works by Turner, a regular guest here, as well as paintings by Blake, Bosch, Titian and Gainsborough.

As you leave the house you are treated to a fascinating glimpse of the medieval manor around which the house was constructed. Opposite are found the servants' quarters, which now display the late Victorian kitchens and house the high-ceilinged tea room.

QUEEN ELIZABETH COUNTRY PARK MAP REF 400 F6

Butser Hill, now bisected by the A3 south of Petersfield, is the highest point on the South Downs. The Country Park gives open access to 1,400 acres (560ha) of woodland and downland within the East Hampshire Area of Outstanding Natural Beauty, with 20 miles (32km) of trails for walkers, cyclists and horse-riders, a demonstration Iron Age farm, an adventure playground and a varied programme of events.

Most of Butser Hill is designated a Site of Special Scientific Interest and since 1998 has been recognized as a National Nature Reserve. It is one of the largest areas of chalky grassland in Hampshire, with yew, beech and conifers providing important additional habitats to a rich population of wild flowers, insects, butterflies and lichens.

UPPARK MAP REF 400 F6

On a hilltop site and the first great house in England to be built without an on-site water supply, Uppark found its geography worked against it in 1989 when the roof caught fire. The wind fanned the flames and water had to be pumped from over a mile (1.6km) away. Over the six-year restoration period builders and craftspeople rediscovered long-lost skills and revived old traditions – such as recording the events of the day on chimney pots. TThe National Trust decided to re-create Uppark as it had been the day before the fire, a seamless join, complete with all the marks of age.

The house itself is built of brick in a Dutch style, and was designed in about 1690 by William Talman. It seems to sit high up on a plateau and is surrounded by landscaped pasture. Children can play ball games on the pleasant South Lawn. Inside, thanks to an extraordinary family history, the restored interiors are almost unchanged since Sir Matthew Fetherstonhaugh and his wife furnished it so lavishly with rich fabrics and exotic mementoes from their honeymoon Grand Tour of Europe in the mid-18th century. Their son, Sir Harry, aged 71, married his 20-year-old dairymaid Mary Ann in 1825 and died 21 years later. Mary Ann lived on with her sister, keeping things as they had been in Sir Harry's heyday. By the 1900s the

next owners had already started work on conserving the fragile textiles, and Uppark passed to the National Trust' in 1954.

The reconstructions are completely convincing; only a look at the photographs in each room will show you where the joins are. Many stewards can relate personal stories of the day of the fire. The basement of spacious kitchens and servants' quarters, which was abandoned in the 1900s, escaped with least damage and seems stranded in time; the butler's room has a water gauge to show when the rooftop tanks need topping up. Also in the basement is the gigantic Uppark Doll's House, with Georgian furniture, glass and silverware. The stable block is more elaborate than the servants' dining hall, and the dairy is positively elegant.

WEST DEAN MAP REF 400 F7

The Weald and Downland Open Air Museum is more like a village of relocated historic buildings rescued from town centre redevelopment, road and reservoir schemes in Sussex, Kent and Surrey – complete with a watermill, ploughed fields and farm animals. It brilliantly promotes public awareness and interest in old buildings and their surroundings.

There's something for everyone, from children who will be fascinated by the low doorways and open fires to the

professional builder or craftsperson. The buildings look as though they have always been there. Most look as they would have been when first built, perhaps as medieval halls, with reproduction furnishings and usually a steward on hand to answer questions. There's a village school from 1895, a carpenter's shop and even an animal pound.

Up in the woods, the pod-like modern gridshell building shows timber framing at its most innovative, and there are tours of the collection of building parts and rural tools kept in store underneath. Special events such as the Heavy Horse and Working Animals Spectacular (June) and Rare Breeds Show (July) are popular and there are demonstrations of flour milling and medieval cooking on most days.

The museum is part of the West Dean estate: you can glimpse the battlemented flint mansion (now West Dean College). Once a playground of King Edward VII, West Dean Gardens run along one side of the seasonal stream of the River Lavant, with walks across downland pasture leading up to an arboretum. The summer-houses and bridges of the Spring Garden are Regency style, while the great pergola with vines, clematis, climbing hydrangea and roses, and the immense walled kitchen garden and glasshouses are from West Dean's Edwardian heyday.

DISTANCE/TIME 11 miles (17.7km) 3h **MAP** OS Explorer 122 South Downs Way: Steyning to Newhaven **START** Free car park by Jack and Jill windmills; grid ref: TQ 304134. Alternative: Ditchling Beacon car park; grid ref: TQ 333131 **TRACKS** Bumpy chalk and grass tracks, some sections on clay **THE PUB** The Bull, Ditchling. Tel: 01273 843147; www.thebullditchling.com

DITCHLING BEACON & THE CHATTRI WAR MEMORIAL

Cycle along one of the most spectacular sections of the South Downs: the route passes two windmills (Jack and Jill), and the Chattri War Memorial

1 Turn left out of the car park, signed 'public bridleway to Ditchling Beacon'. Ignore a driveway, left, to Jack Windmill and another left track. Fork left uphill at a junction, to the South Downs Way. Follow the blue-arrow markers for most of the ride.

2 From Ditchling Beacon car park cross the road and take the South Downs Way opposite. The route climbs up two grassy rises and drops to cross a narrow farm road. Here the clay surface can be sticky after rain.

3 After the next left, a descending fork (which you avoid), look for a track on the right, marked with a blue arrow which leads to the site of Plumpton Plain, a Bronze Age settlement. Carry on along the South Downs Way.

4 Beyond a gate is a National Trust sign for Blackcap. Walk up to the summit by forking left to the trig point. Return via your outward route

5 Unless you want to return to the start along the South Downs Way, turn left at the summit after Ditchling Beacon (where Jack Windmill comes into view). It's marked with a blue arrow and a sign for 'Chattri and the windmills'. Descend at the second gate (waymarked 'Chattri and the windmills' No 13) to detour to the Chattri War Memorial.

6 After the next gate, walk to the war memorial. Return to the junction at the previous gate, turn left: the route bends right (No 44) on a path, left (No 45), then downhill and right leaving the route to 'Chattri and the windmills' (at No 46), which continues ahead. The track crosses the South Downs Way via a farm to the windmills and the car park.

DISTANCE/TIME 12 miles (19.3km) 3h; alternative route 4 miles (6.4km) 1h **MAP** OS Explorer 122 South Downs Way: Steyning to Newhaven **START** Barcombe village centre, roadside parking; grid ref: TQ 418157 **TRACKS** Back lanes, stony track; extension on a track and fields **THE PUB** The Anchor Inn, Barcombe. Tel: 01273 400414; www.anchorinnandboating.co.uk

HAMSEY & BARCOMBE MILLS

Along this route of quiet lanes you'll find everything from Roman sites to wartime defences, and a mill pond and weirs. Off-road sections follow a disused railway track and an ancient 'green lane' that crosses fields and leads to the Lavender Line preserved steam railway.

1 With the Royal Oak pub on your right, go along the main street in Barcombe and turn left in front of the village sign for The Anchor Inn and Newick. At the bottom of the hill turn right on Boast Lane, signposted 'Anchor Inn'. After passing Delves Farm, and just before a house on the right, look for a track beyond a gate on the left, into a triangular field. At the next triangular area, look to your left for a gate with a yellow arrow on it: at the far end of the field a line of hedgerow trees rising up to the top right skyline actually marks the line of a Roman road that ran from London to Lewes. Continue along the track, which later follows the left side of a field and passes a wartime brick pillbox. The route drops to a footbridge. Continue across a meadow to the gate ahead, up over another footbridge and along a track; ignore driveways to the right. At the road T-junction turn right into Isfield. Continue along past the Laughing Fish pub on your left to visit the Lavender Line preserved railway.

2 From Isfield retrace your route across the meadows and back past the pillbox. Turn left on the road to continue to The Anchor Inn.

3 Retrace your route a short distance from The Anchor Inn and, just before Keeper's Cottage on the left, turn left on the old railway track, signposted 'licensed bridleway to Barcombe Mills'.

4 On reaching a road that is opposite the old Barcombe Mills station, take a detour left and then take the first road on the left. Turn right at the junction in front of the driveway to Barcombe House in order to reach the millpond and weirs of Barcombe Mills. Return the same way to the road, cycling past Barcombe Mills station. At the next junction go straight ahead for a short-cut back into Barcombe. For the main route, turn left here, and pass Barcombe church. Carry on along the road, keeping left at the next two junctions towards Hamsey.

5 Just after Hamsey Manor turn left down Whitfeld Lane to Hamsey. Here, there is a lovely half-timbered house called Yeoman's dated 1584; just after the house, turn left at a T-junction. From here the road crosses a former canal via a bridge. After the bridge, you can pick up the keys to Hamsey church from Pine Barn, the first house on the left to look around the church. The road then rises over the old railway to reach Hamsey church, a wonderful example of what medieval country churches used to look like. From this point, return to Hamsey, keeping left at the road junction that is by the canal bridge, and just past a pillbox.

6 Turn right at the T-junction. After Whitfeld Lane joins from the right follow signs for Barcombe to return to the start.

WILMINGTON

Visit the legendary chalk figure, which still puzzles archaeologists and historians. Theories abound about the origin of the Long Man and what he originally looked like. Did he carry a scythe and rake? Was he a fertility figure? How long has he been etched in the hillside? It is possible we will never know for sure.

DISTANCE/TIME 6.25 miles (10km) 2h30 **MAP** OS Explorer 123 Eastbourne & Beachy Head
START Long-stay car park at Wilmington; grid ref: TQ 543042 **PATHS** Downland paths and tracks, stretch of country road; 1 stile **THE PUB** The Giants Rest, The Street, Wilmington.
Tel: 01323 870207

1 Make for the car park exit and follow the path parallel to the road, heading towards the Long Man of Wilmington. Bear left at the stile and take the Wealdway to the chalk figure. Climb quite steeply, curving to the right. Go through a gate, avoid the Wealdway arrow and go straight ahead towards the escarpment, veering right just below the figure of the Long Man.

2 Go through the next gate, cross a track and bear left on reaching a fence. A few paces brings you to a gate and a sign for the South Downs Way. Turn right, pass a small reservoir and follow the track to the road.

3 Turn left and walk down to a signpost for Lullington church, following the path alongside several cottages. After visiting the church, retrace your steps to the road and turn right. Head down the lane and look for Alfriston church on the right. Pass a turning to the village on the right and continue ahead towards Seaford. Look out for a post box and swing left here, signposted 'Jevington'.

4 Follow the bridleway as it climbs steadily between tracts of remote downland. Keep left at the next main junction and there is a moderate climb. Avoid the bridle track branching off to the left and continue ahead

towards Jevington. Lullington Heath National Nature Reserve is on the right now. Pass a bridleway on the right and keep on the track as it climbs steeply. Pass a second sign and also a map for the nature reserve and make for a junction with the South Downs Way.

5 Turn left and follow the enclosed path to a gate. Go straight ahead to walk alongside woodland and pass through a second gate. The path begins a gradual curve to the left and eventually passes along the rim of a spectacular dry valley known as Tenantry Ground. Keep the fence on your left-hand side and look for a gate ahead. Swing right as you approach it to a stile and then follow the path alongside the fence, crossing along the top of the Long Man.

6 Glance to your right and you can just make out the head and body of the chalk figure down below. It's an intriguing view. Continue keeping the fence on the right and descend to a gate. Turn right here and retrace your steps to the car park at Wilmington.

QUEEN ELIZABETH COUNTRY PARK

Follow woodland and downland trails to a unique archaeological farmstead, continue through two of Hampshire's oldest and prettiest villages, Chalton and Buriton, and then climb Butser Hill for all-round views.

DISTANCE/TIME 6.75 miles (10.9km) 3h **MAP** OS Explorer 120 Chichester **START** Pay-and-display car park, Queen Elizabeth Country Park; grid ref: SU 718185 **PATHS** Woodland paths, bridleways and forest tracks; 3 stiles **THE PUB** The Five Bells, Buriton. Tel: 01730 263584

1 From the car park, follow the Woodland Trail (green-booted posts) to the right. On reaching the road, turn right then left and join the gravelled track at a blue-topped horseshoe post. Follow the waymarked bridleway past the maintenance yard, and bear away from the A3 on to a grassy lane.

2 Gently climb between fields, the bridleway soon curving left around woodland, then gradually bear right between fields, noting the 18th-century windmill on the skyline to your right.

3 At the road, turn right for Butser Ancient Farm, otherwise turn left and follow the road (some blind bends) for 0.5 mile (800m) into Chalton. Turn left at the junction, signed 'Ditcham'. Bear right for the Red Lion.

4 Shortly, at a fork, bear left along a byway. Continue between fields and soon descend through trees to join a road. Turn left, walking parallel to the railway for 0.25 mile (400m), to a stile on the right. Bear half-left across a large field, pass under electricity lines, and enter woodland.

5 At a junction of paths continue straight ahead and steadily climb a wide forest track. On the descent fork left, then almost

immediately fork right, down a narrow sunken footpath and continue to a road.

6 Turn right then, in 100yds (91m), take the footpath left and head steeply down through the trees to a stile. Bear half right across a field to a stile by a gate. Follow the path round to the left, passing a pond, into Buriton.

7 Turn left along the High Street then, beside Chapel Cottage, take the footpath left. Go round the village hall and continue past the play area to a gate. Very carefully cross the railway line, go through a gate and keep ahead to a junction with a bridleway. Turn right and steeply ascend to the road. Cross into Hall's Hill car park.

8 Go through a gate and up a wide track (South Downs Way) back into Queen Elizabeth Country Park. Gradually ascend then, just after a track merges from the right, fork right (signed 'South Downs Way walkers and cyclists'). Keep ahead at the barbecue shelter, and descend past a barrier. Pass through Benham Bushes car park, follow a short stretch of metalled road then bear off left with the South Downs Way. Rejoin the road at Gravel Hill car park and turn right, signed 'Hangers Way', and retrace your outward route to the car park.

AROUND THE ARUN VALLEY FROM ARUNDEL

Follow the River Arun to Arundel Park and then tour this handsome Sussex town, dominated by its massive castle. The walk starts down by the River Arun and from here there are teasing glimpses of the castle, but it is not until you have almost finished the walk that you reach its main entrance. Following the river bank through the tranquil Arun valley, the walk reaches Arundel Park. Swanbourne Lake, a great attraction for young children, is located by the entrance to the park, but beyond here the park assumes a rather different character. You may start to feel slightly isolated at this point but don't worry; resume the walk and you will soon be back in the hustle and bustle of Arundel's busy streets.

DISTANCE/TIME 3.25 miles (5.2km) 2h **MAP** OS Explorer 121 Arundel & Pulborough **START** Fee-paying car park, Mill Road, Arundel; grid ref: TQ 020071 **PATHS** Riverside and parkland paths, some road walking; 2 stiles **THE PUB** Black Rabbit, Offham. Tel: 01903 882828

1 From the car park in Mill Road, turn right and walk along the tree-lined pavement. Pass the bowling green and a glance to your left will reveal a dramatic view of Arundel Castle with its imposing battlements.

2 Follow the road to the elegant stone bridge, avoid the first path on the right and cross over via a footbridge; turn right to join the riverside path, partly shaded by overhanging trees. Emerging from the trees, the path cuts across lush, low-lying ground to reach the western bank of the Arun. Turn left here and walk beside the reed-fringed Arun to the Black Rabbit pub, which can be seen standing out against a curtain of trees.

3 From the Black Rabbit, turn left on the minor road back towards Arundel, passing the entrance to the WWT Arundel Wetland Centre. Make for the gate leading into Arundel Park and follow the path alongside Swanbourne Lake. Eventually the lake fades from view as the walk reaches deeper

into the park. Ignore a turning branching off to the left, just before a gate and stile, and follow the path as it curves gently to the right.

4 Turn sharply to the left at the next waymarked junction and begin a fairly steep ascent, with the footpath through the park seen curving away down to the left, back towards the lake. This stretch of the walk offers glorious views over elegant Arundel Park. Head for a stile and gate, then bear immediately right up the bank. Cross the grass, following the waymarks and keeping to the left of Hiorne Tower. On reaching a driveway, turn left and walk down to Park Lodge. Keep to the right by the private drive and make for the road.

5 Turn left, pass Arundel Cathedral and bear left at the road junction by the entrance to Arundel Castle. Go down the hill, back into the centre of Arundel. You'll find Mill Road at the bottom of the High Street.

WALK 42

A CIRCUIT OF DEVIL'S DYKE BY POYNINGS

This is a fine walk with glimpses over the most famous of all the dry chalk valleys. Devil's Dyke is a geological quirk – a spectacular, steep-sided downland combe or cleft. It was probably cut by glacial meltwaters millions of years ago in the Ice Age. Views from this beauty spot stretch for miles in all directions. In good weather the slopes are busy with visitors, while in the skies hang-gliders swoop over the grassy downland. However, away from the car park and chalk slopes the walk heads for more peaceful surroundings.

DISTANCE/TIME 2.75 miles (4.4km) 1h30 **MAP** OS Explorer 122 Brighton & Hove **START** Free car park, Summer Down; grid ref: TQ 269112 **PATHS** Field and woodland paths; 7 stiles **THE PUB** Royal Oak, Poynings. Tel: 01273 857389

1 From the car park go through the kissing gate then veer right. Join the South Downs Way and follow it alongside lines of trees. Soon the path curves left and drops down to the road. Part company with the South Downs Way here, as it crosses to join the private road to Saddlescombe Farm, and follow the verge for 75yds (68m). Bear left at the footpath sign and drop down the bank to a stile.

2 Follow the line of the tarmac lane as it curves right to reach a waymark. Leave the lane and walk ahead alongside power lines, keeping the line of trees and bushes on the right. Look for a narrow path disappearing into the vegetation and make for a stile. Drop down some steps into the woods and turn right at a junction with a bridleway. Take the path running off half left and follow it between fields and a wooded dell. Pass over a stile and continue to a stile in the left boundary. Cross a footbridge to a further stile and now turn right towards Poynings.

3 Head for a gate and footpath sign and turn left at the road. Follow the parallel path

along to the Royal Oak and then continue to Dyke Lane on the left. There is a memorial stone here, dedicated to the memory of George Stephen Cave Cuttress, a resident of Poynings for over 50 years, and erected by his widow. Follow the tarmac bridleway and soon it narrows to a path. On reaching the fork, by a National Trust sign for Devil's Dyke, veer right and begin climbing the steps.

4 Follow the path up to a gate and continue walking up the stairs. From the higher ground there are breathtaking views to the north and west. Make for a kissing gate and head up the slope towards the inn. Keep the Devil's Dyke pub on your left and take the road round to the left, passing a bridleway on the left. Follow the path parallel to the road and look to the left for a definitive view of Devil's Dyke.

5 Head for the South Downs Way and turn left by a National Trust sign for Summer Down to a stile and gate. Follow the trail, keeping Devil's Dyke down to your left, and eventually you reach a stile leading into Summer Down car park.

PETWORTH & AMBERLEY

This tour makes the most of the bewitching scenery of the West Sussex Downs, with glimpses of the distant sea. You can visit Petworth House and Uppark (both National Trust properties), or venture into Europe's largest yew forest at Kingley Vale, and see some of England's finest Roman mosaics at Bignor Roman Villa, discovered in the early 19th century. Learn about the region's traditional building styles at the Weald and Downland Open Air Museum, and find out about the working life of yesteryear in Amberley Museum.

Route Directions

Start the drive at Petworth, where the estate walls of Petworth House extend to the town centre. The house has the finest art collection of any National Trust property, and in addition to its stately rooms, has a huge deer park.

1 From Petworth, take the A272 west and drive through the village of Easebourne to reach the town of Midhurst.

Midhurst's beautifully preserved town centre, especially the section around the church, is well worth exploring.

2 Leave Midhurst by the A272 towards Petersfield. Leave the A272 near Stedham, turning left on a minor road through Elsted (where the delightfully placed Three Horseshoes makes a very pleasant stop) to then turn left through South Harting.

South Harting was once the home of the prolific Victorian novelist Anthony Trollope, author of the Barsetshire novels as well as many more, and has an attractive sloping village street.

3 Fork right on to the B2146. Continue along this road. You will soon pass the entrance to the stately home of Uppark.

This supremely elegant Classical mansion suffered a huge fire in 1989 and the National Trust painstakingly restored it to what it was before the disaster. At West Marden you can divert right to Stansted House, a Georgian mansion in a great park, while at Walderton you can detour left to Stoughton.

4 Beyond Walderton, turn left to stay on the B2146, then take the B2178 towards Chichester. At East Ashling, turn left and continue following the National Nature Reserve signposts.

At North Stoke, a car park gives access to Kingley Vale National Nature Reserve. Follow the path from the car park, and at a path junction go ahead through a gate to follow the circular nature trail through the magical yew grove of Kingley Vale and up to the crest of the Downs, where Bronze Age burial mounds look across Chichester Harbour.

5 From this point, continue heading east and shortly turn left onto the A286 at Mid Lavant.

At West Dean are West Dean Gardens, in the grounds of a prestigious arts college, beautifully set along the River Lavant and looking up to the Downs. Very close by is the Weald and Downland Open-Air Museum, where traditionally constructed buildings from all over southeast England have been re-erected. You can eat at the museum's café, or seek out the Fox & Hounds, a friendly 16th-century pub in Singleton village.

6 Turn right off the A286, beyond West Dean, following the road up to Goodwood racecourse, and fork left towards Petworth.

Beyond 'Glorious Goodwood' you will be able to see the sea at Bognor Regis. Selhurst Park, by the road on the left, is a forest area offering some fine views.

7 Turn left on the A285 towards Petworth. After 3.6 miles (5.8km), just where the road drops from the Downs, turn right at the bottom of the hill on a lane through Sutton to Bignor Roman Villa.

The villa contains magnificent mosaics and has been a tourist attraction since its chance discovery by a ploughman in 1811. You can also divert up on to the South Downs on a little lane ending on Bignor Hill, and explore

Stane Street, a dead straight Roman road now demoted to a track, but well preserved with its agger (ditch) still visible alongside.

8 Carry on through West Burton to Bury. Turn right on the A29, then take the B2139 at the roundabout.

You pass the Amberley Working Museum, in a chalk pit, and home to a community of craftspeople with re-erected buildings recalling earlier working life in the southeast of England. This is a good place to take a break and stretch your legs as you explore the museum.

9 Turn left into the beautiful village of Amberley, with its many thatched houses and the castle overlooking the water meadows. Follow the road that bends right by the Black Horse in Amberley village, and keep left at two junctions to the village of Greatham.

Greatham Bridge is an idyllic place to sit and relax beside the River Arun.

10 Cross the A29 at Coldwaltham, and turn right on to the B2138 to Fittleworth, where the unusual pub sign for the Swan spans the road. Turn left on the A283 and continue to Petworth where you can visit the 17th-century Petworth House (NT).

64 MILES (103KM)

LEWES, WAKEHURST PLACE & ASHDOWN FOREST

This route celebrates Sussex in all its diversity: starting from Lewes, beautifully set in the South Downs, it heads into the Weald. You encounter the primaeval-feeling heathlands and woods of the Ashdown Forest – the landscape of the immortal Winnie-the-Pooh stories – and pass some of the world's greatest gardens and the terminus of the Bluebell Railway, one of Britain's most engaging steam railways. Near the end you can finish in high style by driving up on to the Downs for a view far across southern England. There's no shortage of good pubs and tea rooms along the route where you can stop and take a break and have a bite to eat.

Route Directions

1 Leave the historic county town of Lewes on the A275. Cross the A272 at North Chailey and continue on the A275. You will pass Sheffield Park Station, the southern terminus of the Bluebell Railway on the left. A short distance on is the entrance to Sheffield Park Gardens.

You can detour ahead a short distance to Heaven Farm, on the left of the A275, which is a delightfully informal spot for lunch or tea.

2 Just after the entrance to Sheffield Park Gardens, turn right on a minor road to Fletching, where the Griffin Inn also makes an excellent lunch spot. Carry on to the A272, turn left to Maresfield, left at the A22, and at the next roundabout turn off to the B2026. This climbs over Ashdown Forest, keeping left at a fork with the B2188.

The sandy tracks, rolling heaths and clumps of pine trees make for a remote landscape. It was here that A A Milne set his Winnie-the-Pooh stories, and the scene is instantly familiar from E H Shepard's illustrations. This is vintage territory for picnics (with plentiful car parks), kite flying and bracing walks.

3 At Chuck Hatch you can detour left along a lane for the Poohsticks Bridge, which featured in Milne's stories. Soon you see the entrance to Pooh car park on the right.

The path from the car park goes through the woods, and at a corner of the road, turns right on a bridleway leading to the bridge. Though rebuilt since Milne's time, the bridge looks exactly like the original where Pooh and his friends enjoyed a game of poohsticks.

4 Return to the B2026 and continue to Hartfield. A shop here called Pooh Corner has a wide array of Pooh-related gifts. Take the B2110 west from Hartfield towards Forest Row, then take the second left turn past Coleman's Hatch, keeping forward by the weatherboarded Hatch pub (with a very pretty garden).

You will pass the Ashdown Forest Centre on your right. There is a display and also information about the forest.

5 Cross the A22 and take the minor road opposite, turning left at the next crossroads towards West Hoathly. At the next crossroads detour right past the end of Weirwood Reservoir to Standen house (NT).

This unusual Arts and Crafts house was designed by Philip Webb, a friend and associate of William Morris; the gardens have views over the Weald.

6 Carry on to the B2028, turn left along it, past the entrance to Wakehurst Place, which is maintained by the Royal Botanic Gardens at Kew, and is home to the Millennium Seed Bank. Turn right at Ardingly, towards Balcombe, past Ardingly church and over one arm of Ardingly Reservoir.

This body of water looks almost natural, and provides scope for waterside strolls, as well as fishing and watersports such as canoeing, windsurfing and sailing.

7 Turn left on reaching the edge of Balcombe, and continue on this road towards Haywards Heath.

On the left you see the huge Ouse Valley Viaduct, which carries the London–Brighton railway. A footpath leads from the road and disappears underneath the structure, from which point you can appreciate an extraordinary view through all the oval spaces in the piers.

8 Further along the same road you will find Borde Hill gardens comprising superb parkland and woods.

There is always a spectacular show of blooms at these gardens during the early summer when the colourful rhododendrons and azaleas are out.

9 After Borde Hill gardens, turn left onto a minor road and then take the A272 to Haywards Heath, then the B2112 to Ditchling. The old village of Ditchling nestles at the foot of the South Downs (the Bull makes a welcoming stopping place, or there are a couple of tea rooms). From there head south to Ditchling Beacon.

From the car park at the top you can take a short stroll along the South Downs Way, enjoying the sweeping views over the Weald.

10 Return to Ditchling and then go east along the B2116 to join the A275 just outside Lewes town centre.

South Coast

CLOCKWISE FROM TOP LEFT: EASTBOURNE; SPINNAKER TOWER, PORTSMOUTH; EASTBOURNE; BEACHY HEAD

BEACHY HEAD & SEVEN SISTERS
MAP REF 401 H7

A high rollercoaster of turf-capped white cliffs undulates between Seaford and Eastbourne, rising to seven mini-peaks known as the Seven Sisters. The Channel continues to erode the sheer, crumbling chalk heights. From Seaford Head to Beachy Head to the east, this makes up the longest and most scenic stretch of undeveloped coast in southeast England.

The Seven Sisters Country Park encompasses the western part of the cliffs. Two large car parks either side of the A259 at Exceat give access into Friston Forest to the north and also Cuckmere Haven. This is the only undeveloped estuary in Sussex, with wildlife thriving in the meadows, reed beds and ponds.

Further east is Beachy Head, the highest point on the Sussex coast. This sheer chalk cliff plummets a full 534 feet (163m), with a lighthouse on the shore far below. The views up here are dizzying in the extreme (on a clear day you can see Dungeness to the east and the Isle of Wight to the west), but do be careful as the cliff edge is not stable. From Eastbourne, the South Downs Way leads up – or you can continue along the undercliff closer to the shore before a steep final ascent. From Terminus Road or from the pier in the town centre hop on an open-topped City Sightseeing bus that will take you up the zig-zagging road (not in winter).

BRIGHTON & HOVE MAP REF 401 G7

Brighton is unmistakably cosmopolitan, fun-loving and sophisticated. The cliché that it's a place for romantic frolics has been overtaken by its newer image as a gay capital, an arty vibrant place that keeps going until the small hours.

The beachfront changes in character from one moment to the next. Ornate Victorian lamp-posts, attractive coloured railings and the creamy white stucco frontages characterize one of the finest seaside townscapes in Britain, with bow-windowed Regency and grand Victorian façades. At the middle, ornate Palace Pier has a funfair. Near its entrance, the Brighton Sea Life Centre has displays including a walk-through glass tunnel.

To the east, Brighton Marina is a huge modern complex with outlet shopping, bowling alley, an eight-screen cinema, prestigious apartment complexes and a raft of waterfront restaurants and cafés. West of Palace Pier is the liveliest part of the beachfront. The booths under the esplanade are home to an artistic quarter, with little galleries alongside palmists, cockles and jellied eel stalls, bucket and spade shops, bars, henna tattooists and hair-braiders. Look out for the tiny Mechanical Memories Museum.

At night, the action revolves around the beachfront clubs, plus there are free performances at the Ellipse area, open-air cinema and music on the beach. The

Brighton Centre has shows and gigs, with many big-name bands. By the beach near the ornate bandstand is a free paddling pool and playground. Major plans are afoot to transform the seafront.

Just behind the seafront, the west side of the Palace Pier is The Lanes, an intricate knot of little streets and alleys packed with restaurants, boutiques, and jewellery and clothes shops, with tempting cooking smells wafting from doorways.

Between the railway station and the Royal Pavilion is the North Laine – radically different from The Lanes. Here small streets have evolved into an alternative shopping and promenading area.

Just inland from The Lanes is the heart of Regency Brighton and the astonishing Royal Pavilion. Originally a simple farmhouse, it became a classical 'Marine Pavilion' before John Nash transformed it between 1815 and 1823 for the Prince Regent, later George IV, into an Indian fantasy of domes and minarets. Across the Pavilion Gardens, within the former Pavilion stables and riding school, the Brighton Museum and Art Gallery is one of Brighton's best free sights.

There are delightful hilly streets to the north, rising up to the Montpellier area – site of some of Brighton and Hove's most elegant Regency villas and terraces – and there's more of the same along the seafront. Preston Street, off Western Road, has a concentration of ethnic restaurants.

CHICHESTER HARBOUR
MAP REF 400 F7

Flat farmlands, saltmarshes and mudflats surround this vast natural harbour, where thousands of bobbing masts attest to its status as one of the major yachting havens of the south coast. There are footpaths, but the best way to see this natural wonder is from the water itself.

With West Itchenor as the starting point, Chichester Harbour Water Tours give 1.5-hour cruises on the harbour up to five times a day – with the chance to spot birds such as shelducks, teals and mergansers, as well as seals. Surfers head towards East Wittering and Bracklesham Bay when the conditions are right. On warm summer days it gets very busy at West Wittering, but the crowds soon thin out as you venture on to East Head.

On the western fringes of Chichester are the remains of the largest Roman building yet discovered north of the Alps. It is a huge complex with some 100 rooms and 60 mosaics, believed to be unique in Britain. Fishbourne Roman Palace has become one of the most celebrated archaeological excavations of its time.

Outside, the box hedges are planted in the same intricate patterns as the excavated Roman bedding trenches, and there's an exhibit on Roman gardening. In the impressive Collections Discovery Centre you can take a tour to learn more about the conservation methods.

EASTBOURNE MAP REF 401 H7

Though less obviously trendy than nearby Brighton, Eastbourne scores particularly strongly for its very appealing 4 miles (6.4km) of unspoiled seafront. It retains a gracious atmosphere, with rows of stucco-fronted hotels and guesthouses overlooking the beach. Central to the seafront is the ornate Victorian pier, with its fairy lights strung between lamp-posts and some of the best surviving ironwork and little kiosks of the era, picked out in blue and white paint. The Dome at the end houses a fully restored camera obscura, built in 1901. Near by is the turquoise flattened onion dome of the bandstand.

West from here you can stroll, join the skaters, or take the bus or seasonal hourly Dotto Train past the Wish Tower and the Lifeboat Museum. The promenade ends at the Holywell Tea Chalet. In the other direction, the Dotto Train runs along to Britain's largest man-made marina at Sovereign Harbour. There's a good range of waterfront restaurants and cafés, and harbour boat trips. On the way you'll pass Princes Park, with mini golf, bowls, putting and a model boating lake. On Royal Parade, the Redoubt Fortress is a perfectly intact early 19th-century fort, now the home of the Military Museum of Sussex.

The town's quirkiest attraction has to be How We Lived Then: the Museum of Shops, in Cornfield Terrace, a collection of some 100,000 items of bygone random merchandise set in rooms re-created to mirror times gone by.

NETLEY MAP REF 400 E7

At Netley, a Victorian town on the shores of the Solent, the Royal Victoria Country Park covers more than 100 acres (40ha) of woods, marshes and beach. There is a nature trail, miniature railway and walks.

The ruins of Netley Abbey stand brooding in woodland next to the Solent shore. Netley Castle, on the shore near the abbey and formerly the gatehouse, was one of Henry VIII's gun stations – its tall tower is Victorian, and it has been transformed into a folly with all the panoply of Gothic device (now luxury apartments).

PEVENSEY MAP REF 401 H7

The outer walls of Pevensey Castle enclose a huge oval of grassland. These full-sized walls are late Roman, with some medieval repairs, built to protect the busy port.

The medieval castle is set within a moat at the centre of the enclosure – William the Conqueror put a fort here in 1066, but what you see today is 13th century. Then the castle would still have been on the coast, surrounded by marshes. The castle was abandoned around 1500 after the harbour had silted up. But more than

400 years later it would have been a first defence against a shore invasion in World War II: you can see the rooms used by Canadian soldiers inside the towers, and a gun emplacement looks out over the tea rooms. Pevensey's other historic buildings include Old Mint House Antiques (1342) and the Court House museum.

The extensive shingle beach is at Pevensey Bay, about a mile (1.6km) away. To the north are the Pevensey Levels, a reclaimed marsh with reed-fringed ditches, tiny lanes and isolated farms.

PORTCHESTER CASTLE
MAP REF 400 E7

This is one of the most fascinating historical sites in Britain. The massive, 20-foot (6m) high walls of a 3rd-century Roman fort sit on a little promontory on the northern shore of Portsmouth Harbour, facing directly across it and out to sea. It is the most complete Roman fort remains in northern Europe.

PORTSMOUTH MAP REF 400 E7

Portsmouth has been Britain's foremost naval base since the late 15th century, when it had the first ever dry dock. For a great view over the city, take the lift to the top of the elegant 600-foot (183m) high Spinnaker Tower.

The town's biggest attraction is the collection of historic ships that can be visited in the Naval Dockyard. HMS *Victory*, launched in 1765, was Nelson's flagship at the Battle of Trafalgar in 1805 and is probably the most famous British warship; she is also the oldest commissioned warship in the world. The remains of the *Mary Rose*, which sank off Southsea in July 1545, are housed in a specially designed and constructed building. 'Permanent conservation' is under way, and there is an exhibition of the artefacts found during salvage. HMS *Warrior*, the first 'ironclad', was launched at Blackwall in 1860, the largest, fastest and most formidable warship the world had ever seen. The Dockyard also houses the Royal Naval Museum and 'Action Stations', a thrilling high-tech Royal Naval experience using film and interactive technology.

During World War II Portsmouth was bombed heavily, and it is unfortunate that much of the rebuilding has been particularly uninspired. This being so, hurry through to the historic dockyard and follow the Millennium Promenade (Renaissance Trail) on foot through the bustling Gunwharf Quays shopping complex to The Point. Here is the oldest and most picturesque quarter of Old Portsmouth, where surviving attractive old streets have been restored, and face out on to a pretty little harbour.

The city has more than a dozen museums, including Charles Dickens' Birthplace in Old Commercial Road, but the City Museum and Art Gallery found in Museum Road is probably the best place to start. It features 'The Story of Portsmouth' and will point you in the direction of the other remaining historic buildings around the city, including the Landport Gate of 1760, the Square Tower of 1494 and the Royal Garrison Church. Beyond the tangle of Old Portsmouth's streets to the east, you emerge on to Southsea Common, faced by imposing terraces of 19th-century stucco.

SOUTHAMPTON MAP REF 400 E7

Modern Southampton has been made by its docks. Its famous double tides give prolonged high water, and there's a grand view of the comings and goings of cruise ships and the pleasure craft from Town Quay and Western Esplanade.

This is a sprawling, thriving, working city, with attractions that include some of the best shopping along the south coast, the fine City Art Gallery, a string of leafy green parks, and a little Maritime Museum set in a 15th-century warehouse near the shore, which tells of the great liners built here, and the last, fateful voyage of the RMS *Titanic*. The Solent Sky Aviation Museum, which offers hands-on experience of many of the exhibits, was founded in honour of R J Mitchell, designer of the Spitfire fighter plane which was constructed at Southampton's Supermarine Works.

The most interesting area lies south of the gleaming West Quay shopping centre, and it is worth parking there to explore on foot. The mall leads out on to Above Bar Street, a pedestrianized shopping street and one of several last surviving fragments of the medieval walled city. Stroll down here, passing the Dolphin Hotel where novelist Jane Austen celebrated her 18th birthday in 1793. Next door is the bombed-out Church of the Holy Rood, dedicated to the merchant seamen of the city, and including a memorial to the 500 local crew who died aboard RMS *Titanic* in 1912. Beyond nearby St Michael's, the oldest church in the city, dating to 1070, and the only one undamaged in the war, lie Bugle Street and French Street, with the Medieval Merchant's House of 1290 and the striking timbered Tudor House Museum and Garden. Another little interesting corner to explore is Oxford Street, its mellow old houses now filled with trendy restaurants, and with an Edwardian pub, the London Hotel, at one corner.

On the shore, ferries leave for the Isle of Wight and Hythe, and Ocean Village is a modern marina from where you can take a pleasant cruise of the harbour.

DISTANCE/TIME 13 miles (20.9km) 2h30; shorter route 5.5 miles (8.8km) 1h **MAP** OS Explorer 124 Hastings and Bexhill **START** Pevensey car park (by castle; pay-and-display); grid ref: TQ 646048

TRACKS All on minor roads, except for bridleway at Herstmonceux; the short ride is on roads

THE PUB The Lamb Inn, Wartling. Tel: 01323 832116; www.lambinnwartling.co.uk

A LOOP FROM PEVENSEY TO HERSTMONCEUX

This is a journey between two castles that takes you through the Pevensey Levels in '1066 Country'. Although flat, the Pevensey Levels are full of colour, character and wildlife, while the South Downs rise dramatically in the background. The ride connects the castles at Pevensey and Herstmonceux.

1 From the car park, go to the main street in Pevensey and turn left along it, passing the outer wall of the castle (you can walk in through the gateway, where there is free access, if you don't intend to visit the castle fully later). Just after the Pevensey Castle pub turn right along Peelings Lane, ignoring a minor turn soon on the left. Turn right at a crossroads and follow signs to Hankham.

2 Turn right at a T-junction in Hankham, signposted 'Rickney'. Keep right at the next junction for Rickney (National Cycle Route 2). For a short loop back, at the next junction (in Rickney itself) turn right, then right after 1.5 miles (2.4km). Cross the roundabout and take the road back into Pevensey. To take the main cycle ride, turn left at the junction in Rickney (signposted 'Hailsham'), then take the first right, signposted 'Herstmonceux'. Both the short and full rides afford lovely views across the Pevensey Levels.

3 After 3 miles (4.8km) turn right at the next junction, and then keep right at the next two junctions to reach Herstmonceux Church. Have a look inside for the tomb of Thomas Lord Dacre (died 1553) and his son Sir Thomas Fiennes.

4 Past the church, where the public road ends, go forward, veering left on the bridleway, and follow blue arrows and waymarkers for the 1066 Country Walk. This leads over a surfaced area near college outbuildings and a car park, and through woodland (it can be muddy). It then crosses a field, with a view of Herstmonceux Castle to the left; it is not always open to the public, so enjoy the view from here. Ahead is one of the telescope buildings of the former Royal Greenwich Observatory. Push your bike up some steps and later you will see the other domes of the Herstmonceux Science Centre.

5 Turn right on the road (just to the left is the entrance to the Science Centre and Herstmonceux Castle and grounds) and cycle down to Wartling, keeping right in front of the Lamb Inn. Continue for 2.5 miles (4km) back to the edge of Pevensey.

6 Cross the roundabout carefully, using the cycle crossing points, and take the road into Pevensey to return to the start point.

DISTANCE/TIME 12 miles (19.3km) 4h; shorter route 7 miles (11.3km) 2h **MAP** OS Explorer 123 South Downs Way: Newhaven to Eastbourne **START** Seven Sisters Country Park pay car park; grid ref: TV 518995 **TRACKS** Compacted and forest tracks, road, rough tracks, stony descents

THE PUB The Plough and Harrow, Litlington. Tel: 01323 870632

FRISTON FOREST & CUCKMERE HAVEN

The ride takes you past three wonderful contrasts: the Cuckmere river as it meanders its way to the sea; the tranquil greenery of Friston Forest, planted in the early 20th century over an underground reservoir; and the sweeping views inland and towards the sea from the top of the Downs.

1 From the car park go towards the vehicular entrance, and just before the road turn right on a track signposted 'public bridleway to West Dean'. Look for the bicycle symbols in green, which denote the bike trail you will be following for the first part of the ride.

2 At the first house at West Dean keep heading forward on the track (signposted 'Exceat Hill'), following the green bike symbols. After 1 mile (1.6km) you will reach a junction marked with five tall red-and-white posts.

3 For a short return to West Dean, fork left almost immediatley after, and continue following the green bike symbols, turning right at the hard forest road (to the left you can see the tall red-and-white posts), then soon turn left at another bike symbol. The track rises (at the top a short path leads up right to a viewpoint and then falls). Leave the waymarked trail at a three-way fork, keeping right downhill, past a barrier and houses, then turn left at a road junction into West Dean. Pass the church and rectory and drop to a T-junction by Pond Cottage, then go ahead towards the flight of steps, where you turn right along the track you were following earlier and retrace to the start. For the main route, continue ahead at Point 3 and fork left near some power lines. Go past a barrier, and forward again on joining a metalled road, which becomes less surfaced (ignore side turns). On reaching a road, turn left along it to Jevington.

4 Turn left at Jevington and take the track signposted 'South Downs Way and church'. Continue uphill on the track, which steepens through the woods. Ignore side turns.

5 At the top emerge from the woodland, ignore the South Downs Way to the right and keep forward. There are wonderful views from this track and just to the left is Lullington Heath Nature Reserve. The track later drops steeply and then rises to a junction by a small flint pillar on the left. Carry on downhill, forking left later to Litlington, where the track twists left and then right by farm buildings.

6 At the road turn left through Litlington. The road leads back to the turning to West Dean and the car park at Exceat. To extend the ride, carefully cross the main road through the gate by the bus stop, follow the bike route to the sea and then return.

Windsor & the Thames

CLOCKWISE FROM TOP; WINDSOR CASTLE; FERNS IN KEW GARDENS; RICHMOND PARK DEER; NARROW BOAT ON THE THAMES, HENLEY-ON-THAMES

ASCOT MAP REF 400 F5

This rather small town is a Goliath in the horse racing world, and the Fashion Stakes – not so much a race as a parade of glamorous hats. The first horse racing on Ascot Heath, not far from Windsor, was endorsed by Queen Anne in 1711, and members of the Royal family have continued to attend the June meeting ever since. The Royal Ascot meeting lasts four days and has lent its name to the 'Ascot', a type of broad neck scarf. The principal event is the Ascot Gold Cup, established in 1807 and run over 2.5 miles (4km) by horses over three years old.

A number of distinguished and notable people have lived in AscoT. Sir Edward Richard Henry (1850–1931), Commissioner of Police of the Metropolis, lived in Windsor Road, Ascot. He was responsible for the establishment of the central fingerprint bureau, followed by the development of the habitual criminals register to incorporate fingerprints and the criminal records office. Field Marshall Lord Roberts (1832-1914), soldier and statesman, known as Lord Roberts of Kandahar, lived at Englemere, on Kings Ride.

CLAREMONT & PAINSHILL

MAP REF 401 G5

These two early examples of 18th century picturesque landscapes, manmade but naturalistic, are recognized as important survivors of the English style of landscape gardening. Gardens such as these, Stowe and Stourhead led the movement away from the formal landscape style found throughout Europe.

Conveniently located close to the A307, and not far from Esher, the house and garden at Claremont was designed as a pleasure garden and created over a number of years by Vanbrugh, Bridgeman, Kent and 'Capability' Brown, the most significant landscape gardeners of their day. By 1727 it was described as 'the noblest of any in Europe'.

The Claremont estate was sold to Lord Clive of India in 1769 and he demolished the existing house and replaced it with the mansion that is there today. Claremont became home to many royals during the 19th century, Queen Victoria spent much of her girlhood here but in 1922 the estate was divided and sold. The house and park were bought by Claremont School and the landscape garden was given to the National Trust. After many years of neglect the gardens underwent a full programme of restoration in the 1970's to return the landscaped park to its former glory.

Painshill was created a little later than Claremont but is no less important. Such was the drama of the original design that it is best described as a landscape theatre. The landscape was designed by the Hon Charles Hamilton and included a vast serpentine lake with idyllic scenes and romantic buildings at every turn. These included a ruined Abbey, a gothic temple and tower, waterwheel, grotto and glorious views. During the course of successive ownership the grounds became derelict and overgrown but in 1981 Elmbridge Borough Council bought 158 acres (64ha), almost all of the original acreage, formed the Painshill Trust, and began an ambitious restoration programme that has resulted in a splendid re-creation of the original 18th-century landscape. Painshill is open all year, except Christmas and Boxing Day and has an excellent range of facilities.

COOKHAM & CLIVEDEN

MAP REF 400 F4

Cookham village has an identity crisis; it comprises three villages: Cookham Village, the centre of the original village, with an attractive High Street and a good mix of buildings, little changed over the centuries; Cookham Dean, a desirable and rather expensive area in which to live, and the bit in the middle, Cookham Rise, that has evolved around the village's railway station.

Author Kenneth Grahame who, as a child, lived at 'The Mount' (Herries School) in Cookham Dean, is said to have been inspired by the Thames at Cookham to write *The Wind in the Willows*. Quarry Wood in Bisham, adjoining, is thought to have inspired the original 'Wild Wood'. The famous English painter, Sir Stanley Spencer was born here and many of his works depict villagers and village life. Much of his artwork is in the Stanley Spencer Gallery in the centre of the village, close to where he lived. He is buried in the village churchyard.

East of Cookham, Cliveden, now a private hotel, is a masterpiece, a three-storey Italianate palace built by Sir Charles Barry for the Duke and Duchess of Sutherland. With stunning views across the Thames, Cliveden was the glittering hub of society as the home of Waldorf and Nancy Astor in the early part of the 20th century, and later infamously associated with the 'Profumo Affair'; Henry James, Rudyard Kipling and Winston Churchill were no strangers to Cliveden. The lovely estate with a celebrated parterre, has splendid formal gardens, each with its own character, an outstanding collection of sculpture and statues from the ancient and modern worlds, as well as extensive woodland and riverside walks.

ETON MAP REF 400 F5

The town of Eton, across the Thames from its sibling, Windsor, has an interesting high street, an eclectic mix of the traditional and the contemporary, bringing together antiques and modern art. It is an attractive town dotted with fine historic buildings.

But the town is known primarily for its College, the most famous public school in England. The school was founded in 1440 and still occupies the original buildings.

Eton College was founded by King Henry VI to provide scholars for King's College, Cambridge which was opened the following year. The original name of the school was 'The King's College of Our Lady of Eton beside Windsor'. At the time of the schools endowment it provided free education for poor boys who lived at the school although it also admitted some fee-paying boys who lived elsewhere in the town. The total number of scholars was 70. To fund the school Henry gave it several holy relics and, perhaps more practically, large grants of land.

Life at school for the 15th-century schoolboy was a far cry from today. They were required to study for long hours and comforts were few and far between with only very basic facilities; the boys would have had to wash outside in all weathers using only cold water. From these 70 scholars, the school has expanded to nearly 1,300 boys aged from 13 to 18. No longer the sons of families unable to afford to teach them to read and write, Etons scholars must now pass an entrance examination and Eton College has become one of the most exclusive schools in the world. Not surprisingly, such a long history brings with it much tradition and the School uniform is much as it was in the 1850s. The boys stilll wear a black tailcoat and necktie, a waistcoat and pin-striped trousers. During its long career as an educational institution Eton has educated 18 former British Prime Ministers, including the Duke of Wellington, Walpole, Pitt the Elder, MacMillan and Douglas-Home.

The original school buildings are a wonderful example of the Perpendicular Gothic style with additional buildings added over the next few centuries, notably Lupton's Chapel, finished in 1515. There are guided tours of the College available throughout the summer which offer a fascinating insight into life at the school over the last 600 years. These take you round the Cloisters, the College Chapel, the oldest classroom in the College and the Museum of Eton Life.

HAMPTON COURT PALACE

MAP REF **401 G5**

Get set for an action-packed day at one of the grandest royal palaces in Britain. The magnificent red-brick Hampton Court was built in 1514 by Thomas Wolsey, then Archbishop of York but soon to become Henry VIII's chief minister.

By 1528, Henry had relieved Wolsey of ownership. Until 1737 it was the centre of royal and political life in England and associated with many important events in history. In 1533 Henry VIII honeymooned here with Anne Boleyn and married his sixth wife Catherine Parr in 1543, whilst in 1647 Charles I was held prisoner in the palace by Oliver Cromwell, who lived there in 1653.

The palace has been the scene for many dramas and intrigues throughout history. The palace was opened to the public in 1838 by Queen Victoria and it has been a popular attraction ever since. This is partly because of its range of family-friendly events and exhibitions. There are horse-drawn carriage rides in the summer, ghost-hunting tours, Tudor cookery demonstrations and daily tours of the palace with costumed guides. In the winter an ice rink is formed in the west courtyard (book in advance).

It's worth exploring the palace and its gardens regardless of special events. Henry VIII's State Apartments are the centrepiece of the interior, decorated by woodcarver Grinling Gibbons, painter Antonio Verrio and blacksmith Jean Tijou.

Outside, try to navigate the famous maze or wander along Chestnut Avenue to admire the Diana Fountain.

The Maze is probably the most famous hedge maze in the world. It was planted as part of the gardens laid out for William of Orange between 1689 and 1695 by George London and Henry Wise. It was described with great wit in Jerome K. Jerome's novel *Three Men in a Boat*. Hampton Court Maze continues to attract hundreds of thousands of visitors each year.

HENLEY-ON-THAMES MAP REF 400 F4

A select upper-class town, and home of arguably the world's best-known annual rowing regatta, an event bizarrely emulated in the dry riverbed conditions of the Todd River in Alice Springs in central Australia, Henley lies along a beautiful stretch of the Thames. The town centre is richly endowed with curiosity and antiques shops, and fine buildings from the 15th to 18th centuries. You'll find exceptional examples of architecture along Bell Street, New Street and Hart Street. The Catherine Wheel Hotel in Hart Street (once the St Kathrine of Henley, whom the hotel is named after) is one of the oldest in the town. Charles I stayed at the Red Lion Hotel on New Street during his journey from London to Oxford in 1632.

St Mary's Church is worth a visit to see the churchyard, which contains several interesting tombs, including that of Richard Jennings, a local of Henley, who was renowned as the 'Master Builder' of St Paul's Cathedral under Sir Christopher Wren. In relatively more recent years, the 1960s popular singer Dusty Springfield has a gravesite marker in St Mary's churchyard; her ashes were scattered here, and in Ireland on land at the Moher Mountains.

Beatrice Lilly (Lady Peel), the famous actress, lived at Peelfold, Mill End on Mill Lane, and spent many years at Henley. She was born in Toronto in 1894, and was one of the funniest and most spontaneous women of her generation. Her next-door neighbour was a famous camp cabaret act – none other than Danny La Rue.

Henley Bridge, a pretty five-arched bridge across the Thames which was built in 1786, sits on the river and joins the town to the village of Remenham where the Royal Regatta is actually held. The Henley Royal Regatta is firmly on some social calendars and lasts for four days in late June to early July, and annually rejuvenates a town that probably doesn't need any rejuvenating. The Regatta culminates with a fireworks display, which heralds a degree of partying that can run into the Henley Festival a week later.

Insight
GRINLING GIBBONS

Dutchman and master carver, Grinling Gibbons (1648–1721), was responsible for the beautiful detailed carvings of animals and flowers that can be admired in the King's Apartments at Hampton Court Palace.

Insight
PRINCESS SOPHIA DULEEP SINGH

Princess Sophia Duleep Singh (1838–93) was the youngest daughter of the then Sikh Maharaja Duleep Singh, a favourite of Queen Victoria. Queen Victoria, the Princess's godmother, granted her and her sister, Bamba, a grace-and-favour apartment within Hampton Court Palace. Although the Princess carried an air of refinement, Sophia and Bamba became involved in the Suffragette movement and Sophia was seen selling the published papers of the movement near the palace gates. Sophia later accompanied Emmeline Pankhurst on the suffragettes' march to Parliament in 1910.

KEW GARDENS MAP REF 401 G5

Even if you're not green-fingered, the Royal Botanic Gardens of Kew, to the west of London, are a magical place to spend a day. The gardens were given World Heritage Status in 2003 and have world-class collections of plants displayed in amazing greenhouses, stars themselves.

The Botanic Gardens began as two royal estates. They were combined in 1772 and became a horticultural centre at the time when exotic specimens were brought back from all over the world by sailors, explorers and botanists. That was the science; but there was an art to displaying these plants, for which gardener Lancelot 'Capability' Brown was responsible. In the Western Zone you can see his original design for the Rhododendron Dell.

Be warned: Kew Botanic Gardens cover 300 acres (120ha) so don't expect to see everything in one visit. Highlights include the unmissable Palm House, a multi-layered greenhouse designed by Decimus Burton that took four years to construct. On the opposite side of the Palm House lake, Museum No 1 houses the interactive Plants+People exhibition. In the Pagoda Vista Zone, Burton's Temperate House is the world's largest surviving Victorian greenhouse, home to a Chilean Wine Palm, which is the biggest greenhouse plant in existence, and to the rarest plant at Kew, a cycad from South Africa. There are plenty of inspiring spots to discover, such as Queen Charlotte's Cottage and Gardens, dedicated to British wild flowers. In winter, the largest ice rink in London is established at the gardens.

RICHMOND PARK MAP REF 401 G5

Richmond Park is the largest royal park and the most expansive green space in the capital. In the 17th century it was King Charles I's hunting ground, but the 650 deer that roam the park today have little to worry about. As well as 350 fallow deer, there are 300 majestic red deer. The deer herds, which are free to wander the grassland and the rare oak woodlands, are not difficult to spot. Other mammals living in this National Nature Reserve include nine species of bat and there are 144 species of bird, including a growing group of parakeets.

Although the park's landscape has changed very little over the past three centuries, it has a variety of modern uses. Cyclists and runners do laps of the perimeter; you can hire bicycles in the car park at the Roehampton Gate. There are two golf courses and three rugby pitches, which are sometimes used for polo matches. Fishing in the Pen Ponds requires a permit, while power-kiting needs just a good breeze and nerve.

THE THAMES PATH

Meandering gently from its source in the Cotswolds through several rural counties and on through the bustle of the City of London, the Thames Path follows England's best-known river for 184 miles (296km). On its way, the Path, a National Trail, passes peaceful water meadows rich in wildlife, historic towns and many lovely villages, finishing at the Thames Barrier near Greenwich.

The Thames Valley was first settled by prehistoric people of the New Stone Age, 6,000 years ago, in the region of Runnymede and Staines. Not surprisingly, the valley became an extremely important trading route for hundreds of years and only relatively recently, in the latter half of the 20th century, did the carriage of goods finally come to an end.

The towpath between Lechlade and Putney, along which much of the Thames Path now travels, was established towards the end of the 18th century.

A path along the Thames was among the original list of long-distance routes proposed by the Hobhouse Committee in 1948 and was subsequently supported by the Ramblers' Association, who published the first guide to the route in 1981. It was finally opened as a National Trail in 1996. Of all the National Trails in Britain, the Thames Path especially lends itself to piecemeal consumption, known by some walkers as 'Staggering from one pub to the next', but by others as the perfect way to experience a delightful and historic walk in different seasons.

WINDSOR MAP REF 400 F5

A handsome market town, Windsor sits on the south bank of the River Thames, to the west of London. The town is dominated by Windsor Castle, standing on the outcrop of chalk on which William I (the Conqueror: 1066–87) built the original fortress. Still in regular occupation as a royal residence the Castle is a conspicuous landmark for travellers approaching Heathrow Airport.

KEW GARDENS

AROUND HAMPTON COURT

In just ten years Henry VIII spent more than £62,000 (equivalent to £18 million today) rebuilding and extending the palace. Hampton Court dates back to the early 1200s, when the site was occupied by the Knights Hospitallers of St John of Jerusalem. The world-famous maze and the Great Vine (planted in 1768) continue to delight visitors. Real tennis has been played at Hampton Court by members of the royal family for more than five centuries.

DISTANCE/TIME 4.75 miles (7.7km) 1h45 **MAP** OS Explorer 161 London South **START** Car park in Hampton Court Road; grid ref: TQ 152689 **PATHS** Gravel, tarmac and riverside tracks

THE PUB The King's Arms, Hampton Court. Tel: 020 8977 1729

1 From the car park follow the footpath signposted 'Hampton Court Palace' (HCP), which runs parallel to the road. Cross the road and enter HCP through the main gates. Walk along the wide drive. Just before the palace turn left to pass a gatehouse and then under an arch leading to the walled garden.

2 Turn right just before the tea room, through a gateway and along a path through the gardens. At the end, on the right, is the real tennis court building. Pass through another gateway and turn sharp right to walk alongside the real tennis court and past the entrance to it.

3 Take the central gravel path in front of the palace, past a fountain to ornate railings overlooking the Long Water, an artificial lake nearly 0.75 mile (1.2km) long. Head to a footbridge on the right and go through the wrought-iron gates.

4 After 220yds (200m) a footpath bears left and joins a tarmac track. Follow this, turning left by farm cottages, then the path runs parallel to Long Water. Where the lake ends continue ahead at a crossing of tracks and then bear right along a grassy path to skirt the left side of Rick Pond. Turn left through a metal gate and walk along the enclosed footpath and through another gate to reach the River Thames.

5 Turn left along the riverside path for 0.75 mile (1.2km) to reach Kingston Bridge. Turn left at the bridge to join a road leading to a roundabout.

6 Follow the railings on the left and at a signpost for 'Hampton Court Golf Club' turn left through the Kingston Gate. Immediately after a cattle grid bear right along a grassy path along the left of the boomerang-shaped Hampton Wick Pond. Follow this straight path for 0.75 mile (1.2km) back to Hampton Court Palace.

7 Bear right to cross the footbridge and follow footpath back to the real tennis court, from where you can retrace steps to the car park in Hampton Court Road.

WALK 44

A CIRCUIT OF RICHMOND PARK

Discover London's largest open space at a leisurely pace. At 2,500 acres (1,012ha) Richmond Park has an abundance of wildlife in its hills, woodland gardens and grasslands. Although you will see only a fraction of the park on this walk, you will want to return again and again. The Isabella Plantation was created from an existing woodland and is organically run, resulting in a rich flora and fauna. More than 1,000 species of beetle have been recorded in the park, a National Nature Reserve and a Site of Special Scientific Interest.

DISTANCE/TIME 6.75 miles (10.9km) 2h30 **MAP** OS Explorer 161 London South **START** Car park at Pembroke Lodge in Richmond Park; grid ref: TQ189728 **PATHS** Mainly tarmac paths

THE PUB The White Cross, Richmond. Tel: 020 8940 6844

1 With your back to the information centre in the car park at Pembroke Lodge turn right to follow the Tamsin Trail in the general direction of Ham Gate. The path veers to the right and later runs close to the road.

2 At a crossroads leading to Ham Gate, turn left passing to the right of the Hamcross Plantation. At the next crossroads go right to visit the Isabella Plantation, or continue and turn left at the next main junction, before another plantation. Circle the wood clockwise along a wide track. Take the right fork at the next junction and follow the path to the end of the pond.

3 Turn right along a path between the two ponds (Pen Ponds) and continue ahead. Keep ahead at a car park to reach Robin Hood Gate. Deer are often spotted here but their coats give them good camouflage, especially against a background of bracken.

4 Turn left at Robin Hood Gate. Follow the gravel path of the Tamsin Trail past the Richmond Park Golf Course and on to Roehampton Gate.

5 Continue ahead to cross a footbridge over Beverley Brook and, after a further 500yds (457m), the path winds to pass to the right of Adam's Pond, which is one of the watering holes used by the deer. Follow the path across the upper end of the park, past Sheen Gate, to Richmond Gate.

6 Turn left at Richmond Gate and continue along the path to reach Pembroke Lodge. If you have time, look for the Henry VIII mound, which is at the highest point of the park in the formal gardens of Pembroke Lodge. This prehistoric burial ground is not easy to find (take the higher path to the cottage) but it is well worth the effort, for here is a view of the dome of St Paul's Cathedral 10 miles (16km) away. Henry VIII is said to have stood here while his second wife, Anne Boleyn, was being beheaded at the Tower of London.

London

CLOCKWISE FROM TOP: CHANGING OF THE GUARD, BUCKINGHAM PALACE; KENSINGTON GARDENS

Central

BRITISH LIBRARY

The British Library's new home was completed in 1997 and while the block-like, red-brick exterior (by architect Colin St John Wilson) dismayed some observers, there's no doubting the value of the treasures within. Among them are documents and books that have defined Britain: the Lindisfarne Gospels, the Magna Carta and Shakespeare's First Folio. Editions of global significance include Sultan Baybars' Qur'an, the Gutenberg Bible and the Indian legend the Ramayana. What's more, the British Library is open seven days a week and entry to the galleries is free.

The variety of different exhibits is also surprising: although the library gets a copy of every new book published in the United Kingdom, you might not expect to see so many ancient maps on display or the detailed stamp collection. Musicians can read original music scores written by Bach, Mozart, Beethoven and Handel – and song lyrics by The Beatles. Or you can return to your childhood with the original version of *Alice's Adventures in Wonderland* by Lewis Carroll and first editions of Rudyard Kipling's *Jungle Book*. Special exhibitions are regularly scheduled and renowned writers often give talks.

BRITISH MUSEUM

The British Museum is arguably the finest museum of its kind in the world. It has unparalleled collections of art and antiquities that together document human civilisation across a number of cultures. There is far too much here to see in one day; the best idea is to choose just a handful of galleries at a time.

Most visitors head first for the museum's highlights, which include several Egyptian mummies, kept in a dimly lit room that adds to the eerie atmosphere. Also from Egypt is the Rosetta Stone, a slab of black basalt with text in three different languages that enabled experts to translate Egyptian hieroglyphics. As you might expect, ancient British history is especially well served by the museum. Must-see exhibits include the Mildenhall Treasure, Roman silverware unearthed in a Suffolk field; the Sutton Hoo Anglo-Saxon burial ship, also found in Suffolk; and Lindow Man, the prehistoric corpse of a man preserved in a peat bog.

Visiting the museum is not a dry experience and the curators try hard to interest children. A series of six family trails introduces youngsters to British history, ancient Greece and Egypt, and fantastical creatures. During the school holidays there are activities, workshops and storytelling sessions, all geared to bring the past alive again.

One attraction at the British Museum that would be impossible to overlook is architect Norman Foster's Great Court, an airy, uplifting central courtyard.

BUCKINGHAM PALACE

Although Buckingham Palace is not the most aesthetically pleasing of the royal properties – it's the result of a botched job by architects Edward Blore and John Nash, who began the conversion of the original 1703 house into a royal palace in 1825 – it remains at the heart of London. Today, it is not only the royal family who can enjoy the palace, because during August and September the State Rooms and gardens are opened to the public.

It is fascinating to see not only the extravagant interiors but also how the rooms are organized. The Green Drawing Room is the place where guests gather before they are presented to the Queen, while grand State banquets are held in either the State Dining Room or the vast Ballroom. It is best to book a ticket to see these particular rooms in advance.

The Queen's Gallery, on Buckingham Gate, is open year-round. On display are old masters as well as jewellery, Fabergé eggs and Sèvres porcelain.

CABINET WAR ROOMS & CHURCHILL MUSEUM

It was in this bunker under Whitehall that crucial phases of World War II were planned by Winston Churchill. The rooms are functional yet sparsely furnished. They remain much as they were in 1945, with a map room for plotting troop movements with coloured pins, the Transatlantic Telephone Room for conversations with the President of the United States and a bedroom where Churchill took naps.

You can learn much more about the man himself, including the brand of cigar he smoked, in the Churchill Museum. The interactive Lifeline display allows you to discover what happened on some of the most important dates in his life.

BRITISH MUSEUM

COVENT GARDEN

London's first formal square was designed by the architect Inigo Jones in the 1630s. Bordered on one side by St Paul's Church and by the Royal Opera House on the other, Covent Garden Piazza is no more the quiet residential square that the 17th-century landowner John Russell intended. Instead, it is a tourist nexus, attracting thousands to the arcaded marketplace and the street performers outside. The result is that the lifts at Covent Garden tube station can be very congested: instead arrive at Leicester Square and walk up Long Acre – the distance between Covent Garden and Leicester Square stations is the shortest in the underground network.

The shops within the piazza are carefully selected – no chain stores here. There is still a daily market in the North Hall, with arts and crafts stalls on Tuesday through to Sunday. On Mondays antiques dealers set up their stalls. Jubilee Market, on the corner of Southampton Street, mainly sells cheap and cheerful souvenirs. The surrounding area has also attracted some more prestigious retailers: Floral Street, Henrietta Street and King Street are lined with boutiques, and Southampton Street has a number of stores selling equipment

for outdoor activities. Back on the square, St Paul's Church, also by Inigo Jones, is known as the Actors' Church. Inside there are plaques dedicated to Charlie Chaplin and Vivien Leigh, amongst others. Art historians may be interested to know that woodcarver par excellence Grinling Gibbons was buried here in 1721.

HOUSES OF PARLIAMENT

British political power is concentrated in this majestic Gothic Revival building on the banks of the Thames. The Houses of Parliament, one of the world's earliest parliamentary democracies, are divided into the House of Lords and the House of Commons. The MPs of constituencies across Britain sit and deliberate in the Commons. Legislative proposals are then passed to the Lords for consideration.

During the summer recess, from early August to late September, British citizens can tour the House of Commons. The ticket office is adjacent to the Jewel Tower and is open from late July; tickets are also available online. Security has been tightened, so note what you can and cannot take inside. The 75-minute tour begins at the Norman Porch and enters the Queen's Robing Room, where she

prepares for the annual State Opening of Parliament in November. From here, visitors pass through the Royal Gallery, the Prince's Chamber, the House of Lords Chamber and into the central Lobby, where MPs congregate for TV interviews. The tour concludes in St Stephen's Hall and the 11th-century Westminster Hall.

The medieval Westminster Hall and the Jewel Tower are the only parts of the original Palace of Westminster which survived the fire of 1834. The Jewel Tower, or King's Privy Wardrobe, was built in 1365 to house Edward III's treasures. It is managed by English Heritage and is open to visitors all year round.

NATIONAL GALLERY

You would need to set aside several days, or weeks even, to do justice to the National Gallery's collection of art. Instead of trying to see everything and exhausting yourself, home in on what interests you.

There is such a treasure trove to choose from, with Italian Renaissance art in the Sainsbury Wing a particular strength: there are works by Botticelli, Leonardo and Raphael. Dutch masters, such as Vermeer and Van Dyck, occupy the North Wing, while the French Impressionists,

including Monet, are a big draw for the East Wing. Reynolds, Constable, Turner and Gainsborough are just some of the home-grown artists on show, but as well as drinking in the art, also keep an eye on your surroundings: the building itself is of immense importance, a fact that is confirmed by its Grade I status.

The National Gallery, as befits the country's leading art gallery, also has events, talks, film seasons and performances. Every month there is a full and changing programme of workshops, brunches and evening lectures. Children can create personalized tours of the building in the Micro Gallery or sign up for trails, audio tours and art workshops.

NATIONAL PORTRAIT GALLERY

The National Portrait Gallery owns the world's largest collection of portraits. This surprisingly small space holds a collection of incredible quality and depth, making it a fascinating place for anyone interested in people, art or society. Royalty is represented by the stunning and varied portraits of the royal family in Room 33 and there are paintings of powerbrokers from Elizabethan, Stuart and Victorian times in subsequent rooms. These portraits

HOUSES OF PARLIAMENT

SOMERSET HOUSE

tell the story of art, science, industry and politics through the ages, with the most contemporary characters appearing in the ground-floor galleries. Famous faces here range from modern icon and football player David Beckham (in a video by Sam Taylor-Wood) to one of the most recent additions, a portrait of J K Rowling, author of the phenomenally successful Harry Potter series of novels.

Like the National Gallery, there are frequent talks, films and events at the National Portrait Gallery, which celebrated its 150th year in 2006; visit the gallery's website for more details.

SOMERSET HOUSE

Somerset House is the collective name for three art galleries held in this 18th-century riverside mansion: the Courtauld Gallery, the Gilbert Collection and the Hermitage Rooms. The house was built on the site of the Duke of Somerset's Tudor Palace and changed hands between various government departments and institutions several times during the 20th century. It has certainly embraced its current role with great enthusiasm.

Although the galleries are rather rarefied, Somerset House is a versatile venue for live music (think rock concerts rather than classical recitals) and even ice skating in the winter.

The Courtauld contains examples of art and sculpture from the early Italian Renaissance to 20th-century British pieces. The Gilbert Collection was donated to Somerset House five years before the death of collector Sir Arthur Gilbert in 2001. It is notable for focusing mainly on mosaics and includes some stunning pieces of pietre dure inlay work, but there are also vases, plates and candelabra. The Hermitage, by contrast, is dedicated to biannually changing exhibits from the Winter Palace in St Petersburg.

TATE BRITAIN

With the arrival of its sister gallery Tate Modern, Tate Britain has had much more exhibition space for its collection of 3,500 paintings. But even though it can now focus on British art from 1500 to the present day, the Victorian gallery still shows only a fraction of its vast collection. Rooms 1 to 17 are dedicated to British art from 1500 to 1900 – sporting scenes by Stubbs, Turner's moody landscapes and illustrations by Blake. Turner also appears in several rooms in the Clore Galleries, added in 1987. Rooms 17 to 27 cover British art from 1900 to the present, with one room featuring work by Lucian Freud, Francis Bacon and Reg Butler, and another covering 1960s Pop Art. Talks by art experts and short courses can shed

light on particular artists or periods. Whatever your taste, you should find something to entertain you at Tate Britain; if not, take the Tate boat down the Thames to the newer Tate Modern.

WESTMINSTER ABBEY

The setting for many a royal story, Westminster Abbey dates from 1066, when Edward the Confessor was the first of many monarchs to be buried here. Under the Normans the abbey and its abbot became wealthy and powerful forces. During the Dissolution of the Monasteries in the 16th century the abbey's royal connections spared it the dreadful fate of many of the country's other abbeys. Elizabeth I returned Westminster Abbey to royal control in 1579; her effigy is in the Lady Chapel. The abbey has hosted all but two coronations. The monarch sits on St Edward's Chair during the ceremony.

Burial here is an honour accorded not just to royalty and it is interesting to see the range of people commemorated here, including scientists (Darwin, Newton), actors, politicians and composers. Poets and writers occupy the south transept (Poets' Corner) and include Chaucer, Dickens and Kipling. The busts of the 17th-century poets Dryden, Jonson and Milton are worth seeking out. There are recitals and concerts throughout the year.

Activity
OUTDOOR ICE RINK

Don't forget your ice skates! In the depths of winter Somerset House hosts some of the most popular nights out in the capital with its open-air ice rink. The courtyard is frozen over and skaters take to the ice. The ice rink is in operation from late November to late January and you need to book tickets in advance. It's not London's only open-air ice rink: there are also skating rinks at Hampton Court, the Tower of London, Kew Gardens and even the Natural History Museum.

Visit
ST JAMES'S PARK

The smallest and most central of London's parks is also one of its most appealing. Flanked by the Mall and Horse Guards, St James's Park has no shortage of visitors passing through or relaxing on the grass, making it fine territory for people-watching. You can also spot unusual waterfowl on the lake. From the excellent Inn on the Park, visitors can enjoy the views of Buckingham Palace and the grand old buildings of Whitehall. If you feel the need for more space for a game of Frisbee or cricket, simply head across into neighbouring Green Park.

ST PAUL'S CATHEDRAL

North, Northwest & City

BRICK LANE

Brick Lane is one of the most cosmopolitan streets in London, a pulsating mélange of market stalls, shops, bars and many of London's cheapest (but perhaps not best) curry restaurants, which are mostly run by members from the area's Bangladeshi community. It takes its name from the brick and tile manufacturing workshops that sprang up in the Middle Ages; more recently it lent its name to Monica Ali's novel, *Brick Lane*, about life in London's Asian communities. Brick Lane is best visited on either Sunday morning, for the street market, or in the evening, when it throngs with Londoners hopping from one nightspot to another. Off to the side are some interesting courtyards, such as the Old Truman Brewery, now populated by young artists and designer boutiques.

HAMPSTEAD HEATH

Hampstead Heath is the largest green space in north London. It is now one of London's most welcoming habitats for wildlife and there are birdwatching and bat-spotting walks. Parts of the Heath have been designated Sites of Special Scientific Interest (SSSI).

But the majority of people associate Hampstead Heath with its ponds. There are 25 of them, but the Highgate Ponds for bathing are on the east side, off Millfield Lane. Towards the south of the Heath, Parliament Hill Lido offers more facilities. Close to the Lido there is an athletics track, though most recreational runners will prefer to jog on the Heath itself, among the families, horse riders, cyclists, walkers and kite-flyers.

However, for many the real highlight of Hampstead Heath is its elevated vantage point – from Parliament Hill you can look out across London landmarks.

MADAME TUSSAUDS

Madame Tussauds waxworks collection is still one of London's most popular attractions, drawing in more than 2 million vistors, despite a high entry fee. Famous people know they have made it when their waxwork appears here and, conversely, that their star is shining less brightly when their likeness is melted down to be turned into a more recognisable celebrity.

Strasbourg born Madame Marie Tussaud cannot have envisaged how hugely popular her waxworks would become when she started the collection some 200 years ago. Modern techniques and technology mean that some of the newer exhibits are more interactive than others and it may be your only chance to actually touch stars such as J-Lo, Brad Pitt and Robbie Williams. Set pieces include the Garden Party, the Chamber of Horrors and the Spirit of London, which is a ride through 400 years of the city's history in a black cab.

REGENT'S PARK

Regent's Park, part of Henry VIII's hunting grounds, is perhaps London's most attractive park. It was landscaped by John Nash in the early 19th century and claims London's finest rose gardens, with 400 varieties and 30,000 plants.

The remainder of the 410 acres (166ha) contain 100 acres (40.5ha) of sports pitches and space for activities, including the Regent's Park Tennis Centre, which has courts available for non-members. There is also a Golf and Tennis School, again with practice facilities available to non-members. Netball players can chose from three courts, while runners have a cinder track on the north side of the park.

For a more leisurely time, how about rowing in a hired boat on the lake, dodging the wildfowl? There are several cafés, including the excellent Garden Café in Queen Mary's Garden. If that is too much effort, just sink into a deckchair (summer only) and enjoy the surroundings.

ST PAUL'S CATHEDRAL

St Paul's dome, 354 feet (108m) high – the only cathedral dome in Britain – rises unmistakably above the buildings of the north bank of the River Thames. The cathedral was commissioned after the Great Fire destroyed the original in 1666. Sir Christopher Wren mixed classical and Gothic architecture in its design, although it is the sense of scale that impresses most visitors: the dome is second in size only to St Peter's in Rome; inside, the dome and galleries appear even larger. The interior is a mass of soaring arches, intricate carving and gilding. To the right of the nave, steps lead up to the Whispering Gallery; if you're here early enough and the cathedral is quiet you can hear a whisper from the opposite side of the nave.

Although it is a bit of a hike up the 530 steps to the dome's Golden Gallery, the climb is worth it for the panoramic views across London – they rival those from the London Eye, but are much cheaper! The tombs of the Duke of Wellington (with four lion's heads carved into the block of granite that it sits on), Admiral Nelson and Sir Christopher Wren are in the crypt, as is the cathedral's treasury. The cathedral celebrated its 300th anniversary in 2008.

SIR JOHN SOANE'S MUSEUM

Described as London's best-kept secret, this museum contains the fruit of decades of collecting by Sir John Soane, Professor of Architecture at the Royal Academy. He would open his house to visitors on the day before and the day after one of his lectures, and here they could see a crowded yet fascinating mix of sculpture, paintings, carvings, furniture and curios spread across the floorspace of three town houses. Today the rooms are organized according to Soane's original design.

Highlights include the Picture Room, which has hinged screens to extend hanging space; three Canalettos take pride of place in the New Picture Room. Given the variety of Soane's tastes, it isn't so surprising to come across the 3,000-year-old sarcophagus of Pharaoh Seti I and important Roman marbles and statues. Soane also built up an internationally acknowledged collection of Chinese tiles. It is worth noting that due to the limited space inside and the museum's popularity, there may be queues on Saturdays.

TOWER OF LONDON

The Tower originally came to national prominence in the 13th century, but the oldest building on the site dates from the 11th century. It was initially used as an armoury, fortress and royal residence and only later became a prison. The buildings around Tower Green include the Bloody Tower, where many of the most famous and important prisoners were kept. Traitors' Gate was the place where those accused of treason arrived by boat.

Hourly tours led by Beefeaters are recommended if you have children – the scarlet-clad Beefeaters are experts at bringing the stories to life. The armouries exhibition in the White Tower is an enthralling series of weapons and armour, but the highlight of a visit is seeing the Crown Jewels, on display in the Waterloo Barracks. Although you're herded through on a moving travelator, it's hard to miss the world's largest cut diamond, the Star of Africa, or the Imperial State Crown.

Southeast

CANARY WHARF

When Canary Wharf tower was under construction sceptics suggested that the shiny new offices there would remain forever unfilled. Who, they asked, would relocate their business to the deprived Isle of Dogs, especially since the Jubilee Line tube connecting Canary Wharf to central London had not been finished? The property crash of the early 1990s seemed to confirm the predictions, but step out of Norman Foster's cavernous Canary Wharf tube station today and you'll be confronted by the 800-foot (244m) Canary Wharf tower, and other sparkling glass and steel skyscrapers.

The docks have been landscaped and surrounded by bars, restaurants and shops. Up to 80,000 people now work at Canary Wharf and thousands shop in the underground mall. You can learn to sail in the docks further down the Isle of Dogs, and the London Triathlon takes place on the roads and waterways.

The skyline, while not as awe-inspiring as that of Dubai or many American cities, is a good indication that Canary Wharf is well established as London's centre of business, and the home of many banks and media groups. There are restaurants, health clubs, department stores, bars and cinemas. Development has also spread south and east along the Docklands Light Railway, which runs between central London and Greenwich. Take this railway instead of the tube if you want to see the Docklands in all its glory.

HMS *BELFAST*

The heavily armoured battle cruiser HMS *Belfast* is now tied up alongside City Hall, but in World War II she was patrolling the seas and sinking German warships such as the *Scharnhorst*. Life-size models illustrate what daily life was like for sailors on board and visitors can have a go at targeting the huge six-inch guns. There are also guides on hand to add a little background to the exhibits. Children will seem better suited to the narrow gangways and hatches and they especially enjoy exploring the *Belfast*: weekend activities for families introduce children to other aspects of life at sea.

LONDON DUNGEON

For a gruesome, involving and extremely entertaining journey into the depths of London's dungeons just follow the signs from London Bridge station. This top attraction brings death and misery to life with vivid tableaux, hammy acting from guides in period costume with plenty of fake blood. It's not only London's dungeons and the associated torture and executions that are depicted; other low points in the capital's history, including the Great Plague and the Fire of London, are covered. Children and the squeamish should approach this with caution.

ROYAL OBSERVATORY & PLANETARIUM

Greenwich is at the centre of the world – or at least the world's time zones. At the Royal Observatory you can step from one hemisphere to another before exploring the history of time, space and the scientists who attempted to understand them. It's a fascinating place and well worth visiting, not least for the largest refracting telescope in the country. The Observatory's recent Time galleries explore the various roles that time and timekeeping play in our daily lives.

TOWER BRIDGE

Tower Bridge, which connects the north bank of the Thames at the Tower of London with the south side of the river at the Design Museum, offers those with a good head for heights some excellent views along the Thames.

The bridge's history – it was completed in 1894 after eight years of construction – and workings are well described in the Tower Bridge Exhibition, but the highlight for many is the trip along the upper walkways. Those who make it up there get a great view of Norman Foster's environmentally friendly City Hall, the glassy, helmet-shaped home for London's Mayor. The mechanically minded will also enjoy the engine room, although the Victorian cogs and wheels no longer operate the bridge. If possible, try to time your visit for one of the 900 occasions during the year when the bridge is lifted to allow river traffic to pass below.

TOWER BRIDGE

South Bank & South

IMPERIAL WAR MUSEUM

The Imperial War Museum succeeds in covering conflicts involving Britain or the Commonwealth without sentimentality or jingoism. It presents the apparatus, art and aftermath of war with a combination of scholarly gravity and an instinct for what will interest and intrigue visitors.

In the soaring Large Exhibits Gallery, which opens the collection, World War II fighter planes, including a Spitfire, are suspended above tanks, boats and submarines. Many of the exhibits have stories of heroism attached to them, while others impress through the sheer sense of scale: how did World War II pilots squeeze into those tiny cockpits?

The behind-the-scenes exhibits in the ground-floor galleries are engaging. There are re-creations of the Blitz and trench warfare, while on the second floor you can enter the world of the spy. The next floor offers works from well-known war artists, such as John Singer Sargent, Paul Nash and Stanley Spencer.

But it is the permanent Holocaust Exhibition that provides the numbing counterpoint to the martial display below. The minutiae of death are chilling, while the filmed testimony of Holocaust survivors is very moving. The exhibition is not thought suitable for under-14s.

LONDON AQUARIUM

Learn to tell a conger eel from a moray eel at the London Aquarium, one of Europe's largest aquariums. The 50 displays are arranged according to 14 of the world's watery habitats, with the Atlantic Ocean exhibit forming the centrepiece. Sharks and stingrays patrol the inside of this three-storey tank and are hand-fed by divers daily.

There are 350 species in total at the aquarium and many visitors, children especially, develop a soft spot for the rays, which seem to enjoy being petted at the Touch Pool. However, the tanks with the most eye-catching residents are the Coral Reef and Indian Ocean displays, which contain species seriously endangered by overfishing and global warming.

Other habitats now include tropical freshwater, rivers, ponds, mangroves and rainforest waterways, where you will find catfish, pufferfish and – to the relief of the tank's other inhabitants – a species of piranha (vegetarian!) called pacu. Other species include starfish and jellyfish.

LONDON EYE

It was a publicity coup without equal. In the millennial flurry of new projects and buildings, the London Eye, to the surprise of most observers, stole the show from

the Millennium Dome. Its popularity with Londoners and visitors alike has ensured that the wheel will continue turning on its central site opposite the Houses of Parliament for the foreseeable future.

So, what's the appeal of a 450-foot (137m) big wheel? It's not just the breathtaking views across the capital; views that even on a cloudy day stretch along the Thames to Canary Wharf and on a clear day can extend up to 25 miles (40km). And it's more than admiration for a feat of engineering that keeps 32 space-age glass pods suspended on a giant bicycle wheel of cables, girders and tubes for your half-hour revolution. No, it is perhaps the novelty of seeing some of the world's most recognisable landmarks, such as Buckingham Palace, and the Houses of Parliament from the air.

The genesis of the British Airways London Eye took seven years and was guided by experts from five European

countries. Finally, after the wheel had been pieced together in a horizontal position, it was hoisted upright, using a technique that had been previously employed to erect oil rigs.

Be warned: the Eye is extremely popular during the summer and booking ahead is advised, especially if you're confident of picking a fine day. In the winter months there are night-time 'flights', which offer a different perspective.

SHAKESPEARE'S GLOBE

This superb theatre, brainchild of the late American actor Sam Wanamaker, father of actress Zoë, was completed in 1997. A reconstruction of the theatre where William Shakespeare debuted many of his plays, it is one of London's must-see attractions. It is a work of great craft, thanks in large part to Wanamaker's insistence on building the new Globe Theatre only with tools, materials and

techniques available in Elizabethan times (displays explain the construction process in detail). The original Globe was opened in 1599, but the circular, wooden playhouse burned down shortly afterwards.

Now, not only does the new Globe Theatre look fantastic but, during the busy summer performance season, you can see Shakespeare's work in as authentic a setting as possible. The season normally runs from May to October and the open-air stage means favourable weather is an advantage. It's standing room only in the pit in front of the stage but there are seats for those with less stamina. There are also family events through the year.

It was a popular Elizabethan custom for the 'groundlings' in the pit to heckle the actors, and today the audience is still essential to performances. The Globe provides drama without elaborate sets or props: Shakespeare's words and the building create their own magic.

SOUTHWARK CATHEDRAL

Glowing with the brightness of its recently cleaned and restored stonework, Southwark Cathedral may not look like one of London's oldest Gothic buildings, but it is. The cathedral was a simple priory church (dating from the 13th century) until 1905, when the diocese of Southwark was formed and the church became upgraded to a cathedral. You'll find a monument and window dedicated to William Shakespeare in the south aisle and the tombs of Bishop Lancelot Andrews, translator of the King James version of the Bible, and John Gower, an English poet who died in 1408.

On the north side of the beautiful nave, a finely detailed stained-glass window depicts people associated with Southwark and the cathedral, including preacher John Bunyan and Geoffrey Chaucer, who started his pilgrimage to Canterbury in *The Canterbury Tales* from the Tabard Inn, just off nearby Borough High Street. The Long View of London museum, a garden and a refectory are recent additions.

TATE MODERN

Tate Modern is simply the most important gallery of modern art in Britain. But despite a vast collection that includes some of the biggest names of the 20th century – Henri Matisse, Pablo Picasso, Andy Warhol and Francis Bacon – the art can be dwarfed by the towering architecture of the converted Bankside power station.

The building that the Tate Modern is housed in (unmistakable at the south end of the Millennium Bridge), began life in the 1950s as a power station, designed by the man who also came up with Britain's distinctive red telephone boxes, Giles Gilbert Scott. After the power station was decommissioned, the Swiss architectural firm Herzog & de Meuron was charged with transforming the giant brick-and-steel frame building into a home fit for the Tate Gallery's ever-increasing collection of modern art.

There are two entrances to Tate Modern, at the west and north sides. Both lead into the awe-inspiring Turbine Hall, a vast space that lends itself to whatever monumental sculptures or installations are placed in it. The galleries are spread around the spacious upper levels.

In 2006, Tate Modern rehung its entire fabulous collection around the diverse art themes of Abstract Expressionism, Cubism, and Minimalism and Surrealism, following much criticism that the original organisation according to themes of landscape or history was too subjective and vague. Artists Anish Kapoor and Roy Lichtenstein now have works displayed for the first time at Tate Modern. Other artists, including Juan Muñoz, Thomas Schütte and Mark Rothko now have rooms all to themselves. There are still seasonal exhibitions at the gallery.

One experience you shouldn't miss is a well-earned break in either the café on level two or the more expensive top-floor restaurant – both serve good food and offer excellent views over the Thames.

West & Southwest
CHELSEA PHYSIC GARDEN

You'll have to time your visit to Chelsea Physic Garden carefully: it is open only from Wednesdays to Fridays, Sundays and Bank Holiday Mondays from April through to October. But the wait is worth it because the garden is not only of interest from a scientific and medical point of view, it is also a surprisingly serene place to catch your breath and relax.

The Physic Garden dates from 1673, when it was established to teach students about plants. This, of course, was a time when new plants and cuttings were being brought back to London on ships that had travelled the globe searching for new lands and new peoples to trade with. Its south-facing site on the bank of the Thames was chosen for its temperate climate, in the hope that many of the exotic specimens would survive – one such attraction is Britain's largest outdoor fruiting olive tree. By the 18th century, the garden had set up an international botanic seed exchange system, which continues today.

Most of the garden's plants, numbering some 5,000 species, have medicinal properties. Within the Physic Garden, the Garden of World Medicine is Britain's first garden of ethnobotany and there is also a Pharmaceutical Garden. Other corners are devoted to perfume, aromatherapy and even vegetables.

For more of an insight into the garden's history, guides are on hand to show visitors around, but it is just as rewarding to wander among the unusual shrubs, trees and plants before venturing back into the maelstrom of King's Road.

HYDE PARK

Hyde Park, which adjoins Kensington Gardens, is central London's largest royal park. Although the flat landscape verges on the featureless, there are interesting sights to find. Since Henry VIII bought the park in 1536 it has been the setting for some of London's dramas. Refugees from the slums camped in the park in 1655 in the hope of escaping from the Great Plague. The park was at the heart of disturbances in 1866 between the police and the Reform League, and since 1872 people have been permitted to speak freely at Speakers' Corner to the northwest. The park has become a venue for open-air concerts.

TATE MODERN

Hyde Park is also a much-appreciated green space for Londoners to get out in the fresh air and get some exercise on bicycles and rollerblades. Both skaters and bladers congregate at Hyde Park Corner for a regular Friday-night skate, while cyclists are allowed on the park's roads but not its paths.

Other sporting activities include impromptu games of football and softball, while the Tennis Centre allows non-members to turn up and play. Runners are a common sight and summer sees swimmers take to the water of the Serpentine at the Lido.

KENSINGTON PALACE & GARDENS

Kensington Palace, where she lived, will forever be closely associated with Diana, Princess of Wales. Flowers are still left tied to the black-painted gates to the Gardens on the anniversary of her death, while inside a collection of her dresses forms a permanent exhibition. But there's more to Kensington Palace and Gardens than its most famous resident.

The Royal Ceremonial Dress Collection spans three centuries of regal finery, with the whole process of designing and fitting a dress explained. Upstairs the his-and-hers State Apartments include the understated Queen's Apartment and the over-the-top King's Apartment, where Queen Victoria was baptized. In the gardens, the Orangery is an elegant space in which to have lunch before exploring the gardens. The Sunken Garden is a highlight. However, it won't take you long to find the Serpentine Gallery to the south and the garden's two sculptures: *Physical Energy* and *Peter Pan*.

This just leaves the Albert Memorial on the southern edge of the gardens, a magnificent tribute to Queen Victoria's beloved husband who died in 1861.

SCIENCE MUSEUM

(regarded as the forerunner of the computer), Stephenson's Rocket and Arkwright's Spinning Jenny. The full-size replica of the Apollo 10 command module is a highlight. On the first floor the Who Am I? area investigates the human brain and psychology, while the exhibition on power in the East Hall explores the past and future of energy.

As well as all the interactive computers and exhibits, there's a daily programme of IMAX film screenings and events, including the Science Night Sleepover.

VICTORIA & ALBERT MUSEUM

The third in South Kensington's trio of world-class museums will mesmerize anyone interested in art, culture or society. The V&A's field is the decorative arts, but through this subject it manages to traverse continents and centuries of human history and creativity.

There is too much to take in in one visit, so the best plan of action is to savour just one or two collections at a time. Highlights include the Fashion, Jewellery and Accessories collection, which displays fashionable dress from the 17th century to the present day. The Furniture and Furnishings collection consists of 14,000 items from the Middle Ages onwards, while the Ceramics collection is central to the museum. It includes everything from Egyptian relics to modern industrial ceramics via porcelain, such as the Meissen vulture acquired in 2006.

During school holidays and on most weekends there are events for families. There are also several trails around the museum for children aged 7 to 12 to follow. Best of all, the museum's Back-Packs scheme allows children to borrow one of a series of themed backpacks and use the contents to explore different subjects in a fun and informative way. You don't need to book and the themes include The Emperor's Party and Chinese Treasures as well as Fancy Furnishings.

WELLINGTON ARCH

Decimus Burton's arch was built in 1830 to celebrate the Duke of Wellington's victories over Napoleon's armies. It was relocated to its present site in 1882.

The statue of the Duke on horseback that topped the arch was replaced before World War I with a 38-ton bronze sculpture, the heaviest in Europe, called *Peace Descending on the Quadriga of War*, depicting four magnificent war horses and the Angel of Peace. There are three floors of displays explaining its use over the years, including as a police station; carry on to the top of the arch and take in the spectacular views of Buckingham Palace from the balcony.

NATURAL HISTORY MUSEUM

Where else can you see frighteningly realistic animatronic dinosaurs, as well as Britain's largest collection of fossil remains? Experience the realistically scary tremors of an earthquake, then witness the eruption of a volcano?

The museum does an excellent job of engaging with younger visitors via the use of interactive or multimedia displays such as the Ant Colony, an army of leafcutter

ants, or the Power Within room, in which the effects of the 1995 Kobe earthquake are replicated. Mostly, however, the exhibits don't need any help to enthrall: the creepy crawlies are a perennial favourite and the dinosaur skeleton takes pride of place in the cavernous central hall of the Life Galleries.

The Natural History Museum holds special exhibitions and regular talks and events, including activities for children.

SCIENCE MUSEUM

The Science Museum is practically next door to the Natural History Museum and is similarly successful at stimulating children – thanks to its broad and liberal interpretation of the word science, which manages to include classic computer games and 3D films in its IMAX cinema.

The collections cover the stories behind many of the world's most important inventions: Charles Babbage's Calculator

THE RIVER THAMES, FOLLOWING ITS BRIDGES

Westminster Bridge was built in the 1740s. More than 100 years later, Hungerford Bridge extended the railway into Charing Cross. Work to replace Waterloo Bridge in 1939 took six years. Blackfriars Bridge has five cast-iron arches. Millennium Bridge is the newest crossing and London Bridge is a 20th-century structure.

DISTANCE/TIME 4.5 miles (7.2km) 2h30 **MAP** AA Street by Street London **START** Westminster tube station; grid ref: TQ 302797 **PATHS** Paved streets and riverside walk **THE PUB** The Anchor, 34 Park Street, Bankside. Tel: 020 7407 1577

1 Leave Westminster tube station by Exit 1 to follow signs to Westminster Pier. Walk up the steps to your right and cross Westminster Bridge. Turn left along the riverfront. Ahead are the 32 transparent pods of the London Eye. Just past Jubilee Gardens, on the right, is the next bridge, Hungerford, sandwiched between the Golden Jubilee Bridges.

2 Continue ahead past the Royal Festival Hall and look to the opposite bank of the Thames for Cleopatra's Needle. After the National Film Theatre is Waterloo Bridge.

3 The path bends to the right, past the Royal National Theatre and the Hayward Gallery, before reaching Gabriel's Wharf. Turn right at the Riviera restaurant and walk through the central path lined with wooden sculptures. Turn left at the end into Stamford Street and 100yds (91m) further on take a left turn into Barge House Street.

4 Ahead, the brickwork of the Oxo Wharf shrouds the entrance to the Oxo Tower. Enter the glass doors to catch the lift to the eighth floor for a view of the skyline, or continue along the ground floor to the riverside exit.

5 Pass under Blackfriars Bridge. The former Bankside power station on your right

was made with 4 million bricks. It is now home to the popular Tate Modern.

6 Continue past the Millennium Foot Bridge and Shakespeare's Globe. Beyond this is Southwark Bridge and, 200yds (182m) further on, Cannon Street Rail Bridge. A few paces on are the remains of Winchester Palace. Ahead is a full-size replica of Sir Francis Drake's ship, the *Golden Hinde*. Around the corner is Gothic Southwark Cathedral.

7 Cross London Bridge, descend the steps, following signs for the Thames Path (West).

8 At Blackfriars Bridge the Thames Path joins the pavement next to the river. The first boat you pass on your left is HMS *President*. The next set of buildings to your right after Temple tube station belong to King's College, London. Further along is Somerset House where you can ice skate in winter.

9 After 200yds (182m) the path passes Cleopatra's Needle before arriving at Embankment tube station. Northumberland Avenue is the next road on your right. About 200yds (182m) further on is Horse Guards Avenue. When you reach Westminster Bridge turn right into Bridge Street, to reach Westminster tube station.

WALK 46

CHELSEA

Chelsea is home to the most famous pensioners in Britain. They live in The Royal Hospital, founded by Charles II in 1692 for veteran soldiers. The minimum age is 65 and there is still accommodation for 500. They are easily recognized by their unusual three-cornered hats and their scarlet coats.

DISTANCE/TIME 3.75 miles (6km) 2h **MAP** AA Street by Street London **START** Sloane Square tube station; grid ref: TQ 281787 **PATHS** Paved streets and tarmac paths **THE PUB** The Coopers Arms, 87 Flood Street. Tel: 020 7376 3120

1 From Sloane Square tube walk ahead, crossing Lower Sloane Street. Go past Peter Jones and, a few paces on your left, the Duke of York Square. Turn left into Cheltenham Terrace then bear left into Franklin's Row.

2 Turn right on the Royal Hospital Road. Just beyond the lawns on your right, turn left into the peaceful hospital grounds at Chelsea Gate. A few paces further on the left, a gravel path leads to the Great Hall, chapel and museum. Continue to the end of the road and turn left on to some playing fields. Now head towards the obelisk, bear right and leave through the gates to the Chelsea Embankment.

3 Turn right along the Embankment and right into Tite Street, where Oscar Wilde once lived. At Royal Hospital Road turn left into Paradise Walk. The houses in this narrow, quiet road have window boxes and roof terraces. Turn right and then sharp left towards the Embankment and walk past the Chelsea Physic Garden.

4 At the Albert Bridge traffic lights cross Oakley Street and then bear right to walk along the narrow Cheyne Walk. Turn right

by the Cheyne Walk Brasserie into Cheyne Row, where Thomas Carlyle lived. At the end turn left into Upper Cheyne Row. Turn left again into Lawrence Street – where there is a plaque to mark the Chelsea Porcelain Works – then turn right into Justice Walk. (Don't be fooled into thinking the sign of a red-robed judge is a pub, it merely identifies where the old courthouse used to be!)

5 Turn left into Old Church Street and at the bottom is Chelsea Old Church, with a statue outside of Thomas More, who worshipped here. Walk through Chelsea Embankment Gardens and then cross the Albert Bridge.

6 At a 'Riverside Walk' sign turn left through the gate into Battersea Park. Follow the Thames Path, past the Peace Pagoda in the park, and then continue to reach Chelsea Bridge.

7 Turn left to cross over the bridge and then continue walking ahead, passing Chelsea Barracks on the right before joining Lower Sloane Street. Turn right to retrace your steps back to Sloane Square tube station.

Notting Hill Carnival

Notting Hill's annual summer carnival assaults all of the senses. The spicy aroma of jerk chicken sizzling on a grill gets the mouth watering. The bass from a dub reggae sound system makes your knees wobble and your stomach churn. All around people are jostling, shouting, laughing, drinking Red Stripe beer and dancing, and a gyrating dancer dressed as a 12-foot (3.7m) tall silver butterfly is swaying towards you.

If you don't like large crowds or boisterous parties, then Notting Hill carnival is certainly not for you. But if you do, then block out the August Bank Holiday in your diary and get ready to let your hair down.

The carnival was started in the late 1950s by members of the West Indian community of the West London neighbourhood. The Notting Hill area had seen large-scale immigration from the Caribbean islands during the 1950s – many young Caribbean men and women were recruited to drive buses and do other jobs in a Britain with a decimated post-war population. The newcomers formed communities in the streets around Notting Hill, which was then a considerably more affordable place to live than it is today. Tensions existed between the incoming Caribbean population and indigenous Londoners and a Caribbean-style carnival was proposed as a way of making the Caribbean population feel at home and introduce their culture to curious Londoners.

Surprisingly, the first Notting Hill Carnival took place in 1959 indoors at the St Pancras Town Hall. It wasn't until 1965 that the party took its first steps outside when a parade route was devised around the main Notting Hill streets of Ladbroke Grove, Westbourne Grove and Chepstow Road. Rhuane Laslett and Claudia Jones were seen as the driving forces behind the carnival in its early years, and it remained very much a local event. But from the mid-1960s to the mid-1970s attendance at the carnival, which would become Europe's largest street party by the end of the century, had rocketed from a few thousand to 150,000. Over the years the carnival had to survive riots and a series of crime waves but, by 2000, 1.5 million people turned up to dance, drink and revel in the residential streets of Notting Hill. This temporary influx of vast numbers of people in party mode, obviously, had the potential to cause problems.

While the police usually attend in force, they take a 'live and let live' attitude; it's traditional for at least one photo of an awkward-looking policeman dancing with a gyrating sequined dancer to be published in the weekend's newspapers. But one group of people who really don't enjoy the carnival are Notting Hill's wealthy new residents. Since the 1990s the neighbourhood has changed dramatically, evolving into one of the most sought-after London addresses. The white stuccoed Georgian houses on the narrow streets are inhabited by celebrities and London's movers and shakers, while the Caribbean community which once lived here has moved to the north and west of the city over the years. Residents are not overly enthusiastic about a million people pitching up on their doorsteps every August Bank Holiday. Most opt to escape from the city and spend the weekend in the country or at least away from the packed streets of North London, watching the party unfold on television and perhaps keeping their fingers crossed that their house doesn't feature on the evening news.

While the carnival began as a specifically Caribbean-flavoured event for local residents in the 1960s, it has assumed a broader cultural mantle over the years and many varied communities play a role in planning and staging the event. Caribbean music, such as soca and calypso, is still the heart and soul of the carnival, but it faces loud competition from rap, house music, drum and bass, and reggae. However, despite the forty or so sound systems – mobile music stages staffed by a DJ and sometimes an MC and dancers – the roots of carnival lie in steelpan music. Many of the steelpan drummers who hammered out a tune in the carnivals of the 1960s still continue to play at the parade. Steelpan music itself developed in Trinidad in the West Indies during the 1940s when instruments were fashioned from dustbin lids, paint pots or old oil drums and a rhythm hammered out with sticks of bamboo. The sound became more sophisticated over the years until the sonorous, upbeat steelpan sound of today. At the carnival the steelpan bands compete in the Saturday evening Panorama competition, with the old tunes being as well received as ever. Carnival itself also began in Trinidad in 1833, as a celebration of the end of slavery – many of the stirring songs and tunes of carnival have been as much associated with protest and sorrow as they have with joy.

The weekend gets into full swing on the Saturday evening with the steelpan band competition – the winning band can call themselves the UK Champions of Steel - and a parade of extravagantly decorated floats and (some) outrageously costumed dancers around the 4-mile (6.4km) circuit of Notting Hill. This is the warm-up for the busiest day of the festival weekend, the Bank Holiday Monday. Sunday is children's day dedicated to youngsters, when up to 70 multi-coloured and beautifully adorned floats and steelpan bands, all featuring under-21 year olds, parade along the route from mid-morning onwards. Monday, a national holiday in the UK, is the climax of the carnival with all-day action on the route and surrounding streets. The most popular sound systems tend to be the ones that have a long history with the carnival, such as Good Times, manned by veteran DJ Norman Jay or Sancho Panza, which has staked out a space at the carnival since 1994 with a party-pleasing blend of house music.

With thousands of people milling around and many closed streets in west London, expect a certain degree of travel chaos on this weekend. Tube stations are often closed to minimize crowding and it may be quicker to walk to and from the carnival. However, moves are afoot to take the carnival to Hyde Park, where there will be more space and less disruption for visitors and residents alike. A future parade route would be plotted to wind its way from west London and to finish in the park, but this plan would face fierce resistance from some traditionalists. For the thousands of people that attend the revelry each year, the appeal of carnival lies as much in the ear-ringing sideshows and food stalls that pop up in Notting Hill's streets as the parade itself. Whatever happens to the carnival in years to come, people will always come together on the long, hot August weekend to eat, drink and dance.

TOP Energetic dancers moving to the passionate rhythms that flood the city streets help to create a party atmosphere on this festival weekend in August.

RIGHT The colourful parade winds its way past the crowds - the carnival is now believed to be one of Europe's biggest street parties.

LEFT Spectacular costumes are a much-loved feature of the carnival parade.

DISTANCE/TIME 2.5 miles (4km) 1h **MAP** OS Explorer 173 London North **START** West Carriage Drive car park; grid ref: TQ 269800 **TRACKS** Well-surfaced paths **THE PUB** The Wilton Arms, 71 Kinnerton Street. Tel: 020 7235 4854

DISTANCE/TIME 6 miles (9.7km) 1h45 **MAP** OS Explorer 162 Greenwich & Gravesend **START** Cutty Sark pub, Ballast Quay; grid ref: TQ 389782 **TRACKS** Largely surfaced cycle lanes, some cobbled streets **THE PUB** The Cutty Sark Tavern, 4–7 Ballast Quay. Tel: 020 8858 3146

AROUND HYDE PARK

Henry VIII and his court hunted in Hyde Park and Charles I opened the park fully to the public in 1637. The Serpentine, the vast ornamental lake dominating the park, was created in the 1730s by Caroline, wife of George II. The latest royal connection is the Diana, Princess of Wales Memorial Fountain.

1 From the West Carriage Drive car park, opposite the Serpentine Gallery, cross the road and join the cycle track on the pavement on the west side of West Carriage Drive. The Diana, Princess of Wales Memorial Fountain is on your right.

2 The track drops down on to the road to cross the Serpentine bridge. Once across be sure to look out for the point where the path resumes on the pavement, as the cycle lane on the road surface stops abruptly.

3 At Victoria Gate cross the road and follow the cycle path along The RIng. The path here is on the road but it is often traffic-free.

4 As you appraoch Cumberland Gate and Marble Arch, look for the cycle route sign for Chelsea Bridge and cross the road to pick up the cycle path on Broad Walk. You may need to reduce speed here as the cycle lane can be obstructed by crowds around Speakers' Corner. It then heads south on Broad Walk, a pleasant tree-lined boulevard.

5 On the approach to Queen Elizabeth Gate at Hyde Park Corner, follow signs to the right for Rotten Row to return to the car park at West Carriage Drive. On Rotten Row keep to the left on the fairly narrow path shared with pedestrians and rollerbladers. At West Carriage Drive, use the pedestrian crossing and pick up on the cycle track again on the west side in front of the Serpentine Gallery. (This simple circular ride can be extended eastwards with a foray along Constitution Hill's excellent parallel cycle track to see Buckingham Palace, or to the west to explore Kensngton Gardens. Notices at the park entrances show where cycling is currently permitted.)

EAST FROM GREENWICH ALONG THE THAMES

In the space of just 3 miles (4.8km) of riverside there is at least a millennium's worth of London's industrial, military and seafaring heritage, from maritime Greenwich, which became the site of the prime meridian in 1884, to the Royal Arsenal at Woolwich, via the Thames Barrier and the Millennium Dome.

1 From Cutty Sark Gardens wheel your bike along the riverside walk to the Cutty Sark pub and turn right along Ballast Quay, then bear right into Pelton Road. At the Royal Standard pub turn left into Christchurch Way. As you approach the Alcatel complex, turn right into Mauritius Road. When you reach Blackwall Lane turn left into the bus lane. Just before the traffic lights take the cycle path on the left along the pavement of Tunnel Avenue. At the footbridge look for the green-surfaced track on the left.

2 Cross the footbridge and turn left into Boord Street. At Millennium Way, join the cycle path directly ahead. At West Parkside continue straight on and when you reach the riverside, turn right. Just past the colourful buildings of Greenwich Millennium Village you'll reach the Greenwich Peninsula Ecology Park.

3 The outer boardwalk is always open and considerate cyclists are welcome. Go on along the riverside path, which turns inland to skirt the Greenwich Yacht Club's fenced enclosure. Remain on the riverside past the aggregate recycling works. At the end of that section, stay on the street called Riverside, with the large Sainsbury's depot to your right. Look out for the remains of old dockside railway tracks on your left. At Anchor and Hope Lane take the off-road path to go straight ahead.

4 On reaching the Thames Barrier, the green-surfaced route around the complex is well-signed and quite easy to follow. At the former Thames Barrier Arms pub, go straight ahead along the path which is slightly overgrown and quite narrow. There is a steep slope up to the crossing at Woolwich Church Street. Turn left along the road here and when you reach the roundabout, take the second exit (Ruston Road). Look for the left turn where Ruston Road heads towards the river. Turn left here and turn left again at Harlinger Road. When you reach the T-junction turn right, then right once again.

5 A sign asks cyclists to dismount for the 40yd (37m) section between the road and the riverside. When you rejoin the riverside opposite the Tate & Lyle works on the north bank, turn right. When the pedestrian route uses steps to cross a wall, the cycle path heads inland, where you will find a ramp, and returns to the riverside.

6 At the cannons on the riverside turn inland past the Clockhouse Community Centre. At Leda Road make your way up the slope to join Woolwich Church Street. You may prefer to dismount and push your bike along the pavement to reach the Woolwich free ferry. At the Ferry Approach look for the cycle signs by the ambulance station. Pass the Waterfront Leisure Centre and the entrance to the Woolwich Foot Tunnel. Continue along the riverside to Royal Arsenal Pier, where a large piazza provides access to the revitalized Royal Arsenal complex, including the Firepower museum. From here it is possible to cycle inland to explore the shops, pubs and restaurants of Woolwich centre before you cycle back to Greenwich.

Canterbury
& Kent Downs

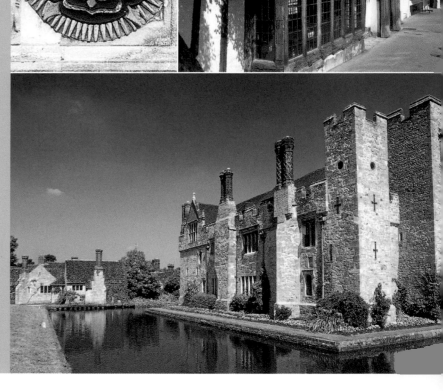

CLOCKWISE FROM TOP LEFT: CANTERBURY CATHEDRAL; TIMBER-FRAMED
CONQUEST HOUSE, CANTERBURY; HEVER CASTLE

CANTERBURY MAP REF 401 K5

Successfully combining modernity with venerable old age, Canterbury may be a place of pilgrimage for those of an historical bent, but it remains a bustling and very much a 21st-century destination of appeal to everyone.

The city stands on the site of Cantii, the capital of an Iron Age kingdom, and from 'Cantii' comes Kent. The city was also an important Roman stronghold, but after the Romans left Britain at the start of the 5th century, the city was left to the local populace until, in the year 602, St Augustine imposed Christianity on the site of a Roman church and so created Christchurch Cathedral. It was an important act that heralded Canterbury's future as the seat of the Archbishop of Canterbury, the spiritual capital of the Church of England and the Mother Church of the Anglican Communion.

Inevitably, the Normans focused their attention on Canterbury, and built a castle here around the year 1100. Within the next 70 years, the greater part of the magnificent cathedral we see today was rebuilt, and then rebuilt again in 1380, and added to around 1500. The cathedral is a truly breathtaking fusion of Romanesque and Perpendicular Gothic styles, and was the infamous place where Archbishop Thomas à Becket was murdered in 1170, if not quite by 'friendly fire' then certainly due to a misunderstanding. This historic incident inspired author Geoffrey Chaucer to write his now well-known literary masterpiece *The Canterbury Tales* in 1387.

So important is Canterbury Cathedral in the scheme of things that along with the modest Church of St Martin, the oldest church in England, and the ruins of the Abbey of St Augustine, a reminder of the saint's evangelising role in the Heptarchy from 597, since 1988 they have collectively enjoyed World Heritage Status.

As you approach Canterbury, the cathedral still dominates the skyline, presenting 21st-century visitors with the same awe-inspiring vision as their medieval counterparts. Making a pilgrimage was an important part of medieval life and thousands of pilgrims flocked to the city to visit the shrine of Thomas à Becket. For some 200 years this was actually the most popular shrine in Europe (outside Rome), and a most sumptuous affair, until it received the unwanted attentions of King Henry VIII's officer during the Dissolution of the Monasteries.

Today, Canterbury still welcomes visitors from around the world and has successfully blended its many ancient buildings with modern shops, bars and restaurants to retain both an old world elegance and a cosmopolitan vitality. The compact city centre is closed to traffic during the daytime to enable the narrow streets to be more easily and safely accessed by visitors.

HEVER MAP REF 401 H6

Tucked away between the villages of Penshurst and Edenbridge, Hever village is most famous for its castle. The castle was begun in 1272, when Edward I allowed a large manor house to be converted by Sir Stephen de Penchester. In the 15th century the then castle was acquired by the Bullen family – later to change their family name to Boleyn.

Hever Castle was home to Anne Boleyn, Henry VIII's wife from 1533 until her execution in 1536. The Boleyn family died out, leaving the castle to Henry VIII who promptly gave it to another of his wives, Anne of Cleeves. The fabric of the castle gave way until it was bought by the Astor family in 1903 and an ambitious programme of restoration was begun. After years of dedicated work, the castle was finally restored to its former glory with the addition of the beautiful grounds and gardens that you see today. American Lord Astor became Viscount of Hever, after being granted British naturalization.

IGHTHAM & IGHTHAM MOTE
MAP REF 401 H5

Ightham is most famous for the nearby medieval moated manor house of Ightham Mote, although the village itself is of even greater antiquity, and an eye-catching place of half-timbered cottages and houses. Ightham is not mentioned in the Domesday Book, although place-name evidence implies derivation from the Saxon 'Ehtaham', 'Ehta' being a personal name, while 'ham' signifies a settlement.

Ightham Mote is a 14th-century manor house, extensively restored by the National Trust in 1989-2004. While still taking in the fact that the dog kennel is a Grade I listed building in its own right, visitors can follow a tour route that includes the Great Hall, Old Chapel, Crypt, Tudor chapel with painted ceiling, drawing room with Jacobean fireplace, frieze and 18th-century wallpaper, and billiards room. There is an extensive garden and interesting walks in the surrounding woodland. Manor houses were the centre of secular village life, and the Great Hall often the scene of the manorial court and the place of assembly of the tenantry.

The House was home to the Selby family from the late 16th century to the middle of the 19th century, and there is a story that Dame Dorothy Selby warned Lord Monteagle not to attend Parliament on 5th November 1605, so leading to the discovery of the Gunpowder Plot. Some supporters of Guy Fawkes blamed Dorothy Selby for its failure, and walled her up in a secret room and left her to die. This may account for the occasional chill you experience on your tour of the house, and it doesn't matter if history prefers to identify Francis Tresham, brother-in-law of Lord Monteagle, as the person who warned him not to attend Parliament.

CANTERBURY

PENSHURST MAP REF 401 H6

This beautiful, quintessentially English village is situated in stunning countryside and falls either side of the River Medway.

The village is famous for its 16th-century grand house, Penshurst Place and its fantastic gardens. The house has some interesting features including an octagonal hearth.

Seat of the Sidney family since 1552, the house owes its current restorative state mainly to the 1st Viscount De L'Isle, William Sidney, who inherited the house at the end of World War II. Penshurst is still in the beloved hands of the Sidney family and has been the home of heir Viscount De L'Isle since 1991.

TUNBRIDGE WELLS MAP REF 401 H6

The cheerful and attractive town of Royal Tunbridge Wells, now included in the borough of Tunbridge Wells, flourished as a spa amid the Wealden forests after a medicinal spring (containing mild chalybeate waters) was discovered by Lord North, a courtier to James I, at the site in 1606. Before the discovery of the waters, the iron content of which was believed to have healing properties, the settlement was little more than a hamlet consisting of a few scattered cottages and farmhouses, with the result that there is nothing of the Tudor period here.

The healthy spa drew added popularity from its location on several hills of The Weald, one of the most scenic stretches of countryside in southern England. The springs, or 'wells', lie at one end of the colonnaded promenade known as Pantiles Parade, first paved in 1700, and, in effect, an 18th-century shopping precinct shaded by lime trees. From then until the early Regency period, Tunbridge Wells was one of the chief resorts of fashionable London society. It reached its height under the dandy and leader of fashion, Richard 'Beau' Nash, and was patronized by novelist William Makepeace Thackeray (who died there), Samuel Johnson and Sir Joshua Reynolds, among others. The Pantiles Parade, with other 17th-century features, is preserved beside the Church of St Charles the Martyr (1684).

Tunbridge Wells added 'Royal' to its name in 1909, after Edward VII officially recognized the popularity of the town amongst royalty and aristocracy by bestowing the official 'Royal' title. Royal Tunbridge Wells is one of only two towns in England to be granted this title, the other is Royal Leamington Spa. Today the town is every bit as charming, a quality it derives from its surfeit of 18th- and 19th-century elegance, most notably seen in Calverley Park and the beautiful buildings you see on Mount Sion.

CANTERBURY

This ancient cathedral city is now a vibrant, cosmopolitan settlement, close enough to the Channel ports and Eurotunnel to reflect a certain continental flavour. The cathedral is forever associated with Thomas à Becket who was murdered there in 1170. He was later canonised. Canterbury's streets have attracted pilgrims for centuries and was the destination of Chaucer's colourful travellers in *The Canterbury Tales*.

1 Go right from Castle Street car park then right again down Gas Street to pass the castle. At the end turn left on Centenary Walk. Where this finishes go right and walk beside the road. Cross a bridge, turn left, go under another bridge and along the river to the other side of the road.

2 Cross some grassland, go over a bridge and through a children's play area. Walk across the car park and turn left up the road to join the Stour Valley Walk.

3 Go under a bridge and continue to a level crossing. Cross the railway, then stroll up past Whitehall Farm. Walk under the bridge, through a gate and over a stream. The path bends round and the main road is on your left. At a junction turn right along the North Downs Way.

4 Go over a bridge and then up a lane. To your left is Golden Hill – from which pilgrims traditionally had their first view of the city. When you come to a track, turn left and then follow it round. Go right along Mill Lane to reach the main road. Take the underpass to cross Rheims Way, walk down London Road, and then turn right into St Dunstans Street.

5 Walk into Canterbury to the Westgate, turn left to walk along Pound Lane and into St Radigunds, where you'll find The Parrot pub situated on your right-hand side.

6 Continue into Northgate, go left then right down Broad Street. You are now walking around the outside of the city walls. Turn right along Broadgate, past a tiny 16th-century building called the Pilgrim's Shop. Soon you come to a pedestrianized area that brings you out at the Butter Market and war memorial. On your right is the entrance to the cathedral.

7 Turn left, then cross over The Parade into St Margaret's Street and turn right down Beer Cart Lane. Turn left into Stour Street and on the right is the city museum, and almost opposite, down Jewry Lane, is Canterbury Wholefoods where you can finish your walk. To return to Castle Street, retrace your steps along Stour Street, turn left along Rosemary Lane and then right.

DISTANCE/TIME 3.75 miles (6km) 1h45 **MAP** OS Explorer 150 Canterbury & the Isle of Thanet **START** Castle Street (several car parks in the city); grid ref: TR 146574 **PATHS** City streets and footpaths **THE PUB** The Parrot, St Radigunds. Tel: 01227 762355; www.theparrotcanterbury.com

WALK 48

HEVER

Hever was in the ownership of the Bullen family when Anne Boleyn, Henry VIII's short-lived wife and mother to Elizabeth I, was born. Anne spent her childhood at this lovely moated castle. After Anne's father died, Henry VIII seized the castle and it became the property of Anne of Cleves after her divorce from Henry. In the early 20th century the buildings and gardens were restored.

1 Walk under the lychgate and go through the churchyard following the Eden Valley Walk. The path goes downhill, across a bridge and soon becomes a path parallel to the road, offering occasional glimpses of the magnificent lake at Hever Castle. The lake might look as if it has always been here, yet it was only created by William Waldorf Astor when he bought the castle in 1903. The path now curves, goes through woodland, across bridge and finally opens out.

2 Pass beside a gate at some houses, bear right and take the Eden Valley Walk to the right of Bothy Cottage. Follow the fenced path to reach the road.

3 Cross the road and then continue along the enclosed path (can get very muddy in wet weather), crossing a stile and footbridge. Ascend some steps, join a gravel path and keep left at the junction, heading down to the gate and track at Hill Hoath.

4 Now turn back to the right and climb a stile by a large gate, so that you seem to be doubling back on yourself. In few paces, cross the stile on your left and follow the path uphill to the next stile. Turn left along the narrow, fenced path, leading into woodland.

5 Keep ahead at a junction of footpaths (can be exceptionally muddy). Continue down the track, passing through two areas of woodland until you reach the road.

6 Turn right here and walk to Wilderness Farm, then take the road that leads to the left opposite the farm. At another road turn right then right again along Pigdown Lane. In another 0.25 mile (400m), cross a waymarked stile on your left and go straight down the field to cross two stiles. Bear right along the field-edge to reach double stiles.

7 Continue ahead, enter the next field, passing left of a pond, and maintain your direction to reach a gate and the road. Turn left and then take footpath on your right. Follow this back into Hever.

DISTANCE/TIME 4 miles (6.4km) 2h **MAP** OS Explorer 147 Sevenoaks & Tonbridge **START** Car park by Hever Castle; grid ref: TQ 476448 **PATHS** Paths, grassy tracks and field-edges, some roads; 19 stiles **THE PUB** King Henry VIII, Edenbridge, Hever. Tel: 01732 862457

PENSHURST

Overlooking the village, Penshurst Place has been in the ownership of the Sydney family since the 16th century. The property was revived after World War II following years of neglect in wartime. It is now the home of the present Viscount De L'Isle and his family. The gardens are simply stunning.

1 Walk up the road away from the village and take the footpath right through a gate. There are great views of Penshurst Place almost immediately and it's well worth taking a photo. The house dates from 1341 and the Great Hall is a fabulous example of medieval architecture. It has a timber roof, a musicians' gallery and an open hearth. There have been some notable visitors to the house over the years: Elizabeth I danced here with Robert Edward Dudley; the Black Prince ate a Christmas dinner here, and the children of Charles I came here after their father was executed. Now bear left to another gate, cross the drive and bear slightly right across parkland, keeping lone oak trees and the lake to your right. Go through a gap in the fence and bear right to pass the lake and reach a stile.

2 The path now veers to the left and goes uphill. Go through a squeeze stile, then walk up an avenue of trees, bearing right at the top. The path levels out with good views of Penshurst Place. You are now following the Eden Valley Walk, a 15-mile (24km) linear walk that traces the route of the Eden from Edenbridge to Tonbridge.

3 Cross a stile and keep walking ahead along a wide, grassy track lined with trees. Exit the trees and follow the path to a stile and gate, joining a track leading down to a road beside Paul's Hill House. Turn right and follow the road (care required) to a bridge.

4 Go through a squeeze stile and follow the waymarked Eden Valley Walk through pasture, along the side of the River Medway which is on your left. Walk by the river for about 0.25 mile (400m), then turn right, away from the water, and head across the pasture to a little bridge. Follow the footpath uphill to a stile which takes you on to a concrete track. Turn right and then left at a junction.

5 Where the track curves sharp left, keep ahead to a stile, then bear left and walk down a path from where there are lovely views of Penshurst Place. Rejoin the concrete track and follow it under an archway, then turn right and walk back into the village.

DISTANCE/TIME 4 miles (6.4km) 2h   MAP OS Explorer 147 Sevenoaks & Tonbridge
START On-street parking in village, also car park for Penshurst Place; grid ref: TQ 525439
PATHS Broad tracks, short section on busy road; 9 stiles   THE PUB Leicester Arms, Penshurst.
Tel: 01892 870551

TUNBRIDGE WELLS

Follow the simple trail through this elegant spa town, discovering the origins of its famous Pantiles and royal patronage. Edward VII conferred the 'Royal' prefix since the town was so popular as a spa with the aristocracy. The Pantiles were originally paved with pantiles and the name has been retained.

1 From the car park behind The Pantiles, turn right and walk up to the main road. Cross over, and then walk up Major York's Road. Just after the car park take the footpath to the left and walk across the common, keeping ahead until you reach Hungershall Park, where you turn left. Keep following the road until you come to a footpath that leads up to the right.

2 Follow this path up through the trees which eventually leads on to a private road. Continue walking ahead and when you reach the top take the track that runs ahead through the trees. After a horse barrier, bear right to pass the churchyard, then turn right and walk around the church and up to the busy main road.

3 Cross over, turn left for a few paces and take the footpath through the trees and across open ground to a road. Turn right, then left along Harmony Street, signed 'Toad Rock'. The road winds down to the rock (it does look rather like a toad, doesn't it?). Return to the junction, turn left then left again at the main road. Continue until you pass Fir Tree Road. On the common, hidden by the trees, are Wellington Rocks.

4 Continue along Mount Ephraim to some cottages on the right that are built into the rock. There are seats here and you get good views over the town. Turn right to walk across the grass and a road to the picturesque old house that was once home to the author William Makepeace Thackeray (it's, unsurprisingly, known as Thackeray's).

5 Go along the path that runs by the left of the house and walk along Mount Ephraim Road. This brings you out in front of a pedestrianized shopping area. Turn right and walk down past the museum and library and the war memorial. Turn left to walk up Crescent Road and continue until you reach Calverley Park, a 19th-century housing development designed by Decimus Burton.

6 Go through the entrance, then in a few paces bear left and walk across Calverley Grounds to go down Mountfield Road, then go right into Grove Hill Road. This brings you down to a roundabout where you turn left and walk along the High Street. At the end go down Chapel Place, pass the Church of King Charles the Martyr, cross the road and then walk along the famous Pantiles and back to the car park.

DISTANCE/TIME 4 miles (6.4km) 1h45   MAP OS Explorer 147 Sevenoaks & Tonbridge
START Car park behind The Pantiles; grid ref: TQ 581386   PATHS Paved streets and tarmac
paths   THE PUB Beau Nash Tavern, Mount Ephraim. Tel: 01892 539350

Oxford & the Chilterns

CLOCKWISE FROM TOP: THE RIDGEWAY; THE BRIDGE OF SIGHS, OXFORD; CHAUCER'S COTTAGE DOOR, WOODSTOCK

BLENHEIM & WOODSTOCK

MAP REF 400 E3

Most visitors to Woodstock come to visit Blenheim Palace, birthplace of Winston Churchill, and while the palace is undoubtedly a magnificent edifice and a stunning part of England's heritage, Woodstock has its own billing, and rightly so. This small town is a happy blend of mellow stone buildings dating from the 17th and 18th centuries, all of which jostle cosily for space alongside shops, pubs, restaurants and hotels.

The palace, built between 1705 and 1722, is one of England's greatest houses. It was intended as a gift to John Churchill, the 1st Duke of Marlborough, from a 'grateful nation' in return for military triumph against the French. But the gratitude was short-lived, and political infighting soon led to Marlborough's exile, and irreparable damage to the reputation of the architect Vanbrugh. Students of architecture will find in Blenheim one of the few buildings designed in the English baroque style, although architectural appreciation of the palace is as subjective today as in the 1720s.

The palace, still home to the Dukes of Marlborough, is open to the public, and contains tourist attractions in the grounds, which in themselves are a delight to explore, not least the avenue of small-leaved limes, but the overall atmosphere is that of a large country house.

Blenheim is a popular choice for film makers and it appears in a number of hits including *Harry Potter and the Order of the Phoenix* (2007), *History of the World Part 1* (1981) and *The Avengers* (1998).

MINSTER LOVELL MAP REF 400 D4

A long, thatched cottage-flanked street beside the River Windrush leads to an attractive 15th-century bridge in the Oxfordshire village of Minster Lovell. Situated along the lovely river bank, Minster Lovell Hall, built in the 1430s, was the home of Viscount Francis Lovell who supported Richard III, the last of the Plantagenet dynasty, against the Lancastrian contender for the crown, Henry Tudor, 2nd Earl of Richmond (later Henry VII). Although Lovell is said by some to have died with King Richard at Bosworth Field, there is a tale that following the battle, Lovell fled to Minster Lovell Hall, where he hid in a secret room. With unfortunate lack of foresight, only Lovell's manservant knew his concealed location. Unfortunately for Lovell, his manservant fell ill and died, taking his location to the grave. Years later, in 1708, Lovell's skeleton was discovered as repairs where being made to the hall.

Now in the care of English Heritage, the ruins of Minster Lovell consist of the great hall, entrance porch and the tower from the south wing. Of the rest of the building only foundations remain.

OXFORD MAP REF 400 E4

Lying just under 60 miles (96.6km) north of London, Oxford is a typical market town situated amid low hills at the meeting point of the River Thames and the River Cherwell. What distinguishes this town from many others like it in England, is its ancient university, with some 38 colleges and six private halls spread throughout the city itself. Places at Oxford University are much sought-after by English students as well as those from abroad. And who can blame them. Apart from its excellent academic reputation is the feeling of following in many famous footsteps along its hallowed halls – among them 26 Prime Minsters, including the Rt Hon David Cameron – the buildings themselves are so ancient and beautiful that many students feel it is a privilege and a pleasure to study here.

There is a mellow ambience of past gentility about Oxford that feeds on the homely blend of amazing architecture and the sprawl of riverside meadows and parkland with their cyclists, punters and rowers. Of course, it's the architecture of the colleges that impresses first; masterpieces that range from the early Gothic of Merton College to the modernism of St Catherine's.

Although the city's origins are lost in time, Oxford has been an established town since the 9th century, with a significant educational influence in the city since 1167, when students who had been expelled from Paris settled here under the patronage of Henry II. But the university's colleges exert palpable influence without entirely dominating city life. Beneath the mantle of education, the city of Oxford still lives and breathes, although, if you stay long enough, you gradually detect a frisson of tension between 'gown' and 'town'.

Within this city of 'dreaming spires' many beautiful, honey-coloured buildings exist, among them the Museum of the History of Science, the Pitts River Museum, and the Ashmolean, England's oldest public museum, founded in 1683, and housing a huge collection of art and antiquity. The Bodleian Library and the nearby Sheldonian Theatre nestle in an area of mainly 17th-century buildings and seem to serve simply to satisfy every new visitor's vision of the city.

Time in Oxford is well spent, and, for the tourist, there is much to detain you; the essence of England seeps from the walls, heritage, pomp and circumstance mingle with student Rag Weeks and the minutiae of daily life in a cosmopolitan setting. The lively covered market is one of Britain's oldest, having been tradng since 1773.

Oxford was also a place of great automobile manufacturing, and is where the Morris Oxford and the T-series MG sports car were created.

Oxford's university population and townspeople exhibit a fascinating contrast of lifestyles. In medieval times this duality led to occasional bloody battles, but although today's students are noted for their often boisterous post-exam antics, Oxford is an eminently civilized place where the traditions of "town and gown" rest side by side. On the one hand Oxford is mildly bizarre and eccentric, on the other it is a 21st-century city in modern times.

The best way to explore is undoubtedly on foot, with serendipity as a guide and frequent stops at coffee shops for on-going refreshment; but there is a range of organized tours by bus or with qualified tourism guides, who deftly deduct aimless wandering from free-range exploration, and substitute knowledge and enthusiasm for one of the finest and most attractive cities in England.

THE RIDGEWAY MAP REF 400 E4

Linking the Chilterns and the North Wessex Downs, the Ridgeway is arguably one of the oldest 'roads' in Britain. Saturated in beauty, it weaves a way for 87 miles (139km) across open chalk downland through secluded valleys and woodlands and passes within strides of the burial mound at Wayland's Smithy beyond which lies the White Horse of Uffington. It largely follows the same chalk ridge route used since prehistoric times by travellers, herdsmen and soldiers. The Ridgeway is a superb way of getting to know the chalk downlands and the Chiltern Hills.

The grasslands which occur on the downs provide some of the most interesting habitats in England, among the richest in terms of plant species that include several types of orchid. Butterflies, especially the many types of blue butterfly, which require particular chalk grassland plants for food, are a key part of the downland natural history. In the Chilterns, red kites, magnificent birds of prey reintroduced from Spain in the 1980s, are now so well established that they far outnumber the buzzard. Fairly commonplace birds such as warblers and finches are found all along the Ridgeway, but skylarks, yellowhammers and corn buntings are especially characteristic of downland. Woodpeckers and nuthatches may well be spotted in the woodlands.

Apart from hundreds of rabbits, numbers of the much larger hare are sometimes found in open countryside; generally solitary animals most active at night. Two species of deer are found on the Ridgeway, roe and fallow, both of which are nocturnal and shy, making early mornings and late afternoons the best time to be out walking the Ridgeway.

OXFORD

OXFORD: CITY STROLL

This famous university city is renowned as the 'city of the dreaming spires'. Its architecture is wonderful, the venerable colleges spread across a large part of the central city. The Thames flows through Oxford where for part of its route it is known as the Isis. The city has long been associated with motor car production, although this has declined from its heyday in the 1960s and 1970s. From unique individual shops and central cafés and restaurants to ethnic outlets and eateries, this is a vibrant, lively place with excellent cultural offerings and happening nightlife.

1 Start at the Carfax, where four streets converge. Walk ahead into St Aldates and head for the visitor entrance to Christ Church, Oxford's largest college, founded in 1525 by Cardinal Wolsey. It became known as Christ Church when the college and cathedral became one. Christ Church has had many notable students, including three Prime Ministers – Robert Peel, William Gladstone and Lord Salisbury. John Wesley, Lewis Carroll and W H Auden also studied here. At the visitor entrance to Christ Church turn right and walk down the tree-lined New Walk. On the left is the green expanse of Christ Church Meadow.

2 At the Thames towpath, swing left and follow the river bank. Keep ahead to reach the confluence of the Thames and the River Cherwell. Avoid the steeply arched footbridge and keep alongside the River Cherwell as it meanders between meadows and sports fields. Leave the river bank and go through wrought-iron gates to walk up Rose Lane.

3 With Magdalen Bridge and Magdalen College bell tower on your right, turn left at

the High Street or 'the High', as it is known in Oxford. Cross Longwall Street and turn right into Queen's Lane. The high perimeter wall of Queen's College is left and right are St Edmund Hall and the former parish church of St Peter-in-the-East. Continue into New College Lane and on the right beyond an arch, is the entrance to New College. Keep along New College Lane to the Bridge of Sighs, a 1913 replica of its Venice namesake, and in front of you is the Sheldonian Theatre.

4 Designed by Sir Christopher Wren and completed in 1669, the theatre was built to hold university meetings and ceremonies. Turn left here for Radcliffe Camera and cross Radcliffe Square towards Brasenose College. Turn right into Brasenose Lane, then right again into Turl Street, cutting between Jesus College and Exeter College. Make for Broad Street and on your right is St Giles, where Charles I drilled his men during the Civil War. Turn left into Cornmarket Street, passing the Church of St Michael at the North Gate. Its Saxon tower is the oldest building in Oxford and originally linked the city wall and the North Gate. Return to Carfax.

DISTANCE/TIME 2.25 miles (3.6km) 1h15 **MAP** OS Explorer 180 Oxford **START** Parking in city centre, or use park-and-ride, or travel by train; grid ref: SP 513062 **PATHS** Pavements, field and riverside paths; 4 stiles **THE PUB** Turf Tavern, 7 Bath Place, Oxford. Tel: 01865 243235; www.theturftavern.co.uk

WALK 52

MINSTER LOVELL: RIVERSIDE RAMBLE

A short distance from Minster Lovell, and a pleasant walk along the river, is the pretty village of Crawley with a river bridge and an old blanket mill. Just to the south of Minster Lovell lie the Charterville Allotments, the subject of a 19th-century social experiment. The 300 acres (121ha) were purchased by an early socialist and offered as smallholdings to poor families, along with £30 and a pig. The experiment failed but some of the cottages remain.

1 Walk up the lane, signposted 'Crawley'. At the end of the village go through a gate, right, and take the footpath diagonally left across the field, also signposted 'Crawley'. Look right for a view of the ruins of Minster Lovell Hall and the dovecote. Go through a gate near a field gate and continue along the path, with a wall to your left. On the horizon is the chimney of Crawley Mill.

2 Go through a gate and ahead up a slight incline. Cross two stiles and continue on the path. Pass above Crawley Mill. At the road turn right and continue into Crawley. At the bottom look left to admire the diminutive village green with its stone cross.

3 Turn right and follow the pavement past Manor Farm, with its huge pond. Cross the humpback bridge over the Windrush – look right for a good view of the old mill house. At the other side of the bridge cross the road and turn left through a gate, signed 'Witney'. Follow the bridleway beside the stream, marked by a line of willows.

4 At the junction of paths by a gate look ahead and left to see New Mill. Turn right

through the gate and walk up the field-edge. Pass a gate and cross the road. Go through the gate and straight on to a second gate, and follow the path down through the woods.

5 At the bottom go through a gate and follow the path along the fence. The wildflower meadows of Maggots Grove lie to your right. Continue through four more gates and bear left beside the trees.

6 Go through a gate into the woods. At a wooden gate bear right, following the arrows, and cross two footbridges. Continue on the path to cross a bridge over the river. Walk up the meadow towards Minster Lovell Hall. Go through two gates to explore the ruins.

7 Leave by the top entrance and walk through the churchyard. Cross a slab stile, continue along a grassy path with the village up to your right. Cross a footbridge, go through a gate and veer to the right. Go through a gate and then another into Wash Meadow recreation ground. Keep right and go through a gate on to the high street, with The Old Swan pub to your left. Turn right and walk up through the village to the car park.

DISTANCE/TIME 4 miles (6.4km) 1h30 **MAP** OS Explorer 180 Oxford, Witney & Woodstock **START** Car park (free) at eastern end of Minster Lovell, above church and hall; grid ref: SP 323114 **PATHS** Meadows, tracks, pavement and lane, woodland; 2 stiles **THE PUB** The Mill & Old Swan Inn, Minster Lovell. Tel: 0870 609 1152; www.devere.co.uk

THE NEW FOREST

■ TOURIST INFORMATION

Christchurch
49 High Street ☎ 01202 471780;
www.christchurchtourism.info

Lyndhurst
New Forest Visitor Information
Centre, Main Car Park
☎ 023 8028 2269;
www.thenewforest.co.uk

■ PLACES OF INTEREST

Beaulieu: National Motor Museum
Palace House, Beaulieu Abbey
☎ 01590 612123; www.beaulieu.co.uk

Bolderwood Deer Platform
Signed from Bolderwood car park
www.forestry.gov.uk/newforest
Fallow deer are fed here.

Breamore Manor House
& Countryside Museum
Near Fordingbridge ☎ 01725 512468;
www.breamorehouse.com

Bucklers Hard
☎ 01590 616203;
www.bucklershard.co.uk

Christchurch Priory Church
Quay Road, Christchurch
☎ 01202 485804;
www.christchurchpriory.org

Eling Tide Mill
The Toll Bridge, Eling, Totton
☎ 023 8086 9575;
www.elingtidemill.org.uk

Exbury Gardens & Steam Railway
Near Beaulieu ☎ 023 8089 1203;
www.exbury.co.uk
A favourite with steam engine fans.

Hurst Castle
Hurst Point, by Keyhaven
☎ 01590 642344; www.hurst-castle.co.uk

New Forest Cider
Littlemead, Pound Lane, Burley
☎ 01425 403589;
www.newforestcider.co.uk

New Forest Museum
Main car park, High Street, Lyndhurst
☎ 023 8028 3444;
www.newforestcentre.org.uk

New Forest Reptile Centre
Emery Down ☎ 023 8028 3141;
www.forestry.gov.uk/newforest

Place Mill
Quay Road, Christchurch
☎ 01202 487626;
www.visitchristchurch.info

Red House Museum
Quay Road, Christchurch
☎ 01202 482860

St Barbe Museum & Art Gallery
New Street, Lymington.
☎ 01590 676969;
www.stbarbe-museum.org.uk

Spinners Garden & Nursery
Boldre, by Lymington
☎ 01590 675488

■ SPORTS & ACTIVITIES

BOATING
Beaulieu River cruises
From Bucklers Hard, 3 miles (4.8km)
south of Beaulieu.

CANOEING & KAYAKING
Mudeford Ferry
Mudeford Quay ☎ 01202 488662;
www.mudefordferry.co.uk

CYCLE HIRE
AA Bike Hire
Fernglen, Gosport Lane, Lyndhurst
☎ 023 8028 3349;
www.aabikehirenewforest.co.uk

Country Lanes Cycle Centre
The Railway Station, Brockenhurst
☎ 01590 622627;www.countrylanes.co.uk

Cycle Xperience Bike Hire
Island Shop, 2–4 Brookly Road,
Brockenhurst ☎ 01590 624204;
www.cyclex.co.uk

Forest Leisure Cycling
Burley ☎ 01425 403584;
www.forestleisurecycling.co.uk

LONG-DISTANCE PATHS
Avon Valley Path
Christchurch to Salisbury Cathedral.

■ ANNUAL EVENTS & CUSTOMS

Beaulieu
Boat Jumble, Apr.
Auto Jumble, Sep.
Fireworks, end Oct.

Brockenhurst
New Forest Show, last week Jul.
www.newforestshow.co.uk

ISLE OF WIGHT

■ TOURIST INFORMATION

Cowes
The Arcade, Fountain Quay
☎ 01983 813818;
www.islandbreaks.co.uk

Newport
The Guildhall, High Street
☎ 01983 813818

Ryde
Western Esplanade ☎ 01983 813818

Sandown
8 High Street ☎ 01983 813818

Shanklin
67 High Street ☎ 01983 813818

Yarmouth
The Quay ☎ 01983 813818

■ PLACES OF INTEREST

Brading Roman Villa
Brading ☎ 01983 406223;
www.bradingromanvilla.org.uk

Carisbrooke Castle & Isle of Wight
Museum
Carisbrooke ☎ 01983 522107; www.
english-heritage.org.uk

Fort Victoria Country Park
Near Yarmouth ☎ 01983 823893;
www.fortvictoria.co.uk

Heritage Museum
11 Spring Hill, Ventnor ☎ 01983 855407;
www.ventnorheritage.org.uk

Isle of Wight Steam Railway
☎ 01983 884343;
www.iwsteamrailway.co.uk

Maritime Museum
Beckford Road, Cowes ☎ 01983 823433

Museum of Island History
Guildhall, Newport ☎ 01983 823366;
www.iwight.com

The Needles Old Battery (NT)
West Highdown, Totland
☎ 01983 754772

The Needles Park
☎ 0871 720 0022 (10p/min from BT
landline); www.iwight.com

Newport Roman Villa
Cypress Road, Newport.
☎ 01983 529720;
www.romans-in-britain.org.uk

Osborne House and Gardens (EH)
East Cowes ☎ 01983 200022

Rosemary Vineyard
Ashey, Ryde ☎ 01983 811084;
www.rosemaryvineyard.co.uk

Shanklin Chine
Shanklin ☎ 01983 866432;
www.shanklinchine.co.uk

Smuggling Museum
Botanic Garden, Ventnor
☎ 01983 853677

Yarmouth Castle (EH)
Yarmouth ☎ 01983 760678

■ FOR CHILDREN

Blackgang Chine
Chale, near Ventnor ☎ 01983 730052;
www.blackgangchine.com

Isle of Wight Zoo
Yaverland Seafront, Sandown
☎ 01983 403883;
www.isleofwightzoo.com

■ PERFORMING ARTS

Medina Theatre
Fairlee Road, Newport ☎ 01983 527020

Ryde Theatre
Lind Street, Ryde ☎ 01983 568 099

Shanklin Theatre
Prospect Road, Shanklin ☎ 01983 862739

■ SPORTS & ACTIVITIES

ADRENALINE SPORTS
First Contact
Yarmouth ☎ 01983 741484;
www.islandactivities.co.uk
Paragliding and fast boats.

Wight Water Adventure Watersports
☎ 01983 404987; www.wightwaters.com

BOAT TRIPS
Needles Pleasure Cruises
From Alum Bay ☎ 01983 761587

CYCLE HIRE
Battersby Cycles
Ryde ☎ 01983 562039

Church Street Cycles
Ventnor ☎ 01983 852232

Top Gear Cycle Hire
Cowes ☎ 01983 299056

FISHING
Scotties Fishing Tackle
11 Lugley Street, Newport ☎ 01983
522115; www.scotties-tackle.co.uk

■ ANNUAL EVENTS & CUSTOMS

Cowes
Cowes Week, late Jul/early Aug.
☎ 01983 295744; www.cowesweek.co.uk
Royal Isle of Wight Agricultural Show,
Aug. ☎ 01983 826275; www.riwas.org.uk

Newport
Isle of Wight Festival, mid-Jun.
☎ 08444 999955;
www.isleofwightfestival.org

Ryde
Carnival, end Aug/early Sep.

Yarmouth
Old Gaffers Festival, early Jun.
☎ 01983 61704;
www.yarmoutholdgaffersfestival.co.uk
Round the Island Race, mid Jun.
☎ 01983 296621;
www.roundtheisland.org.uk

WINCHESTER
& NORTH DOWNS

■ TOURIST INFORMATION

Winchester
The Guildhall, High Street
☎ 01962 840500;
www.visitwinchester.co.uk

■ PLACES OF INTEREST

Gilbert White's House
The Wakes, High Street, Selborne
☎ 01420 511275;
www.gilbertwhiteshouse.org.uk

The Grange
Northington, near Alresford
☎ 01424 775705
www.english-heritage.org.uk

Hospital of St Cross
St Cross Road, Winchester
☎ 01962 851375;
www.stcrosshospital.co.uk

Jane Austen's House
Chawton ☎ 01420 83262; www.jane-
austens-house-museum.org.uk

Mid-Hants Railway (Watercress Line)
The Railway Station, Station Road,
New Alresford ☎ 01962 733810;
www.watercressline.co.uk

Winchester Castle & Great Hall
Castle Avenue ☎ 01962 846476;
www.hants.gov.uk/greathall

Winchester Cathedral
The Close ☎ 01962 857200;
www.winchester-cathedral.org.uk

Winchester City Mill (NT)
Bridge Street, Winchester
☎ 01962 870057

Winchester City Museum
The Square, Winchester
☎ 01962 863064;
www.winchester.gov.uk
Winchester College Tours
College Street, Winchester
☎ 01962 621209;
www.winchestercollege.org

■ FOR CHILDREN
Marwell Wildlife
Colden Common, Winchester
☎ 01962 777407; www.marwell.org.uk

■ PERFORMING ARTS
Chesil Theatre
Chesil Street, Winchester
☎ 01962 867086;
www.chesiltheatre.org.uk
Grange Park Opera
Grange Park, near New Alresford
☎ 01962 868888;
www.grangeparkopera.co.uk
Theatre Royal
21–23 Jewry Street, Winchester
☎ 01962 840440;
www.theatre-royal-winchester.co.uk
Tower Arts Centre
Romsey Road, Winchester
☎ 01962 867986; www.towerarts.co.uk

■ SPORTS & ACTIVITIES
LONG-DISTANCE PATHS
Clarendon Way
A 26-mile (42km) trail from Winchester
to Salisbury.

■ ANNUAL EVENTS & CUSTOMS
New Alresford
Watercress Festival, 2nd Sun in May.
www.watercress.co.uk
Children's activities, farmers market,
celebrity chefs.
Winchester
Hampshire Food Festival, Jul.
www.hampshirefare.co.uk
Culinary events.
Hat Fair 1st weekend of Jul, Thu–Sun.
www.hatfair.co.uk
The UK's longest-running festival of
street theatre with audience participation.
Winchester Festival, Jul.
www.winchesterfestival.co.uk
Arts festival. Guided walks.

SURREY HEATHS
■ TOURIST INFORMATION
Guildford
14 Tunsgate, Guildford, Surrey
☎ 01483 444333;
www.guildford.gov.uk

■ PLACES OF INTEREST
Devil's Punch Bowl
Hindhead, Guildford
www.nationaltrust.org.uk

Guildford Cathedral
Stag Hill, Guildford, Surrey
☎ 01483 547860;
www.guildford-cathedral.org
Hindhead Common
Beside A3, at Hindhead, near crossroads
with A287; www.nationaltrust.org.uk

SOUTH DOWNS
■ TOURIST INFORMATION
Arundel
61 High Street ☎ 01903 882268
Petworth
The Old Bakery ☎ 01798 343523;
www.visitpetworth.com
South Downs National Park Authority
North Street, Midhurst ☎ 0300 3031053;
www.southdowns.gov.uk

■ PLACES OF INTEREST
Amberley Museum
Between Arundel and Storrington,
adjacent to Amberley Railway Station
☎ 01798 831370;
www.amberleymuseum.co.uk
Arundel Castle
☎ 01903 882173;
www.arundelcastle.org.uk
Arundel Museum & Heritage Centre
Mill Road car park ☎ 01903 885708;
www.arundelmuseum.org.uk
Bignor Roman Villa
Bignor ☎ 01798 869259;
www.bignorromanvilla.co.uk
Butser Ancient Farm
Petersfield ☎ 023 9259 8838;
www.butser.org.uk
Ditchling Museum
Church Lane, Ditchling
☎ 01273 844744;
www.ditchling-museum.com
Nymans Garden
Handcross, near Haywards Heath.
☎ 01444 405250;
www.nationaltrust.org.uk
Petworth House & Park
Petworth ☎ 01798 343929;
www.nationaltrust.org.uk
Queen Elizabeth Country Park
Petersfield ☎ 023 9259 5040;
www.hantsweb.org.uk/qecp
Uppark House & Garden
South Harting ☎ 01730 825827;
www.nationaltrust.org.uk
Weald & Downland Open Air Museum
Singleton ☎ 01243 811363;
www.wealddown.co.uk
West Dean Gardens
West Dean ☎ 01243 811301;
www.westdean.org.uk

■ FOR CHILDREN
Arundel Ghost Experience
Old Town Hall, Duke's Path
Entrance, High Street
☎ 01903 889821

Arundel Wetland Centre
Mill Road, Arundel
☎ 01903 883355; www.wwt.org.uk
■ PERFORMING ARTS
Glyndebourne Opera House
☎ 01273 813813;
www.glyndebourne.com

■ SPORTS & ACTIVITIES
BOAT TRIPS
Arundel Boatyard
Mill Road, Arundel ☎ 01903 882609;
www.riveraruncruises.com
HORSE RACING
Fontwell Park Racecourse
Arundel ☎ 01243 543335;
www.fontwellpark.co.uk

■ ANNUAL EVENTS & CUSTOMS
Arundel
Corpus Christi, May/Jun (60 days after
Easter) in the cathedral. ☎ 01903 882297
Arundel Festival, late Aug/early Sep.
www.arundelfestival.co.uk
Petworth
Petworth Festival, Jul/Aug.
☎ 01798 344576;
www.petworthfestival.org.uk

SOUTH COAST
■ TOURIST INFORMATION
Brighton
Royal Pavilion
www.visitbrighton.com
Chichester
29a South Street ☎ 01243 775888;
www.visitchichester.org
Eastbourne
Cornfield Road ☎ 0871 663 0031;
www.visiteastbourne.com
Portsmouth
Clarence Esplanade, Southsea
☎ 023 9282 6722;
www.visitportsmouth.co.uk
Southampton
9 Civic Centre Road ☎ 023 8083 3333;
www.visit-southampton.co.uk

■ PLACES OF INTEREST
Beachy Head Countryside Centre
☎ 01323 737273;
www.beachyhead.org.uk
Brighton Museum
Royal Pavilion Gardens ☎ 03000 290900;
www.brighton-hove-rpml.org.uk
Charles Dickens' Birthplace
393 Old Commercial Road, Portsmouth
☎ 023 9282 7261;
www.charlesdickensbirthplace.co.uk
City Museum & Art Gallery
Museum Road, Portsmouth
☎ 023 9282 7261;
www.portsmouthcitymuseums.co.uk
Explosion! Museum of Naval Firepower
Priddy's Hard, Gosport
☎ 023 9250 5600; www.explosion.org.uk

Fishbourne Roman Palace
Fishbourne, Chichester
☎ 01243 785859; www.sussexpast.co.uk
Maritime Museum
Town Quay, Southampton
☎ 023 8063 5904;
www.southampton.gov.uk
Netley Abbey
Abbey Hill, Netley ☎ 023 9258 1059;
www.english-heritage.org.uk
Portsmouth Historic Dockyard
Victory Gate, HM Naval Base
☎ 023 9286 1512/9766;
www.historicdockyard.co.uk
Redoubt Fortress & Military Museum
Royal Parade, Eastbourne
☎ 01323 410300
Royal Navy Submarine Museum
Haslar Jetty Road, Gosport
☎ 023 9251 0354; www.rnsubmus.co.uk
Royal Pavilion
Church Street, Brighton
☎ 03000 290900;
www.royalpavilion.org.uk
Seven Sisters Country Park
Exceat, near Seaford ☎ 01323 870280;
www.sevensisters.org.uk

■ FOR CHILDREN
Brighton Sea Life Centre
Marine Parade ☎ 01273 604234;
www.sealifeeurope.com
Brighton Toy & Model Museum
Trafalgar Street (underneath railway
station) ☎ 01273 749494;
www.brightontoymuseum.co.uk
Fort Fun
Royal Parade, Eastbourne
☎ 01323 642833; wwwfortfun.co.uk
Indoor and outdoor activities.
Hove Museum & Art Gallery
19 New Church Road, Hove
☎ 03000 290900;
www.brighton-hove-rpml.org.uk

■ PERFORMING ARTS
Bandstand
Grand Parade, Eastbourne
☎ 01323 410611;
www.eastbournebandstand.co.uk
Brighton Centre
Kings Road ☎ 01273 290131;
www.brightoncentre.co.uk
Brighton Dome
Church Street ☎ 01273 709709;
www.brightondome.org
Opera, ballet, orchestral and music.
Chichester Festival Theatre
Oaklands Park ☎ 01243 784437;
www.cft.org.uk
Congress Theatre
Compton Street, Eastbourne
☎ 01323 412000;
www.eastbournetheatres.co.uk
Musicals, comedy, opera, ballet
and concerts.

Devonshire Park Theatre
Compton Street, Eastbourne
☎ 01323 412000;
www.eastbournetheatres.co.uk
Komedia
44–47 Gardner Street, North Lane,
Brighton ☎ 0845 293 8430;
www.komedia.co.uk
Top comedy/cabaret venue.
The Mayflower
Commercial Road, Southampton
☎ 023 8071 1811;
www.the-mayflower.com
New Theatre Royal
20–24 Guildhall Walk, Portsmouth
☎ 023 9264 9000;
www.newtheatreroyal.com
Nuffield Theatre
University Road, Southampton
☎ 023 8067 1771
Royal Hippodrome
112 Seaside Road, Eastbourne
☎ 01323 412000;
www.eastbournetheatres.co.uk
Theatre Royal
New Road, Brighton ☎ 01273 764400;
www.ambassadortickets.com

■ **SPORTS & ACTIVITIES**
BOAT TRIPS
Allchorn Pleasure Boats
The Promenade, Eastbourne
☎ 01323 410606;
www.allchornpleasureboats.co.uk
Blue Funnel Cruises
Ocean Village, Southampton
☎ 023 8022 3278; www.bluefunnel.co.uk
Chichester Harbour Water Tours
☎ 01243 670504;
www.chichesterharbourwatertours.co.uk
SS *Shieldhall*
Berth 29, Eastern Dock, Southampton,
via Dock Gate 4 ☎ 023 8022 3278;
www.ss-shieldhall.co.uk
BUS TOURS
Brighton City Sightseeing
☎ 01273 886200;
www.city-sightseeing.com
HORSE RACING
Brighton Racecourse
Freshfield Road, Brighton
☎ 01273 603580;
www.brighton-racecourse.co.uk
HORSE RIDING
Gleneagles Equestrian Centre
Allington Lane, West End, Southampton
☎ 023 8047 3370
WATER & BEACH SPORTS
The Brighton Watersports Company
West of Palace Pier ☎ 01273 323160;
www.thebrightonwatersports.co.uk
Kayak hire, lessons and equipment.
Chichester Watersports
Coach Road, Chichester.
☎ 01243 776439/ 01243 776712;
www.chichesterwatersports.co.uk

Lagoon Watersports Centre
Hove Lagoon, The Kingsway, Hove
☎ 01273 424842; www.lagoon.co.uk
Powerboat driving, windsurfing, sailing
and water skiing.
Ross Boat Trips
Pontoon 4, Brighton Marina
☎ 07836 262717;
www.rossboattrips.co.uk
Boat trips around the harbour.
SailnetUK
Pontoon 19, West Jetty, Brighton Marina
☎ 01273 628648; www.sailnetuk.com
Sailing for beginners.

■ **ANNUAL EVENTS & CUSTOMS**
Brighton
Brighton Festival, May.
Brighton Pride, Aug. Britain's biggest
gay and lesbian event.
Brighton & Hove Food & Drink Lovers
Festival, Mar and Sep.
Market and other gastronomic delights.
Brunswick Festival, Aug.
Celebration of all things Regency.
Kite Flyers Festival, Jul.
London to Brighton Bike Ride, Jun.
London to Brighton Veteran Car Run,
early Nov. Vintage vehicles attempt the
journey from London, finishing on the
Kemp Town seafront.
Brighton Popular comedy Festival, Oct.
Chichester
Chichester Festivities, Jul.
☎ 01243 5283561; www.chifest.org.uk
Eastbourne
Airbourne, four-day air festival, mid-Aug.
Beachy Head is a good vantage point.
Eastbourne Extreme, Jul. Windsurfing,
parasailing, land yachting, inline skating.
Eastbourne Beer Festival, Oct
AEGON International Magnificent Motors,
May Bank Holiday.
Netley
Fireworks Spectacular, Royal Victoria
Country Park, Nov. ☎ 023 8045 5157
Netley Marsh Steam & Craft Show,
mid Jul at Meadow Mead Farm.
☎ 023 8086 7882;
www.netleymarshsteamandcraftshow.org
Southampton
Kite Festival, mid Jun at Lordshill.
The Big Southampton Boat Show, Sep.
☎ 0870 060 0246

WINDSOR & THE THAMES
■ **TOURIST INFORMATION**
Windsor Castle
The Old Booking Hall, Windsor
☎ 01753 743 909
www.windsor-information.co.uk

■ **PLACES OF INTEREST**
Ascot Racecourse
Ascot, Berkshire ☎ 0870 727 1234 (Ticket
Booking Line); www.ascot.co.uk

Cliveden
Taplow, Maidenhead, Buckinghamshire
☎ 01628 605069/01494 755562;
www.nationaltrust.org.uk
Eton College
Windsor ☎ 01753 671000;
www.etoncollege.com
Hampton Court Palace
East Molesey ☎ 0844 482 7777;
www.hrp.org.uk
Henley Royal Regatta
Regatta Headquarters
☎ 01491 572153; www.hrr.co.uk
Richmond Park
☎ 020 8948 3209;
www.royalparks.gov.uk
Royal Botanic Gardens
Kew, Richmond, Surrey
☎ 020 8332 5655; www.kew.org
Thames Path
A 184-mile (294km) trail following
Britain's best-known river offering
superb easy walks.
www.nationaltrail.co.uk/Thamespath
Windsor Castle
Ticket Sales and Information Office,
☎ 020 7766 7304;
www.royalcollection.org.uk

■ **PERFORMING ARTS**
Theatre Royal
32 Thames Street, Windsor
☎ 01753 853888;
www.theatreroyalwindsor.co.uk

LONDON
Central
■ **PLACES OF INTEREST**
British Library
96 Euston Road, NW1 2DB
☎ 01937 546060;www.bl.uk
Tube: King's Cross/St Pancras
British Museum
Great Russell Street, WC1B 3DG
☎ 020 7323 8000;
www.thebritishmuseum.org
Tube: Russell Square, Tottenham
Court Road
Buckingham Palace
Buckingham Palace Road, SW1A 1AA
☎ 020 7766 7301; www.royal.gov.uk
Tube: Green Park, Victoria
Cabinet War Rooms &
Churchill Museum
King Charles Street, SW1A 2AQ
☎ 020 7930 6961; www.cwr.iwm.org.uk
Tube: Westminster
Covent Garden
www.coventgardenlife.com
Tube: Covent Garden
Houses of Parliament
Parliament Square, Westminster
SW1A 0AA
☎ 020 7219 4272;
www.parliament.uk
Tube: Westminster

National Gallery
Trafalgar Square, WC2N 5DN
☎ 020 7747 2885;
www.nationalgallery.org.uk
Tube: Charing Cross
National Portrait Gallery
2 St Martin's Place, WC2H 0HE
☎ 020 7306 0055; www.npg.org.uk
Tube: Charing Cross, Leicester Square
Somerset House
The Strand, WC2R 1LA
☎ 020 7845 4600;
www.somersethouse.org.uk
Tube: Temple
Tate Britain
Millbank, SW1P 4RG
☎ 020 7887 8888; www.tate.org.uk
Tube: Pimlico
Westminster Abbey
20 Dean's Yard, SW1P 3PA
☎ 020 7222 5152;
www.westminster-abbey.org
Tube: St James Park, Westminster

■ **PERFORMING ARTS**
Adelphi Theatre
Strand, WC2R 0NS ☎ 020 7344 0055;
www.adelphitheatre.co.uk
Tube: Charing Cross
Blockbuster musicals and shows.
Aldwych Theatre
Aldwych, WC2B 4DF ☎ 020 7379 3367;
www.aldwychtheatre.com
Tube: Covent Garden
Donmar Warehouse
41 Earlham Street, WC2H 9LX
☎ 0870 060 6624;
www.donmarwarehouse.com
Tube: Covent Garden
Small-scale theatre that often stages
interesting left-field productions.
Odeon Leicester Square
22–24 Leicester Square, WC2H 7JY
☎ 0871 224 4007;
www.odeon.co.uk
Tube: Leicester Square
Multiplex cinema often used for
film premieres drawing Hollywood stars
and huge crowds.
Ronnie Scott's Jazz Club
47 Frith Street, W1D 4HT
☎ 020 7439 0747;
www.ronniescotts.co.uk
Tube: Leicester Square, Tottenham
Court Road
Jazz gigs that live up to the club's
formidable reputation. Open til 3am
most nights and late shows on Fri
and Sat nights.
Royal Opera House
Bow Street, WC2E 9DD
☎ 020 7304 4000;
www.roh.org.uk
Tube: Covent Garden
The main venue for accomplished opera
and ballet performances.

St Martin-in-the-Fields Church
Trafalgar Square, WC2N 4JJ
☎ 020 7766 1100;
www.stmartin-in-the-fields.org
Tube: Charing Cross, Leicester Square.
Free lunchtime (and occasional evening)
concerts with the focus on baroque
music.

Wigmore Hall
36 Wigmore Street, W1U 2BP
☎ 020 7935 2141;
www.wigmore-hall.org.uk
Tube: Bond Street/Oxford Circus
Amazing acoustics in an attractive and
intimate classical music venue.

North, Northwest & City
■ PLACES OF INTEREST
Brick Lane
Tube: Aldgate East, Liverpool Street
Christ Church
Fournier Street, Spitalfields, E1 6QE
☎ 020 7859 3035;
www.christchurchspitalfields.org
Tube: Aldgate East, Liverpool Street
Madame Tussauds
Marylebone Road, NW1 5LR
☎ 0870 400 3000;
www.madametussauds.com
Tube: Baker Street
Regent's Park
Regent's Park, NW1 4NR
☎ 020 7486 7908;
www.royalparks.org.uk
Tube: Baker Street, Regent's Park
St Paul's Cathedral
EC4M 8AD ☎ 020 7236 4128;
www.stpauls.co.uk
Tube: St Paul's
Sir John Soane's Museum
13 Lincoln's Inn Fields, WC2A 3BP
☎ 020 7405 2107; www.soane.org
Tube: Holborn
Tower of London
EC3N 4AB ☎ 0844 482 7777;
www.hrp.org.uk
Tube: Tower Hill

■ PERFORMING ARTS
The Barbican
Silk Street, EC2Y 8DS
☎ 020 7683 4141; www.barbican.org.uk
Tube: Barbican
Europe's largest arts centre.
Camden Arts Centre
Arkwright Road, NW3 6DG
☎ 020 7472 5500;
www.camdenartscentre.org
Tube: Finchley Road, Hampstead
Exhibitions and performances.
Canal Café Theatre
Delamere Terrace, Little Venice, W2 6ND
☎ 020 7289 6054;
www.canalcafetheatre.com
Tube: Warwick Avenue
Award-winning comedy and theatre.

Electric Ballroom
184 Camden High Street, NW1 8QP
☎ 020 7485 9006;
www.electricballroom.co.uk
Tube: Camden Town
Camden's rock showcase.
Electric Cinema
191 Portobello Road, W11 2ED
☎ 020 7908 9696;
www.electriccinema.co.uk
Tube: Notting Hill Gate
Luxuriously refurbished with a
varied programme.
Gate Picturehouse
87 Notting Hill Gate, W11 3JZ
☎ 0871 704 2058;
www.picturehouse.co.uk
Tube: Notting Hill Gate
Leading art-house cinema.
Hackney Empire
291 Mare Street, E8 1EJ
☎ 020 8985 2424;
www.hackneyempire.co.uk
Train: Hackney Central
This extravagantly decorated Edwardian
theatre is the vital venue for shows,
concerts, musicals and pantomimes in
the East End of London.
Open-air Theatre
Regent's Park, NW1 4NR
☎ 0844 826 4242;
www.openairtheatre.org
Tube: Baker Street, Marylebone,
Regent's Park
Shakespeare on a summer evening.
Sadler's Wells
Rosebery Avenue, EC1R 4TN
☎ 0844 412 4300 (box office);
www.sadlerswells.com
Tube: Angel
Ballet.

Southeast
■ PLACES OF INTEREST
Canary Wharf
Docklands, E14 Tube: Canary Wharf
HMS Belfast
Morgan's Lane, Tooley Street, SE1 2JH
☎ 020 7940 6300;
www.hmsbelfast.iwm.org.uk
Tube: London Bridge, Tower Hill
London Dungeon
28–34 Tooley Street, SE1 2SZ
☎ 020 7403 7221;
www.the-dungeons.co.uk
Tube: London Bridge
Royal Observatory & Planetarium
Greenwich Park, SE10 8XJ
☎ 020 8312 6565 (recorded information
line); www.nmm.ac.uk
Tube: Cutty Sark DLR, Greenwich DLR
Tower Bridge Exhibition
Tower Bridge Road, SE1 2UP
☎ 020 7403 3761;
www.towerbridge.org.uk
Tube: Tower Hill

■ PERFORMING ARTS
East Wintergarden
43 Bank Street, Canary Wharf, E14 5AB
☎ 020 7418 2725;
www.eastwintergarden.com
Tube: Canary Wharf
A variety of events day and night.
Up the Creek
302 Creek Road, SE10 9SW
☎ 020 8858 4581;
www.up-the-creek.com
Train: Greenwich
This comedy club confronts stand-up
comedians, experienced or fresh-faced,
with a raucous crowd.

South Bank & South
■ PLACES OF INTEREST
Imperial War Museum
Lambeth Road, SE1 6HZ
☎ 020 7416 5000; www.iwm.org.uk
Tube: Lambeth North
London Eye
County Hall, Riverside Building,
Westminster Bridge Road, SE1 7PB
☎ 0870 500 0600;
www.ba-londoneye.com
Tube: Waterloo, Westminster
Sealife London Aquarium
County Hall, Westminster Bridge Road,
SE1 7PB ☎ 0871 663 1678;
www.sealife.co.uk/London
Tube: Waterloo, Westminster
Shakespeare's Globe
21 New Globe Walk, SE1 9DT
☎ 020 7902 1500;
www.shakespeares-globe.org
Tube: London Bridge, Southwark
Southwark Cathedral
London Bridge, SE1 9DA
☎ 020 7367 6700;
www.cathedral.southwark.anglican.org
Tube: London Bridge
Tate Modern
Bankside, SE1 9TG
☎ 020 7887 8000; www.tate.org.uk
Tube: St Paul's, Southwark

■ PERFORMING ARTS & GALLERIES
IMAX Cinema
1 Charlie Chaplin Walk, SE1 8XR
☎ 08700 787 2525;
www.bfi.org.uk/imax
Tube: Waterloo
The cinema is accessed by convenient
underground walkways. The screen is
the UK's largest and shows all the latest
releases.
National Film Theatre
South Bank, SE1 8XT
☎ 020 7928 3535/020 7928 3232
(ticket office); www.bfi.org.uk
Tube: Embankment, Waterloo
This is the best venue in the city for
art-house movies.

National Theatre
The Cut, South Bank Centre SE1 9PX
☎ 020 7452 3400;
www.nationaltheatre.org.uk
Tube: Embankment, Waterloo,
or Southwark
The National offers fresh takes on old
classics, as well as putting on new plays
and various exhibitions of photography.
Old Vic
Waterloo Road, SE1 8NB
☎ 0870 060 6628;
www.oldvictheatre.com
Tube: Waterloo
One of London's finest theatres. The Old
Vic's artistic director is American actor
Kevin Spacey.
Purcell Room
South Bank Centre, SE1 8XX
☎ 0844 875 0073;
www.southbankcentre.co.uk
Tube: Embankment, Waterloo
The Purcell Room is used for solo
performances, chamber music and
contemporary music recitals.
Queen Elizabeth Hall
South Bank Centre, SE1 8XX
☎ 0844 875 0073;
www.southbankcentre.co.uk
Tube: Embankment, Waterloo
Second largest concert hall on the South
Bank site and hosts chamber orchestras,
quartets, choirs, dance and opera.
Royal Festival Hall
South Bank Centre, SE1 8XX
☎ 0844 875 0073;
www.southbankcentre.co.uk
Tube: Embankment, Waterloo
This is the permanent base for the
London Philharmonic Orchestra, as
well as the Philharmonia and the
London Sinfonietta. Frequent classical
performances are held in the Festival
Hall's 3,000-seat auditorium.
South Bank Centre
Belvedere Road, SE1 8XX
☎ 020 7921 0813;
www.southbankcentre.co.uk
Tube: Waterloo
The gallery holds some of the most
exciting exhibitions of contemporary
art in London.
Young Vic
66 The Cut, SE1 8LZ
☎ 020 7922 2922; www.youngvic.org
Tube: Southwark, Waterloo
Leading stage for younger directors
and artists – for audiences of all ages.

West & Southwest
■ PLACES OF INTEREST
Chelsea Physic Garden
66 Royal Hospital Road, SW3 4HS
☎ 020 7352 5646;
www.chelseaphysicgarden.co.uk
Tube: Sloane Square

Hyde Park
W2 2UH ☎ 020 7298 2100;
www.royalparks.gov.uk
Tube: Hyde Park Corner, Knightsbridge
Kensington Palace & Gardens
Kensington Gardens, W8 4PX
☎ 020 7937 9561; www.hrp.org.uk
Tube: Bayswater, High Street Kensington
Natural History Museum
Cromwell Road, SW7 5BD
☎ 020 7942 5000; www.nhm.ac.uk
Tube: South Kensington
Science Museum
Exhibition Road, SW7 2DD
☎ 0870 870 4868;
www.sciencemuseum.org.uk
Tube: South Kensington
Serpentine Gallery
Kensington Gardens, W2 3XA
☎ 020 7402 6075;
www.serpentinegallery.org
Tube: Lancaster Gate
Victoria & Albert Museum
Cromwell Road, SW7 2RL
☎ 020 7942 2000; www.vam.ac.uk
Tube: South Kensington
Wellington Arch
Hyde Park Corner, W1J 7JZ
☎ 020 7930 2726;
www.english-heritage.org.uk
Tube: Hyde Park Corner

■ PERFORMING ARTS
Bush Hall
310 Uxbridge Road, W12 7LJ
☎ 020 8222 6955;
www.bushhallmusic.co.uk
Tube: Shepherd's Bush
Wonderful classical and acoustic concerts.
O2 Shepherd's Bush Empire
Shepherd's Bush Green, W12 8TT
☎ 020 8354 3300;
www.2shepherdsbushempire.co.uk
Tube: Shepherd's Bush
An intimate gig and club venue, staging live entertainment for over 100 years.
Royal Albert Hall
Kensington Gore, SW7 2AP
☎ 020 7589 3203;
www.royalalberthall.com
Tube: South Kensington
Classical concerts and other events.

CANTERBURY & KENT DOWNS
■ TOURIST INFORMATION
Canterbury
12/13 Sun Street, Canterbury
☎ 01227 378 100;
www.visitcanterbury.co.uk

■ PLACES OF INTEREST
Canterbury Cathedral
Cathedral House ☎ 01227 762862;
www.canterbury-cathedral.org

Hever Castle & Gardens
Hever, Edenbridge
☎ 01732865224; www.hevercastle.co.uk
Ightham Mote
Mote Road, Ivy Hatch, Sevenoaks
☎ 01732 810378;
www.nationaltrust.org.uk

■ PERFORMING ARTS
Gulbenkian Theatre
University Campus, University of Kent
☎ 01227 769075;
www.kent.ac.uk/gulbenkian/
Theatre, cinema and café, staging drama, dance, comedy and music.
Marlowe Theatre
The Friars, Canterbury ☎ 01865 252200;
www.newmarlowetheatre.org.uk
The New Marlowe Theatre is due to be completed in September 2011. Visit the website to find a list of forthcoming performances and venues of the Marlowe Theatre Team.

OXFORD & THE CHILTERNS
■ TOURIST INFORMATION
Oxford
15-16 Broad Street, Oxford
☎ 01865 252200; www.oxford.org
Wendover Community & Tourist Information Office
The Clock Tower, High Street
Wendover ☎ 01296 696759;
www.wendover-pc.gov.uk/tourism

■ PLACES OF INTEREST
Ashmolean Museum
Beaumont Street, Oxford
☎ 01865 278000; www.ashmolean.org
Blenheim Palace
Woodstock ☎ 01993 811091,
(08700 60 20 80, 24-hour recorded information service);
www.blenheimpalace.com
Bodleian Library
Broad Street, Oxford
☎ 01865 277216; www.bodley.ox.ac.uk
Museum of the History of Science
South Parks Road, Oxford
☎ 01865 270927; www.prm.ox.ac.uk
Pitts River Museum
Broad Street, Oxford
☎ 01865 277280; www.mhs.ox.ac.uk

■ PERFORMING ARTS
New Theatre (Apollo Theatre)
George Street, Oxford
☎ 0844 847 1585 (box office)
Oxford Playhouse
8-12 Beaumont Street, Oxford
☎ 01865 305305;
www.oxfordplayhouse.com
Sheldonian Theatre
University of Oxford, Sheldonian Theatre, Broad Street, Oxford
☎ 01865 277299; www.ox.ac.uk

PUBS
THE NEW FOREST
The East End Arms
Main Road, East End, near Lymington
SO41 5SY ☎ 01590 626223;
www.eastendarms.co.uk
A traditional and comfortable New Forest pub serving brasserie-style food in the lounge bar, with a range of tasty options on the menu such as locally sourced fish and seafood with spectacular dishes such as Porbeagle shark loin with cucumber and dill salad.

The Filly Inn
Lymington Road, Setley, near
Brockenhurst SO42 7UF
☎ 01590 623449; www.fillyinn.co.uk
The bar snacks at this cosy, traditional pub include baguettes and jacket potatoes, and there is a wider menu offering home-baked pies and perhaps 10oz steak. There are vegetarian options and a children's menu as well as a Sunday carvery. Children are welcome and dogs are permitted too.

The Master Builders House Hotel
Bucklers Hard SO42 7XB
☎ 0844 815 3399;
www.themasterbuilders.co.uk
Large grassy areas in front of the pub run gently down to the Beaulieu River, making it a popular spot, especially on summer days. Lemon sole, linguine with crab, roast fillet and belly of pork may appear on the menu, with a good range of light snacks. Also offer an Indian summer barbecue from Easter until the end of September.

ISLE OF WIGHT
The Folly
Folly Lane, Cowes PO32 6NB
☎ 01983 297171; www.thefollyinn.com
Easy access by both land and water makes this unusual Cowes pub a very popular venue in summer. It was constructed in part from the timbers out of the hull of an old barge, and makes good use of its nautical theme throughout. House specialities include venison Wellington, prime British beef and slow-cooked lamb.

The Red Lion
Church Place, Freshwater PO40 9BP
☎ 01983 754925
The pub has a pleasant setting on the River Yar. Everything here is freshly made. Favourites might include rib-eye steak or whole lobster salad. A blackboard lists the day's home-made puds. The garden includes a herb garden – the perfect place to sup a pint of local Goddards ale – and dogs are also permitted here.

WINCHESTER & NORTH DOWNS
The Bell
12 West Street, New Alresford SO24 9AT
☎ 01962 732429;
www.bellalresford.com
An elegant revamp of an old inn with pine tables and a carpeted bar area. Enjoy locally sourced fine food with a pint of local ale or choose from their well-stocked cellar of wine. Sunday roasts with all the trimmings are also served.

Hotel du Vin
Southgate Street, Winchester SO23 9EF
☎ 01962 841414; www.hotelduvin.com
The bistro of this Georgian hotel in the city centre makes an excellent if pricey stop for lunch or coffee. There's a stylish champagne bar and a pretty walled courtyard. The innovative French-style menu changes regularly and dishes might include local trout.

The Wykeham Arms
75 Kingsgate Street, Winchester
SO23 9PE ☎ 01962 853834
The 'Wyk', in an old back street near to Winchester College, is a local institution. It is furnished in part with old desks and ephemera from the school. The food is excellent, with a daily changing menu offering dishes such as the famous Wyk pie supper (new season rack of lamb). There is a choice of wines by the glass.

SURREY HEATHS
The Bat & Ball Freehouse
Bat & Ball Lane, Boundstone GU10 4SA
☎ 01252 792108;
www.thebatandball.co.uk
Nestling at the bottom of the Bourne Valley, this 150-year-old inn is worth making the effort to find. The decor mixes old and new, with oak beams and terracotta floor tiles. The home-made desserts are especially good here.

Red Lion
Shamley Green, Guildford GU5 0UB
☎ 01483 892202;
www.theredlion.uk.com
Situated opposite the village cricket green, this attractive old pub is the perfect place to sit in the pretty rear gardens. Selection of real ales available.

SOUTH DOWNS
Black Horse
High Street, Amberley BN18 9NL
☎ 01798 831552
A convivial place for a drink, lunch or dinner, with a good choice of options for all tastes, including children, this 17th-century tavern has open fires and original flagstones, and a set of sheep bells given to the landlord by the last local shepherd.

The Bull
High Street, Ditchling BN6 8TA
☎ 01273 843147;
www.thebullditchling.com

This inn in the centre of the village was revamped a few years ago, but has kept its character-laden bar much the same and there's usually a large fire blazing. The British menu changes regularly and you can eat in the nicely mellow side rooms or in the bar. It's within striking distance of Ditchling Beacon and the view from the garden might inspire you to venture up there.

SOUTH COAST
Basketmakers Arms
12 Gloucester Road, Brighton BN1 4AD
☎ 01273 689006;
www.thebasketmakersarms.co.uk

A wide array of malt whiskies, several real ales and inexpensive bar food are hallmarks of this friendly back-street pub. The two bare-boarded rooms harbour a fascinating stash of old tins, advertisements, posters and cigarette cards. Not far from the Theatre Royal, this place is open all day.

The Cowherds
The Common, Southampton SO15 7NN
☎ 023 8055 8405

On the A33, at the heart of Southampton Common, this pub was once the haunt of cattle drovers. Food is served all day and it's the perfect spot for lunch or dinner – enjoy tasty sandwiches, grilled rib-eye steak or dishes such as mixed grill, lamb shoulder and duo of pork. There's a patio outside and inside it's cosy with open fires, oak beams and wood panelling.

The Greys
105 Southover Street, Brighton BN2 9UA
☎ 01273 680734; www.greyspub.com

This has the feel of a country pub with its panelled walls and flagstone floors. Choose from real ales or the selection of Belgian beers. The menu changes regularly and features seasonal dishes made with locally sourced produce. Live music one or two days a week; children are not allowed inside.

The Still & West
2 Bath Square, Old Portsmouth PO1 2JL
☎ 023 9282 1567

Located at the top of Broad Street, and close to HMS *Victory*, this nautically themed 1504 pub has great views over the harbour and further out to the Isle of Wight. As you might expect, there's a good range of fish dishes on the menu, including a trademark grill of fresh fish and mussels, and traditional beer-battered fish and chips.

WINDSOR & THE THAMES
The Thatched Tavern
Cheapside, Ascot SL5 7QG
☎ 01344 620874;
www.thethatchedtavern.co.uk

You'll find this great pub just over a mile (1.6km) from the famous racecourse, this attractive 17th-century building features oak beams, flagstone floors and low ceilings. Traditional fare as well as daily specials and fresh fish are offered here, and there is a lovely garden.

LONDON
The Anchor & Hope
36 The Cut SE1 8LP ☎ 020 7928 9898

Considering it is an award-winning gastro-pub, the Anchor & Hope is a remarkably down-to-earth place with reasonable prices. The friendly atmosphere here attracts families and people with dogs are also made welcome. Quality British produce is used in the refreshingly unfussy menu and your meal could be complemented by a glass of good wine or a pint of real ale.

The Belle Vue
1 Clapham Common, Southside
SW4 7AA. ☎ 0207 498 9473

This is a great place to stop and relax, right opposite the green acres of Clapham Common. The lunch and dinner menus both feature fish and shellfish dishes, and the place is a favourite with locals for its Sunday lunches.

The Bleeding Heart Tavern
19 Greville Street EC1N 8SJ
☎ 0207 242 2056;
www.bleedingheart.co.uk

There's been a tavern here since 1746, and, although the promise of 'drunk for a penny, dead drunk for twopence' no longer holds true, plenty of old London spirit has been maintained in this scrubbed-up, contemporary version. Inside is a happy blend of smart and rustic, glass and stone decor that works really well. The menu is a delight for meat-lovers but there are some vegetarian options.

The Cross Keys
1 Lawrence Street, Chelsea SW3 5NB
☎ 020 7349 9111

An upmarket Chelsea pub and restaurant that has been a favourite haunt of the rich and famous for the past 40 years. Food is mainly modern European in style with more traditional dishes available at the bar. The interior has been extensively refurbished with a fully retractable roof in the restaurant and a self-service beer tap table in the bar. There is an excellent wine list.

The Drapers Arms
44 Barnsbury St, N1 1ER
☎ 020 7619 0348;
www.thedrapersarms.com

This is a smart neighbourhood pub with a garden. Enjoy excellent food in the private dining room upstairs or relax on squashy sofas in the open-plan bar area downstairs. The menu offers some interesting main courses and old favourites for dessert.

The Fire Station
150 Waterloo Road SE1 8SB
☎ 020 7620 2226

Close to Waterloo Station and handy for the Old Vic Theatre and the Imperial War Museum, this remarkable conversion of an Edwardian fire station retains many of the building's original features. Choose from an excellent menu of gastro-pub favourites, such as collar of ham, pea and mint risotto or vegetable curry with rice.

The Jerusalem Tavern
55 Britton Street Clerkenwell
EC1M 5UQ ☎ 020 7490 4281

This historic tavern has been in four different locations since it was established in the 14th century. Now situated in one of London's most vibrant corners, the pub features rustic wooden tables, open fires and cosy nooks. Familiar pub fare and bottled beers from St Peter's Brewery complete the experience.

North Pole Bar & Restaurant
131 Greenwich High Road, Greenwich
SE10 8JA ☎ 020 8853 3020

This place gives you three choices in one building – an evening in the Piano Restaurant, a cocktail bar, and a nightclub in the basement. Bar meals and restaurant fare is available along with a selection of wines and draught lagers.

The Queens
49 Regents Park Road, Primrose Hill
NW1 8XD ☎ 0207 586 0408

Enjoy the views of Primrose Hill from the balcony of this Victorian pub. Main courses might include seared calves' liver with bacon and sage mash or roast vegetable Yorkshire pudding. On Sundays, there is a selection of roasts, as well as fish, pasta and salad. Beers include Youngs and guests.

The Round House
2 Northside, Wandsworth Common
SW18 2SS ☎ 020 7326 8580

Although the interior is modern, this has the feel of a real local pub in the heart of Wandsworth. A good selection of food is served until 10pm.

The Seven Stars
53 Carey Street WC2A 2JB
☎ 020 7242 8521

Built in 1602, the Seven Stars pub is one of the oldest ale houses in London. It is one of the few buildings that survived the Great Fire of London while many other buildings around it perished. Popular with the legal fraternity and journalist types because of its close proximity to the Inns of Court, the cosy little pub has a tiny Elizabethan staircase and is furnished in a traditional style. Good quality fare is offered here accompanied by a range of real ales.

CANTERBURY & KENT DOWNS
The Chapter Arms
New Town Street, Chartham Hatch
CT4 7LT ☎ 01227 738340

The Chapter Arms is a pretty, flower-bedecked free house on the Pilgrim's Way, with a lovely leafy garden. The property was once three cottages owned by Canterbury Cathedral's Dean and Chapter – hence the name. Choose from a var ed menu with dishes made from freshly prepared local produce. The outdoor barbecue opens weekends and bank holidays from mid May throughout the summer.

The Dove Inn
Plum Pudding Lane, Dargate ME13 9HB
☎ 01227 751360

Tucked away down a pleasant little lane, The Dove Inn is a picture-postcard village pub, complete with roses round the door outside and simple wooden floors and tables on the inside. The menu has some inspired dishes with a host of inventive main courses that features locally caught game. Bar meals are also served and there is a good range of wines.

OXFORD & THE CHILTERNS
The Anchor
2 Hayfield Road, Walton Manor OX2 6TT
☎ 01865 510282

This is a friendly pub with a relaxed atmosphere. The menu carries a good range of meals including all the favourites, such as fish and chips and sausage and mash.

Turf Tavern
4 Bath Place, off Holywell Street, Oxford
OX1 3SU ☎ 01865 243838

In the heart of Oxford, among the city's winding streets and little alleyways, the Turf Tavern is nestled next to the colleges. The sheltered courtyards provide a quiet haven for a drink in the summertime. You can choose from a selection of real ales and typical pub fare is offered on the menu.

TEA ROOMS
THE NEW FOREST
The Buttery
19–20 High Street, Lymington
SO41 9AD ☎ 01590 672870;
www.thebuttery.org
A well-established and deservedly
popular restaurant and tea room, the
Buttery serves speciality coffees and
teas, sumptuous clotted cream teas,
and a great selection of tasty cakes – all
hand-made on the premises. You can
also get light lunches here, or if you are
particularly hungry after walking in the
Forest, even a full English breakfast.

The Buttery at the Brock & Bruin
25 Brookley Road, Brockenhurst
SO42 7RB ☎ 01590 622958
Delicious home-made cakes and
naughty-but-nice cream teas are top
treats at this restaurant and tea room.
Light lunches are also served daily, and
breakfast too – handy if you're camping.

Montagu Arms Hotel
Palace Lane, Beaulieu SO42 7ZL
☎ 01590 612324;
www.montaguarmshotel.co.uk
An hospitable, 16th-century inn nestling
in the pretty hamlet of Beaulieu, the
Montagu Arms offers finger sandwiches,
loaf cakes, scones, cream tea fancies,
and shortbread. In season, you can enjoy
locally grown strawberries served with
your afternoon tea.

Tasty Pastries Bakery and Tea Room
16A High Street, Lyndhurst SO43 7BD
☎ 023 8028 3448
The perfect place to pause for tea and
cakes, or perhaps to buy freshly baked
pasties, filled baguettes and sandwiches
for a picnic.

ISLE OF WIGHT
God's Providence House
12 St Thomas Square, Newport
☎ 01983 522085
This is the spot where, it is claimed, the
Great Plague of the 1560s came to a halt
– hence the name. Today it's a traditional
tea room, serving coffee, teas, cakes,
snacks and lunches.

Jireh House
St James's Square, Yarmouth PO41 0NP
☎ 01983 760513
This wonderful tea room is located in
a 17th-century house close to the sea
and is the perfect spot for those wanting
to escape the crowds and enjoy a pot
of fine tea in an atmosphere of easy
camaraderie. The service is friendly
and customers can enjoy light snacks,
afternoon tea or a cream tea.

Vineyard Café
Adgestone Vineyard, Upper Road,
Sandown PO36 0ES ☎ 01983 402503;
www.adgestonevineyard.co.uk
The oldest vineyard in Britain serves
some of the best cream teas on the Isle
of Wight, with freshly baked scones, and
home-made cakes. Morning coffee and
light lunches – including wine – are also
available, and check ahead for special
wine-tasting evenings.

WINCHESTER
& NORTH DOWNS
Caracoli
15 Broad Street, Alresford
SO24 9AR ☎ 01962 738730;
www.caracoli.co.uk
With its fresh, modern décor and
courtyard garden, this coffee shop and
food store is a chic place for a light bite.
Ingredients are carefully chosen. There's
also an array of preserves, teas, coffees,
chutneys and wines for sale. Tapas is
served on Friday evenings.

Cassandra's Cup
The Hollies, Chawton GU34 1SD
☎ 01420 83144
On the corner of the street, opposite Jane
Austen's house, and named after her
sister, Cassandra's Cup has a cheerful
interior with floral plates displayed on a
dresser. Light lunches and tea and cakes
are on offer.

Gilbert White's Tea Parlour
The Wakes, High Street, Selborne
GU34 3JH ☎ 01420 511275;
www.gilbertwhiteshouse.org.uk
This tea room overlooking the busy
village street is inside the house of the
naturalist Gilbert White. Much of the food
served here is made from 18th-century
recipes. Try savoury homity pie, seed or
plum cake, accompanied by a good range
of speciality teas.

Tiffin Tea Rooms
50 West Street, Alresford SO24 9AU
☎ 01962 734394
This friendly, traditional tea room with
its blue-and-white striped awning serves
home-made cakes and lemonade, cream
teas and speciality teas and coffees.

The Wessex Hotel
Paternoster Row, Winchester
SO23 9LQ ☎ 0870 400 8126;
www.wessexhotel.co.uk
From the relaxed lounge of this central
hotel you look out on to Winchester
Cathedral. They serve sumptuous
traditional full afternoon teas, with
home-made scones, jam, clotted cream,
sandwiches and cakes.

SURREY HEATHS
Haskett's Tea and Coffee Shop
68B South Street, Dorking RH4 2EW
☎ 01306 885833
Poster art decorates the walls of this tea
and coffee shop, but the Grade II listed
building dates from the 17th century.
Enjoy afternoon tea and light snacks.

SOUTH DOWNS
Belindas Tea Room
13 Tarrant Street, Arundel BN18 9DG
☎ 01903 882977
A white-painted cottage in Tarrant
Street. Go down the steps to an old
English interior, with copper and
brassware on the walls. Belindas serves
breakfasts, cream teas, sandwiches and
jacket potatoes, with a tempting list of
traditional desserts. There is a patio for
fine weather.

Ditchling Tearooms
West Street, Ditchling ☎ 01273 842708
Dolly's is like a cake shop with an
attached warren of low-ceilinged old
rooms in traditional tea shop style.
Alongside cream teas and coffees, enjoy
all-day breakfasts, ploughman's and
lunches, such as quiche and salad. You
can also have a glass of wine or beer with
your meal and enjoy Italian food on Friday
and Saturday evenings.

Tiffins Tearoom
1 Leppards, High Street, Petworth
GU28 0AU ☎ 01798 344560;
www.tiffinstearoom.co.uk
Tea rooms and restaurant with pastel-
painted wooden tables and chairs, and
words of wisdom on the walls. Tiffins
serves breakfasts and light lunches
alongside teas, coffees and delicious
home-made cakes.

SOUTH COAST
Cathedral Cloisters Café
Chichester Cathedral, Chichester
PO19 1PX ☎ 01243 782595
Walk into the cathedral cloisters and
you'll find this splendid café. Airy and
modern in style, it offers a range of
afternoon teas and daily specials, as well
as Sunday lunch.

Mock Turtle
4 Pool Valley, Brighton BN1 1NJ
☎ 01273 327380
Devotees of cream teas have been
tucking into scones and cakes here
since 1972. All the food is home made,
including the jam, with tempting cakes
and meringues, and you can buy a pot of
their jam to take home. Near The Lanes
and the Royal Pavilion, and next to the
National Express bus terminus.

Tower Café Bar
Spinnaker Tower, Gunwharf Quays
Portsmouth PO1 3TT. ☎ 02392 857520;
www.spinnakertower.co.uk
Take your morning coffee or afternoon
tea in style (not at the top!) in
Portsmouth's newest venue. Sandwiches
and cakes give way to wine and beer in
the evenings, as you sit and watch the
sun go down over the harbour.

LONDON
The Dorchester
Park Lane, London W1K 1QA
☎ 020 7629 8888;
www.dorchesterhotel.com
The Dorchester has its own blend of
tea that is offered alongside others like
China Oolong. Afternoon tea here is a
relaxing affair, served by efficient staff
and entertained by the tinkling of piano
music. Beautifully laid tables are set with
bone china groaning with sumptuous
cakes and delicate sandwiches.

The Ritz
150 Piccadilly, London W1J 9BR
☎ 020 7493 8181;
www.theritzlondon.com
Part of the London experience, tea at
the Ritz is an occasion to savour – and
to dress for. Jeans are not welcome
here. From the silver teapots to the
finely cut sandwiches and delicate
cakes and pastries, every detail has
been considered. If tea is not your
preferred beverage then maybe a glass
of champagne will suffice. Make sure you
reserve well in advance.

CANTERBURY
& KENT DOWNS
The Moat Tea Rooms
67 Burgate, Canterbury CT1 2HJ
☎ 01227 784514
These are lovely tea rooms, just a short
walk away from the centre of the city.
In the 16th-century building you'll find
rich, dark furniture and the fireplaces
make it especially cosy in the winter.
For chocolate lovers there is a delicious
chocolate cake or you could try the
Champagne cream tea.

OXFORD & THE CHILTERNS
Old Parsonage Hotel
1 Banbury Road, Oxford OX2 6NN
☎ 01865 310210;
www.oldparsonage-hotel.co.uk
You can take tea in the lovely hotel
restaurant or out on the terrace when the
weather is good. Different blends of tea
are available including the hotel's own
blend, Old Parsonage Blend, which is
served with a range of tasty sandwiches
and scrumptious scones.

Central England

Central England

The oft-called 'heart of England' is made up of two distinct landscapes – one of open fens and flatlands, ribbons of waterways and a coastline buffeted by the North Sea, the other rich with dramatic peaks and deep verdant gorges, and villages of stone cottages built using the power of its rivers.

History as well as nature has helped to sculpt these disparate areas, from the great battles of the Roundheads and the Royalists in the English Civil War, to the life-changing industrial processes and inventions that resulted from the Industrial Revolution.

Not just the cradle of industry, middle England was also the birthplace of its most famous bard, William Shakespeare, born in Stratford-upon-Avon. Other towns, such as the university town and educational mecca, Cambridge, fall within the fold of central England, and many of the towns themselves are blessed with fine architecture. Central England stretches to industrious Staffordshire, which reaches into the Peak District, and to the edge of England where Shropshire nudges into Wales. This really is a beautiful area, separately or as the sum of its parts.

Suffolk Coast

CLOCKWISE FROM TOP: RIVER BLYTH, BLYTHBURGH; ALDEBURGH MOOT HALL; LOBSTERS, ALDEBURGH

ALDEBURGH MAP REF 405 L6

People with an interest in British music will not need to be told about Aldeburgh; the annual Festival of Music and Arts, founded in 1948 by composer Benjamin Britten, singer Peter Pears and librettist Eric Crozier holds world renown, with many of the recitals given in Aldeburgh itself. Others are performed at the nearby Snape Maltings, a site reincarnated from disused malt houses into a concert venue of international acclaim that hosts a year-round programme of concerts.

Aldeburgh has always had an association with fishing and boat-building, one that continues to this day but in a time-honoured fashion, for fishermen still haul their boats onto the shingle beach and sell their catches daily from nearby huts. In fact, the seafront is remarkably little changed since Victorian times, a feature that gives Aldeburgh an infectious charm. For many it is this characteristic that is the attraction.

But things have changed: the early 16th-century Moot Hall, which houses an interesting museum, stands on the sea front but was once at the centre of the town, such has been the serious amount of coastal erosion. And in the lovely 15th-century church there is a bust of local-born poet George Crabbe, although his birthplace at Slaughden has long been lost to the sea along with the remains of the village, originally built here by the Romans. The Suffolk-born scholar Edward Fitzgerald, translator of Omar Khayyám's works, was particularly taken with Aldeburgh, while the English novelist Wilkie Collins holidayed here.

On the shingle bank at Slaughden stands England's most northerly Martello tower, one of 103 towers constructed along the south coast between 1805 and 1812 to defend against invasion by Napoleon.

BLYTHBURGH MAP REF 405 L6

Just inland from the Suffolk Heritage Coast, the Anglo-Saxon village of Blythburgh is set in an Area of Outstanding Natural Beauty and graced with a tidal river, marshes, heathland, small woodlands, pastures and arable fields. The tidal section of the River Blyth flows just to the north of the village, reaching the sea at Southwold. Over the years the sea walls have been breached and the land not reclaimed, creating a tidal lagoon, Blythburgh Water, which is immensely popular with coastal birdlife as a safe habitat.

In August 1577, a bolt of lightning hit and brought down the 15th-century church steeple, and the Devil was blamed. On the same day, Black Shuck, the legendary devil dog of the marshes is said to have run through the church, killing two parishioners. The damage to the roof meant that for a time congregations had to worship beneath umbrellas. The church is sometimes referred to by locals as the 'Cathedral of the Marshes', lending credence to the notion that Blythburgh was once much larger than today, but this is not so. Blythburgh has always been small, although it once had an important medieval priory, and attracted sufficient wealthy piety to build a large church.

DEDHAM MAP REF 401 K3

The Dedham Vale and Stour Valley embraces one of England's most cherished landscapes, one of dignified villages, rolling farmland, rivers, meadows and ancient woodlands; it is what might be thought of as quintessential English lowland landscape. The Area of Outstanding Natural Beauty has a rich history, and has been an inspiration for many writers and artists, not least John Constable who immortalized the vale and the village church tower in his paintings more than 200 years ago. Indeed, this is very much 'Constable Country'. John Constable, born nearby in East Bergholt, attended the local school in Dedham, and both Flatford Mill and Willy Lott's House on the River Stour are recognisable as featuring in many of Constable's paintings.

Pre-dating the Domesday Book, Dedham has prospered for around 1,000 years and in the 14th century was a major wool producer, attracting a colony of Flemish cloth workers seeking refuge from the turmoil on the Continent. As elsewhere, the town's fortunes varied with the wool trade, but revived in the 16th century with the manufacture of new high quality cloths. The wealth created by the wool trade financed the construction of the village church in 1492.

Because much of East Anglia's traditional grassland has been drained and ploughed, the hedgerows and wildflower meadows that remain are among some of England's most vulnerable pastoral landscapes, one enhanced by narrow lanes and characteristic timber-framed and thatched houses.

DUNWICH MAP REF 405 L6

A visit to the coastal village of Dunwich, surrounded by forest and marshland, serves only to demonstrate the destructive force of the sea. In the 7th century, Dunwich was a prosperous city, shipyard and fishing centre, where the first bishop of East Anglia established a Cathedral, in so doing making Dunwich the capital of this part of England. At that time the coastline was a mile (1.6km) further east. Records from the 13th- and early 14th-century give an indication of the size of Dunwich, with a shipping list comprising 11 warships, 36 trading ships and some 24 fishing smacks.

It was in the Middle Ages that the sea began to make significant encroachments into Dunwich, effectively destroying what was once a great port and in the process washing away nine medieval churches and two monasteries. In Dunwich Museum there is a small model showing how the town looked in the 12th century.

In spite of so much of Dunwich being missing, as it were, this remains a lovely place to visit, and the adjacent Dunwich Heath is popular with walkers. Local

VISIT
FLATFORD MILL

Flatford Mill flanks the River Stour in close proximity to the Suffolk-Essex border. The buildings here, particularly the Mill and Willy Lott's House, are instantly recognisable since they feature in numerous paintings by John Constable. Surrounded by lush lowland landscapes, wildlife habitats and places of historic interest, Flatford Mill is a graceful and moving place to visit, although there is no public access to the Mill or to the other buildings in the village. But the National Trust offers guided walks to the sites that Constable painted. There is a tiny 16th-century thatched cottage beside the river, also owned by the National Trust, which houses a permanent exhibition of Constable's work, including several showing the 'Bridge Cottage' and, of course, the famous Hay Wain (now in the National Gallery in London).

FLATFORD MILL

DUNWICH

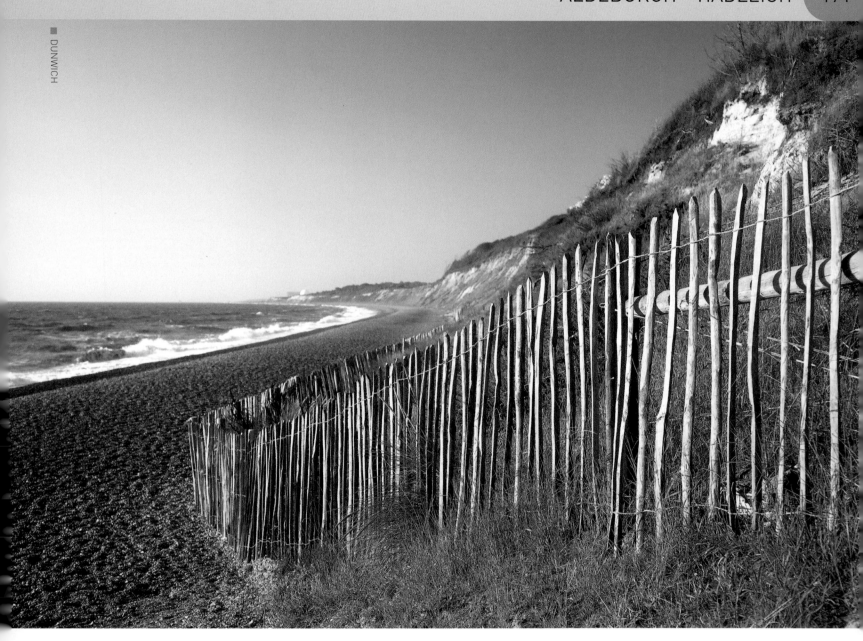

legend has it that on a calm night the long-lost church bells can still be heard tolling deep beneath the waves. It's a starry-eyed story. Believe it or not; but listen, just in case.

FELIXSTOWE MAP REF 405 K7
In the days of press gangs, Felixstowe was not a place to drop your guard; if you did so you risked spending the next few months or years sailing the high seas. Before its development as a container port, Felixstowe was a traditional and truly genteel Edwardian seaside resort, the so-called 'Garden Resort of the East Coast'. Today, in spite of 'containerism', the town is still attractive; it has a long sand and shingle beach, and extensive and beautiful gardens line the promenade; some, like those by the Spa Pavilion and Town Hall, have been listed on the English Heritage Register of Parks and Gardens of National Importance.

A village has stood on the site since before the Norman Conquest, and eventually became a lynchpin in England's

defences. It's vital position was proved when, in 1667, Dutch soldiers landed and failed to capture Landguard Fort.

The town became a major port in 1886. In addition to shipping, tourism increased, and during the late Victorian era it became a fashionable resort, a trend initiated by the opening of Felixstowe railway station, and a visit by the German royal family.

The Landguard Peninsula is a nature reserve, with an historic fort and the Felixstowe Museum as well as a passenger ferry linking Felixstowe with Shotley and Harwich.

FRAMLINGHAM MAP REF 405 K6
Framlingham, with its attractive houses and shops all gathered around the triangular Market Hill, is a place steeped in history. The castle, built by the Earl of Norfolk, Roger Bigod, has an 800-year-old history. It was here at Framlingham Castle, in 1553, that Mary Tudor gathered her supporters around her as she waited anxiously to learn whether she or Lady Jane Grey had been declared Queen.

The castle, one of the most important and beautiful medieval castles, is today in the care of English Heritage, and has one of the earliest curtain walls in England. Unlike other castles, it is possible to walk the full length of the 12th-century battlements. Little remains of the interior, other than a 17th-century poorhouse and medieval stone heads.

In a country surfeited with glorious church architecture, the parish church of St Michael in Framlingham is especially pleasing. The roof is particularly glorious, with intricate fan tracery which conceals superb hammer beams. There is also a splendid collection of 16th-century tombs, belonging to members of the Howard family from the time when they owned the castle. The town also has numerous quaint buildings dating from the 17th, 18th and 19th centuries. You will find many of the best examples on Market Hill.

Framlingham, surrounded by country lanes that are ideal for walking and cycling, is an excellent base from which to explore an unspoiled part of Suffolk.

HADLEIGH MAP REF 405 K7
Hadleigh is a handsome market town at the very centre of the undulating Suffolk countryside. At the heart of Hadleigh, once a royal town for the 9th-century Danish King Guthrum, is a rich and important architectural legacy dating from Saxon times. There are not many towns of such character left in England today, and its medieval charm and architectural styles, ranging from timber-framed to Georgian (with some fine examples of the ornamental plasterwork known as pargeting), are a great attraction for tourists, bolstered by a thriving business and community spirit. Once renowned for its woollen cloth, Hadleigh is an agreeable blend of old and new; 600 years ago Hadleigh was among the most important wool and market towns in England; by the 16th century only Ipswich and Bury St Edmunds were more prosperous. The elegant High Street is lined with those elegant timber-framed houses, as well as a wide range of interesting shops, pubs and restaurants.

SUFFOLK COAST

ORFORD MAP REF 405 L7

To the south of Aldeburgh the isolated castle town of Orford has considerable charm. Its 800-year-old castle is open to the public, and the splendid church of St Bartholomew has hosted many performances over the years of works by Benjamin Britten, including *Noye's Fludde* in 1958 and *Curlew River* in 1964. At the time of the Domesday Book, Orford was little more than a hamlet. Less than 100 years later it had been transformed by Henry II into a busy port, with a magnificent castle both to guard it and defend against unruly barons. Before the castle was built, the area around Orford was dominated by the Bigod family, from their castle at Framlingham. Hugh Bigod was the Earl of Norfolk and one of a group of dissenting barons in the reigns of Stephen and Henry II. Work began on the castle in 1165 and Henry also drained the marshes here making Orford a sheltered port.

When completed, Orford Castle consisted of a curtain wall with flanking towers, and a twin-towered gatehouse surrounding a polygonal keep. Alas, the curtain wall, gatehouse and towers have all decayed and nothing of them survives today. Standing alone and intact is the Great Tower of the original royal castle. It is a remarkable construction and resembles no other in Britain or Ireland, with its basic plan of a circular tower incorporating three great turrets.

Today, the town is sheltered from the penetrating North Sea by the great shingle bank of Orford Ness, the largest vegetated shingle spit in Europe. Not surprisingly, Orford Ness, wild, rugged and remote, is an important nature reserve containing a variety of habitats, including shingle, brackish lagoons, salt marsh, mud flats and grazing marsh. It provides an important habitat for breeding and passage birds as well as for delicate and unusual shingle flora, including a large number of nationally rare species.

SAXMUNDHAM MAP REF 405 L6

With such a delightful name, the market town of Saxmundham is irresistible. It was once an important communication centre between London and Great Yarmouth, and developed with the coming of the railways in the 19th century. The better communication brought industry and attracted a prolonged period of Victorian building, from rows of small cottages to grand 19th-century statements of wealth that belie the much older roots of this ancient community. Saxmundham, or 'Sax', as it is known locally, is an historic market town at the centre of the unspoilt Suffolk Heritage Coast.

Not far from Saxmundham is Minsmere, one of the Royal Society for the Protection of Birds' most famous nature reserves, as it attracts thousands of varieties of migrant and wading birds.

For 'birders' Minsmere is a corner of heaven; it has been a reserve for over 50 years and pioneered the use of observation hides and management of wetland areas.

SUTTON HOO MAP REF 405 K7

A short distance from the town of Woodbridge, at Sutton Hoo, is the Anglo-Saxon royal burial site of King Raedwald, where vast treasure was discovered in a huge ship grave. Sutton Hoo is arguably one of the most vital archaeological sites in Britain, looked on by many as the first chapter of English history. Lying on a low spur of land above the River Deben, one of several large mounds were excavated in 1939 to reveal a warrior's helmet, shield and a collection of gold ornaments in the remains of a burial chamber of a 90-foot (27m) ship. The significance of this important discovery is incalculable.

When, in the early 5th century, the Romans withdrew from Britain, it left the way open for people from Denmark, Germany and the lower Rhine to settle here, displacing and even enslaving the remnant Celtic and Roman people. These early settlers were the Anglo-Saxons, and their language formed the basis of the modern English spoken today. Two hundred years later, new kingdoms were formed: Suffolk and Norfolk becoming the Kingdom of the East Angles, and thereby setting the foundations of England as a country.

Anglo-Saxon custom decreed that important people were buried beneath mounds, often along with precious goods as a sign of their wealth and importance. The burial of an entire ship is unique to East Anglia and Scandinavia, and the burial mound at Sutton Hoo was a prominent and fitting memorial to a powerful leader.

The National Trust exhibition hall at Sutton Hoo houses a full-size reconstruction of the buried chamber and relates the history of how its treasures lay undisturbed for over 1,300 years. The burial mounds form part of a much larger estate, across which there are lovely walks with estuary views, across heathland and along woodland trails.

SOUTHWOLD MAP REF 405 L6

Once a Saxon port, the coastal town of Southwold has an ancient pedigree and is full of interest both for the casual visitor and for historians. The town became a prominent harbour in medieval times, but like so many towns on the east coast, faced the problem of silting, which brought about a decline in the importance of the harbour. In Victorian times it enjoyed a revival of fortunes as an understated seaside resort with none of the 'Kiss-me-quick' silliness of places like Great Yarmouth or Sheringham.

Surrounded by creeks, reed beds and marshes, and with the Blyth Estuary to the south, Southwold is a virtual island,

and reminiscent of a typical seaside resort of the 1920s and 30s. It is an elegant town with some outstanding Georgian buildings, dominated by a 100ft (30m) lighthouse, built in 1890. Southwold's pier was the first to be built in England since the 1950s and this, along with a cliff-top promenade above the beach dotted with brightly coloured beach huts, are all redolent of a bygone age. Elsewhere, pink- and blue-washed cottages and Georgian town houses border a number of greens, intentionally left undeveloped to serve as firebreaks following a disastrous fire in 1659. William Denny's Buckingham House in the High Street is one of the most elegant and interesting; externally it seems to be a classic Georgian town house, but inside it reveals its 16th-century beginnings. Built by a wealthy Tudor merchant, the cellar is now a coffee house, and the ground and first floor an art gallery.

Southwold was granted a market charter in 1489, when it was a prosperous port with a good herring industry. But it was the herring trade that was partly instrumental in starting three vicious naval battles: the first in 1653, off Orford Ness; the second in 1664, just southeast of Lowestoft; and the Battle of Solebay in 1672, which was to be the first battle of the Third Anglo-Dutch War.

Southwold's maritime past, local archaeology, geology and natural history, as well as the history of the Southwold railway, are all portrayed in the museum in Victoria Street, set in a Dutch-style cottage. Incredibly, in 1839 there were 192 boats in Southwold catching herrings, sprats, smelts and shrimps, as well as bigger fish for the London market.

For the literati, each November Southwold stages a literature festival, which has steadily become a popular attraction for artists and writers over the years. Like similar festivals elsewhere in Britain, that at Southwold makes an ideal escape from the bustle of the daily round, a time to engage with books and ideas in a most agreeable setting.

THORPENESS MAP REF 405 L6

The village was originally a small fishing hamlet in the late 19th century, with folklore stories of its role as a route for smugglers into East Anglia. Today, Thorpeness is an agreeably bizarre and whimsical place, and shares an unspoilt beach with neighbouring Aldeburgh. Almost a century ago, the Scottish architect, barrister and playwright, Glencairn Stuart Ogilvie, who had made his money investing on the Russian Railways, created Thorpeness as a neo-Tudor seaside holiday village, among the heather and gorse of the Suffolk coast. His idea was to provide a safe and healthy holiday environment, where children could enjoy the magic and innocence of a traditional seaside holiday, a place for those who wanted to experience life as it was in Merrie England.

Oddly, perhaps, Thorpeness has been voted both as one of 'The Hundred Worst Places to Live in Britain' and as the 'Weirdest Village in England'. Close by, the Meare has islands named after characters in *Peter Pan* by J M Barrie, who was a close friend of the Ogilvies.

Thorpeness Meare is a wildlife-rich and picturesque artificial lake used for fishing and boating, as well as being a haven for wildfowl. At one end of the lake is a mock Norman castle, not surprising given the eccentricity of its surroundings.

WALBERSWICK MAP REF 405 L6

Just a short distance from the rather larger Southwold, Walberswick is a compact village with attractive houses; it is also a pleasant and popular river port. It was the home of the English Impressionist painter, Merseyside-born Philip Wilson Steer. Walberswick was also home to the Scottish designer, artist, architect and exponent of the art nouveau style in Scotland, Charles Rennie Mackintosh, after he left Scotland in 1914.

WOODBRIDGE MAP REF 405 K7

The market town of Woodbridge spreads across the banks of the River Deben, a short distance from Sutton Hoo, the most important Anglo-Saxon site in Britain. With 1,400 years of recorded history, the town has diverse and interesting historical architecture, making it a fascinating town to explore on foot.

What Woodbridge does not have is a wooden bridge; the name derives from the Saxon 'Wode's town'. Its position on the Deben estuary made it a logical place for rope-making, sail- and ship-building industries since the Middle Ages.

WOODBRIDGE

SOUTHWOLD FROM THE PIER

This is a walk around an old-fashioned holiday resort on an island surrounded by the River Blyth, Buss Creek and the North Sea. There is just one road that leads in and out of this quintessentially English village, which prides itself on its lovely beach edged with colourful beach huts and its traditional seaside pier. An exhibition on the pier tells the history of the seaside holiday, complete with saucy postcards, kitsch teapots, palm-readers and old-style arcade machines.

1 Leave the pier and turn left along the seafront, either following the promenade past the beach huts and climbing up some steps or walking along the clifftop path with views over the beach. After passing St James' Green, where a pair of cannon stand either side of a mast, continue along the clifftop path to Gun Hill, where six more cannon, captured at the Battle of Culloden near Inverness in 1746, can be seen facing out to sea.

2 From Gun Hill, head inland alongside the large South Green, then turn left along Queen's Road to a junction with Gardner Road. Cross this road, then look for the Ferry Path footpath, that follows the pleasant stream beside marshes, towards the river. Alternatively, stay on the clifftop path, and walk across the dunes to reach the mouth of the River Blyth.

3 Turn right and walk beside the river, passing Walberswick ferry, a group of fishing huts where fresh fish is sold, and the

Harbour Inn. After about 0.75 mile (1.2km), you reach an iron bridge on the site of the old Southwold-to-Halesworth railway line.

4 Keep straight ahead at the bridge, crossing a stile and following the path round to the right alongside Buss Creek, to make a complete circuit of the island. There are good views across the common to Southwold, dominated by the lighthouse and the tower of St Edmund's Church. Horses and cattle can often be seen grazing on the marshes. Keep straight ahead, going over a stile, through a gate to cross the embankment, then over another stile. Stay on the raised path to reach a white-painted bridge.

5 Climb up to the road and cross the bridge, then continue on a path beside Buss Creek with views of the beach huts in distance. The path skirts the boating lake on its way down to the sea. Turn right and walk across the car park to return to the pier.

DISTANCE/TIME 4 miles (6.4km) 1h30 **MAP** OS Explorer 231 Southwold & Bungay **START** Beach car park (pay-and-display) or free in nearby streets; grid ref: TM 511766 **PATHS** Riverside paths, seaside promenade, town streets, 2 stiles **THE PUB** The Crown, High Street, Southwold. Tel: 01502 722275

WALK 54

DUNWICH LOST CITY

Conjure up visions of a lost city as you stand on the cliffs gazing out to sea. Dunwich is a haunting place, where ghosts of the past assault your senses at every turn. High on the cliff near the start of the walk is the tombstone of Jacob Forster, all that remains of the churchyard of All Saints Church. The other graves have long since sunk without trace and Jacob Forster's bones lie all alone. Who was he, and what did he do to deserve such a fate? How long will it be until he goes too, to join his ancestors beneath the waves?

1 Walk up the road from the beach car park and keep left at the junction. When the road bends, turn left on to a footpath that climbs through the woods to the ruins of Greyfriars Friary. Turn left along the cliff top, go over a set of wooden steps and bear right through the trees on a waymarked path. At the end of this path, turn right along a track to a road.

2 Turn left off the road after 100yds (91m) on a track to the Dairy House. Keep straight ahead on this path as it enters Greyfriars Wood and continues to a road.

3 Turn left and walk along this road for 0.5 mile (800m), passing two caravan sites on the left. As soon as you enter National Trust land, turn left on to a path waymarked with white arrows.

4 Walk around the National Trust's Coastguard Cottages and take the track beside Heath Barn field centre, then bear right on to a sandy path that climbs through the heather. Keep on this path, bearing left and right at a crossing track to follow the Sandlings Walk nightjar waymarks. When

you reach a bridleway, keep straight ahead on a farm track, passing Mount Pleasant farm. Cross the road and keep straight ahead on a concrete lane to Sandy Lane Farm.

5 Turn right for 0.5 mile (800m) on a shady path, to emerge by St James's Church, built in the 19th century when Dunwich's other churches were falling into the sea. For a short cut, keep straight ahead here to return to Dunwich.

6 Turn left at the road and, in 100yds (91m), go right at Bridge Nurseries and Café. Keep to the right around the farm buildings and stay on this track for 1.5 miles (2.4km) beside Dunwich Forest, before turning seawards. Pass through a gate to enter a covert and fork right at a junction around Great Dingle Farm, then follow the path through the reed beds towards the sea.

7 Turn right at a junction when you see an old drainage mill to your left, and follow the flood bank across Dingle Marshes. Turn right to return to Dunwich along the beach, or take the path behind the shingle bank.

DISTANCE/TIME 8 miles (12.9km) 4h **MAP** OS Explorers 212 Woodbridge & Saxmundham and 231 Southwold & Bungay **START** Dunwich Beach car park (free); grid ref: TM 479707 (on Explorer 231) **PATHS** Farm tracks, heathland paths, quiet roads, shingle beach **THE PUB** Ship Inn, St James Street, Dunwich. Tel: 01728 648219

A WARRIOR'S GRAVE AT SUTTON HOO

The discovery of an Anglo-Saxon ship burial at Sutton Hoo in 1939 shed new light on the 'Dark Ages' and opened up a whole new chapter of English history. It all came about when widow Edith May Pretty reported seeing visions of ghostly warriors dancing on the burial mound near her home. An archaeologist was called to investigate and in one of the mounds was found the remains of a wooden ship, which contained a burial chamber. Gold and treasures were found within, although the wood had rotted around it; the only thing missing was a body.

DISTANCE/TIME 7.25 miles (11.7km) 3h **MAP** OS Explorer 197 Ipswich, Felixstowe & Harwich **START** Sutton Hoo National Trust car park; grid ref: TM 290493 **PATHS** Field-edge and riverside paths, farm lanes, short section of busy road **THE PUB** Plough Inn, Sutton. Tel: 01394 411785

1 From the car park, take the signposted blue trail from behind the visitor centre, descending towards the River Deben on a gravel track. Turn left opposite the entrance to Little Haugh and turn right by the map of Sutton Hoo Estate. The path narrows and turns left alongside a fence on its way to the river. Keep left around the meadow and climb the steps to the river bank, with Woodbridge visible on the opposite bank.

2 Turn left along the river bank. The path is overgrown in places and the plank bridges can be slippery but the views are superb. After 400yds (366m), climb steps to the left to leave the river behind and turn left around a turf field. Keep to the field-edge as it swings right and climbs between woodland to the left and a reservoir to the right.

3 Turn right at the top of the rise to follow a bridleway along the field-edge with Deben Wood to the left. At the end of the wood, the path swings half-left across a field, then passes through a hedge on to a lane. Turn left here for a short cut, picking up the walk again in 300yds (273m) at Point **6**.

4 Keep ahead for 0.75 mile (1.2km), crossing the drive to Haddon Hall. At Methersgate Hall bear right around farm buildings, then left on a footpath beside a brick wall. Pass a pair of cannon on the lawn of the hall and continue with the River Deben opening out ahead. Go through a gate and turn left across a field, then go through a gate and turn right along the lane. Stay on this lane for 1 mile (1.6km) as it bends left past Cliff Farm.

5 At the second three-finger signpost turn left along the field-edge track, passing an embankment (right). Keep to the public bridleway as it swings left around woodland. At the end of the woodland, keep ahead between fields and continue as the path becomes a broad grass track through trees, passing cottages to reach a minor lane.

6 Turn right and continue for 1 mile (1.6km) to the main road (B1083). Turn left and walk carefully along the verge for 400yds (364m), soon to take the footpath left, opposite a road junction. When you see burial mounds on the left, turn right to return to the visitor centre on the National Trust permissive path.

WALK 56

FELIXSTOWE FERRY FISH & SHIPS

This walk shows you another side of Felixstowe, well away from the arcades and the sandcastles on the beach. It starts in the small hamlet of Felixstowe Ferry (a great place for excellent fish and chips), with its boatyard, fishing huts and ferry across the river. The walk then leads along the estuary of the River Debden and beside a peaceful stream called the King's Fleet, finally returning to the coast by way of two Martello towers.

DISTANCE/TIME 6.5 miles (10.4km) 3h **MAP** OS Explorer 197 Ipswich, Felixstowe & Harwich **START** Ferry café car park (fee), Felixstowe Ferry; grid ref: TM 328376 **PATHS** Field and riverside paths, country lanes, farm tracks, sea wall; 4 stiles **THE PUB** Ferry Boat Inn, The Ferry, Felixstowe. Tel: 01394 284203

1 Take the tarmac path along the embankment behind the Ferry Café car park. The path passes a boatyard and follows the river wall as you look down on abandoned boats lying moored in muddy flats. Turn right through a squeeze stile to walk beside the Deben Estuary. After 0.5 mile (800m) the path swings left and then right across an inlet at the entrance to King's Fleet.

2 Turn left to descend the embankment and walk along a broad track. You pass an old wind pump and stay on this track as it winds its way between farmland and King's Fleet. After 1 mile (1.6km) the track bends right and climbs to a farm, where it becomes a tarmac lane. Continue to a T-junction.

3 Turn left across the field to climb to a ridge then drop down through the next field to The Wilderness, a belt of trees beside Falkenham Brook. Turn left through the trees and follow this path alongside a stream, then bend right to cross a stile and a meadow. Make for the corner of the hedge opposite and bear right alongside a fence to cross a footbridge and

continue on a grassy path between fields. At the end of the field, turn left and continue to the end of hedge, then turn right to climb on a track to Brick Kiln Cottages.

4 At the top of the track, turn left along the lane and stay on this lane past Gulpher Hall and its duck pond. As the road bends right, walk past the entrance to The Brook and turn left on a field-edge path. The path ascends, then turns right around a field and cuts straight across the field corner, unless it's diverted by crops. Pass through a gate and keep straight on along a lane, then turn left before houses in 150yds (137m) to join another path that runs between fields.

5 At a pillbox, turn right on to Ferry Road. Cross Cliff Road and turn left, walking past the clubhouse and turning half-right across the golf course on a signposted path, to reach the sea wall. Turn left and walk along the wall, passing two Martello towers and some beach huts. Continue to the mouth of the estuary and turn left just before the jetty to return to the Ferry Café.

Cambridge & Fens

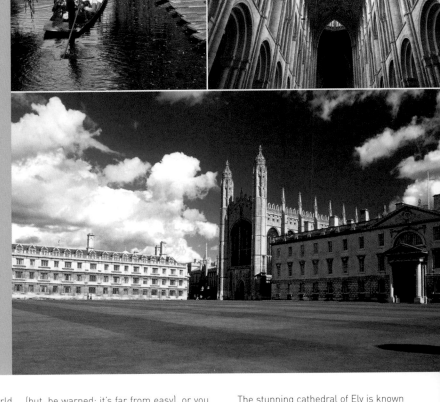

CLOCKWISE FROM TOP LEFT: RIVER CAM, CAMBRIDGE; ELY CATHEDRAL; KING'S COLLEGE, CAMBRIDGE

ANGLESEY ABBEY MAP REF 405 H6

This Jacobean-style house dates from 1600 and is built on the site of a 12th-century Augustinian priory. It contains an idiosyncratic collection of art depicting the tastes of Huttleston Broughton, 1st Lord Fairhaven (1896–1965).

Among the many paintings are works by Claude Lorraine, set alongside fine examples of furniture, silver and tapestries and one of the largest collections of clocks found in any of the properties of the National Trust. The priory is surrounded by a landscaped garden that provides year-round floral interest and an arboretum with more than 100 pieces of sculpture. The watermill has milling days on the first and third Saturday of each month, provided the water levels are adequate.

CAMBRIDGE MAP REF 405 H6

A wonderful and often bizarre synthesis of the everyday and the extraordinary, Cambridge is a pulsating city that has played a major role in the history of England, and reflects the very best of traditional and contemporary life.

Many who have yet to visit Cambridge may well have already experienced its allure; this, after all, is the place that inspired Darwin, Newton, Byron, Tennyson, Wordsworth and, more recently John Cleese, Graham Chapman, Eric Idle and Stephen Hawking. The university in

Cambridge is one of the oldest in the world and one of the largest in Britain. It was formed in 1209 by students who fled here to escape hostile townspeople in Oxford and built a university here. The two cities have been rivals ever since.

The centre of Cambridge is quite small and easily explored on foot; then at least you appreciate just how foremost the university is and the influence it has on the city. King's College Chapel literally dominates Cambridge and is famed for its Christmas carol concerts, a superb choir and its fine fan vaulting. Several of the college buildings are often open to visitors, but the view from the outside, especially the area across the river, is particularly agreeable. This area is known as 'The Backs' because it overlooks the backs of six of the riverside colleges. In the early morning, a thin mist often grazes the river and the college buildings, lending the landscape an eerie half-light. From here you can see the most famous view of Cambridge, embracing King's College and King's College Chapel, with Clare College on the left.

Lending its name to the city, the River Cam flows through the centre of Cambridge, and those in search of relaxation will find several ideal walks along its banks. But the best way to savour the atmosphere is to take a leisurely punt. You can hire a punt and do your own thing

(but, be warned: it's far from easy), or you can let someone else do all the work, and hire a 'chauffeured' punt, leaving you free to admire the college buildings and intriguing bridges.

With such a large student population, there are plenty of pubs, wine bars, eateries and restaurants, perfect places for a coffee break or afternoon tea. And there is a wide range of shops, especially around the market square, which has been the market's location for centuries.

Music, theatre and live entertainment are popular in Cambridge. The Cambridge Corn Exchange and the Cambridge Arts Theatre promote the more traditional arts, the emphasis being on ballet, opera and orchestral concerts. More contemporary works are performed at the ADC Theatre and Drama Centre, the Junction, and the West Road Concert Hall.

ELY MAP REF 405 H6

Ely has its origins in the foundation of an abbey in 673 on the Isle of Ely, which was under the protection of Saint Ethelreda. Destroyed by Danish invaders in 870 and then not rebuilt for over a hundred years, the site was one of the last holdouts in England against the rule of William the Conqueror. Surrounded by treacherous marshlands, known as 'fens', the channels and overgrowing foliage made a labyrinth of the Ely countryside.

The stunning cathedral of Ely is known as the 'Ship of the Fens' for the distant views of its octagonal tower that dominates the surrounding low-lying wetlands. Oliver Cromwell lived in Ely for several years after inheriting the position of local tax collector. His former home dates from the 16th century and is now used as the Tourist Information Office and a museum, with rooms displayed as they would have been in Cromwell's time. Today, Ely has some attractive Georgian buildings and a large park that, together with the cathedral and its history, make this an appealing place to visit.

GRANTCHESTER MAP REF 405 H6

Within walking distance of Cambridge, Grantchester is a lovely village of black-and-white half-timbered buildings, thatched cottages, a pretty church and flower-filled meadows. Its 'Englishness' was immortalized by the poet Rupert Brooke, who was a student at King's College before World War I, in his 1912 poem *The Old Vicarage, Grantchester*, in which he recalls happy days in the idyllic English surroundings of Cambridgeshire.

Grantchester is a favourite amongst both tourists and students, travelling upstream from Cambridge by punt to eat a picnic in the meadows or at the tea gardens called The Orchard, as they have done since the 19th century.

HEMINGFORD GREY MAP REF 405 G6

Spread along a bank of the River Great Ouse, Hemingford Grey is an attractive village that boasts timber-framed cottages and a church with an unusual spire. Also here is a Norman Manor House, once home to author Lucy Boston, which can be visited by appointment.

HOUGHTON MILL MAP REF 405 G6

Set on an island in the Great Ouse, the 18th-century five-storey, weather-boarded mill is the last working watermill on the river, and has intact machinery which is still operated today. Milling takes place on Sundays and Bank Holiday Mondays, with the resulting stone-ground flour for sale, and hands-on exhibits that appeal to all the family. The riverside meadows offer wonderful opportunities for walks, cycling and horse riding.

MADINGLEY MAP REF 405 H6

This unassuming village on the outskirts of Cambridge has two sites of particular interest: Madingley Hall, and the Cambridge American Cemetery and Memorial. Madingley is also mentioned in works by the poet Rupert Brooke.

WANDLEBURY MAP REF 405 H7

An area of beautiful grasslands, chalk slopes and hills that is heaven to walkers and nature lovers. Visitors also come here to see remnants of the Wandlebury Iron Age Hill Fort and the Wandlebury Ring, atop Gog Magog Hill.

WICKEN FEN MAP REF 405 H6

Britain's oldest nature reserve, Wicken Fen, has been managed traditionally for centuries by sedge-cutting and peat-digging to produce a unique fenland habitat rich in wildlife, particularly invertebrates. Wicken Fen is one of only four 'wild' fens which still survive in the Great Fen Basin.

The importance of the fen is demonstrated by the fact that it is not just a National Nature Reserve, but also a Site of Special Scientific Interest, a Special Area of Conservation and a RAMSAR site (an international wetland designation). Wicken is a top site nationally for molluscs, aquatic beetles, rove beetles, caddis flies, bees and spiders.

The nature of the wetland has played an important role in the social and economic life of the area, providing materials for thatch, bedding and animal feed, fish and fowl for food, and peat for fuel.

Today, Wicken Fen is a surviving fragment of the wilderness that once covered East Anglia, and can be explored along traditional wide droves and lush green paths, including a boardwalk nature trail, giving access to several hides.

WICKEN FEN: THE LAST SURVIVOR

Step back in time through an authentic Cambridgeshire fen, virtually the last of its kind left in Britain. Wicken Fen is one of the oldest nature reserves in the country and is one of the most important, too. Over the last 400 years, more than 99 per cent of East Anglia's ancient Great Fen has been drained and converted into farmland, richly productive for agriculture but largely sterile for wildlife. For generations, Wicken peat has been cut for burning, and sedge (a grass-like plant) has been harvested for thatching.

1 From the nature reserve car park, walk up Lode Lane towards Wicken. Before you meet the main road, turn right on to Back Lane and follow this route, which soon becomes a track running behind the houses. At the far end of the lane, just after a windmill, turn right on to a wide track through the fields. (If you have parked in the centre of the village, take the signposted public footpath via Cross Green, just along from and opposite the pub, out to the fields.)

2 Follow this track down to two footbridges. Cross the second bridge and turn right along the bank of Monk's Lode, with St Edmund's Fen opposite.

3 After 550yds (500m) branch left before a fence and gate, for a long straight track, known as a drove, and head out across the fields to Priory Farm. Join the surfaced lane and continue all the way to the end.

4 Turn right by the raised Cockup Bridge and walk along the bank of the Burwell Lode (don't be tempted by the footbridge). Continue for 1.5 miles (2.4km) past Adventurers' Fen,

named after the 17th-century 'Gentlemen Adventurers' who first started draining the fens in earnest.

5 At a high-arched footbridge over Wicken Lode turn right and walk along this bank back towards Wicken Fen, past a National Trust sign. Ignoring paths off into the open fen and fields on your right, continue along the bank until its junction with Monk's Lode. Across the water you pass the lofty thatched Tower Hide.

6 Cross the short bridge by Goba Moorings and continue alongside Wicken Lode, not along Monk's Lode (to the right). The lush vegetation of Wicken Fen is now either side.

7 When you get to the end, turn left to the visitor centre. There is a small admission charge to the reserve itself, which is open daily from dawn to dusk. Near by is the restored Fen Cottage, and a lovely thatched boathouse where the reserve's traditional working fen boat is kept. To return to the car park and village, simply walk back up the lane past the houses.

DISTANCE/TIME 4.75 miles (7.6km) 2h **MAP** OS Explorer 226 Ely & Newmarket **START** Wicken Fen nature reserve car park (pay-and-display) if visiting the reserve, otherwise off Wicken Fen High Street; grid ref: TL 564706 **PATHS** Mostly river banks and farm tracks. Potentially slippery **THE PUB** Maid's Head, 12 High Street, Wicken. Tel: 01353 720727

WALK 58

MANEA FENLAND'S BIG SKIES

An enigmatic landscape links remote Manea with an historic drainage cut. A landscape that is as flat and as bare as the fens may seem an uninteresting prospect for a walk but in fact there is much more to this unique place than first meets the eye, and what you see now isn't the way it looked in the distant past. Ancient tree trunks known as bog oaks are periodically uncovered from the peaty soil, proving that this apparently tree-less country once presented a totally different scene.

1 With the Rose & Crown pub on your left, walk eastwards along Manea High Street and follow it round to the left as it becomes Station Road, then turn right for the public footpath alongside a primary school. At the far end of the football pitch, turn right and pass Manea Wood, planted in 1997. Continue along the path as it bears right and approaches Bearts Farm.

2 Turn left by some old barns and sheds for a wide track out into fields, and bear right at a junction of tracks to reach the attractive reedy lake, known locally as 'the Pit'. This was originally dug for clay, which was then transported across the fields on a light railway to shore up the banks of the nearby Old and New Bedford Rivers. The Pit is now a popular place for fishermen and wildlife alike.

3 At the end of the track turn right on to the lane, with the lake still on your right. Then, when you reach a junction at the corner of the road, turn left, on to Straight Road, and follow this through fields to its end.

4 Turn left on to Purls Bridge Drove, signposted 'Welches Dam' and 'RSPB reserve'. Follow this open lane to Purls Bridge, by the Old Bedford River. Continue along the bank to reach the Ouse Washes Nature Reserve (visitor centre and public toilets).

5 Return along the lane for 440yds (402m) and turn left for a signposted public bridleway by dark wooden sheds. Known as Old Mill Drove, this runs directly across open fields as far as the rusting farm machinery and outbuildings of Boon's Farm. Turn right and walk along dead-straight Barnes's Drove for 1.25 miles (2km) to a road at far end.

6 Turn left and after 150yds (137m) turn off right through a gate to take the public footpath across the fields back into Manea. The route zig-zags between a series of paddocks – just follow the clear yellow waymarks and aim for the fire station tower. At the far side, cross a stile and turn right, past the village stores, to follow the main road back to the centre of Manea and the Rose & Crown pub.

DISTANCE/TIME 6.25 miles (10km) 3h **MAP** OS Explorer 228 March & Ely **START** Roadside parking in centre of Manea; grid ref: TL 478893 **PATHS** Lanes and hard farm tracks, field-edge paths; 1 stile **THE PUB** Rose & Crown, 30 High Street, Manea. Tel: 01354 680 454

Norfolk Broads

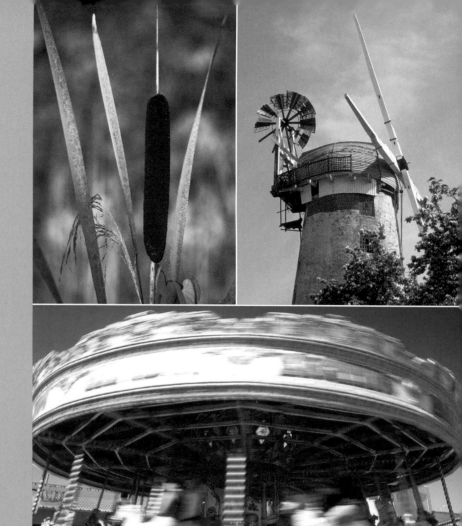

CLOCKWISE FROM TOP LEFT: BULRUSH, BROADS WILDLIFE CENTRE; SUTTON MILL, NEAR STALHAM; GREAT YARMOUTH; BROADS WILDLIFE CENTRE

BECCLES MAP REF 405 L5

Some might argue that the heyday of Beccles was when this market town was a prosperous Saxon port, more than 1,000 years ago. In fact, thinking of Beccles as a port at all is not so easy these days, as it is more than 6 miles (10km) from the sea. But there was a time when Beccles was on the very edge of the coast, and all that could be seen looking east was water. In time, land was reclaimed and wherries came to ply up and down the riverways, and today Beccles has much to attract visitors. It lies at the southernmost extremity of the Broads, although the town itself is rooted across the county border in Suffolk. The name 'Beccles' is in fact a combination of two words: 'beck', a Scandinavian word meaning stream, and 'leas', meaning meadow. In fact, that's what medieval Beccles must have been for many years, largely a beautiful meadow by a stream.

The attractive little parish church of St Michael's has an interesting legend: the church tower has clock faces on only three sides, being blank on the side facing Norfolk, allegedly because the inhabitants of Beccles did not want to give the time for free to their neighbours!

GREAT YARMOUTH MAP REF 405 L5

Northwards along the coast, Great Yarmouth, the chief town and most popular resort on the Norfolk coast, is unashamedly bright, brash and breezy. It is unquestionably focused on seaside holidays and entertainment, the seafront offering a great sweep of arcades, fun fairs, bingo halls, crazy golf and attractions for children; not least 15 miles (24km) of wide, sandy beach from Winterton-on-Sea in the north to Hopton-on-Sea in the south.

The town stands on a peninsula formed by the combined influence of the rivers Bure, Yare and Waveney, and not surprisingly the town developed as a fishing port, from which 'Yarmouth bloaters' earned it international renown. Much of the town's most fascinating architecture was destroyed during World War II, but enough remains, including parts of the original medieval town walls and several of its towers, to provide more than passing interest for visitors.

Great Yarmouth, and the clutch of surrounding villages dotted along the edge of the Norfolk Broads, blends easily with the beautiful countryside in this interesting region, which is steeped in coastal and maritime heritage

LOWESTOFT MAP REF 405 L5

Britain's most easterly town, the first to catch the morning sun, is a delightfully busy holiday resort, significantly less tacky than Great Yarmouth, to the north. Lowestoft was originally a small fishing and farming town perched on a cliff in the northern part of Suffolk. The main street consisted of merchants' houses, shops, schools and pubs while, away from the centre, the town's streets were flanked by breweries, small industries and cottages, many occupied by farm labourers before the western part of the town began to be developed.

Since the 14th century, when that original fishing village began its expansion, Lowestoft evolved into a major fishing port and ship-building centre, and from Victorian times has benefited from its miles of golden beaches, increasing in popularity as a premier seaside resort. The inner harbour, known as Lake Lothing, plugs into Oulton Broad and the River Waveney, the most southeasterly point of the Broads.

There are some strong literary and artistic associations in Lowestoft: Thomas Nashe, the English dramatist, was born here in 1567, as was composer Benjamin Britten (1913–76), probably best known for the *Young Person's Guide to the Orchestra* and his opera, *Peter Grimes*. Oulton Broad is the place to which Norfolk author, George Borrow, returned following his travels, and where he wrote many of his books. He died here in 1881. Nearby Blundelston inspired Dickens' name for David Copperfield's childhood home, and was a place often visited by poet Thomas Gray, warmly remembered as one of the early writers about the English Lake District, after a visit in the late 18th century, and as the author of *An Elegy Written in a Country Churchyard*.

NORFOLK BROADS MAP REF 405 L5

The Norfolk and Suffolk Broads, a tangled network of flooded peat diggings, have transformed into an atmospheric landscape of enchantment and mystery, a place of woodland and fen, of grazing land and convoluted waterways. What is perhaps surprising is that this is a man-made environment, the product of Middle Age industry from the 9th to 14th centuries when peat was dug, almost on an industrial scale, to use as domestic fuel. Over the centuries, as if painstakingly embellished by the hand of some Renaissance artist, the land changed as water levels rose to create a patchwork of shallow lakes, or 'broads'. The result is a place of magic and special appeal. Amazingly, it was not until as recently as the 1960s that man's influence on the landscape was finally proven, so natural has the landscape become.

Some of the broads are flanked by fens, wet areas of reed and sedge that in former times were cut for thatch or to make the ridge along the top of thatched roofs. But as well as a source of building materials, the marshes also provided man with water and food – waterfowl, fish and eels. Then, as the necessity to keep cattle grew, so the fens were drained to provide grazing marshes, a series of open fields laced by a network of dykes, and dotted with wind pumps that provided the power to push the water along the dykes.

In time, this became a unique landscape, threatened for a while in the 1970s as a move to develop arable land gained sway, but finally brought within the embrace of a National Park, which now holds the responsibility for the management and protection of this priceless landscape heritage. In the words of the Norfolk naturalist, the late Ted Ellis, the Broads are 'a breathing space for the cure of souls'. But they are more than that: these sometimes intimate nooks and crannies of reed-fringed pools, sometimes sky-laden expanses of open appeal, are a corner of heaven set aside for lovers of enchantment and the English countryside.

With over two million visitors each year, the Broads cannot compete with the Lake District, Yorkshire Dales or Peak National Parks, nor do they seek to. The Broads hold their own special appeal, and are no less deserving of the protection National Park status brings. Indeed, in some ways, the policies adopted for recreation, focused on promoting 'quiet enjoyment', are more critical than elsewhere because the Broads are also a profoundly important wildlife habitat; Nature's window on a grand scale. Today, wildlife-watching is a popular and inspirational experience best enjoyed by visiting one of the many nature reserves. With such a landscape diversity it is not surprising that other activities are also in demand here – fishing, sailing,

windsurfing, rowing, canoeing, boating and walking – and striking the right balance, one that is sympathetic to the needs of the Broads rather than to the needs of the people, is difficult and on-going.

There are few major centres of population within the National Park, but just beyond the boundaries lie the city of Norwich and the towns of Great Yarmouth and Lowestoft. Here you are on dry land, but the best way to explore the Broads themselves, given that they hug the courses of numerous rivers, is by boat, for it is then that the illusion of remoteness is heightened and the prospect of seeing something rare and wonderful is enhanced by an approach that is slow and quiet. Indeed, the Broads, with over 120 miles (193km) of navigable waterway, have been important for sailing and boating since Victorian times, offering a unique navigation system where special inland sailing craft – wherries – have evolved. Wherries have featured on the Broads for centuries and their use in river trade was instrumental in making Norwich England's second city. The earliest wherry-type vessel was square rigged, but by the early part of the 19th century, the wherry had become single-sailed, and specifically designed for the shallow waters of the Broads.

NORWICH MAP REF 405 K5

The Broads, in the form of the River Wensum, tap a tentative finger at the very gates of Norwich, regarded by 17th-century traveller Celia Fiennes as 'a city walled full round of towers', while George Borrow, better known perhaps for his walk through 'Wild Wales' but who attended King Edwards School here, considered Norwich to be 'a fine old city, perhaps the most curious specimen ... of the genuine old English Town'. Norwich is the county town of Norfolk, at the heart of East Anglia, and has held a regular market since Norman times.

For the curious traveller, Norwich has a wealth of historical architecture to explore and enjoy. The medieval period, a most prosperous time based on the wool trade, is represented by the 11th-century cathedral, 12th-century castle (now a museum) and a large number of interesting parish churches.

During the Middle Ages, founded on the wealth derived from wool, no less than 57 churches stood within the city walls; 31 still remain. This prompted the local saying that Norwich had a church for every week of the year, and a pub for every day. Certainly the overriding impression on visiting Norwich is that of taking a step back in time, in the most agreeable sense. It is a modern city, but the scope for a little self-indulgent time travel is good.

NORWICH CATHEDRAL

Between 1650 and 1750, Norwich was considered to be second only to London in terms of its prosperity, with textiles still the mainstay of the economy. During the 1800s, newer industries appeared, notably printing and the production of leather.

Through the 20th century, Norwich never ceased to evolve. In the 1930s, the city saw the construction of the art deco City Hall, and in the 1960s, in common with cities across England, the University of East Anglia (UEA) admitted its first students. The university brought yet more innovative architecture to Norwich, in the pyramidal shape of Denys Lasdun's Ziggurats, followed in the 1970s by the striking structure of the Sainsbury Centre for Visual Arts, designed by Sir Norman Foster, architect of the famous Millau Viaduct in central France.

POTTER HEIGHAM MAP REF 405 L5

Gateway to the Upper Thurne, and focal point of the northerly Broads, Potter Heigham takes its name from both the pottery that once stood here and the name of the Saxon lord, Heacham, who founded the settlement. This is a popular and busy water resort, with a 14th-century bridge that is regarded by experienced boatmen to be the most difficult bridge to negotiate anywhere on the Broads.

Potter Heigham is the key to Hickling Broad, the largest and wildest of the Norfolk Broads, where there is an abundance of nature trails, boardwalks, sailing opportunities and wildlife. Birdwatchers will find equal pleasure in nearby Horsey Mere, a large triangular shaped broad, with Horsey Mere Nature Reserve on the northern bank.

RANWORTH MAP REF 405 L5

Ranworth is a charming Broadlands village, located on Malthouse Broad (so called because of the old malt houses nearby). Ranworth Broad is a nature reserve and divided from Malthouse Broad by a thick bank. The village itself is dominated by the 14th-century church known as the 'Cathedral of the Broads'. It has some splendid old woodwork, including one of the finest painted rood-screens in England. There is a glorious view from the top of the church tower, which makes the climb worthwhile. With ghostly monks and sightings of the Devil carrying the spirit of a local military man on horseback, Ranworth lays claim to being the most haunted village on the Broads.

The ghost of a traitorous monk is also said to haunt St Benet's Abbey, a short way across the marshes and the River Bure. In the days immediately following the Norman Conquest, the monk betrayed his brethren to the soldiers of William the Conqueror in return for being made Abbot. True to their word, the Normans appointed him Abbot for life, and promptly nailed him to the abbey doors then skinned him alive as reward for his treachery. The Normans had no love for traitors, even Saxon ones. Today, the abbey is in ruins, but it remains a distinctive sight, with a windmill built into the walls of the gatehouse.

From Ranworth, the Broadlands Wildlife Centre can be reached along a nature trail through woods and marshes to an attractive thatched building, floating on pontoons. The upper gallery is a good place from which to observe the amazing diversity of wildlife on the Broads.

SOMERLEYTON MAP REF 405 L5

Somerleyton's pretty red-brick, thatched cottages grouped around a village green, and a gracious sense of calm and tranquility are not the only draw to this village on the Waveney.

Nearby Somerleyton Hall is a lavish pile, built to announce Victorian wealth and grandeur. The Hall was originally a Jacobean manor, remodelled in 1844 into a stunning example of an early Victorian hall in the Anglo-Italian style. Beautiful architecture and antique furniture, trademark Crossley carpets, a distinct and pleasing 'lived-in' feel, and a yew maze of mind-boggling ingenuity gives Somerleyton huge appeal.

The village is named after a Viking, Sumarlithi, a non-aggressive invader who arrived in the 10th century and found the Norfolk countryside much to his liking.

STALHAM MAP REF 405 L4

The pleasant Broadlands market town of Stalham, perfectly placed for exploring Hickling and Barton Broads, still has its original name, derived from 'stal' (a pool of water) and 'ham' (a settlement or village). With its narrow high street and weekly market it retains a worldly 'otherness', a gentle and agreeable place where times gone by linger around every corner.

Stalham was on the Roman road to Caister, and would have been a popular staging post for the Romans heading to Caister and Great Yarmouth. The town is connected to the River Ant by a dyke, with its own staithe, where wherries and other trading vessels could moor.

Pre-dating the Domesday Book by many years, the town was originally divided into four manors. Much building took place over the years, with the church of St Mary built in the 15th century and the Jacobean Manor house, Stalham Hall, in the 17th century.

Progress was steady rather than rapid, and by the 1880s the town, largely self-sufficient, still had a population of only 852. Its economy was mainly based on agriculture and was a base from which to export loads of grain and livestock by road and river.

As elsewhere throughout Britain, the coming of the railway brought new opportunities and prosperity, enabling the community to trade further afield. Today, Stalham, home to one of the principal holiday boat hirers, and with a weekly market and auction on a Tuesday, is a popular Norfolk town.

WROXHAM MAP REF 405 K5

Wroxham is looked on as the capital of the Norfolk Broads, and is the place where boating holidays started in the late 1800s. It has developed commercially over the years, with numerous hotels, tea rooms and gift shops springing up near the river to attract visitors to the village.

Wroxham Bridge is a semi-circular road bridge and has only very low headroom at high water, of key concern for anyone wanting to continue upriver to the limit of navigation at Coltishall.

RANWORTH BROAD

WALK 59

LUDHAM & THE BROADS

Enjoy the windmill-studded skyline in this lovely stroll to the River Ant. No visit to Norfolk would be complete without a trip to the Broads. This is a patchwork of interlinked streams, lakes and channels that wind sluggishly over the flat land to the west of Norwich. Three major rivers – the Bure, Waveney and Yare – supply most of the water to the Broads' meres, ponds and marshes, before entering the tidal basin at Breydon Water and flowing out into the sea at Great Yarmouth.

DISTANCE/TIME 5 miles (8km) 2h **MAP** OS Explorer OL40 The Broads **START** Womack Staithe in Horsefen Road, Ludham; grid ref: TG 391180 **PATHS** Quiet country lanes and grassy footpaths **THE PUB** King's Arms, High Street, Ludham. Tel: 01692 678386

1 Leave the car park and busy marina and walk up Horsefen Road, going the same way that you came in to park.

2 Turn left at the end of Horsefen Road, walking along a footpath that runs inside the hedge next to the road. When you see the King's Arms ahead, turn right up the road towards 'Catfield'. After a few paces, turn left on to School Road. Houses soon give way to countryside. Take the permissive path on the right of a hedge next to the road. Go straight across the next junction, following the sign for How Hill.

3 Turn right along the lane signposted 'How Hill'. This lane winds and twists, and is fairly narrow, which makes for pleasant walking. You will soon reach How Hill House, a sail-less windmill and How Hill nature reserve. There are marked trails through the reserve, if you feel like a pleasant diversion. When you have finished, continue down How Hill Road. Pass Grove Farm Gallery and Studio on your right, and look for a red-brick barn followed by lane, also on your right.

4 Turn right down Wateringpiece Lane. Pass a modern water tower on your left and walk past fields. Look for a public footpath crossing the road. Go left along the bridleway that runs along the field-edge until it ends at a lane.

5 Turn right on Catfield Road and walk along the verge on the right, where there is a footpath. This road can be busy in summer, when thousands of visitors flock to Ludham and How Hill. Ignore the lane on the left, heading to Potter Heigham, and continue walking ahead to reach the crossroads by Ludham Methodist Church.

6 Go straight across, walking a few paces to the next junction, with Ludham church ahead. Turn left along Yarmouth Road, then right into Horsefen Road. This will take you back to the car park.

WALK 60

LODDON BOATS & BULRUSHES

This walk takes you through some of Norfolk's most attractive countryside, giving a taste of the silent and mysterious Broads and peaceful farmland, as well as sampling the delights of watching the boats jostle and jangle on their moorings along the banks of the busy River Chet. If you have time to spare then you can stop for a while at the picnic site, where you can watch novice boatmen steering their crafts nervously towards the wider waterways of the Broads. Collisions are not unknown, and river-watching can be both a relaxing and amusing pastime.

DISTANCE/TIME 5.25 miles (8.4km) 2h 15min **MAP** OS Explorer OL40 The Broads **START** Free car park on Church Plain in Loddon (opposite Holy Trinity Church) or car park near river; grid ref: TM 363987 **PATHS** Footpaths along waterways, farm tracks, paved roads, stiles. Wading required where Hardley Flood meets River Chet **THE PUB** Angel, High Street, Loddon. Tel: 01508 520763

1 Turn right past the library on to Bridge Street and walk down the hill to cross the river into Chedgrave. At the White Horse go right, then start looking for the public footpath on your right, immediately after the row of terraced houses. Meet a residential street, cross it to reach the footpath opposite, that runs between hedges, and continue to Chedgrave church. Follow the footpath until you meet a lane.

2 Turn right, passing a meadow on your left before going through a small gate at the public footpath sign. Continue on the path along the north bank of the River Chet.

3 Continue along the river path. Depending on the growth of reeds you may be able to see that you are on a causeway here, with the Chet on your right and the meres that comprise Hardley Flood on your left. It is well worth pausing here if you are interested in birding, since the Norfolk WildlifeTrust has erected nesting areas in the water, and there is a public hide on the footpath from which you can observe abundant birdlife. Continue

along this path until broad gives way to farmland and you can see Hardley Hall off to your left. The path then goes through a final gate to meet a wide farm track.

4 Turn left on the farm track. Go up a hill, passing Hill Cottage on your right-hand side, then Hardley Hall on your left. The farm track ends here at a lane. Continue straight on a bridleway towards some woodland. Walk along this lane until you reach Lower Hardley Road and a sign pointing left, stating 'Loddon 1.25'. Don't be tempted to take the left-hand footpath further down the road, which heads to Chedgrave Common. Ignore the first turning on the left, signed 'No Through Road', and continue walking to the second.

5 Take this turning, signposted to the church. When you reach the church, look for the grassy footpath to the right, which takes you back to Point **2**, passed earlier in the walk. Retrace your steps along the footpath, go left on the main road, across the river and up the hill to the car park.

Lincoln & Rutland

CLOCKWISE FROM TOP: KNOT GARDEN MAZE, DODDINGTON HALL;
STEEP HILL, LINCOLN

BELTON MAP REF 403 L3

A short distance north of Grantham, the hamlet of Belton is the location of honey-coloured Belton House. Built of limestone in 1685–88 for Sir John Brownlow, the house is a splendid example of Restoration country-house architecture. The interiors house fine Adam-style plasterwork and wood-carving, along with important collections of paintings, furniture, tapestries and silver. Outside, complementing the refined symmetry of the house, the grounds include elegant gardens, the Lakeside Walk, a remarkable landscaped park and the largest children's adventure playground in Lincolnshire.

BELVOIR CASTLE MAP REF 403 L3

The Vale of Belvoir is rich, rolling, English countryside with wooded escarpments, on which stands Belvoir Castle, ancestral home to the Duke of Rutland. It sits high above the village of Belvoir in a superb position on a hilltop and with a breathtaking view across the Vale of Belvoir. Built in a brilliant yellow ironstone with grey stone dressings, the castle is very spectacular, with its towers, turrets, and crenellations, very much the 'beau' ideal of the romantic castle. The name (pronounced 'beever') derives from belvedere, and means 'beautiful view'. The castle houses a large collection of fine art, including a famous Holbein painting of Henry VIII. The Elizabeth

Saloon is by far the most appealing room in the castle, with rich gold decoration and a painted ceiling; the Grand Dining Room also has a superbly decorated ceiling. The surrounding woodlands, and gardens lovingly restored by the 10th Duchess of Rutland, make a superb setting for the castle.

DODDINGTON MAP REF 404 F3

A short distance to the west of Lincoln, the hamlet of Doddington is all but dominated by its hall. Doddington Hall is a breathtaking Elizabethan mansion with walled courtyards and a gabled gatehouse, largely unchanged since it was completed in 1600. The Hall, still very much a family seat, has never been sold and its varied contents reflect 400 years of unbroken family occupation and eclectic collecting, with fine textiles, porcelain and pictures.

GAINSBOROUGH MAP REF 407 K7

Once a strategic and important river port, Gainsborough is a busy market town, with some fine 17th-century red-brick architecture. Gainsborough Old Hall is one of the finest medieval manor houses in the country, built in the 1460s and today buckling inward beneath the weight of age bearing on its oak-framed skeleton.

Nearby Scampton is the home to the Dambusters Heritage Centre that commemorates the renowned 617

'Dambusters' Squadron, who launched raids from the RAF base at Scampton on the Mohne, Eder and Sorpe dams in Germany in May 1943. The centre houses archive material showing how the squadron lived, trained and carried out their mission using the Barnes Wallis's revolutionary bouncing bomb.

LINCOLN MAP REF 404 F3

The triple towers of Lincoln Cathedral are visible for miles around. Closer inspection reveals a structure of bewildering design and complexity set amid an architectural history as good as anything in Britain. Roman ruins, Viking artefacts and cobbled medieval streets that date from Norman times are the elements that brought the makers of *The Da Vinci Code* here for filming, but which have served the local people and visitors for centuries.

The geological prominence of Lincoln invited settlement as far back as Bronze Age times. In fact, so important was this region strategically, that barely two years after the Battle of Hastings, William the Conqueror started work here on a castle, on a site occupied since Roman times, a structure that dominated the skyline until the cathedral was built.

Lincoln held power first as a Norman stronghold and then as a centre for the wool trade with Flanders, until the wool

trade was relocated in neighbouring Boston. Five centuries were to pass before the town fully recovered from this shock to its economy, but gradually the town spread and divided into the 'Up Hill' area – one of middle class respectability – and 'Down Hill', where the grassroots people were based. Today, interest for visitors rests 'Up Hill', around the cathedral.

But while the cathedral and castle are at the heart of a city steeped in the history of England, the surrounding countryside is a perfect partner, dotted with stately homes, castles, hidden gardens, endearing villages and more Norman churches than any other part of Britain. Modern Lincoln is a vibrant and energetic city, a place where history comes to life and rubs shoulders with a very modern community.

LINCOLNSHIRE COAST
MAP REF 405 H3

The lovely, sandy coast of Lincolnshire offers opposing seaside experiences: on the one side there is the happy mayhem of the 'Fun Coast', from Skegness to Cleethorpes; on the other side, a region of unbroken tranquility, the haunt of wildlife and a haven for birdwatchers and conservationists. Great stretches of natural country and coastline, such as The Boston Wash Banks, Gibraltar Point, Far Ings, Snipe Dales and Messingham, are home to birds by the million.

LINCOLN CATHEDRAL

Insight
THE FAMOUS PEOPLE OF LINCOLNSHIRE

Lincolnshire has seen more than its fair share of celebrity:

Henry Bolingbroke, later King Henry IV, was born at Bolingbroke Castle.

John and Charles Wesley, fathers of Methodism, were born in Epworth.

Isaac Newton, scientist, was born at Woolsthorpe Manor.

Alfred Lord Tennyson, Poet Laureate, was a son of Somersby.

Sir Joseph Banks, early botanist in Australia, came from Revesby.

George Bass, explorer of Australia, was born in Aswarby.

Matthew Flinders, cartographer and man who named Australia, was born in Donington, near Spalding.

Lady Margaret Thatcher, first and only British woman Prime Minister, was born in Grantham.

Geoff Capes, Commonwealth Gold Medalist and twice strongest man in the world, was born in Holbeach.

Nicolas Parsons, broadcaster, like Mrs Thatcher, was born in Grantham.

Visit
LINCOLN CATHEDRAL: THE LINCOLN IMP

Visitors to Lincoln's magnificent cathedral may spend a long time hunting within its walls to find a legendary imp. Many stories surround this stone gargoyle tucked away in the cathedral, but all involve the fight between good and evil. According to one of the most told versions of the story, Satan sent an impish creature to Earth to cause trouble. In Lincoln Cathedral the imp caused much damage and was challenged by an angel who turned it to stone.

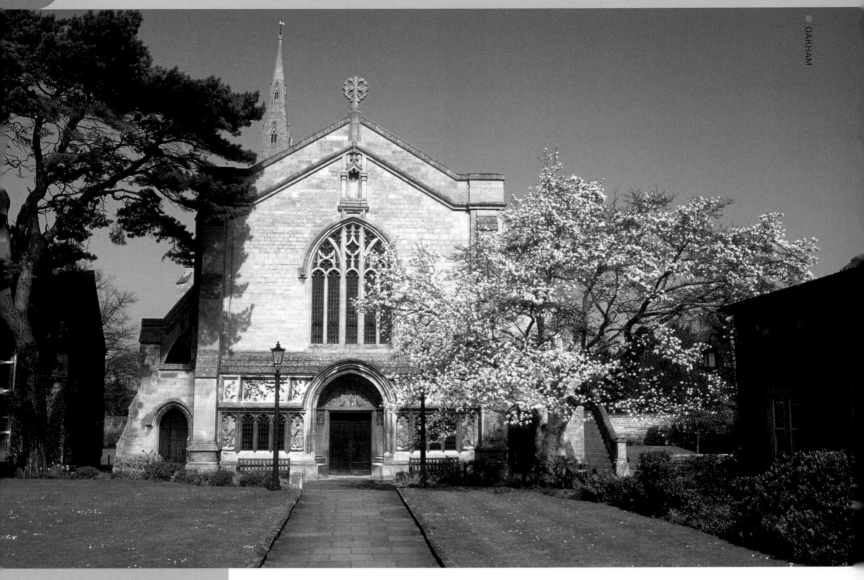

OAKHAM

Insight
GARDENS & GARDENING

In spite of its modest size, Rutland boasts many of England's most spectacular and inspirational garden settings, not least Barnsdale Gardens, designed and developed by the late Geoff Hamilton, which many BBC viewers will remember as the former home to the TV programme *Gardeners' World*, and which comprise 37 individual smaller gardens and features, as well as a nursery.

Somewhat bizarrely, the Clipsham Yew Tree Avenue is surely one of the most eye-catching sights in Rutland, with over 150 tall yew trees clipped into an amazing variety of shapes including animals, a World War II Spitfire and even man landing on the moon. The avenue was once the main thoroughfare through the estate to Clipsham Hall. The topiary was begun in 1870 by Amos Alexander, the estate's Head Forester, who lived in the gate lodge at the foot of the avenue. The clipping is carried out each autumn by the Forestry Commission's local craftsmen.

LITTLE CASTERTON MAP REF 403 M4

The village of Little Casterton is an unpretentious place, playing quiet host to the greatness of nearby Tolethorpe Hall, an early 17th-century manor house in Elizabethan style, built by the Browne family of Stamford on the site of an early 15th-century manor house. The Hall was the birthplace of Robert Browne, who was one of the earliest non-conformist campaigners to split from the established Church of England, of which Elizabeth was the head. The Queen called him 'Trouble-church Browne'. In 1620, Browne and other Separatists were among those who sailed on the *Mayflower*, seeking religious freedom in the New World.

Today, Tolethorpe boasts one of the finest open-air theatres in Europe, the Rutland Open Air Theatre, established in 1977 and now attracting more than 30,000 people to an annual 13-week summer season of Shakespeare plays.

LOUTH MAP REF 407 L7

Nominally the 'capital' of the Wolds, it was in Louth that Alfred Tennyson went to school. Today, this is a bustling market town of fine 17th- and

19th-century buildings, and some unusual associations: St James' Church is a wonderful example of 16th-century architecture, its soaring spire at 295 feet (90m) makes it the tallest parish church spire in England. Equally unique, in Eastgate, a brass plaque marks the Greenwich Meridian of 0 degrees longitude which passes through the town, enabling visitors to stand simultaneously in the western and eastern hemispheres.

OAKHAM MAP REF 403 L4

The ancient county town of Oakham is a traditional market stronghold, bustling, vibrant and energetic, and with a pedigree that pre-dates the Domesday Book. The Market Place holds centre stage, although there seem to have been two market squares in Oakham at some time. Links with the past linger in the form of the stocks, the town pump and the ancient Butter Cross, where dairy produce was traditionally sold.

Near by, Oakham Castle retains a strong link with Norman England, its Great Hall having been a court for over eight centuries, and is without doubt one of the finest examples of late

12th-century domestic architecture in England. It was built by Walkelin de Ferrers, a Norman baron, in about 1180-90. Over 200 horseshoes hang on the walls of the castle and reflect a unique custom that requires every peer of the realm, on their first visit to Oakham, to forfeit a horseshoe to the lord of the manor.

Past associations also find their way into the naming of different parts of the town: 'Deanshold' is a reminder of a time when part of the town was ruled by the Dean and Chapter of Westminster, while 'Lordshold' is the area ruled by the Lord of the Manor, housed in the castle.

In spite of strong links with the past, Oakham is very much a modern place of stylish boutiques and gift shops, designer outlets and markets, not least the traditional Farmers' Market, which is held on the third Saturday of each month.

PICKWORTH MAP REF 403 M4

Devotees of poetry may be drawn to the Pickworth Lime Kiln, an odd destination, perhaps, but it was here that the 19th-century 'peasant' poet, John Clare, renowned for his *Poems Descriptive of Rural Life and Scenery*, worked as a lime burner. The small hamlet of Pickworth lies in a region characterized as the Clay Woodlands of the Rutland Plateau (a Jurassic limestone plateau). In the 13th century, Pickworth was a substantial village, but a hundred years later it was nearly non-existent. It now comprises a small church and a chapel, which services a tiny population.

SEATON MAP REF 403 L4

At the southern edge of Rutland county, the tiny village of Seaton would be relatively unknown but for its spectacular viaduct, long renowned as Britain's longest brick-built railway viaduct, spanning the full width of the Welland Valley. Its 82 arches span the countryside for 0.75 miles (1.2km) and are a truly majestic sight.

STAMFORD MAP REF 403 M4

There is instant delight in simply wandering the streets of Stamford, not least because of the lovely 18th- and 19th-century Lincolnshire limestone buildings that lent themselves to the filming here of George Eliot's *Middlemarch*. The name Stamford derives from Old English and means 'stone ford', and refers to its crossing point of the River Welland.

The town straddles the Welland, although the main centre lies to the north of the river. The fact that this was formerly a wealthy wool town is demonstrated by the large number of interesting churches, dating from the Middle Ages found here. Something of that antiquity lives on in St Martin's Antiques Centre where up to 60 antiques dealers vie for business selling a wide range of collectables.

Delighting in conservation status, Stamford retains much of its old world charm, and is commonly regarded as the finest stone town in England. Amongst its many historic buildings is the 15th-century Browne's Hospital, founded by one of the town's wool merchants, and more famously, the grand Elizabethan Burghley House.

UPPINGHAM MAP REF 403 L4

Perched on a ridge in the south of Rutland, Uppingham is best known for its boarding school (where some of the Harry Potter sequences were filmed), but is home to a host of honey-coloured buildings that give the village a splendid and unique charm. This is an agreeable place of pubs, antique shops, second-hand book shops and tea rooms, a place to unwind and explore at a leisurely pace.

As with Oakham, in Uppingham the Market Place is the focal point, and dates from the 13th century. Uppingham grew to become an important local market town and a convenient coaching stop. There is, too, a history of medieval entertainment here, for Uppingham was a centre for bull baiting (in the Market Place), cock fighting (at the Falcon Hotel) and even dancing bears (off Orange Street). Unacceptable as those practices now are, they do nevertheless illustrate a part of the way of life as it was in medieval England, much like the famous Orange Fair that once met here, selling fruit both for marmalade and as a medicinal cure.

THE WOLDS MAP REF 407 L7

The chalkland area to the northeast of the city, known as the Lincolnshire Wolds, is an Area of Outstanding Natural Beauty. Although intensively farmed, the Wolds are a place of charm, attractive hamlets, villages and market towns. Here, people have lived and worked for centuries, and ancient packhorse trails and salt routes criss-cross the landscape in a telltale network of links that serve only to remind visitors how important this landscape was in the shaping of medieval England.

The notion that Lincolnshire is entirely flat is exploded amid this landscape of rolling hills and gentle valleys, meandering streams and secluded villages. In fact, this is the highest land in eastern England between Kent and Yorkshire, and boasts fine views of the Pennines to the west and the North Sea coast to the east.

In spite of the Wolds being a working landscape with extensive woodland and grassland it is well suited to walking, cycling and the simple enjoyment of wildlife. The heavy incidence of farming invites the suggestion that the Wolds are not conducive to wildlife. But, paradoxically, there is an abundance of clear chalk streams here, and hedgerows and healthy copses that are rich in wildlife and actually benefit from man's constant tending of the landscape.

Neolithic man settled in this part of Lincolnshire more than 6,000 years ago, producing a landscape that by the arrival of the Romans had been extensively cleared and turned to cultivation, the key element in transforming prehistoric man from nomadic hunter-gatherer to settled farmer. In more recent times, the Wolds have become an inspirational landscape to those of the arts' world. Sheffield-born author and critic, A S Byatt set her Booker Prize-winning novel *Possession* in the Wolds, while many views of the Lincolnshire countryside were painted by the English watercolourist, Peter de Wint and can be seen, along with other artists' work, in Lincoln Art Gallery.

Master poet, Lord Tennyson, was born in the Wolds, at Somersby, and many of his poems are based on his life experiences here. Stockwith Mill stands on the River Lymn, in which authorities on Tennyson see *The Brook* (written in 1855), which sparkles 'out among the fern, To bicker down a valley'.

BURGHLEY HOUSE

DISTANCE/TIME 17 miles (27.4km) 3h **MAP** OS Explorer 234 Rutland Water **START** Whitwell car park; grid ref: SK 923082 **TRACKS** Largely smooth tarmac and compacted gravel and tarmac **THE PUB** White Horse, 2 Main Street, Empingham. Tel: 01780 460221; www.whitehorserutland.co.uk

DISTANCE/TIME 9.6 miles (15.4km) 2h **MAP** OS Explorer 223 Northampton & Market Harborough **START** Foxton Locks car park; grid ref: SP 692892 **TRACKS** Smooth gravel, narrow grassy track, road and rutted farm track **THE PUB** Foxton Locks Inn, Foxton. Tel: 0116 279 1515

AROUND RUTLAND WATER

This is a ride around Europe's largest man-made reservoir, at the heart of England's smallest county. The nature reserve is one of the most important bird-watching centres in the UK. Depending on the time of year, Rutland Water is home to as many as 20,000 waterfowl. The dam itself is 1,312yds (1,200m) long and the maximim depth of the reservoir is 111 feet (34m). The reserve also boasts an environmental display, a viewing gallery, 22 hides and a nature trail.

1 From the car park exit opposite the bike shop and climbing tower, turn right and then immediately left into the marina. Follow the road round to the left, away from the water's edge, as it becomes a cycle track. Turn right at the tip of the inlet and continue around the water's edge until you reach another car park. Continue through this car park to reach the dam.

2 After crossing the dam, turn right at the end, through a pair of swing gates, and continue along the obvious tarmac track as far as Normanton Church. Beyond the church, cross a narrow tarmac road and continue straight through an uneven gravel parking area to reach the main Edith Weston car park, with public toilets, snack bar and bike shop. Proceed to the far end of the car park and turn right to continue around the water's edge, past the sailing club and marina.

3 A mile (1.6km) beyond the sailing club, the track delves into a small wood before dropping down a steep hill to a tight bend at the bottom; a sign near the top gives riders plenty of warning that this hill is coming up.

4 At the next road, turn left up a steep hill to reach the B-road between Edith Weston and Manton. Cross the main road with care and then turn right towards Manton, following the cycle lane. At the first junction continue straight on into Manton. Soon after passing a phone box on your left, turn right, following a Rutland Water cycling sign. Bear left past the Horse and Jockey pub, to reach a wide gravel track down to the A6003. Follow a narrow pavement at the bottom beneath the railway bridge (a sign advises riders to dismount for this bit) and stay on this pavement for a further 440yds (400m).

5 Turn right through a swing gate here, following the cycle track around the water's edge until it cuts across the Lax Hill peninsula. This track eventually leads to Egleton. Turn left into the village and then right again after around 200yds (182m). Continue past the church and stay on the road to the main road into Hambleton.

6 Turn left, and then right after 300yds (273m) along a short cycle track, to reach the A606. From here, stay on the rolling pavement for 1.5 miles (2.4km), before heading right, back onto a gravel track and around the water's edge. At the bottom of the next tarmac road, turn left up the short sharp hill before turning right towards Barnsdale Wood car park. After going down and then steeply uphill to reach the car park, continue downhill again to the bottom, far right-hand corner of the car park; delve into Barnsdale Wood here and follow the track all the way back to the start point.

FOXTON LOCKS & THE GRAND UNION CANAL

Enjoy varied and challenging traffic-free riding along one of England's most famous canal systems. The Grand Union Canal actually started its life as lots of separate canals, which were joined to provide a navigable waterway from Birmingham to London. There are 10 locks at Foxton and it takes about 50 minutes for a boat to negotiate all of them.

1 From the car park exit, turn left along a gravel track to get to the bridge over the canal. Cross the bridge and turn right to reach the canal and, after about 330yds (300m), the locks themselves. Cycling isn't permitted on this section so you'll have to walk your bikes down this side of the locks (the Foxton Locks Museum is situated on the far side of the passing pond, and can be reached on foot). Stay to the left at the bottom to reach the shop and café.

2 Continue past the shop to cross a cobbled bridge. On the far side keep going in the same direction. The shingle track along this part of the canal is wide and smooth, although there are one or two places where the left-hand edge has collapsed a little, so it's a good idea to stay right. After 1.5 miles (2.4km), you come to Debdale Wharf. Beyond Debdale Wharf, the path becomes narrow and grassy and, in summer, this section may be overgrown with bulrushes, but it should still be passable. At Gumley Road, the track becomes smoother and wider again, before continuing on to Saddington Road.

3 Just beyond Saddington Road, a short sharp climb takes you up to the right of Saddington Tunnel. A longer but more gentle rise, still on a wide gravel track, then takes you along the top of the tunnel, before an equally gentle descent carries you back down to Kibworth Road. From here it's possible to return the way you came, but what follows is an alternative for those who are still feeling energetic.

4 If the gate is locked here, you'll have to carry your bikes over the narrow stile, before crossing the road with care to reach another, wider stile. Another gradual downhill then takes you to a short, steep slope down to a fence above the canal. This can be ridden but you may prefer to walk it. At the fence, turn left to continue along the canal. The path is quite narrow, and can be slippery in wet weather, so take great care here. At the next bridge, continue past it for about 30yds (27m) to reach a gate – go through this gate to reach the bridge.

5 Cross the bridge and continue to the top of the field ahead, where you'll find an enormous slab of granite welcoming you to Millfield Wood. Go through a gate and continue along a wide bridleway across a field. Follow the track as it bears left to reach Kibworth Road and then cross the road to continue in the same direction along another gravel track.

6 After 1.5 miles (2.4km) of gentle downhill riding on a wide potholed track, turn right at the road to Smeeton, and then first left along Debdale Lane. This rough farm track rises gently, and then more steeply, to reach the canal. At the top of the track, bear left towards Debdale Wharf Farm and then turn right at the farm to regain the towpath. From here, turn left to retrace your tracks back to the start.

Worcester & Malvern Hills

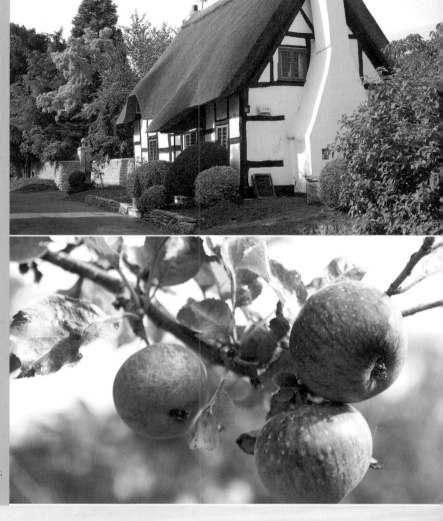

CLOCKWISE FROM TOP: LITTLE COMBERTON; APPLE TREES, LITTLE COMBERTON; GREAT MALVERN

GREAT & LITTLE COMBERTON

MAP REF 403 H6

Great Comberton is a small hamlet south of Pershore, spread across the northern slope of Bredon Hill and the left bank of the River Avon. The village contains a large number of timber-framed 'black-and-white' cottages.

Little Comberton lies in one of the most fertile parts of the county, so it's no surprise that the main industry here is agriculture. The village is small, consisting of just one street of cottages, one of which has an attractive overhanging, timber-framed gable. Opposite the church is the Old Manor House, which dates from the early 17th-century. Nearby Bredon Hill, rising conspicuously from the low-lying Severn Vale, once supported an Iron Age

fort, wherein excavation revealed a large number of mutilated bodies, presumably hacked to pieces in Roman times.

GREAT MALVERN MAP REF 403 H6

Water from the springs on the shapely Malvern Hills has been renowned for more than 300 years, but the village spa of Great Malvern grew only after the 'Water Cure', or hydropathy, was brought to the town from Austria in 1842 by a Dr Wilson. The first water cure establishment in Malvern was the Crown Hotel on Belle Vue Terrace, where one of Dr Wilson's patients made a miraculous recovery.

Today, Great Malvern is a particularly well-preserved Victorian spa town. From the 900-year-old Priory Church, tucked neatly into the hillside, the radiating

roads are lined with an agreeable mix of architectural styles, from elaborate Italianate and Dutch Gabled, to Queen Anne Gothic and austere Scottish baronial.

But what makes the 'Malverns' – Great and Little, North, South, West, Wells and the Link, sometimes known as the 'Seven Sisters' – so appealing is the special relationship they have with the countryside that surrounds them, and in particular the Area of Outstanding Natural Beauty known as the Malvern Hills. More than 500 million years old, these are among the oldest hills in England (being of pre-Cambrian granite), and are embraced like a jewelled necklace by the townships, which themselves are steeped in history.

For those 'in the know', Malvern is a byword for all that is good in performing arts, with festivals of the arts taking place throughout the year, attracting many leading actors, and audiences from across the world. George Bernard Shaw is thought to have founded the first theatre in Great Malvern. Famous British composer Edward Elgar, known to be fond of the Malvern Hills, also lived in Great Malvern and there is a statue in his honour at the centre of the town. For actors there can be no finer theatre in which to perform; nor one more paradoxical – so much is going on here, yet it is so refreshingly relaxing. Purity is in the air; and in the water, of course.

PERSHORE MAP REF 403 H6

Positioned midway between Worcester and Evesham, in the lovely Vale of Evesham, an area important for fruit and vegetable production, the small market town of Pershore is a neat and idyllic gathering of mainly Georgian houses, a place of handsome architecture that contrasts rather abruptly with its rather compact and squat abbey, the remains of a significantly larger Benedictine building which was destroyed at the time of the Dissolution of the Monasteries.

Like most towns and villages in Worcestershire, Pershore is surrounded by beautiful countryside and is a haven for cyclists and ramblers.

WORCESTER MAP REF 403 H5

The city of Worcester clings to the left bank of the River Severn, and, given the propensity of the river to flood, it is not unusual to see large riparian areas, not least the racecourse and car parks, completely flooded. That aside, the city is a glorious mish-mash of architectural styles ranging from delightful timber Tudor buildings to elegant Georgian buildings, although modern developments have done nothing to enhance the historic heart of this ancient city.

Worcester's Norman cathedral is its crowning glory, a superb masterpiece of architectural design and craftsmanship. Among the numerous tombs within the cathedral, that of King John (1199–1216) is the most visited. Also in the cathedral is a memorial to Arthur Tudor, who is buried here. Arthur Tudor was the older brother to the next in line, and subsequent heir to the throne, Henry VIII.

Worcester is a splendid shopping city, with seemingly endless streets of unusual and individual shops located next to larger retail centres. Wandering the streets reveals a plethora of fascinating shops selling quality goods. The Hopmarket hosts a fascinating collection of small stores in an historic courtyard setting. The Shambles is the place to go for fine china, including Royal Worcester, Royal Doulton and Spode. Medieval Friar Street has a number of timbered buildings, and an especially fine example of the architecture of this time is The Greyfriars, a timber-framed merchant's house built in 1480. But perhaps the most intriguing place is tucked away behind the cathedral: the Museum of Worcester Porcelain relates the history of the city's principal industry since the mid-18th century. It adjoins the renowned Royal Worcester Porcelain Works, where Dr John Wall and his associates formed the first Worcester Porcelain Factory.

Links between Worcester and the British Civil War are strong: the Battle of Worcester in 1651 was a key moment in the war, the final crushing defeat for the Royalist cause. The English Civil War ended at nearby Powick Bridge, where it had started nine years previously. Charles II, attempting to regain the throne, was lucky to escape the battlefield and eluded capture until he was able to slip away to safety in France (it was he who hid in an oak tree to evade his pursuers). Oliver Cromwell described Worcester, his last battle as an active commander, as a 'crowning mercy'.

Just outside Worcester, at Lower Broadheath, is the birthplace of the child who was to become one of Britain's most renowned composers, Sir Edward Elgar, best known perhaps for his *Pomp and Circumstance* marches, one of which is commonly called *Land of Hope and Glory*. He also composed the *Enigma Variations*, many evocative symphonies and a beautiful cello concerto.

At the height of his creativity, Elgar was often to be found walking across the nearby Malvern Hills, indeed, near the end of his life he remarked 'If you are walking on the hills and hear music, don't be afraid, it's only me'. He died in 1934, and lies buried in St Wulstan's church in Little Malvern.

WORCESTER CATHEDRAL

MARTLEY THROUGH THE CIDER ORCHARDS

A fruity route from Martley, through beautiful cider-producing apple orchards, up to Rodge's Hill top and returning through the leafy Kingswood Nature Reserve.

DISTANCE/TIME 7 miles (11.3km) 3h15   **MAP** OS Explorer 204 Worcester & Droitwich Spa **START** St Peter's Church, Martley; grid ref: SO 756597   **PATHS** Field paths, lanes, orchard paths, tracks, river meadows, minor roads   16 stiles   **THE PUB** Admiral Rodney Inn, Martley. Tel: 01886 821375; www.admiral-rodney.co.uk

1 Go up through the churchyard to the B4204. Cross to a rough track. In 100yds (91m), walk in trees, parallel to the school. Turn right into a field, then re-enter the grounds. Briefly follow the left edge of the playing fields, then a gate gives on to a field. At the road, turn left. Turn right, signposted 'Highfields'. Beside Lingen Farm go down a track. At the bend take a stile, straight across the field. Cross a stream, then ascend, taking the right-hand gates to reach a minor road.

2 Turn left. At Larkins go ahead, taking two stiles then a field path, not the parallel gravel track. Go ahead for two fields then, at a red sign, don't move right, but forge on, squeezing past a breeze block barn and the driveway of a white bungalow, to walk behind Ross Green's gardens. Cross fields to reach another road. Go straight over, to a partially concealed stile. Walk beside a barn, then in the next field skirt left to a lane. Turn right for a few paces to a fingerpost pointing into an apple orchard before Peartree Cottage.

3 Follow waymarkers carefully through this vast young orchard, descending gently. Emerge at a bridge over a ditch, beside apple-sorting equipment. Go 200yds (182m) up this track, to a gap in evergreens. Turn left, down an orchard ride. At a T-junction turn right, up to just before a gate beside a small house. Turn left, almost back on yourself. Go very

carefully through the orchard, following faded yellow splodges about 1.5ft (45cm) up on the tree trunks, but sometimes obscured by low branches. Leave by a footbridge, crossing fields to the B4197.

4 Turn right for 60yds (55m). Take an excellent track, left, (mostly tarmac) for 0.5 mile (800m) to Rodge Hill's top. Turn sharp left, signed 'Worcestershire Way'. Follow this for 1 mile (1.6km). Steps lead down to a road's hairpin bend.

5 Turn right. In 20yds (18m) turn left, but in only 15yds (14m) turn right again, into conifers. Emerge to drop down steeply. At the B4204 turn right for 30yds (27m). Use a permissive path across two fields to the River Teme. Follow this beautiful riverside walk, later in Kingswood Nature Reserve, for over 0.5 mile (800m). Leave the river when a wire fence requires it. Ascend a path, later a driveway, to a tarmac road.

6 Turn right, uphill; this soon bends left. Near the brow move right (waymarker) to walk just inside the field, not on the road. At the tarmac junction turn left but, in 275yds (250m), walk beside a smart wire fence. Beside fields and allotments, emerge between the Crown and the garage. Pass the telephone box into the village, then turn right to the church and the start of the walk.

WALK 62

WORCESTER CITY SIGHTS & SMELLS

This is a town walk through Worcester, known for Sir Edward Elgar, its battle, its porcelain, its racecourse and, of course, its sauce. But what about its unsung hero? Sir Charles Hastings was a brilliant student, who returned to Worcester Infirmary in order to begin a successful medical career. His dedication and medical observances led to the establishment of the British Medical Association, which still oversees the work of medical practitioners today. It is said that he attended every case during the three cholera outbreaks in 1832, 1849 and 1853.

DISTANCE/TIME 2.5 miles (4km) 1h30   **MAP** OS Explorer 204 Worcester & Droitwich Spa **START** Long-stay pay-and-display car parks at New Road, Tybridge Street and Croft Road (and elsewhere); grid ref: SO 846548   **PATHS** City streets and tarmac riverside path   **THE PUB** Cardinal's Hat, 31 Friar St, Worcester. Tel: 01905 22066

1 The described route begins at the city side of the road bridge, but you can pick it up anywhere – at The Commandery or the Guildhall, for example – depending on where you have parked. Turn left, passing The Old Rectifying House (wine bar). Turn right after the Severn View Hotel, then left, in front of the bus station, following the road round to pass The Butts Dig (archaeological site). Turn left along Farrier Street, right into Castle Street, reaching the northern extremity of the route at its junction with Foregate Street.

2 Go right along Foregate Street, passing the Shire Hall and the Worcester City Art Gallery & Museum. Continue along The Cross and into the pedestrianized area called High Street. Turn left into Pump Street. Elgar's statue stands close to the site of his father's piano shop, at the southern end of High Street. Turn left again, into The Shambles. At a junction, turn right into Mealcheapen Street. Another right turn and you're in New Street (which later becomes Friar Street).

3 Head down this partial time warp as slowly as you can, admiring The Greyfriars (a National Trust property) in particular, for a dual carriageway awaits you at the end. Turn right, then cross over carefully, to visit the cathedral.

4 Leave the cathedral along College Precincts, to the fortified gateway known as Edgar Tower. It is named after the 10th-century King Edgar, but was actually built in the 14th century. Go through this gateway to see College Green. Continue, along what is now Severn Street which, unsurprisingly, leads to the River Severn. Turn right, to complete your circuit, by following Kleve Walk, a leafy waterside avenue; this section floods frequently, as does the county cricket ground opposite, at great cost to the club's revenue.

Stratford & Vale of Evesham

CLOCKWISE FROM TOP LEFT: STRATFORD-UPON-AVON; THE WATER GARDEN, KIFTSGATE COURT GARDENS; ROWING IN EVESHAM

ALCESTER MAP REF 403 J5

The ancient Roman town of Alcester stands at the confluence of two rivers, the Alne and the Arrow. The town owns some fine Tudor buildings and a church that is Gothic externally, but Classical inside, underpinning a fine architectural heritage that somehow works well with the host of independent, family-run shops found here. The town's medieval street pattern survives almost intact, along with ancient properties including the church of St Nicholas with its 14th-century tower, and the 17th-century town hall. Long the focus of attention of Roman scholars, the town is regarded as the best-understood Roman settlement in Britain.

CHARLECOTE PARK MAP REF 403 J5

The home of the Lucy family for over 700 years, the mellow brickwork of Charlecote Park perfectly highlights the essence of Tudor England. Queen Elizabeth and Shakespeare both knew the house well; in fact, the young Shakespeare is said to have been caught in the grounds poaching deer. Notwithstanding a hoard of memorabilia about the British Empire and a uniquely extensive portrait collection, it is the formal garden that is the real delight at Charlecote, opening onto a deer park skillfully landscaped by 'Capability' Brown that bestows a perfect excuse for a family picnic among the deer.

EVESHAM MAP REF 403 J6

Built in a protective loop on the banks of the River Avon, Evesham is an agricultural centre, a market town, situated in the middle of a fertile vale that has become Britain's foremost fruit-growing area. Abbeys like Evesham once dominated this region and were instrumental in developing orchards and gardens for the production of fruit and vegetables.

The medieval town grew up beside the 8th-century Benedictine abbey, one of the grandest abbeys ever built, but of which little survives today. Evesham bell tower is probably England's finest detached bell tower, and along with 14th- and 16th-century gateways and two medieval churches, forms the principal remains of Evesham's once mighty abbey. The churches were originally the abbey chapels and the bell tower was a combined gatehouse and campanile. The bell tower's peal of 12 bells certainly lives up to the grandeur of their setting, and are nationally acclaimed as a benchmark against which other English-hung rings are compared.

One of the abbey buildings houses the Almonry Museum and Heritage Centre, which contains a mock-up Victorian kitchen and exhibits that commemorate the Battle of Evesham (1265), when Simon de Montfort, a thorn in the side of Henry III, was killed by the troops of Prince Edward, later King Edward I. Simon de Montfort, 6th Earl of Leicester, was the leader of the opposition to Henry III. After the rebellion of 1263-1264, de Montfort became de facto ruler of England and called the first directly-elected parliament, securing his place in history as one of the important founders of modern democracy.

ILMINGTON MAP REF 403 J6

Yellow-hued Cotswold limestone houses with pretty, well-tended gardens set amid a tangle of intersecting lanes on the Ilmington Downs, the highest point in Warwickshire, gives this agreeable village the mellow, rustic feel of a true Cotswold village. Less obviously, the village has a strong Morris dancing tradition, often performed in the grounds of the delightful manor house and especially on the annual Gardens Day.

During the summer months the Ilmington Morris Men dance on Wednesday evenings in the surrounding villages. The group was formed in 1974, and, among others, perform up to twenty traditional 'Ilmington' dances collected over the last hundred years. There is evidence of Morris dancing taking place in Ilmington since the 17th century, when dancers from Ilmington performed their sequences around a flag high up on Dovers Hill at Chipping Campden.

SHIPSTON ON STOUR MAP REF 404 D7

Shipston on Stour is a delightful, small market town on the edge of the Cotswolds, and very much a focal point for the surrounding rural communities, with a variety of shops catering for both residents and tourists.

The town was formerly a vital centre for the trade of sheep and grain, and known as the 'Sheep-wash-Town' because in early summer the river was used for washing sheep. From the 14th to the 19th centuries Shipston, lay along the route of the Welsh cattle drovers bound for London. In those days, droving was a thirsty business, so it is not surprising to find that Shipston has many pubs. The inns also served coaches, as this was an important stop.

A three-day fair held in June dates back to the 13th century, while the annual Shipston Proms in June and July promotes a range of music, from classical to rock.

A few miles to the south, and erected more than 4,000 years ago, the Rollright Stones on the Warwickshire-Oxfordshire border, are a sacred site on a hilltop high above the village of Long Compton. The site comprises some 77 chunks of weather-worn limestone: a principal stone circle known as 'The Kings Men', a prominent outlier called 'The King Stone', and the semi-recumbent remains of a megalithic tomb known as 'The Whispering Knights'.

STRATFORD-UPON-AVON

MAP REF 403 J5

There is little in this glorious market town, so steeped in the life and works of one of Britain's most eminent playwrights, to reveal much about William Shakespeare's early career. His birth and baptism are recorded, but other than the fact that 'he had been in his younger years a schoolmaster in the country' (John Aubrey, 1681), he remains a vague personage until he materializes virtually a fully fledged poet and playwright.

That he thereafter spent much of his life in Stratford is more than enough justification for the town to celebrate his presence in a way that, thankfully, is both tasteful and authoritative. For a sense of direction, there is no better place to start than his birthplace, a fine 16th-century building on what was always a busy thoroughfare. Just on the edge of the town centre is Holy Trinity Church, itself an architectural delight, and here Shakespeare lies buried. Not far away, at Shottery on the town's outskirts, is the thatched farmhouse cottage where Anne Hathaway, Shakespeare's wife, grew up. The cottage remained in the possession of Anne Hathaway's descendants until the late 19th century, and still contains numerous items belonging to the family.

There is a world-class quality about Stratford, much of which would have prevailed without the bard as a marketing device, and it is quite a delight to stroll along the streets, inescapably imbued with Shakespeariana, taking in the splendours of medieval craftsmanship and the aura from 16th- and 17th-century England. Among the finest buildings, not least Shakespeare's birthplace, are Thomas Nash's House on Chapel Street owned by the first husband of Shakespeare's grand-daughter, Elizabeth and Hall's Croft in the Old Town, named after Dr John Hall, who married one of Shakespeare's daughters. The most ornate house in Stratford is Harvard House, a splendid example of an Elizabethan town house. Rebuilt in 1596, Harvard House is the home of the Museum of British Pewter. Mary Arden's House and the Shakespeare Countryside Museum is at Wilmcote, 5 miles (8km) north of Stratford; a timbered farmhouse that was the home of Shakespeare's mother before she married John Shakespeare and then moved to Stratford.

Of course, Stratford is internationally renowned as the home of the Royal Shakespeare Company, long recognized as Europe's, and indeed the world's, leading classical theatre company. Its annual repertoire of superb theatre productions features a mix of classical and modern drama and musicals with some of the most distinguished actors and directors in the world performing plays by Shakespeare, his contemporaries, and other classical playwrights, as well as many new plays specially commissioned by the RSC.

Famous for its literary associations, Stratford bustles with culture and history, superb shops and restaurants, and a vibrant Friday market.

Besides Shakespeare there is much to enjoy from a day at Stratford. You could try your luck at the horses at exciting Stratford Races, or take a tour of the city on an open-top bus, make a visit to a butterfly farm or spend the afternoon on a boat trip on the River Avon.

The medieval bridge spanning the Avon greatly contributed to the town's economic prosperity, and still provides a link between the town and the countryside of the Avon that awaits wider exploration.

Visit
STRATFORD'S THEATRES

The most famous theatrical company in the world, the Royal Shakespeare Company, has its home in Stratford-upon-Avon. It draws thespians from around the globe to take part in, and to watch, performances by the great and the good. The three theatres in town provide a variety of stage drama.

The Royal Shakespeare Theatre, or the Royal, has the largest space and was constructed in 1932.

The Swan was built to re-create the space and atmosphere of an Elizabethan theatre, and comes complete with galleries.

The Other Place, which opened for business in 1986, is the smallest and has a more intimate atmosphere.

A donation of land from Charles Flowers in 1875 was the beginning of a successful campaign to bring theatre here. Little did he know that one day Stratford would be so revered.

STRATFORD-UPON-AVON

STRATFORD-UPON-AVON: IN THE BARD'S FOOTSTEPS

This is a tour of theatrical Stratford-upon-Avon, birthplace of William Shakespeare, to see its many sights. But there are other things to see in Stratford-upon-Avon, apart from the Shakespeare heritage. The medieval 14-arched Clopton Bridge forms a splendid gateway to the town. The town hall is a fine Palladian building and Harvard House, in the High Street, dates from 1596. The Falcon Hotel, the ancient guild hall and a row of timbered almshouses are also worth a visit.

DISTANCE/TIME 2.5 miles (4km) 1h **MAP** OS Explorer 205 Stratford-upon-Avon & Evesham **START** Recreation Ground pay-and-display car park; grid ref: SP 205547 **PATHS** Riverside paths and street pavements; no stiles **THE PUB** Dirty Duck, Waterside, Stratford-upon-Avon. Tel: 01789 297 312

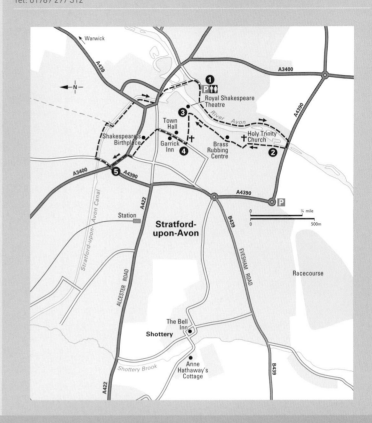

1 From the car park, walk along the banks of the River Avon, opposite the famous Royal Shakespeare Theatre. Continue past the weir until you come to a footbridge over the river, just in front of the A4390 road bridge.

2 Go right over the footbridge and bear right, past flats that have replaced the old watermill, into Mill Lane. Continue up Mill Lane and go through the churchyard of Holy Trinity Church, walking around the church to see the river view. Leave the churchyard through the main gate into Old Town and follow the pavement. Just before turning into Southern Lane, go right into New Place Gardens and walk up to the Brass Rubbing Centre. Continue past the ferry and stroll through the attractive Theatre Gardens by the side of the river, exiting into the Waterside and passing the old theatre building.

3 Go left up Chapel Lane, taking your time to wander through the attractive Knot Gardens on your way up to Chapel Street. At the top of the lane is the Guild Chapel to Shakespeare's Grammar School, with New Place Gardens to your right.

4 Go right along Chapel Street, passing The Shakespeare and Town Hall, into the High Street. Harvard House is on your left, near the black-and-white Garrick Inn. At the end of High Street, bear left around a traffic island into Henley Street and walk along a pedestrianized area that takes you past Shakespeare's Birthplace and Museum. At the top of Henley Street, bear right and then left into Birmingham Road. Cross the road at the pedestrian crossing and go left up to the traffic lights.

5 Head right up Clopton Road for 100yds (91m), then descend to the towpath of the Stratford-upon-Avon Canal at bridge No 66. Follow this, going southeast. Cross the canal at bridge No 68 and continue along the towpath into Bancroft Gardens at the canal basin where you will see colourful narrowboats and the Royal Shakespeare Theatre. Cross the old Tram Bridge to the car park on your right.

CHARLECOTE PARK: AN ELIZABETHAN JEWEL

This is an easy walk into open countryside, starting at Charlecote, about 5 miles (8km) from Stratford-upon-Avon. There is an opportunity to visit the superb Charlecote Park (National Trust), home to the Lucy family since 1247.

DISTANCE/TIME 6 miles (9.7km) 2h15 **MAP** OS Explorer 205 Stratford-upon-Avon **START** National Trust visitors car park for Charlecote Park; grid ref: SP 263564 **PATHS** Field paths and farm tracks; 2 stiles **THE PUB** The Kings Head, Warwick Road, Wellesbourne Tel: 01789 840206

1 From Charlecote Park car park, go left along the grass verge and cross the River Dene. In 100yds (91m), go left along a track that arcs left on to a fenced path by the side of the river and continue for about 1.5 miles (2.4km), passing a sewage farm, via a kissing gate, into Wellesbourne. You will pass a weir and go beneath the A429 before you come to a footbridge near St Peter's Church.

2 Go left over the footbridge and up a fenced path to the left of the church to reach the village via the churchyard gates. Continue up the road to the left of house No 21 – The Kings Head is on the left – then cross the main road and walk up Warwick Road opposite.

3 In about 300yds (274m), just after passing Daniell Road, go right along a tarmac path alongside modern houses. Cross a footbridge and, go through a kissing gate, continue ahead over a cultivated field. Through another kissing gate, continue to cross another over a plank footbridge then along the left side of a hedge. Through a hedge gap take the footpath to the left of the copse of trees, then go right into the woodland. Turn left along the green lane at the top of a hedge of trees. You will emerge from the trees for a short distance and then re-enter again. After you emerge for a second time, look for a hedge gap to the left.

4 Go through the gap and cross a cultivated field to a hedge corner. Continue ahead alongside the hedge to a field corner, then bear right to Middle Hill Farm.

5 At a waymark post go left, between the farm buildings, then go to the right of the farmhouse and walk along the farm access lane for about 0.75 miles (1.2km), passing the entrance to Coppington Farm on the way to the A429. Cross the road with care and go over the stile opposite on to a fenced footpath. After crossing another minor road, continue along a concrete driveway to skirt a brick farm building via three kissing gates.

6 Continue ahead alongside a post and wire fence in pastureland. Bear left at a kissing gate (don't go through it) to a second kissing gate, which leads into a large cultivated field that you walk around by the field hedge, initially alongside a long lake. Go right, through a further kissing gate, and continue to the right of the field hedge until you go through a final kissing gate on to Charlecote Road. Go left along the footway, past a thatched cottage, into the centre of Charlecote, then turn right along the grass verge of the main street. Go past the half-timbered houses and the Charlecote Pheasant Hotel, with St Leonard's Church opposite, to reach the car park.

DISTANCE/TIME 15.5 miles (25km) 3h30 **MAP** OS Explorer 205 Stratford-upon-Avon & Evesham **START** Stratford: Clopton Bridge, grid ref SP 203549 or Seven Meadows car park; grid ref: SP 195540 **TRACKS** Streets, disused railway line with good gravel surface, country lanes and farm track **THE PUB** Masons Arms, Welford Road, Long Marston. Tel: 01789 720586

DISTANCE/TIME 9.75 miles (15.7km) 2h **MAP** OS Explorer 220 Birmingham & Explorer 221 Coventry & Warwick **START** Car park in Brome Hall lane, Kingswood; grid ref: SP 185710 **TRACKS** Quiet lanes and canal towpaths, gravel surfaces **THE PUB** Boot Inn, Old Warwick Road, Lapworth. Tel: 01564 782464; www.thebootatlapworth.co.uk

STRATFORD GREENWAY

Explore the quiet countryside in which England's greatest bard grew up. Whilst Stratford was already a prosperous town before Shakespeare's day, it is probably due to his association that so many of the town's splendid 16th-century buildings have survived.

1 Leave Clopton Bridge along Waterside. Turn left at the end and then go left again into Mill Lane. It finishes in a narrow alley that leads to the river. The continuing path swings beneath a bridge to shadow the main road, shortly passing Seven Meadows car park.

2 If joining the railway track at Seven Meadows, turn right to Milcote picnic area. The way runs beside Stratford's racecourse, then crosses the Avon by a picnic area and the River Stour. Go beyond Chambers Halt and Pearces Crossing to Milcote Station.

3 Through barriers and a parking area, cross a road to a picnic site. The track continues for 2 miles (3.2km), passing crossings at Knobbs Farm and the airfield before reaching Wyre Lane Crossing. Leave right on Wyre Lane into Long Marston and Mason's Arms.

4 To return, either retrace your route, or keep ahead on the road through the village. Turn off right to Dorsington. Carry on for 1.5 miles (2.4km) to a T-junction and go right to another junction in the middle of Dorsington. Take the lane on the right to Welford. Drop to a road and follow that right into modern Welford. Leave after just over 0.5 mile (800m) along Headland Road on the left, which is opposite St Peter's Church.

5 The onward route lies to the right along Church Street. At the end of Church Street by the Bell Inn, take the main road right through the village. Leaving Welford, turn off left to Weston and Clifford Chambers, going left again after 0.5 miles (0.8km) on a narrow lane to Weston-on-Avon.

6 At the bottom, turn right past the church. Keep forward, later passing Milcote Manor Farm. The way disintegrates to dirt as it swings right to meet the disused railway at Chambers Crossing Halt. Follow it left, back to Seven Meadows car park and Stratford.

7 If you began from the town, after passing Holy Trinity Church, carry on past Riverside and instead turn right at the next crossroads into Church Street. Go ahead along Chapel Street and High Street to a roundabout in the town centre, to return to your car park.

BADDESLEY CLINTON & PACKWOOD HOUSE

A ride along towpaths that connect two old houses: Baddesley Clinton, in one of the most picturesque settings in the country, and former Benedictine priory, Packwood House.

1 Join the Stratford-upon-Avon Canal behind the car park. Turn right, past a lock to a bridge where the canal splits. Cross to the spur, which drops through a second lock to another bridge, there dismounting to descend four steps on the far side. Follow the towpath away from the junction, passing a picnic site and going beneath a railway bridge to meet the Grand Union Canal.

2 Cycle along the towpath to the right for some 0.75 miles (1.2km) to the second bridge (No. 63), leaving immediately beyond it for the lane above. Over the bridge, climb away past the Tom O' The Wood pub. At a 'Give Way' crossroads, keep ahead over the B4439, enjoying easy pedalling for a little over 0.5 mile (800km) to the end of the lane.

3 To the left, the way leads past Hay Wood, eventually meeting another junction. Go left again towards Lapworth and Baddesley Clinton, the lane shortly falling to pass the entrance of Baddesley Clinton, which lies opposite Netherwood Lane. Turn in beside the lodge and follow the winding drive to a car park at its end. The National Trust has provided separate facilities for cycles, enabling you to explore the house and nearby church on foot.

4 Returning to the main lane, turn left towards Hockley Heath, soon dropping to a blind humpback bridge spanning the Grand Union Canal. Beyond there, keep going over a railway bridge and, later, ahead at a crossroads beside the Punch Bowl. About 0.5 miles (0.8km) further on, the road turns sharply left. Exercising caution, turn off right onto a narrow lane leading past Packwood House, which stands beside the road only a short distance along.

5 Resuming your ride, carry on for almost another 0.75 mile (1.2km) to the second lane leaving on the left, Vicarage Road. It is signed to Packwood and Hockley Heath. Follow that for 0.5 mile (800km) and then turn left at an unsigned junction. Winding past Packwood's church, St Giles, the lane eventually ends at a main road, the B4439.

6 Turn left towards Lapworth and Warwick, but after 200yds (182m) and just before some white cottages, swing off right onto a gravel track, the entrance to Drawbridge Farm. Meeting the canal a few yards/metres along, follow the towpath left, to the first of a long series of locks (No 2) heralding the canal's descent to Kingswood. Prudent cyclists will then dismount to negotiate the sharp dip and low ridge immediately beyond.

7 The path crosses to the opposite bank over a bridge below lock No 4, remaining on that side to pass beneath a road bridge and shortly reaching lock No 6. Beyond, locks then follow in quick succession, forming a staircase that drops the canal some 70ft (21m) in little over 0.5 mile (800km). The towpath reverts to the north bank below lock No 7, recrossing once more after lock No 14, where The Boot Inn lies, just along a track south of the canal. The final stretch continues along the towpath beneath a road bridge, bending past four more locks and under a final bridge to return you to the car park.

Shrewsbury & Ironbridge

CLOCKWISE FROM TOP LEFT: STATUE OF CHARLES DARWIN, SHREWSBURY LIBRARY; IRONBRIDGE; CHURCH OF ST CHAD, SHREWSBURY

ACTON BURNELL CASTLE
MAP REF 403 G4

Acton Burnell Castle is one of several semi-fortified manor houses located in Shropshire that would have been built for comfort, rather than battle, the most well known and best preserved of these being Stokesay Castle, near Craven Arms (see Shropshire Hills and Stiperstones).

The village of Acton Burnell lies a few miles south of Shrewsbury, and it is puzzling to understand why a castle would be built in such a remote setting, until you realize that its position was very strategic, lying close to Watling Street, an old Roman road linking the city of Viroconium (Wroxeter) with Church Stretton.

What makes the red sandstone remains of Acton Burnell Castle, built in 1284–93 by Bishop Burnell, so historically significant is that the first parliament at which the Commons were formally represented was held here. Parliaments were held here twice, in 1283 and 1285.

ATTINGHAM PARK MAP REF 403 G4

Attingham Park was formerly the ancestral home of the Berwick family, who lived here for more than 160 years. Each generation left its mark on the house, which splendidly recalls the England of Jane Austen. This huge mansion is set in a magnificent deer park, landscaped by the renowned Humphrey Repton. Inside, collections include silver, Italian furniture and Grand Tour paintings collected by the 3rd Lord Berwick. Costumed guides bring Attingham's colourful history to life, including the story of the most corrupt election in the history of British politics.

BUILDWAS ABBEY MAP REF 403 G4

Buildwas Abbey ruins overlook the River Severn, just as the 12th-century Cistercian Abbey did when it was home to a community of monks. It is they who initially built a stone bridge spanning the river at Buildwas.

COALBROOKDALE & IRONBRIDGE
MAP REF 403 H4

Nestled in a valley of the Ironbridge Gorge, Coalbrookdale was one of the places that the Industrial Revolution began. Coalbrookdale furnace produced the first cast iron for railway lines and went on to create the decorative gates for London's Hyde Park.

IRONBRIDGE GORGE
MAP REF 403 H4

Britain has 27 sites considered by UNESCO to have World Heritage Status. The Ironbridge Gorge and its museums were thus designated in 1986.

Ironbridge is renowned throughout the world as the cradle of the Industrial Revolution. Here you discover all the elements of progress that fuelled the rapid development of industry in the 18th century, from mines to railway lines. Near by, in the Museum of Iron, the blast furnace from Coalbrookdale, built in 1708, is a reminder of the discovery of coke, while other elements of a burgeoning industry are found in award-winning attractions like Enginuity, the Jackfield Tile Museum, the Tar Tunnel, the Coalport China Museum and the Broseley Pipeworks, all contributing to an endlessly fascinating exposition of Britain's industrial heritage that will inspire young and old alike.

The amazing bridge at Ironbridge was the world's first bridge built entirely of iron, an event that had a profound influence on developments in the fields of technology and architecture.

SHREWSBURY MAP REF 403 G4

Shrewsbury looks to be on the brink of becoming an island, almost completely surrounded by the River Severn, or as A E Housman put it in *A Shropshire Lad*: 'High the vanes of Shrewsbury gleam, Islanded in Severn Stream'.

As the river is flowing from north to south, the town of Shrewsbury is entirely on what the French would call the Rive Gauche, the Left Bank, an allusion to Paris, where all things traditional and boring are on the right bank, and all things funky on the left. So, it is with Shrewsbury.

Famed for its array of steeples and towers, with the Severn forming a protective moat, Shrewsbury is among England's finest Tudor towns, boasting almost 700 listed buildings, including many stunning black-and-white timber-framed residences, a Norman abbey (home to Ellis Peters' fictional sleuth, Brother Cadfael), a medieval castle, Georgian crescents and churches. The town is networked by 'Shuts' and 'Passages' – a unique maze of narrow alleys which criss-cross the centre in bewildering fashion, and seem purposely designed to draw visitors into further exploration. Shrewsbury is also a floral extravaganza, a place that won the 'Britain in Bloom' Award in 2006; as might be expected from a town where the renowned gardener Percy Thrower was Parks Superintendent for 28 years – there's a massive horticultural legacy to live up to.

Shrewsbury Castle is a Norman red sandstone construction, first built in 1070 on the site of an original Anglo-Saxon fortification that would have guarded the approach to the town and the River Severn. Little of the castle survives today, as much of it was demolished under the reign of Edward I. The castle remained in private hands until 1924, when it was acquired by Shrewsbury Borough Council. Today, the castle houses the informative Shropshire Regimental Museum, including

IRONBRIDGE

spectacular collections of pictures, weapons, uniforms and memorabilia from the 1700s to present times.

In 2009, the town celebrated the birth of its most famous son, Charles Darwin, he of *The Origin of Species*. But rather than leave everything to the last minute, Shrewsbury has been holding a Darwin Festival since 2001, and will do so for years to come.

Everywhere is Art in Shrewsbury, or so it seems. A contemporary arts scene thrives here, particularly in the visual arts featured mainly in the Shrewsbury Museum and Art Gallery, with special exhibitions of Contemporary art; the Real Art Gallery, where contemporary art is spread across two floors and there is a relaxed coffee shop below, and the Bear Steps Gallery – a 15th-century timber hall, which has fortnightly changing exhibitions.

Complementing the visual arts is an invigorating cultural scene, including the Music Hall, the Jazz and Roots Club, Shropshire Music Trust and The Gateway. Nor are shoppers neglected in Shrewsbury; as well as conventional High Street shops, there are a great many that simply aren't, but rather individual outlets for a whole plethora of crafts and goods. Of course, you don't need to shop; just chill out with a Chardonnay or a coffee at one of the many cafés and bars.

TELFORD & THE WREKIN
MAP REF 403 H4
Built as a new town in the late 1960s and early 1970s, Telford absorbed many of the existing villages in this former coal producing area. It is the largest town in Shropshire, partly due to its excellent transport links to the rest of the country. A few miles west of the town is The Wrekin, a hill that rises to 1,335 feet (407m) above the Shropshire Plain.

WROXETER MAP REF 403 G4
Wroxeter (or Viroconium) was the fourth largest Roman city in Britain. At first it was simply a legionary fortress but later acquired a thriving civilian city, peopled by retired soldiers and traders, many of whom decided to stay. Though much remains below ground, the most impressive features of the town today are the 2nd-century bath-houses.

The audio tour is especially revealing and tells how Wroxeter worked, and explains the health and beauty practices of its citizens, who came to number as many as 5,000. Important archaeological discoveries in recent years show what the city was like during the last years of Roman accommodation, and its subsequent adaptation to form the headquarters of a 5th-century British or Irish warlord.

Ironbridge Living Museums & Gorge

Did you know that tar is made from the remains of long-dead animals, and that it used to be used to treat rheumatism and skin complaints such as scurvy? Those are just two of the many fascinating answers to questions you never knew you wanted to ask that will be revealed by a visit to Ironbridge in the Severn Gorge and its award-winning museums in Shropshire.

The Severn Gorge has a long industrial history because of the ready availability of coal, iron ore, limestone and timber, and the proximity of the River Severn, which was used for transport. The monks at Buildwas Abbey were smelting iron in charcoal forges as early as 1200, and iron was made at Coalbrookdale from at least 1500. But, the smelting of iron was dependent on timber, and timber had to be made into charcoal first, and this was a long, slow process. What changed all that was the discovery in 1709 by Abraham Darby that coke could be used for smelting, a discovery that literally changed the world; and it happened here, in the Ironbridge Gorge.

Suddenly, iron could be produced much less expensively, and in far bigger quantities. In 1779, the world's first iron bridge was cast; you can see it still spanning the Severn at Ironbridge. The building of the iron bridge led to an increased use of iron for many areas of engineering, and proved itself in 1795 when flooding damaged every local bridge except one – the iron bridge.

Many of the industrial scars are now healed, and the Severn Gorge is once again a lush and verdant area. But since the 1960s, the relics of such toil and industry that did remain have gradually been transformed into a stunning and award-winning collection of fascinating and innovative museums.

Today, Ironbridge is renowned throughout the world as the cradle of the Industrial Revolution. Here you discover all the elements of progress that fuelled the rapid development of industry in the 18th century, from mines to railway lines. In 1986, Ironbridge Gorge and its museums was awarded UNESCO World Heritage status, one of the first such sites in Britain: this is 'essential' England.

Ironbridge itself is built of warm, mellow brick, its attractive buildings clinging prettily in tiers to the north slopes of the gorge. Although Ironbridge has become a tourist centre, it has lost none of its charm, and it is a delight to explore the steep, narrow streets or walk into the woodlands above.

There are ten museums in the Ironbridge Gorge, and of these Blists Hill Victorian Museum is arguably the most popular. Here, Victorian life is re-enacted by townsfolk dressed in the clothing of the day. Many are ready to demonstrate exactly how tasks would have been done in a small industrial town towards the end of Queen Victoria's lengthy reign. The attractions at Blists Hill include a steam-operated pithead, a Victorian chemist, a squatter's cottage, a schoolhouse and a bank, where you can obtain Blists Hill's own form of money to spend in the town.

The newest museum, Enginuity, brings the story of Victorian industry right up to date. Here you get to play with a vast collection of interactive machinery and indulge in an intriguing array of activities including testing your speed and accuracy against a robot, generating power from water and looking at everyday objects through a powerful giant X-ray machine. The museum is divided into four zones: Materials, Energy, Design, and Systems and Control. Use the latest technology to move a simulated X-ray machine over everyday objects like a guitar, a mobile phone and a teddy bear, and experiment with gizmos used to design things we see and use everyday. This is a wonderful opportunity to give substance to a childhood dream by pulling a five-ton locomotive by hand – strange childhood, strange dream, maybe, but really good fun. If you're feeling especially generous, you can let the children try, too.

Other hands-on experiences can be found at the Coalport China Museum, which houses huge displays of china, produced over two centuries, and is home to nationally important collections of Caughley and Coalport porcelain. Here, in what was one of the country's largest manufacturers of fine china, you can make pottery yourself or watch live demonstrations. Likewise at the Jackfield Tile Museum across the river, a former world centre of the decorative tile industry.

For a history of early iron-making and decorative castings, visit the Museum of Iron, which tells the story of iron-smelting up to the Great Exhibition of 1851. This is where the Coalbrookdale Company showed off its finest work. The Museum of Iron adjoins the original furnace used by Abraham Darby when he first smelted iron ore with coke. The iron produced was used in making cooking pots, rails, wheels and, of course, that rightly celebrated Iron Bridge. The story of the gorge itself is explained in the Museum of the Gorge, housed in a Gothic riverside warehouse where the fine porcelain goods from Coalbrookdale began their journey. The museum has a 40-foot (12m) scale model of Ironbridge as it was in 1796.

If that's not enough, there are the Darby Houses, which offer an insight into the life and times of the Darby family, and Broseley Pipe Works, which saw over 350 years of traditional pipe-making crafts. Then there is the Tar Tunnel, dug from the hillside in 1787 when miners hit an underground spring of thick, treacle-like natural bitumen that became one of the great curiosities of the 18th century. In other parts of Britain such natural seepages are promoted as 'Treacle Mines'. The tar was mainly used to treat ropes and for caulking ships, but some small amounts were processed as 'Betton's British Oil', and peddled as a remedy for 'rheumatic and scorbutic affections'.

As well as Britain's best-known industrial monument, Ironbridge Gorge has also produced a few famous names: Billy Wright, the footballer who captained England in the 1950s, learned his skills on the streets of Ironbridge. On Church Hill, a house called The Orchard was once the home of Captain Matthew Webb, the first man to swim the English Channel. Also born nearby, like Captain Webb, in Dawley, was Edith Pargeter who, as Ellis Peters, became famous for her Cadfael novels, chronicling the adventures of a Welsh monk, set in and around Shrewsbury.

And the museums continue to develop; plans are afoot for the Blists Hill Victorian Town to be improved, adding to the excellence of these 'living' museums. The wonder of it all is that so much can be found in so small a space. You don't come to Ironbridge for just a few hours – think days.

CLOCKWISE FROM TOP LEFT Dressed in Victorian attire, the staff at Blists Hill Victorian Town recreate the day-to-day life of a 19th-century community.

Jackfield Tile Musuem features tiles from 1840 to 1960 by British designers. Here you can learn about the processes involved in making the various types of tile, including encaustic and embossed tiles.

The Victorian Cycle Rally is one of the many popular events held throughout the year at Blists Hill.

OPPOSITE The River Severn runs through the lush green of Ironbridge Gorge, called the Severn Gorge until the construction of Abraham Darby's wonderful feat of engineering.

DISTANCE/TIME 7.5 miles (12.1km) 1h30 **MAP** OS Explorer 242 Telford, Ironbridge & The Wrekin **START** Legge Road car park, Madeley; grid ref: SJ 700043 **TRACKS** Off-road tracks (can be muddy) and lanes, gentle descents and gradual climbs **THE PUB** The Swan, The Wharfage TF8 7NH. Tel: 01952 432306

DISTANCE/TIME 6.5 miles (10.5km) 1h30 **MAP** OS Explorer 243 Market Drayton, Loggerheads & Eccleshall **START** Norbury Village Hall; grid ref: SJ 782235 **TRACKS** Canal towpath (one short grass section) and quiet lanes **THE PUB** Navigation Inn, Newport Road, Gnosall. Tel: 01785 822327

THE SILKIN WAY TO IRONBRIDGE

Pedal back in time to discover what a 'Saggar-maker's Bottom Knocker' did. Although the gorge's natural resources had been exploited since medieval times, the industrial boom only began in 1709 with Abraham Darby's invention at Coalbrookdale, which used coke rather than charcoal to produce large quantities of cast iron cheaply. This pleasant cycle ride cuts through swathes of countryside once industrious in a different way.

1 Leaving the car park, cross the road and climb a set of shallow steps to a tarmac track, called the Silkin Way. Follow the track left, passing Station Road and dropping to curve beneath the main road. Swing right as you emerge and carry on at the edge of a park, later joining the pavement to reach Blists Hill Victorian Town. Keep going down the hill, the cycleway shortly diverging from the road on a gradual tree-lined descent following along the line of an old railway. Through a tunnel, the way courses enjoyably down, later passing beneath the ingenious Hay Inclined Plane. The track eventually ends in front of the Brewery Inn.

2 Cross the road to a gated track left of the pub, which descends past cottages to the riverbank. Bear right as it forks, rising to meet a road. Follow that over the Severn, and then leave immediately down steps on the right, to reach a riverside path. It skirts a picnic area and climbs around to a gate, joining the line of another disused railway. The track continues above the river for just over 0.5 mile (800m) before passing Maws Craft Centre, once the site of a booming tile industry. A little further on as the track ends, keep ahead on the right-most of two roads, which leads past more tile works at Jackfield. These were built by Charles Lynam between 1871 and 1874, for Craven Dunnill & Co, and now house a fascinating museum.

3 Go forward at a junction, but as the road then bends to a reconstructed level crossing, turn off left to regain the line of the railway through Jackfield Sidings. Further on, beyond the Black Swan, pass beneath a skew bridge carrying the road to the Jackfield suspension bridge. It is then not far to the main car park at Ironbridge. Pedal through to the far side and dismount to cross the famous Iron Bridge into the town, where you will find the Malthouse a little way to the left.

4 The route from the bridge, however, is along the main street to the right. At a mini-roundabout, take the right fork ahead, the B4373 to Jackfield and Broseley, leaving the town past the ruins of the Bedlam Furnaces. Where the road later bends to Jackfield Bridge, keep ahead on a narrow, bumpy lane, which undulates along the valley to Coalport. Keep going forward at a later junction, a bridge that takes you over the Hay Inclined Plane, just beyond which, opposite the Shakespeare Inn, you will find the entrance to the Tar Museum. A little further on is the Coalport China Museum.

5 From the museum, go back along the lane a few yards/metres, turning off right onto a track that winds around Coalport Village Hall to an overflow car park. Pass through it, right, to find a track climbing to meet the Silkin Way. Turn left and retrace your outward route past Blists Hill to the car park from which you began. The way is steadily uphill, but the track is well-graded and the climb relatively easy.

THE SHROPSHIRE CANAL

With more miles of canal than any other county, what better way to discover Staffordshire's countryside? The Shropshire Canal was built between 1830 and 1835, under the direction of Thomas Telford, creating a more direct link than hitherto between the industrial towns of England's heartland and the seaports along the Dee and Mersey rivers. The main Shropshire Canal survived and is today busy with leisure boats.

1 Out of the car park, go right and then left to pedal through the village, signed to Oulton and Norbury Junction. Keep with the main lane as it bends right, past a track leading to the striking village church, a large building, dedicated to St Peter, of much weathered sandstone that nestles below a massive brick tower. Leaving the village, go left at a fork signed to Norbury Junction and Gnosall.

2 You will be passing through Norbury Junction on the way back, so for the time being, carry on over the canal bridge and continue along the lane behind the old canal offices and workshops. Beside the lane is a millennium boulder, similar to one just beside the village hall; an erratic boulder stranded as the vast ice sheets that covered this part of the country melted at the end of the last Ice Age, some 10,000 years ago. Beyond cottages, the lane falls towards a wood, there bending sharply right to pass under a bridge (beware of traffic).

3 At the junction beyond, go left towards Gnosall, the lane rising gently along the base of a high wooded embankment upon which the canal runs. After a mile (1.6km), it twists beneath the canal once more (again, watch out for traffic) and climbs to a bend beyond. Keep going with the undulating lane, eventually passing beneath a bridge that once carried the Stafford Newport Railway, to a T-junction with the main road at the end.

4 Turn right, crossing the canal to find The Navigation on the right. If going to the pub, there are steps to the canal towpath from the car park, but an easier way lies down a ramp on the left-hand side of the road. Double back under the bridge and cycle away past the pub beside the canal, shortly going beneath the railway again. The bridge here is very wide, the passage almost tunnel-like, not due to carrying several tracks, but because it is skewed across the canal. Such bridges were disproportionately expensive if built in brick or stone, and it was only the invention of the skew arch that allowed the bridge to be preserved within the width of the upper passage. Shortly emerging from a cutting, there are pleasing views across the open countryside. The way continues to Shelmore Wood, where there is a stop lock, a device inserted periodically along the canal for isolating individual sections so that they could be drained for maintenance. Carry on in trees for another 1.25 miles (2km) to Norbury Junction, there crossing a bridge over the abandoned Wappenshall Branch to reach The Junction pub.

5 Leave the canal for the lane, and retrace your outward route left, back to the car park by the village hall in Norbury.

Shropshire Hills
& Stiperstones

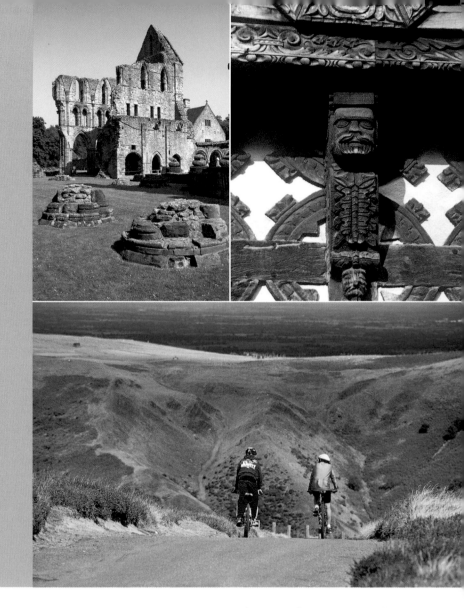

CLOCKWISE FROM TOP LEFT: MUCH WENLOCK PRIORY;
FEATHERS HOTEL, LUDLOW; CYCLING IN LONG MYND

BISHOP'S CASTLE MAP REF 403 G4

Bishop's Castle is a small and ancient town in an Area of Outstanding Natural Beauty, to which it contributes admirably. This unassuming settlement is a unique base for the exploration of the South Shropshire uplands, but is fundamentally a medieval town with a fascinating architectural mélange of styles, including a house built on crutches! Very much a rural market centre, the town sees regular cattle and sheep auctions, and a farmers' market. For almost a millennium, Welsh drovers brought herds of cattle and sheep and flocks of geese along the Kerry Ridgeway to the markets in Bishop's Castle. To cope with the thirst the drovers brought with them, the town has been brewing ale since 1642, and possibly longer.

The main street is disconcertingly steep but is flanked by curio and antique shops, as well as secondhand bookshops, a perfect place for collectors. And while at the top end of town it is worth visiting the old castle for a leisurely tour or picnic.

CHURCH STRETTON MAP REF 403 G4

Nestling into the flanks of Long Mynd and the towering Caer Caradoc, Church Stretton saw brief esteem between 1880 and 1900 as a spa town, a time of a rising passion for neo-half-timbering, which is the hallmark of the town. Today, more prosaically, Church Stretton is a convenient launch pad for the Stretton Hills and Long Mynd, especially Cardingmill Valley; a steep-sided ravine and an historic area of upland heath, where once sheeps' fleeces were combed. With over 30 walking routes and bridleways, this is a pleasant base for walkers and horse riders alike.

There are actually three 'Strettons' – Church Stretton, All Stretton and Little Stretton – all very much focused on those who enjoy outdoor pursuits, including gliding and paragliding – these take to the skies from a base on Long Mynd.

Still happily and rightly clinging to its refined past with streets of individual shops, the lovely market town of Church Stretton has more to offer the visitor than the spa water treatments of old. The town has held a market charter since the reign of King John, and the tradition of the ancient market continues every Thursday, augmented by regular flea markets that draw in visitors from far afield. Many of Stretton's shops still have original frontages, dating from around 1600, when they were rebuilt following a major fire in the town. Church Stretton's church, dedicated to St Lawrence, is Norman and Early English in style and is famed for the sheila-na-gig, an ancient fertility symbol above the north door.

Calcium-rich water from the Stretton Hills is bottled and sold throughout England, and rises from natural aquifers deep in the fragile geological ground on which the whole of this region is based. Sustenance in another form emanates from Church Stretton, which each year hosts an apple fair and a food festival promoting delicious hand-raised pork pies and locally-bred meats, as well as beer from the region's micro-breweries; in fact, in the 1970s, half the brew pubs in England were found in Shropshire.

Close by, in Acton Scott, is one of Britain's leading working farm museums. There are regular demonstrations of historic farming using traditional skills and period horse-drawn machines, milking by hand, butter-making in the dairy, visits from a wheelwright, farrier and blacksmith. In a woodsman's hut, rakes and gate hurdles are made, all part of a setting designed to focus on rural life and the craft skills of estate life more than a century ago.

CLEOBURY MORTIMER
MAP REF 403 H5

Built on the banks of the River Rea, Cleobury Mortimer, the second smallest town in Shropshire, is the epitome of English rural village life. The town is close to the Clee Hills – Brown Clee and Titterstone Clee. Although not especially high, the Clee Hills of Shropshire are just one of only eight sites in England depicted on the 13th-century map of the world, the 'Mappa Mundi', found in Hereford Cathedral. Perhaps the significance is not evident, but without the quarries and mineral wealth of Titterstone Clee in particular, the towns and cities of Victorian England would have been all the poorer.

Cleobury's High Street was described by John Betjeman as a 'long airy curving street'. Nearby Ludlow tends to draw the visitors, but Cleobury Mortimer is every bit as worthwhile a destination, not least because of the church's twisted steeple and its distinctly unnerving state of imminent collapse, which, of course, it isn't about to do. The whole town is a lovely blend of age-old antiquity in the nicest possible sense.

CLUN MAP REF 403 G5

A E Housman considered that 'Clunton and Clunbury, Clungunford and Clun are the quietest places under the sun', and for much of the year that may well be true. But even the quietest places must occasionally go wild, and so each May Day Clun is a-bustle with celebrations, not least the Festival of the Green Man, who confronts Frostie, Queen of Cold, on the ancient bridge and banishes her chilling ways as summer approaches. Clun's Green Man Day is a tradition that today embraces mummers' plays, wandering minstrels, medieval knights and Morris dancers, all performing in the shadow of the impressive Norman castle, although the town largely developed as a kind of staging post along a packhorse trail. The Clun Green Man, like all 'Green Men', personifies centuries of living in harmony with the land.

Clun is difficult to interpret; it is quite simply a comely, agreeable village, seemingly overlooked by the 21st century. But it was once a busy little place and hub of a radiating network of trails that brought Neolithic man, and, later, drovers of herds of cattle and flocks of geese en route to the English market towns and even London. Travellers still pass through Clun, for the village lies on the Shropshire Way.

LUDLOW MAP REF 403 G5

Ludlow, described by John Betjeman as 'England's finest town', is certainly one of Britain's best-preserved medieval and Georgian communities, one that grew in the shadow of its castle. Timber-framed buildings line the narrow streets of the old town centre, not least the stunning Feathers Hotel on Corve Street. Mill Street and Broad Street, by contrast, are lined with superb Georgian houses demonstrating a wide range of Georgian architectural styles. In fact, Ludlow boasts over 500 listed buildings, and the town centre is

a higgledy-piggledy jumble of building styles each leaning companionably on its neighbour for support.

The ancient Buttercross stands at the top of Broad Street, which leads down one of the county's finest streets to the gatehouse. Behind the Buttercross, St Lawrence's church is a dazzling example of the Perpendicular style. Inside are fine collections of medieval glass, and skillfully crafted misericords in the choir that require no religious conviction to appreciate

Ludlow has a less well-known distinction, too. This is the first town in the UK to be admitted to the *Cittaslow* network. *Cittaslow*, Italian for 'slow town', is an international network of towns, with the common aim of improving quality of life. It is about caring for the town and the people who live and work in it or visit it. It is also about protecting the environment, about promoting and using local goods and produce, and about avoiding the 'sameness' that afflicts many towns in the modern world.

Ludlow's commercial heart revolves around the Market Square, at the far end of which stands Ludlow Castle, built in the 11th century, and formerly a major centre of administration – the Court of

the Marches – for the vast tract of border land known as the Welsh Marches. In Tudor times Ludlow Castle was a popular resort patronized by members of the royal family, and it was here that Arthur, Prince of Wales, son of Henry VII, died. Nowadays, it is still a busy centre hosting numerous annual events including a popular vintage car rally, a Christmas Fayre, an annual food festival of international renown, and an excellent open-air Shakespeare production.

The town has grown up on the banks of the River Teme, and the river still plays an important part in the daily life of Ludlow. Linney Park is a lovely place for a picnic or to hire a rowing boat. Near the Millennium Green, the river widens and has a shingle 'beach' that has been a popular paddling spot for generations of Ludlow children. All around, the Shropshire countryside is perfect for walking and cycling, mountain biking, horse riding and canoeing, while the Marches are blessed with country houses, fine gardens and stately homes.

MUCH WENLOCK MAP REF 403 G4

Featured unmistakably in the John Cleese film *Clockwork*, Much Wenlock is a delightful mish-mash of timber-framed

houses, shops and pubs. Today, Much Wenlock's renown rests on the ruins of its fine 7th-century priory, still serenely set amid lush green lawns. The town grew around the priory, a local service industry meeting the daily needs of the nuns and monks. The ornate, timber-framed Guildhall is a 16th-century addition to the town, built over an open market area. Near by, the church of the Holy Trinity is a Norman and medieval masterpiece, something that complements the town's rich legacy of homely architecture, including the ancient, heavily timbered town house called Raynald's Mansion.

But Much Wenlock has another claim to fame, as the inspiration of the modern Olympic Games. Local-born doctor William Penny Brookes introduced a form of Olympic Games in 1850, 49 years before they were revived in Athens. The Much Wenlock Olympics, a mix of conventional athletic sports and events such as 5-a-side football, cricket and volleyball, are held annually in July.

SECRET HILLS MAP REF 403 G5

Unquestionably the finest place to begin an exploration of the Shropshire Hills, Secret Hills, the Discovery Centre, is at

STOKESAY CASTLE

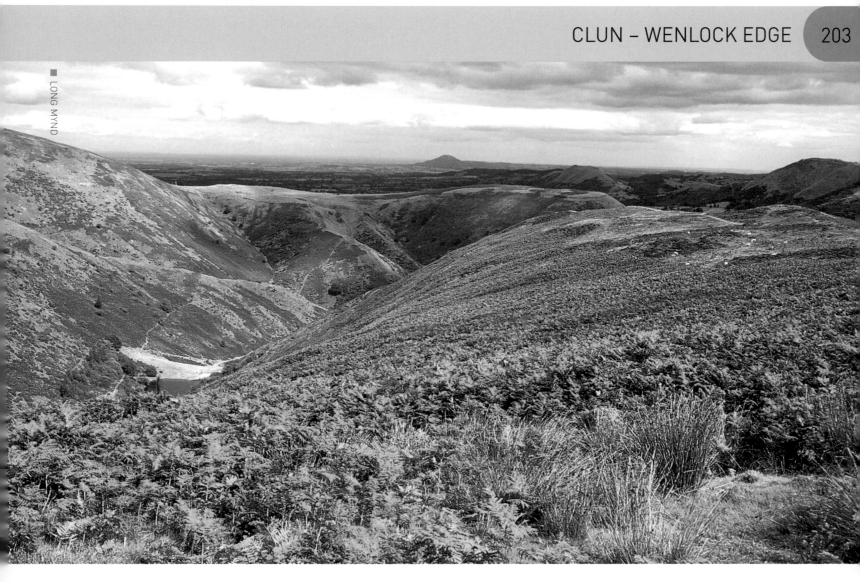

LONG MYND

Craven Arms, and a brilliant way of being transported back in time more than 4,500 million years, or you can just pop in for lunch and a chinwag.

The Shropshire Hills, Housman's 'blue remembered hills', form an Area of Outstanding Natural Beauty, and Secret Hills takes visitors on a balloon flight over the landscape, without ever actually leaving the ground. This is one of the most imaginative concepts, aimed at interpreting an ancient and vital landscape in a way everyone can understand and enjoy. This is a good place to start for another reason: the landscape and underlying geology of Shropshire is so complex, giving rise to so many different formations at surface level, that it is a wise move to try to figure it out first. Here, a single step can cross more than 600 million years in time.

STOKESAY CASTLE MAP REF 403 G5

Stokesay Castle is a truly breathtaking sight, the best preserved 13th-century fortified manor house in England; the name is misleading, as Stokesay is more domestic than military. Set amid the lovely Shropshire countryside, it seems a perfectly composed group of buildings, with its timber-framed gatehouse and parish church destined to set the pulse of photographers racing. Lawrence of Ludlow, a man who made his fortune as a wool merchant, bought the manor in 1281, and built a comfortable residence with defensive capabilities.

The castle has an open-hearthed great hall, with a superb cruck-framed roof, shuttered gable windows and precipitous staircase, little of which has changed since it was built. Across the courtyard stands the equally splendid gatehouse, with ornate timber-framing and elaborate carvings of Adam and Eve.

WENLOCK EDGE, LONG MYND & STIPERSTONES MAP REF 403 G4

Considered to be the finest geological escarpment in Britain, Wenlock Edge was immortalized in literature by A E Housman, author of *A Shropshire Lad*, and by composer Ralph Vaughan Williams, who set Housman's poem to music.

What makes Wenlock Edge so remarkable is its limestone geology, composed of corals, fossilized crinoids, brachiopods, trilobites and shells, formed 425 million years ago. But not here, in what is today Shropshire, but thousands of miles away, south of the Equator, roughly where the Seychelles are today. What makes a visit to this part of England all the more exciting, is that the valley in which Craven Arms and Church Stretton to the north sit, is directly above a crack in the earth's crust that once made this beautiful corner of England one of the most geologically violent. Wenlock Edge is the proof of that; one of the sections of the Silurian Period is even called the Wenlock era. It's all so incredibly confused and confusing, not least because Shropshire is built on rocks from 11 out of the 13 known periods of geology – the smallest area in the world to boast quite so many.

Across that fragile geological divide, the land to the west of Church Stretton rises into the formidable bulk of Long Mynd, a steep-sided uplift of heather moorland that flattens into a wide plateau, penetrated in places by in-cutting valleys formed by streams, of which Cardingmill Valley is the best known.

The Long Mynd, or 'Long Mountain', is a ridge of high ground sandwiched between the Stiperstones to the west, and Wenlock Edge to the east. The highest point of the ridge is Pole Bank, 1,692 feet (516m) above sea level, across which runs an ancient track, the Port Way. Most of Long Mynd was acquired by the National Trust in 1965.

While very attractive in fine conditions, the Long Mynd is treacherous in severe weather, and has claimed many lives. The Rev E D Carr's *A Night in the Snow* describes his experience in 1865 of surviving a winter's night on the Long Mynd, when attempting to walk home after visiting an isolated parishioner. The Long Mynd also features in the poetry of A E Housman, the novels of Mary Webb, and Malcolm Saville's Lone Pine series.

Further west lies Stiperstones, a name to conjure with, to dream up links with the Devil, indeed one of the rock formations is called 'The Devil's Chair'. Stiperstones has far-reaching views and is crowned with a number of rocky tors, said to have been placed there by the Devil in an endeavour to sink Stiperstones into the bowels of the earth so that all of the God-fearing people might perish. According to legend, the ghost of Wild Edric, a Saxon earl who defied the Normans, rides the hills whenever England is threatened by invasion.

Like so many places in Shropshire, Stiperstones features prominently in the works of writers like Mary Webb, who gave Stiperstones the name 'Diafol' in her novel *Golden Arrow*. D H Lawrence paid a fleeting visit, and used Stiperstones and the Devil's Chair as a key element in *St Mawr*. For Lawrence, Stiperstones was the place where 'aboriginal England' could still be felt; many would say it remains so to this day. Stiperstones is a National Nature Reserve and a haven for wildlife and birds normally associated with upland areas, including red grouse, curlew, peregrine falcon and ring ouzel.

WENLOCK EDGE: CLOSE TO THE EDGE

Take a walk along former drovers' roads that link the crest of Wenlock Edge to the fields and meadows of Corve Dale. This great tree-clad escarpment is one of Shropshire's most famous landscape features, partly because it plays a role in A E Housman's collections of poems entitled *A Shropshire Lad* and is also the subject of a choral poem by the composer Vaughan Williams.

DISTANCE/TIME 6.25 miles (10km) 3h **MAP** OS Explorer 217 The Long Mynd & Wenlock Edge **START** Car park/picnic site on east side of unclassified road between Middlehope and Westhope; grid ref: SO 479875 **PATHS** Mostly good but ford on Dunstan's Lane can be deep after rain; 10 stiles **THE PUB** Sun Inn, Corfton. Tel: 01584 861239

1 Turn left from the car park along a lane. At a junction, turn left again, signposted 'Middlehope'. Keep straight on at the next junction, signposted 'Upper Westhope', where the road becomes a track and soon bends left towards house. Enter a gate on the right instead and join a grassy bridleway that soon enters woodland. Keep straight on at two cross paths.

2 The bridleway emerges into pasture; keep straight on along to the corner. Go through a gate and turn right on the field-edge path, which soon becomes a wide track.

3 After passing a cottage, and with some barns ahead, look for blue arrows that direct you sharp right through a gate. Turn immediately left and walk above Corfton Bache, a deep valley, until more blue arrows direct you zig-zagging down into the valley. Follow it to the road at Corfton and cross to a lane, opposite.

4 As the lane degenerates into a track, look on the left for an iron kissing gate. Cross cattle pasture to a prominent stile at the far side. Cross a farm track and walk to the far right corner of an arable field.

5 Go through a gate, then a little way along the left-hand edge of another field until a gate gives access to parkland. Follow the waymarker and St Peter's Church at Diddlebury soon comes into view.

6 Cross two stiles at the far side of the park and go on down. Cross a track to find a footbridge and a path into Diddlebury. Turn right, then left by the church. Join a footpath which passes right of the village hall, then goes diagonally right through a school, to stiles immediately right of the buildings. Cross the fields to a road. Cross to the lane opposite, forking right after a few paces.

7 The footpath leaves the lane on the right, almost opposite Chapel Cottage. Continue up the lane.

8 At a junction at the top of the hill, keep left, still on the lane. As the lane reaches the valley bottom, turn left on a stony track, Dunstan's Lane, soon reaching a ford. Follow it, with waymarks appearing, to Middlehope road and turn left. Keep ahead at a Y-junction. Turn left on the footpath with a Shropshire Way sign. Sometimes muddy, this path leads through woods back to the picnic site.

PAYING HOMAGE AT MUCH WENLOCK

Visit the destination of medieval pilgrims in this peaceful walk in the countryside around Much Wenlock. Much Wenlock has been a market town for at least 700 years. It is a delightful little place, with charming old houses and a real working farm set back just off the High Street.

DISTANCE/TIME 6.25 miles (10km) 2h30 **MAP** OS Explorers 217 The Long Mynd & Wenlock Edge (start), and 242 Telford, Ironbridge & The Wrekin (most of the walk) **START** Car park off St Mary's Lane in Much Wenlock; grid ref: SO 623998 (on Explorer 217) **PATHS** Field paths, couple of boggy patches, 13 stiles **THE PUB** Talbot, Much Wenlock Tel: 01952 727077

1 Go down Burgage Way, left on Mutton Shut to High Street, right to Barrow Street, then left. Pass the church, then turn first right on Bull Ring. Continue past the priory and along a lane (Shropshire Way).

2 Descend past a sewage works. At the bottom, take a footpath on the right, cross a brook and follow the left-hand hedge. Where it bends left, keep straight on to a stile in the far corner.

3 Follow the right edge of the next field then go along the far end to a stile through the hedge. Turn left, pass two big oaks, then bear right to the far corner and a stile. A path climbs through young woodland.

4 Emerge into a field. Follow the left edge, then a short hedged path. Follow a track beside a holly hedge. When it bends right, keep straight on to Arlescott Farm.

5 Right of the farm, two stiles lead into pasture. Turn left, towards Arlescott Cottage, and then climb just to the right of it. Go through a gate on the left and then follow Jack Mytton Way markers; watch for one

pointing down left to a gap in a lower hedge. Turn right and continue walking ahead to reach a lane.

6 Turn right, then left by Manor Farm in Wyke. Turn left again on a lane descending into a wooded valley. Turn left (Shropshire Way marker) on a stony track. Just below a house, bear left on a green track. In the first field, look for a waymark and go left to an isolated oak, then turn right to a stile. In the next field, turn left. Cross another stile. When the rooftops of Bradley Farm appear, bear right towards them.

7 Cross two stiles and follow the access track to a lane. Cross into a green track. Follow a field-edge then a well-trodden path diagonally across pasture. Cross a footbridge, skirt houses at Downsmill and soon meet the lane from Much Wenlock.

8 Go past the sewage works, then keep straight on to join a dismantled railway. Turn left. After 300yds (273m), climb steps on the left to a fenced path, which passes the former station. Emerge near the priory, turn right and return to the start.

STIPERSTONES BACK TO PURPLE

Walk this route to take you from the mining village of Snailbeach to the dragon's crest of Stiperstones. At first sight it looks as though this walk will be all about industrial archaeology, for it begins at Snailbeach, formerly one of the most important lead mines in Britain. Mining ceased long ago and the derelict landscape has been transformed into one of the most fascinating post-industrial sites in the Midlands. But there's another transformation going on nearby. This is the Back to Purple project, which aims to restore Stiperstones to its full glory.

DISTANCE/TIME 4.5 miles (7.2km) 2h **MAP** 216 Welshpool & Montgomery **START** Car park at Snailbeach; grid ref: SJ 374023 **PATHS** Good paths across pasture, moorland and woodland **THE PUB** Stiperstones Inn, Stiperstones, Snailbeach. Tel: 01743 791 327

1 Take Lordshill lane opposite the car park, then join a parallel footpath on left. Rejoining the lane, cross to the site of a locomotive shed, then continue walking up the lane, noticing the green arrows directing you to the main sites.

2 Turn right on the track between the crusher house and the compressor house. A few paces past the compressor house, turn left up some steps. At the top, turn right, then soon turn left up more steps. Turn left to reach the Cornish engine house, then right and continue through woodland. A detour leads to a smelter chimney, or it's uphill all the way.

3 A sign indicates that you're entering Stiperstones National Nature Reserve (NNR). Woods give way to bracken, broom and bramble, before a gate leads to the open hill. The path climbs the slope ahead to a stile and gate at the top.

4 Two paths are waymarked. Take the left-hand one, which runs between a fence and a rim of spectacular dingle on the right.

Climbing away from the dingle, bear right on a grassy ramp before meeting a rutted track. Turn right. As the path climbs you can see the rock tors on the summit. The nearest, isolated from rest, is Shepherd's Rock.

5 Just beyond Shepherd's Rock is a junction marked by a cairn. Turn left here, then, after about 50yds (46m), fork left again. Descend to leave the NNR at a gate and stile. The path runs to the left, shortly bordered by hawthorn hedge. This is an old green lane, variously lined by trees or tumbledown stone wall. It runs through the local nature reserve of Brook Vessons.

6 Keep straight ahead at the NNR sign. At the next junction, fork right to leave the NNR at a gate by a plantation. Go diagonally across the field to a track; turn right, going back across the field, through a plantation, then across pasture on a bridleway.

7 Fork left at the bridleway junction and continue past Lordshill chapel to a lane. Turn right and stay with it as it swings left to reach Snailbeach.

WALK 68

THE LONG MYND: AN ANCIENT SETTLEMENT

The Mynd is a wonderful place and sometimes referred to as the last wilderness in the Midlands. It is liberally dotted with prehistoric remains, including Bronze Age tumuli and dykes, with an Iron Age fort on Bodbury Hill. An ancient road, the Port Way, runs along the top of the Long Mynd and has been in use for 4,000 years.

DISTANCE/TIME 7.5 miles (12.1km) 3h **MAP** OS Explorer 217 The Long Mynd & Wenlock Edge **START** Easthope Road car park, Church Stretton; grid ref: SO 453936 **PATHS** Mostly moorland paths and tracks, 3 stiles **THE PUB** Green Dragon, Ludlow Road, Little Stretton. Tel: 01694 722925

1 Walk up Lion Meadow to High Street and turn right. Turn left at The Square, go past the church and into Rectory Field. Walk to the top left corner, then turn right along a wall and go up into Old Rectory Wood. The path descends to a junction, where you turn right, soon crossing Town Brook. Turn left and climb to a gate on to the Long Mynd.

2 Go forward beside the brook to meet iron railings, then continue in the same direction with the brook on your left. After an almost imperceptible height gain, the path begins to climb more steeply and heads away from the brook. Eventually the path and brook meet up again near the head of the latter.

3 The path crosses the brook. Proceed a further 50yds (46m) to a junction marked by the first in a succession of pink-banded posts. Just follow these posts now, gaining height very gradually again. Ignore branching paths and, after ascending a slight rise, you'll see the summit ahead on the left.

4 Meet an unfenced road about 100yds (91m) left of a junction. Turn left, ignore paths to Townbrook and Little Stretton, and go straight on when the road bends left, joining a bridleway. At the next junction,

turn left to the summit, then keep ahead to the Port Way. Turn right past the site of Pole Cottage.

5 Turn left on a footpath, signposted to Little Stretton. It's a wide rutted track and when it forks, go left – you can see the path ahead, cutting a green swath over the shoulder of Round Hill. Go straight on at a junction, then descend to Cross Dyke (a Bronze Age earthwork). After the dyke, the path ascends briefly but soon levels out, then begins its descent, eventually following a brook to Little Stretton.

6 Cross a footbridge by a ford and turn right on a lane for a few paces. Look out for a footpath on the left. It climbs by a field-edge to the top corner, then turns left, following the top of a steep slope to a pasture. Follow the right-hand edge until the path enters woodland. Descend to Ludlow Road.

7 Immediately join a bridleway next to the footpath. It climbs into woodland, emerging at the far side to meet a track, which soon becomes a road. As it bends to the right there's access left to Rectory Field. Descend to The Square, turn right on High Street and left on Lion Meadow to the car park.

Offa's Dyke

CLOCKWISE FROM TOP LEFT: PONTCYSYLLTE AQUEDUCT, LLANGOLLEN; CASTELL DINAS, DINAS BRAN, LLANGOLLEN; DENBIGH CASTLE; OFFA'S DYKE FOOTPATH AT KNIGHTON

CEIRIOG VALLEY MAP REF 402 F3

'A piece of heaven that has fallen to earth' is how the last British Liberal Prime Minister, Lloyd George, described the Ceiriog Valley. The Ceiriog river, which has its birthplace deep in the heart of the Berwyn Mountains, is a tributary of the Dee. Here, it flows through a pastoral countryside, dotted with farms, that wouldn't go amiss in a Constable landscape. Over the centuries, the valley has provided inspiration for three local bards: Huw Morus (1662–1709), the Reverend Robert Ellis (1812–75) and John Ceiriog Hughes (1832–87).

Glyn Ceiriog is the largest village. It expanded in the 19th century with the mining of slate and other minerals in the area. There are still remnants of a tramway that was built to convey the slate to the main line at Chirk.

Llanarmon Dyffryn Ceiriog is the most beautiful village in the valley, with a church, two old-world pubs and several whitewashed cottages clustering around a picture-postcard square. Lying by the confluence of the Ceiriog and a tributary, the Gwrachen, the village takes its name from the 5th-century missionary, St Garmon. A mound in the churchyard, Tomen Garmon, is a Bronze Age burial mound thought to be the place from where the missionary once stood to preach.

CHIRK MAP REF 402 F3

The border town of Chirk perches on a hillside separating the River Dee from the Ceiriog. It is a 'must' for canal enthusiasts, who can marvel at Thomas Telford's magnificent ten-arched aqueduct, built in 1801 to convey the canal more than 70 feet (21m) above the valley bottom. Alongside, there's an even taller viaduct, built by Henry Robertson in 1840 for the railway. Both were used to carry coal from the once-thriving Flintshire coalfields.

Chirk Castle, which overlooks the town and the Ceiriog Valley, was built in 1310 by Edward I's Justice of Wales, Roger Mortimer, to replace an older, 11th-century wooden motte-and-bailey castle south of the town. The walls have since been decorated by scores of glazed mullioned windows, hiding the stark repressive face those powerful circular towers would have issued.

DENBIGH MAP REF 402 F2

Denbighshire's medieval county town basks in the heart of the Vale of Clwyd, a wide and verdant valley dividing the rolling Clwydian Hills and the foothills of Mynydd Hiraethog's moorland.

Denbigh means 'little fortress', probably referring to the original hilltop castle belonging to the ancient Welsh princes, rather than the large Norman castle you see today. After defeating the Welsh in 1282, Edward I granted the town to Henry de Lacy, who became the first Lord of Denbigh. The castle and its town walls were completed not long afterwards. The fortress would see much action in the years that followed, culminating in a successful six-month siege of Royalist troops during the Civil War. Though the castle was to fall into decay not long afterwards, there's still much to see, including the gatehouse, fronted by two polygonal towers, and walls that give tremendous views of the town, valley and the Clwydian Hills. In the grounds is the 14th-century tower of the otherwise demolished St Hilary's Church, and an old statue believed to be Edward I. It takes very little imagination to conjure up images of how this powerful fortress would have looked.

Beneath the castle, Denbigh has many historical corners and buildings to explore. Narrow ginnels like Back Row thread quietly through the medieval part of the town, revealing buildings from the 15th century. The town also has the remains of a 14th-century Carmelite Friary, and the walls of an unfinished 'cathedral' dreamed up by Dudley, Earl of Leicester, lover of Elizabeth I, but abandoned on his death in 1588.

Denbigh is handily placed for an exploration of the Clwydian Hills, which have long been popular with walkers, who delight in the heather ridges. Moel Famau, which means 'mother mountain', is, at 1,818 feet (554m), the highest of the range. Its summit monument was built in 1810 to celebrate the jubilee of King George III.

KNIGHTON MAP REF 402 F5

Knighton, a country market town, rather affluent in its appearance, lies on the southern bank of the River Teme, surrounded by lovely low, rounded hills. The English border, including the town's hill, Panpunton, lies on the other side of the river. Tref y Clawdd, the Welsh name for Knighton, means town on the dyke, and a motte-and-bailey castle in the heart of town stands squarely on Offa's Dyke, an 8th-century earthwork – the only place where this happens.

The main street ascends gently to a fine Victorian clock tower and then on to Market Street, with Georgian houses and businesses with traditional shopfronts, rather than the brightly coloured plastic panels of the usual high street names.

Knighton has the scant remains of two castles, the open motte at Bryn-y-Castell to the east of town, and the remains of a Norman castle, sacked by Owain Glyndwr, which can just be seen at the back of the fire station. Both are now in private ownership. The town is an excellent base for walking, and the Offa's Dyke Centre can help with information and advice.

For centuries, Welsh warlords had attacked their Anglo Saxon enemies in attempts to force them back across the Marches but in the 8th century, Offa, King of Mercia, decided to settle the disputes. He built a massive earthwork dyke running the full length of Wales, from Prestatyn to Chepstow, intended to mark out the political boundary of his kingdom, beyond which the Welsh were permitted only under strict control. The dyke in these parts is at its grandest, with clear earthwork lines straddling the moors. Today there is a well-established national trail along its length. The Glyndwr's Way, another national trail, also starts here.

LLANGOLLEN MAP REF 402 F3

The self-proclaimed gateway to Wales, Llangollen sits in the fertile and verdant Dee Valley, surrounded by the Llantysilio and Berwyn mountains. The river is at the heart of the town and on any fair day you'll see scores of people congregating around the Elizabethan stone bridge, one of the Seven Wonders of Wales, watching the fast waters bursting over the riverbed rocks.

The bridge was extended in 1863 for the railway line, which linked Wrexham with Barmouth. Following the railway's closure in the 1960s, a preservation society was formed and today steam trains operate the 7.5 miles (12km) to Carrog. The society expects that it will eventually reopen the line to Corwen. Llangollen station is a reminder of days gone by, with its historic steam engines and rolling stock lined up on platforms that are spanned by the original Great Western Railway footbridge.

The Llangollen canal runs parallel to the railway and road. Pioneered by Thomas Telford, it provides another transport leisure link for attractive, horse-drawn narrowboats, which take visitors along the canal and over the Pontcysyllte Aqueduct, where a cast-iron trough carries the canal for 1,007 feet (307m), 120 feet (36m) above the River Dee.

Looking to the skies, you can see the ruffled outlines of castle ruins, once occupied by the Princes of Powys, perched on a limestone knoll above the town. A walk up the hill known as Dinas Bran reveals that the ruins are quite extensive and the views up the Dee Valley are tremendous – far better than the famed Horseshoe Pass, a 4-mile (6.4km) drive away. Behind Dinas Bran are the long, tiered limestone cliffs of Creigiau Eglwyseg. One of the most impressive sights of the region, they stretch to a place called World's End!

Just off the A542 Horseshoe Pass road in the deep, narrow Eglwyseg Valley, lies the ruined abbey of Valle Crucis, a name that means 'valley of the cross'. This was a reference to the cross that used to top the Pillar of Eliseg, a memorial to the 9th-century Prince of Powys. Established in 1201 by Cistercian monks from Strata Marcella near Welshpool, the abbey is sited in fertile pastures beneath a knoll delightfully named the Velvet Hill.

WELSHPOOL MAP REF 402 F4

Set amid Montgomeryshire's rolling verdant hills and wide valley of the River Severn, Welshpool, or Y Trallwng, to give it its Welsh name, has over the centuries become a prosperous and bustling market town. Until 1835 it was known as Pool; some of the old mileposts still refer to it in that way. 'Welsh' was added to the name to distinguish the place from Poole in Dorset. It was the Severn that brought trade to the town, for it was navigable by boat. The Montgomery Canal came to the town in 1797, part of a 33-mile (53km) system from Welsh Frankton in Shropshire to Newtown in Powys. Today's visitor can find out much more at the Powysland Museum and Montgomery Canal Centre, where there is a V-shaped basin used as a winding point and as a base for the Montgomery Canal Cruises.

The pride of Welshpool's town centre is its High Street, a thoroughfare of fine architecture, much dating from the Georgian era, but many much older half-timbered buildings belong to the 16th century. A building with a more dubious past is the Cockpit on New Street, which would have been the popular venue for cockfights until the ban of 1849.

Almost every tourist who comes to Welshpool comes to see Powis Castle, which was built for the warring Princes of Powys in around 1200. A long drive from Park Lane, off the High Street, leads through the fine estate's parklands, past mature oaks and grazing deer to reach the castle. Because of its continuous occupation since 1578, when the ownership passed to the Herbert family, the old fortress has become more of a mansion, with castellated ramparts, tall chimneys, rows of fine leaded windows and fine 17th-century balustraded terraces overlooking manicured lawns and neatly clipped yews. Lead statues of a shepherd and shepherdess keep watch over the many shrubs and perennial borders.

For those wanting to explore the Montgomeryshire hills even further, the Welshpool and Llanfair Light Railway can take you through the picturesque Banwy Valley to Llanfair Caereinion.

HORSESHOE FALLS & THE VELVET HILL

This walk is probably one of the prettiest in North Wales. Though the Horseshoe Falls are an impressive piece of engineering, many visitors feel a bit let down that the falls are just a weir and not nature's own creation. But on Velvet Hill you should see wondrous landscapes in a hundred shades of green.

1 From the car park walk down to the road, turn right for a few paces then descend some steps to the back of the Chain Bridge Hotel. Turn right, to follow the path between the river and the canal. Through a kissing gate at the end of the canal you traverse riverside fields past the Horseshoe Falls. The falls are, in fact, a man-made weir, which was created by Thomas Telford to harness the forceful waters of the Dee in order to feed and control the levels of the Llangollen and Ellesmere canals. From here, climb to Llantysilio church. On reaching the road, turn left through the hamlet of Llantysilio to reach a junction.

2 Continue a few paces further to find a stile on the right and then climb along a rutted track, which keeps a forest to the left, then climbs north on a high pastured hillside.

3 Over a stile at the top of the field, the path swings right, above a plantation. Keep right at a fork and later cross a stile, before eventually descending to cottages at Pen-y-bryn. An enclosed path drops to a stile, which leads out to the Horseshoe Pass road at Britannia Inn.

4 Turn right along the road, then right again when you get to the first junction. At a bend, mount a stile on the left to head south across the fields. Reaching a farm track briefly go right, leaving at a fork over a stile on the left on to a narrow lane. Go left here to meet the Horseshoe Pass road again.

5 Go over a stile on the right-hand side of the road, signposted to the Velvet Hill, and ascend by quarry workings.

6 Later, swing right along a wide grassy track, climbing steeply through bracken to reach the ridge, and go left for the summit.

7 Descend south on a narrow footpath to reach a fence above some woods. Do not cross (as many have done), but follow the fence down, left, to a stile. After crossing the stile go right, along a path that leads back to the lane near the car park.

DISTANCE/TIME 3.5 miles (5.6km) 2h **MAP** OS Explorer 255 Llangollen & Berwyn **START** Picnic site and car park at Llanstysilio Green on minor road north of Berwyn Station; grid ref: SJ 198433 **PATHS** Field paths in valley and on hillside; 10 stiles **THE PUB** Britannia Inn, Horseshoe Pass, Llangollen. Tel: 01978 860144

CEIRIOG VALLEY: IN THE BEAUTIFUL VALLEY

Discover an earthly heaven in one of ancient Clwyd's truly green and pleasant valleys. For 18 miles (29km), from its source on the slopes of Mount Ferna in the Berwyns to its meeting with the Dee, the beautiful Afon Ceiriog meanders through oakwoods, rocky hillsides and fertile cattle pastures.

1 From The Hand, take the eastbound lane past the church and uphill, with a conifer plantation on the right and the pastures of Ceiriog below left.

2 At the far end of the plantation, leave the road for a farm track on the left. This ends at a barn. Keep right of the barn and aim for a gate beyond. Through the gate, maintain your direction, over the shoulder of a grassy knoll, then aim for a stile in the fence ahead. Beyond this, cross another field. Go through a gate, then cross a stile on your right.

3 Bear left, crossing two streamlets to join a track past Ty'n-y-fedw farm. Don't go through the gate, but follow a grass path right, beside a fence, shortly entering a wood.

4 Keep ahead to the far end of the woods. Emerging into a field, follow the grass trod as it curves round to a gate at the top corner. Turn right along a rising farm track, ignoring junctions to reach a lane. Next cross to the ongoing track opposite, which climbs on through high pastures.

5 At a crossroads, turn right along a green track – part of Upper Ceiriog Way. This heads southwest towards a green hill known as Cefn-Hîr-fynydd.

6 After about 300yds (274m) leave the track through a gate on your right. If you head west by the right edge of a rushy area and towards Pen y Glôg's sparse crags, it will be easy to find the small stile in the next fence, then a wooden gate on left soon afterwards. Through the gate head downhill with a faint sheep path to pass a low clump of rocks on your left, and aim for the distant farm of Cyrchynan-isaf.

7 Lower down, a developing grassy track runs on through the valley of Nant y Glôg contouring the lower slopes of Pen y Glôg, eventually reaching a gate.

8 After swinging right with a stream track, it terminates by a lane to the south of Llanarmon Dyffryn Ceiriog. Follow the lane past cottages and a school, to arrive by the Hand Hotel in the village square.

DISTANCE/TIME 3.75 miles (6km) 2h30 **MAP** OS Explorer 255 Llangollen & Berwyn **START** Roadside parking in village; grid ref: SJ 157328 **PATHS** Sketchy paths and farm tracks, 4 stiles **THE PUB** Hand Hotel, Llanarmon Dyffryn Ceiriog. Tel: 01691 600666

Peak District

CLOCKWISE FROM TOP LEFT: ASHFORD IN THE WATER; PAVILION GARDENS, BUXTON; THE OPERA HOUSE, BUXTON; DOVEDALE

Insight
THE RUDDY DUCK

One of Carsington Water's most controversial residents is the American ruddy duck. Just 50 years ago this little duck (it has a big blue bill, white cheeks, a reddish back and a stiff tail) was unknown outside the Wildfowl Trust, but it escaped and is now so widespread that it is threatening to overrun Europe, consequently diluting the genes of its close relative, the European white-headed duck, in the process.

Insight
NATURE RETURNED

Just north of Carsington and Hopton the landscape rises to a 1,000-foot (305m) contour, topped by a stone called King's Chair. This area is pockmarked by old lead mines and limestone quarries, but wild flowers abound on the open limestone and into the Via Gelliae, and in ash woodland there are patches of the rare herb *Paris quadrifolia*.

Visit
CHATSWORTH DEER

The deer at Chatsworth are fallow deer, which were introduced into Britain by the Normans to grace their hunting forests. Fallow differ from the native red and roe deer in having a spotted coat and broad antlers. A visit to Chatsworth's glorious parkland can give the impression of an English version of the African Serengeti, with cattle, sheep and deer instead of wildebeest and impala.

Insight
BILBERRY TIME

Purple bird droppings on moorland walls are a sign that it is bilberry time. Bilberry (blaeberry in Scotland and blueberry in America) grows on the slopes and along the road verges of Beeley Moor. The bell-shaped flowers give way to glorious dark purple berries in July; despite being rather inconspicuous, the fruit bushes are quickly stripped by grouse, foxes and other wild animals.

Activity
WILDLIFE OF THE MOORLAND

Of all the heather moorland in the Peaks the expanse above Beeley is probably the best place for wildlife. This has been due in part to its isolation and lack of access, but now it is possible to explore several of its finest areas without damaging the most sensitive ecological sites.

ASHFORD IN THE WATER
MAP REF 404 D3

Only 2 miles (3.2km) from Bakewell and just off the busy A6, it is a wonder that Ashford in the Water has kept any kind of dignity. In truth it is one of the most attractive and interesting of all the Peak villages, situated on a twist of the River Wye, on the ancient port but bypassed by the new road.

At the middle of Ashford is a green space, called Hall Orchard, once part of the grounds of Neville Hall, a medieval hunting lodge that stood on the eastern side. The space is now a playing field but there are some tall trees, notably limes, and around the rest of the village fine ash trees to offer shelter and shade. 'Oak won't grow in Ashford' goes the local saying, and this has proved true over the years.

The main attraction for visitors to Ashford is the river, crystal clear and full of trout. There is space to wander along the banks, and three bridges, of which two are old. Close to the cricket field, the bridge on the closed road carries an inscription 'M. Hyde 1664'; the brief memorial refers to the Reverend Hyde, who was thrown from his horse and drowned in the river below. Upstream, on an old packhorse trail, is the attractive Sheepwash Bridge; a stone fold on one side shows where the sheep were held before being plunged into the river and made to swim across to clean their fleeces.

BAKEWELL MAP REF 404 D3

Bakewell is always busy with visitors and locals. Its streets are never free of traffic and bustle, but if you accept this from the outset there's every reason to enjoy this town; it is an exciting mixture of old and new, a tourist honeypot that still thrives as a working community.

There are surprisingly few very old buildings considering the rich history of Bakewell (it was granted a market and 15-day fair in 1254), but there are a number of fine 17th-century structures, such as the Market Hall, which serves as the Peak District National Park Information Centre, and the Town Hall. Up the steep road on the west side of the town stands an airy grass-covered knoll on which sits the lovely parish church of All Saints. Like many of the churches in Derbyshire it is broad and low, but with a spire as sharp as a 3H pencil. Inside you will find there are some fascinating fragments of Saxon and Norman stonework, and the famous monument to Sir John Manners and his wife Dorothy, who are reputed to have eloped together from Haddon Hall in 1558. Outside the hall stands the shaft of a 9th-century stone cross, beautifully decorated with vine scrolls and figures.

BUXTON MAP REF 403 J2

Dropping down from the high moors into the elegant spa town of Buxton, on the River Wye, is enough to make anyone blink in disbelief as they find themselves emerging out of the bleak wilderness into a bower of parks and gardens and grand Palladian-style buildings.

Through the centuries health resorts have sprung up in all sorts of unlikely places, and none more so than Buxton. By the 18th century Buxton, in common with other spa towns, was set firmly on the fashion trail. The 5th Duke of Devonshire was responsible for the main wave of building innovation at Buxton. He had been impressed in the 1770s by the Royal Crescent at Bath and was awash with money from his Ecton copper mines. First he had the elegant semicircular Crescent built, complete with 42 pilasters and 378 windows, then the Great Stable with a central court and Tuscan columns, finally followed by Hall Bank and The Square, all built in a grand and imposing style.

In the 19th century the 6th and 7th Dukes carried on the work, so that by late Victorian times the spa in the valley had completely eclipsed the old market town on the upper slope. The Great Stable became the Devonshire Hospital, 'for the use of the sick poor', and was given a massive domed roof 156 feet (47m) across (it is now part of the University of Derby); terraces of hotels and guest houses sprang up to cater for the influx of affluent visitors to the Thermal and Natural Baths; the railways arrived, the beautiful Pavilion Gardens were laid out on the banks of the Wye, and in 1905 the magnificent Opera House was opened.

Surprisingly, the majority of Buxton's fine buildings are still functioning and thriving. The Edwardian Opera House has a full programme, taking advantage of the current renewed interest in opera. Outside is an immaculate square, complete with an ornate Victorian post box, and behind it run the Pavilion Gardens, complete with a Serpentine Walk.

CARSINGTON WATER MAP REF 404 D4

New reservoirs usually take years to blend with a landscape, and sometimes they never do. Carsington, opened by Her Majesty the Queen in 1992, already looks at home in the gently rolling hills southwest of Wirksworth.

Most of the Peak District's many reservoirs gather their water from acid moorland, so they are low in nutrients, and this in turn means they are poor for aquatic plants and animals. However, Carsington is quite different: it is filled largely by water pumped from rivers and so is excellent for wildlife. In the winter there are wildfowl by

the thousand, including wigeon, pochard and tufted duck; in the summer there are great crested grebes and dabchicks; and in the spring and autumn, at migration time, all sorts of waders and seabirds use the reservoir as a rest and refuelling stop on their arduous journeys.

A third of the Carsington shore is set aside as a conservation area, but the rest is accessible by footpath, by bicycle and by horse. The main Visitor Centre is on the west shore, with an extensive car park (pay-and-display) off the B5035.

Hopton village is now dominated by the reservoir, though there is a bypass for the main road. Until 1989, Hopton Hall (not open) was the home of the Gell family, who made their fortune from the nearby limestone quarries, and made their name as scholars, politicians and travellers. Along the limestone rise towards the north runs the Hopton Incline, once the steepest gradient for any standard-gauge railway line in Britain, using fixed engines and cable-haulage to set the High Peak Railway on its journey from Cromford Wharf to Whaley Bridge. It is now the High Peak Trail. Further north again is the Via Gellia, a road created and named by one of the Gells, through flower-rich woodland along a valley west of Cromford.

CHAPEL-EN-LE-FRITH
MAP REF 404 D3

Unfortunately, a pretty name does not always guarantee a pretty, picture-postcard place. The frith, or forest, never really existed here, except to formalize a vast tract of Norman hunting preserve; most of the Derbyshire countryside was open ground rather than woodland.

The most obvious feature of Chapel-en-le-Frith today is its rather dowdy main road, which sweeps south into a hollow and on towards Buxton. A bypass now carries A6 traffic around to the east, but it will take some years for this part of Chapel to brighten up. However, turning off the main road at the white-painted Kings Arms at the top of the town, brings you directly to the market place and a change of character. Lovely cobbled paths and a medieval cross and stocks stand at the heart of the little square, overlooked by a café called The Stocks. Except on market day (Thursday) this is a quiet and out of the way place, perfect for a cup of tea and a wander. Close by is the Roebuck Inn, and a little way further along the street, opposite the church, is what was once the Bull's Head Inn, of which only the sign, a wooden carved life-size shorthorn bull's head, still survives.

St Thomas à Becket Church stands on a grassy knoll overlooking a housing estate. The original chapel in the forest was built here around 1225, but was replaced in the early 14th century by a sturdier structure. Most of what is visible today is from the refurbishment of 1733, but there are hints of antiquity all around; the shaft of a Saxon cross, a weathered sundial, and a view across what must have been glorious hunting country, to the scenic crag-fringed edges of Combs Moss.

CHATSWORTH MAP REF 404 D3

Towards the end of the 17th century, William Cavendish, the 4th Earl of Devonshire and soon to be made the 1st Duke for his part in putting William of Orange on the throne, decided his house needed a radical new look. For a while he tinkered with alterations, but finally knocked everything down and started again. Demolishing one great historic house to build another might seem an odd investment of a lifetime, but in those days great families were judged by their homes and gardens; fashion and taste was everything.

The Chatsworth House that rose from the rubble of the Elizabethan mansion was of a classical, Palladian style, to the duke's own design. It took about 30 years to complete and it set the seal on his new status – even some of the window frames were gilded on the outside. The irony is that he never saw it at its best. Great houses needed great gardens and grounds, and these took decades to establish. In the middle of the 18th century, 'Capability' Brown and James Paine laid the foundations of what we see today by altering the course of the river, building bridges and setting out woodland.

The house is bursting with great works of art in the most superb settings; the Painted Hall is a work of art in itself, with huge, swirling scenes from the life of Julius Caesar, by Louis Laguerre, on the ceiling and upper part of the walls. Splendour follows splendour as you progress through the house (a tour of about a third of a mile/500m), but one of the most engaging features is the wonderful painting of a violin on the inner door of the State Music Room.

None can deny the magnificence of the house itself; from any direction it looks majestic, and from the southwest, approaching Edensor on a sunny evening, it can be breathtaking. On the horizon to the east are the high gritstone moors; in the middle distance are tiers of woodland, melting into ribbons and stands of beech and oak and rolling parkland; and in the foreground winds the Derwent. The front of the house reflects the peach-glow of evening sunlight to perfection; around it are superb formal gardens and the fine Emperor fountain. This is a view that the 1st Duke could only have dreamed about.

The Chatsworth Estate stretches far and wide and includes grouse moors, working farmland and estate villages. Of the villages, Edensor catches the eye first. Until the 1830s, the village stood a little closer to the river but the 6th Duke had it moved further back, out of sight. The new houses were a hotchpotch of styles; Italian, Swiss, almost anything but vernacular English. Only one house of the original village remains, called Park Cottage, but known at one time as Naboth's Vineyard. The biblical reference relates to the owner in 1838, who is supposed to have refused to sell or be relocated. Just 1 mile (1.6km) to the northwest lies Pilsley, more compact than Edensor, with the Chatsworth Farm Shop, a pub and a microbrewery.

Just outside the Chatsworth Estate to the south, but within its influence and historic ownership, lies Beeley. This old working village, tucked neatly away and with many of the elements of a much older settlement, has quite a refreshing character. A tannery once stood beside the brook, and there was an estate-built school and a barn to house the coal wagons that supplied the Chatsworth estate glasshouses with fuel.

DOVEDALE MAP REF 404 D3

Dovedale's Stepping Stones appear on a thousand postcards and attract a million visitors. The Dove flows for 45 miles (72.4km), but only a short section of it is called Dovedale; above the Viator Bridge it becomes Mill Dale, then Wolfscote Dale and then Beresford Dale. But it is to the gorge of Dovedale that the visitors flock, for within the space of a few miles of easy riverside walking, on a broad level path, there are superb craggy rocks and pillars (all named) rising out of dense ash woodland, sweeps of open pasture, banks of flowers, fine cascades of spring water and dark caves. There is no road, and only one main path, following the east (Derbyshire) bank. It is not even necessary to cross the stepping stones upstream from the car park on the Staffordshire side of the river, because there is a footbridge a few yards away.

EYAM MAP REF 404 D3

Disease was a fact of life in medieval England, and many of the Peak villages suffered the horrors of Black Death and plague. What made the weaving village of Eyam special was the attempt by the local rector, William Mompesson, to keep the outbreak in 1665–66 within the confines of the community. The whole village was put in quarantine, entire families tragically perished and Eyam became a byword for tragedy and self-sacrifice.

Eyam today is neither a sad place nor dwelling in the past. It stands on the hill brow between Middleton Dale and Eyam Moor. Visitors are impressed by the Saxon cross in St Lawrence's churchyard and come to enjoy the traditional well dressing and the sheep roast.

BAKEWELL

GLOSSOP MAP REF 404 D2

Textiles breathed life into Glossop; there was water power and coal a-plenty and a workforce who came from Stockport and Manchester. At the turn of the 19th century there were more than 56 mills in the eight townships of Glossopdale; most were cotton mills, but there were also paper mills, ropewalks and woollen mills. Not many thrived; those that did modernized with the times and took to power looms, which were steam-driven and needed more water and more coal.

Glossop suffered disastrously when the cotton industry collapsed in the 1920s, and it took decades to recover. Overspill housing from the 1960s has affected the character of the town too, but there are some fascinating nooks and crannies, hidden away in the fabric of the place.

GOYT VALLEY

Just beyond the housing estate of Gamesley lies the remains of the Agricolan Roman fort of Melandra Castle, whilst to the north of the town, near Howard Park, is Mouselow or Castle Hill, with important Bronze Age and Iron Age associations and the site of a motte-and-bailey built by William de Peverel. Glossop's roads to the east lead to Longdendale and the Snake Pass, whilst only a few miles to the west is the M67 and Manchester.

GOYT VALLEY MAP REF 404 D3

The River Goyt meets the River Tame in Stockport, to form the famous River Mersey. Its upper and middle reaches cleave a deep, gorge-like valley through some of the most accessible moorland in the Peak District. This is an area that is threaded with byroads, pack-horse trails and old railway tracks, a place where Cheshire meets Derbyshire amidst a blaze of heather and bilberry-strewn uplands.

The Goyt River flows from south to north; it rises on the slopes of Cat and Fiddle Moor, a wild and windswept place with a reputation for having the worst weather. The moor is named after the Cat and Fiddle Inn; at 1,690ft (515m) it is the second-highest pub in England. Like other high-altitude hostelries, such as The Snake or Tan Hill, it was built in the turnpike era at the start of the 19th century and is still a welcome sight for traffic on the sinuous A537. There are few other buildings to be seen for miles around, but some facilities are available at Derbyshire Bridge, which is the usual starting point to explore the Goyt Valley. The bridge is closed to traffic on Bank Holidays and Sundays during the summer.

HATHERSAGE MAP REF 404 D3

Stanage Edge divides featureless moorland from the verdant Derwent. Prehistoric pathways, Roman roads and packhorse trails criss-cross the moors and converge below the confluence of the Derwent and the Noe. On the raised south-facing shoulder of the valley lies Hathersage ('Heather's Edge'), a village built on passing trade and farming. Millstones were a speciality in the 18th century, hewn directly from quarry faces. Then came the Industrial Revolution and five mills were built, to make pins and needles. The mills had a short life, as did the men who ground the needle-points and had to breathe in the dust.

The most interesting buildings in Hathersage are along the main road and off School Lane. Past 15th-century Hathersage Hall and Farm, and up the narrow Church Bank, it is possible to walk around Bank Top, a green knoll overlooking the alder-lined Hood Brook and valley. The church crouches on the grassy brow. To the south stands Bell House and The Bell Room, once an inn and barn beside the village green and stocks; to the west stands the Vicarage, and to the east is Camp Green, the ramparts of a 9th-century stockade.

HAYFIELD MAP REF 404 D2

The picturesque name and rural setting disguise Hayfield's industrial past; the village once hummed and rattled to the sound of cotton and paper mills, calico printing and dye works. It has also resounded to marching feet and cries of protest – in 1830 a mob of 1,000 mill workers gathered to demand a living wage and were dispersed by hussars. Eleven men appeared at Derby Assizes as a result, but the cotton industry was in terminal decline and all the anger was in vain. A century later, on 24 April 1932, Hayfield was the starting point for the 'mass trespass' of ramblers onto Kinder Scout. This protest eventually resulted in 'the right to roam'.

Hayfield is a peaceful little village, catering for tourists of all kinds. It has plenty of little cafés and restaurants with quaint and inventive names. One of the most revealing places to while away a few minutes is by the bridge, next to the courtyard of the Royal Hotel, which looks out over the River Sett, from the war memorial to the jumble of cottages and sloping roofs at the back of Church Street. Nearby is St Matthew's Church, built on the foundations of an older church washed away in a flood.

Serious walkers head east out of the village, up and over the green foothills to the russet expanse of the Kinder plateau. Families and other easy-going ramblers head west along the Sett Valley Trail towards New Mills. The car park at the start of this 3-mile (4.8km) trail, separated from the main village by the A624, was once the railway station, and the trail follows the course of the single-track line. In its heyday, thousands of visitors arrived here from Manchester via the New Mills branch line; Hayfield marked the end of the mill towns and therefore the start of the countryside.

HOLMFIRTH MAP REF 407 H7

Before the BBC television series *Last of the Summer Wine* became a national institution, the most famous comic characters to come out of Holmfirth were depicted on postcards published by Bamforths. Saucy seaside cartoons became a serious business for the family firm just after World War I; they had already pioneered lantern slides and the motion picture industry but were outflanked in the end by Hollywood.

The town of Holmfirth is a gem, built at the confluence of the Holme and the Ribble, where the Norman Earl Warren built a corn mill. For several centuries the lower valley was left to the woods and the hilltop towns of Cartworth, Upperthong and Wooldale prospered, combining farming with weaving. There are fine stone farmhouses and cottages on the upper slopes of the valley, often absorbed into the outskirts of the newer town. With the expansion of the cotton mills in the mid-19th century, tiers of three-storey terraced cottages sprang up lower and lower into the valley and eventually cotton mills crowded the riverside.

HOPE MAP REF 404 D3

The Hope Valley is the main access route from the Derwent Valley through to

HOPE

Castleton, Edale and the Dark Peak, so the road is often busy. The little village of Hope lies at the confluence of the Noe and the Peakshole Water, which emerges from the bowels of the earth 2 miles (3.2km) away at Castleton. Hope railway station lies half a mile (800m) out of the village, across the Noe to the east, and is a perfect starting point for a walk up Win Hill, one of the best bracing viewpoints in the whole Peak. Lose Hill, the dark twin of Win Hill and another fine viewpoint, lies due west on the opposite side of the Noe.

Hope Church is in the heart of the village and is a typically squat-spired affair, dating from the 14th century. Inside there are two stone coffin lids bearing hunting horns, the motif of royal forest huntsmen. Outside, next to the porch, is the shaft of a Saxon cross with weathered carvings on its face. Scrollwork on preaching crosses represents the height of Dark Age culture.

LANGSETT MAP REF 404 D2
The northeast corner of the Peaks is probably the least visited sweep of country for 50 miles (80km) around; driving south from Holmfirth or west from Penistone takes you across open moors and plateaux, with the whole of Yorkshire spread out below in a cerulean haze. There are very few villages to catch your immediate attention, but the upper valleys of the Don

and the Porter, which rise up to the same watershed as the Derwent on Howden Moor, are full of interest. The Porter has been dammed in several places above Stocksbridge and there are good access points to the reservoirs and riverside, and high up onto the moors.

Heading out from the car park it is possible to explore the woodlands and shoreline of Langsett Reservoir or walk along the dam wall, past the crenellated valve tower (a miniature of a tower at Lancaster Castle), to the old stone-built hamlet of Upper Midhope.

Above Langsett Reservoir, the Brook House Bridge gives access to the ancient trackway of the Cut Gate, an old drovers' road which started at Derwent and leads all the way to Penistone. The track climbs south over Midhope Moor, which is uncompromising high ground inhabited mostly by mountain hares and short-eared owls, littered with ancient flints and overlooked by the burial mound of Pike Lowe. This is not a good place to get caught in bad weather.

LONGDENDALE MAP REF 404 D2
Above Glossop, a cleft in the most desolate wilderness of Peak moorland runs north by northeast from the little town of Tintwistle to the Derbyshire-Yorkshire border, shielding the A628 as it climbs to

Gallows Moss. Down the cleft runs the River Etherow, a tributary of the Mersey. Over a century ago the valley was dammed to create five reservoirs, and this has so altered the character of the place that it sometimes looks like an oasis in a desert; green woodland and pasture encircles pools of silver, over which white sailing dinghies pirouette and scud.

Longdendale is a favourite place for day trips out of Manchester, and the cultural roots of Tintwistle are entwined with the old Lancashire cotton mills. The waters of the Etherow were harnessed to power the mills and were dammed to provide water for the city. A wealth of railway lines were laid to link the great industrial cities of Manchester and Sheffield, following the valley up to Woodhead and the Prough, a 3-mile (4.8km) tunnel below the moors. But now all that is in the distant past; the weavers' cottages of Tintwistle are now picturesque and the course of the railway is a footpath. Nevertheless, the dale still serves the city in its own way and remains part of its heritage.

The graveyard of lonely Woodhead Chapel, set on a shoulder above the banks of the upper reservoir, contains the last resting place of navvies and their families who died of cholera while the second railway tunnel was being built in 1849. Crowden, above Torside Reservoir,

is a famous youth hostel on the route of the Pennine Way and is a welcome sight for walkers after the rigours of Bleaklow to the south or Black Hill to the north. Apart from a few isolated farms and an Information Centre, there are no other settlements in the valley.

LYME PARK MAP REF 404 C3
Lyme Park (National Trust), on the western edge of the Peak District, is a modest mirror image of Chatsworth. The imposing hall is a leading example of the Palladian style, the work of the Italian architect, Giacomo Leoni, in the 1720s; it featured as 'Pemberley' in the BBC adaptation of Jane Austen's Pride and Prejudice. The interior, a heady mix of Elizabethan and later, houses remarkable Mortlake tapestries and the Lyme Caxton Missal prayer book.

Lyme was the home of the Legh family for 600 years and has sufficient style to make it one of the top visitor attractions in the area, set in a rural idyll of gardens, parkland and moorland, yet only a stone's throw from Stockport. Those who prefer outdoor attractions to the splendours of the stately home will enjoy the wildfowl on the lake and herds of red and fallow deer among the trees. The 1,300-acre (520ha) park also has excellent short walks and viewpoints: a modest alternative to the high hills if the weather is closing in.

MANIFOLD VALLEY

MANIFOLD VALLEY MAP REF 404 D3

The Manifold and the Dove rise within a mile (1.6km) of each other, below Axe Edge. As they head southeast together into limestone country, side-winding like pulled strands of wool, one is transmuted into a Staffordshire valley, the other into a Derbyshire dale.

The difference between the valley and the dale in landscape terms is quite minimal; they both cut a course through superb scenery, meeting finally at the village of Ilam, yet the Manifold Valley escaped all the Victorian hype and the more carnival atmosphere of Dovedale.

Wetton and Warslow villages, on the 1,000-foot (305m) contour on opposite sides of the valley, are the main access points for the most dramatic section of the Manifold. Neither makes very much concession to tourists, though both have good pubs (the Olde Royal Oak and the Greyhound). Warslow has a utilitarian look, as do its medieval iron stocks close to the school. It is an estate village of the Crewe family (of Calke Abbey, south of Derby) and lies at the very foot of the gritstone moors. Access to the moors can be reached by driving along the side road to the northwest. The village of Wetton is on the limestone, surrounded by dairy farms and barns, but its stout church and many of its cottages look as if they really belong amongst the heather.

A steep side road north of Warslow off the B5053 drops down to Ecton, and the most beautiful section of the valley begins. It runs southwards along a thin strip of level meadow, with steep, flower-studded, almost alpine-looking grassland on either side. The road, and what is now the Manifold Trail, follows the route of the Leek and Manifold Valley Light Railway, which opened in 1904 but only survived for 30 years; according to expert judgement it opened too late and closed too soon – if its odd Indian-style engines were still running today, the line would make a fortune!

Close by to Wettonmill, the Manifold usually disappears down swallow-holes, travelling all the rest of the way to Ilam underground. Meanwhile, the Manifold's tributary, the Hamps, heads southwards and the Manifold Trail stays with the old railway line, going along the Hamps to the large village of Waterhouses.

Once out of the depth of the valley, the steep limestone hill slopes are pockmarked with deep caves. The most famous and dramatic is Thor's Cave but Ossom's Cave and Elderbush have been explored or excavated and have produced items from the Stone and Bronze Ages, when this was good hunting country. All the domed hills, which are called Lows, are capped by cairns or barrows and it is very easy on the dry 'karst' hillsides to imagine yourself in another older world.

MATLOCK MAP REF 404 D3

Matlock is a tourist honeypot, but there is more to it than the fairy lights and family attractions. Old Matlock stands on the east bank of the Derwent, before it twists west, under the bridge. St Giles Church, the Rectory and Wheatsheaf House mark an original lead-mining settlement at the meeting of packhorse trails and turnpikes. Next door, Matlock Bath is the home of the Peak District Mining Museum, which incorporates Temple Mine, an old lead and restored fluorspar mine, with a self-guided tour that depicts its geology, mineralisation and mining techniques.

Matlock Bath started as a petrifying well and tufa quarry, but in 1696 a bath was cut into the encrusted limestone and a spa was born. In the 18th and early 19th century, the cream of society took the waters, staying in fashionable hotels on the sides of the gorge. Then, in 1849, the railway arrived and the place was swamped by day-trippers.

MILLER'S DALE MAP REF 404 D3

The River Wye rises at Buxton but then flows east to dissect the limestone plateau. Each reach of the river has its own character, and each section of the narrow valley or dale has its own name. Thus Wye Dale turns into Chee Dale, which gives way to Miller's Dale, then Water-cum-Jolly Dale and Monsal Dale. In many respects

Miller's Dale, to either side of Litton Mill, is the most impressive and complete dale to visit. Not only does the Wye negotiate a barrage of natural obstacles here, side-stepping hills, twisting through gaps and gorges and rock faces, but also there are mill races and weirs where the power of the water has been diverted to drive 19th-century cotton mills (Litton and Cressbrook, a little way further downstream). A recreational footpath, the Monsal Trail, runs the length of the dale, allowing access to the old mill yards (some of the buildings are still in use, but not for weaving). There are footbridges at either end of Miller's Dale, allowing access to convenient car parks.

THE ROACHES MAP REF 404 D3

There are few real peaks in the Peak District (the name is derived from the Old English *pecsaetan*, meaning hill-dwellers), but the most elegant and craggy-topped are in the far west: Hen Cloud, Ramshaw Rocks and The Roaches. They are gritstone outcrops, similar to those in the Dark Peak and Eastern Moors, but here they were more heavily contorted or squashed together, leading to a landscape of misfit valleys, steep slopes and rock faces rather than plateau moorland.

Ramshaw Rocks are probably the best-known outlier of the Roaches, because they tower above the roadside on the A53, north of Leek, and have a face-like formation. The A53 and the quiet winding roads to the west of Axe Edge lead to some interesting places.

Axe Edge itself is too high to be anything but wild. One notable village tucked away just off the main road is Flash. It is claimed to be the highest village in England at 1,518 feet (463m). The River Dane rises nearby, jinking a course between hills and ridges and flowing southwest to Gradbach and Danebridge: this is thoroughly delightful countryside, full of trees and meadows, old barns and cowslip banks.

The Roaches ridge lies a few miles to the southwest of Flash and runs northwest–southeast, its main rock-climbing exposures facing the setting sun. A footpath follows the crest of the ridge, linking with Back Forest, creating a 4-mile (6.4km) ridge walk.

SNAKE PASS MAP REF 404 D2

Weather warnings on television and radio have made Snake Pass famous; when the sun is shining across the rest of the Pennines, Snake Pass (the A57 between Sheffield and Manchester) may be closed because of severe blizzards.

The road from Ladybower and the Woodlands Valley strikes northwest, sheltered on a shoulder of the River

Ashop, but after Lady Clough it has nowhere to hide and crosses a windswept desert at 1,680 feet (512m). Bleaklow lies to the north, Kinder Scout to the south. In places, the peat has been stripped away to reveal a surface of shattered stones, which is how the glaciers left the place after the last Ice Age. It is bleak; there are no trees, no barns and no walls.

Of course, the remote wildness of Snake Pass is irresistible and in fine weather it can be magical. The upper Woodlands Valley is pretty, dotted with old farms and birch-lined cloughs. There are two or three farms and cottages on the Snake Road before you reach the lonely Snake Pass Inn. At the top of Lady Clough, on the highest and most featureless ground, Snake Pass is crossed by the Pennine Way, close to the paved trackway of ancient Doctor's Gate. Travellers have been apprehensively venturing across these moors for thousands of years.

The Snake Inn was built in 1821 as Lady Clough House, when the original medieval track was turned into a turnpike road. If you should need to see how remote this hostelry is, there is a milestone outside the inn that records the 21 miles (34km) to Manchester and 17 miles (27km) to Sheffield. The low stone-built inn is an ideal place to stop for refreshment. Food is served most days of the week and accommodation is available.

STANTON IN PEAK MAP REF 404 D3

Stanton village is a ribbon of cottages on a steep and winding side road, built out of the limestone and below the brow of the gritstone, sheltered from the moor by old quarries and a swathe of tall sweet-chestnut trees. The initials WPT, carved into the lintels of many doorways, refer to William Thornhill, who built most of the village in the 1830s and whose family lived at Stanton Hall. The 18th-century Flying Childers Inn celebrates the greatest racehorse of its day, trained by Sir Hugh Childers for the 4th Duke of Devonshire. Opposite the inn is Holly House, which still has half of its windows blocked up to avoid the 1697 window tax.

Birchover Lane, running to the south of Stanton, follows along the western edge of the moor. Pathways trail through birch scrub and over carpets of heather and bilberry to the Bronze Age landscape. About 70 barrows, or burial cairns, have been identified on the small island of gritstone. The biggest, covering the site of twelve cremations, still stands 5 feet (1.5m) tall, inside a double ring of stones with an outer diameter of 54 feet (16.4m). There are three stone circles or monuments on Stanton Moor; the most famous is the Nine Ladies.

THE ROACHES

ARBOR LOW

Visit
ARBOR LOW'S ANCIENT STONES
Some 3 miles (4.8km) along the Long Rake west of Youlgreave, off the road to the left and easily accessible from a car park, is the famous henge of Arbor Low, probably built by the Beaker People in around 2000 BC. The whole monument, with a rock-cut ditch, a bank and a circle of 47 stones, measures 250 feet (76.2m) across. Although the massive stone blocks are all lying flat and some half buried, Arbor Low is still a powerfully atmospheric place, especially in winter sunlight.

Activity
TEGG'S NOSE
& THE GRITSTONE TRAIL
The best introduction to the Cheshire slice of the Peak landscape is from Tegg's Nose Country Park, along Buxton Old Road to the east of Macclesfield. There are superb views from the Windy Way car park, and walks along a network of tracks and pathways, by the old quarry or down through woodland to the reservoirs above Langley. It is possible at this point to join the Gritstone Trail, a pleasant waymarked footpath running the length of Cheshire, from Lyme Park to Mow Cop.

WHALEY BRIDGE MAP REF 404 D3
This little town grew up with dust on its face and Goyt water in its veins. Coal and textiles provided the only gainful work – both have now gone. These days there is hardly a whisper of past industry and employment is more varied. Visitors call in on their way to the Goyt Valley or the Peak Forest Canal.

The basin in the town is engaging, but the true glory of the waterway is at Buxton, 0.5 mile (800m) to the east, where an extraordinary canal and tramroad interchange has been restored. The canal was built to convey limestone from nearby upland quarries to Manchester, while the rock was processed at Buxton.

South of the town is Toddbrook Reservoir, built to feed the Peak Forest Canal, and tiny Taxal village clustered around its church. Inside St James's are memorials to the Jodrell family, and a monument to Michael Heathcote, 'Gentleman of the Pantry and Yeoman of the Mouth to His Late Majesty King George the Second'. Heathcote lived to be 75 years old, so presumably nobody tried to poison the king during his time as official food-taster.

WILDBOARCLOUGH MAP REF 404 C3
Only a few outbuildings remain of the Crag Mills that once made this valley have the hum of a minor industrial centre, which employed more than 600 people. The mills here specialized in the bleaching, printing and dyeing of cotton, then later carpets.

Along the valley today you'll find that most traces of the village's industrial heritage are camouflaged green. There are shrub-covered foundations, grassy trackways and mossy walls. The stream boasts pretty waterfalls and deep pools and is the territory of dippers and grey wagtails. The impression is of a rural backwater, at the foot of Shutlingsloe, the 'Cheshire Matterhorn'.

YOULGREAVE MAP REF 404 D3
A long, handsome village on the shoulder of Bradford Dale, Youlgreave (known as Pommie by most locals) has one of the most elaborate well-dressing ceremonies in the Peak District, taking place at Midsummer each year, when five wells are dressed (or decorated) with biblical scenes. The White Peak tradition has its roots in the days when wells were essential and were blessed to give thanks for water. However, in the case of Youlgreave the records only go back to 1829, coinciding with the provision of the village's own public water supply via a conduit from the Dale below. The water was gathered in a huge circular stone tank called The Fountain, which stands in the middle of the village. Nearby, on the opposite side of the street, is the Co-op

building, which once had a vital role in the social survival of the area but is now a youth hostel.

On the east side of Youlgreave, by the road which then sweeps down to Alport, stands All Saints Church. Essentially Norman and with an unusually broad nave, the most obvious feature of All Saints is its 14th-century tower, chunky and stylish in the best Perpendicular tradition. Inside are sturdy columns and a 13th-century font, unique in that it has two bowls, and the fine monuments include a tiny effigy of Thomas Cokayne, who died in 1488. The church was restored in 1870 and has some beautiful stained-glass windows by Burne-Jones and Kempe.

Three bridges cross the River Bradford below Youlgreave, including a clapper bridge of stone slabs and also a packhorse bridge, which is now used as a footbridge. The short walk to the confluence with the Lathkill is popular, but by turning southeast, over the main bridge and on to the Limestone Way, you can explore the fine countryside towards Birchover, past the Iron Age hill-fort of Castle Hill and the Nine Stones Close (four stones are still standing tall), to the rock tors of Robin Hood's Stride, Cratcliffe Rocks and Rowtor Rocks. Pagan myths, hermits' caves and a popular dining pub, the Druid Inn, are among the attractions of this magical corner of the Peak.

WOLFSCOTE & A RAILWAY TRAIL

The first part of this very enjoyable walk winds through the scenic Wolfscote Dale and Biggin Dale, and you'll be walking through the heart of the upland limestone country. The return route is an easy-paced one, using the Tissington Trail, which ambles quietly over the high pastures of Biggin and Alsop moors.

DISTANCE/TIME 7.5 miles (12.1km) 4h30 **MAP** OS Explorer OL24 White Peak **START** Tissington Trail pay car park at Alsop Old Station; grid ref: SK 156549 **PATHS** Path can be tricky in wintry conditions. Generally well-defined paths, limestone dale sides can be slippery after rain. Quite a few stiles **THE PUB** Waterloo Inn, Biggin-by-Hartington. Tel: 01298 84284

1 From the car park, cross the busy A515 road and follow Milldale Road immediately opposite. After a junction you are offered a parallel footpath on the left, keeping you safe and away from the traffic.

2 On reaching the bottom of the dale by Lode Mill, turn right along the footpath, tracing the river's east bank through a winding, partially wooded valley.

3 Ignore the footpath on the right at Coldeaton Bridge, but instead stay with Wolfscote Dale, beneath thickly wooded slopes on the right. Beyond a stile the woods cease and the dale becomes bare and rock-fringed, with a cave on the right and the bold pinnacles of Peaseland Rocks ahead. Here, the valley sides open out into the dry valley of Biggin Dale, where this route goes next.

4 The signposted path into Biggin Dale begins beyond a stile in a cross-wall and climbs by that wall. It continues through scrub woodland and beneath limestone screes. Beyond a gate you enter a nature reserve.

5 There's another gate at the far end of the nature reserve. Beyond it the dale curves left and then right, before dividing again beneath the hill pastures of Biggin Grange. We divert left here, over a stile, to follow the footpath signposted to Hartington. On the other side of the wall there's a concrete dewpond.

6 After 200yds (183m) there's another junction of paths. This time ignore the one signposted to Hartington and keep walking straight on, following the path to Biggin. It stays with the valley round to the right, passing a small sewage works (on the left) before climbing out of the dale to reach the road at Dale End.

7 Turn right along the road for a few paces then left, following a road past the Waterloo Inn and through Biggin village.

8 Continue up the road to the old railway bridge and here join the Tissington Trail. Follow this old trackbed southwards across the pastures of Biggin and Alport moors. After 2 miles (3.2km), you reach the car park at the former Alsop Station.

WALK 72

LONGNOR & HOLLINSCLOUGH

Longnor developed as a meeting place on the ancient trade routes and, on this route you ramble over hills and dales once trodden by television's fictitious doctors in the television hit drama from the 1990s, *Peak Practice*.

DISTANCE/TIME 6 miles (9.7km) 4h **MAP** OS Explorer OL24 White Peak **START** Longnor market square; grid ref: SK 089649 **PATHS** Some on road, otherwise good footpaths. Can be muddy **THE PUB** Crewe and Harpur Arms, Longnor. Tel: 01332 700641

1 From the square, take the road towards Buxton. Take the first right to turn into Church Street, and then go immediately left, up a lane and right up steps to the footpath. Follow the waymarkers, behind some houses, over a stile and along a wall. Cross another stile, go downhill and turn left on to a farm road.

2 At a fork, go left, then turn right on to the road. Just before the bend towards the bottom of the hill, take the farm road on the left. At the end, continue through a gate on to the footpath, through a gap stile, downhill, across a bridge and continue straight ahead. Eventually, cross a stile and turn left on to the road.

3 Fork left on to a farm road, following the waymarked path. Cross a bridge by a ford and turn left to follow the river bank to the road. Turn right through Hollinsclough, following the road to the right and uphill. Turn right on to a bridleway, through a gate and downhill.

4 After 50yds (46m) fork left by two stones and continue along the flank of the hill. Cross a stile, then, at a stone wall, fork left and uphill. At the top turn left at a stone gatepost, through Moorside Farm, through a kissing gate to the road. Turn right, then cross a stile to a public footpath on the left.

5 Go downhill to a stream and cross a stile to the left of the ditch. Head uphill, through a stile in the wire fence, through a gap in the wall and round the field to a gap stile. Turn back towards Willshaw Farm, then left on to the well-signposted footpath towards Hill Top Farm.

6 Follow the path over stiles and past the farm to the road. Go left, then take the farm road on the right. Approaching the farm go right, steeply downhill, over a stile and follow the path along the wall. Just before the stream, cross a stile on the left and head uphill to the left of some trees.

7 Continue walking uphill, through a gate in a stone wall to some ruined buildings. Follow the track to the next farm, bear left after the barn, then go left on to a footpath uphill.

8 Go through a stile, follow the wall uphill, over two stiles to the road. Turn left then right towards Longnor. Just before the road bends left, cross a stile on the right, go downhill and over several stiles to a farm road. Turn right and follow this back to the village.

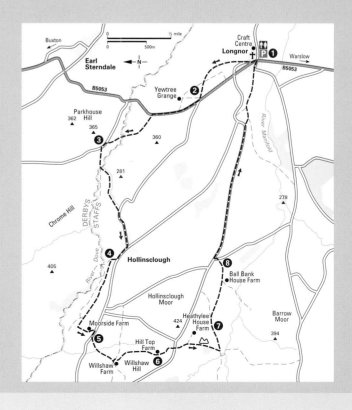

A BUXTON FIGURE OF EIGHT

An attraction in its own right, the town of Buxton lies at the heart of some outstanding countryside. There are high roads with magnificent views that radiate away from the town centre. This tour makes the most of the town's situation with a figure-of-eight route, out on the shoulder of the Goyt, back via Chapel-en-le-Frith and Dove Holes, then out again on the dramatic Axe Edge road and down towards Leek, before returning through quiet rolling farmland.

Route Directions

1 From Buxton, just above the Opera House, take the A5004 uphill towards Whaley Bridge, rising for a mile (1.6km) through woodland and then over moorland. After another half mile (800m) a cairn on the right marks the National Park boundary. Continue for 2.5 miles (4km) along the shoulder of the valley to the Upper Hall lay-by (wonderful views). Drive on for another 2 miles (3.2km), through Fernilee to the outskirts of Whaley Bridge, where you turn right along the B5470, signed 'Chapel-en-le-Frith'. Pass by The Board pub and on for another 3 miles (4.8km), through Tunstead Milton to enter Chapel-en-le-Frith. Turn off at the Kings Arms, on the left, if you want to explore the centre of this old town.

2 Drive along the B5470 through Chapel-en-le-Frith for another mile (1.6km), past the Old Packhorse Inn on the left, then turn left following the sign for the A6 and Buxton. Go under the flyover and then turn right to join the A6, along a wooded valley for 2 miles (3.2km) to Dove Holes.

The workaday quarry village hides the site of a prehistoric henge. Despite the noise from the quarries and traffic from the A6, you'll doubtless find the remains impressive.

3 Continue on the A6 for 3 miles (4.8km) to Fairfield, a pretty village on the outskirts of Buxton. The road descends into the middle of Buxton; at the bottom, follow the signs for the A53 to Leek, via four roundabouts that are well signed, with the landmark dome of the former Devonshire Hospital to your right. Begin the second loop of the tour by following the A53 towards Leek, passing the Pavilion Gardens situated on your left. Continue uphill out of town for 2 miles (3.2km), through traffic lights and out on to open hilltops – the start of Axe Edge. The Dove and Manifold rivers rise here. The road gradually descends past a side road to Flash and out of Derbyshire into Staffordshire, then continues on for about 3 miles (4.8km) to Ramshaw Rocks on the right.

Ramshaw Rocks include a feature which looks like a face; The Winking Man appears to wink at you if you drive north.

4 Continue on the A53 for another 1.5 miles (2.4km), down to Upper Hulme and Blackshaw Moor, and off the high moorland.

In 2 miles (3.2km) pass the delightful Moss Rose Inn on the outskirts of Leek, then in less than half a mile (800m) turn left onto Springfield Road, signed for Ashbourne and Derby. Shortly you will reach a junction with the A523; turn right here to visit Leek or left to continue the tour.

Leek is a thriving market town and antiques centre, with a pretty Market Place. Built on a hill overlooking the River Churt, Leek is also called 'The Queen of the Moorlands' although it is somewhat overlooked now in favour of its much larger neighbouring town, Stoke.

5 Head uphill through rolling pastureland for 2.5 miles (4km) and pass a turn to the RSPB Nature Reserve of Combes Valley, then on for 1.5 miles (2.4km) to Bottom House crossroads and the Green Man Inn. Turn left along the B5053 signed for Longnor and continue for 1.5 miles (2.4km) through Onecote. After 2.5 miles (4km) the road twists down to cross the pretty Warslow Brook, a tributary of the Manifold, then rises for a mile (1.6km) to the village of Warslow. Continue along the B5053 for 4 miles (6.4km), crossing the River Manifold before climbing sharply into Longnor.

Longnor is a compact and attractive village surrounded by farming country. Once an important centre for market trade, Longnor makes a pleasant stop in the Staffordshire Moorlands. It has some interesting buildings, constructed of stone mined locally, which include the Victorian market hall and the Norman church.

6 Go ahead and left, up out of the village (between the stores and The Horseshoe pub), cresting a ridge in 0.5 miles (800m) – beware of the traffic lights – before crossing the River Dove at Glutton Bridge, back into Derbyshire. The landscape changes quite abruptly as the road follows a limestone gorge (Glutton Dale) for half a mile (800m) up to a crossroads (Dalehead to the left, Earl Sterndale to the right). Keep driving ahead here; the road shortly curves to the left across a steep slope and rises to a crest before dropping past the quarries at Hind Low to a T-junction at Brierlow Bar. Turn left along the A515 and drive for just 3 miles (4.8km) to return to Buxton town centre and the start point of the drive.

Howden Moors

Stocksbridge

of industry, New Mills, and the Derbyshire/Cheshire border, away to the right. New Mills was perfectly placed in the 18th century for the water-driven spinning and weaving factories that used the combined force of the River Goyt and the River Sett.

5 In a mile (1.6km) the road drops under a railway bridge to a junction. Turn left, signed 'Chapel-en-le-Frith'. Go under two viaducts and a flyover at Chapel Milton and into Chapel-en-le-Frith; go over a roundabout, still signed 'Chapel-en-le-Frith'. Turn left at a junction signed for the A6; turn left, pass beneath the flyover, and turn right to join the A6 towards Buxton. Continue for a mile (1.6km), then turn left at a roundabout on to the A623, signed 'Chesterfield and Sheffield'.

The landscape is different now; limestone country on a gently rolling plateau. Nestled between the hills of the southern pennines, Chapel-en-le-Frith was important in the early industrial years for it's association with the Peak Forest Tramway, which was essential for moving limestone from local quarries into the towns.

6 After 1.5 miles (2.4km) turn sharp right at The Wanted Inn and continue towards Chesterfield. In 4 miles (6.4km), turn right along the B6049 to Tideswell. Continue beyond the village for 500yds (455m) to a left turn signed (on the right) for Litton. Turn left here and drive through this peaceful little village, reaching a junction with the A623 in 0.75 miles (1.2km). Turn right, continue for a mile (1.6km), passing a garage (closed) and The Three Stags Heads pub. Turn left towards Foolow, then left again to reach the village. Turn right at The Bull's Head Inn and drive the 1.5 miles (2.4km) to Eyam. At the square in the village centre, turn sharp right into The Dale, descending to rejoin the A623; turn left down Middleton Dale into Stoney Middleton. In just 0.75 miles (1.2km), cross over Calver traffic lights, driving 2 miles (3.2km) back to Baslow.

THE SNOW ROAD

This tour begins at Baslow, in the Derwent valley with gritstone cliffs to the east and the White Peak to the west. It heads north to Ladybower Reservoir and then climbs northwest to cross the Dark Peak by the infamous Snake Pass before dropping down to the little mill towns of Glossop and Chapel-en-le-Frith. The return route is over the limestone plateau of the White Peak and down-dale through Stoney Middleton. Always check weather conditions before attempting the Snake Pass.

Route Directions

The tour starts in Baslow, at the roundabout junction of the A619 and the A623. Baslow sits on the edge of Chatsworth Park.

1 Head north towards Manchester on the A623 for 2 miles (3.2km) until you reach the Calver traffic lights. Turn right on the A625, go ahead on the B6001, signed 'Grindleford', for 2 miles (3.2km) into the town. Here, keep ahead on the B6521 and cross the river bridge up into Nether Padley. Continue for 2 miles (3.2km). Pass Longshaw Lodge, right, and sweep up to a T-junction. Turn left onto the A6187, signed 'Hathersage'. The road bears left and there are fine views of Hathersage Moor.

Discarded millstones lie among the birches, close to where they were cut – look for one in a car park on the right.

2 Drop down off the moor for approximately 3.5 miles (5.6km) and drive into the village of Hathersage, ever-popular with hikers.

Hathersage has historical links with the Robin Hood folklore and in the churchyard (on the right up School Lane and Church Bank) is Little John's grave.

3 Drive through Hathersage, then continue along the A6187 for a mile (1.6km) towards Castleton before turning right at traffic

lights on to the A6013, signed for Bamford and Ladybower. Continue for 2 miles (3.2km), past the dam wall of Ladybower Reservoir, to a T-junction. Turn left on the A57, signed for Glossop. Continue for another 14 miles (22.5km); going up Woodlands Valley, along Ladybower, then past The Snake Pass Inn.

Snake Pass is one of the most exposed and lonely places in England, and the road really does snake its way over the dome of moorland before descending to Glossop.

4 Head into Glossop, turn left at traffic lights onto the A624, signed 'Chapel-en-le-Frith'. Continue for 4 miles (6.4km) to Little Hayfield, then on to Hayfield, with the village on the left and the start of the Sett Valley Trail on the right. Continue ahead for 2 miles (3.2km), past the Lamb Inn.

Here, there is an imposing sweep of green hills and gritstone walls to the left and a hint

DISTANCE/TIME 15 miles (24.1km) 4h; shorter route 9 miles (14.5km) 2h30 **MAP** OS Explorer OL1 Dark Peak **START** Fairholmes Visitor Centre, Upper Derwent Valley; grid ref: SK 176894 **TRACKS** Tarred lanes and rough mountain roads **THE PUB** Yorkshire Bridge Inn, Bamford. Tel: 01433 651361; www.yorkshire-bridge.co.uk

DISTANCE/TIME 8 miles (12.9km) 3h30 **MAP** OS Explorer OL24 White Peak **START** Carsington Water Visitor Centre; grid ref: SK 241515 **TRACKS** Compacted gravel, sand and earth tracks, with some back lanes **THE PUB** Red Lion Inn, Ashbourne. Tel: 01335 370396; www.redlionhognaston.co.uk

THE UPPER DERWENT VALLEY RESERVOIRS

This is a long and challenging cycle route around the stunning chain of reservoirs in the Upper Derwent Valley.

1 Head north from the Fairholmes Visitor Centre, rising to the level of the dam top of Derwent Reservoir. Easy cycling takes you past a memorial.

2 Dipping in and out of Ouzelden Clough, the road passes close to the site of Birchinlee, or 'Tin Town'. Passing beside Howden Dam, the route circuits a long arm of Howden Reservoir to the turning circle at Kings Tree, the end of the tarred road. This is a good place to turn around (9 mile/14.5km round trip); the next section is more challenging.

3 Beyond the gate the route becomes a rough forest road that climbs through the woods above Howden Reservoir. At a fork, keep right to drop to the old packhorse bridge at Slippery Stones. Just above the bridge, swing sharp right to climb the roughening track along the eastern shore of the reservoir.

4 The going is rough for a mile (1.6km) or so, before a well-graded service road heralds the approach to Howden Dam. A steep, rougher descent follows, before the route comes close to the reservoir edge where steep, grassy banks drop into the water, so take care. The track improves as the route nears Derwent Dam. Passing close to one of the towers, the way develops into a tarred lane and passes the first of some isolated houses.

5 You can cut short the ride by turning right to pass the foot of Derwent Dam, to return to Fairholmes (9.5 miles/15.3km). The main route continues south past St Henry's Chapel, becoming rougher again as it rounds an inlet to an interpretation board.

6 At a gateway, join the tarred lane and drop to the main road. Turn right along the wide cycle path across Ashopton Viaduct, and right again at the far end. At a gateway, join the tarred lane and drop to the main road. Turn right along the cycle path across Ashopton Viaduct, and right again at the far end. Head back to the visitor centre along the approach road you took to reach the car park earlier.

AROUND CARSINGTON WATER

Discover picturesque hamlets and abundant wildlife at one of England's largest reservoirs as you cycle this interesting route.

1 From the car park at the visitor centre, look for the fingerposts pointing the way to the wildlife centre; this will bring you to the start of a compacted track, just below the coach park. These initial stages are an easy settling-in section, with a few short hills and descents. The track is partly shared with walkers and partly designated as a horse and cycle route, so be prepared to stop and obey any instruction signs.

2 The track joins a tarred farm access road, shortly passing by the Sheepwash car park. Take extra care here as you join the car park access road before arriving at the main road. The way is diagonally across to the left and along the road for Carsington.

3 There's a steady climb before the lane descends into Carsington. The lane undulates gently through the village and the neighbouring hamlet of Hopton. Pass beside the wall surrounding the Hopton Hall Estate, a wavy barrier of bricks with square towers and rounded bays. At the far end of Hopton, pass by Henmore Grange before looking right for the waymarked, fenced path that drops steeply down to a gate on to the B5035.

4 Cross carefully here, go left signed for Millfields, and turn right along the track beyond a further safety gate. You're at the extremity of the reservoir here, with views down the length of the lake. The first of a long series of hills is soon encountered, leading to a gate into woodlands with a wealth of wild flowers, and many short descents and longer inclines. You rise high above the waterline here before cresting a final summit to reveal views towards the dam and valve tower, and a steep hill down, passing by a wooden carving, just one of the sculptures dotted around the reservoir. When you eventually reach a short section of tarred farm lane, turn up along this to a waymarked gate, right, back on to the track.

5 Further ups and downs bring you past a stone shelter; take a peek inside to find some inventive wooden carvings. Just past here, turn up the old lane. Pass by the farmhouse before looking right for the waymarked gateway back on to the cycle track. From here, you're once again on a dedicated cycle/horse track that brings you to a gateway on to a wide grass verge by the main road. Turn right down the verge and right again into Millfields.

6 The waymarking is confusing here. Take the marked cycle path past the entry barriers and then go sharp left along a track. Go round a bend and along a short straight section, then dogleg left then right along a sandy track to reach the dam. At the far end head back to the visitor centre.

DISTANCE/TIME 8 miles (12.9km) 3h; shorter route 5.25 miles (8.4km) 1h15 **MAP** OS Explorer OL24 White Peak **START** Bakewell Old Station; grid ref: SK 223690 **TRACKS** Railway trackbed and lanes **THE PUB** Monsal Head Hotel, Monsal Head. Tel: 01629 640250; www.monsalhead.com

DISTANCE/TIME 13 miles (21km) 3h30 **MAP** OS Explorer OL24 White Peak **START** The Manifold Inn; grid ref: SK 108593 **TRACKS** All on-road apart from a short section of the Manifold Trail at the end **THE PUB** Manifold Inn, Hulme End, Hartington Buxton. Tel: 01298 84537; www.themanifoldinn.co.uk

BAKEWELL & THE MONSAL TRAIL

An easy ride from the town of Bakewell, with its railway heritage, which loops through a picturesque limestone village and riverside hay meadows.

1 Access to the trackbed is via the gap at the left side of the imposing structure. Turn left along the level track which, beyond some industrial units that occupy the former goods yard, runs initially through thin woods. After passing beneath the main road, Bakewell is soon left behind.

2 Beyond the warehouse here, the trees thin and become less constricting. The old trackbed passes under and over several roads, before reaching the impressive buildings at Great Longstone's old station.

3 A sign warns you that there is no exit for cyclists beyond this point, however it is worth cycling 0.25 miles (400m) to the end of the useable track for great views across towards the River Wye in its deep valley. You can simply retrace your route back to Bakewell from here, a distance of 5.25 miles (8.4km) or return to Great Longstone Station and take the steep flight of steps, left, to a minor road. Turn left along this road for an easy, level ride to the village centre at Great Longstone.

4 At the market cross and village green, fork right along either of the lanes. Both wind down to the main street to reach the White Lion. Just beyond this, take Church Lane, left to the parish church. The road bends to the right here along Beggarway Lane, offering views up to Longstone Edge and odd glimpses back towards the buildings Bakewell.

5 In 0.75 miles (1.2km), turn right along the lane at a left-hand bend. Fork left just before the bridge, up a gravelly ramp to regain the old railway. Turn left here to return to Bakewell. To extend the route you can then cycle across the car park and take Station Road downhill. On reaching the junction at the bottom of the road, turn sharp left along Coombs Road, passing the car park entrance. This peaceful, level lane runs for about a mile (1.6km) to a high-arched viaduct crossing.

6 Immediately before the viaduct, look for the Monsal Trail board, left, indicating a short, sharp incline, up which you wheel your bicycle to the old railway. Turn left to return to Bakewell and enjoy the good views across the town.

THE STAFFORDSHIRE MOORLANDS

Cycle this lovely, undulating, on-road route, through countryside where the White Peak meets the Dark Peak.

1 Take the B5054 outside The Manifold Inn to a junction on the left signposted 'Sheen & Longnor'. This winding lane initially descends before starting a gradual climb between limestone walls. Sight-lines on this section are not good, but they improve after a slightly steeper pitch brings the route to the straggling village of Sheen.

2 Passing by the village inn, The Staffordshire Knot, then the church, the way again steepens slightly as it rises through a few bends to level out past Harris Close farm, with Sheen Hill to the left. A long, easy ride follows, cresting to fall down a sharp hill with bad sight lines. At the junction, keep ahead to reach Longnor.

3 At the heart of Longnor is the Market Square. This route crosses straight over the junction here, in front of the Horseshoe pub and along a lane signposted 'Royal Cottage and Leek'. Once out of the village, there's a steep descent to a bridge over the River Manifold and the start of a climb up the valley side. In 0.5 miles (800m) the route levels to reach a left turn signposted 'Fawfieldhead and Newtown'. Follow this through to a T-junction and turn right along an undulating lane with pleasing views.

4 At a telephone box turn left along a lane signposted 'Warslow'. Soon you'll pass by the little chapel at Newtown (built 1837) off to your right. This is an airy, easy cruise along a high road, with the distinctive limestone hills at Ecton the main feature off to your left beyond Reaps Moor. Beyond a house called Hayshead, the lane starts a long, gradual climb before levelling out beside Lum Edge and Warslow Moor.

5 Go straight across the crossroads, bear left at the junction, joining a road that rises gradually, soon crossing a cattle grid. Cresting another rise, there's a long descent into Warslow. Continue, to pass the Greyhound Inn, and to a junction with the B5053.

6 Turn left along this road and remain on it for about 200yds (182m) to find a lane on the right, signposted 'Unsuitable for Heavy Goods Vehicles'. Carefully turn into this, which drops increasingly steeply as a narrow, winding lane. Keep right, to descend to a bridge across the Manifold. Just beyond this, turn left along the Manifold Way and follow this to Hulme End. Rejoin the main road and turn right to return to the nearby Manifold Inn and the start of the ride.

Sports in the Peaks

The Mass Trespass onto Kinder, the highest point in the Peak District, in 1932, is hailed as a landmark in a hard-fought campaign for access to moorland in Britain, at a time when open moorland, 'grouse' moorland, was keenly guarded to meet the demands of the game keeping interests of the landed gentry.

There is a tendency to celebrate the Kinder Trespass as the first demonstration against the closure of moorland walking areas. While the Kinder episode was undoubtedly a major catalyst, there was an earlier mass trespass onto the West Pennine Moors around Bolton almost 40 years before, in 1896, which may well have fuelled the minds of the 20th-century protagonists. The moors of the West Pennines and the Peak District formed a natural rural escape for the workers in industrial towns and cities, and continue to do so today. Some latter-day researchers attribute to the Peak District a sense of manliness, and the identification of masculine values with a certain type of landscape, especially during the inter-war years.

Today, the Peak District, the first designated national park in Britain, provides opportunities for a wide range of outdoor activities. A network of paths and long-distance trails, stretching for more then 1,800 miles (2,900km) in total, as well as large open-access areas, are available for hill-walking. Bridleways, intended originally for horse riding, are now also legally used by that new adrenalin-fuelled phenomenon, mountain-biking. Some of the longer trails, such as the Tissington Trail and the Monsal Trail, re-use former railway lines.

Although the ability to climb rocks was a key component of mountaineering in the French and Italian Alps, it is generally accepted that the 'sport' of rock-climbing, where the climbing took precedence over reaching summits, began in Britain in the Lake District. But it was only a short step before the many Peakland gritstone outcrops, such as Stanage and the Roaches, were recognized as some of the finest rock-climbing sites in the world. Climbing has been practised all over the Peak District since the late 19th century; James W. Puttrell is generally credited with starting the sport. Historically, gritstone crags – Laddow Rocks and Castle Naze – were the first to be explored, and others where access was not restricted by gamekeepers. This continued until the 1950s, when a post-war generation emerged and public access to crags became more widely available. The number of climbers increased, led by legendary figures such as Nat Allen, Joe Brown and Don Whillans.

Some of the Peak's large reservoirs, for example Carsington Water, with the relaxation of water catchment restrictions, have become centres for water sports, including sailing, fishing and canoeing. A variety of small sailboats is available for hire from sailing centres here, on production of the appropriate RYA level competence certificates. Powerboats are also evident on Carsington Water and centres around the lake run training courses for these vessels, in accordance with the RYA National Powerboat Scheme (for over 16s only). But one of the more peculiar sports in the Peak, and generally throughout the north of England and Scotland is that of fell-running, or mountain-racing. Although the sport is strongly competitive, it has a very introspective element; most fell runners compete against themselves or the clock, and the sport demands incredible running strength and agility. The sport has much in common with cross-country running, but differs in its readiness to race over high mountains, not always on established paths, and often requiring navigational skills of the highest order. Moreover, the courses followed by fell-runners are considerably longer and vastly more demanding. Some routes over open moorland and rocky crags can be punishing both physically and mentally and it takes a certain strength and perseverance to endure the course.

The varied landscape of the Peak also lends itself to a sport pursued by that species of humanity that delights in throwing itself off high cliffs in the hope that a cat's cradle of thin cord and a pair of over-sized lady's undergarments will bring them safely back to earth, known to enthusiasts as paragliding. Soaring effortlessly and virtually soundlessly along the Peak ridges, suspended below a brightly coloured 'wing', making the most of up-currents, is a scintillating mix of hope, terror and avid, unabashed pleasure. Mam Tor to the west of Castleton is a hugely popular launch site. As a form of flying, paragliding is controlled by the Civil Aviation Authority, who have accepted a self-regulatory system controlled by the British Hang Gliding and Paragliding Association. To become a hang-glider or paraglider pilot you must join an affiliated club and undergo training at a licensed school, of which there are several in the Peak.

Those people who like to drift across the skies paragliding have an equally adventurous cousin in the potholer. Potholing, the 'sport' of losing oneself underground in often damp, dangerous and flooded subterranean passageways, is a pursuit which has relatively fewer adherents compared to walking, or even rock-climbing. But the Peak is an ideal place to practice this minority sport. Unlike the limestone areas of Yorkshire, for example, there are few natural potholes in the Peak. However, the Peak abounds with natural caves, of which Peak Cavern is the largest and most important. This and other 'showcase' caverns were a major tourist attraction in the 19th century when the 'Grand Tour' of Europe was less popular with the upper classes.

The proximity of the national park to major conurbations – and, with improved high-speed road networks, much further afield – means the number of visitors to the park has grown enormously in recent years. This poses unique challenges to those who manage the area. The Peak National Park Authority, the National Trust, and other landowners, work tirelessly to keep the upland landscape accessible to visitors for recreation, while at the same time protecting it from intensive farming, natural erosion and pressure from visitors themselves. An unavoidable strain exists between the needs of the residents of the Peak, the millions of people who visit annually, and the conservation needs of the area. The uneven distribution of visitors creates further stresses. Dovedale alone receives 2 million visitors annually; other highly-visited areas include Bakewell, Castleton, Chatsworth, Hartington and the upper Derwent valley. Like many of the national parks, the Peak has become a victim of its own success.

With its sombre gritstone walls, rough-and-tumble heather moorlands and benign limestone dales, the Peak District is one of Britain's best-loved landscapes. Fashioned by man over thousands of years, this is still a 'living landscape', one that supports a rich diversity of wildlife, culture and heritage. But that's quite another story.

OPPOSITE, CLOCKWISE FROM TOP LEFT Kinder Scout is a popular challenge for hikers. This large rocky outcrop, in the Peak District National Park, stands at around 1,970 feet (600m) above sea level.

The approach to Peak Cavern is dramatic but the cave itself is awesome. Once home to a community of rope-makers, the cave is beautifully lit to show off its geological splendours and the chambers also have superb acoustics.

The gritstone escarpment of the Roaches attracts rock-climbers of all abilities from around the world.

Hang-gliders hoping to catch that perfect thermal launch from the verdant hills in Staffordshire's Manifold Valley.

LEFT Spanning 85 acres (34ha), spring fed Errwood Reservoir in the Goyt Valley makes a great spot for fly fishermen keen to hook brown and rainbow trout.

MILLER'S DALE

The walk starts in Tideswell Dale, takes in Miller's Dale, passes Litton Mill and continues into Water-cum-Jolly Dale to follow the River Wye.

1 Follow the path south from beside the car park's toilet block into Tideswell Dale, taking the right-hand fork to cross a little bridge.

2 On entering Miller's Dale, go left along the lane and continue to Litton Mill. Go through gateposts on to a concessionary path through a mill yard. Beyond the mill, the path follows the River Wye, as it meanders through the steep-sided dale.

3 The river widens out in Water-cum-Jolly Dale and the path, liable to flooding here, traces the wall of limestone cliffs before reaching Cressbrook. Do not cross the bridge on the right, but turn left to pass in front of Cressbrook Mill and on to a road.

4 Turn left along the road, then take the right fork which climbs steadily into Cressbrook Dale. Where the road doubles back uphill leave it for a track going ahead into the woods. Beyond a gate, the track becomes a narrow path that emerges in a clearing high above the stream. Follow it downhill to reach a footbridge over a stream, then take the right-hand fork path up the valley side to reach a stile in the top wall.

5 Don't cross the stile. Instead take the downhill path to the dale bottom and

a junction of paths. Take the path that recrosses the stream on stepping stones, and climbs into Tansley Dale.

6 The path turns right at the top of the dale, and follows a tumbledown wall before crossing it on a step stile. Head for the wall corner in the next field, then veer right through a narrow enclosure to reach a walled track just south of Litton village.

7 Turn left along the track, which emerges on a country lane at the crown of a sharp bend. Keep straight on down the lane but leave it at the next bend for a cross-field path to Bottomhill Road. Across the road, a further field path descends to a road at Dale House Farm. Turn left along the pavement, then right on a lane marked 'unsuitable for motor traffic', into the centre of Tideswell.

8 Head south back down the main street, then turn right on to Gordon Road, which then also heads south.

9 Where this road ends, continue down a stony track ahead, parallel with the main road. At the far end, take a gated footpath on the left, down to walk along a road into Tideswell Dale. Turn right along the road, back to the car park.

DISTANCE/TIME 6 miles (9.7km) 4h **MAP** OS Explorer OL24 White Peak **START** Tideswell Dale pay car park; grid ref: SK 154743 **PATHS** Generally well-defined paths and tracks. Path in Water-cum-Jolly Dale liable to flooding. Quite a few stiles **THE PUB** The George Hotel, Commercial Road, Tideswell. Tel: 01298 871382; www.thegeorge-hotel.tideswell.co.uk

WALK 74

THROUGH MONSAL DALE

From Ashford's streets the route climbs to high pastures and continues over a viaduct, descends to Monsal Dale and the River Wye, then heads westwards through woodland to eventually return to Ashford.

1 From Ashford-in-the-Water car park, walk out to the road and turn right to walk along Vicarage Lane. After 100yds (91m), a footpath on the left doubles back left, then swings sharp right to continue along a ginnel behind a row of houses. Beyond a stile the path enters a field.

2 Head for a stile in the top left-hand corner, then veer slightly right to locate a stile allowing the route to go on to Pennyunk Lane. This walled stony track winds among high pastures. At its end go left uphill along a field edge. At the top it joins another track, heading north (right) towards the rim of Monsal Dale. The path runs along the top edge of the deep wooded dale to reach the car park at Monsal Head.

3 Take the path marked 'Viaduct and Monsal Trail' here – this way you get to walk across the viaduct. On the other side of the viaduct go through a gate on the left. Ignore the path climbing west up the hillside, but descend southwest on a grassy path raking through scrub woods down into the valley. This shouldn't be confused with the steep eroded path plummeting straight down to the foot of the viaduct.

4 Now you walk down the pleasant valley. The right of way is well away from the river at first but most walkers trace the river bank to emerge at Lees Bottom and a roadside stile.

5 Cross the A6 with great care and go through the White Lodge car park on the path the other side, where the route back to Ashford begins. Beyond the gate carry on along the path, ignoring the turning to Toddington. Go over a wall stile and then up to a rocky path, forking left for the path into Great Shacklow Wood, signposted 'Ashford'.

6 The path now climbs steeply through the trees and stony ground to another gate. Ignore the turning right for Sheldon and continue straight ahead, following a fine ledge path along the steep wooded slopes. Eventually the path comes down to the river, past an old mill, before joining a minor road at the bottom of Kirk Dale.

7 Turn left along the road, down to the A6 and turn right towards Ashford. Leave the road to cross Sheepwash Bridge. Turn right along Church Street, then left along Court Lane to the car park.

DISTANCE/TIME 5.5 miles (8.8km) 3h30 **MAP** OS Explorer OL24 White Peak **START** Ashford-in-the-Water car park; grid ref: SK 194696 **PATHS** Well-defined paths and tracks throughout, lots of stiles **THE PUB** The Bull's Head, Ashford in the Water. Tel: 01629 812931

WALK 75

PENNINE WAYS ON KINDER SCOUT

One end of the Pennine long-distance trail ascends to the craggy outcrops of the Kinder Plateau. An edge walk goes round the chasm of Grindsbrook and passes the gritstone sculptures of Grindslow Knoll to the ravine of Crowden Brook. The route descends by the brook passing waterfalls then crosses the fields of Edale.

DISTANCE/TIME 5 miles (8km) 3h30 **MAP** OS Explorer OL1 Dark Peak **START** Edale pay car park; grid ref: SK 125853 **PATHS** Rock and peat paths, some steep and rough **THE PUB** Old Nags Head, Hope Valley. Tel: 01433 670291

1 Turn right out of the car park and head north along the lane into Edale village, under the railway and past The Old Nags Head. At the end, turn right and follow the path across the footbridge over Grinds Brook.

2 Leave the main Grindsbrook Clough path by the side of a barn, taking the right fork that climbs up the lower hillslope to a stile on the edge of open country. Beyond the stile the path zig-zags above Fred Heardman's Plantation then climbs up the nose of The Nab to the skyline rocks. Where the path divides, take the right fork to the summit of Ringing Roger.

3 Follow the edge path left, rounding the cavernous hollow of Grindsbrook past Nether Tor. The old Pennine Way route is met on the east side by a large cairn.

4 Ignoring the left fork heading for the outlier of Grindslow Knoll, follow the paved footpath westwards to the head of another deep hollow, the clough of Crowden Brook.

5 Cross over Crowden Brook, and then immediately leave the edge to follow a narrow level path traversing slopes on the left beneath the imposing outcrop of Crowden Tower. Below the tower, fork left for a steep and, at first, rough track down to the banks of the brook. The path now follows the brook, fording the water on several occasions.

6 Cross a stile at the edge of open country and then go across a footbridge shaded by tall rowans to change to the west bank. From here the path threads through woodland before descending in steps to the road at Upper Booth. You now need to follow the Pennine Way path back to Edale.

7 Turn left along the road and then left again into the farmyard of Upper Booth Farm before exiting at the top right corner. After following a track to a gateway, bear left uphill to a stile by an old barn. Here the Way traverses fields at the foot of Broadlee Bank before joining a tree-lined track into the village. Turn right along the road back to the car park.

WALK 76

OVER WIN HILL

This walk from Hope to Win Hill threads through pastures above the River Noe passing Roman earthworks and there are views of Ladybower Reservoir, while the gritstone tors of Kinder Scout, the Derwent Edge, and Bleaklow fill the horizon.

DISTANCE/TIME 8.75 miles (14.1km) 5h **MAP** OS Explorer OL1 Dark Peak; **START** Hope pay car park; grid ref: SK 149829 **PATHS** Paths can be slippery after rain, quite a few stiles **THE PUB** Cheshire Cheese, Edale Road, Hope Tel: 01433 620381

1 Turn left out of the car park along the main street. At the far end of the village turn right on a walled stony lane and continue along a well-defined path accompanying Peakshole Water. Cross the railway with care and continue along the path to its end at Pindale Road.

2 Turn left here, then right at the next junction. After 200yds (182m), go over a stile by a gate on the left and follow the path running roughly parallel to the lane at first, then the River Noe, to reach the site of the Roman fort of Navio. Beyond the earthworks go over a stile in a fence and bear half right across another field to reach the B6049 road at Brough.

3 Turn left through the village and cross the footbridge over the River Noe. Go left over a stile and head northwest to the A6187. Turn left along the road for 200yds (183m) to a small gate just beyond a cottage. Follow the hedge and dyke on the right to pass to the right of some houses.

4 Turn left along the lane heading towards the railway station, then go right on a narrow path, leading to a footbridge over the line. Cross the bridge and turn right at its far end, then left over a stile to cross yet more fields, this time keeping the fence on your right.

5 When you reach Aston turn left along the road, then almost immediately turn right along a narrow, surfaced lane, signposted 'To Win Hill and Hope Cross'.

6 Beyond Edge Farm an unsurfaced track on the left takes the route along the top edge of some woods to a path junction above Twitchill Farm. Now climb right on a well-used path to Win Hill's summit.

7 From the summit retrace your steps back to the junction above Twitchill Farm. This time descend left past the farm on a tarmac drive, to the railway.

8 Turn left under the railway tunnel for the lane via Kilhill Bridge to Edale Road. Turn right along the road, under the railway bridge, then left by a postbox on a field path.

9 By a cottage turn right on a path climbing towards Lose Hill. Take the left fork, which is signposted 'Castleton' to follow a waymarked route westwards to Spring House Farm.

10 In front of the farm, turn right to walk along a track behind Losehill Hall. Where the lane swings left, leave it to follow a cross-field path, which joins a rough lane. After passing the outdoor centre, turn left along Hollowford Road into Castleton.

SUFFOLK COAST

■ TOURIST INFORMATION

Aldeburgh
High Street ☎ 01728 453637;
www.suffolkcoastal.gov.uk/tourism
Felixstowe
91 Undercliff Road West ☎ 01394 276770;
www.suffolkcoastal.gov.uk/tourism
Woodbridge
The Station ☎ 01394 382240;
www.suffolkcoastal.gov.uk/tourism

■ PLACES OF INTEREST

Bridge Cottage
Flatford, East Bergholt
☎ 01206 298260;
www.nationaltrust.org.uk
Dunwich Museum
St James Street, Dunwich
☎ 01728 648796;
www.dunwichmuseum.org.uk
Framlington Castle
☎ 01728 724189;
www.english-heritage.org.uk
Landguard Fort
Viewpoint Road, Felixstowe
☎ 07749 695523; www.landguard.com
Orford Castle
☎ 01394 450472;
www.english-heritage.org.uk
Sutton Hoo
☎ 01394 389700;
www.nationaltrust.org.uk

■ PERFORMING ARTS

Snape Maltings Concert Hall
Snape, Saxmundham
☎ 01728 687110; www.aldeburgh.co.uk

■ SPORTS & ACTIVITIES

NATURE RESERVES
Dunwich Heath
☎ 01728 648505;
www.nationaltrust.org.uk
Orford Ness National
Nature Reserve
☎ 01728 648024;
www.nationaltrust.org.uk
RSPB Minsmere Nature Reserve
Westelton, Saxmundham
☎ 01728 648281; www.rspb.org.uk

■ ANNUAL EVENTS & CUSTOMS

Aldeburgh
Aldeburgh Literary Festival, Mar.
Aldeburgh Easter Festival, Apr.
Alderburgh Festival, Jun.
Snape Proms, Aug.
Britten Festival, Snape Maltings,
mid Oct.
Felixstowe
Easter Fair, Apr.
Historic Vehicle Rally, May.
Felixstowe Carnival and Fair, Aug.
Framlingham
Framlingham Gala, May.

Walberswick
Walberswick Crabbing Competition, Aug.
Woodbridge
Horse Show, May.
Suffolk Folk Festival, Jun.

CAMBRIDGE & FENS

■ TOURIST INFORMATION

Cambridge
The Old Library, Wheeler Street,
☎ 0871 226 8006;
www.visitcambridge.org

■ PLACES OF INTEREST

Anglesey Abbey Gardens & Lode Mill
Lode ☎ 01223 810080;
www.nationaltrust.org.uk
Ely Cathedral
Chapter House, The College
☎ 01353 667735; www.elycathedral.org
Superb cathedral with a rich history.
Houghton Mill
Houghton, near Huntingdon
☎ 01480 301494;
www.nationaltrust.org.uk
This is the last working watermill that
exists on the River Ouse. A visit here is a
wonderful day out.
Oliver Cromwell's House
29 St Mary's Street, Ely
☎ 01353 662062;
www.visitely.eastcambs.gov.uk

■ FOR THE CHILDREN

Cambridge Uncovered
Live The City Ltd, The Old Crown Court,
Market Hill, Cambridge
☎ 0871 226 8006; www.livethecity.com
A self-guided tour with treasure hunt
clues to keep everyone entertained.

■ SPORTS & ACTIVITIES

GARDENS
Clare College Gardens
Trinity Lane, Cambridge
☎ 01223 333200; www.clare.cam.ac.uk
A beautiful example of a 20th-century
English garden.
The Orchard Tea Gardens
Mill Way, Grantchester
☎ 01223 845788;
www.orchard-grantchester.com
NATURE RESERVES & COUNTRY PARKS
Wicken Fen National Nature Reserve
Lode Lane, Wicken, Ely
☎ 01353 720274; www.wicken.org.uk

NORFOLK BROADS

■ TOURIST INFORMATION

Great Yarmouth
Maritime House, Marine Parade
☎ 01493 846345;
www.great-yarmouth.co.uk
Lowestoft
East Point Pavilion ☎ 01502 533600;
www.visit-sunrisecoast.co.uk

Norfolk Broads National Park
Broads Authority, 2 Gilders Way,
Norwich ☎ 01603 610734;
www.broads-authority.gov.uk
All information about the waterways.
Norwich
The Forum, Millennium Plain
☎ 01603 213999; www.visitnorwich.co.uk

■ PLACES OF INTEREST

St Benet's Abbey
Ludham
Derelict wind pump and Benedictine
monastery ruins on the edge of the
River Bure.
Somerleyton Hall
☎ 01502 734901;
www.somerleyton.co.uk
Victorian extravaganza, with gardens,
garden trail, maze, Viking fort, children's
farmyard, pony treks and cycle trail.

■ SPORTS & ACTIVITIES

ANGLING
Wroxham Angling Centre
Station Road ☎ 01603 782453;
www.anglingdirect.co.uk
BOAT TOURS
Beccles
Waveney Stardust ☎ 07817 920502;
www.visitnorwich.co.uk
Hoveton/Wroxham
Broads Tours ☎ 01603 782207;
www.broads.co.uk
Norwich, River Wensum
City Boats, Thorpe Saint Andrew
☎ 01603 701701; www.cityboats.co.uk
Oulton Broad
Waveney River Tours, Mutford Lock,
Bridge Road, Lowestoft ☎ 01502 574903
CANOEING
Wroxham
Barnes Brinkcraft, Riverside Road
☎ 01603 782625
All levels of experience catered to on
the Broads and it's feeder rivers.
NATURE RESERVES
Hickling Broad
Reserve open daily ☎ 01692 598276
Boarded walkway for easy walks and
visitor centre.
Ranworth Broads Wildlife Centre
Floating Broads Wildlife Centre open
Apr–Oct

LINCOLN & RUTLAND

■ TOURIST INFORMATION

Lincoln
9 Castle Hill, Lincoln ☎ 01522 545458;
www.lincoln.gov.uk
21 Cornhill, Lincoln ☎ 01522 873256;
www.lincoln.gov.uk
Lincolnshire Tourism, Beech House,
Waterside South, Lincoln
☎ 01522 526450;
www.visitlincolnshire.com

■ PLACES OF INTEREST

Barnsdale Gardens
The Avenue, Exton, Oakham
☎ 01572 813 200;
www.barnsdalegardens.co.uk
Belton House
Near Grantham ☎ 01476 566116;
www.nationaltrust.org.uk
Belvoir Castle
Near Grantham ☎ 01476 871002;
www.belvoircastle.com
Burghley House
Stamford ☎ 01780 752451;
www.burghley.co.uk
Clipsham Yew Tree Avenue
Kesteven Forest, Clipsham
1 mile to the west, is the nearest town or
village; grid ref: SK 980169.
Gainsborough Old Hall
Parnell Street ☎ 01427 612669;
www.gainsborougholdhall.co.uk
Lincoln Castle
Castle Hill, Lincoln ☎ 01522 511068;
www.lincolnshire.gov.uk/lincolncastle
Lincoln Cathedral
☎ 01522 561600;
www.lincolncathedral.com
Oakham Castle
& Rutland County Museum
☎ 01572 758440; www.rutland.gov.uk
All enquiries to Rutland County Museum,
Catmose Street, Oakham
Rutland Open Air Theatre
(Shakespeare)
Tolethorpe Hall ☎ 01780 754381;
www.stamfordshakespeare.co.uk

■ SHOPPING

Lincoln
St Mark's Shopping Centre,
off High Street, Lincoln
www.stmarks-lincoln.co.uk

■ SPORTS & ACTIVITIES

BOAT TRIPS
Lincoln Boat Trips
Brayford Pool ☎ 01522 881200;
www.lincolnboattrips.com
CYCLING
Rutland Water Cycling
Whitwell Leisure Park, Bullbrigg Lane,
Whitwell, near Oakham
☎ 01780 460705;
www.rutlandcycling.com
GOLF
Rutland Water Golf Course
Lodge Farm, Oakham ☎ 01572 737525;
www.rutlandwatergolfcourse.co.uk
HORSE RIDING
Stretton Riding Centre
Stretton Manor Bungalow Farm
☎ 01780 410323
WATERSPORTS
Rutland Watersports
Rutland Water, North Shore
☎ 01780 460154; www.rutnet.co.uk

ANNUAL EVENTS & CUSTOMS
Burghley
Burghley Horse Trials, Sep.
☎ 01780 752131 (not all year);
www.burghley-horse.co.uk
Oakham
Oakham Festival, Jun/Jul.
☎ 07826 733374;
www.oakhamfestival.co.uk
Oakham's annual art festival includes
poetry, music, comedy, theatre, dance
and film events.

WORCESTER & MALVERN HILLS
TOURIST INFORMATION
Malvern
21 Church Street ☎ 01684 892289;
www.visitthemalverns.org
Pershore
Town Hall, 34 High Street
☎ 01386 556591;
www.visitpershore.co.uk
Worcester
The Guildhall, High Street
☎ 01905 726311;
www.visitworcestershire.org;
www.visitheartofengland.com

PLACES OF INTEREST
Elgar Birthplace Museum
Crown East Lane, Lower Broadheath
☎ 01905 333224; www.elgarmuseum.org
Great Malvern Priory
Church Street ☎ 01684 561020;
www.greatmalvernpriory.org.uk
The Greyfriars
Friar Street, Worcester ☎ 01905 23571;
www.nationaltrust.org.uk
Superb 15th-century timber-framed
house.
Malvern Hills
Malvern Hills Conservators, Manor
House, Grange Road, Malvern
☎ 01684 892002;
www.malvernhills.org.uk
Pershore Abbey
☎ 01386 552071;
www.pershoreabbey.org.uk
Royal Worcester Visitor Centre
Severn Street, Worcester
☎ 01905 746000;
www.royalworcesterfactoryshops.co.uk
Worcester Cathedral
☎ 01905 732900;
www.worcestercathedral.org.uk
Worcester Porcelain Museum
Severn Street ☎ 01905 21247;
www.worcesterporcelainmuseum.org
Decorate china in the 'Paint a Plate' area.

FOR CHILDREN
The Ghost Walk of Worcester
City Centre ☎ 01905 611427
Guided evening walks for 5–11 year olds.
Every Saturday in the winter months.

SHOPPING
Worcester Antiques Centre
Reindeer Court, Mealcheapen Street
☎ 01905 610680
Friar Street, New Street and Charles
Street have many shops and galleries.

SPORTS & ACTIVITIES
ANGLING
Leigh Sinton Farm Fishing Lake
Lower Interfields, Near Malvern
☎ 01886 832305;
www.fisheries.co.uk/leighsinton
BOAT CRUISES
Worcester River Cruises
North Quay, Worcester
☎ 01905 611060;
www.worcesterrivercruises.co.uk
GOLF
Ravenmeadow Golf Centre
Hindip Lane, Claines, Worcester
☎ 01905 757525;
www.ravenmeadowgolf.co.uk
The Vale Golf Club
Hill Furze Road, Bishampton, Pershore
☎ 01386 462781; www.thevalegolf.co.uk

ANNUAL EVENTS & CUSTOMS
Autumn in Malvern Festival, Oct.
☎ 01684 892277 (tickets)
Worcester Christmas Fayre, early Dec.
☎ 01905 726311

STRATFORD & VALE OF EVESHAM
TOURIST INFORMATION
Stratford-upon-Avon
Bridgefoot ☎ 0870 160 7930;
www.shakespeare-country.co.uk

PLACES OF INTEREST
Anne Hathaway's Cottage
Cottage Lane, Shottery ☎ 01789 204016;
www.shakespeare.org.uk
Hall's Croft
Old Town, Stratford-upon-Avon
☎ 01789 292107;
www.shakespeare.org.uk
Elegant house of Shakespeare's
daughter.
Nash's House & New Place
Chapel Street, Stratford-upon-Avon
☎ 01789 204016;
www.shakespeare.org.uk
See where Shakespeare died in 1616.
Shakespeare's Birthplace
Henley Street, Stratford-upon-Avon
☎ 01789 204016;
www.shakespeare.org.uk

FOR CHILDREN
Stratford-upon-Avon Butterfly Farm
Swan's Nest Lane, Stratford-upon-Avon
☎ 01789 299288;
www.butterflyfarm.co.uk
Plenty to enjoy for all the family.

Stratford-upon-Avon Mini Golf
The Recreation Ground, Swan's Nest
Lane, Stratford-upon-Avon
☎ 07703 883904
18-hole putting course by the peaceful
River Avon.

SPORTS & ACTIVITIES
BOAT CRUISES
Avon Boating
The Boathouse, Swans Nest Lane,
Stratford-upon-Avon ☎ 01789 267073;
www.avon-boating.co.uk
Bancroft Cruisers
Holiday Inn Hotel, Bridgefoot,
Stratford-upon-Avon ☎ 01789 269669;
www.bancroftcruisers.co.uk
HOT-AIR BALLOONING
Wickers World
The Hawthornes, Tolldish Lane,
Great Haywood ☎ 01889 882222;
www.wickersworld.co.uk
Hot-air balloons flights giving superb
views of the countryside.

SHREWSBURY & IRONBRIDGE
TOURIST INFORMATION
Ironbridge
Museum of the Gorge,
The Wharfage ☎ 01952 884391;
www.shropshiretourism.co.uk
Shrewsbury
Rowley's Hall, Barker Street
☎ 01743 281200;
www.visitshrewsbury.com

PLACES OF INTEREST
Acton Burnell Castle
Shrewsbury ☎ 0870 333 1181;
www.english-heritage.org.uk
Attingham Park
Shrewsbury ☎ 01743 708162;
www.nationaltrust.org.uk
Ironbridge Gorge Museums
The Ironbridge Gorge Museum Trust,
Coach Road, Coalbrookdale, Telford
☎ 01952 884391; www.ironbridge.org.uk
Shrewsbury Abbey
Abbey Foregate ☎ 01743 232723;
www.shrewsburyabbey.com
Wroxeter Roman City
☎ 01743 761330;
www.english-heritage.org.uk

SHOPPING
The Parade Shopping Centre
St Mary's Place, Shrewsbury;
www.paradeshops.co.uk
Plenty of upmarket shopping and
specialized boutiques.

ANNUAL EVENTS & CUSTOMS
Shrewsbury
Darwin Festival, Feb. ☎ 01743 281281;
www.darwinshrewsbury.org

Shrewsbury Children's Bookfest, May.
☎ 01743 281200;
www.shrewsburybookfest.co.uk
A popular festival with little people in
mind, featuring all types of children's
books and publications.
Shrewsbury Folk Festival, Aug.
☎ 01743 281281;
www.shrewsburyfolkfestival.co.uk
Shrewsbury International Cartoon
Festival, Apr. ☎ 01743 281200;
www.shrewsburycartoonfestival.com
Shrewsbury Flower Show., Aug.
Exhibits for all floral preferences.
☎ 01743 234050;
www.shrewsburyflowershow.org.uk

SHROPSHIRE HILLS & STIPERSTONES
TOURIST INFORMATION
Church Stretton
Church Street ☎ 01694 723133;
www.churchstretton.co.uk
Ludlow
Castle Street
☎ 01584 875053
Much Wenlock
The Museum, High Street
☎ 01952 727679
Shropshire Tourism
Grove House, 8 St Julian's
Friars, Shrewsbury ☎ 01743 261919;
www.shropshiretourism.co.uk

PLACES OF INTEREST
Ludlow Castle
Castle Square
☎ 01584 873355;
www.ludlowcastle.com
Stokesay Castle
☎ 01588 672544;
www.english-heritage.org.uk

FOR CHILDREN
Acton Scott Historic Working Farm
☎ 01694 781306; www.actonscott.com
Traditional farming skills displays.
Location for the BBC 2 television series,
Victorian Farm.

SHOPPING
Antique and Flea Markets
Castle Square, Ludlow on 1st
& 3rd Sun of the month.
☎ 01588 638379
Bishop's Castle – 1st Sat of the month.
Farmers Markets
Ludlow – 2nd & 4th Thu of the month.
Bishop's Castle – 3rd Sat of the month.
Church Stretton – 2nd & 4th Fri of
the month.
Traditional markets
Ludlow – Mon, Wed, Fri, Sat.
Church Stretton – Thu and alternate
Fridays and Saturdays.
Bishop's Castle – Fri.

■ SPORTS & ACTIVITIES
CYCLING
Wheely Wonderful
Petchfield Farm, Elton, Ludlow
☎ 01568 770755;
www.wheelywonderfulcycling.co.uk
GOLF
Elm Lodge Golf Course
Fishmore, Ludlow ☎ 01584 872308;
www.elm-lodge.org.uk
HORSE RIDING
North Farm Riding Establishment
Whitcliffe, Ludlow ☎ 01584 872026;
www.northfarmludlow.co.uk
QUAD TREKKING & MOUNTAIN BOARDING
The Edge
Opposite Walton Cottages, Much Wenlock
☎ 01952 727491; www.ridetheedge.co.uk

OFFA'S DYKE
■ TOURIST INFORMATION
The Offa's Dyke Centre
Knighton, Powys ☎ 01547 528753;
www.offasdyke.demon.co.uk

PEAK DISTRICT
■ TOURIST INFORMATION
Bakewell
The Old Market Hall, Bridge Street
☎ 01629 816558
Buxton
The Pavilion ☎ 01298 25106;
www.visitbuxton.co.uk
Holmfirth
49–51 Huddersfield Road
☎ 01484 222444;
www.pennineyorkshire.com
Matlock
Crown Square ☎ 01629 583388;
www.visitpeakdistrict.com

■ PLACES OF INTEREST
Blue John Cavern
1 mile (1.6km) west of Castleton via
Winnats Pass ☎ 01433 620638;
www.bluejohn-cavern.co.uk
Chatsworth House
☎ 01246 565300;
www.chatsworth.org
Magnificent mansion and home to the
Duke and Duchess of Devonshire. Child
and adult audio tours are available of
both the house and the grounds.
Eyam Museum
☎ 01433 631371;
www.eyammuseum.demon.co.uk
The museum tells the story of the
bubonic plague, how it reached Eyam
and was contained there.
Haddon Hall
Bakewell ☎ 01629 812855;
www.haddonhall.co.uk
A splendid house that has remained
virtually untouched by the passage of
time. Topiary gardens.

Heights of Abraham
Matlock Bath ☎ 01629 582365;
www.heights-of-abraham.co.uk
Last of the Summer Wine Exhibition
30 Huddersfield Road, Holmfirth
☎ 01484 681408;
www.summerwine-holmfirth.co.uk
Lyme Park
Disley ☎ 01663 762023;
www.nationaltrust.org.uk
Nine Ladies Stone Circle
Stanton Moor. Free.
Old House Museum
Bakewell ☎ 01629 813642; www.old
housemuseum.hammerdesign.co.uk
Peak District Mining Museum
The Pavilion, Matlock Bath
☎ 01629 583834; www.peakmines.co.uk
Peak Rail
Matlock Station ☎ 01629 580381;
www.peakrail.co.uk
Peveril Castle
Castleton ☎ 01433 620613;
www.english-heritage.org.uk

■ FOR CHILDREN
Chatsworth Farm & Adventure Playground
☎ 01246 565300; www.chatsworth.org
Gulliver's Kingdom
Temple Walk, Matlock Bath
☎ 01629 580540;
www.gulliversfun.co.uk
Theme-park fun including rollercoasters.
Matlock Farm Park
Darley Moor, Matlock ☎ 01246 590200;
www.matlockfarmpark.co.uk

■ SHOPPING
Bakewell
Market on Mon, includes cattle, except
Bank Holiday Mons when a general
market is held.
Buxton
Market, Tue and Sat. Farmers markets
first Thu of month.
Chapel-en-le-Frith
Market, Thu.
Matlock
General market, Tue and Fri.
Glossop
Indoor market, Thu; indoor and outdoor
market, Fri and Sat.
Holmfirth
Craft market, Sat and Bank Holiday
Mons.
Farmers Market, 3rd Sun of the month.
General market, Thu.
LOCAL SPECIALITIES
Bakewell Puddings
Original Bakewell Pudding Shop,
The Square, Bakewell ☎ 01629 812193;
www.bakewellpuddingshop.co.uk
Bloomers Original Bakewell Puddings,
Water Lane, Bakewell
☎ 01629 814844

Craft Workshops
Glossop Craft Centre, No 1 Smithy Fold,
off High Street East, Glossop
☎ 01457 863559;
www.glossopmaycrafts.co.uk
Pork Pies
Connoisseurs Deli, Water Street, Water
Lane, Bakewell ☎ 01629 812044

■ PERFORMING ARTS
Buxton Opera House
Water Street ☎ 0845 1272190;
www.buxtonoperahouse.org.uk

■ SPORTS & ACTIVITIES
ANGLING
Fly
Carsington Water ☎ 01629 540478;
www.carsingtonwater.com
Coarse
Combs Reservoir, Whaley Bridge
☎ 01663 762393
BOAT HIRE
Carsington Water ☎ 01629 540478;
www.carsingtonwater.com
CYCLE HIRE
Hayfield
Old Railway Station
☎ 01663 746222; www.peakdistrict.org
Manifold Valley Bike Hire
Old Station Car Park, Earlsway,
Waterhouses ☎ 01538 308609;
www.visitpeakdistrict.com
Peak District National Park Centre
Waterhouses ☎ 01298 84493
GUIDED WALKS
Buxton
From Tourist Information Centre
☎ 01298 25106
Derbyshire Dales Countryside Service
Planning and Development Services,
Town Hall, Matlock
☎ 01629 761326
Full guided walks service.
National Park Walks with a Ranger
Peak District National Park
☎ 01629 816200;
www.peakdistrict.gov.uk
Professional Blue Badge Guides
☎ 01629 534284;
www.blue-badge-guides.com
HORSE RIDING
Buxton Riding Centre
Fern Farm ☎ 01298 72319; www.
fernfarmcottages.co.uk
Haddon House Riding Stables
Over Haddon, Bakewell
☎ 01629 813723;
www.haddonhousestables.co.uk
LONG-DISTANCE FOOTPATHS & TRAILS
The High Peak Trail
Middleton Top Countryside Centre
☎ 01629 823204
Follows the former High Peak Railway
from High Peak Junction (Cromford) to
Dowlow (south of Buxton).

Manifold Trail
Manifold Valley Visitor Centre, Hulme End
☎ 01298 84679
Traces a former narrow-gauge railway
from Hulme End to Waterhouses
ROCK-CLIMBING
**Rock Lea Activity Centre,
Peak Activities Ltd**
Station Road, Hathersage
☎ 01433 650345; www.iain.co.uk
Outdoor activity specialists.
WATERSPORTS
Carsington Sports & Leisure
Carsington Water ☎ 01629 540478;
www.carsingtonwater.com

■ ANNUAL EVENTS & CUSTOMS
For the full programme visit
www.visitpeakdistrict.com
Well dressing in Chapel-en-le-Frith,
Buxworth and Buxton, Jul.
Ashford in the Water
Well dressing, late May/early Jun.
Blessing of the Wells Trinity Sunday, May.
Bakewell
Well dressing, late Jun/early Jul.
Carnival, early Jul.
Bakewell Show, early Aug.
Buxton
Antiques Fair, May.
Brass Band Festival, May
Buxton Festival, Jul.
Buxton Fringe Festival, Jul.
International Gilbert & Sullivan Festival,
Jul/Aug.
Chatsworth
Tudor Fair, May.
Horse Trials, mid/late May.
Horticultural Show, late Aug.
Country Fair, early Sep.
Music events, spring/autumn.
Dovedale
The Dovedale Dash, a 4.25-mile (6.8km)
run from Thorpe Pastures, early Nov.
Eyam
Well dressing and demonstration, Aug.
Plague Commemoration Service, last
Sunday in Aug.
Carnival, Aug/Sep.
Glossop
Jazz Festival, mid Jun.
Carnival and Country Fair, early Jul.
Victorian weekend, early Sep.
Well dressing and Padfield Plum
Fair, Sep.
Hayfield
Well dressing, mid July.
Sheepdog Trials, Sep.
Holmfirth
Folk Festival, early May.
Matlock
Carnival, Aug
Matlock Bath
Illuminations, late Aug/Oct.
Youlgreave
Well dressing, late Jun.

PUBS

SUFFOLK COAST

The Crown Hotel
High Street, Southwold IP18 6DP
☎ 01502 722275;
www.hotelsadnams.co.uk
This is a smart, no smoking old hotel with the emphasis on good food and good beer. The elegant beamed bar has a relaxed atmosphere with high-backed settles, kitchen chairs and bar stools. The smaller oak-panelled 'locals' bar has more of a traditional pubby atmosphere.

CAMBRIDGE & FENS

The Anchor
Silver Street, Cambridge CB3 9EL
☎ 01223 353554
Situated at the end of a medieval lane that borders Queens' College, the Anchor is set by the bridge over the River Cam. In fine weather this is an ideal spot to enjoy one of a range of fine ales or sampling a choice of hearty meals that includes lasagne, home-made pies and roast beef.

The Cock
47 High Street, Hemingford Grey
PE28 9BJ ☎ 01480 463609
A recent refurbishment has transformed this attractive little establishment into a gastro-pub. Expect blazing log fires in winter and a pretty garden in summer. Plenty of special ales and beers on hand pump, and a good choice of wines by the glass. The stylish restaurant serves lunches at sensible prices.

Dyke's End
8 Fair Green, Reach CB5 0JD
☎ 01638 743816; www.dykesend.co.uk
The pub takes its name from the nearby Devil's Dyke, and attracts visitors from Cambridge and Newmarket. But the inn is very much a destination in its own right, with a reputation for fine food, wines and home-brewed real ales.

The Pheasant Inn
Keyston PE28 0RE ☎ 01832 710241;
www.thepheasant-keyston.co.uk
The Pheasant Inn has an immaculate oak-beamed bar with a cosy atmosphere, open fires, simple wooden tables and chairs. They have a fine wine list and the food here has a high reputation, too.

NORFOLK BROADS

The Buckinghamshire Arms
Blickling NR11 6NF ☎ 01263 732133
This 17th-century former coaching inn serves good food, has a pretty garden and attractions of the Elickling Hall estate on the doorstep. The pub oozes character, and is a delight to visit, while the menu includes traditional and modern dishes.

King's Arms
Westgate Street, Blakeney NR25 7NQ
☎ 01263 740341;
www.blakeneykingsarms.co.uk
This attractive old inn just a stroll from the harbour gets crowded at times but is worth visiting. The simply furnished rooms have low ceilings, with some of the rooms offering wonderful views over the marshes. Excellent range of inexpensive food, and a good range of speciality beers.

The Old Ram
Ipswich Road, Tivetshall St Mary
NR15 2DE ☎ 01379 676794;
www.theoldram.co.uk
The Old Ram, a former coaching inn has a long tradition of tending to the needs of man and beast. In those former days the inn was a-buzz with visitors, and nothing seems to have changed, except the replacement of coach and four with the modern motor car. This is still a great attraction for discerning diners and those who know a good pint when they see one.

Walpole Arms
Itteringham NR11 7AR ☎ 01263 587258;
www.thewalpolearms.co.uk
The large open-plan bar in this attractive 18th-century dining pub has exposed oak beams, stripped brick walls, little windows, a mix of dining tables, and quietly chatty atmosphere. Choose from locally brewed ales, wines by the glass, cider, and local apple juice. There is a two-acre landscaped garden and vine-covered terrace to sit and relax on warm days, and a choice of meals is served.

LINCOLN & RUTLAND

The Blue Pig
9 Vine Street, Grantham NG31 6RQ
☎ 01476 563704
This is an attractive, jettied Tudor pub, with open fire, low beams, panelling, stripped stone and flagstones, and lots of pig ornaments, prints and bric-a-brac. They serve a good range of interesting changing ales and simple lunchtime food. No children or dogs.

WORCESTER & MALVERN HILLS

The Bear & Ragged Staff
Station Road, Bransford WR6 5JH
☎ 01886 833399;
www.bearatbransford.co.uk
Laden with accolades, this was Worcestershire Dining Pub of the Year in 2007, 2006 and 2004. Real ales and a comprehensive wine list complement local produce, such as Herefordshire steak, breast of pheasant or chargrilled leg of lamb. There is a garden for those warm summer days.

The Nag's Head
Bank Street, Malvern WR14 2JG
☎ 01684 574373;
www.nagsheadmalvern.co.uk
The Nag's Head keeps an astonishing range of real ales on hand pump. They also keep a fine range of wines by the glass, malt whiskies and Belgian beers.

The Swan
Whittington WR5 2RL ☎ 01905 351361;
www.swanatwhittington.com
Lovers of quality pub food have been dining here for years, during which the Swan has built an enviable reputation as the 'Pub with Food'. This popular country pub serves food with a Mediterranean tang, enhanced by a sun patio.

STRATFORD & VALE OF EVESHAM

The Bell
Alderminster, Stratford-upon-Avon
CV37 8NY ☎ 01789 450414;
www.thebellald.co.uk
With an enviable reputation for fine dining, perfect for Sunday lunch with the kids, it is easy to forget that The Bell is also an excellent pub, and 18th-century coaching inn.

The Four Alls
Binton Bridges, Welford-on-Avon,
Stratford-upon-Avon CV37 8PW
☎ 01789 750228;
www.fouralls.greatpubs.net
Open daily and offering inexpensive, quality bar meals, The Four Alls has a riverside pub garden and eating area, and a light, spacious interior.

SHROPSHIRE HILLS & THE STIPERSTONES

The Armoury
Victoria Quay, Victoria Avenue,
Shrewsbury SY1 1HH ☎ 01743 340525
Superb bar food is a hallmark here. The open plan interior, with arched windows, is housed in a former 18th-century warehouse. The pub is bright and light, with eclectic décor and a lively buzz. There is a great stone fireplace at one end, lots of old prints on brick walls, and Colonial-style ceiling fans whirring away. The comprehensive menu ranges from light meals and snacks to main meals. Typical dishes are chilli and coriander crab cakes, wild boar and apricot sausages, and pan-fried salmon with crab risotto.

Three Fishes
Fish Street, Shrewsbury SY1 1UR
☎ 01743 344793
Voted Pub of the Year 2010 by CAMRA, take the opportunity to enjoy a pint of real ale here. Cask Marque and CAMRA

2007 *Good Beer Guide* recommended. This lovely pub serves home-cooked food daily.

PEAK DISTRICT

The Barrel Inn
Bretton, near Eyam S32 5QD
☎ 01433 630856
Derbyshire's highest pub, The Barrel Inn stands right on the lip of Eyam Edge. Expect beers from Hardys and Hansons brewery and good-size portions of tasty, but unpretentious pub food, served in comfortable surroundings of antique seats, age-smoothed flagged floors and an oak-beamed bar. Sit outside on the front terrace or in the covered courtyard at the rear.

Cheshire Cheese Inn
Edale Road, Hope S33 6ZF
☎ 01433 620381
A compact, cheerful local with a warm welcome guaranteed. They stock beers from Peak District microbreweries and offer an ever-changing menu using local produce whenever possible. B&B accomodation available.

The Lathkil Hotel
Over Haddon, Bakewell DE45 1JE
☎ 01629 812501; www.lathkil.co.uk
This long-established inn's guests tuck into a mix of simple bar meals, inventive, top-notch dishes, and beers from Peak District breweries, including Peak Ales, Horbeam and Black Hole.

The Pack Horse Inn
Crowdecote, near Buxton SK17 0DB
☎ 01298 83618;
www.packhorseinn.co.uk
At the Pack Horse Inn, fine hand-pulled real ales compliment the excellent, locally sourced food. Accommodation is also available in 12 well-appointed, en-suite bedrooms.

Quiet Woman
Earl Sterndale, Buxton SK17 9SL
☎ 01298 83211
Enjoy a pint from a good range of well-kept real ales. You can also purchase local produce, such as cheese and eggs, from the pub, which is reputed to be more than 400 years old.

The Swan Inn
Macclesfield Road, Kettleshulme,
High Peak SK23 7QU ☎ 01663 732943;
www.the-swankettleshulme.com
Rescued from closure by a consortium of passionate and loyal villagers, this tiny pub is a champion of local brewery beers, complementing the range of largely locally sourced food. It's the perfect place to unwind after a good walk.

TEA ROOMS
CAMBRIDGE & FENS
Elevens West
11 Burleigh Street, Cambridge CB1 1DG
☎ 01223 369157
In the centre of Cambridge, this café is unpretentious and serves inexpensive snacks, sandwiches, coffee and tea.

Peacocks
65 Waterside, Ely CB7 4AU
☎ 01353 661100;
www.peacockstearoom.co.uk
Light meals include Norfolk ham salad and home-made cakes, available all day, including scones served with Cornish clotted cream. The choice of teas is remarkable, with over forty listed. The Special Afternoon Tea includes finger sandwiches, scones with jam and cake.

NORFOLK BROADS
Mary Janes Fish and Chips Restaurant
27–29 Garden Street, Cromer NR27 9HW
☎ 01263 511208
It is unthinkable to visit Norfolk and not to head for the seafood delights of Cromer. In Cromer they pride themselves on serving only the best and freshest fish and chips. Mary Jones is both a take-away and an eat-in place, and isn't restricted to fish.

LINCOLN & RUTLAND
Sam's Place
11–12 St Mary's Street, Stamford PE9 2DE ☎ 01780 766511
This traditional, friendly tea room is located above a china shop, and offers a good range of teas and coffees, and freshly baked scones.

Uncle Henry's Farm Shop & Café
Grayingham Grange, Grayingham, Gainsborough DN21 4JD
☎ 01652 640308;
www.unclehenrys.co.uk
Uncle Henry's is a farm shop, but set in a converted 19th-century barn in a picturesque farmyard complete with duck pond and animals. This local food hub is well worth visiting if you have children. As a bonus, the farm shop has the freshest fruit and vegetables, home-produced pork and meat from local suppliers.

Mount Pleasant Windmill Tearooms
North Cliff Road, Kirton in Lindsey, Gainsborough DN21 4NH
☎ 01652 640177;
www.trueloafbakery.co.uk
A chance for a quiet bite in a windmill. Mount Pleasant offers welcoming tea rooms serving light lunches, scones, cream teas and a delicious range of home-baked cakes made with the organic flour from the windmill. There is also a wholefood shop with quality chutneys, pickles and jams.

Tealby Tearooms
12 Front Street, Tealby, Market Rasen LN8 3XU ☎ 01673 838261;
www.tealbytearooms.co.uk
Savour a friendly atmosphere while enjoying cream teas with home-made cakes and Lincolnshire Plum Loaf with either butter or cheese. Salads, sandwiches and snacks are also available or you can pick up locally made Lincolnshire ice cream. Home-made desserts include fruit pie with cream.

The Rutland Coffee House
10 Crown Walk, Oakham LE15 9QB
☎ 01572 722216
This traditional tea room and restaurant in a small arcade, just off the High Street offers a good range of all things calorific in the centre of this bustling little town.

WORCESTER & MALVERN HILLS
Cathedral Café
7 Severn Street, Worcester WR1 2ND
☎ 01905 745680
Perfect for light meals (including vegetarian dishes), lunch, snacks, tea, coffee, wine and beer. Children are welcome and high chairs are available.

The Elms
Abberley, Worcester WR6 6AT
☎ 01299 896666;
www.theelmshotel.co.uk
The Elms is a country house hotel set in well kept gardens and lawns. The Queen Anne house has ornate moulded ceilings, carved fireplaces and stained glass windows. There are more than ten different varieties of tea served alongside a light lunch menu with snacks, sandwiches, cakes and afternoon tea.

STRATFORD & VALE OF EVESHAM
The Café Within
All Saints Parish Church, Royal Leamington Spa CV31 1AA
☎ 01926 429169;
www.allsaintsleamington.org.uk
Open lunchtimes from Wednesday to Saturday, this cafe serves soup, light lunches, snacks, cakes, tea and coffee at reasonable prices. Children are welcome.

Bensons
4 Bard's Walk, Stratford-upon-Avon CV37 6EY ☎ 01789 261116;
www.bensonsrestaurant.co.uk
At Bensons you can pamper yourself with a Champagne breakfast or merely enjoy a pot of Earl Grey. Enjoy English breakfast muffins with butter and jam, Danish pastries, smoked salmon and lightly scrambled eggs or eggs Benedict.

Hathaway Tea Rooms and Bakery
19 High Street, Stratford-upon-Avon CV37 6AU ☎ 01789 292404
The building dates back to 1610, but has been used for this family business only since 1971. On entrance to the tea rooms you are greeted with a quaint bakery with delicious-looking cakes, all of which are baked on the premises. The tea rooms are on two floors.

Henley Ice Cream
152 High Street, Henley-in-Arden B95 5BT ☎ 01564 795172
Although this famous 16th-century establishment has been producing traditional premium dairy ice cream for over 65 years, it also does a good line in morning coffee and home-made cakes, hot or cold light lunches and afternoon cream teas, and is worth tracking down.

Thomas Oken Tea Rooms
20 Castle Street, Warwick CV34 4BP
☎ 01926 499307
Formerly a dolls museum, this tea shop is brimming with historic ambience and Englishness. Choose from Oken's afternoon tea, Oken's cream tea or Warwick cream tea, all served with a giant scone, strawberry preserve and clotted cream. There is a delicious range of sandwiches and light snacks as well.

SHROPSHIRE HILLS & STIPERSTONES
Rock Cottage
Abcott, Clungunford SY7 0PX
☎ 01588 660631;
www.rockcottagetearooms.co.uk
The Rock Cottage was awarded the Tea Guild's Award of Excellence 2010, and people come from far and wide for its 1940s interior, cottage garden, home-made cakes and light lunches.

De Grey's
5–6 Broad Street, Ludlow SY8 1NG
☎ 01584 872764; www.degreys.co.uk
De Grey's is located behind an attractive beamed bakery. Afternoon tea includes a sandwich, fancy cake, and fruit scone with jam and cream. Also available are teacakes, pastries, scones and buns. Meals are served throughout the day.

PEAK DISTRICT
Cauldwell's Mill
Rowsley, near Bakewell, Matlock DE4 2EB ☎ 01629 733185;
www.cauldwellsmill.couk
Cauldwell's Mill, built in the 19th century, is a complex of craft workshops and a working water-powered mill where you can take tea while enjoying the lovely view. Everything is made on the premises using freshly milled flour. They offer ten varieties of tea alongside a lunch menu of snacks, sandwiches and set teas.

The Coffee Shop
Lyme Park, Disley, SK12 2NR
☎ 01663 762023;
www.nationaltrust.org.uk
In the shadow of magnificent Lyme Hall, this unpretentious and welcoming coffee shop is a convenient place for a refreshment break and offers simple, filling fare.

Eyam Tea Rooms
The Square, Eyam S32 5RB
☎ 01433 631274;
www.eyamtearooms.co.uk
Overlooking the pretty square this tea room has a reputation for fine home-made soups, cakes and pastries, light lunches and snacks.

Grumbley's
Church Street, Hayfield SK22 2JE
☎ 01663 741444; www.grumbleys.com
This modern café-bar and bistro is popular with walkers to Kinder. Renowned for its inventive cooking, there's also a good range of snacks, pastries, cakes and more substantial meals; in the evenings it is a restaurant.

The Original Bakewell Pudding Shop
The Square, Bakewell DE45 1BT
☎ 01629 812193;
www.bakewellpuddingshop.co.uk
Above the shop where Bakewell's famed recipe was recreated, this comfortable, air-conditioned restaurant serves teas, coffees, snacks and three-course meals. Don't miss out on a generous helping of Bakewell Pudding. In the evenings, you can watch the pudding makers in action or make one yourself

Woodbine Café
Castleton Road, Hope S33 6RD
☎ 01433 621407
A welcoming, homely stone terraced cottage, with a sheltered tea garden, not far from Hope's distinctive church. The café offers an interior that is cosy and tranquil. They also offer B&B.

The Wrinkled Stocking Tea Room
Huddersfield Road, Holmfirth HD9 2JS
☎ 01484 681408;
www.wrinkledstocking.co.uk
Pastel walls and crisp tablecloths – just what Nora Batty would expect! Indulge in home-made hot and cold food plus speciality cakes and good Yorkshire tea.

Wales

Wales

Wales has always been, and remains today, a country within a country, which has for centuries passionately defended its identity and still proudly uses its Celtic mother tongue as a first language in some remote parts of the interior.

Blessed with some of natures finest gifts, Wales can boast dramatic mountain ranges, verdant pastureland, beautiful lakes and some of the most stunning coastline in Britain. Wales' western edges reach out into the Gulf Stream and consequently benefit from the balmy influence of the warm waters.

The people of this ancient land fought many long and bloody battles to keep their individuality and despite it becoming part of the Union in 1536, once you cross the border from England to Wales, it is apparent that you are entering a proud and different country.

Cardiff

CLOCKWISE FROM RIGHT: THE MILLENNIUM STADIUM;
BUTE PARK, FROM CARDIFF CASTLE

CARDIFF CITY CENTRE
MAP REF **399 H3**

Much of Cardiff's history is encompassed within its castle, which stands proudly in the heart of the city. The moated Norman castle was built on the site of the Roman fort – some of the Roman foundation walls can still be seen. The castle was left ruinous by Owain Glyndwr, but eventually it was rebuilt by Richard Beauchamp, the Earl of Warwick and continued as a residence for several centuries.

The powerful Bute family, who were descendants of the royal Stuarts, took possession of the castle by marriage in 1797. It was the 3rd Marquis of Bute who commissioned William Burges to redevelop the living quarters into the gothic Victorian style you see today. No expense was spared: the interiors were opulent, using marble, gold leaf and fine hardwoods from around the world. Many of the rooms have amazing decorated ceilings, stained glass windows, murals of historical and mythological figures and fine works of art on the walls.

The city centre buildings are a mix of modern, Victorian and Edwardian. The Venetian style Morgan Arcade with its glass gable roofs and elegant balustrades is a particularly fine example of the Victorian shopping arcades to be found in the city. The Butes were responsible for most of the 19th-century civic buildings, including the majestic City Hall, the Law Courts, and the National Museum, which are divided by long tree-lined avenues and the lawned gardens of Cathays Park. Built from gleaming Portland stone, the City Hall has a 200 feet (60m) high clock tower and a large dome topped by a Welsh dragon. Its fine Marble Hall with stained glass windows provides a magnificent setting for the series of Serraveza marble statues of the 'Heroes of Wales'.

The buildings look across to the broad open spaces of Bute Park, once part of the grounds of Cardiff Castle, which you can see peeping through the trees. The 130-acre (52ha) park with its ornamental trees extends to the banks of the River Taff, where you look across to Sophia Gardens and the Glamorgan County Cricket ground. Also on the banks of the Taff are the two stadiums of Cardiff Arms Park. One is the home of Cardiff rugby club: the other, the gigantic Millennium Stadium. Seen from the river the gleaming stadium resembles the bridge of an ocean liner. You'll get the best view if you catch a waterbus from the Bute Park jetty and cruise to the waterfront of Cardiff Bay.

CARDIFF BAY MAP REF **399 H3**

Cardiff's prosperity and rise to importance came with the Industrial Revolution. The discovery of coking coal allowed the iron smelting industry to boom in the valleys to the north and Cardiff became the obvious choice for a port. The Bute family enlarged the docks and made Cardiff into one of the world's largest coal - and iron - exporting ports. Tiger Bay, the area between dock and city became one of the roughest but most lively multicultural centres in the world. Pubs with names like the Bucket of Blood and the House of Blazes were patronized by sailors from all corners of the globe.

By the 1970s, when the coal industry had been decimated, Cardiff's waterfront had become an industrial wasteland, an area of deprivation and decay. Tiger Bay had lost its soul. With this in mind the presiding Welsh Secretary, Nicholas Edwards announced the establishment of the Cardiff Bay Development Corporation. Its mission was to put Cardiff back on the international map and to create a thriving maritime city. The harbour at Cardiff had one of the world's most expansive tidal ranges: up to 46 feet (14m) – low tide rendered it inaccessible for up to 14 hours a day. The idea of a barrage that created a 494-acre (200ha) freshwater lake out of the bay solved the problem but brought out vehement opposition from Friends of the Earth, the RSPB and local residents, who believed this would be an ecological disaster for the thousands of birds whose wetland and mud-flat habitat would be submerged beneath the lake. The Welsh Office believed that the scheme would be the catalyst for a complete dockside development and persisted with the plans. In 1993 the Cardiff Barrage Act was passed. The £220-million project included three locks for ships to pass through, sluice gates to control the water level in the lake, and a fish pass to allow the sea trout and salmon to access their spawning area in the Taff and Ely rivers. To compensate for the loss of wildlife habitat 1,000 acres (40ha) of farmland were flooded in the Gwent Levels 15 miles (24km) to the east to create a freshwater marsh.

The 0.75-mile (1.2km) long barrage, completed in 1997, and the 0.5-mile (800m) long sand and stone embankment provided an 8-mile (13km) waterfront in the bay. Besides picnic spots there's a sail-like structure with a wooden viewing platform where visitors can gaze out across the Bristol Channel to the distant West Country coastline. The bay is still

CARDIFF BAY WATERFRONT

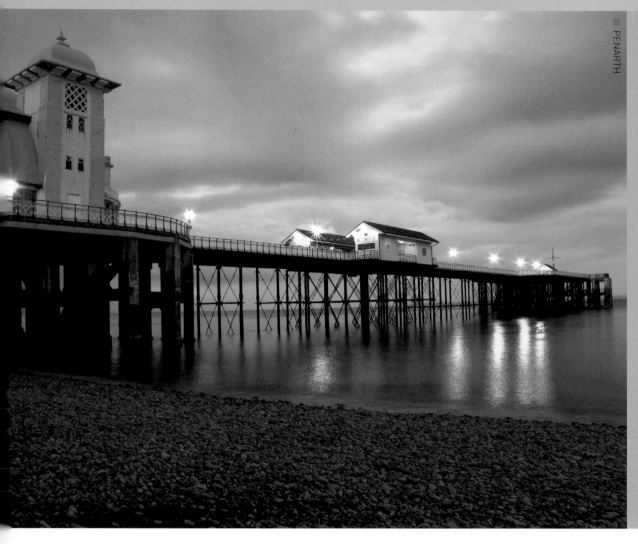

PENARTH

Visit

CASTELL COCH – THE RED CASTLE

This fairytale castle a few miles north of Cardiff echoes those found in Bavaria, with its circular red sandstone towers and conical roofs. Built on a limestone outcrop on wooded hillslopes, the original Norman castle had fallen into disrepair, but the 3rd Marquis of Bute commissioned William Burges to refurbish the structure to the same extravagant standards that he lavished on Cardiff Castle.

Visit

NATIONAL MUSEUM CARDIFF, CATHAYS PARK

Housed in one of the magnificent Portland-stone buildings of the Civic Centre A fascinating 'Evolution of Wales' discovery tour of Wales from the dawn of time, through the Iron Age and the Industrial Revolution to the present day. The collection of dinosaurs, both big and small, and a 'moving' woolly mammoth that roars are particularly memorable. The museum also exhibits one of the finest Impressionist art collections in Europe and includes work by Cezanne, Renoir and Monet.

good for birdwatching. Long-legged waders like the grey heron, the egret, a small white heron-like bird, and the cormorant, another heron-like bird with a black coat, can be seen waiting patiently and silently for their fish suppers to swim by. The wetland reserve by the Taff Estuary hosts great crested grebe and snipe.

Cardiff's regeneration continued with Tiger Bay and the dock area. The pristine waters of the new lake were far easier on the eye than the tidal mud flats and it wasn't hard to sell the idea of luxury apartments in the bay. The National Assembly of Wales decided that they would build their Senedd Building in the heart of the development. Designed by Richard Rogers, the revolutionary building was constructed with energy conservation in mind – its renewable energy systems aim to cut running costs by nearly a half. Not far from the Senedd building is the Millennium Centre, which showcases the performing arts. Built from local slate it has a bilingual inscription: 'In these stones horizons sing' and *Creu gwir fel gwydr o ffwrnais awen*, which in English means 'creating truth like glass from the furnace of inspiration'.

Old and modern mingle on the waterfront with the terracotta Pierhead Building lying right next to the Millennium

Centre. Built by the Bute family in Gothic style, the Grade 1 listed old port headquarters now houses a permanent interactive exhibition that gives an insight into the workings of the National Assembly for Wales. Not far away, the Norwegian Church, which was built in 1869 as a place of worship for the large number of Scandinavian sailors, had fallen into disrepair by the 1960s. A trust set up by the author Roald Dahl, who was baptized here, financed the rebuilding of the church on the present site. The attractive spired timber building painted gleaming white is now a coffee shop and art gallery.

LLANDAFF MAP REF 399 H3

Although it's just a couple of miles from Cardiff's centre and officially part of the city these days, the ancient city of Llandaff has a long history of its own. Here, by the banks of the Taff, the 6th-century Celtic saint, Dyfrig, founded one of Britain's earliest Christian communities. All that remains of the original church is an old stone cross, which can be seen by the Chapter House. Early in the 12th century the building of a much larger Norman cathedral was instigated by Bishop Urban, and during the next couple of centuries the proud building took shape in a mix of Norman and Early English styles. The Reformation

saw the cathedral fall into neglect and it is said that it was used at various times as a beer house and a cattle shed. Later two towers collapsed and the roof of the nave caved in. Llandaff was described as 'a miserable village of mean cottages'. In 1734, however, the restoration began, first under John Wood who envisaged an Italian temple, then under J F Seddon and John Pritchard. The cathedral suffered more devastation during World War II when it was wrecked by a German bomb. Once again it was rebuilt. Under the guidance of architect George Pace it became an intriguing mix of ancient and modern. A huge arch bearing Sir Jacob Epstein's aluminium statue, *Christ in Majesty*, dominates the interior.

PENARTH MAP REF 399 H3

Sited on high headland overlooking the south bank of the Ely Estuary and Cardiff Bay, Penarth was for centuries a small fishing village that grew to prominence as a coal shipping port. However, the cliff-lined shingle beach, the fine outlook across the Bristol Channel and the clean sea air attracted wealthy coal and iron merchants, who built fine villas. Tourism was introduced by the Victorians, who constructed a long esplanade on the south shore, then added a pier and acres

of flower-decked gardens and parkland. Penarth became known as The Gardens by the Sea. The town's fortunes flourished with the regeneration of Cardiff Bay and it can easily be reached by waterbus, car or train. The old coal harbour has been replaced by an attractive yacht marina, and the modern architect-designed waterfront contrasts with the classic Victorian buildings and leafy parks.

One of the town's skyline landmarks on Penarth Head, the Victorian parish church of St Augustine's, has a splendid 90-foot (27m) saddle-back tower.

ST FAGANS CASTLE MAP REF 399 H3

Very much at the heart of St Fagans is the National History Museum. Sited in the grounds of St Fagans Castle, an Elizabethan manor house given over to the people of Wales by the Earl of Plymouth. Since its opening in 1948, more than 40 original buildings from different ages have been re-erected in the 100-acre (40ha) parkland, including a woollen mill from Brecknockshire, a pretty timber-framed Montgomery cottage (c1600), an 18th-century Unitarian chapel of the Teifi Valley and a longhouse from Radnorshire. Craftsmen demonstrate their skills in the mill and workshops, giving visitors a real taste of Welsh folklore and bygone days.

South Wales & Pembrokeshire

CLOCKWISE FROM TOP LEFT: OFF FISHGUARD; A LIFEGUARD STATION AT TENBY;
A SEAL ON THE ROCKS; RED-AND-WHITE DECKCHAIRS ON TENBY'S SOUTH BEACH

FISHGUARD MAP REF 402 C6

Built in 1906 as a rival to the great shipping ports of Liverpool and Southampton, Fishguard never did fulfill that potential but remains a busy port and is the main sailing place in North Pembrokeshire.

Lower Fishguard was used as a location for the film adaptation of Dylan Thomas' *Under Milk Wood* in 1971 starring Richard Burton and Elizabeth Taylor. This area of the village makes up a third of the place, with Upper Fishguard and Goodwick completing the rest. All parts, however, cling to the shores of Fishguard Bay and have attractive fishermen's cottages sprinkled through the village streets.

Apart from its movie fame, Fishguard is also known for being the target of a failed and quite hopeless invasion attempt by the French in the late 18th century. In 1797 four vessels carrying French convicts and mercenaries, actually led by William Tate, an American, attempted to land at Fishguard Bay but were driven on by the cannon fire from Fishguard Fort. They went further around the coast to Carregwastad and came ashore only to get drunk on the local brew and to try to steal poultry. They were efficiently gathered up by the local farmers' wives and made to surrender in the local hostelry, the Royal Oak Inn, where evidence of this ridiculous saga can still be seen today.

The Royal Oak still plays an important part in village life today and is one of the venues for the Fishguard Folk Festival held each year. During the day, performances at this excellent event are perfect for families, while the more raucous performances take place at the pub in the evenings. The festival atmosphere is great and people can take part in music masterclasses.

HAVERFORDWEST & ST BRIDES BAY MAP REF 402 B7

Sited on the Western Cleddau, one of the two wide rivers that flow into the Milford Haven, Haverfordwest was, before the arrival of the railways, a thriving port with barges, small steamships and coasting vessels regularly docking on the quayside. The castle, which was built by the 1st Earl of Pembroke, Gilbert de Clare in the 12th century, dominates the town from its position atop a lofty crag above the river. Being a Norman stronghold, Haverfordwest was attacked and burned to the ground by Llywelyn the Great, but the castle survived, as it did when besieged in 1405 by another Prince of Wales, Owain Glyndwr. However, Oliver Cromwell ordered its destruction during the Civil War. The substantial walls and keep remain today and are still an impressive sight – second only to Pembroke in this region.

ST BRIDES BAY

Today, Haverfordwest is a thriving market town, the principal shopping centre for the area, with many stores by the quayside. It's worth a visit to the town museum, which is housed in the castle off Church Street. Also worth seeing are the recently excavated ruins of the Augustinian Priory of St Mary and St Thomas the Martyr, a short walk from the centre.

Haverfordwest is an excellent base from which to explore Pembrokeshire's West Coast and St Brides Bay. Facing west to the Atlantic, most of the St Brides beaches are exposed to the prevailing winds. These whip up the surf and makes the coast here extremely popular for watersports such as surfing, windsurfing and, the new phenomenon, kite-surfing. The most northerly of the beaches is Newgale Sands, where golden sands stretch 2 miles (3km) from Newgale village in the north to the rocks of Rickets Head. A shingle bank separates the beach from the village. Patrolling lifeguards designate the safe swimming areas.

There's another long sandy beach at Broadhaven, a lively resort with a good range of facilities. It's worth exploring the northern end to see natural rock arches and stacks. To the south lies Little Haven. This pretty village with a slipway, used by the lifeboat, and a beach, is a popular place with sea-anglers.

Most spectacular is Marloes Sands where violent earth movements thrust up the rock strata to form steeply angled rocky cliffs that resemble yacht sails caught in a great gust of wind. Marloes village is a 0.6-mile (1km) walk from the isolated sandy beach.

INLAND GOWER MAP REF 398 F3

Back in 1956, the Gower Peninsula was designated Britain's first Area of Outstanding Natural Beauty, and it certainly lives up to that description. As well as this, a third of the area is a Site of Special Scientific Interest, not forgetting that a large stretch of the Gower coastline has been recognized as a Heritage Coast.

The Gower Peninsula's landscape is diverse and encompasses wooded valleys and soaring limestone cliffs on its southern coast, in complete contrast to the salt marshes and mud flats near to the northern coastline. Inland, you'll find heath, grazing land and farmland that is broken up into tiny parcels of fields. Each terrain is important to wildlife and the mud flats are especially vital to a great variety of wild birds (consequently the area is also very popular with twitchers).

Inland, there is a smattering of little villages, such as Reynoldston, situated on the Cefn Bryn ridge from where there are far-reaching views of the peninsula. Also of interest on inland Gower are the ruins of the 14th-century Weobley Castle. It's fortifications are indicative of its defensive position, and there were modifications made to strengthen them in the 15th and 16th centuries. However, the castle was used in later years as a farmhouse and there is an exhibition on site tracing its history within the building.

SOUTH WALES & PEMBROKESHIRE

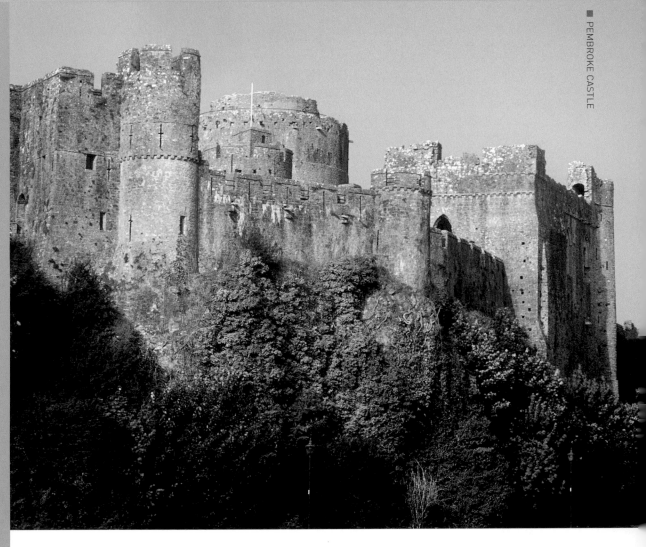

PEMBROKE CASTLE

Visit
SKOMER

There's a summer ferry (not Mondays) to Skomer Island from Martin's Haven on the headland west of Marloes. On the short voyage you may see porpoises and dolphins, or even a basking shark. You'll almost certainly see some puffins peeping from their burrows. Like much of the mainland Skomer Island is girt with dark volcanic cliffs, which accommodate southern Britain's largest colony of nesting seabirds. On the pink thrift and sea campion-decked clifftops are the remnants of an Iron Age settlement – a standing stone, burial cairns, ancient field boundaries and the earthworks of hut circles. Footpaths criss-cross the island. Do not stray off the paths.

Visit
BURIAL CROMLECH

Pentre Ifan is probably the finest example of a Neolithic burial cromlech in Wales. It dates back to around 3500 BC and its huge capstone measures over 16 feet (5m), poised on three 8-foot (2.5m) uprights, which seem to frame and capture Carn Ingli's mystical outlines to perfection, especially when the sun is low in the sky. The cromlech can be accessed free of charge and is well signposted from the A487 east of Newport and the B4329 Preseli road at Brynberian.

Visit
THE GUN TOWER MUSEUM

Built in 1851 to protect the Royal Naval Dockyard at Pembroke, the Gun Tower houses a museum illustrating Pembroke's military heritage. You can learn about life as experienced by one of Queen Victoria's soldiers who waited for an invasion that never came, see models of the old navy dockyard where more than 200 ships were built, and learn about the World War II flying boats – Pembroke was the world's largest flying boat base.

Activity
RAMSAY ISLAND

You can take the regular Ramsay Island boat from the slipway at St Justinian's, 3 miles (5km) west of St David's and you will be transported across the fast-flowing Sound and infamous reef known as the Bitches to a haven for wildlife. Ramsay Island's rugged coastline, with its 300-foot (91m) cliffs and isolated rock coves, is home to the largest colony of grey seals in southwest Britain.

MANORBIER MAP REF 402 C7

Overlooking the South Pembrokeshire Heritage Coast, Manorbier draws visitors for its beautiful sandy beach or to marvel at its magnificent castle.

Manorbier Castle was begun in the 12th century and managed to evade attack from both the Welsh and Cornwell's armies, surviving intact. The castle is still the baronial home of the Barri family.

MILFORD HAVEN MAP REF 402 B7

'It's one of the world's finest harbours,' Admiral Lord Nelson claimed as he gazed admiringly across the vast blue waters of Milford Haven. And this lovely sheltered estuary has provided one of Britain's most important maritime strongholds since the days of the Tudor kings. And yet Milford Haven the town is a more recent affair, built and planned in the late 18th century by Sir William Hamilton, the husband of Nelson's mistress, Emma. In the 1960s the big ships arrived – carrying crude oil for processing in new refineries. Of these, only the Texaco plant now survives. Today Milford boasts a pleasant harbour front and marina, overlooked by the Georgian buildings of Hamilton Terrace. In 1991 memories were rekindled when the Tall Ships Race came to town.

MYNYDD PRESELI
MAP REF 402 C6

The Mynydd Preseli rise from Cardigan Bay at Fishguard and Newport. They reach their peak at Foel Cwmcerwyn, 1,760 feet (536m) above sea level. They're not that high by Welsh standards but these peaks have always been synonymous with all things spiritual.

Buried beneath your feet are the settlers from pre-history: the Neolithic tribes who were here before the 'true Welsh', the Celts, came from across the sea. Cromlechs, the earthwork and stone remains of fortress walls and hut circles, are liberally scattered across the map for you to discover. Stonehenge in Wiltshire was built from rocks hewn from the Preselis. The rock that the monoliths were carved from, an igneous spotted dolerite, is exclusive to Carnmenyn on the eastern side of the range.

If you've first visited the county's English-speaking south coast you may be surprised when you arrive at Rosebush, a tiny village that lies to the south of Foel Cwmcerwyn, for this friendly place is Welsh-speaking. The little village, which is the starting point for the best Preseli walks, has a campsite and one of the best inns in Wales, Tafarn y Sinc.

NEWPORT MAP REF 399 H3

While its neighbour Fishguard is bustling with cars and lorries rushing to make the ferry to Ireland, life in little Newport, tucked away in the far northwest corner of Pembrokeshire, chugs along at a more relaxed pace. Here the distinctive crag-topped Carn Ingli ('Angel Mountain') rises from the back gardens of the villagers' cottages, while small boats bobble from their moorings or lean against the sandbars of the Nevern Estuary. Although only 1,138-feet (347m) high, Carn Ingli is distinctively rugged and its cloak of heather and gorse is capped by jagged outcrops of dolerite. The ramparts that remain from an Iron Age fort ring the summit of the hill, which is scattered with the foundations of many of those early settlers' circular huts.

Newport Castle is part fortress, part manor house – it has been inhabited as a private dwelling for the past 150 years. Built in the 13th century by Norman baron William Fitzmartin, the castle was held for centuries by the powerful lords of Cemaes. As can be seen from its ruined battlements, the fortress was involved in bloody conflict, first in 1215 when captured and sacked by Llewelyn the Great, Prince of Wales, then by Owain Glyndwr. Fitzmartin also established St Mary's Church, whose impressive Norman square tower vies for dominance with the castle.

The River Nevern divides Newport's two beaches. On the north side there's an excellent sandy beach with safe bathing away from the currents of the river mouth. Parrog beach on the south side is for walkers who can stroll along the clifftops, past thickets of colourful gorse.

PEMBROKE MAP REF 402 C7

Pembroke is an attractive walled town with a 900-year history dating back to its Norman castle, which overlooks the town from its perch on a limestone crag. Surrounded by water on three sides, the castle, built by the Earls of Pembroke, was one of the biggest and most powerful in Wales. The walls of the keep are 7 feet (2m) thick and 75 feet (23m) high. A secret underground passage burrows beneath the Great Hall to the harbour. Harry Tudor, the grandson of John of Gaunt and a descendant of Llewelyn the Great, was born in the castle. On returning from exile he advanced with an army that defeated Richard III at Bosworth Field, after which he was crowned King Henry VII.

In 1977 Pembroke was designated an Outstanding Conservation Area. In the bustling main street, lined with both Georgian and Tudor buildings there are some fascinating shops, and good cafés and restaurants. If it's peace you're after, a stroll by the river and Mill Pond will take you around the castle walls.

RHOSSILI MAP REF 398 F3

This delightful town enjoys an enviable position at the end of Rhossili Bay, a beautiful golden beach, and the village backs on to open downland of Rhossili Down, complete with many archaeological wonders. The downs rise up to The Beacon which climbs to 632 feet (193m) and from which there are great views. This hill is also popular with avid hang-gliders and is now under the ownership of the National Trust.

Of historical note are the Bronze Age burial mounds on the downs and the Neolithic burial chambers. The chambers can be found just north of the Beacon at Sweyne's Howes.

Just past Rhossili to the west is Worm's Head, the most westerly point on the Gower Peninsula. A set of rocks takes you to the outer point, but take care.

ST DAVID'S MAP REF 402 B6

Set on a windswept plateau, St David's, Britain's smallest city, is as isolated from urban life as is possible. Flanked by the dolerite crests of Carn Llidi and Carnedd-lleithr, this looks and feels as if it is an inhospitable corner of the world. And so it was when Dewi, a 6th-century Celtic preacher who was later to become St David, patron saint of Wales, sailed from Ireland to set up his monastery here.

When you arrive in St David's and walk up the High Street past the gift shops, cottages, the boat-trip vendors' offices and the cafés, there are no signs of the grand ecclesiastical buildings. They're hidden in the hollow of the Alun Valley behind Cross Square, and it's only when you descend down the Pebbles to the Bell Tower that they appear. At first glance the cathedral appears as austere as the surrounding landscape, yet the purple-hued sandstone and perfect proportions give it quite an impressive presence. Inside, the cathedral is light and airy, with striking ornamental Norman arches and the slightly leaning piers of the nave lead your gaze to a splendid roof constructed of Irish oak.

The oldest part of the current cathedral, the nave, dates back to 1180 – the original tower collapsed in 1220. In the early 14th century Bishop Henry de Gower raised the walls of the aisles, inserted much grander windows and built the south porch, transept chapels and Lady Chapel. A century later Bishop Vaughan built the tower up to its present height and added the splendid roof.

In 1862 George Gilbert Scott renovated the cathedral. While doing so he discovered two skeletons, believed to be St David and his friend St Justinian, now kept in an oak chest in the Holy Trinity Chapel.

For around nine days in May and June each year, St David's Cathedral holds a festival of classical music. St David's three cathedral choirs attend, as well as many top musicians from around the world.

Across the Alun stream the large and magnificent ruins of the Bishop's Palace make a good venue for concerts and plays. There are permanent exhibtions.

SAUNDERSFOOT MAP REF 402 C7

Once a small fishing village, which flourished with finds of high-quality anthracite coal, Saundersfoot has since been caught up in near-neighbour Tenby's popularity. It's not hard to see why. Set at the foot of a pleasant wooded valley, the village has an attractive harbour alongside wonderful golden sands. The village is a popular centre for fishing, sailing and all manner of watersports.

From Saundersfoot you can easily get to Amroth and the start of the lengthy Pembrokeshire Coastal Path.

RHOSSILI

TENBY

There's another National Trust car park (fee) at Stackpole Quay near to the site of Stackpole Court. The mansion was demolished in 1963 when punitive taxes forced the Cawdors to dispose of their Welsh assets. The quay, a tiny inlet with a stone-built harbour pier, marks a clearly visible transition between the old red sandstone cliffs of Manorbier and the limestone of southwest Pembrokeshire. A short walk across fields and clifftops leads to some steps down into Barafundle Bay, a traffic-free golden sandy beach ideal for swimming or a spot of sunbathing. Further sojourns through the pines and sycamores at the far end of the bay take you to the cliffs, arches and stacks of Stackpole Head.

If you time your visit for when the military are not training, you can take the minor road leading south from Bosherton to St Govan's car park. Steps lead down to the 13th-century St Govan's Chapel, a tiny building wedged into a fissure at the base of the cliffs on the site of a Celtic hermit's cell. St Govan, an 11th-century saint, is believed to be buried beneath the altar.

TENBY MAP REF 402 C7

Tenby, by far the biggest and most successful of Pembrokeshire's resorts, is surrounded by caravan sites and it's often buzzing with coach parties and holiday-makers from all backgrounds. On Bank Holidays the town feels like it's going to burst with the weight of its own popularity. But Tenby has undeniable beauty. Brightly colour-washed cottages wrap themselves around a small sandy beach, framed by the pier of the lifeboat station, the harbour and the small boats in the bay. Take an after-dinner stroll along the promenade with those cottages and the old castle floodlit against the night sky.

Tenby has two distinct parts. Within the largely intact medieval town walls many of its ancient narrow streets have been cobbled to re-create their authenticity, but outside these walls, overlooking the large South Beach, the Victorian influence is there in the traditional seaside terraces.

Castle Hill looks down on both the old and new towns, but little remained of the castle after its destruction in the Civil War. Much of the town's history from the Stone Age to present times can be traced by visiting the Tenby Museum and Art Gallery on Castle Hill. This includes charters and privileges granted by the Tudors and the Earls of Pembroke.

A devised town trail visits the walls and many of the historic buildings, including the Tudor Merchant's House (National Trust), which is fitted out with authentic furnishings and has three walls with the remains of early frescoes.

SOLVA MAP REF 402 B6

Three miles (5km) east of St David's is Solva, a village of two parts. The more modern upper village lines the A487 coast road, while in the lower, more attractive part, cottages, small shops and restaurants cluster around the harbour at the sheltered head of a long, winding tidal inlet. These days Solva is a busy little tourist trap but it was founded on maritime traditions. A thriving port until the arrival of the railways, it had warehouses and a dozen or so limekilns. Solva once boasted a passenger service to New York. Unusually, the passengers would have to bring their own food for the voyage!

Though it's a fine place for pottering about and having a spot of lunch, Solva is one of the best bases for a coastal walk, maybe to St David's (get the bus back), or just a stroll along the Gribin, where there's an Iron Age settlement and a perfect view back to the village.

STACKPOLE MAP REF 402 C7

The 2,000-acre (810ha) Stackpole estate, which was once owned by the powerful Scottish Cawdor family but now managed by the National Trust, is situated between Bosherton, Stackpole and St Govan's Head. It encompasses some of Pembrokeshire's finest coastal scenery.

Bosherton, a tiny village at the western end of the estate, is well placed for a visit to the Bosherton Lily Ponds. These were created by flooding three limestone valleys. It has been claimed that this was the home of the Lady of the Lake and from where King Arthur gained his sword, Excalibur. It's certainly a magical place for nature lovers, who can wander through the woodland at the waters' edge to reach the seashore at Broad Haven beach. A June visit will reveal water lilies on the waters of the Western Arm. Visitors include the cormorant, grey heron, kingfisher, coot and moorhen, and you're likely to see dragonfly on the lakes.

STRUMBLE HEAD: AN INVIGORATING TRUNDLE

The headland cliffs tower above the pounding Atlantic surf, the path cuts an airy, at times precarious, line across their tops and the sky is alive with the sound of seabirds. Atlantic grey seals, porpoises and even dolphins are regularly spotted in the turbulent waters.

DISTANCE/TIME 8 miles (12.9km) 3h30 **MAP** OS Explorer OL35 North Pembrokeshire **START** Car park by Strumble Head; grid ref: SM 894411 **PATHS** Coast path, grassy, sometimes muddy tracks, rocky paths, 13 stiles **THE PUB** Lighthouse Ferryboat Inn & Restaurant, Goodwick. Tel: 01348 874747

1 Walk back up the road and cross a gate on the left on to the coast path. Pass above the bays of Pwll Bach and Pwlluog, then drop steeply to a footbridge behind the pebble beach of Porthsychan.

2 Follow the coast path waymarkers around Cnwc Degan and down to another bridge, where a couple of footpaths lead away from the coast. Continue along the coast, passing a cottage on the right and climbing and dropping a couple of times, before you reach the obelisk at Carregwastad Point.

3 Follow the main path inland and cross a stile on to a farm track, where you turn right, away from the coast path. Continue with this path, which is vague in places, up through the gorse to a wall, then turn right on to a good track. Take this through a succession of gates and around a left-hand bend.

4 Ignore a track to the right and continue up the cattle track, eventually bearing right into the farmyard where you follow a walkway past livestock pens before swinging left, after the buildings, to the road. Turn right and follow the road past a large house to a waymarked bridleway on the left. Pass Trenewydd and go through a gate on to a green lane. Follow this up to another gate and on to open ground.

5 Turn right here and follow the wall to yet another gate. This leads to a walled track which you follow to the road. Turn left and climb up to the car park beneath Garn Fawr. Turn right, on to a hedged track, and follow this up, through a gap in the wall, and over rocks to the trig point.

6 Climb down and cross the saddle between this tor and the other, slightly lower, one to the south. From here head west towards an even lower outcrop and pass it on the left. This becomes a clear path that leads down to a stile. Cross this and turn left, then right on to a drive that leads to the road.

7 Walk straight across and on to the coast path. Bear right and cross a stile to drop down towards Ynys y Ddinas, the small island ahead. Follow the coast path north, over Porth Maenmelyn and up to a cairn.

8 Continue along the coast, towards the lighthouse, until you drop to a footbridge above Carreg Onnen Bay. Cross a stile into a field, then another back on to the coast path and return to the car park.

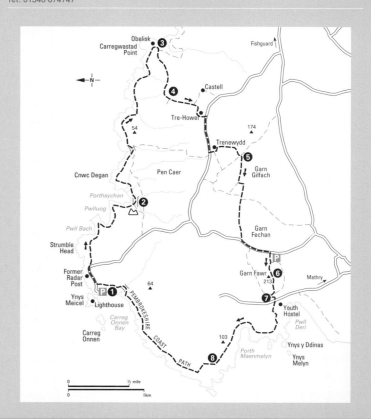

WALK 78

MARLOES ISLAND VIEWS

The Marloes Peninsula forms the westernmost tip of the southern shores of St Brides Bay. The paddle-shaped headland is a popular place to walk, due to the narrow neck that affords minimum inland walking for maximum time spent on the coast. It is famous for its stunning scenery, which includes two of the Pembrokeshire Coast National Park's finest and least-crowded beaches, some secluded coves that are often inhabited by seals, and wonderfully rugged coastline.

DISTANCE/TIME 6 miles (9.7km) 2h30 **MAP** OS Explorer OL36 South Pembrokeshire **START** National Trust car park above Martin's Haven, near Marloes village; grid ref: SM 761089 **PATHS** Coast path and clear footpaths, short section on tarmac; 9 stiles **THE PUB** Lobster Pot, Marloes. Tel: 01646 636233

1 From the bottom of the car park, walk down to the bottom of the hill. Bear around to the left, then go through the gate straight ahead into Deer Park. Turn left and follow a path along to a gate and out on to coast.

2 With the sea to the right, continue easily along over Deadman's Bay to a stile. The next section cruises along easily, passing the earthworks of an Iron Age fort on the left and crossing another stile as you approach Gateholm Island.

3 It is possible to get across to the island at low tide, but care is needed to scramble over the slippery rocks. To continue the walk, follow the coast path, above the western end of beautiful Marloes Sands until you drop easily to the main beach access path. If you're taking this walk in the spring or summer you'll be impressed by the pretty small flowers that carpet the cliff tops. These are sea campion (white) and thrift (pink).

4 Turn left and climb up to the road; turn right here. Follow the road along for around 0.75 mile (1.2km) to a hedged bridleway on the left. Follow this down and then turn left into Marloes village.

5 Pass the Lobster Pot on left and continue ahead to leave the village. Ignore a few tracks on the right, as the road bends around to the left, and continue out into open countryside where you'll meet a footpath on the right.

6 Walk down the field edge and bear around to the left to drop back down on to the coast path above Musselwick Sands. Turn left and follow the path west for over 1.5 miles (2.4km) to Martin's Haven. From here, in the summer months, a boat departs every morning (returns in the afternoon) to Skomer. As well as the wildlife and relics of ancient civilizations, there's also some fine walking on the island. Please note that dogs are not allowed on the island. Meet the road and climb past the information centre back to the car park.

GOWER PENINSULA: THE ROCKY ROAD

This route takes you on a linear trek along the most scenic stretch of the Gower Coast – and you get to make your return journey by bus. The limestone cliffs of the Gower coast are justly popular with rock climbers. Along this section are a number of well-known routes that span from easy beginners' climbs to high-grade test pieces. If it's fine, you're almost bound to spot some climbing activity as you follow the coastline along to Rhossili.

DISTANCE/TIME 6.5 miles (10.4km) 3h **MAP** OS Explorer 164 Gower **START** Large car park in Port-Eynon (buses provide logistical links on this linear route); grid ref: SS 467851 **FINISH** Grid ref: SS 416881 **PATHS** Coast path for the whole distance; 8 stiles **THE PUB** The Ship, Port Eynon. Tel: 01792 390204

1 Follow the path past the car park and through a gate to the Youth Hostel, which you keep left to continue on a caravan park drive to the ruins down left. From here, follow the track along the coast until, in the centre of the rocky bay to your left, the path splits. Take the right-hand fork and climb past a quarry to the monument on the hilltop.

2 Follow the cliff tops until the path drops to a gate. Cross this and walk behind the rocky beach. When the path forks, keep right to climb slightly, then drop left, down steps to a gate. Keep ahead to follow the path as it squeezes between limestone cliffs and steep scree. You'll hurdle a rocky terrace and drop beneath more crags. The path sneaks between more rocky outcrops before heading down to a broken wall.

3 Turn right here and follow it steeply upwards to meet a good path. Turn left and follow the wall. Keep ahead in the dip and climb steeply back up. Continue along the wall and through a gate. After 200yds (182m), next to a wooden gate (right), fork left. Don't be drawn to the coast; instead continue until you join the wall again and drop to a stile.

4 Cross and bear left back out on to the cliff top. A wall splits the ramparts; cross this by a stile and follow the coast around to a fence. Follow the fence to the head of a huge hollow. Go behind it and continue along the line of the wall. As the wall turns sharp right, keep ahead to a steep path that drops awkwardly into Mew Slade.

5 At the bottom of the dip, go through the gate and turn left to follow a grassy path to a small cove, hidden behind outcrops and covered almost completely by the sea at high tide. A narrow path heads west from the beach and contours around the steep hillside to rejoin the main coast path. Bear left on to the path here and follow it around to another dip, where a path to the left has been closed due to cliff erosion. Keep high to round the head of the valley and then drop down, with the wall on your right, towards Tears Point.

6 Leave the wall to head back up a grassy down to the cliff tops where you veer around to the right to follow the cliffs along. To continue on to Rhossili, keep walking past the car park to a bus stop by St Mary's Church, to catch a bus to the start.

WALK 80

ST DAVID'S HEAD: A ROCKY RAMBLE

St David's Head is steeped in legend and peppered with the evidence of ancient civilisations. It would be difficult to imagine a more atmospheric place but for its full effect visit at sunset and watch the sky turn red over the scattered islets of the Bishops and the Clerks, located on the west of the headland. St David's Head itself is magnificent and if you spend some time exploring here you will find a series of rocky terraces where you can shelter from the wind and again enjoy the fine views out to sea and to Ramsay Island.

DISTANCE/TIME 3.5 miles (5.6km) 2h **MAP** OS Explorer OL35 North Pembrokeshire **START** Whitesands Beach; grid ref: SM 734271 **PATHS** Coast path, clear paths across heathland; 1 stile **THE PUB** The Farmers Arms, 14–16 Goat Street, St David's. Tel: 01437 721666; www.farmersstdavids.co.uk

1 From Whitesands Beach head back up the road, pass the campsite, and a track on the left, and then take the second track on the left. Bear right where it splits and continue around a left-hand bend to walk up to the buildings. Keep left to walk between the houses, then carry on to a gate.

2 Turn right on to the open heathland and follow the footpath along the wall beneath Carn Llidi. Pass the track that drops to the youth hostel on the right and continue around to where the path splits. Take the higher track and keep going in the same direction until, at the corner of a wall, a clear track runs diagonally left towards the coast.

3 Follow this to the coast path, where there's a large fingerpost, and turn left to hug the cliff tops. At Porth Long, the path bears right to climb to a cairn. The headland is a labyrinth of paths and tracks, but for maximum enjoyment try to stick as close

to the cliff tops as possible as you round a number of narrow zawns. The official coast path doesn't go as far as the tip of the peninsula, but plenty of other tracks do, so follow one as far as you wish.

4 From the tip, turn left and make your way through the rocky outcrops on the southern side of the headland. As you approach Porthmelgan, you'll pick up an obvious path that traverses the steep hillside down into a valley, which shelters a small stream.

5 Cross the stream and climb up the steps on the other side. Continue to a kissing gate, where the National Trust land ends, and maintain your direction. Pass Porth Lleuog and the distinctive rocky promontory of Trwynhwrddyn, which is worth a visit in its own right.

6 The path then drops steeply down to the road at the entrance to Whitesands Beach.

MILFORD HAVEN: ITS TWO FACES

The peninsula offers some challenging walks, including this interesting circular route. The outward leg, as far as the sands of Freshwater West, is about as tough as coast-path walking gets, dipping and climbing on narrow, often exposed, paths. The return leg is a little more civilized, tracking around Angle Bay and following field edges out on to the headland.

DISTANCE/TIME 9 miles (14.5km) 4h **MAP** OS Explorer OL36 South Pembrokeshire **START** Car park at West Angle Bay; grid ref: SM 854031 **PATHS** Coast path and easy tracks over agricultural land, short road section; 9 stiles **THE PUB** Old Point House Inn, Angle. Tel: 01646 641205

1 Facing the sea, walk left out of the car park and pass between the café and the public conveniences to a waymarked gate. Follow the field edge along, passing through further gates, and eventually leading out on to the coast, where a right fork drops to a ruined tower on a slender headland.

2 Continue back up from this, pass through further gates and then go down to a footbridge. Climb up from this and pass Sheep Island on your right.

3 Continue along the coast, dropping steeply into a succession of valleys and climbing back up each time. As you reach the northern end of Freshwater West, keep your eye open for a footpath waymarker to the left.

4 Cross a stile and walk up the floor of the valley, swinging left to a stile at the top. Cross the next field, and another stile, and continue to the road (B4320). Turn left on to the road and walk past a cluster of houses to a right-hand turn. Follow this all the way down to the coast and turn left on to the coast path to merge on to a drive.

5 Take the drive to a bridleway sign on the right. If the tide is low, you can cross the estuary here and continue along the bank of pebbles to the road on the other side. If it's not, carry on along the drive to join a road that leads into Angle village and bear right by the church to follow a dirt track over a bridge and around to the right.

6 Continue around, pass the Old Point House Inn on your left and follow field edges to the gravel turning point above the lifeboat station on your right. Keep straight ahead, through a gate, and continue through a succession of fields into a wooded area.

7 You'll join a broad track that runs around Chapel Bay cottages and fort. Keep straight ahead to follow the narrow path back above the coast. This eventually rounds the headland by Thorn Island.

8 As you descend into West Angle Bay, the path diverts briefly into a field to avoid a landslide. Continue downwards and bear right on to a drive that drops you back to the car park.

WALK 82

MYNYDD PRESELI: ROMANCING THE STONES

This walk forms a contorted, narrow figure-of-eight that scales the most spectacular hill on the ridge, traces the line of the famous dolerite outcrops, or cairns, and then makes an out-and-back sortie to an impressive stone circle. Convoluted it may be, but it's packed with interest. When you reach Foeldrygarn (which means 'bare hill of three cairns'), you will see the remains of three Bronze Age burial cairns, as well as the ruins of an Iron Age fort.

DISTANCE/TIME 5.5 miles (8.8km) 2h30 **MAP** OS Explorer OL35 North Pembrokeshire **START** Small lay-by on lane beneath Foeldrygarn; grid ref: SO 165331 **PATHS** Mainly clear paths across open moorland; no stiles **THE PUB** Pendre Inn, Cilgerran. Tel: 01239 614223

1 Walk to the left out of the lay-by on the lane from Crymych, then turn right up a stony track. When you reach the gate, keep going straight ahead for another 100yds (91m) or so, and then fork left on to a grassy track, which soon becomes clearer as it winds its way up the hillside. Follow this all the way to the rocky cairns and trig point on Foeldrygarn.

2 Bear left at the summit and locate a grassy track that drops steeply to the south. Cross the heather-clad plateau beneath, aiming for the left-hand corner of a wood. When you meet the main track, turn right to walk with the edge of the wood on your left.

3 Leaving the wood, the path climbs slightly to some rocky tors. The second of these, the one that's closest to the track, has a sheepfold at its base. Shortly after this, the path forks and you follow the left-hand track down to the nearest of the group of outcrops to your left.

4 This is Carn Gyfrwy. Continue on faint paths to the larger outcrops ahead, then curve right away from the stones and drop slightly to Carn Menyn, the lowest of the bunch, perched precariously on the edge of the escarpment. The path becomes clearer here and drops slightly into a marshy saddle that can be seen ahead.

5 In the saddle you'll meet the main track. Turn left and follow it steadily up towards Carn Bica, which is visible on the hillside ahead of you. Just before this, you'll cross the circle made by the stones of Beddarthur.

6 Turn around and retrace your steps back to the saddle. Climb slightly to pass the tor with the sheepfold and stay on this main path to walk beside the plantation once more, now on your right. At the end of this, drop on a grassy track, down to the gate. Turn right on to the lane and continue walking back to the car park.

A TOUR OF NORTHERN PEMBROKESHIRE

From Norman Haverfordwest we cross the Landsker into the land of the Celts and Neolithic tribesmen. This tour follows the ancient pilgrims to St David's Cathedral, visits Pembrokeshire's most picturesque coastal village, and seeks out one of Britain's largest and best preserved burial chambers at Pentre Ifan before climbing onto the mysterious Mynydd Preseli, where the blue obelisks of Stonehenge were hewn out of the mountains.

Route Directions

1 From Haverfordwest quayside, head north past Castle Square to reach a roundabout. Take the A487 signed 'St David's'. Across rolling pastureland you'll see Roch Castle perched on a rocky outcrop.

Built by the Normans in the 13th century, Roch Castle is one of the Landsker castles used to repress the Welsh-speaking people and keep them contained in the hills. Nowadays, it offers self-catering holidays.

2 The road drops to the sands at Newgale, where there are often surfers or windsurfers enjoying the waves. After climbing around the headland, the road descends into the wooded valley sheltering Solva, one of Pembrokeshire's prettiest coastal resorts.

Detour left to see the older lower village and harbour, where there's a good-sized car park. There are plenty of cafés here for morning coffee and a bite to eat, or you could take a short walk over the Gribin to reach the sea cliffs on the headland.

3 Return to the main road, which climbs past the upper village and across more pastures to reach St David's.

The pay car park lies at the entrance to the attractive village. The cathedral and the extensive ruins of the Bishop's Palace are unmissable sights.

4 Veer right in the village centre, still following the A487, now signed to Fishguard. After 6 miles (10km), once you are in the hamlet of Croes-goch ('the red cross'), take the second turning on the left, a minor road passing through Llanrhian where you go straight ahead at the crossroads to return to the coast at Porthgain.

Once a busy port exporting slate and granite around the world, Porthgain's harbour is now the domain of small fishing craft and pleasure boats. If you've worked up an appetite, then stop off at the historic Sloop Inn for lunch – relics and old photos lining the walls give an insight into the history of the village.

5 Return to the A487 and turn left for Fishguard. The road first drops to the coast at Goodwick, from where the coastal A40 road passes the head of the deep water harbour before doubling back left at the large roundabout to enter Fishguard. On reaching the bustling town centre stay with the A487, signposted 'Cardigan', and descend to the more attractive lower town.

You can park here and walk along the quayside, taking in all the water-borne activity of the harbour.

6 Beyond Lower Fishguard the A487 climbs from the harbour and heads for Newport, a small seaside resort, which is dominated by the ruffle topped Mynydd Carn Ingli.

If a spot of sunbathing would fit the bill, the best beach lies across the Nevern Estuary and is reached using narrow and circuitous lanes. Closer at hand is Parrog, where you could stretch your legs along the clifftops. There's also the rather good Morawelon Café Bar if you want more relaxation (turn left on the Parrog Road in Newport's centre).

7 Continue along the A487 signed 'Cardigan', until you see signs for Pentre Ifan on the right. These lead up country lanes to the Iron Age burial cromlech (free). Continue on the lane going straight over at the crossroads

to Brynberian. Once through the village turn right on the B4329, which climbs the northern slopes of the Preseli Hills to a high pass (1,330ft/405m) along the main ridge.

It's only a short walk up the hill to the right (west), Cerrig Lladron, where there's a view indicator to highlight the superb western panoramas of the Pembrokeshire and Cardigan Bay coastlines.

8 The B4329 descends all the way back to return to Haverfordwest, but if you're looking for somewhere for supper, turn left at the first crossroads, then left again through the little hamlet of Rosebush to the Tafarn Sinc, a wonderful old-fashioned pub.

CA 187

Snowdonia National Park

CLOCKWISE FROM TOP LEFT: OGWEN VALLEY; TRYFAN, OGWEN VALLEY; A CAMPSITE AT THE BASE OF TRYFAN; CONWY CASTLE

ABERDYFI MAP REF 402 D4

In the most southwestern corner of the Snowdonia National Park, Aberdyfi is the finest of Merionydd's coastal resorts. Rows of picturesque, pastel colour-washed cottages, shops and inns, and the small harbour are tucked between the steep grassy slopes of the Tarren Hills and the sancs of the Dyfi Estuary and Cardigan Bay. Those beaches extend northwards for almost 4 miles (6.4km) to Tywyn. Besides swimming, sunbathing and sandcastle building, Aberdyfi is popular for many watersports, including sailing. On most weekends hundreds of yachts with a multitude of colourful sails can be seen gliding across the waves.

Inland from Aberdyfi, the Happy Valley delves into the Tarren Hills. Its river, the Afon Dyffryn-gwyn, flows from Llyn Barfog, which means the Bearded Lake. Some say that the name Barfog could relate to Barfog, the colleague of King Arthur. Tales abound about Arthur slaying the mythical beast, Afanc, here, and there's even a nearby summit rock named Carn March Arthur, 'the cairn of Arthur's horse'. Could it be more simple, that the rushes growing along the lake's edge form the beard?

On the other side of the Happy Valley Lane the Tarrens proper begin. These superb, grassy whalebacks span some 10 miles (16km) to the Dysynni Valley and offer some of the best wilderness ridge-walking in this part of Wales. Although covered by conifer forests in places, there are many Neolithic cairns and stunning views of mountain coast and estuary, especially at sunset.

BALA MAP REF 402 E3

Bala's jewel is its lake, Llyn Tegid, the largest natural lake in Wales. This beautiful lake, surrounded by the Aran and Arenig Mountains, is popular for watersports, and with anglers too; pike, perch, trout, salmon and roach are plentiful.

The town is dominated by the wide main street, whose austere architecture is camouflaged by the brightly coloured signs of cafés, gift shops and inns. Bala has notable religious roots, a fact reinforced by the number of chapels and the statue of Dr Lewis Edwards, founder of the Methodist College, and, opposite the White Lion, a statue of the Reverend Thomas Charles, one the founders of the British and Foreign Bible Society.

BARMOUTH MAP REF 402 D4

The Snowdonia National Park borders bypass Barmouth on the side of the Rhinog Mountain. The largely Victorian resort built into the rocks is quite touristy. When walking the promenade past the funfair and the fish-and-chip cafés visitors could be forgiven for thinking they were on the Fylde Coast, and Barmouth has been blessed with the same wonderful sands. Those who look for more than a beach holiday and who choose to explore a little further, will find true beauty and majesty in the surrounding mountains and the Mawddach Estuary. The Rhinogydd range, which rises from the backyards of the resort, features some of the finest mountains in Wales.

A fascinating web of stairs and alleyways leads from the High Street up to Hen Bermo, the old town, built almost vertically and haphazardly up the cliffs. Eventually you will come to Dinas Oleu ('the Fortress of light'), donated to National Trust by the local Talbot family.

As there wasn't enough room to squeeze the main road from Harlech between the foothills and the sea, all roads climbed inland, over the Rhinog mountain passes.

However, in the mid-19th century a coast road was built borrowing ground from the beach area. In 1867 the railways followed, crossing over the Mawddach Estuary on a half-mile (800m) new bridge which had a swing section to allow shipping to pass. The new breed of Victorian tourist flocked here for the sea air, the beaches and the bathing. One of those visitors was William Wordsworth, who described the view across the estuary towards Cadair Idris as sublime and equal to any in Scotland.

BEDDGELERT MAP REF 402 D3

Beddgelert has a location to die for, tucked away near the confluence of the Glaslyn and Colwyn valleys, and beneath the lusciously wooded lower crags and bluffs of Snowdon. The centrepiece of the village is a pretty twin-arched stone bridge over the lively Glaslyn. Huddled around the bridge are the stone-built cottages, inns, and cafés. Beddgelert and the area around it once made it to Hollywood, for scenes from Ingrid Bergman's film, *The Inn of the Sixth Happiness*, were shot here.

Beddgelert, which means 'Gelert's grave', takes its name from the Celtic saint, Kelert. Some tourist literature would have you believe that Gelert was Llywelyn the Great's faithful dog, killed by his master, who mistakenly believed it had butchered his child. The myth and subsequently the building of the grave were ploys by David Pritchard, the first landlord of the Royal Goat Hotel, built in 1803, to bring more visitors to his hotel.

The Sygun Copper Mines to the north of Beddgelert are well worth seeing. You'll go on foot on a self-guided audio-visual tour through winding tunnels to see the veins of copper ore in chambers that are coloured by a fascinating array of stalactites and stalagmites.

Looking downwards onto the copper mine from Snowdon's slopes is Dinas Emrys, a rocky wooded knoll capped with the ruins of an old fort, possibly from the Iron Age and probably used in the time of Llewelyn the Great. Legends tell that it was the refuge of Arthurian magician Merlin, and of Vortigern, a 5th-century British king who was fleeing from the Danes. Access to the area is difficult, sometimes even dangerous, and is not advised.

To the south of the village the A498 Porthmadog road enters the Aberglaslyn Pass, where the flanks of Moel Hebog and the 700-foot (213m) splintered cliffs form a cavernous rocky gorge, through which the waters of the River Glaslyn transform into white torrents as they pound the boulders of the riverbed. There's an adventurous riverside path here, close to the Welsh Highland Railway track.

BALA LAKE

Visit
UNDERGROUND TOURS

At the award-winning Llechwedd Slate Caverns at Blaenau Ffestiniog, visitors can take a miners' tramway into the heart of the slate mountain, where a miner guides them around spectacular 19th-century caverns of cathedral-like proportions. There's also a Deep Mine tour starting with Britain's steepest railway (1:1.8), where a 25-minute underground walk reveals the social condition in which the miners lived as told by 'the ghost of a Victorian miner'. Re-created Victorian shops plus a licensed restaurant and a pub complete this interesting experience.

Visit
CAER LLEION FORT

Conwy Mountain forms the backdrop to the town and its castle. High on the hillside are the remains of a much older civilisation, for here lies Caer Lleion fort. Evidence shows that boundary walls surround more than 50 Iron Age hut circles. The walls have almost, but not quite, crumbled into the hillside from which they came. Sadly, the huts, with their roofs thatched with rushes and reeds, have not survived.

BETWS-Y-COED

BETWS-Y-COED MAP REF 402 E2

Betws-y-Coed, pronounced 'betoose ee koyd', is the most popular of all the Snowdonian resorts and on most days, especially during the busy summer months, its main street, the A5, will be choc-a-bloc with traffic. Sheltered by enormous hillside forests and sited near to the confluences of the Conwy and two of its tributaries, the Lledr and the Llugwy, Betws-y-Coed is renowned for its waterfalls. One flows beneath the Pont-y-Pair ('the bridge of the cauldron'), which was built in 1468 at the heart of the village. This is always popular with sunbathers who lounge on the crags that line the banks. The Swallow Falls, best viewed from the north bank of the Llugwy, is a spectacular torrent, lying some 2 miles (3.2km) west up the road, while the Conwy Falls can be found on the Penmachno end of the village, accessed from the car park of the Otter Restaurant and Café.

Every day walkers and climbers gather before and after their mountain adventures. There are more gear shops for them to browse than food stores. Nightlife tends to centre on the Royal Oak's Stables Bar – those wanting a seat have to get there early most weekends. One of the popular visitor attractions is the motor museum.

Created from the private collection of the Houghton family, it includes several exotic and rare cars such as Bugatti, Aston Martin, Bentley and the Model T Ford.

Lead played a big part in the popular town's early development and if you take one of the forest walks up to Llyn Parc you'll see many of the relics from the old mines. Further east is Llyn Crafnant, a beautiful mountain lake reached by narrow winding lanes from Betws or on foot along a bridleway from the next village west, Capel Curig.

Capel Curig is the true gateway to the big mountains of Snowdonia and as such is considered to be the best-placed resort for weekend mountain walkers and climbers who want an early start.

BLAENAU FFESTINIOG
MAP REF 402 E3

Arrive at Blaenau Ffestiniog on a rainy day and you'll see nothing but slate. The houses are built from it, they're roofed with it and their gardens and backyards are piled up with it – great slag heaps that disappear into the low slate-grey clouds. Slate is Blaenau's heritage and they're proud of it. The slate has been mined and quarried from the Moelwyn and Manod mountains that lie either side of the

900-foot-high (275m) valley head where the town stands. When the cloud lifts, the mountains reveal themselves to be finely sculpted with distinctive shapes.

This slate town has its ghostly relics. Take a look at the valley of Cwmorthin, just beyond the suburb of Tanygrisiau. A slatey track climbs beneath the Moelwyn crags past a forlorn-looking lake into a valley that has been devastated by quarries and mines. Beyond the high-chimneyed shell of the old barracks, you can also see the rusting pulley wheels and the bogies of the old slate carts.

Blaenau lies at the end of the narrow-gauge Ffestiniog Railway from Porthmadog, a splendid journey around the Moelwyn and through the beautiful oak woods and pastures of the Ffestiniog Valley. The journey takes you past Tanygrisiau's lake and power station. These form part of a hydroelectric scheme where cheap-rate power is used to pump water up to the higher tarn, Llyn Stwlan, whose head of water is then stored until needed at peak periods.

Blaenau's smaller neighbour, Llan Ffestiniog, is a typical Welsh village with a small square and a large chapel, surrounded by verdant scenery. Roaring deep in the valley, below the village

church, are the waterfalls known as Rhaeadr Cynfal, plunging into a 200-foot (61m) craggy ravine. The large, dominant rock pillar that stands at the top of the falls, Huw Llwyd's Pulpit, was named after a 17th-century warrior and poet who lived in the village.

CONWY MAP REF 402 E2

Few rivers can match the Conwy for true beauty. Its source, Llyn Conwy, lies high in moorland known as the Migneint but soon it is tumbling down the mountainsides to Betws-y-Coed. Here, it calms, passing through pastures before meandering across sandbars and mudflats out into the estuary between Conwy and the headland of Llandudno's Great Orme.

Conwy, the town, is one of the great treasures of Wales; a place where history parades itself around every corner. Three fine bridges, including Thomas Telford's magnificent suspension bridge of 1822 and Stephenson's tubular railway bridge, cross the estuary beneath the castle, allowing both road and the railway into this medieval World Heritage Site.

Conwy Castle is the traditional design and shape we expect from our fairy-tale castles. It dates back to 1287 when the powerful English king, Edward I, built it as part of his 'iron ring' to repress the rebellious troops of Llywelyn the Great, who had given him a great deal of trouble in his conquest of Wales. A statue of the revered Welsh prince dominates Lancaster Square.

Great town walls 6-feet (1.8m) thick and 35-feet (10.7m) high with three original gates and numerous towers still encircle the old town. The walkway along the top of these walls offers splendid views of the castle, the Conwy Estuary and the rocky knolls of Deganwy. At the wall's end, steps descend to the quayside where fishermen sort their nets and squawking seagulls watch out for the scraps. In summer there is a good selection of boat trips, some just around the estuary; others further afield to Anglesey.

Conwy has many fine old buildings to admire including the half-timbered Aberconwy House (National Trust), which has origins in the 14th century, although most of its structure belongs to around 1500. The equally impressive Plas Mawr is a large mansion, which was built for the Wynne family in 1576. Now in the hands of CADW, the building has exceptionally fine interior plasterwork.

St Mary's Church occupies a central but quiet position in the town, on the site of a Cistercian Abbey of which it was once a part; the abbey was moved to this location by Edward I in order to acquire its former setting for his castle.

DINAS MAWDDWY MAP REF 402 E4

Dinas Mawddwy, a small village just off the main highway (A470), lies sheltered from the westerly winds by the high pass, Bwlch Oerddrws, in a sylvan hollow close to the valleys of the Cerist and the Dyfi rivers. It's a centre for walkers and climbers who flock to Cwm Cywarch where gigantic crags soar to the Aran ridges. The Dyfi valley is simply delectable in these parts. The sleek profiled velvety hills with a patchwork of heather, bracken and moor grass, are mellowed by hedgerow, oak woods and whitewashed farm cottages – this is truly God's country. Indeed it used to be the stamping ground of St Tydecho, cousin of St Cadfan and one of three saints sent from Brittany in the 6th century to introduce Christianity to Wales.

DOLGELLAU MAP REF 402 E4

Dolgellau sits snugly among pastureland that rises from the banks of the Mawddach and Wnion to the great cliffs of Cadair Idris. An impressive seven-arched bridge, Y Bont Fawr, built in 1638 but heavily modified in subsequent centuries, crosses the Wnion and leads into the market town. Narrow, austere streets of stone and slate buildings lead into a large central square.

Dolgellau's origins as a village lie in the 12th century when it was attached to the Cistercian monastery at Cymer Abbey. Very little remains in the town from that period – even the old Parliament building, Cwrt Plas yn Dre, where Owain Glyndwr plotted the downfall of the English in 1398, was pulled down in 1881. The town grew during the 13th and 19th centuries from the proceeds of a large wool industry – celebrated every year in the local Wool Race – and a gold rush of the same era. At its peak, more than 500 men were employed in the gold and copper mines in the hills around Dolgellau.

Come to Dolgellau early on a Sunday morning and you'll see scores of walkers, stocking up with bread, cakes and soft drinks in readiness for a trip up Cadair Idris. Steeped in Celtic legends and myths, Cadair Idris, The Seat of Idris, is the most romantic of Welsh peaks. Though not quite reaching the heights of central Snowdonia, Cadair has all the grandeur of Snowdon and a little bit more – fine crag-bound tarns, sheer rockfaces and wide-sweeping views across what seems like the whole of Wales. It is set in a green, fertile landscape of oak woods, dashing streams and pretty stone cottages dotted across pastoral foothills. The main starting points for Cadair are Minffordd, which lies just north of Tal-y-llyn, and Pont Dyffrydan car park on the Old Cader Road, the start of the well-worn route known as the Pony Path.

HARLECH MAP REF 402 D3

Harlech Castle stands on a great 200-foot (61m) crag defiantly watching out over Tremadog Bay. It's one of the most dramatic castles in the United Kindgom. Although the outer walls are badly damaged, the majestic inner curtain wall and the great round corner towers are well preserved. Built for Edward I around 1280, the castle would have been protected by what were then sea cliffs (the sea has since receded to reveal coastal plain and sand dunes), while a deep moat protected the rear landward side. The castle kept the Welsh at bay until 1404 when it was taken by the Welsh leader Owain Glyn Dwr, who then had himself crowned here as Prince of Wales, witnessed by noblemen from Scotland, France and Spain. A long siege here during the Wars of the Roses inspired the famous Welsh marching song 'Men of Harlech'

Harlech village is quite small. The old quarter lies on the hillside by the castle, while the holiday quarter, including a hotel, campsites, apartments and the railway, spreads across the plains. Visitors come here for the magnificent beaches whose position, with the mountains of Snowdonia spanning the skyline across Tremadog Bay, is quite spectacular.

Behind the village, narrow country lanes wind through the impressive Rhinog Mountains, a range that consists of thick beds of gritstone and shale formed in the Cambrian era – some of the world's oldest surface rocks. The gnarled and faulted crags are riven by deep transverse canyons that create repeated obstacles to those wanting to walk along the 'ridge'. Boulders and scree from the eroded gritstone slabs are frequently covered with knee-deep heather. Early roads, paths and tracks all ran east–west, following the natural lie of the land.

LLANBERIS & SNOWDON

MAP REF 402 D2

The successes and failures of Llanberis have always been linked to its mountains. From the moment in the late 18th century that they decided to quarry the slate from Elidir Fawr, Llanberis was transformed from a tiny village into a bustling lakeside town, as it is today. In its prime the Dinorwig Quarry employed 3,000 men, many of whom travelled from far afield. When the slate quarry finally closed without warning in August 1969, mountain tourism was ready to take its place.

The Snowdon Mountain Railway, Britain's only rack-and-pinion railroad, opened in 1896. Unfortunately, the first day proved disastrous, for an out-of-control descending train derailed itself before tumbling down steep slopes. One passenger who had jumped from a falling carriage was killed. Today many thousands of passengers listen to the running commentary as their steam engine travels through woodland and over a viaduct before puffing up the mountain. A sleek new summit station, visitor centre and cafeteria, Hafod Eryri, opened in 2009.

The slate industry lives on through the town's Welsh Slate Museum, which occupies the same Dinorwig site on the northeast shore of Llyn Padarn. At the museum you can get an insight into a miner's life and his work, watch a craftsman split the rock into fine tiles and see the largest waterwheel on mainland Britain. The enormous wheel, some 50 feet (15.2m) in diameter, was built by the De Winton company in 1870 and harnessed the power of the water that had been piped from the slopes of Mount Snowdon to turn the slate machinery in towns below.

LLANRWST MAP REF 402 E2

Llanrwst has always flirted with tourism but has never stepped out of the shadow of its neighbour Betws-y-Coed. It is claimed that the three-arched bridge over the Conwy was designed by Inigo Jones, and although there's little evidence of this, it certainly is elegant. But the 16th-century bridge is extremely narrow and allows single-file traffic only. The 15th-century ivy and Virginia creeper-clad cottage of Ty Hwnt i'r Bont next to the bridge is a National Trust tea house.

A few miles north down the Conwy Valley at Caerhun, is the site of a Roman fort, Canovium, established soon after the invasion of Wales under Cnaeus Julius Agricola, between AD 75 and 77. The Roman cohorts marched into the hills, tamed the Ordovices tribesmen who farmed the high Carneddau slopes, and constructed a surfaced road over Bwlch y Ddeufaen, which would link with their fort at Segontium (Caernarfon).

RHINOG MTS (ROMAN STEPS)

MAP REF 402 E3

From the Mawddach Estuary in the south, the Rhinog range, the Rhinogydd, pushes its way northwards to the Vale of Ffestiniog across 15 miles (24km) of the most unrelenting and roughest country in Wales. The hard Cambrian gritstone favours the growth of heather above all else and, with the profusion of huge boulders buried in peat, give the whole area an appealing rugged splendour.

SWALLOW FALLS MAP REF 402 E2

Swallow Falls, near Betws-y-Coed, is the most renowned and popular display of water power in Snowdonia, and is easy to access from the adjacent A5. Here, the beautiful Afon Llugwy rages and roars down from the mountains through tree-girt, granite chasms, until it smashes itself against the jagged rocks and crags that divide its flow into foaming cascades tumbling downwards between thickly wooded banks to a pool below.

59 MILES (95KM)

5 Drive through Llanberis, passing the scenic lake of Llyn Padarn on your right, before leaving the mountains for the fantastic coast and castle at Caernarfon.

Here a visit to the royal Caernarfon Castle is a must. Also worth seeing are the ruins of the Roman fort Segontium, which is situated on the outskirts of the town.

6 Follow the coast road (A487) east towards Bangor, just before which you join the A55 dual carriageway signed to Conwy and Betws-y-Coed. If it's fine, and there's a spare hour or so, take the turning signed 'Abergwyngregyn'. Take this minor road south to a forestry car park, which lies just beyond the bridge over the Afon Rhaeadr-fawr. A very gentle but superbly scenic there-and-back walk takes you through a verdant upland glen to the spectacular Aber Falls.

At the Aber Falls, the fantastic Afon Goch tumbles hundreds of feet down impressive cliffs of quartz-streaked Cambrian granophyre. The glen is now part of the Coedydd Aber National Nature Reserve, which was set up in 1975 by the Nature Conservancy Council (now English Nature), as an important ecological site and example of a broad-leaved woodland habitat.

7 Return to the A55 and head back to Conwy, tracking the coastline that runs to your left until you turn inland for Conwy.

THROUGH THE MOUNTAINS OF SNOWDONIA

The first part of the route skirts the edge of the Snowdonia National Park, passing through small villages in the fertile Vale of Conwy, before reaching Betws-y-Coed and Capel Curig, nestling in the foothills of Moel Siabod. The route climbs to the high Pass of Llanberis and passes a couple of lakes before reaching the coast. There is an opportunity to visit the Aber Falls, before returning to Conwy.

Route Directions

This tour starts and ends at the historic town of Conwy. The castle here is one of the finest of Edward I's 'iron ring' and walking along the town walls offers splendid views over the rooftops, the pretty Conwy Estuary and Great Orme. The harbour always echoes to the sound of the seagulls that follow the fishermen at work.

1 From Castle Square, right in the centre of Conwy, take the B5106 road south through a narrow gate in the town wall and under the railway. Once through the outskirts of town, the road winds through very pleasant countryside with tidal waters of the Afon Conwy in the wide pastoral valley on your left and the sprawling Carneddau mountains, right. Continue to Trefriw.

Those interested in textiles and fabrics might want to visit the Trefriw Woollen Mills, established in 1859 alongside Afon Crafnant.

2 Continue south along the B5106 and turn right a couple of miles (3.2km) south of Trefriw. Pass the manor house Gwydir Castle, and continue ahead to reach Betws-y-Coed. Turn right along the A5 in Betws, following the signs to Capel Curig. Soon you will reach Swallow Falls.

In Betws there's a picturesque waterfall right in the village centre, and a very good range of shops for tourists. It's worth stopping at the falls, which can be seen from near the roadside, though a walk along the north bank offers a more spectacular view.

3 The next village on the A5, Capel Curig, is the gateway to the mountains of Snowdonia. Take the left fork (A4086) by the Pinnacle Café to pass Llynnau Mymbyr, two lovely windswept lakes set amid wild surroundings beneath the barren slopes of Moel Siabod. The Snowdon massif soon appears ahead.

If you want a huge all-day breakfast or a good mug of tea, you'll find the Pinnacle Café, popular with both walkers and climbers, is a good choice. But if you prefer a bar meal, then try Cobdens.

4 At a junction take the right fork (A4086) at the Pen-y-Gwryd Hotel and follow the road through the rugged Pass of Llanberis, which squeezes between Snowdon the highest mountain in Wales, and the rocky Glyderau range. At the bottom of the pass lies Nant Peris, a village shoehorned into narrow pastures between the mountainsides. At the entrance to the larger village of Llanberis is the massive round tower of 13th-century Dolbadarn Castle, overlooking Llyn Peris. Llanberis has a wealth of tourist attractions and time demands that you will have to choose. If there's at least 2.5 hours to spare, you could take the scenic Snowdon Mountain Railway to the highest summit in Wales.

The fascinating Welsh Slate Museum is situated in Padarn Country Park. Alternatively, you might enjoy a visit to Electric Mountain and take a tour bus to the hydroelectric pump-storage power station built into the heart of the mountain of Elidir Fawr.

LLYN CRAFNANT: THE TWIN LAKES

Llyn Crafnant is serenely beautiful, and it's only five minutes from the car to its northern tip. Here, at the head of the 'valley of garlic', is a lake surrounded by woodland, lush pasture and craggy hills. The walk is easy too, on an undulating forestry track that gives a slightly elevated view of the lake. The lower pastures are dotted with pretty, whitewashed cottages and the hill slopes at the head of the valley are tinged with heather and the golden grey of the crags on the ridge.

1 Turn right out of the car park and follow the lane to the north end of Llyn Crafnant. Turn right again here, and follow the forestry track along the northwest shores of the lake, before taking the lower left fork.

2 Ignore a stile on the left, and instead climb with the forestry track. Keep watching for a later waymarked footpath on which you should descend left to cross a stream by a cottage, Hendre Bach. Turn left down a track passing a couple of modern chalets.

3 Turn left along the road which heads back towards the lake. Leave this at a telephone box for a path, signposted 'Llyn Geirionydd' and waymarked with blue-capped posts. This climbs through the conifer forests and over the shoulder of Mynydd Deulyn.

4 Descend with the main winding forestry track, still following the obvious blue-capped posts. Ignore the track forking to the right – it leads to Llyn Bychan.

5 On reaching the valley floor, leave the track to go over a step stile on the left. The path crosses a couple of meadows beneath Ty-newydd cottage before tracing Llyn Geirionydd's shoreline. At the northern end of the lake the path keeps to the right of a wall and meets a farm track.

6 Turn left and immediately right to reach the Taliesin Monument on a grassy mound. Descend to a green path heading north towards the Crafnant Valley.

7 Veer left to cross a ladder stile and follow the undulating path ahead over wooded rock and heather knolls.

8 The path eventually swings left to reach an old mine. Here, take the lower track on the right which descends back to the valley road and the forest car park.

DISTANCE/TIME 5 miles (8km) 3h **MAP** OS Explorer OL17 Snowdon **START** Forestry car park, north of Llyn Crafnant; grid ref: SH 756618 **PATHS** Clear paths and forestry tracks; 5 stiles

THE PUB The Old Ship, Trefriw. Tel: 01492 640013

OGWEN – THE DEVIL'S KITCHEN

If you come here when the damp mountain mists swirl in and out of the blackened mossy crags, and waterfalls drop from those mists like plumes of steam, you will experience the atmospheric menace, and perhaps understand the legend and the shepherds' folklore that says Idwal is the haunt of demons and damned water. However, sunshine can paint a very different picture, with golden rocks and small mountain birds flitting through the grasses.

1 The lovely Cwm Idwal nature trail starts to the left of the toilet block at Ogwen and climbs up the hillside to pass the impressive waterfalls, before turning right and then continuing up the hill.

2 Go through the gate in the fence, that marks the boundary of the National Nature Reserve, and turn left along the side of Llyn Idwal's eastern shores. A clear footpath then climbs into the dark shadows of Cwm Idwal.

3 Now leave the nature trail, which turns right to complete the circuit around the lake. Instead, ascend beneath the rock-climbing grounds of Idwal Slabs and across the stream of Nant Ifan, beyond which the footpath zigzags up rough boulder ground to the foot of Twll Du – Devil's Kitchen. If the weather, and the forecast too, are fine climb to Llyn y Cwn at the top of this impressive defile, if not, skip this bit and go to Point **6**. The rich soils on the crags around Twll Du allow many species of Arctic plants to flourish free from grazing animals. Collectively, the foliage seems to flow down the rocks and you can see why it is called the Hanging Gardens

4 To ascend Twll Du climb the engineered path as it angles left up the rock face, which will now be on your right-hand side, above an extensive area of scree and boulder. At the top reach a relatively gentle (by comparison) grassy hollow between the rising summits of Y Garn, to the right, and Glyder Fawr, to the left.

5 Just beyond the first grassy mounds is the small tarn of Llyn y Cwn – dog lake – which makes a great rest and picnic spot. Now retrace your steps carefully to the bottom of Twll Du.

6 Among the huge boulders, the path forks and the left branch heads down to run above the western shore of Llyn Idwal, then rounds its northern end to meet the outward route at Point **2**. Follow the route of your outward journey back to the car park at Ogwen.

DISTANCE/TIME 3 miles (4.8km) 2h **MAP** OS Explorer OL17 Snowdon **START** Small car park at Ogwen; grid ref: SH 649603 **PATHS** Well-defined paths **THE PUB** Cobdens Hotel, Capel Curig. Tel: 01690 720243

CAPEL CURIG: AN ALPINE JOURNEY

This superb walk rounds the valley, where the rocks and mountains provide challenging ground for today's climbers and mountaineers, and takes in the huge sweep of mountains that surround Capel Curig and LLugwy Valley. There's an optional scramble to Capel's very own pinnacle, Y Pincin, where you can see the five distinctive peaks of Snowdon reflected in the twin lakes of Mymbryr.

DISTANCE/TIME 4 miles (6.4km) 2h **MAP** OS Explorer OL17 Snowdon **START** Behind Joe Brown's shop at Capel Curig; grid ref: SJ 720582 **PATHS** Generally clear and surfaced but can be wet in places, 9 stiles **THE PUB** Ty'n y Coed, Capel Curig. Tel: 01790 720331

1 The path begins at a ladder stile by the war memorial on the A5 and climbs towards Y Pincin, a large craggy outcrop cloaked in wood and bracken. Cross another stile and keep to the left of an outcrop. Those who want to go to the top should do so from the northeast, where the gradients are easier. It's fun, but take care! You'll need to retrace your steps to the main route.

2 Continue walking east through the woods and then across marshy ground, keeping well to the right of the great crags of Clogwyn-mawr. At two ladder stiles, ignore the footpath, on the right, back down to the road, but maintain your direction to walk across the hillside.

3 Just beyond a footbridge over Nant y Geuallt, leave the main footpath and follow the less well-defined one, with marker posts, across marshy ground. The path veers southeast to cross another stream before coming to a prominent track.

4 Turn right along the track, go over a ladder stile, then, at a four-way meeting of paths, head left. Follow the path descending into some woods. Take the right-hand fork descending to a road near Ty'n y Coed Inn.

5 Turn left down the road, then right, along the lane over Pont-Cyfyng. Go right again beyond the bridge to follow the footpath that traces Llugwy to another bridge opposite Cobdens Hotel. Don't cross this time, but scramble left over some rocks before continuing through the woods of Coed Bryn-engan, where the path soon becomes a wide track.

6 After passing a cottage (Bryn-engan), the track comes to a bridge at the head of Mymbyr lakes. Turn right across it, then go left along the road for a short way.

7 Cross the road to reach a ladder stile and then take the track straight ahead, soon swinging right to hug the foot of the southern Glyder slopes.

8 Beyond Gelli farm turn right to follow a cart track back to the car park.

WALK 86

ROMAN STEPS WITH THE DROVERS

Cwm Bychan is one of the treasures of Snowdonia and the Roman Steps one of its oldest highways. The road from Llanbedr into Cwm Bychan is a joy, passing through oak woods, by the banks of a bubbling stream and beneath the small rocky castles of the Rhinog foothills. Drovers used this track too on their way to market with their cattle.

DISTANCE/TIME 7 miles (11.3km) 5h **MAP** OS Explorer OL18 Harlech, Porthmadog & Bala **START** Llyn Cwm Bychan; grid ref: SH 646314 **PATHS** Rocky paths, tracks and boggy moorland; 9 stiles **THE PUB** Castle Cottage Restaurant, Y Llech, Harlech. Tel: 01766 780479

1 Go through the gate at the back of the car park at Llyn Cwm Bychan and over the paved causeway across the stream. Beyond a stile the path climbs up through squat woodland.

2 Over another stile you leave woodland behind and cross a stream on a small bridge. The path, always clear, climbs steadily to a gate. Now slabbed with 'the steps', it climbs through a heather-clad rocky ravine and on to the cairn marking the highest point along the rocky pass of Bwlch Tyddiad.

3 From the col, the path descends into a grassy moorland basin beneath Rhinog Fawr, then, beyond a stile, enters the conifers of the Coed-y-Brenin plantation. A well-defined footpath tucks away under the trees and eventually comes to a wide flinted forestry road, along which you turn left.

4 After about a mile (1.6 km), the road swings away to head east; watch out for a waymarked path on the left just beyond the turn. Waymarks guide the route left, then right, to pass the ruins of Hafod-Gynfal. Beyond this you head north to go over a ladder stile and out of the forest.

5 Go straight ahead from the stile, heading north across the grassy moor of Moel y Gwartheg. The ground gets wet as you descend, but it's wetter still further right. You're heading for the isolated cottage of Wern-fâch, which stands a little to the left of a small patch of conifers, but for now aim towards the green fields of Cefn Clawdd.

6 You meet a fence, which guides you down to Wern-fâch. Cross a stile, then just above the cottage turn left and go over two ladder stiles. Follow the main stream (Afon Crawcwellt) to Wern-cyfrdwy (house), pass behind it, then join the walls and fences that shadow the stream. These give the least wet line across the sodden moorland.

7 The going firms up as the ground steepens, climbing to the lonely col of Bwlch Gwylim, a narrow pass between Clip and Craig Wion. Descending the far side, Cwm Bychan and the start of the walk come back into view. The footpath now descends to the southwest, through heather and bracken. After a ladder stile, look for a small waymark where you turn left down steep slopes back to reach the car park.

DISTANCE/TIME 13.5 miles (21.7km) 3h30 **MAP** OS Explorer OL13/14; OS Landranger Sheet 161 **START** Skenfrith Castle, Monmouth; grid ref: SO 457202 **TRACKS** Quiet B-road and country lanes **THE PUB** The Angel Inn, Grosmont. Tel: 01981 240646

A TRAIL OF TWO CASTLES: SKENFRITH & GROSMONT

This cycle tour passes through lovely countryside, passing two forgotten fortresses, and country pubs and cafés which are dotted along the route.

1 Skenfrith is a delightful place in summer. The low-lying castle ruins include a keep surrounded by a four-towered curtain wall. Beautifully sited between the village green and the banks of the Monnow, sunny summer days see the castle surrounded by picnickers, many eating ice creams from the shop opposite. Leave Skenfrith on the narrow northbound lane, passing St Brigit's church, where the road winds past the last of the cottages. The very narrow road lined by hedgerow wends it way through streamside farm pastures, before coming to a T-junction with the B4347.

2 Turn left here, then right at the next junction along the B4521 signed Abergavenny. Beyond the scattered hamlet of Walson the road climbs steadily uphill. Stay with the B-road at the next crossroads, ignoring the right turn to 'Dawn of the Day'. Beyond this there's a winding downhill section into the hamlet of Cross Ash.

3 At Cross Ash leave the B4521 by a bus shelter on a sharp left-hand bend and turn right for Grosmont. Take the wider left fork at the next junction, heading steadily uphill with the partially wooded hill of Graig Syfyrddin up on the right.

4 Take the left fork, dropping past Grosmont Wood Farm. Views have opened out to show the distinctive craggy outlines of Ysgyryd Fawr (the Skirrid), then sweeping panoramas of the long ridges of the Black Mountains across the fields of the Monnow Valley. A lane joins in from the left, then you keep straight ahead at the next junction.

5 The road passes an old chapel and a cluster of houses at the junction with the Llanfihangel Crucorney road. Turn right here by the phone kiosk and continue, now following the undulating lane signed for Grosmont. After 2.5 miles (4km) turn right along a narrow lane, again signed to Grosmont, to descend into the village.

6 Turn right along the B4347 through the attractive award-winning village, whose cottages have lovely gardens. The whitewashed Angel Inn, which is set back from an unusual sandstone village hall, offers a choice of tasty bar meals and West Country ales and has a pleasant beer garden to the rear. Gentle Jane's Tearoom is just down the road near the spired church. The castle, which is off to the left at the end of a short narrow lane overlooking the River Monnow, is surrounded by a deep moat – dry these days – and the skeletons of its ruined curtain walls, three towers and a gatehouse look rather gaunt against their verdant backdrop.

7 Returning to the B4347, continue past the campsite, ignoring the minor right fork lane. The route has now entered the Monnow Valley. If you want a food stop, the Part y Seal tea room is a well-signposted short detour on the left. Beyond the tea room the lane climbs right on the north side of Graig Syfyrddin. Ignore the minor right fork and leave the Monnow Valley behind. The road meets the outward route at Point 2, where you turn left and continue on the narrow lane back to Skenfrith.

DISTANCE/TIME 16 miles (25.7km) 2/3h **MAP** OS Explorer 200; OS Landranger Sheet 147 **START** Car park at Cwmdauddwr off B4518 west of Rhayader; grid ref: SN 966677 **TRACKS** Railway track and country lane **THE PUB** The Elan Valley Hotel, Elan Village. Tel: 01597 810448

THE ELAN VALLEY TRAIL

An easy reservoir and railway route with a little extra. It's a pleasant ride on well-surfaced paths and railway tracks through stunning scenery. The superb Victorian dams on the route are a bonus, especially when the headwaters are thundering down them. Benches near the dams offer a place to rest.

1 The trail starts on the opposite side of the road to the car park, you can't miss the sculptured wooden gate and gateposts by the artist Reece Ingram. Note the carved red kite on the gate. The tarred course of the old railway leads across fields. After about 500yds (455m) the track bypasses the old railway tunnel, now part of the Radnorshire Wildlife Trust Reserve. The tunnel has been modified as a habitat for hibernating bats.

2 Beyond the tunnel the route comes to the former junction with the Mid Wales Valley line, part of the Cambrian Railway (and later the Moat Lane and Brecon section of the GWR). Beyond this the track draws closer to the roadside again.

3 Around 2.5 miles (4km) from the start, the trail joins the road for a short distance turning left at a T-junction. From here you can either follow the road downhill to the visitor centre, which has a café, or cross the road to continue along the trail, which soon comes to the Caban-y-Coch dam.

4 If you need a rest there's the first of many sculptural benches just beyond the dam – they're at 0.6 miles (1km) intervals and were the work of artist Dominic Clare. The track now runs beside the reservoir with the rock-fringed slopes of Craig y Foel soaring above you on your right-hand side.

5 After curving, the track approaches the viaduct and submerged dam between the reservoirs of Garreg-Ddu and Caban-y-Coch. On the upstream side of the dam is the Foel Tower, where water is drawn and conveyed by tunnel to the filter beds, to eventually reach Birmingham which is 75 miles (121km) away. The submerged dam helps maintain a level sufficient to keep the Foel Tunnel charged with water, whilst the lower Caban-y-Coch lake would be used to discharge into the Afon Elan the mandatory 29,000 gallons (131,837 litres) a day required to keep the ecological status quo. The track continues past the Foel Tower along one of the most scenic parts of the route – lined by birch trees, and with the cliffs and screes of Craig Dolofau ahead.

6 The trackbed climbs to the road, which should be crossed (with care) before continuing on an incline through trees. It soon swings left to the top of the Pennygarreg dam, one of Elan's most spectacular sights when the foaming overspill waters are tumbling to the river below. You're on the level again now as the track passes beneath woods and through a section exploded through huge crags.

7 The trail ends at the fine 13-arched Craig-Goch Reservoir dam where you can stop before retracing your route. A better option is to cross to the other side of the dam and then turn left along the road as it winds high above Pen-y-Garreg Reservoir, before descending through the woods beneath its dam. You now join the outward route at the bottom of the incline (Point 6) and then follow the track all the way back to Rhayader.

DISTANCE/TIME 6 miles (9.7km) 2h30 **MAP** OS Explorer: either 255 or 256; OS Landranger Sheet 117 **START** Llangollen Wharf; grid ref: SJ 215423 **TRACKS** Canal towpath, hilly country lanes **THE PUB** The Britannia Inn, Llangollen. Tel: 01978 860144; www.britinn.com

DISTANCE/TIME 14 miles (22.5km) 2h30 **MAP** OS Explorer 17 Snowdonia, Snowdon & Conwy Valley **START** Slate quarry car park, Caernarfon; grid ref: SH477627 **TRACKS** Gravel cycle trail, quiet country lanes **THE PUB** The Harp Inn, Tyn'llan, Llandwrog. Tel: 01286 831071

ACROSS THE LLANGOLLEN SKYLINE

Enjoy Llangollen's beautiful valley on a lofty skyline ride. The Dee Valley is one of Wales' most beautiful places. Verdant hills and a still-lively meandering river contrast with the extensive crags and screes of the Trefor Rocks. Although the ride is strenuous on the climbs, the route offers exquisite lofty views of the landscapes.

1 Fed by the waters of the River Dee, diverted at the Horseshoe Falls east of Llangollen, Thomas Telford's 43-mile (69km) narrowboat canal was completed in 1805. For many years barges carried slate and lime from the town and brought in coal from the nearby Ruabon coalfields. Today it is one of the best loved and most scenic of leisure canals. From Llangollen Wharf take the eastbound towpath past the narrowboat moorings. Through the trees there will be lovely views of the Dee Valley on the right and the castle-topped hill of Dinas Bran on the left. The canal passes under the Llangollen road.

2 Watch out for the whitewashed Sun Trevor pub on the left. When you see it, follow the exit track just preceding the canal bridge. Through a kissing gate the track climbs away from the towpath, before turning left over the bridge to the main road. Cross the road with care before following the lane opposite behind the inn. The climb is steep at first but it steadies as height is gained. Soon the lane is raking over the hillslopes high above the Dee and beneath limestone crags. A lane joins in from the right as you pass beneath Trevor Rocks. You are now following Offa's Dyke. The road descends for a while, with the domed knoll of Dinas Bran dominating the view ahead.

3 There's a footpath to the summit of Dinas Bran starting from a narrow lane on the left, and if there's time it would be a good idea to secure the bikes and detour on foot to the extensive castle ruins. When you get to the top, the ruins are large and impressive. The castle was almost certainly built for the Princes of Powys, but you can still see the embankment of a much earlier Iron Age fort. The Welsh castle's demise isn't known for certain, but it was probably laid waste by Edward I. Back on the cycle route, the high lane, which is lined by twisted hawthorn trees, climbs steadily beneath the tiered limestone cliffs with the rocks of Creigiau Eglwyseg ahead.

4 The views are so wide-sweeping and magnificent that it seems a shame to come down, but to avoid using busy main roads the route turns left on a lane signed to Llangollen. After passing Garth Wood the narrow lane descends steeply (take care).

5 Turn left at the next T-junction, Dinbren Road and then right at a crossroads by Tower Farm Campsite (Tower Road). This brings you down to the A542 after crossing the Llangollen canal.

6 Don't cross the road but turn left along the pavement, then go left through the smaller of two gates on to the canal towpath. This route leads back to Llangollen Wharf, where the café awaits to offer refreshments.

BETWEEN THE MOUNTAINS & THE MENAI STRAITS: CAERNARFON

This ride is a delight for cyclists looking for a gentle ride with just a few hills. The route takes you through an old railway trail and quiet country lanes as you peddle through through the countryside, enjoying views of majestic Snowdonia to the east and across to Anglesey to the west.

1 From Slate Quay car park, pass the Harbour Offices to join a road between the railway line and warehouses. In 300 yards (273m) join the old trackbed on the left and pass beneath the impressive Lon Eifion cycle route sign. With the Welsh Highland railway to your left, gradually climb above the harbour and leave the town. Cross a lane by a house , signposted 'Hendy', continue to cross another road and keep to the trail to reach Bontnewydd, where you cross the Afon Gwyrfai. Gently ascend through a cuttting, pass Dinas station to reach a road at Llanwnda, with the village church to your left.

2 If you wish to continue south on the traffic-free trail (returning to Llanwnda), go round the gate opposite. Otherwise, go right along the narrow lane for 2 miles (3.2km) ignore a turning on the right and soon drop down to the waters of the Afon Carrog. Climb to a junction. go right and then left at the next junction to reach Llandwrog. Turn right by the Harp Inn; the road descends to a junction in 0.5 mile (800m). Go right for Dinas Dinlle and soon reach the seafront.

3 Retrace your route to Llandwrog and turn left before the Harp Inn, still on your outward route. Keep to this lane for 0.75 mile (1.2km) to cross the Afon Carrog and pass a small cluster of buildings (telephone box). Continue to a sharp right bend and bear off left along a quiet narrow road leading to Foryd Bay. The lane bears right close to the water's edge, eventually reaching a crossroads. Go left here through the hamlet of Saron.

4 The road descends to a bridge at Pont Faen, crossing the Afon Gwyrfrai, and rises to a junction, just before the Llanfaglan village sign. Turn left and continue for less than 0.5 mile (800m) to the water's edge at Foryd Bay, with excellent views across the Isle of Anglesey. This delightful lane hugs the coast and passes the small windswept Llanfaglan church, isolated in a field to your right. The road bears right and runs along the front of the harbour at Caernarfon. Wheel your cycle across the Aber footbridge and retun to the castle and the start point of the ride.

Brecon Beacons
& Central Wales

CLOCKWISE FROM TOP: RIVER USK AND BLACK MOUNTAINS; PENNYWORT,
LLYN BRIANNE RESERVOIR; LLANGORSE LAKE; MAEN LLIA (LLIA'S STONE),
FOREST FAWR

ABERGAVENNY MAP REF 399 H2

Abergavenny, which is by far the largest town in the upper Usk Valley, occupies a large basin surrounded by three very distinctly shaped mountains: the cone-shaped Sugar Loaf Mountain and the craggy Ysgyryd Fawr in the north; Blorenge in the south. It's also well situated as a base to explore the Black Mountains and the Brecon Beacons.

Although it took a pounding after the Civil War, Abergavenny's Norman castle is still worth seeing, as is the museum next door. There's no shortage of castles in the surrounding area too. Raglan lies 10 miles (16km) east along the A40, while the lesser-known 'three castles' of Grosmont, Skenfrith and White Castle are hidden away in low, rolling hills a few miles to the east. Along some of the narrowest country lanes imaginable in the beautiful Vale of Ewyas, lie the romantic ruins of Llanthony Priory founded by Augustinian canons early in the 12th century.

For visitors who find Abergavenny a little too busy – they do get traffic jams here – Crickhowell, up the Usk Valley, is a picturesque village that is well sited for many of the attractions in the area.

BRECON & PEN Y FAN

MAP REF 402 F6

Although the Romans made their home here, Brecon's roots date back to the 5th century when it was governed by the Celtic chieftain, Brychan, who gave his name to the town. Situated at the confluences of three rivers, the Usk, Honddu and Tarell, the town grew in importance during Norman times when a Benedictine monastery, a castle and formidable town walls were built. In the Act of Union of 1536 Brecon was listed as one of four local capitals and in 1542 Henry VIII set up a chancery here, installing the exchequer in the castle.

In modern Brecon the once-important castle's remains are no more than a battlemented wall set in the gardens of the Castle of Brecon Hotel, while only fragments of the town wall still stand near Captains Walk.

St John's Church, part of the monastery, survived Henry VIII's Dissolution and in 1923 it was elevated to cathedral status. The impressive old, red sandstone building was extensively refurbished in 1872 by Sir Gilbert Scott, whose finest work is the chancel's vaulted ceiling.

The town centre's buildings are a mix of Georgian, Jacobean and Tudor, with a network of narrow streets leading off the Bulwark. The 19th-century Shire Hall with its Athenian-style columns, houses the lively and fascinating Brecknock Museum and Art Gallery, while Brecon's military history is well recorded and celebrated at the Museums of the Royal Regiment of Wales in the Barracks.

Each August, Brecon swings to its own jazz festival – one of Britain's premier jazz events. For those who like old steam railways, the Brecon Mountain Railway puffs 7 miles (11.3km) from Pant just north of Merthyr Tydfil, into the foothills of the Brecon Beacons. You can see the repair workshop for the locomotives at Pant.

Seemingly always in view from the town and riverbanks, the Beacons' twin peaks, Pen y Fan (2,907feet/886m) and Corn Du (2,863feet/873m) display their angular outlines, finely sculpted northern cliffs and shadowy cwms to perfection. The proliferation of walking gear shops in the town shows that many visitors come to walk and there's no finer place than Brecon to explore southern Britain's highest mountains, the Black Mountains.

Visit
DEVIL'S BRIDGE

The Vale of Rheidol narrow-gauge railway takes passengers on an hour-long journey to Devil's Bridge. At Devil's Bridge, coin-operated turnstiles allow access to paths into a spectacular wooded gorge where you'll see three bridges, one on top of another (legend has it that the lowest one was built with the help of the Devil) and the Mynach Falls.

Visit
PLYNLIMON

Plynlimon (Pumlumon in Welsh) [2468ft/752m], at the heart of the Cambrian Mountains, is a swathe of moors, ridges, vales and lakes. George Borrow, a 19th-century writer, loved the mountain, and sipped the water from the sources of its rivers, the Severn, the Wye and the Rheidol. Two corners of this wild mountain worth visiting are Llyn Llygad Rheidol to the north of the main summit, and Glaslyn, a high windswept lake reached by car from the Machynlleth–Llanidloes mountain road.

PEN Y FAN

Visit
WATERFALL COUNTRY

Four streams, the Nedd, Pyrddin, Mellte and Hepste, tumble from the moors of Fforest Fawr to cut deep gorges through the more permeable limestone rocks. They create a series of spectacular waterfalls in the woods north of Pontneddfechan. All are approachable by footpath from car parks south of Ystradfellte.

Visit
LLANTHONY PRIORY

A little road climbs south from Hay over the Gospel Pass before descending into the beautiful Vale of Ewyas, where the romantic ruin of Llanthony Priory basks in the beauty of its surroundings and the backdrop of the Black Mountains. The Priory was established in 1103. After an attack by Owain Glyndwr the priory was left ruinous, but there are still substantial arches, walls and towers to explore. Unusually, you can enjoy the view over a pie and a pint, as there's a pub in the grounds.

Visit
CENTRE FOR ALTERNATIVE TECHNOLOGY

The Centre for Alternative Technology was founded in 1973 and utilized the disused Llwyngwern slate quarry, 2 miles (3.2km) north of Machynlleth. The centre now has a workforce of 90 permanent staff and volunteers on the 7-acre (2.8ha) site. Visitors can get up the hill on an amazing water-powered cliff railway. They will see exciting interactive displays along with some practical ideas for their own homes.

Insight
HAY-ON-WYE LITERARY FESTIVAL

The Hay Festival was likened to a cult music event which took place in the 1960s, by former American President Bill Clinton in 2001, when he referred to the festival as 'The Woodstock of the mind'. Renowned throughout the world as 'the' place to be at the end of each May by bibliophiles, the festival draws speakers from the worlds of publishing and politics as well as people from the performing arts. The festival is open to everyone and attracts families with small children. The event is the brainchild of Richard Booth, who opened a secondhand bookshop in the little town in 1961 and the idea of a festival began. Today, Hay-on-Wye is also known as Booktown.

GLYNTAWE & UPPER SWANSEA VALLEY MAP REF 402 E7

The transition from stark industrial landscapes to rural ones happens very suddenly in the Swansea Valley. One minute you're in Ystradgynlais on the edge of the old coalfields, the next you've turned the corner past Abercraf into the magical garden-like landscapes of Glyntawe and you're staring across the River Tawe up to the limestone crags of Cribarth, a southern outlie- of the Black Mountain. Glyntawe, a sprawling village, is one of the best starting points for a climb on the Fan Hir escarpment to the highest Black Mountain summit, Fan Brycheiniog.

The limestone geology of the valley has left it with its major attraction, the Dan yr Ogof Caves, discovered in 1912. This is Wales' largest subterranean cavern system extending to 10 miles (16km), where visitors can enter a weird world of impressive stalactites, stalagmites and underground waterfalls brought to life with lighting and music.

The south side of the valley is dominated by Craig y Nos Castle, once home to world-famous Victorian opera singer Adelina Patti. This Gothic mansion, now a grand hotel, is surrounded by superb riverside gardens with mature woodland fringing meres and meadows, which now form a valuable part of the Craig y Nos Country Park.

HAY-ON-WYE MAP REF 402 F6

Hay-on-Wye lies in the northeast corner of the Brecon Beacons National Park by the sleepy banks of the River Wye, and sheltered by the sweeping slopes of the majestic Black Mountains. With the flower-decked meadows and rolling green hills of Radnorshire in the north, spring and summer in Hay are delightful times to get outdoors for a walk or ride.

The name 'hay' comes from the Norman word *haie* meaning 'enclosed place'. It's known that there was a settlement here when King Offa of Mercia built his dyke here in the 8th century. There are only fragmented remains of the old Norman town walls in the Newport Street area, but this would have been a heavily fortified border town since the 13th century when William de Breos built his castle. The baron soon fell out with King John and was forced to flee to France, where he died in poverty; it's believed that after sacking the castle King John's men starved the baron's wife and child to death. Further attacks and destruction came at the hands of Llywelyn the Great and Owain Glyndwr, and by fire as late as 1977.

Today Hay is a vibrant market town known for its 30-plus secondhand and antiquarian bookshops, and tourists come from all over the world to visit the annual literary festival. Among a maze of narrow streets you'll discover many fascinating

old buildings around the town to admire, including the colonnaded 19th-century butter market and the attractive Victorian clock tower.

LLANDOVERY & TYWI VALLEY MAP REF 402 E6

Llandovery, known here as Llanymyddfri – 'the church amongst the waters' – was described by the 19th-century writer, George Borrow, as 'the pleasantest little town in which I have halted in the course of my wanderings'.

The area was once occupied by the Romans, whose fort, Alabum, was sited near to St Mary's Church by the Afon Bran to the north of the town. The castle, which was built for the Norman baron Richard Fitz Pons in the 12th century, was captured by the Welsh in the Glyndwr Revolts. It changed hands several times over the centuries. In 1532 its owner, Rhys-ap-Gruffydd, was executed at the behest of Henry VIII for treason and, in an act of revenge by the Welsh, the castle was destroyed, never to be rebuilt. A recently erected statue of Llywelyn ap Grufydd stands guard on the grassy mound beneath the remains of the castle keep.

Across the car park from the statue you'll find the Heritage Centre where you can get information about the many walks in the area, and discover the myths and history of the region.

LLANGORS

Llandovery's history is intertwined with the fortunes of the cattle drovers. When thieves made travelling on Wales' rugged roads a hazardous exercise, the local farmers hired the drovers to drive cattle to the more lucrative markets of England and to settle accounts for them with non-local people. This meant that drovers needed to handle large sums of money and led to the introduction of banking systems, some of them even issuing bank notes. One of the most successful of these was David Jones' Black Ox Bank, which was taken over at the turn of the 20th century by Lloyds.

To the south of Llandovery, the Black Mountain (or Mynydd Du as it is known in Wales) lies at the western end of the Brecon Beacon Range, rising in grand escarpments of old red sandstone. Glacial action has formed magnificent cliffs on the northern and eastern faces of the group and also provided two lovely tarns: Llyn y Fan Fawr and Llyn y Fan Fach. Myddfai, which is sheltered in the northern foothills of the Black Mountain, is a particularly picturesque village.

The nearby Epynt Military Range is encircled by a pleasant recreational bridlepath and footpath.

LLANGORS MAP REF 402 F6

The little village of Llangors is delightful in itself, but what makes it a real gem are the magnificent views of the Brecon Beacons that can be had from its superb location. Not only is the village blessed with such a grand vista, but, is also a only couple of miles (3.2km) away from the largest natural lake in South Wales.

Llangors lake stretches for a mile (1.6km) in length and half a mile (800m) in width, and covers an area of 327 acres (132ha), although to walk around its circumference would be a 5-mile (8km) trek. The lake has drawn settlers since ancient Celtic times and was mentioned in the 12th century by Gerald of Wales, who commented that the beautiful lake had plenty of waterfowl.

A striking feature of the lake is the crannog, or man-made defensive island, at its centre. The island is thought to date back to AD 889–893. It is also thought to have been one of the royal sites of medieval Brycheiniog, one of the kingdoms of medieval Wales.

Today, Llangors draws people still and every year the village is full of enthusiastic musicians who come to take part in and

enjoy, its popular music festival, which features folk-rock, jazz and even an experienced ceilidh band. There are also children's entertainments laid on and the atmosphere is relaxed and welcoming.

The lake draws a different crowd and is the perfect place for watersports lovers and anglers (coarse fishing). All types of boating fun takes place here including sailing, canoeing and water-skiing, and the surrounding countryside and mountains are delightful for walking and hiking. Those with equine interests can horse ride in the area or you can get a birds-eye view of the dramatic landscape if you go up in a glider from the Black Mountains Gliding Club. The excellent Llangorse Rope Centre is the place to go to practice your climbing skills for later adventures in bouldering or pot-holing.

Llangors lake is a site of Special Scientific Interest mainly because it is naturally eutrophic. This means that the water is naturally high in nutrients which tends to make it appear slightly murky. It also means, however, that the habitat is highly productive which goes a long way to explain why this expanse of water is so popular with waterfowl.

Visit
THE DINAS NATURE RESERVE
This RSPB reserve, which lies 10 miles (16km) north of Llandover, has a footpath over wetlands and through oak woodland to the steep slopes of Dinas. There's a cave in the crags here, where Twm Sion Catti, the Welsh Robin Hood, hid from his enemies. Red kites can often be seen soaring above the trees and in summer you can also see dippers, pied flycatchers, common sandpipers and grey wagtails.

Visit
GIGRIN FARM RED KITE FEEDING STATION
Gigrin Farm, an upland sheep farm on the A470, 0.6 mile (1km) south of Rhayader, is an official RSPB feeding station for red kites. It's fascinating to see first the noisy crows arriving on the scene, then the red kites and buzzards swooping down to foil the smaller birds. The number of kites visiting here can vary from a dozen to around 400 or so. Feeding the birds takes place every afternoon.

Machynlleth Alternative Technologies

Home to a proud nation of people, a place of verdant valleys and numerous rugged and rather splendid mountains, Wales, the central part of the country in particular, is also home to the interesting Centre for Alternative Technology (CAT), an award-winning eco-centre, and a living example of what we can each do to make the world a cleaner, much more pleasant place and to help our environment to last longer. Quite early on in your visit to CAT you are told that the 'earth is one big creature working together; if we don't interfere, it should last forever'. Wishful thinking, perhaps, but this is what the Centre is all about: making you think.

CAT is dedicated to exploring and demonstrating 'globally sustainable, whole and ecologically sound technologies and ways of life'. It explains and teaches sustainable development, but despite its name does not give undue attention to alternative technology, focusing instead on general environmentalism. The Centre is open to visitors throughout the year, holds residential courses, and publishes information on organic farming, gardening, and ecologically friendly living. Rather than the doom and gloom, or off-beat view of things normally associated with 'alternative' anything, the Centre takes a constructive and elevating approach, demonstrating all kinds of environmental technologies in an interesting and informative way.

Without actually going there you might be forgiven for thinking that the Centre is some time-warp hippie and idealist-populated drop-out manifestation. In fact it's a hugely pleasurable and thought-provoking visitor attraction – and there's no sign of sackcloth, ashes, incense or sandals, or even doing without meat. The Centre is based on realism and embraces all forms of positive change.

CAT was the brainchild of and was founded by old Etonian businessman-turned-environmentalist Gerard Morgan-Grenville. It was opened in 1974. The centre utilizes the disused Llwyngwern slate quarry near Machynlleth, where it occupies a 7-acre (2.5ha) site. When the quarry was operational, the slate was sent via the narrow gauge Corris railway to Machynlleth where it was then transferred for onward shipment via the mainline railways to help supply the building trade throughout the country.

Some 12 people live permanently at CAT, and they and all the facilities are largely self-sustaining. This is achieved with a good supply of solar-and hydro-power, productive fruit and vegetable gardens, a reed-bed sewerage system and free-range hens for fresh eggs. The on-site restaurant is, as you might expect, notoriously but wholesomely vegetarian. Facilities include a water-balanced funicular railway, solar-, hydro- and wind-power, a low-energy house, a site-wide electricity grid powered by renewable energy (any excess is sold to the national grid), displays of organic gardening methods, a hydraulic ram pump and straw-bale and rammed-earth buildings.

This is not some ramshackle ghetto of tents, lean-to's and life-style protesters, but an in-depth, well-researched, thoughtful and highly sophisticated illustration of green technology at work. The funicular railway that greets your arrival is powered by water; you climb into the bottom car, making it heavier, and water is released into tanks in the top car to balance it out. When there is sufficient weight above, the top car descends, hauling the bottom one up. The site now occupied by the water-operated funicular was formerly the quarry incline with two parallel tracks. The weight of the loaded wagons coming down was used to haul up the returning empties with a wood and cast-iron winding drum at the top controlled by a braking system to prevent runaways.

Water-balanced funicular technology was very widespread in the 19th century, but most of the funiculars were progressively replaced by electrically operated systems. The CAT railway is the only modern, water-operated funicular.

There are around 20 buildings in all, with different examples of low impact eco-buildings like the straw bale theatre. But they are all practical visions of ecologically benign living, showing, in this world-climate-conscious era, how heat, power, water, food and waste can be handled with a minimal eco-footprint.

On the face of it, you might think that CAT would be all too sophisticated for children. But quite the contrary. Specifically catering for children there are activities that explain solar wind and wave power, an adventure playground, a maze, and a smallholding with farm animals – but there is an important message too. The Centre has its own reservoir and water supply in an old slate quarry, and its own sewage systems. In fact the treatment of sewage is one of the Centre's most famous pioneering achievements, using composting toilets and reed beds, although you may not want to investigate this splendid achievement too closely.

Adults will find the Centre immensely edifying, intentionally so, with illustrations of sustainable architecture in cut-away houses that explain how much more environmentally friendly our lifestyles might be. The Centre is also a reliable source on almost any aspect of organic gardening and sustainable living. There's lots of information available on energy conservation, compost-making and other important aspects of gardening organically. Equally important are the way we do things – like avoiding chemicals when gardening, achieving more with less, and not excluding nature from our living and working spaces.

In the final analysis, CAT expounds a belief in valuing communities, and their right to control their immediate environments. The Centre for Alternative Technologies is one of the very few places in the UK where you can get holistic advice covering every aspect of energy use and environmental impact. They can help with everything from changing light bulbs to building a new house. In this way, the knowledge and experience gleaned from the Centre's 30 years of existence and research can be passed on in simple, practical ways so that everyone can feel that they are contributing in some small ways to avoiding the slow pollution and destruction of the environment.

For those who want to consider these topics to a higher degree, the Centre is also home to a successful MSc course in Advanced Environmental and Energy Studies. Run by the University of East London, the course is based entirely at CAT and covers many aspects of environmental science and its business applications.

There is also a regular programme of short- and long-term volunteer placements for those who wish to get involved with the work of The Centre for Alternative Technologies, covering specific tasks and building work as well as administrative duties. Contact CAT or visit www.cat.org.uk for information and details.

LEFT FROM TOP Solar panels fitted to the Information Centre roof play a vital part in the self-sustaining power supply here.

Rich, nutrient loaded compost is used throughout the gardens at CAT.

This innocent-looking hut contains the Rocket Composter – an innovative device that turns kitchen and restaurant waste into nutrient-rich soil ready to use for vegetable growing, all in a couple of weeks. The clever design features a well-insulated chamber in which the vegetable matter is turned over by a screw every day, so accelerating the decomposing process.

RIGHT FROM TOP The eco-cabins blend easily into the environment and are powered by their own renewable energy system. Cabins also have monitoring systems so that residents can monitor their input and output of energy.

Wind-power is a vital 'clean' energy source and this community turbine in the Dyfi Valley is thought to save some 70 tonnes of carbon dioxide emissions each year.

Insight

THE PHYSICIANS OF MYDDFAI

Llyn y Fan Fach at the northern foot of the Black Mountain is an eerie place to be when the mists swirl around the gullies, and it's not surprising that there's some mystery and legend lurking beneath its waters. From its depths a flaxen-haired fairy appeared and enchanted a local farmer's boy, Rhiwallon. After altercations with her husband the fairy returned to the waters. However, the couple sired three sons, who would learn from their mother about medicine. The boys became the first in a line of Physicians of Myddfai, the last was Dr C Rice Williams of Aberystwyth, who died in 1842.

Visit

FOREST FAWR GEOPARK

The area in the Brecon Beacons known as Forest Fawr was designated a Geopark in October 2005 by UNESCO. Forest Fawr is the Welsh translation for 'Great Forest' and it is within this great forest that you will find some of the great natural wonders of Wales. The Geopark encompasses the Welsh National Snow Caves and the Brecon Beacons' mighty reservoirs.

MACHYNLLETH MAP REF 402 E4

Machynlleth shelters on high ground to the south of the wide valley of the Dyfi, where the mountains of Snowdonia give way to the rolling foothills of Plynlimon. A fine 17th-century four-arched stone bridge spans the river on the road leading into this small market town. An 80-foot (24m) Victorian clock tower of an extremely ornate design forms the hub of this town centre and looks down on a wide Maengwyn Street, where the weekly Wednesday markets are held. Here you'll also find Parliament House, a medieval town house standing on the site of the building where Owain Glyndwr held the last independent Welsh Parliament in 1404. It now hosts an Owain Glyndwr interpretative centre. The 14th-century Royal House at the junction of Garsiwn Lane and Penrallt Street is so called because Charles I stayed here in 1644.

North of the town, the Dulas Valley threads past the Centre for Alternative Technology into a countryside of streams, forests and fractured mountains where slate was mined for centuries. At Corris, a narrow gauge railway (closed 1948) is being resurrected; further into the hills, hamlets crouch beneath spectacular landscapes, a paradise for the path-finding rambler.

Today Machynlleth has an appealing mix of all things Welsh, Celtic mysticism, and green idealism. The unusual shops and the wholefood café are a testament to this, as is the Centre for Alternative Technology. The townsfolk were a bit dubious when the 'hippies' first set up the alternative living centre, but their fortunes are now intertwined.

RHANDIRMWYN MAP REF 402 E6

Once an important old lead-mining village, Rhandirmwyn lies in the valley of the Upper Tywi, 9 miles (14.5km) north of Llandovery. This is a real haven for those who like riverside walks, angling and bird-spotting. Two fine bird reserves are set among the riverside crags, where the boisterous Tywi and Doethie rivers twist between rocky, oak-clad peaks. Beneath the conical hill called Dinas, the rivers converge in a violent cauldron of foam.

A short way upstream, where the Doethie meets the Pysgotwr, is one of the wildest gorges in Mid Wales. A few miles north of Rhandirmwyn along winding lanes, Llyn Brianne Reservoir is among plantations of spruce and larch in the narrow valleys of the Tywi and Camddwr.

RHAYADER MAP REF 402 F5

Rhayader's full Welsh name is Rhaeadr Gwy, meaning 'waterfall on the Wye'. The waterfall to which it refers was actually blown up in 1780 to make way for the bridge over the river.

Dominated by its opulent Victorian clock tower, which lies at the crossroads in the centre of the village, Rhayader is a very pleasant town set among some of the finest river scenery in Mid Wales. The poet Percy Shelley was drawn to these parts in 1809. He lived in the cottage of Nantgwyllt in the Elan Valley, then a famed beauty spot. However, the planned flooding of the Elan Valley was to change the nature of the scenery forever.

In the first part of the scheme, four reservoirs, the Craig-Goch, Peny-Garreg, Garreg-ddu and Caban-Coch were created. Nantgwyllt was among the dwellings submerged by the reservoirs. A church, chapel, school and numerous farms were submerged when the scheme was completed in 1904. A fifth reservoir, the Claerwen, was completed in 1952. Some one hundred years later the reservoirs have blended almost seamlessly with their surroundings and the power of the dams, and the white waters thundering down them, adds great character to the landscape. The visitor centre gives an intriguing insight into the construction of the dams, the railway built to supply them and the lives of the construction workers involved in the project. The old railway trackbed now forms the Elan Valley Trail, which is a marvellous facility for waterside walking or cycling.

RHANDIRMWYN

PORTH YR OGOF, ALONG THE WATERFALLS

You could start or end this walk with a visit to the Porth yr Ogof caves. The route takes in lovely riverside scenery and four waterfalls created as the inland rivers rush through the mountainous area. At Sgwd yr Eira you can walk behind the waterfall (take care as the path here can be slippery).

DISTANCE/TIME 4 miles (6.4km) 2h **MAP** OS Explorer OL12 Brecon Beacons National Park Western & Central areas **START** Park car park at Porth yr Ogof, near Ystradfellte; grid ref: SN 928124 **PATHS** Riverside paths and forest track. Some rough sections and steps; no stiles **THE PUB** The New Inn, Ystradfellte, Aberdare. Tel: 01639 720211

1 Cross the road at the entrance to the car park and head down the left-hand of two paths, waymarked with a yellow arrow. Ignore the right fork marked 'Cavers Only' and follow the main path through a kissing gate and on to the river bank. Now keep the river to the right to follow a rough footpath through two more kissing gates and then on to reach a footbridge.

2 Don't cross but continue walking ahead, to climb steeply up to a fence. Stay with the path, with a wooden fence now on your right for a few paces to reach a junction of footpaths marked with a large fingerpost. Bear sharp left on to a well-surfaced track, waymarked to Gwaun Hepste, and follow this for a short distance to another junction, where you should turn right (waymarked 'Sgwd yr Eira').

3 Continue walking along this waymarked forest trail until your see another fingerpost directing you to the right and downhill. Follow this to the edge of forest and then bear around to the right. This track leads to the top of some wooden steps, on your left.

4 Go down the steps to Sgwd yr Eira (Waterfall of the Snow) and then, having edged along the bank and walked behind the falls (waterproofs recommended), retrace your steps up to the edge of the wood. Turn left and continue, still following the red-banded posts, to a fork marked with another fingerpost.

5 Turn left here (waymarked to Sgwd Isaf Clun-gwyn) and descend to the riverside. Turn left again to Sgwd y Pannwr (Fullers Falls), then turn around to walk upstream to Isaf Sgwd Clun-gwyn (Lower Waterfall of the White Meadow). Take care, the ground is very steep and rough around the best viewpoint.

6 Retrace your steps downstream to reach your original descent path and then turn left to climb back up to the fork at top. Turn left and follow the red-banded waymarkers along to Sgwd Clun-gwyn, where there's a fenced viewing area. From here, continue along the main trail to the place where you split off earlier.

7 Drop back down to the footbridge and continue along river bank to Porth yr Ogof.

WALK 88

PEN Y FAN: THE BEACONS HORSESHOE

This is the connoisseur's way up to the high ground of Pen y Fan, the highest summit in the Brecons. Pen y Fan, with its twin summit of Corn Du, and Cribyn and Fan y Big, form a 'horseshoe' around the head of a river. The going is steep from the car park on to the head of the remote Cwm Gwdi where the path then follows rocky old quarry tracks before it passes on to the grassy spur that leads on to Cefn Cwm Llwch, a good walk where you will be rewarded with magnificent views.

DISTANCE/TIME 7 miles (11.3km) 4h **MAP** OS Explorer OL12 Brecon Beacons National Park Western & Central areas **START** Car park at end of small lane, 3 miles (4.8km) south of Brecon; grid ref: SO 025248 **PATHS** Well-defined paths and tracks, short distance on quiet lanes; 5 stiles **THE PUB** The Felin Fach Griffin Inn Brecon. Tel: 01874 620111

1 Walk uphill from the car park and pass an information plinth before crossing a stile. Walk along the right-hand side of the field towards the top right-hand corner and then bear left to continue along the fence to reach another stile.

2 Follow the broad but faint grassy track straight on. As it reaches steeper ground, it becomes a better-defined stony track that swings slightly left and climbs the hillside. Continue ahead, up towards the head of Cwm Gwdi, and keep ahead, ignoring a few right forks, until the path eventually levels out on Cefn Cwm Llwch.

3 Continue along the ridge towards the summit ahead. As you reach the foot of the peak, the track steepens considerably, offering a viewpoint over a perilous gully that drops into Cwm Sere on the left. Continue to climb steeply over a few rocky steps to reach the summit cairn on Pen y Fan.

4 Bear right to follow the escarpment edge along and then drop into a shallow saddle beneath the rising crest of Corn Du. Continue climbing up on to this summit, then bear left for a few paces to locate a steep path that

drops down through rocky outcrops on to easier ground below. Bear right and drop past the summit.

5 Continue down the hill and pass the Tommy Jones obelisk with the steep crags of Craig Cwm Llwch on your right-hand side. Above the lake, the path forks; take the right-hand option and drop steeply, around a dog-leg and over moraine banks to the lake shore.

6 A clear track leads north from the lake – alongside the outflow; follow it over easy ground to cross a stile that leads on to a broad farm track. Take this down to a gate in front of a building and climb the stile on the left. Cross the compound and climb another stile to follow waymarker posts around to the right on to another track, beyond the building.

7 Bear left on to this track and follow it down, over a footbridge, to a parking area. Keep straight ahead, through a gate to a T-junction, where you turn right. Cross the bridge and continue for over a mile (1.6km) to another T-junction. Turn right and walk uphill back to the car park.

A STROLL AROUND THE PRECIPICE

One of the finest short walks in Wales, the Precipice Walk follows a balcony route with spectacular views of valley, mountain and estuary. The route starts high so there's little ascent. The walk starts by crossing woodland and farm pastures, but from here, the route becomes more exciting as you walk along a terrace high above the river before descending to the shores of Llyn Cynwch.

DISTANCE/TIME 3 miles (4.8km) 2h **MAP** OS Explorer OL18 Harlech, Porthmadog & Bala **START** Coed y Groes car park on Dolgellau–Llanfachreth road; grid ref: SH 745211

PATHS Stony tracks and good paths, occasionally rough; 4 stiles **THE PUB** The Stag, Bridge Street, Dolgellau. Tel: 01341 422533

1 From the top end of the Coed y Groes car park turn right on to a level footpath which curves around to join another wide track. The Precipice Walk is a private path around the Nannau Estate, but its use has been authorized by the estate owners since 1890, on the basis that all walkers observe the country code. It's probably one of the finest short routes in Wales and, as such, has been one of Dolgellau's most famous attractions since those early days when Victorian tourists came for their constitutional perambulations. The track then swings right at the edge of some fields.

2 Where the track comes to an estate cottage, Gwern-offeiriaid, turn left off it. Follow a clear path leading to the hillside north of Llyn Cynwch. There you see the grand mansion of Nannau, built for the Vaughans in 1796.

3 At a footpath signpost fork right. The path climbs the hillside and turns northwards by the side of a dry-stone wall.

4 Beyond a stile the footpath curves around a crag-studded hill, with open slopes that give fine views across a green valley below to the village of Llanfachreth and the rugged mountainsides of Rhobell Fawr and Dduallt that lie behind. The footpath edges rounds Foel Cynwch and passes the Sitka spruce woodlands of Coed Dôl-y-clochydd. Ignore a path signed to Glasdir and keep left, reaching the dramatic, but even ledge path traversing the high hill slopes above the Mawddach Valley. Where the slopes finally ease, there's a promontory on the right, with a bench placed to enjoy the view. The path now arcs round to the southern side of Foel Faner, drops to the lake and turns sharp left to follow the western shore.

5 The path meets the outward route by the hill footpath sign. Retrace the outward route past the estate cottage of Gwern-offeiriaid and through the woods back to the car park.

CAERFANELL VALLEY SKYLINE WALKING

Spectacular escarpments above a wild and remote valley, this walk sums up everything good about walking in the Brecon Beacons. In only 5.5 miles (8.8km), it encapsulates almost every sort of landscape found in the National Park. The route also passes a memorial to the Canadian airmen who crashed here in 1942.

DISTANCE/TIME 5.5 miles (8.8km) 3h **MAP** OS Explorer OL12 Brecon Beacons National Park Western & Central areas **START** Car park, 3 miles (4.8km) west of Talybont Reservoir; grid ref: SO 056175 **PATHS** Clear mountain, river and forest tracks; some mud and peat; 3 stiles

THE PUB Travellers Rest, Talybont-on-Usk. Tel: 01874 676333; www.travellersrestinn.com

1 Walk back out of the car park, either crossing the cattle grid or a stile to the left of it, then turn immediately right on to a stone track that heads uphill, with the stream on your left. Follow this track steeply up to the top of the escarpment and keep straight ahead to cross the narrow spur, where you bear around, slightly to the left, to follow the escarpment.

2 Stay on the clear path, with the escarpment to your right, for about 1.5 miles (2.4km), till you meet a number of paths at the head of the valley.

3 Take the sharp right turn to follow a narrow track slightly downwards, around the head of the valley, towards the cliffs that can be seen on the opposite hillside. Keep left at a fork and continue to the crash memorial.

4 Almost directly above the memorial, you'll see a rocky gully leading up on to the ridge. On the left-hand side of this, as you look at it, is a faint track that climbs steeply up. Take this to the top and turn right on to a narrow but clear track. Follow this track easily above the crag, to a distinctive cairn at the southern end of the ridge. Just north of the cairn you'll see a small stream.

5 Follow this down for 10ft (3m) to join a clear grassy track that trends leftwards at first, then follows a clear groove down the spur. This becomes an easy footpath that crosses a broad plateau and then leads to a junction at a wall. Turn right here and drop down to the Afon Caerfanell.

6 Cross the stile on your left at the bottom and follow the narrow footpath downstream, past a number of waterfalls. Eventually you'll pass the largest of them and come to a footbridge.

7 Cross the footbridge and then a stile to follow the track into the forest. Pass some ruined buildings on your right, and before you cross the small bridge, turn right on to a clear path that leads uphill into the forest with waterfalls on your left.

8 Continue uphill on the main track, taking optional detours to the left and right to see other waterfalls. Eventually you'll meet a broader forest track where you turn left and then right to return to the car park.

NEUADD RESERVOIRS IN THE BRECON BEACONS

This is a fine way to visit the area's highest ground as any, or all, of the big peaks can be bypassed if required. It's also an easy way to gain the tops, as it starts at an altitude over 1,300ft (396m) and, with the exception of two short but stiff sections, the climbing remains gentle to the point of being almost undetectable. Walkers can also glimpse the seldom-visited valley of Cwm Crew.

DISTANCE/TIME 7.5 miles (12.1km) 4h   **MAP** OS Explorer OL12 Brecon Beacons National Park Western & Central areas   **START** At end of lane leading north from Pontsticill; grid ref: SO 032179   **PATHS** Clear paths, boggy patches, rocky track, no stiles   **THE PUB** Travellers Rest, Talybont-on-Usk Tel: 01874 676333; www.travellersrestinn.com

1 Continue up the lane to a small gate, which leads into the grounds of the reservoir. Bear slightly left on to a narrow path that drops to cross a concrete bridge spanning the outflow. Climb up on to the bank opposite and bear left to walk along its top. This will take you to a gate that leads out on to open moorland.

2 Go through this and keep straight ahead, taking the left-hand of the two tracks, which leads easily uphill towards the edge of a mainly felled forest. Follow the clear track up, with the forest to your left, and then climb steeply up a stony gully to the top of the escarpment.

3 Once there, turn right on to the obvious path and follow the escarpment along for over 2.5 miles (4km). You'll eventually drop into a distinct saddle with the flat-topped summit of Corn Du directly ahead. Where the path forks, keep straight ahead and climb easily up on to the summit. Follow the escarpment edge along and then drop down into another saddle, where you take the path up on to the next peak, Pen y Fan.

4 Again, from the summit cairn, follow the escarpment around and drop steeply, on a rocky path, down into a deep col beneath Cribyn. Keep straight ahead to climb steeply up to the cairn on the narrow summit. Note: this climb can be avoided by forking right and following another clear path that contours right around the southern flanks of the mountain and brings you out at Point **6**.

5 From the top, bear slightly right and follow the escarpment around to the southeast. After a long flat stretch, you'll drop steeply down into a deep col known as Bwlch Ar y Fan.

6 Turn right on to the well-made track that leads easily down the mountain. Go through a gate and follow this for over 1.5 miles (2.4km), until it starts to swing slightly to the left and drops steeply into a rocky ravine. Turn right here on to a track and take it down to a gate. Go through this, turn left and follow the track to its end. Turn right in front of the gate on to another track that leads back to gate at the head of the lane. Go through the gate and follow the lane back to the start.

WALK 92

CRAIG CERRIG-GLEISIAD: BACK TO NATURE

This is one of many possible walks in the 156-acre (63ha) National Nature Reserve but it is the closest to the National Park Visitor Centre on Mynydd Illtud Common, near Libanus. It is a great source of information about the National Park, hosts some great displays and has a programme of guided walks.

DISTANCE/TIME 4 miles (6.4km) 2h   **MAP** OS Explorer OL12 Brecon Beacons National Park Western & Central areas   **START** Pull-in by small picnic area on A470, 2 miles (3.2km) north of Storey Arms; grid ref: SN 972221   **PATHS** Clear footpaths and broad stony tracks, 2 stiles   **THE PUB** Tai'r Bull Inn, Libanus. Tel: 01874 625849

1 There's a bridge and a small picnic area at the southern end of the lay-by. Walk towards this and go through the adjacent kissing gate (signposted to Twyn Dylluan-ddu and Forest Lodge). Head towards the crags, following a clear footpath, until you come to a gap in the next wall.

2 Pass through this and turn right to follow a dry-stone wall north. Much of the outward leg follows the line of a pristine dry-stone wall. Although changes in farming practices in the hills haven't altered as radically as they have in many lowland areas, the hedgerows and walls that once divided the land are expensive to maintain and have been slowly replaced by wire fences. The National Park Authority provides free consultation to landowners wishing to keep the more scenic traditional crafts alive. Head down into a small valley, cross the stream, then a stile to continue in the same direction. Drop into another, steeper, valley and climb out, still following the track. Continue through the bracken to a stile.

3 Cross and turn left on to a stony track. Follow this up to a gate and a stile and continue through rough ground, churned

up by mining, until it levels on a dished plateau. Bear right here to the whitewashed trig point of Fan Frynych, then turn sharp left to return to the main track above the escarpment.

4 Turn right on to the main track again and continue past more rough ground before dropping slightly into a broad but shallow valley. Near the bottom, go over a stile on the left (signed 'Beacons Way').

5 Follow the obvious path straight ahead and cross the top of the steep hillside to a cairn. Turn right here to drop steeply all the way down into the heart of the nature reserve, following regular waymark posts.

6 As the ground levels, bear around to the right to follow a signed diversion and continue alongside the stream to the gap in the wall you passed through earlier. Go through again and follow the outward path back to the car park.

CARDIFF
■ TOURIST INFORMATION
Cardiff
The Old Library, The Hayes
☎ 029 2087 3573; www.visitcardiff.com
Cardiff Bay
The Tube ☎ 029 2046 3833
Penarth
Penarth Pier, The Esplanade
☎ 029 2070 8849

■ PLACES OF INTEREST
The Boat House
Dylan's Walk, Laugharne
☎ 01994 427420;
www.dylanthomasboathouse.com
Caerphilly Castle
Market ☎ 029 2088 3143;
www.caerphillycastle.com
Cardiff Castle
Castle Street ☎ 02920 878100;
www.cardiffcastle.com
Castell Coch
Castle Hill, Tongwynlais
☎ 029 2087 8100/2081 0101;
www.cadw.wales.gov.uk
Llandaff Cathedral
The Cathedral Close, Llandaff, Cardiff
☎ 02920 564554;
www.llandaffcathedral.org.uk
National History Museum
St Fagans, Cardiff
☎ 029 2057 3500;
www.museumwales.ac.uk/en/stfagans
National Museum Cardiff
Cathays Park ☎ 029 2039 7951;
www.museumwales.ac.uk/en/cardiff

■ SHOPPING
Plenty of choice and opportunites
for shopping in a safe, traffic-free
environment. Several Victorian arcades
full of small independent shops and
many of the larger chain stores selling
a wide range of Welsh-made crafts and
goods including jewellery.

■ PERFORMING ARTS
Chapter Arts Centre
Market Road, Canton Cardiff
☎ 029 2031 1050; www.chapter.org
Millennium Centre
Bute Place, Cardiff
☎ 029 2063 6400;
www.wmc.org.uk
St David's Hall
The Hayes, Cardiff ☎ 029 2087 8444;
www.stdavidshallcardiff.co.uk

■ SPORTS & ACTIVITIES
BOAT TRIPS
Bay Island Voyages
Lock Keeper's Cottage, Britannia Park,
Cardiff ☎ 01446 420692;
www.bayisland.co.uk
Cruises around Cardiff Bay and the coast.

■ ANNUAL EVENTS & CUSTOMS
Cardiff
Worldport Festival, Jul.
www.worldport-festivals.com
Live music at various venues in the city.
Part of the Cardiff Summer Festival.
Cardiff Summer Festival, Jul/Aug.
www.cardiff-festival.com
Local, national and international events.

SOUTH WALES & PEMBROKESHIRE
■ TOURIST INFORMATION
Fishguard
Town Hall, Market Square
☎ 01437 776637;
www.visitpembrokeshire.com
Fishguard Harbour
Ocean Lab, Goodwick ☎ 01348 872037;
www.visitpembrokeshire.com
Haverfordwest
19 Old Bridge Street ☎ 01437 763110
Newport
2 Bank Cottages, Long Street
☎ 01239 820912
Pembroke
Commons Road ☎ 01437 776499
St David's
Oriel y Parc ☎ 01437 720392
Saundersfoot
The Barbecue, The Harbour
☎ 01834 813672
Tenby
Unit 2, Upper Park Road ☎ 01834 842404

■ PLACES OF INTEREST
Caldey Island
Off Tenby ☎ 01834 844453;
www.caldey-island.co.uk
Boat trips from Tenby to the Benedictine
monastery. Good walking and beaches.
Castell Henllys
Off the A487 between Newport
(Pembrokeshire) and Cardigan.
☎ 01239 891319;
www.castellhenllys.com
One of many prehistoric Iron Age
promontory hill forts in Pembrokeshire
National Park, now an award-winning
interpretative archaeological site.
Dinosaur Park
Gumfreston, Tenby ☎ 01834 845272;
www.thedinosaurpark.co.uk
A 1-mile (1.6km) long walk complete with
prehistoric monsters and woodland trail.
The Gun Tower Museum
Pembroke Dock ☎ 01646 622246;
www.guntowermuseum.org.uk
Pembrokeshire's naval heritage.
Pembroke Castle
☎ 01646 684585;
www.pembrokecastle.co.uk
Impressive ruins with well-preserved
remains of the 14th-century town walls
and plenty of passages, tunnels and
stairways to explore.

St David's Bishop's Palace
☎ 01437 720517; www.cadw.wales.gov.uk
Extensive and impressive ruins next to
cathedral. The entry fee includes 'Lords
of the Palace' exhibition.
St David's Cathedral
The Close, St David's ☎ 01437 720202;
www.stdavidscathedral.org.uk
Built on the site of St David's
6th-century monastery.
Tenby Museum & Art Gallery
Castle Hill, Tenby ☎ 01834 842809;
www.tenbymuseum.org.uk
The interesting and informative displays
here include the archaeology, geology
and maritime and social history of the
town, plus various exhibits of the work
of local artists.
Tudor Merchant's House
Quay Hill, Tenby ☎ 01834 842279
Re-creates the atmosphere of family life
in Tudor times, including a small garden
filled with herbs and plants used during
Tudor times.

■ FOR CHILDREN
Folly Farm
Begelly, Kilgetty ☎ 01834 812731;
www.follyfarm.co.uk
A family adventure park with an indoor
fun fair, theatre, play barn, exotic
animals, restaurant and coffee shop.
Winner of the best family day out in
Pembrokeshire.
Oakwood Theme Park
Narberth ☎ 01834 891373;
www.oakwoodthemepark.co.uk
Roller coasters and more.
Teifi Valley Narrow Gauge Railway
Henlan, Llandysw ☎ 01559 371077;
www.teifivalleyrailway.co.uk
Pleasant scenic train journeys through
stunningly wooded countryside, where
there is also a choice of delightful
woodland walks.

■ SHOPPING
Markets
Fishguard, farmers market weekly, Sat.
Haverfordwest, fortnightly.
Pembroke Dock, Fri.
St David's, weekly Women's Institute
market, Thu.
Tenby, indoor market, Mon, Tue, Thu–Sat.
Narberth
A popular centre for antiques shops.

■ PERFORMING ARTS
Theatr Gwaun
West Street, Fishguard ☎ 01348 873421;
www.pembrokeshire.gov.uk
Cinema, jazz and youth theatre.
Torch Theatre
St Peter's Road, Milford Haven
☎ 01646 695267; www.torchtheatre.co.uk
Cinema, music, drama, opera and dance.

Queens Hall
High Street, Narberth ☎ 01834 861212;
www.thequeenshall.org.uk
Live music, gallery, cinema, comedy.

■ SPORTS & OUTDOOR ACTIVITIES
ANGLING
Boat Fishing
Short trips or day-long deep-sea fishing
trips from many harbours.
Tenby
☎ 07974 623542; www.tenbyfishing.co.uk
Solva
☎ 01437 720053; www.solva.net
Neyland
☎ 01646 600313; www.celticwildcat.com
Coarse Fishing
Yet-y-Gors Fishery, Manorwen, Fishguard
☎ 01348 873497; www.yet-y-gors.co.uk
Two coarse lakes plus still-water fly-
fishing for trout.
Holgan Farm, Narberth
☎ 07796 517586; www.fisheries.co.uk
Carp and tench lakes.
BEACHES
Always take note of safety instructions.
Broadhaven, St Brides Bay
Another long sandy beach popular
for watersports.
Dale
A shingle beach well known for yachting,
diving and windsurfing.
Freshwater West
Big Atlantic waves make this sand and
shingle beach ideal for surfers.
Little Haven, St Brides Bay
Small sheltered cove next to the village
of Little Haven.
Manorbier
A busy beach, popular with surfers,
swimmers and families.
Marloes Sands
This crescent-shaped sandy beach has
interesting rocky outcrops.
Newgale Sands, St Brides Bay
Exposed beach especially popular for
surfing and kite surfing.
Saundersfoot
Popular sandy beach beyond the harbour.
Tenby North
The little sandy beach is overlooked by
the harbour and town's old quarters.
Tenby South
A good expanse of sandy beach, very
popular with bathers.
Whitesands, St Davids
Fine long sandy beach with safe
swimming and surfing areas.
BOAT TRIPS
Tenby to Caldey Island
☎ 01834 844453;
www.caldey-island.co.uk
Day trips from Tenby Harbour
**Neyland/Martin's Haven to Grassholm,
Skokholm and Skomer**
☎ 01646 603110; www.dale-sailing.co.uk

St David's to Ramsey Island
www.ramseyisland.co.uk
www.thousandislands.co.uk
www.aquaphobia-ramseyisland.co.uk
For trips to Ramsey and wildlife-watching.
Cardigan Bay
☎ 01239 623558;
www.baytoremember.co.uk
Cetacean watching and leisure trips from the Teifi Estuary.

WATERSPORTS
Coasteering
St David's ☎ 01437 721611; www.tyf.com
Kitesurfing
Newgale Beach ☎ 07816 169359;
www.bigbluekitesurfing.com
Sea Kayaking
☎ 01348 837709;
www.preseliadventure.co.uk
Surfing
Newgale, Manorbier, Freshwater West
☎ 01646 680070;
www.outerreefsurfschool.co.uk

CYCLING
Old railways, reservoir roads, byways, coastal and hill tracks. For general info visit www.cyclepembrokeshire.com
Cycle Hire
Newport
☎ 01239 820773;
www.newportbikehire.com)
Haverfordwest
☎ 01437 760068; www.mikes-bikes.co.uk
Fishguard
☎ 01348 874170;
www.pembrokeshirebikes.co.uk

HORSE RIDING
Dunes Riding Centre
Cotts Lane, Martlewy, Narberth
☎ 01834 891398;
www.dunes-riding.co.uk
East Nolton Riding Stables
East Nolton Farm, Nolton Haven, Haverfordwest ☎ 01437 710360;
www.noltonstables.com
Havard Stables
Trewyddig Fawr, Dinas Cross, Newport
☎ 01348 811452
Llanwnda Riding & Trekking
Penrhiw Fach, Llanwnda, Goodwick
☎ 01348 873595

LONG-DISTANCE PATHS
Pembrokeshire Coast Path
☎ 01437 764551; www.pcnpa.org.uk
For information about this long distance path and other walking routes.
For timetables and information about the year-round coastal bus services visit www.pembrokeshire.gov.uk/coastbus.

■ ANNUAL EVENTS & CUSTOMS
Fishguard
Folk Festival, May.
International Music Festival, Jun.
Jazz festival, Sep.

Narberth
Winter carnival, early Dec.
Newport/Preseli
Walking Festival, May.
St David's
Cathedral festival, May/Jun.
Tenby
Arts festival, late Sept.

SNOWDONIA NATIONAL PARK
■ TOURIST INFORMATION
Aberdyfi
The Wharf Gardens ☎ 01654 767321
Bala
Pensarn Road ☎ 01678 521021
Barmouth
Station Road ☎ 01341 280787
Beddgelert
Carnolfan Hebog ☎ 01766 890615
Betws-y-Coed
Royal Oak Stables
☎ 01690 710426; www.nwt.co.uk
Blaenau Ffestiniog
Unit 3, High Street ☎ 01766 830360
Conwy
Conwy Castle
☎ 01492 592248;
www.visitllandudno.org,uk
Dolgellau
Eldon Square ☎ 01341 422888;
www.visitmidwales.co.uk
Harlech
Llys y Graig ☎ 01766 780658
Llanberis
41b High Street
☎ 01286 870765 (seasonal);
www.visitsnowdonia.info

■ PLACES OF INTEREST
Aberconwy House
Castle Street, Conwy
☎ 01492 592246;
www.nationaltrust.org.uk
Fourteenth-century merchant's house – one of the finest examples of its kind you will find in Wales.
Chirk Castle
Chirk, near Wrexham
☎ 01691 777701;
www.chirk.com/castle
Magnificent medieval fortress on the Welsh Marches.
Conwy Castle
Castle Street, Conwy
☎ 01492 592358; www.cadw.wales.gov.uk
A masterpiece of fascinating medieval military architecture.
Conwy Valley Railway Museum
Betws-y-Coed Station Yard
☎ 01690 710568;
www.conwyrailwaymuseum.co.uk
Miniature steam train railway rides in picturesque countryside.
Denbigh Castle
☎ 01745 813385; www.cadw.wales.gov.uk

Striking ruins crowning a steep hill above the town.
Electric Mountain
Llanberis ☎ 01286 870636;
www.electricmountain.co.uk
Informative and lively guided tours around an underground hydro-electric power station.
Great Orme Mines
Great Orme, Llandudno
☎ 01492 870447;
www.greatormemines.info
Fascinating Bronze Age copper mines to explore.
Llechwedd Slate Caverns
Blaenau Ffestiniog
☎ 01766 830306;
www.llechwedd-slate-caverns.cc.uk
A tour of the underground world of the slate miner.
Motor Museum
Betws-y-Coed
☎ 01690 710760;
www.betys-y-coed.co.uk/attra/motor.htm
Exhibits include Bugatti, Aston Martin, Bentley, Bullnose Morris, Ford T and British motorbikes.
Plas Mawr
High Street, Conwy.
☎ 01492 580167
Built between 1576 and 1585, this is possibly the best-preserved Elizabethan townhouse in Britain.
Quaker Heritage Centre
Ty Meirion, Sgwar Elson, Dolgellau
☎ 01341 424680
Tells the story of the local Quaker community that lived here, of their persecution and finally, their emigration to Pennsylvannia.
Rhuddlan Castle
Near Rhyl
☎ 01745 590777;
www.cadw.wales.gov.uk
Rhuddlan's massive twin-towered gatehouse immediately catches the eye.
Rhyl Sky Tower
Rhyl Promenade
www.rhylsuncentre.co.uk/
A 240-foot (73m) modern tower whose observation car rotates to give birds-eye views of the North Wales Coast.
Snowdon Mountain Railway
Llanberis ☎ 08443 4938120;
www.snowdonrailway.co.uk
Enjoy a more leisurely route up Snowdon, the highest mountain in England and Wales on Britain's only rack-and-pinion railway.
Trefriw Woollen Mills
Trefriw ☎ 01492 640462;
www.t-w-m.co.uk
The mill specializes in the manufacture of magnificent Welsh double weave (tapestry) bedspreads (carthenni) and beautiful tweeds. Visitors can tour the

mill and see goods being made or buy from the shop.
Welsh Slate Museum
Padarn Country Park, Llanberis
☎ 01286 870630;
www.museumwales.ac.uk
The museum, housed in old Victorian buildings, gives an insight into the day-to-day goings on of a miner's life.

■ FOR CHILDREN
Alice in Wonderland Centre
3 & 4 Trinity Square, Llandudno
☎ 01492 580648;
www.wonderland.co.uk
Alice in Wonderland story and its connection to Llandudno.
Harlequin Puppet Theatre
Rhos on Sea Promenade, Colwyn Bay
☎ 01492 548166; www.puppets.uk.com
Opened in 1958, this is Britain's only remaining puppet theatre devoted solely to marionettes.
Rhyl Sun Centre
East Parade, Rhyl ☎ 01745 344433;
www.rhylsuncentre.co.uk
An indoor tropical water park, with 'white rollers' to surf and daredevil waterslides to thrill and to scare.
SeaQuarium
East Parade, Rhyl ☎ 01745 344660;
www.seaquarium.co.uk
An excellent acquarium where you come face to face with a huge variety of sea creatures.

■ SHOPPING
Trefriw Woollen Mill and Meirion Mill at Dinas Mawddwy have lovely Welsh fabrics and tapestries.
MARKETS
Bangor, farmers' market, fortnightly Sun.
Blaenau Ffestiniog, Tue.
Barmouth, Thu and Sun in summer.
Colwyn Bay, farmers' market, Thu.
Conwy, Wed
Llanrwst, Tue.
Prestatyn, Tue, Fri, Sun.
Ruthin, last Sun of the month
Wrexham, 3rd Fri every month.

■ PERFORMING ARTS
Clwyd Theatre
Mold ☎ 0845 330 3565;
www.clwyd-theatr-cymru.co.uk
The Dragon Theatre
Jubilee Road, Barmouth
☎ 01341 281697;
www.dragontheatre.co.uk
Theatr Harlech
☎ 01766 780667;
www.theatrharlech.co.uk
Theatr Colwyn
Abergele Rd, Colwyn Bay
☎ 01492 532668;
www.theatrcolwyn.co.uk

Venue Cymru
Promenade, Llandudno
☎ 01492 872000; www.venuecymru.co.uk

■ SPORTS & OUTDOOR ACTIVITIES

ANGLING

Bala Lake
Llyn Tegid (Bala Lake), Wales's largest natural lake, holds large pike, also perch, roach, trout and eel.

Crafnant Fishery
Llyn Crafnant, above Conwy Valley near Trefriw ☎ 01492 640818
Quiet lake with brown and rainbow trout.

Llandudno, Colwyn Bay, Rhos, Deganwy, Rhyl, Mostyn Docks
Shore fishing.

Llyn Brenig
Permits from The Visitor Centre, Brenig Reservoir, Cerrigydrudion.
☎ 01490 420463
Day permits from machines.
Fly fishing lake filled with rainbow trout.

BEACHES

Aberdyfi
A sandy beach, ideal for families.

Abergele
A good beach popular with windsurfers and canoeists. Good car parking.

Barmouth
Long sandy beach away from the estuary, ideal for sunning, sandcastles or beach games.

Colwyn Bay
A lively pier and a good arcing sandy beach sheltered by the Little Orme.

Conwy
Good beach with sand dunes a mile (1.6km) west of the town, just beyond the marina.

Fairbourne
Good sandy beach, ideal for swimming and playing beach sports.

Harlech
A straight beach with miles of golden sand, ideal for swimming.

Llandudno
Two excellent sandy beaches popular with families either side of the Great Orme. The West Beach has a pier and many activities for children, such as Punch and Judy shows.

Prestatyn
A 4-mile (6.4km) bar of sand, very popular with families.

Rhyl
6 miles (9.6km) of sandy beach, good for families.

Tywyn
Cobbles with good sand at low tide, popular beach for families.

CYCLING
☎ 01341 440728 www.beicsbrenin.co.uk
Huge mountain biking area, with challenging routes and beginners' trails. Cycle hire at Forest Visitor Centre

Gwydyr Fores
☎ 01690 710766 www.bikewales.co.uk
Forestry, miner's tracks and byway routes at Betws-y-Coed. Cycle hire from Beics Betws

GOLF

Chirk Golf Club
Chirk, near Wrexham
☎ 01691 774407;
www.chirkgolfclub.co.uk.
18 holes.

Ffestiniog Golf Club
Y Cefn, Festiniog
☎ 01766 831829; www.ffestinioggolf.org
9 holes.

Llanymynech Golf Club
Pant, near Oswestry
☎ 01691 830983;
www.llanymynechgolfclub.co.uk
18 holes.

Old Colwyn Golf Club
Woodlands Avenue, Old Colwyn
☎ 01492 515581;
www.oldcolwyngolfclub.co.uk
9 holes.

Rhos-on-Sea Golf Club
Glan-y-mor Road, Penrhyn Bay, Llandudno
☎ 01492 549641; www.rhosgolf.co.uk
18 holes.

Tyddyn Mawr Golf Club
Crawia Road, Llanrug, Caernarfon
☎ 01286 674919;
www.welshgolfcourses.com/north/tyddynmawr.php
9 holes.

HORSE RIDING

E Prichard Pony Trekking
Felen Rhyd Fach,
Maentwrog ☎ 01766 590231

Gwydyr Stables
Penmachno,
Near Betws-y-Coed
☎ 01690 760248;
www.horse-riding-wales.co.uk

Ruthin Riding Centre
Cae Coch Farm, Ruthin
☎ 01824 703470;
www.ruthinridingcentre.co.uk

Sychdyn Riding Centre
Tai Cochion, Alltami Road, Sychdyn, Mold
☎ 01352 840284

The Trekking Centre
Abergwynant Farm, Penmaenpool, Dolgellau
☎ 01341 422377

Tynllwyn Riding Stables
Tynllwyn Farm, Bryn-y-Maen, Colwyn Bay ☎ 01492 580224;

SAILING CENTRES

Aberdyfi
Harbourmaster, The Quay
☎ 01654 767626

Barmouth
Harbourmaster, The Quay
☎ 01341 280671

Conwy
Harbourmaster, The Quay
☎ 01492 596253

SKIING

Llandudno Ski and Snowboard Centre
Wyddfyd, Great Orme, Llandudno
☎ 01492 874707;
www.jnllandudno.co.uk

WALKING
This area is the best in Wales and offers a variety of walks. Snowdon, the Glyderau and the Carneddau ranges are the most popular for walking. Check the weather forecast before setting out.

WHITE WATER RAFTING

Canolfan Tryweryn
Frongoch, Bala
☎ 01678 521083; www.ukrafting.co.uk

■ ANNUAL EVENTS & CUSTOMS

Conwy
Conwy River Festival, early Aug.
☎ 01492 596253;
www.conwyriverfestival.org

Llanberis
Llanberis Film Festival, various venues, early Mar.
☎ 01286 871534; www.llamff.co.uk

Ruthin
Ruthin Festival, Jun/Jul.
☎ 01286 871534; ruthinfestival.co.uk
Music festival.

BRECON BEACONS & CENTRAL WALES

■ TOURIST INFORMATION

Abergavenny
Swan Meadow, Monmouth Road
☎ 01873 857588;
www.visitabervagenny.co.uk

Aberystwyth
Terrace Road ☎ 01970 612125;
www.tourism.ceredigion.gov.uk

Brecon
Cattle Market Car Park
☎ 01874 622485;
www.tourism.powys.gov.uk

Brecon Beacons National Park
Visitor Centre, Libanus, Brecon
☎ 01874 623366;
www.breconbeacons.org

Hay-on-Wye
Oxford Road ☎ 01497 820144;
www.hay-on-wye.co.uk

Llandovery
Heritage Centre, Kings Road
☎ 01550 720693

Llandrindod Wells
Old Town Hall, Memorial Gardens
☎ 01597 822600

Machynlleth
Owain Glyndwr Centre
☎ 01654 702401

Rhayader
The Leisure Centre, North Street
☎ 01597 810591; www.rhayader.co.uk

■ PLACES OF INTEREST

Brecon Cathedral
Cathedral Close ☎ 01874 623857;
www.breconcathedral.org.uk
Magnificent 11th-century cathedral.

Carreg Cennen Castle
Trapp, near Llandeilo
☎ 01558 822291;
www.carregcennencastle.com
Thought by many to be Wales' most spectacularly sited castle on high cliffs overlooking the Tywi Valley.

Centre for Alternative Technology
Machynlleth ☎ 01654 705950;
www.cat.org.uk
See some of the solutions being used to the combat the environment challenges facing Earth.

Ceredigion Museum & Coliseum Gallery
Coliseum, Terrace Road, Aberystwyth
☎ 01970 633088;
pilgrim.ceredigion.gov.uk
A fine collection of historic objects including the furniture, archaeological finds, agriculture, seafaring and lead mining industries of the people of Ceredigion.

Dan-yr-Ogof Showcaves
Abercrave, Swansea ☎ 01639 730284;
www.showcaves.co.uk
Visit the underground world of stalagmites, stalactites, waterfalls, a museum, Iron Age farm and the dinosaur park.

Dinas Nature Reserve
Rhandirmwyn ☎ 02920 353000
RSPB reserve with beautiful walk and shop/information centre. Charge for car park for non-members.

Dolaucothi Gold Mines
Pumpsaint, Llanwrda Carmarthenshire (Site off A482 between Lampeter and Llanwrda.) ☎ 01558 650177;
www.nationaltrust.org.uk
Free for National Trust members only (excludes underground tour). The only known Roman gold mine in the UK.

Gigrin Farm Kite Feeding Station
South St, Rhayader ☎ 01597 810243;
www.gigrin.co.uk
A fantastic opportunity to see the rare bird of prey, the red kite.

National Cycle Collection
The Automobile Palace, Temple Street, Llandrindod Wells ☎ 01597 825531;
www.cyclemuseum.org.uk
Boneshakers, penny farthings and modern bikes; 250 machines on display and themed exhibitions.

National Library of Wales
Penglais, Aberystwyth.
☎ 01970 632565; www.llgc.org.uk.
Entry here includes a number of exhibitions (some free of charge), there is also a cinema, shop and a restaurant. Disabled access.

■ FOR CHILDREN

Brecon Mountain Railway
Pant Station, Merthyr Tydfil
☎ 01685 722988;
www.breconmountainrailway.co.uk
A narrow-gauge steam line.

Vale of Rheidol Railway
Park Avenue, Aberystwyth
☎ 01970 625819;
www.rheidolrailway.co.uk
One of the Great Little Trains of Wales.

■ SHOPPING

Markets
Abergavenny, Farmers market, 4th Thu
of month.
Aberystwyth, 1st and 3rd Sat of the
month.
Brecon, Tue and Fri.
Cardigan, Farmers market every Sat from
mid Jul to late Sep.
Hay-on-Wye, Thu.
Lampeter, alternate Tue.
Llandrindod Wells, Fri. Farmers market
last Thu am of the month.
Llanidloes, Sat.
Machynlleth, Wed.

■ PERFORMING ARTS

Aberystwyth Arts Centre
Aberystwyth University, Penglais Campus
☎ 01970 623232;
www.aberystwythartscentre.co.uk

The Tabernacle
Hoel Penrallt, Machynlleth
☎ 01654 703355;
www.momawales.org.uk

Theatr Brycheiniog
Canal Wharf, Brecon ☎ 01874 611622;
www.brycheiniog.co.uk

Theatr Hafren
Llanidloes Road, Newtown
☎ 01686 625007; www.theatrhafren.co.uk

■ SPORTS & OUTDOOR ACTIVITIES

ANGLING

Freshwater
There are numerous opportunities
for fishing on farms, lakes and rivers,
including the Clywedog Reservoir near
Llanidloes, the Beacons Reservoir at
the head of the Taff Valley and the River
Tawe in Carmarthenshire. Permits
and licences are available from tackle
shops and most Tourist Information
Centres.

BOAT TRIPS

New Quay Boat Company
Pier Slip, New Quay ☎ 01545 560800;
www.newquayboattrips.co.uk
Pleasure and fishing trips.

CYCLING

Cycle Routes
Taff Trail (from Cardiff to the Brecon
Beacons through a variety of landscapes
– urban and open moorland).

The shore of Lake Llangors is a very
important habitat for water-based bird
and wildlife.

GOLF

Borth & Ynys Golf Club
Aer y Mor, Borth
☎ 01970 871202
18 holes.

Cradoc Golf Club
Penoyre Park, Cradoc, Brecon
☎ 01874 623658;
www.cradoc.co.uk
18 holes.

Machynlleth Golf Club
Newtown Road, Machynlleth
☎ 01654 702000;
www.machynlletgolf.weebly.com
9 holes.

Rhosgoch Golf & Leisure Club
Rhosgoch, Builth Wells
☎ 01544 370286;
www.rhosgoch-golf.co.uk
18 holes.

St Idloes Golf Club
Trefeglwys Road, Llanidloes
☎ 01686 412559;
www.stidloesgolfclub.co.uk
9 holes.

HORSE RIDING

Cantref Riding Centre
Cantref, Brecon
☎ 01874 665223; www.cantref.com

Underhill Riding Stables
Underhill Farm, Dolau,
Llandrindod Wells
☎ 01597 851890;
www.underhillridingstables.co.uk

LONG-DISTANCE PATHS

The Beacons Way
100 miles (160km) through the Brecon
Beacons.

Glyndwr's Way
132 miles (212km) between Knighton and
Welshpool, via Machynlleth.

■ ANNUAL EVENTS & CUSTOMS

Brecon

BreconJazz Festival, mid Aug.
☎ 0870 9901299; www.breconjazz.co.uk
Great event for jazz lovers with top
performers.

Hay

Hay Festival, end May to early Jun.
☎ 01497 822629l; www.hayfestival.com
World-famous literary festival.
International Walking Festival, mid Sep.
www.visitmidwales.co.uk

Aberystwyth

Musicfest Aberystwyth, end Jul.
www.aberfest.org

Builth Wells

Royal Welsh Show, mid to end Jul.
☎ 01982 553683; www.rwas.co.uk
Agricultural show with plenty of interest
for all the family.

PUBS

CARDIFF

Caesars Arms
Cardiff Road, Cardiff CF15 9NN
☎ 029 2089 0486;
www.caesarsarms.co.uk
The Caesars Arms attracts a well-heeled
clientele to its heated patio and terrace
looking out over the lovely gardens and
surrounding countryside. The inn prides
itself on its vast selection of fresh fish,
seafood, meat and game, and its friendly,
relaxed atmosphere. Draught ales are
somewhat overshadowed by a massive
wine list, which has many selections
available by the glass.

SOUTH WALES & PEMBROKESHIRE

Cambrian Inn
6 Main Street, Solva SA62 6UU
☎ 01437 721210
The Grade II-listed 17th-century inn
at the entrance to Lower Solva offers
both restaurant and bar meals in cosy
surroundings. Expect to see pasta dishes,
steaks and vegetarian dishes with real
ales such as Brains Reverend James.
No children under 10 or dogs in the bar.

Ferry Inn
Pembroke Ferry, Pembroke Dock
SA72 6UD ☎ 01646 682947
Once the haunt of smugglers, this fine
16th-century inn is set on the banks
of the Cleddau River, with good views
across the estuary from the nautical-
themed bar and waterside terrace. The
menu changes regularly but always offers
a range of fresh local fish, such as sea
bass, monkfish and lemon sole.

The Georges Restaurant/Café Bar
24 Market Street, Haverfordwest
SA61 1NH ☎ 01437 766683;
www.thegeorges.uk.com
This remarkable 18th-century building
incorporates many original features in
its restored vaulted cellar and eating
areas. Its delightful walled garden, which
enjoys spectacular views over the ruins
of 12th-century Haverfordwest Castle,
has outdoor heating for those chillier
evenings. An extensive range of good
home-cooked food is served all day, and
there are plenty of fish dishes.

The Stackpole Inn
Jasons Corner, Stackpole SA71 5DF
☎ 01646 672324;
www.stackpoleinn.co.uk
The 17th-century Stackpole Inn is popular
with walkers and locals. The extensive,
award-winning bar and restaurant menu
includes fresh locally caught fish that
appear on the 'just in' specials board and
old favourites such as Welsh lamb.

SNOWDONIA NATIONAL PARK

The Castle Hotel
High Street, Conwy LL32 8DB
☎ 01492 582800;
www.castlewales.co.uk
A rather grand 16th-century coaching inn
adorned with many antiques and some
fine paintings by Victorian artist John
Dawson-Watson, who it is said painted to
pay for his lodgings here. You can dine in
Dawsons restaurant and bar or there's a
popular bar serving excellent meals, but
be early to grab a table.

Dovey Inn
Seaview Terrace, Aberdyfi LL35 0EF
☎ 01654 767332; www.doveyinn.com
This historic inn, on the estuary of the
River Dovey, is only 20 yards from the
sea and the fine sandy beach. The village
clings to the hills above the estuary,
once a major slate port and now a sailing
centre. An extensive seafood menu
includes Thai spiced shark steak, fish
pie, Bantry Bay mussels, chargrilled
swordfish and tuna steak with red wine
fish gravy. There are plenty of other
delicious options on offer, including
sandwiches, light bites, vegetarian
dishes, meat dishes, pasta and pizza.

The Groes Inn
Tyn y Groes, Conwy LL32 8TN
☎ 01492 650545; www.groesinn.com
Dating back to 1573, the Groes Inn,
overlooking the scenic Conwy Valley,
became the first licensed inn in Wales.
A traditional but luxurious inn, garlanded
with delightful flowerboxes in summer,
it retains beamed ceilings and log
fires. Anything from a light snack to
gourmet meals (with seafood specials)
can be enjoyed in the bar or restaurant.
Childrens menu also available.

Stables Bistro Bar
Betws-y-Coed LL24 0AY
☎ 01690 710219
In an extension to Betws-y-Coed's largest
hotel, the Stables Bistro Bar efficiently
produces tasty bar meals time after time,
even though the bar is usually extremely
busy. On summer evenings there's a
large outside dining area where you can
eat under the trees and the stars.

White Horse Inn
Capel Garmon, Betws-y-Coed LL26 0RW
☎ 01690 710271
A cosy 400-year-old inn in the village
of Capel Garmon: one with beamed
ceilings, log fires and a panoramic view
of the Conwy Valley and the mountains of
Snowdonia. The inn is well known for its
fine food. It also serves a wide selection
of fine wines and real ales.

BRECON BEACONS & CENTRAL WALES

Clytha Arms
Clytha, Abergavenny NP7 9BW
☎ 01873 840206
This family-run free house has an outstanding reputation for its food and real ales. Bass, Felinfoel and Hook Norton ales are joined by an ever-changing selection of guest beers, and there's also a good choice of wines by the glass. As for food, the owner cooks up a storm on his new oak-fired grill, starting the day by baking his own bread and muffins. The menu offers something for every taste, from rabbit and cider pie to bacon, laverbread and cockles. Treacle pudding to finish is a must. Raglan's famous 15th-century castle is near by, while Cardiff, with its historical attractions and superb shopping, is a 40-minute drive.

The Felin Fach Griffin
Felin Fach LD3 0UB
☎ 01874 620111
Felin Fach Griffin is a country inn in a quiet valley on the edge of the Brecon Beacons National Park. At the pub's heart are comfortable, deep leather sofas surrounding a large newspaper-strewn farmhouse table, and a warming open fire, (nearly always alight). The food is simple but delicious and all tastes are well catered for.

Kilvert's Hotel
The Bull Ring, Hay-on-Wye HR3 5AG
☎ 01497 821042; www.kilverts.co.uk
This attractive ivy-clad Georgian free house is popular with the local community and tourists alike, and has a small flagged outdoor terrace area in the front, and a charming rustic oak-beamed bar serving real ales such as Kilvert's Gold Ale, alongside a range of favourite bar meals like braised Welsh lamb, pizzas and pastas. The elegant restaurant specializes in classic dishes such as French onion soup, steak and ale pie, Welsh sirloin steak and slow-roasted organic lamb. There are also vegetarian dishes available.

Kings Head Inn
1 Market Square, Llandovery
SA20 0AB ☎ 01550 720393;
www.kingsheadcoachinginn.co.uk
A comfortable 16th-century former coaching inn and drovers' bank situated in the centre of town. The exposed stone walls, wood beams and cosy welcoming fires combine to give the inn a warm and convivial atmosphere. The excellent food is based on fresh and wholesome Welsh produce.

TEA ROOMS
CARDIFF

The Bay Bistro & Coffee House
Rhossili, Gower SA3 1PL
☎ 01792 390519;
www.thebaybistro.com
Enjoy magnificent views across Rhossili Bay whilst indulging in hot chocolate with marshmallows, a laver-bread burger or a baked Camembert; great cream teas and cakes too! Evening meals include the freshest local fish.

Crema Coffee Shop
Millennium Centre, Cardiff CF10 5AL
☎ 029 2048 4884
This is a stylish modern venue in the buzzing heart of the arts centre serving mouth-watering cakes, including a wicked chocolate fudge cake, with a wide range of coffees and teas.

Norwegian Church
Harbour Drive, Cardiff Bay, Cardiff
CF10 4PA ☎ 029 2087 7959
Built in 1869 as a place of worship for Scandinavian sailors in Cardiff, this attractive white wooden building has a popular tea room where you can indulge yourself with excellent calorific cakes and a range of snacks.

SOUTH WALES & PEMBROKESHIRE

Morawelon Café Bar & Restaurant
Parrog, Newport, Pembrokeshire
SA42 0RW ☎ 01239 820565
Set on the Parrog beachfront, you can indulge yourself here with many varieties of tea or coffee and delicious cakes, or you can tuck into a mouth-watering meal that might include freshly caught local crab, washed down with a glass of wine. Also open Thursday, Friday and Saturday evenings.

The Old Printing House
20 Main Street, Solva SA62 6UU
☎ 01437 721603
The award-winning tea room/restaurant is located at the heart of the village of Solva, in an 18th-century house and paper mill with beamed ceilings and stripped stone walls. The tea room is noted for its eight blends of tea, freshly baked bread and cakes, home-made soups, vegetarian dishes, chutneys and traditional cream teas. It's an ideal place to stop after a walk on the coastal path.

Tudor Lodge Restaurant
Jameston, Manorbier SA70 7SS
☎ 01834 871978;
www.tudorlodgerestaurant.co.uk
This restaurant has a clean, modern style with walls hung with contemporary paintings and a good atmosphere, but

with traditional, blazing log fires for when the sun cools. The food is excellent and prepared using fresh local produce wherever possible, whether it is for light lunches or evening meals.

SNOWDONIA NATIONAL PARK

Badgers Café and Patisserie
The Victorian Centre, Mostyn Street,
Llandudno LL30 2RP ☎ 01492 871649
Here, delicious teas, coffees and cream cakes are served by Victorian-costumed waitresses known as Badgers' Nippies. Welsh treats such as bara brith and Welsh cakes are on the menu, along with Welsh rarebit, swan meringues and dragon eclairs.

Cemlyn Restaurant and Tea Shop
High Street, Harlech LL46 2YA
☎ 01766 780425;
www.cremlynrestaurant.co.uk
An award-winning tea shop serving over 20 varieties of teas, along with coffees, delicious home-made cakes and sandwiches. All the food is made on the premises. Try local specialities such as bara brith or fruit cake, perhaps on the sun terrace with its spectacular views of Harlech Castle, Royal St David's Golf Course, Cardigan Bay and the Snowdonian mountains. There's a patio for outdoor seating in fine weather, and bed-and-breakfast is also available.

Lyn's Café and Teagarden
Liverpool House, Church Street,
Beddgelert LL55 4YA ☎ 01766 890374
Sited by the attractive River Colwyn in picturesque Beddgelert, the cosy café has a splendid riverside garden where you can relax with a coffee or tea. Alternatively, choose from a menu of breakfast items, snacks, light meals, clotted cream teas and evening meals. The café is licensed in the evening.

Pete's Eats
40 High Street, Llanberis LL55 4EU
☎ 01286 870 117; www.petes-eats.co.uk
This café is (perhaps) one of the best chippys, and, if you're in a mood to be self-indulgent, look no further. It's lively and popular among the climbers and hillwalkers who mix with the locals.

The Plas
High Street, Harlech LL46 2YA
☎ 01766 780204
After clambering over the castle or a bracing walk along the sands, set aside a long, languid afternoon for savouring the atmosphere of this lovely house and its delicious afternoon tea, where you can enjoy the view while you tuck into the sandwiches, cakes and scones.

BRECON BEACONS & CENTRAL WALES

The Angel Hotel
15 Cross Street, Abergavenny
NP7 5EN ☎ 01873 857121;
www.angelhotelabervagenny.com
Enjoy afternoon tea in comfort and style, in this refurbished hotel. There is an interesting selection of artisan speciality cakes and pastries from specialist baker, Sally Lane, are served, and whether you choose to take tea in the restaurant, sitting room or outdoors in the courtyard, the service is friendly and welcoming. There are also many speciality teas to try – perfect with a slice of cake.

Giglios Coffee Shop
10 Bethel Square, Brecon LD3 7JP
☎ 01874 625062
A modern licensed coffee shop and restaurant in the heart of Brecon. Excellent cream teas, gateaux and sandwiches, such as smoked salmon and cream cheese, Thai green chicken, or salmon with dill mayonnaise. A wide variety of teas and coffees is on offer.

The Granary
20 Broad Street, Hay-on-Wye HR3 5DB
☎ 01497 820790
This splendid licensed café has a cosy bistro style interior with outside tables looking across to the town's Victorian clocktower. Food includes sandwiches, jacket potatoes and warming soups, as well as full main meals.

Nant y Bai Mill
Rhandirmwyn, Llandovery SA20 0PB
☎ 01550 760211
A wonderfully situated country café/restaurant/B&B in the beautiful Tywi Valley, the old mill serves light lunches (sandwiches, jacket potatoes, Welsh rarebit), afternoon teas and excellent evening meals in a cosy atmosphere.

Pilgrims Tea Rooms & Restaurant
Brecon Cathedral Close, Brecon
LD3 9DP ☎ 01874 610610;
www.pilgrims-tearooms.co.uk
This charming tea room and restaurant can be found in Brecon Cathedral Close, next to Brecon's magnificent cathedral. The tea room still has the look and feel of the 15th-century barn next to it. In good weather, customers can sit outside and enjoy the delightful aroma from the beautifully laid out herb garden, and spend the afternoon relaxing in the cloisters while they sip their tea. Meals are created using locally grown produce and the premises are fully licensed so, if you wish, you can have a glass of wine with your lunch instead of a cup of tea

Northern England

Northern England

The northern reach of England is famous for its diverse landscape that is home to many of the country's beautiful National Parks.

The rolling green of the Yorkshire Dales is in stark contrast to the craggy mountains of the Lake District or the broad sandy beaches of the west coast, and a myriad hills and dales in between, all with their individual sense of drama and beauty. Even the climate seems to change from the rugged and wild west coast to the calmer and milder eastern shores, both providing a home to many important species of birds and plants.

The influence of the Industrial Revolution is evident still on the land in this beautiful region and in its cities. Great tracts of land once used for heavy manufacturing and engineering plants have been redeveloped and there are many excellent museums here to celebrate the area's industrial heritage.

Lake District

CLOCKWISE FROM TOP: LAKE CONISTON; WAST WATER; LANGDALE

AMBLESIDE MAP REF 406 E4

At the northern tip of lake Windermere, Ambleside is a convenient base for touring the central Lakes, with Grasmere and the Langdale valleys a short drive away. The town has adopted this role with gusto; it seems that every other shop sells walking boots and outdoor clothing.

The Romans first saw the strategic potential of this site, and built a fort they called Galava close to where the rivers Brathay and Rothay flow into Windermere. Centuries later, during Queen Victoria's reign, the town gained fame and prosperity through the growth of tourism.

Ambleside won its market charter in 1650, and a few buildings, including a watermill, survive from this time. However, the best-known building in Ambleside is also the smallest: Bridge House is built on a little bridge that spans the beck of Stock Ghyll. It now serves as a diminutive National Trust shop.

It is just a short walk from the centre of Ambleside to the lake at Waterhead. Like a Bowness Bay in miniature. It has a short stretch of beach, dinghies for hire and ever-hungry ducks. The steamers *Swan*, *Tern* and *Teal* call in at Waterhead on their round-the-lake cruises.

BARROW-IN-FURNESS
MAP REF 406 E5

Even the most loyal locals would hesitate to describe Barrow as beautiful. Until the mid-19th century there was just a tiny fishing village here. What made it grow at an astonishing rate were the iron- and steel-making industries, closely followed, logically, by the construction of ships.

The shipbuilding company of Vickers became almost synonymous with Barrow, and even today the docks and shipyards are an impressive sight. For a fascinating overview head for the popular Dock Museum on North Road. The museum tells how, within a generation, Barrow had become a major force in maritime engineering. Other exhibits focus on older shipbuilding traditions and its pioneers.

A surprise awaits visitors who drive past the museum – a road bridge links Barrow with the Isle of Walney. A glance at the map shows this to be a geographic oddity shielding the tip of the Furness peninsula, and Barrow itself, from the ravages of the sea. The southern tip of the Isle of Walney is a haven for wildlife.

Between Barrow and Dalton, in the 'Vale of Deadly Nightshade', is Furness Abbey. Now an evocative ruin of weathered, salmon-coloured sandstone, it was, in its heyday, second in importance only to Fountains Abbey in North Yorkshire. Parts of the abbey (now in the hands of English Heritage) still stand to their full height, in a romantic wooded setting.

BORROWDALE MAP REF 406 E3

This glorious wooded valley, which runs south from Derwent Water, contains two of the Lake District's most dramatic natural features – the Bowder Stone and the Jaws of Borrowdale. The Stone is signposted along a path east of the B5289 Borrowdale road, south of the village of Grange. Why stop to look at a stone? Well this one weighs about 2,000 tons and appears to be balanced, ready to topple over. A set of steps leads up to the top of its 36 feet (11m), and despite the attempts of almost everyone who visits to give it a push, it hasn't fallen yet. It was put into place by a glacier, which later melted around it.

Here, too, are the so-called Jaws of Borrowdale, where the high crags on either side of the valley almost meet, squeezing the road and the river (the B5289 and the River Derwent) together as they both try to get through. Both do, and the road then swings round to the west, through the village of Seatoller, to climb through the equally dramatic Honister Pass, which links Borrowdale with Buttermere.

BUTTERMERE & CRUMMOCK WATER MAP REF 406 E3

These two lakes in the Buttermere valley, separated only by a half-mile (800m) strip of meadowland, were probably one lake originally. Buttermere is perhaps the more beautiful, although Crummock Water is twice its size and claims one of the most impressive waterfalls in the Lakes. Scale Force, on its western side, plunges 172ft (52.4m) on its way to the lake. The path to Scale Force, however, begins in tiny Buttermere village, and is a rough walk to the tree-lined gorge through which Scale Beck plummets. Buttermere is also surrounded by high hills, such as the 2,126-ft (648m) Fleetwith Pike which guards the Honister Pass and the 1,959ft (597m) Hay Stacks. The easy two-hour walk around Buttermere is an impressive one, with superb views in all directions. To the northwest are the Derwent Fells, crossed only by the Newlands and Whinlatter passes, while to the west above Burtness Wood stands another range of dramatic crags and fells.

Visit
THE ARMITT COLLECTION

Ambleside's museum was founded as a library in 1909 by the Armitt sisters. This fine small museum illustrates the life and work of writers and artists such as John Ruskin and Beatrix Potter. The collection includes most of Beatrix Potter's scientific illustrations as well as pictures by artists such as William Green and J B Pyne.

Visit
TRADITIONAL SPORTS

At Ambleside Lakeland sports are held on the Thursday before the first Monday in August, including fell racing, hound trails, and Cumberland and Westmorland wrestling.

Activity
W2W CYCLE ROUTE

The Walney to Wear Cycle Route was inspired by the success of the Coast to Coast route, which runs from St Bees. The W2W, Sustrans regional route 20, crosses the Lake District peninsulas in easy stages to Kendal, before heading up the Lune Gorge, then over the Eden Valley and across the Pennines. Its total route is 151 miles (243km) from Walney Island to Wearmouth, near Sunderland.

BOWDER STONE

CONISTON

CARLISLE MAP REF 406 E2

If you want to begin with the history of Carlisle, the award-winning Tullie House Museum and Art Gallery in Castle Street with its interactive displays is the place to start. It traces the history of Carlisle from before the Romans to the railways and beyond, via the reivers, Robert the Bruce and the Roundheads. It also has very good natural history displays.

Linked to the museum by the Millennium Gallery, Carlisle Castle dates from 1092. The keep dates from the same time, but many of the distinctive rounded battlements were added by Henry VIII to house artillery. Rooms in the gatehouse are decorated in medieval style, while a warren of chambers and tiny passageways in the castle can be explored. Also here is the Museum of the Border Regiment. Its collection of weaponry, uniforms, medals and other items reveal many tragic and heroic stories from the wars in which the regiment has been involved.

Carlisle Cathedral was founded in 1122. It was first a priory but became a cathedral in 1132 and can claim to have held a daily service for almost 900 years. Inside, the first thing to strike the eye is the magnificent high ceiling. Its stained glass dates from the 14th to the 20th centuries. Do not miss seeing the buildings opposite the main entrance.

The Fratry was a monastic common room in the 13th century and now contains the cathedral library and the Prior's Kitchen Restaurant. Across from the Fratry, the 13th-century Prior's Tower was used, among other things, as a place of refuge. Inside the tower, which can be seen by arrangement, is a ceiling with 45 panels, hand-painted in 1510.

Slightly overshadowed by the cathedral, but worth a visit, is St Cuthbert's Church, which was also built in the 12th century, although the present buildings date from the 1700s. Its most unusual feature is a moveable pulpit, mounted on rail tracks.

The city walls give some idea of the extent of the place in Roman times, as they were built around the remains of the Roman town and fort. The West Walls which were completed in 1200 and run behind St Cuthbert's and around the cathedral, are the best surviving examples.

CARTMEL MAP REF 406 E5

First-time visitors will wonder why a village as small as Cartmel should have such a large and magnificent church. In the 12th century when Cartmel (along with Carlisle and Lanercost) was chosen as the site for an Augustinian priory, the original endowment stipulated that local people should always have the right to worship in the priory church.

Much of the stone from the priory was re-used to build what is now the village of Cartmel, and the only other tangible relic of monastic times is the gatehouse (now a private residence in the care of the National Trust). The stepped market cross stands near by, but the markets themselves are long gone. The Cartmel of today is a pretty little village, worth exploring in its own right as well as for its gem of a church.

To the south of the village is Holker Hall, the home of the Cavendish family and the Hall itself retains the feel of a family home. The 25 acres (10ha) of gardens and woodland are justifiably renowned. Features to look for include the Ice House, where ice was stored in Victorian times to serve the great house. The gardens are renowned for their rhododendrons and the great Holker Lime, one of the largest trees of its kind in Britain.

CONISTON MAP REF 406 E4

Overlooked by the huge bulk of the Old Man of Coniston and near to the northern tip of Coniston Water, the village enjoys a superb setting. A little off the beaten track, Coniston caters best for those who want to explore the magnificent range of peaks that rise up behind the little grey town.

It was these mountains, and the mineral wealth they yielded, that created the village of Coniston. While copper had been mined in this area since the Roman occupation, the industry grew most rapidly during the 18th and 19th centuries. The story of copper mining, slate quarrying and farming, as well as the lives of celebrities such as John Ruskin, Arthur Ransome and Donald Campbell, are told in the Ruskin Museum.

A short stroll from the centre of Coniston brings you to the shore of the lake where a public slipway allows the launching of boats (no powered craft).

Few houses enjoy a more beautiful setting than Brantwood, in an estate on the eastern shore of the lake. From 1872 to 1900 this was the home of John Ruskin, artist, poet and social reformer, who became the most influential and controversial art critic of his time. The grounds are an attraction in their own right, and the house is filled with many of Ruskin's drawings, watercolours and other items recalling the man whose ideas influenced such intellectual giants as Mahatma Gandhi and Leo Tolstoy. Ruskin is buried in Coniston churchyard.

Tarn Hows is a short drive from Coniston off the B5285 Hawkshead road. Just yards from the National Trust car park, you can gaze across the tarn, studded with islands, surrounded by gorgeous conifer woodland and the most beautiful backdrop of rolling hills.

DERWENT WATER MAP REF 406 E3

South from Keswick spreads Derwent Water. It is the lakeland's widest lake at 1.25 miles (2km) and is attractively dotted with islands. These include, in the very centre, St Herbert's Island, named after the saint who lived here as a hermit in the 7th century. Derwent Isle was once home to German miners who came to work around Keswick and the Newlands Valley in the 16th century. With Borrowdale closing in to the south, and crags on either side of the lake's southern half, Derwent Water is a popular favourite. Popular too is the way in which it can be explored by using the ferries that run between the seven landing stages around the lake, allowing visitors to get off and walk the many footpaths through the surrounding woods and up to the various viewpoints.

The eastern side is rich in waterfalls, such as the spectacular Lodore Falls in the southeastern corner, which is one of the ferry stops. Much of the land here is owned by the National Trust. This is largely due to the efforts of Canon Hardwicke Rawnsley, vicar of Crosthwaite, the parish church of Keswick. He was Secretary of the National Trust from its formation until his death in 1920. The beautiful Friar's Crag, on the

northern shore of Derwent Water close to the Keswick boat landings, was given to the National Trust (along with Lords Island and Calf Close Bay) to be his memorial. The view from here was deemed by Ruskin 'to be one of the finest in Europe'

ESKDALE MAP REF 406 E4

Here is another beautiful valley that remains relatively quiet when so many other places are busy with tourists. The reason is inaccessibility; to explore Eskdale most people will have to negotiate the twists, turns and hairpin bends of the Hardknott and Wrynose passes, or else take the long way round, meandering through south lakeland. All the better, then, for those who venture this far west, for Eskdale is well worth the effort.

Hardknott Pass, rising 1,000 feet (305m) out of Eskdale in little more than a mile (1.6km), is one of the most spectacular roads in the country; a few of the hairpin bends are as steep as 1-in-3 (33%). The steep ascent holds few terrors for car drivers these days; most problems arise at peak holiday times. But if the road is icy, or you are towing a caravan, you shouldn't even consider it!

However, when you gaze down from the remains of the fort at the western end of the Hardknott Pass it is easy to see why the Romans chose this site. Hardknott Castle Roman Fort (owned by English Heritage) enjoys a commanding position above the green valley of Eskdale.

This is excellent walking country, with plentiful rights of way and room to roam. For more than 30 years the Ravenglass and Eskdale Railway has enabled sightseers and hikers to venture into the heart of Eskdale without blocking up the narrow road with their cars. This delightful narrow-gauge railway used to carry iron ore from the Eskdale mines to the coast; now the engines carry passengers up the valley. There are seven stations along the line, all offering opportunities for scenic walks with the option of taking a later train back down to Ravenglass.

The terminus, at Dalegarth, is just a short walk from Boot, a tiny village with a friendly pub, the Boot Inn. Just up the valley, the Woolpack recalls a time when this was a watering hole for the men who drove packponies heavily laden with fleeces down to the coast. Beyond a packhorse bridge spanning Whillan Beck is the delectable grouping of tiny buildings that

comprise Eskdale Mill. Cereals have been ground here since 1578, but milling ended during the 1920s. The overshot waterwheel was adapted to supply electricity to upper Eskdale; the valley was connected to the mains in 1955.

GRANGE-OVER-SANDS
MAP REF 406 E5

Looking out over Morecambe Bay is the charming resort of Grange-over-Sands, with its ornamental gardens, promenade and relaxed ambience.

Thanks to the Gulf Stream, Grange enjoys a mild climate, a factor which helps to explain why so many people find this a pleasant place for their retirement years. Springtime is reckoned to be warmer in Grange than anywhere else in the north. Gardeners with green fingers are encouraged by the climate, and plants grow here that would be unlikely to survive elsewhere on the west coast.

GRASMERE MAP REF 406 E4

The village of Grasmere is central, geographically and historically, to the Lake District. Set in a valley surrounded by hills, and a short stroll from Grasmere lake, the village is a gem.

Literary pilgrims have flocked to Grasmere since the days when William Wordsworth's 'plain living and high thinking' produced some of the finest romantic poetry. It was during a walking tour of the Lake District, with his lifelong friend Samuel Taylor Coleridge, that Wordsworth first spied the little house that would become his home for eight of his most productive years.

Despite its size, the house was filled with the artistic luminaries of the day, and it was here, between 1799 and 1808, that Wordsworth composed some of his best-known poems. He knew the house as Town End. It was years later, after the poet's death, that it was christened Dove Cottage. The house is open to the public, and an adjacent coach house has been converted into the Wordsworth Museum with a collection of manuscripts and books. The attached Jerwood Centre is used for academic studies.

By the time Wordsworth's wife, Mary, was expecting their fourth child, Dove Cottage was too small to house them adequately. The family moved first to Allan Bank and the Rectory (both in Grasmere, and now private homes), before making one last move to Rydal Mount.

GRIZEDALE FOREST MAP REF 406 E4
The Grizedale estate, between the lakes of Coniston Water and Windermere, was the first forest owned by the Forestry Commission, and was used to encourage recreational activities. The forest was opened to the public in the 1960s, and Grizedale is now the largest forest in the Lake District. The Grizedale Forest combines two roles: woodland recreation and the commercial production of timber.

Your first stop should be the visitor centre, where you can get a guide to the many waymarked trails.

An imaginitive move brought art into the forest. Sculptors were sponsored to create works in woodland settings; more than 80 original sculptures nestle among the trees or stand on hilltops.

KENDAL MAP REF 406 F4
For motorists coming from the M6, the first sight of Kendal, in the valley below, means that the Lakes are 'only just round the corner'. Though some motorists drive on the bypass, impatient to reach Bowness or Windermere, others prefer to see what Kendal has to offer. The one-way traffic system can be frustrating so it's better to explore on foot and investigate Kendal's numerous 'yards' or alleyways.

Catherine Parr, sixth wife of Henry VIII, was born in Kendal Castle, whose splendid view over the town repays the climb, though the castle is in ruins.

Near the parish church is Abbot Hall. This elegant Georgian house is now an equally elegant art gallery, showing works by the many artists – including Ruskin and Constable – who were inspired by the Lakeland landscape. The Museum of Lakeland Life and Industry, also at Abbot Hall, brings recent history to life, with reconstructed shops, room settings and a farming display. The study of Arthur Ransome, author of *Swallows and Amazons* and many other children's books, has been painstakingly recreated.

At the opposite end of town, close to the railway station, the Kendal Museum has fascinating displays of geology, archaeology and natural and social history, based on the collection of 'curiosities' first exhibited by William Todhunter in 1796. He charged 'one shilling per person; children and servants 6d each'. There are displays of wildlife, both local and global (though the case full of iridescent humming birds seems gross by today's standards).

One of Kendal's best-known adopted sons was Alfred Wainwright (1907–91), whose seven guides to the Lakeland hills became classics in his own lifetime. You can see Wainwright's little office in Kendal Museum, where he held the post of honorary curator for many years. A hand-drawn map reveals that his interests were already in place at the tender age of ten. However, it wasn't until he was 45 that he began the mammoth task of writing his Pictorial Guides, which were indispensable reading for many years to come. Other books about his beloved North Country followed, until his death in 1991.

KESWICK MAP REF 406 E3
Keswick is a natural centre for mountain climbers, country walkers and more leisurely tourists alike. It is small, with a population of under 5,000, but is said, for its size, to have more beds for guests than anywhere else in the country. This gives an idea of how busy it can get here.

If now reliant on tourism, in the past mining kept it alive. The industry flourished in the 16th century with the formation of the Company of Mines Royal. Expert miners came from Germany and settled on Derwent Isle. But as mining declined by the second half of the 19th century, so in 1865 the Cockermouth–Penrith railway line was built, bringing mass tourism.

Graphite is the reason the Cumberland Pencil Museum exists here today. A delightfully quirky specialist collection, it shows that even the humble pencil has a fascinating history. The first was made locally in the 1550s, though you can see modern production methods too, and the largest pencil in the world!

Even if you are not mad on cars, you'll find that the Cars of the Stars Motor Museum is a fascinating collection. Some are merely interesting vehicles, such as a Fiat from 1972 painted to look like the Noddy Car. The 'Star Cars' range from one of the Reliant Robins used in *Only Fools and Horses*, to a Morris 8 Tourer driven in *All Creatures Great and Small*, and a selection of cars used in the James Bond films, including several Aston Martins.

One of the oldest museums in the county, the Keswick Museum and Art Gallery has a good display on Lakeland's literary connections. This covers the poet Robert Southey in particular, who moved to Greta Hall in Keswick (now part of a school) to join his brother-in-law, Coleridge, and remained there for over 40 years until his death in 1843. He became Poet Laureate in 1813. There is also a fine period scale model of the Lake District as it was in the early 19th century. The geology collection is of national importance and contains mineral examples from the Caldbeck Fells. Geology is also the key to the Keswick Mining Museum. As well as mineral collections, there is an excellent bookshop of books on industrial archaeology.

On the northern edge of Keswick at Crosthwaite is the Church of St Kentigern, whose best-known incumbent, Canon Rawnsley, was the first Secretary of the National Trust. He was also an author, journalist, educationalist and orator, and his influence pervades almost every corner of Keswick and Cumbria.

CASTLERIGG

Visit
CASTLERIGG STONE CIRCLE
Just 2 miles (3.2km) east of Keswick is one of the most dramatic and atmospheric stone circles in Britain. It dates from about 2000 BC, but its purpose remains unknown, adding to its enigmatic qualities. The 38 stones in the circle itself, with a further 10 set in the centre, are surrounded by high fells, with Helvellyn to the southeast. The stones are made of volcanic Borrowdale rock, brought here by the glaciers of the Ice Age. The construction is actually oval in shape, 107 feet (33m) across at its widest point, and the name means 'the fort on the ridge', though no evidence of any fort exists here. Castlerigg Stone Circle is in the hands of the National Trust.

THE LANGDALES

MAP REF 406 E4

The Langdales are considered to be two of the most beautiful valleys in the Lake District. They are no secret, as you will find if you try to make the circular drive around Great Langdale and Little Langdale on a weekend in summer. The road is very narrow so it's best to park at Skelwith Bridge or Elterwater, and then you can tackle the area on foot. There are climbs and scrambles here to challenge the sure-footed, as well as lowland rambles if you just want to enjoy the view.

At Skelwith Bridge, where the B5343 Langdale road branches off from the A593, is Skelwith Force. The path to the waterfall continues to Elter Water, where you can enjoy one of the many views that seems to typify the Lake District – the distinctive silhouette of the Langdale Pikes, popular with walkers. The twin humps of Harrison Stickle (2,415ft/736m) and Pike of Stickle (2,323ft/708m) can be glimpsed from many different points.

Beyond the village of Chapel Stile, the Great Langdale valley opens up. The valley floor is divided by stone walls, dotted with farmsteads and surrounded by a frieze of mountain peaks. The valley road meanders past the Old Dungeon Ghyll Hotel. After a steep climb the road drops, with views of Blea Tarn, into the Little Langdale valley. Though not as stunning as the main valley, it is delightful and has good footpaths. From Little Langdale a minor road branches west, to become first Wrynose Pass and then Hardknott Pass – exciting driving if your brakes are in good order!

LOWESWATER MAP REF 406 E3

One of the smaller lakes but no less delightful for that, Loweswater (National Trust) is often less crowded than those lakes with an easier access. To reach it involves a short drive on the B5289 down Lorton Vale from Cockermouth, but many motorists simply continue down the main road that leads to nearby Crummock Water and Buttermere. If you plan to explore Loweswater, take a turning through Brackenthwaite, leading along the north shore of the lake with parking at either end. Swimming is not allowed.

Loweswater village is little more than a church, a village hall and a pub, with a scattering of whitewashed farm buildings surrounded by woodland and meadows. The woods offer many leafy footpaths and are cared for by the National Trust.

NEAR SAWREY MAP REF 406 E4

Beatrix Potter first came here on holiday in 1896, fell in love with the place and used the royalties from her first book, *The Tale of Peter Rabbit* (1901), to buy Hill Top. It was in this unpretentious little 17th-century farmhouse that she wrote many of the books that have delighted readers throughout the world.

The success of the books allowed Beatrix Potter to buy up farms and land: all her properties were bequeathed, on her death in 1943, to the National Trust. Her will decreed that Hill Top should remain exactly as she had known it. Visitors will recognize details from the pictures in her books and even the adjacent inn, the Tower Bank Arms, will be familiar to readers of *The Tale of Jemima Puddleduck* (1908). Despite its unprepossessing exterior, Hill Top is chock full of Beatrix Potter memorabilia, including original drawings. Hill Top is so popular that it is best avoided at peak holiday times. The Beatrix Potter Gallery at Hawkshead and The World of Beatrix Potter at Bowness also hold lots of interest for 'Potterphiles'

THE LANGDALES

ULLSWATER MAP REF 406 E3

On the western shores of Ullswater, a series of splendid waterfalls tumbles down through the wooded gorge of Aira Beck, which flows into the region's second largest lake, some 7.5 miles (12km) long. The falls are known by the name of the largest, the 70-ft (21.3m) drop of Aira Force, on land owned by the National Trust. There's also an arboretum, a café and a landscaped Victorian park.

Back in 1802, the falls didn't just feed the waters of Ullswater, they fed the imagination of William and Dorothy Wordsworth. The poet and his sister were walking near by, when Dorothy observed the 'daffodils so beautiful...they tossed and reeled and danced.' Her words were transformed into one of the best-loved of English poems, William Wordsworth's 'Daffodils'. Aira Force itself is also the setting for another of William Wordsworth's poems, 'The Somnambulist'.

It is appropriate that the poet was inspired by what, for many people, is the lake among lakes, indisputably beautiful. The southern tip of its slim shape falls below the shoulders of Helvellyn to the west, and is reached through the dramatic Kirkstone Pass, which rises to 1,489 feet (454m). Near here is the Kirkstone Pass Inn, third highest pub in the country.

At Pooley Bridge on the lake's northern tip, a fish market used to be held in the main square, and this area is still rich in trout and salmon. A short walk up to Dunmallard Hill reveals Iron Age remains among the trees. Below, at the pier near the 16th-century bridge, two 19th-century steamers, *Lady of the Lake* and *Raven*, leave to take visitors down the lake. They call at Howtown, roughly halfway along Ullswater's eastern shore, then travel on to Glenridding at the southern end. A popular option is to combine a cruise with a walk, and no finer walk is reputed to exist in the Lakes than that between Howtown and Glenridding.

There is no road through this steep-cliffed southeastern shore of the lake. The cruise boat could be rejoined at Glenridding. The lake's length may be only 7.5 miles (12km), but that is also roughly the distance by foot from Howtown to Glenridding. The curve of its crescent shape accounts for the rest, with an extra stretch round the bottom loop of the lake.

ULVERSTON MAP REF 406 E5

Ulverston, on the fringe of Morecambe Bay, is sufficiently off the beaten track to maintain an unhurried air, though Thursdays and Saturdays find the market square thronged with stalls. On top of Hoad Hill, overlooking the town, is a 90-ft (27.4m) copy of the Eddystone Lighthouse.

ULLSWATER

It is no help to ships, however, but a monument to Sir John Barrow, Ulverston-born in 1764. A founder member of the Royal Geographical Society, his story is told in the town's heritage centre.

In Upper Brook Street the Laurel and Hardy Museum is an attraction for those who still can't hear the 'Cuckoo Waltz' without thinking of the much-loved bowler-hatted buffoons of the silver screen. It is not so much a museum as a haphazard collection of Laurel and Hardy memorabilia, assembled here because Stan Laurel (the shorter one) was born in Ulverston in 1890. No souvenir is deemed too trivial for inclusion in the displays

and visitors can watch clips from some of the pair's 105 films in a tiny cinema shoehorned into a corner of the museum.

WASDALE & WAST WATER
MAP REF 406 E4

The bleakly beautiful valley of Wasdale must be approached from the west, and for most visitors that involves a lengthy drive. The reward is that Wasdale will be spectacularly empty when the Lakeland honeypots are thronged with visitors.

If the view up to the head of the valley seems familiar, it's because the National Park Authority created their logo from this view of Wast Water and the three peaks,

Yewbarrow, Great Gable and Lingmell, whose symmetry frames the view. Scafell Pike, near the valley head is, at 3,210ft (978m), the highest peak in England.

Although it is just 3 miles (4.8km) long, Wast Water is the deepest lake in England. The screes that dominate the southern shore continue their descent fully 250ft (76m) into the cool clear waters.

The road hugs the water's edge until you reach Wasdale Head; communities don't come much smaller or more welcoming than this. At the Wasdale Head Hotel walkers and climbers congregate. Ensconced in a comfortable chair you can forget that you are miles from anywhere...

Activity
CONSERVING CUMBRIA

Visitors can do a lot to help the environment simply by parking their cars and using the waymarked walks or seeing the beautiful countryside by cycling along some of the marked cycle routes. Other environmentally friendly modes of transport include taking the local trains, buses, minibus tours, or one of the launches on the lakes. During the summer an open-top bus service operates between Bowness, Windermere, Ambleside and Grasmere. The Coniston Rambler links Windermere, Ambleside, Hawkshead and Coniston, and a service from Keswick leaves for Borrowdale and Buttermere. Minibus tours are a popular way of seeing the high passes; their main centres are Windermere and Keswick.

WINDERMERE

WHITEHAVEN MAP REF 406 D3

In the middle of the 18th century Whitehaven was the third largest port in Britain, after London and Bristol, thanks to the local industries. Today, Whitehaven has a small fishing fleet, and its harbour is a conservation area, with several monuments to its mining industry, which finally died out in 1986. Your first stop in Whitehaven should be The Beacon, on West Strand, which offers an insight into the history of the town and harbour through audio-visual presentations and exciting displays. On the top floor is the Weather Gallery, full of high-tech equipment. On the headland above The Beacon is the winding gear and engine house of the Haig Colliery Mining Museum. Haig was the town's last deep pit. Now it records the often tragic stories of the town's mining past, in which more than 1,200 men, women and children died.

The town boasts many handsome Georgian buildings and has two churches that are worth seeking out. St Begh's, from around 1868, is striking as it was built from white stone with a red stone dressing. St James' is slightly older, from 1753, with Italian ceiling designs and a very moving Memorial Chapel. It was dedicated first to those who lost their lives in the two world wars, and later also to local people who were killed in mining accidents. A miner's lamp serves as the Sanctuary lamp.

Book lovers should note that Whitehaven has the largest antiquarian bookshop in Cumbria, and one of the largest in the north of England. Michael Moon's Antiquarian Bookshop in Roper Street claims to have 100,000 books on its mile (1.6km) of shelving, with room for at least a hundred book browsers.

WINDERMERE & BOWNESS-ON-WINDERMERE MAP REF 406 E4

To many visitors, a visit to the Lakes implies nothing more strenuous than mooching around the shops of Windermere and Bowness, and a relaxing boat trip on the lake. It cannot be denied that these twin towns (almost joined into one these days) attract a disproportionate number of holiday-makers. Though traffic congestion is a problem around the area, walkers can escape the crowds surprisingly quickly, even on the busiest bank holidays.

The popularity of Windermere and Bowness is largely historical. Windermere is as far into the heart of the Lake District as the railway was ever driven. William Wordsworth lamented the coming of the railway; he foresaw that his beloved Lakeland would be spoiled irretrievably by an influx of visitors. Certainly the railway opened up the area to working people.

It may seem a bit odd that it is Windermere, rather than Bowness at the water's edge, that takes its name from the lake. This was to provide the railway station with a more appealing name; until the branch line opened in 1847, Windermere was known as Birthwaite.

Bowness offers its visitors a warm welcome, and is continually developing new enterprizes for their pleasure. A few years ago it was hard to find a decent place to eat; now you can take your pick from a wide array of good bistros, cafés, Indian restaurants, pizza parlours and the ever-popular fish and chip take-aways.

The water of England's longest lake laps on the beach at Bowness Bay. Swans and ducks, fed by visitors, enjoy an indolent lifestyle. Sleek clinker-built dinghies can be hired by the hour. The less energetic can enjoy a lake-long cruise, via Waterhead and Lakeside (linking to the steam trains of the restored Lakeside–Haverthwaite Railway), on the cruise ships Tern, Teal and Swan. Since 2005, when the National Park Authority's contested 10mph water speed limit took effect, Windermere has become a more peaceful lake.

Opposite Bowness Bay is Belle Isle. In 1774, when notions of the 'romantic' and 'picturesque' were at their height, a Mr English built an eccentric residence. Its round design brought so much ridicule on his head that Mr English was prompted to sell his unusual home.

The island site was earlier occupied by a manor house, which was besieged by troops of Roundheads while the Royalist owner was busy fighting in Carlisle. Archaeological finds reveal Belle Isle was also occupied during Roman times. It was bought in 1781 as a present for Mrs Isabella Curwen, and renamed in her honour. While most of Windermere's little islands are now owned by the National Trust, Belle Isle is still privately owned.

At the bottom of Bowness Hill is The Old Laundry, which caters for visitors and locals alike. As well as a theatre, there is a regular programme of exhibitions and events. Here, too, you'll find the World of Beatrix Potter, which uses the latest technology to bring to life the stories of Peter Rabbit, Jemima Puddleduck and many other much-loved characters.

Just 1.5 miles (2.4km) from the centre of Bowness is a house of exquisite beauty. Completed in 1900 for the Manchester brewing Mogul Sir Edward Holt, Blackwell was designed by Mackay Hugh Baillie Scott as an astounding expression of the Arts and Crafts movement. Restored after years of neglect, almost all the decorative features have remained intact and furnished with items from the period. Throughout the house, you will find delightful details and interplays of light, accentuated by the majestic backdrop of the lake and distant fells.Blackwell is also an important exhibition space for contemporary ceramics, textiles, jewellery and furniture. The house is managed by the Lakeland Arts Trust, who are currently restoring the Lakeland Steamboat Museum on the Bowness to Windermere road.

A further 2.5 miles (4km) north along the Ambleside road brings you to Brockhole, a fine house with gardens that shelve down to the lake shore. The house has, since the late 1960s, been the National Park Visitor Centre, with gardens, displays, exhibitions, an adventure playground and a range of events.

The eastern shore of Windermere is, for much of its length, in private hands. Mill owners bought up plots of land to create tranquil oases with stunning views of the lake. Thus it is that the drive along the lake (on the A592) can be disappointing; there are few public access points to the water's edge. However, the less-populated western shore, much of it managed by the National Trust, offers lakeside walks.

For an elevated view of the lake, take a path to the left of the Windermere Hotel. Within a few minutes you will have a glorious view of the lake and the southern Lakeland fells from Orrest Head. Another excellent viewpoint is the rounded hill called Gummer's How, which can be approached via a minor road just north of Newby Bridge. From the top (half an hour's walk from the car park) you will be able to see almost the length of Windermere.

OVER HAMPSFELL FROM GRANGE-OVER-SANDS

A walk through woods, gardens and over open fell above a charming seaside resort which retains a refined air of quiet dignity. The town has many fine and interesting buildings and its ornamental gardens, complete with ponds, provide suitable solitude in which to relax and enjoy a picnic.

DISTANCE/TIME 4 miles (6.4km) 2h **MAP** OS Explorer OL7 The English Lakes (SE) **START** Car park below road and tourist office, central Grange; grid ref: SD 410780 **PATHS** Paths and tracks, can be muddy in places, 7 stiles **THE PUB** Commodore Hotel, Grange-over-Sands. Tel: 015395 32381

1 Join the main road through Grange and go right (heading north), to pass the ornamental gardens. Cross the road and continue along the pavement to the roundabout. Go left along Windermere Road rising to round the bend, and find steps up to a squeeze stile on the left, signed 'Routon Well/Hampsfield'.

2 Take the path rising through Eggerslack Wood. Cross over a surfaced track and continue to pass a house (left). Steps lead on to a track. Cross this diagonally to follow a track, signed 'Hampsfell'. The track zig-zags right (with a house left) and continues up through the woods to a stile over the wall.

3 Cross the stile to leave the wood and follow the path directly up the hillside. Pass sections of limestone pavement and little craggy outcrops until the path levels and bears left to a stile over a stone wall. Cross the stile and go right along the wall. Continue, following a grassy track, to pass ancient stone cairns and up to the square tower landmark of the Hospice of Hampsfell.

4 Leave the tower, head south and follow the path over the edge of a little limestone escarpment (take care here). Continue over another escarpment and descend to find a stile over the wall. Descend to the bottom of the dip and rise directly up the green hill beyond. Cross over the top and descend to find a stile over the wall. Although the path bears diagonally left at this point it is usual to continue to the cairn on Fell End. At the cairn, turn sharp left and descend to pick up a grassy track leading left round a little valley of thorn bushes to a gate and a road.

5 Cross the road, take the squeeze stile and descend diagonally left across the field to a gate on to a road by Springbank Cottage. Descend the surfaced track to enter a farmyard and continue left over a stile. Go over the hill, following the path parallel to the wall then take the stile into a ginnel. Follow this, with a high garden wall, right, round the corner and descend to a junction. Go left on a private road/public footpath, and then bear right at the fork. At the next junction turn right to descend the track and at the following junction go left down Charney Well Lane. At a junction, turn left below the woods of Eden Mount to a junction with Hampsfell Road; turn right. At the junction with a larger road go left and pass the church before descending to pass the clock tower and junction with the main road (B5277). Go left then right to the car park.

WALK 94

FROM ELTERWATER TO LOUGHRIGG TARN

Elter Water and Loughrigg Tarn are amongst the prettiest stretches of water in the region, with bluebell woods, swans and a waterfall. Each season delights, with daffodils by Langdale Beck in spring, bluebells in Rob Rash woods in May, yellow maple in Elterwater in October and shades of green, everywhere, all summer.

DISTANCE/TIME 4 miles (6.4km) 2h **MAP** OS Explorer OL7 The English Lakes (SE) **START** National Trust pay-and-display car park, Elterwater; grid ref: NY 328048 **PATHS** Grassy and stony paths and tracks, surfaced lane; 4 stiles **THE PUB** The Britannia Inn, Elterwater. Tel: 01539 437210; www.britinn.net

1 Pass through a small gate to walk downsteam above Great Langdale Beck. Continue to enter the mixed woods of Rob Rash. A little gate leads through the stone wall; the open foot of Elter Water lies to the right. Continue along the path through the meadows above the river. Note that this section can be wet and is prone to flooding. Pass through the gate and enter mixed woods. Keep along the path to pass Skelwith Force waterfall down to the right. A little bridge leads across a channel to a viewing point above the falls. Keep along the path to pass through industrial buildings belonging to Kirkstone Quarry.

2 Touchstone Gallery is on the right, as the path becomes a small surfaced road. Continue walking to intercept the A593 by the bridge over the river where there are picnic benches. Turn left to pass the hotel. At the road junction, cross over the Great Langdale road to a lane that passes by the end of the cottages. Follow the lane, ascending to intercept another road. Turn right for a short distance and then left towards Tarn Foot farm. Bear right along the track, in front of the cottages. Where the track splits, bear left. Through the gate carry on walking along the track to overlook the beautiful Loughrigg Tarn. At a point half-way along the tarn cross the stile over the iron railings on the left.

3 Follow the footpath down the meadow to traverse right, just above the tarn. The footpath swings off right to climb a ladder stile over the stone wall. Follow the grassy track leading right, up the hill, to a gate and stile on to the road. Turn left along the road, until a surfaced drive leads up to the right, signed 'Public Footpath Skelwith Bridge'. Pass a small cottage and keep on the track to pass a higher cottage, Crag Head. A little way above this, a narrow grassy footpath leads off right, up the hillside, to gain a level shoulder between the craggy outcrops of Little Loughrigg.

4 Cross the shoulder and descend the path, passing a little tarnlet to the right, to intercept a stone wall. Keep left along the wall descending to find, in a few hundred paces, a ladder stile leading over the wall into the upper woods of Rob Rash. A steep descent leads down to the road. Cross this directly, and go through the gap in the wall next to the large double gates. Descend a track to meet up with the outward route. Bear right to return to Elterwater village.

DISTANCE/TIME 12 miles (19.3km) 2h **MAP** OS Explorer OL4 The English Lakes (NW) **START** Bowness Knott car park; grid ref: NY 109153 **TRACKS** Good forest roads, occasionally bumpy **THE PUB** Shepherd's Arms Hotel, Ennerdale Bridge. Tel: 01946 861249; www.shepherdsarmshotel.co.uk

DISTANCE/TIME 7 miles (11.3 km) 1h15 **MAP** OS Explorer OL4 The English Lakes (NW) **START** Near Little Town, south of Skelgill; grid ref: NY 232194 **TRACKS** Lanes, mostly quiet **THE PUB** Swinside Inn, Newlands. Tel: 01768 778253; www.theswinsideinn.com

WILD ENNERDALE

A superb ride through the forest beyond Ennerdale Water. This route, entering the heart of the high fells, joins the world of the mountaineer, the fell-runner and the long-distance walker. The Forestry Commission and National Trust own large tracts of woodland and the lakeshore. There is no road alongside Ennerdale Water, but this cycle route gives you some wonderful views of this clear water, which is a reservoir for some Cumbrian towns.

1 Turn left from the car park, rolling down to the shores of Ennerdale Water. The track runs beside the lake for about 1 mile (1.6km), then continues through the forest above the river, here called Char Dub. 'Dub' is a common dialect word for a pool, while 'char' refers to a species of fish. Continue past Low Gillerthwaite Field Centre and then the youth hostel at High Gillerthwaite.

2 Just past the youth hostel the track forks. Keep right (really straight ahead). The track goes up and down more than you might expect. Take care on fast downhill bends where the surface is loose. Above all, don't grab the brakes. At the next fork 1 mile (1.6km) further on, a sign to the right points to Pillar. Save the Pillar road for the return and keep straight on – in fact, this track straight ahead gives the best views of the Pillar Rock. The way climbs gradually to a more level stretch with open views across the valley to Pillar directly opposite. Pillar Rock is the centrepiece of a mass of crags strewn across the north face of the mountain. At this point you could turn back.

3 As Pillar falls behind, the valley head opens up. There's a space where you may find vehicles and then the main track curves down right.

4 Straight ahead through a gate is a much rougher track leading 400yds (364m) to Black Sail Hut – many people may prefer to walk for some or all of it. You can make yourself tea or coffee (leave a suitable donation). Return to the gate. The bridleway going up right climbs to Scarth Gap Pass and then descends to Buttermere. Ignore it, and go back through the gate and down left to the River Liza.

5 Splash through the ford and swing round right. Now keep straight ahead along the track, mostly downhill, ignoring branches off the track up and left until it swings down to the river.

6 Cross the bridge and go up to the 'Pillar' signpost. Rejoin the main track of the outward route to return to your car at the car park.

MEANDERING IN NEWLANDS

This classic Lakeland cycle route, west of Derwent Water, is surrounded by scenery that, even by Lakeland standards, is stunning, although you will catch glimpses of only one lake – Bassenthwaite.

1 From the parking place head up the steep hill to Little Town. Once through Little Town, relax and enjoy a fine winding, mostly downhill, run through the valley to Stair and a junction at the bottom of a hill.

2 Turn sharp right on to a narrow lane. The sign says 'Skelgill – Narrow Gated Road'. Climb again, with the hill of Cat Bells ahead. The lane steepens as it twists through Skelgill, reaching a gate just above. To the left of the isolated Swinside Hill, to the north, the stretch of water you can see is Bassenthwaite Lake. The lane passes a small parking area before reaching a T-junction on a bend. Turn left, downhill, over a cattle grid and round another sharp bend. The road levels out, then climbs to a junction.

3 Go left; the junction proves to be triangular. Go left again. As the road swings round to the right there are fantastic views up the valley and to the surrounding fells: Dale Head, Hindscarth, Maiden Moor and Robinson. Just beyond is the Swinside Inn. Turn right beside the pub on a narrow lane signed to Ullock and Braithwaite. Keep left where a road branches right to Ullock.

4 Cross a stone arched bridge over Newlands Beck and begin a short climb, steep at the start. As it levels out there's another fleeting glimpse of Bassenthwaite Lake. At a T-junction turn sharp left. The road runs south, generally level along the base of the steep slopes, and just high enough above the valley floor to give open views. Dip down to a small bridge. Just beyond is the start of the principal walkers' path up Causey Pike; you may well see figures struggling up the initial steep slope of Rowling End. A little further on, keep straight on past a sharp left turn (for Stair, Portinscale and Grange). There are wonderful views of the beautiful Dales from here.

5 Very shortly, a steep stony track drops off to the left to a ford. Those seeking a moment's mountain-bike excitement can choose this track – it merely cuts off a short corner of the road. Alternatively, continue more sedately, round over a bridge to a wooden house. Turn left (signed to Newlands Church, Little Town) and drop down, then swing round, heading straight up the valley with its glorious range of fells ahead.

6 As you come right down into the valley bottom, turn right on the no-through-road to Newlands Church – closer even than the advertised 0.25 mile (400m). Retrace your route to the last junction and turn right, where it's only a few more pedal strokes to the bridge and the car park just beyond.

DISTANCE/TIME 8.75 miles (14.1km) 1h   **MAP** OS Explorer OL5 The English Lakes (NE) **START** Village car park, Askham; grid ref: NY 513237   **TRACKS** Quiet lanes   **THE PUB** The Queens Head, Askham. Tel: 01931 712225

DISTANCE/TIME 11 miles (17.7km) 2h (off road); shorter route 6.5 miles (10.4km) 1h   **MAP** OS Explorer OL5 The English Lakes (NE) and OL315 Carlisle   **START/FINISH** Armathwaite village; grid ref: NY 504461   **TRAILS/TRACKS** Lanes with two optional off-road sections **THE PUB** The Duke's Head, Armathwaite. Tel: 016974 72226

AROUND ASKHAM & BAMPTON

This pleasant road circuit has few steep gradients and is away from the main tourist routes. It begins and ends in Askham.

1 From the car park follow the main road south through the village past greens left and right. Keep on along this road, enjoying the generally easy gradients and views down the valley to the Shap Fells. Across the valley on the left is the sharp profile of Knipe Scar.

2 After just over 1 mile (1.6km), on the boundary of Helton, branch off right on a loop road to go through the village. The extra climb is worth it for the pretty cottages and flowery verges. Ease back to rejoin the valley road and continue, with limestone walls and small fields flanking the road on the right. As the road starts to descend, two lanes branch off to the right from a shared junction.

3 Follow the left-hand lane for 400yds (364m) to a cattle grid. Continue until the lane reaches open fell. There are good views here and you may find fell ponies grazing. Retrace to the road at the start of Point 3 and turn right to continue, now descending. At the bottom go right over Beckfoot Bridge and continue along the valley floor, passing pretty cottages at Butterwick. Climb to the edge of Bampton, and go into the village.

4 The post office and village shop has a café attached. Over the bridge opposite the shop, it's just a short way up the lane to the pretty Mardale Inn. (For a longer ride continue up this lane for 2 miles/3.2km to Naddle Bridge and Haweswater.) Continue along the main valley road towards Bampton Grange, swinging left into the village over a bridge crossing the River Lowther, and past the Crown and Mitre pub.

5 On the edge of the village, turn left, signposted 'Knipe, Whale'. Cross a cattle grid on to open fell. Look up to the right to the low crags of Knipe Scar. The lane climbs gently, with great views of the valley and the fells to the west. Descend to a junction by a phone box and turn right through a gate. Climb steeply to another gate, beyond which the road continues to climb gradually. The going levels off for a stretch before beginning to descend. Whizz back down into the valley, keeping straight on at a junction, and down to the river at Crookwath Bridge.

6 The climb away from the river is gentle but quite sustained. It then levels off just before a T-junction. Emerge with care as some traffic moves quite fast here, and almost immediately go right at the T-junction then left back into Askham.

THE EDEN VALLEY FROM ARMATHWAITE

Discover an unsung but lovely corner, with two exciting off-road options. Armathwaite is a pretty settlement, with a small pele tower on the shore of the River Eden, now a country house.

1 Head north through the village and past the church. Continue along this lane, before a dip alongside a railway viaduct. Now climb, in two stages, to the level crossing at Lowhouse Crossing. Bump across the line and continue less steeply to a junction near Froddle Crook. The old, rusty signpost has lost one arm.

2 For the shorter ride, turn left here and follow the lane beside the High Stand Plantation, with fine views, to the crossroads at Blackmoss Pool. Go straight across to rejoin the longer route. For the longer route, go straight ahead at Froddle Crook for 1.5 miles (2.4km) to a turning on the left signed to Cotehill.

3 To stay on tarmac turn left here and follow the road for 1 mile (1.6km) to the crossroads in Cotehill village, then turn left. For the off-road alternative, continue ahead to a bridge over the railway and then pass a small wood on the left. At the end of the wood follow a bridleway sign left through a gate and down a short track. Where this bends left into a farmyard continue ahead, through an awkward gate, and follow field edges. At the bottom of the second field, just below the railway line, bear right on a short track to a gate and out on to the tracks. Cross with care. Go through the gate on the other side and straight out along the green track, rounding a bend to reach a clearer track. Follow this more easily, to emerge on to a road. Turn left for a short climb into Cotehill. At a crossroads, go straight across to rejoin the road alternative.

4 Carry straight on, signed to Armathwaite. Climb to Stand End, then on beside High Stand Plantation to the crossroads at Blackmoss Pool (more marsh than open water).

5 Turn right, signed to Aiketgate and Low Hesket. The tree-lined lane runs dead straight, first down, then up. A view of the fells opens up as the road dips to a T-junction. Turn left, signed to Nunclose and Armathwaite, and make a short climb into the hamlet of Aiketgate. A fork in the road, opposite the phone box, offers another off-road option.

6 To stay on the tarmac, keep right, and then bear left at the next fork. The lane begins a descent and the off-road alternative rejoins half-way down, at Windy Nook. For the off-road adventure, take the left fork at Point 6. The tarmac lane leads into a stonier track, climbing steeply. The gradient eases, but the track continues stony up to the crest. The descent ahead is on a much greener track. Go through the gate and on downhill, curving right. The final 100yds (91m) before the road are steep and tricky: consider walking. Rejoin the road at Windy Nook and turn left (pass the turning for Nunclose). The road goes towards a railway viaduct. Go left at a junction and into Armathwaite.

OVER MUNCASTER FELL

Muncaster Fell is a long and knobbly fell of no great height. The summit rises to 758 feet (231m), but is a little off the route described. A winding path negotiates the fell from end to end and this lovely linear walk takes you from Ravenglass to Eskdale Green, returning or Laal Ratty, a narrow-gauge train.

DISTANCE/TIME 6 miles (9.7km) 2h30 **MAP** OS Explorer OL6 The English Lakes (SW) **START** Car park at Ravenglass, close to station; grid ref: SD 085964 **FINISH** Eskdale Green Station; grid ref: SD 145998 **PATHS** Clear tracks and paths, muddy after rain; 1 stile **THE PUB** The Ratty Arms, Ravenglass. Tel: 01229 717676

1 Leave the car park by crossing the mainline and miniature railway line, using the footbridges, then follow a narrow path to a road junction. Turn right on a footpath by the side of a narrow road, signposted 'Walls Castle'. The bathouse is soon on the left.

2 Continue along the access road and turn left along a track signposted 'Newtown'. Turn left again before the cottage and follow another track up a little wooded valley. Go through four gates, following the track from the wood, across fields and into another wood. Turn left to reach Home Farm and a busy main road.

3 Cross the road and turn right, passing Muncaster Castle car park and the Muncaster Guest House. The road leads up to a bend, where Fell Lane is signposted uphill. Ascend the clear track, cross a little wooded dip, then fork right and left, noticing Muncaster Tarn on the left. Go through a gate at the top of the lane to reach Muncaster Fell.

4 A path forges through boggy patches along the edge of a coniferous plantation, then the path runs free across the slopes of Muncaster Fell. A path rising to the left leads to the summit, otherwise keep right to continue.

5 Views develop as the path winds about on the slope overlooking Eskdale. A panorama of fells opens up as a curious structure is reached at Ross's Camp. Here, a large stone slab was turned into a picnic table for a shooting party in 1883.

6 Continue along the footpath, looping round a broad and boggy area to reach a corner of a dry-stone wall. Go down through a gateway and bear in mind that the path can be muddy. There is a short ascent on a well-buttressed stretch, then the descent continues on a sparsely wooded slope, through a gate, ending on a track near another gate.

7 Go through the gate and then turn left, crossing a field to reach a stone wall seen at the edge of Bankend Wood. Walk on keeping to the right side of the wall to reach a stile and a stream. A narrow track continues, becoming better as it draws close to a road. Turn left at the end of the road to reach The Green Station.

SEATHWAITE & THE DUDDON VALLEY

William Wordsworth loved the Duddon Valley so much that he wrote many sonnets about it. Follow in his footsteps by a chattering beck and through a gorge, where little has changed since his day. There's tarmac on those winding, walled lanes, but the byres and woods and lively stream are still untouched.

DISTANCE/TIME 5 miles (8km) 3h **MAP** OS Explorer OL6 The English Lakes (SW) **START** Seathwaite: roadside pull-off, grid ref: SD 231975; limited roadside parking near pub; grid ref: SD 228960 **PATHS** Paths, tracks, can be muddy below Seathwaite Tarn; 9 stiles **THE PUB** The Newfield Inn, Seathwaite. Tel: 01229 716208; www.newfieldinn.co.uk

1 From the Newfield Inn at Seathwaite in Dunnerdale follow the main valley road past the little church, then turn right on the tarmac lane towards Turner Hall Farm. Leave this and follow a track on the left through a gate marked 'High Moss'. Where the track ends, keep to the left-hand side of the farm, go through the top gate and follow the field path out to the Walna Scar Road.

2 Turn right along the road, then left on to the utility company's access road to Seathwaite Tarn. This pleasant track climbs steadily to the reservoir dam.

3 Retrace your steps for around 200 paces to a waymarking post highlighting a downhill path that weaves through rock and rough pasture. Crossing over a tiny beck it continues down to a gate, leading to a boggy field. On the far side of this, another gate leads to a ladder stile on the right.

4 Cross the stile and footbridge over Tarn Beck. On the opposite bank turn left and follow an obvious, wet, path through a gate and on along the edge of a wood. Pass behind a lovely cottage and continue in the wood past a barn on the left until the path rises to enter open country. Continue on this marshy way to the road.

5 Across the road follow the signed bridleway to the Fickle Steps, huge boulders, which allow you to cross the River Duddon. (Caution: if the river is in spate here and the steps are underwater, return by the road.)

6 To continue on the route, turn left, go over the footbridge across Grassguards Gill, then climb along a waymarked path above the tight wooded Wallowbarrow Gorge. The footpath descends again to cross boulder-strewn terrain on the bank of the River Duddon.

7 When you reach a tall one-arched footbridge, cross over to the other side of the river and turn right along the path, now tracing the eastern bank of the Duddon. Go over the footbridge spanning a tributary, Tarn Beck, before following a path out to the road. Turn left to walk back to your car in Seathwaite village.

KESWICK'S WALLA CRAG ABOVE DERWENT WATER

At the foot of Borrowdale – often referred to as the most beautiful valley in England – the northern head of Derwent Water opens to Keswick and the northern fells with dramatic effect. The highlight of this walk is undeniably the panoramic views from the heights of Walla Crag to the surrounding fells.

DISTANCE/TIME 5.25 miles (8.4km) 3h **MAP** OS Explorer OL4 The English Lakes (NW) **START** Lakeside car park, Keswick; grid ref: NY 265229 **PATHS** Good paths and tracks. Steep ascent and descent; 3 stiles **THE PUB** Lake Road Inn, Keswick. Tel: 01768 77240

1 Proceed down the road to Derwent Bay. Go left opposite the landing stages, past the toilets, to take a track through Cockshot Wood. Exit the wood on to a fenced lane across the field to Borrowdale road. Cross the road and climb stone steps to enter Castlehead Wood. Take the path that trends left to ascend the shoulder. In little way a steeper path climbs right, to the rocky summit of Castle Head and a fine viewpoint.

2 Descend by the same route to reach the shoulder then bear right to locate a kissing gate into an enclosed lane. Follow this to Springs Road and turn right. At Springs Farm, cross the bridge and take the track up through Springs Wood. Bear right at a junction and follow the edge of wood up past a TV mast. Ignore the turning on the right and continue to the footbridge on the left to join Castlerigg Road. Turn right along the road and walk up past Rakefoot to another footbridge on the right.

3 Cross the footbridge over a stream and follow the path, ascending by a wall. Go through a gate, and walk out on to the open shoulder of fell, ascending a steep grassy

nose. The going levels until a gate on the right, through a wall, leads to a path which follows the edge of a crag. Caution – there is a steep unfenced drop. To stay away from the cliff edge take the higher stile. Follow the path across the head of a gully, to climb on to the polished rock cap of Walla Crag where the views are superb.

4 Continue along the main ridge path down to a stile over a wall. Cross and go right, down the hill following a grassy path which becomes increasingly steep and stepped into the gorge of Cat Gill. Entering Great Wood continue steeply downwards, passing a bridge before leaving a beck to head into the wood. Bear left down the hill, across a wooded car park and on, to find a wall gap on Borrowdale Road. Cross to the wall gap opposite and continue walking to reach the attractive lakeshore.

5 Bear right, following around Calfclose Bay, by Stable Hills, around Ings Wood and then Strandshag Bay to the Scots pine on Friar's Crag. Continue easily back to Derwent Bay and take the footpath along road to the car park.

WALK 98

BIRKRIGG COMMON'S DISTANT PAST

This is a superb outing on Birkrigg Common; a wonderful open expanse of bracken, grass and low limestone scars, which is and strewn with ancient remains.

DISTANCE/TIME 8 miles (12.9km) 3h **MAP** OS Explorer OL6 The English Lakes (SW); OL7 The English Lakes (SE) **START** Small car parks between coast road and shore at Bardsea; grid ref: SD 301742 (on Explorer OL7) **PATHS** Paths and tracks, some muddy field paths; 10 stiles **THE PUB** The Braddylls Arms, Bardsea Tel: 01229 869707; www.braddyllsarms.co.uk

1 Follow the shore to Sea Wood. At the far end of the wood turn right, through its inside edge to the road. Turn left for 400yds (364m), then right at a gate into Sea Wood again.

2 Turn left to follow a path around the top edge of the wood, then left again to leave the wood at a gate. Cross a road and follow a grassy path through bracken on Birkrigg Common. Turn left to a wall corner then walk a few paces to a stone circle on your right. Follow any grassy path through the bracken to the high skyline.

3 Pass a bench and take a path to the right down to a road. Cross and walk parallel to another road as the common tapers out to a cattle grid. Continue along the road and make a right turn along a walled track.

4 Cross a stile at the end of the track and bear right past a stone trough and the site of an ancient homestead. Keep left of a wall to cross a stile at a gate. Bear left to find a path down a valley to a gate. Turn right before the gate, cross a stile, then follow a hedgerow across a slope to a house. Cross a stile leading down to a road, and then turn left to pass farm buildings at Holme Bank.

5 Turn right signposted 'Public Footpath Church Road'. Cross a ladder stile and footbridge, then take a path to a village hall

and road. Cross the road and turn right to pass a school. Pass the parish church and village store in Great Urswick.

6 Turn right at the Coot on the Tarn to follow another road. Watch for Clint Cottage on the left and Tarn House on the right, then turn left up a steep track. This is flanked by hedgerows and reaches two gates. Go through the gate on the left and walk straight ahead, keeping right of a low hill; the site of an ancient fort.

7 A wall leads to another gate, then straight on again. Cross a stile on the right, and on the other side of a gate, cross a stile on the left. Walk straight on, crossing two more stiles to reach a road junction. Turn right, walk through a crossroads and to the next farm.

8 Turn right at Far Mount Barrow along a track signposted 'Bardsea Green'. Cross a stile by a gate and keep left to cross a road on Birkrigg Common. Turn left again for Bardsea Green, along an obvious path parallel to the road, then parallel to a wall.

9 At a corner of the wall, go through a gate and follow a track downhill to a road and cross a dip. Keep left at a junction up into Bardsea, then right at the Braddylls Arms and follow a road down to the shore.

FROM PATTERDALE BY ULLSWATER

Ullswater is undoubtedly one of the loveliest lakes. It was the sight of golden daffodils amongst the trees and beside the shore that inspired Wordsworth's most widely known poem, 'I wandered lonely as a cloud' (1807). This walk takes you along the shores of Ullswater to Silver Point, a spectacular viewpoint.

DISTANCE/TIME 4 miles (6.4km) 1h30 **MAP** OS Explorer OL5 The English Lakes (NE) **START** Pay-and-display car park, Patterdale; grid ref: NY 396159 **PATHS** Stony tracks and paths, no stiles **THE PUB** Patterdale Hotel, Patterdale. Tel: 01768 482231; www.patterdalehotel.co.uk

1 From the car park walk to the road and turn right towards the shore of Ullswater. Pass the school to a track leading off right, through the buildings. Follow the unsurfaced track over a bridge and continue through the buildings of Side Farm to join another unsurfaced track.

2 Turn left along the undulating track, with a stone wall to the left, and pass through mixed woodland, predominantly oak and ash, before open fellside appears above. Proceed along the path above the campsite and pass a stand of larch before descending to cross a little stream above the buildings of Blowick, seen through the trees below. The path ascends again to crest a craggy knoll above the woods of Devil's Chimney. Make a steep descent following the path through the rocks before it levels to traverse beneath the craggy heights of Silver Crag. A slight ascent, passing some fine holly trees, gains the shoulder of Silver Point and an outstanding view of Ullswater. A short there-and-back to the tip is worthwhile.

3 Follow the path, which sweeps beneath the end of Silver Crag and continue to pass a small stream before a steep stony path, eroded in places, breaks off to the right.

Ascend this, climbing diagonally right, through the juniper bushes. Gain the narrow gap which separates Silver Crag to the right from the main hillside of Birk Fell to the left. This little valley is quite boggy and holds a small tarnlet.

4 If you don't care for steep, exposed ground, follow the high narrow path to make a gradual descent south in the direction of Patterdale. But for those with a head for heights, a short steep scramble leads to the top of Silver Crag and a wonderful view. Care must be exercised for steep ground lies in all directions. Descend back to the ravine and the main path by the same route. The path is easy though it traverses the open fellside and may be boggy in places. Pass open quarry workings, where there is a large unfenced hole next to the path (take care), and continue on, to cross over the slate scree of a larger quarry. Bear right to descend by a stream and cross a little footbridge leading to the gate at the end of a track.

5 Go left through the gate and then follow the lane which leads through the meadows. Cross over the bridge and join the road. Bear right to walk through Patterdale and return to the car park.

KIRKBY LONSDALE TO WHITTINGTON

From the old market town to Whittington village, on the Cumbria/Lancashire border, this circular walk goes over rolling hills, through farmland and woods, returning to the village of Whittington along the banks of the lovely Lune. The walk passes close to Sellet Mill, reputedly the second largest waterwheel in Britain.

DISTANCE/TIME 4.75 miles (7.6km) 2h30 **MAP** OS Explorer OL2 Yorkshire Dales – Southern & Western **START** Devil's Bridge car park, Kirkby Lonsdale; grid ref: SD 615782 **PATHS** A little overgrown and indistinct in patches, quiet lanes and tracks; 12 stiles **THE PUB** Dragon's Head, Whittington. Tel: 015242 72383

1 From the west river bank, just down from Devil's Bridge, go diagonally across the park to a kissing gate. Cross the A65, go through a meadow and between houses; cross the B6254. Enter a meadow, go uphill, keeping the walled wooded area left. Yellow markers show your route. Keep over the brow of hill and ahead through two kissing gates to a gate near houses. Bear left to a signpost.

2 Cross a farm track and in front of Woodend Cottage to a walled path, rough in places. Lower down, the stream comes in from the left; head right to drier ground before the millpond of Sellet Mill. Continue past some sheds to a farmyard.

3 Turn right over a stile and walk up a field, fence to your left, to just past the end of a garden. Go left through a yellow marked gate and across a field to a marked gate followed by a stream. Turn right round Sellet Bank, aiming first for the corner of a hedge under power-lines. Continue with the hedge right.

4 As the hedge begins to bear left, cross it through a yellow marked stile (right), then skirt round a wooded area. Facing Sellet Hall, turn right adjacent to a fenced driveway following marker arrows, then keep on over

the corner of the field to cross a stile, down two steps to a road at a T-junction. Turn left along Hosticle Lane towards Whittington.

5 The lane is sunken in places and quiet. The descent steepens as you approach the outskirts of Whittington.

6 Go left at the T-junction for a few paces, then cross the road and turn right over the mosaic entrance to the church. Keep the bell tower left and descend stone steps, then cross a stile and the graveyard. Follow the hedge to a gate in the left corner and keep ahead to a stone stile into a walled path that leads on to Main Street. Turn right and walk past the village hall and the Dragon's Head.

7 At a sharp right bend on the edge of the village, turn left along a gritty track, passing a farm and tennis courts. Follow the lane between fields, eventually crossing a cattle grid and running out at an anglers' hut beside the Lune. Follow the river bank upstream on the route of the Lune Valley Ramble. The route is obvious back to the A65 bridge at Kirkby Lonsdale. Go through a gate and up the steps to the left of the parapet. Cross the road and drop down the other side to cross the park at the start of the walk.

58 MILES (93KM)

The town was the site of Holme Cultram Abbey. Some of its buildings survived to become the splendid parish church. Robert the Bruce's father was buried here in 1294, 25 years before his son sacked the abbey.

7 Leave Abbey Town on the B5302, then just beyond Waverbridge turn left on to an unclassified road, signed to Aikhead and Station Hill. On reaching the A596, turn left, then right into Wigton and then right again into the town centre.

A feature of this town is the gilded granite fountain, erected in the 19th century. /it shows four fine bronze reliefs of the Acts of Mercy.

8 Leave Wigton by going left in the town centre signed 'B5305' and then soon B5304. After about a mile (1.6km) cross the A595 and the continue ahead for 7 miles (11.2km) on an unclassified road, to arrive in Caldbeck on the B5299.

To visit the village, park in the car park by the bridge and walk beside the river to a little bridge giving access to the Church of St Kentigern.

9 Leave Caldbeck in the same direction by which you entered the town, but bear left on to the B5299 (to the left of the Oddfellow's Arms). After driving for about 3 miles (4.8km), at a fork keep to the B5299 and then continue for another mile (1.6km) to a sign for Ireby. Turn left and then descend into the village where you should turn left again and follow the signs for Bassenthwaite.

Here you enter the Lake District National Park, where there are 14 'lakes'. It is one of the remaining places in Britain that the red squirrel still inhabits.

10 Continue to a junction where a road from Uldale comes in on the left. Continue down to meet the A5291. Turn right, then left in front of the Castle Inn Hotel on to the B5291. Keep ahead on the B5291, cross Ouse Bridge and turn left to a parking area.

This is a good place to stop and take a stroll.

11 Keep on the B5291 for about half a mile (800m) to meet the A66, turn right and drive back along it to reach Cockermouth.

FROM THE MOUTH OF THE CROOKED RIVER

This tour starts at Cockermouth, famous as the town where William Wordsworth was born. The route continues to the coast at Maryport, before heading north, hugging the coastline and passing through small fishing villages and an Area of Outstanding Natural Beauty. It then turns inland, taking in small villages and pretty market towns, crossing the boundary of the Lake District National Park and finally returning to Cockermouth.

Route Directions

In Cockermouth explore and breathe in some of its character – visit Wordsworth House (the poet's birthplace) in Main Street. The 13th-century Norman castle is partially ruined but a section is still occupied by the Egremont family; however, the castle is rarely open.

1 Take the A594 out of Cockermouth and drive for approximately 7 miles (11.2km) until you get to Maryport.

A port in Roman times, Maryport was developed in the 18th century by Humphrey Senhouse. Visit the interesting harbour, pretty marina, excellent Maritime Museum and Aquarium, then go up the hill to the Roman Museum and enjoy the superb view over the town.

2 Continue on the main route, passing King Doniert's Stone on the left (where there is parking). At the next junction, turn right, signed 'Draynes, Golitha Falls'. After 300 yards (273m), a left turn over a bridge leads to a car park with toilets.

From here, it is a short walk to the spectacular Golitha Falls, a favourite beauty spot and National Nature Reserve that lies alongside the River Fowey. The reserve covers an area of 18 hectares of woodland with the River Fowey running through it and creating several pretty cascades along its way.

3 From here, head towards the right, with the coastline to your left, and continue along the main route to Allonby.

Allonby retains much of its appeal from its days as a Georgian and Victorian bathing resort. Just across the Solway lies Scotland, and the Galloway hills.

4 From Allonby continue to drive north for 6 miles (9.6km) on the B5300 to Silloth, keeping the coast on your left.

Until 1857 Silloth was a fishing village; it expanded as a port when linked by rail with Carlisle; the town still preserves its charming Victorian spa atmosphere.

5 Continue straight on past the green and drive for about 1.5 miles (2.4km) to the village of Skinburness.

This is a designated Area of Outstanding Natural Beauty, with a wonderful coastline and stunning views across the sea to Dumfries and Galloway.

6 Drive on a narrow road from Skinburness for another 2 miles (3.2km). Turn left on to the B5302 and go through Calvo to reach Abbey Town.

THE REIVERS' TOUR

From the 4th to the late 17th centuries, the land around Carlisle, on the hazy border between England and Scotland, was one of the most lawless places in Britain. Reivers were the villainous families who lived on either side of the border and who plundered each other's property and cattle, killing each other into the bargain. There was even a reiving thieving season, beginning in August and lasting for three months, until the law courts reconvened. Today the quiet, countryside gives no indication of how awful this area must have been for its inhabitants. Reiving has left its dreadful mark on the English language with the word 'bereaved'

Route Directions

The length of this tour is 68 miles (109km). It begins at Carlisle, the county town of Cumbria and the largest city in the area. There has been a settlement here since Celtic times, followed by the Romans, the Romano-Celts, Anglo-Saxons, Danes, Normans, Scots and English. Carlisle's imposing castle, which now houses a Regimental Museum, is a reminder of this constant conflict. The cathedral, built by the Normans, is also an indication of their search for peace after creating mayhem in the district, as they did in the rest of Britain. Visit the Reivers Exhibition at Tullie House to gain an accurate picture of the wild time and events, before starting out on your journey into the past.

1 Leave Carlisle on the A7. Drive round Hardwicke Circus roundabout and cross the River Eden. Shortly go right along the B6264 towards Hexham and Newcastle.

This is the area through which cattle, sheep and vegetables were brought to Carlisle. As Carlisle had been the traditional market centre for miles around and as roads were practically non-existent, the people had very little choice in where they could go to get the best prices.

2 Cross the M6 and meet a roundabout, where you take the 2nd exit on to the A689. Pass the airport runway and then turn left with the sign to the airport and Irthington. Continue through Irthington.

Here in Irthington village only a grassy mound indicates the probable remains of the Norman castle that once stood here.

3 About a mile (1.6km) after Irthington, turn right on to the A6071 and keep ahead. After crossing the bridge, turn left to Walton.

The course of Hadrian's Wall passes through the village. There was once a fort at Castlesteads, in the trees up to your left as you enter. There is little to see in the way of remains here, but the Wall's National Trail passes through.

4 Keep forward through Walton and at the junction with the B6318 turn right, signposted 'Gilsland and Greenhead'. Just after a mile (1.6km) turn left for Askerton Castle and Bewcastle church. At Bewcastle turn right up to the church and the cross.

Bewcastle is very close to the Scottish border and this proximity was one of the reasons that made it the focus for reiving activity – consquently there were many tracks leading through the area. In 1582 Thomas Musgrave, Captain of Bewcastle, and his tenants lost 700 cattle, 300 sheep, and crops and buildings were burnt. The history of Bewcastle goes back much further – to Celtic and Roman times. During the 2nd and 3rd centuries AD there were around 1,000 Roman soldiers stationed here. In the churchyard the Bewcastle Cross is an excellent example of Anglo-Saxon sculpture and a very early Christian memorial, as the majority of Anglo-Saxons were still pagans at this time. During the time of the reivers, it was said that only women were buried in the churchyard, because all the men were hanged in Carlisle.

5 At Bewcastle, turn left, and then at the junction take the right fork. Go right at the T-junction on to the B6318, which bears left. Continue for 4 miles (6.4km) to where the B6318 turns left. Do not take this left turn but continue straight ahead on a minor road, then bear right at the next junction, heading for Newcastleton. You are now in Scotland.

In Newcastleton take the opportunity to visit the Liddesdale Heritage Centre and Museum. This history museum and genealogical research facility houses a large collection of artefacts. A commemorative bicentenary tapestry created by local needleworkers is a unique exhibit. The museum also includes a superb collection of railway memorabilia in connection with the Waverley line, which had a station here.

6 Return south on the B6357 and after Canonbie join the A7 to return to England through Longtown and Carlisle.

On the edge of Longtown, Arthuret church overlooks the site of an important battle in the 6th century AD. According to Welsh poems, 30,000 were slain on the field and the wizard Merlin (Myrddin) was driven to madness by the death of his lord Gwenddoleu here.

Yorkshire Moors

CLOCKWISE FROM BELOW LEFT: ROBIN HOOD'S BAY; ROSEBERRY TOPPING; ST HILDA'S ABBEY, WHITBY; STANDING STONE, FRYUPDALE

AMPLEFORTH MAP REF 407 J5

Best known for its public school and Benedictine monastery, Ampleforth is a linear village of handsome houses that overlooks the Howardian Hills. French monks, fleeing religious persecution in their homeland in 1793, found sanctuary in England and patronage from the Fairfax family, settling at Ampleforth in 1802. As theirs had been a teaching order, they built a school within the monastery. The oldest school buildings date from 1861, while the monastery dates from 1894–98. But both establishments have been extended up to the present day.

Just after the end of World War I, headmaster Father Paul Nevill, who was also the parish priest, commissioned Robert Thompson of Kilburn to make a wooden cross for the churchyard in the village. Father Nevill was so impressed by the woodcarver's craftsmanship that Thompson was asked to make furniture for the school. The library remains one of Robert Thompson's most ambitious commissions. The present abbey church

is a new addition, built between 1922 and 1961 to a design by Sir Giles Gilbert Scott; it too contains fine examples of woodwork and carvings by Robert Thompson.

BRANSDALE MAP REF 407 J4

The unspoiled valley of Bransdale drives deep into the moors, but most visitors pass by. For a delightful drive, leave Helmsley along the A170 towards Kirkbymoorside looking out on the left for a signpost to Carlton (and Helmsley Youth Hostel). The road loops around Bransdale and then returns to the A170 about 5 miles (8km) further east at Kirkbymoorside.

Beyond the houses that comprise the village of Carlton, the views open up dramatically. To the left is unenclosed heather moorland; to the right the valley bottom is divided up by neat drystone walls either side of Hodge Beck. This pattern is punctuated by a handful of farmsteads. The moors, with barely a tree to be seen, echo to the evocative calls of the curlew, red grouse and lapwing; sheep graze the grassy verges and wander across the

road. Unenclosed for the majority of the way, the road heads north; look out left for examples of inscribed milestones.

Flour was ground for centuries at Bransdale Mill (National Trust, but not open to the public), accessible, on foot only, from either side of the valley head. The present building, dating from 1811, was built by William Strickland and his son, Emmanuel, the vicar of Ingleby Greenhow. Stones inset into the mill walls are inscribed with 'improving' texts in Hebrew, Latin and Greek.

The road then makes a broad sweep to the right, before continuing the circuit of Bransdale. Here sturdy farmsteads with fanciful names – Cow Sike, Toad Hole and Spout House – gaze down into the bottom of the valley. Before arriving in Kirkbymoorside, you can visit Gillamoor and Fadmoor, a pair of typical moorland villages barely half a mile (800m) apart.

BROMPTON MAP REF 407 K4

Motorists on the A170 tend to drive straight through Brompton in their haste to get to the Yorkshire coast. The pretty little village is set around a small lake, into which the church doors were thrown during the Civil War; they were later recovered and re-hung. The poet William Wordsworth took the time to get to know the village, for he courted Mary Hutchinson, a local girl who lived at Gallows Hill Farm. They were married, in 1802, in Brompton's church.

The village has a unique (though sadly little-known) place in the history of aeronautics. Everybody knows it was Wilbur and Orville Wright who made the first manned flight, in their flimsy craft, *Kittyhawk*. Yet a remarkable 50 years before that memorable occasion, an unsung squire of Brompton Hall quietly set about building a flying machine.

Brompton Hall (now a school and not open to the public) had been the home of the Cayley family since Stuart times, and Sir George Cayley (1771–1857) developed an unquenchable scientific curiosity. His inventions included caterpillar tracks and a new form of artificial limb, prompted by an accident to one of his estate workers.

But the prospect of flight remained Sir George's passion. Even before the 18th century was out he was designing gliders – continuing to refine the craft's aerodynamics until he had a controllable machine that could carry a man. His various experiments proved that a contoured wing could provide much greater lift than a wing with a flat profile.

Though an inscription in the church porch acknowledges Sir George as the 'Father of Aeronautics', his pioneering efforts are largely overlooked. Facing the main road through the village is the

six-sided building, the summerhouse, now boarded up, unfortunately, where Sir George worked on his flying machines.

CASTLETON MAP REF 407 J4

The castle is long gone from Castleton; only the name and a mound to the north of the village remain – a lot of the stone from the ruined castle was probably used to build Danby Castle. Castleton used to have regular markets and a goods yard on the railway; the markets have long gone, but the village still has its passenger station on the Esk Valley railway line.

The River Esk, which rises at Esklets in Westerdale to the south, is joined at Castleton by a tributary, Commondale Beck. To the north of the village is an expanse of moorland, but the landscape is very different from that of the south, with a selection of minor roads, tracks and footpaths exploring a landscape of great variety. Two routes 'take the high road' over Castleton Rigg, enjoying panoramic views down into Westerdale and Danby Dale, and on to Ralph Cross (used as the National Park emblem) and the head of beautiful Rosedale. This is moorland scenery at its best; valley bottoms divided up into neat fields by drystone walls, the pattern interrupted by little copses.

COXWOLD MAP REF 407 J5

Coxwold, about 3 miles (4.8km) south of Kilburn, has a 15th-century village church, with an eight-sided tower, overlooking the handsome houses lining the broad main street, which include almshouses dating back to the reign of Charles II.

Shandy Hall opposite the church was once the home of Laurence Sterne (1713–68). As a writer Sterne was a relatively late developer, not picking up his quill until the ripe age of 46. The publication of his picaresque novel, *The Life and Opinions of Tristram Shandy, Gentleman*, happened as he became the vicar of Coxwold. Literary success was immediate, and Sterne was able to indulge his taste for high living. He contracted pleurisy and died in 1768. His skull is buried in Coxwold churchyard. Dilapidated Shandy Hall was renovated in the 1960s, filled with manuscripts and first editions and opened to the public.

To the south of Coxwold is Newburgh Priory, which was designed and built as an Augustinian house in 1145. After the Dissolution of Monasteries, Henry VIII rewarded his chaplain, Anthony Bellasis, by giving him the building. He, and the owners who followed him, transformed the priory into a fine country house.

The beautiful setting of Byland Abbey (English Heritage) wasn't the first site chosen by the band of Cistercian monks who came here from France. They had

CROPTON FOREST

DANBY

settled briefly near Old Byland, but it was reckoned to be unsuitable because the monks were confused by hearing the bells of nearby Rievaulx Abbey. Finally, in 1177, work began on Byland Abbey. The dramatic west facade, with its 26-ft (8m) diameter window, still stands to its full height, and gives an impression of just how huge the nave used to be.

CROPTON FOREST MAP REF 407 J4
The extensive moors are continually evolving, and one of the most dramatic changes of the 20th century was the creation of large-scale conifer plantations. The Forestry Commission began this in the 1920s; now the area comprises one of the most extensive man-made forests in the country. Cropton Forest occupies a large area of the North Riding Forest Park between Rosedale in the west and Newtondale to the east.

The woodlands are now reaching maturity, and upwards of 120,000 tons of timber are felled every year to meet consumer demand. More recently, care has been taken to ensure that plantings harmonize with their surroundings. Areas of broadleaved and mixed woods provide a more varied habitat for wildlife.

Cropton Forest provides plenty of outdoor activities – there is a campsite, forest cabins and educational outdoor activity centres set out amid the trees, and opportunities for walking and biking. The North Yorkshire Moors Railway, from Pickering to Grosmont, passes through the eastern edge of the forest, and stations at Levisham and Newtondale provide easy access for visitors to the woodland.

Roman roads are not hard to find, on the map at least. The Roman road, commonly known as Wade's Causeway, across Wheeldale Moor and immediately to the north of Cropton Forest, is still that rare thing – a Roman road which is still visible on the ground.

There are Roman remains at Cawthorn Camp, believed to have been used as a training camp, which is signposted from the minor road between the villages of Cropton and Newton-on-Rawcliffe. From the purpose-built car park the waymarked path, no more than a mile (1.6km) long, guides you around them. The well-preserved earthworks reveal a camp, two forts and an annexe wedged side by side on a plateau, which enjoys panoramic views to the north across to the moors.

DANBY MAP REF 407 J4
The lovely village of Danby lies on a crossroads; blink and you've missed it. But it was to this little village that John Atkinson came, at the age of 36, as minister of the parish. He was Essex-born and until the end of his long life retained the natural curiosity of the newcomer. One of his major passions was prehistory, and the moors, with their burial mounds, standing stones and wayside crosses, provided much to excite his mind.

There are a number of interesting features in the immediate vicinity, and the easiest way to see them is to park up at the National Park's Visitor Centre, just half a mile (800m) from the village on the road to Lealholm. The Moors Centre represents the public face of the National Park. Here you can discover what makes the North York Moors so special and the unique habitats that the moors support. The Moors Centre hosts exhibitions and events, including guided walks. The evolution of the moorland landscape is explained, and those whose needs extend no further than tea and a slice of cake are equally well catered for. The Moors Centre sits in 13 acres (5.2ha) of land, close to the Esk, a lovely spot to enjoy a picnic or a stroll along the riverside on a gloriously sunny day. There are waymarked walks to help you explore the area; longer walks start from the car park.

EGTON BRIDGE MAP REF 407 J4
Egton and Egton Bridge are two villages separated by both the River Esk and a steep descent. Egton appeared in the Domesday Book as Egetune, meaning 'the town of the oak trees'. The oaks are gone, as are the annual hiring fairs, when farmers would look to employ farm labourers. The village is important as the venue, every August, for one of the area's largest agricultural shows.

A new bridge, built in 1993, spans the River Esk at Egton Bridge. The stone arch replaces an ugly metal structure that was itself merely a replacement for the original bridge, which was swept away in floods in the 1930s.

Egton Bridge was the birthplace in 1599 of Father Nicholas Postgate, who ministered to his Catholic flock at much danger to himself. In 1678 he was sentenced – in his 80s – to be hanged, drawn and quartered. In remaining staunchly Roman Catholic, Egton Bridge became known as 'the village missed by the Reformation'. The impressive Catholic Church of St Hedda contains relics of Father Postgate's ministry. Half-way up the hill to Egton is a house with a tiny chapel hidden in the roof, reached by a secret passage. The room was rediscovered 150 years after Postgate's death, since when it has been known as the Mass House.

Ramblers alight at Egton Bridge, a stop on the Middlesbrough to Whitby line, and walk along the Esk Valley to Lealholm to catch the next train home.

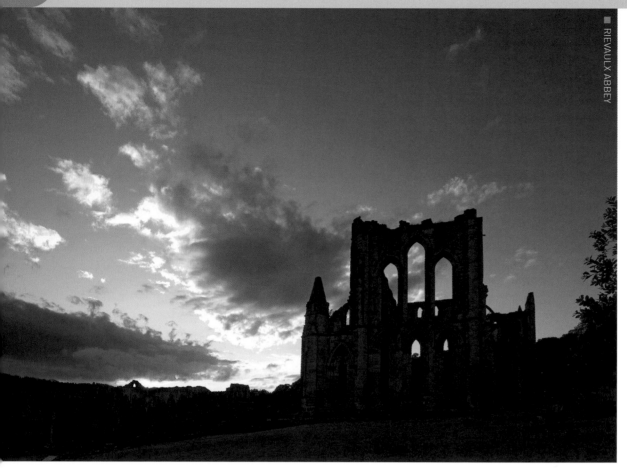
RIEVAULX ABBEY

RAVENSCAR MAP REF 407 K4

Great things were planned for Ravenscar. A developer named John Septimus Bland decided to build a holiday resort that he thought would rival Whitby and Scarborough. A station was built, Bland laid out the town's network of roads and began to build shops and houses. But Bland's company went bankrupt, and work stopped. Despite the panoramic sea views, this exposed site was clearly unsuitable for such a development. It is geologically unstable, and visitors would have been faced with an awkward descent to the stony beach far below.

You can see Ravenscar's street layout today, though grass is growing through where the buildings ought to have been. When the Raven Hall Hotel was built in 1774, it was simply Raven Hall. The hotel was to have been the centrepiece of the resort; now it stands alone, its mock battlements a landmark for miles around.

The Romans built a signal station here; its foundations and an inscribed stone (on display in Whitby's Pannett Park Museum) were found when Raven Hall's own foundations were being laid. The signal station relayed warnings of Anglo-Saxon invaders to military bases.

This part of the coastline (in the care of the National Trust, visit their Coastal Centre in Ravenscar) was exploited for alum, used in dyeing to fix colours permanently. Remains of the quarries and buildings can be found near the town.

RIEVAULX ABBEY MAP REF 407 J4

A short drive (or pleasant stroll) from Helmsley is one of Yorkshire's finest treasures. Today the setting of Rievaulx Abbey (English Heritage) is sheltered and inviting, but when Walter l'Espec dispatched a group of French monks to find a suitable site on which to build a new community it was reported to be fit only for 'wild beasts and robbers'.

In 1131, the monks began to build the mother church of the Cistercian Order in England. Many people today consider Rievaulx to be the pre-eminent Cistercian abbey in the country. The nave is Norman, while the rest of the abbey was built in the Early English style.

The monks may have started out with a strictly ascetic attitude towards wealth and lifestyle, but the 140 monks and nearly 600 lay brothers of Rievaulx Abbey succeeded in creating great influence. By 1538, at the Dissoution of Monasteries, the monks had become very wealthy indeed.

Cut into the hillside above the abbey is Rievaulx Terrace (National Trust), a curved grassy promenade that is more than a match for the landscaped terrace at nearby Duncombe Park. The terrace at Rievaulx offers strollers tantalising glimpses of the abbey between groups of trees, with fantastic views of the Rye Valley and Hambleton Hills. There are temples, one in the Ionic style, with a fine sumptuous interior, the other Tuscan, to mark both ends of the terrace.

ROBIN HOOD'S BAY MAP REF 407 K4

Robin Hood's Bay vies with Staithes for the title of the prettiest fishing village on Yorkshire's coastline. Both communities have to juggle the demands of tourism with the needs of local people. To visit Robin Hood's Bay leave your car at the top of the hill, where there are two large car parks. The road down to the beach is a cul-de-sac and visitors' cars are barred.

Apart from the access road, the houses, clinging precariously to the side of the cliff, are reached by narrow alleyways and steps. A jumble of whitewashed cottages and red-tiled roofs lead down the main street and almost into the sea. A story tells of a ship which came so close to shore at high tide that its bowsprit knocked out the window of a pub!

There is no harbour. Where once there were more than a hundred fishing boats, there are now just a handful, and they are launched down a slipway. Many of the old fishermen's cottages are now holiday homes. There is a good stretch of sandy beach and a rocky foreshore; children love to investigate the little rock pools left in these scars by the receding tide. Take care; it is easy to get cut off by the tide when it starts coming in again.

Robin Hood's Bay has had its share of wild storms, their effects exacerbated by the softness of the rock that forms the cliffs. A sea wall helps to blunt the worst of the buffeting, though every winter still brings memorable storms.

ROSEDALE MAP REF 407 J4

Rosedale is a lovely tranquil valley. City visitors will feel a long way from the noise and grime of Yorkshire's industrial heartlands. But just one hundred years ago the scene was very different: Rosedale was a veritable moorland 'Klondike'.

Ironstone had been mined here, sporadically, since the Iron Age. During the 13th century mining added to the wealth of the monks of Byland Abbey; but it was only in the middle of the 19th century that the extent of Rosedale's subterranean wealth was realized, with the discovery of massive quantities of top-grade iron ore. The Industrial Revolution brought a huge demand for iron and the blast furnaces on the rivers Tees and Tyne needed a constant supply for building ships, railways and general engineering.

The transport of ore was difficult from isolated Rosedale. In 1861 the North Eastern Railway Company built a line from Battersby Junction on the Stockton–Whitby line, over the bleak moorland to Rosedale West. In 1865 a branch was built around the head of Rosecale to the east mines, joining the original line at Blakey Junction, just below the Lion Inn on Blakey Ridge. To reach Teesside the wagons, now laden with ore, were winched down the descent of the Ingleby Incline.

The Rosedale railway was closed in 1929, by which time the valley's mining boom was over. The route of this line is used today by walkers, cyclists and horse riders. The valley is quietly 'going back to nature', but the massive calcining kilns (where ironstone was roasted to reduce its weight) have been preserved in memory of Rosedale's mining past.

SCARBOROUGH MAP REF 407 K4

The resort of Scarborough can claim to be one of the oldest in the country. Its prosperity goes back to the occasion in the year 1620, when a visitor, Mrs Elizabeth Farrow, was drinking a glass of spring water. Finding the water acidic in taste, she came to the natural conclusion that something that tasted so unpleasant must surely have medicinal qualities too.

Promises of miraculous cures have always had willing ears. Scarborough's spring water was said to cure many ills, even hypochondria. Scarborough's spring water certainly contains Epsom salts and a cocktail of minerals. The taking of the waters was soon put on a more commercial footing. Scarborough became known as a spa town; a name borrowed from the Belgian resort. Scarborough was put firmly on the map as a place where the well-heeled might come to recuperate. A local doctor also started to extol the health-giving properties of sea bathing.

Scarborough Castle has dominated the town with an air of fortress-like impregnability for the best part of a millennium. On its headland, between the North and South Bays, it enjoys an uninterrupted view over the town and out to sea. Remains of earlier defences have been unearthed, including an Iron Age settlement and a Roman signal station.

Scarborough has enough attractions to keep visitors coming back for more. Cricket lovers eagerly anticipate the Scarborough Festival, traditionally held towards the end of the season. Playwright Sir Alan Ayckbourn keeps faith with local theatre-goers by premiering most of his plays here in his Stephen Joseph Theatre. The miniature North Bay Railway runs for just under a mile (1.6km) between Peasholme Park and the Sealife Centre at Scalby Mills where you can see a colourful Caribbean-style coral reef.

STAITHES MAP REF 407 J3

It is easy to miss the Staithes turning off the main A174 coast road. Nor is the first sight of the village very promising. You have to drive half a mile (800m), park in the pay-and-display car park and proceed on foot if you want to see the place.

This perfectly preserved Yorkshire fishing village is divided into two by Cowbar Beck and the steep-sided gorge through which it runs. For centuries the people of Staithes coped with the twin problems of an inhospitable site and the ravages of the North Sea. The Staithes we see today is a village that would be immediately familiar to the young James Cook, who spent an impatient 18 months working at the counter of a draper's shop in the village before realising his ambition to go to sea. The whitewashed houses, pantiled roofs, fishing cobles and lobster pots would make him feel at home.

STOKESLEY MAP REF 407 J4

Stokesley maintains the unhurried character of a market town. The broad verges of West Green create a little space between the Georgian façades of the houses and the main street that winds through the town. Stokesley still has markets every Friday on the cobbled edges of the main street. Each September, the market town is the site of one of the largest agricultural shows in the area.

The big open spaces include College Square and the market square. Behind them is Levenside, where the River Leven, little more than a stream at this point, follows its tranquil winding course between grassy banks and underneath a succession of little bridges. The oldest of these is the handsome arch of a fine old packhorse bridge; near by is a ford.

WHITBY MAP REF 407 K4

Those who take a leisurely stroll along the pleasant harbour front may be forgiven for thinking of Whitby as just another resort. But Whitby has a long, illustrious and genuine history as one of the country's most important seaports.

Whitby's setting itself is dramatic, with houses clinging on to the steep slopes on either side of the River Esk. Whitby has always gazed out to sea. By the 18th century it was a major port, with shipbuilding, fishing and whaling. The fine Georgian houses at the west end of the town, built by wealthy shipbuilders and fleet owners, attest to this success.

Elsewhere, more traditional cottages, whitewashed and with red-tiled roofs, housed the fishermen. Space was at a premium, so their houses were built in close proximity, mostly up the steep inclines on the eastern side of the Esk. They are linked by ginnels and steps. Leave your car in one of the long-stay car parks near the marina; Whitby's narrow streets were not built for cars.

The town was prosperous during the 17th and 18th centuries with the mining and refining of alum. Coal was brought here to fire the cauldrons that separated alum from rock, and stone was needed for building; this increase in trade required the building of a better harbour. In 1753 a company was set up in the town to undertake whaling expeditions, using the sturdy ships already being built here.

Smaller boats sailed out of Whitby to net herring, and the fish market was one of the busiest. The men still fish, but on a much reduced scale.

In AD 655 King Oswy of Northumbria celebrated a victory in battle by promising his daughter as a bride of Christ. He founded a monastery on Whitby's eastern cliff, much where the later abbey's ruins stand today. The first abbess was Hilda and for her goodness and piety she was recognized as a saint. St Hilda's abbey was destroyed by Viking raiders. The abbey that replaced it was begun in the 11th century; this is what we see today.

Sharing the abbey's site is St Mary's Church. St Mary's parishioners have to tackle the 199 steps up to the church. At the bottom of Church Steps is the oldest part of town. If those 199 steps have taken their toll enjoy a drink in one of the harbour-side pubs.

On Grape Lane, by the harbour, you will find the home of ship owner and Quaker, Captain John Walker, to whom the young James Cook was apprenticed in 1746, before enlisting in the Royal Navy. Today the building houses the Captain Cook Memorial Museum, with fascinating room sets and exhibits about his life.

STAITHES

ROSEBERRY TOPPING & CAPTAIN COOK COUNTRY

Climb Roseberry Topping, once mined for ironstone, for views of the countryside. After the descent from the summit, and the climb again to the woodland, the track descends over Great Ayton Moor. Ahead, the Captain Cook Monument, a stone obelisk 52ft (15.8m) high, dominates the view. The explorer was born in 1728 within sight of Roseberry Topping at Marton (then a village, but now a suburb of Middlesbrough) and went to school at nearby Great Ayton. After you have gone through the gate after Point 5, the dips and hollows in the ground to the left are the remains of an ironstone mine, Ayton Banks. Further on you'll pass by Gribdale Terrace, a row of cottages built to house the iron miners and their families.

1 Take the rough lane that runs beside the car park, which heads towards Roseberry Topping. The path goes through a gateway and then rises to a second gate at the start of woodland.

2 Go through a gate into National Trust land and then turn left. Take a well-worn, mostly-paved, path to reach the summit. It is a stiff climb to the trig point on the hill top.

3 From the summit, walk east from the trig point, past two iron poles in a rock, and then straight on along a paved way. Go steeply downhill. At the bottom, bear right up a track that bends right around the corner of woodland to reach a gate.

4 Go through the gate and then take the path alongside the wood, following yellow waymarkers. Continue walking on the path until it follows a wall and then descends hillside to reach a road.

5 Turn right, cross a cattle grid and bear left between two benches, then go right, along the fence line, at first parallel with the road. Go down a field, through a gate and cross a stile into a lane. Walk past cottages to a road and go straight ahead.

6 At the crossroads go right, on Aireyholme Lane. Follow the lane past houses, then take a signed footpath left over a stile. Follow the fence to two gates into woodland. After 0.5 mile (800m), go right at a National Trust sign, up a path through the woods to a signposted stile. Cross, turn left to another stile, then, go right along the edge of woodland. Bend left to a gate near a house.

7 Walk across two fields to a stile, then continue uphill to a tower. Beyond it, take the grassy path left down a gully, to a gate into woodland. Follow the path downhill through the woods to return to the gate at the top of the lane leading to the car park.

DISTANCE/TIME 5.5 miles (8.8km) 2h30 **MAP** OS Explorer OL 26 North York Moors – Western **START** Car park at Newton under Roseberry; grid ref: NZ 570128 **PATHS** Hillside climb, then tracks and field paths; 5 stiles **THE PUB** The Royal Oak Hotel, Great Ayton. Tel: 01642 722361

A LOOP FROM SWAINBY TO WHORLTON

From the once-industrial village of Swainby, this walk takes in fine views from the northern edge of the North York Moors plateau. The route then passes through Whorlton village, deserted since it was devastated by the plague in the 14th century and the survivors moved away.

1 With the church left, walk down the street to the right of the stream. Continue past a sign 'Unsuitable for Buses and Coaches' and go straight ahead uphill. As the road bends to the right, follow the bridleway sign to Scugdale, up the track that lies ahead.

2 Go through a gate and turn left to join the waymarks for the Cleveland Way National Trail. Walk through the woodland, turning left, just after a seat, down to a gate. The footpath goes half right, towards blue-topped posts and downhill to another gate. Cross the stream on the footbridge to reach a lane, with another footbridge, over Scugdale Beck. Turn left.

3 Follow the lane past Hollin Hill Farm to a T-junction with telephone and post boxes. Cross the lane and go through a Cleveland Way signed gate. Walk up the path beside woodland to a gate.

4 The path beyond bends right to a stile and goes on to a paved track in the wood. Go straight ahead at a crossing track to another gate, and continue to follow the paved path up to the heather moorland, passing a cairn. After the first summit, the path descends beyond a large and a small cairn into a dip.

Just before the paved path ends, look out for a narrow path off to the left, down through the heather.

5 After about 100yds (91m) you reach a concrete post. Bear left and follow the path down the gully to a fence beside a wood. Turn left to a signpost. Go straight on, eventually crossing a spoil heap to a gate on your right.

6 Through the gate, go straight down the hill through woodland. At the bottom, bear right, then left to cross a stile by a gate and go down the lane. Just after the first house on the left, take a footpath over two stiles.

7 Walk up through the woodland on to a grassy track. Turn left, and left again at another track. At a T-junction, turn left again and follow the track downhill to a stile. Turn left to go over another stile. Go straight ahead along the signed track.

8 Go over a stile beside a gate and follow the track along the hillside. Over a stile with steps beyond, turn left at the bottom and follow the field-edge. Go through a gateway beside a paddock to another gateway on to a metalled lane. Follow the lane past Whorlton church and castle back to Swainby village.

DISTANCE/TIME 6 miles (9.7km) 3h **MAP** OS Explorer OL 26 North York Moors – Western **START** Roadside parking in Swainby village; grid ref: NZ 477020 **PATHS** Tracks and moorland paths, lots of bracken; 6 stiles **THE PUB** The Black Horse, Swainby. Tel: 01642 700436; www.theblackhorseswainby.co.uk

BYLAND ABBEY & OLSTEAD OBSERVATORY

This is a gentle walk from the romantic ruins of Byland Abbey through some lovely woodland to an old observatory at the highest point of the walk. The lumps and bumps of the final field you cross are the remains of the monks' ponds, some used for breeding fish.

DISTANCE/TIME 5 miles (8km) 2h30 **MAP** OS Explorer OL26 North York Moors – Western
START Car park behind Abbey Inn in Byland Abbey; grid ref: SE 548789 **PATHS** Woodland tracks, field paths; 8 stiles **THE PUB** The Abbey Inn, Byland Abbey. Tel: 01347 868204; www.theappletree.org

1 Visit the abbey, then start your walk from beside the ticket office and turn right along the abbey's north side. Opposite a public footpath sign, go left through a gateway and after 10yds (9m) right, over a stile. Cross the field to a second stile, then bear half left uphill to a waymarked gate behind a bench. Go through two more gates and on to a metalled lane.

2 Turn left. At the top of the lane go through a gate signed 'Cam Farm, Observatory'. The path climbs then leaves the wood edge to rise to a terrace. After a stile, take the left-hand path, following Cam Farm. Go straight on at two junctions, uphill, to reach a large open space.

3 Turn right and, just before a waymarked metal gate, turn left along the wood edge. Follow the path to Oldstead Observatory, bearing left through the wood. Pass to the left of the Observatory, go down a slope and follow the path running steeply downhill to reach a signpost.

4 Turn right on the track, signed 'Oldstead'. Follow the track as it curves left to become a metalled lane. Turn left at the T-junction, and left again on to the road by a seat. Just before the road narrows sign, turn left.

5 Go through some gateposts and over a cattle grid. Then, as the avenue of trees ends, take a signposted footpath to the right, uphill. Climb up to a stile, bending around to the left beside the woodland to a gate. After the next gate, go straight ahead, through two more gates and on to a metalled road.

6 Turn right then, just beyond the road sign which indicates a bend, take a track to the left by the Oldstead Grange sign. Pass the house and go between barns and through a gateway. Bear right downhill on the track, bending right on a track to a gateway with a waymarked tree.

7 Immediately after the gateway, turn left and go through the wood to a Byland Abbey signpost. Follow the path ahead as it bends left by another sign, go over a stile and down the field with the hedge on your left, bending left then right at the end to another signpost. Go through an opening beside a metal gate and along the field with a hedge right.

8 Go over two stiles then bear slightly left to another stile. Go across the field to a signpost in the hedge by a metal gate. Follow the fence, then go on to the road by a wooden stile. Turn left back to the car park opposite the abbey.

WALK 104

OUT ON THE TILES AT BOLTBY & THIRLBY BANK

The western boundary of the North York Moors National Park passes just outside Boltby. It is a delightful place, with a tiny 19th-century chapel and stone-built houses. Our route passes Tang Hall and Southwoods Hall, before going through Midge Holme Gate and into woodland. On the top of Boltby Scar, as you begin the descent from the Cleveland Way you pass the remains of a Bronze Age hill fort.

DISTANCE/TIME 5.25 miles (8.4km) 2h **MAP** OS Explorer OL26 North York Moors – Western
START Roadside parking in Boltby village; grid ref: SE 490866 **PATHS** Mostly easy field and woodland paths; very steep and muddy climb up Thirlby Bank, 4 stiles **THE PUB** The Carpenter's Arms, Felixkirk. Tel: 01845 537369; www.carpentersarmsfelixkirk.com

1 From the humpback bridge in the village centre, follow the signed public footpath along a stream to reach a gate, and through three more gates to cross a footbridge to a stile. Continue following the stream; cross a gated footbridge, go over a stile and then through a gate, then bear left over a stream and right to reach a gated footbridge.

2 Cross the bridge and then continue over two stiles, then go straight on, beside a hedge, to go through two gates on to a metalled track at Tang Hall.

3 Turn left and, at the end of farm buildings, turn right by a sign to Southwoods and through a gate to go diagonally left across a field; the route is marked by stones. At the field end, go through two gates then continue with the wire fence on the right. The path veers left and then descends to a gate.

4 Continue along a track to a handgate. Go ahead on the track, confusingly named Midge Holm Gate. Follow the track to another gate beside a cottage, Southwoods Lodge, and then go on to a metalled lane.

5 Turn left to follow a track, signposted 'Bridleway to Gormire'. At a signpost go ahead on a bridleway, up Thirlby Bank. This steep, often muddy, track ascends the ridge; bear right at a fork part way up. Eventually reach a Cleveland Way sign on the ridge top.

6 Turn left and follow the Cleveland Way footpath for 1 mile (1.6km) along the ridge, to reach a bridleway sign to Boltby on your left. Descend to a gate then go ahead on a woodland ride, crossing a track to a gate. Continue ahead down the field, through a gate, and follow the track to the right, along the edge of the wood.

7 At a signpost, turn right towards Boltby, to continue to gate. Pass a tree stump with a mosaic of a toadstool and descend to a gate leading on to a lane. Follow the lane through another gate. Cross a stream by a footbridge and continue up a metalled lane. At a T-junction in the village, turn left back to the humpback bridge at the start.

LASTINGHAM & HUTTON-LE-HOLE

From Lastingham and St Cedd's monastery the walk reaches Spaunton before leading on to Hutton-le-Hole clustered around an irregular green and along the banks of a beck. The route passes through fields and woodland on the return leg.

DISTANCE/TIME 4.5 miles (7.2km) 2h **MAP** OS Explorer OL26 North York Moors – Western **START** Village street in Lastingham; grid ref: SE 729905 **PATHS** Farm tracks and field paths; 2 stiles **THE PUB** The Blacksmiths Arms, Lastingham. Tel: 01751 417247

1 Begin by The Green and follow signs to Cropton, Pickering and Rosedale, past the red telephone box. Where the road swings left, go right to wind over a small bridge and beside a stream. Ascend to a footpath sign, and go right, uphill, through a gate and through woodland to a handgate on to a road. Turn right, signed 'Spaunton'.

2 Follow the road through Spaunton, and bend right at the end of the village, then turn left, by the public footpath sign, over the cattle grid into the farmyard. The waymarked track curves through the farm to reach another footpath signpost, where the track bends left. After 100yds (91m), at a barn, the track bends left again.

3 After about 200yds (182m), follow a public footpath sign right and walk on to follow another sign as the track bends to the left. After 100yds (91m), take a footpath to the right, down the hill and into woodland. Follow the track as it bends to the left, then go right, following the waymarks, down a steep grassy path into the valley. Descend to a gate beside a stream, and on to the road through Hutton-le-Hole.

4 Turn right up the main street and then right again at a footpath signpost opposite the Village Hall. Follow the waymarked route along the field-edges and through five waymarked gates to a kissing gate before a footbridge. Follow the path through woodland to a gate and follow the grassy track to the road.

5 Turn right and follow the road for 0.5 mile (800m). Turn left at a footpath sign just before the road descends to a stone bridge. Continue on the grassy path, going over a stile, and follow the track towards a farm.

6 Follow the waymarked posts, bending left alongside the wall beside a clump of trees and descending into a valley. Cross over the stream and follow the wall on your right-hand side uphill. You will reach a bench and then a carved stone with a cross and a three-pointed sign nearby.

7 Take none of the directions indicated by the sign, but turn right, downhill through a gate and on to the metalled road. Follow the road downhill back into the village of Lastingham.

WALK 106

THE IRON VALLEY OF ROSEDALE

Rosedale is a peaceful valley that pushes northwest into the heart of the North York Moors. Yet little more than 100 years ago the village of Rosedale Abbey had a population ten times its present size. The reason was the discovery of ironstone in the 1850s. The remains of the Rosedale East Mines can be seen during the walk.

DISTANCE/TIME 3.5 miles (5.7km) 1h30 **MAP** OS Explorer OL26 North York Moors – Western **START** Roadside parking near road junction northeast of Rosedale Abbey, near Sycamore Farm sign; grid ref: SE 717970. **PATHS** Mostly field paths and tracks, 7 stiles **THE PUB** White Horse Farm Hotel, Rosedale Abbey. Tel: 01751 417239; www.whitehorserosedale.co.uk

1 From your parking place take the lane downhill by a Sycamore Farm sign. It bends right. Follow the waymarkers to turn right through Low Bell End Farm gateway. Follow the track through two gates and continue downhill. Near a gate on the left, the track bends right, following a stream. After going through another gateway, bend left towards the stream to cross a footbridge with stiles at each end. Follow the waymarked footpath half left, uphill, towards farm buildings. The route passes through buildings and on to a farm track. Follow the track uphill, forking right to a reach lane. Turn right.

2 Continue up a metalled lane through Thorgill. Beyond buildings the metalled lane becomes a track. Follow the track for 0.75 mile (1.2 km), going through a wooden gate near Medd Farm and continuing downhill. Pass Seven Side caravan site and then the track begins to rise again. Almost opposite High House Farm on the left, go right over a waymarked stile beside a gate.

3 Walk down the slope beside a fence and cross the River Seven on a gated footbridge. At the end, turn left to go up a short, steep

slope. At the top, the path goes above a stream, running parallel with it. Continue through the gate into a field and walk ahead. Go through another gate and continue up the field with fence on the left. Go through a metal gate into Craven Garth Farm yard. Go through another gateway and pass between buildings to reach a metalled country lane at a T-junction.

4 Turn right to follow the lane; just before former ironworkers' cottages, look for the Rosedale parish notice board on the left. Turn up a track beside it. Along the track, before the farm, look for a gate across the track to Clough House.

5 Go over a stile beside a gate and follow the track down towards a wood. The track bends right just before Clough House, then bends left to pass in front of the house. Opposite to the building, go through a waymarked gate on the right and walk down a field towards houses. Leave the field by a gate, and follow the track to a road. Turn left and follow the road back to the start.

DISTANCE/TIME 7.4 miles (12km) 2h **MAP** OS Explorer OL26 North York Moors – Western **START** Sutton Bank Visitor Centre; grid ref: SE 516831 **TRACKS** Good level lanes followed by undulating bridleways on the edge of the escarpment **THE PUB** The Hambleton Inn, Sutton Bank. Tel: 01845 597202; www.hambletoninn.co.uk

DISTANCE/TIME 6miles (9.7km) 2h **MAP** OS Explorer OL27 North York Moors – Eastern **START** Car park at Adderstone Field, Dalby Forest; grid ref: SE 883897 **TRACKS** Forestry roads and several narrow paths, mostly well graded **THE PUB** New Inn, Thornton le Dale. Tel: 01751 474226

THE HAMBLETON HILLS

Enjoy some of northern England's best views and experience a bit of adventure with a ride along the edge of the escarpment. The long tarred lane that takes you north from Sutton Bank seems unremarkable, but there's a history dating back to the Iron Age tribes who settled here around 400 BC. They would have used the route long before the Romans followed in their footsteps.

1 Before you leave Sutton Bank Visitor Centre, take a look at the panoramas to the south and west. From here you can see for miles across the flat fields of the Vales of Mowbray and York. Alf Wight, alias the fictional vet James Herriot, believed this view to be the finest in England. Apparently, both York Minster and Lincoln Cathedral are discernible on a clear day. From the visitor centre car park, turn left up the lane signed to Cold Kirby and Old Byland. Then take the left fork past Dialstone Farm and its tall communications mast, before heading north on an ever-so-straight lane through cornfields and pastures.

2 The lane comes to a T-junction by a triangular wood, called the Snack Yate Plantation. This is a popular starting point for serious mountain bikers who will swoop down on rough tracks through Boltby Forest. Your route turns left down the lane. It's a gentle downhill for a short distance. Just before the road dives off the edge, turn left through a gate on to a grassy bridleway to cycle along the escarpment's edge. You are now riding on the Hambleton Hills. The first stretch is slightly uphill, but the track is firm and the views wide-sweeping. You'll see a small reservoir surrounded by forestry and the little village of Boltby huddled beneath a pastured hill.

3 The bridleway climbs to the top of the hill at High Barn, an old stone ruin shaded by a fine stand of sycamore. The going eases at this point and the cliffs of an old quarry appear up ahead. Here the bridleway goes through a gate on to a walled track for a short way. Ignore the bridleway on the left (it goes back to the Hambleton Road), and stay with the edge path to the hill above the rocks of Boltby Scar. This is the highest point of the ride. Note the wind-warped larch trees here – they add to the views across the Vale of Mowbray.

4 The trees of the Boltby Forest now cover the west slopes, almost right up to the summit. Beyond the next offshoot bridleway, which you should ignore, the path becomes much narrower with a few embedded rocks in some places. The difficulties are short-lived, but the younger and less experienced riders might prefer to dismount and walk for a bit here. The riding gets easier again as the bridleway arcs right above South Wood. At the end of this arc you turn left to a sign that tells you that the continuing edge path is for walkers only. This is a fine spot to linger and admire the views. To the south the half-moon-shaped Gormire Lake lies in a nest of broad-leaved woodland and beneath the sandy-coloured Whitestone Cliff.

5 When you've rested for a while, turn left on a bridleway to Dialstone Farm. This heads east across large prairie-like fields. Beyond a wood, the High Quarry Plantation, you will see the hurdles of the equestrian centre. Past the large farm, turn right along the tarred lane, then right again, back to the visitor centre car park.

DALBY FOREST

This is a short ride through the forest to seek the wildlife – if you stay quiet and look hard enough, you'll see it in abundance. Roe deer happily inhabit the forest and you may be very lucky and see a badger if it is late in the day. Besides the common blue tits, you're quite likely to see a wading heron, or a tiny warbler. The forest is made up of a variety of trees including the many broad-leaf species such as oak, alder and hazel, but is mostly pine and spruce.

1 The green cycle route begins beyond the trees at the southeast end of the large Adderstone Field (the furthest from the visitor centre). Here you turn left along a narrow slightly downhill track. Ignore the two lesser, unsigned left fork tracks.

2 Turn right along a much wider forestry track which takes a winding course round the afforested valley of Worry Gill. Where the more demanding red route goes off on a rough track to the right, your green route goes straight on, still using a well-graded track.

3 Where a track doubles back, go straight on up a steady hill before meeting up with the forest drive again. Cross this with care – it can be busy – before turning right along it for 200yds (182m). Turn left along a narrow path signed with red and green waymarkers and just before a 30mph speed limit sign.

4 The path reaches a flinted road at the southeast edge of the forest. Turn right along this, then turn left at the next junction. To your left the rougher high pastures of Ebberston Low Moor decline to the greener, more fertile fields of the Vale of Pickering.

5 Turn right just before Givendale Head Farm along a rutted farm track which has a disitinctive grassy island in the middle of it. Turn right at the next junction (Post B) continuing on a downhill section, followed by an uphill one where you're joined by a farm track coming in from the left.

6 A long hill follows to a wide junction where you go straight on along a tarred lane. A sign tells you that you're now at the head of Flax Dale. Stay with the tarred lane at the next bend and junction. Turn right at the crossroads along a long sandy track (Post A), then turn right again at the next junction. Note the linear earthwork to both left and right – nobody seems to know the exact origins of these.

7 After going straight on at the next junction past a fine stand of Scots pines, you get fine views over the farm pastures of High Rigg to reach Levisham Moor. Here, there's another downhill section followed by an uphill one. Take a right fork at Newclose Rigg. Where the red route goes straight on, your green route veers right along the main track. There's a downhill left curve beyond where you take the upper right fork, which brings the route back to the forest drive opposite Adderstone Field.

DISTANCE/TIME 11.25 miles (18.1km) 2h **MAP** OS Explorer OL27 North York Moors – Eastern **START** Roadside parking on way into Ravenscar; grid ref: NZ 980015 **TRACKS** Almost entirely on well-surfaced old railway track; short street sections at Ravenscar and Robin Hood's Bay **THE PUB** The Laurel Inn, Robin Hood's Bay. Tel: 01947 880400

DISTANCE/TIME 9.3 miles (15km) 2h **MAP** OS Explorer 300 Howardian Hills and Malton **START** Roadside parking in the main street, Terrington; grid ref: SE 670706 **TRACKS** Country lanes with some hills **THE PUB** Bay Horse Inn, Terrington. Tel: 01653 648416

FROM RAVENSCAR TO ROBIN HOOD'S BAY

The former railway line between Whitby and Scarborough can now be followed, in its entirety, on two wheels. The full distance is 20 miles (32.2km) one way, so this ride picks out probably the finest section, looping around Robin Hood's Bay. It is a little confusing that the name of the bay and the much-photographed village are exactly the same, but the ride gives great views of the former and a chance to visit the latter.

1 Descend the road until it bends sharply right. Turn left, past the National Trust Coastal Centre, and continue on an obvious descending concrete track. A rougher section needs more care, but lasts less than 100yds (91m). Now swing left and go through a gate on to the old railway trackbed and a much easier surface.

2 The track now runs below the scarred face of the alum workings, with some ups and downs that clearly don't match the original rail contours exactly. After this section, take care crossing a steep concrete track that runs down to a farm.

3 Pass under an arched bridge. Note more quarried cliffs up on the left, while looking down to the right – if the tide is not too high – there are extensive rocky platforms in the bay, with conspicuous parallel strata. There's a short cutting and the sea views are hidden by tall gorse and broom, then it becomes more open again as the track swings gradually inland. A tall embankment crosses a steep wooded valley. Go under a bridge and then make a sharp left turn on to a lane.

4 Go up 20yds (18m), then sharp right to continue on the track. Keep right at a fork and the track resumes its steady gentle descent, then starts to turn uphill for the first time on the ride. As you come out into the open after a tunnel of trees, the direct way ahead is again blocked (unless you're Evel Knievel!). Here slant down left, cross a lane, and then climb back up on to the continuing trackbed.

5 Pass a cricket ground, next the back of a caravan site, then a farm. Cross the rough farm track and keep straight on ahead, through a gate where the surface changes to tarmac, on the outskirts of Robin Hood's Bay. Go through another gate and drop down to a road. Turn right down this road for 100yds (91m) then go left on a lane signposted to the Station Workshops. At the top of the rise is the old station building and just beyond it is a large car park. (It is, of course, possible to descend the road all the way into the village of Robin Hood's Bay, but it's a very steep climb back. An alternative is to lock the bikes at the car park and head down on foot.)

6 Continue alongside the car park, drop down to a road, turn left and almost instantly go right (very nearly straight across) on to Mount Pleasant. Follow this to its end then bear left up a short gravelled ride to regain the railway path. Continue for about 0.5 mile (800m). You will have some good views back now over Robin Hood's Bay to the cliffs near Ravenscar. Look for a National Trust sign for Ness Bay. There is open access on foot so you could leave your bikes and walk down to the headland, a great spot for a picnic, especially on a fine day. This makes as good a turnaround point as any, though the track continues into Hawsker and on to Whitby.

TERRINGTON & CASTLE HOWARD

This is a ride through Yorkshire's most magnificent estate. The house was severely damaged by fire in the middle of the 20th century but was rebuilt to its former glory and is now one of England's most popular houses to visit. It has collections of paintings, sculpture, ceramics and more. The grounds include a range of gardens and the estate comprises farms and woodland.

1 Terrington is a peaceful little village with fine sloping greens either side of the main street, giving the place a spacious feel. The cottages, which are largely Victorian, are built with local limestone. Above them, just off the main street, stands the church, a square-towered building that dates back to Saxon times – there's an interesting Anglo-Saxon window in the south aisle. Much of the church's structure is 13th-century but it was modernized around 1860. Heading east past the ivy-clad Bay Horse Inn towards Castle Howard is a slightly downhill stretch, a nice start – although the tea rooms tempt you straight away. If it's hot, a splendid avenue of trees on the way out of the village will offer some welcome shade.

2 Take the right fork, signed 'Ganthorpe, York', 0.5 mile (800m) out of the village. Now you pay for your downhill as the road climbs to the top of Cross Hill, where there's a good view back to Terrington. The lane levels out as it passes through the stone cottages and farms of Ganthorpe. This hamlet was the birthplace of the historian Arthur Toynbee (1886–1975) and the botanist Richard Spruce (1817–93), who travelled to places like the Andes and the Amazon in search of specimens for scientific research. There's another short downhill section as the lane bends right by Sata Wood, then it's uphill again.

3 Turn left at the T-junction, where you get glimpses of a couple of the Castle Howard domes, then left at the crossroads following the directions to Slingsby and Castle Howard. The road, known as The Stray, is straight ahead and madly undulating like a Roman road, with wide verges and avenues of trees lining the way. Some of the traffic is speedy so take care! Soon you pass beneath the extremely narrow stone arch of the Castle Howard estate's Carmire Gate, which is flanked by castellated walls, then you come upon the gate house with its pyramidal roof. There's a roundabout next to a 100ft (30.5m) obelisk of 1714 dedicated to Lady Cecilia Howard. Here, you need to decide whether or not to visit the palace (highly recommended).

4 Continuing down the Stray you'll pass the Obelisk Ponds, which are enshrouded by woodland, then the Great Lake, across which you can get a great view of the magnificent palace and its many domes.

5 Turn left for 'Terrington' at the crossroads just beyond the lake. The lane soon swings right and climbs through the trees of Shaw Wood. If you have mountain bikes and are experienced riders you could take the bridleway at the next bend (South Bell Bottom) then double back on the track over Husket and Ling Hills to meet the lane further west. If not, continue along the lane, which winds downhill across Ganthorpe Moor to meet the outward route by the first T-junction east of Terrington. Though you've still got the trees for shade, the downhill is now an uphill so you'll probably deserve that refreshment at the Bay Horse Inn.

THROUGH SCARBOROUGH'S RAINCLIFFE WOODS

Just outside Scarborough, a walk through woodland to the rare remains of a glacial lake. The steep hillside of Raincliffe Woods overlooks a deep valley carved out in the Ice Ages. Although mostly replanted in the 1950s and 60s, the woods in places retain remnants of ancient oak and heather woodland – look out for the heather and bilberry bushes beneath oak trees that will show you where. Throughout the walk you will come upon humps and banks, depressions and pits that show that this hillside has been a hive of human activity in the past.

DISTANCE/TIME 5 miles (8km) 2h   **MAP** OS Explorer OL27 North York Moors – Eastern   **START** Hazelhead picnic site on Mowthorpe Road, near road junction; grid ref: SE 984875   **PATHS** Field tracks, woodland paths, some steep, 2 stiles   **THE PUB** Ox Pasture Hall Country Hotel, Throxenby. Tel: 01723 365295

1 From the car park, turn left on the road, then right at the junction. Go downhill, and after the woodland ends, pass houses on the right. Opposite a bungalow, No. 5, turn right down a track to Thorn Park Farm. Follow the track as it bends left by the farm buildings, then right past a cottage to a metal gate. Continue to follow the track, which bends left then right, then through two gateways.

2 Just before the next gateway, turn right and walk up the field side to go through a gateway, which takes you on a short path to the road. Turn left, follow the road and continue to the next car park on the right.

3 Go up through the car park, bearing left towards a signboard, then go uphill on the path ahead. Where the main path bends right, go ahead, more steeply, to a crossing, grassy track. Turn left and follow the path. Where it forks, take the right-hand path.

4 After 500yds (455m) look out for a faint path on the left, which bends right over a drainage runnel. The path goes down into a valley. Turn left, downhill, then follow the path

as it bends right again, past an old quarry. The path descends to reach Throxenby Mere. Turn right along the edge of the Mere – this part of the path is on boardwalks.

5 Just before you reach a picnic place, go through a gate and immediately turn right. Follow the path which goes up steeply, ignoring all joining paths until it reaches a track at the top of the hill.

6 Turn right and go beside a gate, then follow the path for a mile (1.6km), parallel with first a fence and then a wall. It passes through a gateway with a stile by it and eventually reaches a gate with a public bridleway sign.

7 Don't go through this gate into fields, but turn right and continue beside the wire fence on the edge of the woodland. Where the main path swings left and another goes right, go straight ahead, steeply downhill. When the path joins another go left, down steps and along a boardwalk to meet a crossing path.

8 Turn right and follow the path, which soon descends to the car park.

WALK 108

EARLY WARNINGS AT FYLINGDALES & LILLA CROSS

The past and the future come together on this walk on the North Yorkshire coast. Unlike in most of upland Britain, the most important roads and tracks in the North York Moors follow the ridges between the valleys. The tracks are often marked by standing stones or crosses. The most impressive and ancient of the Moor's crosses is Lilla, commemorating an act of bravery in AD 626, when Lilla died protecting King Edward of Northumbria. Dominating the middle section of the walk is the improbably large sandcastle that houses the Fylingdales early warning system.

DISTANCE/TIME 6.75 miles (10.9km) 3h   **MAP** OS Explorer OL27 North York Moors – Eastern   **START** May Beck car park; grid ref: SX 106836   **PATHS** Forest tracks and moorland paths; 3 stiles   **THE PUB** The Birch Hall Inn, Goathland. Tel: 01947 896245

1 Walk up the wide track opposite the approach road. Where the track bends round to the right, go left down a signed footpath, descend to go over a bridge and bear right to continue along the green track. Go through a kissing gate and up the valley, eventually swinging away from the stream and into the forest.

2 On reaching a forest road turn right, passing a flooded quarry on your right. At the next junction of forest roads bear right. After about 0.25 mile (400m), turn up a track to the left.

3 Go up the track, leaving forest for moorland. Continue past the base and shaft of York Cross. At a track going left, near a waymarked post, turn sharp left.

4 Walk along the track, bearing left at the Foster Howes tumuli, and continue with the fence on your right. Pass Ann's Cross to your right and 0.5 mile (800m) beyond you'll reach a T-junction. Turn right through a gate and take the track to the left.

5 When you reach a crossroads with a signpost, turn right along the track to visit Lilla Cross. Return to the crossroads, and go straight ahead, following the Robin Hood's Bay sign. Follow the path, which goes parallel with the forest edge, for 2.5 miles (4km), eventually heading for a lone tree to the right of the wood's end.

6 Bear right when you reach a post with the number 9 on it. Pass posts 8 and 7, going left when you reach a trail sign.

7 Pass post 6, (by the remains of John Cross) and go through a gate, to continue walking downhill on a track. After 50yds (46m), go left off the track and walk parallel with the woodland to a waymarked stile near the ruins of a building.

8 Go to the left of the building and ahead to another stile. Follow the obvious footpath downhill through the bracken, passing two public footpath signs, down to the road. Turn left to return to the start.

Yorkshire Dales

CLOCKWISE FROM TOP: KNARESBOROUGH; THORNTON FORCE;
PEN-Y-GHENT; COW AT SWALEDALE

DENT HEAD VIADUCT

BOLTON ABBEY MAP REF 407 G5

Bolton Abbey Estate is owned by the Duke of Devonshire and is an enjoyable amalgamation of recreational, historical and geographical, with guests at the Devonshire Arms enjoying the comforts of one of the best hotels in the country, as well as being one of the region's best restaurants. For most people, though, Bolton Abbey is a day out in the car, within easy reach of Bradford and Leeds, with ample parking and plenty to see and do.

The first people to enjoy the site were the Augustinian monks who moved here from Embsay in 1154 to found a new priory. It was finished by the next century and now lies in evocative ruins by the banks of the River Wharfe. The adjoining priory church of St Mary and St Cuthbert is far from ruined, however, and is one of the finest churches in the Dales. Built in 1220, it escaped the Dissolution of the Monasteries, only to fall victim to a dwindling congregation. Now restored, the priory church has breathtaking stained-glass windows.

If you drive along the B6160 to one of the car parks (day tickets allow you to move between several car parks) you will pass under a narrow stone archway, part of an aqueduct that once carried water to the mill, of which little now remains.

There are many good walks to be had around the estate, including marked nature trails near the river and through Strid Wood, which is a Site of Special Scientific Interest. A leaflet showing the colour-coded walks is handed to visitors at the car park entrance.

DENT MAP REF 406 F4

If there were ever a vote for the most attractive village in the Dales, it would hardly be surprising if Dent won first prize. It is a beautiful cluster of pretty whitewashed cottages and cobbled streets nestling in the lush green valley that is Dentdale. As a result it is extremely busy in the holiday season, and is perhaps best visited at other times if possible.

Dent is on the Settle–Carlisle Railway line and is the highest mainline station in Britain, at 1,150ft (351m), but if you are planning to travel by train, be warned that the station is 5 miles (8km) from the village itself. There is only a connecting bus service on Saturdays (a Wednesday service goes once a day from Cowgill, about half a mile/800m down the valley).

Dent boasts a flourishing artistic community, from practitioners of Dent's knitting tradition to painter John Cooke, musician Mike Harding and photographers John and Eliza Forder, whose books on life in the Dales are sold in the local shops. On the road to Sedbergh you will find the Dent Crafts Centre, a display of local and not-so-local arts and crafts, which also has a café and opens as a restaurant on weekend evenings. In Dent there are cafés and pubs and a good choice of accommodation and souvenir shops.

Adam Sedgwick was born in Dent in the Old Parsonage in 1785, attended the local grammar school and went on to become the Woodwardian Professor of Geology at Cambridge. The pink Shap granite memorial fountain in the main street marks his career as a geologist. This was not always merely a memorial, as it also provided the town's main water supply until the 1920s. In 1985, to commemorate the 200th anniversary of his birth, the National Park Authority created the Adam Sedgwick Geology Trail, near Sedbergh. Leaflets are available at National Park Centres and tourist information centres.

Near the Sedgwick Stone stands St Andrew's Church, which has a Norman doorway, although most of the church was rebuilt in the late 19th century. Inside are some unusual Jacobean box-pews and flooring of Dent marble. Both black and grey marble were quarried near here. The Stone House Marble Works flourished in the 18th and 19th centuries at Arten Gill, southeast of Dent Station, where you will also find the Dent Head Viaduct, yet another of the marvellous constructions on the Settle–Carlisle Railway line.

FOUNTAINS ABBEY MAP REF 407 H5

To describe Fountains Abbey as a ruin does it a disservice, and even the term 'remains' does not prepare the visitor for the awesome and graceful sight of the best-preserved Cistercian abbey in Britain. It looks as if it may have been only a few years ago that the monks finally moved out. Fountains Abbey was designated a World Heritage Site in 1986, and is one of the largest monastic ruins in Europe.

Fountains Abbey was founded in 1132 by a group of monks who left a Benedictine abbey in York because the order was not strict enough for them. The buildings you see today were mostly constructed in the years from 1150 to 1250, though the North Tower, which looms up into the sky, is a 16th-century addition.

A visitor centre caters for the 300,000 people who visit the site each year. It incorporates an auditorium, a restaurant and kiosk and the largest National Trust shop in Britain. You can also see the restored monastic mill, and some rooms in Fountains Hall, the 17th-century home of the subsequent owners of the abbey.

The adjoining grounds of Studley Royal were created in the 18th century and then merged with Fountains Abbey in 1768. They were the work of John Aislabie, and his son, William. The landscaping took 14 years and another decade for the buildings. There are several paths around the gardens, through which the River Skell flows, and acquiring a map is probably a good idea as there is a great deal to see including temples and water cascades.

GRASSINGTON MAP REF 407 G5

Grassington may look as if it has always been a small, sleepy Dales town, but this is not the case. With the discovery of large lead deposits on the surrounding moors, it was a thriving industrial town from the 17th to the 19th centuries.

Modern Grassington is the major tourist centre in Upper Wharfedale, with guesthouses, shops and eating places radiating out from its cobbled square. It also has a National Park Centre, near the village centre, and the Upper Wharfedale Folk Museum, a tiny, enjoyable collection which explores the history of mining here.

Five miles (8km) southeast, off the B6160 road, is Appletreewick village, where the hillside Parcevall Hall Gardens, which were laid out from 1927, are planted with specimen trees and shrubs from western China and the Himalayas. The gardens have formal terraces, a glorious rose garden, rock garden, woodland walks, orchards, a 15th-century farmhouse and wonderful views of Wharfedale.

Six miles (9.6km) to the southeast of Grassington on the B6160, is Barden Tower, a medieval hunting lodge that was renovated and used by Lady Anne Clifford in the mid-17th century. Lady Anne was an admirable woman whose name you will encounter throughout the Yorkshire Dales. She built charitable institutions and renovated buildings, including Barden Tower. She also restored Brougham Castle at Penrith in Cumbria, where she died.

The Lady Anne Clifford Trail, which was established in 1990, commemorates the 400th anniversary of her birth in Skipton Castle, where the trail begins. This 100-mile (161km) long-distance path leads through the Yorkshire Dales and the Upper Eden Valley to Brougham Castle.

Visit
THE STRID

As the River Wharfe flows through the Bolton Abbey Estate, in one place it thunders through a narrow ravine just a few feet across – little more than a stride, or strid. If you feel a desire to jump across, bear in mind that several people have been killed doing just this, as they slipped on the rocks and fell into the fast-flowing river, which is up to 30 feet (9m) deep in places. One of the leaflets handed to visitors asks them to 'remember that anything that goes into the Strid rarely surfaces for several days'.

You have been warned!

Activity
ROLL OUT THE EGGS

Parents of young children might like to know that an earlier Easter Monday egg-rolling tradition was revived at Fountains Abbey in the 1980s, at the suggestion of an estate worker who recalled the tradition from his own childhood there. Hard-boiled eggs are thrown or rolled down a hill, a prize being given to the one that goes the furthest before finally disintegrating completely. In some areas, children would decorate their eggs and put them on display, before rolling them down the nearest slope and finally eating any eggs that remained edible.

Activity
TAKE THE HIGH ROAD

Drive south out of Hawes through Gayle, heading for Kettlewell, and you will cross Wether Fell and Fleet Moss Pass, reaching a height of 1,857 feet (566m). This is the highest road in the Yorkshire Dales, and one of the highest in all England.

Visit
THE NORBER BOULDERS

Follow the bridleway between Clapham and Austwick and you will see a signpost to the Norber Boulders. This scattering of boulders, each on its own little pedestal of rock, at first glance looks as if it ought to be of some human significance, but in fact is a natural occurrence. The boulders, also called the Norber Erratics, are several hundred million years old and were deposited in their present location by the actions of a glacier about 25,000 years ago during the last Ice Age. They are made of Silurian gritstone, the type of rock found in Crummack Dale about half a mile (0.8km) to the north.

HARDRAW MAP REF 407 G4

Hardraw is a hamlet that would probably be visited only by those passing through on the Pennine Way if it was not for the existence of Hardraw Force. At 96 feet (29m) it has the longest free drop of any waterfall in England – above ground, at least – and was painted by Turner on his travels through the Yorkshire Dales. Another unusual feature is that to reach it you must pass through the Green Dragon pub, paying a small entrance fee as you do so. The volume of water from the fall is not great, and it is therefore best visited after heavy rain. Those who do not mind a slight splashing can walk round behind the fall, although care must be taken on the wet rocks as they are slippery. In 1739 and 1881, the falls froze completely to produce an impressive 100ft (30.5m) icicle.

The Force falls into a pool in a natural amphitheatre, and the acoustics here are such that an annual brass band contest takes place every September, a tradition that goes back to 1885. Past winners include famous names such as the Black Dyke Mills Band and Besses o' the Barn. The contests once included choirs who stood on the ground above the Force and sang with the bands. This was not, however, a raging success because they could not actually hear each other. The contests died out but their revival is proving to be a great attraction once more.

HARROGATE MAP REF 407 H5

Although not within the Yorkshire Dales National Park, Harrogate is by far the largest town on their fringes, and a magnet for anyone with serious shopping – or just window-shopping – to be done. It is an attractive and lively place with theatres, cinemas and good restaurants, and a plethora of new hotels and conference centres created by the hospitality industry. Harrogate has plenty of history and charm, and the spa town that developed after the discovery of a mineral spring in 1571 is still plainly visible.

An important feature of Harrogate is its lush greenery, especially the wide swathes of grass and flower beds, known as the Stray, that sweeps right through the town. These 200 acres (81ha) are protected under an ancient law, which ensures that residents and visitors alike are entitled to enjoy these facilities. There are more pretty flowers as well as a boating pond, playground, crazy golf and plenty of other activities in the Valley Gardens, Harrogate's main park. Its entrance is close to the Royal Pump Room Museum.

Flower lovers will not want to miss a visit to the Royal Horticultural Society Garden at Harlow Carr on the outskirts of Harrogate off the B6162. This was the HQ of the Northern Horticultural Society (until its merger with the RHS in 2001) and is set in 68 impressive acres (28ha), a lovely mix of the formal and informal, with a gardening museum, plant and gift shops, and places for refreshments. Several courses, demonstrations and practical workshops are held in the Study Centre.

Harrogate's origins can be traced in the octagonal Royal Pump Room Museum, which was built in 1842 in order to enclose the old sulphur well on this site. In addition to serving up local history, the museum serves up cups of the pungent spa water that first made the town so famous. It claims to be the strongest sulphur water in Europe, so some visitors may prefer Perrier, or to refresh the palate with a visit to Betty's tea rooms, a real Yorkshire institution, which offers delicious cream cakes and Yorkshire fat rascals.

Not quite a Yorkshire institution is a visit to a Turkish baths. Harrogate is one of the few places where you can enjoy a Turkish bath in all its original 19th-century splendour at the Turkish Baths and Health Spa in the Royal Baths Assembly Rooms. Its Victorian exterior masks a beautifully renovated tiled interior, which includes a cold plunge bath, hot rooms, a steam room, massage room and a relaxing rest room for when the ordeal is over. There are both male and female sessions, so check first if you are thinking of going.

HAWES MAP REF 407 G4

Local family businesses make up the shops in the main street in Hawes, and it is certainly the place to stock up on good local produce, especially on the busy Tuesday market day when packed stalls line the streets and farmers conduct their business at the livestock market along the Leyburn road.

For a taste of Wensleydale cheese, and the chance to watch it being made, head for the Wensleydale Creamery. This factory has a flourishing visitor centre which includes a museum, video display, licensed restaurant, shop, free cheese-tasting and viewing platforms.

A more conventional museum is the fascinating Dales Countryside Museum, in the Station Yard. The arrival of a railway link in 1877 boosted Hawes' fortunes. The trains no longer run but Hawes is now well established as the main town of Upper Wensleydale. The museum (which also contains a Tourist Information Centre and a National Park Centre) has first-class displays on life in the Dales, particularly on small local industries such as knitting and peat-cutting. Its collection is enhanced by the inclusion of material donated by the local authors and historians, Marie Hartley and Joan Ingilby.

HUBBERHOLME MAP REF 407 G5

With its riverside setting, surrounded by trees in the valley floor, there are fewer more picturesque villages to be found than Hubberholme. It is not surprising, then, to discover that it was the favourite place of J B Priestley. This Bradford author, who wrote *The Good Companions* and many other books and stage plays, loved Hubberholme and visited it often. He drank in the village pub, and a plaque in the local church commemorates his great affection for the tiny village where he chose his ashes to be scattered.

The Church of St Michael and All Angels, one of the delights of the Dales, was originally a chapel in the Norman hunting forest of Langstrothdale Chase. A major attraction is its rood loft from 1558, which only survives thanks to Hubberholme's isolation. In 1571 an edict was issued in the York Diocese to destroy all rood lofts in the region, but Hubberholme's was one of only two in Yorkshire to escape destruction. Look also for the wooden mouse symbol of Robert Thompson, who made much of the church's more recent woodwork.

INGLEBOROUGH MAP REF 406 F5

There are several ways of approaching Ingleborough on foot, from Clapham, Ingleton, Horton in Ribblesdale and Chapel-le-Dale, and each is an energetic but rewarding climb to the top of the peak's 2,373ft (723m). Until accurate measurement of hills became possible, Ingleborough was long believed to be the highest point in Yorkshire. We now know that it is surpassed by both Whernside and Mickle Fell. At the top of Ingleborough is a wide plateau, with a triangulation point and a stone windbreak, and of course grand views. An Iron Age fort once stood here, and horse races have been run in more recent memory, with large bonfires still lit occasionally for special celebrations.

The path from Chapel-le-Dale is the shortest and the steepest approach, giving a daunting impression of the challenge to come as you look up at Ingleborough's heights. From Clapham the walk is about 4 miles (6.4km) one-way, passing Ingleborough Cave. Ingleborough's slopes have a lot of potholes, so you need to take care if you stray from the path.

South of the summit of Ingleborough you'll see the Gaping Gill pothole, though to describe it as a pothole is like calling Westminster Abbey a parish church. In fact you could probably fit the abbey inside Gaping Gill: some mathematician has certainly worked out that you can fit York Minster Cathedral inside the main cavern. This is about 120ft (37m) high and 500ft (152m) long, and the stream

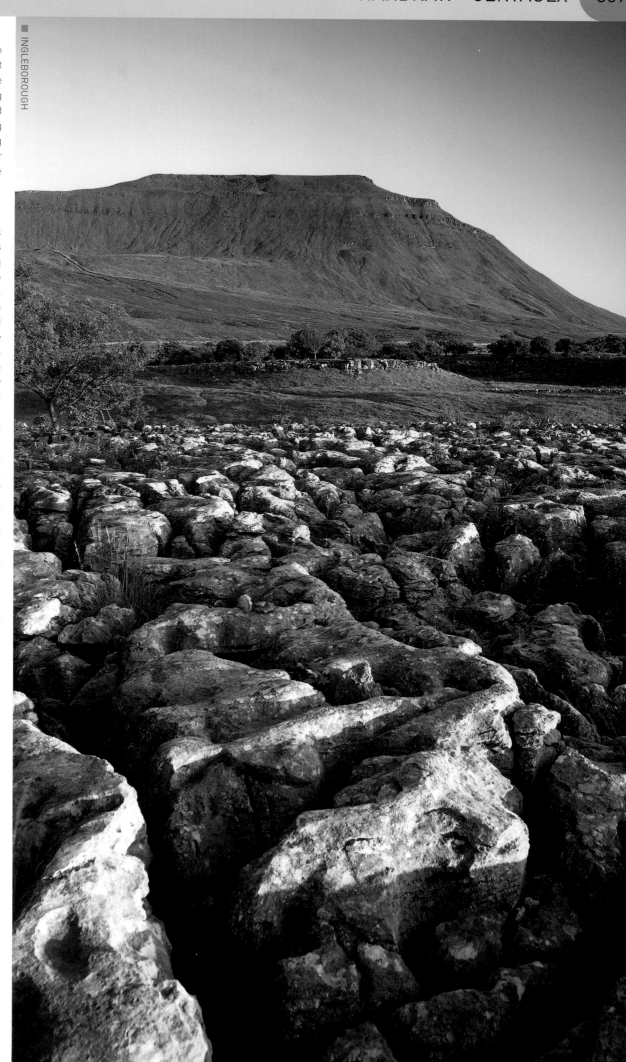

INGLEBOROUGH

of Fell Beck plunges down into it from the surface, making it one of the highest waterfalls in Britain at 364ft (111m). The breathtaking sight of the interior of Gaping Gill is normally reserved for experienced potholers, but twice a year, on spring and summer bank holidays, local caving clubs set up a winch and bosun's chair and allow members of the public to share the experience.

INGLETON MAP REF 406 F5

Ingleton has too much modern sprawl to be called a pretty village, but it has an attractive centre with steep winding streets going down to the gorge where its celebrated Waterfalls Walk starts. Before the arrival of the railway in the late 19th century, bringing the visitors and walkers who heralded much of the new development, Ingleton relied on its woollen and cotton spinning industries, and before that coal mining and stone quarrying. Now instead of mill-workers' cottages there are guesthouses, shops and several pubs, though the rock quarry is still one of the largest in the Dales.

The Church of St Mary the Virgin is in a dominating position, and has been rebuilt several times, though the 15th-century tower remains. Its oldest feature is a Norman font, which was rediscovered in 1830. It had been hidden in the river below during times of religious persecution. The church also has what is known as the 'Vinegar Bible', so-called because of a misprint in 1717 in what should have been the Parable of the Vineyards.

On the B6255 to the northeast of Ingleton is the White Scar Cave, the best show cave in the Dales. With rivers and waterfalls, there are exhilarating subterranean guided tours.

JERVAULX ABBEY MAP REF 407 H4

This superb Cistercian monastery, now mostly in ruins, is a truly evocative place, filled in summer with the scent of the glorious wild flowers that grow around the crumbling grey stones. The abbey was founded in 1156 and eventually owned much of Wensleydale. Sheep, cattle and horses were bred by the monks, who were the first to make Wensleydale cheese.

Despite the fact that the buildings are in a ruinous state there is still plenty to see, such as the staircase, which is known as the Night Stairs, which led from the monks' upstairs dormitory to night services in the church. Other abbey remains which can be identified include the cloister, the infirmary, and the kitchen as well as the parlour. Jervaulx is on private land but open access is allowed, with an honesty box for admission money. There is a car park, a tea room and souvenir shop.

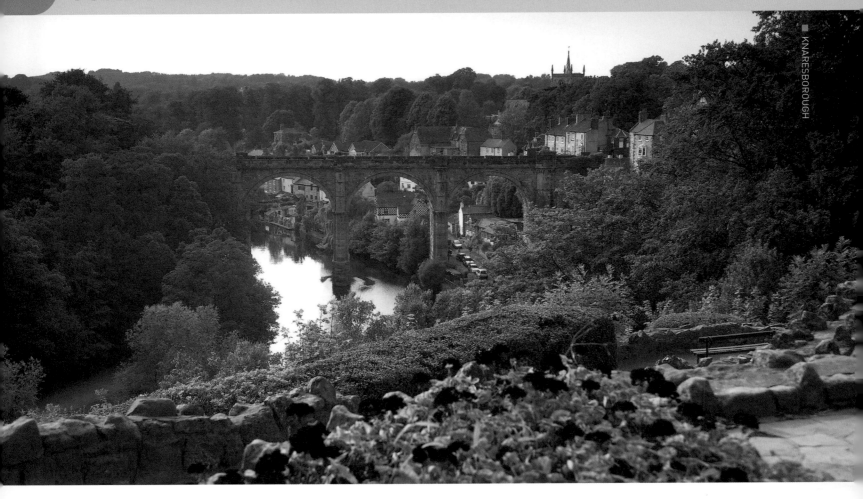

KIRKBY LONSDALE MAP REF 406 F5

This tiny market town stands just over the border in Cumbria and marks the far western limit of the Yorkshire Dales. It is a delightfully unspoilt place, whose charms have been recognized by artists and authors, from Constable and Turner to Ruskin and Wordsworth, all of whom have sung its praises over the years.

A Roman fort has been excavated at Burrow, just 2 miles (3.2km) south of the town, and in 1227 King Henry III granted a market charter which allowed for a weekly market and an annual fair. The fair died out in the 19th century, but the market still thrives every Thursday in Market Place. Here the lovely butter cross dates from the early 20th century.

The Church of St Mary the Virgin is a most impressive building. It is thought to date from the late 11th and early 12th centuries, and a Norman archway beneath the solid square tower is a beautiful construction. It has some fine stained glass and a carved pulpit. Outside, near the north entrance, is a tower which can be seen in J M W Turner's famous painting of 1822, *Kirkby Lonsdale Churchyard*, which serves as another reminder of the timeless nature of this attractive little town.

On the edge of town, the medieval Devil's Bridge spans the River Lune. It is one of the town's most notable features with three graceful arches striding over the water and is a very popular meeting place

for bikers. Its date is not certain, though records from the late 14th century tell of repairs to a bridge in the town. The bridge is now open for pedestrians only. A short way down the river is a piece of limestone, known as the Devil's Neck Collar, through which a hole has been worn by the action of the water.

KNARESBOROUGH MAP REF 407 H5

Knaresborough is considered to be one of the most picturesque market towns in the Dales, much of it perched on ridges of rock rising above the River Nidd, on which rowing boats are usually bobbing about. A viaduct crosses high above the river, while old houses peek through the trees on one side, looking across at the parkland and woods that conceal Mother Shipton's Cave on the opposite bank.

In the time of Mother Shipton, the Yorkshire prophetess, this land was a large hunting forest, and Knaresborough must have looked even more beautiful. Mother Shipton, said to have been born in the cave in 1488, gained a reputation as a prophet. It is claimed that she foretold the attempted invasion and subsequent defeat of the Spanish Armada in 1588, and predicted the devastating Great Fire of London in 1666. You can visit the cave as part of a self-guided audio tour, along with the Petrifying Well – in which minerals in the water turn any object placed inside it to stone – and a small museum.

The town's official museum is up in the Old Courthouse in the grounds of Knaresborough Castle. It houses local items and a gallery devoted to the Civil War in Knaresborough, but is enjoyable not least because Knaresborough seems to have had more than its fair share of rather odd characters over the years, and their doings are well chronicled.

In addition to Mother Shipton there was Robert Flower, who lived in a cave on the riverside and was known locally as St Robert because of his alleged powers as a healer; Eugene Aram, a schoolmaster who murdered a shoemaker in St Robert's cave and escaped justice for 13 years; and John Metcalfe, who went blind at the age of six, but later went on to enjoy various careers including, quantity surveyor, road building pioneer, accomplished violinist and part-time smuggler!

These days, Knaresborough Castle is much reduced, but it has also seen its fair share of characters over the years. The murderers of Thomas á Becket sought refuge here for a time, and royal visitors included Edward III, King John and Richard II, who was imprisoned here in 1399. The dungeon remains just as it was. There are knowledgeable guides on hand to answer questions, and regular tours of the sallyport (a secret access to the moat). With a small park around the remains, this is a popular spot to sit and enjoy the lovely views over the river.

At the market place, as well as a bustling Wednesday market, you will find the oldest chemist's shop, or apothecary, in Britain, thought to have been here since the 13th century, but trading continuously since 1720. The market is first mentioned in 1206, but is known to have been held each and every Wednesday since 1310, the day fixed by Edward II's charter.

The Church of St John contains some Norman remains, and a Tudor font with a lockable cover to prevent witches stealing the holy water. By the church, a street named Water Bag Bank drops steeply down to the river. The name arose because the town's water supply was once brought up here on horseback in leather bags.

MALHAM MAP REF 407 G5

Malham is a magnet for visitors to the Dales. Malham Cove is one of Britain's most impressive natural features and consequently the area has become almost too popular for its own good. At busy times the National Park Centre car park overflows and the roadside verges disappear under the wheels of parked cars. There are a number of cafés, pubs, outdoor shops and guesthouses to accommodate the crowds.

The half-mile (800m) walk to Malham Cove is signed from the village centre. The limestone rock face seems to tumble down the 250ft (76m) cliffs, and extends for about 1,000ft (305m). Try to picture the water that once flowed over the cliff face, helping create what has been aptly described as a 'dry waterfall'. This natural amphitheatre is simply the most visible part of the Craven Fault. It is a steep climb up man-made steps to the top, but your reward is a view over the moors around Malham, north to Malham Tarn and over the limestone pavements. It is in these pavements that some of the area's wide variety of unusual plants can be found.

Malham Tarn, north of the village, is in the care of the National Trust and the Field Studies Council. It is 1,229ft (374m) above sea level, and the tarn and surrounding area have been declared a Site of Special Scientific Interest. A track leads down past Tarn House, where the Field Studies Council run regular courses on the natural history of the area. It is a particularly important area for plant life and as a breeding ground for many birds: a hide is open to the public to enable views of parts of the lake that can't be accessed on foot. Tarn House was also the home of Walter Morrison whose visitors included Charles Darwin, John Ruskin and Charles Kingsley, author of *The Water Babies*.

PATELEY BRIDGE MAP REF 407 H5

The main attraction at Pateley Bridge is the Nidderdale Museum, but the town is also a good base for visiting nearby places of interest. Many of the buildings date from the 18th and 19th centuries though as they are built with gritstone the town can appear to be a rather dour place in gloomy autumnal weather.

There is nothing dour, though, about the award-winning Nidderdale Museum, housed in the town's former workhouse. Founded in 1975, it grew from just a very small collection to one which today provides all the information you need about life in Nidderdale, from the spread of religion and the development of transport to collections of cameras and razors that have been owned by local people. Some of the most enjoyable exhibits are the reconstructed shops and offices. All have fascinating memorabilia, and the museum is much loved and well looked after.

To the north of Pateley Bridge, near Lofthouse, is How Stean Gorge, also known as Yorkshire's 'Little Switzerland'. The ravine of up to 80ft (24m) deep was hacked out in the Ice Age. Pathways lead by the

HOW STEAN GORGE

fast-flowing river through ferns and by lush, dank undergrowth; there are bridges on different levels and fenced galleries on rocky ledges. There are also a few caves, the best known being Tom Taylor's Cave, with a 530ft (162m) walk underground (take a torch).

PEN-Y-GHENT MAP REF 407 G5

The lowest of this region's Three Peaks, Pen-y-ghent in profile looks like a face, thrusting its jaw out defiantly as if challenging anyone to climb to the top of its 2,277ft (694m). In its capacity as the third highest of the Three Peaks, many people assume it is the third highest peak in the Yorkshire Dales. This honour, in fact, goes to Buckden Pike.

Unusually, for this most distinctive of Yorkshire's hills, Pen-y-ghent carries a Celtic name, meaning 'hill of the border', once marking the edge of one of the English tribes' kingdoms. For those who want to tackle its challenge, the most common route is a 3-mile (4.8km) hike from Horton in Ribblesdale, following the signs for the Pennine Way, which passes right over the top of the hill.

At the end of the track out of Horton, just beyond the point where the route turns sharp right towards the hill, there are two potholes. The larger is the huge gaping hole known as Hull Pot, into which Hull Pot Beck disappears. Treat these potholes with extreme caution.

The climb up to the summit of Pen-y-ghent is steep in places, with a little bit of scrambling. At the top, walkers can revel in views across to the other peaks, north across the fells of Langstrothdale Chase, and south over Ribblesdale and Lancashire's Forest of Bowland.

RICHMOND MAP REF 407 H4

To approach Richmond from Swaledale is to see the importance of the town to the dale. The road winds through lovely wooded valleys, eventually revealing Richmond Castle standing high on its hill above the river. The castle, now cared for by English Heritage, dates from the Norman period and inside is Scolland's Hall, which dates from the 11th century and claims to be the oldest hall in England. The panoramic views down the river and over the surrounding area are splendid.

Behind the castle is Richmond's huge cobbled Market Place, with its Market Cross and the unusual sight of Holy Trinity Church: unusual because there are shops and a museum built into the base of the building, which was almost destroyed several times and then later restored, since its construction in around 1150. The curfew bell sounds from the church's clock tower, at 8am and 8pm every day.

The museum in the church is that of the Green Howards, one of Yorkshire's proudest regiments. Inside are smart modern displays, but this is actually only one of three museums in Richmond. The Richmondshire Museum itself is a typical collection of historical items.

Richmond's best museum, however, is the Georgian Theatre Museum. The theatre, built late in the 18th century, is the only one in the world that still survives in its original state. As well as attending a show in the evenings, visitors should take one of the guided tours to have a glimpse behind the stage, into the dressing rooms and inside the original box office. Volunteer guides make the place come alive.

A mile (1.6km) southeast of the town centre, via a walk along the banks of the Swale, is Easby Abbey (English Heritage). The ruins of this medieval monastery are impressive. They certainly make a fitting destination for a pleasant walk, though, where Swaledale comes to an end.

RIPON MAP REF 407 H5

In AD 672 St Wilfrid built a church on the site of what is now Ripon Cathedral, and the crypt of that church can still be visited, making it the oldest complete Saxon crypt in any English cathedral. The west front of this cathedral dates from 1220, the east front from 1290, and inside there are 500-year-old woodcarvings, a 16th-century nave and some exceptional stained glass work. A building not to be missed.

Close by, in St Mary's Gate, visitors move from God to the godless, in the Ripon Prison and Police Museum. Housed in the cell block of what was first the Ripon Liberty Prison and later its Police Station, the museum tells the vivid story of Yorkshire law and disorder. It has some chilling but never gruesome displays. It's one of a series of sites making up the Yorkshire Law and Order Museums. The city's Law and Order Trail will also take you to the Old Workhouse Museum and the Courthouse Museum.

All around Ripon attractions vie for attention. The Lightwater Valley Theme Park, with its enormous rollercoasters and other rides, is high on the list for families. There are lots of eating places and gift shops, and the Lightwater Village, with factory, fashion and food shops.

Just 2 miles (3.2km) east of Lightwater Valley is Norton Conyers, a lovely country house which dates back to the mid-14th century. Visitors will hear the legend of the Mad Woman, a story also heard by Charlotte Brontë when she visited the house in 1839. The character possibly inspired the mad Mrs Rochester in *Jane Eyre*, written eight years later, but there are other claimants to this honour.

FROM ADDINGHAM TO ILKLEY

This walk takes you from the extended village of Addingham, which grew as the textile trades expanded, through rolling country and along a stretch of the lovely River Wharfe to the spa town of Ilkley. During the reign of Queen Victoria, the great and the good came to Ilkley to take the medicinal waters.

DISTANCE/TIME 5.5 miles (8.8km) 2h30 **MAP** OS Explorer 297 Lower Wharfedale **START** Lay-by at eastern end of Addingham, on bend where North Street becomes Bark Lane by information panel; grid ref: SE 083498 **PATHS** Riverside path and field paths, some road walking; 7 stiles **THE PUB** The Fleece Inn, Addingham. Tel: 01943 830491

1 Walk 50yds (46m) up the road, and take stone steps down to the right, (signed 'Dales Way'). Bear immediately right again, and cross the River Wharfe on a suspension bridge. Follow a metalled path along a field edge. Turn over a stream at the end and follow a farm track left to emerge on the bend of a minor road. Go right here; after about 0.5 mile (800m) you reach Nesfield.

2 About 100yds (91m) beyond the last house, and immediately after the road crosses a stream, bear left up a stony track (signed 'High Austby'). Immediately take a stile between two gates. Cross to a gate in the far-right corner. There is no obvious path, but follow the right-hand boundary, heading towards Low Austby Farm. Approaching the buildings, waymarks indicate the path dog-legging left and right outside the boundary wall, passing under an oak towards a wood.

3 Cross a footbridge over a stream; beyond a stile you enter woodland. Follow a path downhill, leaving the wood by another step stile. Bear right across the slope of a field to a stile at the far end, to enter more woodland. Follow an obvious path through the trees, before reaching a road via a wall stile. Go right, downhill, to reach a road junction. Go

right again, crossing Nesfield Road, and take a path to the left of an electricity sub-station. You have a few minutes of riverside walking before you reach Ilkley's old stone bridge.

4 Cross the bridge and turn right, on to a riverside path. At its end, keep ahead along a drive to Ilkley Tennis Club. Beside the clubhouse, bear off left through a kissing gate and follow an obvious path across a succession of pastures, which eventually returns you to the River Wharfe. Cross a stream on a footbridge, and enter woodland. Cross another stream to meet a stony path. Go right, downhill to the river. Through a kissing gate, walk the length of a riverside meadow before joining the old A65 road.

5 Follow the road by the riverside. After almost 0.5 mile (800m), go right, just before a row of terraced houses, on to Old Lane. Carry on between the houses to a riverside path at the far side. Once you have passed the Rectory on the left, and the Old Rectory on your right, look for a gate on the right. Take steps and follow the path to a tiny arched bridge. Swing left across a pasture, in front of the church. Cross a drive to an arched bridge, walking out between stone cottages onto North Street in Addingham.

WALK 110

RIVER & WOODLAND AT BOLTON ABBEY

This walk takes you over moorland and alongside the Strid to the romantic Bolton Abbey. The route also passes through woodland where information boards explain the birds and plants, including sessile oak. Characteristic of the area, sessile oak is distinguished from the pedunculate oak by its acorns that have no stalks.

DISTANCE/TIME 6.75 miles (10.9km) 2h **MAP** OS Explorer OL2 Yorkshire Dales – Southern & Western **START** Main pay car park in Bolton Abbey village; grid ref: SE 071539. **PATHS** Field and moorland paths, then riverside tracks, 3 stiles **THE PUB** Devonshire Arms Hotel (Brasserie), Bolton Abbey. Tel: 01756 710441; www.thedevonshirearms.co.uk

1 Leave the car park at its north end, by the Village Store. Turn right and walk to the B6160. Turn left and follow the road under an archway. Opposite the battlemented Bolton Hall, turn left on a signed track. At the top of the track, go through a gate on the right with a bridleway sign. Walk under a power line to a signpost. Go past two pools to a gate, then bear right to another gate into woodland.

2 Follow the rising track through the wood, with several signs, to another gate. Follow blue waymarks, most painted on rocks, across fields. At a crest bear left to a gate in a corner, then turn left along the wall. The path climbs more steeply onto Hare Head, which has wide views. Descend gently to a gate, and 20yds (18m) beyond, take a path downhill, trending right lower down, to a signpost.

3 Turn right on a path, parallel to the road, to another signpost 'FP to B6160'. Follow the track to a stile, then take the left fork, going roughly level across the moor, to a wall corner. Continue to the next wall, then turn right along it, following an improving track to a signpost.

4 Turn left over a stile and follow the wall down to the road. Turn right for a few paces then enter the car park. Pass beside the Strid Wood Visitor Centre and follow tracks, signed 'The Strid', down to reach the river close to its narrowest part of The Strid.

5 Follow wide tracks downstream until you reach an information board and gateway near the Cavendish Pavilion. Bear left by the café and cross the footbridge.

6 Immediately after the bridge turn right, signed 'Bolton Abbey'. The path briefly joins a vehicle track to cross a side-stream then bears right. When the path forks, take either branch (the higher has better views of the priory). Descend to a bridge beside stepping-stones near the priory.

7 Cross the bridge and walk straight on. Climb steps to a gateway – the Hole in the Wall. Go through to the road, left a few paces, then right to the car park.

WALK 111

A CIRCULAR WALK TAKING IN MALHAM COVE

The noble Malham Cove is the majestic highlight of this limestone Dales walk. As you begin the walk, the stream from Malham Tarn suddenly disappears in a tumble of rocks. This is the aptly named Water Sinks. The now-dry valley of Watlowes, just beyond Water Sinks, was formed by water action. It was this stream in fact that produced Malham Cove, and once fell over its spectacular cliff in a waterfall 230ft (70m) high. It is 200 years since water reached the cove.

DISTANCE/TIME 6.25 miles (10.1km) 3h **MAP** OS Explorer OL2 Yorkshire Dales – Southern & Western **START** At Water Sinks, Malham Tarn, near gateway across road; grid ref: SD 894658 **PATHS** Well-marked field and moorland paths. More than 400 steps in descent from Malham Cove; 5 stiles **THE PUB** The Buck Inn, Malham. Tel: 01729 830317; www.buckinnmalham.co.uk

1 From your car parking space, walk through a gate, then turn left through a kissing gate at a Malham Cove sign. Keep left at the next signpost, following the Pennine Way down a dry valley until the path bends sharp right, overlooking another dry valley.

2 Turn left, cross a stile and descend steeply into the lower valley. Walk down the level valley to a stile at its end. Just beyond is a limestone pavement at the top of Malham Cove. Turn right and walk along the pavement. Take care here, both of the sheer drop down to the left and the gaps in the limestone pavement (known as grikes). Turn left to descend beside a stone wall; go through a gate, then descend more than 400 steps to the foot of Malham Cove.

3 At the bottom, fork left to visit the base of the cliff, then follow an obvious track beside the river. On reaching a road, turn left and follow it into Malham village centre. Turn left to cross the bridge.

4 Turn immediately right on a track past houses then continue along a gravelled path. Follow it left at a sign to Janet's Foss.

Eventually the footpath enters woodland, then climbs beside a waterfall (Janet's Foss) to a kissing gate. Turn right along the road, towards Gordale Scar.

5 At Gordale Bridge (two bridges), go through a gate to the left. (To visit Gordale Scar, continue ahead here. Take the signed gate to the left and follow the path through a field into a gorge. Continue to the waterfall and then follow the same route back to the bridge.) On the main route, follow a signed public footpath uphill through three gates. Climb alongside the lane before emerging on to it.

6 Turn right and follow the lane uphill for 600yds (546m), to a ladder stile on the left. Follow the track to a footpath fingerpost.

7 Bear left and walk over broad open moor before descending to some small pools. Turn right at the sign for Malham Tarn, go over a ladder stile, then take the left-hand path to reach the start again.

WALK 112

A CIRCUIT FROM LOFTHOUSE

This is a pleasant walk from Lofthouse to Ramsgill and Middlesmoor in the valley of the River Nidd, across the rich farmland and moorland landscape. Nidderdale is a designated Area of Outstanding Natural Beauty.

DISTANCE/TIME 7 miles (11.3km) 3h **MAP** OS Explorer OL30 Yorkshire Dales – Northern & Central **START** Car park by Memorial Hall in Lofthouse; grid ref: SE 101734 **PATHS** Mostly field paths and tracks, may be muddy; 18 stiles **THE PUB** Crown Hotel, Middlesmoor. Tel: 01423 755204

1 Walk down past the Crown Hotel. At the main road turn left. Just beyond a track to High Lofthouse farm go right, through a stile. Follow a track bending left to a waymarked stile, then bear left to another. Continue down to a slightly raised track (the old railway) and bear left to rejoin the road.

2 Cross the road and go through a gate, signed Bouthwaite. Bear left off the track to a stile and ascend a grassy ramp. Bear left to climb more steeply, then right towards a plantation. Follow a path just below the plantation. Pass a house then join a track and follow it past a gate and Nidderdale Way sign to a fork. Bear left, still parallel to the plantation, then turn right over a stile. Descend left of a farmhouse, then bear left to a ladder stile. Continue, with the wall right, down into a valley. Ignore a stile (right) and go through a waymarked gate, over a bridge, through a gate and ahead. Bear right past a house down a gravelled track to a lane.

3 Turn right to a T-junction. Turn left, over the bridge. Turn right by the green, then right again, signed 'Stean'. Follow the track until it bends left up to Grindstone Hill House.

4 Go over four stiles. At West House Farm go over a stile between the farm and a bungalow, cross the farm road, follow waymarked posts

(Nidderdale Way) and continue along a track, eventually descending to a signpost near a barn. Follow the obvious track into a valley and over a bridge.

5 At a T-junction of tracks, turn left. Follow the walled track uphill, bending right. As the main track bends left to Moor House, keep along a grassy track. Another track joins from the left. Just beyond this, after crossing a stream, turn right. Bend left by a farm and follow the track over a ford into Stean.

6 Follow the lane right, then take a stile on the left signed 'Middlesmoor'. Descend into How Stean Gorge, down steps, over a bridge and up steps, then follow signs to the road. Turn left into Middlesmoor. Turn right beside the Wesleyan chapel to the gateway of the parish church.

7 Turn right before the gate, through a stile signed 'Lofthouse'. Follow the path to Halfway House farm. Go through the farmyard to a gate and follow the right side of two fields then bear left across the third to a gate in the corner. In the lay-by go left through a gate, then along the path beside the cricket ground. Cross the lane and go over a bridge, then bear right to emerge near the Market Cross in Lofthouse. Turn left to return to the car park.

DISTANCE/TIME 8 miles (12.9km) 2h **MAP** OS Explorer 289 Leeds **START** Sicklinghall Road, Wetherby; grid ref: SE 397483 **TRACKS** Well-compacted gravel railway trackbed lanes and smooth bridleways **THE PUB** The Castle, Spofforth. Tel: 01937 590200

DISTANCE/TIME 9.75 miles (15.7km) 1h30; extension 12.5 miles (20.1km) 2h **MAP** OS Explorer OL30 Yorkshire Dales – Northern & Central **START** Small car park on A684, Aysgarth; grid ref: SD 995889 **TRACKS** Grassy tracks; short rough sections. Return can be muddy **THE PUB** The Wheatsheaf Hotel, Carperby. Tel: 01969 663216; www.wheatsheafinwensleydale.co.uk

THE HARLAND WAY

The meandering Harland Way forms the basis of a delightful rural ride following in the tracks of the old steam trains and visiting one of Yorkshire's most fascinating Norman castles situated at Spofforth. Lying among the peaceful pastures of the Crimple Valley, Spofforth is an idyllic backwater for a Sunday afternoon ride.

1 With your back to the car park entrance, turn right along the railway trackbed, highlighted by a Harland Way fingerpost. The old line has been exploded through the bedrock to reveal limestone crags, and is now hung with lovely woodland that offers plenty of welcome shade on hot sunny summer days.

2 Take the left fork at the road junction that used to be known as the Wetherby Triangle. You are soon joined from the right by another branch of the line and then together the routes head west towards Spofforth. Half-way along the track you have to dismount to get through a metal gateway and almost immediately again at another gate. The trackbed forges ahead through an avenue of beech, hawthorn, ash and rowan before coming out into the open. Now you'll see thickets of wild roses and bramble, with scabious and purple vetch among the numerous wild flowers of the verges. Here there are wide views across cornfields, and soon the tower of Spofforth church comes into view ahead.

3 The Harland Way ends beyond a gate just short of the village. Take a gravel path which veers right across a green on to East Park Road. This threads through some modern housing to come to the main road where you should turn right. If you have young children it might be better to dismount here to cross over the road, and use the pavements to get to The Castle inn.

4 Just beyond the pub, where the road bends to the right, take the lane on the left, leading to the castle. When you've explored the 14th- and 15th-century remains of Spofforth Castle retrace your route past the pub then turn right along Park Road. Beyond the houses this becomes a stony bridleway, which rises gently across the fields.

5 Ignore all turn-offs until you come to Fox Heads Farm. Turn left along the track here, passing left of the farmhouse. The dirt and stone track descends to a bridge over a stream, then climbs again past an old quarry. Though there are a few climbs the track is still quite easy, being smooth-surfaced and reasonably well drained. Often it's lined with bramble, ferns and foxgloves, and the odd tree. Just beyond the summit of a hill the track bends to the right. After being joined from the right by a second farm track it comes to the road, just to the west of Sicklinghall village.

6 Turn left along the road into the village. On the right there's a pond with lilies and coots, then on the left there's another pub, the Scott Arms. The winding road makes a long but gradual descent towards Wetherby, passing the upmarket Linton Springs Hotel on your right. Beyond the hotel, ignore the right turn 'to Linton'. After passing through some housing in the Wetherby suburbs watch out for the blue cyclists' sign. This marks the access road back to the car park.

GREEN WAYS OF WENSLEYDALE

This route follows a magical green ribbon of a bridleway along a broad terrace high above the valley. You start in Aysgarth, best known for the Aysgarth Falls and can stop and visit Castle Bolton.

1 Cross the footbridge and follow a tarmac path out to a wider lane. Bear right, up to a road and turn right. After 2 miles (3.2km) Carperby is a left turn signed for Castle Bolton. Pass under the corner of one of the castle towers and at the top turn left.

2 Where the lane swings up into the car park, go ahead through a gate and along a track. Follow this through several gates and go to the left of some farm sheds. After going through the next gate, the track winds left through another gate and then right again. The track beyond is distinctly rougher; dismount and walk here.

3 At the next gate bear left above the wall. After some lawn-like grass, dip to a ford to more grassy going. At the next gate bear half left on to a smooth green track, following signposts to Askrigg and Carperby. After 0.5 mile (800m) you will reach Low Gate.

4 At Low Gate go up the hill on a green track, signed for Askrigg. Level out and descend to a gate where Peatmoor Lane crosses. Follow the green track ahead, across a level grassy plateau, until it descends to Oxclose Gate. From here the track skirts left of conspicuous bare ground and the spoil heaps on the site of a former lead mine.

5 Opposite this area the track has a gritty surface, and descends to a gate, with a ford beyond. Dismount and wheel the bikes across this ford and beware of the drop just below. Follow the stony track through another gate. Go up to another gate, swing left through it and down 50yds (46m) to a signpost.

6 For the shorter of the two loops, descend the steep track to Woodhall. The surface is loose in places, and inexperienced riders should dismount and walk down. Turn left on the wider road for an easy run, back to the start. For the extension, turn right and then climb the steep track. After two gates the gradient eases. Go through a gate alongside a small plantation. Beyond is the final climb, very tricky in places with bare rock and large loose stones. Over the top there's smooth grass, then a final section of rutted track leads to a gate by a barn. The track beyond soon descends, getting steeper and rougher. At a junction turn sharp left, almost immediately meeting tarmac. Follow the steep lane, down into the hamlet of Nappa Scar and turn left on to the wider road.

FROM ARNCLIFFE TO KETTLEWELL

You'll need good boots for this walk through rocky hillside, moorland and meadows from Arncliffe to Kettlewell, returning alongside the River Skirfare. Arncliffe sits on a spit of gravel above the river's floodplain. Before the bridge was built, a ford allowed travellers an easy crossing for the many ancient tracks that meet here.

DISTANCE/TIME 6.5 miles (10.4km) 3h30 **MAP** OS Explorer OL30 Yorkshire Dales – Northern & Central **START** Arncliffe, near church; grid ref: SD 932719. **PATHS** Mostly clear, some rocky sections. May be muddy; 16 stiles **THE PUB** Blue Bell Inn, Kettlewell. Tel: 01756 760230

1 From the car park, cross the bridge and turn immediately right, over a gated stile. Walk parallel with the river, cross the road via two stiles, then bear right and follow the footpath uphill over a stile and through a gate. Continue up in the same direction through the woods of Park Scar, with one short zig-zag near the top, to a stile.

2 Bear right and follow the footpath to another stile. Keep on the same heading to pass a signpost, a tumbled wall and then another signpost. The path bears left, crosses a line of shakeholes and continues via a stile to another stile on the ridge.

3 Descend on the same heading. The path passes more shakeholes and descends beside a wall to a ladder stile. Follow the path down, descending steeply to a signpost. Cross a track and reach another signpost above a limestone scar overlooking Kettlewell. Descend a narrow cleft (The Slit), then descend to a track. Turn right and walk to the road.

4 Turn right for 300yds (273m), then go right through a gate by a fingerpost, bearing right again at another sign. Climb through woodland, go through a gate, then bear right

and up to a small ruin. Continue along the edge of trees and round to a gateway beside a stile. Bear left to reach another stile then ascend the grassy path, keeping right where it forks, along a broad shelf. Eventually reach another stile and begin to descend, bending right by a cairn.

5 At a track junction continue ahead, with a wall on your left. The track leads down into Hawkswick village. On the outskirts go left, curve right between buildings and descend to the lane.

6 Cross the bridge and follow the lane round right. Just before farm buildings on the left, turn right towards a footbridge; turn left before it at the 'Arncliffe' sign. Follow the river to a footbridge over a side-stream and continue to a double gate. The path bears slightly away from the river to a gate. Cross the field beyond, skirting a steep bank above the river, to another footbridge.

7 Walk past a barn and through a gate, then bear left to a squeeze stile and cross a track. From the next stile bear slightly right to rejoin the river. Follow the path, with plentiful waymarks and signs, to emerge by the churchyard and return to the start.

WALK 114

ALONG LANGSTROTHDALE FROM HUBBERHOLME

This lovely walk takes you from J B Priestly's favourite Dales village, along Langstrothdale and back via a limestone terrace. The popular literary figure enjoyed supping the local ale at the George, in Hubberholme, and the churchyard there is the resting place for his ashes. The church itself has a wonderful wooden rood loft and the pews bear the 'mouse' trademark of craftsman Robert Thompson.

DISTANCE/TIME 5.25 miles (8.4km) 2h **MAP** OS Explorer OL30 Yorkshire Dales – Northern & Central **START** Beside river in Hubberholme, opposite church (not church parking; grid ref: SD 927782. **PATHS** Field paths and tracks. Steep after Yockenthwaite; 11 stiles **THE PUB** The George Inn, Hubberholme. Tel: 01756 760223; www.thegeorge-inn.co.uk

1 Enter the farmyard beside the church and then turn left immediately through a Dales Way signed gate. Take the lower path, signed 'Yockenthwaite', alongside the churchyard. Walk beside the river for 1.25 miles (2km); the clear Dales Way path is never far from the river. Approaching Yockenthwaite, go up steps to a little gate and left to a gate and signpost.

2 Follow the track towards a bridge but, before it, go sharp right up a farm track, which swings back to the left to a sign to Cray and Hubberholme.

3 Go up to find another signpost and then follow the obvious track slanting right and up. Part-way up the hill, go right at a footpath sign through a gate.

4 Follow the near-level path to a signpost, then bear left and up a rough section to another signpost. Turn right and follow the obvious path, descending very gently along a beautiful natural terrace until the path goes left and up to enter a wood by a footbridge over a miniature gorge.

5 Walk through the wood then continue, level again, to a small side valley above a house. A signpost above the house points towards the Cray. Go up slightly, over the rocks, then along another green terrace path for 1 mile (1.6km) to reach a footbridge. Cross, then ascend slightly to a barn; bear right to a gate then follow a marked path across meadow land. Pass a house to a junction of tracks on the edge of Cray.

6 Go sharp right, down to a footpath sign to Stubbing Bridge. Descend between walls and through a gate and on to the grassy hillside. Pass another footpath sign and continue downhill to meet a stream.

7 Follow the streamside path past waterfalls and pools, crossing a bridge over a side-stream. Cross a stile and continue past a barn to reach the road. Turn right to return to your parking place in Hubberholme.

Tea Room Traditions

One of the great British pleasures, one that few other nations quite understand and even fewer adequately replicate, is the ritual of taking tea. The popularity of a 'cuppa' was a strong economic incentive throughout Britain, and prompted the evolution of often quaint and intimate salons everywhere – the National Trust alone boasts tea rooms at almost 200 of its sites, and few public attractions these days survive without the almost obligatory tea room.

Yet tea, that most vital of English beverages, is a latecomer to Britain. The custom of drinking tea originated in China 5,000 years ago, and it was not until the mid-17th century that the beverage first appeared in England.

A tea room is a form of café or tea house peculiar to Britain, but these days also present in other Commonwealth countries. They tend to be small establishments, sometimes occurring in the most improbable places to serve visitor needs, but in their heyday tea rooms played a widespread and significant role in British social life.

With an observance bordering on ritual, tea rooms provide a delightful core service, offering customers cream tea, or Devonshire tea, in some cases served from silver teapots and poured into china cups, and a scone with jam and clotted cream. However, this pleasant experience is far more widely available these days than Devonshire clotted cream might suggest – you can even get Devonshire Teas in Australia, presumably a touch of nostalgia for many expats living there. In Scotland, teas are usually served with a variety of scones, pancakes, crumpets and other cakes. And almost every part of Britain serves its own regional specialities – Yorkshire parkin, Lancashire Eccles and Chorley cakes, the ubiquitous carrot cake and muffins, Bakewell puddings (they don't call them 'tarts'), Banbury cakes, Dundee cake – there are just so many of them.

In the 18th century, tea was expensive and heavily taxed, a luxury only the well-to-do could afford, and the rich were not for sharing the pleasure. Doubts arose about the suitability of tea for 'persons of an inferior rank', but the increasing concern within the Temperance movement over the habitual drunkenness of the working classes led to the promotion of tea as an alternative. From the 1830s, many new cafés and coffee houses opened up as a temperance alternative to pubs and inns.

The tea room itself was developed towards the end of the 19th century, when Catherine Cranston opened the first of what became a chain of Miss Cranston's Tea Rooms in Glasgow, providing elegant, well-designed social venues that enabled well-to-do and unchaperoned women to socialize without male company. They were an instant success. The 'birth' of the seemingly very English tradition of the tea room in Glasgow may surprise people, but Miss Cranston was keen to engage a new breed of talented designers, and became a patron of the distinctly unique Charles Rennie Mackintosh, who designed the complete building of The Willow Tearooms in Glasgow, contrasting a strikingly modern exterior with intriguing interior designs.

From the 1880s, fine hotels began to offer tea service in tea rooms and tea courts, and by 1910 they had begun to host afternoon tea dances as the dance craze swept the country. By the 1950s, tea rooms of all kinds were widespread in Britain, but in the years to come, cafés became more fashionable, and tea rooms, as such, less common, though the distinction is often blurred. Country tea rooms offering cream teas, such as are found throughout Yorkshire especially, are a hearty tourist attraction in many areas, and many book publishers produce books of 'Tea Shop Walks' so that walkers can conclude their day out in a time-honoured British manner.

Because tea was highly valued, it was kept by the lady of the house and not entrusted to the care of the housekeeper, and it was also always the lady of the house who would serve the tea. But eventually, the beverage became generally affordable and the growing middle class imitated the affluent and privileged and found that the meal 'tea' was an economical way of entertaining friends. Thus afternoon tea quickly became the norm in many households.

Traditionally, 'afternoon tea' is a light meal taken around four o'clock, and although few these days actually take afternoon tea, as such, it is still available in high quality hotels, and follows a long-established template: loose tea is to be served in a previously warmed teapot, with milk and sugar to be added according to taste. This is accompanied by various sandwiches (customarily cucumber, egg and cress, fish paste, ham or smoked salmon), scones (with butter, clotted cream and jam), and often with cakes and pastries (such as Battenberg or Victoria sponge), usually served on a tiered stand.

TOP LEFT The Bakewell Pudding Shop, in the Peak District National Park, Derbyshire. Here you can buy cakes, preserves and Bakewell puddings – also erroneously called Bakewell 'tarts' in other parts of England.

BELOW LEFT Traditional scones - best served warm with strawberry jam and clotted cream, accompanied by a refreshing cup of tea.

BELOW Light, fluffy Victoria sponge layered with strawberries and cream often appears on afternoon tea menus.

OPPOSITE Silver cutlery, delicate bone china crockery and opulent surroundings create the perfect setting for this most English of traditions.

The story is probably apocryphal, but afternoon tea is said to have originated with the 7th Duchess of Bedford, who in the early 1800s hit on the idea of having tea in the late afternoon to bridge the gap between luncheon and dinner, which in such lofty social circles would not be served until well into the evening.

'High tea' is an early evening meal, taken usually between five and six o'clock as a substitute for both afternoon tea and the main evening meal. The actual term 'high tea' comes from the meal being eaten at the 'high' or table of the house. High tea would typically provide cold meats, eggs or fish, cakes and sandwiches, and is an informal meal served in many families. For agricultural workers however, high tea was traditionally a meal that combined both daily meals and was eaten just after nightfall.

In the north of England, 'tea' is the main evening meal, even if no-one is actually drinking tea. It is traditionally eaten at five o'clock or later, sometimes as late as 9pm. Tea as a meal is synonymous with supper in the south of England, and the midday meal is sometimes termed dinner, rather than lunch. It's all a little confusing, but part of the on-going and agreeable idiosyncrasy of the North-South divide so ably described in Stuart Maconie's best-selling book *Pies and Prejudice*.

To ensure that the highest standards are observed in British rural tea shops, there is now a Tea Council, dedicated to maintaining traditions and quality, and each year it distinguishes a worthy tea room with an award. And while the attendant cakes and sandwiches, although no doubt delicious, may not always be as healthy as we might like, latest research has shown that your daily cuppa provides you with antioxidants, and contributes successfully to your daily fluid target.

SEMER WATER MAP REF 407 G4

Yorkshire's largest natural lake was formed in Raydale during the Ice Age when a retreating glacier left behind a huge clay dam, and another was blocked in by a glacier in Wensleydale. The resultant melt water formed Semer Water, which is now a very popular place. It is usually busy at all times with anglers, boaters, watersports enthusiasts, nature lovers, swimmers, walkers and those who simply want to stop and admire the splendid views.

It's possible to walk all the way round the lake, which is ringed by three pretty little villages – Countersett, Marsett and Stalling Busk – with a fourth settlement said to be lying on the bed of the lake! Another explanation for the lake's origins claims that a beautiful city once stood here. An angel, disguised as a beggar, went round the city asking for food and drink, but was turned away at every home. The angel left the city and finally found food and shelter in the home of a poor man and his wife. On leaving the next morning, the angel turned to the city and said:

Semerwater rise – Semerwater sink,
And cover all save this lile house
that gave me meat and drink.

The waters did rise to create the lake, and beneath its surface you may just hear the occasional sound of bells from the long-drowned city. The poor man's cottage survived, and is said to be at Low Blean, on the eastern edge of Semer Water.

SETTLE MAP REF 407 G5

The day to visit Settle is Tuesday – market day – when busy stalls are crammed into Market Square and visitors jostle with locals from the surrounding farms and villages. Settle is quite a lot smaller than nearby Skipton, but it is still a great place for shopping, with some old-fashioned family-run stores adding to the appeal of its 18th- and 19th-century buildings.

The composer, Edward Elgar, had a very good friend in Settle, a Dr Buck. Elgar stayed with him often, in his house overlooking the Market Square, where a plaque commemorates the connection. Also overlooking the square is a two-storey row of shops known as the Shambles. In the 17th century this was an open market hall, which later became a butcher's shop. Arches and cottages were added in the 18th century, and the second storey was built above the cottages in 1898. In front of the Shambles is a fountain pillar erected in 1863 to replace the former market cross, and in front of this is a café with one of the most unusual names: Ye Olde Naked Man Café. Take a look behind Ye Olde Naked Man and you will see Bishopdale Court, typical of the many old yards and alleyways in Settle's streets.

One of the important natives of Settle is Benjamin Waugh, who founded the National Society for the Prevention of Cruelty to Children (NSPCC). He was born in a saddler's shop in what is now Lloyds TSB Bank, off the Market Square. Perhaps Settle's most unusual building is Richard's Folly, on School Hill, close to the Market Square. The house was built in 1675 for a local tanner, Richard Preston. He called it Tanner Hall, but it earned its 'folly' nickname because it stood empty long after Richard's death. It has since been restored and houses a museum.

West of Settle you'll find the rather oddly named Giggleswick. The village is renowned for its public school founded in 1553, and a much quieter place than Settle for visitors to wander around. Russell Harty, broadcaster and author, once worked as a teacher at the school.

To the west of Giggleswick, on the A65, is the Yorkshire Dales Falconry and Conservation Centre, with a collection of birds of prey from around the world. The outdoor aviaries are built from local limestone and are very attractive.

SKIPTON MAP REF 407 G5

Skipton buzzes with life, a bustling market filling its main street with stalls four days out of seven. It has modern shops, ancient inns, churches, a museum, restaurants and hotels, as well as a Norman Castle, over 900 years old but still in a superb state of preservation.

Skipton Castle is one of the most complete and well-preserved medieval castles in England. It was the birthplace of the indomitable Lady Anne Clifford and bears the Clifford family motto of 'Desormais' (Henceforth) in large lettering above the splendid main entrance gate. The castle's huge appeal to visitors is indicated by the fact that there are tour sheets in several languages. Take one to find your own way around its warren of rooms. Some of the original Norman building remains, but most dates from the 13th century, later damaged during the Civil War but renovated by Lady Anne Clifford in the mid-17th century.

Beside the castle is the Holy Trinity Church, which dates mainly from the 14th and 15th centuries, although there was a church here in the 12th century. It contains the tombs of many members of the Clifford family (though not Lady Anne), and a fine Tudor roof and screen.

Castle and church stand at the top of the High Street; half-way down is the Craven Museum, housed in Skipton's Town Hall. There is a small exhibition relating to one of Skipton's most famous sons, Thomas Spencer, of Marks and Spencer, who co-founded the company; other more conventional exhibits depict life ancient and modern in Skipton and the surrounding Craven area. One of the exhibits is a simple piece of cloth that was discovered in one of the Bronze Age graves near by. It is believed to be the oldest piece of cloth to be discovered in Britain. The museum is a good place to browse, wet or fine.

SEMER WATER

SWALEDALE

The oldest building in Skipton's High Street is the Red Lion Inn. It was built in the late 14th or early 15th century and was once partly a farm. It is said to have been owned by Richard III. Still visible in the forecourt is a bear-baiting stone.

But the town of Skipton, like Settle, is a place whose back streets need to be explored. There are also pleasant walks to be enjoyed along the canal-side towpaths. The Leeds and Liverpool Canal passes through town joining the Ellerbeck and Springs Canal, adding to the atmosphere that Skipton, for centuries, really has been the 'Gateway to the Dales'.

SWALEDALE VILLAGES
MAP REF 407 G4

Swaledale names are mostly short and sharp, from their Norse origins: Muker, Keld, Thwaite, Reeth, Angram. Even the longer ones are spat out with those same short Norse vowels: Gunnerside, Arkengarthdale. Most of the villages in this area are short and sharp too, strung out along the B6270, but they welcome tourists and offer lots of places to shop, stay and eat, and a range of local craft studios. Beyond Keld, the 'knots' end, the lonely road crosses the fells to Nateby and Kirkby Stephen at the northern end of the valley of Mallerstang, as it opens out into the lovely Vale of Eden.

Travelling from Reeth, Gunnerside is the first sizeable community you reach. It is an appealing place with grey stone cottages, which were once the homes of lead miners, looking down on the River Swale with high-rising moors. Norse settlers were attracted by its sheltered location at the confluence of Gunnerside Gill and the larger river. Later, lead mining brought prosperity, and the remains of mines can be found just a short distance from the centre of the village. Another walk is to the unusual Ivelet Bridge.

Beyond Ivelet is Muker, a collection of stone cottages clustered in jigsaw streets that zig-zag steeply up from the main road. Plaques on the church wall commemorate Richard (1862–1928) and Cherry (1871–1940) Kearton, brothers who were born in Thwaite and went to school in Muker. They devoted their lives to watching wildlife and became early pioneers of wildlife photography. There is also a Literary Institute, an echo of the Norse origins of its unusual name, for Muker means 'a cultivated plot'.

Scarcely a mile (1.6km) west of Muker is Thwaite, where the cottage in which the Kearton brothers were born still stands. This idyllic place hides the tragedy of the flood of 1899 when the waters of Thwaite Beck swept down and almost wiped out the community. It is said that flowers washed from Thwaite's cottage gardens were later found growing in Muker.

The last Swaledale village is Keld, quietly going about its business, set back from the main road in a dead end that leads down to the River Swale and some of Swaledale's most impressive falls. The Pennine Way passes the edge of Keld before heading northwards up Stonesdale to the lonely outpost of Tan Hill. The Swaledale road goes west through some of the most dramatic scenery in the Yorkshire Dales before arriving at Nateby, just outside the boundary of the National Park, in the valley of Mallerstang

WENSLEY MAP REF 407 G4

Wensley is one of the small villages that many people pass through on their way to the dale that took the village's name. It is hard to imagine that this was once the main settlement in Wensleydale, the first place to receive a market charter, in 1202, with the only market in the dale for the following 100 years. Wensley flourished until plague struck in 1563, when the focus of Wensleydale life shifted a mile (1.6km) to the east, to Leyburn, and later westward to Askrigg and then Hawes.

The Church of the Holy Trinity remains as a reminder of that former importance, with parts of the building dating from 1240. Its attractive pale stone tower was built in 1719, and inside you will find an 18th-century pulpit and a 17th-century font. There's also a memorial to the Scrope family, from Castle Bolton who had close connections with the church. When the Scropes built Bolton Hall in 1678 Wensley began its regrowth as an estate village.

Near the church is the gate that leads to Bolton Hall, and also near here is the river on which there is a small waterfall and also Wensley Mill. Today the mill houses the White Rose Candles Workshop.

HAWES & HARDRAW

These popular settlements both have something to offer visitors and walkers – Hawes is famous for Wensleydale cheese and motorcyclists, who gather here on summer weekends, and Hardraw for its spectacular waterfall. The walk in-between takes in farmland and moorland scenery.

1 From the car park turn left. Just before the Creamery turn right between houses. Follow the left side of the field to a stile at the top. Keep straight on past a barn and across a lane. After passing a ruined barn, bear right to the B6255. Turn left, then right through a gate signed 'Thorney Mire House'. Follow the path, which bears left between parallel walls, for 0.5 mile (800m) to meet a lane. Turn right and follow this to the A684 at Appersett.

2 Turn left over the bridge. Continue over another bridge to a junction, turn right and go straight over a stile, signed 'Bluebell Hill'. Bear slightly right to a gate and over a bridge, then bear left uphill to reach a gate. Continue past waymarks to a signpost.

3 Turn right and walk to a stile (Bob's Stile) then bear slightly right to a prominent ladder stile. Walk straight ahead and Hardraw soon appears. Continue down over a stile, then over a ladder stile into a lane.

4 Turn right, then left at the main road. Hardraw Force entrance is through the Green Dragon pub. Immediately after the pub, turn left, then right through a signed gap in the wall and through a courtyard. Follow a flagged path and steps uphill to

a house. Turn right behind it, pass right of the stables, then bear slightly left to pass below the grounds of Simonstone Hall Hotel, joining its drive.

5 Walk down to a road and turn left. Almost immediately turn right through a stile signed 'Sedbusk'. Follow the track past farm buildings to a ladder stile, then continue straight ahead. Skirt below a house and continue over more stiles, along a flagged path and between houses into Sedbusk.

6 Turn right along the road, bend left near the postbox and descend. Go right, over a stile signed 'Haylands Bridge'. Cross the field, bear right below a wall-corner to a stile, then descend to a stile by the right end of a line of trees. Cross the lane to a stile and follow the path across a stream. Descend to a humpback bridge and continue to a road.

7 Turn left and cross Haylands Bridge. About 200yds (182m) beyond, go right through a kissing gate signed 'Hawes'. Follow the path to a track, turn left a few paces, then right on to the main road. At the junction, cross the first road, then turn right past the post office. Follow the main road through Hawes. Immediately before the public toilets, turn left up steps to the car park.

DISTANCE/TIME 5 miles (8km) 2h **MAP** OS Explorer OL30 Yorkshire Dales – Northern & Central **START** Pay car park off Gayle Lane at west side of Hawes; grid ref: SD 870898 **PATHS** Field and moorland paths. May be muddy; 35 stiles **THE PUB** Green Dragon Inn, Hardraw. Tel: 01969 667392; www.greendragonhardraw.co.uk

WALK 116

FROM WEST BURTON TO AYSGARTH

This pleasant walk travels between two typical Dales villages, and back, via the famous Aysgarth Falls on the River Ure and some unusual farm buildings.

1 Leave the Green near the village shop. Opposite 'Meadowcroft' go left, signed 'Eshington Bridge'. Cross the road, turn right, then left through a gate and down steps. Go through a gate beside a barn and continue to a stile at the bottom right of the field. Cross two more stiles, then bear right to meet a stone wall. Follow this then continue in the same direction to a road.

2 Turn left, cross the bridge and go up a narrow lane to a bend. Go ahead through a stile, signed 'Aysgarth'. Climb past another stile and left of a barn. Continue up the field and bear left to a gate near the corner, then diagonally across the next field. Keep left of an obvious wall gap to a stile by another gap. Descend to a stile and footpath sign.

3 Continue in the same direction and up to a signpost. Follow the Aysgarth direction to a gateway and stile. Cross the field half left to a stile onto a lane. Turn left, then right, signed 'Aysgarth'. Go through three stiles to a road.

4 Turn right, into the village. Go past the George and Dragon then straight ahead to the Methodist Church and bear right along the lane. Cross a stile by Field House. Follow the wall and continue along a short track, then follow a path through eight stiles to finally reach a road.

5 Enter the churchyard, pass right of the church and leave by a stile. Cross a field and go through a wood. Follow the path downhill, descending steps to the river bank. Take a signed stile right.

6 Follow the path by the river to a signpost. Bend right across a field to the main road. Turn left, cross a bridge, then turn right into woodland, signed 'Edgley', soon bearing left, uphill, to a stile. Bear right across a field to a gate in the far corner and join a road.

7 Turn right. About 150yds (137m) along, go left over a stile, signed 'Flanders Hall'. Walk towards the follies, then bear right just below the ridge, passing Sorrelsykes Park to your right. Cross a track and bear left past a waymark to a signpost. Turn right to a stepped stone stile, then follow the bottom edge of the field to reach a gate opposite a stone barn.

8 Descend through this and two more gates, then bear left along the field edge to a stile. Continue ahead to a lane. Turn right, cross a bridge and join the village road. Turn left, back to the Green.

DISTANCE/TIME 4 miles (6.4km) 1h30 **MAP** OS Explorer OL30 Yorkshire Dales – Northern & Central **START** Centre of West Burton, by (but not on) the Green; grid ref: SE 017867 **PATHS** Field and riverside paths and tracks, 35 stiles **THE PUB** The George & Dragon, Aysgarth. Tel: 01969 663358; www.georgeanddragonaysgarth.co.uk

WALK 117

FROM KELD TO MUKER

This is a classic walk in Upper Swaledale from Keld to Muker along Kisdon Side and backed by the River Swale. Keld – its name is the Old Norse word for a spring – is one of the most remote of the Dales villages. Set at the head of Swaledale, its small cluster of grey stone cottages is a centre for some of the most spectacular walks in North Yorkshire. It is worth taking some time to explore the village of Muker when you get there. Like many of the Swaledale settlements, it rapidly expanded during the 18th and 19th centuries because of the lead-mining industry.

1 Walk back down the car park entrance road, and straight ahead down a gravel track, signed 'Muker'. Continue along at the upper level, ignoring a path downhill to the left. Go through a gate, pass a sign to Kisdon Upper Force, and continue along the path below crags to a signpost.

2 Turn right, following the Pennine Way, and go up to a gap in a wall and another signpost. Go left and follow a rough but mostly level path along Kisdon Side, first above woodland then across more open slopes. Cross a ladder stile as the path starts to descend. Go down to a signpost and then bear right to reach another signpost, where the Pennine Way goes right.

3 Bear left down a walled track, marked 'Muker'. The track becomes gravelled and then metalled, finally descending into a walled lane on the edge of the village. Continue to a T-junction.

4 Turn left and in a few paces left again by a sign to Gunnerside and Keld. Follow the paved path through six gates to the river. Turn sharp right and walk downstream to reach a footbridge.

5 Ascend steps beyond the footbridge and turn left, signed 'Keld'. Follow a clear track up along the valley, until it curves right into Swinner Gill. Cross a footbridge by the remains of lead workings, and go up to a wooden gate.

6 Go straight ahead up the hill and through woodland. The track levels out, then starts to descend, winding left round a barn then swinging back right. Continue steadily downhill to reach a gate above East Gill Force.

7 Fork left by a wooden seat, at a sign to Keld. Follow the path down to a footbridge then bear right, uphill, to a T-junction, where you turn right and follow the track back to the car.

DISTANCE/TIME 6 miles (9.7km) 2h30 **MAP** OS Explorer OL30 Yorkshire Dales – Northern & Central **START** Signed car park at west end of Keld near Park Lodge; grid ref: NY 892012. **PATHS** Field and riverside paths and tracks; 5 stiles **THE PUB** The Farmers Arms, Muker. Tel: 01748 886297

WALK 118

LANGTHWAITE IN ARKENGARTHDALE

Follow a route around an austere valley where lead workers once toiled leaving a mine-scarred moorland landscape with evocative remains of industry. One of the most northerly of the dales, Arkengarthdale runs northwards from Swaledale into dark moorland, with the battle-scarred Stainmore beyond its head.

1 Leave the car park, turn right, then right over the bridge into Langthwaite. Climb the narrow lane between cottages. The lane becomes a track. Ignore two left forks and continue to the hamlet of Booze. Go straight through the yard of Town Farm and follow a rutted track up and left to a gate.

2 Continue ahead on a green track slanting down through spoil heaps and past ruined Sleigill House to the stream. Walk up the valley, go through a gate and cross the stream near a limekiln.

3 Climb the steep bank, go through new tree-plantings and follow green paths through the heather. Pass a wooden hut and turn left on a broad track. Follow the main track through a slight valley, then bearing left over the moor and down to a T-junction with a wall just below. Where this falls back, go down, right, to a gate in the corner.

4 Follow the small gully downhill and past waymarks to a level track. Turn right and follow the track, traversing the hillside until it bends sharp left to meet a stony track. Turn left to a house then bear right, through the garden and down a slanting green track, eventually entering woodland.

5 Emerge alongside Scar House. Follow the drive downhill and over a bridge. Bear right on a walled track, then turn right through gateposts and walk to a road. Turn left, uphill, to a T-junction. Turn right and follow the road for 0.5 mile (800m). Opposite a barn, turn left on an obvious track.

6 Turn right at the far side of a gravelled area, cross a grassy area and slant uphill towards a prominent flat-topped spoil heap. Just before this, the track bends sharp left then winds uphill to reach a T-junction near the crest. Turn left and follow the clear track, along the ridge then bearing right down to a road.

7 Turn left. Pass above a farm (Bouldershaw), then turn right at a bridleway sign. Turn left just before the farmyard and go straight down a green track. At The Ghyll, join its access track but as it bends right bear left and down to a stile in the bottom right corner of the field. Go down to the road. Turn left back to the car park.

DISTANCE/TIME 8 miles (12.9km) 3h15 **MAP** OS Explorer OL30 Yorkshire Dales – Northern & Central **START** Pay-and-display car park in Langthwaite; grid ref: NZ 005024 **PATHS** Mostly clear tracks, some heather moor; 4 stiles **THE PUB** The CB Inn, Arkengarthdale. Tel: 01748 884567; www.cbinn.co.uk

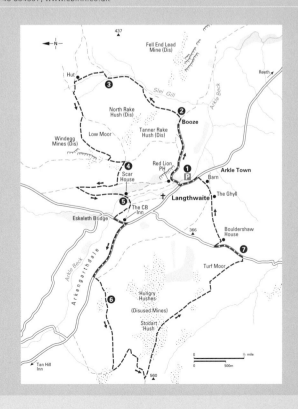

MAJOR PEAKS & MINOR DALES

This drive takes you through some of the minor but most beautiful dales such as Ribblesdale, Dentdale, Mallerstang, Deepdale and Kingsdale, and passes on the way the Three Peaks: Whernside, Ingleborough and Pen-y-ghent. You'll also be able to see the marginally smaller but equally dramatic hills of Wild Boar Fell and High Seat, on the northern boundary of the National Park.

Route Directions

1 From Settle take the B6480 north to its junction with the A65. Turn right on to the A65 travelling towards Kirkby Lonsdale. Turn right on to the B6255 to reach Ingleton, and its unique Waterfalls Walk.

Ingleton is a small but friendly place with some steep streets, tourist shops and a fine parish church. Follow the signs for 'Village Centre' and then the 'Waterfalls Walk'.

2 At the start of the Waterfalls Walk, which is marked by a large sign, the road swings sharply left and then right again. Watch for the right turn along here signposted 'Dent'. Follow this road through Thornton in Lonsdale and turn sharp right by the church, still following signs for Dent. This is a narrow, gated, but glorious road through Kingsdale, following Kingsdale Beck and then climbing, with the summit of Whernside at 2,415ft (736m) on your right-hand side before descending steeply into Deepdale. Turn left at the next junction going towards Sedbergh. Continue left through the cobbled streets of Dent, which are delightful but not designed for drivers looking in vain for signposts, until you emerge on the other side. Continue towards Sedbergh, passing through the very green Dentdale and following the road round to the right. Bear left over the bridge at Millthrop and follow the road signed 'Town Centre'. Go straight on at the roundabout and turn right on to the main street in front of the Reading Room.

Sedbergh has a Wednesday market and there is also a monthly farmers' market, where you can buy locally produced goods and crafts.

3 At the far end turn left, following the signs for Hawes, Kirkby Stephen and Brough. Follow the A683 alongside the River Rawthey all the way out of the National Park with the Cautley Spout and the Howgill Fells to your left. From the moors the road descends towards Kirkby Stephen. Turn right on to the A685 into this unspoiled town between the Yorkshire Dales and the Lake District.

One attraction is its parish church of St Stephen, with 18th-century bread shelves and a 10th-century Norse stone cross.

4 In Kirkby Stephen turn right on to the B6259 for Nateby, staying on the road through Nateby and down through the valley

of Mallerstang, with Wild Boar Fell on your right and Mallerstang Edge and High Seat, left. Wild Boar Fell rises to 2,323ft (708m) (higher than Pen-y-ghent at 2,274ft/693m), and gets its name because the last wild boar in England was said to have been killed here. Its ruggedness remains.

5 At the T-junction by the Moorcock Inn, turn left on to the A684 towards Hawes but before you reach the centre of Hawes; turn right on to the B6255 heading towards Horton in Ribblesdale and Ingleton.

This lovely winding road passes through Widdale and up and over Gayle Moor, bringing into view the magnificent sight of the Ribblehead Viaduct, carrying the Settle–Carlisle Railway line. The railway was built in the late 19th century, and is one of the most impressive feats of engineering. It is the most beautiful route in England, driving both under and over the Dales. Overlooking the railway line is Whernside, the largest of the Three Peaks, followed by Ingleborough and finally Pen-y-ghent. Though the smallest of the peaks, the brooding face of Pen-y-ghent has a special appeal.

6 Just before the viaduct, turn left on to the B6479 to pass through Horton in Ribblesdale, Stainforth and on to Settle. This road runs through Ribblesdale with Ingleborough, right. Next, you'll see the unmistakable looming shape of Pen-y-ghent on your left. The road then runs along the banks of the River Ribble and back down into Settle.

TO SMALL TOWNS & LARGE VILLAGES

Middleham, with its market, splendid Norman castle and horse racing stables, is the smallest town in the Yorkshire Dales – much smaller than many villages. This drive takes in some of the attractive places that hover between town and village, such as Kettlewell, Grassington, Leyburn and Pateley Bridge, where the tour starts, and some of the finest scenery the Dales have to offer.

Route Directions

The drive starts in Pateley Bridge, a lively market town in the heart of Nidderdale with its own fascinating local museum, good shopping and a tourist information centre.

1 From the centre of Pateley Bridge take the minor road that leads north from near the bridge itself, towards Ramsgill and Lofthouse. Pass Gouthwaite Reservoir on your right. In Lofthouse turn right and take the steep road out of the village, over the moors towards Masham. Continue for about 6 miles (9.7km), passing two more reservoirs on your right. Take the third left turning, as you approach Healey, heading towards Ellingstring. Turn left at the crossroads, continue to the junction with the A6108 and turn left to Leyburn passing the remains of Jervaulx Abbey, right.

Founded in 1156, the abbey is in complete contrast to grand and busy Fountains Abbey, yet in its day Jervaulx was one of the most important Cistercian abbeys in Yorkshire.

2 Continue on the A6108 and drive through Middleham, with its quaint cobbled market squares, its cottages built of grey stone and its racing connections.

Middleham is considered to be 'the Newmarket of the north', with its 16 or so racing stables. The impressive castle ruins was the much-favoured home of King Richard III, whose son Edward was born here in 1473.

3 Continue to Leyburn, a busy Wensleydale town with many tea shops for visitors as well as a wealth of everyday shops. In Leyburn turn left, then right following the signs 'A6108 Richmond'. Drive through Bellerby, turn right then left, still with the A6108. The road first takes you over upland pasture then along the wooded Alpine-like slopes of Swaledale towards Richmond. At this point you can choose to take a detour and continue into Richmond, which stands at the foot of Swaledale, for a leisurely visit.

Richmond's castle commands an impressive position above the river. The town has a large cobbled square, a church with shops in its side, riverside walks and three good museums.

4 If you are not taking the detour, continue as before and as you reach Richmond pass a right turn to Catterick, turn immediately left

up Hurgill Road, past a car park on the left. This road takes you back along the Swale but climbs high above the river, before dropping steeply down to Marske. Cross the bridge and turn right towards Reeth, then turn left on to the B6270 to Grinton. In Grinton turn right on to a minor road and take the right fork following the signs for Redmire. You are now on an impressive high moorland road passing disused lead mines. When the road finally descends, take the first turning on the right for the village of Castle Bolton then turn right for Carperby. Take a left turn to visit Aysgarth Falls – a very popular beauty spot. Although they consist of three different sections, only the Upper Falls are visible from the road. Near by are a mill, a carriage museum and tea rooms, while Aysgarth village itself is another half-mile (800m) away, on the main Wensleydale road.

5 Beyond Aysgarth Falls turn left on to the A684 signposted 'Leyburn' and then take the second turning on the right on to the B6160 following the signs into West Burton.

This has been described as the prettiest village in the Dales. It has a large village green, on which horses graze and children play. There is a pub and a pottery, but no church or market. Burton Force waterfall is a short stroll away.

6 Rejoin the B6160 to drive along the lovely Bishopdale, and over Kidstones Pass to Buckden in Wharfedale. Pass the small town of Kettlewell on the left.

Kettlewell is a centre for walkers tackling nearby Great Whernside. It is also on the Dales Way long-distance footpath, and was once a centre of the lead-mining industry.

7 Continue ahead and look out for Kilnsey Crag on your right, easily identified as it juts out dramatically towards the main road. Kilnsey Crag is popular with climbers, filmmakers and peregrine falcons.

8 Continue on the B6160 then turn left to reach the centre of Grassington, a popular village for people who appreciate stalactites and stalagmites amongst other things.

This is an attractive, large village with cobbled streets, 17th- and 18th-century houses, pubs and a museum of Upper Wharfedale life.

9 Drive around the centre of Grassington, and leave on the B6265 and then make the return journey to your starting point at Nidderdale and Pateley Bridge.

Northumbria & Coast

CLOCKWISE FROM TOP: A PUFFIN, FARNE ISLANDS; HOUSESTEADS FORT,
HADRIAN'S WALL; DUNSTANBURGH CASTLE

FOUNTAINS AT ALNWICK

Visit
ALNWICK FOLK

If you're in Alnwick in early August, don't be surprised if you come across groups of brightly dressed Eastern Europeans or Scandinavians. They will be part of the Alnwick International Music Festival that takes place in the town each year. It is an opportunity for folk musicians and dancers from around the world to show and celebrate their skills.

Visit
AYDON CASTLE

Aydon Castle is really a very early fortified manor house, built at the end of the 13th century and given its battlements in 1305. Where it was most vulnerable, to the north, it has an irregular outer bailey, and behind that a small, open courtyard, with the living quarters to one side. Instead of a keep there was a hall and a solar with a fine fireplace and beautifully detailed windows – don't miss the bearded face staring out from above the northern one.

ALNWICK MAP REF 409 L6

Alnwick (pronounced 'Annick') has been the stronghold of the Percy family since 1309. They went on to become the Earls of Northumberland, then in the 18th century, the Dukes of Northumberland. Alnwick Castle's strong walls and round towers, although altered over the centuries, owe their outline to the Normans. Its barbican, the best surviving in Britain, and the impressive gateway, with stone figures mimicking an ever-watchful garrison, were added when the Percys arrived.

The medieval interior was transformed into a Renaissance palace by the 4th Duke in the 19th century. It glows with fine woodwork and marble and is filled with treasures, including paintings by Titian, Canaletto, Van Dyck and Andrea del Sarto. There are two stunning cabinets made for Louis XIV, and two Meissen dinner services. The castle grounds are famous as Hogwarts in the Harry Potter films.

The park was landscaped by the renowned designer 'Capability' Brown, a Northumberland man. It is now home to the spectacular new gardens created by the Duchess, complete with a restored great cascade, hundreds of fountains and the world's biggest tree house.

Alnwick Castle does not dominate the attractive stone-built town, but its influence is apparent. The 15th-century parish church lies near the castle, while at the other end of town is a survivor of the town walls begun in 1434, the narrow Hotspur Gate, named after the most famous member of the Percy family, Shakespeare's Harry Hotspur. Alnwick's cobbled market place bustles with life, and there are shops selling local produce, crafts and antiques.

The pastures below the castle are the scene for a mammoth Shrove Tuesday football match, which uses the Lion and Denwick bridges as goals.

ALWINTON MAP REF 409 K6

This small village lies in the Upper Coquet Valley and is set between the Cheviots and the more rugged Harbottle Hills, making it a good base. Sir Walter Scott stayed at the popular Rose and Thistle while researching his heroic tale, *Rob Roy*.

Alwinton church is on the hillside south of the river, and from its large churchyard there are wonderful views. Each October the village hosts the last of the season's traditional country shows – the Border Shepherds' Show – with sheep, fell racing and sheepdog trials.

At Chew Green, 8 miles (12.9km) west of Alwinton, is one of Britain's best Roman earthworks. The remains of a fort and camp are visible among the hills. Drive to the site from Redesdale when the army firing ranges are not in use – with superb views along the Roman Dere Street.

BAMBURGH MAP REF 409 L5

Bamburgh for many means the castle, dominating both the village and the coast. It looks so medieval that film crews use it as a backdrop. Yet the castle is both more and less historical than it looks. The great Whin Sill crag has been defended since the Iron Age and became the site of a fort for the Anglians in AD 547 and was given by King Ethelfrith to his wife Bebba; Bebba's burgh became Bamburgh.

An eventful progress through the centuries ensued until the castle fell to the Normans, who began the stone castle we now see. Additions were made in later centuries, creating a castle that was virtually impregnable until its defeat in 1464 during the Wars of the Roses.

The shattered remains passed to the local Forster family and they held it – but largely left it in a derelict state – until the early 18th century, when Lord Crewe, the Bishop of Durham, undertook repairs and left the castle as a charitable trust.

The castle was sold in 1894 to Lord Armstrong, an eminent inventor and industrialist. He restored the castle to its present appearance. The State Rooms now appear late Victorian, and they are palatial, particularly the Great Hall with its impressive roof and musicians' gallery.

Bamburgh village can be extremely busy at the height of the tourist season, but it is a pleasant place for a stroll. Its parish church stands on the site of the chapel used by St Aidan and has a beautiful early 13th-century chancel and Forster family monuments, as well as the much-visited grave of the Victorian heroine Grace Darling in the churchyard. Bamburgh also has an attractive sandy beach. Budle Bay, an area of wetland west of Bamburgh, is a nature reserve visited by many wildfowl – information boards will help you to identify a good number of them.

BELLINGHAM MAP REF 409 K7

St Cuthbert's Church, a fascinating early 13th-century building, was rebuilt in the early 17th century, when it was given its stone-vaulted roof, probably to protect it from the frequent Scots' raids.

Outside Bellingham's Town Hall is more evidence of fierce warfare – a gun captured at the Boxer Rebellion in China in 1900 – and the presence of army training areas is felt here today. For ten years from 1838 the town was a thriving iron and coal centre, but the industry was killed by competition from foundries nearer Newcastle upon Tyne and on Teesside.

Bellingham hosts an agricultural show in August and is a good base for exploring the Kielder area and the Northumberland National Park. Some 7 miles (11.3km) northwest of Bellingham, in the Tarset Burn valley, is Black Middens Bastle, one of very few which are open to the public.

BERWICK-UPON-TWEED

MAP REF 409 K4

Berwick-upon-Tweed was a Royal Burgh of Scotland until William the Lion surrendered it to the English in 1174. Over the next 300 years it changed hands 11 times, became a free town in 1482 and an independent state in 1502. It became part of Northumberland only in 1974.

Such a turbulent past gives Berwick its own gritty individuality. A fascinating town, it holds a unique place in both British and military history. In the Middle Ages it was protected at its north end by the castle, first mentioned in 1160 and rebuilt at the end of the 13th century. Its White Wall plunges from the castle to the river, protecting precipitous steps known locally as 'The Breakynecks'. The Constable's Tower is impressive, and you can see part of the northwest wall from the station platform – much more was demolished when the railway arrived.

Berwick had medieval town walls – the best remaining stretch lies alongside the cliffs between Meg's Mount and the railway bridge – but more important are its Elizabethan ramparts. Built between 1558 and 1569, when the Scots and the French were threatening England, they are unique in Britain. The walk along them should not be missed, to see the 22ft high (6.7m) stone-faced walls, 12ft (3.6m) thick at the base and topped with grassed mounds. They were never

properly finished. In 1568 Mary, Queen of Scots, fled to England, thus removing some of the Scottish threat – and when Scottish King James VI became James I of England in 1603 they were redundant.

Berwick remained a military town, however, and Britain's earliest barracks, dating from the early 17th century, held nearly 600 men. They now house the King's Own Scottish Borderers Museum and the town Museum and Art Gallery, which, alongside exhibits of local history, has something of a surprise – outstanding works of art, including paintings by Degas and Daubigny, medieval carvings and Chinese ceramics. Modern art is displayed at the Gymnasium Gallery, on the Parade.

Opposite the Barracks is Berwick parish church – built in the 1650s, during the Commonwealth. Oliver Cromwell, a friend of the benefactor, hated bells, so there is no tower. Bells did arrive here, but were hung in the mid-18th century Guildhall, Berwick's most prominent building, with its tall tower and spire.

Among Berwick's landmarks are its bridges. Early wooden bridges were swept away. Without one for 200 years, Berwick put up another wooden bridge in Tudor times, but it was King James VI, going to London in 1603, who demanded, and eventually paid for, the magnificent 1,164ft (355m) long Old Bridge. It remained the only road bridge in the town until the Royal Tweed Bridge was built in 1928,

but the most spectacular bridge, Robert Stephenson's Royal Border Bridge, 2,152ft (656m) long on 28 high arches, was built for the railway in 1846.

CHILLINGHAM MAP REF 409 K5

Chillingham village, with its Tudor-style houses, was built by the Earls of Tankerville, related by marriage to the Grey family. In the church the tomb of 15th-century Sir Ralph Grey has some rare figures of saints that escaped later religious destruction. The Greys fought against the Scots and, often, the Percys of Alnwick. Their fortress, Chillingham Castle, was started in 1245, but much of its present appearance dates from 1344.

All was nearly lost when the castle was left empty after the contents were sold in 1933. There was a fire during the time that soldiers were billeted here in the 1940s and rot ravaged the rest, until Sir Humphrey Wakefield, related to the Greys, bought the castle in the 1980s and began its triumphant restoration.

Visitors can see the splendid Great Hall, with banners and armour, as well as antique furniture, tapestries and restored plaster- and metalwork, carving and masonry. There is even a torture chamber, suitable for a place reputed to be 'the most haunted castle in England'. The gardens, revived after years of neglect, include woodland walks and a topiary garden on the site of the tournament ground.

CORBRIDGE MAP REF 407 G2

The first Roman fort to stand at Corbridge – Corstopitum – was built around AD 90, more than 30 years before Hadrian's Wall, to guard the bridge where Dere Street crossed the Tyne. The Stanegate, built earlier by Agricola's troops, also crosses the fort on its way into Carlisle. As a vastly important junction, Corstopitum had a succession of forts – the one we see today is the fourth, built about AD 140 as the Romans occupied Scotland. It was an important military headquarters, depot and supply base, even after the Romans finally gave up on Scotland towards the end of the 2nd century. By degrees it changed into a town, much of which is still buried, though its stones are found in many Corbridge and Hexham buildings.

The excellent museum is full of finds from the site, including inscriptions and some small, often personal objects. The tour takes you past the granaries, perhaps the most memorable part of the fort, and the best preserved in Britain, with floors of stone slabs on low walls.

The square courtyard to the north of the main street (part of Stanegate) was never finished and no one is quite sure what it was. Opposite are the military compounds, where you can trace the workshops and officers' houses before descending into the former strongroom to see where soldiers and locals worshipped both Roman and local gods.

The town suffered from invasion by Danes and Scots. Not surprisingly, there are two defensive pele towers in Corbridge. One, at the end of Main Street, dating from the 13th century was converted into a house in about 1675. The other, the Vicar's Pele, is made from Roman stones and was probably put up in the 14th century.

St Andrew's Church, too, uses some Roman stones – between the tower and the nave is a whole Roman archway. The tower's lower parts were probably built before AD 786, and there is more Saxon work in the walls, as well as a Norman doorway and a 13th-century chancel.

CRASTER MAP REF 409 L5

A picturesque village that seems almost to tumble into the sea, Craster became a haven for fishing in the 17th century, although its harbour, today used by pleasure craft and traditional cobles, was given its present form in the 1900s. It was built by the local landowners, the Crasters. The harbour was used to export whinstone (used for roads and kerbs), and you can still see the concrete arch that once supported the chipping silos. The quarry is now the National Trust car park, a good starting point for walks to Dunstanburgh Castle.

CHILLINGHAM CASTLE

DURHAM MAP REF 407 H3

Even without the great cathedral and castle that dominate its skyline the city of Durham would be spectacular. The River Wear does a huge loop, in a deep ravine, coming almost to meet itself. From this superb defensive position the city developed, down the hill and outwards, but from whichever side you approach – and especially if you arrive at the station by rail – Durham is a magnificent sight.

The city is a place for visiting on foot. Gently climbing from the market place up Saddler Street you will see elegant Georgian houses from one of Durham's most prosperous times, interspersed with small specialist shops and university departments. Owengate leads into Palace Green, dominated by the cathedral's north side and surrounded by fine university buildings, with the castle to your right.

It was in Durham that St Cuthbert's bones finally ended their century-long journey from Holy Island in AD 995, but the present cathedral building, with its three massive towers, dates from 1093. Enter by the north door with its replica sanctuary ring (a 12th-century door-knocker). The original is in the Treasury.

The main effect of the interior is of enormous strength. Huge columns, alternate ones patterned with bold geometric incisions hold up the earliest Gothic roof anywhere. The east wall is dominated by a rose window, and below it is the Neville Screen, made from creamy stone. Beyond this is the 13th-century Chapel of the Nine Altars, with its tall lancet windows, overlooked by St Cuthbert's tomb which has just a simple stone slab. In the choir, the Bishop's throne is the highest in Britain.

In about 1170, the monks built a Galilee Chapel at the west end, perched precariously over the ravine. The tomb of the Venerable Bede is here. Off the cloisters, try not to miss the Monks' Dormitory, with its huge wooden roof, and the Treasury, full of silver, pre-Conquest embroidery and manuscripts, and relics of St Cuthbert. To get the classic cathedral view, go to Prebends' Bridge, reached from South Bailey.

The castle, begun in 1072, now houses University College, and its 18th-century gatehouse has a Norman core, as does the massive keep, which was rebuilt in 1840. The highlight of a tour around the castle is a visit to the splendid Norman gallery and the Norman chapel.

College buildings cluster in the streets around the castle and cathedral. The churches – particularly St Oswald's, near the elegant Kingsgate Bridge – are worth exploring. The Heritage Centre at St Mary-le-Bow, North Bailey, vividly tells

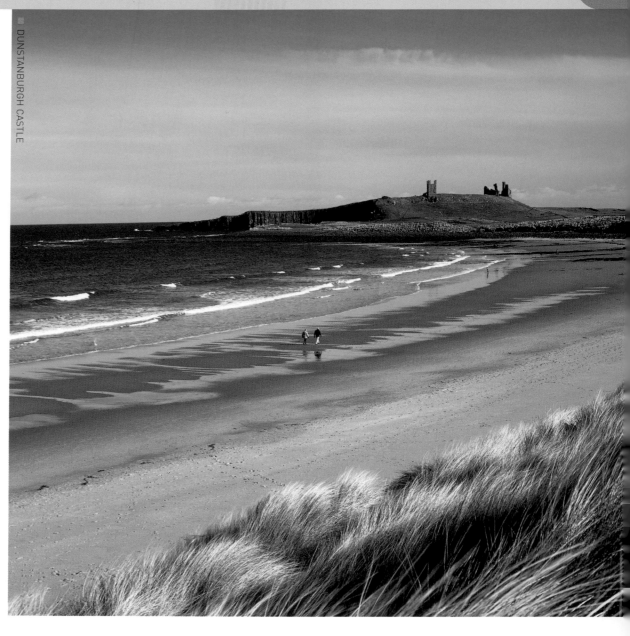

DUNSTANBURGH CASTLE

the history of Durham, while Durham University Oriental Museum, off Elvet Hill Road, is full of Chinese porcelain and jade. The Durham Light Infantry Museum reflects the military past of the regiment and the city. It also houses an art gallery.

A good way to see the best the city has to offer is to take this 2.5-mile (4km) walk. Start in the Market Place, and from the statue of Lord Londonderry on his horse, walk along Silver Street to descend to Framwellgate Bridge. Immediately at the end of the bridge turn left down the steps by the Coach and Eight pub to reach the river bank, going straight ahead with the castle and cathedral across the river. Now walk behind the riverside buildings to Prebends' Bridge, begun in 1772 with funds from the Canons (Prebendaries) of the cathedral. Do not cross the bridge, but continue alongside the river. On the opposite bank you will see the charming Grecian-style Count's House.

Walk along the riverside path until it ascends into St Oswald's churchyard. Turn left into Church Street and at the end

of the buildings, go left over Kingsgate Bridge, then up the steps at the end and into Bow Lane. At the top, turn left along North Bailey (if the cathedral is closed, turn right here and then take the first left on to Palace Green). After about 100 yards (91m) go right through the 16th-century archway leading to the informal little square called The College. Follow the wall on the right and turn right again at its end to go through a tunnel that leads into the cathedral cloister. Go left and right, around the cloister and then into the cathedral.

Leave the cathedral by the south door and walk towards the castle. At the end of the first building go left, signed Museum of Archaeology, past the house where J M Falkner, the author of *Moonfleet*, lived. Continue down to a crossing path, turn left and follow the main path downhill to the east end of Prebends' Bridge.

Turn sharp right along the river bank, past the Museum of Archaeology and up the steps on to Silver Street. Turn right here and after a few yards take another right turn to go through a narrow opening

into Moatside Lane. Follow the passage to emerge in Saddler Street and then turn left into the Market Place.

ELSDON MAP REF 409 K6

Elsdon by the River Rede was the capital of the remote Middle March – one of three protective areas set up in 1249 along the Scottish border. The attractive triangular green is surrounded by mainly 18th- and 19th-century houses. From early in the 12th century the village was guarded by Elsdon Castle; its motte-and-bailey earthworks are very well preserved.

The 14th-century Elsdon Tower, once a defensive pele for the vicars of Elsdon, stands near the church. The church, another St Cuthbert's, said to be one of the places where his body rested during its wanderings, is isolated on the green. Its bell-turret dates from 1720, but most of the building is from the 14th century. Inside are narrow aisles and thick walls. More than 1,000 skulls and bones were found here – bodies of soldiers who fell at the Battle of Otterburn in 1388.

Insight
ROMAN STOPS ON HADRIAN'S WALL

CARVORAN Magnis fort at Carvoran was built before Hadrian's Wall, to guard the junction of the Stanegate and the Maiden Way. The only stones still visible are part of the northwest tower. Adjoining the fort is the exciting Roman Army Museum, with finds from Magnis and other sites along the Wall, and a large-scale model of the fort. To the west, there is a fine stretch of the *vallum*, and further beyond this lies 14th-century Thirlwall Castle, beside Tipalt Burn.

HOUSESTEADS Housesteads – Roman Vercovicium – is the most visited fort on Hadrian's Wall due to its spectacular site, impressive remains and access to one of the best parts of the wall. Visit the museum first, then climb to the remains of town buildings by the South Gate. The gate itself was rebuilt as a bastle in the Middle Ages. Through it, to the right, you can visit the communal latrines, where 12 soldiers could sit. Walk along the wall westwards to Milecastle 37 – the views are wonderful – and on, if you can, to Steel Rigg, to see how the military structures of Rome have been absorbed into the landscape.

CARRAWBURGH Brocolitia, the fort here at Carrawburgh, remains largely unexcavated, though it is known to have been added in around AD 130. Near by are the remains of the most complete Mithraic temple to be found in Britain. The uninitiated gathered in a small ante-room. Beyond this was the temple, with three altars (those you see today are replicas) and statues of Mithras' attendants; Cautes, with his torch raised to represent light, and Cautopates, torch down for darkness.

CHESTERS Where Hadrian's Wall crossed the North Tyne, the Romans built a wooden bridge guarded by Cilurnum fort, now called Chesters. Near by are remains of the bridge, but they are better preserved over on the opposite bank, reached by a footpath from the bridge at Chollerford. In the river you can see an original pier, which carried the wooden pedestrians' bridge, as well as a later stone bridge built in about AD 206 to carry vehicles; two of its three piers can still be seen when the river is low.

HADRIAN'S WALL

HADRIAN'S WALL MAP REF 409 K7

Around AD 80 the Romans constructed a road – Stanegate – south of the Great Whin Sill. It went from Corbridge, where Dere Street crossed the River Tyne, to Carlisle. Guarded by forts, it was not originally a frontier, for Roman troops were active far into Scotland. But in about AD 100 Emperor Trajan withdrew to the Stanegate, building new forts and watchtowers on the Whin Sill. Trajan's successor, Hadrian, visiting in AD 122, ordered the construction of a wall which would be the limit of the empire and would offer protection from the tribes in the north that resisted Roman invasion.

Running 80 Roman miles – 73 modern miles (117.5km) – the Wall was built of local sandstone and ran between the Tyne and the Irthing; further west turf was used, later replaced by stone. It began 10 Roman feet – 9.5ft (3m) – wide, later reduced to 8ft (2.4m), or sometimes 6ft (1.8m). The *vallum*, a high-banked ditch south of the Wall to control civilians at the frontier, was another modification.

The Wall was probably around 21 feet (6.4m) high. Regular crossing points gave the Romans control: the barbarians could pass through into the Empire, but only to approved markets, unarmed and with a military escort. Later, in more troubled times, some of the gates were blocked.

When Hadrian died, the new emperor, Antoninus Pius, abandoned the Wall, pushed into Scotland and built the Antonine Wall (of turf) from the Forth to the Clyde. But the troops retreated to the Whin Sill in AD 160, when a new route – the Military Way – was built between the Wall and the *vallum* to improve access.

By around AD 407 the empire was breaking up; at this time the British army chose its own emperor, Constantine III, who went off to win Rome, leaving Britain undefended. The auxiliaries at the Wall drifted away, and it became a quarry for local farmers. Hadrian's part in the Wall's construction was forgotten until 1840, and it has only been in the 20th century that the site has gained legal protection.

HALTWHISTLE MAP REF 409 J7

Haltwhistle Burn flows into the South Tyne east of the town of Haltwhistle, and there are pleasant walks alongside the burn up to Hadrian's Wall. Haltwhistle is also a good place from which to explore the north Pennines. But don't neglect the attractive town centre, its stone streets radiating from the market place giving it a slightly stern, Scottish air. Some of its Victorian station buildings, including the stationmaster's house, waiting room and ticket office, date from as early as 1838.

The Red Lion Inn is based on a defensive tower, probably of the 17th century, when Haltwhistle was still at the mercy of Scottish raiders. The town was under the protection of the powerful Ridley family.

The church is one of the best in Northumberland, at least on the inside – its exterior is rather unprepossessing. It is mostly Early English in style, with long, thin lancet windows, and was carefully restored in 1870, when the wonderful stained glass, made by William Morris's company, was put in the east windows. Haltwhistle was once a thriving centre of industry (there are still manufacturing plants in and around the town), and by the burn you can see the remains of woollen mills, collieries and brickworks.

HEXHAM MAP REF 409 K7

St Etheldreda made a gift of Hexham manor to her spiritual adviser, Wilfrid, for supporting her against her husband King Egfrith. Wilfrid built the priory – it was never an abbey – in about AD 674. Wilfrid's crypt, reached from the new nave built in 1907, was built of Roman stones from Corstopitum (Corbridge), many still with carvings or inscriptions.

The rest of the priory is impressive, too, especially the early 13th-century choir, the north transept with fine lancet windows and, in the south transept, the Night Stair for the Augustinian canons to descend from their dormitory for night prayers. Look out for the nearby Roman tombstone of standard-bearer Flavius.

The priory was kept apart from the town by a row of houses set towards the market place, with its stone-columned Shambles, still used by traders. Be sure to visit 14th-century Moot Hall, a miniature castle with an archway tunnelling through it, which now houses the gallery. Through the arch, in Hallgate, is another fearsome tower, the Archbishops' Gaol. Built about 1330, it houses the Border History Museum and Library.

HOLY ISLAND MAP REF 409 K5

Holy Island has been known by this name since the 11th century, although its Celtic name, Lindisfarne, is just as familiar. The island was given to St Aidan in AD 635 by the King of Northumbria, and it became respected throughout Europe. Even more famous and influential was St Cuthbert, whose life and teaching drew pilgrims. He died in AD 687 and was buried in the church. When it was sacked during Danish raids in AD 875 the monks fled with his bones, searching for a safe and permanent home for them. The remains arrived in Durham more than 100 years later.

Lindisfarne seems an ideal setting for the monastic life – bare, windswept and flat, surrounded by sands covered by the sea twice daily. Before crossing to the island via the causeway, check the tides and note any warnings. A refuge is provided for the foolhardy who don't.

South of the square is St Mary's Church. Near by in the Heritage Centre there is an electronic copy of the famous Lindisfarne Gospels (with 'turnable' pages) – the original is in the British Museum. It was illuminated here in AD 698. Just offshore St Cuthbert's Island was used by the saint when he needed total solitude.

Next to the church are the remains of Lindisfarne Priory, built of beautiful red sandstone. It was founded by the Bishop of Durham in 1083, and finished by 1140. Its columns are patterned with zig-zags and chequers. The remaining rib of the crossing, known as the rainbow arch, shows that it once had a strong tower. Part of the cloister remains – in contrasting grey stone – but there is not much more, except a gatehouse and defensive walls against the Scots. The nearby museum tells the story of the island.

Stones from the Priory were used in the 1540s to build a fort on Beblowe, a rocky crag on the south shore. The fort's purpose was to defend the harbour, where part of Henry VIII's fleet had taken shelter in 1543 and where today the boats of the lobster and crab fishermen mingle with the pleasure craft. These defences were never tested before peace with the Scots came 60 years later. It was neglected until Edward Hudson, founder of *Country Life* magazine, bought it in 1902 and commissioned architect Edwin Lutyens to adapt it for use as a home. Lutyens' gardening collaborator Gertrude Jekyll designed the tiny walled garden 500 yards (455m) north of the castle.

OTTERBURN MAP REF 409 K6

Otterburn has had a place in military history since the Battle of Otterburn, on 19 August 1388, brought together the son of the Earl of Northumberland, Harry Hotspur, and Earl Douglas, who commanded a Scots raiding party. Versions of the battle vary, but most people agree that the Scots raiders beat Hotspur, that Douglas was killed and Hotspur was captured and later ransomed. The Percy Cross, in a plantation northwest of the village, is traditionally where Douglas died. Modern soldiers have practised live firing on the Otterburn Ranges to the north since 1911. There is public access along rights of ways and roads – but not when the red flags are flying. Check locally or call the Range Control on 01803 520569.

At the picturesque Otterburn Mill, built in the 18th century, you can purchase fine tweeds and woollens.

ROTHBURY MAP REF 409 K6

One of the main tourist centres of Northumberland, Rothbury, the capital of Coquetdale, is an attractive town, with stone buildings spreading outwards from an irregularly shaped green and a medieval bridge over the River Coquet.

The town was harried by William Wallace's army in the 13th century, and proclaimed the Old Pretender as James III in the 18th, but since the 19th century it has developed as a holiday centre.

The parish church underwent a Victorian restoration, which destroyed a Saxon tower and left little of the rest, but it is worth visiting for a glimpse of the font whose bowl dates from 1664, but stands on part of the 9th-century Rothbury Cross, decorated with Celtic-inspired designs.

East of Rothbury the Coquet rushes through a narrow gorge at The Thrum – you can reach it by a footpath from the bridge. In places no more than 5 feet (1.5m) wide, the river has scoured the sandstone here into contorted shapes.

Cragside (National Trust), east of Rothbury, is a major tourist attraction, but with a country park and gardens, it is usually easy to find a quiet corner. Built for the 1st Lord Armstrong by the architect Norman Shaw, it is a fantastic creation, a cross between an English manor house and a Bavarian *schloss*. It hangs over the wooded gorge of Debdon Burn in a sea of trees and its interior is full of heavy, late-Victorian atmosphere, though parts are dark and cramped. Spectacular exceptions include the fine library and the drawing room, with its huge alabaster fireplace.

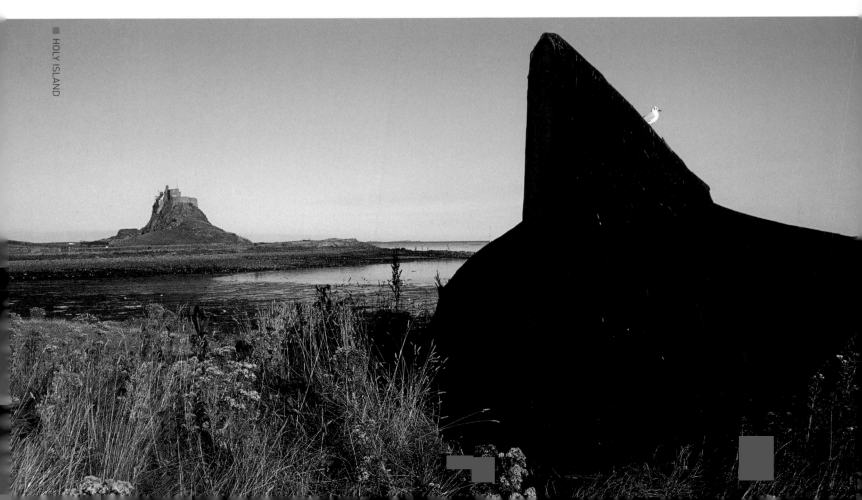

HOLY ISLAND

Kielder Water

Tucked away at the top of Northumberland, close by Hadrian's Wall and the Scottish Border, Kielder Water, with a 27-mile (43km) shoreline, is by far the largest man-made lake in Europe, and sits at the heart of the equally impressive Kielder Forest, Britain's largest forest, covering an area of over 153,140 acres (62,000ha). The lake is the reason why water shortages are unheard of in Northumberland, except on the national news, even though the county is one of the driest in Britain.

Kielder Forest, is also one of Britain's biggest nature reserves, where the hills, rivers and open areas add to the rich diversity of the forest making it an ideal habitat for some 6,000 roe deer, and one of the few places in England still home to native red squirrels, rather than the American grey variety. There is a tranquil beauty here, enhanced by activities such as sailing and other watersports, fishing and ferry cruises. The lake fringes and forest glades are best explored on foot, on a bicycle or on horseback.

Sitka spruce is the main species at Kielder, a tree that thrives best in the hostile upland environment, accounting for around three-quarters of the forest area: 12 per cent is Norway spruce, 9 per cent lodgepole pine plus a small percentage of larch, broadleaf and the once-ubiquitous Scots pine. And if the sometimes sombre aspect of a dense pine plantation is not your thing, then the on-going planting of natural broad-leaved trees, taking the percentage of hardwoods from just 1 per cent in the original forest to 8 per cent by 2020, will eventually make a real difference.

At the end of the day, Kielder's main purpose is commercial timber production. Half the timber produced here is taken straight to the saw mills in the north of England and southern Scotland for construction timber, fencing and packaging. The remaining half,

consisting of small round wood cut from smaller trees and the tops of much bigger trees, goes to a paper mill at Workington in Cumbria, and is turned into carton board, cereal packets and boxes.

Central to the area stands Kielder Castle. Built in 1775 as a hunting lodge for the Duke of Northumberland, the Castle is dressed with mock fortifications and is now the focal point for visitors to the forest. The Castle itself houses a series of exhibitions about birds, wildlife, history and the daily working of the Forest. The grounds include picnic sites, a children's playground, walking trails, cycling routes (cycle hire on site), a mountain bike skills loop, and orienteering routes. Within the grounds of the Castle is a work of art, one of a few at Kielder, called Minotaur, which is a maze built of basalt stone and glass. The Castle, now one of Kielder Forests visitor centres, houses a Forest Enterprise exhibition.

Kielder Water Birds of Prey Centre at Leaplish Waterside Park, offers a direct 'hands on' experience during which you meet all the northern indigenous owls, as well as birds of prey and other owls from around the world. It is one of the largest and most fascinating collections of birds of prey in the north of England, boasting over 60 birds and 28 species. Weather permitting, flying demonstrations take place three times a day.

Free-range birdwatching at Kielder can be difficult because of the density of trees, but birds of prey are the star attractions, and Forest Enterprise have created a raptor viewpoint at Bakethin, about a mile (1.6km) from Kielder Village. Kestrels are seen regularly, and there is always a chance of seeing merlin, peregrine or goshawk. Nor are sparrowhawks uncommon; indeed the Forest Information Centre at Kielder Castle has seasonal video footage of a nearby sparrowhawk nesting site. Bakethin Reservoir has been declared a nature reserve, and attracts ospreys as well as sizeable numbers of wildfowl and gulls at all times of the year. In the main conifer forest, the elusive crossbill flits through the tree canopy, whilst the more deciduous areas of the North Tyne Valley attract pied flycatcher and redstart especially during the breeding season.

With over 372 miles (598km) of waterways in the forest, and the reservoir at its centre, otters are increasingly a common (if secretive) inhabitant, but there are now signs that otters are using all the major waterways in the area. The European otter is part of the same family as badgers, weasels, stoats, pine marten and mink, and is listed in the International Union for the Conservation of Nature (IUCN) Red Book as 'vulnerable to extinction'. The number of otters in Britain is not known, but they are on the increase in some areas, and the steps being taken at Kielder to maintain and improve their habitat are vital to the future well being of this amphibious and charismatic creature. Being at the top of the food chain, otters are predators, hunters rather than being hunted, and have a diet mainly of fish, small mammals and birds. The main threat to otters is from humans through the destruction of their habitat and from pesticides running off farmland and polluting watercourses.

The remarkable diversity of Kielder is shown in the fact that here there are no fewer than nine Sites of Special Scientific Interest. Embracing some 18,500 acres (7,500ha), this represents 4 per cent of the total SSSI area in England alone, and sites include ancient woodland, fossil trees, geological sites, moorlands and the extensive Border Mire peat bogs. Access to part of the mires has been improved by the completion of a boardwalk, which just happens to surround one of the best ponds for dragonflies in Northumberland.

Cycling, walking, sailing, birdwatching and simple relaxation and enjoyment with the family are all major attractions at Kielder, and are enjoyed by many through the balmy days of summer. But above all else, away from the main centres of sports and activities, there is a serenity and tranquility that belies the man-made nature of this stunning place, where herds of silent deer slip through the serried ranks of spruce like shadows in springtime, and the wind seems forever tangled in the trees.

TOP LEFT Budding mountainbikers get ready to test their brakes on a skills coaching course in Hamsterley Forest.

TOP RIGHT *Skyspace* at Cat Cairn in Kielder Forest, is an underground chamber that is accessed by a tunnel. The 10ft (3m) circular opening in the top allows natural light to shine in and create a changing pattern of light on the inside throughout the day.

ABOVE LEFT A Ruppell's Griffon vulture at the Kielder Water Birds of Prey Centre.

ABOVE RIGHT Husky racing has been taking place at Kielder for many years. The rigs use wheels for most of the year and skis during snowy weather conditions.

OPPOSITE Kielder Water, surrounded by Kielder Forest. The Forestry Commission owns all of the forest land on this side of the border, excluding Kielder Reservoir and a 50 metre strip of trees that surrounds it. This strip of land is largely unplanted and owned privately.

SEAHOUSES & FARNE ISLANDS
MAP REFS 409 L5

Seahouses has a prosperous air, geared to the tourist industry. In the town there are some pleasant fishermen's cottages around Craster Square and a busy harbour, built in the 18th century but much enlarged in the 19th. At the harbour you can get boat trips to the Farne Islands, and there are fine sands to the north and south of the sheltering Snook Point.

St Aidan spent each Lent on Inner Farne, one of the 28 Farne Islands (or 15, if you count at high tide), and St Cuthbert lived here from AD 676 to AD 685. His cell on Inner Farne was surrounded by an embankment so that all he could see was heaven. St Cuthbert's Church on Inner Farne, near the site of his hermitage, dates mostly from about 1370 and has 17th-century woodwork, brought here from Durham Cathedral.

To the west, Prior Castell's Tower may have held a lighthouse from the days when there were Benedictine monks on the island. Today's white-painted lighthouse, which is open to visitors, was built in 1809. Further out, beyond Staple, is Longstone, a rather uninviting, low, bare rock with a red-and-white striped lighthouse, built in 1826. This was where the Darling family lived, and from where Grace and her father set out on their rescue mission.

For many visitors the attraction of the Farne Islands is their wildlife, especially the birds and the seals. Egg collectors caused unprecedented damage in the 19th century, and the Farne Islands Association, set up in 1880, employed watchers to protect the breeding birds. The National Trust has owned the islands since 1925, and permits to land on Inner Farne and Staple Island must be bought from the Wardens. Check, too, that your boatman is licensed to land his passengers. During the breeding season, from May to July, landing is restricted – and if the weather is bad you may not be able to land at all. There are nature walks on both these islands.

The delightful little puffins are always favourites with visitors, but you may also see fulmars, petrels, razorbills, ring plover, rock pipits, eiders (known locally as St Cuthbert's – or Cuddy's – Chicks), kittiwakes, cormorants, terns, guillemots, shags, oystercatchers and, of course, gulls. The boat trips usually pass near enough to see their nesting sites, and on Staple and Inner Farne you can walk, with care, among their nests.

VINDOLANDA MAP REF 409 J7

Agricola had a turf fort at Vindolanda in the AD 80s to guard the Stanegate, and part of the paved road, as well as a Roman milestone, can still be seen here. Another fort was built before Hadrian's time, and when the wall was put up, the fort was rebuilt in stone, then almost totally rebuilt 100 years later, with its usual rectangular shape. The layout of the headquarters and parts of the gates are clearly visible.

Vindolanda also has the biggest civilian settlement that can be seen on the wall. Visit the mansion (an inn for travellers) with its bathhouse, and the large 'corridor' house, part of which was a butcher's shop. At the town bathhouse hairpins and a child's sandal were found in the drains. You can see some of the pink waterproof plaster that lined the walls and floors.

Children visiting Vindolanda usually make for the reconstructions of parts of Hadrian's Wall. The Turf Wall shows what the original part of the wall was like before it was rebuilt in stone. More impressive is the Stone Wall, nearly 23 feet (7m) high, with battlements, turret and ditch.

Vindolanda's waterlogged soil has helped to preserve many details of daily life – the museum shows some of them, including leather shoes, textiles and ornaments. There is also a replica of a Roman kitchen. Most important are the wooden writing tablets, with gossip, invitations, letters asking for new underwear, and accounts of food stores, bringing the people vividly to life.

WARKWORTH CASTLE MAP REF 409 L6

Shakespeare, who set three dramatic scenes of *Henry IV* here, called the ruins of Warkworth Castle 'this worm-eaten hold of ragged stone'. Actually, the huge keep is one of the most spectacular in Britain. Set in a loop of the River Coquet on the site of the original motte, its plan is a cross superimposed on a square, and it stands to its full height, partly restored in the 19th century for the Duke of Northumberland. The original 11th-century structure was replaced by a stone castle before 1158 and was sacked by the Scots in 1174. The Percys lived at Warkworth rather than Alnwick until the 16th century and the Lion Tower carries their crest.

The Percy Lion is also carved on the keep wall that dominates the little town, where the medieval street plan is still evident. Georgian and Victorian houses lead down the hill to the church and the fortified bridge. The Old Pretender was proclaimed here in 1715, his army dined at the Masons' Arms and in the church his Catholic chaplain said prayers.

The church has a 14th-century spire but inside is almost all Norman, with a stone-vaulted chancel, its roof ribs decorated with zig-zags. This church was the scene of a massacre in 1174, when the Scottish army killed most of the population of Warkworth, seeking refuge inside.

VINDOLANDA

AROUND DRURIDGE BAY

This walk takes in a nature reserve, country park and beach. The biggest attractions here are the birds. Resident species are joined by those migrating between the summer feeding and breeding grounds in the north and Africa, where many over-winter. Wimbrel, dunlin and sanderling are among the migrating species, whilst redshank, plover and bar-tailed godwit winter here. You will also see whooper and Bewick swans plus favourites such as tits, finches, blackbirds and robins.

DISTANCE/TIME 5.5 miles (8.8km) 1h45 **MAP** OS Explorers 325 Morpeth & Blyth; 332 Alnwick & Amble **START** Car park at Hauxley Nature Reserve; grid ref: NU282024 (on Explorer 332) **PATHS** Paths and tracks, with good walk on beach, no stiles **THE PUB** Widdrington Inn, Morpeth. Tel: 01670 760260

1 A waymarked footpath beside the car park entrance winds between the nature reserve and a caravan site towards the coast. Through a gate at the bottom, turn right on a track, which shortly passes two gates that give access to hides overlooking the lake.

2 Leaving the reserve, continue a little further along a tarmac track to an informal parking area on the left, where there is easy access on to the beach. Now, follow the shore past Togston Links, across a stream and on below Hadston Links.

3 After 1.25 miles (2km), wooden steps take the path off the sands on to the dunes. Cross a tarmac track and continue over a marshy area into pinewood. Beyond the trees, emerge by a car park and walk across to the Druridge Bay Country Park visitor centre, where there is a café and toilets.

4 A footway to the left winds around Ladyburn Lake, soon passing a boat launching area. Keep to the lower path, which soon leads to stepping-stones across the upper neck of the lake. If you would rather not cross here, continue around the

upper edge of a wooded nature sanctuary above the water to a footbridge higher up. Over the bridge, turn immediately right, through a gate into a nature sanctuary. Follow the river bank back through another gate to reach the far side of the stepping-stones.

5 This side of the lake has a more 'natural' feel, the path winding through trees to emerge beside a lushly vegetated shoreline where swans like to feed. After crossing a bridge over the lake's outflow, carry on back to the visitor centre.

6 Retrace your steps to the beach and turn back towards Hauxley, but when you reach the point at which you originally dropped on to the sands, remain on the shore towards Bondi Carrs. Seaweed can make the rocks slippery, so be careful clambering over them as you round the point, where Coquet Island then comes into view ahead. Not far beyond there, after passing a look-out post and approaching large rocks placed as a storm defence, leave across the dunes, retracing your outward path the short distance back to the car park and the start of the walk.

WALK 120

THE ANCIENT SPIRIT OF THE SIMONSIDES

This walk visits a hill that had religious significance to early settlers and is now a rock climbers' playground. Many sites show evidence of human activity that dates back 5,000 years to the Iron Age. Conifer forests now cover the lower reaches of the hills, but the summit crags remain clear. As a sport, rock climbing began in Northumberland in the late 19th century and the crags of Simonside were among the first to be developed.

DISTANCE/TIME 5.5 miles (8.8km) 3h **MAP** OS Explorer OL42 Kielder Water & Forest **START** Large car park at forest picnic area; grid ref: NZ 037997 **PATHS** Generally good, but steep and muddy in places **THE PUB** The Queen's Head Hotel, Townfoot, Rothbury. Tel: 01669 620470; www.queensheadrothbury.com

1 From the notice board in the picnic area, go through the gate on to the broad forest road. Follow this gently uphill, swinging to the right round the long hairpin bend, then back left at the top of the hill. When the road splits, take the right-hand fork, past the communications mast and go gently downhill. When you get to the next junction, take the left-hand fork and follow the road past the sign indicating a detour to Little Church Rock.

2 When you come to a marker post, where a narrow track leads to the left, ignore this and continue along the broad track, which now becomes grassy. After passing a huge, heavily overgrown boulder, continue to the small cairn which marks the start of a subsidiary track on the left. Follow this track uphill through the forest and out on to the heather-covered hillside. You will now see Simonside's crags 0.5 mile (800m) away to your left.

3 Continue up the narrow track to join the broader one at the edge of the upper forest and follow this left for about 275yds (250m) to the corner of the trees. A rough track,

sometimes quite muddy in places, picks its way through boulders up the hillside. Follow this, keeping the crags on your left-hand side, on to the plateau and walk on the paved route along the top of the crags to the large cairn on the summit, which is probably a burial mound.

4 Away from the summit, the track splits into two. Follow the right fork, still paved across boggy ground for a third of a mile (500m). Climb the short rise keeping the wonderfully wind-sculpted Old Stell Crag to your left and move round on to the summit and another large cairn.

5 Take the narrow path down to join the lower track. This joins the paved route again in 0.5 mile (800m), by the cairn on Dove Crag. Now descend a rocky staircase and cross a ladder stile, keeping your direction along the broad ridge path uphill to The Beacon cairn. Continue downhill for 0.5 mile (800m) to join the road at Lordenshaws car park.

6 Turn left and follow the road for 1 mile (1.6km) until you arrive back at the forest picnic area at the start of the walk.

The gated narrow road needs care as it winds for 7 miles (11.5km) – wide verges allow passing. The road drops into North Charlton. At the A1 turn left and after a mile (1.6km), turn right, signed 'Preston Tower, Ellingham'. After about 2 miles (3.2km) you will see the 1392 Preston Tower.

This has a medieval Border life display. With its robust 7ft (21m) thick walls, this original Pele tower has retained two of its fine turrets.

6 At the T-junction just beyond, turn left to 'Beadnell, Seahouses'. Go over the level crossing at Chathill, continue for 3.5 miles (5.6km) past Beadnell and along the coast on the B1340, into Seahouses. At the first roundabout turn right, at the next roundabout turn left, following the 'Coast' signs to ancient Bamburgh with its wonderful coastline.

Bamburgh has a huge, square Norman castle, visible for miles around atop a 180ft (549m) basalt crag. The castle walls were impregnable until the War of the Roses, when cannon fire proved too much for its fortifications.

7 Go round Budle Bay and at the T-junction in Waren Mill turn left to 'Belford, Wooler'. In 2.5 miles (4km) turn right on the A1 and left to Belford. Just before the church go left on the B6349 to 'Wooler'. In 2.5 miles (4km), turn right on a narrow unclassified road signed 'Hazelrigg, Lowick'.

There are spectacular views of the Cheviots to be had from here. For environmental scientists, Hazelrigg has a significant weather station.

8 Turn right at a T-junction after 2 miles (3.2km), to 'Holburn, Berwick'. A little way along here is the track to St Cuthbert's Cave. After 5 miles (8km) cross the B6353, then after 0.5 mile (800m) turn right to 'Kentstone, Beal'. At the A1 go straight over to visit Holy Island, checking the tides for your return journey first.

Lindisfarne has a ruined priory, a Tudor castle and a heritage centre. As well as the Holy Island scriptures to see, the heritage centre pays tribute to the bravery of its seafaring islanders.

9 Otherwise, turn left towards Berwick, passing Haggerston Castle. In 4.5 miles (7.2km) go right at the roundabout along the A1167 to 'Scremerston, Berwick'. At the next roundabout go straight on, over the bridge and into the town centre.

NORTHUMBERLAND'S COAST & HILLS

Castles, spectacular views of the Cheviots, wild moorland and the coastal islands are among the highlights of this circular drive from England's most northerly town. Extend the drive by 10 miles (16km) if you visit Holy Island, but before you set out be sure to check on the tides.

Route Directions

Start at the historic town of Berwick-on-Tweed. Fought over by the Scottish and the English for centuries, Berwick is England's most northerly situated town and lies almost equidistant between Newcastle and Edinburgh.

1 From the centre go over the Royal Tweed Bridge, signed 'Newcastle, A1' and go right, signed 'Coldstream A698'. Head right at the first roundabout and then straight on at the second, following Coldstream signs. After 3 miles (4.8km), turn right along an unclassified road signed 'Horncliffe, Norham Castle'. In 2 miles (3.2km) pass the ruins of Norham Castle to enter Norham.

Norham Castle was one of the strongest border castles and saw much fighting until the union of the Scottish and English crowns removed the need for defence here.

2 Follow the road past the cross and at the T-junction turn left, signed 'Berwick', on the B6470. After 0.5 miles (800m) turn right along an unclassified road. At the T-junction turn left on the A698, to Berwick, then fast right on to an unclassified road, signed 'Felkington'. Follow this winding road for 4 miles (6.4km), following signs for Etal and Ford, to reach the B6354, where you turn right. Follow the road for 3 miles (4.8km) through Etal to Ford.

In Ford, visit Lady Waterford Hall, with murals depicting locals in biblical scenes. The pretty building, with its two front gables, was originally used as the village school.

3 Just before Ford church go right, signed 'Kimmerston'. After 1.5 miles (2.4km) turn right at the T-junction, signed 'Milfield'. Go over Redscar Bridge and straight on to meet the A697, where you turn left towards Wooler and Morpeth. Follow the main road through Akeld and at a junction a mile beyond turn right (signed 'Wooler light traffic only') then continue into the centre of Wooler.

This bustling market town is popular with walkers heading to the Cheviots. Once made prosperous by the wool trade from the Cheviot sheep, Wooler is a popular stop along the long-distance path St Cuthbert's Way.

4 At the end of the main street turn left by the church then cross the main road on to the B6348, signed 'Chatton', 'Belford' and 'Chillingham Castle, Wild Cattle'. After 2.5 miles (4km) there is a sharp right-hand bend at the top of a hill. Beyond this, follow the main road for 2.5 miles (4km) to Chatton. Turn right at the 'Chillingham, Alnwick' sign. Follow the road past the entrance to the Wild Cattle Park and the castle.

5 At the brow of the hill turn left to 'Hepburn Wood Walks'. Follow the road through Hepburn and then uphill, past Ros Castle.

70 MILES (112.6KM)

THREE DALES

This is a spectacular drive that takes you to the valleys of the Tyne, Wear and Tees and across some of England's wildest and most remote moorland. Much of the route is within the officially designated North Pennines Area of Outstanding Natural Beauty. Note: Some of the route passes over unfenced, high moorland. You should not attempt this drive in bad weather or when visibility is low.

Route Directions

Hexham is a good town to explore on foot, with its attractive Victorian shop-fronts, fine medieval buildings and 7th-century abbey.

1 From the centre of Hexham take the B6305 west towards Allendale turning left at the traffic lights by the Fox Inn. Follow the main road, signed 'Allendale', to Catton. Go through Allendale town.

Allendale's centre has an attractive square surrounded by stone houses. The market town became prosperous in the 17th century due to the success of its lead mines.

2 Continue down the valley of the River East Allen for 7.5 miles (12.1km) through spread-out Sinderhope and on into Allenheads, once an important lead-mining centre. After driving 1.5 miles (2.4km) beyond the village, cross the County Durham border and then descend into Weardale. The B6295 joins the A689 as you reach Cowshill. At the junction you can divert from the main route by turning right for 2.5 miles (4km) to visit Killhope Wheel & Lead Mining Centre.

A discovery trail leads visitors through the site, devoted to the local lead-mining industry, or you can take a guided tour and go underground

3 On the main route, turn left to go through Cowshill and Ireshopeburn and into the centre of St John's Chapel, with its 18th-century church and the only Town Hall in a Durham village. Turn right up a narrow entry, Harthope Road, signed 'Langdon Beck'. The unclassified road eventually crosses a cattle grid and climbs steeply on to Harthope Moor. This is one of the highest roads in England, attaining an altitude of 2,057ft (627m).

Do not attempt this route in bad weather or limited visibility. The road is marked by tall, narrow poles, indicating the route when the road itself is covered by snow.

4 Follow the road for 5 miles (8km), to descend, with wide views of the valley, into Teesdale. At the junction with the B6277 turn left, signed 'Langdon Beck, Middleton'. After half a mile (800m) of driving a road to the right leads to Cow Green Reservoir and Cauldron Snout. Continue along the B6277 for 3 miles (4.8km) to reach the spectacular High Force waterfall.

One of the highest single-drop waterfalls in England, this is where the Tees plunges over Great Whin Sill.

5 In 1.5 miles (2.4km) is Bowlees Visitor Centre, and then the road enters the former lead-mining centre of Middleton-in-Teesdale. Immediately after crossing the bridge into Middleton turn sharp left, up a steep hill signed 'Stanhope'. After half a mile (800m) turn right, again signed 'Stanhope'. After 4.5 miles (7.2km) pass over a cattle grid, go round a sharp right-hand bend and turn left immediately, then left again on to the B6278. The road goes over moorland with spectacular views.

6 After 8.5 miles (13.7km), descend into Weardale. Just before the river the road bends left and then right over a bridge to join the A689. Turn right into the centre of Stanhope and turn left, signed 'B6278 Edmundbyers', just beside the Grey Bull pub. Go up the steep hill through Crawleyside and after 2.5 miles (4km), where the main road goes slightly right, continue ahead on an unclassified road, signed 'Blanchland'. Follow this road for 5.5 miles (8.8km) across open moorland and descend into the valley of Beldon Burn at Baybridge. Go over the bridge, crossing back into Northumberland, and follow the road into Blanchland.

The honey-coloured, mainly 18th-century houses in the centre of Blanchland are set around two informal squares separated by an archway of the monastic gatehouse.

7 In the village take the road straight ahead beside the abbey tower, signposted 'Corbridge, Hexham'. As the road ascends there are views over Derwent Reservoir. The road then passes through Slaley Forest and descends to the very narrow Linnels Bridge over Devil's Water, and 2 miles (3.2km) further on takes you back into the centre of Hexham town.

THROUGH THE GORGE OF THE RIVER COQUET

This is a fairly demanding but spectacular walk through some of Northumberland's geological history. Nowhere is this geology better laid out to view than it is around the gorge of the River Coquet, west of the village of Alwinton. To the north are the volcanic Cheviot Hills, while to the south are the fell sandstones. And in the gorge itself, at Barrow Scar, the layers of the cementstones lie fully exposed.

1 Turn right, out of the car park and follow the road for 700yds (637m) to a gate on the left to Barrow Mill. Go through the gate and down to the farm, passing the remains of a corn-drying kiln (1812). Go through another gate into a field, cross this and go through a gate to the river bank. Ford the river. After a period of rain, this will involve getting your feet wet. If the water is too high, go back to Alwinton and walk along the main road to the bridge over the Coquet. A few yards beyond, look for a stile on the right and follow the path across meadows to the ruin at Barrow.

2 Enter the field and follow the fence to the right to a gate. Go through this or over the stile about 20yds (18m) away to the left and continue to the derelict farm buildings. Follow the track up the hillside to the right-hand corner of the conifer forest.

3 About 50yds (46m) before reaching a signpost marking the edge of a military firing range, follow a less well-defined track across the heather-covered hillside to the right, rising slightly, until you come to a wire fence. Follow this over the top of Barrow Scar, keeping the fence on your right. When you meet a second fence, follow this

to a stile. Cross the stile and go down to an obvious loop in the river. In late summer, the track may be obscured by bracken.

4 At the river bend, cross a stile, then another after 100yds (91m). Cross the field and a stile into the farmyard at Linshiels. Go through the farmyard, across two bridges and join the road. Turn left and follow the road until just past the farm buildings, to a signpost pointing to Shillmoor.

5 Go up the hillside, over a stile and follow the track overlooking the gorge and its waterfalls. For a short distance, the slopes below are precipitous and care is needed, though the track is good. Continue alongside the river, descending eventually to some sheep pens and a ford. Continue ahead, now ascending a larger path to intersect a bridleway. Turn right and double back, crossing a stream and passing through a series of gates before ascending the hillside on a broad sweeping path.

6 At the top of the slope continue across level ground, then descend to a stile. Cross this and follow the track, over another stile and down to the road. Follow the road for 1 mile (1.6km) back to Alwinton.

DISTANCE/TIME 4.5 miles (7.2km) 3h **MAP** OS Explorer OL16 The Cheviot Hills **START** Car park at Alwinton; grid ref: NT 919063 **PATHS** Mostly hill footpaths, some narrow with severe drops on one side. River forded at one point; 8 stiles **THE PUB** The Rose and Thistle, Alwinton. Tel: 01669 650226; www.roseandthistlealwinton.com ❶ Close to MoD artillery range over Barrow Scar. When red flags flying, walk may be inadvisable

WALK 122

TARSET BURN & NORTH TYNE

The area around Lanehead is called Tarset but there is no Tarset village – only the burn in its valley, a name and the scant remains of a castle. The walks leads to the hamlet of Thorneyburn, which consists mainly of the church and the former rectory. The farmhouse at Redhaugh probably began as a fortified bastle house.

1 At a staggered crossroads at Lanehead turn right, signed 'Donkleywood'. At Redmire cottages turn right through a gate, and cross the yard to leave it by two more gates. Cross a field, passing through a gap to reach a handgate. Bear left, descending to reach a kissing gate by the river. Follow the river bank right, through some gates before rising to a final gate and dropping to a bridge. Cross Tarset Burn and follow the path down a ramp to join a farm track. Turn left along this track to reach the farmyard.

2 Go though the farmyard and ascend on a track on the far side. As it bears left, go ahead past a waymarker and down to cross a stream. Pass a waymarker post and go through a gateway. Bend right and go through a handgate. Turn left along the fence, then, at a stile, bear half right across the open moor towards some woods and a church. Keep left of a ruined wall, aiming for a dilapidated shed and wall descending to a bridge over the burn.

3 Cross the stream. Veer left on the opposite bank to locate a gate at the side of a garden. Go through this and follow the track beside a

churchyard to reach the road. Turn right and at a T-junction turn left. Follow the lane past Redheugh farm and a 'Forestry Commission Sidwood' sign to the Sidwood Picnic Area, near white-painted buildings.

4 Follow the path into the wood on your left, but soon look for a right turn, crossing a burn and continuing uphill. Cross a forest track and then continue uphill through a clear fell. Maintain your direction as the route levels, now with a ditch to your right. On descending, the forest gives way to moorland on the left and you reach a gate. Continue walking down through the enclosure, crossing a burn then rising to a crossing track. Turn left and follow the track down to cross the burn with care at Slaty Ford.

5 Continue on a prominent enclosed track to reach a gate. Beyond the gate, follow a minor road for 1 mile (1.6km) along the flank of the North Tyne valley passing through a gate after 0.5 mile (800m) to reach a junction. Keep ahead, over a cattle grid and down to a bridge over Tarset Burn. Continue on the lane as it ascends the bank to the main road. Turn left to return to the car park.

DISTANCE/TIME 7.5 miles (12.1km) 3h **MAP** OS Explorer OL42 Kielder Water & Forest **START** Lanehead Village Hall car park; grid ref: NY793858 **PATHS** Burnside and moorland paths and tracks. Some wet areas **THE PUB** The Hollybush Inn, Greenhaugh, Hexham. Tel: 01434 240391

SMUGGLERS & THE LIGHT OF MARSDEN BAY

You will walk along the coast near South Shields, and inland to the Cleadon Hills, passing two windmills. The first, in Marsden, retains its sails; the other was built in the 1820s, but was later damaged in a storm. In World War II it housed Royal Observer Corps members who scanned the North Sea for enemy aircraft. The 1871 Souter Lighthouse protected ships from the rocks called Whitburn Steel.

DISTANCE/TIME 5.5 miles (8.8km) 2h   **MAP** OS Explorer 316 Newcastle upon Tyne **START** Whitburn Coastal Park car park; grid ref: NZ412635 **PATHS** Roads, tracks, field and coastal paths **THE PUB** The Marsden Grotto, Coast Road, Marsden. Tel: 0191 455 6060

1 Leave the car park at its southern end, following the gravel track toward the houses. The path winds and goes past a sign for Whitburn Point Nature Reserve. Follow the track ahead to go through a gap in a wall and turn right. The path bends right, left and right again to join a road into houses. Go straight ahead to join the main road.

2 Cross the road and turn left. Walk down the road until you reach the windmill. Turn right to enter the grounds of the windmill. Go up the slope on the path, then between houses. Bear left, then turn right to reach a T-junction.

3 Go straight ahead on a path that goes to the right of house No. 99. When you reach another road turn left. Just after the first bungalow on the right, turn right along a signed track. Follow the track towards the farm. Go through the farmyard over two stiles and follow the lane beyond, with a hedge to your right. Where it ends, turn right over a stile.

4 Follow the path along the field-edge. Go over another stile, gradually ascending. The path bends left then right, still following

the field edge. Go over another two stiles. The path will bring you to the tower of Cleadon Windmill.

5 Go to the right of the windmill, following the wall on your right. Go right through a kissing gate, then bear slightly right (a brick tower to your left). Go parallel with the wall on your right. Cross a track and go through a wire mesh fence at right angles to the wall. Follow the path through scrubland to emerge by a yellow post by the golf course.

6 Cross the course, following yellow posts and looking out for golfers. Cross a stile and turn right along a signed footpath, following the wall on your right. The path eventually descends beside houses to a road.

7 Cross and take the footpath almost opposite, to the right of a caravan site, heading towards the sea. Carefully cross the busy A183, then turn right, following the sea edge. Marsden Rock is near by, and the Marsden Grotto to your left as you cross the road. Follow the coast as it bends left to Lizard Point. After visiting Souter Lighthouse, continue ahead on a path slightly inland from the coast, which returns you to the car park.

WALK 124

ALONG HADRIAN'S WALL

The Romans built the Wall to repel the Picts and Britons. It was planned to span the land between the River Irthing at Thirlwall and Newcastle, but added a turf wall that would extend to the west coast at Bowness on the Solway Firth. After the Romans left Britain the Wall decayed and its masonry was re-used.

DISTANCE/TIME 8 miles (12.9km) 4h   **MAP** OS Explorer OL43 Hadrian's Wall **START** Steel Rigg (pay) car park; grid ref: NY750677 **PATHS** Mainly well-walked National Trails; 16 stiles **THE PUB** The Milecastle Inn, Military Road, near Haltwhistle. Tel: 01434 321372; www.milecastle-inn.co.uk

1 From the car park descend to a grassy depression beneath Peel Crags. The path arcs left and climbs back to the ridge in a series of steps before following the cliff tops past Turret 39a and Milecastle 39.

2 There's another dip, then a climb to Highshield Crags, which overlook Crag Lough. Beyond the lake the footpath climbs past Hotbank farm.

3 At the next dip, Rapishaw Gap, turn left to cross over a ladder stile and then follow the faint but waymarked Pennine Way route across undulating moorland. The first stile lies in the far right corner of a large rushy enclosure. A clear cart track develops beyond a dyke and then climbs to a ridge on Ridley Common where you turn half left to descend a grassy ramp.

4 The path slowly arcs right to meet and cross a fenced cart track at Cragend. Here a clear grass track zig-zags down to a moorland depression with Greenlee Lough in full view to your left. At the bottom the ground can be marshy and the path becomes indistinct in places. A waymark points a sharp right turn but the path loses itself on the bank above it. Head north here, keeping

the farmhouse of East Stonefolds at ten to the hour. The next stile lies in a kink in the cross wall.

5 Beyond this, turn half left over a field then cross a ladder stile and turn left along a farm track to pass through East Stonefolds. The track ends at West Stonefolds. Walk through the farmyard, heeding the plea from the residents not to intrude on their privacy.

6 Past the house continue, with a wall left, along a grassy ride, and go over a step stile to a signposted junction of routes. Go ahead on the permissive path signposted to Greenlee Lough Birdhide. The path follows a fence down to the lake. Ignore the stile and continue alongside the fence.

7 Cross a stile then wetlands on a duckboard path, which soon swings right to a gate. Beyond this continue on the path, climbing northwest, guided by waymarker posts to the farm track by the clearfelled stumps of the Greenlee Plantation.

8 Turn left along the track and follow it past Gibbs Hill farm. Past the farmhouse a tarmac lane leads back towards the wall. Turn left at the T-junction to the car park.

DISTANCE/TIME 13 miles (20.9km) 2h30 **MAP** OS Explorer OL42 Kielder Water & Forest **START** Falstone car park; grid ref: NY723874 **TRACKS** Minor roads, lanes and tracks **THE PUB** The Pheasant Inn, Stannersburn, Falstone. Tel: 01434 240382

DISTANCE/TIME 12 miles (19.3km) 2h **MAP** OS Explorer OL43 Hadrian's Wall **START** National Park Visitor Centre pay car park at Once Brewed; grid ref: NY752668 **TRACKS** Roads and country lanes **THE PUB** Twice Brewed Inn, Once Brewed, Bardon Mill. Tel: 01434 344534

BOTH SIDES OF THE TYNE

This cycle ride takes you along both banks of the River North Tyne which has its source on Deadwater Fell in the nearby Cheviot Hills. It then flows into Europe's largest artificial lake at Kielder Water before emerging at Falstone then flowing south to join the River South Tyne at the 'meeting of waters' near Hexham. From here it continues as the River Tyne into the city of Newcastle. This is a very peaceful route through some splendid scenery. At Kielder Water there is a range of family-friendly activities including watersports and walking trails and at this point there is the opportunity to extend this route to include some of the many cycle trails through Kielder Forest. It is also worth spending some time exploring Falstone village. The Victorian schoolroom is part of the Tynedale Renewable Energy Trail and has been converted into an excellent tea room, while the village churchyard has several interesting gravestones from the early 18th century. Look out for one depicting a girl holding hands with a skeleton. Part of the run out from Falstone takes you along the disused line of the old Borders County Railway that once ran from Riccarton Junction to Hexham. It now forms part of the Reivers Cycle Route before disappearing under water at Kielder Dam.

1 Exit the car park at the start and turn right on to a lane. Continue along it to cross a bridge by a church. The lane turns right and away from the river then forks at Mouseyhaugh. Keep left here, crossing a cattle grid, then go through a gate.

2 Cross another bridge and go through another gate then continue along the track to High Hawkhope Farm. Go through a gate and circle to the right of the farmstead to reach a crossroads. Turn left on to Regional Cycle Route 10, The Reivers Route.

3 Head uphill on this broad track passing through a forestry plantation. Just before the top of the hill the trees stop and you can see along Kielder Water. On the left is a memorial erected to commemorate the opening of the reservoir by Her Majesty the Queen on 26 May 1982.

4 Continue cycling to the top of the hill and then turn left to head down to and along the road across the dam. At a T-junction with the road turn left and keep on this route, passing the Pheasant Inn to reach the Tyne Bridge after 4.5 miles (7.2km).

5 Cross the bridge and head uphill to the hamlet of Lanehead. At a junction turn left on to a narrow lane signposted to Donkleywood. This is The Reivers Route, which meanders along the edge of the Tyne valley going through several gates.

6 At one point you will cross over the old railway line at what was a level crossing, still with well-preserved gates. Beyond Donkleywood, climb to the highest point of the route before descending into Falstone. Go under a railway bridge then turn right opposite the Blackcock Inn to return to where you started.

AROUND HADRIAN'S WALL & THE STANEGATE

This cycle route takes you along the finest section of Hadrian's Wall, past two Roman forts and along an ancient Roman road. Hadrian's Wall became a World Heritage Site in 1987 and in 2005 the name was changed to the Frontiers of the Roman Empire WHS. The site was extended to include some remains of the Roman frontier between the rivers Rhine and Danube. The Roman Empire had conquered as far as Mons Graupius in Northern Scotland by AD 83 but unable to hold their gains the Romans gradually withdrew to a line stretching from the Solway Firth to the Tyne. There they built a chain of forts along the road known since medieval times as the Stanegate. Emperor Hadrian decided to consolidate the frontiers of his empire and in AD 122 had a wall built close to the line of Stanegate to 'separate the Romans from the barbarians' in the north who refused to accept Roman dominion. The ride takes in Housesteads fort, the most visited on the Wall, so in order to avoid the crowds try not to plan your ride for a weekend falling in high summer. Along the route the views of the Wall and the surrounding countryside are spectacular and the temptation to dismount and explore will be strong.

1 Exit the car park and turn left. At a T-junction turn right on to the B6318. (A turn almost immediately to the left heads uphill to reach a car park at Steel Rigg, where a footpath leads walkers along one of the finest sections of Hadrian's Wall.)

2 Continue along the B6318. This is a straight, undulating road with a superb view of the Wall. After cycling approximately 2 miles (3.2km) pass a turn-off signed for Bardon Mill on your right and in another 0.5 mile (800m) pass the car park for Housesteads fort.

3 Housesteads is the most complete Roman fort in Britain and you may want to spend some time exploring here. Afterwards continue along the road for another 1.7 miles (2.7km) then turn right at a sign for Haydon Bridge. The building on the corner here has a tea room and is built on the site of a Roman signal station.

4 Head along this narrow lane cycling downhill at first, followed by a short, energetic pull up to the top of the next hill. Just past Grindon Hill Farm take a right turn at the crossroads on to Cycle Route 72, heading towards Bardon Mill. This is the line of the Stanegate, an important Roman road that ran from Corbridge to Carlisle.

5 Keep ahead on 'Cycle Route 72' with a grand view of the Wall on your right and over Thorngrafton Common on your left. There is a great view of Housesteads and, further on, Vindolanda. After a downhill section make a right turn, still continuing on Cycle Route 72, following signs for Vindolanda.

6 Head downhill to reach the museum entrance. Pass by the entrance then continue uphill, passing the top car park and a thatched cottage before reaching a T-junction. Turn right on to Pennine Cycle Route 68 and keep on it to reach the start.

LAKE DISTRICT
■ TOURIST INFORMATION
Ambleside
Central Buildings, Market Cross
☎ 01539 432582; www.golakes.co.uk
Barrow-in-Furness
Forum 28, Duke Street ☎ 01229 876505;
www.golakes.co.uk
Bowness-on-Windermere
Glebe Road, Bowness Bay
☎ 01539 442895; www.golakes.co.uk
Coniston
Ruskin Avenue ☎ 01539 441533;
www.golakes.co.uk
Grange-over-Sands
Victoria Hall, Main Street
☎ 01539 534026; www.golakes.co.uk
Kendal
Town Hall, Highgate ☎ 01539 725758;
www.golakes.co.uk
Keswick
Moot Hall, Market Square
☎ 01768 772645; www.golakes.co.uk
Lake District Visitor Centre (Brockhole)
On the A591, Windermere
☎ 01539 446601; www.lakedistrict.gov.uk
Ullswater
Main car park, Glenridding
☎ 01768 482414; www.golakes.co.uk
Ulverston
Coronation Hall, County Square
☎ 01229 587120; www.golakes.co.uk
Whitehaven
Market Hall, Market Place
☎ 01946 598914; www.golakes.co.uk
Windermere
Victoria Street ☎ 01539 446499;
www.golakes.co.uk

■ PLACES OF INTEREST
Abbot Hall Art Gallery and Museum of Lakeland Life & Industry
Kirkland, Kendal ☎ 01539 722464;
www.abbothall.org.uk
The Beacon
West Strand, Whitehaven
☎ 01946 592302
Beatrix Potter Gallery
Main Street, Hawkshead
☎ 01539 436355
Brantwood
Coniston ☎ 01539 441396;
www.brantwood.org.uk
Cars of the Stars Motor Museum
Standish Street, Keswick.
☎ 01768 773757;
www.carsofthestars.com
Cartmel Priory
Cartmel, Grange-over-Sands.
☎ 01539 536261
Castlerigg Stone Circle
Atmospheric remains located 2 miles
(3.2km) east of Keswick.
Cumberland Pencil Museum
Southey Works, Carding Mill Lane,
Keswick ☎ 01768 773626

Dock Museum
North Road, Barrow-in-Furness
☎ 01229 876400;
www.dockmuseum.org.uk
Dove Cottage
Grasmere ☎ 01539 435544
Eskdale Mill
Boot ☎ 01946 723335;
www.eskdalemill.co.uk
Furness Abbey
Barrow-in-Furness ☎ 01229 823420
Extensive remains of the Cistercian abbey
built in 1147.
Haig Colliery Mining Museum
Kells, Whitehaven ☎ 01946 599949
Hardknott Castle Roman Fort
Hardknott Pass. Remains of the Roman
fort can be seen at the western end of
Hardknott Pass.
Hill Top
Near Sawrey ☎ 01539 436269
Holker Hall and Gardens
Cark-in-Cartmel, Grange-over-Sands
☎ 01539 558328
Includes the popular Lakeland Motor
Museum.
Kendal Museum of Natural History & Archaeology
Station Road, Kendal ☎ 01539 721374
Keswick Mining Museum
Otley Road, Keswick ☎ 017687 80055
Mining memorabilia and geology plus
an exceptional bookshop devoted to the
history of the Lake District geology and
industrial archaeology.
Keswick Museum and Art Gallery
Fitz Park, Station Road, Keswick
☎ 01768 773263
Displays of letters and manuscripts; also
local geology and natural history.
The Lakes Discovery Museum @ the Armitt
Rydal Road, Ambleside
☎ 01539 431212
Laurel & Hardy Museum
Brogden Street, Ulverston
☎ 01229 582292;
www.laurel-and-hardy.co.uk
Ravenglass & Eskdale Railway
Ravenglass ☎ 01229 717171
Steam and diesel trains run along a
7-mile (11.3km) track from Ravenglass
to Dalegarth.
Ruskin Museum
The Institute, Coniston ☎ 01539 441164
The World of Beatrix Potter
The Old Laundry, Bowness-on-
Windermere ☎ 01539 488444

■ FOR CHILDREN
The Aquarium of the Lakes
Lakeside, Newby Bridge ☎ 01539 530153
Lakeside and Haverthwaite Railway
Lakeside, Newby Bridge ☎ 01539 531594
Trotters World of Animals
Coalbeck Farm, Bassenthwaite

☎ 01768 776239; www.trottersworld.com
A conservation-oriented zoo, with feeding
displays and a soft play area.

■ PERFORMING ARTS
The Brewery Arts Centre
Kendal ☎ 01539 725133
Civic Hall
Whitehaven ☎ 0845 095 2130
Coronation Hall
Ulverston ☎ 01229 582610;
www.corohall.co.uk
Forum 28 Theatre & Arts Centre
28 Duke Street, Barrow-in-Furness
☎ 01229 820000
The Old Laundry
Crag Brow, Bowness-on-Windermere
☎ 01539 488444
Rosehill Theatre
Moresby, Whitehaven ☎ 01946 692422
Theatre by the Lake
Lakeside, Keswick ☎ 01768 774411

■ SPORTS & ACTIVITIES
ANGLING
Bassenthwaite Lake
Permits from Keswick TIC
☎ 01768 72645
Derwent Water
Permits from Keswick TIC
☎ 01768 72645
BOAT HIRE
Derwent Water
Derwent Water Marina, Portinscale
☎ 01768 772912
Keswick Launch
☎ 01768 772263
BOAT TRIPS
Coniston
Coniston Ferry Services, Pier Cottage,
Near Sawrey, Ambleside.
☎ 01539 436216
Steam Yacht Gondola, Gondola Pier,
Coniston ☎ 01539 441288
Derwent Water
Keswick Launch ☎ 01768 772263
Regular passenger service.
Ullswater
Ullswater Steamers ☎ 01768 482229
Windermere
Windermere Lake Cruises, Newby
Bridge, Ulverston ☎ 01539 531188
CYCLE HIRE
Ambleside
Biketreks, Rydal Road ☎ 01539 431505
Keswick
Keswick Motor Co, Lake Road
☎ 01768 772064
Keswick Mountain Bike Centre, Southey
Hill Estate ☎ 01768 775202
Whitehaven
Haven Cycles, Preston Street
☎ 01946 63263
Windermere
Windermere Cycle Hire, Country Lanes,
the Railway Station ☎ 01539 444544

CYCLING
Coast-to-Coast (C2C) Cycle Route
A 140-mile (225km) route linking
Whitehaven, Workington and Sunderland.
The Eskdale Trail
The Ravenglass and Eskdale Railway is
a virtually traffic-free route. Details from
stations at Ravenglass or Dalegarth.
The Reivers Cycle Route
A 190-mile (306km) cycling route
which runs from Tynemouth as far
as Whitehaven.
Wear to Wear (W2W) Cycle Route
This superb trans-Pennine route
(Sustrans Regional Route 20) begins
on Walney Island and traverses the
southern lakes on its 151-mile
(243km) path northeast.
GOLF COURSES
Barrow-in-Furness
Barrow Golf Club, Rakesmoor Lane,
Hawcoat ☎ 01229 825444;
www.barrowgolfclub.co.uk
Furness Golf Club, Central Drive,
Isle of Walney ☎ 01229 471232;
www.furnessgolfclub.co.uk
Keswick
Keswick Golf Club, Threlkeld Hall
☎ 01768 779324;
www.keswickgolfclub.com
Whitehaven
Whitehaven Golf Club, Red Lonning
☎ 01946 591144;
www.whitehavengolfclub.com
HORSE RIDING
Kendal
Holmescales Riding Centre,
Old Hutton ☎ 01539 729388;
www.holmescalesridingcentre.co.uk
Windermere
Lakeland Pony Trekking, Limefitt
Park, Troutbeck ☎ 01539 431999
www.lakelandponytrekking.co.uk
LONG-DISTANCE PATHS
The Cistercian Way
This 33-mile (53km) walking route goes
from Grange-over-Sands to Roa Island,
near Barrow-in-Furness.
Coast-to-Coast Walk
A 190-mile (306km) walk from
St Bees Head to Robin Hood's Bay
in North Yorkshire.
The Cumberland Way
An superb 82-mile (132km) crossing
of the Lake District from Ravenglass
to Appleby.
The Furness Way
A 71-mile (114km) walk from Arnside
to Ravenglass and crossing the
Furness Peninsula.
The Pennine Way
The country's premier National Trail
(all 268 miles/431km of it) crosses the
high Pennine ridge between Dufton
and Alston; www.nationaltrail.co.uk/
pennineway

The West Lakes Way
A 70-mile (112km) walking route from Whitehaven to Millom.

SAILING

Bassenthwaite
Bassenthwaite Sailing Club
☎ 01768 776341;
www.bassenthwaite-sc.org.uk

Crummock Water
Woodhouse, Buttermere ☎ 01768 770208
Permits and boats for hire.

■ **ANNUAL EVENTS & CUSTOMS**

Ambleside
Rushbearing Ceremony, first Sat in Jul.
Ambleside Sports, late Jul.
Lake District Summer Music Festival,
early to mid Aug.

Barrow-in-Furness
Barrow Flower Show, Jul and Oct.

Bassenthwaite
Sailing Week, late Jul/early Aug.

Borrowdale
Borrowdale Shepherds' Meet and Show,
mid-Sep.

Buttermere
Buttermere Shepherds' Meet and Show,
mid Sep.

Cartmel
Cartmel Steeplechases, Spring Bank
Holiday.
Agricultural Show, early Aug.
Cartmel Races, Aug Bank Holiday.

Coniston
Coniston Water Festival, early Jul

Eskdale
Eskdale Tup (ram) Show, late Sep.
Eskdale Show, late Sep.

Grange-over-Sands
Edwardian Festival, mid Jun.
Lakeland Rose Show, Jul.

Kendal
Kendal Torchlight Procession, mid Sep.
Westmorland County Show, early Sep.

Keswick
Keswick Literature Festival, early Mar.
Keswick Jazz Festival, mid May.
Keswick Mountain Festival, May.
Carnival, mid-Jun.
Keswick Convention, late Jul–early Aug

Loweswater
Loweswater Show, mid Sep.

Ulverston
North Lonsdale Agricultural Show,Jul.
Lantern Procession, Sep.

Whitehaven
Copeland Carnival, early Jul.

YORKSHIRE MOORS
■ **TOURIST INFORMATION**

Guisborough
Priory Grounds, Church Street
☎ 01287 633801;
www.visitnortheastengland.com

Hutton-le-Hole
Ryedale Folk Museum ☎ 01751 417367

North York Moors National Park
The Moors Centre, Lodge Lane,
Danby ☎ 01439 772737;
www.northyorkmoors.org.uk

Scarborough
Brunswick Shopping Centre,
Westborough ☎ 01723 383636;
www.discoveryorkshirecoast.com
Harbourside, Sandside ☎ 01723 341000
(seasonal)

Whitby
Langborne Road ☎ 01723 383637

■ **PLACES OF INTEREST**

Byland Abbey
Coxwold ☎ 01347 868614;
www.english-heritage.org.uk

Captain Cook Memorial Museum
Grape Lane, Whitby ☎ 01947 601900;
www.cookmuseumwhitby.co.uk

Gisborough Priory
Guisborough ☎ 01287 633801

National Trust Centre
Ravenscar ☎ 01723 870138/870423

The Moors Centre
Lodge Lane, Danby ☎ 01439 772737;
www.northyorkmoors.org.uk

Rievaulx Abbey
Rievaulx ☎ 01439 798228;
www.english-heritage.org.uk

Rievaulx Terrace
Rievaulx ☎ 01439 798340;
www.nationaltrust.org.uk

Robin Hood's Bay Museum
Fisherhead; www.museum.rhbay.co.uk

Ryedale Folk Museum
Hutton-le-Hole ☎ 01751 417367;
www.ryedalefolkmuseum.co.uk

Scarborough Castle
☎ 01723 372451;
www.english-heritage.org.uk

Shandy Hall
Coxwold ☎ 01347 868465
www.shandean.org

Tocketts Watermill
Skelton Road, Guisborough
☎ 01287 610182; www.tockettsmill.co.uk

Whitby Abbey
East Cliff, Whitby ☎ 01947 603568;
www.whitbymuseum.org.uk

■ **PERFORMING ARTS**

Futurist Theatre & Cinema
Foreshore Road, Scarborough
☎ 01723 365789/374500;
www.futuristtheatre.co.uk

Spa Entertainment Complex
South Bay, Scarborough
☎ 01723 376774
www.scarboroughspa.co.uk

Spa Theatre
South Bay, Scarborough
☎ 01723 357869

Stephen Joseph Theatre
Westborough, Scarborough
☎ 01723 370541; www.sjt.uk.com

Whitby Pavilion Theatre
West Cliff, Whitby
☎ 01947 604855/820625

■ **SPORTS & ACTIVITIES**

ANGLING

Fly fishing
The Mere, Scarborough ☎ 01723 507588
Tickets on site.

Sea fishing
Staithes & Whitby.
Ask at the harbour, or the TIC.

BOAT TRIPS

Whitby
Trips round the bay leave from the
West Pier.

CYCLE HIRE

Oswaldkirk
Golden Square Campsite, Oswaldkirk
☎ 01439 788269

GOLF COURSES

Scarborough
North Cliff Golf Club, North Cliff Avenue
☎ 01723 360786; www.ncgc.co.uk
South Cliff Golf Club, Deepdale Avenue
☎ 01723 365150;
www.southcliffgolfclub.com

HORSE RIDING
Farsyde Stud and Riding Centre
☎ 01947 880249;
www.farsydefarmcottages.co.uk

LONG-DISTANCE PATHS

The Cleveland Way
A 110-mile (177km) walk from Helmsley
to Filey Brigg; www.nationaltrail.cc.uk

The Esk Valley Walk
Scarborough to Whitby Railway Trail;
www.eskvalleyrailway.co.uk/walking
Route for walkers and cyclists follows the
old railway line. (Cycle hire at Hawsker.)

■ **ANNUAL EVENTS & CUSTOMS**

Castleton
Castleton Show, Sep.

Coxwold
Coxwold Fair, Jun.
Agricultural Show, mid Aug.

Danby
Agricultural Show, mid Aug

Egton
Egton Show, late Aug.

Egton Bridge
Gooseberry Show, early Aug.

Helmsley
Ryedale Festival, Jul/Aug.

Robin Hood's Bay
Folk Festival, Jun.

Rosedale
Rosedale Show, Aug.

Scarborough
Scarborough Fayre, Jun–Jul.
International Music Festival, Jun–Jul.
Scarborough Cricket Festival, end Aug/
Sep.

Stokesley
Stokesley Show, Sep.

Whitby
Planting of the Penny Hedge,
Ascension Eve, May.
Morris Dance Festival, Jun.
Blessing of Boats, mid Jul.
Whitby Angling Festival, Jul.
Whitby Folk Festival, Aug.
Whitby Regatta, mid Aug.

YORKSHIRE DALES
■ **TOURIST INFORMATION**

Grassington
National Park Centre, Colvend, Hebden
Road ☎ 01756 751609;
www.yorkshiredales.org.uk

Harrogate
Royal Baths, Crescent Road
☎ 01423 537300

Ingleton
The Community Centre ☎ 015242 41049

Kirkby Lonsdale
24 Main Street ☎ 015242 71437

Knaresborough
9 Castle Courtyard ☎ 0845 3890 177

Pateley Bridge
8 High Street ☎ 0845 3890 179

Richmond
Friary Gardens, Victoria Road
☎ 01748 828742

Ripon
Minster Road ☎ 0845 3890 178

Settle
Town Hall, Cheapside ☎ 01729 825192

Skipton
35 Coach Street ☎ 01756 792809

■ **PLACES OF INTEREST**

Bolton Abbey Estate
☎ 01756 718009; www.boltonabbey.com
Visitor centres and gift shops.

Craven Museum & Gallery
Town Hall, High Street, Skipton
☎ 01756 706407; www.cravendc.gov.uk

Dales Countryside Museum
Station Yard, Hawes ☎ 01969 666210;
www.thedales.org.uk/countryside
museum
Superb and informative displays and
exhibitions about the National Park

Dent Village Heritage Centre
Dent ☎ 015396 25800;
www.dentvillageheritagecentre.com

Easby Abbey
Richmond; www.english-heritage.org.uk
Medieval abbey remains set beside the
River Swale.

**Fountains Abbey & Studley Royal
Water Garden**
Ripon ☎ 01765 608888;
www.fountainsabbey.org.uk
World Heritage Site managed by the
National Trust.

Georgian Theatre Royal
Victoria Road, Richmond
☎ 01748 823710;
www.georgiantheatreroyal.co.uk

Dating from 1788, the theatre was restored and extended in 2003. It is still used for live productions.

Green Howards Regimental Museum
Trinity Church Square, Market Place, Richmond ☎ 01748 826561; www.greenhowards.org.uk
The military history of the Green Howards is illustrated here, together with displays of uniforms, weapons and medals.

How Stean Gorge
Near Lofthouse, Pateley Bridge ☎ 01423 755666; www.howstean.co.uk

Ingleborough Cave
Clapham ☎ 015242 51242; www.ingleboroughcave.co.uk
Tours of cave formations and streams.

Ingleton Waterfalls Trail
The Falls, Ingleton ☎ 015242 41617; www.ingletonwaterfallswalk.co.uk
A 4.5 mile (7.2km) circular trail on boardwalks in the gorge and through meadows and woodland.

Jervaulx Abbey
Jervaulx ☎ 01677 460226; www.jervaulxabbey.com

Knaresborough Castle
Knaresborough ☎ 01423 869274

Mother Shipton's Cave
Knaresborough ☎ 01423 864600; www.mothershiptonscave.com

Nidderdale Museum
Pateley Bridge ☎ 01423 711225; www.nidderdalemuseum.com

Norton Conyers
Ripon ☎ 01765 640333

Old Courthouse Museum
Castle Yard, Knaresborough ☎ 01423 869274

Parcevall Hall Gardens
Skyreholm, Skipton ☎ 01756 720311; www.parcevallhallgardens.co.uk

Parson and Police Museum and the Courthouse Museum
Ripon Museum Trust, The Workhouse Museum, Allhallowgate ☎ 01765 690799; www.riponmuseums.co.uk

RHS Garden Harlow Carr
Crag Lane, Otley Road, Harrogate ☎ 01423 565418; www.rhs.org.uk

Richmond Castle
Richmond ☎ 01748 822493; www.english-heritage.org.uk
Occupying a stunning position overlooking the River Swale, the castle is now in ruins, but visitors can see the keep, two towers and Scolland's Hall.

Richmondshire Museum
Ryder's Wynd, Richmond ☎ 01748 825611; www.richmondmuseum.org.uk
Museum of local history.

Royal Pump Room Museum
Crown Place, Harrogate ☎ 01423 556188

Skipton Castle
☎ 01756 792442; www.skiptoncastle.co.uk
Very well-preserved medieval castle.

Stump Cross Caverns
Greenhow Hill, Pateley Bridge ☎ 01756 752780; www.stumpcrosscaverns.co.uk

Upper Wharfedale Folk Museum
Grassington Square, Grassington ☎ 01756 752801; www.grassingtonfolkmuseum.org.uk
Exhibits relating to Upper Wharfedale all housed in 18th-century former lead-miners' cottages.

Wensleydale Creamery Visitor Centre
Gayle Lane, Hawes ☎ 01969 667664; www.wensleydale.co.uk

Wensleydale Railway
Leeming Bar Station ☎ 08454 505474; www.wensleydalerailway.com

White Scar Cave
☎ 015242 41244; www.whitescarcave.co.uk
Britain's largest show caves, with tours to falls and rivers, on B6255 to Hawes.

Yorkshire Dales National Park Centre
Malham ☎ 01969 652380; www.yorkshiredales.org.uk
Local literature, displays on the natural history, the local community and the work of conservation bodies. 24-hour information screen.

■ FOR CHILDREN

Lightwater Valley Theme Park & Village
North Stainley ☎ 0871 720 0011; www.lightwatervalley.co.uk
Family entertainment with rides and activities for children.

■ SPORTS & ACTIVITIES

ANGLING
Fly fishing
Ingleton
Trout fishing on local rivers. Permits available from Village News, Main Street, Ingleton ☎ 015242 41683

Pateley Bridge Scar House Dam
Day tickets from Lofthouse Post Office. ☎ 01423 755203; www.harrogate.gov.uk
Skipton
River Aire in and around Skipton. Contact Tourist Information Centre in Skipton ☎ 01756 792809

BOAT HIRE
Knaresborough
Blenkhorns Boat Hire, 2 Waterside, High Bridge ☎ 01423 862105
Various rowing boats, punts and canoes for hire.

Skipton
For information about boat hire contact Skipton Tourist Information Centre. ☎ 01756 792809

BOAT TRIPS
Skipton
Various companies operate boat trips along the Leeds and Liverpool Canal, including Pennine Boat Trips, from Skipton, Waterside Court, Coach Street ☎ 01756 790829
Details of other operators are available from Skipton TIC ☎ 01756 792809

CYCLE HIRE
Skipton
Dave Ferguson Cycles, 3 Albion Yard ☎ 01756 795367; www.davefergusoncycles.com

CYCLING
The Yorkshire Dales
Cycleway
This is a 130-mile (209.2km) circular cycling route that starts and finishes in Skipton.

GUIDED WALKS
Several guided walks in the area are organised by the National Park Authority, Friends of Dalesrail and Dalesbus Ramblers. For more information contact the Tourist Information Centre in Settle ☎ 01729 825192
Week-long as well as other short break holidays for walkers in the Yorkshire Dales are organized by H. F. Holidays Limited, Catalyst House, 720 Cetennial Court, Elstree, Herts ☎ 0845 470 7558; www.hfholidays.co.uk

HORSE RACING
Ripon
Boroughbridge Road ☎ 01765 530530; www.ripon-races.co.uk

HORSE RIDING
Pateley Bridge
Bewerley School of Horsemanship, Bewerley Old Hall ☎ 01423 712249

HOT-AIR BALLOONING
Skipton
Airborne Adventures, Old Burton Croft, Rylstone ☎ 01756 730166; www.airborne.co.uk

LONG-DISTANCE PATHS
The Dales Way
A fantastic 81-mile (130km) lowland walk through the heart of the Yorkshire Dales connecting Ilkley in the south with Bowness-on-Windermere in the north.

The Nidderdale Way
This 53-mile (85km) walk tours the moors and gritstone outcrops of the lovely valley of Nidderdale, starting and finishing in Pateley Bridge.

The Pennine Way
The mother of all long-distance walks enters the area west of Skipton, before heading off over the fells from Malham.

The Six Dales Hike
A superb 42-mile (67.6km) walk through North Yorkshire from Settle to Skipton.

The Yorkshire Water Way
This 41-mile (66km) reservoir-themed walk enters Upper Nidderdale from Kettlewell, before crossing to the Washburn Valley on its way to Ilkley.

■ ANNUAL EVENTS & CUSTOMS
Fountains Abbey
Egg-rolling, Easter Mon.
Grassington
Grassington Festival, mid to late Jun.
Hardraw
Hardraw Brass Band Festival, contact The Green Dragon, Hardraw ☎ 01969 667392
Harrogate
Harrogate International Youth Music Festival, Easter.
Performances throughout the region including at Ripon Cathedral.
Spring Flower Show, late Apr.
The Great Yorkshire Show, mid Jul.
Harrogate International Festival, late Jul to early Aug.
Trans-Pennine Run for vintage vehicles, from Manchester to Harrogate, 1st Sun in Aug.
Autumn Flower Show, mid Sep.
Hawes
Hawes Gala, late Jun.
Hubberholme
On 1st Mon of the year the 'Hubberholme Parliament' sits in the George Inn after a church service.
Ingleton
Annual Fellsman Hike, Ingleton to Threshfield, early May.
Gala and mountain race, mid Jul.
Horticultural Show, early Sep.
Jervaulx
Jervaulx Horse Trials, early Jun.
Malham
Malham Show, late Aug.
Pateley Bridge
Nidderdale Show, late Sep, held in Bewerley Park.
Reeth
Reeth Show, late Aug.
Richmond
The Richmond Meet, Spring Bank Holiday weekend.
The 'Poor Old Horse' Mummers' Play takes place around Christmas.
Ripon
Setting the Watch by the Ripon Hornblower every evening in the market place by the Obelisk at 9pm.
International Festival, mid-Sep.
St Wilfrid's Feast Procession, Sat before the first Mon in Aug.
Settle
Maypole celebrations at Long Preston, Sat after May Day.
Skipton
Skipton Gala, mid Jun.
Game Fair, held at Broughton Hall, late Jun.
Medieval Festival, early/mid Dec.

NORTHUMBRIA & COAST
■ TOURIST INFORMATION

Alnwick
The Shambles ☎ 01665 510665;
www.welcomenorthumberland.co.uk

Bellingham
Fountain Cottage, Main Street
☎ 01434 220616

Berwick-upon-Tweed
106 Marygate ☎ 01289 330733;
www.welcomenorthumberland.co.uk

Corbridge
Hill Street (seasonal) ☎ 01434 632815

Durham
2 Millennium Place ☎ 0191 384 3720;
www.thisisdurham.com

Haltwhistle
Railway Station ☎ 01434 322002

Hexham
Wentworth Car Park ☎ 01434 652220;
www.visitnortheastengland.com

Northumberland National Park Headquarters
Eastburn, South Park, Hexham
☎ 01434 605555; www.northumberland-national-park.org.uk

■ PLACES OF INTEREST

Allenheads Heritage Centre
☎ 01434 685568

Alnwick Castle
☎ 01665 510777; www.alnwickcastle.com

Aydon Castle
Corbridge ☎ 01434 632450;
www.english-heritage.org.uk

Bamburgh Castle
☎ 01668 214515;
www.bamburghcastle.com

Barnard Castle
☎ 01833 638212;
www.english-heritage.org.uk

Bellingham Heritage Centre
Station Yard, Woodburn Road
☎ 01434 220050

Berwick Castle
Berwick-upon-Tweed
www.english-heritage.org.uk

Border History Museum, The Old Gaol
Hallgate, Hexham ☎ 01434 652349;
www.tynedaleheritage.org

Bowes Castle
☎ 0191 269 1200;
www.english-heritage.org.uk

Brinkburn Priory
Longframlington
☎ 01665 570628;
www.english-heritage.org.uk

Chillingham Castle
☎ 01668 215359;
www.chillingham-castle.com

Coquet Island, RSPB Reserve
☎ 01665 712313/711975

Durham Dales Centre
Castle Gardens, Stanhope
☎ 01388 527650;
www.durhamdalescentre.co.uk

Farne Islands & Longstone Lighthouse
Inner Farne and Staple Island
☎ 01665 721099;
www.nationaltrust.org.uk

Grace Darling Museum
Radcliffe Road, Bamburgh
☎ 01668 214910

Heatherslaw Corn Mill
Ford ☎ 01890 820488;
www.ford-and-etal.co.uk

High Force
Near Middleton-in-Teesdale
☎ 01833 640209; www.rabycastle.com
England's highest waterfall.

Killhope Lead Mining Centre
☎ 01388 537505;
www.durham.gov.uk/killhope

Lady Waterford Hall
Ford ☎ 01890 820503;
www.ford-and-etal.co.uk

Lindisfarne Centre
Marygate, Holy Island ☎ 01289 389004;
www.lindisfarne-centre.com

Lindisfarne Priory
Holy Island ☎ 01289 389200;
www.english-heritage.org.uk

Moot Hall & Gallery
Market Place, Hexham
☎ 01434 652351

Paxton House
Paxton ☎ 01289 386291;
www.paxtonhouse.co.uk

Rokeby Park
Rokeby, Barnard Castle
☎ 01833 637334; www.rokebypark.com

Vindolanda (Chesterholm)
Bardon Mill ☎ 01434 344277;
www.english-heritage.org.uk

■ FOR CHILDREN

Fenton Centre
West Fenton, Wooler
☎ 01668 216216; www.fentoncentre.com
Working farm with an educational
conservation centre.

Kielder Water Bird of Prey Centre
☎ 01434 250400; www.kwbopc.com

Marine Life Centre & Fishing Museum
Main Street, Seahouses
☎ 01665 721257

Otterburn Hall (YMCA)
☎ 01830 520663;
www.otterburnhall.com
Forest walks and rare breeds.

■ PERFORMING ARTS

Alnwick
Playhouse ☎ 01665 510785;
www.alnwickplayhouse.co.uk

Berwick-upon-Tweed
The Maltings Theatre and Arts
Centre, Eastern Lane ☎ 01289 330999;
www.maltingsberwick.co.uk

Hexham
The Queen's Hall Arts Centre, Beaumont
Street, Hexham ☎ 01434 652477

■ SPORTS & ACTIVITIES
ABSEILING, CAVING & CLIMBING
Kingsway Adventure Centre, Alston Road,
Middleton-in-Teesdale ☎ 01833 640881;
www.kingswaycentre.co.uk

ANGLING
Coarse fishing
North Tyne River
Tyne Angling permits from Tyne Rivers
Trust ☎ 01434 611817

Fly fishing
Kielder Water Visitor Centre
☎ 01434 251000
Permits from Leaplish Waterside Park
or Tower Visitor Centre.

Sea angling
Alnmouth: enquire at harbour.
Berwick-upon-Tweed: Shore fishing is
restricted because of seals. For boat
fishing, enquire at Berwick harbour.

ARCHERY
Kingsway Adventure Centre, Alston Road,
Middleton-in-Teesdale ☎ 01833 640881
www.kingswaycentre.co.uk

CANOEING
Teesdale Canoe Club, Barnard Castle.
☎ 01833 650691
Kingsway Adventure Centre, Alston Road,
Middleton-in-Teesdale.
☎ 01833 640881
www.kingswaycentre.co.uk

CYCLE HIRE
Alnwick
Alnwick Cycles, 24 Narrowgate.
☎ 01665 606738;
www.alnwickcycles.co.uk

Bamburgh
Cyclelife, 10 Oak Drive, Lionheart
Enterprise Park ☎ 01605 602925;
www.cyclelifealnwick.co.uk

Kielder
Purple Mountain Bike Hire Centre,
Kielder Castle ☎ 01434 250532;
www.purplemountain.co.uk
The Bike Place, Station Garage, Kielder
☎ 01434 250457; www.thebikeplace.co.uk

Wooler
Haugh Head Garage ☎ 01668 281316

CYCLE ROUTES &
LONG-DISTANCE PATHS
Coast & Castles Cycle Route
A 200-mile (320km) ride, from Newcastle
to Edinburgh.

Coast to Coast the Roman Way
This 150-mile (240km) cycle ride takes
you from the Cumbrian coast to the
North Sea.

Hadrian's Wall Path
An 84-mile (134km) walk from Wallsend
to Bowness-on-Solway.

The Northumbrian Coastline
A 61-mile (98km) walk, from Berwick
to North Shields.

Pennine Cycleway
A 355-mile (571km) ride from Derbyshire
to Berwick.

Pennine Way
A 270-mile (434km) path from Kirk
Yetholm in the Scottish Borders to Edale
in Derbyshire.

Reivers Cycle Route
A 187-mile (301km) ride from Tynemouth
to the Scottish borders and Whitehaven.

St Cuthbert's Way
A challenging 62-mile (100km) path
that runs all the way from Melrose to
pretty Lindisfarne

■ ANNUAL EVENTS & CUSTOMS

Alnwick
Shrove Tuesday Football.
Fair, late Jun–early Jul.
International Music Festival, late
Jul–early Aug.
Northumbrian Gathering, Nov.

Alwinton
Border Shepherds' Show, mid Oct.

Barnard Castle
Meet Weekend, late May.
Steam Fair, late May.
Tractor Pull, Apr, late Dec.
Truck Show, late Aug.

Bellingham
Bellingham Show, late Aug.

Berwick-upon-Tweed
Border Marches, May.
Riding the Bounds, early May.
May Fair, last Fri in May.
Northumbrian Gathering, weekend
after Easter.

Bowes
Agricultural Show, early Sep.

Corbridge
Northumberland County Show, Spring
Bank Holiday Mon.

Durham
Durham Miners' Gala, early Jul.
Durham County Show, mid Jul.
Egg Rolling at Penshaw Monument,
Easter weekend.
Kite Festival, early Jul.
Children's kites to competition types.

Eggleston
Eggleston Agricultural Show,
mid Sep.

Haltwhistle
Walking Festival, Spring and Autumn.

Hexham
Abbey Festival, mid Sep.
Folkworks Hexham Gathering, late May.

Kielder Castle
Kielder Forest Festival, early Aug.

Otterburn
Otterburn Festival, Jul.

Rothbury
Traditional Music Festival, mid Jul.

Stanhope
Agricultural Show, early Sep.

Whittingham
Whittingham Show, Aug.

Wooler
Glendale Show, late Aug.

PUBS

LAKE DISTRICT

Black Bull
1 Yewdale Road, Coniston LA21 8DU
☎ 015394 41335;
www.conistonbrewery.com
Built around 400 years ago, this coaching inn is supplied by the excellent brewery to its rear. Quality bar meals are served all day and the restaurant is superb.

Boot Inn
Boot, Eskdale CA19 1TG
☎ 019467 23334; www.bootinn.co.uk
Located in the centre of Boot village, this is a popular pub, which is also good for families. The conservatory dining area has enviable views of the surrounding fells and the garden in the summer.

Bridge Hotel
Buttermere CA13 9UZ ☎ 017687 70252;
www.bridge-hotel.com
An 18th-century former coaching inn surrounded by the Buttermere Fells. There are wonderful walks right from the front door. Good food and real ales are served in character bars.

Drunken Duck
Barngates, Ambleside LA22 0NG
☎ 015394 36347;
www.drunkenduckinn.co.uk
This pub is a popular place with walkers and cyclists. Here you can get excellent beer and food, and enjoy the fine views.

Golden Rule
Smithy Brow, Ambleside LA22 9AS
☎ 015394 32257
Considered by many to be one of the few true pubs, this is a haven of good craic in front of real log fires. Beers are from Robinsons, and the food is rather limited, but the welcome is warm.

YORKSHIRE MOORS

The Black Swan Inn
Oldstead, Coxwold YO61 4BL
☎ 01347 868387;
www.blackswanoldstead.co.uk
This is a traditional country pub with a welcoming atmosphere. As you'd expect there is real ale in the Drovers Bar, with its flagged floor, comfy chairs and a bar made by Robert Thompson's craftsmen in nearby Kilburn. There's a pretty garden, and views of woodland and hills. The food is freshly prepared from local ingredients and with plenty of choices for all tastes.

Duke of Wellington Inn
Danby YO21 2LY ☎ 01287 660351;
www.dukeofwellingtondanby.co.uk
An attractive inn, in the scattered village of Danby with wide views of the village

in its moorland setting. Inside, the décor is warm, welcoming and traditional, and there is a good selection of whiskies and local beers. Good standard fare is served at lunchtimes and the evening with dishes, such as braised lamb shank and venison pie as well as vegetarian dishes.

Laurel Inn
New Road, Robin Hood's Bay YO22 4SE
☎ 01947 880400
Situated near to the bottom of the winding main street, this pub has a cosy, traditional atmosphere, with a welcoming open fire. It offers real ales and simple but wholesome food – including tasty thick soups in the winter.

The Mallyan Spout Hotel
The Common, Goathland YO22 5AN
☎ 01947 896486;
www.mallyanspout.co.uk
Relax with a pint of real ale or a coffee in front of a roaring fire in winter or outside in the garden in summer. The food is excellent too with the dishes created from local produce, including fresh fish from Whitby and local speciality cheeses. If you like puddings, don't miss the superb sticky toffee pudding.

Moorcock Inn
Langdale End, Scarborough YO13 0BN
☎ 01723 882268
This remote Moors pub has a tiled floor and an assortment of benches set out in two small rooms. Stop by here and you're guaranteed a decent drink, with a changing selection of beer from local, regional and microbreweries. Excellent, home-cooked food is available and in the summer, you can sit outside in the garden and enjoy the view.

YORKSHIRE DALES

The Angel
Hetton, Skipton BD23 6LT
☎ 01756 730263;
www.angelhetton.co.uk
The reputation of this fine pub stretches far. A string of awards, including some from the AA, reflect its prominence as one of the best dining pubs in the north of England. The emphasis is on modern British food, freshly cooked and using local beef, lamb, pork and cheese. The fish is delivered fresh daily.

The Bridge Inn
Low Wath Road, Pateley Bridge,
Harrogate HG3 5HL ☎ 01423 711484
The Bridge may look like a traditional Dales pub, but it has only been open since 2003. In that short time it has established a reputation for excellent, locally sourced food and reliable beers.

George Inn
Hubberholme, Skipton BD23 5JE
☎ 01756 760223;
www.thegeorge-inn.co.uk
The George Inn was a favourite of the writer J. B. Priestley. The 'Hubberholme Parliament' still sits here at New Year, but year round it is popular with visitors who come for the locally sourced lamb, pork and beef dishes. Lighter dishes might include home-made soup.

Green Dragon Inn
Hardraw, Hawes DL8 3LZ
☎ 01969 667392;
www.greendragonhardraw.com
Even without the access to Hardraw Force behind the pub, you would still want to visit the Green Dragon for its hand-pulled ales, traditional game casserole and home-made steak pie.

Lister Arms
Malham, Skipton BD23 4DB
☎ 01729 830330; www.listerarms.co.uk
An old coaching inn that caters well for the summer hordes while retaining a villagey feel inside. Diners will find a mix of Tex-Mex and traditional food, and there's a children's menu. Beer lovers may be tempted by the dazzling array of Belgian beers as well as the reliable stock of British cask and bottled ales.

Royal Oak
36 Kirkgate, Ripon HG4 1PB
☎ 01765 602284;
www.royaloakripon.co.uk
The Royal Oak is just a few steps away from Ripon's Market Square. Expect tasty, freshly cooked food created from fresh local produce with a wide selection of dishes available and there's an excellent wine list with more than 40 wines. Premium draught lagers include Timothy Taylors and hand-pulled ales.

Sun Inn
Main Street, Dent, Sedbergh LA10 5QL
☎ 01539 625208
This charming pub in the heart of the Yorkshire Dales has peaceful public rooms, coal fires and a fascinating collection of local photographs. The excellent bar food, served lunchtimes and evenings, includes plenty of flavoursome home-made dishes.

The Woolly Sheep Inn
38 Sheep Street, Skipton BD23 1HY
☎ 01756 700966;
www.woollysheepinn.co.uk
At the foot of Skipton's main shopping street, this is a Taylor's pub has a friendly atmosphere and serves excellent beer and 'hearty food for healthy appetites'.

The menu and daily specials boards offer a good selection of well-cooked traditional and international dishes.

NORTHUMBRIA & COAST

The Cheviot Hotel
Bellingham NE48 2AU ☎ 01434 220696;
www.thecheviothotel.co.uk
The Cheviot Hotel is a great place to relax, either in the bar or the restaurant. Using locally sourced ingredients, the hotel's menu includes traditional dishes, lighter snacks and a carvery on Sundays.

Victoria Inn
86 Hallgarth Street, Durham DH1 3AS
☎ 0191 386 5269;
www.victoriainn-durhamcity.co.uk
The Victoria Inn opened its doors in 1899 and the interior has changed very little since then. In this Victorian gem there are real ales – an ever changing selection – and more than 70 types of whisky (and whiskey). Comfortable B&B accommodation is also available.

Milecastle Inn
Military Road, Cawfields, near
Haltwhistle NE49 9NN ☎ 01434 321372;
www.milecastle-inn.co.uk
Only a few hundred yards from one of the best bits of Hadrian's Wall, the stone-built Milecastle Inn is a traditional pub serving home-cooked food and real ales. Local game is a strong suit of the menu, and people travel miles just to sample one of the speciality pies – try the Poacher's Pie, with beef and venison, or the wild boar and duckling pie.

Dipton Mill Inn
Dipton Mill Road, Hexham NE46 1YA
☎ 01434 606577; www.diptonmill.co.uk
Dipton Mill Inn is a country pub standing a few miles from Hexham, beside a trickling stream. In the summer you can sit outside in the garden. The pub offers good bar meals, but its secret is that round the back there is the Hexhamshire microbrewery that produces its own real ale including tipples with such interesting names as Devil's Water, Whapweasel and Old Humbug.

Twice Brewed Inn
Bardon Mill, Hexham NE47 7AN
☎ 01434 344534;
www.twicebrewedinn.co.uk
The Twice Brewed Inn is not far from both the Roman sites at Vindolanda and Housesteads. This inn is a wonderful place to relax after marching up and down Hadrian's Wall. In the bar there is always a great selection of real ales, including their own bitter, and you can eat well in both the bar and restaurant.

TEA ROOMS
LAKE DISTRICT

The Apple Pie Eating House and Bakery
Rydal Road, Ambleside LA22 9AN
☎ 015394 33679
Bestselling Bath buns are just one of the favourites here. With views over Bridge House and the hills, it's the ideal spot to enjoy the delicious treats, baked dishes or just a cappuccino.

Fellbites
Dalegarth Station, Boot, Eskdale CA18 1SW ☎ 01229 717171;
www.ravenglass-railway.co.uk
At the valley terminus of 'laal Ratty' the Fellbites café can serve a trainload of hungry and thirsty passengers at a time with freshly cooked food and hot tea and coffee. They use locally sourced ingredients in the preparation of their inviting food wherever possible.

Grange Bridge Cottage Tea Shop
Grange in Borrowdale, Borrowdale CA12 5UQ ☎ 017687 77201
Just a few yards from the famous double bridges, this 400-year-old cottage is home to a favourite on the Borrowdale tea shop trail. Home-baked cakes, cream teas and light lunches are served in the beautiful Riverside Tea Garden.

Hazelmere Café & Bakery
1 Yewbarrow Terrace, Grange-over-Sands LA11 6ED ☎ 015395 32972;
www.hazelmerecafe.co.uk
Expect at least 28 types of tea from around the world at this award-winning tea shop. Bread, cakes, pâtés and preserves are all made on the premises, and offered alongside local pheasant burgers, Cumbria lamb tattie pot, and Stalker's casserole. Teatime specialities include Cumberland Rum Nicky, vanilla slices and scones made with apricots and yoghurt. Enjoy the open fire in winter or eat on the Victorian verandah in summer.

Low Sizergh Barn Farm Shop & Tea Room
Low Sizergh Farm, Sizergh, Kendal LA8 8AE ☎ 015395 60426;
www.lowsizerghbarn.co.uk
Low Sizergh Barn, on an organic dairy farm near the Lake District National Park, has everything from a tea room and farm shop to a craft gallery and farm trail. Enoy a cup of tea and then head out to watch the cows being milked!

Stone Close
Main Street, Dent ☎ 01539 625231;
www.dentdale.com/stoneclose
Stone Close is popular with locals, writers, walkers, talkers – in fact, with everyone who chances upon this convivial 17th-century cottage, with its cast-iron range and flagstone floor. The delicious afternoon spread comes with a sumptuous array of home-made cakes and organic leaf and herbal teas or Fairtrade coffee. For High Tea, there is a selection of toast toppers, followed by crumpets, teacake or scone and jam. B&B accommodation available.

YORKSHIRE MOORS

Abbey Tea Rooms & Store
Rosedale Abbey YO18 8SA
☎ 01751 417475
As well as plain, fruit and cheese scones, the tea rooms also serve cherry scones, scones made with treacle, scones made with blueberries and ginger...and you can spread them with blueberry and lavender jam. If you're more peckish, try the Yorkshire Ham afternoon tea.

Coxwold Tea Rooms
School House, Coxwold YO61 4AD
☎ 01347 868077;
www.coxwoldtearooms.co.uk
You can eat in either of the two rooms, one very cosy and the other airy, or outside in the tea garden. You can treat yourself to afternoon tea with home-baking, or sample the delights of Yorkshire ham and eggs.

Elizabeth Botham & Sons
35/39 Skinner Street, Whitby YO21 3AH
☎ 01947 602823; www.botham.co.uk
The tradition of fine baking, begun in 1865, is still going strong in this superior first-floor café. The excellent menu includes tea breads, cream teas and scones as well as a lunch special.

Gisborough Hall Hotel
Whitby Lane, Guisborough TS14 6PT
☎ 0870 400 8191;
www.macdonaldhotels.co.uk/gisborough
For a taste of luxury, in truly elegant surroundings, treat yourself to tea at Gisborough Hall. As well as the traditional scones with jam and cream, there's the traditional full afternoon tea with sandwiches, cake and scones, or the celebration tea where your scones and fruitcake are accompanied by a glass of fizz. Tea is served midday until 6pm.

The Old Bakery Tea Rooms
Chapel Street, Robin Hood's Bay YO22 4SQ ☎ 01947 880709
A lovely, traditional tea room in the heart of the village. The bread and cakes are produced in the attached bakery. Scones with home-made preserves are a favourite, along with the chocolate and coffee cakes.

YORKSHIRE DALES

Abbey Tea Rooms
Jervaulx, Ripon HG4 4PH
☎ 01677 460391;
www.jervaulxabbey.com
Just across the road from the abbey ruins, the Abbey Tea Rooms do swift trade with visitors using the car park. Sit in the garden and enjoy the delicious home-made honeycakes, or scones, or sit inside for something more substantial.

Betty's
1 Parliament Street, Harrogate HG1 2QU
☎ 01423 814070; www.bettys.co.uk
The story of this noble Yorkshire institution began here in 1919, and you can still choose from more than 50 varieties of tea and coffee, and more than 300 breads, cakes and chocolates if you visit even now. The glorious art nouveau interior was designed by Charles Spindler's studio in Alsace in the 1930s.

Cavendish Pavilion
Bolton Abbey, Skipton BD23 6AN
☎ 01756 710245;
www.cavendishpavilion.co.uk
Bolton Abbey has a number of tea rooms but this one has the best setting, between the priory ruins and The Strid. Here, you can enjoy breakfast, morning coffee, afternoon tea and sandwiches.

Hazel Brow Farm
Low Row, Richmond DL11 6NE
☎ 01748 886224; www.hazelbrow.co.uk
With tray bakes, fresh scones, carrot cake and perhaps a 'Hazelbrowman's lunch', the café also offers sandwiches made with local produce.

The Old Granary
17 High Street, Pateley Bridge, Harrogate HG3 5AP ☎ 01423 711852;
www.oldgranary.net
You'll find The Old Granary in the centre of delightful Pateley Bridge. It's the perfect place for a quick bite or a light lunch. As well as various teas and coffees, the tasty home-made apple crumble is always popular. The menu includes vegetarian, gluten-free and dairy-free dishes.

Pen-y-ghent Café
Horton-in-Ribblesdale, Settle BD24 0HE
☎ 01729 860333;
www.horton-in-ribblesdale.com
An institution amongst walkers, cyclists and runners who take up the Three Peaks Challenge, this is more than just a place for a mug of tea and a piece of home-made cake (although it is excellent for both). The weekend safety service ensures walkers can log in and log out.

Ye Olde Naked Man
Market Place, Settle BD24 9ED
☎ 01729 823230
This busy tea shop and bakery in the Market Place takes its rather revealing name from a peculiar relief carved above the doorway dated 1663. Inside sample tempting cakes or pastries or try one of the tasty savoury pies. The shop also sells the café's produce, including delicious breads.

NORTHUMBRIA & COAST

The Almshouses
Palace Green, Durham DH1 3RL
☎ 0191 386 1054
The Almshouses, a tea room with a fine view, hobnobs with Durham Castle on one side and the cathedral on the other. It's a handy place for an afternoon tea and a piece of home-made cake or for a choice of something more substantial at lunchtime. All the food is home-prepared and the menu changes daily.

Copper Kettle Tea Rooms
21 Front Street, Bamburgh NE69 7BW
☎ 01668 214315;
www.copperkettletearooms.com
On the main street which runs from the church to the castle, the Copper Kettle Tea Rooms is a delightful, cosy building, with panelled walls, arched windows and a pretty garden. As well as its famous cream teas, the café offers light meals and snacks, including excellent home-made soup.

Café Beangoose
Selby House, Holy Island, Berwick-upon-Tweed TD15 2RX ☎ 01289 389083
You'll find the Café Beangoose near to the Heritage Centre and the Priory, and it is a real treasure. Take tea either inside the pretty white building or in the attractive garden. There is a wide range of specialist teas and a choice of cakes – perfect on a summer's afternoon.

Grannies
18 Narrowgate, Alnwick NE66 IJG
☎ 01665 602394
You'll be tempted into Grannies by the aroma of freshly baked bread and cakes in the shop. Take your tea in the quirky downstairs tea room.

Harley's Tea Rooms
Bridge Street, Rothbury NE65 7SE
☎ 01669 620240
In the heart of Rothbury, this is a friendly family-run café is housed inside an old stone building. Harley's can provide you with a full afternoon tea, a light snack or choose from more substantial lunch and dinner dishes.

Scotland

Scotland

As the ideal destination for active holidays, the Scottish Highlands were first 'discovered' at the end of the 18th century, when fear of wilderness and mountains gave way to the Romantic movement that celebrated the majesty and wonder of the natural landscape. Visitors came first to gaze in awe, and thrill to major events of recent history that included a doomed Jacobite monarchy and the last gasps of the feudal clan system. By the time Queen Victoria fell in love with the Scottish Highlands in the mid-19th century, grand sporting estates were taking hold, and the country was perceived by some as a limitless playground for the pursuits and pleasures of hunting, shooting and fishing.

Today, those traditional, monied sports still play an important part in the economy of the Highlands, but most visitors are drawn here for other activities. These include walking, mountain biking, birdwatching, and adventure sports and watersports such as quad biking, sea-kayaking, mountaineering and white-water rafting. The opportunities for getting out there and enjoying the landscape are boundless.

Edinburgh

LISTINGS 391

CLOCKWISE FROM TOP LEFT: PRINCES STREET; HOLYROOD PALACE;
FORTH RAIL BRIDGE, SOUTH QUEENSFERRY; SALISBURY CRAGS

Visit
ROYAL BOTANIC GARDEN

The largest collection of Chinese plants to be found outside China grows in the Royal Botanic Garden in Edinburgh. The Chinese Hillside is just one of the many delights to be explored in this beautiful green oasis, which has 5,000 plants in the rockery garden alone. The gardens cover 70 acres (28ha) of landscaped and wooded grounds in the north of the city and hide an art gallery, a café and shop.

Visit
UNDERGROUND EDINBURGH

Edinburgh's Old Town is thickly piled – upon itself. For an atmospheric and rather creepy insight into the living conditions here in the mid-18th century, you can visit Mary King's Close, a narrow alleyway opposite St Giles Cathedral, preserved when the City Chambers were built straight over the top. More of these buried streets riddle the foundations of the Old Town, and can be seen in the Tron Kirk, on the Royal Mile.

Visit
GREYFRIAR'S BOBBY

Edinburgh's favourite statue is much less imposing than the Scott Monument on Princes Street, and stands at the top of Candlemaker Row, opposite the Museum of Scotland. It depicts a Skye terrier, and was raised in 1873 in memory of a loyal little dog who slept faithfully on his master's grave in the nearby Greyfriars Kirkyard for 14 years after the man's death. Local people fed him on scraps each day as he kept his lonely vigil.

GREYFRIAR'S BOBBY

SCOTT MONUMENT

EDINBURGH MAP REF 409 H4

Edinburgh grew up in medieval times as a warren of narrow streets around the ancient castle. Wealth led to expansion in the 18th century and the gracious development of the New Town. Today, it is the grand home of the new Scottish Parliament, and is the financial, legal and tourism hub of Scotland. Its annual arts festivals are world renowned, and in 2005 the city was declared the first ever literary capital of Europe because of its numerous connections with esteemed writers over the centuries, from Walter Scott, Robert Louis Stevenson and Arthur Conan Doyle to today's writers, J K Rowling and Alexander McCall Smith.

Central Edinburgh is relatively compact, and divides into two halves: the narrow, steep, curving streets of the Old Town to the south of Princes Street Gardens, and the neat grid-patterned, broad boulevards and crescents of the New Town to the north of Princes Street.

The Old Town is built along a ridge of rock that stretches from the castle for around a mile eastwards to Holyrood Palace, which lies in the shadow of the tilted volcanic hill of Arthur's Seat. All the main streets run parallel to this line – Queen Street, George Street (great for designer shopping) and Princes Street (good high

street shopping) to the north; Castle Street, Lawnmarket, High Street and Canongate (which together form the famous 'Royal Mile') run along the top of the ridge; and Grassmarket, Cowgate and Chambers Street (home to the Royal Museum and Museum of Scotland) less regularly to the south.

The best places to get your bearings are from the top of Calton Hill, at the east end of Princes Street, or standing at the castle esplanade. Views extend north to the Firth of Forth, the Forth bridges and the hills of central Scotland, south to the Pentland Hills, and east to the conical mound of Berwick Law.

The main highlight of the Old Town is magnificent Edinburgh Castle, a solid symbol of the Scottish nation which has withstood centuries of battering. It was mostly destroyed during the Lang Siege of 1567–1573, but was rebuilt by James Douglas, Earl of Morton, regent to the young James VI. Edinburgh's role in modern times as a garrison fortress is celebrated each summer with a military tattoo, with regimental displays and pipe bands from places around the world. The greatest treasures on display here are the royal crown and sceptre, with the Stone of Destiny, on which loyal Scottish kings were once crowned.

The Museum of Scotland is housed in a strikingly modern building in the Old Town. This is where you can see Scottish treasures including the famous Lewis chess pieces, the exquisite 1st-century Hunterston brooch and the beautiful 8th-century Monymusk Reliquary. The comprehensive collections at this fine museum help to explain Scottish history from its earliest times to the present.

Edinburgh's still-named New Town covers an area of about 1 square mile (318ha) to the north of Princes Street, and is characterized by broad streets of spacious terraced houses with large windows and finely detailed ornamental door arches. Until the mid-18th century, Edinburgh had been neatly contained on the ridge between Arthur's Seat and the castle. Conditions became overcrowded and insanitary and, as a new age of scientific advance and intellectual enlightenment dawned, so the need for expansion became clear. A competition was held in 1766 to design a new city to the north. The winner was unknown architect James Craig (1744–1795), and within three years the first house was ready. The first New Town was so successful that a second one was laid out in 1802, extending north towards Leith. While Princes Street has lost its shine in the glare of modern

commerce, the broad Charlotte Square, with its fine preserved Georgian House, is the epitome of the planners' intentions.

The North Bridge was needed to enable pedestrians to reach the new city without foundering in the (then) muddy valley. A second link, the Mound, came about by accident, when 'Geordie' Boyd, a clothier in the Old Town, started to dump earth rubble in the marsh. Soon the builders from the New Town joined in, as they dug out foundations for the new buildings and dumped the residue. It took 2 million cartloads of rubble to complete the job, and the causeway became the Mound, later home to the National Gallery. This superb collection of paintings includes works by talented Scottish painters such as Henry Raeburn, Allen Ramsay, David Wilkie and William McTaggart, in addition to international masters including Vermeer, Van Dyke, Raphael and Monet.

The tour buses that congregate on Waverley Bridge, by the main railway station, offer the easiest and most efficient introduction to the city, with a choice of four different routes taking in the main attractions and linking you to the sites outside the city centre such as the Botanical Gardens and the old port of Leith. From 2012, a regular tram service will run to Leith.

EDINBURGH CASTLE

Fife & Stirling

CLOCKWISE FROM TOP: WEST SANDS, ST ANDREWS; STIRLING; CRAIL HARBOUR

EAST NEUK VILLAGES MAP REF 409 J3

A 'fringe of gold' is how James II described the coastal villages of this eastern corner (and 'neuk' is a Scots word for corner) of Fife, way back in the 15th century. However, he was referring to the area's many prosperous little fishing communities rather than golden beaches, although these can be found, too, at Elie and around Largo Bay.

Most of this shoreline is rocky, and the villages that cluster around their diminutive harbours seem to be packed in as tightly as sardines huddled against the rising land. They are characterized by neat harbours piled with lobster pots and fishing nets, buildings with pantile roofs and whitewashed, crow step gables, thick stone walls and small windows to fend off the elements – little fisher houses clustered along winding narrow lanes that grew up long before motorised vehicles were dreamed of.

In fact, you could drive through Fife on the A917 and overlook these little gems completely, but approach from the sea or on foot along the route of the Fife Coastal Path and it is a different matter.

The East Neuk villages are strung out in line: Elie, St Monans, Pittenweem, Anstruther and Crail. Each has its own character. Picturesque Pittenweem, for instance, was once the main fisheries port for the area, and had a priory in the 13th century which was dedicated to Fillan, a 7th-century saint who lived in a cave and spent his life converting the local Picts to the Christian faith.

Anstruther was a herring port and has the feel of a resort town complete with fish and chip shops. It also has a darker side, as an historic centre for smuggling. A chief attraction today is the Scottish Fisheries Museum, an extensive and fascinating collection of fishing craft and stories down the ages. St Monan's, dominated by the squat tower of its 14th-century Auld Kirk, was noted for ship-building as well as fishing in the 19th century.

Elie, with its golden sands, became a popular seaside holiday resort in the 19th century. A causeway leads to a rocky islet, with panoramic views across the Firth of Forth, and a watersports centre. And Crail, the most easterly of the villages, had particularly strong trading links with the Low Countries, which is reflected in its architecture and in the tolbooth bell, which came from Holland in 1520.

ST ANDREWS & FIFE

MAP REF 409 J2/H3

The broad sweeps of golden sands that lie to the north of St Andrews attracted the attention of Adolf Hitler during World War II, who saw them as the perfect landing site for a planned invasion force. Although his plans came to nothing concrete anti-tank defences may still be seen along the tree line. The undulating turf between the beaches and the more fertile farmland is known in Scotland as the links, a term which has become almost synonymous with golf courses. St Andrews is where the game is said to have originated, and it has six of them, of which the Old Course of the fine Royal and Ancient Golf Club, founded in 1754, is the most famous.

The town itself received its royal charter in the mid-12th century, and the spectacular ruined cathedral set above the harbour dates from then. St Andrews retains its medieval street plan, with North Street, South Street and Market Street the main arteries spreading west from the cathedral. Before the building's destruction during the Reformation in the 16th century, this was known as the ecclesiastical heart of Scotland, and a major pilgrimage site. The castle in its present form dates from around 1390, but was originally constructed by the bishops as essential defence. Its most remarkable features lie underground: the chilling bottle dungeon, 24ft (7.3m) deep and hewn from solid rock under a tower, from which no prisoner could escape. A mine and counter mine are legacies of an attempt to break a siege of 1546–1547 by the Duke of Argyll. His men tunnelled towards the castle but were thwarted when the defenders dug out a counter-mine and headed them off.

Today, what might have become simply an elegant and sleepy resort town is kept wide awake by its thriving and ever-more popular, university – Scotland's most venerable – which dates from 1413, and where Prince William attended.

The National Trust for Scotland owns two properties on the eastern tip of Fife. Both show the hand of the Arts and Crafts restorer, Robert Lorimer (1864–1929).

In the rolling hills to the south of the bustling town of Cupar lies the Hill of Tarvit Mansionhouse, an Edwardian house filled with elegant furniture and fine paintings, and surrounded by formal gardens. In contrast, by a peaceful corner to the south, just inland from St Monans, lies beautiful Kellie Castle, dating from 1360, and restored with eccentric charm by the Lorimer family. The castle is set beside an interesting, rambling, walled Arts and Crafts garden.

St Andrews secretly also played a part in monitoring the security of Great Britain for many years, but evidence of this is now common knowledge. A hole, 131ft (40m) deep, in the ground between St Andrews and Anstruther was the secret location of Scotland's Nuclear Command Centre, built in the 1950s as fear of the Cold War was growing. It is eerie to think that, in the event of nuclear attack, a self-supporting military community of around 300 people could have survived in the cramped conditions of this concrete-lined shelter. In 1994 the bunker opened its doors to the public as Scotland's Secret Bunker, a preserved time-capsule of a fearful age.

STIRLING MAP REF 408 F3

This ancient royal burgh grew up around a strategic crossing point of the River Forth before the waterway widens to the east and eventually becomes impassable. The Old Bridge, at the northern end of the town, once carried the only route north on this side of the country. Because of this Stirling remained the key to the north and was in a powerful geographical position up until the Kincardine Bridge opened to the southeast in 1936.

However, the town's most spectacular landmark is its castle, set high above the once-marshy plain on a rocky crag, and fought over by Scots and English in the 13th and 14th centuries. It was later remodelled as a royal palace favoured by Stuart kings, becoming the birthplace of James II and James IV, temporary home to an infant Mary, Queen of Scots, and the chosen site of James VI's coronation. Visitors can tour the castle and see the exhibition in the Queen Anne Casemates. Don't miss the recreated kistchens and the tapestries project in the Queens Inner Hall, which recreates the seven medieval tapestries in the 'Hunt of the Unicorn'.

Fabulous views from the castle's Esplanade extend to the Campsie Fells in the west and the start of the brooding Highland hills to the north. Several magnificent 17th-century buildings can be seen in the old town, including Argyll's Lodging (once used as a military hospital), before Victorian developments take over at the bottom of the hill.

Stirling's other great landmark is the imposing National Wallace Monument, the tower which crowns Abbey Craig. It was constructed during a revival of nationalist sentiment in 1869, to commemorate the Battle of Stirling Bridge in 1297, when William Wallace won a profound victory against Edward I's English forces, killing thousands and hounding the wounded into the marshes to die. The structure now houses this patriotic hero's broadsword, and you can climb the 246 steps to the top for views to the distant Forth bridges.

Just to the south of Stirling, the battlefield of Bannockburn was the site of a major Scots victory in their wars against English oppression in 1314. King Robert the Bruce took on the superior forces of Edward II and won decisively. Stirling was

the last English stronghold north of the River Forth, and while its fall was only a stage in the fight for independence (which would continue to rage on for another 14 years), this great victory consolidated the power of Robert I, effectively silencing any rival claimants to the Scottish throne. For the first time, the Scots were able to present a united front against their old enemy, the English and their Crown.

As well as monuments to bloody battles fought and won, or rebuilt strongholds showing the might of Scottish warlords, there are also peaceful structural tributes. Southeast of Stirling, near the village of Dunmore, sits a distinctive folly, a rare example of architecture inspired by fruit. It's the Pineapple, a garden retreat built to adorn Dunmore Park in 1761 by John Murray, the 4th Earl. The rendered stone foliage tops an octagonal Gothic tower. Nobody knows quite why it was built, but pineapples were considered a rare and exotic delicacy at the time. The attractive gardens and surrounding parkland are owned by the National Trust for Scotland, and the Landmark Trust lets out the folly as holiday accommodation.

Visit
THE ISLE OF MAY

The Isle of May is a rocky outcrop in the Firth of Forth, 6 miles (9.7km) offshore and clearly visible from the villages of the East Neuk. It is accessible in summer by boat from Anstruther. Now in the care of Scottish Natural Heritage, it is given over to wildlife, which includes breeding colonies of terns and puffins, eider ducks, and a small resident colony of grey seals.

Visit
FRUITFUL FOLLY

Southeast of Stirling, near the village of Dunmore, sits a distinctive folly, a rare example of architecture inspired by fruit. It's the Pineapple, a quirky garden retreat built to adorn Dunmore Park in 1761 by John Murray, the 4th Earl. Nobody knows quite why it was built, but pineapples were considered a rare and exotic delicacy at the time. The attractive gardens and surrounding parkland are owned by the National Trust for Scotland.

STIRLING

DISCOVER A ROMAN WALL & THE CANAL AT FALKIRK

A stroll along Scotland's old canal system to see the striking 21st-century Falkirk Wheel – the world's first rotating boat lift. It was designed in order to reconnect the Forth & Clyde canal with the Union canal and so restore a centuries-old link between Glasgow and Edinburgh.

DISTANCE/TIME 2 miles (3.2km); 4 miles (6.4km) with monument 1h **MAP** OS Explorer 349 Falkirk, Cumbernauld & Livingston **START** Car park Lock 16, by The Union Inn; grid ref: NS 868800 **PATHS** Canal tow paths and town streets **THE PUB** The Union Inn, Lock 16, Falkirk. Tel: 01324 626697

1 Start at the Union Inn by Lock 16. Turn right now, away from the canal, then go right along the road. Turn right along Tamfourhill Road and go through the kissing gate on the left-hand side of the road. Alternatively, don't turn up Tamfourhill Road yet, but continue walking uphill to go under the viaduct. Keep walking all the way up until you come to a monument on the left. Retrace your steps, under the viaduct, turn left into Tamfourhill Road, and left through the kissing gate on the left-hand side of the road.

2 This takes you to a section of the Roman Antonine Wall – there's a deep ditch and a rampart behind it. Walk along here, going parallel with Tamfourhill Road. When you reach the point where you can go no further, climb up the bank on the right-hand side and go down the steps to join the road by a kissing gate.

3 Go left to continue along the road – you'll soon see another kissing gate on the left leading you to another, much shorter, section of the wall. Leave the wall, rejoin the road and maintain direction to reach a mini-roundabout. Turn left here, along Maryfield Place. When you reach the end, join the

public footpath signed to the canal towpath and woodland walks. Follow this track as it winds up and over the railway bridge, then on to reach the Union Canal.

4 Don't cross the canal but turn right and walk along the tow path. This is a long straight stretch now, popular with local joggers. Eventually you'll reach Roughcastle tunnel – but remember that it currently closes at 6pm to protect the Wheel from the risk of vandalism.

5 Walk through the tunnel – it's bright and clean and dry. This will bring you out to the new Falkirk Wheel (and yet another section of the Antonine Wall). You can walk on as far as the Wheel, then walk down to the visitor centre at the bottom. Bear right here to cross the bridge over the Forth and Clyde Canal.

6 Turn right now and walk along the tow path. Lots of dog walkers and cyclists come along here (so take care if you are walking with a dog), while people frequently go canoeing along the canal. Keep walking until you come back to Lock 16, then turn right and cross the canal again to return to the start of the walk at the Union Inn.

SOLDIERS & SAINTS ON THE PENTLANDS

A lovely bracing walk that takes you across the hills and past Edinburgh's huge reservoirs. Although this walk starts from Edinburgh's busy city bypass, you'll soon think you're miles from the city. The Pentlands are an uncompromising range of hills, which clasp the city in their craggy, green arms. Their peaks rise 1,500ft (457m) above the sea and offer many great walks.

DISTANCE/TIME 7 miles (11.3) 3h **MAP** OS Explorer 344 Pentland Hills **START** Car park at the end of Bonaly Road, beyond Bonaly Tower; grid ref: NT 212679 **PATHS** Wide firm tracks, short stretches can be muddy, 3 stiles **THE PUB** The Spylaw Tavern, Colinton. Tel: 0131 441 2783

1 From the car park, go through the gate and take the right-hand path, signposted 'Tordruff Reservoir'. Beyond a wooden gate, the path crosses over the reservoir dam to intersect with a tarmac lane.

2 Turn left along the lane, keeping Tordruff Reservoir on your left-hand side. When you reach the top of the reservoir, walk over the little bridge and follow the metalled track as it bends round to the right beside a waterfall. Walk under a line of electricity pylons, and go over a small bridge, passing a water chute on your left-hand side, and continue past Clubbiedean Reservoir.

3 Your path now bears right, with fields on either side. Pass under another line of pylons and walk to Easter Kinleith farm. Now follow the lane as it bends back to the left, signposted 'Harlaw'. Pass a sign for Poets' Glen and continue ahead, over a bridge and on to a large white house on the left-hand side called Crossroads.

4 Turn left. Follow the track past a conifer plantation on your left-hand side, then go through a small gate. Continue walkingstraight ahead until you reach an

intersection. Turn left to go through a gate, which is signposted to Glencorse.

5 Follow the path across the moor and up into the hills, where you cross a stone stile. Continue in the same direction until you come to a copse of conifers on the right-hand side, with Glencorse Reservoir ahead. Turn left at this point, following the sign to Colinton by Bonaly.

6 Walk uphill and maintain direction to go through a metal gate. The track now narrows and takes you through the hills, until it eventually opens out. Continue in the same direction to reach a fence encircling conifers. Keep the fence on your left and walk down to a gate on the left-hand side.

7 Turn left through the gate. Walk past Bonaly Reservoir, then through a kissing gate and walk downhill, getting good views over Edinburgh as you descend. When you reach a wooden gate, go through and continue ahead, walking downhill, with trees on either side. Go through another kissing gate and follow the tarmac path ahead to return to the car park.

A FISHY TRAIL IN FIFE

Take a bracing linear coastal walk through the villages of Fife's East Neuk. This corner of the east coast is dotted with picturesque fishing villages, which nestle close together yet retain their own distinctive character.

DISTANCE/TIME 4 miles (6.4km) 1h30   **MAP** OS Explorer 371 St Andrews & East Fife   **START** On street in Crail; grid ref: NO 613077   **FINISH** Grid ref: NO 569034   **PATHS** Ancient streets and golden sands   **THE PUB** The Golf Hotel, 4 High Street, Crail. Tel: 01333 450206

1 From the tourist information centre in Crail, walk down Tolbooth Wynd. At the end turn right and, where the road divides, you bear left (a sign says 'no vehicular access to harbour'). You'll now be walking beside the old castle wall to a lookout point over the picturesque harbour. Bear right and then walk on to reach the High Street.

2 Turn left and walk along the road out of the village, passing the two white beacons, which help guide boats into the harbour. Turn left and walk down West Braes, following the signs for the Coastal Path. When you reach Osbourne Terrace turn left down a narrow path, then go down some steps, through a kissing gate and on to a grassy track by the shore.

3 From here you follow the path as it hugs the shoreline. You should soon see cormorants perched on rocks to your left and will also get views of the Isle of May. Go down some steps, over a slightly boggy area, and continue walking until you reach two derelict cottages – an area known as The Pans.

4 Walk past the cottages and continue along the shore, then hop over a stone stile. You'll now pass flat rocks on the left, which are covered with interesting little rock pools. Cross the burn by the footbridge – you'll now

be able to see the Bass Rock and Berwick Law on your left and the village of Anstruther ahead, and will soon reach some caves.

5 Pass the caves, then cross a little stone stile on the left-hand side then a footbridge. Your track is narrower now and takes you past fields on the right, then maritime grasses on the left. Stone steps lead to another stile. Climb over it to reach Caiplie.

6 Go through the kissing gate to pass in front of houses, follow the wide grassy track, then go through another kissing gate to walk past a field. The path now runs past a free-range pig farm and up to a caravan park.

7 Continue along the shore, on a tarmac track to reach a play area and war memorial on the right. Maintain direction now as you enter the village of Cellardyke and continue to the harbour. Pass the harbour and The Haven restaurant and continue along John Street, then James Street.

8 At the end of James Street maintain your direction, then follow the road as it bends down to the left. You'll walk past a guiding beacon and will come into Anstruther's busy little harbour. You can now either retrace your steps back to Crail or take the bus which leaves from the harbour.

WALK 128

A LEISURELY CIRCUIT OF CULROSS

An easy walk that ends on the cobbled streets of an historic town, where a prosperous trading history is reflected in the stylish buildings.

DISTANCE/TIME 3.5 miles (5.6km) 1h30   **MAP** OS Explorer 367 Dunferline & Kirkcaldy   **START** Culross West car park; grid ref: NS 983859   **PATHS** Generally firm paths, some muddy woodland tracks   **THE PUB** The Red Lion Inn, Low Causeway, Culross. Tel: 01383 880 225; www.redlionculross.co.uk

1 From the car park, take the steps up to reach a tarmac path that runs alongside the railway and then turn right. Just beyond a reed bed to the right, turn right down steps and follow the path to the road. Cross over to the entrance to Blair Castle, now a convalescent home for miners.

2 Walk up the tarmac drive, which is lined with magnificent rhododendron bushes. Walk ahead until you can see Blair Castle on the left. Before you reach it, take the right-hand turning in the trees and follow it as it bears to the right. Continue until you reach Blair Mains farmhouse, which you'll find on the left.

3 Continue following the track, with fields on either side. Walk ahead until you reach the trees and continue following this track until you reach a metal gate on the left-hand side, just beyond a line of pylons. Look carefully and you should spot a wooden fence post on the right-hand side, with the words 'West Kirk' and 'grave' painted on it in faint white. Take the narrow right-hand path immediately before it, which runs through the trees.

4 Follow this path to go through a kissing gate and continue walking ahead, with trees on your left and fields on your right. Go

through another kissing gate, and continue in the same direction. When you reach a crossing of paths, continue ahead along the track and walk under a line of pylons. You will soon pass the remains of a church on the left-hand side.

5 Continue ahead, past the old cemetery, and walk in the same direction until the track joins a tarmac road. Walk in the same direction until you reach a junction. Turn right here and head downhill – watch out for traffic now as the road can be busy. You will soon reach Culross Abbey on the left-hand side.

6 It's worth stopping at this point to visit the abbey. You can then continue to walk on downhill, down Tanhouse Brae, and will soon reach the Mercat ('old Market') Cross, with The Study on the right-hand side. Continue walking in the same direction, down Back Causeway, until you reach the main road.

7 Turn right, walk past the tourist information centre, past the Tron (the old burgh weighing machine), then past the large ochre-coloured building on the right, which is Culross Palace. To reach the starting point and the car park, continue walking in the same direction – the car park is on the left-hand side, just past the children's play area.

Trossachs & South

CLOCKWISE FROM TOP LEFT: SCOTT'S SHIP RRS *DISCOVERY*, DUNDEE; BLAIR CASTLE; CALLANDER

ABERFELDY MAP REF 409 G1

Born in Ireland, General George Wade (1673–1748) served as Commander-in-Chief of North Britain from 1724 to 1740, and left his long-lasting mark on the Scottish Highlands in the form of almost 250 miles (400km) of military roads and some 40 bridges to go with them. Today, one of his finest bridges still carries the traffic of the A827 over the River Tay at Aberfeldy, a pleasant stone-built town in the heart of Perthshire. The bridge's elegant structure, with its four obelisks and five graceful spans, was designed for Wade by the architect William Adam. On the bank nearby stands a monument to the Black Watch Regiment.

Signs in the town point the way to walking trails that lead to the Birks of Aberfeldy, birchwoods celebrated by the poet Robert Burns. On the edge of the town, the Dewar's distillery offers a visitor centre and tour, culminating in a tasting. Outside you might see native red squirrels. To the west, at Weem, is the 16th-century stronghold of Castle Menzies, a restored Z-plan tower house. One of the rooms used by Bonny Prince Charlie has been furnished and decorated in the style he would have known.

Loch Tay lies 5 miles (8km) to the west of Aberfeldy, with the picturesque village of Kenmore at its eastern end. A splendidly spired gateway marks an entrance to Taymouth Castle, now privately owned. The town also has a great watersports centre, but its most unusual attraction has to be a replica round-house or crannog, set low over the waters of the loch.

This is part of the Scottish Crannog Centre, the visitor centre for an on-going project that is exploring and excavating the 18 or so similar Iron Age dwellings that once lined these shores. Crannogs were community dwellings built on wooden stilts. The cold, peaty water of the loch has helped to preserve timber, plant and food remains and even scraps of cloth, and the discoveries made here reveal much about the way of life of the crannog builders. Visitors are able to watch, and take part in, demonstrations of ancient crafts.

Shortly before it reaches Aberfeldy, the Tay is joined by the waters of the River Lyon. This river flows down from one of Scotland's most beautiful valleys, Glen Lyon, which lies sandwiched between Loch Tay and Loch Rannoch. Entry to the glen is through the dramatic and steep-sided pass at Fortingall, or over the mountain pass by Ben Lawers.

CALLANDER MAP REF 408 F3

Callander straddles the A84 northwest of Stirling, and is the eastern gateway to the Trossachs. During the 19th century it was a flourishing resort town, and the grandeur of the Victorian buildings along its main street bears this out.

On a summer's day the little town is packed out with visitors, keen to enjoy the varied shops and tea rooms, and to track down the history of Rob Roy, a folk hero. Rob Roy MacGregor (1671–1734) took refuge with his people in the local hills, and his story is told at the visitor centre in the former church on the main square. His grave is in the churchyard at Balquhidder. There are several good walks from the town centre, leading to Bracklinn Falls and the Callander Crags.

The Hamilton Toy Collection in Main Street has toys from the 19th century onwards, including dolls, teddy bears, model train sets, toy soldiers, books, jigsaws and games. It is as popular with adults eager to relive their childhood days, as with children.

To the west of the town, beyond the woollen weaving mill and display at Kilmahog, is the scenic spot of the Pass of Leny, with the Falls of Leny accessible from the roadside car park. Of interest to cycling enthusiasts, the Callander to Strathyre Cycleway runs past here too, following the route of the former railway line from Callander up the western shore of Loch Lubnaig towards Killin.

To the southwest of Callander lies the Lake of Menteith, where you can hire a boat and fishing tackle and try casting for rainbow trout. Alternatively, a ferry goes out to the lovely tree-covered island where the romantic ruins of Inchmahome Priory stand. Augustinian monks made it their home in 1238, and the infant Mary, Queen of Scots was hidden here for three weeks in 1547 after the Battle of Pinkie Cleugh before she was eventually smuggled to safety in France.

Southeast of Callander on the A84 lies the rural village of Doune, with a substantial ruined castle at its heart, hidden amid the trees on a curve of the River Teith. Built by the powerful regent of Scotland, Robert Stewart, Duke of Albany, in the late 14th century, it is comparatively simple in construction, with a main block of buildings set within a courtyard and contained by a mighty curtain wall. The fabric of the castle is maintained by Historic Scotland. You can climb to the top of this for panoramic views of the village and the surrounding countryside, and there are lots of little stairways as well as chambers to explore. Its medieval austerity and imposing stature gave the castle a starring role in the film *Monty Python and the Holy Grail*.

CRIEFF MAP REF 409 G2

The old spa town of Crieff lies above the meandering River Earn west of Perth, on the edge of the Highlands. For a time in the 17th century it took the alternative name of Drummond, in honour of local patrons, but the original name was restored in the 18th century, after the town was burned down by Jacobite rebels.

Crieff grew up as a centre for cattle drovers, who passed through here on their way south to England or north to the Highlands. The linen and tanning industries thrived for a while, but were overtaken by the growth of the Lowland factories. Today Crieff is an industrious service town, celebrated for the quality of its schools, and as a main hub for activities including fishing, cycling, and water sports on Loch Earn. There is good walking through the hills, too, with a signposted trail from the town centre north to Knock Hill offering great views.

The Drummonds had their castle 3 miles (4.8km) south of the town, and while the castle itself is still private, the fabulous formal 17th-century garden has been restored to its former state and is open on summer afternoons. The burial chapel of the Drummonds stands beside the Innerpeffray Library. Founded in 1691 it is the oldest lending library in Scotland.

To the north of Crieff a narrow road leads up the remote Glen Turret to Loch Turret, passing the scenic beauty spot at the waterfalls of the same name. Begun in 1775, Glenturret Distillery is home to

the Famous Grouse Experience, which is entertaining and offers a glimpse into the serious business of making whisky.

DUNDEE MAP REF 409 H2

Dundee was founded on a 19th-century industrial base which, over time, was famously reduced to the three 'J's: jam, jute and journalism. Today it is busy reinventing itself as a lively centre for the arts and hands-on science, and celebrating its maritime and industrial heritage. The main focus of rejuvenation has been along the waterfront, where the three-masted Royal Research Ship *Discovery* is now berthed; she was built here in 1900–1901, and her maiden voyage was to the Antarctic. In 1902 she became trapped in the pack ice, and survived two timber-crunching winters before breaking free and sailing home. The modern museum alongside tells her story. Nothing beats exploring the ship herself, however, and witnessing the cramped conditions of the brave men who crewed her.

Moored nearby, the frigate *Unicorn* was built in 1824 and is the oldest British warship afloat. In the same corner is

Sensation: a state-of-the-art celebration of science geared to children, centred on the five senses.

Wool and flax were both woven in Dundee, long before the important advent of jute in the early 19th century caused a boom in the town's growth. The plant fibre was imported from India and softened with whale oil before being spun and woven. By the 1870s most Indian mills were undercutting Dundee prices, and the industry had to scale down. It was hit hard again by the post-World War I recession. A fascinating survivor is the Verdant Works, which explains how Dundee developed so quickly, and why more women than men were employed by the jute industry.

D C Thomson (1861–1964), son of a Dundee shipping entrepreneur, founded the newspaper company that still bears his name in 1906. *The Sunday Post* and the *Weekly News* are still produced here, along with many local papers, but the company's best loved creations were its popular comics for children, the *Beano* and *Dandy*. Statues of the characters Minnie the Minx and Desperate Dan can be seen on the High Street.

Insight
PONTIUS PILATE
The pretty hamlet of Fortingall is claimed by some to be the birthplace of Pontius Pilate. It is said that he was born here, the son of a Roman soldier and a local girl, before rising to become the Roman prefect of Judea and Samaria. The Fortingall connection seems to have arisen from a headstone in the churchyard, marked simply 'PP'.

Insight
WHO PAYS THE FERRYMAN?
Until 1535, anybody wishing to cross the River Teith at Doune had to pay a ferryman to be rowed across. One day James Spittal was refused passage when he showed up without any money. Spittal was the wealthy tailor to James IV, and took the slight personally. It is said that, out of spiteful anger, he paid for the building of a bridge here to permanently deprive the ferryman of his living. The bridge is still standing, though it was modified in 1866.

DRUMMOND GARDENS

DUNKELD MAP REF 409 G2

A picturesque little 18th-century town with a tiny Gothic cathedral, Dunkeld lies surrounded by glorious woodland on the banks of the River Tay. Everything here, bar the cathedral, was destroyed by the Jacobites after their 1689 victory at Killiecrankie. When it was rebuilt, terraced cottages were squeezed into a compact centre of just two main streets: Cathedral Street and High Street, with a neat little square, called The Cross. The pleasing uniformity of Dunkeld owes much to this rebuilding by the Dukes of Atholl, and more to the carefully done restoration of around 20 houses by the National Trust for Scotland since the 1950s. The Trust has a shop in the main square, in a building distinctive for the iron 'ell' mounted on its exterior. The ell was a unit of measurement equivalent to 37 inches (92.5cm). The graceful stone bridge which links Dunkeld to Inver, much favoured as a subject by painters, was a masterpiece in 1809 of the great engineer Thomas Telford.

Dunkeld's ruined cathedral stands in a picturesque, shady setting on the banks of the river, and the crumbled building dates back to the 13th century, although its history as a monastic site goes back to the 6th century. Kenneth MacAlpin, the first king of Scotland, brought St Columba's bones here from Iona in around 850, thereby making it an important medieval ecclesiastical centre. The most substantial part left standing today is the choir, which still serves as the parish church. Close by the end of the cathedral furthest from the main entrance, look out for a sign indicating the 'Parent Larch'. This particular tree was imported from Austria in 1738, and became the source of many trees in and around nearby forests, planted up by the Dukes of Atholl between 1738 and 1830.

There are plenty of good circular signposted walks in the woods around here and along the river bank, with carpets of bluebells in late spring, and red squirrels to look out for – a leaflet from the tourist office gives full details. One walk leads through mixed woodland along the River Braan and up to the folly of the Hermitage, or Ossian's Hall, set above the Black Linn Falls.

Little Dunkeld is the last resting place of the great Scottish fiddler, Neil Gow (1727–1807), who composed many dance tunes and fine airs and was famous throughout Britain for his skill. His violin is on display at Blair Castle

KILLIN MAP REF 408 F2

The village of Killin is set beneath the hills where the River Dochart tumbles over an extensive waterfall and into the western end of Loch Tay. Once home to the MacNabs, it is at the heart of the ancient district of Breadalbane, and has now become a popular walking, fishing and touring centre. The Breadalbane Folklore Centre located in St Fillan's Mill shares its premises with the local tourist office, and offers an intriguing insight into Scottish legends of kelpies, brownies and other mythical creatures. The mill originally powered machines for the weaving of tweed. The ruins of 16th-century Finlarig Castle, a Campbell stronghold, stand at the head of the loch. It has what are said to be the only surviving remains in the country of a beheading pit, reserved especially for the execution of the gentry.

The National Trust for Scotland is noted for its preservation of some grand castles, but lists some more modest dwellings, too. One of the humblest is along the narrow Glen Lochay Road, just north of Killin. Moirlanich Longhouse is a long, low 19th-century farmhouse, built with a cruck frame. At least three generations of the Robertson family lived here, until the 1960s, and the house has been preserved, complete with a 'hingin' lum' (suspended chimney) and traditional wooden box beds.

The view from Killin up Loch Tay is dominated by the bulk of Ben Lawers, 1,214m (3,984ft), the highest mountain in the area. It is known for its delicate alpine flora, and with the neighbouring Tarmachan range, is a popular focus for walkers. The area is a national nature reserve. The 79-mile (126km) Rob Roy long-distance path passes through the town and so it is a popular stopping-off point for walkers.

KIRRIEMUIR MAP REF 409 H1

Kirriemuir is the gateway to the great Glens of Angus, the long valleys which stretch north into the open moorland of the Grampian Mountains, forming the southern edge of the mighty Cairngorms National Park. The range includes Glen Esk, Glen Clova and Glen Prosen, and they all offer superb hill-walking, with Glen Clova giving access to remote Glen Doll. The glens are all home to red and black grouse, golden eagles, ptarmigans and capercaillies, red and roe deer. Antarctic explorer Robert Falcon Scott and Edward Wilson, the expedition's doctor and artist, came to the area to plan their ill-fated voyage to the South Pole, and are commemorated by a fine memorial cairn in Glen Prosen.

Kirriemuir itself is an industrious red sandstone town, built on the revenues of weaving and farming. The town hosts an annual walking festival in May and June, but its main claim to fame is its associations with the playwright and novelist J M Barrie. The creator of *Peter Pan* was born here in 1860, the son of a weaver and one of ten children, and his birthplace is now an evocative museum. The wash-house round the back of the property served as Barrie's first theatre, and may have inspired the Wendy House in *Peter Pan* (1904). Although he lived for most of his life in London, Barrie wrote with great affection about the small-town life of Kirriemuir, disguised as 'Thrums' in his tales. In 1930 Barrie presented the community with a novel gift after they had honoured him with the freedom of the town: a camera obscura on nearby Kirrie Hill, for far-reaching views over the surrounding countryside (check back at the birthplace for opening times).

About 5 miles (8km) to the south of Kirriemuir lies Glamis Castle, family seat of the Earls of Strathmore and Kinghorne, and the childhood home of the late Queen Elizabeth, the Queen Mother. With its multiple turrets and fairytale battlements Glamis Castle (pronounced 'Glahms') is the archetypal vision of what a Scottish castle should look like, and the interior is equally fabulous too, with moulded plaster ceilings and fine panelling. At its core is a medieval tower house, dating back to around 1372.

The surrounding parkland is well worth exploring, with its formal Italian garden and a pinetum. For a total contrast, six 18th-century cottages n the nearby village house the Angus Folk Museum, showing how the rural community lived.

DUNKELD

THE TROSSACHS

PERTH MAP REF 409 G2

The Roman settlement of Perth was founded on the banks of the River Tay in the 1st century; in the Middle Ages it became the capital of Scotland. Today it is a lively city at the centre of a thriving and established farming community, its compact core offering great shopping and bohemian cafés that spill out onto the pavements. With its theatre, City Hall, a concert hall and other venues, not to mention galleries and cinemas, Perth is an active centre for music and the arts, culminating in a lively festival in May.

Perth's extensive parks are headed by the North Inch and the South Inch, beside the river, and there are several gardens to explore in the area, including Branklyn, which is specially noted for its blue Himalayan poppies (Meconopsis).

In recent years Perth has developed as the adventure capital of Scotland, with an ever-longer list of adventure sports and activities to take you out and about across the region. So if the more traditional sports of fishing, golf, pony trekking, mountain biking and hill-hiking seem tame, you can get your adrenalin rush by quad biking, off-road driving, abseiling, canoeing, waterskiing, cliff-jumping, white-water rafting or even paintballing. The local tourist information office has more details about where you can do these activities.

PITLOCHRY MAP REF 409 G1

This bustling town in the wooded valley of the River Tummel is based around one long main street, running parallel with the river, and lined with shops and eating places. The geographical heart of Scotland, it first appeared on the map when General Wade built a military road through here, and it has been a popular holiday resort since the 19th century.

A footbridge leads across the river to the Festival Theatre, with its Explorers' Garden, opened in 2003 to celebrate 300 years of botanical exploration and a collection of artefacts from around the world by Scots. There is also an ever-changing programme of drama and concerts at the theatre. There is a view from the footbridge to the salmon ladder, which was installed as part of a hydroelectric dam system along the river and which also created Loch Faskally, a local beauty spot. Learn more at the Scottish Hydroelectric Visitor Centre, which gives access to an observation window where you can watch the wild salmon jumping (usually between April and October). Pitlochry also has two distilleries, Blair Atholl and Eradour.

Just to the north of the town is the conservation village of Moulin, with its 17th-century church and ruined castle in the shadow of Ben Vrackie. The writer Robert Louis Stevenson stayed here in 1881, and described it as a 'sweet spot'.

Some three miles (4.8km) north of Pitlochry is the narrow, wooded gorge of Killiecrankie, on the River Garry. This was the site of a battle in 1689 when a Jacobite army defeated government troops. Continue north and you'll reach Blair Castle, a white-painted mansion in a majestic setting of trees and gardens, with hills behind. It's been the ancestral home of the Dukes and Earls of Atholl for more than 700 years, and can claim its own private army. Bonnie Prince Charlie slept in the now tartan-clad tower room in 1745. The exterior of the castle reflects a Victorian make-over in 1863 and inside are wonderful artefacts and paintings.

THE TROSSACHS MAP REF 408 F3

The Trossachs is an Area of Outstanding Natural Beauty in central Scotland, now with protected status as the main sector of the Loch Lomond and the Trossachs National Park. Scotland's first such designated park, its land stretches for 720 square miles (1,865 sq km) from the Argyll Forest Park in the west over to Callander in the east, and from Killin and Tyndrum up in the north to Balloch in the south, at the foot of Loch Lomond. The Trossachs is the region lying to the east of Loch Lomond which was first 'discovered' by travellers in the late 18th century, and was popularized for a wider audience as a thrilling backdrop to the novels of Sir Walter Scott (1771–1832). Scott's famous poem, 'The Lady of the Lake' (1810), was set in identifiable and accessible places across the Trossachs, and attracted many tourists to the area.

The village of Aberfoyle is the key to this region, giving easy access to the wooded hills of the Queen Elizabeth Forest Park and the peak of Ben Venue (2,319ft/729m), as well as Loch Katrine to the north. There are great opportunities for walking and cycling, including a pretty cycle route that runs through the Forest Park and along the shores of Loch Venachar and Loch Lubnaig to Balquhidder, Lochearnhead and Killin. The Trossachs Discovery visitor centre in Aberfoyle is a mine of information about activities in the area. The Scottish Wool Centre behind it offers an entertaining Sheepdog School Show, as well as a chance to see lambs and sheep shearing in season.

Reintroducing Species

What little remains of a once huge Caledonian Forest is today being eroded by the ever-increasing population of red and sika deer. The only way to restore the balance, many claim, is to reintroduce the deer's natural predator, the wolf, to the wilds of Scotland. Without such action the forest and its ecosystem is in increasing danger of disappearing forever.

For millions of years, Scotland was covered in trees – a pristine wilderness of birch, rowan, aspen, juniper and Scots pines. When the Romans arrived a mere two millennia ago, they called Scotland 'Caledonia', meaning 'wooded heights'. Today, only one per cent of that mighty Caledonian Forest remains, and attempts to revive the forests by restocking are thwarted by the very icon of Scotland, the red deer. With no natural predators except for man in the short hunting season, deer populations have simply grown out of hand. Ironically, of the six species of deer in Scotland, only two are native. But the red deer in particular is threatening the very existence of both the remaining forest and the animals that depend upon it.

When the forest was rich in flora, it was rich in wildlife too. Now, with the beaver, wild boar, lynx, moose, brown bear and wolf all gone, only a few birds – the capercaillie, crested tit and endemic Scottish crossbill – remain.

Thankfully, steps are now underway to reintroduce some of Scotland's native species of wildlife. Duncan Horwood's book *The Stonor Eagles* relates the passing of the last of the white-tailed eagles from Scotland. But these magnificent birds were reintroduced in the 1970s, and have now become locally widespread, notably on the islands of Mull, Rhum and Skye. In fact today, Mull is fast becoming one of the prime wildlife tourism destinations in Scotland, and the opportunity to see golden and sea eagles is one of the main attractions on offer.

Capercaillie are the largest and by far the most impressive of the grouse family. Sadly, it was their dependency on woodland which was in juxtaposition with man's intense forest felling, that led to their extinction in Britain in the 18th century. They were reintroduced in 1837, initially with considerable success, but the demands for timber during two world wars once more pushed this interesting creature into decline. They continue to struggle, but have limited strongholds in Scotland, and a poor breeding record is once again making them vulnerable.

Staying with birds, if you take the road from Castle Douglas down to Loch Ken in Dumfries and Galloway there is a better than average chance that there will be a red kite circling above, marked out by its distinctive reddish-brown colour and forked tail. This road is a favourite foraging ground for the 100 birds which have been released into the area since 2001 and have become a popular local attraction.

Until recently red kites were a rare site in Scotland. By 1879 they had been wiped out in Scotland, mainly as a result of poisoning and egg collecting. The birds were reintroduced in 1989 and releases continued to 2004 at three sites around the country, as part of a joint project between SNH and RSPB Scotland.

For our prehistoric ancestors, the sight and sound of beavers along the rivers of Britain would have been familiar, though the story of the beaver today is less happy. Due to hunting, European beaver became extinct in England and Wales in the 12th century, and only survived in Scotland until the 1600s. By the 18th century, beaver were close to extinction across most of Europe, but since the 1920s, successful reintroductions have taken place in twenty-three European countries, but sadly not Britain.

As an effort to reintroduce beaver into Scotland, in 1998, a public consultation was undertaken by Scottish Natural Heritage (SNH), to consider the trial reintroduction of European beaver. The results showed the Scottish people to be overwhelmingly in favour of the proposal. In February 2005, SNH, who wanted a licence to reintroduce beaver to Forestry Commission land at Knapdale in Argyll, wrote to the Scottish Executive asking for ministerial approval to proceed and to issue a licence for the trial. Seven months later, the Scottish Executive said no.

Wild boar is increasingly appearing in butchers' shops, supermarkets and restaurant menus, but sadly not in the wild. Unlike many extinct British species, wild boar existed in Britain long after the Roman occupation. Under Norman rule, punitive laws were passed forbidding anyone to kill them, but they nevertheless became extinct in Britain in 1683, as a result of hunting and absorption into domestic herds. The ultimate omnivore, eating anything and everything, wild boar have recently re-established themselves in southern England, largely as escapees from farms. Glen Affric is just one of a number of Scottish locations that have been the scene of an experiment with wild boar to help regenerate the Caledonia forest by eating invasive bracken shoots, and other estates in Scotland have small herds of wild boar in enclosed areas.

Throughout history, pine martens have been regarded as the most beautiful of British mammals, with a fur so soft only kings might wear it. These lithe, ferret-like animals have impressive speed and agility which, alas, allows them to chase down red squirrels. Their taste for game birds made them unpopular with game estates, and the marten has suffered widespread persecution. They are now a protected species, and their numbers are increasing rapidly in Scotland.

The iconic native species in Scotland, red squirrel, has suffered greatly from habitat loss, persecution and competition from the introduced grey squirrel. The red squirrel is most at home in the dense coniferous forests of Scottish plantations.

It is not all doom and gloom: plans exist to see the long-term introduction of rare species to the Alladale wilderness, 40 miles (64km) north of Inverness. The plans are still plans, but within the confines of a 37-mile (59km) electric fence, packs of wolves, a dozen European brown bears, lynx, boar and European elk may well, one day, roam wild.

LEFT FROM TOP Wild boar forage once again in the pine woodland of Glen Affric.

The windswept hills of Glen Falloch are home to the scant remains of the once-great Caledonian Forest, which at one time covered the area in thick woodland.

A fine red stag in the Glengoulandie Deer Park – the tips of its antlers are known as 'points'. In March and April the stags shed their antlers as new bone grows.

Pine martens have made a rapid come-back in the wild now that they are a protected species. The animals' bushy tails grow to half the length of their bodies.

RIGHT FROM TOP The large capercaillie is still fighting for survival as a breed due to its diminished natural woodland habitat.

Sightings of pretty crested tits are now more frequent in the Cairngorms.

Some 15 miles (24km) from Loch Ness, Glen Affric's lake and rivers create a romantic picture when the mists roll down from the surrounding hills.

ABOVE CALLANDER

Steep wooded paths lead you through the crags for superb views of the Trossachs. Known unofficially as the eastern gateway to the Highlands, Callander is a great place to strike out from and explore the breathtaking surrounding countryside with its snow-clad mountain backdrop.

1 From the Riverside car park, walk back to the main road, then turn left. Follow this, then turn right along Tulipan Crescent. Just in front of some modern flats, turn left and follow the wide track. Where the track splits, take the path on the left that is signposted 'The Crags'.

2 Your path now winds steeply uphill through the trees and can get slippery if there's been a lot of rain. Keep following the path and cross a footbridge. Climb to reach a wall on the left-hand side, after which your path narrows. Follow it to pass a large boulder.

3 Continue following the path, which eventually bears left, up some steps to a fence. Cross another footbridge, scramble over some rocks and go through a metal kissing gate. You eventually come to a memorial cairn, created in 1897 for Queen Victoria's Diamond Jubilee. On a clear day there are stunning, panoramic views of the surrounding countryside from here.

4 Leaving the cairn, your path now begins to wind downhill. It's rocky in places and you'll need to take some care as you descend. Follow the path down to the road.

5 Turn right along the road – you'll see the Wallace Monument near Stirling in the far distance. You'll soon pass a sign on the right-hand side for the Red Well, where the water runs a distinctly reddish colour owing to the presence of iron traces in the local rock. Continue until you reach a car park on your left. You can make a detour here to see the Bracklyn Falls.

6 After the car park, stay on the road for about 0.25 mile (400m) passing a track up to a reservoir on your right, then turn right into the Forestry Commission car park (signposted 'The Crags').

7 Continue to walk through a car park on to a broad Forestry Commission track. Continue walking past telecommunications next to the end of the track. At the end of the track, turn left and then walk downhill until you reach a wooden seat and a footbridge.

8 Take the path that runs to the right of the seat (don't cross the footbridge). Follow the path as it runs downhill and takes you back to the place at which you entered the woods. Turn right, then go left along the main road and walk back into Callander to the car park at the start of the walk.

DISTANCE/TIME 4 miles (6.4km) 2h30 **MAP** OS Explorer 365 The Trossachs **START** Riverside car park; grid ref: NN 625079 **PATHS** Forest tracks and some rocky paths **THE PUB** The Lade Inn, Kilmahog, just west of Callander. Tel: 01877 330152

WALK 130

FROM BALQUHIDDER TO CREAG AN TUIRC

A forest walk to a cairn at the summit of a knoll and a bench where you can rest and enjoy the far-reaching views of the River Balvag, Loch Voil and the atmospheric Braes of Balquhidder. This is Rob Roy country, where the 17th-century outlaw lived and died. Immortalized in the 19th century by Sir Walter Scott in his novel *Rob Roy* (1817), the romantic myth of Rob Roy MacGregor's turbulent life was retold in the 1995 film of the same name starring Liam Neeson and Jessica Lange. The Old Kirk at Balquhidder is the final resting place of Roy alongside his beloved wife Mary and two of his four sons. A surrounding bronze rail marks the grave.

1 From Balquhidder church, walk along a dirt track, go past a shed and turn on to a path on the right-hand side which gives access into the forest. Follow the direction arrows on the green signposts pointing to Creag an Tuirc, along a forest track and heading up the hill.

2 Continue on this obvious trail for about 0.5 mile (800m) and then turn right, alongside a green building, again following the signposted and waymarked route along a forest road. After 0.5 mile (800m) go through a gate on the right-hand side, go slightly downhill on stone steps and across a stream.

3 The path now heads uphill on some stone steps, through old pine trees and on towards the summit of a knoll. Here is a cairn erected by the Clan Maclaren Society in 1987 to commemorate their 25th anniversary. The plaque proclaims that this place is the ancient rallying point of their clan.

4 A seat below the cairn is a grand place to rest after the climb up here. Sit for a

while and enjoy the magnificent views over the meandering line of the River Balvag and the length of Loch Voil with the Braes of Balquhidder rising steeply above it. You can see the route that Rob Roy's funeral procession would have taken from Inverlochlarig down to the village itself, and the churchyard where his body lies. From here, retrace your steps back down the hill but before reaching the top of the stone steps on which you came up, take the path to the left signposted 'Forest Walk'. This continues downhill following waymarked poles, down some steps and across a small bridge. The path goes through some bracken, over a small stream and then across a stile. Eventually it will pass through a small wood of young native trees before emerging on to the forest road.

5 Turn left here and retrace your steps back downhill over the stile and then turn left to return to reach the car park. From here enter the churchyard and turn left. Rob Roy's grave is on the left in front of the ruins of a pre-Reformation church.

DISTANCE/TIME 2.5 miles (4km) 2h **MAP** OS Explorer 365 The Trossachs **START** Car park at Balquhidder church; grid ref: NN 536209 **PATHS** Forest roads and hillside, 2 stiles **THE PUB** Monachyle Mhor, Balquhidder. Tel: 01877 384622; www.monachylemhor.com

WALK 131

THE BRAES O' KILLIECRANKIE

A deeply wooded riverside walk leads from the famous battlefield to Loch Faskally. When James II was ousted from England in a bloodless coup in 1688, the Scots Parliament (the Estates) voted to replace him with William of Orange. The Stuarts had neglected and mismanaged Scotland, and had mounted a bloody persecution of the fundamentalist Protestant (Covenanters) of the Southern Uplands.

DISTANCE/TIME 8.75 miles (14.1km) 4h **MAP** OS Explorer 386 Pitlochry & Loch Tummel **START** Killiecrankie visitor centre; grid ref: NN 917626 **PATHS** Wide riverside paths, minor roads, no stiles **THE PUB** Old Mill Inn, Pitlochry. Tel: 01796 474020

1 From the back corner of the visitor centre steps, signed 'Soldier's Leap', lead down into the wooded gorge. A footbridge crosses the waterfall of Trouper's Den. At the next junction, turn left ('Soldier's Leap'). Ten steps down, a spur path on the right leads to the viewpoint above the Soldier's Leap.

2 Return to the main path, signed 'Linn of Tummel', which runs down to the River Garry below the railway viaduct. After 1 mile (1.6km) the path reaches a footbridge.

3 Don't cross, but continue ahead, signed 'Pitlochry', along the riverside under the South Garry road bridge. The path bears left to a footbridge. Cross and turn right, signed 'Pitlochry', back to the main river. The path runs around a huge river pool to a tarred lane; turn right. The lane leaves the lochside, then passes a track on the right, blocked by a barrier. Ignore this track; shortly afterwards turn right at a signpost, 'Pitlochry'.

4 Immediately bear left to pass along the right-hand side of Loch Dunmore, following red-top posts. A footbridge crosses the loch, but turn away from it, half right, on to a small path that becomes a dirt track. After 270yds (246m) it reaches a wider track. Turn left, with a white/yellow waymarker. After 220yds (201m) the track starts to climb; here the white/yellow markers indicate a smaller path on the right, which follows the lochside to a point below the A9 road bridge.

5 Cross Loch Faskally on the Clunie footbridge below the road's bridge and turn right, on a quiet road around the loch. In 1 mile (1.6km), at the top of the grass bank on the left, is the Priest Stone. After you pass the Clunie power station, you reach a car park on the left. Here a sign indicates a steep little path down to the Linn of Tummel.

6 Return to the road for 0.5 mile (800m), to cross a suspension bridge on the right. Turn right, downstream, to pass above the Linn. A spur path back right returns to the falls at a lower level, but the main path continues along the riverside (signed 'Killiecrankie'). It bends left and goes down wooden steps to the Garry, then continues upstream and under the road bridge. Take the side path up on to the bridge for river views, then return to follow the descending path signed 'Pitlochry via Faskally'. This runs down to the bridge, Point **3**. Return upstream to the start.

WALK 132

THE MYSTERIOUS STONES OF ABERLEMNO

This walk takes you through agricultural land once inhabited by the Picts, a fascinating ancient British tribe. Had history turned out differently you would have been doing this walk in Pictland, not Scotland. The Picts inhabited this northern part of Britain for thousands of years, yet we know little about them. Neither their language nor manuscripts have survived, and their culture remains a mystery.

DISTANCE/TIME 5 miles (8km) 1h45 **MAP** OS Explorer 389 Forfar, Brechin & Edzell **START** Car park by school in Aberlemno; grid ref: NO 522558 **PATHS** Quiet agricultural land and ancient carved stones **THE PUB** Royal Hotel, Castle Street, Forfar. Tel: 01307 462691

1 If you want to see the Pictish stones, you will find them opposite the car park. Take a good look at the wonderful carvings on the stones. No one truly understands the symbols carved on Pictish stones, but they seem to represent an early writing system. Stones are carved with scenes of warriors and battles; with spirals and complex patterns; with simple geometrical shapes; with wild creatures, such as stags, wolves and eagles; and even everyday objects, such as combs. Later stones include crosses. From the car park, turn right and walk along the road, then go first left, signed 'Aberlemno church and stone'. Walk past the church – another Pictish stone is found in the churchyard. After the church, follow the road as it bends round to the right, then continue until you reach a T-junction.

2 Turn right and follow this road, passing the entrance to Woodside on the left. At the corner, follow the road as it bends right. Walk down to join the B9134, turn right and follow this a short distance until you reach a turning on the left.

3 Turn left along this road, signed 'Finavon Hill'. The road winds uphill, past several outcrops, then under a line of pylons. Continue on this road as it skirts a hill.

4 Continue following the road uphill, passing a small loch half-hidden in woodland to the left. Shortly after this, you reach an old stone wall on your right. Just beyond a rusty gate in the corner of a field, you will see a section of the wall has collapsed. Hop over here, taking care to avoid the strand of wire.

5 Head uphill now to explore the turf-covered ramparts of Finavon vitrified fort. Dating from the Iron Age (1000 BC), the hilltop stronghold had walls built of stones that were fused together by tremendous heat. As you walk around the summit, keep a sharp eye out for vitrified material found in the bank.

6 From the hilltop, return to the road and turn left to retrace your steps back to the start of the walk in Aberlemno.

Aberfoyle is surrounded by the pine trees of the Queen Elizabeth Forest Park, and the visitor centre, situated a mile (1.6km) to the north has comprehensive information about the area's walking and cycling routes. The Scottish Wool Centre in Aberfoyle attracts many visitors.

6 Continue on the A821 and the A81. At the intersection with the A811, turn right to pass Drymen, and then go through Gartocharn.

Quiet little Gartocharn is best known for the wonderful view up Loch Lomond from the hill, Duncryne (462ft/141m), known fondly to locals as the 'Dumpling' behind the village.

7 Continue on the A811 through Balloch and turn right at the A82. Lying near the foot of Loch Lomond, Balloch has an ultra-modern shopping mall with fantastic views of the loch. Pass Inverbeg where you can catch a ferry across the loch to the isolated settlement of Rowardennan. Follow this main route north, and after about 9 miles (14.5km) pass the turning to the pretty village of Luss. Continue on by the west shore of the Loch as it narrows.

8 Rejoin the A82 and keep travelling up the west shore of the loch. After Ardlui, the mountains become more rugged as you continue up Glen Falloch to Crianlarich. Turn right here on to the A85. Go through Glen Dochart. Pass Loch Lubhair on the left, with Ben More (3,842ft/1,171m) on the right. Turn left at the A827 to return to Killin.

TROSSACHS TRAIL

Starting from attractive Killin village, with the Falls of Dochart on its doorstep, this drive explores the varied and magnificent scenery of Scotland's first designated national park of Loch Lomond and the Trossachs. The route takes in the Duke's Pass where there are spectacular views of the surrounding countryside.

Route Directions

1 Leave the hill-walking centre of Killin on the A827, and follow this northeast for 17 miles (27km) to Kenmore. As you pass Loch Tay on the right, the big, bare-looking mountain of Ben Lawers (3,984ft/1,214m) looms up to your left.

The area is now a National Nature Reserve and is celebrated for its variety of Arctic and alpine flora, which thrives on the lime-rich soils. Look for mountain hares on the high ground. The National Trust for Scotland has a visitor centre, signposted from the road. Kenmore supports a watersports centre and on the loch is the Scottish Crannog Centre.

2 Continue along the A827 for a further 6 miles (10km) until you get to Aberfeldy. Pass a stirring memorial of 1887 to the men of the Black Watch on the southern side of the bridge.

The Black Watch regiment was enrolled into the British Army in 1739, and took its name from the soldiers' dark tartan, which was carefully selected to differentiate them from the Guardsmen, or 'Red Soldiers'. The Black Watch served as a famous regiment from 1739 to 2006 when, due to military reorganisation, it became a battalion within the new Scottish Regiment.

3 Leave by the A826, and follow this wild road up over the high moors. Turn right at the A822, then right at the A85 and follow this into Crieff. Continue on the A85 for 19 miles (31km) through Comrie to Lochearnhead.

This small town at the tip of Lochearn grew when the railway was built through Glen Ogle, which lies to the north and links up with Killin, passing to a height of 948ft (289m). Edinample Castle, a castellated mansion of 1630, lies where the Burn of Ample runs into the loch.

4 Leave by the A84 and follow it for 14 miles (22.5km) southward to Callander, passing a turning right to Balquhidder, where outlaw Rob Roy MacGregor (1671–1734) is buried in the churchyard. After visiting Callander, return along the A84 then turn left at the A821. After passing the Trossachs Hotel, follow signs (right) to Loch Katrine. Leave your car in the parking area at the end and take a walk or bicycle ride beside this loch, 9 miles (14.5km) long, whose island-studded beauty became legendary after Sir Walter Scott's description in 'The Lady of the Lake'.

While recreation is to the fore as visitors come in droves to enjoy the scene and take a ride on the steamer, the loch also has a serious practical function, supplying central Glasgow with fresh water via an underground pipeway some 35 miles (56km) long.

5 Return to the A821 and turn right. Follow the A821 for 7 miles (11km) over the hills on the Duke's Pass, and continue through the dense Achray Forest to the little town of Aberfoyle. The Achray Forest forms a quarter of Queen Elizabeth Country Park.

106 MILES (171KM)

EAST OF INVERNESS

Legend and history come to life in this scenic Highland tour which takes you to the east of Inverness. It's a reasonably long distance to drive so you may want to stay overnight en route and take a couple of days to complete the drive. The tour starts at Culloden, a name most people will be familiar with from history lessons on the great battle here. You continue on to two castles, Cawdor and Brodie, and on to the religious community and eco-village at Findhorn. This innovative village, opened in 1985, features 55 ecologically efficient buildings and four wind turbines.

Route Directions

1 From the Culloden Battlefield & Visitor Centre head west on the B9006 to reach the A9. Join the A9 and follow it to Inverness.

Inverness, 'the Capital of the Highlands' is a working city but also a tourist hub, and, for many, the gateway to Loch Ness.

2 Drive out of Inverness on the A96, travelling through the flatlands south of the Moray Firth. Turn left onto the B9039 to reach the small fishing village of Ardersier, then take the B9006 to Fort George, a distance of 12 miles (19km).

Fort George was constructed between 1748 and 1769 on a narrow spit of land which protrudes out into the Moray Firth, facing Chanonry Point on the Black Isle. With many landward defences, the site originally covered 12 acres (29.6ha), and was designed to accommodate a garrison of over 2,000 men. The fort, named after George II, was set here to protect Inverness from seaward attack, and as part of the violent backlash to subdue the Highlands after the bloody battle of Culloden. It is unaltered, a superb example of an artillery fort.

3 Drive the 12 miles (19km) back to Ardersier, then follow the B9006 and the B9090 to Cawdor Castle.

This 14th-century castle is associated with the play *Macbeth*. Kilravock Castle (private) stands to the west, the 15th-century family seat of the Roses and in the shadow of its more famous neighbour. It can number both Bonnie Prince Charlie and his nemesis, the Duke of Cumberland, among its visitors in the hours before Culloden (1746)

4 Leave Cawdor Castle and continue on the B9090. Stay on this road and follow it until you get to Nairn.

Silent-movie star and famous comic actor Charlie Chaplin (1889–1977) liked to take his holidays at this prosperous resort town, with its fine beach, good golf course and variety of activities for all the family. Villas and hotels spread back from old Fishertown by the shore, where the former little fishermen's cottages are tightly packed together. The attractive little harbour is lovely for a stroll and dates

from 1820, and was designed by Victorian engineering legend Thomas Telford.

5 Leave by the A96, passing Auldearn, site of a major battle between Covenanters and Royalists in 1645. Drive down this road through the shady plantation of Culbin Forest. Turn left for a visit to Brodie Castle.

A Z-plan tower house dating back to 1567, Brodie Castle is set in attractive parkland that is famous for its spring show of daffodils. Remodelled into a comfortable home in the 19th century, it remained in the private hands of the Brodie family until 1980, after which it passed to the National Trust for Scotland. The family's collection of fine art, books and furniture is outstanding, and includes many works from the 17th century, from that of the Dutch masters to the Scottish Colourists.

6 Regain the A96, and stay on this road into Forres. Continue on the A96, then turn left at the B9011 and follow this road to Findhorn.

Ever vulnerable from the sea and shifting sand dunes, this is the third village on the site to be called Findhorn – the first village was buried by sand in 1694, the second washed away in 1701. Once a major port, the harbour is now given over to pleasure craft. In 1962 the Findhorn Community was founded here by Peter and Eileen Caddy and Dorothy Maclean to create a more spiritual and sustainable way of living. This thriving community now has more than 400 permanent residents, and supports an extensive holistic education programme and also boasts an eco-village.

7 Return along the B9011 and A96 to Forres. Head south on the A940 and join the A939 for Grantown-on-Spey, a total distance here of 27 miles (43km).

Grantown-on-Spey lies at the edge of the Speyside whisky country, and makes a useful touring centre. The village was planned in the late 18th century by Sir James Grant, and the arrival of the railway in 1863 heralded its popularity as a health resort. The railway was lost in the 1960s, but the town is still popular with walkers and anglers, and in winter accommodates some of the overspill of skiers from nearby Aviemore.

8 Leave on the A95 towards Aviemore, and at Dulnain Bridge turn on to the A938 to Carrbridge, noted for its picturesque old bridge of 1717, and the Landmark Forest Heritage Park. Continue on the A938 and join the A9, heading towards Inverness. Just after Daviot, turn right onto the B851. Turn left at the B9006 and follow it to the major battle site of Culloden Moor where the tour started.

Just east of Culloden, a minor road (B9091) passes Clava Cairns, three of the most important chambered cairns in the country, dating from the Bronze Age (free access). The two outer ones are passage graves, topped with a massive flat slab. The perimeters of all three cairns are marked by a ring of standing stones, often carved with 'cup' marks.

Argyll, Mull & West

CLOCKWISE FROM TOP LEFT: CHARLES RENNIE MACKINTOSH DESIGNS AT
HOUSE FOR AN ART LOVER, GLASGOW; ABBEY CLOISTERS, IONA; TEMPLE WOOD
STANDING STONES, KILMARTIN; BOATS MOORED AT CRINAN

CRINAN CANAL

ARDNAMURCHAN & MORVERN
MAP REF 408 C1

You can go no further west on mainland Britain than Ardnamurchan Point, with its spectacular views over to Mull, Coll and Tiree. The whole peninsula, with its rocky hills and desolate moorland, gale-blown trees and pretty heather-capped promontories, has an 'end-of-the-world' feeling. The main road mostly hugs the northern shore of Loch Sunart, rich in birdlife, and you can take a minor road to Ardnamurchan's north coast as the main road passes round Beinn nan Losgann, or continue to the little crofting village of Kilchoan, where a ferry goes to Tobermory on Mull. The 13th-century Mingary Castle, built on sheer rock to guard the entrance to Loch Sunart, is the place where King James IV finally accepted the submission of the Lord of the Isles in 1495; Hanoverian troops built barracks inside the castle 350 years later.

Morvern, across Loch Sunart, is a rugged land with gentler green glens. Lochaline, a popular yachting haven, is reached either by road along Glen Gleann, or by ferry from the Isle of Mull. The remains of Ardtornish Castle lie east of the village. The silica sands at Lochaline have been quarried commercially for manufacturing optical glass. Fiunary, along the Sound of Mull, was the birthplace of George Macleod, founder of the Iona Community. Caisteal nan Con is a small fortress guarding the Sound of Mull. The road ends some 4 miles (6.4km) beyond, near Drimnin, with views towards Tobermory.

ARRAN, ISLE OF MAP REF 408 D5

Generations of Clydesiders have enjoyed holidays on this attractive island, caught between the Ayrshire coast and the Kintyre Peninsula, yet it remains unspoiled. The Highland Boundary Fault runs through the island, and while the mountain of Goat Fell (874m/2,867ft) dominates the skyline to the north, the south is much more level. This reflects the geology of the country as a whole, and Arran is often tagged 'Scotland in Miniature'. Glen Rosa offers fairly easy walking, while Goat Fell and Glen Sannox are more rugged, and there are plenty of opportunities for a range of other outdoor activities, including golf and pony trekking, around the island. Brodick is the biggest town, with villages catering for visitors scattered round the 56-mile (90km) coastline.

The red sandstone Brodick Castle is the island's biggest single attraction, with its extensive collection of porcelain and silver, some 19th-century sporting pictures and trophies, and a beautiful country park of meadows and woodland. The gardens include a world-renowned collection of rhododendrons. The seat of the Dukes of Hamilton, the estate has a history that dates back 800 years.

The legacy of much earlier settlers may be seen in the chambered cairns at Clachaig, Whiting Bay and other sites, and also in the stone circles on Machrie Moor. These stones date from the Bronze Age but there is also evidence that the site was previously occupied in the Neolithic era.

In recent years the island has developed a name for its food produce, which includes cheese and smoked meats. Around the courtyard of Home Farm, just north of Brodick, you can see the cheese being made at the Island Cheese Company, and you can purchase delicately smoked fish, rich game and free-range poultry next door at Creelers Smokehouse. The fragrant soaps of Arran Aromatics share the same site. Arran Fine Foods, at Lamlash, sells a range of locally produced mustards and preserves.

Ferries sail to Arran from Ardrossan (year-round) and Claonaig, by Skipness (summer). The Ayrshire coast between here and Prestwick Airport is famous worldwide for the quality of its golf courses, centring on Troon.

CRINAN CANAL MAP REF 408 D3

In 1847 Queen Victoria and Prince Albert sailed the 9 miles (14.5km) of the Crinan Canal aboard the barge *Sunbeam* – a journey followed later in the century by MacBrayne's steamers in order to sell 'Royal Route' excursions from Glasgow to Oban. Today you are most likely to see pleasure craft negotiating the canal's 15 locks, but its original purpose was to enable merchant traffic to and from the Western Isles to avoid the hazardous voyage around the Mull of Kintyre. Two famous engineers worked on the Crinan Canal, which finally opened in 1801. John Rennie was responsible for the original engineering work, and Thomas Telford masterfully solved all of the problems with the water supply.

From the basin at Ardrishaig, where it leaves Loch Fyne, the canal hugs the wooded hillsides as it climbs up to its highest point of 64 feet (19.4m). On the hills above Cairnbaan are reservoirs that constantly replenish the water down in the canal as it descends underneath the unusual hand-wound rolling bridge at Dunardry. Beyond this the landscape then opens out into the flat marshland near to the River Add estuary. The canal ends at the picturesque haven of Crinan Harbour, with beautiful views over the Sound of Jura. Enjoy a drink and a snack at the Crinan Hotel. With some luck you may find a 'puffer' in the harbour to remind you of the canal's past glories.

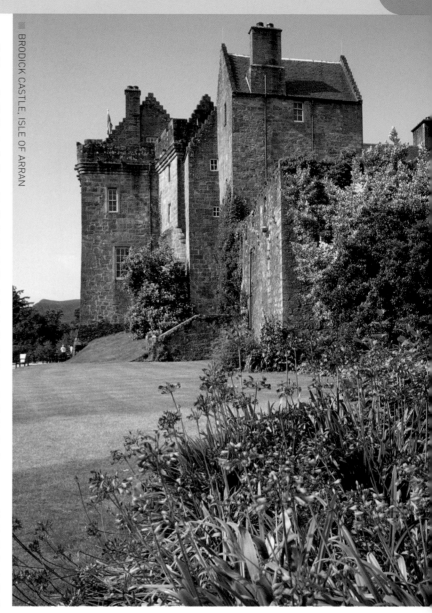
BRODICK CASTLE, ISLE OF ARRAN

DUNOON MAP REF 408 E4

Paddle steamers used to bring huge crowds from Gourock to Dunoon, and there are still regular ferry services here. On the grassy headland between the town's two bays are the remains of the 13th-century royal castle, largely destroyed in 1685. Below is the 1896 statue of Burns's love, Highland Mary, erected to mark the centenary of the poet's death. Dunoon is busiest each year during late August for the Cowal Highland Gathering, when pipe bands gather from all over the world.

Morag's Fairy Glen, off the road south from Dunoon, has shaded walks along the Berry Burn, but for more expansive views, continue onward to Toward Point lighthouse (not open) at the southern end of the A815, where you can look out across the water to Bute and down to Largs. In the grounds of the 19th-century Castle Toward stands ruins of a 15th-century tower house. This is where the Campbells of Ardkinglas besieged the Lamonts, who were Stuart loyalists. Although guaranteed safety, 36 Lamont men were taken to Dunoon and hanged.

This area is rich in ancient sites. Near Sandbank, on the shore of Holy Loch, are the huge stones forming Adam's Grave, a remaining Neolithic burial chamber, and you can take a trail from near Ardnadam Farm to see the ancient field boundaries and the site of a prehistoric enclosure.

Bute has been the holiday playground for generations of Glaswegians, most of whom arrive at Rothesay on the ferry from Wemyss Bay. Standing on the Firth of Clyde, Rothesay has a late 19th-century atmosphere created by its solid, mostly Victorian houses and decorative Winter Gardens (now housing a visitors centre), but much more ancient are the ruins of the moated and circular 13th-century Rothesay Castle.

The island largely consists of green and fertile hills, with superb views across the narrow Kyles of Bute to the mainland and to mountainous Arran. Just off the east coast road is one of Bute's hidden gems, the extraordinary Victorian Gothic Mount Stewart House, surrounded by extensive and superbly planted gardens that lead down to the shore.

GLASGOW

Insight
BRUCE & THE SPIDER

In 1307, on his way back from exile on Rathlin Island, off Northern Ireland, Robert the Bruce mustered his troops in Glen Cloy, on Arran, before heading to the Scottish mainland to try once more to oust the English and claim the throne. According to legend, he was roused from despair and inspired to fight once more – and succeed this time – by watching a spider, spinning its web and succeeding only on the seventh attempt to attach its thread. In another version of the story, he watched the spider in a cave near to Blackwaterfoot on Arran, known still as the King's Caves.

Activity
GOING DOWNHILL FAST

Glen Coe's skiing may not be as fashionable as Klosters, but it can be just as exciting. From White Corries at the top of the glen, where the fascinating Museum of Scottish Skiing and Mountaineering puts the sport into perspective, a chairlift takes skiers (and summer visitors) high into the mountains, where there are superb views to Rannoch Moor and beyond. There are 15 runs catering for all abilities, some with intriguing names – Fly Paper, for example, and Mug's Alley. Instruction is available. If hurtling downhill doesn't appeal, the Glen Coe area offers cross-country skiing, ski mountaineering, snowboarding, speed skating, and even paragliding.

Insight
SPANISH TREASURE

There is a fascinating old treasure map, now on display at Inveraray Castle, showing the location of the wreck of a Spanish galleon that sank in Tobermory Bay in 1588. After the defeat of the Armada, many Spaniards attempted to get home via the north of Scotland. The legend goes that one such vessel was given food and other supplies by the people of Mull, but the Spanish refused to pay, and even locked up Donald Maclean, who had come to collect the payment. He managed to escape, and blew up the ship, which sank in the bay. Confusion reigns as to whether the ship was a troop carrier, the *San Juan de Sicilia*, or a treasure ship, the *Florida*. Treasure hunters still dive here in search of a shower of golden ducats, yet so far only a few coins and cannon have been raised.

GLASGOW MAP REF 408 F4

Scotland's second city, Glasgow grew on the back of the tobacco trade with the New World to become one of the major industrial and engineering centres of Britain in the 19th century. In the 20th century its fortunes changed, as shipbuilding and manufacturing slumped after World War II. In recent years, however, it has reinvented itself as a vibrant and stylish place to be, making the most of its Victorian heritage of buildings, celebrating the designs of its most famous son, Charles Rennie Mackintosh (1868–1928), and investing in daring new projects that include the 'Armadillo' Scottish Exhibition and Conference Centre and the titanium-clad Science Centre. The trendy bars, cafés and restaurants spill out onto the pavements, and the city is known across the world for its classy shopping, with malls selling everything from top quality modern furniture to luxury chocolate, and bold, cutting edge designer fashion, in addition to hand-crafted jewellery.

Glasgow is full of things to do and see. Highlights include the treasures on show in the Kelvingrove Museum, which includes a Mini-Museum for under-5s and hands-on exhibits; the Science Centre, with around 500 interactive exhibits to explain everything from the structure of the Forth Bridge to the movement of an artificial limb; and the People's Palace

– the red-brick museum of local life on Glasgow Green which captures the wit, eccentricity and gritty character of the city, telling its history through familiar objects and quotes from real people. South of the city centre, in leafy Pollok Park, is Glasgow's outstanding art collection, made by shipping magnate William Burrell, and displaying a small range of exquisite pieces – from original paintings and Chinese porcelain to some medieval tapestries and stained glass – in a small, purpose-built gallery. Musts on the Mackintosh trail include Glasgow School of Art, the House for an Art Lover, the Mackintosh House at the university's Hunterian Museum, and the famous Willow Tea Rooms. The Kibble Palace, a vast Victorian glasshouse in the Botanic Gardens of the West End, is the perfect escape on a wet or chilly day.

GLEN COE & RANNOCH MOOR
MAP REF 408 E1

On 13 February 1692 the Campbell clan defied the age-old traditions of Highland hospitality and massacred 38 members of the Macdonald clan in Glen Coe. Alastair Macdonald, like many clansmen reluctant to accept William and Mary as ruling monarchs, failed to get papers attesting his loyalty to a magistrate by the deadline, the end of 1691, though they did arrive in Edinburgh in the new year. However, the papers were secretly suppressed by the

Under Secretary of State, who then told Campbell of Glenlyon that the Macdonalds 'must all be slaughtered'. Campbell and his men, pretending to be delayed on a trip, were accommodated by the Macdonalds in Glen Coe for a fortnight, then cold-bloodedly slaughtered their hosts.

The atrocity took place in the lower glen by Glencoe village, where the now heather-roofed Folk Museum offers displays of real Highland life. The most dramatic part of Glen Coe is higher up. From the roof of the National Trust for Scotland Visitor Centre there is a fine view of outstanding mountain scenery of stark peaks and glittering waterfalls. You can get details about the many exhilarating walks from the Visitor Centre; there is challenging climbing here too.

Southeast of Glen Coe, Rannoch Moor is a vast expanse of peat bog, treacherous even in the driest season. Rannoch actually means 'watery' in Gaelic. The finest view is perhaps from the railway as it crosses on its way north to Fort William, but the best approach by car is along Loch Rannoch. On its south side is the Black Wood of Rannoch, native Caledonian forest of ancient pines and groves of alder, birch and juniper. Just beyond Bridge of Gaur is a house built as barracks for Hanoverian troops after Culloden – a bleak posting. Rannoch Station is the end of the road, but you can walk on from here on old tracks.

INVERARAY MAP REF 408 D3

Inveraray, on the shores of Loch Fyne, is as fine an example of town planning as you will find, created by the 3rd Duke of Argyll in the 1740s to sit at the gates of his grand new home. It seems a great deal of trouble to go to, just to move your ancestral home by 0.5 mile (800m), but this was, after all, the extravagant 18th century. The little town that the Duke created is stylish, with a wide main street of white-painted houses running up to the classical kirk. Down at the waterfront are brilliant white arches, one of which leads up to All Saints Episcopal Church – climb the bell-tower for a wonderful view of the town, the castle, the loch and the hills.

Inveraray Castle, now home to the 13th Duke and his family, is a neo-Gothic building with pointed sash windows and battlements. Inside, its most spectacular feature is the Armoury Hall, the tallest room in Scotland, which is dramatically adorned with pikes, axes, swords and muskets.

Moored on the loch side is the three-masted vessel *Arctic Penguin*, upon which you can take a turn at steering, ring the ship's telegraph, visit the engine room and watch archive film of old sailing and steam ships. Inveraray Jail, near the kirk, is open to visitors, where you can be part of the crowd hearing a trial, and in the 19th-century cells you can try out canvas hammocks and turn the crank machine.

KILMARTIN GLEN MAP REF 408 D3

The waters of Loch Awe once flowed southwards through the glacier-formed Kilmartin Glen, depositing sediment on the valley floor. The area was occupied by farmers from early prehistoric times, and the concentration of monuments that they left behind makes this one of the richest archaeological areas in Scotland. At Achnabreck is the largest group of cup-and-ring marked rocks in Britain, but even more impressive remains are to be found further north.

The tall, flat-faced Ballymeanoch standing stones and a line of burial cairns stretch towards Kilmartin village. Ri Cruin is a crescent of boulders in a grove, and carvings of axeheads and, possibly, a boat's keel can be seen on the stones. The three Nether Largie cairns are higher – especially the most southerly, with its large chamber topped by huge stone slabs. Central to the site is Temple Wood Circle, begun around 3000 BC and modified several times up to 1200 BC. To get the most out of this fascinating area visit the superb interpretative museum in Kilmartin village. Carnasserie Castle, further up the valley, is a well-preserved fortified house from the 16th century.

KINTYRE MAP REF 408 C5

At the north end of Kintyre and 38 miles (61km) from Campbeltown, the pretty fishing port of Tarbert has rows of colour-washed houses as well as the remains of a 15th-century tower house built on the site of a former royal castle. The Campbeltown road follows the wind-swept west fringe of Kintyre, with wide views over to Jura and Islay, and then the hills give way to a gentler landscape towards the handsome harbour of Campbeltown. By the waterfront is the 15th-century Campbeltown Cross, and near by is an unexpected delight – the 1913 art deco front of the 256-seat Picture House. Davaar Island, reached on foot at low tide, shelters the harbour, and on its south side is a restored cave-painting of the crucifixion, originally created by Archibald MacKinnon in 1887.

St Columba landed near Southend at the foot of the peninsula – a ruined chapel and two footprints carved in a nearby rock mark the spot. A winding road eastwards goes to the Mull of Kintyre, with its lighthouse – a stark, windswept place, only 12 miles (19.3km) from Ireland. A single-track, hairpin road with breathtaking views over Arran follows the western coast back to Campbeltown; alternatively retrace your route up the B842, diverting west to the sands of Machrihanish, where the golf course is on the bay's edge.

To the north of Campbeltown, the east coast route is slow and winding, with tree-lined glens and fertile valleys. Up the valley from the battlemented castle at Saddell (now let by the Landmark Trust) are the remains of Saddell Abbey, with its impressive collection of carved gravestones (open access). Carradale, further up the coast, is a small rural village beside a beautiful sandy bay. You can catch the summer ferry from Claonaig to Lochranza on Arran, and at Skipness you can explore the fine castle ruins or wander around the 13th-century Kilbrannan Chapel.

LOCHGILPHEAD MAP REF 408 D3

Lochgilphead was once the centre of herring fishing on Loch Gilp, with a wooden pier stretched across the bay, but the fish mysteriously vanished before World War I. Mills and dyeworks also disappeared, and, besides tourism centred around the Crinan Canal, the main employer is now Argyll and Bute Council, which has its headquarters at Kilmory Castle.

The castle gardens, which are now open to the public, were partly laid out by Mr Joseph Hooker, first director of Kew Gardens. A little further to the north is Auchindrain township, a former crofting settlement which now gives visitors an experience of Highland life.

Glacial action reversed the waters of Loch Awe, to the north of Lochgilphead, to flow through the dramatic Pass of Brander instead of through Kilmartin Glen. The longest loch in Scotland – measuring nearly 25 miles in length – it is very narrow, and the north end is dominated by the peak of Ben Cruachan.

INVERARAY

LOCH LOMOND MAP REF 408 E3

Part of Scotland's first National Park (Loch Lomond and the Trossachs National Park was established in 2002), Loch Lomond has two very distinct characters – the narrow upper loch is hemmed in by mountains, and stretches up into the heart of the Highlands, while the broad, island-speckled southern end is bordered by fertile farmland. Here, within easy reach of Glasgow, are some of the loch's most popular attractions.

Balloch, with its modern castle, country park and opportunities for boat cruises, sits astride the only natural outlet from the loch, and is a popular centre. The Loch Lomond Shores Visitor Centre includes an information centre and shopping outlets. Along the west side, just off the well-used A82, is Luss, a smart estate village which was the setting for the television series, *Take the High Road*.

Lomond's east side is much quieter, offering walking and outdoor pursuits. From Balmaha there are some good views over several of the loch's 38 named islands – especially Inchcailloch, once the site of a nunnery, and now part of the Loch Lomond National Nature Reserve. Much of the eastern shore is within the 50,000-acre (20,000ha) Queen Elizabeth Forest Park.

The narrow road ends at Rowardennan, from where there is a stiff climb up the 3,192 feet (973m) of Ben Lomond. To visit the beautiful Inversnaid, approach from Aberfoyle or by ferry come from Inveruglas – unless you are energetic enough for the walk along the West Highland Way approach from Rowardennan.

It is on the shores of Loch Lomond that the 95-mile (153km) West Highland Way, Scotland's first long-distance footpath, makes the transition from easy lowland walking to the harder going rugged terrain of the Highlands. Starting from Milngavie (pronounced Mull-guy) on the outskirts of Glasgow, the route makes its way north to Fort William, often using ancient and historic routes. These include old drove roads that were once used by cattle dealers to get their animals to market (like the Devil's Staircase out of Glen Coe), military roads instituted by General Wade to aid in suppressing the clans, some old coaching roads and even discarded railway lines. Walk all the way if you wish – experts recommend going south to north, to build up stamina for the hills – or take a short walk along the route; there is no shortage of breathtaking sections, and you may see red deer and, just possibly, golden eagles on the way.

MULL & IONA MAP REF 408 C2 & 408 B2

Take the time to properly explore and discover Mull and you will find it full of interest and beauty. Craignure is the main arrival point, and from Old Pier Station the Mull and West Highland Narrow Gauge Railway runs the extremely scenic 1.25 miles (2km) to Torosay Castle. This line boasts a real rarity – a modern steam locomotive, built in Sheffield in 1993.

Torosay Castle is actually a Victorian mansion, set in 12 acres (5ha) of superb gardens. The house is full of character and is enthusiastically shared with all visitors by its resident owner – you are positively encouraged to sit on chairs, peer into cupboards and browse through the family scrapbooks. Nearby, on a craggy point with wonderful views along the Sound of Mull, is 13th-century Duart Castle, centre for the Clan Maclean.

Mountains give way to pretty pastoral scenery on the way to the little island's capital, Tobermory, with its houses painted in jolly colours around the bay – a familiar sight to fans of TV's *Balamory* for young children. Tobermory's tourist attractions – the Mull Museum and the distillery – are tiny. Calgary, further on, has an interesting sculpture trail and the best sandy beach on the island.

West of Ben More, Mull's highest mountain, is the Ardmeanach peninsula, the tip of which is only accessible by an arduous 5.5-mile (8.8km) path. Its main sight is MacCulloch's Tree, 50 feet (15m) high and engulfed in lava more than 50 million years ago. Boat trips round Mull sometimes give passengers a view of it. Mull's main road is mostly single track and traverses the moorland from the east coast to Loch Scridain, and on across the Ross of Mull to Fionnphort, for the Iona ferry. South of the road is fine walking country, with a coastline of basalt stacks and sea arches – wild and lonely, and full of fascinating wildlife.

Iona is a magical place. Most visitors make straight for the abbey, but you should spare time for the remains of the 13th-century priory, built for the use of Augustinian nuns. St Columba founded his monastery in AD 563 where the abbey now stands, and from it the teachings of Christianity radiated throughout Europe. The monks compiled a library of magnificently illuminated manuscripts including the *Book of Kells*, now on show in Dublin's Trinity College Library. Columba's foundation ended in AD 806 when Vikings slew 68 monks at Martyrs' Bay. Later a church and

OBAN

Insight
FERRY CONVENIENT

You can't get far in Western Scotland without needing to catch a ferry at some point, especially if you want to visit any of its 130 or so inhabited islands. Many of the shorter routes are operated by local owners and provide an excellent service, but Caledonian MacBrayne – CalMac – is undoubtedly the name you will come across most. The company was formed in 1973 when MacBraynes, operators of shipping services mostly to the Western Isles since 1851, joined forces with the Clyde-based Caledonian Steam Packet Company, founded in 1889. CalMac sails to 22 islands and operates more than 29 ferries in a huge range of sizes, from the largest vessels working the Ullapool to Stornoway route, capable of taking 690 passengers and 123 cars, to the six-car ferries that ply from Oban to Lismore and from Ballycastle in Northern Ireland to Rathlin Island.

Insight
LANGUAGE OF THE LAND

In Scotland lakes are lochs, and 'ben' means mountain. Like many Highland place names, these are Gaelic words, and the words often give an idea of the kind of place they refer to – 'kin' (Gaelic ceann), for example, means head, so Kinloch means the top of a lake, while 'inver' (inbhir) denotes an outlet – Inverness is where the River Ness meets the sea. 'Tarbert' (or 'Tarbet') means isthmus or crossing place. Other pointers include 'ard', a height, 'ban' meaning white; 'beg', confusingly meaning little, and 'more', meaning great. It all adds another dimension to the landscape.

buildings erected there by 12th-century Benedictine monks were left in ruins after the Reformation, until restoration began in 1910. Currently the home of the Iona Community, founded in 1938, the abbey welcomes pilgrims from around the world. Right beside it is the ancient burial ground of the Scottish kings, among them notably Macbeth and Duncan. The abbey does get busy with visitors at times, but although the island is small, it is possible to escape the crowds quickly and enjoy walks across the fine sands and through the rocky landscape wild wild flowers and birds in abundance, and far-reaching sea views .

Many visitors will know of Staffa because of composer Mendelssohn's 'Fingal's Cave' overture. He came to this extraordinary island in 1829, to visit the cavern on its south side. Here, the dark volcanic basalt has cooled and formed its characteristic six-sided columns, making it look like a massive cathedral organ. The enormous interior of Fingal's Cave is also like a cathedral; weather permitting, visitors can land from some of the boat trips in the area.

OBAN MAP REF 408 D2

To experience the true splendour of Oban, you should climb at dusk to MacCaig's improbable Gothic Coliseum and watch the glorious sunset over the Firth of Lorne and the mountains of Morvern and Mull.

MacCaig engaged a group of unemployed stonemasons to work on his spectacular tower from around 1897, and though it was never finished, it is Oban's most notable landmark. At the foot of the tower, the pretty bay, sheltered by the nearby island of Kerrera, is alive with pleasure craft of all types, especially in summer.

Much of the broad harbour front is dominated by a bank of hotels. Ferries bound for the Hebrides depart from Railway Quay. Oban Distillery, in the heart of the town, welcomes visitors, and near by you'll find Geoffrey (Tailor) making his famous tartan kilts.

Northwards, the soaring tower of St Columba's Cathedral dominates the bay,

and beyond it are the haunting remains of Dunollie Castle. A few miles further on, Dunstaffnage Castle, a mostly ruined stronghold with gatehouse, two round towers and 10ft (3m) thick walls, stands on a rocky outcrop, and was once the prison of Flora Macdonald.

Across the Connel Bridge in Barcaldine located among the beautiful pine clad shores of Loch Creran is the Scottish Sea Life Sanctuary, where you can see a huge variety of British marine life, including rescued and common seals, at close quarters. Drive south out of the town and you'll reach Arduaine Garden with its wonderful views to the Isle of Jura.

ALONG THE CRINAN CANAL & AROUND MÒINE MHÒR

A lengthy but easy stroll along the 19th-century Crinan Canal, the walk passes through Mòine Mhòr (managed by Scottish Natural Heritage), Scotland's last wild peat bog and a birdwatchers' paradise as the curlew returns here each spring.

DISTANCE/TIME 8.25 miles (13.3km) 5h. **MAP** OS Explorer 358 Lochgilphead & Knapdale North **START** Dunardry Forest car park; grid ref: NR 824908 **PATHS** Canal towpath, country roads and farm tracks **THE PUB** The Cairnbaan Hotel & Restaurant, Cairnbaan, by Lochgilphead. Tel: 01546 603668

1 From the car park go down some steps, cross the road and turn left. Keep going to reach a white cottage on your right. Turn right and on to a dirt track that runs behind the cottage then go through a gap between the fence and a wall. Cross the canal over Dunardry Lock and turn left on the tow path.

2 Head along the tow path as far as Bellanoch Bridge and then turn right on to the road. Cross over Islandadd Bridge and on to the B8025. This narrow, but not busy, road is long and straight and runs right through the Moine Mhor. Keep going ahead for nearly 2 miles (3.2km) then turn right on to an unclassified road signposted for Drimvore.

3 Follow this for about 1.75 miles (2.8km) as it runs through the National Nature Reserve and passes the farms of Dalvore and Drimvore. Finally reach a T-junction with the A816 and turn right. After 0.5 mile (800m) an Historic Scotland fingerpost will point you in the direction of Dunadd Fort.

4 Turn right here on to a long straight farm road and keep on it, passing the farm of Dunadd, until your reach the Historic Scotland car park. Make your way towards the hill on a well-trodden path, go past the

house on the left and through a kissing gate. Continue on the path, following the direction arrows, to emerge through a gap in some rocks within the outer ramparts.

5 Continue from here to the summit and after you have admired the views, seen the carvings and tried your own foot in the carved footprint, return by the same route to the car park. Leave it and turn right on to a farm track. Go through a gate then, almost immediately, go left through another gate and follow it as it curves left.

6 Another gate is encountered just before the road turns right and heads uphill. Continue following the road going through a gate to the steading of Dunamuck farm. Turn left through the steading, go through a gate and head downhill on a farm road, continuing along it to a T-junction with the A816.

7 Turn right on the road and follow it for about 0.5 mile (800m), then turn right on the road signposted for Cairnbaan and Crinan. After 0.25 mile (400m) turn right towards Crinan. As the road turns left across the swing bridge keep ahead and on to the canal tow path. Follow this back to Dunardry Lock and retrace your steps to the car park.

THE CARBETH HUT COMMUNITY

A short walk in the shadow of the Campsie Hills, to discover the Carbeth hut community established after World War I by the unemployed seeking an escape into the countryside. The first hut was built in 1919 and by the 1930s there were more than 30 dwellings, built from free or extremely low cost materials.

DISTANCE/TIME 3 miles (4.8km) 2h30 **MAP** OS Explorer 348 Campsie Fells **START** The Carbeth Inn (check beforehand with landlord if you wish to park here); grid ref: NX 524791 **PATHS** Roads, access tracks and footpaths, 1 stile **THE PUB** The Carbeth Inn, Blanefield. Tel: 01360 770002

1 From the car park at the Carbeth Inn turn right on to the A809. Walk for 0.25 mile (400m) and then take the first turning right on to the B821. Continue along this road for another mile (1.6km), passing a collection of huts on the left and ignoring a public footpath sign to the right.

2 Turn right at the signpost for the West Highland Way. There's also a Scottish Rights of Way Society signpost beside this pointing to the Khyber Pass Road to Mugdock Country Park. This was the favoured route of the early walkers heading out of Glasgow to the Campsie Fells and beyond.

3 Go through a gate and continue along a well-surfaced access road. Ignoring the Khyber Pass turn-off, keep right to follow the West Highland Way along the access road to more huts. After passing the first of the huts and reaching a left bend in the path, look out for a partially concealed public path signpost on the right beside a West Highland Way marker post.

4 Turn right here on to a narrow but well-surfaced footpath and continue along it, passing Carbeth Loch on the right-hand side,

to reach the junction with the drive leading to Carbeth House. This is a private house and is not open to the public. Turn left, pass a house and some huts on the right then take the next turning on the left.

5 Continue along this lane, then head uphill to reach another grouping of the Carbeth huts. Follow the main route through the huts and when it forks, keep left.

6 Keep on this road as it passes through the main part of the Carbeth huts, an extraordinary assortment of small dwellings, shanties and shacks. Ignore all of the smaller tracks branching off this road. They allow access to individual huts or other parts of the settlement.

7 Eventually reach a T-junction. Turn right and follow the lane as it winds downhill to reach the junction with the A809 beside the Carbeth Inn. Turn left and return to the car park.

INTO THE LOST VALLEY

A rugged waterfall walk into the hidden hollow where the MacDonalds hid their stolen cows for centuries until the massacre of 1692, when the rightful owners came storming in over the Moor of Rannach with torch and claymore.

1 From the uphill corner of the parking place, a faint path slants down to the old road, which is now a well-used wide path. Head up the valley for about 650yds (591m). With the old road continuing as a green track ahead, your path now bends down to the right. It has been rebuilt, with the bog problem solved by scraping down to the bedrock. The path reaches the gorge where the River Coe runs in a geological dyke. Descend here on a steep wooden step ladder, to cross a footbridge.

2 The ascent out of the gorge is on a bare rock staircase. Above, the path runs through regenerating birch wood, which can be very wet on the legs; sheep and deer have been excluded from the wood with a temporary fence. Emerge from this through a high gate. The path, rebuilt in places, runs uphill for 60yds (55m). Here it bends left; an inconspicuous alternative path continues uphill, which can be used to bypass the narrow path of the main route.

3 The main route contours into the gorge of the Allt Coire Gabhail. It is narrow with steep drops below. Where there is an alternative of rock slabs and a narrow path just below, the slabs are more secure. You will hear waterfalls, then two fine ones come into view ahead. After passing these, continue between boulders to where the main path bends left to cross the stream below a boulder the size of a small house. (A small path runs on up to right of the stream, but leads nowhere useful.) The river here is wide and fairly shallow. Five or six stepping stones usually allow dry crossing. If the water is above the stones, then it's safer to wade alongside them; if the water is more than knee-deep the crossing should not be attempted.

4 A well-built path continues uphill, now with the stream on its right. After 100yds (91m) a lump of rock blocks the way. The path follows a slanting ramp up its right-hand side. It continues uphill, still rebuilt in places, passing above the boulder pile that blocks the valley, the result of two large rockfalls from under Gearr Aonach opposite. At the top of the rockpile the path levels, giving a good view into the Lost Valley.

5 Drop gently to the valley's gravel floor. The stream vanishes into the gravel, to reappear below the boulder pile on the other side. Note where the path arrives at the gravel, as it becomes invisible at that point. Wander up the valley to where the stream vanishes, 0.25 mile (400m) ahead. Anywhere beyond this point is more serious hillwalking than you have done up to now on this walk. Return to the path and follow it back to the start.

DISTANCE/TIME 2.75 miles (4.4km) 2h15   **MAP** OS Explorer 384 Glen Coe & Glen Etive

START Lower of two roadside parking places opposite the Gearr Aonach (middle one of Three Sisters); grid ref: NN 168569   **PATHS** Rugged and stony, stream to wade through.

THE PUB The Clachaig Inn, Glencoe. Tel: 01855 811252

WALK 136

THE NEOLITHIC MONUMENTS OF KILMARTIN GLEN

A short walk back in time to the stones and monuments in the valley of the ghosts. In around 5000 BC, nomadic hunter gatherers frequented this area but left little evidence of their presence other than piles of bones and shells in caves. In the Iron Age, warring tribes ringed the glen with hill forts and it is one of these, at Dunadd, that the Scotti tribe from Ireland founded their capital in the 6th century AD. St Columba came to Kilmartin during this century and is believed to have established the first Christian church here.

1 From the car park visit Kilmartin church to see the stones and the Kilmartin Cross. Leave the church, turn left and walk along the road past Kilmartin House. Leave the village and then head downhill towards a garage on the left. Just before the garage turn left, go through a kissing gate and then head across a field to Glebe Cairn.

2 From the cairn head half right, across a field to cross over a stile. In wet weather this can be very boggy so stout footwear is advisable. Cross over the stream using the bridge. Go through a gate and turn left on to an old coach road. Follow this to the next cairn. Go left over a stile and follow the path to visit the cairn.

3 Return to the coach road and then turn left, continuing to reach the next cairn. After exploring, follow the coach road to Kilmartin school, where the route becomes a metalled road. Go through the crossroads, past Nether Largie farm and, ignoring a cairn on left, continue a short distance to Temple Wood ahead on the right.

4 Go through a gate on the right into Temple Wood, then return by the same route. Turn right on to a road and continue until you reach a T-junction. Turn left and walk along the road to a sign on the right for Ri Cruin Cairn. Cross a wall via a stile and proceed along the well-defined path to reach an ancient monument.

5 Return by the same route and turn right on to the road. Follow it to a T-junction then turn left and keep ahead to the car park at Lady Glassary Wood. Opposite this take the path to the left signposted to Temple Wood. Cross the bridge, go through a gate and head towards the standing stones.

6 Turn right and walk across a field away from stones towards a wood. Go through the gate and follow the fenced path to Nether Largie Cairn. From here continue along the fenced path, go through another gate and turn right on to a road. Continue past Nether Largie farm and Kilmartin school and retrace your steps to reach Kilmartin church and the car park.

DISTANCE/TIME 3.5 miles (5.6km) 3h   **MAP** OS Explorer 358 Lochgilphead & Knapdale North

START Car park outside Kilmartin church; grid ref: NR 835988   **PATHS** Boggy fields, old coach road and country lanes; 3 stiles   **THE PUB** Horseshoe Inn, Kilimichael Glassary, Lochgilphead. Tel: 01546 606369

THE SHORES OF LOCH KATRINE

Glasgow's water supply in the heart of the Trossachs, Loch Katrine, takes its name from the Gaelic 'cateran', a Highland robber – a fitting place then for the birthplace of Rob Roy MacGregor, the bandit, who was born at Glengyle at the western end of the loch. This is the heart of MacGregor country and one of their clan graveyards lies near the head of the loch. Rob Roy's lasting fame is due to a novel of the same name written by Sir Walter Scott and the loch, too, owed its early popularity to one of Scott's poems, *The Lady of the Lake*. First published in 1810, Scott's description of the dramatic scenery encouraged tourists to visit the Trossachs.

1 From the car park follow the road back towards the B829 and take the second turning on the left. This is an access road for Scottish Water vehicles only. Continue along the access road until you come to a cattle grid with green gate posts at a building known as Royal Cottage. Turn right just before this on to a rough gravel track that heads through some dense bracken.

2 As the path emerges on to open hillside you see the first of several ventilation shafts and beyond it, on a hill, a strange obelisk. Follow the path along this line. At the obelisk be sure to look back for a magnificent view over Loch Katrine below and across to the hills with their narrow passes. This is where Rob Roy and his men moved from Loch Katrine to Balquhidder and beyond, moving cattle or escaping from the forces of law and order. Continue following the line of ventilation shafts towards a chimney-like structure on top of the hill. Skirt this hill to the aright and then continue around its left-hand side, following a forestry track.

3 Follow this well-defined track past another ventilation shaft. Keep left at the shaft. It can be very muddy on this short stretch. Continue on the path until it intersects a forest road by a stream. Cross the road and look for a faint track continuing downhill in the same direction. In the summer, the path may be difficult to find because it's hidden by bracken. In this case follow the line of telephone poles. Eventually, after working downhill through more woodland, the track emerges on to the B829.

4 Turn right here and follow the road. It will eventually emerge from Loch Ard Forest into open countryside. Loch Arklet can be seen on the left; it is now connected to Loch Katrine by an underground pipeline. When the road reaches a T-junction with Inversnaid road, turn right. When the road forks, turn right again and return to the car park at Stronachlachar Pier.

DISTANCE/TIME 6.75 miles (10.9km) 4h30 **MAP** OS Explorer 364 Loch Lomond North and 365 The Trossachs **START** Car park at Stronachlachar Pier; grid ref: NN 404102 (on explorer 364)

PATHS Water board roads, hill tracks **THE PUB** The Forth Inn, Aberfoyle. Tel: 01877 382372

WALK 138

ARIUNDLE OAKWOODS

On the way to the lead mine and waterfalls of Strontian Glen, the walk passes through the Ariundle National Nature Reserve. In the mountains, the native wild wood of Scotland was the Scots pine. Here on the warm, damp sea coast, the wild wood is of oak. The Ariundle oakwood owes its survival to human interference. The destructive livestock and deer of Scotland's forests were kept out so that the oaks could be coppiced – harvested on a seven-year cycle.

1 From the car park, continue along the track into oakwoods. After 0.25 mile (400m), ignore a pony path on the right. In another 0.25 mile (400m) a footpath turns off right. It crosses the Strontian River and heads upstream. After a pleasant 0.75 mile (1.2km) it recrosses the river, following a duckboard section to rejoin the oakwood track.

2 Turn right, away from the car park, to a high gate in a deer fence. The track immediately forks. Take the downward branch on the right to emerge into open grazings at river level. The track passes through a high gate and ends at a gateway and stream.

3 Ford the stream on to a rough path. This crosses two more small streams, then forks (small cairn). The lower, right-hand branch continues alongside the Strontian River, but take the left-hand one, which is quite faint. It slants up to the left to a solitary holly tree. Here it turns straight uphill for 50yds (46m), then bends right to slant up as before, passing 200yds (182m) below a bare rock knoll. The remains of wooden steps are in the path and a few cairns stand beside it. It steepens slightly to pass below a small crag

with rowan, hazel and oak growing out of it. With a large stream and waterfalls ahead, the path turns uphill to the brink of the small gorge. Above the waterfalls, the slope eases. Just above, the path reaches the broken dam wall of a former reservoir.

4 A green path runs across the slope just above. You can turn right on this, heading up beside the stream for about 0.25 mile (400m). Here you will find a spoil heap; a heather bank marks the entrance to an adit – a mine tunnel running into the hill.

5 Return along the green path past Point **4**, with the remains of the Bellsgrove Lead Mines above and below. The path improves into a track, following a stream down a small and slantwise side valley. As this stream turns down to the left, the track contours forward, to cross a wooded stream valley by a high footbridge above a waterfall.

6 A wide, smooth track continues ahead through a gate. After 0.5 mile (800m) it rejoins the outward route at the edge of the nature reserve. Follow the track back to eventually reach the car park.

DISTANCE/TIME 7 miles (11.3km) 3h45 **MAP** OS Explorer 391 Ardgour & Strontian

START Nature Reserve car park at Ariundle; grid ref: NM 826633 **PATHS** Good through woodland, sketchy on open hill, no stiles **THE PUB** Ariundle Centre, Strontian. Tel: 01967 402279; www.ariundle.co.uk

Cairngorms & Central

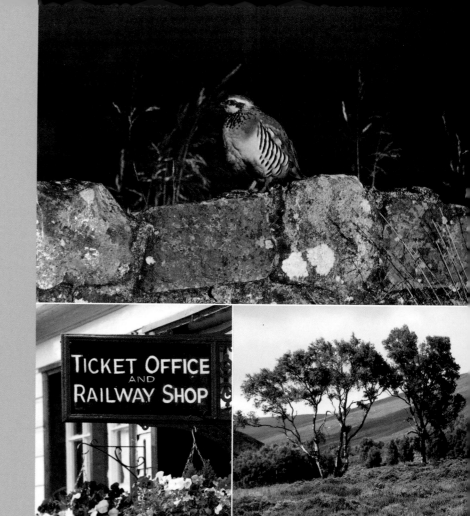

CLOCKWISE FROM TOP: PARTRIDGE IN THE CAIRNGORMS;
HEATHER, GLEN ESK; LOCH MORLICH, AVIEMORE; BOAT OF GARTEN

Visit
SANTA'S HELPERS

This area of ancient forest is associated with rare native creatures such as wildcats, red squirrels, pine martens and capercaillies. Since the 1950s, however, it has also been home to a herd of handsome, horned interlopers originating in Sweden: reindeer. Visit a herd of them at the Cairngorm Reindeer Centre in Glenmore Forest Park, where they graze on the hillside.

Insight
CLOOTIE DUMPLING

The Clootie Dumpling is a suet pudding, or dumpling, traditionally wrapped and boiled in a cloth – the word 'clout' is the broad Scots for a cloth. The puddings are usually sweetened, and contain some raisins and currants, orange peel and spices. They are particularly associated with Hogmanay, or New Year. The dumpling can be served hot after it has been boiled, or the cooled pudding can be sliced up and the wedges fried in butter.

AVIEMORE MAP REF 411 H6

The once-sleepy, remote railway station settlement of Aviemore was developed in the 1960s as a ski destination, and while it has never been able to rival the brash attractions of the Continental ski resorts, it manages to hold its own as an activities centre for the Cairngorms National Park. Its arcaded main street is a hang-over from an earlier time, but there is now a good range of outdoor shops and places to eat and relax.

The Rothiemurchus Estate, 1.5 miles (2.4km) to the south, has belonged to the Grant family since the 16th century. Elizabeth Grant's very readable account of her early life there, *Memoirs of a Highland Lady*, gives a captivating insight into the workings of the land here some 200 years ago, when timber was sawn by hand and floated down the Spey, and the idea of sustainable forestry was barely in its infancy. Today the estate offers an amazing variety of outdoor pursuits in the beautiful setting of mountains, lochs and Caledonian pine forest. This is the remains of the Old Wood of Caledon which once covered the whole country, harbouring wolves and bears, but was long since cleared for

timber, fuel and farmland. Try your hand at anything from clay pigeon shooting to off-road driving, or more peaceable activities of birdwatching, cycling, fishing and horse trekking. Don't miss the local cheeses and estate venison in the farm shop.

To the south, a good walk lasting about 1.5 hours leads around lovely Loch an Eilean, with its picturesque remains of a 15th-century castle.

Loch Morlich, 7 miles (11.3km) east of Aviemore, is perfect for water-based activities including sailing, windsurfing and canoeing. There is a very popular camping site, and Glenmore Lodge is a training centre for mountaineers.

Situated just to the north of Aviemore, at Carrbridge, the popular Landmark Forest Adventure theme park has displays on local history and wildlife as well as a treetop walk, adventure playgrounds, a maze and water slides.

Another point of interest at Carrbridge is the old Packhorse Bridge, which straddles the fast-flowing River Spey. Following serious flooding in the area in 1829, the bridge was damaged and what remains is a perfect – yet fragile – stone arch to the west of town.

BOAT OF GARTEN MAP REF 411 H6

Boat of Garten is an attractive little Victorian village on the west bank of the River Spey, between Aviemore and Grantown, and gets its name from the ferry that once operated here (replaced by a more convenient bridge in 1898). It is a key stop on the now preserved and restored Strathspey Steam Railway, and its station was once the point where Highland and Great North of Scotland rail companies swapped trains. The railway currently runs from Aviemore all the way to the little country station at Broomhill, which found unlikely fame as 'Glenbogle' station in the TV series, *Monarch of the Glen*. The town also has a challenging golf course, which has been described by some in the golf fraternity as a miniature version of Gleneagles.

Two miles (3.2km) to the east lie the still waters of Loch Garten, in the Abernethy Forest, where ospreys have nested since 1959. The RSPB has a hide there, overlooking the distant nesting site, and from where you can watch the activities of the birds in intriguing close up via a video-link. There are walking trails all through the woods around the loch.

BRAEMAR

CAIRNGORMS

Abernethy, a National Nature Reserve, is the biggest Scots pine forest remaining in Britain and home to other interesting birds such as crossbills and capercaillies.

Just to the north, the resort village of Nethy Bridge is set amid heather-clad hills and native woodland, with the ruins of 13th-century Castle Roy close by and visible from the road. The walls stand up to 25ft (7.6m) high.

Northeast of Boat of Garten, off the A95, lies the pretty little village of Dulnain Bridge. Its chief attraction is the Speyside Heather Visitor and Garden Centre at Skye of Curr, where you can purchase display heathers. There is also a garden centre, an antique shop, an art gallery, and an interesting restaurant dedicated to the Clootie Dumpling.

BRAEMAR & DEESIDE MAP REF 411 J7
When, in 1852, Queen Victoria and her consort Prince Albert picked an estate between Ballater and Braemar on which to build their holiday home, the entire Dee Valley acquired a cachet which it has never quite lost. Members of the royal family still spend their summer holidays at Balmoral Castle, enjoying country pursuits in the hills and forests. The Braemar Gathering in September is the most famous Highland games, predating Queen Victoria's arrival by some 20 years.

Braemar itself is a bustling place,

spread over the banks of the Cluny Burn. Braemar Castle lies to the east, an L-plan tower house, converted to a star-fort and barracks in the mid-18th century to guard an important military road. It has been recently reopened to visitors thanks to the local community.

To the west, a narrow road leads upstream to the Linn of Dee, where the river plunges down between polished rocks into foaming pools. This is part of the 72,598-acre (29,380ha) Mar Lodge Estate, managed by the National Trust for Scotland. There are signposted walks. The road ends near the Earl of Mar's Punchbowl, where, it is said, the Earl brewed punch in a natural bowl in the rocks before the Jacobite uprising of 1715. A long-distance walk from here heads into the Lairig Ghru pass to Speyside.

From Braemar the A93 follows the meandering of the river as it flows for 60 miles (96km) to the coast at Aberdeen. Ballater is a small granite-built spa town, once the terminus of a railway branch line. This is celebrated at the Old Royal Station, now an information centre which recalls the days when famous guests would alight here on their way to Balmoral. It also has some interesting little shops and an excellent tea room. To the east lies Glen Tanar, with birch woods at the Muir of Dinnet, and good walking over the Grampian hills to the Glens of Angus.

CAIRNGORMS NATIONAL PARK
MAP REF 411 H6
In 2003 the Cairngorms were designated Scotland's second national park, which covers a wide area of upland to the east of, and including, the Spey Valley. Over to the south the boundary continues from Dalwhinnie right across to the Glens of Angus, taking in Glen Esk before turning north to pass east of Ballater and up to Glenlivet. The centre of the national park is made up of the high granite plateaux of the Cairngorm mountains, riven by steep-sided glens and deep corries, creating a sub-Arctic environment that is unique in Britain. An estimated half the area of the national park has been cleared of trees over the centuries, and it is now open heather moorland, managed for grouse shooting. Around the margins, ancient areas of native woodland survive, the original forests have been felled and replanted for their timber many times.

The park takes in two great river valleys, the Spey and the Dee, and it is along these that most of its small population of about 14,000 live and work, their numbers swelled in summer by visitors looking for outdoor adventure, and in winter by snow-sports enthusiasts.

There's an extensive network of paths in the glens and forests around the Cairngorms, from starting points such as Nethy Bridge, Rothiemurchus, Aviemore,

Glenmore, Grantown-on Spey, Tomintoul, Ballater, Braemar and glens Tanar, Doll and Feshie. More experience is needed to tackle the heights such as Ben Macdhui (4,295ft/1,309m), Cairn Gorm (4,085ft/1,245m) and Cairn Toul (4,242ft/1,293m). There are plenty of great opportunities for cycling, fishing and golf, and watersports are focused on Loch Insh or Loch Morlich. There are ski centres at Cairngorm, the Lecht and Glenshee, and a funicular railway runs to the summit of Cairngorm for the views (for conservation reasons there is no access beyond the summit station during the summer).

Signs of the earliest settlers may be seen in the hummocks of hill forts such as Dun da lamh, near Laggan, and the mound of a crannog on Loch Kinnord. Queen Victoria was enchanted by this romantic landscape and built her holiday home, Balmoral Castle, at Braemar in 1853, popularising the region and also beginning a royal connection that still holds strong to this day. The castle sits amongst more than 50,000 acres of beautiful countryside, and was once described by Queen Victoria as a 'paradise in the Highlands'. In many of the local towns you will find royal paraphernalia, but one of the oddest memorials associated with her is the crown-shaped monument that was built over a spring in remote Glen Mark, known as the Queen's Well.

DISTANCE/TIME 14 miles (22.5km) 3h **MAP** OS Explorer 403 Cairn Gorm & Aviemore **START** Inverdruie car park; grid ref: NH 902109 **TRACKS** Decent tracks and woodland trails, some sections of road **THE PUB** The Old Bridge Inn, 23 Dalfaber Road, Aviemore. Tel: 01479 811137; www.oldbridgeinn.co.uk

DISTANCE/TIME 11 miles (17.5km) 2h **MAP** OS Explorer 365 The Trossachs **START** The Forth Inn (ask permission to park); grid ref: NN523010 **TRACKS** Road, forest tracks (good condition), some quite steep rises **THE PUB** The Forth Inn, Main Street, Aberfoyle. Tel: 01877 382372; www.forthinn.com

ROTHIEMURCHUS ESTATE

The Rothiemurchus Estate is set right on the edge of the remarkable Cairngorm Mountain massif, the vast mountain plateau that was recently designated the UK's largest national park. The estate lies just outside the resort town of Aviemore, the self-styled 'Adventure Capital of the Highlands'. Rothiemurchus is one of best places in Scotland to enjoy swathes of indigenous Caledonian woodland on a ride that steers through Scots pine, birch and juniper forest on an undulating trail that also scoops around a brace of wood-shrouded lochs. There is a real sense of being somewhere genuinely unspoilt and pristine here, with clear evidence of how the land was formed during the last Ice Age 10,000 years ago, such as rounded hillocks (known locally as 'drumlins'). Wildlife abounds on the route – look out for everything from red squirrels and crossbills, through to capercaillie and pine marten.

1 From the visitor centre car park make your way southwards on a route that quickly takes you into the lush Caledonian forests. En route to the first loch of this cycle ride you pass an old croft (small farm holding).

2 Loch an Eilein, one of Scotland's prettiest lochs, unfurls after you pass by the car park (the car route comes in further to the west). The 'Loch of the Island' is named after the small islet that nestles in the middle of the silvery blue water, which is topped off with a picturesque old abandoned castle. Cycle right around or just skirt the northern fringes if you are short on time.

3 Breaking east, the trail delves on into a thick forest that is alive with lots of little lochans. One of the most charming is Lochan Deo, which is set just south of the main forest track between the two main lochs. Hop off your bike for five minutes and take a peak at a lochan that is usually deserted.

4 The trail is now deep within the Caledonian forest. Take time to stop and listen to the singing of the birds and for rustles amongst the trees as this is deer country with myriad other wildlife also to be found in the woodland undergrowth.

5 Cross the Cairngorm Club Footbridge, the footbridge which sweeps you over Am Beanaidh. It is a pleasant spot with the water rushing below. The rocky banks make a good place to relax for a moment before pushing on to Loch Morlich.

6 Loch Morlich is a popular place for watersports and draws many waterskiing and boating enthusiasts. From here there are stunning views of the Cairngorm mountains on a clear day. There is a beach on the eastern shores of the loch by the watersports centre. From Loch Morlich turn left and the route breaks back west following the road to Inverdruie, with patches of cycling trail offering an alternative along the way.

QUEEN ELIZABETH FOREST PARK

The Loch Ard Forest in the hilly Trossachs region of Central Scotland is part of the Queen Elizabeth Forest Park. The route soon leaves the tourist-friendly village of Aberfoyle and rambles through thick forests and around the hills that pepper this area, known affectionately by many Scots as the 'foothills of the Highlands'. Look out for grazing red and roe deer, capercaillie, wood ants and stunning barn owls.

1 From The Forth Inn head towards Aberfoyle's main car park behind the inn and then turn right past the cars looking towards a small exit. Take a right turn here and head up the minor road to a junction where you make a left turn on to an even quieter road that meanders west in search of Loch Ard.

2 Before going into the hamlet of Milton leave the road to take the track to the left, which curls around towards the loch. You are now in the forest proper so take care on the looser woodland tracks as you head west, snatching tempting glimpses of the beautiful loch as you cycle along.

3 After a short section deep inside the forest, the track then drops back down to the loch at Couligarten. Keep a sharp look out for a left turn just past Couligarten – if you get all the way to the aqueduct you have gone too far.

4 The path rises up through the forest cutting and tracks between a series of low wooded hills that lie to the left of Duchray Water. You cross over the waterway at the Duchray Bridge after a zig-zag section. Continue on the trail as it starts to curve back towards Aberfoyle village.

5 After tracking a section that traverses some old mine shafts you then pick up the Bofrishlie Burn (burn is Scots for stream), which tumbles down towards Aberfoyle; avoid the smaller tracks that break off the main route as they lead deeper into the forest and you run the risk of getting lost.

6 As the route leaves the forest behind it becomes surfaced and passes to the west of Doon Hill (the 'hill of the fairies') just before The Covenanters Inn hotel comes into view on the left. The Forth Inn is only a short cycle away now across the River Forth, accessible via the right turn into the main village car park from where you set out.

SUENO'S STONE, FORRES

CULLODEN MAP REF 411 G5

The fierce Battle of Culloden finally marked the end of Stuart ambitions to reclaim the throne of Britain from the Hanoverians. On this bleak and desolate moorland east of Inverness, 5,000 Highlanders under the command of the Young Pretender – Bonnie Prince Charlie – faced 9,000 troops led by the Duke of Cumberland. It was 16th April 1746, a day of bitter cold, with snow flurries. The Highlanders, used to short skirmishes, were no match for the disciplined and well-armed soldiers, and despite courageous fighting were swiftly defeated. Cumberland ordered that no prisoners should be taken.

Although it can be very crowded in summer, Culloden remains a moving place. The 1,200 Highlanders who died were buried in clan graves, marked by small, weathered stones. The 76 English dead lie in the Field of the English. Coloured flags fly over the battlefield to mark the disposition of the armies. The focal point of the area is a 19th-century memorial cairn, built where the fighting was most ferocious. The excellent Visitor Centre has clear explanations of the battle, its causes and its aftermath.

FORRES MAP REF 411 H5

The ancient market town of Forres, lying on the River Findhorn, was once plagued by witches. William Shakespeare made full use of this in *Macbeth* (c1606), when he set scenes with the three 'weird sisters' in the area. Three more witches, burned to death, are commemorated with an iron-bound stone in the town. Sueno's Stone, on the eastern outskirts, is a Pictish cross-slab which stands 20ft (6m) tall and is believed to date from the 9th or 10th centuries. The sandstone is intricately carved in five sections with vivid scenes from an unidentified and bloody battle. Southeast of the town, Cluny Hill is the highest point, topped by an octagonal tower, raised in 1806 to commemorate Lord Nelson. It is believed to be the first such monument in Britain, and provides a magnificent viewpoint. To the south of Forres, the Dallas Dhu Historic Distillery is preserved by Historic Scotland.

Remarkably, Pluscarden Abbey is the only medieval foundation in Britain still used for its original purpose. Just east of Forres, the monastery is home to 21 Benedictine monks, and a haven of spiritual retreat for both men and women. The monastery was founded in 1230 by Alexander II, and during the Reformation in the 16th century was gradually abandoned. In 1943 restoration began and, in 1974, it was granted abbey status. Today the white-habited monks work here and care for the abbey buildings.

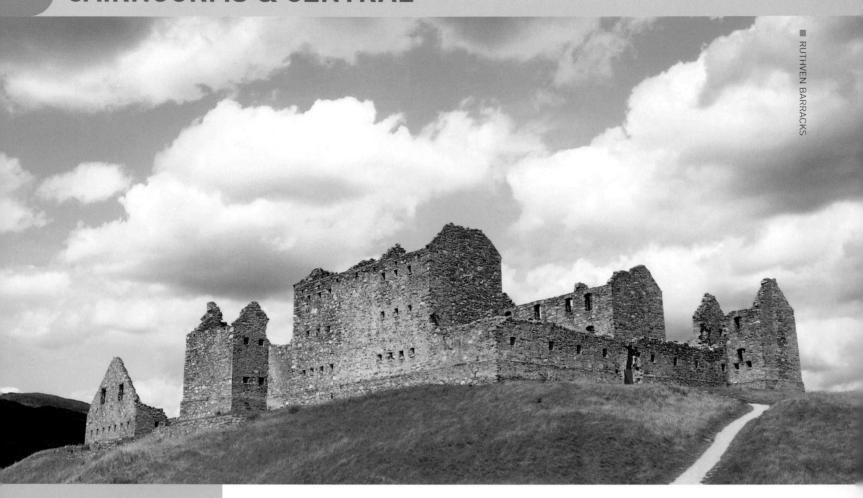

RUTHVEN BARRACKS

Insight
SHINTY
Kingussie is known as a stronghold of the Gaelic sport of shinty. It's a team game similar to hockey, and the highlight of the shinty players' year is the Camanachd Cup Final, held in mid June at different venues across the country.

Visit
THE COOPER'S CRAFT
None of the distilleries of Strathspey could thrive without the wooden barrels or casks in which the spirit is left to mature. For an insight into the cooper's skill, you can visit the family-run, fully working Speyside Cooperage just south of Craigellachie. Nowadays, oak for the barrel staves is largely imported from the US, and the cooperage produces around 100,000 casks a year for shipping worldwide – oak is preferred for its qualities of 'breathing'

Visit
EARLY CAIRNS
The fascinating Clava Cairns near Culloden open a window on our remote ancestors. They were probably built between 2000 and 1500 BC. Clava Cairns is part of a series of such historic monuments found only in the region of the Moray Firth

KINGUSSIE MAP REF 411 H6
The little town of Kingussie lies in the beautiful Spey Valley, once the capital of the ancient area of Badenoch, and with a history that dates back to pre-Pictish times. Today it is best known as home to the Highland Folk Museum, a place with fascinating indoor and outdoor exhibits. In fact, the museum occupies two sites, the other being situated at Newtonmore, to the south. The main house here contains traditional furniture and bygones, and a representation of a Highland kitchen; in the grounds you will find a reconstructed Hebridean mill and a salmon smokehouse in addition to a primitive blackhouse from Lewis. There are regular craft demonstrations during the summer.

Southeast of Kingussie are the impressive Ruthven Barracks, dramatically set on a grassy mound, formerly the site of a castle, and built in 1718 in order to subdue the Highlands, following the 1715 rebellion. Despite being set on fire by the fleeing Jacobite army in 1746, there are still considerable remains. The garrison here guarded General Wade's military road, leading from Glen Truim.

The adjacent Insh Marshes Reserve (RSPB) has hides and nature trails. There is also a guided tour. You can walk from here to beautiful Glen Tromie.

Just to the north of Kingussie, off the B9152, is the noted Highland Wildlife Park, an extensive reserve and exhibition

of themed habitats dedicated to Scottish wildlife, and part of the Royal Zoological Society of Scotland (the owners of Edinburgh Zoo). A driving tour takes in herds of red deer, as well as ancient breeds of bison and horse, before you explore the rest on foot. Look out for otters, owls, boars, Arctic foxes, wildcat and eagles. You can also take a guided tour. The centre is perhaps best known for its collection of wolves, and a raised walkway takes visitors safely into the heart of their (well-fenced) enclosure. The last wild wolf in Scotland was killed in 1743. The centre's newest arrival is a polar bear, named Mercedes, originally rescued from Churchill in Canada.

The nearby village of Kincraig is the access point for Loch Insh, popular for watersports, and its ski school has a dry ski slope (60m/200ft). A church on the loch shore reputedly stands on a site where worship has been continuous since the 6th century. Kingussie is just 12 miles (20km) from Aviemore ski resort and so is a popular stop for winter holidaymakers.

SPEYSIDE MAP REF 411 J5
The Spey is one of the foremost salmon rivers in Scotland, flowing northeast from its source on Craig a' Cleat, in the Monadhliath Mountains along a broad strath, or valley, finally reaching the sea at Spey Bay, to the west of Buckie. Although it starts in the mountainous Highlands, its

lower reaches are more characteristic of lowland scenery. Along its course, it is fed by streams from high in the Cairngorms, including the Feshie and the Nethy.

The river itself is unnavigable, but the Speyside Way long-distance footpath follows its route for 84 miles (135km) from the police station at Aviemore to the coast, passing Grantown-on-Spey, Cromdale and the Craigellachie Forest, with spur paths joining from Tomintoul and Dufftown.

The Spey Valley is equally renowned for its malt whisky – you'll not have to travel far before spotting the distinctive pointed chimney-caps of a distillery, for there are more than 30 along the river and its tributaries. Pick up the official 75-mile (120.7km) Malt Whisky Trail for a tour of some of Scotland's finest. Some distilleries that welcome visitors include Glenfiddich, founded by William Grant in 1887 at Dufftown, and the Aberlour Distillery (Walkers Shortbread is also made in Aberlour).

Grantown-on-Spey is one of the largest settlements along the riverbank. The township was planned out in 1765, and has a spacious, genteel feel. Its creator was James Grant, and the arrival of the railway here in 1863 heralded the town's popularity as a health resort. The railway folded in the 1960s, and the town is now much better known as a centre for anglers, and walkers keen to explore the Cairngorms. Its story is told in the local museum.

A WALK TO LOCHAN A' CHOIRE

A fairly challenging linear walk, which takes you sometimes over fairly rocky and rugged ground, through areas of regenerating clusters of woodlands leading to the outflow of Lochan a' Choire. From here there is a stunning view of the old crag walls of looming Coire Ardair.

DISTANCE/TIME 8 miles (12.9km) 4h15 **MAP** OS Explorer 401 Loch Laggan & Creag Meagaidh **START** Nature reserve car park at Aberarder track end beside Loch Laggan, grid ref: NN 483872 **PATHS** Very good, rough around the loch, no stiles **THE PUB** Monadhliath Hotel, Laggan. Tel: 01528 544276; www.laggan.com/Monadhliath.htm

1 From the car park, take the new path that runs alongside the grey gravel track, leading to Aberarder farm. Here there's an information area and a bench under a roof. Pass to the right of the buildings following a footprint waymarker on to a rebuilt path.

2 The well-built path rises through bracken, then crosses a boggy area. It heads up the valley of Allt Coire Ardair, keeping a little way up the right-hand side, becoming steeper as it ascends through an area of regenerating birch trees. Now the crags of Coire Ardair come into sight ahead. The path crosses many small streams – here it is still being reconstructed. It bends left, slightly downhill, to join the main river. Tiny rowan trees can be seen attempting to regenerate among the heather. Wild flowers in the boggy ground include the pink or white pyramids of the heath spotted orchid (the leaves have the spots). The path winds gently near the stream, then suddenly to the outflow of Lochan a'Choire.

3 The outflow is a fine viewpoint for the crag walls of Coire Ardair. These walls are too loose and overgrown for rock climbing, but when covered in snow and hoarfrost give excellent sport for winter mountaineers.

The circuit of the lochan is considerably more rugged than the path up the glen, and could be omitted if the outflow stream is too full, or if a picnic is preferred. Cross the outflow stream near where it emerges from the lochan and follow a trace of path round the shore to the notable clump of boulders marked by a stretcher box. (The stretcher is used for removing mountain casualties from the foot of the crags.) One of the boulders forms a small cave, with a spring running through it. A vigorous rowan tree, seeded where deer can't get at it, shows that without grazing pressure this glen would be wooded even at this altitude of 2,000ft (610m).

4 After the boulder cave you must cross rocks and scree. This short section is awkward. Once past the head of the lochan, slant up away from the shore. A path descends from high on the left, coming out of the notch called the Window. Join this and turn down to the loch's outflow (Point **3** again). Quite clearly there's no way out of this dead-end valley that doesn't involve serious mountain walking – or one of those winter climbs up the icy gullies. Return down the valley by the outward path.

LOCH AN EILEIN'S CASTLE & ORD BAN

A relatively easy walk, around Loch an Eilein and its castle, surrounded by ancient pines and with the mountains rising majestically behind. Walk quietly and you may see some of the unique birdlife that exists in the forest including the small crested tit and the stout Scottish crossbill.

DISTANCE/TIME 4.25 miles (6.8km) 1h45 **MAP** OS Explorer 403 Cairn Gorm & Aviemore **START** Estate car park near Loch an Eilein; grid ref: NH 897084 **PATHS** Wide smooth paths. Optional steep hill with high ladder stile **THE PUB** The Old Bridge Inn, Dalfaber Road, Aviemore. Tel: 01479 811137; www.oldbridgeinn.co.uk

1 From the end of the car park, a made-up path leads to the visitor centre. Turn left to cross the end of Loch an Eilein, then turn right on a sandy track. The loch shore is on the right. Small paths lead down to it if you wish to visit. Just past a red-roofed house, a deer fence runs across, with a gate.

2 The track becomes a wide, smooth path close to the loch. After a bridge, the main track forks right to pass a bench backed by a flat boulder. A smaller path on the left leads into the hills and through the pass of Lairig Ghru, eventually to Braemar. After crossing a stream at a low concrete footbridge, the path bends right for 120yds (109m) to a junction. Just beyond you'll find a footbridge with wooden handrails.

3 To shorten the walk, cross this footbridge and continue along the main track, passing Point **4** in another 170yds (155m). For the longer walk, turn left before a footbridge on to a narrower path that will pass around Loch Gamhna. This second loch soon appears on your right. Where the path forks, keep right to pass along the loch side, across its head

(rather boggy) and back along its further side, to rejoin a wider path around Loch an Eilein. Turn left here.

4 Continue around Loch an Eilein, with the water on your right, to a reedy corner of loch and a bench. About 55yds (50m) further on, the path turns sharply right, signposted 'footpath'. After a gate, turn right to the loch side and a memorial to Major General Brook Rice who drowned here while skating. Follow the shore to a point opposite to the castle, then back up to the wide track above. A deer fence on left leads back to the visitor centre.

5 From here, the stiff climb (500ft/152m) can be made on to the rocky little hill of Ord Ban. Cross a ladder stile immediately to the right of the toilet block and follow the deer fence to the right for 150yds (137m), to a point behind the car park. Just behind one of the lowest birches on slope, a small indistinct path zig-zags up a steep slope. It slants to the left to avoid crags, then crosses a small rock slab (take care if wet) and continues on to the summit. Descend by the same path.

Moray Firth Dolphins

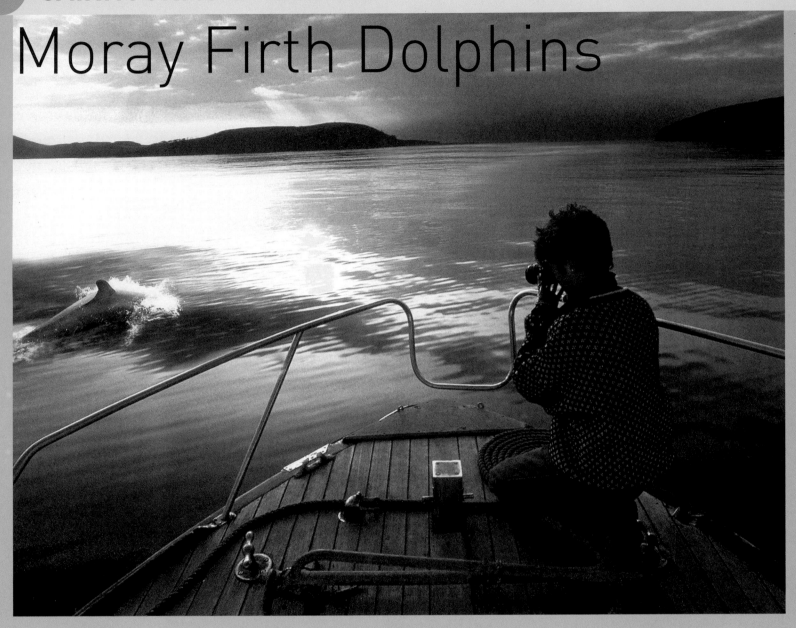

Bottlenose dolphins (*Tursiops truncates*) have been living in and around the Moray Firth in the northeast of Scotland for years, and as a result they have become a major tourist attraction. Moray Firth dolphins are larger than other populations of bottlenose dolphins, a significance that is attributed to the cold water of the Firth.

Experts from the Whale and Dolphin Conservation Society (WDCS) near Inverness, however, fear that expansion of the off-shore drilling industry beyond the Moray Firth is threatening to drive the dolphins away. With fewer than 130 remaining, data collected from the Firth predicts an annual decline of almost 6 per cent in the dolphin population; in short that means extinction in a little less than 50 years.

Also known as grey porpoise, black porpoise and cowfish, bottlenose dolphins grow to between 10 and 12 feet (3–4m) and live for up to 30 years (although some females have been known to reach the grand old age of fifty!). They are highly sociable mammals, living together in groups or 'pods' and communicating through high-pitched clicks or whistles. It has been suggested by some experts that bottlenose dolphins can stun their prey by producing very loud noises.

Bottlenose dolphins are very active and often seen bow-riding, surfing, lobtailing – slapping its fluke up and down on the surface of the water – and breaching – leaping completely out of the water, often twisting and then falling sideways back into the water. They can easily leap several yards, and are sometimes seen playing 'games' with seaweed, coral or other animals. Bottlenose dolphins sometimes bow-ride in front of large whales like the humpbacks, as they are pushed along by the pressure wave. The easiest way of recognising a bottlenose dolphin is to look out for an obvious dark and curved-back dorsal fin.

When a calf is first born, a bottlenose dolphin mum whistles repeatedly so that her calf learns her particular call and is always able to find her, even among whole gatherings of mothers and calves. A bottlenose mother's milk contains 14 per cent fat which is over four times the amount of fat in human or cow's milk.

The Moray Firth (like Cardigan Bay in Wales) is one of the key sites in Britain for whales, dolphins and porpoises (cetaceans). The species most commonly spotted from the shore are bottlenose dolphins and harbour porpoises. There are several locations around the coastline of the firth that are perfect for dolphin and porpoise-watching.

But the Moray Firth is not just about dolphins. Minke whales are often seen in the outer Firth during late summer and autumn. Whereas dolphins and porpoises have teeth to catch their prey, the minke whale has plates of baleen in its mouth – what look like long, furry combs – and takes huge mouthfuls of water, straining it out through the baleen leaving the food behind in its mouth – ingenious, and a bit messy in restaurants, but it works for the whale.

Orcas (killer whales – *Orcinus orca*) also occasionally enter the Firth, travelling in small family pods. They are actually the largest member of the dolphin family. Easy to spot with their black and white markings and the distinctively tall dorsal fin of the males. The huge dorsal fin of the bull orca can reach a height of 6 feet (1.8m, as tall as a man, and taller than many). Adults can range from 18–25 feet (5.5–10m), and weigh anything from 2.5 to 9 tonnes. Orcas have a fearsome reputation as killers, and have a diet of fish, squid, seabirds, turtles, sea lions, seals and other cetaceans. A typical orca eats about 5 per cent of its body weight a day, as much as 880lbs (400kg) of food, or the same as 40 large supermarket bags of potatoes.

Whales and dolphins do not sleep in any commonly understood sense, but simply rest on the surface of the sea, or nap briefly while swimming. Remarkably, each side of the brain takes turns to 'switch off', while the other half remains alert and keeps the animal breathing. Two kinds of seal also live in the Moray Firth: common seals and grey seals. Grey seals have long, straight 'Roman' noses, while common seals have a face rather like a dog. Over 1,500 common seals live along the Firth and can often be seen lounging on sandbanks. In fact, the Moray Firth is the only place in Europe where seals can be watched from a main road: at low-tide from the A9 Cromarty Firth bridge. As many as 500 grey seals visit during the summer months.

The protection and conservation of whales and dolphins around the British coastline is vitally important, and no more so than along the beautiful waters of the Moray Firth. Here the Whale and Dolphin Conservation Society has a Wildlife Centre, based at the mouth of the River Spey on the south side of the Moray Firth. It is about an hour's drive from Inverness. Here, the River Spey, the second longest river in Scotland, flows rapidly into the Firth after a 100-mile (161km) journey from the Monadhliath Mountains all the way to the west of Laggan.

The Moray Firth Centre was converted from a former salmon fishing station that has existed on the site since 1768, but today houses an excellent visitor exhibition and a series of education and public awareness initiatives. Now managed by the WDCS the centre exists primarily to contribute to the protection and conservation of the Moray Firth dolphins and their habitat. But as well as being famed for the dolphins, the Centre's location is also within a wonderful wildlife haven, home to other fascinating species such as ospreys, grey and harbour seals, otters, wildfowl and waders, all part of a large nature reserve that forms part of the largest vegetated shingle habitat that exists in Scotland.

That such a range of whale, dolphin and porpoise species naturally exists around the coastline of Britain is not widely known, and people need to realize that not all cetaceans are exotic species of warmer waters. And while you may want to travel to warmer countries every now and then you can't really use dolphins as an excuse: they are part of the natural heritage of Britain.

TOP Swimming in pods, dolphins can be seen leaping from the water in what appear to be spectacular performances laid-on for human entertainment, but are in fact natural behaviours for dolphins in the wild.

ABOVE Moray Firth's waters are home to many creatures including a large population of grey seals. Males can grow up to 6.5 feet (2m) long and can weigh up to 47 stone (300kg), while females develop to a maximum length of 6 feet (1.85m) and a maximum weight of 16 stone (100kg). Males are distinctly different to females and have darker coats while females have lighter coats with dark spots. Grey seal pups, of course, are easily distinguished by their white, soft downy fur that changes colour as the seal matures.

OPPOSITE Dolphin-watching boat trips are a must here on the 2000 square miles (5,120sq km) of the Moray Firth. However, not all the dolphin-watching boats sortie just for pleasure. Some of the boats, like the one operated by Aberdeen University, have been collecting data about the bottlenose dolphin population here since 1990, and many individual dolphins have been recorded.

MOORLAND ON MORRONE

The hill at the back of Braemar gives a taste of the Cairngorms. Coming down the back of Morrone Hill, descend through several different plant zones, and the home ground of two distinctive Grampian birds – the grouse and the ptarmigan. The ptarmigan turns white in the winter, but an easy way to recognize it is by where it lives – a grouse above the heather line is actually a ptarmigan.

DISTANCE/TIME 6.75 miles (10.9km) 4h15 **MAP** OS Explorer 387 Glen Shee & Braemar **START** Duck pond at top of Chapel Brae, Braemar; grid ref: NO 143911 **PATHS** Well-made but fairly steep path, track, 1 stile **THE PUB** The Fife Arms, Braemar. Tel: 01339 741644

1 Take the wide track uphill, to the right of the duck pond at the top of Chapel Brae, bearing left twice following blue waymarkers to Woodhill house. The house can be bypassed by taking a small footpath on the right which rejoins the track just above. When the track forks again, bear left to a viewpoint indicator.

2 Cross a track diagonally to a hill path marked 'Morrone'. The path has been rebuilt with rough stone steps. Higher up, it slants to the right along a line of rocky outcrops, a geological dyke of harder rock. At the top of this it turns directly uphill, passing five sprawling cairns. These are the turning point in the Morrone Hill Race that is part of the Braemar Games. The wide, stony path runs up to the radio mast and other ugly constructions on top of the summit.

3 The summit, if you turn your back on the buildings, has fine views across Deeside to the high Cairngorms. On the main tops, Ben Macdui and Beinn a'Bhuird, snow may show right through the summer. To the east you will see Loch Callater and the White Mounth plateau. A notable hump is Cac Carn Beag, one of the summits of Lochnagar. Morrone's

summit area is bare stones, but if you go past the buildings you'll find the start of a wide track. It runs down to a shallow col and climbs to the cairn on the low summit beyond. Here it bends left towards a lower col, but before reaching it, turns left again down the side of the hill. A gentle zig-zagging descent leads to the road by the Clunie Water.

4 Turn left, alongside the river, for 1.5 miles (2.4km). Ben Avon with its row of summit tors fills the skyline ahead. After a snow gate and golf clubhouse comes a road sign warning of a cattle grid (the grid itself is round the next bend). Here a track, back up to the left, has a blue-topped waymarker pole.

5 Go up between caravans to a ladder stile with a dog flap. A faint path leads up under birches, bearing right and then becoming clearer. After a gate in a fence the path becomes quite clear, leading to a Scottish Natural Heritage signboard and blue waymarker at the top of the birchwood. The path becomes a track with a fence on its right and, in 220yds (201m), reaches the viewpoint indicator, Point **2**. From here you can return to the duck pond and the start of the walk at Braemar.

CROMBIE WATER & THE WHISKY HILLS

A walk through a green valley and bare heather moor in the smugglers' country of Glenlivet. Long before the coming of licensed distilleries, whisky was part of the economy of the Highlands. After the hard work of the barley harvest came the quieter occupation of mashing and distilling. The draff (dregs) from the mash-barrel went to feed the cows, while the spirit itself warmed the crofter through the harsh storms and bitterly cold snows of winter.

DISTANCE/TIME 6.25 miles (10.1km) 3h15 **MAP** OS Explorer 420 Correen Hills & Glenlivet **START** Quarry car park, up track opposite the church at Tombae; grid ref: NJ 218257 **PATHS** Waymarked, muddy and indistinct in places; 11 stiles **THE PUB** Glen Avon Hotel, The Square, Tomintoul. Tel: 01807 580 218; www.glenavon-hotel.co.uk **NOTE** Grouse shooting in August/September – consult Glenlivet Ranger Service at Tomintoul

1 At Tombae church, turn left for 330yds (300m) to a stile on the right. The track leads down into the woods. Bear right at a waymarker and follow the main track to reach a bridge and cross River Livet. After 60yds (55m), turn right to another bridge, now over Crombie Water. Turn half left, up to a stile beside a field gate. The route follows the top of a low wooded bank above Crombie Water to a footbridge (grid ref 226245).

2 Across the footbridge, a small path runs across a meadow into a wood, slanting up to the right to reach a green track. Turn right and continue walking up through the wood, then bend left on to attractive heather moorland. Below the abrupt hill of The Bochel, the track forks. Keep ahead, with the waymarker. The way becomes a peaty path. At the top of the first rise is stile with a gate. The path, with waymarker, leads to a gateway in another fence. Don't go through, but turn right, with the fence on your left, to reach a stile with a signpost.

3 Just before a house, turn right at another signpost and follow the track towards Bochel

farm. The main route goes over The Bochel itself. Across a stile, turn uphill on sheep paths to reach the summit cairn. Turn left, to descend towards Braeval distillery below the Ladder Hills. As the slope steepens, you'll see Bochel farm below. Head down the left-hand edge of the nearer wood to join a rough track leading into a farm.

4 At once, a gate on the right leads to a faint path into a plantation. This soon becomes a green track running just above the bottom edge of the wood. It becomes more well-used and then runs out to the road.

5 Turn right, over a bridge to a waymarked gate on the right. The track rises to open fields above the river. At its highest point, a waymarker points down to the right. Go down to the fence, with the waymarked stile on your left, then through the heather with the fence on your left. Turn downhill to a stile at the bottom. Cross this and then turn left, ignoring another stile on the left, to reach a footbridge, Point **2**. Retrace the first part of walk back to Tombae.

WALK 143

THE PASS OF RYVOAN & THE THIEVES' ROAD

Following cattle thieves and drovers to the lochan used by the fairies for their laundry. The Pass of Ryvoan has all the atmosphere of a classic Cairngorm through-route. It's a scaled down version of the famous and fearsome Lairig Ghru that cuts through the Cairngorm range southwards to Aviemore. You pass from the shelter of the forest to a green lochan, trapped between two high and stony mountainsides. Once through the narrow gap, you're in different country. Here you will find wide moors and a ring of peaks around the horizon.

DISTANCE/TIME 5 miles (8km) 2h15 **MAP** OS Explorer 403 Cairn Gorm & Aviemore **START** Bridge just south of Glenmore village; grid ref: NH 980095 **PATHS** Smooth tracks. One steep ascent, no stiles **THE PUB** The Winking Owl, Grampian Road, Aviemore. Tel: 01479 810646

1 Head upstream on a sandy track to the left of the river. Interpretation signs explain the flowers of the forest you may come across, many are ferns and mosses. After 550yds (500m), turn left on a wide smooth path with blue/yellow waymarkers. Ahead is a gate into Glenmore Lodge rifle range; here the path bends right, to a wide gravel track.

2 Turn right, away from Glenmore Lodge, to cross a bridge into the Caledonian Reserve. Immediately keep ahead on a smaller track (blue waymarker) as the main one bends right. The track narrows as it heads into the Pass of Ryvoan between steep wooded slopes of pine, birch and scree. Here, the path turns left, with a blue waymarker, which you take in a moment. Just beyond, steps on the right lead down to Lochan Uaine. Walk round to the left of the water on a beach. At the head of a loch, a small path leads back up to a track. Turn sharp left, back to the junction already visited; now turn off to the right on to a narrower path with a blue waymarker.

3 This small path crosses a duckboard and heads back down the valley. Very soon it starts to climb steeply to the right, up rough stone steps. When it levels, the going is easier, although it's still narrow with tree roots. The path reaches a forest road at a bench and waymarker.

4 Continue to the left along the track. After a clear-felled area with views, the track re-enters trees and slopes downhill into Glenmore village. Just above the main road turn right, through a green barrier, to reach Glenmore Visitor Centre. Pass through its car park to the main road.

5 Cross to Glenmore shop. Behind the post-box, steps lead down to a campsite. Pass along its right-hand edge to a path into the woods. Head left across a footbridge to the shore of Loch Morlich and follow the beaches until another river blocks the way. Turn left along the river bank. Ignore a footbridge, but continue on a wide path with the river on the right. Where the path divides, a smaller branch continues beside the river through bushes to the car park.

WALK 144

SIR JAMES GRANT'S TOWN

In about 1750, young Mr James Grant decided that Speyside could do with some grand architecture as he'd seen in Edinburgh and persuaded his father, Sir Ludovic to help. The town was to be supported by a linen factory. Sadly, the linen factory floundered and it wasn't until Queen Victoria visited the town in 1860 that it was really admired, but the handsome town has been attracting tourists ever since.

DISTANCE/TIME 7 miles (11.3km) 3h **MAP** OS Explorer 419 Grantown-on-Spey **START** Grantown-on-Spey museum; grid ref: NJ 035280 **PATHS** Tracks and smooth paths; 1 stile **THE PUB** Grant Arms Hotel, The Square, Grantown on Spey. Tel: 01479 872526

1 Go down past the museum. Turn left into South Street, then right into Golf Course Road. A tarred path crosses the golf course to a small gate into Anagach Wood.

2 The wide path ahead has a blue/red waymarker. At a junction, the blue trail departs to the right; turn left, following a Spey Way marker and red-top poles. Keep following the red markers, turning left at the first junction and bearing left at the next. When the track joins a new fence and a bend in a stream is on the left, keep ahead, following a Spey Way marker.

3 The track emerges into fields. After crossing a small bridge, turn to the right through a new hunting gate. A path on its left leads to a track near the River Spey.

4 Turn sharp right on this track, alongside the river. At a fishers' hut it re-enters forest. About 0.75 mile (1.2km) later it diminishes to a green path and slants up past the cottage of Craigroy to join its entrance track.

5 At Easter Anagach, a grass track on the right has red waymarkers and runs into a birch wood. With a barrier ahead, follow marker poles to the left, on to a broad path beside a falling fence. At the next junction, turn right, following red poles, over a slight rise. Descending, turn left just before a blue-top post, on to a smaller path with blue and red posts. This runs along the top of a ridge, to a bench above a lane. To the left down the lane is the stone bridge built by Major Caulfield as part of the military road system.

6 The path bends right, alongside the road, to meet a wide track which is the former military road. Turn right, to a path on the right with green-top posts. At a small pool, the main path bends left for 150yds (137m), with blue and green posts; take the path ahead, with green posts. A very old tree in the middle of the path was once used for public hangings. Once at a five-way junction bear left to find the next green post. At the edge of the golf course turn left to a small car park and information board.

7 Follow the tarred street uphill, past the end of the golf course, to Grantown's High Street. Turn right to The Square. Just past the Grant Arms Hotel, a sign points right, to the museum.

Skye & North

CLOCKWISE FROM TOP LEFT: CAVELL GARDENS, INVERNESS; ULLAPOOL; CUILLIN HILLS, ISLE OF SKYE

APPLECROSS MAP REF 410 D5

Looking north from the picture-postcard village of Plockton, the rugged hills of Applecross fill both the view and the imagination. Until the last century this peninsula was almost as isolated as Knoydart. Rough tracks linked the old settlements along the coast down to Toscaig, and access up from the south was via the breathtakingly spectacular Bealach-na-Ba pass, which rises to some 2,050ft (624.8m). In 1965 a road was started around the northern margin from Shieldaig, making it a pleasant circular driving route around this remote and beautiful place.

An Irish saint established a religious community here in the 7th century, but it was destroyed in a Viking raid. Today it is hard to believe that 3,000 people once thrived with their cattle in the green, fertile valley around the quiet village of Applecross itself – cleared from the land when the Mackenzies sold it off for a sporting estate; only the outlines of their deserted cottages remain.

Applecross Bay is a welcoming curve of pinkish sand, with an excellent little inn noted for its fresh seafood.

BLACK ISLE MAP REF 411 G4

The Black Isle is the fertile spit of land between the Cromarty and Moray Firths. The central forested ridge carries the peninsula's older name of Ardmeanach,

and was part of lands gifted by Mary, Queen of Scots to her husband (and cousin), Lord Darnley.

Cromarty, set on the northeastern tip of the peninsula, is a delightfully built 18th-century town, an important centre of fishing and commerce until the 19th century, when it was bypassed by the railways. The white-washed Courthouse Museum tells the town's story, with the aid of computer-controlled, animated figures. Hugh Miller, a 19th-century geologist, social commentator and also writer, lived in the little thatched cottage next door. The cottage is now in the care of the National Trust for Scotland. The fossil beach where he worked is 2 miles (3.2 km) away at Eathie.

The Moray Firth is also the best place to go to spot dolphins. Bottlenose dolphins found around the Scottish mainland are some of the largest in the world, and in the Moray Firth area there is currently one of only two resident populations in Britain, with at least 88 individuals identified. Cromarty has become the best place in Britain to see bottlenose dolphins in the wild – boat trips run by Dolphin – Ecosse are available throughout the year. There are also whale-watching trips in August and September.

Fortrose looks out across the Moray Firth. The cathedral was completed in the 15th century, but in the 16th was then unroofed, before Cromwell plundered its

sandstone blocks to build the fortifications in Inverness. On the other side of the spit (once a popular spot for witch-burning but now dedicated to golf) lies Rosemarkie, notable for the magnificent remains displayed at the Groam House Museum and carvings.

The mudflats of the Beauly Firth attract a large number of birds – over-wintering greylag and pink-footed geese graze the fields around, and a variety of sea ducks, including goldeneye and scoter, may be spotted near the Kessock Bridge.

In the graveyard of the parish church of Avoch, near Rosemarkie, lie the remains of the great Scottish explorer Sir Alexander Mackenzie (1755–1820). Mackenzie travelled to Canada in 1779 and was soon trading furs for the North West Company. Based at Fort Chipewyan on Lake Athabasca, he set out with a team of native Canadian Indians in 1789 to discover a route across the continent, but found instead a long river, which would be named after him, leading up to the Arctic Ocean. In 1793 he became the first caucasian man to cross the Rockies and finally reach the Pacific.

CANNICH MAP REF 410 F5

The broad Strath Glass from the north leads to the modern village of Cannich where four valleys meet. Eastwards, down Glen Urquhart, is the prehistoric Corrimony Cairn, still with its stone roof

and eleven standing stones. Dramatic Glen Cannich is entered by a winding road between bare mountain tops, with groves of birch and alder. It widens towards Loch Mullardoch and its dam, 9 miles (14.5km) west of Cannich, at 2,385ft (729.7m), is the longest in Scotland.

The approach to Glen Affric, perhaps the most beautiful of Scottish valleys, passes the popular Dog Falls. Along this 6-mile (9.7km) stretch of Loch Beinn a'Mheadhoin are parking spots, many with fine walks starting from them. On the opposite side is one of the largest remnants of the ancient Caledonian Pine Forest, fenced to keep out deer and allow regeneration. Beyond the loch the road ends, but you can walk on to Loch Affric – a magical scene of clustered hills, birch and pine forest; during the autumn there is dazzling colour and a hint of snow on the peaks. You can also follow the old track up through the mountains to Sheil Bridge in Kintail.

Today, local employment in the town is provided by the many hydroelectricity plants in the area and the forestry industry, as well as conservation and tourism.

FORT WILLIAM MAP REF 410 F7

Fort William's greatest asset is its close proximity to Ben Nevis, Britain's highest mountain, which stands sentinel over the Nevis range about 7 miles (11.3km) to the north. The town, the biggest in the

Western Highlands, is also at the southern entrance to the Great Glen and at the head of Loch Linnhe, with routes to Badenoch and Skye. But this is not just a place to venture from – it has its own delights too. The idiosyncratic West Highland Museum, famous for the Jacobite collections held there, lives up to its description as 'an old-fashioned museum – it is full of information and surprises' with an eclectic range of displays, including natural history, Highland clothing and crofting. Housed since 1926 in what was once the British Linen Bank, the museum is thought by many to be the best museum dedicated to the Highlands in the whole of Scotland. Treasures of the Earth, at Corpach to the west of town, is a fascinating and huge collection of rare gemstones, crystals and fossils, including Europe's largest uncut emerald – a thing of great beauty. Visitors can also discover how amethyst crystals take a quarter of a million years to grow just 1 inch (3cm).

Until recently the tops of Scotland's mountain ranges were the exclusive preserve of the athletic, but now everyone can experience breathtaking views without so much as getting out of breath. Panoramic vistas to the upper slopes of Aonach Mor (4,000ft/1,219.2m) open up from enclosed gondola cable cars which cover about 1.5 miles (2.4km) in their climb to an altitude of 2,150ft (655.3m). The ascent takes about 15 minutes and at the top, in addition to the views across Loch Lochy, the Great Glen, Loch Eil and the Inner Hebrides, you will find a restaurant, a sports shop, telescopes, interpretative plaques and slide presentations. There are a number of walks but do keep to the paths, both for your own safety and for conservation. Two recommended walks are to Sgurr Finnisg-aig (taking about 20 minutes each way) and to Meal Beag (taking about 30 minutes in each direction).

Until well into the 19th century everyone thought that soaring Ben Macdhui in the Cairngorms and, in fact, not Ben Nevis, was Britain's highest mountain. It was the peak everyone climbed, including Gladstone and even Queen Victoria. The then Queen wrote in her journal, 'Nothing could be grander or wilder; the rocks are so grand and precipitous, and the snow on Ben Macdhui has such fine effect.' Like Everest, only recognized as the world's highest mountain in the 19th century, Ben Nevis remained unrecognized until accurate measurement was finally made by the Ordnance Survey in 1846 and the issue was resolved – Ben Nevis is the highest at 4,406ft (1,343m), and Ben Macdhui is a close runner-up at a height of 4,296ft (1,309m).

THE GATE OF FORT WILLIAM

Visit
THE PARALLEL ROADS

In a quiet valley 18 miles (29km) to the northeast of Fort William is a geological phenomenon that is unique in Britain. Glen Roy and its side valleys are marked by three strange parallel lines known as the 'Parallel Roads', not roads at all, but the shorelines of an ancient glacial loch. Towards the end of the last Ice Age, some 10,000 years ago, the valley was dammed with ice that melted in three stages, leaving these strange horizontal ridges along the valley slopes. Scottish Natural Heritage explains it all on an interpretative board above the car park. To get to Glen Roy from Fort William, go north on the A82, turn right on to the A86 at Spean Bridge, then left on an unclassified road at Roy Bridge.

Visit
EILEAN DONAN CASTLE

One of the most photographed and romantic castles in Scotland, Eilean Donan is perched on a rock just offshore in Loch Duich, linked to the mainland and a modern visitor centre by a stone bridge. There has been a fortification here since the 13th century and its 14-foot (4.26m) thick walls have withstood the onslaught of both men and the elements; in 1719 the castle came under fire from Government warships and was subsequently abandoned as a wreck after the attack. The castle owes its appearance today to restoration between 1912 and 1932, by Lt Col John MacRae-Gilstrap, who had a vision of how it should look.

Visit
CONCRETE BOB'S VIADUCT

The West Highland Railway gives wonderful views down Loch Shiel from the Glenfinnan Viaduct, and the viaduct itself is impressive. It was built when the line from Glasgow, which had struggled across Rannoch Moor to Fort William by 1894, was extended to Mallaig in 1902. Curving over 1,000 feet (305m) over the River Finnan, its 21 concrete arches are up to 100 feet (30.5m) high. The viaduct was designed for Robert MacAlpine (later Sir Robert, founder of the civil engineering firm) whose nickname was Concrete Bob. Legend has it that buried within the Glenfinnan Viaduct are a horse and cart that fell headlong into the concrete before it was set.

GAIRLOCH MAP REF 410 E4

This popular holiday village with its excellent Heritage Museum is spread around a sunny, sandy bay, with the heights of the delightfully named Flowerdale looming behind. There are superb views out to the islands, and Gairloch lies at the heart of a fine scenic area which takes in the incomparable Loch Maree. West from the village, the road winds around the bay and eventually turns into a track, leading to the former lighthouse at Rubha Reidh. Beyond sheltered Badachro the road passes sandy bays to end at Redpoint, but energetic walkers can take the long path to Diabaig on Loch Torridon.

Behind Gairloch the A832 leads to Loch Maree, famous for its fishing. It is surrounded by high mountains and scattered with islands. The highest peak on the northern shore is Slioch (3,219ft/981m), while to the south Beinn Eighe, with its cap of white quartzite, lies at the heart of Britain's first National Nature Reserve. Find out about nature trails and picnic spots at the visitor centre at Aultroy, towards the eastern end of the loch.

Isle Maree, by Letterewe, was the site of a 7th-century hermitage, and may even have had much older, druidical connections. Queen Victoria fell in love with the whole area when she visited in 1877, giving her name to the waterfall that plunges down near Talladale.

GLENELG MAP REF 410 E6

The old military road that leads up to Glenelg rockets off the main Kyle of Lochalsh road, climbing rapidly up the Mam Ratagain pass to a fine viewpoint offering stunning views of the lovely Five Sisters of Kintail above Loch Duich. There follows a gentler descent into Glen More, where a side road goes to the six-car turntable ferry that is a romantic summer alternative to the modern bridge to Skye. The Glenelg road passes the gaunt remains of Bernera Barracks, built in 1722 for Hanoverian troops (ruins fenced off for safety reasons). Continue for 2.5 miles (4km) into Glen Beag for Glenelg's most famous sight – its two brochs. Close by at Sandaig, was the home of *Ring of Bright Water* author Gavin Maxwell.

GLENFINNAN MAP REF 410 E7

Glenfinnan will always have a special place in Scottish history, for it was here that the event which Winston Churchill called 'one of the most audacious and irresponsible enterprises in British history' began – the 1745 Jacobite Rising. The monument tower of 1815, with its 1834 figure of a Highlander, may not be on the exact spot where Bonnie Prince Charlie unfurled his father's white and red silk banner, yet it is most romantically set at the head of Loch Shiel, overlooking the wooded Eilean Glean Fhianin and the mountains of Sunart and Moidart. Climb the tower for the best views of the loch.

The clan chiefs were dismayed that the Prince had brought only seven followers, not the French troops they had expected. They were persuaded to join him only by the example of Cameron of Lochiel, who brought 700 men to Glenfinnan for the Prince. So on 19 August 1745 the banner was set flying, the Old Pretender was proclaimed King James III & VIII, with the Prince as his Regent, and the army – still only 1,200 strong – began its campaign. Capturing Edinburgh easily and defeating General Cope in the 15-minute battle at Prestonpans on 21 September, the determined men set out for London. But with little English support and no hope of French help, they turned back at Derby that December and met their doom at Culloden in April 1746.

GLENFINNAN VIADUCT

GAIRLOCH

The story is vividly told in the Visitor Centre near by, which also traces the Prince's journeys through the Western Highlands and Islands after Culloden.

INVEREWE MAP REF 410 E4

Surrounded by barren peat bogs, rocks and water lies Inverewe, one of Britain's most remarkable gardens, and a must-see for plant-lovers from all over the world. Lying on the same line of latitude as Moscow and Hudson's Bay, the site must have seemed a daunting challenge when Osgood MacKenzie inherited the Inverewe Estate in 1862 from his step-father. Osgood possessed every skill and quality necessary in order to create this wonderful oasis – imagination, vision, perseverance and patience.

First he planted a shelter belt of pines and firs, carted out the rocks and replaced them with hundreds of tonnes of garden soil. Once protected against strong winds, Inverewe could benefit from the warming effects of the North Atlantic Drift. Rhododendrons were planted in profusion, and still provide one of the most spectacular attractions in the early summer. Paths meander between the blooms and beneath the pines, and pass an almost bewildering array of rare and exotic plants, collected from all over the world. Rock gardens are bright with

alpines, including many species from New Zealand, and the area named 'Japan' is planted with a rich and unusual variety of tree ferns and palms.

There are wonderful views along the loch from the tip of the garden at Cuddy Rock, and also from the front of the house, built in 1937 after fire destroyed Osgood's original building. Mackenzie died in 1922, and his daughter Mairi, who had maintained and developed his vision, presented the garden to the National Trust for Scotland in 1952.

INVERNESS MAP REF 411 G5

Inverness is known as the 'Capital of the Highlands', Scotland's newest city (designated in 2000) and a popular holiday centre, set on the banks of the River Ness at the eastern extremity of the Great Glen. Commanding the east–west facing corridor to Moray and Aberdeen as well as the main north–south route through Scotland, its location has given the town a strategic importance that has resulted in a much-chequered history. Inverness was probably well established by the time of St Columba's visit in AD 565. Certainly King Duncan (c1010–1040), notably of Shakespeare's *Macbeth*, had his castle in the town, and various clan chiefs and disaffected Jacobites have stormed through the town over the centuries.

Today Inverness is a busy administrative centre for the Highlands and Islands and presents a mostly 19th-century face. Even the dominating red sandstone walls of Inverness Castle were rebuilt during Victoria's reign as a Sheriff Court and jail, with a monument to Flora Macdonald on the castle esplanade. On the opposite side of the river loom the two massive towers that top St Andrew's Episcopal Cathedral, which contains an interesting collection of Russian icons. The recently refurbished Inverness Museum and Art Gallery, has fine examples of Highland artefacts and displays on the archaeology, social as well as the natural history of the Highlands. The museum hosts various exhibitions, performances and talks.

From the museum you can see Craig Phadrig, a vitrified Iron Age fort on a wooded hill west of the River Ness, reached by a steep forest trail from Leachkin Brae. In Huntly Street next to the river you can visit the largest kilt-making workshop in Scotland – Highland's House of Fraser's Scottish Kiltmaker.

INVERPOLLY MAP REF 410 F3

North of Ullapool the habitation is sparse and the landscape becomes altogether bigger and wilder, with giant, bare mountains looming out of bleak, bitter moorland. The Inverpolly National Nature

Reserve, managed by Scottish Natural Heritage, offers access to this fine, dramatic countryside in all its glory, and the visitor centre at Knockan is a good place to start. The diversity of habitats in the region is revealed, including bogs, lochs and patches of ancient woodland, with a corresponding diversity of flora. A geology trail here illuminates the formation of the Assynt area, and part of the 'Moine Thrust' can be seen in the rocks of Knockan Cliff. There are excellent views from the top of the mountains of Coigach. Of these, Stac Pollaidh (2,008ft/612m) is the most popular, and a relatively easy walk leads up from the minor road by Loch Lurgainn. Look out for deer and birds of prey, and you may even see signs of wildcats in the area. To the north on a clear day you can see the familiar form of Suilven (2,402ft/732m), but this peak is strictly for experienced mountaineers.

There is a further extensive nature reserve at Inchnadamph. From this point the road leads round the shores of Loch Assynt, past the rocky ruins of Ardvreck Castle. Beyond this place is the popular harbour of Lochinver (this links up with a narrow and very scenic road from Loch Lurgainn). Up the coast, just north of the hamlet of Clachtoll, the circular remains of a broch from the first century AD can be seen on the shoreline.

LOCH NESS MAP REF 411 G6

It would be difficult for anyone but the most hardened sceptic to gaze out over the waters of Loch Ness without just the small hope of seeing something which might be interpreted as a 'sighting'. Mentioned in writing as long ago as the 7th century, when St Adamnan's *Life of St Columba* tells of the saint calming the creature down after an apparent attack on a monk, the Loch Ness Monster – or, familiarly, Nessie – has become the focus of the tourist industry here. Drumnadrochit is the main centre for this, offering the Original Loch Ness Visitor Centre with a large-screen cinema, exhibition and sonar scanning cruises, and the Official Loch Ness Monster Exhibition with audio-visuals and a 'life-size' model of Nessie.

Monster or no, Loch Ness is beautiful and it contains more water than all the lakes and reservoirs in England and in Wales put together. The loch is 24 miles (38.6km) long, 1 mile (1.6km) wide and 750 feet (228.6m) deep, making it one of the largest bodies of fresh water in Europe. The loch forms a major part of the Caledonian Canal, which links the west coast with the Moray Firth, and follows the line of the dramatic Great Glen, cutting Scotland in two halves. This spectacular geological fault has provided a way through the mountains for centuries of travellers and is tracked today by the A82 between Fort William and Inverness.

MALLAIG MAP REF 410 D6

This small, busy fishing harbour, facing the Isle of Skye across the Sound of Sleat, stands at the end of the A830 from Fort William, more romantically known as the 'Road to the Isles'. The term comes from the cattle-droving days, before the railway arrived in 1901, but it holds the evocative promise of a special destination for today's travellers. It is also the last stop on the famous West Highland Line, and ferries from Mallaig can take you on to Skye, Rum, Eigg, Muck and Canna. The town has a heritage centre with displays anout the fishing industry of the town. The old steam train *Jacobite* runs from picturesque Fort William to Mallaig, passing Morar on the way.

A couple of miles outside Mallaig, at Morar, the waters of Scotland's deepest freshwater loch tumble and cascade down a spectacular waterfall and into a beautiful sandy bay. One of the long, white-sand beaches along here provided the setting for the film *Local Hero*. A leisurely drive southwards is enchanting, passing through mixed woodland, with fine views to the islands. Allow yourself plenty of time – it's a slow, winding road and mainly single track until you reach the little church above Lochailort.

SHIELDAIG & TORRIDON
MAP REF 410 E5

The villages around Loch Torridon are picturesque, but cannot compete with the grandeur of some of the finest mountain scenery in Scotland. The road east from Shieldaig, a whitewashed, 18th-century planned village overlooking the pine-clad Shieldaig Island, gives views over Upper Loch Torridon to the huge mountain mass dominated by Ben Liathach.

Of red Torridonian sandstone, 750 million years old and 3,359ft (1,024m) high, Liathach has a row of seven peaks topped with shining white quartzite from 150 million years later. It forms part of the National Trust for Scotland's 16, 100-acre (6,520ha) Torridon Estate. The Trust's Countryside Centre in Torridon village shows the best routes in the mountains, but guided walks are recommended for the 5-mile (8km) ridge between Liathach's peaks. The Deer Museum has a herd of wild deer, and information about their life on the hills.

Further on, Beinn Eighe presents a forbidding face to the traveller, but like the other mountains has impressive corries to the north. Britain's first National Nature Reserve was founded here in 1951 to protect the native Caledonian pine forest on its slopes.

The road north of Loch Torridon, with wonderful views over to the Applecross peninsula, passes through Fasag, built to house families displaced in the clearances, and through several crofting settlements to end at Lower Diabaig, from where you can walk to Redpoint, far out on the coast of Wester Ross

SKYE, ISLE OF MAP REF 410 C5

Skye is the largest and most famous of the Inner Hebrides, dominated from every view by the high peaks of the Cuillins. The jagged gabbro (igneous rock, like basalt) of the Black Cuillins and the mystical-looking pink, scree-covered granite of the Red Cuillins have proved an irresistible challenge for mountaineers – the most inaccessible peaks were only conquered at the end of the 19th century. Located to the north, on the Trotternish peninsula, is an extraordinary broken ridge, jutting out from which are jagged peaks and pillars that loom eerily on misty days.

Road signs written in Gaelic as well as English quickly tell you that you're in a different culture, and Skye retains a strong Gaelic identity, encouraged at the college, Sabhal Mòr Ostaig, in Sleat. At the Aros Centre, just south of Portree, a forest walk illustrates the letters of the Gaelic alphabet. There are crofting museums at Colbost and Kilmuir, with several reconstructed homesteads.

Portree is the island's capital. This little town was named after a royal visit in 1540 by James V – *port righ* means king's harbour – and its formal square is a miniature delight. The town is the gateway to the Trotternish peninsula. Taking the road up the eastern side, look out for the column of the Old Man of Storr and other strange rock formations up on your left, and for the columnar formations and dramatic waterfall at the Kilt Rock on the coast to your right, just before Staffin. There are marvellous views from here across to the blue hills of the mainland.

Heading west from Portree brings you to the wilder side of the island, with the Waternish and Duinish peninsulas like two long fingers reaching out towards the Outer Hebrides. At Carbost, the Talisker Distillery produces a distinctive peaty, smoky malt whisky. Dunvegan is the family seat of another powerful Skye clan, the MacLeods, and claims to be Scotland's oldest inhabited castle, being occupied since the 13th century.

Broadford is the main centre for exploring the south of the island, and if the weather is clear, drive over to Elgol to experience some of Britain's most magnificent scenery. The road winds below the mighty Red Cuillins and beside Loch Slapin before descending an alarmingly steep road into Elgol (not suitable for caravans). You can see across to the island of Soay, with Canna, Rum and Eigg to the south.

After the barrenness of the mountains, Sleat seems a veritable Garden of Eden. Lovely Armadale Castle Gardens and the Museum of the Isles are well worth a visit. There are excellent exhibitions about Clan Donald, genealogical research facilities, guided walks, a restaurant and more.

Skye is an unlikely crossroads among the islands. You can reach it by ferry from Mallaig (about 40 minutes), or across the strong currents by Glenelg (summer only), or across the new bridge at Kyle of Lochalsh. The bridge provoked controversy when it was built, but is low enough to be unobtrusive. Ferries to the outer islands leave from the harbour at Uig, on the Trotternish peninsula, and sail over to Raasay from Sconser.

STRATHPEFFER MAP REF 411 G5
Once hailed as 'the Harrogate of the North', Strathpeffer is a curious phenomenon to find above the Highland line – a genteel, attractive little spa town, complete with Victorian architectural twirls such as verandahs and ornamental barge-boards.

Locals had known about the curative properties of the mineral springs here for centuries, but thanks to a serious scientific analysis of the water in 1819, Strathpeffer became a boom town. Inevitably, tastes change, and Strathpeffer's popularity declined after World War II. Many of the spa buildings have disappeared, and the old wooden railway station now houses a museum of childhood. There are several good places to walk here, including the ridge of Knock Farril to the south, and through the woods to the Falls of Rogie to the west. Salmon may be seen in the Blackwater River here, and there are pleasant picnic sites between the trees.

ULLAPOOL MAP REF 410 F3
As you approach on the A835, the pretty little whitewashed town of Ullapool is neatly laid out before you on a spit of land curving into Loch Broom. The tidy grid-plan of the streets reveals that this is a model town laid out to a plan developed by the British Fishery Society in 1788.

The site was chosen to provide a fishing harbour, and to squeeze out the Dutch herring vessels which had taken advantage of the lack of local boats. The herring did not last, however, and, without the railway, the settlement declined.

The Fishery Society had chosen their site well, however, and in the first half of the 20th century boats came from the east coast and fortunes revived. Until the mid-1990s, the local economy was given a boost by the 'Klondyker' factory ships from Eastern Europe, processing the catches of east coast trawlermen in the loch's sheltered waters. Sadly, the collapse of the Russian economy saw them disappear and now tourism is the main industry. Learn more about crofting, fishing and emigration at Ullapool's good, small museum, set in a former church.

Ullapool is the gateway to the remote northwestern tip of Scotland and a designated geopark, as well as the main ferry port for Stornoway, in the Outer Hebrides. Around the coast at Achiltibuie is the Hydroponicum, a scientific delight, where bananas and other exotic plants thrive without soil – seeing is believing! At the head of Loch Broom, take time out to stop and see the dramatic Corrieshalloch Gorge, and the impressive suspension bridge just below the Falls of Measach.

ISLE OF SKYE

TO FLOWERDALE FALLS

On most summer days, either the harbour porpoise or common dolphin – or possibly both – can be seen, given a little patience, in Loch Gairloch. A loch cruise is the best way to see these creatures. After walking along the Gairloch shoreline, take the fairly easy route up a rocky valley to Flowerdale Waterfall.

DISTANCE/TIME 5.25 miles (8.4km) 2h45 **MAP** OS Explorer 433 Torridon – Beinn Eighe & Liathach or 434 Gairloch & Loch Ewe **START** Beach car park, southern end of Gairloch; grid ref: NG 807756 **PATHS** Tracks and smooth paths, mostly waymarked, no stiles **THE PUB** The Old Inn, Gairloch. Tel: 01445 712006/0800 542 5444; www.theoldinn.net

1 Cross the road and head up to the right of the newer cemetery. Turn left at its corner, going into trees to reach a path above. Turn right until a footbridge leads on to a wide path that soon runs downhill. The main path bends right (green-top waymarker) and then runs down to reach a tarred driveway.

2 Turn left along the tarred track to pass Flowerdale House. The track passes to the left of a barn and then turns right at a waterfall sign to pass Gairloch Trekking Centre. In about 0.25 mile (400m) you pass a timber-surfaced bridge on the right.

3 Follow the main path ahead, still to the left of the stream to reach a footbridge built by the Royal Engineers, just before you get to Flowerdale Waterfall.

4 The path leads past a waterfall to cross a footbridge above. It runs up into a pine clump, then turns down into the valley. After another footbridge it joins a rough track. Pass the memorial to the blind piper of Gairloch, just before a forest road beside Point **3**. Turn left, away from the timber-surfaced bridge, to walk through a felled forest that's regenerating naturally.

5 Blue-topped pole marks the path to the right with a footbridge. It leads through scrub birch and bracken with blue waymarker poles. The path bends right at an old fence cornerpost and down to pass above and to the left of an enclosed field. Turn right underneath two large oak trees and cross a small stream to reach an earth track.

6 Turn left for a few steps, until a bracken path runs up right past the waymarked power pole. The path bends left under oaks, then drops to rejoin an earth track. This soon meets a larger track (the old road from Loch Maree to Gairloch). Turn right, through two gates, to reach the Old Inn at Charlestown.

7 Cross the old bridge, and then the main road, heading towards the pier. Turn right at a signpost for the beach, to a stepped path to the left of Gairloch Chandlery. The tarred path passes to the left of a pine wood, then turns right into trees. It bends left and emerges to run along the spine of a small headland. Just before being carried out to sea, it turns sharp right and crosses above a rocky bay to fort (An Dun). A duckboard path runs along back of the beach, then turns right to the car park.

SEA EAGLES AT PORTREE BAY

While walking beside Portree Bay, keep at least one eye looking out to sea; you may spot the sea eagles that nest in the cliffs at Portree. The Aros Experience, just south of Portree, has the RSPB's closed-circuit TV link with the sea-eagle nest. Most nest action occurs between April and July (the young hatch in April), and the 'nest cams' give a magical insight into eagle chick behaviour and allows people to witness the moment when a chick tentatively takes to the air for the first time.

DISTANCE/TIME 3.5 miles (5.6km) 1h15 **MAP** OS Explorer 409 Raasay, Rona & Scalpay or 410 Skye – Portree & Bracadale **START** Portree on main A855 above harbour; grid ref: NG 485436 **PATHS** Smooth, well-made paths, farm track, 3 stiles **THE PUB** Well Plaid, The Royal Hotel, Portree. Tel: 01478 612525; www.royal-hotel.skye.com

1 Turn off the A855 on to a lane signed 'Budh Mor'. Walk to the shoreline and then continue to a small parking area. A tarred path continues along the shore past a slipway. After a footbridge, it passes under hazels. The path passes below a viewpoint with flagpoles and then rounds the headland to reach the edge of a level green field called The Bile.

2 A wall runs up the edge of The Bile. A sign points up left for Scorybreck but ignore it and go through the small gate ahead. This rough path leads into a corner of The Bile field. Go up its left edge and turn across its top, to a stile just above a field gate. Cross the top of the next field on an old green path, to a stile at its corner. You'll be able to see the track just beyond.

3 Turn sharp left, up the track. At the top it passes through two gates to reach a stony road right of Torvaig. Turn left past a house and cross the foot of a tarred road into a gently descending track. It runs down between two large corrugated sheds and then through to a gate with a stile.

4 The grassy path ahead leads down into Portree, but you can take a short, rather rough, diversion to Dun Torvaig (ancient fortified hilltop) above. For the dun, turn left along the fence, and left again on a well-made path above. It leads to a kissing gate above two sheds. Turn sharp right along the fence for a few steps, then bear left around the base of a small outcrop and head straight up on a tiny path to the dun. Remnants of dry-stone walling can be seen around the summit. Return to the well-made path, passing above Point **4** to join a wall on the right. The path leads down under goat willows into a wood where it splits; stay close to the wall.

5 At the first houses (The Parks Bungalow 5), keep downhill, walking along a tarred street. On the left is the entrance to the Cuillin Hills Hotel, if you're in need of refreshment. A few steps later, fork right on to a stony path. At the shore road, turn right across the stream and at once right again on a path that runs up for 60yds (55m) to a craggy little waterfall. Return to the shore road and turn right to reach the start.

WALK 147

SKYE & NORTH 389

STRATHPEFFER & THE FALLS OF ROGIE

A fairly easy riverside and forest walk from the Victorian spa town of Strathpeffer to the Falls of Rogie. If you stand on the suspension bridge at the falls between July and September, when the river is fairly full, you might glimpse leaping salmon.

DISTANCE/TIME 10 miles (16.1km) 5h **MAP** OS Explorer 437 Ben Wyvis & Strathpeffer
START Main square, Strathpeffer; grid ref: NH 483582 **PATHS** Waymarked paths and track, no stiles **THE PUB** Achilty Hotel, Contin. Tel: 01997 421355; www.achiltyhotel.co.uk

1 Head along the main road towards Contin. At the edge of the town, turn right at a metal signpost for Garve then, at a bend in the lane, turn left, following another signpost.

2 Follow the track to the left of Loch Kinellan. As it bends right, keep ahead up a path beside tall broom bushes to the corner of a plantation. Here you join a larger track leading into the forest. Continue for 0.5 mile (800m) until it reaches a signpost.

3 Turn left for View Rock on a good path with green waymarkers. At View Rock, a side-path diverts to the right for the viewpoint, then rejoins. After a long descent, ignore a green path turning off to the left and follow green waymarkers downhill. At a forest road go straight over beside a signpost. The path crosses two more forest roads to Contin Forest car park.

4 At the end of the car park pick up a wide path signed 'River Walk'. Where red waymarkers turn back right, keep ahead on a rougher path with deer markers. It bends up right beside a stream to a forest road. Turn left, signposted 'Garve', and in 80yds (73m) bear left, heading slightly downhill.

5 Go on for 600yds (546m), when a small track on the left is signed 'Rogie Falls Bridge'. At its foot, cross a spectacular footbridge below the falls and turn right, upstream. The path has green waymarkers and after 0.25 mile (400m) bends left away from the river. It crosses rocky ground to a junction. Turn up right, to Rogie Falls car park.

6 Leave the car park through a wooden arch and follow green waymarkers back to the bridge. Retrace the outward route to Point **5** and turn sharp left up another forest road. It leads uphill to where a much fainter track crosses.

7 Turn right down the smaller track to pass between obstructing boulders, to a signpost. Turn left, signed 'Strathpeffer'. After 600yds (546m) it reaches the signpost at Point **3**. Keep ahead and retrace the outward route to Point **2**. Turn left on the tarred lane, which becomes a track. At Kinloch house bear right, then turn left through a kissing gate, with a second one beyond leading into a plantation with a signpost for Strathpeffer.

8 Follow the main path ahead until you see Strathpeffer down on the right. At the next junction bear right down the wood edge and turn right into the town. The street on the left leads past a church with a square steeple, where you turn down right to the main square.

WALK 148

LOOKING OVER THE SEA TO SKYE

This is a bracing coastal walk along Loch Alsh, with stunning views of Skye, the sea and a fish farm. Fish farming is a tough life: mending a net that's 3ft (90cm) underwater is not comfortable when the water is still, but it invariably breaks on the day of a howling gale – hauling the cages out of the water for cleaning is the toughest job of all. Yet because of depleted fish stocks we are reliant on these farms for much of the salmon we consume.

DISTANCE/TIME 8.5 miles (13.7km) 4h **MAP** OS Explorer 413 Knoydart, Loch Hourn & Loch Duich
START Above pier of Glenelg ferry; grid ref: NG 795213 **PATHS** Grassy shoreline, minor road; 4 stiles **THE PUB** The Glenelg Inn, Glenelg. Tel: 01599 522273; www.glenelg-inn.com

1 The track runs out of the car park, signed 'Ardintoul and Totaig'. It descends through two gates, then goes up through a third into a plantation. With power lines above, the track forks. Take the left-hand one, downhill, passing an arrow made of stones. The track runs between the feet of a pylon and climbs again to contour through the wood. It runs in and out of a stream gorge, then descends towards the shore. On the other side of Loch Alsh, Balmacara is ahead.

2 At the shoreline, the track disappears into an open field strip. Follow the short grass next to a shingle beach, passing a salmon farm just offshore. When the trees once more run down to the sea, a green track runs next to the shore to reach an open field below a small crag with birches. Keep along the shore, walking outside the field walls, and sometimes taking to the stripy schist shingle, towards a square brick building on the point ahead. As you pass the end of a birch crag, you come to a wall gap. Here the track, that's simply a pair of green ruts, runs directly inland through a grey gate to meet a gravel track. Turn left, away from the

abandoned Ardintoul farm passing sheds and a house to regain the shoreline at Ardintoul.

3 The track runs along the shoreline, then turns inland to climb the hill behind. The steeper uphill sections are tarred. Below on the left, Allt na Dalach runs into Loch Alsh, with an example of a gravel spit where the river debris runs into tidal water. The track enters plantations, crosses over a stream and bends right to complete the climb to Bealach Luachrach.

4 Divert here to Glas Bheinn – a tough little hill, but a fine viewpoint. (Grading and timing don't take account of this side-trip.) From the road's high point, turn right up a wet tree gap to open hillside. Follow the remains of an old fence up the first rise. Where it bends right, continue ahead up to the summit, returning by same route. The old fence makes a useful guide back into the tree gap. Continue downhill from Point **4** on an unsurfaced road, which reaches a tarred road 1 mile (1.6km) north of Glenelg village. The grassy shoreline, then a road, leads back to the ferry pier.

FARIGAIG FOREST & LOCH NESS

This is a delightful walk that has wonderful views overlooking Loch Ness and takes you past the home of a different monster, the Beast of Boleskine. With so many fine sights in Scotland, it's a shame that such large numbers of people still flock to try to see the one that doesn't actually exist.

DISTANCE/TIME 4.25 miles (6.8km) 2h15 **MAP** OS Explorer 416 Inverness, Loch Ness & Culloden **START** Forest Enterprise car park; grid ref: NH 522237 **PATHS** Waymarked paths and tracks, no stiles **THE PUB** Craigdarroch House Hotel, Lower Foyers. Tel: 01456 486400

1 From the car park follow yellow waymarkers uphill near a stream. After 100yds (91m), a path on the right has a yellow-top waymarker. After a bench, the path contours briefly then turns up left, to a higher viewpoint. It then turns back sharply right and descends on earth steps through a little crag to a forest road. Turn right for 200yds (182m).

2 Turn up left on a footpath with more yellow waymarkers. The path has a low, heavily mossed wall alongside as it bends up to a higher forest road. Turn right and walk for about 150yds (137m) until you reach a sharp left-hand bend. Turn off right here, on a small footpath walking through an area of small self-seeded trees, then go steeply up to the left underneath mature trees. At the top, bear left along a little ridge, dropping gently downhill to a fine viewpoint.

3 Return for 100yds (91m) and bear left down the other side of the ridge. The path now descends steeply until it reaches a forest road. A sign indicates Lochan Torr an Tuill, near by on the left, with a picnic table.

4 Return along the forest road, past where you joined it. It climbs gently and then descends to the sharp right bend where you turned off earlier – the waymarker says 'to Car Park' on the side now facing you. After 150yds (137m), at another 'to Car Park' waymarker, turn left down the path with the low mossed wall to the forest road below (Point **2**). Turn left, past a red/green waymarker. The track kinks left past a quarry.

5 Where the main track bends right, downhill, keep ahead on a green track with a red/green waymarker. It emerges from the trees at a signpost. Follow this down to the right towards Easter Boleskine house. Green waymarkers indicate a diversion to the left of the house, to join its driveway track below. Follow this down to the B852.

6 Turn right for 50yds (46m). Below the left edge of the road is a tarred track. Turn down a faint path between the trees to cross this track, with a blue waymarker leading into a clearer path beyond. This passes down to the right of electricity transformers. At the foot of the slope, the main path bears right with a blue waymarker. It runs above the loch shore and joins a gravel track just below Lower Birchwood House. At a tarmac turning circle, a jetty on the left is great for monster-watchers. The tarred lane ahead leads up to the B852, with the car park just above right.

WALK 150

HEART OF THE CUILLINS

The Black Cuillin Hills, seen through Skye's moist Atlantic air, appear blue and under romantic sunset light almost purple. This land is like nowhere else, even in Scotland, for crag, boulder and jagged horizon. The special quality of Skye is obvious to the eye, but even more so to the foot. The black rock grips the foot like Velcro. This is gabbro, formed in the magma chamber of a massive volcano that stood here 50 million years ago.

DISTANCE/TIME 5.75 miles (9.2km) 4h **MAP** OS Explorer 411 Skye – Cuillin Hills **START** Pull-off before gate into Glenbrittle campsite; grid ref: NG 409206 **PATHS** Mountain paths, one boggy and tough; 2 stiles **THE PUB** Sligachan Hotel, Sligachan. Tel: 01478 650204

1 From the parking area, the track leads on through Glenbrittle campsite to a gate with a kissing gate. Pass left of the toilet block to cross a stile. Turn left along a stony track just above, which runs gently downhill above the campsite, to rejoin the Glenbrittle road.

2 Keep ahead to cross a bridge with the white Memorial Hut just ahead. On the right are some stone buchts (sheep-handling enclosures) and here a waymarked path heads uphill to reach a footbridge which crosses the Allt Coire na Banachdich.

3 Cross the footbridge and head up to the right of the stream's deep ravine, with a great view of the waterfall at its head. Its Gaelic name, Eas Mor, means simply 'Big Waterfall'. Above, the path bears right, to slant up the hillside. Below the spur of Sgurr Dearg the path forks. Here keep right, aiming for the right-hand of the two corries above, which is Coire Lagan. The path passes above Loch an Fhir-bhallaich. After a short steepening, the rebuilding works currently end and the path becomes rough. It rounds a shoulder into the lower part of Coire Lagan and meets a much larger path at a big cairn.

4 Turn uphill on this path, until a belt of bare rock blocks the way into the upper corrie. This rock has been smoothed by a glacier into gently-rounded swells, known as 'boiler-plates'. A scree field runs up into the boiler-plate rocks. The best way keeps up the left edge, below a slab wall with a small waterslide, to the highest point of the scree. Head up left for 50ft (15m) on bare rock, then back right on ledges to an eroded scree above the boiler-plate obstruction. Look back down your upward route to note it for your return. The trodden way slants up to the right. With the main stream near by on the right, it goes up to the rim of the upper corrie.

5 The boiler-plate slabs at the lochan's outflow are excellent for picnics. Walking mainly on bare rock, it's easy to make a circuit of the lochan. For the return journey, retrace your steps to Point **4**. Ignoring the right fork of the route you came up by, keep straight downhill on the main path. It runs straight down to the toilets at Glenbrittle campsite. Turn left over a rustic footbridge to finish along the beach.

EDINBURGH
■ TOURIST INFORMATION
Edinburgh & Scotland Information Centre
3 Princes Street ☎ 0845 2255 121;
www.edinburgh.org
Forestry Commission Scotland
Silvan House, 231 Corstorphine Road,
☎ 0845 367 3787;
www.forestry.gov.uk/scotland
Historic Scotland
Longmore House, Salisbury Place
☎ 0131 668 8800;
www.historic-scotland.gov.uk
Holyrood Palace
Canongate, The Royal Mile
☎ 0131 556 5100;
www.royalcollection.org.uk
National Trust for Scotland
Wemyss House, 28 Charlotte Square
☎ 0844 493 2100; www.nts.org.uk
Royal Museum
Chambers Street ☎ 0131 247 4422;
www.nms.ac.uk
Scottish Natural Heritage
12 Hope Terrace ☎ 0131 447 4784;
www.snh.gov.uk
Scottish Wildlife Trust
Cramond House, 3 Kirk Cramond
☎ 01131 312 7765; www.swt.org.uk

■ PLACES OF INTEREST
Edinburgh Castle
☎ 0131 225 9846;
www.edinburghcastle.gov.uk
Georgian House
Charlotte Square ☎ 0131 226 3318;
www.nts.org.uk
Museum of Scotland
Chambers Street ☎ 0131 225 7534;
www.nms.ac.uk
National Gallery of Scotland
The Mound ☎ 0131 624 6200;
www.nationalgalleries.org
Royal Botanic Garden
20A Inverleith Row ☎ 0131 552 7171;
www.rbge.org.uk

■ SHOPPING
In Edinburgh, there are plenty of shops on George Street as well as Victoria Street. As well as the national chains, Edinburgh has many speciality shops where you can buy all manner of Scottish paraphernalia, some more authentic than others.
Harvey Nichols
30–34 St Andrew Square
☎ 0131 524 8388;
www.harveynichols.com
Jenners
48 Princes Street ☎ 0844 800 3725;
www.houseoffraser.co.uk
Ocean Terminal
Ocean Drive, Leith ☎ 0131 555 8888;
www.oceanterminal.com

■ SPORTS & ACTIVITIES
CYCLE HIRE
Biketrax
Tollcross ☎ 0131 228 6633;
www.biketrax.co.uk

■ ANNUAL EVENTS & CUSTOMS
Edinburgh
International Festival and Fringe Festival, Aug.
Military Tattoo, Aug.
Hogmanay, 31 Dec.

FIFE & STIRLING
■ TOURIST INFORMATION
St Andrews
70 Market Street, Stirling
☎ 01334 472021; www.visitfife.com
Stirling
41 Dumbarton Road ☎ 01707 200620;
www.visitscottishheartlands.com

■ PLACES OF INTEREST
Argyll's Lodging
Castle Wynd, Old Town, Stirling
☎ 01786 431319;
www.historic-scotland.gov.uk
Bannockburn Visitor Centre
Glasgow Road, Stirling. 2.5 miles (4km) southeast of Stirling
☎ 01786 812664; www.nts.org.uk
Hill of Tarvit Mansionhouse
2 miles/3.2km south of Cupar off A916
☎ 01334 653127; www.nts.org.uk
Kellie Castle
Pittenweem ☎ 0844 493 2184
www.nts.org.uk
National Wallace Monument
Stirling ☎ 01786 472140;
www.scottish.heartlands.org
Old Town Jail
St John Street, Stirling
☎ 01786 450050; www.oldtownjail.com
The Pineapple
Dunmore Park, Dunmore
☎ 01324 831137
Scottish Fisheries Museum
Harbourhead, Anstruther
☎ 01333 310628;
www.scotfishmuseum.org
St Andrews Cathedral and Castle
The Scores ☎ 01334 477196;
www.visit-standrews.co.uk
Stirling Castle
Upper Castle Hill ☎ 01786 450000;
www.historic-scotland.gov.uk

■ FOR CHILDREN
Scotland's Secret Bunker
Crown Buildings, Troywood, near St Andrews ☎ 01333 310301;
www.secretbunker.co.uk
A tunnel leads to the fascinating secret underground command rooms used by government Secret Service personnel during the Cold War.

Scottish Deer Centre
Bow-of-Fife, by Cupar ☎ 01337 810391;
www.tsdc.co.uk
More than 140 deer, bird of prey demonstrations, tree-top walkway and more.

■ SPORTS & ACTIVITIES
ADVENTURE SPORTS
East Neuk Outdoors
Cellardyke Park, Anstruther
☎ 01333 311929;
www.eastneukoutdoors.com
Cluny Clays
Cluny Mains Farm, Kirkcaldy
☎ 01592 720374; www.clunyclays.co.uk

TROSSACHS & SOUTH
■ TOURIST INFORMATION
Perth
West Mill Street ☎ 01738 450600;
www.visitperthshire.co.uk
Trossachs Discovery Centre & Aberfoyle Tourist Information Centre
Main Street, Aberfoyle ☎ 08707 200604;
www.lochlomond-trossachs.org

■ PLACES OF INTEREST
Angus Folk Museum
Kirkwynd, Glamis ☎ 01307 840288;
www.nts.org.uk
J M Barrie's Birthplace
9 Brechin Road, Kirriemuir
☎ 0844 493 2142; www.nts.org.uk
Bell's Blair Atholl Distillery
Pitlochry ☎ 01796 482003
Bells Cherrybank Gardens
Perth ☎ 01738 472800;
www.welcometoscotland.com
Blair Castle
Blair Atholl, just off A9 ☎ 01796 481207;
www.blair-castle.co.uk
Branklyn Garden
116 Dundee Road, Perth
☎ 0844 493 2193; www.nts.org.uk
Castle Menzies
Weem, Aberfeldy ☎ 01887 820982;
www.menzies.org/castle
Dewar's World of Whisky
Aberfeldy Distillery, Aberfeldy
☎ 01887 822010; www.dewarswow.com
RRS Discovery
Dundee ☎ 01382 201245;
www.rrsdiscovery.com
Doune Castle
☎ 01786 841742;
www.historic-scotland.gov.uk
Drummond Castle Gardens
Muthill, Crieff ☎ 01764 681433;
www.drummondcastlegardens.co.uk
Edradour Distillery
Pitlochry ☎ 01796 472095;
www.edradour.co.uk
Famous Grouse Experience
The Hosh, Crieff ☎ 01764 656565;
www.thefamousgrouse.com

Glamis Castle
☎ 01307 840393;
www.glamis-castle.co.uk
Hamilton Toy Collection
Main Street, Callander
☎ 01877 330004
The Hermitage
2 miles (3km) west of Dunkeld
☎ 01350 728641
Inchmahome Priory
Port of Menteith ☎ 01877 385294;
www.historic-scotland.gov.uk
Killiecrankie Visitor Centre
3 miles (5km) north of Pitlochry
☎ 0844 493 2194
Kirriemuir Aviation Museum
Bellies Brae, Kirriemuir
☎ 01575 573 233; www.kamrafa.co.uk
Loch of the Lowes Visitor Centre
Off A923 northeast of Dunkeld
☎ 01350 727337; www.swt.org.uk
Moirlanich Longhouse
Near to Killin ☎ 01567 820988
Perth Museum & Art Gallery
78 George Street, Perth
☎ 01738 632488; www.perthshire.com
Rob Roy and Trossachs Visitor Centre
Callander ☎ 01877 330342
Scone Palace
Scone, Perth ☎ 01738 552300;
www.scone-palace.co.uk
Scottish Crannog Centre
Loch Tay, near Aberfeldy
☎ 01887 830583
Scottish Hydro Electric Visitor Centre
Pitlochry ☎ 01796 473152;
www.scottish-southern.co.uk
Learn about the power of water here.
Scottish Wool Centre
Aberfoyle ☎ 01877 382850;
www.scottishwoolcentre.co.uk
HMS Frigate Unicorn
Victoria Dock, Dundee ☎ 01382 200900;
www.frigateunicorn.org
Verdant Works
West Henderson's Wynd, Dundee
☎ 01382 226659; www.verdantworks.com

■ FOR CHILDREN
Sensation: Dundee
Greenmarket, Dundee ☎ 01382 228800;
www.sensation.org.uk
Hands-on science centre that puts the fun back in to physics. Six themed zones take you through the science behind the senses and there are interactive exhibitions galore.

■ SHOPPING
Perth Farmers' Market, First Sat each month.
Continental Market, regular markets featuring continental produce.
Gardener's Market, for info on market dedicated to all things for the garden.
Art on the River, art market with works of

art displayed along Tay Street.
Craft Market, Scottish crafts at their best
covering some 30 stalls.
For all markets check online at
www.perfectperth.com for details.

■ PERFORMING ARTS
Dundee Contemporary Arts
152 Nethergate ☎ 01382 909900;
www.dca.org.uk
Dundee Rep Theatre
Tay Square, Dundee ☎ 01382 223530;
www.dundeereptheatre.co.uk

■ SPORTS & ACTIVITIES
ADVENTURE SPORTS
Highland Adventure Safari
Drumdewan, Aberfeldy ☎ 01887 820071;
www.highlandadventuresafaris.co.uk
BOAT TRIPS
SS Sir Walter Scott
Trossachs Pier Complex, Loch Katrine
☎ 01877 376316; www.lochkatrine.co.org
CYCLING
Escape Route
3 Atholl Road, Pitlochry ☎ 01796 473859;
www.escape-route.biz
GOLF
Crieff Golf Course
Ferntower, Perth Road ☎ 01764 652909;
www.crieffgolf.co.uk
Gleneagles Hotel & Resort
Auchterarder ☎ 01764 662231;
www.gleneagles.com
Pitlochry Golf Course
Golf Course Road, Pitlochry
☎ 01796 472792;
www.pitlochrygolfclub.co.uk

■ ANNUAL EVENTS & CUSTOMS
Blair Castle
Glenfiddich Piping Championships,
end Oct.
Atholl Gathering and Highland Games,
end May.
Crieff
Highland Gathering, Aug.
Kirriemuir
Angus Glens Walking Festival, early Jun.
Perth
Festival of the Arts, May.
Highland Games, Aug.
Pitlochry
Highland Games, Sep.

ARGYLL, MULL & WEST
■ TOURIST INFORMATION
Inveraray
Front Street ☎ 08707 200616/
01499 302063; www.inveraray-argyll.com
Isle of Arran
The Pier, Brodick ☎ 01770 302140;
www.ayrshire-arran.com
Mull
The Pier, Craignure ☎ 01680 812377;
www.visitscottishheartlands.com

Oban
Argyll Square, Oban ☎ 01631 563122;
www.visitscottishheartlands.com

■ PLACES OF INTEREST
Arduaine Garden
20 miles (32km) south of Oban, on A816
☎ 0844 493 2216;
www.arduaine-garden.org.uk
**Ardnamurchan Lighthouse Visitor
Centre**
Ardnamurchan Point ☎ 01972 510210;
www.ardnamurchanlighthouse.com
Botanic Gardens
Great Western Road, Glasgow
☎ 0141 276 1614
Brodick Castle, Garden & Country Park
Brodick, Isle of Arran ☎ 0844 493 2152
Burrell Collection
Pollok Country Park, Glasgow
☎ 0141 287 2550;
www.glasgowmuseums.com
Carnasserie Castle
2 miles (3km) north of Kilmartin, off A816
www.historic-scotland.gov.uk
Duart Castle
1.5 miles (3km) from Craignure, Mull
☎ 01680 812309; www.duartcastle.com
Dunadd Fort
Kilmartin Glen
www.historic-scotland.gov.uk
Dunstaffnage Castle
4 miles (6.5km) north of Oban, off A85
☎ 01631 562465
Glasgow School of Art
167 Renfrew Street, Glasgow
☎ 0141 353 4526; www.gsa.ac.uk
Glencoe & North Lorn Folk Museum
Glencoe, Ballaculish ☎ 01855 811664
Glencoe Visitor Centre
Glencoe ☎ 0844 493 2222;
www.glencoe.nts.org.uk
House for an Art Lover
Bellahouston Park, 10 Dumbreck Road,
Glasgow ☎ 0141 353 4770;
www.houseforanartlover.co.uk
Inveraray Castle
☎ 01499 302203;
www.inveraray-castle.com
Island Cheese Company
Brodick, Arran ☎ 01770 302788;
www.islandcheese.co.uk
Isle of Arran Distillery Visitor Centre
Lochranza, Arran ☎ 01770 830264;
www.arranwhisky.com.
Tours and tastings.
Kelvingrove Art Gallery & Museum
Argyle Street, Glasgow ☎ 0141 276 9599;
www.glasgowmuseums.com
Kilchurn Castle
Loch Awe
www.kilchurncastle.com
Beautifully sited castle on a loch.
Kilmartin House Museum
Kilmartin ☎ 01546 510278;
www.kilmartin.org

Kilmory Castle Gardens
Lochgilphead ☎ 01546 602127;
www.argyll-bute.gov.uk
Loch Lomond Shores Visitor Centre
Benlomond Way, Balloch
☎ 01389 751033
Discover the history of the Loch and
much more
Mount Stewart House
Rothesay, Bute ☎ 01700 503877;
www.mountstewart.com
Mull Museum
Main Street, Tobermory, Mull
Oban Distillery
Stafford Street, Oban ☎ 01540 672219;
www.malts.com
Tours and tastings.
People's Palace
Glasgow Green, Glasgow
☎ 0141 554 0223;
www.glasgowmuseums.com
Rothesay Castle
Castlehill Street, Rothesay, Bute
☎ 01700 502691
Scottish Sealife Sanctuary
Loch Creran, Barcaldine, Argyll
☎ 01631 720386;
www.sealsanctuary.co.uk
Torosay Castle and Gardens
Mull. One mile (1.6km) south of Craignure
☎ 01680 812421

■ FOR CHILDREN
**Arctic Penguin (Inveraray Maritime
Experience)**
The Pier, Inveraray ☎ 01499 302213;
www.inveraraypier.com
A three-masted schooner that has many
items of maritime memorabilia including
some touching mementoes from former
seamen to their loved ones.
Cowal Bird Garden
Lochan Wood, Sandbank Road, Dunoon
☎ 01369 707999
With donkeys, goats, owls, pigs and
rabbits, this small animal park is
especially suited to families and those
with small children.
Glasgow Science Centre
50 Pacific Quay, Glasgow
☎ 0141 420 5000; www.gsc.org.uk
Set in its amazing space-age building,
the museum inside does not disappoint.
State-of-the-art technology is used to
translate theory to reality in a fun way. The
IMAX theatre adds to its appeal.
Inveraray Jail
Church Square, Inveraray
☎ 01499 302381; www.inverarayjail.co.uk
A top visitor attraction where real people
portray life in a 19th century prison.
Visitors can interact with costumed
prisoners and wardens, watch trials
or even sample punishments and
experience life in the cells. There's also
an exhibition of prison artefacts.

■ SHOPPING
Arran Fine Foods
The Old Mill, Lamlash, Arran
☎ 01770 600606;
www.paterson-arran.com
Creelers Smokehouse
Home Farm, Brodick, Arran
☎ 01770 302797; www.creelers.co.uk
Dunoon Ceramics
Pot Shop, 162 Argyll Street, Dunoon
☎ 01369 702662
Geoffrey (Tailor) Kiltmakers & Weavers
309 Sauchiehall Street, Glasgow
☎ 0141 331 2388;
www.geoffreykilts.co.uk
Island Cheese Company
Home Farm, Brodick, Arran
☎ 01770 302788;
www.islandcheese.co.uk
Loch Lomond Shores
Ben Lomond Way, Balloch
☎ 01389 721500;
www.lochlomondshores.com
Tiso Glasgow Outdoor Experience
50 Couper Street, Glasgow
☎ 0141 559 5450; www.tiso.com

■ SPORTS & ACTIVITIES
BOAT TRIPS
Cruise Loch Lomond Ltd
The Boat Yard, Tarbet, Loch Lomond
☎ 01301 702356;
www.cruiselochlomond.co.uk
Waverley Excursions Ltd
33 Lancefield Quay, Glasgow
☎ 0845 1304647;
www.waverleyexcursions.co.uk
GOLF
Cowal Golf Club
Dunoon, off A815 at Kirn
☎ 01369 705673;
www.cowalgolfclub.com
18-hole course.
Tobermory Golf Club
Erray Road, Tobermory, Mull
☎ 01688 302741;
www.tobermorygolfclub.com
9-hole course.
HORSE RIDING
Argyll Adventure
Dalchenna, Inveraray.
☎ 01499 302611; www.horserides.co.uk
LONG-DISTANCE PATHS
Isle of Arran Coastal Way
Circular route, 65 miles (104km).
www.coastalway.co.uk
Kintyre Way
New footpath developed to run from
Tarbet to Southend, 90 miles (60km)
www.kintyre.org
West Highland Way
This is Scotland's most famous long-
distance trail. The trek stretches from
Glasgow to Fort William, and is 95 miles
(150km) long.
www.west-highland-way.co.uk

WILDLIFE TOURS
Discover Mull
Ardrioch Farm, Dervaig, Mull.
☎ 01688 400415;
www.discovermull.co.uk
Island Encounter
Arla Tir, Aros, Mull.
☎ 01680 300441;
www.mullwildlife.co.uk
Wildlife tours of the island, including
eagles, owls, otters and more. Advance
booking essential.
Sea.fari
Easdale Harbour, Seil, by Oban
☎ 01852 300003; www.seafari.co.uk
Wildlife-spotting safaris in rigid
inflatables.
Turus Mara
Penmore Hill, Dervaig, Mull
☎ 01688 400242/08000 858786;
www.turusmara.com.
Cruise tours from Ulva Ferry, Mull, or
Oban, to Treshnish Isles, Staffa and Iona;
times vary.

WINTER SPORTS
Glencoe Ski Centre
Kingshouse, Glencoe ☎ 01855 851226;
www.glencoemountain.com

■ ANNUAL EVENTS & CUSTOMS
Dunoon
Cowal Highland Gathering, late Aug.
Glasgow
Celtic Connections, folk music
festival, Jan.
International Jazz Festival, Jun
World Pipe Band Championships,
mid-Aug.
Inveraray
Highland Games, mid-Jul.
Oban
Kilmore and Kilbride Highland
Games, Jul.
Argyllshire Highland Gathering,
late Aug.
Taynuilt
Taynuilt Highland Games, late Jul.
Tobermory, Mull
Mull Music Fest, last weekend Apr.
Tour of Mull Car Rally, mid Oct.

CAIRNGORMS & CENTRAL
■ TOURIST INFORMATION
Aviemore
Grampian Road, Aviemore
☎ 0845 2255121
Cairngorms National Park Authority
☎ 01479 873535;
www.cairngorms.co.uk

■ PLACES OF INTEREST
Aberlour Distillery
High Street, Aberlour.
☎ 01340 881249
Balmoral Castle
Ballater ☎ 013397 42534;
www.balmoralcastle.com

Cairngorm Mountain Railway
Cairngorm Ski Area, by Aviemore
☎ 01479 861261;
www.cairngormmountain.co.uk
Dallas Dhu Historic Distillery
South of Forres
☎ 01309 676548
Glenfiddich Distillery
Dufftown ☎ 01340 820373;
www.glenfiddich.com
Highland Folk Museum
Kingussie Road, Newtonmore
☎ 01540 673551; www.highlandfolk.com
Loch Garten Osprey Centre
Abernethy
☎ 01479 831476; www.rspb.org.uk
Mar Lodge Estate
Braemar ☎ 0844 493 2172;
www.marlodgeestate.org.uk
Pluscarden Abbey
Pluscarden, Elgin
☎ 01343 890257;
www.pluscardenabbey.org
Speyside Cooperage
Dufftown Road, Craigellachie
☎ 01340 871108;
www.speysidecooperage.co.uk
**Speyside Heather Visitor
& Garden Centre**
Skye of Curr, Dulnain Bridge
☎ 01479 851359;
www.heathercentre.com
Strathspey Steam Railway
Aviemore, Boat of Garten
☎ 01479 810725;
www.strathspeyrailway.net

■ FOR CHILDREN
Cairngorm Reindeer Centre
Reindeer House, Glenmore
☎ 01479 861228;
www.cairngormreindeer.co.uk
See Britain's only herd of reindeer living
free in the Cairngorms.
Highland Wildlife Park
Kincraig, by Kingussie
☎ 01540 651270;
www.highlandwildlifepark.org
Breeds of naturally wild animals
including elk and Highland cattle can
all be seen here. Interesting and makes
for a good day out.
Landmark Forest Adventure Park
Carrbridge ☎ 01479 841613/
0800 731 3446;
www.landmarkpark.co.uk
Superb living museum with authentically
dressed 'Highlanders' showing how life
was in days gone by.

■ SHOPPING
Lamont Sporrans Ltd
8 Invercauld Road, Braemar
☎ 013397 41404;
www.sporrans.net
Full range of kilts and Highland dress.

■ SPORTS & ACTIVITIES
ADVENTURE SPORTS
Active Outdoor Pursuits
Grampian Road, Aviemore.
☎ 01479 780000;
www.activepursuits.com
Full On Adventure
24 Cairngorm Avenue, Aviemore.
☎ 07885 835838;
www.fullonadventure.com
Glenmore Lodge
8 miles (12.8km) from Aviemore.
☎ 01479 861256;
www.glenmorelodge.org.uk
Rothiemurchus Estate
By Aviemore.
☎ 01479 812345;
www.rothiemurchus.net
FISHING
Fishdee
Fishpal Ltd ☎01573 470612;
www.fishdee.co.uk
Glen Tanar Estate
Brooks House, Glen Tanar, Aboyne
☎01339 886451;
www.glentanar.co.uk
GOLF
Aberneythy Golf Club
Nethybridge ☎ 01479 821305;
www.abernethygolfclub.com
9 holes.
Grantown-on-Spey Golf Club
Golf Course Road
☎ 01479 872079;
www.grantownonspeygolf.co.uk
18 holes
Kingussie Golf Club
Gynack Road, Kingussie
☎ 01540 661600;
www.kingussie-golf.co.uk
18 holes.
LONG-DISTANCE PATHS
Speyside Way
This trek takes you from Aviemore to
Buckie, 65 miles (104km).
www.speysideway.org
WATERSPORTS
Loch Morlich Watersports Centre
Glenmore Forest Park, near to Aviemore
☎ 01479 861221; www.lochmorlich.com
WILDLIFE TOURS
Speyside Wildlife
Garden Office, Inverdruie House,
Inverdruie, Aviemore ☎ 01479 812498;
www.speysidewildlife.co.uk
WINTER SPORTS
Aviemore Ski & Snowboard Hire
Unit 4 Myrtlefield Shopping Centre,
Grampian Road ☎ 01479 811711;
www.osatravel.co.uk
Experienced winter sports outfitter for all
your skiing and snowboarding needs.
Glenshee Ski Centre
Cairnwell, by Braemar
☎ 013397 41320;
www.ski-glenshee.co.uk

■ ANNUAL EVENTS & CUSTOMS
Abernethy
Highland Games, Aug.
Grantown-on-Spey
Highland Games, Aug.
Speyside
Spirit of Speyside Whisky Festival, end
Apr to May.

SKYE & NORTH
■ TOURIST INFORMATION
Fort William
Cameron Centre, Cameron Square
☎ 01397 703781
Glenfinnan
National Trust of Scotland, 18 miles
(29km) west of Fort William
☎ 01397 722250
Inverness
Castle Wynd, Inverness
☎ 01463 234353
Portree
Bayfield Road, Portree, Skye
☎ 01478 612137

■ PLACES OF INTEREST
Aonach Mòr Gondola Ride
Torlundy
☎ 01397 705825;
www.nevisrange.co.uk
**Armadale Castle Gardens and Museum
of the Isles**
Armadale, Sleat, Skye
☎ 01471 844305; www.clandonald.com
Aros
Viewfield Road, Portree, Skye
☎ 01478 613649; www.aros.co.uk
Beinn Eighe Visitor Centre
Aultroy. ☎ 01445 760254
Caledonian Canal Visitor Centre
Ardchattan House, Fort Augustus
☎ 01320 366493; www.waterscape.com
Colbost Croft Museum
Colbost, by Dunvegan, Skye
☎ 01470 521296
Dunvegan Castle
Skye ☎ 01470 521206;
www.dunvegancastle.com
Eilean Donan Castle
Loch Duich, Kintail
☎ 01599 555202;
www.eileandonancastle.com
Fortrose Cathedral
Cathedral Square, Fortrose
☎ 01667 460232
Open access.
Gairloch Heritage Museum
Achtercairn, Gairloch
☎ 01445 712287;
www.gairlochheritagemuseum.org.uk
Glenfinnan Monument
Glenfinnan ☎ 0844 493 2221
Groam House Museum
High Street, Rosemarkie
☎ 01381 620961;
www.groamhouse.org.uk

Highland Wineries
Moniack Castle, Kirkhill
☎ 01463 831283;
www.moniackcastle.co.uk
Wines, liqueurs, sauces and preserves
are all sold in this castle.

Hugh Miller's House
Church Street, Cromarty
☎ 01381 600245

Hydroponicum
Achiltibuie, north of Ullapool
☎ 01854 622202;
www.thehydroponicum.com

Inverewe Garden
Poolewe ☎ 0844 493 2225

Inverness Museum & Art Gallery
Castle Wynd, Inverness
Tel:01463 237114;
www.invernessmuseum.com

Knockan Visitor Centre
Inverpolly National Nature Reserve, off
A835 north of Ullapool.
☎ 01854 613418

**Loch Ness 2000: Official Loch Ness
Monster Exhibition Centre**
Drumnadrochit
☎ 01456 450573;
www.loch-ness-scotland.com

Mallaig Heritage Centre
☎ 01687 462085;
www.mallaigheritage.org.uk

Original Loch Ness Visitor Centre
Drumnadrochit
☎ 01456 450342;
www.lochness-centre.com

St Andrews Cathedral
15 Ardross Street, Inverness
☎ 01463 233535

Skye Museum of Island Life
Kilmuir, by Portree, Skye
☎ 01470 552206;
www.skyemuseum.co.uk

Talisker Distillery
Carbost, Skye
☎ 01478 614308;
www.malts.com

**Torridon Visitor Centre
& Deer Museum**
The Mains, Achnasheen
☎ 01445 791221

Treasures of the Earth
Corpach, by Fort William
☎ 01397 772283;'
www.treasuresoftheeath.co.uk

Ullapool Museum
7–8 West Argyle Street, Ullapool
☎ 01854 612987;
www.ullapoolmuseum.co.uk

Urquhart Castle
Drumnadrochit, Loch Ness
☎ 01456 450551

West Highland Museum
Cameron Square, Fort William
☎ 01397 702169;
www.westhighlandmuseum.org.uk
Fascinating displays and exhibitions.

■ **FOR CHILDREN**
Bright Water Visitor Centre
The Pier, Kyleakin, Skye.
☎ 01599 530040; www.eileanban.org
This is an informative and fun centre
ostensibly to educate about the island
and conservation.

Jacobite Steam Train
Operates between Fort William
and Mallaig
☎ 01524 737751
Follow the West Highland Line on Harry
Potter's Hogwarts steam train. The full
84-mile (135km) journey starts from the
highest mountain in Scotland, passes
the deepest loch, goes near the most
westerly railway station and passes
the shortest river in Britain. It truly is a
journey of extremes and a great day out.

Kylerhea Otter Haven
Kylerhea, Skye ☎ 01320 366322
The mixed conifer plantation here is
home to a colony of otters. If you look up
you may be lucky enough to see golden
eagles circling above.

Skye Serpentarium/Reptile World
The Old Mill, Harrapool, Broadford, Skye
☎ 01471 822209;
www.skyeserpentarium.org.uk
Snakes, lizards, frogs and other reptiles
are all here, and there are regular
handling sessions for those who like to
touch as well as look.

■ **SHOPPING**
Castle Gallery
43 Castle Street, Inverness
☎ 01463 729512;
www.castlegallery.co.uk
Modern art.

Crocks and Rocks
2 Wentworth St, Portree, Skye
☎ 01478 612670;
www.hebridean-jewellery.co.uk
Jewellery in Celtic designs.

**Hector Russell Scottish Kiltmaker
Visitor Centre**
6-8 Bridge Street, Inverness
☎ 01463 713 083;
www.hector-russell.com

Highland Stoneware
North Road, Ullapool
☎ 01854 612980;
www.highlandstoneware.com

Holm Mills Shopping Village
Holms Woollen Mills, Dores Road,
Inverness ☎ 01463 223311
Weaving exhibitions.

Inverness Farmers' Market
Eastgate Precinct, Inverness
☎ 01309 651206

Nevisport
High Street, Fort William
Tel:01397 704921; www.nevisport.com
Outdoor adventure sports equipment
and clothing.

Skye Batiks
The Green, Portree, Skye
☎ 01478 613331;
www.skyebatiks.com
Colourful items crafted to island patterns
and styles.

Spean Bridge Mill
Spean Bridge, 10 miles (16km)
north of Fort William
☎ 01397 712260
Weaving mill.

■ **SPORTS & ACTIVITIES**
ADVENTURE SPORTS
Raasay Outdoor Centre
Raasay House, Raasay, off north Skye
☎ 01478 660266;
www.raasayoutdoorcentre.co.uk
Sailing, cycling, climbing, kayaking and
much more. This centre has an excellent
reputation worldwide and is staffed by
experienced instructors.

Whitewave: Skye's Outdoor Centre
Kilmuir, Skye
☎ 01470 542414;
www.white-wave.co.uk
Rock climbing, kayaking, guided walks
and more. All activities are catered to and
there are instructors on hand to help.

BOAT TRIPS
Bella Jane Boat Trips
Elgol, Skye
☎ 0800 731 3089; www.bellajane.co.uk
Explore Loch Coruisk, the Small Isles and
Skye wildlife. Advance booking essential.

Calum's Seal Trips
32 Harbour Street, Plockton
☎ 01599 544306;
www.calums-sealtrips.com
Boat trips out to see the local population
of grey seals in their native habitat.

Cruise Loch Ness
Knockburnie, Inchnacardoch,
Fort Augustus
☎ 01320 366277;
www.cruiselochness.com
Cruise the loch aboard the *Royal Scot*
which is fitted with a special 3D imaging
system to show you what's going on in
the deep.

Dolphin Ecosse
Cromarty
☎ 01381 600323;
www.ecoventures.co.uk

Inverness Dolphin Cruises
Shore Street Quy, Inverness.
☎ 01463717900;
www.inverness-dolphin-cruises.co.uk
Boats leave Inverness harbour and sail
into the Moray Firth where there is the
best chance of seeing dolphins as well as
many types of birds.

Summer Isles cruises
From Ullapool ☎ 01854 612472;
from Achiltibuie ☎ 01854 622315;
www.summerqueen.co.uk

These day cruises take you to the outlying
islands and unusual rock formations off
the mainland. There is a one-hour stop
on an island featured on each cruise.

CYCLING
Highland Cycles
16A Telford Street, Inverness
☎ 01463 234789;
www.highlandcycles.co.uk

Island Cycles
The Green, Portree, Skye
☎ 01478 613121; www.isbuc.co.uk
Cycle hire here as well as fishing tackle
hire for anglers.

GOLF
Inverness Golf Club
Culcabock Road, Inverness
☎ 01463 239882;
www.invernessgolfclub.co.uk
This par 69 course welcomes visitors
and has a variety of tee times available
throughout the week.

Isle of Skye Golf Club
Sconser, Skye
☎ 01478 650414;
www.isleofskyegolfclub.co.uk
9-hole course that is open year round.

Loch Ness Golf Course
Fairways, Castle Heather, Inverness
☎ 01463 713335;
9- and 18-hole courses; also large
leisure complex.

Strathpeffer Spa Golf Club
Golf Course Road, Strathpeffer
☎ 01997 421219;
www.strathpeffergolf.co.uk
18-hole course established 1888.

HORSE-RIDING
Highland Riding Centre
Borlum Farm, Drumnadrochit
☎ 01456 450220; www.borlum.com

Skye Riding Centre
Suledale, by Portree, Skye
☎ 01470 582419;
www.skyeridingcentre.co.uk
Pony trekking for all abilities, plus
disabled facilities.

LONG DISTANCE PATH
Great Glen Way
73-mile (118km) trail from Fort William
to Inverness, then cycle trail.
www.greatglenway.com

WINTER SPORTS
Nevis Range
Torlundy, north of Fort William
☎ 01397 705825;
www.nevisrange.co.uk
Ski and snowboarding centre for all
abilities and experience levels.

■ **ANNUAL EVENTS & CUSTOMS**
Inverness
Tattoo, Northern Meeting Park,
late Jul

Portree
Skye Highland Games, Aug

PUBS

EDINBURGH

Doric Tavern
15–16 Market Street, Edinburgh
EH1 1DE ☎ 0131 225 1084;
www.thedoric.co.uk
A good public bar, bistro and wine bar offer something for everybody in this comfortable and authentic popular Old Town hostelry, a short way from the castle. There is a full range of seafood, game, meat and vegetarian dishes on the bistro menu, including Scottish old favourites such as Cullen skink and haggis. More traditional pub food is on offer downstairs in the Doric Bar which oozes with atmosphere.

The Shore Bar & Restaurant
3 Shore, Leith EH6 6QW
☎ 0131 553 5080; www.theshore.biz
Overlooking the Water of Leith and close to the port, this is a great place to come for good seafood and game. Refurbished in 2010, there is a friendly bar for pre-dinner drinks and a cosy dining room to eat in or an outside seating area for warmer weather. Not just an evening venue, the Shore Bar serves a good range of sandwiches at lunchtime as well as roasts on Sundays.

FIFE & STIRLING

Clachan Inn
2 Main Street, Drymen, Loch Lomond
G63 OBG ☎ 01360 660824
The Clachan Inn is reported by some to be the oldest alehouse in Scotland, with a license dating to 1734. Many walkers use this inn as a pit stop as they make their way along the West Highland Way.

Cross Keys Hotel
Main Street, Kippen FK8 3DN
☎ 01786 870293
Kippen is a small village in the Fintry Hills, some ten miles (16km) west of Stirling and just off the A811. Close by, lovely Burnside Wood is managed by people from a local community group, and is perfect for walking and nature trails. This friendly pub, dating from 1703, on the high street offers excellent home-made food, including a full lunch and dinner menu. Beers include Deuchars and IPA. Children and dogs welcome.

The Settle Inn
91 St Mary's Wynd, Stirling FK8 1BU
☎ 01786 474609
Licensed from the 1700s, this atmospheric inn is in a great position near to Stirling Castle and happens to be the oldest alehouse in Stirling. The Settle is a traditional Scottish inn serving a wide range of real ales.

The Ship Inn
The Toft, Elie KY9 1DT ☎ 01333 330246;
www.ship-elie.com
Elie is a perfect place to stop in the picturesque East Neuk villages. On the busy waterfront at Elie Bay, The Ship has been here since 1838. Activities such as beach cricket, live music and summer Sunday barbecues all add to the friendly, relaxed atmosphere. The full menu makes the most of good local suppliers, including fish from St Monans and traditionally made haggis from nearby Crail. The wide range of beers served here include Bellhaven Best, and the wine list is also extensive if even a little eclectic. Children and dogs are both made welcome here.

TROSSACHS & SOUTH

Lade Inn
Kilmahog FK17 8HD ☎ 01877 330152;
www.theladeinn.com
Set in its own grounds on the Leny Estate west of Callander, this white-painted free house was built as a tea room in the 1930s and first licensed three decades later. The cosy bar has a welcoming open fire decorated by a collection of brasses, and serves real ales. The restaurant offers high-quality Scottish cooking. Expect haggis, neeps and tatties, whole baked Trossachs trout or penne pasta wild mushroom sauce. The pub's own shop stocks over 120 ales from Scottish mircrobreweries.

Monachyle Mhor
FK19 8PQ. On A84, 11 miles (18km) north of Callander ☎ 01877 384622;
www.monachylemhor.com
This small, award-winning farmhouse hotel has dramatic loch and mountain views and Rob Roy's resting place is not far away. The interiors are resplendent with open fires, antique furniture and sporting prints mixed with original modern art. Excellent menus change daily and reflect the seaons, with ingredients coming from the hotel's own organic garden, as well as the rivers, lochs and hills of the Trossachs. There are several golf courses nearby, or you can just enjoy the views with tea and scones on the lawn.

Moulin Hotel
11–13 Kirkmead Road, Moulin, Pitlochry PH16 5EH ☎ 01796 472196
Moulin's summer courtyard and garden, and winter log fires and pub games make it popular with walkers, tourists and locals all year round. There is a choice of real ales from its own micro-brewery, and the Gaelic fare on a lengthy all-day menu are a big plus.

ARGYLL, MULL & WEST

Cairnbaan Hotel
Cairnbaan, by Lochgilphead PA31 8SJ
☎ 01546 603668; www.cairnbaan.com
Situated at lock 5, almost half-way along the Crinan canal, this former 18th-century coaching inn serves lighter meals, such a ciabattas, in the lounge bar and conservatory, with lots of locally produced seafood and game on the menu, but other choices too, such as Cajun spiced chicken Caesar salad.

Craignure Inn
Isle of Mull PA65 6AY ☎ 01680 812305;
www.craignure-inn.co.uk
The present bar makes good use of the original stables at this former drovers' inn. The inn has a great atmosphere and regularly features live music from folk bands to jigs and reels to blues. The bar menu has many traditional dishes and some special local delicacies, such as Mull cheddar and smoked trout.

Crinan Hotel
Crinan PA31 8SR ☎ 01546 830261;
www.crinanhotel.com
The hotel is set by the little harbour, basin and lock at the end of the Crinan Canal, and offers the choice of the bar or restaurant. In both the seafood is excellent, offering such delights as a warm tart of local scallops with smoked bacon and a goat's cheese cream, or steamed Loch Etive mussels.

CAIRNGORMS & CENTRAL

The Old Bridge Inn
Dalfaber Road, Aviemore PH22 1PU
☎ 01479 811137;
www.oldbridgeinn.co.uk
A cosy, friendly Highland pub overlooking the River Spey, with an attractive riverside garden as a bonus for high summer. Bar meals include lamb chops with redcurrant jelly, Aberdeen Angus steaks, or perhaps chicken breast marinated in lime, yoghurt and coriander. There's also a large selection of malt whiskies to sample.

Tipsy Laird
68–70 High Street, Kingussie, Highland
PH21 1HZ ☎ 01540 661334;
www.thetipsylaird.co.uk
If you want to try something really tasty then look out for the venison burgers. Other equally appetising choices include soup of the day served with home-made bread, and sandwiches or toasted ciabattas on the light lunch menu. This is a popular walkers' and outdoor enthusiasts' pub, so it can get quite busy at times. There is hostel-style accommodation available.

SKYE & NORTH

Applecross Inn
Shore Street, Applecross IV54 8LR
☎ 01520 744262; www.applecross.co.uk
Overlooking Skye and the Cuillins, this traditional white-painted inn standing on the shore of the remote and lovely Applecross peninsula is known for its imaginative menu. Local fish and game appear on the menu, but it's the seafood that is usually outstanding, from the simplest prawn tails with Marie-Rose dip, to king scallops cooked in garlic butter with lemon, herbs and crispy bacon. Puddings are tempting too, with fruit crumble or raspberry cranachan on the list.

Glenelg Inn
Glenelg IV40 8JR (from Shiel Bridge
(A87) take unclassified road to Glenelg)
☎ 01599 522273; www.glenelg-inn.com
The inn is a conversion of the 200-year-old stables set in a large attractive garden stretching down to the sea, with stunning views across the Sound of Sleat. Folk singers and musicians are frequent visitors to the bar. In addition to the cosy bar, there is a guests' private morning room and an atmospheric dining room. The menu offers a range of traditional Scottish fare based on outstanding local produce, including plenty of fresh fish and seafood.

Moorings Hotel
Banavie, PH33 7LY ☎ 01397 772797;
www.moorings-fortwilliam.co.uk
Situated right next to the tricky-to-navigate Neptunes Staircase set of locks on the Caledonian Canal, this is a modern hotel that serves excellent food and has a good selection of wine. Not only can you watch the comings and goings on the water, but you can enjoy views of Ben Nevis and Aonach Mor from the upstairs rooms. The menu changes every four or five days and choices for dinner might include Aberdeen Angus steak, but the specialities of the house are its superb fish dishes.

The Old Inn
Carbost, Isle of Skye IV47 8SR
☎ 01478 640205; www.carbost.f9.co.uk
Stone walls and wooden floors characterize this former croft house, now a popular inn favoured by walkers and climbers. At one time rents from farming tenants were collected here. Nowadays the inn serves traditional and hearty Scottish food. The daily specials might include oysters, crispy confit of duck, Scottish sirloin steak or homemade beefburger. The patio terrace overlooks Loch Harport.

TEA ROOMS

EDINBURGH

Always Sunday
170 High Street, Edinburgh
EH1 1QS ☎ 0131 622 0667;
www.alwayssunday.co.uk
This lovely café offers a little bit of Sunday afternoon relaxation every day of the week. Sit and sip a fair-trade coffee or tuck into all-day deli dishes, share a pot of tea and munch on a slab of delicious home-made cake. A bright city place to have afternoon tea.

Balmoral Hotel – Palm Court
1 Princes Street, Edinburgh EH2 2EQ
☎ 0131 556 2414;
www.thebalmoralhotel.com
A harpist plays gentle music on the balcony of this very elegant setting with its Venetian chandelier and palm trees. The Balmoral tea is served with sandwiches and home-made scones prepared by the Balmoral bakery together with tempting cakes and pastries. Accompany your meal with one of 20 teas or a glass of Champagne.

George Inter-Continental
19–21 George Street, Edinburgh
EH2 2PB ☎ 0131 240 7100
Afternoon tea is celebrated in refined elegance at this gracious New Town hotel, designed by Robert Adam. Pass through the marble-floored foyer and look up at the detailed plasterwork and fine chandeliers. The lobby lounge serves tea and snacks throughout the day. Choose from a traditional Highland tea, served from 3pm, with finger sandwiches and Dundee cake, or Georgian tea with champagne and millionaire's shortbread, or perhaps dip into gravadlax and Belgian waffles from the à la carte menu.

FIFE & STIRLING

Kind Kyttock's Kitchen
Cross Wynd, Falkland KY15 7BE
If you're exploring in Fife, let the aroma of freshly baked scones and pancakes entice you to this comfortable, well-established tea room in the historic village of Falkland. The preserves and cakes are home-made, too, and a small selection is offered for sale. Soups, sandwiches, salads and sweets are also served at lunchtime.

TROSSACHS & SOUTH

The Gleneagles Hotel
Auchterarder PH3 1NF
☎ 01764 662231; www.gleneagles.com
With an international reputation for high standards and its championship golf course, this grand hotel, close to the A9, is one of the finest in Scotland. It's

main restaurant has a coveted four AA rosettes, but if dining here seems a little over the top (or beyond your budget), why not treat yourself to an afternoon tea. Perhaps if the standard package with delicious cakes, sandwiches, pastries and scones isn't enough, try the champagne version or even sample a whisky-taster's tea! Reservations are essential if you want to come here at weekends.

Perthshire Visitor Centre
Bankfoot, Perth PH1 4EB
☎ 01738 787696; www.macbeth.co.uk
Lying some 7 miles (11.3km) north of Perth on the A9, this busy centre is based around quality shopping. Stock up on Loch Fyne fresh salmon and oysters, Macsween's tasty, renowned haggis and locally made fruit wines before relaxing in the 120-seater restaurant, which serves a tempting combination of home baking and locally sourced produce.

The Watermill
Mill Street, Aberfeldy PH15 2BG
☎ 01887 822896;
www.aberfeldywatermill.com
This extensive complex now includes a bookshop, music shop and art gallery all in a converted watermill, infused with the aroma of freshly brewed coffee. Enjoy a fruit smoothie on the terrace, or a speciality coffee with your cake – all the products are locally sourced or organic where possible. And the old waterwheel is still used to power the lighting!

ARGYLL, MULL & WEST

The Coach House Coffee Shop
Loch Lomond Trading Co Ltd, Luss
G83 8NN ☎ 01436 860341;
www.lochlomondtrading.com
Gaelic music, log fires and a kilted proprietor set the scene at this friendly coffee and gift shop in the pretty village of Luss, on Loch Lomond's western shore. The perfect spot for a light meal or tea stop, it offers home-made rolls and soup, and speciality fruit cake baked with ale and studded with crystallised ginger.

Kilcamb Lodge Hotel
Strontian, Highlands PH36 4HY
☎ 01967 402257;
www.kilcamblodge.co.uk
If you're looking for a place to stop on the Ardnamurchan Peninsula, then seek out this fabulous and friendly, 300 year-old stone-built hotel just outside the village of Strontian. Basic afternoon tea includes mouth-watering home-baked shortbread, while a full afternoon treat includes sandwiches and scones with jam and cream. Here, the main restaurant has a great reputation, too.

Tchai-Ovna House of Tea
42 Otago Lane, Glasgow G41 3LP
☎ 0141 357 4524; www.tchaiovna.com
Relax inside or out at this beautiful tea room in the bustling city of Glasgow. There are no cream cakes on offer here but the huge choice of teas range from realtively well-known tastes such as Darjeeling to unknown blends from Nepal. The emphasis is on the tea and the relaxing experience. As in Middle Eastern and European tea houses, you can buy healthy food snacks such as falafel and vegetarian delicacies to accompany your choice of brew.

The Willow Tea Rooms
217 Sauchiehall Street, Glasgow
G2 3EX ☎ 0141 332 0521;
www.willowtearooms.co.uk
Above a jewellery shop, this is one of Kate Cranston's original tea rooms designed by famous Charles Rennie Mackintosh in 1903. The food served here is more than a match for the striking interior, and afternoon tea is a popular ritual with the city's visitors. Sip your tea or coffee and tuck into cakes, sandwiches and scones in the elegant surroundings of the Room de Luxe, with its wall-panelling, stylish stained glass and distinctive silver chairs.

CAIRNGORMS & CENTRAL

Brodie Countryfare
Brodie, Forres IV36 2TD
☎ 01309 641555;
www.brodiecountryfare.com
On the A96 close to Brodie Castle, this busy shopping complex offers a food hall and good delicatessen full of rich aromas. Only the best local ingredients are served up in the restaurant, whether it's freshly baked scones with your cup of tea or a more substantial meal.

The Clootie Dumpling
Speyside Heather Garden & Visitor Centre, Skye of Curr, Dulnain Bridge PH26 3PA ☎ 01479 851359;
www.heathercentre.com
Tea, coffee, sandwiches, speciality soups and other traditional home-made foods are available all day – but the highlight has got to be the Clootie Dumpling, which is served in 21 different ways.

Culloden Visitor Centre
Culloden Moor, Inverness IV2 5EU
☎ 01463 790607
This is a great place to stop and refuel when you have been out on the moor, especially if the weather is inclement. The lovely café/restaurant here serves light lunches and snacks, including vegetable soups complimented by freshly baked cheese scones.

The Station Restaurant
Station Square, Ballater
AB35 5QB ☎ 013397 55050
Walk where Queen Victoria once walked and visit the special waiting room built especially for the Queen's use. Then complete your day's visit to the handsomely restored Old Royal Station by tucking into some excellent home baking at this excellent café, with its good Italian-style coffees. For light meals choose from freshly made soups, toasties and paninis.

SKYE & NORTH

The Ceilidh Place
14 West Argyle Street, Ullapool IV26 2TY
☎ 01854 612103;
www.theceilidhplace.com
An Ullapool institution since it opened in 1970, this unique complex combines several different places to sit back and relax: an all-day coffee shop, a bar and a restaurant with a bookshop, art gallery and performance venue. For cake-lovers, freshly baked cakes are part of the appeal of the all-day menu. The main menu offers more substantial dishes and you might try a dish of locally caught fish. For good weather days you can eat outside and dogs are permitted in the garden.

Inverlochy Castle Hotel
Torlundy, by Fort William PH33 6SN
☎ 01397 702177;
www.inverlochycastlehotel.com
For a memorable Scottish afternoon tea with a stunning backdrop of a loch and high mountains, it would be hard to beat this luxurious castle hotel just north of Fort William. There's a wide variety of teas on offer to accompany the tempting array of sandwiches, scones, cakes, pastries and biscuits, served in the majestic Great Hall or the stunning drawing room which overlooks the loch.

The Torridon
Torridon IV22 2EY ☎ 01445 791242;
www.thetorridon.com
How do you fancy a high tea in every sense of the word? Using all the polished silverware and the very best china, pots of tea or coffee freshly brewed to accompany the delicately cut cucumber sandwiches, fluffy light scones with scrumptious fruit jam and spoonfuls of thick cream and calorific home-made cakes – but all taken on the top of a mountain, and led by a mountain guide? This is one of the most unusual options available at this delightful Highland hotel situated on the shore of Loch Torridon. You can have all this at sea level too, or opt for coffee and fresh shortbread and enjoy the views.

Administrative Boundary

A Road - Single Carriageway

Primary Route - Single Carriageway

Other Town

Primary Route - Dual Carriageway

Motorway

Motorway Junction

A Road - Dual Carriageway

National Park

Heritage Coast

Featured location

Certain county, county borough or council area names are abbreviated on the maps as follows:

Aber C	Aberdeen City	E Duns	East Dunbartonshire
C Edin	City of Edinburgh	E Rens	East Renfrewshire
C Glas	City of Glasgow	Myr Td	Merthyr Tydfil
Clacks	Clackmannanshire	Oxon	Oxfordshire
Dund C	Dundee City	W Duns	West Dunbartonshire

Scale of mapping pages 398 - 411   1:1,000,000

0   20   40   60   80   100 kilometres

G   H   J   K   L   M

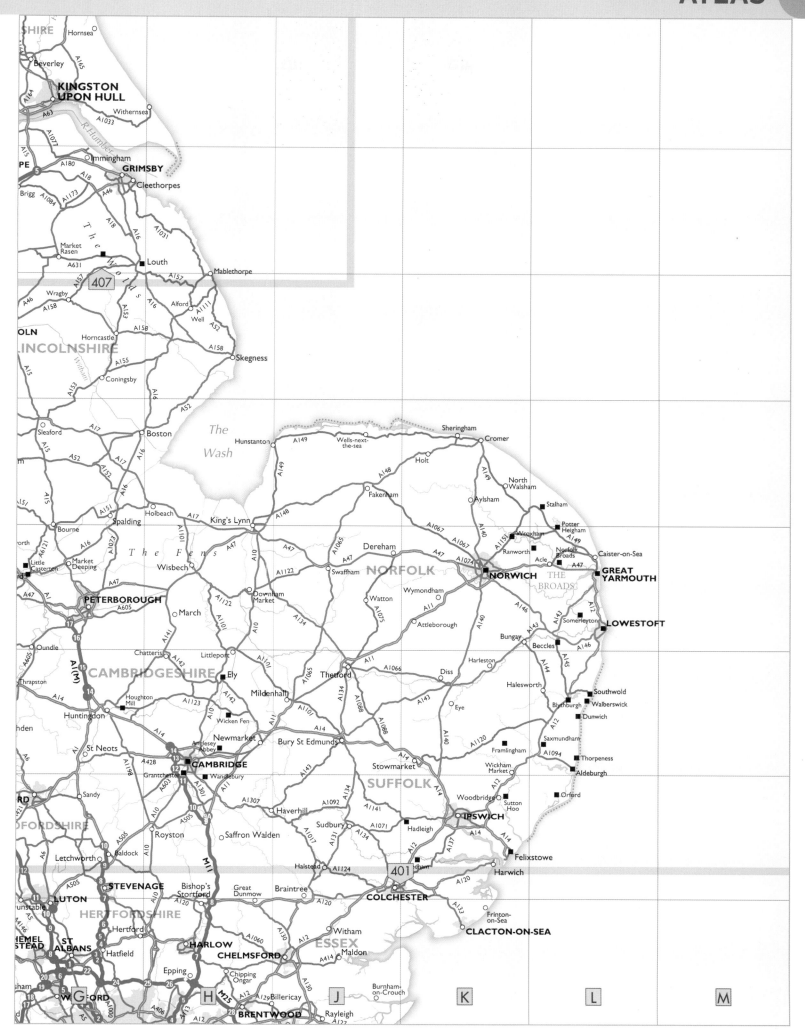

SHIRE
Hornsea
Beverley
A165
KINGSTON
UPON HULL
Withernsea
A63
R. Humber
A1033
PE
A15
Immingham
A180
GRIMSBY
5
Brigg
A1084
A1173
A46
Cleethorpes
A18
A16
A1031
Market
Rasen
The Wolds
A631
A157
Louth
407
Mablethorpe
A46
A158
Wragby
A16
Alford
A1111
A153
Well
A52
OLN
Horncastle
A158
A158
LINCOLNSHIRE
A155
Skegness
A15
Withorn
A153
Coningsby
A15
A16
A52

The
Wash

Sheringham
Hornsea
Sleaford
A17
Boston
Hunstanton
A149
Wells-next-
the-sea
Cromer
A17
A149
Holt
A148
North
Walsham
Stalham
A149
Bourne
A16
A151
Holbeach
A17
King's Lynn
A148
Fakenham
A1067
Aylsham
A140
A151
Spalding
The Fens
A47
A47
A1065
Dereham
A47
A1067
Wroxham
Potter
Heigham
A149
Little
Easterton
Market
Deeping
Wisbech
A1122
Swaffham
NORFOLK
Ranworth
Acle
Norfolk
Broads
Caister-on-Sea
PETERBOROUGH
A605
A1122
Downham
Market
Watton
Wymondham
NORWICH
THE
BROADS
A47
GREAT
YARMOUTH
17
March
A101
A10
A134
A1075
Attleborough
A140
A146
Somerleyton
LOWESTOFT
16
Oundle
A141
Bungay
A143
Beccles
A146
A505
A1(M)
15
Chatteris
A142
Littleport
A1101
A1065
Thetford
A11
A1066
Diss
Harleston
A144
A145
Thrapston
CAMBRIDGESHIRE
Ely
Halesworth
14
Houghton
Mill
A1123
A142
Mildenhall
A134
A1088
Eye
A143
Southwold
A12
Blythburgh
Walberswick
Huntingdon
A10
A11
A14
A1088
Dunwich
A14
Wicken Fen
Saxmundham
A1094
Thorpeness
St Neots
A14
Newmarket
Bury St Edmunds
Framlingham
A140
A1120
A6
Anglesey
Abbey
14
13
CAMBRIDGE
A143
Stowmarket
Wickham
Market
A12
Aldeburgh
12
Grantchester
11
A603
Wandlebury
A11
SUFFOLK
A14
Woodbridge
Sutton
Hoo
Orford
RD
Sandy
A10
10
A505
A1307
Haverhill
A1092
A1141
A137
IPSWICH
Royston
9A
Sudbury
A1071
Hadleigh
A12
FOLDSHIRE
A505
Baldock
Saffron Walden
A1017
A131
A134
A12
Felixstowe
Letchworth
10
Halstead
A1124
401
Harwich
12
11
Luton
8
7
STEVENAGE
Bishop's
Stortford
Great
Dunmow
Braintree
A120
COLCHESTER
A133
Frinton-
on-Sea
Dunstable
A5
10
HERTFORDSHIRE
Hertford
A120
A130
Witham
ESSEX
CLACTON-ON-SEA
9
ST
ALBANS
Hatfield
HARLOW
A1060
A130
A414
Maldon
HEMEL
STEAD
8
Epping
CHELMSFORD
20
19
5
W G FORD
22
24
25
26
H M25
Chipping
Ongar
J
Burnham-
on-Crouch
K
L
M
18
A5
A406
A13
A12
BRENTWOOD
A129 Billericay
Rayleigh
A127

Inner He

Muck

Sound of Arisaig

Glenfinnan A830

Fort William

Loch
Ericht

Grampian

Ardnamurchan
Peninsula

Acharacle

A861

Kinlochleven

Loch
Rannoch

1

Coll

Arinagour

Tobermory

410

A861

A82

A861

A884

Loch Linnhe

A828

South
Ballachulish

Glen
Coe

A82

Tiree

Scarinish

Morvern

Lochaline

A848

Sound of Mull

Loch
Tay

Lyon

Loch
Tay

A827

2

Ulva

Iona

Fionnphort

Isle of Mull

A849

Oban

A85

A816

Firth of Lorne

A85

Dalmally

Tyndrum

Crianlarich

Killin

A85

Locheamhead

LOCH LOMOND AND
THE TROSSACHS

3

Colonsay

Scalasaig

Oronsay

Scarba

Luing

Loch
Awe

A819

ARGYLL &
BUTE

Inveraray

A83

The Trossachs

Loch
Katrine

A821

A81

Callander

A873

STIRLING

STIRLING

11
10
9

Kilmartin
Glen

Crinan Canal

Lochgilphead

A816

A83

A815

A814

A82

A811

A875

M80

4

Port Askaig

A846

Islay

A847

A846

Jura

Sound of Jura

A83

Tarbert

Kennacraig

Claonaig

Gigha

A8003

Dunoon

Colintraive

Rothesay

A886

A815

Helensburgh

A8

DUNS

E DUNS

Kilsyth

A803

M80

A801

A803

A80

M73

GREENOCK

INVERCLYDE

Dumbarton

A82

GLASGOW

PAISLEY

RENFREWSHIRE

30

31

29

28

A737

A761

25

21

15

11

10

Portnahaven

Port Ellen

Kintyre

Largs

Kilbirnie

Beith

Stewarton

A78

A760

A737

A736

NORTH
AYRSHIRE

Kilwinning

Ardrossan

Irvine

A736

A759

A77

A719

HAMILTON

EAST
KILBRIDE

M77

A723

A726

A71

KILMARNOCK

A719

Galston

A71

SOUTH L

Strathaven

5

Saddell

A83

Arran

Brodick

Lamlash

A841

Firth of
Clyde

Troon

Prestwick

Ayr

A70

Cumnock

A76

A70

Campbeltown

Sound
of Bute

A841

Kilbrannan Sound

Maybole

A713

EAST
AYRSHIRE

6

Girvan

A77

SOUTH
AYRSHIRE

A713

o u t

A702

7

North Channel

Ballantrae

A714

New Galloway

A712

A713

A762

Loch Ryan

A77

406

Newton Stewart

A75

8

Stranraer

A718

A75

A716

Wigtown

A75

Gatehouse
of Fleet

A755

Castle
Dougla

Portpatrick

A77

A716

Luce Bay

A746

A747

Wigtown
Bay

Kirkcudbright

A711

Drummore

Whithorn

A   **B**   **C**   **D**   **E**   **F**

N O R T H

S E A

ANGUS

PERTH & KINROSS

FIFE

CLACKS

FALKIRK

EAST LOTHIAN

MIDLOTHIAN

WEST LOTHIAN

BORDERS (SCOTTISH)

LANARKSHIRE

DUMFRIES & GALLOWAY

NORTHUMBERLAND

TYNE & WEAR

DURHAM

Blair Atholl
Pitlochry
Aberfeldy
Dunkeld
Blairgowrie
Coupar Angus
Kirriemuir
Forfar
Brechin
Laurencekirk
Inverbervie
Montrose
Arbroath
Carnoustie
Perth
Crieff
Auchterarder
DUNDEE
Newport-on-Tay
St Andrews Bay
St Andrews
Newburgh
Auchtermuchty
Cupar
Crail
Falkland
East Neuk Villages
Pittenweem
Kinross
Glenrothes
Leven
Loch Leven
Alloa
Kincardine
DUNFERMLINE
Kirkcaldy
North Berwick
Falkirk
Cumbernauld
LIVINGSTON
EDINBURGH
Haddington
Dunbar
East Linton
Dalkeith
Penicuik
Lammermuir Hills
Eyemouth
Berwick-upon-Tweed
Lanark
Biggar
Peebles
Lauder
Greenlaw
Holy Island
Innerleithen
Galashiels
Melrose
Coldstream
Bamburgh Castle
Farne Islands
Kelso
Seahouses
Moffat
Selkirk
Wooler
Chillingham Castle
Craster
Hawick
The Cheviot Hills
Alnwick
Thornhill
Alwinton
Warkworth Castle
Amble
Rothbury
Otterburn
Elsdon
Ashington
Lochmaben
Lockerbie
Bellingham
Kielder Water
Morpeth
Bedlington
Blyth
Dumfries
Hadrian's Wall
Dalbeattie
Annan
Gretna
Longtown
Vindolanda
Corbridge
NEWCASTLE UPON TYNE
Tynemouth
SOUTH SHIELDS
Brampton
Haltwhistle
Hexham
GATESHEAD
Carlisle
Wigton
Alston
Consett
SUNDERLAND
WASHINGTON
Chester-le-Street
Seaham
Maryport
Durham
Peterlee
Workington
Cockermouth
Crook
HARTLEPOOL
Keswick
Derwent Water
Ullswater
Penrith
Bishop Auckland
Newton Aycliffe
STOCKTON-ON-TEES
MIDDLESBROUGH
Staithes
Appleby-in-Westmorland
Loweswater
Lowestoft

406

411

407

1

2

3

4

5

6

7

8

A   B   C   D   E   F

Port Nis
(Port of Ness)
A857

A858
Carlabhagh (Carloway)   A857
Broad Bay
Stornoway
(Stornoway)
A858   A866
A859
Isle of Lewis
Scarp
WESTERN ISLES
The Minch
Scourie
A894
Lochinver   A837
Inchnadamph
Inverpolly National
Nature Reserve   A835
A835
A837

Taransay   A859
Tairbeart
(Tarbert)   Shiant
Islands   Ullapool
A859
Harris
(Hearadh)   A859

Pabbay
Berneray
(Bearnaraigh)   Sound of Harris
Uibhist a Tuath
(North Uist)   Loch nam Madadh
(Lochmaddy)
A865   A867
A865
The Little Minch   Inverewe
A832   Loch
Maree
Gairloch
A832   Loch
Fannich
Uig   Rona   Kinlochewe   A832
A832   A835
Beinn Na Faoghla
(Benbecula)
A855   Sound of Raasay   A896   Achnasheen
Sheildalg   A896
Torridon
Dunvegan   A850
A87   Applecross   A890
Isle of
Skye   Portree   Inner Sound   A896   Loch
Monar
Uibhist a Deas
(South Uist)
A865   A863   Raasay
Scalpay
Drynoch   A863   A890   Cannich
A87   Loch
Mullardoch
Loch Baghasdail
(Lochboisdale)
A865   Kyle of
Lochalsh
Soay   Glenelg   A87
HIGHLAND
Sound of Barra   A851
Cuillin   Ardvasar   Sound of Sleat   A87   Fort
Augustus   A887
Eriskay (Eiriosgaigh)
Canna   A87   Invergarry
Barraigh
(Barra)   Rum   Sound   Mallaig   Loch
Lochy
Eigg   Loch Morar   Loch
Arkaig
Bagh a Chaisteil
(Castlebay)
Sandray   Muck   Sound of Arisaig   A830   Spean Bridge   A86
Glenfinnan   A830   A82
Mingulay   Inner Hebrides   A861   Fort William
A82
Coll   Acharacle   Kinlochleven
Ardnamurchan
Peninsula   A861   A82
Tiree   Arinagour   Tobermory   408   South
Ballachulish   Glen
Coe   A82
Mor   A884
Scarinish   Ulva   Isle of Mull   Lochaline   Loch Linnhe
A848   Sound of Mull   A849   Oban   A85   Tyndrum

Outer Hebrides

North West Highlands

Durness
A838
Bettyhill
A836 Melvich A836
Tongue
A836
Loch Loyal
Naver
A897
Altnaharra
Loch Naver
A836
A838
Loch Shin
Lairg
A839 A839
A836
Golspie A9 Brora
Bonar Bridge
A836
A949 Dornoch
Tain

Scrabster
Thurso A836 John o' Groats
Island of Stroma
Pentland Firth
South Ronaldsay
A961
A9
A836
A9
A882 Wick
A9 A99
Dunbeath Lybster
A9
Helmsdale

Carron

Alness
Invergordon
Cromarty Firth
Cromarty
Moray Firth
Strathpeffer Dingwall
Black Isle
Fortrose
A862 A9
A832
Muir of Ord A96
A831 A862
A833 Inverness Culloden
A82
A831
Drumnadrochit
Loch Ness
Invermoriston
Monadhliath Mountains
A9
Aviemore
Kingussie
Newtonmore
A86
Spey
A889
A9
Loch Laggan
Loch Ericht

Nairn
A96
Forres
A96 A939 A940
MORAY
Rothes
Aberlour
A95 Speyside
A939
Grantown-on-Spey
A938
Carrbridge A95
Boat of Garten
A939
Tomintoul
CAIRNGORMS
Braemar
River Dee
Grampian Mountains
Loch Rannoch
Blair Atholl
Pitlochry A9
Aberfeldy A827
A827
Loch Tay
Lyon
Killin
G

Lossiemouth
A941
Elgin A96 Buckie A942 Cullen Portsoy
A96 A98 Banff
Spey A96
Keith
A941
Dufftown A920
A941
Huntly
A920
A944
Kildrummy Castle
A944
Alford
A980
A93
Ballater Aboyne
Dee
Banchory
A93
A93
A924
Blairgowrie
A923 Dunkeld A984
Coupar Angus
Tay
A93
PERTH &
H

Aberchirder
Turriff
A95 A97
A97
A96
Oldmeldrum
Inverurie
Kintore
A96
A944
A980
A957
A90

Fraserburgh
A98 A981
A981 A950
A952
A96
A920 Ellon
A90 A947
Dyce
ABE ABERDEEN
A944
ABERDEENSHIRE
Stonehaven
Laurencekirk
A90 A937 A92 Inverbervie
Brechin
A933 A935 Montrose
Kirriemuir A926 409 A932 A934
A926 Forfar
A94 A933
A923 A90 Arbroath
A92
Carnoustie
DUNDEE
J K L M

Peterhead
A975
A946

ANGUS

Drumochter
A9
A86

ACKNOWLEDGEMENTS

The Automobile Association would like to thank the following photographers and companies for their assistance in the preparation of this book.

Abbreviations for the picture credits are as follows:
(AA) AA World Travel Library; (t) top; (b) bottom; (c) centre; (l) left; (r) right

1 AA/T Mackie; 3 AA/R Coulam; 4 AA/J Smith; 6 AA/A Burton; 7 AA/A Burton; 8 AA/JM Moody; 9 AA/A Burton; 11cl AA/J Wood; 11cc AA/J Wood; 11cr AA/J Wood; 11b AA/J Wood; 12 AA/J Wood; 13 AA/J Wood; 14 AA/J Wood; 15 AA/J Wood; 16 AA/C Jones; 19 AA/C Jones; 20 Ben Foster/Eden Project; 21cl AA/J Wood; 21c AA/J Wood; 21r Simon Burt/apexnewspix.com; 21b R Moltmaker/ Eden Project; 22 AA/A Burton; 23 AA/J Wood; 24 AA/A Burton; 25 AA/A Burton; 31tc AA/N Hicks; 31tr AA/C Jones; 31cr AA/N Hicks; 31cl AA/N Hicks; 31cc AA/N Hicks; 31b AA/N Hicks; 32 AA/C Jones; 33 AA/A Burton; 34 AA/N Hicks; 35tl AA/N Hicks; 35tr AA/N Hicks; 36 AA/C Jones; 37 AA/N Hicks; 38 AA/N Hicks; 43tc AA/N Hicks; 43tr AA/N Hicks; 43c AA/N Hicks; 43b AA; 44 AA/N Hicks; 45 AA/N Hicks; 46 AA/N Hicks; 51tr AA/N Hicks; 51cl AA/J Tims; 51c AA/J Tims; 51cr AA/N Hicks; 51b AA/N Hicks; 52 AA/N Hicks; 53l AA/J Tims; 53tr AA/J Tims; 53cr AA/J Tims; 54 AA/N Hicks; 58tr AA/J Tims; 58cl AA/J Tims; 58cr AA/J Tims; 59 AA/J Tims; 60 AA/J Tims; 61 AA/J Tims; 63tr AA/M Jourdan; 63cl AA/N Hicks; 63cr AA/M Jourdan; 63b AA/A Burton; 64 AA/A Burton; 65 AA/M Jourdan; 66 AA/A Burton; 69tc AA/E Meacher; 69r AA/J Tims; 69cl AA/J Tims; 69cc AA/J Tims; 70t AA/J Tims; 70b AA/E Meacher; 71tr AA/D Hall; 71cr AA/D Hall; 71cl AA/H Palmer; 71cc AA/D Hall; 71b AA/D Hall; 72 AA/S Day; 73 AA/D Hall; 74 AA/D Hall; 75 AA/D Hall; 76 AA/D Hall; 78 AA/D Hall; 85l AA/H Williams; 85r AA/A J Hopkins; 86 AA/I Burgum; 87l AA/S Day; 87r AA/C Jones; 88 AA/C Jones; 89 AA/C Jones; 95 AA/A Burton; 97tr AA/A Burton; 97c AA/A Burton; 97b AA/A Burton; 98 AA/A Burton; 99 AA/A Burton; 100 AA/A Burton; 101 AA/A Burton; 105cl AA/W Voysey; 105cr AA/T Souter; 105cl AA/S & O Mathews; 105b AA/A Burton; 106 AA/A Burton; 107 AA/S McBride; 108 AA/A Burton; 110 onEdition; 111tl onEdition; 111tc onEdition; 111tr onEdition; 111c onEdition; 111br onEdition; 113tc AA/M Moody; 113tr AA/M Moody; 113cl AA/S Day; 113cr AA/M Moody; 113b AA/M Moody; 114 AA/M Moody; 115 AA/M Moody; 116 AA/M Moody; 119tr AA/J Miller; 119cl AA/J Tims; 119c AA/J Tims; 119cr AA/J Tims; 120 AA/J Tims; 122tr AA/M Moody; 122cl AA/J Miller; 122cr AA/J Miller; 122b AA/J Miller; 123 AA/J Miller; 124 AA/J Miller; 125 AA/J Miller; 126 AA/J Miller; 132tc AA/J Miller; 132r AA/A Burton; 132cl AA/J Miller; 132cc AA/J Miller; 135t AA/J Tims; 135cl AA/J Tims; 135cc AA/N Setchfield; 135r AA/N Setchfield; 136 AA/J Tims; 137 AA/R Turpin; 138 AA/N Setchfield; 140t AA/M Jourdan; 140c AA/M Jourdan; 141 AA/N Setchfield; 142 AA/J A Tims; 143 AA/M Jourdan; 144 AA/N Setchfield; 145 AA/J A Tims; 146 AA/J A Tims; 147 AA/N Setchfield; 148 AA/N Setchfield; 150 Jon Arnold Images/Alamy; 151t Getty Images; 151b Robert Harding Picture Library Ltd/Alamy; 153tc AA/M Birkitt; 153tr AA/P Baker; 153cr AA/M Busselle; 154 AA/M Birkitt; 157tr AA/Bob Johnson; 157c AA/D Hall; 157cr AA/C Jones; 158 AA/C Jones; 167 AA/T Mackie; 169tr AA/T Mackie; 169cl AA/T Mackie; 169bl AA/T Mackie; 170 AA/T Mackie; 171 AA/T Mackie; 172 AA/T Mackie; 173 AA/T Mackie; 176tc AA/C Coe; 176tr AA/T Mackie; 176c AA/C Coe; 177 AA/T Mackie; 179tc AA/T Mackie; 179tr AA/A Baker; 179c AA/T Mackie; 179b AA/T Mackie; 180 AA/C Coe; 181 AA/R Ireland; 182 AA/T Mackie; 184t AA/T Mackie; 184c AA/T Mackie; 185c AA/T Mackie; 185br AA/J A Tims; 186 AA/M Birkitt; 187 AA/M Birkitt; 189t AA/M Moody; 189c AA/M Moody; 189b AA/M Moody; 190 AA/M Moody; 193tc AA/M Moody; 193tr AA/D Hall; 193c AA/M Moody; 194 AA/M Moody; 196tc AA/C Jones; 196tr AA/M Hayward; 196c AA/C Jones; 197 AA/M Hayward; 198 AA/J Welsh; 199tl Ironbridge Gorge Museums; 199tr Ironbridge Gorge Museums; 199c Ironbridge Gorge Museums; 201tc AA/M Short; 201tr AA/R Surman; 201c AA/M Hayward; 202 AA/C Jones; 203 AA/M Hayward; 206tc AA/N Jenkins; 206tr AA/N Jenkins; 206c AA/I Burgum; 206b AA/C & A Molyneux; 209tc AA/T Mackie; 209tr AA/T Mackie; 209c AA/T Mackie; 209b AA/T Mackie; 211 AA/T Mackie; 212 AA/T Mackie; 213 AA/T Mackie; 214 AA/T Mackie; 215 AA/T Mackie; 216 AA/T Mackie; 222tl AA/T Mackie; 222tr AA/M Birkitt; 222bl AA/T Mackie; 222br AA/T Mackie; 223 AA/T Mackie; 231 AA/M Bauer; 233cl AA/I Burgum; 233cr AA/N Jenkins; 234 Billy Stock/PhotolibraryWales; 235 Jeff Tucker/PhotolibraryWales; 236tcl AA/M Moody; 236cl AA/M Moody; 236b AA/M Moody; 236r AA/M Moody; 237 AA/C Warren; 238 AA/N Jenkins; 239 AA/M Moody; 240 AA/M Moody; 245 AA/W Voysey; 246tc AA/S Watkins; 246tr AA/S Watkins; 246cr AA/S Watkins; 246bl AA/G Matthews; 247 AA/N Jenkins; 248 AA/C Jones; 249 AA/G Matthews; 250 AA/M Bauer; 256tr AA/C & A Molyneux; 256cl AA/C & A Molyneux; 256c AA/N Jenkins; 256b AA/N Jenkins; 257 AA/N Jenkins; 258 AA/N Jenkins; 259 AA/N Jenkins; 260tl Centre for Alternative Technology; 260cl Nick Turner/Centre for Alternative Technology; 260bl Centre for Alternative Technology; 261tr Centre for Alternative Technology; 261br Centre for Alternative Technology; 262 AA; 271 AA/M Kipling; 273tr AA/A Mockford & N Bonetti; 273cr AA/A Mockford & N Bonetti; 273bl AA/A Mockford & N Bonetti; 274 AA/A Mockford & N Bonetti; 275 AA/A Mockford & N Bonetti; 276 AA/A Mockford & N Bonetti; 277 AA/T Mackie; 278 AA/T Mackie; 279 AA/A Mockford & N Bonetti; 280 AA/A Mockford & N Bonetti; 289cl AA/M Kipling; 289c AA/M Kipling; 289cr AA/M Kipling; 289bl AA/M Kipling; 290 AA/M Kipling; 291 AA/M Kipling; 292cl AA/M Kipling; 292bl AA/M Kipling; 292c/r AA/M Kipling; 293 AA/M Kipling; 294 AA/M Kipling; 295 AA/M Kipling; 304tc AA/T Mackie; 304tr AA/T Mackie; 304c AA/T Mackie; 304bl AA/T Mackie; 305 AA/T Mackie; 307 AA/T Mackie; 308 AA/T Mackie; 309 AA/T Mackie; 314 AA; 315tl AA/T Mackie; 315cl AA/J Freeman; 315br AA/J Freeman; 316 AA/T Mackie; 317 AA/T Mackie; 322tr AA/R Coulam; 322cr AA/R Coulam; 322bl AA/R Coulam; 323 AA/R Coulam; 324 AA/R Coulam; 325 AA/R Coulam; 326 AA/R Coulam; 327 AA/C Lees; 328 AA/R Coulam; 329tl Forestry Commission; 329tr Forestry Commission; 329cl Kielder Water Birds of Prey Centre; 329cr Forestry Commission; 330 AA/R Coulam; 343 AA/David W Robertson; 345tc AA/J Smith; 345tr AA/J Smith; 345cl AA/J Smith; 345cr AA/J Smith; 346bl AA/K Paterson; 346c/r AA/J Smith; 347 AA/R Elliott; 348tr AA/J Smith; 348cl AA/M Taylor; 348cr AA/S Day; 349 AA/S Whitehorne; 352tc AA/K Paterson; 352tr AA/J Smith; 352c AA/S Anderson; 353 AA/J Smith; 354 AA/J Smith; 355 AA/S Day; 356tl Pete Cairns/Nature Picture Library; 356cl AA/S Day; 356bl AA/H Williams; 356br Laurie Campbell; 357tr Laurie Campbell; 357tc Pete Cairns/Nature Picture Library; 357br AA/S Anderson; 362tc AA/S Whitehorne; 362tr AA/R Elliott; 362c AA/S Anderson; 362b AA/D Hardley; 363 AA/K Paterson; 364 AA/S Whitehorne; 365 AA/S Whitehorne; 366 AA/S Anderson; 367 AA/S Anderson; 371t AA/J Smith; 371c AA/J Smith; 371cr AA/J Smith; 371b AA/S Anderson; 372 AA/J Smith; 373 AA/J Smith; 375 AA/S Anderson; 376 AA/J Smith; 377 Scottish Viewpoint/Alamy; 378t Charlie Phillips; 378cr AA/M Moody; 382tc AA/S Anderson; 382tr AA/S Whitehorne; 382c AA/S Whitehorne; 383 AA/J Carnie; 384 AA/J Carnie; 385 AA/S Whitehorne; 386 AA/J Smith; 387 AA/S Whitehorne

Every effort has been made to trace the copyright holders, and we apologise in advance for any unintentional errors. We would be pleased to apply any corrections in any future edition of this publication.